# RESEARCH HANDBOOK ON URBAN SOCIOLOGY

RESEARCH HANDBOOKS IN SOCIOLOGY

**Series Editor:** Hans-Peter Blossfeld, *Professor of Sociology, University of Bamberg, Germany*

The Research Handbooks in Sociology series provides an up-to-date overview on the frontier developments in current sociological research fields. The series takes a theoretical, methodological and comparative perspective to the study of social phenomena. This includes different analytical approaches, competing theoretical views and methodological innovations leading to new insights in relevant sociological research areas. Each *Research Handbook* in this series provides timely, influential works of lasting significance. These volumes will be edited by one or more outstanding academics with a high international reputation in the respective research field, under the overall guidance of series editor Hans-Peter Blossfeld, Professor of Sociology at the University of Bamberg. The *Research Handbooks* feature a wide range of original contributions by well-known authors, carefully selected to ensure a thorough coverage of current research. The *Research Handbooks* will serve as vital reference guides for undergraduate students, doctoral students, postdoctorate students and research practitioners in sociology, aiming to expand current debates, and to discern the likely research agendas of the future.

For a full list of Edward Elgar published titles, including the titles in this series, visit our website at www.e-elgar.com.

# Research Handbook on Urban Sociology

*Edited by*

Miguel A. Martínez

*Professor of Housing and Urban Sociology, Institute for Housing and Urban Research, Uppsala University, Sweden*

RESEARCH HANDBOOKS IN SOCIOLOGY

Cheltenham, UK • Northampton, MA, USA

© Miguel A. Martínez 2024

Cover image: Miguel A. Martínez (editor), Utrecht, 2023.

All rights reserved. No part of this publication may be reproduced, stored in a retrieval system or transmitted in any form or by any means, electronic, mechanical or photocopying, recording, or otherwise without the prior permission of the publisher.

Published by
Edward Elgar Publishing Limited
The Lypiatts
15 Lansdown Road
Cheltenham
Glos GL50 2JA
UK

Edward Elgar Publishing, Inc.
William Pratt House
9 Dewey Court
Northampton
Massachusetts 01060
USA

A catalogue record for this book
is available from the British Library

Library of Congress Control Number: 2024930509

This book is available electronically in the Elgaronline
Sociology, Social Policy and Education subject collection
http://dx.doi.org/10.4337/9781800888906

ISBN 978 1 80088 889 0 (cased)
ISBN 978 1 80088 890 6 (eBook)

Printed and bound by CPI Group (UK) Ltd, Croydon, CR0 4YY

# Contents

| | | |
|---|---|---|
| *List of contributors* | | viii |
| *Acknowledgements* | | xxiii |
| *List of abbreviations* | | xxv |
| 1 | Introduction to the *Research Handbook on Urban Sociology*<br>Miguel A. Martínez | 1 |

PART I   SOCIETY, STATE, CAPITALISM, AND CITIES

| | | |
|---|---|---|
| 2 | Social and critical features of urban sociology<br>Miguel A. Martínez | 26 |
| 3 | The capitalist local state, urban change, and social conflict<br>Özlem Çelik | 50 |
| 4 | The city in class perspective<br>Ibán Díaz-Parra and Beltrán Roca | 65 |
| 5 | The global city and other fetishes: financial foundations of a mirage<br>Mariana Fix | 80 |
| 6 | Rentier and homeowner cities: a long-run comparative history of urban tenure<br>Sebastian Kohl | 98 |
| 7 | The flaws of urban financialization and rentierism: not distribution, but exploitation<br>Ismael Yrigoy | 110 |

PART II   REVISITING DEBATES IN URBAN SOCIOLOGY

| | | |
|---|---|---|
| 8 | Renewing sociological research on the urban with Bourdieu<br>Virgílio Borges Pereira | 120 |
| 9 | Urban social ecology and neighbourhood effects revisited<br>Ngai-Ming Yip | 135 |
| 10 | Questioning the foundations: the embedded racism in urban sociology theorization<br>Miguel Montalva Barba | 151 |
| 11 | Sociology of gentrification<br>Andrej Holm | 167 |

| 12 | Feminist urban sociology and social reproduction<br>Bahar Sakızlıoğlu | 188 |
| --- | --- | --- |
| 13 | Who cares? The moral architecture of urban conflict<br>Tino Buchholz and Jere Kuzmanić | 202 |
| 14 | Planetary urbanisation reloaded: a radical theory for the burning issues of our time<br>Max Rousseau | 219 |
| 15 | Inhabiting the right to the city<br>Margherita Grazioli | 236 |

## PART III  SOCIO-SPATIAL SEGREGATIONS

| 16 | Social mix and its critics: reflections on housing policies<br>Marie-Hélène Bacqué and Éric Charmes | 252 |
| --- | --- | --- |
| 17 | Producing and closing rent gaps: political and social dimensions<br>Defne Kadıoğlu | 269 |
| 18 | School choices and gentrification in late capitalist cities: the neighborhood as a distinction strategy of the middle class<br>Carlotta Caciagli | 285 |
| 19 | Use and abuse of the ghetto concept in Chilean urban sociology<br>Nicolás Angelcos | 299 |
| 20 | Processes of urban hyper-marginalisation under climate change: examples from Angola and Mozambique<br>Cristina Udelsmann Rodrigues | 314 |
| 21 | Crime, policing, and youth orientations towards urban futures<br>Naomi van Stapele and Samuel Kiriro | 326 |
| 22 | Feminist urban planning: women transforming territories through participatory action methods<br>Blanca Valdivia and Sara Ortiz Escalante | 341 |

## PART IV  THE HOUSING QUESTION

| 23 | Financialization and the rescaling of large developers: the built environment and national business groups<br>Ivana Socoloff | 360 |
| --- | --- | --- |
| 24 | How Airbnb and short-term rentals push the frontier of financialisation through housing assetisation<br>Javier Gil | 380 |

| 25 | From social housing to upscale regeneration: the pitfalls of residents' participation in Dublin<br>*Valesca Lima* | 398 |
|---|---|---|
| 26 | Resisting the destruction of home: un-homing and homemaking in the formation of political subjectivities<br>*Dominika V. Polanska* | 412 |
| 27 | Migrants, markets, movements: immigrants and housing as commodity and right in Madrid<br>*Sophie Gonick* | 428 |
| 28 | Socially and culturally produced boundaries in housing access in relation to sexuality<br>*Myrto Dagkouli-Kyriakoglou* | 444 |
| 29 | Urban squatting movements, the right to the city and solidarity networks: the case of the metropolitan region of Belo Horizonte, Brazil<br>*Clarissa Cordeiro de Campos* | 457 |
| 30 | Urban commons in practice: housing cooperativism and city-making<br>*Lorenzo Vidal* | 472 |

PART V   SOCIALLY SHAPED CITIES

| 31 | Structures and agents: re-scaling citizen participation in urban regeneration<br>*Luca Sára Bródy* | 492 |
|---|---|---|
| 32 | Temporalities and everyday lives of Filipina domestic workers in Hong Kong<br>*Maren K. Boersma* | 508 |
| 33 | Urban public space and biopolitical social control<br>*Jorge Sequera* | 523 |
| 34 | The logic of informality in shaping urban collective action in the Global South<br>*Sonia Roitman and Peter Walters* | 538 |
| 35 | Rethinking China's urbanisation through informal politics<br>*Yunpeng Zhang* | 552 |
| 36 | University as the nexus between the urban and the social<br>*Do Young Oh* | 567 |
| 37 | Looking forward: a research agenda for contemporary urban sociology<br>*Mika Hyötyläinen and Miguel A. Martínez* | 583 |

| Index | 608 |
|---|---|

# Contributors

**Nicolás Angelcos** (BA Sociology, University of Chile; MA-PHD Sociology, École des Hautes Études en Sciences Sociales, France) is Assistant Professor in the Sociology Department of the University of Chile. He is also Associate Researcher at the Centre for the Study of Conflict and Social Cohesion (COES). His PhD dissertation (2015) examined the political subjectivation of low-income people in the context of the housing conflict in Chile. He currently studies political participation at the neighbourhood level and sociological theory. His work has been published in journals such as *Social Movement Studies, Latin American Research Review, Latin American Perspectives*, and *Scripta Nova*. He is the editor of *Vivir con dignidad: transformaciones sociales y políticas de los sectores populares en Chile* (Fondo de Cultura Económica, 2023). Webpage: https://facso.uchile.cl/sociologia/cuerpo-academico/nicolas-angelcos-gutierrez.

**Marie-Hélène Bacqué** (BA Architecture, ENSA Paris La Villette; MA Urban Planning, Université Paris 7; MA Social Sciences, EHESS; PhD Urban Studies, École des Hautes Études en Sciences Sociales, Paris; PhD Architecture, ENSA Paris La Villette) is Professor of Urban Studies at Paris Nanterre University (France). Previously she held teaching positions in sociology and urban studies in different universities in France. She was visiting scholar at the Center for European Studies, Harvard University (Boston, USA), and the Institut National de la Recherche Scientifique (Montreal, Canada). Her PhD dissertation (1994) studied the transformations of the Paris 'red suburb'. Her research focuses on urban segregation, working-class neighbourhoods, and community development in France and North America. In particular, she has analysed participatory processes in these contexts. Her publications have appeared in journals such as *International Journal of Urban and Regional Research, Cities, Scripta Nova, Actes de la Recherche en Sciences Sociales, Sociologie, Revue française de sociologie*, and *Sociologie et sociétés*. She is author and coauthor of several books including *The Middle Classes and the City. A Study of Paris and London* (Palgrave, 2016), *L'empowerment, une pratique émancipatrice?* (La Découverte, 2013) (translated into Spanish as *El Empoderamiento*, Gedisa, 2014), and *Retour à Roissy, un voyage sur le RER B* (Le Seuil, 2019).

**Maren K. Boersma** (BSc-MSc Human Geography and Planning, Utrecht University, The Netherlands; PhD Public Policy, City University of Hong Kong, Hong Kong S.A.R.) is MSCA Postdoctoral Fellow (Marie Skłodowska-Curie Actions, Horizon Europe) at the Institute for Housing and Urban Research (IBF), Uppsala University (Sweden). Previously, she held a teaching position in Human Geography at Utrecht University, The Netherlands, and a research position in social welfare services for vulnerable groups at the Dutch Organisation of Applied Scientific Research. Her PhD dissertation (2016) studied time in the everyday lives of Filipina domestic workers in Hong Kong. She currently studies how temporalities contribute to urban social processes, extending her dissertation on Filipina domestic workers with empirical material from policy-makers and ex-domestic workers in Manila. Her publications have appeared in journals such as the *Journal of Ethnic and Migration Studies* and *Time & Society*.

**Virgílio Borges Pereira** (BA, MA, PhD, and habilitation in Sociology, University of Porto, Portugal) is Professor of Sociology at the Department of Sociology of the Faculty of Arts and Humanities of the University of Porto and Researcher at the Institute of Sociology of the University of Porto. He is also an invited Professor at the Faculty of Architecture of the University of Porto. His research combines sociological, historical, and ethnographic approaches and focuses on the production of social and cultural inequalities in different spatial contexts in northern Portugal, with a special interest in the study of the sociological legacy of Bourdieu's work. He has written extensively on the constitution of social spaces, class cultures, territorial stigma, social housing, and construction industry. His publications have appeared in journals such as *City*, *Poetics*, *Environment and Planning A*, *The Sociological Review*, *Politix*, *Actes de la recherche en sciences sociales*, and *International Journal of Urban and Regional Research*. He is the translator of the Portuguese version of P. Bourdieu's and L. Wacquant's *Invitation to Reflexive Sociology* (University of Porto Press, 2022). Among his recent publications in English is the co-authored chapter 'Class formation and social reproduction strategies in the Portuguese construction industry. Elements for a relational sociological analysis' in the edited book *Class Boundaries in Europe. The Bourdieusian Approach in Perspective* (Routledge, 2022). He is co-editor of *Hidden in Plain Sight: Politics and Design in State-subsidized Residential Architecture* (Park Books, 2021).

**Luca Sára Bródy** (MSc Sociology and Economics, Corvinus University of Budapest, Hungary; MSc Social Problems and Social Policy, University of Amsterdam, the Netherlands; PhD Urban Studies, Gran Sasso Science Institute, Italy) is a Postdoctoral Research Fellow at the Centre for Economic and Regional Studies (KRTK) in Budapest, Hungary. Previously, she was a research fellow at the Periféria Policy and Research Centre in Budapest. She held also a visiting doctoral scholar position at the University of Barcelona and at the Central European University. Her research has mainly taken place in Hungary, while her previous work also focused on the cities of Barcelona, and Amsterdam. Her PhD dissertation (2019) explored the political economy of citizen participation in urban regeneration, involving comparative research between Barcelona and Budapest. She is currently working on social movements and citizen mobilisation, state–civil society relations, urban–rural divides, local development, and food sovereignty initiatives. Her publications have appeared in journals such as *Local Environment*, *Territorio*, and other Hungarian journals. She has also co-authored and co-edited scientific booklets on topics involving household debt, local self-government, and the power of civic ecosystems. She is a member of the HerStory Collective, a Budapest-based feminist food-related research collaborative. More on her current research project can be found at: http://sustainaction.org.

**Tino Buchholz** (BA-MA Spatial Planning, University of Dortmund, Germany; PhD Urban Planning, University of Groningen, the Netherlands) is Assistant Professor at the Institute of Urban Planning and Design, Dept. of Planning Theory and Practice, University of Stuttgart, Germany. He has held visiting fellowships at Leibniz Institute IfL Leipzig, AISSR Amsterdam, and Rostov-on-Don State University. He also works as director and producer of documentary films. His PhD dissertation (2016) addressed the urban question of justice as struggles for recognition and decent housing in Amsterdam and Hamburg and conceptualised local struggles for local recognition with their consequences of resignation, resistance, and relocation. Working at the intersection of urban sociology, moral geography, and urban planning he focuses on rights to place, space, and the city; urban conflict and human agency for planning theory; and planning ethics, with a special focus on the insurgent self-confidence of architects, planners, and movements for institutional change. His academic publications and films target privileges and conflicts involving property-led urbanisation, morality, and cynicism; the limits of solidarity movements; and informal self-organisation in cities (e.g. squatting) between resignation and hope. Selected writings and films can be found online: https://tuniproductions.com/.

**Carlotta Caciagli** (BA-MA Philosophy, University of Pisa, Italy; PhD Political Science, Scuola Normale Superiore of Pisa, Italy) is currently Junior Researcher at the Department of Architecture and Urban Studies (Dastu) of Polytechnic of Milan (Italy). She previously held research fellowships in urban sociology, political science, and political participation at the Scuola Normale, Polytechnic of Milan, and Luiss in Rome. Her PhD dissertation (2018) focused on housing movements and squatting practices in Rome, Italy. Her fields of study are urban transformations under late capitalism, housing, welfare policies, and socio-spatial inequalities in contemporary cities. In particular, she investigates how processes of class distinction foster urban dynamics and vice versa, concentrating on the analysis of residential and school segregation. Her publications have appeared in journals such as *Antipode*, *Critical Sociology*, *Voluntas*, and *Partecipazione e Conflitto*. She is author of two books: *Housing Movements in Rome. Resistance and Class* (Palgrave, 2022), and *Movimenti Urbani* (Mondadori, 2021).

**Clarissa Cordeiro de Campos** (BA Architecture and Urban Design, Universidade Federal de Minas Gerais (UFMG), Brazil; MA Architecture and Urban Design, Universidade de São Paulo, Brazil; PhD Architecture and Urban Design, UFMG, Brazil) is Adjunct Professor of Architecture and Urban Design at Universidade Federal de Minas Gerais (Brazil). Previously, she conducted part of her PhD studies, and later worked as a visiting post-doctoral researcher at the Institute of Housing and Urban Research, Uppsala University (Sweden). She also held teaching positions at Pontifícia Universidade Católica de Minas Gerais and Universidade Federal de São João del-Rei (Brazil), and was employed as an architect at different public administration offices in the city of Belo Horizonte, Brazil. Her PhD dissertation (2020) discussed urban squatting movements in the Metropolitan Region of Belo Horizonte (RMBH), Brazil, the city of Madrid, Spain, and six municipalities of the Basque Country, within Spanish territorial limits. She currently studies propositional and transdisciplinary methods of urban research that can contribute to the design of practical responses to complex problems in large urban centers. Her main focus is the RMBH, Brazil. Her publications have appeared in journals such as *Territorios*, *Revista V!rus*, *International Journal of Housing Policy*, and *Housing Theory & Society*. She is co-editor of *Não são só quatro paredes e um teto: uma década de lutas nas ocupações urbanas da Região Metropolitana de Belo Horizonte* [Not Just Four Walls and A Roof: A Decade of Struggles in the Urban Occupations of the Metropolitan Region of Belo Horizonte] (Cosmópolis, 2020). Most of her publications are available at: https://ufsj.academia.edu/ClarissaCampos.

**Özlem Çelik** (BA Urban and Regional Planning, Mimar Sinan Fine Arts University, Turkey; MA Sociology, Middle East Technical University, Turkey; PhD Urban Studies and Planning, University of Sheffield, UK) is Collegium Fellow at Turku Institute for Advanced Studies (TIAS) and the Department of Sociology, University of Turku (Finland). Previously, she held research and teaching positions in Political Science, Human Geography, Sustainability

Science, International Relations, and Global Development Studies in different universities in Turkey, Sweden, and Finland. She was also a visiting scholar in the University of Sheffield. Her PhD dissertation (2013) studied the role of the state and the power of resistance in urban regeneration projects in three working-class neighbourhoods in Istanbul, Turkey. She currently studies financialisation of housing and local governments from political economy and political ecology perspectives. In particular, she investigates financialisation of housing, housing movements, the urban commons, the local state, and green financialisation in Turkey and Sweden. Her publications have appeared in journals such as *Housing Studies*, *Antipode*, and *Journal of Urban Affairs*. Most of her publications are freely available at: https://researchportal.helsinki.fi/en/persons/%C3%B6zlem-celik/publications/.

**Éric Charmes** (BA-MA in engineering, Ecole Centrale de Paris, France; PhD in urban planning, Ecole Nationale des Ponts et Chaussées, France) is a research director at ENTPE (Vaulx-en-Velin) where he works with the Laboratory of Interdisciplinary Research on City, Space and Society (RIVES, University of Lyon, UMR CNRS 5600). Previously, he held a teaching and research position at Institut Français d'Urbanisme (University Paris 8). His PhD dissertation (2000) was about the transformation of suburban residential streets in Bangkok. Since then, he has undertaken research in urban studies, urbanism, and planning, with focuses on various issues, including social mix, gated communities, periurbanisation, and sprawl. His publications have appeared in various journals, including: *Urban Studies*, *International Journal of Urban and Regional Research*, *Journal of Urban Design*, *La vie des idées*, and *Fonciers en débat*. He has published several books, including *Métropoles et éloignement résidentiel* (Autrement, 2021); *La Revanche des villages* (Seuil, 2019); *Quitter Paris?* (with Stéphanie Vermeersch, Lydie Launay, and Marie-Hélène Bacqué, Créaphis, 2019); *Mixité sociale et après?* (with Marie-Hélène Bacqué, Presses universitaires de France, 2011); *The Middle Classes and the City. A Study of Paris and London* (with Marie-Hélène Bacqué, Gary Bridge et al., Palgrave, 2015); and *La Ville émiettée. Essai sur la clubbisation de la vie urbaine* (Presses Universitaires de France, 2011). Webpage: https://umr5600.cnrs.fr/fr/lequipe/name/eric-charmes/.

**Myrto Dagkouli-Kyriakoglou** (BA Management Science and Technology, Athens University of Economic and Business, Greece; MAs Social Environment and Development, and Urban and Regional Planning, National Technical University of Athens, Greece; PhD Urban Studies, GSSI, Italy) is an inter-departmental postdoc researcher between Gender Studies (Tema G) and Visualisation Studies (MIT) at Linköping University (Sweden). Previously, she was a postdoc researcher in the Institute for Urban Research at Malmö University (Sweden) and held teaching assignments at Malmö and Lund Universities. She was also a research assistant appointed by Leeds University School of Geography, Durham University's Department of Geography, and ICS-ULisboa in projects about housing, displacement, urban struggles, and austerity. Her PhD dissertation (2019) critically explored the dimensions of gender, sexual orientation, and ethnic background and the impact of austerity on the housing strategies of young people in the aftermath of the financial crisis in Athens, Greece, during 2017–8. Her research centers around housing and welfare with a special focus on the dimensions of gender and culture and the impact of multiple crises in the context of Southern Europe and Nordic countries. Currently, she is also working on her interdisciplinary project bridging data visualisation with critical geography and cartography with a focus on politics, cultural patterns, and gendered imaginaries. Her publications have appeared in journals such as *Housing Studies, Social & Cultural Geography, European Journal of Women's Studies, Critical Housing Analysis*, etc.

**Ibán Díaz-Parra** (BA and MA degree in Geography, University of Seville, Spain, and Social and Cultural Anthropology, National University of Distance Education, Spain; PhD in Geography, University of Seville, Spain) is Associate Professor in the Department of Human Geography at the University of Seville (Spain). His 2011 PhD dissertation studied gentrification in the historic centre of Seville. He has conducted extensive post-doctoral research at the National Autonomous University of Mexico and the University of Buenos Aires (Argentina). In 2018 he was one of the promoters of the Ibero-American Research Network on Urban Policies, Movements and Conflicts, of which he was the coordinator until 2021. His lines of research are focused on the area of urban studies, dealing with different socio-spatial processes, such as socio-spatial segregation, gentrification, and touristification, and their relationship with public policies and protest movements. His most recent book is *Vender una ciudad. Gentrificación y turistificación en los centros históricos* (University of Seville, 2023).

**Mariana Fix** (Professional degree in Architecture and Urbanism, University of São Paulo (USP), Brazil; MA in Sociology, USP; PhD in Economics, University of Campinas (Unicamp), Brazil; postgraduate diploma in Economics, USP) is Professor at the Architecture and Urbanism School, USP. Previously, she was Professor at the Economics Institute, Unicamp; Fellow at the Israel Institute for Advanced Studies (2019–20); Visiting Scholar at CUNY (New York, USA, 2012–13) with an Urban Studies Foundation Fellowship; and Lecturer at the Wohnungsfrage Academy/The Housing System, WKW, Berlin (2015). Her PhD dissertation (2011) 'Financialization and recent transformations of the real estate circuit' was awarded Best PhD Dissertation by Coordination for Higher Education Staff Development (CAPES). Her MA dissertation (2003) 'São Paulo global city: Financial foundations of a Miragem' was awarded Best Master Thesis by ANPUR. Her current studies are on real estate, land rent, finance, and financialisation; public–private partnerships; the housing question; urban struggles, and the right to the city. Her publications have appeared in journals such as *Urban Studies, Estudos Avançados* (USP), and *Revista de Economia Política* (REP). She is author of the books *Parceiros da exclusão* (Boitempo 2001) and *São Paulo Cidade Global* (Boitempo 2007). Additional information: http://lattes.cnpq.br/2947005633726248.

**Javier Gil** (BA Political Science, University Complutense of Madrid, Spain; MA Political Science, National University of Distance Education (UNED), Spain; PhD Sociology, UNED, Spain) is Post-doctoral Researcher in Sociology at the Faculty of Political Science and Sociology at UNED (Spain). Previously, he was researcher at the Institute for Housing and Urban Research (IBF), Uppsala University (Sweden). His research focuses on housing financialisation, short-term rentals, urban politics, housing movements, and platform capitalism. His publications have appeared in journals such as *Housing Studies*; *International Journal of Housing Policy*; *Cities*; *Housing, Theory and Society*; *Current Issues in Tourism*; etc.

**Sophie Gonick** (AB, Harvard University, United States; MCP and PhD, University of California, Berkeley, United States) is Associate Professor of Metropolitan Studies in the Department of Social & Cultural Analysis, New York University (NYU) (United States). Previously, she was a post-doc at the Center for European and Mediterranean Studies, also at NYU. Her dissertation (2015) was an ethnographic and historical analysis of the intersection of homeownership, immigration, and social movements in Madrid, Spain. She continues to research questions of housing and immigration, in addition to property relations, urban politics, and anti-racist and feminist grassroots mobilisations. Her work has appeared in *Antipode*; the *International Journal of Urban and Regional Research*; *International Labour and Working Class History*; *Society and Space*; and *Territory, Politics, Governance*, among other journals. Public scholarship has appeared in *Jackson Rising Redux* (PM Press, 2023), and Public Books, where she is also the urban editor. She is the author of *Dispossession and Dissent: Immigrants and the Struggle for Housing in Madrid* (Stanford University Press, 2021).

**Margherita Grazioli** (BA in Political Sciences, University of Milan, Italy; MA in Political Studies and International Relations, University of Bologna, Italy; PhD degree at the School of Business, University of Leicester, UK) is a postdoctoral research fellow in Economic Geography in the Social Sciences Area of the Gran Sasso Science Institute (L'Aquila, Italy). Previously, she was a graduate teaching assistant at the School of Business of the University of Leicester (UK). Her dissertation (2018) was entitled 'The "right to the city" in the post-welfare metropolis. Community building, autonomous infrastructures and urban commons in Rome's self-organised housing squats'. She currently studies geographies and infrastructures of habitability in urban and non-urban peripheral areas in the Abruzzo region; grassroots housing practices and squatting in Rome; and multilevel housing policies and their responsiveness to conflict-driven, grassroots social innovation. Her publications have appeared in journals such as *City*, *Radical Housing Journal*, and *Citizenship Studies*. She is the author of the book *Housing, Urban Commons and the Right to the City in Post-Crisis Rome Metropoliz. The Squatted Città Meticcia*, (Palgrave Macmillan, 2021). Most of her publications can be freely accessed at: https://gssi.academia.edu/MargheritaGrazioli.

**Andrej Holm** (Diploma and PhD in Social Science, Humboldt University Berlin, Germany) is Senior Researcher at Humboldt University Berlin (Germany). Previously, he held teaching and research positions in different universities in Germany and Austria. His PhD dissertation (2004) studied the power relations in urban renewal areas in East Berlin. He currently studies in the field of housing, housing policies, and social urban movements. His publications have appeared in journals such as *International Journal for Urban and Regional Research*, *CITY*, *Social Justice*, *Urbanisicatre*, *sub/urban*, *Espace et Société*, *Arch+*, etc. He is author of *Objekt der Rendite. Zur Wohnungsfrage und was Engels noch nicht wissen konnte.* (Dietz Berlin, 2021) and co-editor of *The Berlin Reader. A Compendium on Urban Change and Activism* (transcript, 2013). Additional information: https://www.sowi.hu-berlin.de/de/lehrbereiche/stadtsoz/mitarbeiterinnen/copy_of_a-z/holm and https://gentrificationblog.wordpress.com/.

**Mika Hyötyläinen** (BA Sociology and Cultural Studies, University of Sussex, UK; MA Social Sciences and PhD Public Policy and Urban Studies, University of Helsinki, Finland) is Postdoctoral Fellow at the Institute for Housing and Urban Research (IBF), Uppsala University (Sweden). He has worked as a postdoctoral researcher at the University of Helsinki and was a visiting researcher at the Federal University of Minas Gerais, Belo Horizonte, Brazil. His doctoral dissertation (2019) explored changes in Finnish land and housing policies and how they affect urban inequalities. He develops this work in his monograph *Urban Inequality in Finland: Land, Housing and the Nordic Welfare State* (2024, Edinburgh University Press). He is also the editor of a collection of works on the political economy of land (2022) published by Routledge and his articles on topics like housing policy, cooperative housing and public real estate policy have featured in journals such as *Acme*, *International Journal of Housing Policy* and *Geoforum*. His current and future research is focused on comparing land value capture policies across Nordic capital cities and local state rentierism in the context of a transforming welfare state.

**Defne Kadıoğlu** (BA Social Sciences, Heinrich-Heine University Dusseldorf, Germany; MA Human Rights, University of Essex, UK; PhD Political Science and International Relations, Boğaziçi University, Turkey) is a researcher at the Institute for Urban Research at Malmö University (Sweden). Previously, she has been a postdoctoral researcher at the same institute, a research fellow at Istanbul Policy Center (Turkey), and a visiting doctoral researcher at the Berlin Graduate School of Social Sciences at Humboldt University (Germany). She has also held teaching positions at various universities in Turkey. Her PhD dissertation (2015) studied the nexus between migration, racism, and gentrification in Berlin. She currently studies processes of financialisation in the rental housing sector, as well as the financialisation of urban and social policy in Germany and Sweden. Her publications have appeared in journals such as *Housing Studies*, *Ethnicities* and the *Journal of Race, Ethnicity & the City*. Most of her publications are open access and can be found at www.iuresearch.se.

**Samuel Kiriro**, a devoted social worker and social justice advocate, has dedicated his life to uplifting marginalised communities in Mathare, Nairobi. As the founder of Ghetto Foundation, he has pioneered community-led research and action to address the challenges faced by residents of informal settlements in Nairobi, thus fostering positive change in the lives of countless individuals over three decades now. Born and raised in Mathare, Samuel experienced first-hand the hardships and inequality prevalent in his community. Driven by a deep sense of empathy, he pursued a Social Work diploma at a local college in 2012, equipping himself with the knowledge and tools needed to co-found the social justice movement. Samuel established Ghetto Foundation in 2013 to work with marginalised youth in community-led education, urban planning, and social justice work against police violence. Under Samuel's leadership, Ghetto Foundation's programs have provided educational scholarships, vocational training, and mentorship opportunities to marginalised youth. He co-founded the social justice movement against police violence in 2018 and he also started the Mathare Special Planning Research Collective to pursue people-driven urban planning in Nairobi and beyond. More about his work is available at: www.ghettofoundation.org and https://www.sjc.community/.

**Sebastian Kohl** (MA Economics & Sociology, University of Cologne, Germany; PhD Sociology, Sciences Po, Paris, France) is currently Professor of Sociology at Berlin's Free University (JFK Institute). Previously, he worked as a senior researcher at Cologne's Max Planck Institute for the Study of Societies. He was a Kennedy Fellow at the Center for European Studies at Harvard (USA) and worked at the Sociology Department and the Institute for Housing and Urban Research (IBF) in Uppsala University (Sweden). His PhD dissertation (2014) studied historical long-run differences in countries' homeownership rates. His current research focus is on the political economy of housing and the insurance sector, both in historical-comparative perspective. His research appeared in journals such as *Housing Studies*, *Urban Studies*, *Review of International Political Economy* and *Socio-Economic Review*. His book *Homeownership, Renting, and Society* appeared with Routledge in 2017. More information at: www.sebastiankohl.com.

**Jere Kuzmanić** (BA Architecture, Landscape Design and Urban Planning, University of Zagreb, Croatia; MSc Urbanism, Delft Technical University, the Netherlands; PhD candidate, Universitat Politècnica de Catalunya, Spain) is Department Member at Departament d'Urbanisme, Territori i Paisatge (DUTP), Barcelona. Previously, he held a teaching position at the Faculty of Civil Engineering, Architecture and Geodesy in Split, Croatia. His PhD dissertation (started 2021) reconstructs the historical continuity of the anarchist roots of the urban planning movement. He currently studies radical histories of urban planning culture(s) with a broader interest in social and environmental justice, direct action and cooperation in urbanism, and urban degrowth. His publications have appeared in journals and books, such as a chapter in *European Planning History in the 20th Century: A Continent of Urban Planning* (Routledge, 2023). Most of his publications are freely available at: https://upc.academia.edu/JereKuzmanic.

**Valesca Lima** (PhD, University College Dublin, Ireland) is Assistant Professor in Politics at Dublin City University. Previously, she held a research fellow position at Maynooth University (Maynooth, Ireland) and postdoctoral positions at University College Dublin. She was also a visiting scholar at the University of Lisbon, Hokkaido University, and the Scuola Normale Superiore in Florence. She currently studies social movements, housing policy, citizen engagement, and political participation, paying special attention to the impact of social mobilisation on policymaking, changes in housing policy, participatory democracy, and the inclusion of vulnerable groups in the political arena. Her research interests involve locations in both Latin America and Europe, such as Ireland, Portugal, Brazil, and Chile. Her publications have appeared in journals such as *Housing Studies*, *International Journal of Housing Policy*, *Social Movement Studies*, *Urban Studies*, *Third World Quarterly*, *Comparative European Politics*, and *Latin American Politics and Society*. She is the author of *Participatory Citizenship and Crisis in Contemporary Brazil* (Palgrave, 2020) and co-editor of *The Consequences of Brazilian Social Movements in Historical Perspective* (Routledge, 2023). She is also editor of the *International Review of Public Policy* (IRPP), the open-access journal of the International Public Policy Association (IPPA); co-director for Women in Research Ireland, a registered charity working for better representation of women and under-represented groups in academia; and co-convenor of the Political Studies Association of Ireland's Participatory and Deliberative Democracy Specialist Group. Most of her research is available with open access on ResearchGate.

**Miguel A. Martínez** (BA-MA Sociology and Political Science, University Complutense of Madrid, Spain; PhD Political Science, University of Santiago de Compostela, Spain) is Professor of Housing and Urban Sociology at the Institute for Housing and Urban Research (IBF), Uppsala University (Sweden). Previously, he held teaching positions in sociology, political science, and urban studies in different universities in Spain, Portugal, and Hong Kong. He was also a visiting scholar in universities in Colombia, China, Portugal, the United States, Bulgaria and the Netherlands and has conducted empirical fieldwork in cities such as Porto, Vigo, Madrid, Hong Kong, Medellín, Chicago, Beijing, Berlin, Amsterdam, Buenos Aires, and Belo Horizonte. His PhD dissertation (2000) studied cases and scales of citizen participation in urban matters. He currently studies social movements and urban phenomena from a sociological perspective. In particular, he investigates housing activism in Spain, Europe, and Latin America. Other topics covered by his research include squatting, urban politics, housing policies, segregation, migration, sustainability, labour, social structures, and activist research. His publications have appeared in journals such as *Sociology*, *Housing Studies*, *Antipode*, *Urban Studies*, *International Journal of Urban and Regional Research*, *International Journal* of *Housing Policy*, *Social Movement Studies*, *Interface*, *Partecipazione e Conflitto*, *Revista Española de Investigaciones Sociológicas*, etc. He is the author of *Squatters in the Capitalist City* (Routledge, 2020), editor of *The Urban Politics of Squatters' Movements* (Palgrave, 2018), and co-editor of *Contested Cities and Urban Activism* (Palgrave, 2019). Most of his publications are freely available at: www.miguelangelmartinez.net.

**Miguel Montalva Barba** (Dual BA Sociology and Music, California State University, Los Angeles, United States; MA Sociology, California State University, Los Angeles, United States; PhD Sociology, Northeastern University, Boston, United States) is Assistant Professor at the University of Massachusetts Boston (Boston, USA). Previously, he held an assistant professorship in Sociology and the Latinx Student Success Faculty Fellowship at the Center of Justice and Liberation in Salem State University (Salem, USA). His PhD dissertation (2019) studied White resident narratives of gentrification in Jamaica Plain, Massachusetts. He currently studies the racialised narratives that White residents utilise to make sense of racialised extractive practices in Boston. His work aims to infuse the study of urban sociology and the sociology of racism and race. His publications have appeared in journals such as *Critical Sociology* and *Urban Studies*. He is the author of *White Supremacy and Racism in Progressive America: Race, Place, and Space* (Bristol University Press, forthcoming).

**Do Young Oh** (BSc Architectural Engineering, Yonsei University, South Korea; MSc International Planning, University College London, UK; PhD Regional and Urban Planning, London School of Economics and Political Science, UK) is Assistant Professor at Seoul National University, South Korea. Previously, he held research and teaching positions at Pusan National University (South Korea), Lingnan University in Hong Kong and the London School of Economics and Political Science in the UK, where he finished his PhD in 2018 with a thesis investigating the evolving university–city relationship through a comparative analysis of East Asian urbanisation processes. His research interests focus on comparative urbanism and postcolonial urbanism in East Asia. His publications have appeared in journals such as *Geoforum*, *Cities*, and *Journal of Urban History*. He is co-editor of *COVID-19 in Southeast Asia: Insights for a Post-pandemic World* (LSE Press, 2022).

**Sara Ortiz Escalante** (BA Sociology, Universitat Autònoma de Barcelona, Spain; MA Urban Planning, University of Illinois at Urbana-Champaign, USA; PhD Planning, University of British Columbia, Canada) is a member of Col·lectiu Punt 6, a cooperative of sociologists, planners, and architects applying an intersectional feminist perspective in urban planning. Based in Barcelona, Col·lectiu Punt 6 has more than 17 years of experience working nationally and internationally. It develops urban planning and architecture projects, participatory processes, capacity building, teaching, and research. Previously, she has worked on addressing gender-based violence and gender transformation in El Salvador, Mexico, and the USA. Her PhD dissertation was titled 'Planning the everyday/everynight: A feminist participatory action research with women nightshift workers'. She has also published multiple materials and guides to apply a feminist perspective in different aspects of design and planning. She is co-author of *Urbanismo Feminista. Por una Transformación Radical de los Espacios de Vida* (Virus, 2019).

**Dominika V. Polanska** (BA and MA Sociology, Södertörn University, Sweden; PhD Sociology, Stockholm University, Sweden) works as Senior Lecturer in Social Work and is Associate Professor in Sociology at the School of Social Sciences at Södertörn University

(Sweden). Previously, she held the position of Research Fellow at the Institute for Housing and Urban Research (IBF) at Uppsala University (Sweden) and at the Sociology Department at the University of Gothenburg (Sweden). Her PhD dissertation (2011) studied the emergence and popularity of gated communities in Poland. She currently studies urban social movements, urban transformation, housing policy, and housing activism in Sweden and Central and Eastern Europe. Her publications have appeared in journals such as *City*, *Housing Studies*, *Interface*, *International Journal of Sociology and Social Policy*, *Journal of Urban Affairs*, *Partecipazione e Conflitto*, and *Radical Housing Journal*. She is the author of *Contentious Politics and the Welfare State: Squatting in Sweden* (Routledge, 2019). Most of her publications are freely available at www.dominikavpolanska.se.

**Beltrán Roca** (BA and PhD Social Anthropology, University of Seville, Spain) is Professor of Sociology at the University of Cádiz (Spain). Previously, he held teaching and postdoctoral positions in sociology and social anthropology in the University of Seville and the University Pablo de Olavide (Spain). He was also a visiting scholar at City University of New York (USA), Yale University (USA), the London School of Economics (UK), and CONICET (Argentina). He leads the research group Transformations and Conflicts in Contemporary Societies (SEJ-657) at the University of Cádiz. His research interests are trade unions, social movements, and migrant workers, employing a socio-spatial perspective. He has conducted research on labour conflicts among shipyard workers, metro workers, Spanish migrants in Berlin, and worker centres in New York. He is currently Principal Investigator of a research project on the spatiality of trade union action in the logistics industry. His publications have appeared in journals such as *Environment & Planning A*, *Antipode*, *Transfer*, *Employee Relations*, *Journal of Industrial Relations*, *Labor History*, *Critical Sociology*, *Revista Española de Investigaciones Sociológicas*, etc. He is the co-author, with Ibán Díaz-Parra, of *El espacio en la teoría social* (Tirant, 2021) and co-editor of *Migrant Organising: Community Unionism, Solidarity and Bricolage* (Brill, 2021) and *Challenging Austerity: Radical Left and Social Movements in the South of Europe* (Routledge, 2017).

**Sonia Roitman** (BSc (Hons) Sociology, National University of Cuyo, Argentina; PhD Urban Planning, University College London, UK) is Associate Professor in Development Planning at the University of Queensland (Australia). She previously held research positions in London (Bartlett School of Planning, UCL), Berlin (Latin American Institute, Free University Berlin) and Mendoza, Argentina (National Scientific and Technical Research Council). Her PhD dissertation (2008) studied gated communities and segregation in Mendoza, Argentina. Her contributions to the field of development planning and urban sociology include influential research on urban inequalities and how these manifest in cities. Her research interests include housing and poverty alleviation policies; the role of grassroots organisations in urban planning; disaster planning and informal practices; and gated communities, segregation, and planning instruments in Global South cities. Her main research locations are Indonesia, Uganda, Argentina and Australia. She has served on the Board of the Research Committee of the Sociology of Urban and Regional Development, International Sociological Association (RC21 Committee) since 2014. Her publications have appeared in journals such as *Urban Studies*, *Housing Studies*, *Cities*, *Journal of Planning Education and Research*, and *Revista INVI*. Her most recent publication is *The Routledge Handbook of Urban Indonesia* (2023, Routledge) co-edited with D. Rukmana.

**Max Rousseau** (BA Geography and Political Science, University of Nancy and Sciences-Po Grenoble, France; MA Philosophy and Political Science, University of Hull, UK and University of Paris 1, France; PhD Political Science, University of Saint-Étienne, France) is a geographer and political scientist at the CIRAD (Montpellier, France). Previously he was a junior lecturer in political science at the University of Saint-Étienne. From 2014 to 2020 he was an assistant professor in sociology at the Rabat Institute of Urban Planning and Development (Morocco), where he conducted research projects (on the control of urban sprawl, on food governance, etc.) and acted as a technical assistant in urban planning for international organisations and various local authorities. His PhD dissertation (2011) studied the history of industrial cities in France and the UK. He currently studies the mutations of declining areas and extended urbanisation in both the Global North and the Global South. His publications have appeared in journals such as *International Journal of Urban and Regional Research*, *Urban Studies*, *Urban Geography*, *Geopolitics*, *Critical Sociology*, *Theory, Culture & Society*, *Environment and Planning E*, *Cities*, *International Planning Studies*, *DisP*, etc. He is the co-editor of *Déclin urbain* (with N. Cauchi-Duval and V. Béal, Croquant, 2021) and co-author of *Plus vite que le cœur d'un mortel* (with V. Béal, Grevis, 2021) and *Gentrifications. Views from Europe* (with M. Chabrol, A. Collet, M. Giroud, L. Launay, and H. Ter Minassian, Berghan, 2022). Many of his publications are freely available at https://cv.hal.science/max-rousseau?langChosen=fr.

**Bahar Sakızlıoğlu** (BA Business Administration and MA Sociology, Middle East Technical University, Turkey; PhD Human Geography, Utrecht University, the Netherlands) is Assistant Professor of Urban and Housing Studies at the Institute of Housing and Urban Development Studies, Erasmus University (the Netherlands). Previously, she had teaching and research positions in sociology and human geography at different universities in Turkey, the UK, and the Netherlands. Her PhD dissertation (2014) studied displacement experiences of low-income residents living in gentrifying neighbourhoods of Amsterdam and Istanbul. Her post-doctoral research (2019) focused on gendered gentrification and was financed by the H2020 Marie Curie Individual Research Fellowship. She currently studies social reproduction in relation to displacement, gentrification, and migration in the Netherlands and Turkey. Her publications have appeared in journals such as *Tijdschrift voor Economische en Sociale Geografie*, *Environment and Planning A: Economy and Space*, *City and Community*, and *International Journal of Urban and Regional Research*. Most of her publications are available at: https://eur.academia.edu/baharsakizlioglu.

**Jorge Sequera** (PhD Sociology, University Complutense of Madrid, Spain) is Lecturer at the National University of Distance Education (UNED), Spain, Director of the Critical Urban Studies Group (GECU), and Principal Investigator (PI) of the project 'ONDEMANDCITY: Platform capitalism, digital workers and techification of everyday life in the contemporary city' (PID2021-122482OB-I00; 2022-2025) funded by the Spanish Ministry of Science and Innovation. He has also been PI of the projects 'LIKEALOCAL: Socio-spatial effects of AIRBNB. Tourism and transformation in 4 cities in Spain' (RTI2018-093479-A-I00; 2019-2021), funded by the Ministry of Spanish Science, Innovation and Universities; 'Tourism and urban transformations in contemporary Lisbon' (FCT Portugal; 2017-2018); and 'Gentrification, new lifestyles and socio-spatial marginalisation in the ludic city. A comparative geographical perspective: Madrid and Lisbon' (UAM-UNL; 2016). His lines of research address key phenomena of post-Fordist society and the metropolis, such as consumption, lifestyles, new middle classes, residential segregation, social exclusion, social control, gentrification, touristification, platform urbanism, and digital capitalism.

**Ivana Socoloff** (BA Sociology, University of Buenos Aires, Argentina; MA 'Territory, Space and Society', École des Haute Études en Science Sociales, France; PhD Social Sciences, University of Buenos Aires, Argentina) is Tenured Researcher for Argentina's National Research Council (CONICET) based at the Institute of Latin American Studies (IEALC-UBA). Previously, she held teaching positions in urban sociology, geography, and urban studies in different universities of Argentina, Brazil, and France. She was also a visiting scholar in universities of Brazil, France, Belgium, and Sweden. Her PhD dissertation (2013) studied the history and role of a large real estate developer in Argentina and Latin America. She currently studies the way in which financialisation is transforming the role of different actors in the spatial production of cities in Argentina and Latin America, including the political and economic organisation of large developers and business groups. Her publications have appeared in journals such as *Housing Policy Debate*, *INVI*, *Scripta Nova*, *Territorios*, *Ciudades*, etc. She is currently co-editing volumes on real estate and financialisation to be published by Teseo and Edward Elgar Publishing. Most of her publications are freely available at: https://conicet-ar.academia.edu/IvanaSocoloff.

**Naomi van Stapele** (BA-MA with Honours Non-Western History of Society, Erasmus University Rotterdam, the Netherlands; PhD with Honours Anthropology, University of Amsterdam, the Netherlands) is Associate Professor in Inclusive Education at the Centre for Expertise Global and Inclusive Learning at The Hague University of Applied Sciences (THUAS). Previously, they held Assistant Professor positions in Anthropology and Development and in Urban Governance and Development at Radboud University and the International Institute of Social Science (the Netherlands). Their PhD thesis (2015) studied how notions of gender, work, and criminality interact in the formation of gangs in Nairobi. They were a visiting scholar in Kenya and in Ethiopia and conducted numerous ethnographic research projects for over 20 years in Kenya, Ethiopia, and the Netherlands. In particular, their research focus is on criminalisation, marginalisation, gangs, gender, (higher) education, urban activism, and social justice movements. Their publications have appeared in journals such as *Africa*; *Conflict, Security and Development*; *The European Journal of Development Research*; and *Environment and Planning D—Society and Space*. At present, they conduct research together with members of marginalised and criminalised groups as co-researchers in order to counteract dominant power relations and work towards transformative education and community organising. Their current research projects include working with undocumented students, young (queer) refugees, young sex workers, young delinquents, and many other groups that are racialised, classed, and in other ways othered, minoritised, and excluded in and from (higher) education in many different places in the world.

**Cristina Udelsmann Rodrigues** (BA Anthropology, Nova University, Portugal; MA African Studies, ISCTE-IUL University Institute of Lisbon, Portugal; PhD Interdisciplinary African Studies, ISCTE-IUL University Institute of Lisbon, Portugal) is Senior Researcher at the Nordic Africa Institute (Uppsala, Sweden). Previously, she held teaching positions in Urban Sociology, African Sociology, and Development and Globalisation in Portugal and research positions as Principal Investigator in several research projects. She has conducted research and fieldwork in urban settings in Angola, Mozambique, Guinea-Bissau, Cape Verde, Sao Tome, and Principe. Her PhD dissertation (2004) studied urban formal and informal work in Luanda and families' strategies. She currently studies urbanising temporary settlements in Angola, the DRC and Zambia (former refugee camps, slums, and mining boomtowns) at the intersection of residents' agency and state policies. Other topics covered by her research are urban–rural dynamics and migration, secondary cities, social stratification and segregation, climate change and sustainability, and mining towns. Her publications have appeared in journals such as the *International Journal of Urban and Regional Research*, *Journal of Southern African Studies*, *Africa Today*, *Journal of Modern African Studies*, *Journal of Contemporary African Studies*, *Urban Forum*, *Environmental Practice*, *African Studies Review*, *African Studies Quarterly*, *The Extractive Industries and Society*, *Social Dynamics*, *International Journal of Urban Sustainable Development*, and *City*. She is the co-editor of *Transformations of Rural Spaces in Mozambique* (Bloomsbury Publishing, 2022) and author and co-editor of other books published in Portuguese.

**Blanca Valdivia** (BA Sociology, University Complutense of Madrid, Spain; MA Urban Management and Valuation, Technical School of Catalonia, Spain; PhD Urban and Architectural Management and Valuation, Technical School of Catalonia, Spain) is a member of Col·lectiu Punt 6, a cooperative of sociologists, planners, and architects applying an intersectional feminist perspective in urban planning. Based in Barcelona, Col·lectiu Punt 6 has more than 17 years of experience working nationally and internationally. It has developed more than 400 projects in urban planning and architecture, participatory processes, capacity building, teaching, and research. Previously, she was a researcher at the Center for Land Policy and Valuation of the ETSAB in Barcelona, Spain. Her PhD dissertation (2021), 'The caring city: Quality of urban life from a feminist perspective', studied the relation between care, urban configuration, and quality of life from a feminist perspective. She currently studies the link between health, care, and environment from a feminist urban planning approach. Her publications have appeared in journals such as *Urban Planning and Development* and *Habitat y Sociedad*. She is co-author of *Urbanismo Feminista* (Virus, 2019) and multiple materials and guides to apply a feminist perspective in urban spaces. Most of her publications are freely available at www.punt6.org.

**Lorenzo Vidal** (BA Philosophy, Politics and Economics, University of Warwick, United Kingdom; MA International Economics and Development, Complutense University of Madrid, Spain; PhD Political Science, Public Policies and International Relations, Autonomous University of Barcelona, Catalonia) is a Marie Skłodowska-Curie Individual Fellow at the Institute for Housing and Urban Research (IBF), Uppsala University, Sweden. Previously, he held postdoctoral research positions at the Institute of Government and Public Policy in the Autonomous University of Barcelona and the CIDOB-Barcelona Centre for International Affairs. His PhD dissertation (2018) studied housing cooperativism and the housing question in Denmark and Uruguay. He currently studies urban political economy, with a focus on housing, property, and digital transformations. His publications have appeared in journals such as the *International Journal of Urban and Regional Research*, *Environment and Planning A*, *Housing, Theory and Society*, and the *International Journal of Housing Policy*.

**Peter Walters** (BA Economics and Political Science, University of New South Wales, Australia; MSc Social Psychology, London School of Economics, UK; PhD Sociology, University of Queensland, Australia) is Senior Lecturer and Sociology Program Convenor in the School of Social Science at the University of Queensland, Australia. His PhD dissertation (2008) examined the role of property developers in constructing community in new outer suburban residential estates. He is an expert in urban community in all its forms. His research encompasses the outer suburbs in Australia, the gentrifying inner city and informal communities in cities in the Global South including Bangladesh, Indonesia, Solomon Islands, and India. His publications have appeared in journals such as *Urban Studies*; *Housing, Theory and Society*; *Geoforum*; and *Space and Culture*.

**Ngai-Ming Yip** (BSocSc Social Work, University of Hong Kong, Hong Kong; PhD Social Policy, University of York, UK) is Professor of Housing and Urban Studies at the City University of Hong Kong. He currently studies the neighbourhood, spatial segregation, and activism of homeowners in Hong Kong and Mainland China, as well as urbanisation in Vietnam. His publications have appeared in journals such as *Urban Studies*, *British Journal of Sociology*, *Housing Studies*, *Geoforum*, *Journal of Urban Affairs*, etc. He is editor of *Neighbourhood Governance in Urban China* (Edward Elgar Publishing, 2014) and co-editor of *Contested Cities and Urban Activism* (Palgrave, 2019), *Young People and Housing: Transitions, Trajectories and Generational Fractures* (Routledge, 2014) and *Housing Markets and the Global Financial Crisis: The Uneven Impacts on Households* (Edward Elgar Publishing, 2012). He has been involved in policy and professional communities and served as a committee member of the Hong Kong Housing Authority (2014–23), member of the Task Force on Tenancy Control of Sub-divided Units in Hong Kong (2019–21), chairman of the Chartered Institute of Housing Asian Pacific Branch (2013, 2014), and Asia Editor of *Housing Studies* (2015–23).

**Ismael Yrigoy** (BA Geography, University of the Balearic Islands, Spain; MA Territorial and Population Studies, Autonomous University of Barcelona, Spain; PhD Geography, University of the Balearic Islands, Spain) is Ramón y Cajal Research Fellow at the University of Santiago de Compostela, Spain, and Research Fellow at Uppsala University. Previously he was employed as a distinguished researcher and as Juan de la Cierva postdoctoral researcher at the University of Santiago de Compostela and as a Wallanderstipendiat postdoctoral researcher at Uppsala University. He has also been a visiting scholar at the universities of Lund (Sweden) and Málaga (Spain). His PhD dissertation, defended in 2015, studied the origins of investments in the unfolding of tourism urbanisation in Majorca, Spain. He currently carries out research on the political economy of Swedish lifestyle migration in Spain and on asset managers' use of global and local regulations to invest in real estate markets, with an emphasis on Southern Europe. His publications have appeared in journals such as *Antipode*, *International Journal of Urban and Regional Research*, *Urban Studies*, *Geoforum*, *Environment and Planning A*, *Cities*, *Tourism Geographies*, and *Journal of Sustainable Tourism*, amongst others.

**Yunpeng Zhang** (BSc Management, Shanghai Normal University, China; MSc Urban Management and Development, Erasmus Universiteit Rotterdam, the Netherlands; PhD Geography, University of Edinburgh, UK) is Assistant Professor in Regional and Urban Planning at the School of Architecture, Planning and Environment Policy, University College Dublin (Ireland), and affiliated researcher at the Division of Geography and Tourism, KU Leuven (Belgium). Previously, he was a postdoctoral research fellow based at KU Leuven, funded by Fonds Wetenschappelijk Onderzoek – Vlaanderen (grant numbers: 12T2418N and 12T2421N). He was a visiting researcher at several universities in China and has a sustained interest in China's urban-centric transformations and resulting injustice. His PhD thesis (2014) investigated mega-urban projects and the destruction of people's homes, or 'domicide'. His current research involves two lines – one on Chinese investments in mega-urban projects outside China and the other on the platformisation–urbanisation nexus in China. Other topics covered by his research include displacements, land grabbing, gentrification, the everyday state, financialisation, and contentious politics. His work has been published in *International Journal of Urban and Regional Research, Antipode, Urban Geography*, and a few edited volumes on urban studies and geography.

# Acknowledgements

The commission of this *Handbook* came to me in difficult times in late 2020 with the Covid-19 pandemic still hitting hard, social isolation, and, in my case, a new appointment as Director of Research Studies in the Department of Sociology at Uppsala University (Sweden), in addition to the usual heavy workload of teaching, writing academic papers, organising academic meetings, supervising postgraduate students, and the like. So, after a few months of trying to identify and contact potential contributors to the *Handbook* among hundreds of scholars, I experienced severe stress and the first burnout of my life, as far as I remember. While slowing down with all my work, I was helped to get out from that unhealthy situation first of all by my partner Alba Folgado, to whom I am immensely grateful. I also enjoyed the warm support of some colleagues at both the Department of Sociology and the Institute for Housing and Urban Studies (IBF) in Uppsala.

The *Handbook* kept moving but not as fast as desired. As all the contributors know, the more than two-year span for the production of this *Handbook* is not uncommon, but in this case, it took longer due to my approach of requiring a thorough and perhaps too picky peer review of all the chapters. Hence, I thank all the authors not only for their rigorous research and writing here but also for their attentive reading and helpful comments given to the assigned texts. Most of the contributors were also responsive with the deadlines and guidelines, which made my life easier and allowed the volume to be finished within a reasonable period of time. Particularly, I would like to mention Mika Hyötyläinen for his effort in joining this project once it was already ongoing, reviewing my texts, reading the preliminary versions of the chapters, and leading the writing of the final conclusions and research agenda. I am equally grateful to other initial contributors who helped with the reviewing process, despite their withdrawal of their own chapters due to different reasons: Karen Coelho, Kathleen Dunn, and Lisa Kings. Likewise, my own chapter benefited from comments during an IBF seminar by my always helpful colleagues Mats Franzén, Susanne Urban, and Nils Hertting.

One of my old mentors who had given me intellectual advice many times in the past, Chris G. Pickvance, also offered his sharp comments on my initial framing of the *Handbook*, just a few months before he sadly passed away. Needless to say, I always appreciated very much his insights about urban sociology and social movements, so I just wish this *Handbook* can continue his legacy. Margit Mayer also kindly shared her feedback and support for this book project once I told her about it. I have always followed her work on urban and political affairs, which I hope has been at least partially manifested in the decisions regarding topics and perspectives I made here.

Over the last year (2022–23), I was lucky to enjoy a sabbatical leave granted by my home employer (IBF) that allowed me to conclude this *Handbook*. First, I stayed as a visiting researcher in the Centre for Advanced Studies Sofia (CAS) in Sofia (Bulgaria) for four months, with an in-residence fellowship. Next, I joined the Human Geography, Planning and International Development (GPIO) Department at the University of Amsterdam (UvA), the Netherlands, for eight months, thanks to a Riksbankens Jubileumsfond (RJ) Sabbatical Grant. In Sofia, I appreciated very much the interesting conversations with Dimiter Dimov, Nikola Venkov, and Rositsa Kratunkova. In Amsterdam, where I completed the last reviews of chapters of the *Handbook*, I was warmly welcomed and intellectually inspired by many colleagues, especially Justus Uitermark, Mieke Lopes Cardozo, Nanke Verloo, Rivke Jaffe, Dominic Teodorescu, Cody Hochstenbach, Wouter van Gent, Willem Boterman, Federico Savini, Carla Huisman, Ceylin Idel, and Richard Ronald.

Additionally, recent funded research projects allowed me to work with brilliant researchers and attend academic meetings where I could discuss urban matters with other outstanding scholars. The projects included: 'The intersectional and sustainable impacts of housing movements: The Spanish case' (FORMAS, the Swedish Program for Sustainable Spatial Planning, Ref. 2019-00349, which I led, but I am especially grateful to Javier Gil for all his contributions to this project, and also to other outstanding collaborators: Lorenzo Vidal, Ángela García-Bernardos, Luisa Rossini and Inés Gutiérrez-Cueli), 'Renovation and participation: Towards an ecologically, socially and economically sustainable Million Program?' (FORMAS, Ref. 2018-00191, led by Håkan Thörn), and 'Urban struggles for the right to the city and urban commons in Brazil and Europe' (STINT, the Swedish Foundation for International Cooperation, Ref. BR2018-8011, co-led with Rita Velloso and Dominika Polanska). Among the post-pandemic meetings were: the RC21 (Research Committee 21 of the International Sociological Association (ISA), whose large Board I joined a few years ago, which became a great and inspiring source for understanding the profession of urban sociology with a global perspective) in Athens (2022); the RN37 (Research Network 37 of the European Sociological Association (ESA)) in Berlin (2022); the Urban Sociological Summer School in Naples (2022); the Nordic Geographers Meeting (NGM) in Joensuu (Finland) (2022); the Spanish Federation of Sociology (FES) in Murcia (2022); the *Sociologidagarna* in Uppsala (2022); and the International Nertwork of Urban Research and Action (INURA), also an amazing synergy of critical urban scholars from whom I learned a lot, in Zurich (2023).

To be fair, I should be no less grateful to many other people and social conditions, such as public education systems and libraries, grassroots activists, new and second-hand bookshops, and the free scientific publications provided by Sci-Hub, Libgen, and open-access journals. Finally, I thank Daniel Mather, Emily Passmore, Natasha Rozenberg and others from Edward Elgar Publishing for their technical guidance and support along this much-harder-than-expected (but highly satisfactory at the end of the day) editorial process.

# Abbreviations

| | |
|---|---|
| AI | Artificial Intelligence |
| ANRU | Agence Nationale pour la Rénovation Urbaine [National Urban Renewal Agency, France] |
| BCPA | Budapest City Protection Association |
| BID | Business Improvement District |
| BL | Boligselskabernes Landsforening [Common Housing Federation, Denmark] |
| CEDU | Cámara Empresaria de Desarrolladores Urbanos [Entrepreneurial Chamber of Real Estate Developers, Argentina] |
| CENU | Centro Empresarial Nações Unidas [United Nations Entrepreneurial Centre, Brazil] |
| CEO | Chief Executive Officer |
| CEPAC | Certificado de Potencial Adicional de Construção [Certificate of Additional Building Rights, Brazil] |
| CESP | Companhia Energética de São Paulo [São Paulo Energy Company, Brazil] |
| CIAM | International Congress of Modern Architecture |
| COPOL | Coordinadora de Pobladores en Lucha [Coordination of Residents in Struggle, Chile] |
| CPTED | Crime Prevention Through Environmental Design |
| CRT | Critical Race Theory |
| CT | Cultural Turn |
| DCC | Dublin City Council |
| EU | European Union |
| FAUUSP | Faculdade de Arquitetura e Urbanismo da Universidade de São Paulo [Faculty of Architecture and Urban Planning, University of São Paulo, Brazil] |
| FDI | Foreign Direct Investment |
| FUCVAM | Federación Uruguaya de Cooperativas de Vivienda por Ayuda Mutua [Federation of Mutual-Aid Housing Cooperatives, Uruguay] |
| GCRR | Global Critical Race and Racism |
| GDP | Gross Domestic Product |
| GFC | Great/Global Financial Crisis |
| GIS | Geographical Information System |
| GPS | Global Positioning System |
| HEA | Human Ecology Approach |
| HIV | Human Immunodeficiency Virus |
| Hong Kong SAR | Hong Kong Special Administrative Region |
| HOPE VI | A program of the United States Department of Housing and Urban Development intended to revitalise public housing projects |
| IDB | Inter-American Development Bank |

| | |
|---|---|
| ILGA | International Lesbian, Gay, Bisexual, Trans and Intersex Association |
| IMF | International Monetary Fund |
| ISIS | Islamic State of Iraq and Syria |
| IT | Information Technologies |
| LBF | Landsbygefonden [National Building Fund, Denmark] |
| LEED | Leadership in Energy and Environmental Design |
| LGBTQI+ | Lesbian, Gay, Bisexual, Transexual, Queer, Intersexual, and Other Non-heterosexual and Non-normative Sex Orientations |
| MCA | Multiple Correspondence Analysis |
| MLB | Movimento de Luta nos Bairros, Vilas e Favelas [Movement of Struggles in Neighbourhoods, Villages, and Favelas, Brazil] |
| MPE | Marxist Political Economy |
| MST | Movimento dos Trabalhadores Rurais sem Terra [Landless Rural Workers' Movement, Brazil] |
| MTST | Movimento dos Trabalhadores Sem Teto [Roof-less Workers' Movement, Brazil] |
| NGO | Non-Governmental Organisation |
| NYSE | New York Stock Exchange |
| OUC | Operações Urbanas Consorciadas [Urban Operations Consortium, Brazil] |
| PAH | Plataforma de Afectados por las Hipotecas [Platform for People Affected by Mortgages, Spain] |
| PPP | Public–Private Partnership |
| REITs | Real Estate Investment Trusts |
| RFID | Radio-Frequency Identification |
| RMBH | Região Metropolitana de Belo Horizonte [Metropolitan Region of Belo Horizonte, Brazil] |
| SRA | Strategic Relational Approach |
| STRs | Short-Term Rentals |
| UNICEF | United Nations Children's Fund |
| WGS | World Global Systems |
| WSF | World Social Forum |
| WTC | World Trade Centre |
| WTO | World Trade Organisation |
| YUPPs | Young Urban Professional Parents |

# 1. Introduction to the *Research Handbook on Urban Sociology*

## Miguel A. Martínez

In this introductory chapter my aim is to answer these two questions: Why am I editing this *Handbook*? What are its main contributions and contents? I jointly address them in the following six sections.

## TRANSDISCIPLINARY URBAN SOCIAL SCIENCES

This *Handbook* responds, above all, to my interest in emphasising and revealing the contributions of sociology to urban scholarship. In so doing, one first needs to map which other disciplines are related to the study of urban phenomena and the implications of this plurality for urban sociology.

For some colleagues, 'urban sociology' is an outdated and fuzzy designation of a research sub-discipline within the broader fields of sociology and urban studies, respectively. Urban sociology is concerned with housing, public spaces, and social life in cities, to name a few of its usual research topics. Other academic disciplines, however, are equally interested in the investigation of topics like these. Urban studies have always been quite interdisciplinary, or better, 'transdisciplinary', as all urban disciplines can potentially nurture each other, not just sit side by side in the same train. Sociologists are only one of the groups of passengers, all helping to keep the train moving, together with, for example, geographers, anthropologists, economists, architects, urban planners and designers, historians, political scientists, social psychologists, social workers, educators, legal scholars, ecologists, philosophers, and artists. Journalists and writers such as Lewis Mumford and Jane Jacobs could also be named as salient figures in the history of urban theorisation.

To some extent, this is a healthy and win-win development. Multiple academic insights and traditions contribute to the production of knowledge around cities and urban phenomena. We all learn from each other, at least potentially, although there is always the risk of only achieving a 'mediocre compromise' (Lefebvre 2003: 54).

Transdisciplinary cooperation has been meaningful inasmuch as urban studies has been capable of amalgamating all that scholarship within the umbrella of social sciences as 'urban social sciences'. The situation changed once natural scientists also jumped in and broadened the scope of challenges. The old dream of bridging the domains of natural and social sciences (the positivist unity of all sciences, according to Auguste Comte) has recently been revived with the labels 'urban science' and 'the science of cities' (Batty 2013, Gleeson 2013, Parnell & Robinson 2017, West 2017). The rise of so called 'smart cities' and urbanism shaped by digital platforms or the environmental impacts of urban life, for example, have called in hardcore scientists such as engineers, mathematicians, biochemists, physicists, big data analysts, and health scholars. Pressing issues related to transport, energy consumption, climate warming, digital platforms, and pandemics certainly suggest that social scientists would need to cooperate with natural scientists, sooner or later. Otherwise, absurd fragmentation and mutual ignorance will keep sustaining disciplinary strongholds: 'economists advise on city growth strategies, sociologists on urban race and youth issues, and engineers on how to build bridges' (Parnell & Robinson 2017: 15).

This *Handbook* does not go that far. It remains within the transdisciplinary domain of urban social sciences. However, while an enlarged transdisciplinary cooperation is not necessarily a problem, the neutralisation or annihilation of the perspective provided by social sciences is. Often, the dominant epistemological paradigm in natural-experimental sciences imposes a set of assumptions that differ from those embraced by most social sciences. I would label the former as 'simplified positivism' when it consists of: exclusive quantitative measurement, claims of absolute objectivity, and the search for universal and mono-causal laws (Steinmetz 2005, Wyly 2011). My contention, then, is that if urban studies become subsumed into a broader 'urban science', they may likely be forced to comply with the rule of simplified positivism.

Social sciences produce scientific knowledge of a particular kind. On the one hand, their theories, methods, and findings follow general principles shared by all sciences (e.g. accuracy, validity, reliability, integrity, rigour, and accountability), despite these and related criteria being subject to endless epistemological disputes. On the other hand, social scientists have to observe and interpret the specific complexity and the unique features of social phenomena (Sayer 2000, Tilly 2008, Wilden 1987). Hence, theoretical consistency, appropriate choice of research methods, and sound interpretation of the empirical evidence—three additional common bases for all sciences—need to be informed by the particular structures and powers of social life, including the reflexive effects produced by the production and circulation of scientific knowledge. In a nutshell: animals, plants, minerals, and atoms do not react to the researchers' goals and to the publication of scientific findings, but human beings do. These particularities should not be downplayed when compared to the prevailing epistemological model (and modelling trends) within natural sciences—simplified and akin modalities of positivism—even in the rare cases of cooperation between social and natural sciences.

Given that sociology is one of the key disciplines in the historical foundation of social sciences, a sociological angle to urban phenomena also makes a difference within urban studies. Positivism has enticed some sociologists over time, more in their practice than explicitly justifying it (Turner 1985). Most sociologists, however, place themselves at different points of the epistemological and theoretical spectrum, usually away from the simplified version of positivism: logical positivists, post-positivists, and critical realists, increasingly farther; constructivists, relativists, and postmodernists, on the opposite pole. I will return to these differences later. For now, it is worth remembering that not all academic disciplines in urban studies adhere to the principles of producing scientific knowledge and systematic theories as sociology does. This would be the case for the arts, journalism, philosophy, and legal studies, except when their practitioners borrow and strictly follow scientific procedures. Furthermore, regardless of how welcome transdisciplinary partnerships are, urban sociologists will at least always ask a crucial question that may be overlooked by other urban scholars: what is the 'social' dimension of urban phenomena?

As will be noted, the contributors of this book are not only sociologists by training, education, or professional standing. My commission of the chapters insisted particularly in stressing the social aspects of the examined topics, independently of the disciplinary background of each contributor. I anticipated a lack of consensus regarding the definition of the 'social' and what a sociological perspective means. To soothe the confusion, I wrote a preliminary draft of my own views and circulated it around for the contributors' perusal and as a general framing of the *Handbook*, without demanding any compulsory adherence to it. Previously, I had asked for initial advice and comments from Margit Mayer and Chris Pickvance, who, together with my doctoral supervisor Tomás R. Villasante, were my main mentors and scholarly beacons in urban studies.

My conviction is that urban sociology does not represent a minor, insignificant, or too narrow discipline in urban studies, rather the opposite. It is well-located in the origins of contemporary reflections on cities (Madoo & Niebrugge-Brantley 2002) and it has also evolved in many fruitful directions throughout the decades, usually in close dialogue and with regular liaisons with various germane disciplines (Chen et al. 2013, Gottdiener et al. 2019, Harding & Blokland 2014). I also think that the use of the term 'social'—or 'sociological' to this effect—in urban studies demands rigorous concepts and theories. Sociology has traditionally provided such a repertoire, despite the manifold and competing strands of approaches within the discipline (Bourdieu et al. 1991, Patel 2010, Turner 2006). Furthermore, vagueness, abuse, and inconsistency when referring to the 'social' dimensions of urban phenomena undermine the credibility of urban studies as a social science. Consequently, some remedy is needed. Sociological schools of thought and research, without claiming exclusive rights over the subject, may well serve the purpose.

An obvious implication of this approach is that research in urban sociology entails neither threat to nor enmity with other urban disciplines. Rather the contrary: all contributions to clarify, scrutinise, and explain the 'social' in its relation with the 'urban' are welcome regardless of their home discipline or their preferred methods (Verloo & Bertolini 2020). Hence, the selection of contributors to this book intends to underscore how researchers adopt a sociological angle to investigate urban phenomena, irrespective of their academic backgrounds, trajectories, and institutional affiliations. My goal was thus to unearth different contributions to contemporary sociology that are engaged with urban issues in original and virtuous ways. Nevertheless, urban studies are as plural as all the social sciences, so the pretension of leading them with one scientific domain at the expenses of the others seems to me arrogant and likely doomed to fail (Lefebvre 2003: 45–76) (see Figure 1.1 as a metaphor of this idea). Whether we like it or not, we are sitting on the same train. Fruitful conversations and a good party on board—while working to make the train move—is a highly beneficial way of looking at this coexistence.

## THE SOCIAL AND THE URBAN

In addition to the contents of my own chapter, I here introduce a brief note on the definitions of the social and the urban and their mutual relations.

I first assume that a sociological perspective of urban phenomena implies, above all, a fundamental knowledge of the existing social structures and social processes. Different social groups and categories, their practices and discourses, their mutual and conflictual relations, their material living conditions, and the emergent properties of their aggregations over time are key concerns for all sociologists. Urban sociologists pay specific attention to the interplay of all these social phenomena with particular physical spaces, especially those that we designate

*Source:* Miguel A. Martínez.

*Figure 1.1    View of Amsterdam from the Eye Film Museum (2023)*

as 'urban' because they are related to the configuration and dynamics of cities. People live in cities but also migrate to and from cities, commute daily to and from cities, freely move or are forcibly displaced within cities, produce them materially and symbolically, reproduce urban life and their own means of subsistence through urban facilities, and change cities according to their available resources, social needs, cultural influences and aspirations, economic interests, and political agendas. In Bourdieu's terms, the aim of urban sociology would be to investigate the relations between the 'symbolic space' (mental categories), the 'social space' (the positions of social groups according to economic, cultural, social, symbolic, and political capitals), and 'physical space' (the material built environment), but also 'the rules, internal history, and specific struggles' of each space (Wacquant 2023: 6–10, 53).

The sociological perspective that I advocate places the understanding of the social production of physical space before the understanding of the constraints exerted by the built environment over people's behaviours (Saunders 1986: 173–174). Hence, the material dimensions of urban spaces are not taken for granted, but shaped by social forces involving economic, political, and cultural struggles. Although I defend that urban research is focused on cities, we cannot assume that the boundaries, contents, and conceptions of cities are the same for everyone or uncritically accept those determined by administrative or second-hand statistical definitions. Urban phenomena, additionally, have effects beyond the social life of cities, deeply influencing non-urban or extra-urban spaces. The old and intuitive, but also problematic, term 'rural' can hardly capture the multiple compounds of people and space beyond urban areas and with different degrees of urbanisation, including airports, suburbs, agricultural areas, industrial zones, roads, rail-tracks, etc., which recently triggered discussions on the notion of 'planetary urbanisation' (Schmid 2018). Natural ecosystems, beyond and within cities, in addition call for a primary focus on how urban life impacts their sustained reproduction or collapse, which is a pressing issue in current anthropogenic times (the so-called 'Anthropocene').

My perspective also leads to conceiving of the research units of urban socio-spatial phenomena as encompassing more than spatial or localised units (houses, buildings, shops, gyms, libraries, jails, streets, hospitals, power and water infrastructures, neighbourhoods, parks, districts, cities, metropolitan areas, etc.), ranging from specific social activities and groups in relation to various types of locally rooted spaces to socio-spatial networks (involving global or supra-local connections as well), processes of socio-spatial change, flows of resources, local governments and politics (from street and district to metropolitan and regional levels), and multiple socially made temporalities (Jessop et al. 2008, Lefebvre 2003). Not least, urban sociology, in order to fully pursue its scientific goals, also demands a reflexive turn, which entails critical reflections about the social consequences of the knowledge it produces and the contextual circumstances that enable its production and dissemination (Wacquant 2023).

In the form of general premises, I would summarise my approach to urban sociology as follows:

(1) All social phenomena have a spatial and temporal dimension, but urban sociology only investigates those phenomena when the urban space is one of its key aspects. The location, emplacement, or spatial distribution of social phenomena, for example, are not necessarily relevant spatial dimensions of all sociological studies, unless those spatial aspects themselves become significant for, or contested and shaped by, the involved actors. The same applies to other spatial features of the built environment, especially when related to cities and their dialectic with non-urban spaces. According to Saunders, the substantial questions at stake here are: 'Why identify space as peculiarly significant for social analysis? What makes location something more than simply one variable among many which need to be taken into account when developing explanations of why and how social phenomena develop as they do?' (Saunders 1986: 193).

(2) The interplay of society and physical space is at the core of urban sociology research. On the one hand, the social structures (made of social groups and relations) and processes of change (reproducing or transforming social structures over time) interact with space in specific ways that should allow researchers to justify their relevance. On the other hand, the interaction is asymmetrical since there are no absolute powers in physical spaces that determine social life, unless we refer to the forces of nature that are independent from the socially built environment.

(3) Space is sociologically significant when it is socially produced, shaped, transformed, used, appropriated, conceived, represented, imagined, contested, and interconnected. Some spatial configurations can even be socially framed as basic social needs (e.g. housing). These and other spaces can also be the main target of capital investment and industrial location. Unique buildings or squares can be recognised as iconic landmarks of a city. All in all, urban sociology mainly studies how specific social groups produce

the urban space. The latter, in turn, becomes a key constituent component of the social processes involved in its production.
(4) Once spatial features of the urban built environment become significant, if not crucial, in the development of social structures and processes, spatialities can have particular and situated effects in social phenomena (e.g. a one-bedroom and 40 square metre apartment will severely affect the accommodation and cohabitation of a household made of ten people). If interpreted as significant, then, the physical space can crucially mediate in the development of social relations, or even partially structure them. However, the features of physical spaces alone can hardly be the ultimate explanatory factor in sociological interpretations; social structures and processes (or, in some cases, a socio-spatial compound) should be at the core of explanation (Pickvance 1995, 2001).

In sum, following one of the Marxist epistemological cornerstones, if human beings 'make their own history, but not of their own free will; not under circumstances they themselves have chosen but under the given and inherited circumstances with which they are directly confronted' (Marx & Engels 1974: 103), we can also assume that human beings make their own cities under the circumstances they have inherited. Note that history is not simply natural time but socially constructed time and cities are not simply physical spaces but particular socially made spaces. Likewise, social agency ('free will') and collective identities are not left out of sight but just generally limited by the contextual conditions, which mostly are a result of previous collective human-made actions.

These are very general statements and guidelines that just lead to asking more specific questions of how and why certain socio-spatial phenomena occur, as the following chapters elaborate.

## THEORETICAL CONSISTENCY

When urban scholars privilege the social dimensions of urban life they necessarily adhere to one or another theoretical perspective in social sciences before they subscribe to specific theories in urban studies—even if this ascription is reluctantly stealthy. Textbooks of sociological theory provide manifold distinctions among this diverse tradition. Some, for example, distinguish strictly speaking micro-sociological analysis (including symbolic interactionism and constructivism) from other approaches that combine micro- and macro-analysis (rational choice, social capital, exchange theory, institutionalism, postmodernism, and the sociology of race and gender), in addition to highlighting the main premises of key sociological thinkers (Foucault, Giddens, Habermas, and Bourdieu) (Calhoun et al. 2002). Other attempts emphasise the opposition between micro-level (interactionism, role and identity theory, conversational ethnomethodology, emotions) and macro-level analyses (functionalism, systems theory, sociobiology, Marxism, Weberianism, structuralism, network analysis), leaving gender/feminist analysis, postmodernism, or the dichotomy between structure and agency in a more ambiguous status (Turner 2006). The focus on relevant and previously overlooked thinkers (Perkins Gilman, Du Bois, Simmel, Mead, Hill Collins, etc.) guides other compilations (Appelrouth & Desfor 2021).

An obvious and canonical classification consists in going back to the roots of the conventional modern founders of sociology: Marx–Engels, Durkheim, and Weber. Each inaugurated highly distinct branches of sociological theorisation. Turner, for example, embraces the Durkheimian ideal that sees 'sociology as a natural science that would discover the laws of human organization' whereas he discredits both the Marxist approach 'as a critique and as a call for action' and the Weberian quest of 'sociological "explanation" as revolving around interpreting empirical events in terms of analytical schemes consisting of categories describing classes of empirical phenomena' (Turner 2006: 2). Although there has not been much progress in establishing those general laws of society, it should be recognised that Durkheim contributed to defining the epistemological foundations of sociology with a solid demarcation of social phenomena with their own emerging properties, apart from psychology and biology. His approach led Turner to reasonably claim that sociological theories have 'to justify their importance vis-à-vis other theories… [and] be tested against empirical facts' (Turner 2006: 1–2).

My own theoretical stance and guideline to navigate social sciences, however, is more inclined to follow Marxist and Weberian assumptions in order to provide critical and reflexive explanations of the major conflicts in society. This approach gives priority to the macro-structural, material, and historical contexts that constrain the practices and ideas of social groups and individuals and the crucial contentious role of the antagonism between capital and labour: class struggles (Burawoy & Wright 2006). Nonetheless, I agree with Turner that

> social reality does indeed unfold along micro, meso, and macro dimensions; that each of these levels reveals its own emergent properties; that these properties are driven by forces distinctive to each level; that theory is to be about the dynamics of the forces operating at each level; and that theoretical integration will always be about how the properties of one level load the values for the unique forces operating at other levels. (Turner 2006: 6)

Likewise, Alford & Friedland (1985), with the aim of developing a sociological theory of the state, proposed an illuminating classification of three broader perspectives of inquiry: pluralist, managerial, and class. Each perspective sets different social phenomena as their analytical priority. On the one hand, each 'contains incompatible world views' (Alford & Friedland 1985: xiii). On the other hand, each perspective 'has a distinctive but limited "power": a home domain of analysis' (Alford & Friedland 1985: xiv). This framework sharply indicates that acute conflicts exist between these theoretical approaches: indeed, their proponents tend to neutralise and dominate the rival theories or pretend to describe and explain the same issues as their competitors, albeit with their own language and interpretive logic. Alford and Friedland also suggest a possible complementarity since pluralists (and functionalists) emphasise individuals and the democratic aspect of the state; managerial (including Weberian, elitist, and institutionalist) scholars stress social organisations and the state's bureaucratic dimension; and the class (Marxist) perspective helps explain societies broadly (including disruptive social movements and revolutions) and the state's capitalist dimension. Different theories of urban politics have unfolded or combined these three umbrella paradigms with more nuance (Davies & Imbroscio 2008, Judge et al. 1995, Mossberger et al. 2012).

In the field of urban sociology, the first comprehensive reviews of theoretical approaches (Castells 1972, Saunders 1986) were regularly updated (Gottdiener et al. 2019, Harding & Blokland 2014, Lin & Mele 2013, Savage & Warde 1993, Scott & Storper 2014, Storper & Scott 2016, Tonkiss 2005). One of the most recent contributions (Wacquant 2023: 2–5) distinguishes six main clusters in the interdisciplinary world of today's urban studies, albeit not all the strands take a clear sociological stance:

(1) Marxist-inspired critical scholars (also adding followers of Foucault and Deleuze) focused on global cities (Sassen), planetary urbanisation (Brenner and Schmid), critical political economy of neoliberalism (Harvey, Peck, Theodore, Mayer), and urban political ecology (Kaika, Swyngedouw);
(2) Scholars strongly inclined to ethnographic research on neighbourhoods, communities, social capital (Blokland), ethnicity (Patillo, Small), gender, and sexuality, with micro-sociological and phenomenological lenses;
(3) Positivist scholars mainly coming from the fields of economics and planning (Glaeser, Florida) dealing with the 'social problems' as conventionally defined by city elites and state officials;
(4) Urban scientists from the fields of data science, engineering, environmental design, and planning who investigate environmental impacts and digital technologies in urban management (Batty, Bettencourt, West);
(5) Post/decolonial researchers centred on Global South urbanisms such as informal settlements, citizenship, cultural innovation, and violence (Roy, Robinson, Simone);
(6) Urban historians (Tilly) concerned about every urban topic going back to centuries ago.

Other approaches such as feminism, postmodernism, actor–network theory, assemblage theory, and posthumanism are not easily placed within the above categories but, for Wacquant (2023: 1), they have also come to replace the 'lost hegemony' of human ecology (the Chicago school), Marxism, and Weberianism. Wacquant declares that his adaptation of Bourdieu's theoretical skeleton to urban theory is situated 'at the intersection of the first two clusters, high theory and institutionalism' (Wacquant 2023: 5).

Other urban scholars may also find it attractive to build their theories as one or another form of intersection, assuming that the above grid of cages is exhaustive. The above theoretical mapping and similar attempts (Leitner et al. 2019) indicate that the current challenges to unify these multi-disciplinary and theoretically plural academic domains are as utopian as in Lefebvre's times. No approach has debunked all the rest. Even more, there are sufficient traces that the three founding sociological ones are still very much alive and kicking.

This *Handbook* has no intention to represent all the above clusters but nor did I circumscribe my choices to solely represent critical Marxist and Weberian perspectives. At most, 'radical approaches' (Harding & Blokland 2014: 38–47) enjoy here a greater share than in other edited compilations. The goal was not to promote a vague eclecticism either. First, I expected that all the contributors would examine the implications of their theoretical choices—even the eclectic ones—especially in relation to their notions of the social in urban matters. Neither is the *Handbook* a mere collection of empirical findings about a necessarily limited sort of urban topics. Although some chapters are intentionally more theoretically elaborated than others (especially in Part II), even the case studies are meant to include coherent theoretical overviews. Second, my rule of thumb is to ensure clarity in the concepts and arguments, consistency among them, and justification of the choices, sources, and the probable empirical productivity to interpret urban socio-spatial phenomena beyond common sense and obvious descriptions and explanations. This approach implies a certain continuity and development to make the theoretical scaffolding robust. The subsequent corollary is that researchers should be faithful to their theoretical elaborations when they analyse and interpret their empirical data and disclose the contradictions that may arise, leading them to change their theoretical assumptions accordingly if needed.

## CRITICAL AND SELECTIVE APPROACHES TO URBAN AFFAIRS

This *Handbook* is also motivated by my interest in fostering critical approaches in urban studies in particular (Brenner et al. 2009, Mayer 2020, Slater 2021) and in social sciences in general (Calhoun 2006). As mentioned before, the crudest contrast to critical science is 'simplified positivism'. The latter does not only hold an idealistic, and thus unrealistic, notion of social science, but it usually backs technocratic and bureaucratic power relations: only scientific experts would know how the world works and what to do in order to fix the problems; state authorities should only follow their indications and implement them in a top-down manner (Wyly 2011). Accordingly, normative concerns and political utopias would be fully left out from the research process—let alone from its policy consequences. Critical science, on the contrary, sets a research agenda that aims at responding to social problems not as defined by the ruling elites, but according to widely socially agreed upon (deliberated, negotiated) goals and ideals, such as the general interest, solidarity (reciprocity, contributions to communities, care), equality (socialism in its material and radical approach focused on outcomes; equality of rights and opportunities in its more formal and liberal approach), freedom (the emancipation from all forms of oppression and the autonomous self-organisation and self-determination of the oppressed in its republican stance; the flourishing of human capacities within the rule of law and according to others' freedoms in its liberal stance), human rights, social needs, democracy (from direct to participatory and representative), social and environmental justice, and peace. The traditional anti-capitalist claims of the working class (through communism, socialism, anarchism, and autonomist struggles), feminist, anti-racist, and anti-colonial movements also crucially nurture critical approaches in social sciences. The lack of consensus on those ideals and their implications and the existing conflicts between different social groups often lead researchers to take sides in their scientific activities, but this political positionality should not betray the methodological and theoretical rigour of science.

When social scientists do not take a critical stance by discussing the political motivations and impacts of their work, they may easily fall prey of the vested interests of powerful groups who co-opt them and use their research in order to manipulate people's resources, thoughts, and decisions. The corporatist constraints of academic institutions experienced by most scientists during their professional careers may add up to the lip service they are requested to pay for the sake of authoritarian modes of government, for-profit business, and the unscrupulous spread of false ideas. Urban sociologists in particular and urban scholars more generally may find jobs in private urban planning firms, real estate marketing and management corporations, retail companies, state departments, statistical agencies, and conservative think tanks attacking measures such as rent controls, social housing, desegregation policies, affirmative action, rights for domestic workers and migrants, the minimum wage, and the right to strike and protest. The researchers' employability does not necessarily mean that they produce reliable and relevant science or, if they do, that their findings are used for the common good. A reflexive critical approach thus invites us to disclose the practical effects that our knowledge produces, not only to appraise its quality and validity compared to alternative explanations. For instance, pioneering scholarly networks such as International Network of Urban Research and Action (INURA) have advocated engaged urban research for decades and paved the way to collectively and practically counter the trends of mainstream neoliberal academia.

In my professional life I have worked with many different social scientists including architects and urban planners, in a municipal housing office, and with various grassroots organisations, on top of several university appointments and some precarious jobs. I thus noticed that it is possible to speak out and advocate for social change from within state and academic institutions, or even as an employee in private firms, though rarely. Collective support, mutual aid, unions, and organising are beneficial platforms in this respect. However, it is from my involvement in progressive (leftist) social movements that I have been more motivated to take critical approaches when conducting sociological research. All in all, we should always identify the limitations at play and push them to expand the cracks of possibilities in every particular setting that allows us to productively unfold social science research, including urban studies, with a critical standpoint.

This spirit has also nurtured the decisions made about the authors of the chapters and the topics they cover. In terms of the latter, one classical source of inspiration has always been the Athens Charter from 1933, published a few years later by Le Corbusier as the main manifesto of the Modern Architecture International Conference (CIAM). In that document, cities were supposed to accomplish four main functions: dwelling, work, recreation, and transport. In other words, urban studies should be mainly focused on housing (social reproduction), productive activities in all the economic sectors, quality of life (from leisure to environmental health), and spatial mobility (within, to, and from cities). To some extent, the CIAM approach reflected key claims of the workers' movements of the time (eight hours for waged work, eight hours for domestic work and reproductive activities, and eight hours for rest every day, which evolved to paid holidays and four days' work per week later on). The well-known criticism of the underlying assumptions of that manifesto (preference for high-rises, hierarchical planning and government, zoning or functional socio-spatial segregation, the hegemony of motorised mobility and private automobiles, etc.) or its virtues (low-cost production of housing to decently accommodate the working class, health and environmental concerns in housing design, a cry for rational, comprehensive, and redistributive urban planning, etc.) do not amend the fact that they were pointing to crucial socio-spatial phenomena (for a critical assessment of both the 1933 and the updated 2003 version of the Athens Charter from a gender perspective, see Tummers and Zibell (2012)) (see Figure 1.2 as a reminder of the city where the 1933 Charter was formulated).

If we look beyond the Athens Charter, we find that the number of topics investigated by urban scholars has proliferated exponentially over the last 100 years (Bridge & Watson 2000, Burdett & Sudjic 2011, Harding & Blokland 2014, Knox 2014), which indicates the need for a more nuanced thematic organisation for urban studies.

(1) Housing issues concern not only cost, aesthetic design, and mass construction but also tenure, finance, affordability, welfare provision of social housing or subsidies, central and peripheral (or suburban) locations, distance to workplaces and public facilities, overcrowding and substandard dwellings, homelessness, squatting, home evictions, informal settlements, short-term touristic rentals, urban planning for residential construction, etc. The so-called 'housing question' under capitalism is as acute today as it was in times of Engels's and Proudhon's pioneering analyses, although many of its traits and contexts have changed. Chapters included in Part IV align with these debates.

(2) Industrial production has been widely expelled from most city centres (sometimes to overseas urban and non-urban areas), but many other formal and informal activities sustain the inner economic life of cities, from outdoor markets and street vending to retail, private and public services, state administration, construction, domestic work,

*Source:* Miguel A. Martínez.

*Figure 1.2    View of Athens (2022)*

        banking, cultural and touristic industries, low-scale manufacturing, headquarters of transnational corporations, platform companies, special economic zones, logistics, assemblage of technology, laboratories, etc. The socio-economic processes of goods and services (and information) production, extraction, trade, finance, and construction are thus cornerstones to understand the general socio-spatial forms of segregation as well as the relations between socio-spatial phenomena with the state and the capitalist global market. Chapters comprising Parts I and III engage with these insights.

(3) Urban life certainly goes beyond leisure and recreation, including the use of public spaces, the provision and quality of education and health, crime and safety issues, racial and class segregation, gentrification, police racial profiling, gender discrimination, community organising, sport facilities, social proximity and supporting networks, job opportunities, democratic participation in urban development and renewal, pollution, place attachment and appropriation, and so on and so forth. Chapters in Part V are related to this comprehensive knowledge of socially shaped urban spaces.

(4) It would be restrictive to talk about mobility by merely focusing on all the means of transport involved (cars, motorbikes, all forms of public transit, cycling, walking, skating, electric kick-scooters, etc.), the policies, environmental implications, physical and digital infrastructures, and concerned social groups and reasons to move without also thinking about the spatial moves of newcomers to cities, migrants, refugees/asylum seekers, regional commuters, tourists, temporary visitors for work or leisure-related matters, etc., with all their class, gender, and racial conflicts at play. There is no special part in the *Handbook* to cover these topics, but many of them intersect with chapters in the other large sections of the volume.

The four main urban functions seem to have exploded during a century of massive urbanisation worldwide. As is easily deducted, most of the abovementioned issues are related to each other and urban spaces are key constitutive dimensions of the social relations, structures, and processes that they indicate. This socio-spatial complexity, after all, demands focused theoretical and empirical analyses in order to make sense of contemporary urban life without missing the main social conflicts across those topics within every historical period.

As a consequence, first, many chapters of the *Handbook* deal with the key issues of the social production of urban space and the spatial conditions for the social reproduction of the labour force and urban life, while looking at the core of those processes—social struggles between dominant and dominated groups. Second, these should be manifested in specific domains of socio-spatial conflict but framed according to significant historical contexts, especially the development of neoliberal urbanism, globalisation, and neo-authoritarianism since the 1970s. Therefore, there was no intention to imitate here encyclopaedic ambitions, neither in terms of urban issues nor by discussing all the expressions of urban theory (Orum 2019).

## THE ART OF ACADEMIC CURATING

Within the word-length limit set by the publisher, I just navigated my academic networks of affinity and even went beyond previous mutual knowledge in order to call for contributions to the *Handbook*. I thus searched in my social circles (mainly through email lists, Facebook groups, Twitter, Mastodon, publications in academic journals, books, presentations in conferences, university and research centres' websites, and by asking colleagues directly) for sociologists who had already contributed to the topics I initially proposed. I also identified urban scholars who were not sociologists strictly speaking but had some affinity with the approach taken for this volume.

Retired scholars were dismissed because I assumed their work has already been influential such that other scholars are probably digesting it and producing more novel outputs. Active senior scholars do not populate most of the chapters either, although their experience has also been called in and is always appreciated in order to illuminate key tenets of the discipline. So-called 'early-career researchers' (ECRs) were thus the primary target. In addition, I am aware that women, LGBTQ+ people, ethnic minorities, and academics from the Global South and the many 'peripheries' of the Global North experience marginalisation and discrimination in many academic instances, while they may happen to be experts on many socio-spatial topics, included those related to the oppressions they or their peers experience. Therefore, the casting needed to take all this into account as much as was possible and feasible. In so doing, one of the selection criteria was to include as many scholars from the most subordinated categories as possible on the grounds that they had previously produced outstanding quality publications, even if only a PhD dissertation or a few articles I was familiar with. Craftwork and post hoc quotas, rather than an a priori distribution of the assignments, thus guided my pursuit.

I was also open to suggestions. Other colleagues in this series of handbooks opted for open calls for chapters. I took an alternative route, albeit equally painful. In a form of snowball sampling, many contributors named brilliant scholars who could fit the book proposal. These additions obliged me to check their profiles and read some of their publications in case I did not know them. Some were scholars whom I had come across in the past, in conferences or books, but I had forgotten about. Others had not published much in the English language, so it was not always easy for me to judge unless I was lucky to be fluent in their native language.

Concerning the North–South divide alone, I am especially sensitive about some peripheral areas in between, such as Southern and Central Eastern Europe, because of my own intellectual curiosity and academic trajectory (with starting positions in Spain and Portugal, followed by my involvement in European academic–activist networks, visiting Latin American cities and Beijing for short periods, moving later to Hong Kong and Sweden with recent research stays in Sofia and Amsterdam). I am aware that my Spanish origin and mother tongue constrained (and enabled) many of my opportunities to remain in academia. However, English has ascended to be the *lingua franca* in the scientific world. All the high-ranked indexed journals (according to the arbitrary status manufactured by some for-profit corporations) in urban studies are written in English and led by academics from US and UK universities. Reference books and conferences follow suit. Despite the fact that I was educated with a mostly Spanish academic literature in my undergraduate studies, when struggling to write in English I tend to cite works written in the English language, assuming that an international audience may access them easier. Notwithstanding the above, I always hope that there is some space in books like this to mention outstanding research in languages other than English.

Moreover, social scientists usually need to gather thick descriptions and rich narratives that help us in making sense of what people mean, intend, and do, with careful attention to the subtle contents, local connotations, and intertextuality of every discourse in the speakers' own preferred language. Translation from languages other than English is therefore inevitable—at least if we aim to know the whole world beyond the rather limited English-speaking one. Hence, stories from every corner of the world are recommended to be picked up and interpreted in a consistent manner, attending to global as well as local concerns. This includes accounts from different world regions, as I intended to cover, to some extent, in this volume.

In sum, the publication of a collective book entails careful work of curating. This means that the editor suggests, guides, gives support and feedback, advises, and establishes productive conversations with the authors as much as needed. Similarly to art exhibitions, there is always a triggering *concept* for gathering the commissioned works, but it is the artists' final say and responsibility that determines the substance of the outcome. Scientific curating may be a little more contentious since rational argumentation and academic research standards come to the fore in various rounds of critical review performed by academic peers (two other contributors to the book and the editor in our case)—not to mention the controversial differences in terms of epistemological or theoretical assumptions that may underlie the reviewers' criticism. In my view, a well-curated academic book should preserve a healthy and constructive peer-review culture in order to ensure high academic quality so all who are involved gain intellectual satisfaction. Likewise, the editor should be respectful with the chosen allies as much as fully motivated with the whole project. With this statement at the forefront, I participated in the review of all the chapters and invited other contributors to jump in. I cannot claim the resulting book is a fully collectively self-organised *artwork* although I do hope that many readers understand that the editor was immersed in the same troubled waters as the contributors in order to keep the project afloat.

## CONTENTS OF THE CHAPTERS

This *Handbook* is organised according to five general parts.

Part I, Society, state, capitalism, and cities, examines theoretical debates and some empirical illustrations that mainly frame urban sociology inquiry according to macro-historical circumstances. The global expansion of capitalist markets and forms of social domination are at the core of these analyses, which lead to highlighting class relations, social reproduction through housing, the capitalist constraints over the local state, and the rise of neoliberalism and financialisation.

Part II, Revisiting debates in urban sociology, continues with the review of some of the major theoretical approaches in urban sociology. The included chapters discuss approaches to the study of gentrification, neighbourhood effects, race, and gender, and the contributions of authors such as Pierre Bourdieu, Henri Lefebvre, and Axel Honneth. Authors also include some references to their own research that help reinforce their views of the debates.

Part III, Socio-spatial segregations, encompasses chapters dealing with both theoretical overviews and empirical case studies about the manifold expressions of urban inequalities. Marginalisation, discrimination, violence, gentrification, and social mixture represent some of the social conflicts that have a crucial spatial component. These topics are tightly related to other socio-spatial phenomena such as gender, race, policing, schooling, informal settlements, and environmental issues.

Part IV, The housing question, places the production of dwelling and the capitalist speculation with the social needs of housing at the centre of urban inquiry. While some chapters investigate the role of real estate developers, landlords, and housing authorities, other chapters reveal collective actions of residents, tenants, migrants, non-binary people, squatters, and housing commoners.

Part V, Socially shaped cities, provides a broader view of urban life. It covers processes of citizen participation in relation to local policies, informality in both Global North and Global South cities, the hardships experienced by migrant domestic workers in a global city, the effects of neoliberalism in the configuration of public urban spaces, and the social role of universities in cities.

A final brief introduction and summary of each chapter follows.

Chapter 2 argues that urban sociology is concerned, above all, with the study of social structures and processes of social change in the production, reproduction, and transformation of cities. Class and other social conflicts, urban movements, the state, and capitalism are thus situated at the core of socio-spatial phenomena. Additionally, an 'interdependent' approach between epistemology and politics guides my critical standpoint, which leads science to pursue the emancipation of the oppressed by revealing hidden forms of domination and social contradictions.

Chapter 3 deals with the theories of the 'capitalist local state'. The author, Özlem Çelik, introduces capitalism and social conflicts in the discussion of urban politics. The analysis of the local state focuses on the development of capitalism, whether at the secondary circuit of real estate investment, production, and consumption in the local realm or in relation to the world market. Hence, urban politics has to be explained by centrally examining how local governments operate in relation to capital and class struggles. Who actually rules and how? How do different social groups and organisations interact with local governments in order to influence capitalists' interests? Çelik critically reviews pluralist, elite, managerial, and structuralist frameworks in order to shed light on the above questions.

Chapter 4 offers a review of the class perspective in urban studies. The authors, Ibán Díaz-Parra and Beltrán Roca, discuss different notions of class and suggest three key areas of urban research where the class perspective has been central. First, they present the main rationale behind the studies on urban location and socio-spatial segregation patterns according to class dimensions. Second, they take the class approach to discuss its influence in the analysis of the social production of cities in capitalist times. Third, they recall the analysis of labour issues and contention by taking into account their spatial dimensions.

Chapter 5 critically presents Saskia Sassen's 'global city' theory by interrogating how it was translated into urban policy and planning in the city of São Paulo (Brazil). Mariana Fix argues that it easily changed from an analytical perspective to a normative prescription in urban planning and policy making with the help of Borja and Castells's promotion of 'strategic city planning' and inter-urban competition. Fix shows that globalisation processes have been present at the origins of most major cities even before the 'informational age' was accelerated with the expansion of neoliberal restructuring since the 1980s, which was not different in São Paulo. By studying how growth coalitions have operated in this city in order to foster uneven urban development, the chapter reveals the justification role played by some academic discourses.

Chapter 6 shows the significance of housing tenure to investigate crucial economic and social dimensions of urban life over time. Sebastian Kohl traces back the history of homeownership and rental housing in cities across the world, which is an often overlooked perspective due to the conventional use of national statistics. The latter tend to disregard the comparison between urban and non-urban areas. According to Kohl's analysis, homeownership has seldom occurred in most cities over many centuries, although it rose significantly and steadily from the second half of the 20th century onwards. Conversely, peasants and farmers tended to own their living spaces especially after the Middle Age and the trend is still ongoing despite the massive exodus to urban areas throughout the last century. This evidence calls for attention to the well-established forms of rentierism in cities over long periods of time before the decline of the welfare state and the onset of urban neoliberalism in the 1970s. The negative effects of homeownership, especially when it is achieved through high rates of indebtedness, should not leave aside questions regarding who profited from rentals before as well and who profited from the overwhelming aspirations to own property in the last decades.

Chapter 7 discusses two of the topics that have recently worried urban scholars influenced by Marxist critiques of political economy—financialisation and rentierism. The Marxist tradition in urban sociology emphasises that the dominance of the capitalist system is rooted in basic processes of labour exploitation in which the owners of the means of production manage to grab the surplus value. This profit-making economic model prevails over other non-profitable economic, social, cultural, and political activities. The outcomes of such a model are well-known: gigantic social inequalities in terms of wealth distribution, conflicts and struggles—more or less visible—between social classes, the promotion of infinite growth, and the devastation of natural resources. Capitalist social relations have also serious consequences for the reproduction of the labour force in terms of supply and quality of food, housing, transport, health, education, leisure, and culture. In this chapter Ismael Yrigoy engages with these discussions in urban studies in order to question how accurate the current views on the processes of financialisation and rentierism are, which substantially affect how the built environment and urban life change. Yrigoy argues that the debate has focused too much on the distribution of surplus value and the unproductive nature of financialisation and rentierism. Instead, more attention has to be paid to the 'secondary' forms of labour exploitation.

Chapter 8 addresses Pierre Bourdieu's theoretical approach, which is often missing in the dominant strands of urban sociology. Although this scholar seldom discussed issues related to urban spaces, he coined key concepts that are deemed essential or at least have become commonplace for contemporary sociology, such as 'capitals', 'field', 'habitus', and 'symbolic violence'. These concepts, in addition to some of his original theoretical and epistemological assumptions, have influenced a significant number of urban scholars, especially those using ethnographic methods and topological representations of the 'social space' in relation to the 'physical space'. In this chapter Virgílio Borges Pereira recalls some of the key tenets and insights provided by Bourdieu and shows how he and other colleagues systematically applied them to study the metropolitan area of Porto (Portugal) over various decades. He disentangles the lifestyles, everyday spaces, and complexity of class dimensions that undergirded the social conditions of life of those subject to specific housing policies and the reproduction of socio-spatial segregation in this urban setting.

Chapter 9 revises the influence of the 'urban ecology' tradition from the early Chicago school into contemporary studies around 'neighbourhood effects'. The former is a conventional milestone in the foundations of urban sociology as a discipline. Many of the concepts that the male and female urban scholars from late 19th and early 20th centuries in Chicago borrowed from natural sciences (biology, ecology) are still in use, although often with different terms. Their notions about 'natural areas', 'urban communities', and 'neighbourhoods' according to patterns of social and spatial organisation in an ever changing urban life have given birth to abundant studies to date, mostly following an ethnographic approach. Despite the radical critique that this school has been subjected to by Marxist and Weberian sociologists since the 1960s, their main assumptions experienced a new life with the rise of 'neighbourhood effects' scholarship. Ngai-Ming Yip thoroughly reviews these theoretical debates and reveals the flaws and potential virtues of those approaches to the neighbourhood as a particular socio-spatial scale of study. He also points out the policy constraints and aspirations that these strands of research have experienced, despite their limited capacity to explain urban and social phenomena that always interplay with phenomena at other socio-spatial scales.

Chapter 10 examines problematic approaches and missing questions of race, racism, and whiteness in different strands of theorisation in urban sociology. Miguel Montalva Barba thus critically reviews the human ecology approach, neo-Marxist political economy, world/global systems theory, and the cultural turn in order to disclose how racist and colonial biases are ingrained in their explanations of urban phenomena. He supports his claims with global critical race theory and invites urban sociologists to reveal how whiteness operates in the social production of the city and how it draws socio-spatial boundaries.

Chapter 11 introduces the reader to the main academic debates about gentrification in urban studies while emphasising its most remarkable sociological features. Andrej Holm reviews the main theoretical contributions, discusses the definitions and explanatory powers of these approaches, and suggests a research agenda in order to overcome the main identified flaws. As the chapter shows, there is often confusion between the full-fledged understanding of urban change processes, among which gentrification might be identified as a special case, and some of their social consequences, such as the displacement of working-class or low-income residents. In addition, sociological engagements in the study of gentrification have often merely focused on in-depth descriptions of the residents' and gentrifiers' experiences, leaving aside other actors' strategies and structural political and economic dynamics. Holm also questions the neighbourhood scale as an appropriate one to study gentrification once this phenomenon has been generalised at much larger scales across cities and countries worldwide.

Chapter 12 takes a feminist and social reproduction approach to discuss gentrification research. Bahar Sakızlıoğlu unfolds the main categories and assumptions of such an approach by addressing the global crisis of care, the class contradictions of gendered experiences in gentrified neighbourhoods, and the impacts of gentrification for natural ecosystems and non-human species. She also suggests to investigate everyday experiences of social reproduction in connection to macro structural processes of accumulation by dispossession.

Chapter 13 looks back to three classical authors in sociology (Tönnies, Durkheim, and Simmel) in order to recall the debates on the key features of highly urbanised societies. Tino Buchholz and Jere Kuzmanić argue that questions regarding who cares for what, whom, and why are at the core of sociology and also nurture urban sociology since shared spaces are essential in social values, practices, and relations of solidarity. They then turn to review Axel Honneth's theory of conflict and justice, which is considered illuminating for understanding the urban struggles for recognition and the challenges of urban planning. The chapter also questions the limits of communicative planning while introducing anarchist insights that bring norms, forms, and scales in the discussion of privilege, property, and housing.

Chapter 14 revives one of the key theoretical contributions of Henri Lefebvre: planetary urbanisation. Max Rousseau first reviews contemporary debates around the phenomena covered by that notion. Second, he discusses the 2020–22 Covid-19 pandemic from the same more-than-urban approach. Empirical research from the Global South and attention to global processes also help in understanding the political implications of such a theoretical approach, especially in times of devastating ecosystemic catastrophes and social inequalities fostered by capitalist development.

Chapter 15 engages with Lefebvre's notion of 'the right to the city'. Lefebvre drew upon a Marxist framework of analysis but his theses on the social production of space and the relevance of urban struggles, among other topics, developed those assumptions even beyond the 'new urban sociology' of the 1960s and 1970s. Margherita Grazioli interprets the main contents of the right to the city both as a political proposal and analytical insight and uses her own research on the housing rights movements based in Rome (Italy) as an illustration of the heuristic capacity of such a notion. Particularly, she discusses the questions of centrality, the claims for equal forms of recognition of urban inhabitants, the everyday routines of housing struggles, and the spatio-temporal features of self-organisation. Her focus on the squatting of vacant buildings for housing purposes, especially involving international migrants as dwellers and activists, and the historical background of the current housing precarity and urban segregation add a critical perspective when it comes to interpreting specific urban struggles in the light of Lefebvre's inspirations.

Chapter 16 discusses the notion of social mix in relation to housing policies mainly by contrasting France and the United States of America. Marie-Hélène Bacqué and Éric Charmes first review the arguments expressed in two seminal studies from the 1960s. Secondly, they scrutinise the political and normative dimensions that underpin arguments in favour of and against social mix policies. Despite the negative effects of social mix policies found by academic research, the authors of this chapter think that there are still valuable ideological bases to support such an approach. When debunking the promises of social mix, scholars have revealed the higher benefits reaped by middle and upper classes and the permanence of multiple social cleavages at different spatial scales and across different social groups, not necessarily defined by class. Nevertheless, the discrepancy between academic and policy discourses points to a broad social consensus, for example around the need to increase the production of social housing, especially with mandatory proportions or zoning regulations in new urban developments. Allegedly, measures such as the latter may counter socio-spatial segregation, although the actual impacts in this matter are largely poor.

Chapter 17 presents the concept of 'rent gap' coined by Neil Smith with the intention to explain gentrification processes from a production-side perspective within cycles of capital disinvestment and investment. The author of the chapter, Defne Kadıoğlu, not only reviews the conceptual debates around the explanatory capacity of the rent gap theory but also contributes with an illustration of two case studies in Berlin and Stockholm where the main issues are clearly at stake. Kadıoğlu helps clarifying the social and political dimensions of gentrification processes in particular, and uneven urban development more broadly. She first argues that rent gaps are produced, widened, and closed, which entails a refined conceptual view of the theory when facing its critics. She also advocates for an extension of the understanding of gentrification processes to include an analysis of the state, social structures, and political configurations. In so doing, Kadıoğlu highlights the role of territorial stigmatisation processes at play and warns that the displacement of former low-income residents may not occur in the short-term, although they are likely to be subject to overcrowding and worse living conditions.

Chapter 18 takes a specific approach to understanding gentrification processes: the role of school choices made by some factions of the middle class. Carlotta Caciagli takes a demand-side approach and discusses the main tenets and findings from the relevant literature in order to explore a particular case in the city of Milan (Italy). She suggests that the focus on the middle class may reveal how socio-spatial mechanisms play out in relation to class reproduction. In particular, the distance to the school in the examined case appears to be less important than the proximity to gathering places that foster close social ties. Likewise, the high academic reputation of the schools is considered less desirable than tolerated degrees of racial diversity. The availability of both public and private schools also allows the middle class to easily move in or out within the neighbourhood, despite the crucial weight of the local proximity in their preferences. This contrasts with the limitations of working-class and poor migrant parents who face many more constraints in terms of both residential mobility and school choices.

Chapter 19 criticises the use of the ghetto concept in the context of Latin American urban sociology in general and Chilean urban sociology in particular. Nicolás Angelcos follows international discussions about the segregation of the urban poor and finds that the negative assessments of their social problems go beyond objective descriptions. In addition to omitting significant social practices and groups that do not match the ethnic and housing homogeneity or the overwhelming experience of crime and broken social networks, those experts' descriptions have the effect of increasing the stigmatisation of these urban areas. In addition, Angelcos shows that the political organising of poor urban and metropolitan dwellers is systematically overlooked by the analytical approaches merely focused on the traits of socio-spatial segregation and marginalisation. Grassroots struggles for the right to housing and the right to the city are thus prominent in the poor Chilean neighbourhoods examined by the author, as in the revival of previous movements of '*pobladores*' decades ago, although with different protest repertoires and relations with the political parties.

Chapter 20 revolves around contemporary debates on climate change and its consequences for marginalised urban populations living in risk-prone settlements while focusing on examples from Africa. The author of this chapter, Cristina Udelsmann Rodrigues, argues that the increasing and devastating effects of climate change are worsening the living conditions of slum dwellers, hence increasing their job and residential precarity, social vulnerability, socio-spatial segregation, and many other additional hardships. This is an urgent issue for large numbers of inhabitants in the urban Global South, which is hardly addressed by most mitigation and adaptation systems foreseen in urban planning, let alone by sociological analyses of urban inequalities. The examination of two cases from the cities of Luanda (Angola) and Maputo (Mozambique) confirms the cumulative consequences of climate change in terms of social hyper-marginalisation.

Chapter 21 recalls a traditional topic in early urban sociology, crime, but with an entirely different approach and by empirically looking at the deprived outskirts of another African city, Nairobi (Kenya). Naomi Van Stapele and Samuel Kiriro investigate in depth, from an engaged positionality, the social complexity of criminality in the Mathare neighbourhood, where both police killings and youth gangs operate in a context of local social divisions, corrupt national politics, and a devastated and dependent economy. The authors of the chapter focus on the social construction of time by the youths who aim at getting away from a daily social environment of violence, given the socio-spatial ties they hold with their neighbourhood and their poor economic prospects. The notions of 'anticipations' and 'aspirations' are thus highlighted in order to understand how these youths navigate frequent violent encounters, participate in grassroots organising, and collectively shape future possibilities for improving their lives.

Chapter 22 offers a theoretical and practical view of feminist urbanism according to the experiences of sociologists who are developing it on a regular basis. Blanca Valdivia and Sara Ortiz Escalante, members of the cooperative Col·lectiu Punt 6, present both the main goals of feminist urban planning and the methodological principles that guide their participatory research practice. They assume an intersectional approach that goes beyond gender and questions the usual limitations of institutional participatory processes in urban affairs. Hence, all stages and aspects of urbanism, according to the authors, should challenge intersectional exclusions and discriminations and incorporate the lessons of feminist scholarship regarding social reproduction needs in both private and public spheres.

Chapter 23 invites us to look at the upper and dominant classes who crucially produce the city in general and residential developments in particular. Ivana Socoloff takes a political economy approach that makes it possible to follow the money of real estate firms and corporate businesses, their multi-scalar or rescaling moves, their sources of funding, their links with state power, and their tax evasion strategies over time. By focusing on the city of Buenos Aires (Argentina), Socoloff shows how these companies promote urban development according to the context of global financialisation in order to reproduce and expand capital accumulation.

Chapter 24 presents an original argument in relation to the burgeoning literature that has been produced on Airbnb, short-term rentals, urban tourism, and housing financialisation since the 2008 great financial crisis. Javier Gil contends that the rapid expansion of Airbnb has deeply affected housing markets and class relations. New types of corporate landlords, online platform tools, and tenants have triggered residential displacements and increased for-profit and speculative operations around housing. Gil interprets these phenomena according to one main driver: the assetisation of housing which, in turn, reactivates rentierism. If the rise of homeownership was at the core of housing financialisation and neoliberal urban policies, the rise of rentierism has opened up new profitable investment avenues in the aftermath of the financial crisis. Although wealthy homeowners and landlords, tourists, and global nomads may enjoy this more diverse supply of housing, the inflationary effects and the dispossession of most tenants are serious concerns that should not be overlooked by housing policies.

Chapter 25 examines a case involving the regeneration of social housing estates in Dublin, which was very controversial because of the private interests involved and the eventually failed participation of the residents in the process. Valesca Lima thus scrutinises the dominant top-down model of urban regeneration at play despite the many attempts by tenants and some local councillors to have a say in the plans and achieve more affordable housing with a central location in the city. The collapse of the real estate developers, the relocation of tenants in other urban areas, and the long time span of the regeneration process were among the many circumstances that prevented the satisfaction, or even serious negotiation, of the residents' demands in a context of neoliberal policies and gentrification pressure in the city centre.

Chapter 26 offers a novel angle on the sociology of housing and broader urban phenomena such as large renovations of social rental estates in Sweden, with the consequence of rent rises and dramatic pressures on and socio-spatial displacement of vulnerable social groups. Dominika V. Polanska not only discusses how post-welfare and increasingly neoliberal Sweden is translated into worsened housing affordability, tenure security, and social life in neighbourhoods where the state massively invested in social housing some decades ago, but also reveals how tenants contest and resist processes of 'renoviction' (i.e. the forcible displacement due to rent rises resulting from the renovation of previously affordable rental housing). Tenants' organising thus lies in a process of political formation of subjectivity (or collective identity), which is socially, spatially, and temporally based. In so doing, discontented and organised tenants produce and recreate homes, not only with the material defence of their residential conditions and housing but also by including political meanings and the community in struggle in their symbolic notion of 'homemaking'.

Chapter 27 deals with similar issues of forcible home evictions, but adds two interrelated questions: migration and homeownership. In her analysis of the post-2008 financial crisis in Madrid (Spain), Sophie Gonick follows the migrant former homeowners who were among the first devastated by unemployment and the subsequent inability to pay their mortgages off. They became syphoned off into the homeownership market due to multiple sources of social pressure and also because of the experience of racist and xenophobic rejections from the meagre rental options available before 2008. A careful examination of access to housing as private property and commodity in this context leads to questioning it as a limited, weak, and risky social integration strategy for immigrants. Remarkably, Gonick also stresses that some of those financially broken migrants who faced home evictions became key activists at the forefront of housing struggles in Spain.

Chapter 28 investigates the housing question from the perspective of non-heteronormative sexual orientations in another South European context, Greece. Myrto Dagkouli-Kyriakoglou provides a detailed portrait of the challenges that LGBTQ+ people face when trying to access housing. They first disrupt the dominant patriarchal attitudes pervading constitutional statements and a very influential Orthodox Church and thus every single household. Family conflicts regarding sexual orientations and identities can exacerbate the hardships of LGBTQ+ people in accessing housing in Greece due to the weak welfare state and the robust mechanisms of class reproduction through the main family asset, which is housing. Differences between villages and large cities are also crucial for non-heteronormative identities when it comes to navigating all these social conflicts. Hence, Dagkouli-Kyriakoglou examines the major contextual forces that constrain housing pathways and choices in relation to sexuality by combining insights from the macro and micro spheres of social life.

Chapter 29 presents a case study of the squatting movement in a Brazilian metropolitan region, and discusses its right to the city features as well as its social networking practices. Clarissa Cordeiro de Campos addresses the issue of squatting for housing in that Global South context by distinguishing different forms of land and building occupations, their relationship with the city and metropolitan centre, and their solidarity ties that make them a prominent urban and housing movement, despite rarely being recognised as such. The chapter also engages with a comparative analysis of squatting movements in various geographies and reveals crucial features of the political economy of Brazil and the intersectionality of housing activism.

Chapter 30 remains focused on the housing question, but this is now approached from the angle of housing cooperatives as specific forms of urban commons. Lorenzo Vidal examines the cases of Copenhagen (Denmark), Montevideo (Uruguay), and Barcelona (Spain) and interrogates the main social dimensions. Housing cooperatives are democratic and usually affordable ways of access to housing for non-wealthy social groups, although different forms of capital mobilised within specific social networks, community building processes, and negotiations with the state are crucial dimensions in order to assess their performance. Tensions with housing markets and gentrification processes are also at the centre of the decommodification attempts of these cooperatives in order to sustain full or restricted urban commons. In this regard, the studied cases show different outcomes and historical developments. Vidal thus scrutinises the political and economic contexts in which housing cooperatives operate, but also the organisational structures and decisions that the involved dwellers take in order to keep the cooperatives away from the dominant capitalist urban dynamics.

Chapter 31 returns to key sociological questions in the analysis of urban phenomena such as the structure and agency debate. In particular, the author of this chapter, Luca Sára Bródy, approaches the debate from a cultural political economy perspective and offers an empirical investigation of how it can be deployed in the analysis of citizen participation in urban regeneration processes in the city of Budapest (Hungary). Although both structural and constructivist approaches are considered analytically valuable, Bródy emphasises that each one may take priority according to long-term historical periods and the specific interactions between experts and citizens. The developments of neoliberalisation, Europeanisation, and authoritarianism in Hungary, coupled with the poor results of institutional participatory processes, allow the author to also highlight how contesting groups, even as outsiders, became significant in a full understanding of urban regeneration in Budapest.

Chapter 32 focuses on topics that have been largely neglected in urban sociology such as spatio-temporalities and gendered migrant domestic work. Maren K. Boersma first reviews an often overlooked body of research regarding the social production of space and time and the bounced effects that the resulting spatialities and temporalities have in everyday urban life. These processes are not mere conditions of social life, but widely determined by the development of global capitalism and its manifestations in cities. To illustrate this topic, Boersma presents her analysis of the living conditions of Filipina domestic workers in Hong Kong. The particular labour regime that applies to them reveals time and spatial restrictions that make them subject to a wide range of human rights violations. Their abusive employers' practices additionally exacerbate the constraints that these female migrants experience in their relations with their decisions to stay or return to their home countries and in their regular time-management decisions while navigating housing, public spaces, legal institutions, and supportive organisations in the city.

Chapter 33 revises current trends in the mechanisms of social control through the planning and management of urban public spaces. Jorge Sequera argues that critical perspectives on the analysis of public spaces should consider the deployment of biopolitical power and knowledge devices such as video surveillance, state regulations that target and exclude vulnerable social groups, and crime prevention measures. Urban sociology is thus confronted with both normative discourses regarding the interactive and inclusive nature of public space on the one hand and the actual practices of social repression, segregation, and contestation across different urban public spaces on the other.

Chapter 34 suggests a nuanced and contextualised approach to the urban informality in which most of the impoverished working-class people of the Global South are daily entangled. Sonia Roitman and Peter Walters, drawing on their own studies in Indonesia and Bangladesh, respectively, first distinguish the different and overlapping domains of informality. Next, they discuss the theoretical approaches to the formal and informal, either as a continuum or in opposition. In this regard, the authors of this chapter propose to consider the boundaries between the formal and the informal porous and contingent through time and space. In their analysis, the agency and social organisation of informal dwellers, and the latter's interactions with formal authorities and the formal city when dealing with extreme necessity, are at the forefront.

Chapter 35 also deals with the topic of informality but this time in the context of new urban developments in China and by including state agents, real estate developers, and small land owners. Yunpeng Zhang investigates the complexity of these intra- and inter-group relations, the flexible interpretations of the law, their negotiations and economic compensations for land transfers, and also the illicit and even criminal activities involved in the process of building a new city. Contrary to stereotypes of how an authoritarian state such as China works, Zhang reveals that urban politics are subject to different formal and informal collective strategies, pro-growth coalitions, and rules emanating from various state levels.

Chapter 36 focuses on one specific urban facility, the university (either public or private), in order to reveal its relationship with the rest of the city, its historical and spatial contexts, and its role in broader social transformations. The author of the chapter, Do Young Oh, uses the growth machine theory and evidence beyond the Western context and Global North to observe global patterns of using universities in urban and regional competition, next to other key developments such as convention centres, sports stadiums, and large-scale shopping malls.

Chapter 37 concludes with a general overview of the topics covered by this *Handbook* and their implications for future research. Hence, Mika Hyötyläinen and I propose paths to continue with some of the theoretical strands presented before, while also indicating neglected topics that would deserve more priority in the research agenda of contemporary urban sociology.

# REFERENCES

Alford, R. & Friedland, R. (1985) *Powers of Theory. Capitalism, the State, and Democracy.* Cambridge: Cambridge University.
Appelrouth, S. & Desfor, L. (eds.) (2021) *Classical and Contemporary Sociological Theory: Text and Readings.* Thousand Oaks, CA: Sage.

Batty, M. (2013) *The New Science of Cities*. Cambridge, MA: MIT.
Bourdieu, P. et al. (1991 [1973]) *The Craft of Sociology. Epistemological Preliminaries*. Berlin: de Gruyter.
Brenner, N. et al. (2009) Cities for people, not for profit. *City* 13(2–3): 176–184.
Bridge, G. & Watson, S. (eds.) (2000) *A Companion to the City*. Oxford: Blackwell.
Burawoy, M. & Wright, E. O. (2006) Sociological Marxism. In Turner, J. (ed.) *Handbook of Sociological Theory*. New York, NY: Springer, 459–486.
Burdett, R. & Sudjic, D. (eds.) (2011) *Living in the Endless City*. London: Phaidon.
Calhoun, C. (2006) The critical dimension in sociological theory. In Turner, J. (ed.) *Handbook of Sociological Theory*. New York, NY: Springer, 85–111.
Calhoun, C. et al. (eds.) (2002) *Contemporary Sociological Theory*. Oxford: Blackwell.
Castells, M. (1972) *The Urban Question: A Marxist Approach*. Cambridge, MA: The MIT Press.
Chen, X. et al. (2013) *Introduction to Cities. How Place and Space Shape Human Experience*. Chichester: Wiley-Blackwell.
Davies, J. & Imbroscio, D. (eds.) (2008) *Theories of Urban Politics*. London: Sage.
Gleeson, B. (2013) What role for social science in the 'urban age'? *International Journal of Urban and Regional Research* 37(5): 1839–1851.
Gottdiener, M. et al. (2019) *The New Urban Sociology*. New York, NY: Routledge.
Harding, A. & Blokland, T. (2014) *Urban Theory*. London: Sage.
Jessop, B. et al. (2008) Theorizing sociospatial relations. *Environment and Planning D: Society and Space* 26: 389–401.
Judge, D. et al. (eds.) (1995) *Theories of Urban Politics*. London: Sage.
Knox, P. (ed.) (2014) *Atlas of Cities*. Princeton, NJ: Princeton University Press.
Lefebvre, H. (2003 [1970]) *The Urban Revolution*. Minneapolis, MN: University of Minnesota Press.
Leitner, H. et al. (eds.) (2019) *Urban Studies Inside/Out: Theory, Method, Practice*. London: Sage.
Lin, J. & Mele, C. (eds.) (2013) *The Urban Sociology Reader*. Abingdon: Routledge.
Madoo, P. & Niebrugge-Brantley, J. (2002) Back to the future: Settlement sociology, 1885–1930. *The American Sociologist* Fall: 5–20.
Marx, K. & Engels, F. (1974 [1848]) Manifesto of the Communist Party. In *Collected Works Vol. 6*. London: Lawrence and Wishart.
Mayer, M. (2020) What does it mean to be a (radical) urban scholar-activist, or activist scholar, today? *City* 24(1–2): 35–51.
Mossberger, K. et al. (eds.) (2012) *The Oxford Handbook of Urban Politics*. New York, NY: Oxford University Press.
Orum, A. (ed.) (209) *The Wiley Blackwell Encyclopedia of Urban and Regional Studies*. John Wiley & Sons.
Parnell, S. & Robinson, J. (2017) The global urban: Difference and complexity in urban studies and the science of cities. In Hall, S. & Burdett, R. (eds.) *The SAGE Handbook of the 21st Century City*. London: Sage, 13–31.
Patel, S. (2010) *The ISA Handbook of Diverse Sociological Traditions*. London: Sage.
Pickvance, C. (1995) Comparative analysis, causality and case studies in urban studies. In Rogers, A. & Vertovec, S. (eds.) *The Urban Context. Ethnicity, Social Networks and Situational Analysis*. Oxford: Berg Publishers, 35–54.
Pickvance, C. (2001) Four varieties of comparative analysis. *Journal of Housing and the Built Environment* 16: 7–28.
Saunders, P. (1986) *Social Theory and the Urban Question*. (2nd edition). Abingdon: Routledge.
Savage, M. & Warde, A. (1993) *Urban Sociology, Capitalism and Modernity*. London: Macmillan.
Sayer, A. (2000) *Realism and Social Science*. London: Sage.
Schmid, C. (2018) Journeys through planetary urbanization: Decentering perspectives on the urban. *Environment and Planning D: Society and Space* 36(3): 591–610.
Scott, A. J. & Storper, M. (2014) The nature of cities: The scope and limits of urban theory. *International Journal of Urban and Regional Research* 39(1): 1–15.
Slater, T. (2021) *Shaking up the City. Ignorance, Inequality, and the Urban Question*. Oakland, CA: University of California Press.

Steinmetz, G. (ed.) (2005) *The Politics of Method in Human Sciences: Positivism and Its Epistemological Others*. Durham, NC: Duke University Press.

Storper, M. & Scott, A. (2016) Current debates in urban theory: A critical assessment. *Urban Studies* 53(6): 1114–1136.

Tilly, C. (2008) *Explaining Social Processes*. New York, NY: Routledge.

Tonkiss, F. (2005) *Space, the City and Social Theory: Social Relations and Urban Forms*. Cambridge: Polity.

Tummers, L. & Zibell, B. (2012) What can spatial planners do to create the 'connected city'? A gendered reading of the Charters of Athens. *Built Environment* 38(4): 524–539.

Turner, J. (1985) In defense of positivism. *Sociological Theory* 3(2): 24–30.

Turner, J. (ed.) (2006) *Handbook of Sociological Theory*. New York, NY: Springer.

Verloo, N. & Bertolini, L. (eds.) (2020) *Seeing the City. Interdisciplinary Perspectives on the Study of the Urban*. Amsterdam: University of Amsterdam.

Wacquant, L. (2023) *Bourdieu in the City. Challenging Urban Theory*. Cambridge: Polity.

West, G. (2017) *Scale. The Universal Laws of Growth, Innovation, Sustainability, and the Pace of Life in Organisms, Cities, Economies, and Companies*. New York, NY: Penguin.

Wilden, A. (1987) *The Rules Are No Game. The Strategy of Communication*. New York, NY: Routledge.

Wyly, E. (2011) Positively radical. *International Journal of Urban and Regional Research* 35(5): 889–912.

# PART I

# SOCIETY, STATE, CAPITALISM, AND CITIES

# 2. Social and critical features of urban sociology
## Miguel A. Martínez

Urban scholarship is an increasingly transdisciplinary and cross-fertilising field in which its 'social' dimensions are seldom distinct. Furthermore, 'critical' stances in urban studies are rarely identified beyond a vague or underlying leftist alignment among scholars. Due to the multi-paradigm landscape that social sciences face in epistemological, theoretical, and methodological terms (Alford & Friedland 1985), the aim of defining the social and critical features of urban sociology may thus seem a pyrrhic attempt. However, both sociologists and urban scholars keep nurturing critical thinking in present times. In this chapter I intend to shed light on the meaning of social and critical approaches in urban studies as a response to their increasingly blurred or contradictory formulations. In particular, what should a reconceptualisation of critical urban sociology look like? My main contribution is to combine both discussions in a coherent framework in which the urban space is a key dimension in social structures and processes driven by substantial conflicts and struggles, which are, in turn, the object of critical scrutiny that centrally takes into account the emancipatory claims and practices of the oppressed social groups in relation to the production, reproduction, and transformation of cities. In so doing I engage with classic and recent theorisations of these issues with the purpose of reinvigorating the particular perspective of urban sociology.

Burawoy (2005: 6–7), for example, has argued that sociology has experienced a drift to critical approaches since the 1960s international protest wave while society has moved in the opposite direction, with 'ever-deepening inequality and domination ... expansive markets and coercive states ... in what has commonly come to be known as neoliberalism'. For him, critical sociology should 'examine the foundations—both the explicit and the implicit, both normative and descriptive—of the research programs of professional sociology... [and] make professional sociology aware of its biases, silences, promoting new research programs built on alternative foundations' (Burawoy 2005: 10). Critical sociology would therefore consist of reflexive work interrogating who benefits from sociological knowledge and what values underlie its scientific production. However, it would mainly address academic audiences. If critical sociologists would engage in dialogue, mutual education, and political action with extra-academic publics, it should turn into 'organic public sociology' (Burawoy 2005: 7–8) and follow 'participatory action research' methodologies (Fals-Borda & Rahman 1991).

In the same vein, Mayer (2020) contends that critical scholars are, above all, expected to address the major ecological, economic, and political 'tipping points' of our current times. They should focus 'on the contestations, resistance and emerging alternatives to the destructive and unjust effects of the growth paradigm and seeks to spell out versions of de-growth that connect democratically-led shrinking of production and consumption with the aim of social justice and ecological sustainability' (Mayer 2020: 45). She argues that critical scholarship starts with the study of emancipatory struggles and their political proposals. It should also engage with grassroots activists while discussing how well those political alternatives work and how they could be strengthened and scaled up. She also suggests revealing their side effects and contradictions (Mayer 2020: 47).

Scholars such as Harloe (2018) have offered an insider's account of the trajectory of critical urban sociology. On the one hand, it became an innovative and interdisciplinary response to the urban problems triggered by Fordism (mass production and mass urbanisation) and post-Fordism (deindustrialisation, welfare state cuts, neoliberalism, and globalisation) throughout the 20th century. On the other hand, it had a bitter development through reformist institutionalisation and mainstream scholarship.

Against the backdrop of these insights, in the first section of this chapter I argue that urban sociology comprises, above all, the study of social structures and processes of social change in the production, reproduction, and transformation of cities. According to the critical and materialist approach inaugurated by the 'new urban sociology', the focus on size, density, and diversity is both insufficient and misleading when studying urban phenomena. I thus suggest investigating the social production of the urban space according to its spatiotemporal conditions and the significant contexts defining the relations between people (e.g. specific social relations, groups, and processes) and spaces (e.g. locations, boundaries, and scales of both urban and extra-urban spaces). Furthermore, a critical approach in urban sociology has to question its practical alliances with specific social groups and the effects of the knowledge it produces.

In the second section I contend that critical social sciences would benefit from an 'interdependent' approach between epistemology and politics by reflecting on the opportunities and constraints provided by the latter in relation to the former, but also from their relative autonomy. In line with this approach, critical theory highlights that science should pursue the emancipation of the oppressed above all, while situated epistemologies emphasise the key properties of science in contributing to progressive politics. I then show that some approaches in sociology and urban studies have fruitfully incorporated the legacies of interdependent critical inquiry.

## URBAN SOCIOLOGY RELOADED

Urban sociology is conventionally singled out as the main origin of contemporary urban studies. The first significant contributions in the Western world can be traced back to Friedrich Engels' *The Condition of the Working Class in England* (1845) and *The Housing Question* (1872), written away from academic institutions and disciplines. These works were followed by a plethora of surveys on urban poverty and rural-to-urban migration in parallel with the rise of industrial capitalist urbanisation. In 1892, the Chicago school of sociology led by Robert E. Park and Ernest W. Burgess (Park et al. 1925)—including often forgotten feminist and reformist scholars such as Jane Addams (Deegan 1988)—inaugurated an influential tradition of research on urban communities, ethnicity, and so-called 'social disorganisation', with human ecology and symbolic interactionism as their main theoretical frameworks (Wirth 1938). On the European side, Max Weber's posthumously published *The City* (1921) stressed the socio-spatial dynamics of cultural history, social stratification, local markets, and state power (Isin 2003, Saunders 1986). In the mid-20th century, Ruth Glass—who pioneered the 'gentrification' approach—defined urban sociology as the study of 'social phenomena seen in their mutual influence in a historical, social and physical setting of varying range' (Glass 1955: 7).

Although not intending an appraisal of these legacies here, it is worth noting that they were deeply criticised by Marxist scholars in the 1970s, such as Manuel Castells (1972) and David

Harvey (1973), often in overt or implicit dialogue with Henri Lefebvre's (1970) work. These 'new urban sociology' and 'radical geography' schools prompted the rise of the 'critical' label in urban studies but also tended to circumscribe it to Marxist-inspired approaches (Milicevic 2001, Walton 1993, Zukin 1980). Some renewed Weberian concerns, epitomised by Ray Pahl's thesis on the 'urban managers', were also incorporated into the critical strand in the 1970s onwards (Saunders 1986). In particular, Pahl defined cities as 'the products of the society… reflecting in their physical structures the institutions and social patterns of social stratification of the societies which created them' (Pahl 1968: 3–4).

A remarkable work in this combination of Weberian and Marxist approaches was Logan and Molotch's (1987) analysis of the 'political economy of place' and elites' coalitions as 'growth machines' (Le Galès 2017). Since the 1990s, due to a significant geopolitical restructuring of the world market in the aftermath of the Cold War, critical scholarship in sociology and urban studies has shifted focus toward globalisation, neoliberal urbanisms, financial capitalism, gender, race, and Global South topics above all (Aalbers 2019, Abu-Lughod 1999, Brenner 2019, Garrido et al. 2021, Nicholls 2010, Parnell & Oldfield 2014, Rolnik 2019, Rossi 2017, Sassen 2001, Yrigoy 2018).

Seminal academic outlets *Antipode* (founded in 1969) and the *International Journal of Urban and Regional Research* (IJURR, established in 1977 by the same people who founded the Research Committee on Urban and Regional Development (RC21) within the International Sociological Association in 1970) stood out as the main hosts of critical urban scholarship in the English language and even became top-ranked and very profitable later on. *Espaces et Sociétés* (founded in 1970) was also a reference for critical urbanists in the French language (Harloe 2018). Other journals followed suit in more recent times and were also opened to diverse critical viewpoints (feminism, post/decolonial theory, activist research, political ecology, etc.). Nowadays, urban sociology can be found across all kind of urban studies and sociology journals, with very few only focused on this sub-discipline (*City & Community*, for example, established in 2002) and even fewer journals explicitly associated with Marxism(s) or critical political economy (*Critical Sociology* would count among the exceptions). US and UK academics dominate the editorial boards and institutional locations of most journals in urban studies and sociology. The predominance of the English language as the international standard for academic publishing and the evaluation of scholars' performance has thus relegated journals in other languages to the bottom of this global hierarchy of academic reputation (Müller 2021).

Given that the sociological approach has enjoyed ups and downs in its academic popularity and that competing disciplines have engaged with social issues in very different manners throughout the development of urban studies in the last decades, in the remainder of this section I build on the tradition of the new urban sociology and outline its key features by emphasising the focus on social structures and processes of change in the production of urban spaces. I also engage with recent reflections about the state of the art of urban sociology and discuss its implications.

**Social Structures and Processes**

When urban scholars make use of the adjectives 'social' or 'socio-spatial' they seldom specify what they mean. To address this shortcoming we should go back to the roots of sociology and its original aim of producing scientific knowledge about 'social structures' and 'social change'.

On the one hand, 'social structures' consist of different types of social relations involving social groups; i.e. sets of individuals according to specific social categories of both material and cultural belonging. Social relations may be broadly identified by their economic (wealth), political (power), or cultural (status, information) nature, as well as their contingent combinations (Tilly 1999, Wright 2015). The examination of class, gender, ethnicity, age, ability, and many other cleavages in social relations (Collins 2019) is crucial to determine the main problems at play in a given society. In addition, conflicts, inequalities, and oppressions implying social relations of both vertical (top-down and bottom-up) and horizontal (among relatively equal but different people) character (Boltanski 2011), within and beyond state boundaries, determine how social structures are shaped and reproduced. For most Marxist-inspired urban and housing scholars, socioeconomic inequalities and class structures based on the ownership of the means of production exert the most powerful constraints over urban life, despite their crucial intersections with other sources of power and divisions (Bhattacharya 2017, Holgersen 2022, Jacobs et al. 2022).

On the other hand, 'social change' essentially refers to the dynamic processes of social relations and structures over time, highlighting the major historical shifts that they experience. Industrialisation and migration to cities, for instance, have been often identified as social processes driving urban change over the last two centuries, albeit other phenomena additionally determined the history of cities throughout time (Isin 2003). The historicity of the modern state and the different stages of capitalism are likewise processes that contribute to revealing the major pressures exerted on both individual and collective actions (Martineau 2016). It follows that social scientists need to historically contextualise not only the interpretation of the social phenomena under scrutiny but also the historical development of the concepts they mobilise to know society (Passeron 2006).

Furthermore, social scientists would assume that the ultimate explanation of social phenomena rests in other social phenomena. Neither individuals alone (nor their psychological, emotional, and bodily features) nor extra-social phenomena (from the physical and biological realms, material space included) can suffice to grasp the main social relations, structures, and processes under examination. 'Social facts' must thus be theoretically and reflexively constructed as significantly distinct from the objects of non-social sciences (Bourdieu et al. 1973). Nevertheless, despite the foundational value of this Durkheimian legacy, we do not need to accept social institutions, integrative functions, and symbolic representations as the main matter of sociology. On the contrary, following Marxist insights, I assume that the actual practices and the material living conditions of human beings hold—depending on their dimensions and contextual circumstances—a more constraining power over individuals and groups than values, norms, ideologies, and subjectivities. The latter, however, can exert certain bottom-up influence in social life inasmuch as they help in shaping, reproducing, and modifying social structures. Language and discourse, for example, may also enjoy a performative capacity and enforce social behaviours if certain political, economic, and cultural conditions are met (Bourdieu 1991, Therborn 1980).

Hence, sociology encompasses the study of both structures and agency while assuming that the former mainly constrains and enables the latter, but without the meanings and actions performed by individuals-as-group-members and collective actions, social analysis would be incomplete (Alford & Friedland 1985). Both social structures and social agency include material and symbolic dimensions, but the material aspects will always set more powerful limitations on the expression of social practices, without necessarily determining them entirely. Furthermore, the agency of social groups involves emergent properties that cannot be reduced to their members' features, as well as strategic interactions among peers and between insiders and outsiders. In this critical realist approach, social agents behave in order to cope with structural constraints and opportunities over different historical periods and circumstances (Bhaskar & Callinicos 2003, Sayer 2000).

**The Social Production of Cities**

How does the sociological approach apply to the study of the urban, then? First, it needs to define the urban, which encompasses, in broad terms, all the social phenomena that have to do with the formation, development, and transformation of cities. Cities may be understood as human settlements with relatively high concentrations of people, resources, and buildings. Since cities are lived in and built, planned, managed, and transformed by people, urban phenomena are intrinsically social. Yet the specific merging of the social and spatial features of a city in comparison to other relatively bounded geographical units or scales needs to be specified above all.

The classic formula coined by the Chicago school defined cities as spatial areas with large size and high density, diversity of groups and activities, and social interdependence in terms of a highly developed economic division of labour, as well as between governmental bodies and abundant civil society organisations (Wirth 1938). This conceptualisation of an extraordinary concentration and aggregation of households, economic units, networks of communication, and links with surrounding areas, in addition to international connections and dependencies, has been theoretically refined and contested periodically (Brenner 2019, Saunders 1986, Scott & Storper 2014). On the one hand, the boundaries of cities, and especially of mega urban regions (such as the Pearl River Delta in China, the major European economic corridors, the Mexican Federal District, or the large agglomerations around Cairo and Lagos in Africa), are often difficult to draw. In addition to the different administrative jurisdictions they may incorporate, there are multiple social relations across different spatial scales (peripheries, inner districts, and peri-urban and ex-urban spaces) and types of land use through commuting, the mobility of goods, and political conflicts that contribute to defining the specific central places of an urban area. Hence, the 'socially produced' boundaries of cities are continuously drawn by people's practices and have to be identified and revealed by urban sociologists. On the other hand, the size and growth of urban populations are very superficial indicators when it comes to understanding the social production, reproduction, and transformation of the urban space, which requires special attention to all its material living conditions beyond demographics. Different social groups use, appropriate, influence, and represent urban spaces in diverse—though patterned—manners, in tight intersection with the social structures of wealth, power, and status, and their historical processes of change, that constrain and enable their actions.

The very concept of 'urbanisation' merely indicates three phenomena: 1) rural-to-urban movement of people; 2) demographic characteristics that are highly different from non-urban areas; 3) all human activities affecting any given space, urban or not. In contrast, the notions of 'urbanism' and 'urbanity' denote specific ways of inhabiting and building cities, always in comparison with an outsider extra-urban other (Wirth 1938). Urbanism may also be employed with the strict meaning of urban planning around the organisation of land use as a technical skill usually performed by architects, engineers, and urban designers. As a consequence, where people live and work, how they move within and beyond the city, and what people do in cities even without residing there are key components of the urban as a social phenomenon. Regardless of the main term that is chosen (urbanisation, urbanism or urbanity), all suggest an investigation of socio-spatial phenomena in relation to specific cities, urban sites, and city centre–periphery dialectics by taking into account how spatial locations, boundaries, and scales (among other spatiotemporal categories) are socially produced.

**Spatiotemporal Phenomena and Contexts**

Urban sociology may thus be simply defined as the study of the 'social' aspects of the production, reproduction, and transformation of cities (Gottdiener et al. 2019, Hall & Burdett 2017). In accordance with the premise that 'the social explains the social', the social configuration of space—whether urban or not—is always the result of the interplay of social structures, categorical groups, and historical processes of social change or continuity. This entails an entirely different epistemological logic when compared to spatial (or environmental) determinism. I thus assume that spatial features alone (location, distance, boundaries, scales, places, territory, volumes and materials of construction, etc.) do not suffice to explain urban phenomena. On the contrary, specific social groups with their available resources, power, and knowledge ultimately produce spaces, taking into account that these, once materially and symbolically produced, erect material structures that in turn may constrain and enable social action. The same applies to temporalities such as events, phases, rhythms, ephemerality, memory, path dependence, planning the future, etc., which are likewise socially constructed in urban life and as historical processes in interaction with the natural features of time (Harvey 2006, Martineau 2016).

All social phenomena are thus constituted by spatiotemporal coordinates but these—to the extent that they are social products and not mere physical entities—can hardly explain the origin, development, and consequences of the qualified social phenomena. Space and time are socially shaped, appropriated, used, interpreted, negotiated, planned, and governed. The urban manifestation of time and space is also above all material. Social groups with their own contradictory interests and different needs make them urban, not the other way around. As Gans (2002: 329–330) noted, 'natural space becomes a social phenomenon, or social space, once people begin to use it, boundaries are put on it, and meanings are attached to it'. Mobility practices across urban spaces, commuting to and from cities and the opening hours of public and retail facilities, for example, illustrate how natural time becomes a socio-spatial phenomenon as well. Put differently, 'The question "what is space?" is therefore replaced by the question "how is it that different human practices create and make use of different conceptualizations of space?"' (Harvey 2006: 275); or, as Haila (2016) suggested, we should 'analyse the historical relationships between social classes, the social and political conditions and consequences of using land, and … interrogate the origin of rent' (xxiv).

Another corollary of the above assumptions is that the sole occurrence of social phenomena in the scenario or location of cities (their emplacement) does not entitle them to be 'urban' unless those phenomena contribute to shaping, reproducing, and altering the city in a substantial manner. As Saunders noted, Marx, Durkheim, and Weber's 'analyses were not aspatial, for they understood how spatial proximity could, for example, help foster a sense of class consciousness among city-based factory workers, or could aid the erosion of a powerful collective morality, but they were non-spatial, in the sense that the explanations for such phenomena were located in changes current in the society as a whole which were not specific to cities or any other form of human settlement' (Saunders 1986: 169). Topalov provided a striking illustration of the same rationale. He stressed that from the 1990s onwards urban scholars in France were called to help in fixing issues such as 'the problem of the *banlieue* [marginalised suburbs in French urban regions]' but the definition of the problem was not necessarily 'urban': 'a social question has been transformed into a spatial or urban question, and relationships between social groups have been redefined as relationships between groups and spaces… Mention is rarely made of unemployment, the lack of job security, low wages, racism, police violence and denial of justice, failing schools, or the impossibility of starting up a business' (Topalov 2015: 6–7).

Contrary to Saunders' conclusions leading to a full-fledged non-spatial urban sociology (Saunders 1986: 194–195, 202–203), I contend that urban sociology is defined by the study of social phenomena for which the physical space is more relevant than other intervening dimensions. For instance, the social claims to access housing and the decisions about planning specific land uses for different parts of the city all involve social relations, structures, and processes in which determined spaces are key and contested dimensions. Saunders, however, is correct when he introduces—following Massey (1984)—the additional ontological need for spatial aspects to be at the core of socio-spatial phenomena as their key constituents (Saunders 1986: 190–192, 201). This argument demands the interpretation of empirical contingencies in order to discern whether spatial features crucially structure social phenomena once they have been socially produced or because of their physical conditions. In short, urban sociology studies the interplay of people and urban space but two additional warnings are needed. First, neither part of the equation must be superficially defined—we need to study these features with thick descriptions and dialectical and historical approaches. Second, there is not equal weight for each part—the social becomes primary when it comes to explaining socio-spatial phenomena as a whole, in a non-deterministic manner. What people do, think, produce, and shape, for example, in relation to (urban) space represents the ultimate echelon of explanations in a chain of constraints of the people over the space, including the feedback of spatial constraints once space is appropriated, created, or used in certain ways. The people as well as the urban are the product of specific social structures and processes that need to be disclosed and explained. In these dual relations not all people and not all urban spaces need to be included at once in every set of the phenomena under examination.

Furthermore, different contexts drive the interpretation of urban phenomena in different directions (Pickvance 1995, Therborn 2017). Neoliberal urbanism, for example, since the 1970 and 1980s has caused a considerable shift in our social understanding of many cities worldwide, both in liberal democratic and authoritarian regimes (Mayer 2016, Rossi 2017). In the urban sphere neoliberal policies entailed measures promoting inter-city competition to attract capital investment, especially in post-industrial areas; the privatisation of municipal property and services or the entire suppression of welfare benefits; various forms of deregulation of capital flows and urban management (of housing and planning, energy supplies, waste disposal, etc.); legitimation strategies with extreme symbolic inflation and spectacle (exclusionary processes of citizen participation, city-branding, mega events and buildings, etc.); suburban expansion at the same time as processes of gentrification (Lees et al. 2016) and concentration of corporate capital in the city centre; and increasing trends of urban touristification (Novy & Colomb 2017, Gil & Sequera 2022) and commodification of urban goods. At least until the 2008 global financial crisis and the 2020 Covid-19 pandemic, the hegemony of neoliberal urbanism represented a historical period of intensified state transfers to capital via intertwined state–market operations such as public–private partnerships and deteriorating conditions for labour epitomised in the disciplinary repression of international migrants (Nicholls & Uitermark 2017) (and internal migrants too in India, China, Brazil, Russia, and South Africa) and precarious workers of 'digital platforms'. These conditions have also favoured the rise and increasing dominance of financial capital, especially manifest in the urban housing sector where state authorities retrenched. According to the literature, cities and states subject to neoliberal rule have also facilitated capital accumulation through the increasing indebtedness of the working-class residents and inhabitants (via mortgages or rentierism, for example (Aalbers 2019, Christophers 2021, Gil & Martínez 2023, Yrigoy 2018)) and the unsustainable consumption of scarce natural resources aiming at extreme rates of uneven and unlimited growth.

**Contemporary Crossroads for Urban Sociology**

The legacies of the new urban sociology are slightly hidden in urban studies (Harding & Blokland 2014, Lin & Mele 2013, May & Perry 2005: 344), especially when there are not clear distinctions between the social groups, structures, and processes of change at play in the study of urban phenomena. Let me summarise those legacies and their current implications for consistent and fruitful theoretical frameworks for critical urban sociology.

According to Castells (2002), different approaches in urban sociology were responses to the problems of each historical period. Topalov (2015) however suggests that the rise of the new approaches in the 1960s and 1970s was mainly a result of the theoretical and political debates of their times. Regardless of who is right, each theoretical approach has its own theoretical powers and limitations (Alford & Friedland 1985, Le Galès 2005: 351). Marxist criticisms towards the Chicago school are a case in point (Harvey 2001: 68–89). In particular, Castells (1968, 1972) attacked the ideological bases and the lack of conceptual rigour—according to his reconstruction of Marxist categories—of the approach with 'social integration… of recent rural immigrants' and 'urban culture' (Castells 2002: 9–10) as its prime concerns.

Castells' own contributions on 'state-mediated consumption processes' (Castells 2002: 11) and 'social groups with conflicting interests and alternative projects' and 'urban social movements' (Castells 1983, 2002: 10–11) also questioned 'culturalist' critics such as Lefebvre and Mumford, despite some reconciliation with them in his next salient work on urban movements targeting the 'meaning'—next to spatial forms and social structures—of the city (Castells 1983, Gottdiener 1984). Thus, 'cities became redefined as the points of contradiction between capital accumulation and social redistribution, between state control and people's autonomy' (Castells 2002: 11). Castells' approach of giving theoretical priority to class conflicts, urban movements, and state-led capitalism in shaping cities has been one of the most influential critical approaches in urban sociology to date, despite some specific weaknesses (Fainstein & Hirst 1995, Martínez 2020a, Mayer 2006, Miller 2006, Pickvance 1985).

The rise of the new urban sociology in countries such as Italy, France, and the UK responded to the effects of mass production (Fordism), the migration of a low-wage labour force from agriculture to cities, and rapid urbanisation and social conflicts in the aftermath of the Second World War: 'for example, inner city urban renewal led to the destruction of communities and the removal of their residents to the periphery. And, on the periphery, large public housing estates, with poor facilities and limited access to employment, were another source of urban struggles' (Harloe 2018: 30). State authorities thus demanded the services of radical urban scholars to formulate and evaluate urban policies. These scholars in turn wished to promote socialist alternatives with their analyses, both in state institutions and academic departments. Despite the dominance of structuralist Marxism in this school, some of these researchers had a more nuanced understanding of the historical cycles of capitalism, its globalising trend, the fragmentation of the working class, and the increase in urban poverty (Massey 1984, Mingione 1991).

Nevertheless, Castells himself admitted that his Marxist urban sociology 'became obsolete vis-à-vis its new urban context, marked by the early stages of the Information Age' (Castells 2002: 11). According to him, urban sociologists of our times should be concerned again with the old topics of social integration and urban culture, although with an updated terminology: 'cities [are] communication artifacts... the challenge is the sharing of the city by irreversibly distinct cultures and identities... how messages are transmitted from one group to another, from one meaning to another in the metropolitan region' (Castells 2002: 14–15). Intertwined online and offline communities, networked spatial mobility ('homes and offices on the run' (Castells 2002: 16) and geosatellite maps and navigation), mass tourism, international migration, 'people's strategies to overcome the constraints of a gendered built environment' (Castells 2002: 17), and, not the least important, the 'lingering questions of urban poverty, racial and social discrimination, and social exclusion' (Castells 2002: 17) would be some of the key topics to investigate. This agenda encompasses various relevant phenomena, as well as novel concepts such as 'time-space regimes' and 'glocal social movements', but in my view, and according to some critics, Castells' theoretical framework risks a lack of attention to the central social processes, power structures, and relations that derive from the capitalist political economy of cities, and neoliberal urbanism in particular (Marcuse 2002: 137).

Why did these changes take place? How were they possible? Who won and who lost? By specifying the social relations, groups, structures, and processes at play, urban sociologists hold a distinct vantage point to explain these phenomena in their old and new dimensions. Socio-spatial segregation and unaffordable housing, for instance, are regular urban problems, although subject to different forces and grassroots responses in every historical period (Madden & Marcuse 2016, Rolnik 2019, Slater 2021).

Following this line of inquiry, Zukin reminds us that one of the 'crucial findings' of the critical school of urban sociology in the 1960s to the 1980s

> was that space is produced; it doesn't just appear or develop *naturally*. As it is a social product that requires specific laws like zoning and often serious financial subsidies from the state, and also has the potential to move people around against their will, the production of space always represents forces of capital, always implicates political elites, and sometimes also provokes collective resistance. (Zukin 2011: 10)

This implies investigating the 'social production of the space' according to social contradictions and contentious processes as well as the engendered forms of social life. The empirical concerns of urban sociology would be clearly oriented toward knowing 'what kinds of social structures are created in one place but not in another, and why. The science of urban sociology needs to make comparisons' (Zukin 2011: 14).

On a supplementary note, Sassen's plea for urban sociology insists on studying cities in order to understand 'the broader social transformations under way' (Sassen: 2005: 353).

She departs from cities, different urban spaces, and places in their physical materiality and proximity but without necessarily being bounded: 'a city is traversed by a variety of global or trans-urban circuits that produce new types of fragmentations alongside the old ones ... [and] strategic sites for the enactment of important transformations in multiple institutional domains' (Sassen 2005: 354–355). Therefore, instead of asking what sociology can offer to the city (or urban studies), Sassen is rather inclined to ask what the study of cities can offer to sociology—to the knowledge of societal change at large.

More explicitly, Mayer (2020: 40–41) pointed out that contemporary critical urban studies should be concerned with global capitalism, its ecological 'tipping point... and the emergence of growing numbers of "superfluous" people [which] are creating unprecedented social upheaval'. Within this contemporary context, an urgent research question would be: who controls and who resists the dominant organisation and governance of cities—and why, how, and with what consequences?

Moving beyond Marxism, other critical scholars such as Harding and Blokland, for example, have defended a pluralistic view of urban studies 'as a result of the acute visibility of inter- and intra-urban inequalities, related to deindustrialization, migration and segregation' (2011: 5). They suggested getting rid of ethno- and Western-centric analyses by paying more attention to cities and urban phenomena in the Global South, which have certainly been increasingly reported in urban journals and book series in the present century.

Similarly, Le Galès proposed manifold research topics engaging with old and new trends in urban affairs worldwide. According to him,

> Research on gated communities, the rise of fantasy cities, transnational migrations, poverty, global cities and the governance of local economies, are being debated and researched in every continent... There is only a limited amount of urban sociology research done on major cities such as Manila, Djakarta, Tehran, Nairobi or Seoul. In that perspective, both classical questions about inequalities, segregation, social mobility, food riots, the making of social and political order and new questions about transnational migrations or the 'global local problematic' are central to the development of urban sociology. Urban sociologists are at the forefront of this trend because they easily think beyond national frontiers and beyond the nation state. (Le Galès 2005: 349)

He also calls to investigate the different types of urban models, sites, and 'mixes of social, political, economic, cultural and economic structures' (Le Galès 2005: 349). Hence, his approach is not only about the necessity of knowing the different meanings of the city, its distinct urban areas, and the social groups involved in their production, consumption and transformation but also their relation to broader metropolitan, global, and social structures.

## Urban Sociology for Whom?

A final issue to discuss here relates to the practical effects of urban sociology. How useful is urban sociology for policy reforms, urban planning, and urban activism? Should its contributions serve to advance urban reforms within the capitalist system or to propose radical programmes capable of overcoming the dominant capitalist social relations in the production of the urban space?

Topalov, for example, has summarised these dilemmas and splits in the French schools of urban sociology. On the one hand, some 'clearly defined an urban sociology that deliberately positioned itself in such a way as to ensure better-informed planning on a more humane scale.... with the aim of improving things gradually' (Topalov 2015: 3, 8) On the other hand, others tried to pursue a more radical agenda by 'analysing the capitalist production of the city, the urban policies of central government and the social movements that contested these policies' (Topalov 2015: 3). The latter were also engaged in specific projects with progressive local authorities in order to foster radical changes; however 'without realizing it, [they] remained fascinated by the state at the same time' (Topalov 2015: 8). Therefore, rather than radical change, reforms are more likely to happen when urban sociologists are highly dependent on state funds and political constraints, which end up in the policy-driven definition of urban phenomena and problems such as the *banlieues*. This development was mainly due to the 'neoliberal conservative revolution' and the collapse of urban planning where urban sociologists found their main allies (Topalov 2015: 9). Such a risk may be mitigated when sociologists ally with progressive grassroots urban movements or bridge their struggles with responsive state authorities.

Zukin (2011) also advocates a reflexive self-criticism of the discipline, warning against its submission to powerful funders whose interest in 'urban problems' and 'solutions' often leads scholarly work to reinforce social control and superficial policy reforms and fuel ongoing capitalist urbanisation according to exploitative business as usual.

As a consequence, it seems inevitable to investigate to what extent the knowledge produced by urban sociology is efficiently used, above all in policy-making, local administration, urban planning, and housing management, and what their benefits and side effects are (Slater 2021). Real estate developers, investors, public–private partnerships, and other for-profit private businesses can take advantage of the views provided by urban scholars, which would demand an even more critical questioning of this sponsorship given the exploitative dynamics that are entailed in most of those businesses. No less critical evaluations should be conducted to grasp how urban sociology is applicable to the solidarity and cooperative branches of the urban economy (Ferreri & Vidal 2021), and the strategic choices of urban movements (Martínez 2019, 2020a).

## WHEN EPISTEMOLOGY MEETS POLITICS

Standard and mainstream notions of science claim that politics is—and ought to be—in an entirely separate realm of social reality. If there is any mutual influence between science and politics, this is just an object of investigation for certain academic disciplines, not a feature that defines scientific work. Epistemology—the analysis of the conditions of possibility and validity of knowledge—should be free of political concerns, it is claimed. Conversely, a critical approach to social sciences, such as the one examined earlier when discussing urban sociology, takes those encounters between science and politics at the core of their epistemological assumptions, albeit in specific ways that I aim to present in this section. Critical social science, in short, aims at revealing the structures, causal powers, and contexts of social phenomena (Sayer 2000: 11–13), including—reflexively—the social conditions and effects of scientific knowledge (Calhoun 2006). In particular, the openness of social phenomena to historical change and their dialectical or conflictual nature (Harvey 1996, Wilden 1987), rather than approaches focused on the social order and atomistic phenomena, present an invitation to place power and politics at the core of scientific investigations (Fraser 2003).

I suggest distinguishing two kinds of critical inquiry: 'subaltern' and 'interdependent'. Subaltern critical science means that every scientific operation is highly constrained by the environment of power relations and the ideological views of the researchers and other participants in the social processes of knowledge production. Politics as well as other social, economic, and cultural interferences eventually undermine the scientific project, including any claim of objective truth. Epistemology becomes equal to politics. Science becomes subaltern in relation to politics. Therefore, power relations contaminate all the moments of the scientific process and hinder its independent flourishing. Constructivist and relativist epistemologies often account for these limitations. Both full-fledged partisan (i.e. 'organic') and fatalist attitudes may guide scientists who take this stance.

The 'interdependence' of science and politics means that the latter offers both constraints and opportunities for the former. Political goals crucially motivate scientists. Political—as well as social, economic, and cultural—circumstances and institutions make science possible and socially acceptable or the opposite—science is not always subordinated to politics. Epistemology thus consists of joint reflection on politics and science in order to scrutinise their interdependence or relative independence and to determine the most desirable combination of both. Rather than assuming the entire subordination of science to politics, the researchers have relative autonomy at some stages of the process of knowledge production. It is thus claimed that scientists hold a logical-rational or technical expertise that makes a difference compared to other social and political skills. Nevertheless, scientific knowledge is always partial, situated, and provisional, subject to further improvement (Calhoun 2006). Scientists working within specific social structures also become critical when they are both aware of the social structures in which they work and aim to change them if deemed politically, ideologically, and morally intolerable. Scientific scepticism and non-dogmatic political commitment go hand in hand without partisan conflation.

In the remainder of the section I argue that the 'interdependent' standpoint represents a more robust and fruitful critical approach to urban sociology than the 'subaltern' one, despite the possibility that they may not entirely be mutually exclusive. In addition, I acknowledge that some Marxist traditions (Burawoy & Wright 2006, Skeggs et al. 2022) have been crucial in the articulation of both branches. However, they rarely provide a united view of the nature of science and the direction of emancipatory politics.

**From Critical Theory to Situated Epistemology**

To clarify my view, I assume that all sciences should be critical in at least three dimensions: 1) they should have the capacity to question common sense, myths, and beliefs, especially irrational and religious ones; 2) they should disclose hidden aspects, structural patterns, causal and contingent associations, constraining contexts, and spatiotemporal dynamics of reality; 3) scientists should be expected to counter facts, findings, explanations, and arguments generated by other scientists if proved wrong. Social sciences are no different (Steinmetz 2005). However, social and political worldviews have much more influence in the social sciences when it comes to selecting research topics, adhering to specific theories, and interpreting data compared to natural and experimental branches of science. As a result, struggles between different epistemological paradigms in social sciences are much more strident.

For the purpose of this chapter there are two milestones that foreground these disputes. First, there is Marx and Engels's critique of conventional political economy up to the 19th century, which naturalised and fetishised the exploitation of labour. Second, there is the critical theory elaborated by key figures of the Frankfurt school (Theodor Adorno, Max Horkheimer, Herbert Marcuse, etc.) and diffused throughout the 20th Century, especially after the 1968 uprisings. I focus on the latter because it originally engaged with Marx's famous exhortation: 'Philosophers have hitherto only interpreted the world in various ways; the point is to change it' (Marx & Engels 1845: 123).

In its early formulations, critical theory held the following rationale. Theory (preferred by them to 'science') entails rational knowledge and explanatory—not merely descriptive or exploratory—interpretations of reality, albeit only by taking a holistic perspective, including macro and micro phenomena together. Social research encompasses both the unmasking of justifications of the capitalist society as well as precise knowledge of its inherent contradictions, mainly as class struggles. However, knowledge alone does not suffice. It should also instigate a certain kind of politics—the emancipation of the proletariat from capitalist exploitation and alienation. In Horkheimer's words, this particular form of science/theory seeks to satisfy 'the needs and powers of men [and women]' (Horkheimer 1972: 246).

This overarching programme consisted of an investigation of all forms of social domination—in both the infrastructural realm of production and the superstructural realm of ideology—in relation to the historical rise and global rule of capitalism. At the same time, it suggested practical ways to overcome them according to the potentialities and political utopias of the oppressed human beings—socialism and communism, although in a more democratic fashion than implemented by the Soviet Union and its satellite regimes. According to my initial categories, they took a 'subaltern' position regarding the relations between epistemology and politics.

However, this specific articulation of Marxism did not amend the three main critical dimensions of all sciences, as expressed above. On the contrary, it attempted to move social sciences further toward a comprehensive theory able to synthesise knowledge and emancipatory politics. On the one hand, this ambition held substantial benefits. Critical scholars would give priority to research with the potential to serve emancipatory purposes. Even non-self-identified critical scientists ought not to keep silent or unreflective regarding the practical implications of their empirical inquiries, questions, and results. The critical warning was that any scientific endeavour may be used for violating the scientists' moral beliefs and political preferences. On the other hand, a synthesis as such had the obvious risk of making science entirely subordinated to partisan political goals in a way that may discard any alleged autonomy of science. Adorno and Horkheimer, indeed, were severe opponents of hardcore positivist science for it may be used as another myth and form of domination, even leading to war and fascism (Pombo et al. 2011: 2).

A healthy corollary follows—critical approaches are also required to be subject to criticism. Their interpretations can be insufficient, wrong, or simply outdated in relation to the historical mutations of capitalism and political regimes. Likewise, critical scholars' political proposals might be dogmatic, authoritarian, or rejected by those they intend to emancipate. In support of the 'interdependent' approach, it is worth recalling that critical theory was questioned early on in the 1930s by Otto Neurath, a socialist member of the Vienna Circle (the cradle of various positivist strands). Neurath criticised Horkheimer's anti-science attitude and argued exactly the contrary—that scientific knowledge can contribute to social and political progress because it eliminates superstition through testable theories and the interdisciplinary cooperation of scientists (Neurath 1937, Pombo et al. 2011). Neurath unambiguously adhered to the

Enlightenment project—the rule of reason but also the moral imperatives of human rights and the political triad of equality, solidarity, and freedom. This implied, for him, the need of theoretical and methodological pluralism as well as open discussion for the sake of scientific advancement first and political progress later. The ulterior dominant versions of positivism were much less plural though (Steinmetz 2005).

Neurath's defence of 'interdependence' illustrates alternative notions of a critical social science. In general, positivism has often been portrayed as a caricature exclusively comprising quantitative measures and political conservatism (Steinmetz 2005, Wyly 2011). In urban scholarship there is justification for this image. The 'positivist city hall' (Wyly 2011: 893–895) in urban planning, for example, exacerbates the exclusive rule of an experts' technocracy, with false assertions of neutrality and objectivity and biased notions of the general interest. Thus, as Wyly argues, critical urban scholarship would not be trusted as an alternative to this scientific and political hegemony if it did not provide solid and credible scientific knowledge based on traits such as accuracy, validity, reliability, integrity, rigour, and accountability. Depending on the research questions and the complexity of the topics, different methods may be used or wisely combined. Moreover, not all social phenomena can be precisely or meaningfully measured, so qualitative inquiry and interpretation may be more appropriate in those cases.

Given various controversial epistemological issues concerning replicability, prediction, generalisation, universal laws, models of causality, and absolute objectivity, some critical social scientists prefer to call for 'hybrid', 'situated', or 'strategic' positivism (Wyly 2011: 906) in a fashion not so different from plain non-positivist epistemologies such as dialectical materialism and critical realism (Bhaskar & Callinicos 2003, Harvey 1996). For either strand, science should not be subordinated to politics despite the guidance and inspiration provided by the latter. The point is to produce 'objective, real truths in particular contexts of time, place and human understanding' (Wyly 2011: 905) by resorting, at the least, to theoretical consistency, clearly defined concepts, appropriate and accountable methods, and a coherent match between explanations and empirical evidence. In another concise formulation: 'doing sociology in a critical way means looking beyond appearances, understanding root causes, and asking who benefits' (Buechler 2014: 12). This is especially urgent in times of accelerated climate change, pandemics, forced displacements, fake news, flat-earth believers, and devastating financialised capitalism. In this context, the ruling class may easily dismiss science altogether or make it up according to its material interests and ideological goals. Both are deplorable alternatives.

In my view, if critical scholars want to address social injustice, inequalities, and all forms of oppression (in the realms of wealth misdistribution and the misrecognition of identities (Fainstein 2010, Fraser 2003)), good social science practiced according to at least the above criteria is one of their main weapons to wield. Yet critical theory has shown that the social responsibility of scientists and their political commitment to the emancipation of the oppressed social groups is a guiding beacon for all who participate in the production of significant and valid knowledge. Scientific skills can be as useful as those of lawyers, journalists, or musicians when there are chances to contribute to protest campaigns, workers and residents' organising, policy change, or revolutions. A common ground for all engaged experts could be 'do not serve the masters' or 'do not empower all the stakeholders alike'. It also follows that normative notions such as 'the right to the city' (Marcuse 2009, Mitchell 2003, Grazioli 2021), 'urban commons' (Martínez 2020b), 'the just city' (Fainstein 2010), or 'real utopias' (Wright 2010) add a useful political direction to scientific research and are themselves legitimate matters of critical theoretical and empirical scrutiny.

## Public Sociology

Critical sociology has also drawn on the above legacies, which is manifest, for example, in the work of Wright Mills (1959) when he tried to debunk the flawed functionalist paradigm of Parsons, and its 'abstract empiricism' companion provided by Lazarsfeld, prevailing in the academy and among policy-makers until the 1960s. Wright Mills explicitly advocated for the values of reason and freedom, for workers' control of production, and for participatory democracy in a similar fashion to what is known today as 'public sociology' (Burawoy 2005). In terms of my previous discussion, Wright Mills would match the 'interdependent' approach to critical scholarship, manifested in his statements in favour of independent researchers rid of the constraints of state and corporate powers. However, regarding the scope of his contributions it is worth noting that he did not pay attention to structural issues of race, gender, and grassroots social movements (Burawoy 2008). Indeed, 'knowing the power of social structures is just as likely to paralyze as to mobilize' (Burawoy 2008: 369). This knowledge is just a necessary step in order to be engaged, talk, and work with oppressed communities and marginalised social groups (Burawoy 2008: 372–373).

Burawoy's 'public sociology' programme has also been at the centre of heated debates. For example, some disagree with his claim that 'public sociology' can peacefully coexist and be compatible 'in a reciprocal interdependence' (Burawoy 2005: 15) with mainstream 'professional' and 'policy' sociology (Feagin et al. 2009: 72). Without an enduring struggle against mainstream sociology, critical/public sociologists concerned with social justice and human rights will not achieve more than 'subaltern positions': 'We see no evidence that professional sociology has ever made the major ideas of feminism, Marxism, and critical race theory central to its concerns' (Feagin et al. 2009: 76). In another rubric, Feagin et al. (2009) suggest looking beyond the exclusive focus on the three main categorical inequalities along class, gender, and race lines in order to heed oppressions and discriminations related to heteronormativity, homophobia, transphobia, ageism, ableism, citizenship, nationality, carcerality, housing, religion, caste, coloniality, etc. (Collins 2019, Fraser 2003). Nevertheless, the demarcation of social phenomena also calls for the scrutiny of what kind of categorical inequality and oppression is more influential in given spatiotemporal parameters according to the social groups involved and the main traits of the dominant politico-economic context (Bhattacharya 2017).

Another challenge for critical/public sociology is that it can also be practised by scholars who espouse conservative or far-right agendas (e.g. anti-abortion and anti-immigration advocates). Hence, more unequivocal normative development is always needed to supplement scientific research. Additionally, the time dedicated to public exposure and political engagement by scientists may damage their actual income and prospects of academic promotion, unless they are tenured, hired as lucrative consultants or media commentators, or authors of bestselling books (Glenn 2009). By the same token, their activism may risk ending in a type of political involvement and raising public statements without the support of rigorous sociological research or conclusive evidence (Glenn 2009: 141–144).

Critical social scientists are thus prone to become activists and perform the role of 'organic' or 'public intellectuals', defined as those who 'identify with the trouble-making assertions of power by groups at the bottom of society, or groups at the cultural margins… when we commit ourselves to the more troubling sorts of demands that advance the interests and ideas of groups that are at the margins of public life, the people who are voiceless, degraded and exploited' (Piven 2010: 807–808).

The study of emancipatory struggles and their political proposals (Grazioli 2021, Jacobsson 2015, Martínez 2020a, Polanska & Richard 2021, Thörn 2020) thus represents a privileged entry point for engaged scholarship, though not necessarily conducive to progressive outcomes unless scholars collaborate with activists in the research process and the popular dissemination and appropriation of the research outcomes (Fals-Borda & Rahman 1991). As Bourdieu (2002: 1) stressed, a scholar in social movements

> is not dispensing lessons—like certain organic intellectuals who, unable to peddle their wares on the harshly competitive scientific market, resort to playing the intellectual among non-intellectuals, all the while denying the intellectual's very existence. A scholar is neither a prophet nor an intellectual guru. [S/]He must invent a very difficult new role: [s/]he must listen, search and create; [s/]he must try to help the organisations that have taken up the mission of resisting neoliberal politics.

**Critical Urban Studies**

In the interdisciplinary field of urban studies, the canon of the critical approach led by Marxist political economy has often been questioned by assemblage, planetary urbanism, post/decolonial, and communicative planning approaches (Aalbers 2022, Bhambra 2014, Brenner 2019, Chibber 2013, Fainstein 2010, Holgersen 2022, Leitner et al. 2020, Rossi 2017, Scott 2022, Storper & Scott 2016). Despite many of them sharing the common ground of critical and radical orientations in politics, the degree and nature of the latter and their epistemological assumptions have been highly disputed, which nonetheless seems a healthy academic development, at least to clarify each standpoint. Reviews or collections from specific world regions beyond the West and Anglo-Saxon academic dominance—especially from the often-ignored Global South(s) and East(s), or low- and middle-income countries and cities in the UN's preferred language—along with the visibility of their urban phenomena and the scholars' engagement with the struggles that take place there, not to mention significant comparisons, have enlarged and enriched the above discussions over the last two decades (Aalbers 2022, Coelho & Sood 2022, Fix & Arantes 2022, Lancione & McFarlane 2021, Marrengane & Croese 2021, Vilenica 2023). However, these contributions have not sufficed to settle durable agreements between the different theoretical interpretations and the political implications at play.

More often than not, critical scholars target other less radical academics and think tanks as opponents. This also contributes to the critical reflexivity of sociology beyond, before, or simultaneously with its public engagement. Take as an illustration Wacquant's criticism of three urban ethnographies for 'their eager embrace of the clichés of public debate (albeit in inverted form), the pronounced discordance between interpretation and the evidence they offer, and the thick coat of moralism in which their analyses are wrapped' (Wacquant 2002: 1469). This criticism stands on the shoulders of critical appraisals of the 'culture of poverty' studies that are time and again revived with media and political stereotypes alike (Wyly 2011: 895). As Wacquant notes, the reviewed books treat the black proletariat as 'paragons of morality… in an effort to attract sympathy for their plight' (Wacquant 2002: 1470). However, according to him, the 'task of social science… is to dissect the social mechanisms and meanings that govern their practices, ground their morality (if such be the question), and explain their strategies and trajectories, as one would do for any social category, high or low, noble or ignoble' (Wacquant 2002: 1470). This lack of both political and theoretical reflexivity leaves 'U.S. sociology… tied and party to the ongoing construction of the *neoliberal* state and its "carceral-assistential complex" for the punitive management of the poor' (Wacquant 2002: 1471).

Following Wacquant's steps, Slater (2021) has revealed the vested interests and pernicious politics for the working class that lie behind policy-driven research on urban resilience, new urbanism, gentrification, neighbourhood effects, the creative class, rent control, and the ghetto. His 'agnotological' approach thus interrogates the categories, rationales, and political implications of the 'ignorance' produced in that body of urban research, often under the guidance of policy and corporate agenda-setting alien to thorough, theoretically based questions. Conversely, against those scholarly and think tanks discourses he opposes more relevant empirical evidence based on, for example, the examination of 'territorial stigmatisation' processes that activate rent gaps. On the political side, Slater advocates for specific policy proposals such as rent controls that have been proved beneficial to address the reproduction of inequalities and the socio-spatial displacement of the urban poor, racialised groups, and women. In sum, he envisions critical urban scholarship as going 'against the grain of established research orthodoxies to dissect multiple aspects of urban divisions, to diagnose and challenge the hegemonic economic and political order of the metropolis, and to critique the categories of urban research that serve the interests of state elites and big business' (Slater 2021: 3).

In the same vein, Brenner et al. proposed five indications to move forward in the critical approach to urban studies, which represent a useful guideline beyond the 2008 global financial crash that contextualised their formulation:

(a) to analyze the systemic, yet historically specific, intersections between capitalism and urbanization processes;
(b) to examine the changing balance of social forces, power relations, sociospatial inequalities and political–institutional arrangements that shape, and are in turn shaped by, the evolution of capitalist urbanization;
(c) to expose the marginalizations, exclusions and injustices (whether of class, ethnicity, 'race', gender, sexuality, nationality or otherwise) that are inscribed and naturalized within existing urban configurations;
(d) to decipher the contradictions, crisis tendencies and lines of potential or actual conflict within contemporary cities, and on this basis;
(e) to demarcate and to politicize the strategically essential possibilities for more progressive, socially just, emancipatory and sustainable formations of urban life. (Brenner et al. 2009: 179)

Another source of critical insights in urban studies can be traced back to the foundation of the IJURR. Its editors aimed to counter the hegemony of the Chicago school and micro-community studies for they 'led to a strong functionalist emphasis, attributing conflict to individual pathology rather than tracing it to structural bases' (Harloe et al. 1998: i). The journal thus privileged a macro sociological approach and questions concerning the 'class interests which are affected by planning and state intervention, the accumulation and circulation of capital in the regional system, the ownership of land and other economic determinants of the urbanization process, and urban social movements as spatial reflections of the class struggle' (Harloe et al. 1998: ii). After two decades of consolidation of the journal, there was also an openness to micro and bottom-up approaches because they 'may be very useful, and are in fact the necessary complement of more macro approaches' (Harloe et al. 1998: iv).

In this development, the IJURR editors added three guidelines: 1) scientific research defined by its explicit theoretical statements subjected to empirical control; 2) interdisciplinary confrontation and mutual enrichment inspired by Marxism (but in a heterodox fashion, 'to be treated as an intellectual approach like any other' (Harloe et al. 1998: iv)); and 3) an international scope through comparative urban research beyond Western ethnocentrism. For them, 'being critical may seem slightly tautological for an academic journal, since social science is supposed to refuse to accept established representations of society' (Harloe et al. 1998: i). Consequently, the first obligation of a critical scholar is to produce science that is epistemologically, theoretically, and methodologically sound—and critical with regard to previous knowledge on a given matter when justified.

Remarkably, the IJURR promoters chose the stance to leave politics and 'advocacy' in 'other arenas of expression… [because] research should not be subordinated to politics. Rather, research should develop its own independent scientific criteria and would thereby make its best possible contribution to politics—"*seule la vérité est révolutionnaire*"' (Harloe et al. 1998: iii). In my view, the truth may also be revolutionary when established through cooperation and critical dialogue with those struggling for their emancipation. However, I concede that the vantage point of the proletariat and other oppressed groups does not guarantee any access to the truth. Furthermore, the official truths of their alleged representatives (trade unions, political parties, organic intellectuals, movement organisations) who never scrutinise how the subjugated people actually live and think have also experienced historical defeats in terms of substantial advancement towards a leftist hegemony and a fairer society (Hoffman 2019).

A controversial point in discussion has become the corporate ownership of academic journals, including those born with a radical orientation. Scholars who run the journals made compromises with the transnational capital that is increasingly concentrated in academic publications, critical and non-critical alike, while imposing its profit-seeking logics on researchers working unpaid as editors, reviewers, and authors. Their rewards are mostly symbolic in the form of reputation and scientific credibility, which can be converted into economic benefits like a promotion in their academic career or paid invitations to give keynote speeches, evaluate research and policy programmes, etc. The growing neoliberalisation of universities (Harvie et al. 2022) has engendered more competitive and casualised labour environments, so urban studies journals with a critical orientation have struggled to strike a balance between their high-quality standards and the cash-making pressure of publishers aiming to increase the number of released articles, paywall downloads, institutional subscriptions, and for-profit trades of big data. A backlash to these trends is manifested in alternative initiatives taken by other self-managed publications (*ACME, Radical Housing Journal, Interface, Ephemera, Sociologica, Partecipazione e Conflitto, Culture Unbound, tripleC*, etc.) and activist research networks, collectives, and projects (INURA,[1] SqEK,[2] CRUSH,[3] Conflictos Urbanos,[4] Beyond Inhabitation,[5] Anti-Eviction Mapping Project,[6] Common City,[7] etc.).

## CONCLUSIONS

This chapter has discussed key concepts and theoretical assumptions that underpin critical urban sociology. The legacy of the 'new urban sociology' from the 1960s and 1970s was examined by emphasising the materialist and realist connections between social and spatiotemporal phenomena, particularly in their manifestations in cities. Rather than spatial determinism, I have argued that space is socially, culturally, politically, and economically organised, produced, reproduced, and transformed in interaction with its natural/physical features. It is people, divided into specific social groups with different resources, who build, shape, plan, change, and use space while living, performing activities, and establishing social relations with particular spatio-temporal dimensions. People also talk about space, give different meanings and symbolic forms to different spaces, and appropriate and live in spaces that are unevenly allocated—albeit these practices are often subordinated to the constraints exerted by the material living conditions and the prevailing politico-economic regimes. Urban sociology should thus ask above all how and why social processes and structures occur in relation to space (and time). A sociological perspective is also expected to primarily question who is involved in socio-spatial and socio-temporal phenomena and understand their effects; e.g. who wins and who loses from urban change. The explicit definition of social groups, categorical inequalities, and power relations would render the focus on the 'social' properties of urban phenomena more fruitful than just taking them for granted.

Moving beyond the classic tenets of urban sociology, critical approaches also focus on intersectional social conflicts in relation to the production and reproduction of space (and social relations of production and livelihood), the constraints of historical contexts on urban phenomena, and the reflexivity regarding the social and political effects of sociological knowledge. In this regard, the second part of the chapter advocated for an 'interdependent' approach between epistemology and politics, building upon the tradition of a critical theory that centrally addresses the actual and potential emancipation of oppressed people from all forms of domination. This approach requires relative autonomy for science with a 'situated epistemology' when setting the standards of knowledge quality. Science is always critical inasmuch it debunks irrational beliefs and superstitions, but it also is a human activity subject to corporate and political pressures. Politics, in turn, can guide, inspire, and enable the agenda-setting of science, but the legitimacy and social usefulness of the latter lies in its supply of theoretical consistency and clarity, appropriate and accountable methods, and coherent matches between explanations, interpretations, and empirical evidence. Critical urban sociology thus engages with this tradition above all when it addresses inequalities, injustice, and marginalisation issues in socio-spatial phenomena. This entails paying attention to class struggles as well to other crucial social conflicts and divides and the grassroots activism and policy debates that intervene in those matters. As argued before, the trajectories of neoliberal and financialised capitalism over the last decades in particular have forged a context of social and urban problems that is unavoidable for today's engaged urban sociology.

In line with this analysis I expect further theoretical and empirical contributions to the critical urban sociology programme. More systematic accounts and appraisals of urban scholarship stressing its social, critical, and reflexive features are thus very welcome. Likewise, engaged urban sociology in tight connection with emancipatory activism and progressive politics might make more explicit its positionality, participatory procedures, and achievements. Finally, dialogues and cooperation between different critical approaches in the transdisciplinary field of urban studies may pave the way for determining more robust theoretical and methodological guidelines.

## NOTES

1. International Network for Urban Research and Action: https://www.inura.org/v2/.

2. Squatting Everywhere Kollective: https://sqek.squat.net/. For a description of its trajectory, see: https://radicalhousingjournal.org/2019/sqek/.
3. This network was active between 2014 and 2020: https://www.iuresearch.se/research/housing/crush/.
4. Red Iberoamericana de Investigación en Políticas, Conflictos y Movimientos Urbanos: www.conflictosurbanos.org.
5. https://beyondinhabitation.org.
6. https://antievictionmap.com/.
7. https://commoncity.net/.

## REFERENCES

Aalbers, M. (2019) Financial geography II: Financial geographies of housing and real estate. *Progress in Human Geography* 43(2): 376–387.
Aalbers, M. (2022) Towards a relational and comparative rather than a contrastive global housing studies. *Housing Studies*. doi: 10.1080/02673037.2022.2033176.
Abu-Lughod, J. (1999) *New York, Chicago, Los Angeles. America's Global Cities*. Minneapolis, MN: University of Minnesota Press.
Alford, R. & Friedland, R. (1985) *Powers of Theory. Capitalism, the State, and Democracy*. Cambridge: Cambridge University.
Bhambra, G. (2014) *Connected Sociologies*. London: Bloomsbury.
Bhaskar, R. & Callinicos, A. (2003) Marxism and critical realism. *Journal of Critical Realism* 1(2): 89–114.
Bhattacharya, T. (ed.) (2017) *Social Reproduction Theory. Remapping Class, Recentering Oppression*. London: Pluto.
Boltanski, L. (2011) *On Critique. A Sociology of Emancipation*. Cambridge: Polity Press.
Bourdieu, P. (1991) *Language and Symbolic Power*. Cambridge: Polity Press.
Bourdieu, P. (2002) Toward politically engaged scholarship. *Le Monde Diplomatique*. https://mondediplo.com/2002/02/20scholarship.
Bourdieu, P. et al. (1973) [1991] *The Craft of Sociology. Epistemological Preliminaries*. Berlin: de Gruyter.
Brenner, N. (2019) *New Urban Spaces: Urban Theory and the Scale Question*. New York: Oxford University Press.
Brenner, N. et al. (2009) Cities for people, not for profit. *City* 13(2–3): 176–184.
Buechler, S. (2014) *Critical Sociology*. Boulder, NY: Paradigm.
Burawoy, M. (2005) For public sociology. *American Sociological Review* 70: 4–28.
Burawoy, M. (2008) Open letter to C. Wright Mills. *Antipode* 40(3): 365–375.
Burawoy, M. & Wright, E.O. (2006) Sociological Marxism. In Turner, J. (ed.) *Handbook of Sociological Theory*. New York, NY: Springer, 459–486.
Calhoun, C. (2006) The critical dimension in sociological theory. In Turner, J. (ed.) *Handbook of Sociological Theory*. New York, NY: Springer, 85–111.
Castells, M. (1968) [1976, 2007] Is there an urban sociology? In Pickvance, C. (ed.) *Urban Sociology. Critical Essays*. Abingdon: Routledge, 33–59.
Castells, M. (1972) *The Urban Question: A Marxist Approach*. Cambridge, MA: The MIT Press.
Castells, M. (1983) *The City and the Grassroots. A Cross-Cultural Theory of Urban Social Movements*. Berkeley, CA: University of California Press.
Castells, M. (2002) Urban sociology in the twenty-first century. In Susser, I. (ed.) *The Castells Reader on Cities and Social Theory*. London: Blackwell.
Chibber, V. (2013) *Postcolonial Theory and the Specter of Capital*. London: Verso.
Christophers, B. (2021) Class, assets and work in rentier capitalism. *Historical Materialism* 29(2): 3–28.
Coelho, K. & Sood, A. (2022) Urban studies in India across the millennial turn: Histories and futures. *Urban Studies* 59(13): 2613–2637. doi: 10.1177/00420980211056773.
Collins, P.H. (2019) *Intersectionality as Critical Social Theory*. Durham, NC: Duke University Press.

Deegan, M.J. (1988) *Jane Addams and the Men of the Chicago School, 1892–1918*. New Brunswick, NJ: Transaction.
Engels, F. (1845) [1974] *The Condition of the Working Class in England*. London: Panther.
Engels, F. (1872) [1969] The housing question. In Marx, K. & Engels, F. *Selected Works*. Moscow: Progress Publishers.
Fainstein, S. (2010) *The Just City*. Ithaca: Cornell University Press.
Fainstein, S. & Hirst, C. (1995) Urban social movements. In Judge, D. et al. (eds.) *Theories of Urban Politics*. London: Sage, 181–204.
Fals-Borda, O. & Rahman M.A. (eds.) (1991) *Action and Knowledge. Breaking the Monopoly through Participatory Action-Research*. Bogotá: CINEP.
Feagin, J. et al. (2009) Social justice and critical public sociology. In Jeffries, V. (ed.) *Handbook of Public Sociology: Toward a Holistic Sociology*. Lanham, MD: Rowman & Littlefield, 71–88.
Ferreri, M. & Vidal, L. (2021) Public-cooperative policy mechanisms for housing commons, *International Journal of Housing Policy* 22(2): 149–173. doi: 10.1080/19491247.2021.1877888.
Fix, M. & Arantes, P. (2022) On urban studies in Brazil: The favela, uneven urbanisation and beyond. *Urban Studies* 59(5): 893–916. doi: 10.1177/0042098021993360.
Fraser, N. (2003) Social justice in the age of identity politics: Redistribution, recognition, and participation. In Fraser, N. & Honneth, A. *Redistribution or Recognition? A Political-Philosophical Debate*. London: Verso, 7–109.
Gans, H. (2002) The sociology of space: A use-centered view. *City & Community* 1(4): 329–339.
Garrido, M. et al. (2021) Toward a global urban sociology: Keywords. *City & Community* 20(1): 4–12. doi: 10.1111/cico.12502.
Gil, J. & Martínez, M. (2023) State-led actions reigniting the financialization of housing in Spain. *Housing, Theory & Society* 40(1): 1–21. doi: 10.1080/14036096.2021.2013316.
Gil, J. & Sequera, J. (2022) The professionalization of Airbnb in Madrid: Far from a collaborative economy. *Current Issues in Tourism* 25(20): 3343–3362. doi: 10.1080/13683500.2020.1757628.
Glass, R. (1955) Urban sociology in Great Britain: A trend report. *Current Sociology* 4(4): 5–19.
Glenn, N. (2009) Some suggested standards for distinguishing between good and bad public sociology. In Jeffries, V. (ed.) *Handbook of Public Sociology: Toward a Holistic Sociology*. Lanham, MD: Rowman & Littlefield, 135–150.
Gottdiener, M. (1984) Debate on the theory of space: Toward an urban praxis. In Smith, M.P. (ed.) *Cities in Transformation. Class, Capital and the State*. London: Sage, 199–218.
Gottdiener, M. et al. (2019) *The New Urban Sociology*. New York, NY: Routledge.
Grazioli, M. (2021) *Housing, Urban Commons and the Right to the City in Post-Crisis Rome. Metropoliz, The Squattted Città Meticcia*. Cham: Palgrave.
Haila, A. (2016) *Urban Land Rent. Singapore as a Property State*. Oxford: Wiley-Blackwell.
Hall, S. & Burdett, R. (eds.) (2017) *The SAGE Handbook of the 21st Century City*. London: Sage.
Harding, A. & Blokland, T. (2011) Comment on Sharon Zukin/1. From 'strict' urban sociology to relaxed but engaged urban theories. *Sociologica* 3: 1–8.
Harding, A. & Blokland, T. (2014) *Urban Theory*. London: Sage.
Harloe, M. (2018) A child of its times: the 'new urban sociology' in context and its legacy. In Andreotti, A., Benassi, D. & Kazepov, Y. (eds.) *Western Capitalism in Transition. Global Processes, Local Challenges*. Manchester: Manchester University Press.
Harloe, M. et al. (1998) IJURR: Looking back twenty-one years later. *International Journal of Urban and Regional Research* 22(1): i–iv.
Harvey, D. (1973) *Social Justice and the City*. Athens, GA: University of Georgia.
Harvey, D. (1996) *Justice, Nature and the Geography of Difference*. Cambridge: Blackwell.
Harvey, D. (2001) *Spaces of Capital. Towards a Critical Geography*. New York, NY: Routledge.
Harvey, D. (2006) Space as a keyword. In Castree, N. & Gregory, D. (eds.) *David Harvey. A Critical Reader*. Oxford: Blackwell, 270–293.
Harvie, D. et al. (2022) Public university. The political economy of the public university. In Maisuria, A. (ed.) *Encyclopaedia of Marxism and Education*. Leiden: Brill, 606–623.
Hoffman, M. (2019) *Militant Acts. The Role of Investigations in Radical Political Struggles*. Albany, NY: State University of New York Press.

Holgersen, S. (2022) The urban. In Skeggs, B. et al. (eds.) *The Sage Handbook of Marxism*. London: Sage, 1503–1518.
Horkheimer, M. (1972) [2002] *Critical Theory. Selected Essays*. New York: Seabury Press.
Isin, E. (2003) Historical sociology of the city. In Delanty, G. & Isin, E. (eds.) *Handbook of Historical Sociology*. London: Sage, 312–325.
Jacobs, K., Atkinson, R. & Warr, D. (2022) Political economy perspectives and their relevance for contemporary housing studies. *Housing Studies*. doi: 10.1080/02673037.2022.2100327.
Jacobsson, K. (ed.) (2015) *Urban Grassroots Movements in Central and Eastern Europe*. Farnham: Ashgate.
Lancione, M. & McFarlane, C. (eds.) (2021) *Global Urbanisms. Knowledge, Power and the City*. Abingdon: Routledge.
Lees, L. et al. (2016) *Planetary Gentrification*. Cambridge: Polity.
Lefebvre, H. (1970) [2003] *The Urban Revolution*. Minneapolis, MN: University of Minnesota Press.
Le Galès, P. (2005) Interesting times for urban sociology. *Sociology* 39(2): 347–352.
Le Galès, P. (2017) The political sociology of cities and urbanisation processes: Social movements, inequalities and governance. In Hall, S. & Burdett, R. (eds.) *The SAGE Handbook of the 21st Century City*. London: Sage, 215–235.
Leitner H. et al. (2020) *Urban Studies Inside/Out. Theory, Method, Practice*. London: Sage.
Lin, J. & Mele, C. (2013) *The Urban Sociology Reader*. Abingdon: Routledge.
Logan, J. & Molotch, H. (1987) *Urban Fortunes. The Political Economy of Place*. Berkeley, CA: University of California Press.
Madden, D. & Marcuse, P. (2016) *In Defense of Housing. The Politics of Crisis*. London: Verso.
Marcuse, P. (2002) Depoliticizing globalization: From Neo-Marxism to the network society of Manuel Castells. In Eade, J. & Mele, C. (eds.) *Understanding the City. Contemporary and Future Perspectives*. Oxford: Blackwell, 131–158.
Marrengane, N. & Croese, S. (eds.) (2021) *Reframing the Urban Challenge in Africa. Knowledge Co-production from the South*. Abingdon: Routledge.
Martineau, J. (2016) *Time, Capitalism and Alienation. A Socio-Historic Inquiry into the Making of Modern Time*. Chicago: Haymarket.
Martínez, M. (2019) Framing urban movements, contesting global capitalism and liberal democracy. In Yip, N. et al. (eds.) *Contested Cities and Urban Activism*. Singapore: Palgrave, 25–45.
Martínez, M. (2020a) *Squatters in the Capitalist City. Housing, Justice, and Urban Politics*. New York: Routledge.
Martínez, M. (2020b) Urban commons from an anti-capitalist approach. *Partecipazione e Conflitto* 13(3): 1390–1410.
Marx, K. & Engels, F. (1845) [1976] *The German Ideology*. London: Lawrence & Wishart.
Massey, D. (1995) [1984] *Spatial Divisions of Labour. Social Structures and the Geography of Production*. London: Macmillan.
May, T. & Perry, B. (2005) Continuities and change in urban sociology. *Sociology* 39(2): 343–347.
Mayer, M. (2006) Manuel Castells' *The City and the Grassroots. International Journal of Urban and Regional Research* 30(1): 202–206.
Mayer, M. (2016) Neoliberal urbanism and uprisings across Europe. In Mayer, M. et al. (eds.) *Urban Uprisings. Challenging Neoliberal Urbanism in Europe*. New York: Palgrave MacMillan, 57–92.
Mayer, M. (2020) What does it mean to be a (radical) urban scholar-activist, or activist scholar, today? *City* 24(1–2): 35–51.
Milicevic, A. (2001) Radical intellectuals: What happened to the new urban sociology? *International Journal of Urban and Regional Research* 25(4): 759–783.
Miller, B. (2006) Castells' *The City and the Grassroots*: 1983 and today. *International Journal of Urban and Regional Research* 30(1): 207–211.
Mingione, E. (1991) *Fragmented Societies: A Sociology of Economic Life Beyond the Market Paradigm*. Oxford: Blackwell.
Mitchell, D. (2003) *The Right to the City. Social Justice and the Fight for Public Space*. New York, NY: The Guilford Press.
Müller, M. (2021) Worlding geography: From linguistic privilege to decolonial anywheres. *Progress in Human Geography* 45(6):1440–1466.

Neurath, O. (1937) [2011] Unity of science and logical empiricism: A reply. In Symons, J. et al. (eds.) *Otto Neurath and the Unity of Science*. London: Springer, 15–28.
Nicholls, W. (2010) The Los Angeles school: Difference, politics, city. *International Journal of Urban and Regional Research* 35(1): 189–206.
Nicholls, W. & Uitermark, J. (2017) *Cities and Social Movements. Immigrant Rights Activism in the United States, France, and the Netherlands, 1970–2015*. Chichester: Wiley-Blackwell.
Novy, J. & Colomb, C. (eds.) (2017) *Protest and Resistance in the Tourist City*. New York, NY: Routledge.
Pahl, R. (ed.) (1968) *Readings in Urban Sociology*. Oxford: Pergamon Press.
Park, R. et al. (1925) [1984] *The City. Suggestions for Investigation of Human Behavior in the Urban Environment*. Chicago: University of Chicago Press.
Parnell, S. & Oldfield, S. (eds.) (2014) *The Routledge Handbook on Cities of the Global South*. Abingdon: Routledge.
Passeron, J.C. (2006) [2013] *Sociological Reasoning. A Non-Popperian Space of Argumentation*. Oxford: Bardwell.
Pickvance, C. (1985) The rise and fall of urban movements and the role of comparative analysis. *Environment and Planning D: Society and Space* 3: 31–53.
Pickvance, C. (1995) Marxist theories of urban politics. In Judge, D. et al. (eds.) *Theories of Urban Politics*. London: Sage, 253–275.
Piven, F. (2010) Reflections on scholarship and activism. *Antipode* 42: 806–810.
Polanska, D. & Richard, Å. (2021) Resisting renovictions: Tenants organizing against housing companies' renewal practices in Sweden. *Radical Housing Journal* 3(1): 187–205.
Pombo, O. et al. (2011) Neurath and the unity of science: An introduction. In Symons, J. et al. (eds.) *Otto Neurath and the Unity of Science*. London: Springer, 1–11.
Rolnik, R. (2019) *Urban Warfare. Housing Under the Empire of Finance*. London: Verso.
Rossi, U. (2017) *Cities in Global Capitalism*. Cambridge: Polity.
Sassen, S. (1991) [2001] *The Global City: New York, London, Tokyo*. Princeton: Princeton University Press.
Sassen, S. (2005) Cities as strategic sites. *Sociology* 39(2): 352–357.
Saunders, P. (1986) *Social Theory and the Urban Question*. 2nd edition. Abingdon: Routledge.
Sayer, A. (2000) *Realism and Social Science*. London: Sage.
Scott, A.J. (2022) The constitution of the city and the critique of critical urban theory. *Urban Studies* 59(6): 1105–1129. doi: 10.1177/00420980211011028.
Scott, A.J. & Storper, M. (2014) The nature of cities: The scope and limits of urban theory. *International Journal of Urban and Regional Research* 39 (1): 1–15.
Skeggs, B. et al. (eds.) (2022) *The Sage Handbook of Marxism*. London: Sage.
Slater, T. (2021) *Shaking up the City. Ignorance, Inequality, and the Urban Question*. Oakland: University of California Press.
Steinmetz, G. (ed.) (2005) *The Politics of Method in Human Sciences: Positivism and Its Epistemological Others*. Durham, NC: Duke University Press.
Storper, M. & Scott, A. (2016) Current debates in urban theory: A critical assessment. *Urban Studies* 53(6): 1114–1136.
Therborn, G. (1980) *The Ideology of Power and the Power of Ideology*. London: Verso.
Therborn, G. (2017) *Cities of Power. The Urban, the National, the Popular, the Global*. London: Verso.
Thörn, C. (2020) 'We're not moving': Solidarity and collective housing struggle in a changing Sweden. In Krase, J. & DeSena, J. (eds.) *Gentrification around the World. Vol. I*. Palgrave, 175–196.
Tilly, C. (1999) *Durable Inequality*. Berkeley, CA: University of California Press.
Topalov, C. (2015) Thirty years of urban sociology. A French viewpoint. *Metropolitics* 30: 1–11.
Vilenica, A. (ed.) (2023) *Decoloniality in Eastern Europe: A Lexicon of Reorientation*. Novi Sad: New Media Center_kuda.org.
Wacquant, L. (2002) Scrutinizing the street: Poverty, morality, and the pitfalls of urban ethnography. *American Journal of Sociology* 107(6): 1468–1532.
Walton, J. (1993) Urban sociology: The contributions and limits of political economy. *Annual Review of Sociology* 19: 301–320.
Weber, M. (1921) [1958] *The City* (edited by D. Martindale & G. Neuwirth). New York: Free Press.

Wilden, A. (1987) *The Rules Are No Game. The Strategy of Communication*. New York: Routledge.
Wirth, L. (1938) Urbanism as a way of life. *American Journal of Sociology* 44(1): 1–24.
Wright, E.O. (2010) *Envisioning Real Utopias*. London: Verso.
Wright, E.O. (2015) *Understanding Class*. London: Verso.
Wright Mills, C. (1959) [2000] *The Sociological Imagination*. New York: Oxford University Press.
Wyly, E. (2011) Positively radical. *International Journal of Urban and Regional Research* 35(5): 889–912.
Yrigoy. I. (2018) State-led financial regulation and representations of spatial fixity: The example of the Spanish real estate sector. *International Journal of Urban and Regional Research* 42(4): 594–611.
Zukin, S. (1980) A decade of the new urban sociology. *Theory and Society* 9(4): 575–601.
Zukin, S. (2011) Is there an urban sociology? Questions on a field and a vision. *Sociologica* 3: 1–17.

# 3. The capitalist local state, urban change, and social conflict
## Özlem Çelik

What is the relationship between different social groups at the local level and decision-makers? To what extent does the state play a role in urban change? How does power get exercised and contested? These are long-term debates and are still open to further discussions in human geography, political science, and urban sociology disciplines among others. There has been a growing interest in the local state throughout the social sciences since the late 1960s, due in large part to the urban crises and the urban struggles in late- and early-capitalist countries (around employment, housing, transport, and public services). Through Cockburn's (1977) ground-breaking work on Lambeth, London, the first steps towards local state research were laid. In line with Marx's discussion of the state in capitalist society (Miliband 1969), Cockburn argued that the local state is not simply a governmental activity of the central state, nor does it simply represent the state locally (Cockburn 1977: 47). The local state is entwined with the central state, but it is also enmeshed with contradictions between capital and labour that are specific to the local scale (Cockburn 1977: 55). Local states are viewed as complex webs of relations among local government functions, social and civic organizations, and local business interests. I discuss debates in local state theory in this chapter, which provides a framework for understanding local governance and decision-making dynamics rather than municipalities, which are specific administrative entities with legal authority and responsibilities for local government.

The various approaches to the local state are directly connected to broader discussions of state theory. These include: (i) pluralist, (ii) managerialist, (iii) elite, and (iv) structuralist approaches. The diverse approaches to state theory are presented in this chapter in terms of three characteristics that cut across all the approaches: growth, localism, and social struggle. In all approaches, growth has a central role, since cities and city regions are increasingly the primary sites of capital accumulation and growth. Localism carries importance in each approach in positioning the role of local actors, institutions, and the local scale of the state. The aspect of social struggle sheds light in understanding how the conflicts between different actors and groups take place, how the impacts of local struggle by urban social movements shape decision-making processes, and how power is exercised.

The discussion below unfolds as follows: by adopting growth, localism, and struggle as lenses, four approaches to state theory are explained. Firstly, I elaborate the more agency-oriented approaches: (i) pluralist, where the state is seen as a neutral actor that is equally open to the influence of all social groups; (ii) managerialist, which emphasizes the role of local officials in shaping policy outcomes according to their own values and goals; and (iii) elitist, which underlines that small, powerful ruling groups can and do govern and that they form the power coalition at the local level (Dunleavy & O'Leary 1991). Pluralism emphasizes the role of negotiation and compromise among various social groups, while managerialism focuses on the agency of local officials. Elitism, on the other hand, highlights the concentration of power among a select few. My second focus is on structuralist approaches that illuminate how structures and agency interact. These approaches include classic instrumentalist and structuralist Marxist perspectives. Classic instrumentalist approaches view structures as tools or instruments that individuals use to achieve their goals. Structuralist Marxist approaches highlight the inherent conflicts and contradictions within capitalist societies, emphasizing the role of class struggle and exploitation in shaping structures. In this chapter I also introduce the strategic relational approach (SRA) as one of the key strands of structuralist approaches, which examines how social actors strategically navigate and negotiate social structures.

The fifth section delves into two new debates in local state theory; namely, new municipalism and degrowth. What is new beyond the classical theories of the local state is the influence of feminist, Lefebvrian, commons, and libertarian theories. The chapter concludes by highlighting possible new avenues for the financialization debate and new formulations of local state theory.

## PLURALISM

Pluralism has been vastly influential in urban politics for and against it. It has played a vital role in inspiring social movements and yet has been a driving force for institutionalists to regulationists, who accept the plurality of organizations as an expression of urban politics (Judge 1995: 13). The main characteristics of pluralism are: 1) power is seen as fragmented and decentralized; 2) all groups have some resources to articulate their case, even if their demands are not always met or are not successfully implemented; 3) there will be different outcomes in different policy sectors as a result of different processes, actors, and power distributions; and 4) politics extends beyond formal institutions such as elections and representative bodies (Judge et al. 1995).

According to pluralists, in a liberal democracy the state operates in a neutral manner, remaining equally receptive to the influence of all social groups. This inclusivity extends to various stakeholders, such as employers, workers, students, and organizations. The state's interaction with these groups occurs both explicitly through elections and implicitly through lobbying or through the existence of corporatist structures. In this approach, the state is often viewed as a site of conflict that reflects the pressures of interest groups. As a result of differing pressures, the policies reflect the interests of everyone involved in the decision-making process (Smith 2006). In a pluralist understanding, politics is a constant negotiation process and the resolution of conflicting interests. Therefore, the central questions of the pluralist understanding are 'who governs' in an urban community, who is involved in making decisions, and how are decisions made. As Dahl (Judge 1995: 14–17) points out, there is no single model of pluralism that can answer these questions. Rather than being an abstract concept, pluralism serves as a 'descriptive empirical' analysis of decision-making processes. It operates within the framework of a polyarchy or urban pluralism, as described by Dahl, as no minority group is permanently excluded from the political arena (Judge 1995: 14–17).

A progressive perspective on urban pluralism provides a distinct viewpoint. In adapting Habermas's concept of communicative rationality, Patsy Healey (1997) developed a new understanding of urban planning, in which it is placed at the center of how to govern local politics, through the link between institutionalism and pluralism. The institutionalist perspective reframes planning from being solely an individual or interpersonal activity to being a part of governance. Healey (1997) highlights this shift and expands the scope of planning beyond the realm of public planning and the state. The institutionalist perspective asserts the significance of institutions in society and argues that they offer valuable insights into human behavior. Moreover, this perspective considers planning itself as a form of institution, conceptualized as a social structure (Healey 1999). According to Healey, our understanding of the material world is shaped by our social perceptions, as well as by our moral reasoning and emotional feelings. Nevertheless, this does not mean that people's interests determine their preferences: they are formed through interactions (Healey 1997: 29). In a shared space, everyone has a range of interests and expectations; how can public policies be crafted to accommodate everyone's needs? According to Healey (1997: 29–30), communicative or interpretive planning theory operates in a collaborative consensus-building manner rather than through competitive interest bargaining. As a result, she sees public policy-making taking place within a 'social context' where everyday practices take place. Healey's approach to the local state provides an agent-based analysis opposed to an analysis of material relations (Healey 1997: 37).

Specifically, Healey (1997) claims that in that culture of diversity, priorities and strategies for collective action are determined by interaction when all interest groups achieve a certain degree of collaboration and reciprocity. A conversation open to a wide range of people can lead to shared values if knowledge and understanding are exchanged. Planning practice and the role of urban planners are crucial in Healey's work. Healey's approach to urban governance demonstrates how interest groups and planners can work together to reach a consensus by using a process of interactive collective action. Healey, applying the normative side of pluralism to a pluralist local state theory, argues that planners and planning bring power relations into play and planners also have the power to transform them (Healey 1997). Thus, Healey places planning at the center of urban growth, where the local scale takes center stage and social struggle is embedded within a pluralistic actor-based context.

A pluralist approach views power as fragmented and decentralized, allowing every group to participate in local decision-making. Nevertheless, this approach is not without its limitations, both methodologically and theoretically. Firstly, simply demonstrating the potential for participation in decision-making fails to adequately address historical and structurally embedded social relations and inequalities. Additionally, such analyses begin from a practical level of specificity rather than treating states as abstract concepts. The pluralist approach presents itself as an analysis that prioritizes governments and governmental systems rather than the state or its organizational structure (Smith 2006). When referring to the state, the pluralist approach views it as distinct entities, such as state institutions, courts, and the civil service (Dunleavy & O'Leary 1991). This perspective gives rise to inquiries like 'who possesses power in a polyarchy?' instead of focusing on the nature of the state itself (Dunleavy & O'Leary 1991: 42). Furthermore, according to the pluralist approach, policy-makers are seen as operating within a consensus of values that is politically impartial and emerges from various interests (Smith 2006). Nonetheless, even in cases where consensus is achieved, it can be argued that it embodies the tensions and contradictions inherent in class struggle (Eisenschitz & Gough 1998: 93).

## FROM MANAGERIALISM TO ENTREPRENEURIALISM

Managerialist theory sees the state as an institution distinctly separate from society, aiming to reproduce its own power. This autonomy is not embedded in the demands and interests of classes or groups in civil society: rather, it is rooted in the self-interest of state officers. The approach's emphasis on the power of state officers might be seen as similar to the elite approach; however, the state is not seen as captured by any powerful group outside the state as is accepted in the elite approach. The state elite have an autonomous power embedded in their own self-interests (salary, prestige, etc.), which is different from other groups or classes in society (Mann 1984, Skocpol 1985). Developed through Rex and Moore's concept of 'urban managerialism', managerialist local state theory emphasizes the role of important managers within bureaucratic state institutions that manage the provision of services, mainly collective consumption. These managers, also known as gatekeepers, have a critical role to play in distributing resources in the city (Saunders 1981, Savage et al. 1993). The core ideas of urban managerialism have been discussed by Ray Pahl in his collection of essays asking the question 'whose city?' (Pahl 1970). Pahl was interested in finding out how the owners of the city—capitalists and managers—reproduced ownership, appropriating rents and profits from the city. His study identified the various 'urban managers' employed by state authorities and local municipalities in charge of allocating public goods and services; namely, local economic development and growth. In this way, Pahl was able to demonstrate how 'urban managerialism' produced territorial inequalities and social exclusions, a breakthrough for critical urban sociology for its time.

Early forms of managerialism had a significant flaw based on the assumption that the state is an institution separate from society with autonomy in its operations (Savage et al. 1993). According to this assumption, state power is revoked by officers owing to the bureaucratic governing of the state. Consequently, the first weakness stems from disentangling state bureaucrats from the historical and structural context of the governing process and institutions (Savage et al. 1993), which neglects the class nature of the state (Das 1996). Therefore, the idea of the powerful bureaucrat became implausible. Since then, managerialism has appeared in neoliberal ideologies as an enemy or barrier to local growth—for example, local planners would stifle economic development because they are overly bureaucratic.

Traditionally, urban managerialism (Kujawa 2016: 1) has been viewed as a phase of urban governance in which state actors have engaged in a series of public–private partnerships since the 1970s (Harvey 1989) that led to entrepreneurial local governing. This shift was driven by the new role cities played as economic generators in the global market. Cities compete to bring various sources of funding, direct investment, and new employment opportunities by cooperating with private enterprises. Thus, urban entrepreneurialism is a new form of urban management that places public–private partnerships at the core of its governing process, stimulating all forms of economic growth through the speculative construction of place rather than by addressing collective consumption and other social needs within a given area. The new developments based on urban entrepreneurial logic target developers, investors, and tourists through the exploitation of local advantages for the production of goods and services, the development of new mass consumption activities, and the attraction of corporate command and control functions (Phelps & Miao 2020).

However, the shift from managerialism to entrepreneurialism also played a role in state rescaling. Urban managerialism had delivered innovations in order to fit the purposes of mass consumption and thus was universalized across national territories (Phelps & Miao 2020: 306). Urban entrepreneurialism is more associated with the city scale, where promotion, marketing, and branding of cities' innovativeness and speculative ventures involving public–private partnerships happen (Phelps & Miao 2020: 309). According to Phelps and

Miao, urban speculation is less likely to be driven by urban public services but rather by land redevelopment and land exchange surpluses. There is no doubt that urban speculation continues around basic infrastructure and services, even though it may be true of cities in the United States where redevelopment agencies have accrued surplus tax revenues normally earmarked for affordable housing and services (Jonas 2020). Thus, urban speculation has a wider impact that extends beyond the local scale. Interurban competition and the collaboration among urban elites at (often) transnational levels brings global- to local-scale actors into play (Phelps & Miao 2020: 316).

It is likely that disadvantaged groups will be ignored or inadequately addressed where interurban competition drives speculative local growth. The question of social conflict in entrepreneurial local governing concerns not only that between the urban elite and entrepreneurs; the majority of city dwellers take their share from the uneven spatial and social consequences of speculative projects. Discussions of counter-movements against entrepreneurially induced speculative projects have been increasing in the literature (Thompson et al. 2020, MacLeod 2002).

## ELITE THEORY OF THE STATE: GROWTH MACHINES AND URBAN REGIMES

Elite approaches can be classified in three groups: classic, technocratic, and radical.

The classic elite approach is based on a hierarchical conception of society and focuses on the relations between the rulers and the ruled or the powerful and the powerless. The ruled need decision-makers (e.g. leaders) for complex decision-making processes (Dunleavy & O'Leary 1991: 138–141, Judge et al. 1995). The technocratic elite approach largely adopts Max Weber's understanding of state organization as a bureaucracy. Power is in the control of those who have the commanding positions within society's leading bureaucracies (Dunleavy & O'Leary 1991: 141–143, Judge et al. 1995). Lastly, the radical elite approach sees the state as dominated by a new managerial elite formed of sections of business and powerful committees in the state. This approach has a particular focus on the governing of cities with a specific critique of the pluralist approach to governing. Thus, according to elitist approaches, the major decisions are made by only a handful of people, rather than in the interests of diverse groups or classes, such as sections of business, senior government officials, wealthy individuals, media owners, or sections of the middle class, independent of democratic election processes (Dunleavy & O'Leary 1991: 137).

The elite theory of the local state is characterized by a critique of classic elite theory. The growth machine (Jonas & Wilson 1999, Logan & Molotch 1987) and urban regime (Stone 1987) are the well-known strands that see the local state as captured by a coalition of powerful groups, primarily businesses, to foster local economic growth.

Harding argues that the growth machines are more concerned with 'who has the greater influence over the physical restructuring of places, why, and with what effect' (Harding 1995: 44) rather than 'who rules'. Growth machines are coalitions of powerful social groups that become entrepreneurs in a particular area; e.g. local media, banks, universities, and property investors. As a result of the close and relatively permanent relationship between these coalition members and public officials, elite groups are able to exert systematic and long-term power and influence public policy. Local governments may or may not be essential members of the coalitions, but they do strongly support them (Harding 1995: 43). Coalition members are often active members of local government. As an example, elected council members get involved in the coalition to pursue their interests directly (Jonas & Wilson 1999, Logan & Molotch 1987, Savage et al. 1993, Stone 1987); however, there is a controversial plural understanding of the power within the coalition, and business leaders are not seen as omnipotent (Harding 1995).

The growth machine approach to local government faces criticism for failing to define the 'local state' in terms of 'how or why local government employs its autonomy' (Clarke 1991). Growth is thus viewed ideologically since local governments and business community act as growth machines for their localities; e.g. the city. Logan and Molotch focus only on one aspect of local growth: property development (Harding 1995: 44). They have a one-sided analysis where they emphasize the ownership of property as the key conflict (Harding 1995: 44). However, a critique of seeing growth machines as a form of property development reminds us that investors and developers do not only look for low-cost sites in the property market. The growth machine coalitions are also interested in regional skills; ongoing relationships between employers and workers, including unions; training opportunities; and suitable local networks of suppliers and business services and their level of involvement in communication technologies (Eisenschitz & Gough 1998).

The second approach in elite local state theory in the *urban regime* is one of the prevailing approaches, including several variations. Regardless of the form, there is a formal or informal mode of collaboration between the public and private sectors (Mossberger 2009: 40) and an interest in understanding the issue of power (Stoker 1998: 54). The definition of an urban regime is a set of governance arrangements, including the ability of a group to access resources and exert significant influence over urban policy and management. A regime is defined by Stone (1989: 4) as an 'informal, yet relatively stable, group with access to institutional resources that enable a sustained role in making governing decisions'. There tends to be an institutional base of power among regime participants in a particular area. However, the regime is an informal basis for coordinating different participants without having an 'encompassing structure of command' (Stoker 1998: 59). In a market-economy society, this approach's liberal underpinnings make collaboration between business and government inevitable. According to urban regime theory, in a liberal political economy officials are popularly elected to control local government institutions to a certain extent with the involvement of the private sector channeling investment decisions (Stone 1993: 2).

Regimes do not have a single focus of direction and control; they do not operate according to a formal hierarchy one can find within an institution. Stoker (1998) explains the non-single focus by arguing that regime members operate as a network rather than engaging in open-ended bargaining like pluralists. The cooperation created within a regime is based on the principles of solidarity, loyalty, trust, and mutual support (Stoker 1998: 59). Participants in regime coalitions aim to establish a long-term relationship rather than achieving an immediate goal or a focus on growth. Nevertheless, these collaborations create both fragmentations of authority and interdependence between elected institutions' policy-making capacity and market-economy resources that generate growth (Mossberger 2009: 41). Therefore, unlike growth machine theory, which posits a single coalition acting together, urban regime approaches suggest that different social groups have different significant impacts on the local state. Diversity arises from the complexity of social relations in controlling and managing local development (Stoker 1998, Stone 1987). As a result, regime theory explains how a political system with diversity and complexity can develop a capacity to govern (Stoker 1998: 57).

There are two main limitations of the approach. Firstly, urban regimes are viewed as a means of integrating societal demands and class struggles. This stems from the belief that coalitions have strong capturing capacity with regard to the local state. Nevertheless, capitalist relations encounter impasses as a result of their contradictory nature. Class and other social conflicts are sometimes embedded covertly at the local level (Cox & Mair 1989). A second concern is that the urban regime approach correctly states that the influential coalition of groups is locally dependent; however, it does not link the local scale of the state with other scales and the relations constructed at those scales. In other words, both growth machines and urban regimes are regarded as 'essentially localist' (Harding 1997). A critique of this approach refers to the lack of recognition of the importance of higher levels of government or external structures, such as investors. Furthermore, it is argued that the varied forms of growth machines are generally the results of effective city leadership and strong networking (Jessop et al. 1999). As Stoker (1998) argues, both of the approaches disregard the conflicts between different levels of the state and the contradictions of the demands of different interest groups at different levels (see Figure 3.1).

*Source:* Miguel A. Martínez.

*Figure 3.1* Istanbul (2014)

## STRUCTURALIST THEORY

Marxist theories of urban politics, namely the instrumentalist and the structuralist view, regard the role of the state in capitalist societies as twofold: (i) a role in capital accumulation to secure the reproduction of capitalism by providing general prerequisites of production (i.e. legal and monetary systems, transportation, a healthy labour force); and (ii) a role in maintaining legitimation to maintain social order by establishing institutions and policies that provide concessions to certain groups, as well as controlling them to repress possible social conflicts and uprisings (Pickvance 1995).

While sharing the twofold role of the state in capitalist societies, Marxist approaches differ in terms of who controls the autonomy in relation to the dominant classes where the state needs to accomplish accumulation and legitimation and to what degree. Instrumentalist and structural approaches differ in understanding the autonomy of the state regarding the dominant classes, the conflicts between state institutions, and how and by whom urban politics are designated.

The instrumentalist approach sees the state as an 'instrument' that serves the general interest of the dominant classes and has a minimal autonomy in relation to those classes. According to instrumentalists, the state acts as a unity and the conflicts among state institutions are minimal. The local state is thus seen as a reflection of the national interest of dominant classes without real power but offering participation at the local level (Pickvance 1995: 254).

The structuralist theory offers an alternative approach to how the state performs accumulation and legitimation. For the accomplishment of these functions both the state institutions and the dominant classes share autonomy. The main emphases of the view are the divisions among different fractions of the capitalist class and how the power of the working class can be tamed and controlled by concessions. Thus, state institutions have a greater role in responding to conflict pressures. The local state then has some autonomy to reconcile local and national class interests.

The structuralist theory of the local state, which we focus on in this chapter, is the strategic relational approach (SRA), which departs from two discussions: strategic selectivity and rescaling of the state. The state is considered the strategic site and center of the exercise of power in the SRA: an organization of the dominant class in relation to the dominated classes (Poulantzas 1978: 148). As opposed to the elite approach, the state is not a subject that obtains power for itself nor is it an instrument of the dominant classes but rather a social relation that is the terrain, the source, the result, and the crystallization of political strategies (Jessop 1985, Poulantzas 1978). No group, class, or individual can control the outcomes of the conflict-laden processes of micro-power games (Jessop 1985: 129). The SRA considers the Marxist state theories as being either capital-theoretical, 'which subsumes different patterns of accumulation under general economic laws' (Jessop 1991: 142), or class-theoretical, which reduces patterns of accumulation and state forms to 'specific "economic corporate" struggles' (Jessop 1991: 142) (e.g. the political structuralist approaches). The SRA calls for linking capital- and class-theoretical approaches through 'strategic-relational' middle-range concepts (Jessop 1991: 142) for a more adequate and concrete approach. The SRA combines the structural selectivity of the state debate with a strategic political approach. In the structural selectivity of the state (Offe 1974), the state is sorted according to its selective principles. This selectivity has four main principles:

(1) The state excludes or includes certain groups or fractions by using its political power over the economic power of various capital interests.
(2) The state secures its maintenance by guaranteeing its mandate for securing the general interest of capital.

(3) The state apparatus and state personnel act according to the maintenance of capital accumulation.
(4) A legitimate selection process is essential for the unity of society.

Thus, state policy formulation is complex, incoherent, and chaotic, reflecting a class struggle in the internal divisions and contradictions within and between different state apparatuses and branches. Further, the role of the state organization is to impose a general line over micropolitics, including the strategies and tactics of various classes and factions. A general line of analysis is what is known as the 'structural selectivity' of the state, characterized by the state's apparatuses and personnel, conflicts and contradictions between fractions and classes, and a more or less successful overall strategy. Structural selectivity is not reducible to any of these; rather, it emerges from clashes between the state personnel, conflicts between different capital fractions, and the power of the working class in making demands (Jessop 1985: 126–127, Poulantzas 1978: 132–136). Therefore, the concept of 'strategy' is crucial for understanding the nature of the state and its interventions, as well as for developing middle-range concepts that bridge the gap between capitalist- and class-theoretical approaches. Based on the SRA's concept of strategic selectivity, the strategies of the state refer not only to the institutional matrix, which reflects the political dominance embodied in the state's institutional materiality (Jessop 2007: 125), but also to the tactics and strategies of the fractional classes.

State hegemony is achieved by using spatial selective mechanisms; namely, privileging and articulating differentiated state policies for specific zones and scales. Jones (1999: 237) defines spatial selectivity as 'the privileged scales, places, and spaces that the state favors through accumulation strategies (economic policy) and ideology'. Thus, geographical privileging can be understood in material and ideological forms and occurs in crises 'to achieve political and ideological control, as class, social, and interest groups must be mobilized in order to secure support for particular economic and ideological policies' (Jones 1999: 237). This can include providing concessions in various forms to specific groups or fractions (such as tax cuts) or crisis displacements when the state's existing accumulation strategy is inadequate to resolve tensions between different capital fractions. It is the displacement of crisis in the political sphere rather than in the economic sphere that opens capital accumulation to new accumulation strategies, new hegemonic projects, and alternative state projects including a variety of forms of representation (Jones 1999: 238–239).

In a similar manner to Jones (1997, 1999), Brenner (2004: 89) states that spatial selectivity is 'never permanently fixed but, like all other aspects of state structure, represents an emergent, selective, and politically contested process'. This theory assumes that 'the state's organizational coherence and functional unity are never pre-given' (Brenner 2004: 89) but are determined by historically specific political strategies. Industrial policies, spatial planning programs, and housing policies are all part of state spatial strategies. At different scales, these strategies are manifested in territorial differentiation of policy regimes. State policies may be geographically variable and uneven, promoting divergent, context-specific impacts at diverse scales and locations (Brenner 2004: 93). Thus, the geographies of statehood in capitalism can be seen as reflecting the dialectical interaction between past 'partitioning and scaling of political space' and contemporary state spatial projects/strategies that aim to reshape capitalism (Brenner 2004: 93). This 'selective' character of the state travels across different scales and varies across different geographies, leading to the state debate's rescaling in the SRA.

The second strand of the local state debate in the SRA is based on Brenner's (2004) emphasis on the importance of the rescaling of the state thesis under neoliberalism. Spatial arrangements have a competitive nature under neoliberalism, seeking global capital flows for particular localities. Selective mechanisms of the state can and may create spatial privileging by providing public investments and incentives in terms of labour, land, financial processes, training, and employment regimes. As a result, those privileged areas will prosper in terms of economic growth and become more competitive than those left behind. With the neoliberal turn in economic growth, there has been increased competition among states and, more important, cities and city regions within states, which leads to uneven urban development. Various regulations and institutions have been introduced by national, regional, and local governments to encourage investment in certain areas. The creation of new urban governing bodies, development boards, training, and enterprise councils is intended to strategically promote local economies for a 'good business environment' (Brenner 2019: 194). For Western European local governments, welfare service provision and state-financed consumption have started to diminish and have been replaced by new tax concessions and financial incentives for transnational capital (Brenner, 2019). In essence, the deregulation of welfare services, the spatially selective investments in infrastructure, and the marketing of urban spaces support the neoliberal policies by rescaling the development process. The rescaling of the state leads to uneven development by fragmenting national space into competing urban and regional economies, resulting in territorial inequality and socio-spatial exclusion. Brenner (2019: 247) moves a step forward despite criticisms by arguing that growth machine and urban regime approaches can also be reinterpreted as multiscalar analyses of urban development. According to the three analytical standpoints of the approach—1) structural features of a state's spatial and institutional organization; 2) historically specific regimes of urban spatial policy; and 3) conjunctural struggles over urban spatial development—the urban scale is attributed as an institutional site for growth (Brenner 2019: 245–271).

In both strands of the SRA, the conjunctural analysis of critical theory emphasizes how and to what extent rescaling and selective strategies are taking place. The SRA indicates that an accumulation strategy establishes a general strategy appropriate to the realization of a specific 'growth model' for a given conjuncture. This does not imply that there is only one hegemonic strategy. Conjunctural analysis frames various tactics within a given accumulation strategy as well as the plurality of strategies at a given period. Therefore, there is a margin of maneuver for non-hegemonic fractions and dominated classes. Although such tactics might threaten the realization of the hegemonic accumulation strategy, they also create a negotiating arena for counter-interests within the framework of the given hegemonic strategy (Jessop 1991: 205). The conjunctural analysis results in the periodization of Marxist analysis, such as feudalism, commercial and colonial capitalism, and in some geographies Fordism and post-Fordism. Peck, for example, adopts late entrepreneurialism as a manifestation of neoliberal global urbanism in his conceptual framework: 'conjunctural urbanism' (2017). In line with this framework, the call that Harvey made to analyze cities in the entrepreneurial period is taken up by Peck and Theodore (2019) in order to examine hegemonic projects (such as tourism, urban regeneration, and flagship projects) in the context of neoliberal globalization in cities.

The SRA is widely used by scholars in urban studies but also has been criticized due to its shortcomings. Firstly, this approach does not take into account the contradictions and limits of the various state apparatuses, fractions of capital, and institutions of the state at various levels. Such limitations and contradictions emerge from a conjunctural analysis of a particular period associated with an accumulation strategy and a hegemonic project that lacks a broad, comprehensive, and adequate analysis of capitalism and capitalist relations as a whole. The method explains only part of the whole by separating a particular period from the contradictions through which capital develops, including the spatial ones (Cox 2009: 933). Furthermore, the functionalist explanation of the approach lacks an explanation of the process of selectivity as a result of class struggle (Cox 2009: 933).

## ALTERNATIVES: NEW MUNICIPALISM AND DEGROWTH DEBATES

In recent years, there have been new directions in the local state debate influenced by feminist, Lefebvrian, commons, and libertarian municipal approaches, among which I will focus on two: new municipalism and degrowth. New municipalism is a global social movement aimed at transforming local governments and economies by democratic means. The advent of this new approach to democratization of municipalism is regarded as a renaissance in local political and economic life. The local state is called back to experiment with new forms of co-production, shifting from regulatory to enabling roles and cultivating worker-owned cooperative ecosystems (Thompson 2021: 1). Urban activism that reclaims the right to the city, urban commons, and self-organization models lead the democratic transformation of the local state for just and equal cities. According to Thompson (2021), new municipalism adds a fresh perspective to the local state debate by giving rise to novel forms of institutionalization that embody urban and not state logics. The new municipalism therefore extends beyond state-centric approaches by both pushing the boundaries of state reform at the local level and prefiguring a different kind of polis rooted in the urban. It developed as a response to austerity measures after the 2008 global financial crisis. In many countries, the Occupy and Square movements (which occurred in the Arab Spring and expanded across the globe) have given rise to new political potentials beyond traditional party politics. At the time of occupations, citizens of different cultures and classes engaged in different forms of self-organization and novel horizontal democratic institutional forms to claim the right to the city and the commons. In everyday urban politics, spaces are reshaped and re-appropriated in a temporary manner, forming alternative networks to fulfill social needs and reproduce people; i.e. community gardens, social centers, cooperatives.

It has been challenging to implement sustainable institutional forms of democratic governing (e.g. alternative economic spaces, DIY urbanism) at a sufficiently large scale to challenge traditional logics. In this sense, the new municipalism allows for the development of innovative municipal institutions for seeding, promoting, and protecting their development (Thompson 2021). This is represented by three types of new municipalism: platform-based, autonomously based, and management-based (Thompson 2021). Platform municipalism works in, against, and beyond the state by forming new citizen platforms through civil society mobilization. The institutional form of the new local state is a composition of digital platforms, participatory budgeting, and popular assemblies. The autonomous municipalism aims for a stateless city governed through self-organizing that is nourished by feminism, degrowth, ecosocialism, libertarian municipalism, and communalism. The institutional forms of the autonomous model are represented by the confederation of autonomous self-governing communes and cooperatives. Managed municipalism targets the democratization of urban economies via technocratic projects under the influence of cooperativism and a pluralist commonwealth (Thompson 2021:

11–12). These new attempts at local governing and the transformation of the local state renew and redefine what a local state can be. The novel forms of local economy, bottom-up democratization, degrowth in relation to the state (D'Alisa & Kallis 2020), and degrowth machine politics (Schindler 2016), as well as other possibilities of alternative intra- and inter-scale solidarities between and within municipalities, promise new futures for social and economic sustainability.

## CONCLUSIONS

There is a great deal of diversity in understanding, revealing, and conceptualizing the local state. The above discussion illustrates that there are a number of ways to solve the puzzle of how the local state functions. However, three basic characteristics of the debate cut across all approaches: growth, localism, and struggle. In all approaches, the issue of growth is at the center, since cities are increasingly the primary sites of capitalist accumulation, production, and reproduction at a global scale. With the shift in how growth is pursued, managerialism, entrepreneurialism, and degrowth have been offered as alternative forms of municipalism and its institutions. Localism is at the core of most debates (pluralist, elitist, and Marxist) about the local state, whether it is an ontological position or an empirical scale, relation, and entity. The scale debate draws attention to the question of whether local state debates isolate the local scale from broader political economy analysis, structures, and forces. Lastly, struggle penetrates all approaches; however, except for alternative novel approaches, they do not take into account the impact of social movements on reshaping the state. Former approaches focus more on the conflicts between actors within and outside of the state and the struggle between different capital fractions.

For the future directions in local state theory, the deepening and expanded impacts of financialization at the national and local scales and a new turn towards an entrepreneurial shift in urban governance are worth mentioning. Current research on new forms of urban entrepreneurialism (Beswick & Penny 2018, Knox-Hayes & Wójcik 2020, Peck & Whiteside 2016) delves into the relationship between debt-based financing and the global financial markets, calling on the local state to help to facilitate and create markets and illustrating how global financial capital can make its way to local markets (Gotham 2009). This discussion's turning point was the shifting position of the local state in different waves of roll-back and roll-out neoliberalism, bringing cities to the forefront of local growth and fostering a local entrepreneurial state (Van Loon et al. 2019, Lauermann 2018). Beswick and Penny (2018) conceptualized this shift as 'financialized municipal entrepreneurialism', which incorporates speculative residential development and a greater interest in capital markets. Municipal financialization refers to the role of real estate and housing as the driving force behind entrepreneurial governance: not as a by-product of it but as an item to be evaluated on a financial basis (Beswick & Penny 2018, Christophers 2017). In fact, market forces are the initiators of financialization, but the state facilitates and enables the necessary conditions to make financialization possible. When the state allows the land to be treated as a purely financial asset, it prepares the necessary conditions for obtaining rent from the land, which previously had a privileged value based on its use (Beswick & Penny 2018, Hyötyläinen & Haila 2018). In the same vein, Çelik (2023) argues that the state has an additional deliberate role as a developer in treating land as a financial asset. Its roles include: (i) introducing new legislation, (ii) creating financial frameworks to encourage domestic and international capital to speculate on land and housing as assets, (iii) enclosing public land, (iv) leveraging revenue-sharing urban regeneration projects, and (v) using coercive legal and penal force to criminalize informal development and to quell resistance to state-led regeneration. As a result, the financialization of the local state has also been well-integrated with sustainable goals and green boosterism at the local level, for which further research on the local state is required.

## REFERENCES

Beswick, J. & Penny, J. (2018) Demolishing the present to sell off the future? The emergence of 'financialized municipal entrepreneurialism' in London. *International Journal of Urban and Regional Research* 42(4): 612–632.

Brenner, N. (2004) *New State Spaces: Urban Governance and the Rescaling of Statehood*. Oxford: Oxford University Press.

Brenner, N. (2019) *New Urban Spaces: Urban Theory and the Scale Question*. Oxford: Oxford University Press.

Çelik, Ö. (2023) The roles of the state in the financialisation of housing in Turkey. *Housing Studies* 38(6): 1006–1026.

Christophers, B. (2017) The state and financialization of public land in the United Kingdom. *Antipode* 49(1): 62–85.

Clarke, S. (1991) Marxism, sociology and Poulantzas's theory of the state. In S. Clarke (ed.) *The State Debate*. New York, NY: Palgrave Macmillan, 70–108.

Cockburn, C. (1977) The local state: Management of cities and people. *Race & Class* 18(4): 363–376.

Cox, K. R. (2009) *New State Spaces*. Oxford: Oxford University Press.

Cox, K. R. & Mair, A. (1989) Urban growth machines and the politics of local economic development. *International Journal of Urban and Regional Research* 13(1): 137–146.

D'Alisa, G. & Kallis, G. (2020) Degrowth and the state. *Ecological Economics* 169: 106486.

Das, R. J. (1996) State theories: A critical analysis. *Science & Society* 27–57.

Davies, J. (2021) *Between Realism and Revolt: Governing Cities in the Crisis of Neoliberal Globalism*. Bristol: Policy Press.

Dunleavy, P. & O'Leary, B. (eds.) (1991) *Theories of the State*. London: Macmillan.

Eisenschitz, A. & Gough, J. (1998) Theorizing the state in local economic governance. *Regional Studies* 32, 759–768.

Gotham, K. F. (2009) Creating liquidity out of spatial fixity: The secondary circuit of capital and the subprime mortgage crisis. *International Journal of Urban and Regional Research* 33(2): 355–371.

Harding, A. (1995) Elite theory and growth machines. In D. Judge, G. Stoker & H. Wolman (eds.) *Theories of Urban Politics.* London: Sage, 35–53.

Harding, A. (1997) Urban regimes in a Europe of the cities? *European Urban and Regional Studies* 4(4): 291–314.

Harvey, D. (1989) From managerialism to entrepreneurialism: The transformation in urban governance in late capitalism. *Geografiska Annaler: Series B, Human Geography* 71(1), 3–17.

Hay, C., Lister, M. & Marsh, D. (eds.) (2006) *The State: Theories and Issues*. Basingstoke: Macmillan.

Healey, P. (1997) *Collaborative Planning: Shaping Places in a Fragmented Society*. Basingstoke: Macmillan.

Healey, P. (1999) Institutionalist analysis, communicative action, and shaping places. *Journal of Planning Education and Research* 19(2): 111–121.

Hyötyläinen, M. & Haila, A. (2018) Entrepreneurial public real estate policy: The case of Eiranranta, Helsinki. *Geoforum* 89: 137–144.

Jessop, B. (1985) *Nicos Poulantzas: Marxist Theory and Political Strategy: Marxist Theory and Political Strategy*. London: Macmillan.

Jessop, B. (1991) Accumulation strategies, state forms and hegemonic projects. In S. Clarke (ed.) *The State Debate*. London: Palgrave Macmillan, 157–182.

Jessop, B. (2007) *State Power*. Cambridge: Polity Press.
Jessop, B., Peck, J. & Tickell, A. (1999) Retooling the machine: Economic crisis, state restructuring, and urban politics. In A. Jonas & D. Wilson (eds.) *The Urban Growth Machine: Critical Perspectives Two Decades Later*. New York, NY: Sunny Press, 141–159.
Jonas, A. E. (2020) The new urban managerialism in geopolitical context. *Dialogues in Human Geography* 10(3): 330–335.
Jonas, A. E. & Wilson, D. (eds.) (1999) *The Urban Growth Machine: Critical Perspectives, Two Decades Later*. New York, NY: Sunny Press.
Jones, M. R. (1997) Spatial selectivity of the state? The regulationist enigma and local struggles over economic governance. *Environment and Planning A* 29(5): 831–864.
Jones, M. R. (1999) *New Institutional Spaces*. London: Jessica Kingsley Publishers.
Judge, D. (1995) Pluralism. In D. Judge, G. Stoker & H. Wolman (eds.) *Theories of Urban Politics*. London: Sage, 13–34.
Judge, D., Stoker, G. & Wolman, H. (eds.) (1995) *Theories of Urban Politics*. London: Sage.
Knox-Hayes, J. & Wójcik, D. (eds.) (2020) *The Routledge Handbook of Financial Geography*. London: Routledge.
Kujawa, R. S. (2016) Urban managerialism. In D. Richardson (ed.) *International Encyclopedia of Geography: People, the Earth, Environment and Technology*. New York, NY: Wiley-Blackwell, 1–3.
Lauermann, J. (2018) Municipal statecraft: Revisiting the geographies of the entrepreneurial city. *Progress in Human Geography* 42(2): 205–224.
Logan, J. R. & Molotch, H. (1987) [2007] *Urban Fortunes: The Political Economy of Place*. Oakland, CA: University of California Press.
MacLeod, G. (2002) From urban entrepreneurialism to a 'revanchist city'? On the spatial injustices of Glasgow's renaissance. *Antipode* 34(3): 602–624.
Mann, M. (1984) The autonomous power of the state: Its origins, mechanisms and results. *Archives of European Sociology* 25: 185–213.
Miliband, R. (1969) *The State in Capitalist Society*. New York, NY: Basic Books.
Mossberger, K. (2009) Urban regime analysis. In J. S. Davies & D. L. Imbroscio (eds.) *Theories of Urban Politics*. London: Sage, 40–54.
Offe, C. (1974) Structural problems of the capitalist state. In K. von Beyme (ed.) *German Political Studies (Vol. 1)*. London: Sage, 104–129.
Pahl R. E. (1970) *Whose City? And Other Essays on Sociology and Planning*. London: Longmans.
Peck, J. (2017) Transatlantic city, part 1: Conjunctural urbanism. *Urban Studies* 54(1): 4–30.
Peck, J. & Theodore, N. (2019) Still neoliberalism? *South Atlantic Quarterly* 118(2): 245–265.
Peck, J. & Whiteside, H. (2016) Financializing Detroit. *Economic Geography* 92(3): 235–268.
Phelps, N. A. & Miao, J. T. (2020) Varieties of urban entrepreneurialism. *Dialogues in Human Geography* 10(3): 304–321.
Pickvance, C. (1995) Marxist theories of urban politics. In D. Judge, G. Stoker & H. Wolman (eds.) *Theories of Urban Politics*. London: Sage, 253–275.
Poulantzas, N. (1978) *State, Power, Socialism* (2nd ed.). London: Verso.
Saunders, P. (1981) *Social Theory and the Urban Question*. London: Hutchinson.
Savage, M., Warde, A. & Ward, K. (1993) *Urban Sociology, Capitalism and Modernity*. London: Macmillan.
Schindler, S. (2016) Detroit after bankruptcy: A case of degrowth machine politics. *Urban Studies* 53(4): 818–836.
Skocpol, T. (1985) Bringing the state back in: Strategies of analysis in current research. In P. B. Evans, D. Rueschemeyer & T. Skocpol (eds.) *Bringing the State Back In*. New York, NY: Cambridge University Press, 3–37.
Smith, M. (2006) Pluralism. In H. Colin, M. Lister & D. Marsh (eds.) *The State: Theories and Issues*. Basingstoke: Palgrave Macmillan, 21–38.
Stoker, G. (1998) Theory and urban politics. *International Political Science Review* 19(2): 119–129.
Stone, C. N. (1987) Summing up: Urban regimes, development policy, and political arrangements. In C. N. Stone & H. T. Sanders (eds.) *The Politics of Urban Development*. Lawrence: University Press of Kansas, 269–290.

Stone, C. N. (1989) *Regime politics: Governing Atlanta, 1946–1988*. Lawrence: University Press of Kansas.
Stone, C. N. (1993) Urban regimes and the capacity to govern: A political economy approach. *Journal of Urban Affairs* 15(1): 1–28.
Thompson, M. (2021) What's so new about New Municipalism? *Progress in Human Geography* 45(2): 317–342.
Thompson, M., Nowak, V., Southern, A., Davies, J. & Furmedge, P. (2020) Re-grounding the city with Polanyi: From urban entrepreneurialism to entrepreneurial municipalism. *Environment and Planning A: Economy and Space* 52(6): 1171–1194.
Van Loon, J., Oosterlynck, S. & Aalbers, M. B. (2019) Governing urban development in the Low Countries: From managerialism to entrepreneurialism and financialization. *European Urban and Regional Studies* 26(4): 400–418.

# 4. The city in class perspective
*Ibán Díaz-Parra and Beltrán Roca*

The class perspective has been very present throughout the history of urban studies and practically from its very beginning in its modern version. The tradition of urban studies in Europe and America dates to the last third of the 19th century and the beginning of the 20th century, linked to urban hygienist concerns. The growth of cities gives rise to the emergence of problems such as socio-spatial segregation, the degradation of living conditions in poor neighborhoods, social conflict, etc. The criticism of these situations has been translated into the world of artistic representation: in Doré's engravings of London; the novels of Zola, Blasco Ibañez and Dickens; and Riis's photographs of New York. It also generates the need for intervention in the physical environment of the city itself, either from reactionary positions, from Haussmann to Moses, or from reformist or utopian perspectives, from Howard to Mumford, through the models of the garden city (Hall 1994). The policy interventions around this broad issue required empirical information and theory regarding how the city operated.

Whether correct or not from today's perspective, this general problematic was interpreted primarily in relation to the fractioning of society into social classes, antagonistic for some and reconcilable for others. On the one hand, the reformist spirit accompanies Charles Booth's cartographies of London (1892), as well as the tradition initiated by the Chicago School (Park & Burgess 1967). On the other hand, anarchists and socialists took the city as an example of the contradictions and injustices of the capitalist system that represented the need for social revolution, with key references in the figures of Friedrich Engels (1997) and Élisée Reclus (2013). For much of the 20th century, class perspectives continued to play a major role in liberal and critical currents of thought; in the case of the latter, with a certain boom in the 1970s, when a growing interest in urban issues coincided with a great diffusion of Marxist perspectives in urban sociology and geography.

From the 1980s, liberal scholars have attacked class perspectives, considering them as obsolete for explaining postmodern society (Beck 1983). Inequality may still be a relevant problem in contemporary society, but it is no longer seen as a class-based phenomenon (Clark & Lipset 2001, Kingston 2000, Pakulski 2015). The thesis of the disappearance of social class as a basis of political behavior was significantly expanded from the 1980s on (and questioned by Wright (2015: 17)). Many critical sociologists and urban scholars of the 1960s and 1970s also moved away to some extent from class analysis in more recent decades. In this framework, the study of social movements and identity politics tended to displace class as a key category (Castells 1983, Touraine 1981). In urban studies, at the end of the last century, Schteingart complained about the abandonment of theorization of socio-spatial structure or land rent, which has been replaced by studies of urban actors, social movements and urban poverty. Case studies of informal slums abound, but those theorizing the general dynamics that structure the city as a whole are scarce (Schteingart 2001). More recently, Ward and Aalbers (2016) also complained about the abandonment of rent theory and the theorization of the capitalist remaking of geography in the English-speaking academy. Other authors have blamed postmodern thought for its disdain regarding general theorization and political economy concepts in urban studies

(Delgadillo 2013) and social theorization in general (Eagleton 1997). There is little doubt that social class and political economy perspectives have lost some of the attention they had a half-century ago from social and critical theory.

Our main objective here is to highlight the current relevance of class perspectives for urban studies, bringing into dialogue different ways of relating social class and the city and examining the possibilities of connecting them for a complex approach to the problem (Díaz-Parra & Roca 2021). This is not an exhaustive bibliographical review of the topic of social class and the city, which would be so extensive that it would require a whole book.

We defend the interest of a class perspective in current urban studies, and class theory and its relationship with urban studies is our exclusive focus in this chapter. In no way does this mean that we try to render invisible other categories and perspectives. In this chapter, we thus limit our focus to class.

In short, if we are to approach urban problems from a class perspective, we need to be aware of the theoretical traditions and debates regarding class, as well as its relationship with urban studies. Thus, to begin with we synthesize debates in social class theory that we consider most relevant to the current context of urban studies. This is followed by a discussion of perspectives in urban studies related to specific debates on social class. First, there are studies on socio-spatial segregation, which have a long tradition in urban studies and are evidently connected to sociological studies on social stratification. Second, the study of the material and symbolic production of urban space continues to represent a key explanatory element regarding the agents of production, their class character, their interests and their conflicts around the appropriation of land rent. Third, class perspectives remain a fundamental contribution to understanding the dynamics of urban conflict. The very contemporary idea of social class in critical studies makes no sense without this contentious dimension.

These three aspects – socio-spatial segregation, the capitalist production of urban space and contentious politics – have their own risks and weaknesses. Studies of segregation or urban conflict can easily be reduced to naive empiricism when ignoring their relationships with general strategies of capitalist urbanization. Similarly, works that focus on capital flows can become so abstract as to ignore their foundation in concrete strategies and geographies. Our proposal is that in order to enrich urban studies from a class perspective, these three dimensions should be understood as interrelated, as well as always being informed by the broader debates in social theory.

## FROM SOCIAL STRUCTURE TO SOCIO-SPATIAL STRUCTURE: THREE KEY DEBATES FROM THE 20TH CENTURY

There have been two main debates on class theory in the 20th century that we must take into account when examining the current class content of urban studies. The first concerned the very understanding of class from different perspectives, from the gradational scale of prestige of liberal and functionalist sociologists to the relational conception of neo-Weberian and neo-Marxist approaches. The second was the opposition between structuralist approaches, where class emerges mechanically from capitalist structures, and historicist approaches, with class as the result of concrete process of political struggle. We would add a third debate here introduced by social space thinkers on the relation between social structures and spatial structures, as well as the related prioritization of production or reproduction in class conflict.

Ossowski (1963) in his famous book on social classes opposed two main traditions in class analysis, the liberal one dominant in the US and the Weberian and Marxist ones in Europe. On the one hand, liberal perspectives on class mainly pay attention to individuals and their position on a scale of prestige or accumulation of a resource, such as rent. On the other hand, Marxist and Weberian analyses 'both start from the problem of the social relations that determine individuals' access to economic resources' (Wright 2015: 48). In the Marxist case, this would be established in terms of exploitation and domination in the relations of production and in the Weberian case in terms of inequality in exchanges. Classes here have a determining explanatory power in the development of human societies, which Wright has argued might have been overambitious at times (Wright 2005). Goldthorpe (neo-Weberian) and Wright (analytical Marxist) developed complex schemas of class adapted to late capitalist societies based on status and relation with property and exploitation, respectively (Erikson et al. 1979, Goldthorpe 1996, Wright et al. 1982).

A common criticism of relational perspectives is that classes as overly abstract categories do not correspond to empirically observable reality; for example, in public statistics. The Durkheimian tradition was at some point proposed as an alternative to the decline of Marxist and Weberian class analysis (Gurski 2005), which is based on the analysis of institutionalized categories in the labor market. However, this type of analysis has limitations like those of liberal approaches in terms of its descriptive character. In this type of study, we could speak more of strata than of social classes (Ossowski 1963). Bourdieu's class theory lies somewhere in between some of these positions, as it follows the gradational logic of accumulation of various types of resource (capitals) while at the same time being concerned with relations of oppression (Bourdieu 2010). In any case, while pure descriptive works may be of interest, the main interest of class in social theory is related to its explanatory character.

With respect to the conception of class as a determining theoretical concept in explaining the political processes of society, the debate between structuralist and historicist perspectives within Marxism is one of the most relevant in the second half of the 20th century. The debate concerns the tension between a mechanical/objective interpretation of class and an interpretation focused on agency and concrete historical processes. This was mostly a debate between structuralist/positivist Marxism (such as Althusser, Harneker, Poulantzas, and the young Laclau) and cultural/humanist Marxism (such as Williams, Hall, and Thompson). On the one hand, Althusser's perspective is usually linked to an economic conception of class, where cultural, ideological, or political arenas are reduced to mere epiphenomena. Social classes are determined by their place in the production process, which is the main dimension of the economic sphere. On the other hand, in the interpretation of Thompson (1966) it is political conflict that creates a class, which is always politically constituted throughout a historical process. The perspective of Thompson implies a revalorization of subjectivity, culture, and political will in historical processes. However, as Camarero (2009) points out, if historicist criticism of structuralism was necessary, the subjective character in class construction should not make us abandon the valuation of objective conditions and long-standing paths in capitalism. Some interpretations of Thompson's positions seem to go toward antitheoretical positions, compatible with arguments advocating the abandonment of class analysis. If, as Lefebvre said (1963), the problem is not the structures but structuralism, the solution is to elucidate ways of articulating the relationship between structure and agency.

Another key debate among 1970s and 1980s radical scholars was about the role of space in social theory. Space in class analysis has usually been little more than a metaphor. Social structure has tended to appear in all systems as something rather abstract that develops independently from its environment. Some of the critiques since the 1970s have tended to reintroduce concrete space into sociology and political economy as an alternative to previous excessive abstraction. Perhaps the most representative manifestation of this debate is the polemic between Lefebvre and Castells.

Castells polemicizes against Lefebvre, whom he accuses of constructing a spatial ideology that supports the hypothesis of the substitution of the problem of industry and production with a problem of urbanization and habitat. This implies shifting the focus from questions of production to social reproduction and from the working class to inhabitants. Castells' position here is still close to structuralism, as in the work of Pradilla Cobos (1984). Concrete social space is determined by industrialization forces and production relations. Harvey (1973) gives greater significance to space as an independent structure but he also criticizes the excess of the Lefebvrian hypothesis. Neil Smith's (1984) early works were also concerned with Lefebvre's emphasis on reproduction as opposed to production. The 'reproductionist thesis' has much to do with postwar capitalism, the expansion of mass consumption, and state direction of the economy, especially in the more developed Western world. This results in the struggles of the 1960s and 1970s being based more on community and neighborhood relations than on the workplace, which does not mean that the reproduction of the social relations of production has become the most determining function. Smith questioned the extent to which this is a structural change in capitalism or just a conjuncture (Smith 1984: 125). Nevertheless, classes in their Marxist sense continued to play a determining role in Lefebvre's work on the city (1969, 1976, 2013). Rather than a substitution, one could understand the Frenchman's work as an extension of interest from production to reproduction, integrating both into the notion of reproduction of social relations of production.

## THE CITY AS A SOCIAL MOSAIC: SOCIAL CLASS AND THE SEGREGATION OF GROUPS IN URBAN SPACE

The study of the city as a social mosaic is linked to the very origin of urban studies and is perhaps one of the perspectives in this field that is more frequently connected to the concept of social class. Social differences are expressed in space in the form of forced segregation and self-segregation, ghettos, housing discrimination, socio-spatial injustice, degraded habitats, forced displacement, gated communities and many other processes that are based in tendencies toward spatial separation of different social groups. The seminal works of modern urban studies focused on this issue. The works of Charles Booth (1892), Park (Park & Burguess 1967) and Hoyt (1939) focused on the separation of social groups from different perspectives. However, when dealing with this kind of research, two key questions arise in relation to previous debates on social structures and spatial structures. First, what conception of class are we dealing with when researching socio-spatial segregation? Second, what is the role of space in this process of social segregation?

The work of the Chicago school of urban sociology on urban segregation was usually very descriptive and naturalistic, close to a journalistic approach, answering to a typical functionalist and liberal theoretical approach despite their political concern with social reform. The rise of quantitative studies in the second half of the 20th century led to the development of socio-spatial segregation indicators (Duncan & Duncan 1955), factorial analysis (Ocaña 2005) and more recently cluster analysis (Martori & Horberg 2008). Much of this work is a spatial and generally cartographic counterpart of sociological surveys on the structure of classes and/or social strata and should consider carefully the reflections and debates on categories and strata that take place in this field. Empirical research on socio-spatial segregation in multiple cities continues to capture the interest of researchers. Most of America's research tends to discuss class- and race-based segregation, as this is a key historical element of the social structures of American and Latin American societies.

On the other hand, in Europe ethnic or racial elements have been less relevant until relatively recently (Andersen 2019). In these cities, income is not the only segregation-driven factor, but it is still the main factor (Musterd et al. 2017, Tammaru et al. 2014). Beyond these differences, these types of segregation studies continue to attract attention as the increase in inequalities is one of the most relevant aspects in the changes in Western societies in recent decades (Piketty 2014), resulting in the rise of urban segregation (see Tammaru et al. 2014), although this relation between inequality and segregation has been challenged by other scholars (Maloutas & Fujita 2016). In any case, most of these works are focused on a gradational perspective or socio-occupational categories determined by public statistics. Thus, many of the studies are purely descriptive and would be better understood as studies of social stratification rather than class-based analyses. Generally, in these studies, the idea of class in political terms does not play an explanatory role.

Another related problem addressed by different scholars is the exclusive focus on poverty and slums. Maloutas and Fujita (2016) have criticized this focus on poor neighborhoods when segregation is something that involves all social groups and the whole urban space. Urban segregation is not only a question of the ghetto but a multidirectional problem, and a rich enclave is as much segregated as an ethnic minority one (Nel-lo 2021). The supposed revitalization of segregation studies through innovative categories like the underclass has the same problem (Maloutas & Fujita 2016). The focused interest of segregation research on lower socio-economic strata and discriminated ethno-racial groups, even though in most cases it is the higher social groups that are the most segregated, exonerates broader mechanisms in the opinion of Maloutas and Fujita (2016).

Liberal and functionalist explanations fit better with a perspective based on social strata and individual households making location decisions. However, it would be much more interesting to understand strata and class as interrelated (Wright 2015). A segregation analysis does not need to be invalid from this perspective, but we should go beyond studying mechanisms conditioning individual households making decisions and socio-ethnic strata patterns of location. Most Marxist scholars focus on rent theory and class strategies for understanding these problems (see the next section). The key question here is that, as interesting as descriptive approaches to socio-spatial segregation are, if we do not connect to the class-based process that generates this segregation, we are losing all the explanatory and political potential of class theory.

There is still another debate on the effects of space, usually referred to as the neighborhood effect. It refers to the extent that we conceive socio-spatial segregation as an expression of socio-spatial structure or like a relatively autonomous process (Nel-lo 2021). Engaging with Lefebvre's critiques of structuralism, many authors have stressed the effects of space itself in the reproduction of inequalities (Soja 1996). Madden and Marcurse (2016) are very critical of Engels's *The Housing Question* as an example of the orthodox thesis of housing problems as an epiphenomenon of exploitation in the production sphere. In the opinion of Madden and

Marcuse, housing provision can be improved in a way relatively independent from the production arena. These relative improvements are historical facts in the Western world. However, the hypothesis that the housing problem cannot be completely solved in a way independent from production (Harvey 1973) is still solid, and many scholars have pointed to the way urban renewal and mixture policies are strategically used for provoking gentrification (Davidson 2008) or as a means of social control for dangerous classes (Wacquant 2009). These later works invite us to search away from the world of appearances that predominates in the housing and land markets and to introduce ourselves to the world of production, not just manufacturing production but also the production of the whole space (see Figure 4.1).

*Source:* Miguel A. Martínez.

*Figure 4.1* *Miraflores park in Seville (2004)*

## THE CITY AS FIX AND SOCIAL CAPITAL: CLASS IN THE PRODUCTION OF SPACE AND URBAN POLICY

Class analysis in the city goes much further than the description and explanation of socio-spatial segregation. For critical political economy, the city is overall a part of the circuits of capital and social space is a main mediation of class strategies. Different factions of the dominant class, guided by the logic of accumulation for accumulation's sake and particular interests, develop class coalitions, antagonisms, strategies and ideologies. The ultimate result is the production of social space itself. In contrast with the description of labor strata, here we have the social class organized politically and functioning theoretically as an explanatory factor for broader political and socio-economic processes. As opposed to the descriptive tendency of the previous group of academic works, here we can situate a series of studies with a more theoretically oriented perspective. However, as the poststructuralist critics would complain, to what extent do these works fall into excessive abstraction, economicism, or mechanicism, losing sight of concrete processes?

Despite earlier works of Engels, according to Pradilla Cobos (1984) much of the Marxist approach to the city began anew with Lefebvre's *Right to the City* (1969). Marxists and radical scholars during the first two thirds of the 20th century were mostly focused on a very abstract political economy or sociology. The arrival of Lefebvre at the city had to do with his criticism of this type of thought, especially Marxist structuralism. The urban is an opportunity to appreciate concrete practices and experiences in concrete spaces. At the same time, it does not mean abandoning class perspectives. The production of space is mainly the result of class strategies oriented toward the reproduction of social relations of production. It means the organization of space for production and consumption, as well as for disciplining and reproducing the workforce (Lefebvre 1969, 1976, 2013).

However, subsequent developments of Marxist perspectives on the city in the 1970s were initially closer to structuralism. From the class perspective shared by these works, social space is mainly a result of the production process, connecting it with the Marxist theory of value. Moraes and Dacosta (1984) speak about social space production as a valorization process. Harvey (1973) describes the city as a deposit of social surplus product in space, which requires the division of work and exploitation. For Lefebvre (2013) and for Harvey (1982) the spatialization of capitalism is a class strategy oriented toward overcoming the structural tendency of capitalism toward crisis. This perspective is present in current debates on gentrification (Hackworth & Smith 2001, Smith 1996) and planetary gentrification (López-Morales 2015, Slater 2017). Rent theory has been another key element connecting urbanization with class interests, guiding strategies for rentiers and coercing working-class subjects in the market. This was a key theme in the work of Topalov (1979, 1984) and the early work of Harvey (1973, 1982). These themes have kept attention in Latin America through the works of Samuel Jaramillo (2008) from a Marxist perspective and Pedro Abramo (2011) from a non-Marxist approach.

However, some of the work on the production of spaces and rent theory can be seen as excessively abstract, disconnected form practical reality, economistic or even mechanistic. Criticisms of the work of geographers such as Harvey or Smith again bring up an old debate on class theory: the questioning of the deterministic character of structuralist perspectives. Most of the criticism of Jessop (2006) and Massey (1991) regarding Harvey's early theory of capitalist urbanization was that it paid little attention to questions such as culture and social diversity in political economy. Perhaps as a response to this criticism, most of the systemic and class perspectives on the process of urbanization have tended to use regulation theory (Aglietta 1979, Boyer 1989). Some of the later works by Harvey (1989) have paid much more attention to cultural and political issues, analyzing relations between economic structure, cultural theory and regulation theory.

The focus on political issues as a way of avoiding excessive economicism justifies the current focus on urban neoliberalism (Brenner 2004, Peck et al. 2018) as class strategy. The work of Harvey is again key in this trend, dealing with the entrepreneurial city, monopoly rent and accumulation by dispossession in relation to neoliberal urbanism as the result of the excessive power of capital over labor after the 1970s. From them on, urban politics turned from redistribution issues to competitive policies as the capitalist class gained political influence (Harvey, 2001). This is a long-term trend, from the governance discourses of the 1990s to current smart-city policies (Rossi 2016). Jäger (2003) introduced basic concepts from regulation theory into the analysis of class strategies around rent appropriation, where the deregulation of rent controls in neoliberalism is analyzed as a class strategy to support capital accumulation, whilst Sassen (2013) pointed to polarization of skilled and unskilled workers as a result of concentration of capital and power in global cities.

One of the most recurrent neoliberal urban strategies has been cultural politics (Harvey 2001). Within this strand of the literature, the work of Richard Florida (2005) on the creative class has become very popular. This is also a good example of the misuse of the concept of class as vaguely referring to a social stratum, at the same time being unsupported by empirical evidence (Rossi 2016). The main problem with this type of vague use of class is that it potentially renders invisible the true class strategies of rentiers and developers using cultural policies for capital accumulation through urbanization. The open and tolerant spaces to which Florida refers are fundamentally gentrified urban centers of large cities. We can find the inverse of this creative class theory in Smith's notion of the revanchist city (Smith 1996), where the attraction of creative class members and the consequent increases in income and housing prices at a neighborhood level tend to gentrify lower- and middle-class areas and produce marginalization and exclusion of long-term residents (Ponzi & Rossi 2009).

The current problematization of the financialization of the economy, specifically the financialization of urbanization and housing, is derived from this type of historical-structural analysis from a class perspective. Financialization has continued as a main topic of research for Harvey, but also for many critical economists and historians (Arrighi 1978, Boyer 1989, Naredo 2003). In relation to urbanization, there has been growing attention paid to the work of the geographer Manuel Aalbers on the financialization of housing (Aalbers & Christophers 2014, Fernández & Aalbers 2016). Moreover, Ward and Aalbers (2016) have reasserted the necessity of paying renewed attention to rent theory, understanding rent as a class relation. Currently, there is a growing body of literature on current rentierism and its effect on urbanization; for example, the effects of short-term rentals on current capitalist urbanization from a class perspective (Sadowski 2020, Yrigoy et al. 2022).

Still, a key criticism of historical and structural perspectives on class and the urban has revolved around the idea of false generalization. Most of the criticisms from postcolonial and decolonial perspectives focus on false generalization from a few European and American examples. This criticism is old enough and affects both class theory and capitalist urbanization theory (Robinson 2016). First, the questioning came from dependency theory. American dependentists began to criticize work that took for granted that peripheral capitalism would take the same forms as core societies in social structure and urban development (Castells 1973). Pradilla Cobos (1984) made a relevant attack on the French school of urban sociology for not taking into account the diversity of economic and social development in its theorization of urban development. This accusation of false generalization has also been directed against Sassen's global cities theory (Maloutas & Fujita 2016).

Most current studies on the production of spaces and neoliberal urbanization consider this criticism. There is a general acceptance of modes of regulation as sets of policies and institutions that can vary extremely in diverse contexts (Peck et al. 2018). There is also an effort in both the English- and Spanish-speaking academies to understand how concrete processes of political diffusion connect very different urban realities and reproduce similar policies and strategies that can result in diverse outcomes (Jajamovich 2013, Lees 2012).

However, these theoretically, historically and political economy-anchored perspectives give little space for urban conflict, as if there were only a capitalist class acting in the production of space. How can we articulate all these reflections on capitalist urbanization strategies with the analysis of spatial practices of urban conflict and labor movements?

## SPACE IN CLASS ORGANIZATION AND LABOR CONFLICT

Workers' organizing, the creation of their institutions and their protests have had a privileged setting in the urban sphere with an impact on urban sociology. However, since the 1980s the idea of class conflict has been replaced by the more vague idea of social movements. Although Thompson's studies were firmly anchored in the class perspective, the idea of class as a historical political construct taken to its extreme can become independent of the socio-economic bases that gave it meaning in the first place. If the very term 'social movements' was sociologically popularized by Touraine, it is worth noting how he moved from a sociology in which class plays a central role to referring to class society as a historical, contingent image created in 19th century Europe and disappearing in the second half of the 20th century (Touraine 1981). One of his most advanced disciples, Manuel Castells, who is more closely linked to urban issues, makes a similar transition from *The Urban Question* (1977) to *The City and the Grassroots* (1983), where he concludes by discarding the class origin of urban conflicts and later abandoning the radical perspectives that had characterized his first stage. In geography, authors such as Soja (1996) and Massey (1991) also moved progressively from Marxist perspectives to poststructuralist ones, where the contingency and diversity of the subjects mobilized in the conflict take precedence.

There seem to be good reasons for not addressing urban conflict from a class perspective, including the decadence of the labor movement from the last third of the 20th century. However, it is worth asking to what extent current urban conflicts are class conflicts. Does the usual focus on social reproduction like housing force us to abandon class perspectives? Are labor conflicts independent of urban and spatial dynamics? For this to make any sense, it is first necessary to distinguish between class-based and non-class-based conflicts. Let us tentatively accept Harvey's (2019) division between opposition movements and class movements. Opposition movements can be characterized basically by demands for rights and justice without questioning of the political and economic structures of capitalist society, in contrast to class conflict emerging from contradictions constitutive of these structures. Harvey's differentiation is not based on a particular subjectivity or sociological description of a human group, but on the type of conflict and its relation to the more macro-economic processes of urban capitalist development that we discussed in the previous section. This avoids falling into the error of confusing the class relation with the labor stratification of the protagonists, although this should not be left completely aside either. Mayer (2016) points out that articulating this division is very complicated. The boundaries between these types of struggles are indeed porous. Nevertheless, it is possible to at least identify whether or not of a class component exists in each urban struggle.

Madden and Marcuse's (2016) book begins by criticizing positions that posit specifically urban problems as an expression of class struggle, thinking first of Engels' pioneering work.

Madden and Marcuse seem concerned to make housing movements and policies autonomous from the realm of production. For these authors, the political subject here would not be so much a social class as the inhabitants. However, we would say that class perspectives would be an interesting way of addressing housing struggles, providing a way of not artificially separating production and reproduction spheres as if they were completely autonomous.

One of the problems most commonly addressed from a class perspective is that of tenants. This topic has appeared in work on urban social history practically forever. Property as a means of extraction of rent and its absence determine the social roles of tenants and landlords as antagonistic classes (Gray 2018). The practices of landlords have changed enormously over time; for example, through the rise of platform capitalism and new rentierism (Yrigoy et al. 2022). However, the relations of exploitation remain the same. Some processes derived from the last real estate crises have resulted in an increase in households in tenancy relations (Carmona 2022) and therefore also an intensification of the forms of organization and struggle of tenants (Bradley 2014, Martínez & González 2021), entailing the capacity to act politically as a class. The profiles of tenants do not necessarily coincide with a typical classification of social classes in the production process. However, fights about rent appropriation and tenant–landlord conflict can be easily understood using the logics of class relations and exploitation and are always conditioned by the roles of the individual households in the production process. Something similar can be said of the struggles around mortgage execution, where the conflict derives from exploitation of the borrower household by lender institutions (Colau & Alemany 2014). Displacement from central areas, touristification and gentrification also do not affect the population independently of their class position. Studies show that tenants and manual workers form the households that are more subject to displacement (Díaz-Parra & Barrero 2022).

Class perspectives are not only alien to social reproduction struggles. In addition, social reproduction in concrete spaces can be the basis for class politics. Harvey (1996) identifies the origin of class organization in the solidarities created in the local under concrete historical and geographical conditions, what he calls, following Williams (1989), militant particularism. This work was highly criticized from poststructuralist perspectives, with accusations that Harvey privileged class over other categories that were supposedly reduced to particularisms (Featherstone 1998, McDowell 1998). However, this concrete and local base for the wider (universalist) policies of the labor movement has been a very common topic in geographical studies following the 1980s. Scott and Storper (1986), in this line, note that class phenomena should be studied in terms of specific local/regional forms of social life with which work and capital accumulation take place and in relation to other forms of social division. The formation of localized communities of workers is a necessary condition for the rise of class consciousness and struggle. This idea has been present in much of the sociology and the anthropology of work, which have studied class conflict and trade unionism in relatively homogeneous working-class communities structured around industries that require high geographical concentration of the workforce (such as in docks, mines, shipyards or automobile plants) (Bottiglieri & Ceri 1987, Moreno 1990, Palenzuela 1995).

This connects with the debate about the strategy of community unionism and the complex relations between trade unions and social movements. The idea of community unionism implies a substantial change in the spatial practices of the labor movement: primarily, not limiting itself to the workplace but broadening the geographical areas in which workers develop their family and collective lives (McBride & Greenwood 2009, Roca 2020, Wills & Simms

2004). Addressing demands that go beyond strictly labor issues has been part of the effort to revitalize trade unionism in recent decades (Milkman 2013). However, this has involved sharing the limelight (and competing) with other organizations that have also represented segments of the working class. In this sense, part of the specialized literature has highlighted the tendency towards the convergence between unions and social movements (Kelly 1999), while other research has identified very significant tensions and rivalries (Roca & Díaz-Parra 2017).

Greenberg and Lewis (2017) stress that activists and trade unionists are adopting increasingly sophisticated geographical thinking. Strike action, they argue, remains the central tactic in the dispute between labor and capital, but urban social movements seek to paralyze economic activity through tactics that disrupt traffic on highways, avenues, bridges or squares. Occupations of buildings and public spaces, encampments, mass assemblies, barricades and street theatres are part of the repertoire of protest that can be used for this purpose. Thus, streets, neighborhoods, infrastructures and urban commons have (at least in part) displaced workplaces as the epicenter of class conflict. Underlying this current is the Lefebvrian idea (Lefebvre 2013) of the production of space as a class strategy. Through organization and collective action, workers demonstrate their own knowledge of the socio-spatial organization of capitalism, which materializes in concrete practices aimed at disrupting spatial fixes or influencing certain scales of political and economic power where they can find answers to their demands (Herod 2001).

## CONCLUSIONS

The present chapter has tried to emphasize the interest and strength of class perspectives for urban studies through a dialogue between class theory and social space theory. Most of the work on social class and urbanization shares elements of the three perspectives exposed in the sections above: the understanding of social-spatial segregation and derived phenomena as outcomes of class divisions; the study of the structure of the agents of the production of space, their class interest and strategies; and spatiality as a main factor in class politics, organization and conflict. However, the three have been separated as part of an analytical process. Analytical thought needs to disentangle its object of study and it also needs to recompose it to some extent.

Analysis of socio-spatial segregation without considering the process of political conflict tells us more about social strata than about class issues, at least in Marxist terms. Moreover, the tendency to reduce segregation to studies of poverty or ghettos eliminates the relational conception that makes the category of class analytically rich. The perspective focused on the production of space as a class strategy is based on agents with the capacity to transform that space. It runs the risk of leading to the opposite problem; that is, pretending that only the capitalist class and its interests exist, ignoring relational and conflict perspectives on class. A radically constructivist position, defining class exclusively in terms of conflict, can lead to ignoring the material basis of the processes behind the conflict, leaving the social transformation that has been the basis of class theory to a certain kind of political voluntarism. A class conflict analysis ignoring wider processes of capitalist production of space may end up being myopic and talking about something else.

Can we treat spatial segregation, class conflict and capitalist production of space together then? Implicitly at least yes, even if we focus on one aspect while considering the existence of the others. However, even doing so, there is also a risk of not paying enough attention to the complex relations among them. Putting together the three perspectives without analyzing their interrelations could even undermine the attempt to achieve a better understanding of urban affairs. These three fields connect in multiple ways. Class strategies and circulation of capital shape cities, concentrating surplus at some points and generating uneven geographical development. Class strategy and ideology valorize and devalorize urban space, transforming land use and the conditions for reproduction of the entire society. One can describe and even quantify the social mosaic of the city, but one cannot understand it without examining the class agency and antagonism behind the capital and symbolic flows in the built space. Investments in space and uneven development are the basis for the growth of new cultures of labor and the decay of others. Investment and disinvestment and industrial relocation destroy everyday local productive systems while developing new ones. At the same time, labor culture and class conflict condition and shape concrete niches of labor created by the specialization of the economy. Furthermore, socio-spatial segregation and an urban mosaic pave the ground for the development of militant particularism and class-based communities, while labor culture and militancy intervene against socio-spatial segregation and derived processes, such as gentrification or touristification.

Studies on socio-spatial segregation must take into account the way in which the urban structure transforms and changes, giving rise to certain configurations. The analysis of capital flows must observe the actions, lives and conflicts of concrete people and groups so as not to fall into speculative theorizing. The analysis of conflicts must accompany the analysis of the dominant forms of capitalist urbanization and consider the social conditions related to the production and reproduction of the people who inhabit the city.

A class-based approach to urban issues, well-informed by class theory debates, is nowadays fundamental for politicized critical urban studies. Not every notion of class is valid for this purpose. We adhere here to a relational conception of class, giving an explanatory role to political and socio-economic processes. In this trend, urban scholars continue to develop insightful perspectives for the study of the urban phenomena, overcoming long-lasting dilemmas such as the agency–structure one and the problem of the recognition of culture and political subjectivities in the making of class.

## REFERENCES

Aalbers, M. & Christophers, B. (2014) Centering housing in political economy. *Housing Theory and Society* 31(4): 373–394.

Abramo, P. (2011) *La ciudad caleidoscópica. Coordinación espacial y convención urbana: una perspectiva heterodoxa para la economía urbana*. Bogotá: Universidad del Externado de Colombia.

Aglietta, M. (1979) *Regulación y crisis del capitalismo: la experiencia de los Estados Unidos*. Madrid: Siglo XXI.

Andersen, H. S. (2019) *Ethnic Spatial Segregation in European Cities*. Oxon and New York: Routledge.

Arrighi, E. (1978) *La geometría del imperialismo*. Madrid: Siglo XXI.

Beck, U. (1983) Jenseits von Stand und Klasse? In Kreckel, R. (ed.) *Soziale Ungleichheiten. Soziale Welt*. Sonderband: Gottingen, 35–74.

Booth, C. (1892) *Life and Labor in the People in London. Vol. 1*. London/New York: Macmillan.

Bottiglieri, B. & Ceri, P. (1987) *Le culture del lavoro*. Bolonia: Il Mulino.

Bourdieu, P. (2010) *Distinction: A Social Critique of the Judgement of Taste*. London/New York/New Delhi: Routledge.

Boyer, R. (1989) *La teoría de Regulación. Un análisis crítico.* Buenos Aires: Área de Estudios e Investigaciones Laborales de la SECYT.
Bradley, Q. (2014) *The Tenants' Movement. Resident Involvement, Community Action and the Contentious Politics of Housing.* New York: Routledge.
Brenner, N. (2004) *New State Spaces: Urban Governance and the Rescaling of Statehood.* Oxford: Oxford University Press.
Camarero, H. (2009) Las concepciones de E. P. Thompson acerca de las clases sociales y la conciencia de clase en la historia. *Espacios de Crítica y Producción* 40: 136–142.
Carmona, P. (2022) *La democracia de propietarios. Fondos de inversión, rentismo popular y la lucha por la vivienda.* Madrid: Traficantes de Sueños.
Castells, M. (1973) *Imperialismo y urbanización en América Latina.* Barcelona: Gustavo Gili.
Castells, M. (1977) *The Urban Question.* Boston: The MIT Press.
Castells, M. (1983) *The City and the Grassroots.* Berkeley: University of California Press.
Clark, T. N. & Lipset, S. M. (2001) *The Breakdown of Class Politics.* Baltimore: John Hopkins University Press.
Colau, A. & Alemany, A. (2014) *Mortgaged Lives. From the Housing Bubble to the Right to Housing.* Los Angeles: Journal of Aesthetics & Protest Press.
Davidson, M. (2008) Spoiled mixture: Where does state-led 'positive' gentrification end? *Urban Studies* 45(12): 2385–2405.
Delgadillo, V. (2013) América Latina urbana: la construcción de un pensamiento teórico propio. Entrevista con Emilio Pradilla Cobos. *Andamios* 10(22): 185–201.
Díaz-Parra, I. & Barrero, M. (2022) Clase, gentrificación y trabajo: La experiencia del doble desplazamiento de los trabajadores productivos en Sevilla. *Ciudades* 26: 123–141.
Díaz-Parra, I. & Roca, B. (2021) *El espacio en la teoría social. Una mirada multidisciplinar.* Valencia: Tirant.
Duncan, O. D. & Duncan, B. (1955) A methodological analysis of segregation indexes. *American Sociological Review* 41: 210–217.
Eagleton, T. (1997) *Las ilusiones del posmodernismo.* Buenos Aires: Paidós.
Engels, F. (1997) *The Housing Question.* Moscow: Progress Publishers.
Erikson, R., Goldthorpe, J. H. & Portocarero, L. (1979) Intergenerational class mobility in three Western European societies: England, France and Sweden. *The British Journal of Sociology* 30(4): 415–441.
Featherstone, D. (1998) Some versions of militant particularism: A review article of David Harvey's *Justice, Nature, and the Geography of Difference*. *Antipode* 30(1): 19–25.
Fernández, R. & Aalbers, M. (2016) Financialization and housing: Between globalization and varieties of capitalism. *Competition and Change* 20(2): 71–88.
Florida, R. (2005) *Cities and the Creative Class.* New York: Routledge.
Goldthorpe, J. H. (1996) Class analysis and the reorientation of class theory: The case of persisting differentials in educational attainment. *British Journal of Sociology* 47(3): 481–505.
Gray, N. (2018) *Rent and its Discontents: A Century of Housing Struggles.* London: Rowman & Littlefield.
Greenberg, M. & Lewis, P. (eds.) (2017) *The City Is the Factory. New Solidarities and Spatial Strategies in an Urban Age.* New York: Cornell University Press.
Gurski, D. (2005) Foundations of a neo-Durkheimian class analysis. In Wright, O. (ed.) *Approaches to Class Analysis.* Cambridge. Cambridge University Press, 31–81.
Hackworth, J. & Smith, N. (2001) The changing state of gentrification. *Tijdschrift voor Economische en Sociale Geografie* 92: 464–477.
Hall, P. (1994) *Ciudades del mañana: Historia del urbanismo del siglo XX.* Barcelona: Ediciones del Serbal.
Harvey, D. (1973) *Social Justice and the City.* Athens: University of Georgia Press.
Harvey, D. (1982) *The Limits to Capital.* London: Verso.
Harvey, D. (1985) *The Urbanization of Capital.* Oxford: Basil Blackwell.
Harvey, D. (1989) *The Condition of Postmodernity.* Oxford: Basil Blackwell.
Harvey, D. (1996) *Justice, Nature and the Geography of Difference.* Oxford: Blackwell.
Harvey, D. (2001) *Spaces of Capital. Towards a Critical Geography.* London/New York: Routledge.
Harvey, D. (2019) *Rebel Cities. From the Right to the City to the Urban Revolution.* London: Verso.

Herod, A. (2001) *Labor Geographies: Workers and the Landscapes of Capitalism*. New York: Guilford Press.
Hoyt, H. (1939) *The Structure and Growth of Residential Neighborhoods in American Cities*. Washington: Government Printing Office.
Jäger, J. (2003) Urban land rent theory: A regulationist perspective. *International Journal of Urban and Regional Research* 27(2): 233–249.
Jajamovich, G. (2013) Miradas sobre intercambios internacionales y circulación internacional de ideas y modelos urbanos. *Andamios* 10(22): 91–111.
Jaramillo, S. (2008) *Hacia una teoría de la renta del suelo urbano*. Bogotá: Ediciones Uniandes-Universidad de los Andes.
Jessop, B. (2006) Spatial fixes, temporal fixes, and spatio-temporal fixes. In N. Castree (ed.) *David Harvey: A Critical Reader*. New York: Blackwell, 142–166.
Kelly, J. (1999) *Rethinking Industrial Relations: Mobilization, Collectivism and Long Waves*. London: Routledge.
Kingston, P. W. (2000) *The Classless Society*. Stanford: Stanford University Press.
Lees, L. (2012) The geography of gentrification: Thinking through comparative urbanism. *Progress in Human Geography* 36(2): 155–171.
Lefebvre, H. (1963) Reflexiones sobre el estructuralismo y la historia. *Cuadernos Internacionales de Sociología* 35: 136–172.
Lefebvre, H. (1969) *El derecho a la ciudad*. Barcelona: Península.
Lefebvre, H. (1976) *Espacio y política*. Barcelona: Península.
Lefebvre, H. (2013) *La producción del espacio*. Madrid: Capitán Swing.
López-Morales, E. (2015) Gentrification in the Global South. *City* 19(4): 564–573.
Madden, D. & Marcuse, P. (2016) *In Defense of Housing*. New York: Verso.
Maloutas, T. & Fujita, K. (2016) *Residential Segregation in Comparative Perspective. Making Sense of Contextual Diversity*. New York: Routledge.
Martínez, M. & González, R. (2021) Acción colectiva durante la crisis pandémica en España (2020–2021). In Fundación Betiko (ed.) *Anuario de Movimientos Sociales 2020*. Bilbao: Fundación Betiko.
Martori, C. C. & Horberg, K. (2008) Nuevas técnicas de estadística especial para la detección de clústeres residenciales de población inmigrante. *Scripta Nova* 12: 261.
Massey, D. (1991) Flexible sexism. *Environment and Planning D: Society and Space* 9(1): 31–57.
Mayer, M. (2016) Neoliberal urbanism and uprisings across Europe. In Mayer, M. et al. (eds.) *Urban Uprisings. Challenging Neoliberal Urbanism in Europe*. New York: Palgrave, 57–92.
McBride, J. & Greenwood, I. (eds.) (2009) *Community Unionism: A Comparative Analysis of Concepts and Contexts*. Basingstoke: Palgrave Macmillan.
McDowell, L. (1998) Some academic and political implications of *Justice, Nature and the Geography of Difference*. *Antipode* 30(1): 3–5.
Milkman, R. (2013) Back to the future? US labour in the new gilded age. *British Journal of Industrial Relations* 51(4): 645–665.
Moraes, A. C. R. & Da Costa, W. M. (1984) *Geografía crítica. La valorización del espacio*. Ciudad de México: Itaca.
Moreno, I. (1990) Cultura del trabajo e ideología: el movimiento anarquista campesino andaluz. In *Actas del IV Congreso sobre el Andalucismo Histórico*. Sevilla: Fundación Blas Infante, 77–93.
Musterd, S., Marcińczak, S., Van Ham, M. & Tammaru, T. (2017) Socioeconomic segregation in European capital cities. Increasing separation between poor and rich. *Urban Geography* 38(7): 1062–1083.
Naredo, J. M. (2003) *La burbuja inmobiliario-financiera en la coyuntura económica reciente (1985–1995)*. Madrid: Siglo XXI.
Nel-lo, O. (2021) *Efecto barrio. Segregación residencial, desigualdad social y políticas urbanas en las grandes ciudades ibéricas*. Valencia: Tirant lo Blanch.
Ocaña, C. (2005) Microanálisis sociodemográfico de espacios urbanos. *Boletín de la AGE* 40: 5–34.
Ossowski, S. (1963) *Class Structure in the Social Consciousness*. New York: The Free Press of Glencoe.
Pakulski, J. (2015) Fundamentos de un análisis de clases posclasista. In E. O. Wright (ed.) *Modelos de análisis de clases*. Valencia: Tirant, 211–248.

Palenzuela, P. (1995) Las culturas del trabajo: una aproximación antropológica. *Sociología del Trabajo* 24: 3–28.
Park, R. E. & Burgess, E. W. (1967) *The City*. Chicago: Chicago University Press.
Peck, J., Brenner, N., Theodore, N., Cahill, D., Cooper, M., Konings, M. & Primrose, D. (2018) Actually existing neoliberalism. In Cahill, D., Cooper, M, Konings, M. & Primrose, D. (eds.) *The Sage Handbook of Neoliberalism*. London: Sage, 1–15.
Piketty, T. (2014) *The Capital in the XXI Century*. Harvard: Harvard University Press.
Ponzi, D. and Rossi, U. (2009) Becoming a creative city: The entrepreneurial mayor, network politics and the promise of an urban renaissance. *Urban Studies* 47(5): 1037–1057.
Pradilla Cobos, E. (1984) *Contribución a la crítica de la teoría urbana*. México: Universidad Autónoma Metropolitana Xochimilco.
Reclus, E. (2013) *Anarchy, Geography, Modernity: Selected Writings of Elisée Reclus*. Oakland: PM Press.
Robinson, J. (2016) Thinking cities through elsewhere: Comparative tactics for a more global urban studies. *Progress in Human Geography* 40(1): 3–29.
Roca, B. (2020) Socio-spatial strategies of worker centres: An ethnography of alt-labour in NYC. *Antipode* 52(4): 1196–1215.
Roca, B. & Díaz-Parra, I. (2017) Blurring the borders between old and new social movements: The M15 movement and the radical unions in Spain. *Mediterranean Politics* 22(2): 218–237.
Rossi, U. (2016) The variegated economics and the potential politics of the smart city. *Territory, Politics, Governance* 4(3): 337–353.
Sadowski, J. (2020) The internet of landlords: Digital platforms and new mechanisms of rentier capitalism. *Antipode* 52(2): 562–580.
Sassen, S. (2013) *The Global City: New York, London, Tokyo*. New Jersey: Princeton University Press.
Schteingart, M. (2001) La división social del espacio en las ciudades. *Perfiles Latinoamericanos* 19: 13–31.
Scott, A. J. & Storper, M. (eds.) (1986) *Production, Work, Territory. The Geographical Anatomy of Industrial Capitalism*. Boston/London/Sydney: Allen & Unwin.
Slater, T. (2017) Planetary rent gaps. *Antipode* 49(1): 114–137.
Smith, N. (1984) *Uneven Development: Nature, Capital and the Production of Space*. London: Verso.
Smith, N. (1996) *The New Urban Frontier. Gentrification and the Revanchist City*. London: Routledge.
Soja, E. (1996) *Thirdspace: Journeys to Los Angeles and Other Real and Imagined Places*. Oxford: Blackwell.
Tammaru, T., Marcińczak, S., Van Ham, M. & Musterd, S. (2014) *Socio-economic Segregation in European Capital Cities*. Abingdon: Routledge.
Thompson, E. P. (1966) *The Making of the English Working Class*. New York: Vintage.
Topalov, C. (1979) *La Urbanización Capitalista. Algunos Elementos para su Análisis*. México: Edicol.
Topalov, C. (1984) *Ganancias y Rentas Urbanas. Elementos Teóricos*. México: Siglo XXI.
Touraine, A. (1981) New social movements. *Telos* 49: 33–37.
Wacquant, L. (2009) *Punishing the Poor. The Neoliberal Government of Social Insecurity*. Durham: Duke University Press.
Ward, C. & Aalbers, M. B. (2016) 'The shitty rent business': What's the point of land rent theory? *Urban Studies* 53(9): 1760–1783.
Williams, R. (1989) *Resources of Hope*. London: Verso.
Wills, J. & Simms, M. (2004) Building reciprocal community unionism in the UK. *Capital & Class* 28(1): 59–84.
Wright, E. O. (2005) *Approaches to Class Analysis*. Cambridge: Cambridge University Press.
Wright, E. O. (2015) *Understanding Class*. London and New York: Verso.
Wright, E. O., Costello, C., Hachen, D. & Sprague, J. (1982) The American class structure. *American Sociological Review* 47(6): 709–726.
Yrigoy, I., Morell, M. & Müller, N. (2022) Why do middle-class positions matter? The alignment of short-term rental suppliers to the interests of capital. *Antipode* 54(3): 959–978.

# 5. The global city and other fetishes: financial foundations of a mirage

*Mariana Fix*

This chapter investigates the reception and reach of the global city hypothesis in urban planning and in the urban planning literature, presenting the emblematic case of São Paulo, the largest metropolis of Latin America.

Global cities became one of the most popular topics in urban studies and urban planning practice during the 1990s. The global city concept 'bewitched authors, professors, publishers, journalists and consultants' (Maricato 2007) with slogans such as 'São Paulo has the vocation to become a "global city"',[1] disseminating its normative and ideological form as a kind of 'badge of honour' that cities desperately wanted to get, at the height of the advance of the neoliberal agenda in the country (Carvalho 2000, Ferreira 2007, Villaça 2007). However, to what extent was this global cities construct originally formulated in the field of urban studies really influential in urban planning with concrete repercussions on the social production of the built environment in São Paulo?

It is important to clarify that although the analytical hypothesis of the global city is known mainly in the formulation of Saskia Sassen (2001),[2] in Brazil it has often been disseminated side by side with the new normative urban planning model, the so-called 'strategic planning of cities', associated with the then-known Barcelona model (Arantes 2000). This model has added weight to the shift already underway in the urban planning approach and mindset in São Paulo, in its own way incorporating and reverberating with the crisis of modern urbanism and the advancement of urban entrepreneurialism (Compans 2005), which presented public–private partnerships as a kind of magic formula to make urban interventions feasible in the context of the state's fiscal crisis (Fix 2004).

To answer the main research question, this chapter is structured in four sections, in addition to this introduction and the conclusions. In the first section, I briefly review texts on global cities that have influenced the research agenda and policies in Brazil, not only through their academic production but also through their presence in debates inside and outside the university and/or by offering consultancies on the subject. I also bring up some of the discussions raised in the international literature.

In the second section, I discuss how Brazilian authors reacted to the inclusion of São Paulo in the list of global cities, albeit in the second rank, as well as how the concept went on to become detached from the hypothesis of the global city, becoming an influential but diffused reference lacking the cohesion of a full project.

In the third section, aiming at reflecting on the context in which the rapid assimilation of this theory took place in São Paulo, I examine some critical approaches to the concept of globalisation that contributed to the understanding of the structural change that capitalism was undergoing at that moment in time and how that changed the characteristics of the processes of dependence and underdevelopment (Brandão & Siqueira 2000). We will also see how the critique of globalisation went beyond academia and mobilised social movements and civil society organisations.

In the fourth section I propose investigating the articulation behind the production of a skyline that mimics those of the so-called global cities, setting out to identify interests, conflicts, contradictions, and resistance movements at play. These interconnections are also discussed by means of empirical evidence obtained through field research conducted since 1995, when I closely observed the expansion of one of the main fronts of the São Paulo real estate market (see Figure 5.1) (Fix 2001, 2007).

*Source:* Mariana Fix.

*Figure 5.1*     *View from the helipad of the largest business centre in the 'global city' of São Paulo*

Hence, rather than revisiting a debate that has been partially worn out by time, this chapter seeks to discuss some of these contradictions, which remain relevant and current but are already in their decline, with greater historical distance (Fiori 2023) and a geographically situated standpoint from a Latin American metropolis.

Although the relationship between cities and the world economy was elaborated long ago (Braudel 1977), it is worth pointing out that the global city hypothesis was widespread at the height of the debate on globalisation. This was before the concept of globalisation had undergone several rounds of scrutiny, many of them motivated by political resistance to commercial and financial liberalisation, labour market flexibilisation, state reform, and privatisation in countries such as Brazil.[3] The global city never carried the same weight as globalisation in the ideological sense of the term. Still, it has significantly impacted urban planning.

It is also worth recognising that the unequal structure of the intellectual division of labour marks the formulation and dissemination of hypotheses, conferring greater visibility and validation to the so-called developed (or central) countries and, among them, to the Anglo-American hub due to the hegemony of the English language, among other reasons. Therefore, as suggested by Erminia Maricato, we need to be doubly careful not to absorb any concept that is in vogue without mediations, however good it may be, as we risk disregarding the specificities of the Brazilian socio-spatial formation and the reality of Brazilian cities (Maricato 2000).

## THE GLOBAL CITY AS AN 'ASPIRATION'

'Countless cities today aspire to be the globalised centre of the world economy': this was one of the mottos adopted in celebration of the work *The Global City* (Sassen 1991) in early 2022 owing to its 30th anniversary at a roundtable discussion organised by the Melbourne Centre for Cities and published on its website (Melbourne Centre for Cities 2022).

As the notion of global city was rapidly disseminated in academia and in local governments, it also developed a life of its own. For this reason, it is worth recalling that Sassen's hypotheses gained relevance by questioning the common sense of the time while the concept of globalisation was spreading swiftly. She was responding to a very common notion that location has ceased to matter due to the development of electronic exchanges made possible by the increasing digitalisation of financial activity and by the fact that financialisation generates a dematerialised and hyper-mobile product.

The point of departure for the book is that

> the combination of spatial dispersal and global integration has created a new strategic role for major cities... [as] highly concentrated command points in the organisation of the word economy... as key locations for finance and for specialised service firms... as sites of production, including production for innovations... and as markets for the products and innovations produced. (Sassen 2001: 3)

On several occasions Sassen explains why she chose the term 'global', instead of 'world': 'I did so knowingly – it was an attempt to name a difference: the specificity of the global as it gets structured in the contemporary period' (Sassen 2005: 28). In this article, the author traces the origins of the term 'world cities': 'Originally attributed to Goethe, the term was re-launched in the work of Peter Hall, *The World Cities* (1966), and more recently re-specified by John Friedmann and Wolff Goetz, *World City Formation: An Agenda for Research and Action* (1982)' (Sassen 2005: 41).

Initially presented in 1986, the world city hypothesis was taken up by Friedman in 1993 for a conference that resulted in the book *World Cities in a World-System* (Friedmann 1997). 'Without being too precise about their specific role in the global economy', the class of cities associated with the term global or world cities was presented through five 'agreements' (Friedmann 1997: 22). Among them was the understanding of world cities as command nodes in the global system, which 'can be arrayed in a hierarchy (of spatial articulations) on the basis of the economic power they command' (1997: 23). For the author, assigning a hierarchy was less important (given the volatility of the world economy) than recognising the existence of differences in position and investigating the articulations of particular world cities with each other. Since hierarchical relations are essentially power relations, world cities are 'driven by relentless competition, struggling to capture ever more command and control functions that compromise their very essence. Competitive angst is built into world city politics' (Friedmann 1997: 23). In this text, Friedman tells how the world city 'had become a badge of status, just as "growth poles" in an earlier incarnation' (1997: 36). It is worth recalling that competition between cities was a theme that had already been addressed by David Harvey, when discussing Baltimore in *The Condition of Postmodernity* (1989), as a phenomenon that intensified from the 1970s onwards in the context of 'deindustrialization and restructuring that left most major cities in the advanced capitalist world with few options except to compete with each other, mainly as financial, consumption, and entertainment centers' (1989: 92). This was therefore fertile ground for the diffusion planning models that encourage competition, as we shall see.

For now, it is important to emphasise that Sassen has clarified that the term global cities 'may be reductive and misleading if it suggests that cities are mere outcomes of a global economic machine' (2001: 4). Put differently, the internal dynamics and social structure of global cities do matter. In brief, she argues that the key structure of the world economy is necessarily situated in cities, hence the importance of studying them for understanding the global order.

Sassen upholds that territorial dispersal of current economic activity creates a need for expanded central control and management (2001: 4) and that top-level control and management of the financial industry has become concentrated in a few leading financial centres (2001: 5). The results of her research indicate that the expansion in the volume of financial transactions has increased the impact of these two trends. Sassen also identifies the re-concentration of a considerable share of foreign direct investment and the formation of an international property market in these cities.

For the author, global cities are more than nodal points for the coordination of process relations. They are particular sites for production of (1) specialised services 'needed by complex organizations for running a spatially dispersed network' and (2) financial innovations and the making of markets, 'both central to the internalisation and expansion of the financial industry' (Sassen 2001: 5). The focus on the power of large corporations (which was at the centre of globalisation research at the time) and the big banks (with the proliferation of financial institutions and the rapid internationalisation of financial markets after 1982) was 'insufficient to explain the capability for global control' (Sassen 2001: 6–7).

Sassen examines the changes in the organisation of work in the USA and identifies an increasing polarisation of workers' income and occupation distribution. Major growth industries show a greater incidence of jobs in the lowest and two highest quintiles of income (Sassen 2018: 241). She then offers an explanation for the rapid growth verified since the 1970s and its concentration in a few cities of service producers and finance as a need created by what has been called the 'global assembly line' (Sassen 2001: 10). The author sets out to refine the face-to-face explanation by suggesting that 'concentration arises out of the needs and expectations of the high-income workers employed in these firms. They are attracted to the amenities and lifestyles large urban centres can offer and are more likely to live in central areas than in suburbs' (Sassen 2001: 11–12).

An important argument put forward by Sassen is that the possibility of such centralised control 'needs to be produced', i.e. it includes the production of a 'vast range of highly specialised services and of top-level management and control functions' (Sassen 2001: 331). Hence, I argue for the relevance of integrating the production of the built environment and investigating the (active) role real estate plays in these processes: 'The social and physical landscape of an urbanized capitalism is far more... than a mute testimony to the transforming powers of capitalist growth and technological change... How does capital became urbanized, and what are the consequences of that urbanization?' (Harvey 1985: 222, 185). These are key questions that, particularly in the case of global cities, must go through the examination of the coalitions and conflicts behind the strategies involving landlords and property owners, developers and financiers, urban governments, the media, etc.

The combination of these agents makes the city a kind of 'growth machine', an entrepreneurial type of organisation aimed at increasing the volume of aggregate income through the intensification of land use (Logan & Molotch 1987). Logan and Molotch offered the hypothesis that 'all capitalist places are the creation of activists who push hard to alter how markets function, how prices are set, and how lives are affected' (Logan & Molotch 1987: 3).

The belief that 'the contemporary urban built environment did not represent an uncomplicated response to demand but rather that developers both moulded demand and respond to public-sector initiatives and regulation' guided the research of Susan Fainstein on London and New York (Fainstein 1994: x).[4] More than that, architecture and urban form, while physically configuring spaces, give us the perception we have of the city. In this sense, they are the materiality and the symbolic expression of a city (Zukin 1993).

Sassen formulates and discusses questions she considers strategic for an understanding 'from the perspective of the world economy' (Sassen 2001: 15). In this sense, she asks: 'what moment in the global accumulation process is contained by or located in major cities'? (Sassen 2001: 15). The author clarifies that the new urban spatiality that is produced is 'partial in a double sense: it accounts for only part of what happens in cities and what cities are about, and it inhabits only part of what we might think of as the space of a city' (Sassen 2001: xii). Sassen's books are full of empirical evidence to support her thesis. It is also worth mentioning that Sassen never neglected to examine new forms of inequalities underway in terms of race and income (Sassen 2018: 235–272),[5] so her work has nothing apologetic about it, unlike appropriations of it by other authors or governments.

For our purposes of examining the topic in a Latin American framework, it is important to note that although the author works with an informed view of transformations in the world economy, she declares her preference for the concept of the 'Global South versus Global North divide' and nomenclature such as 'developing countries' (Sassen 2018: 7). These classifications pay a heavy price to the tradition of geographical regionalisation (Ortiz 2022, which is based on homogeneities. In contrast, the centre–periphery approach emphasises relationships (Vainer 2022: 57). From a different perspective, authors such as Anibal Quijano have pointed out that 'coloniality is a fundamental element of modernity and of the capitalist system, which in turn is born global, with centre–periphery relations as its structuring element' (Vainer 2022: 57).

The framework developed by Sassen grew out of an 'ocean of often contradictory data and established "truths"', as the author explains in the preface to a new edition (Sassen 2001). Sassen has revised and refined her hypotheses over time after the initial effort of comparing three cities as distinct and distant as London, Tokyo, and New York, extracting from this analysis more general aspects of the transformations taking place. It is beyond the limits of this chapter to recapitulate this author's long investigative journey and the dialogues and debates developed in different parts of the world, which have been reviewed and discussed by various authors (Brenner & Keil 2006: 257–266), as well as the alternative approaches suggested.

Marcuse and van Kempen, for example, have argued that the term 'globalizing cities' would do more justice to 'the changes in the spatial order since globalization is a process, not a state' (Marcuse & van Kempen 2000).

Robinson suggests the concept of the ordinary city 'rather than develop[ing] a regulatory fiction of the powerful global city' (Robinson 2006: 113). For her, 'an ordinary city perspective will start from the assumption that all cities can be thought of as diverse and distinctive with the possibility to imagine (within the constraints of contestations and uneven power relations) their own futures and their own distinctive forms of cityness' (Robinson 2006: 113). Robinson's concern with the powerful discursive effect, in both academic and policy circles, produced by the global city hypothesis (Robinson 2006: 97) seems similar to that which has moved academic debate and production in São Paulo since the mid-1990s. However, for several of the responses produced in São Paulo, understanding how globalisation or financialisation (Paulani 2021) have redefined centre–periphery relations while maintaining the hierarchies that have structured capitalism since its inception is paramount and a matter of debate.

## SÃO PAULO, A GLOBAL CITY?

In the 1990s, various authors including the well-known Brazilian geographer Milton Santos sought to understand the transformations in cities during globalisation. The articulation between global and local became one of the centres of debate in the social sciences and particularly in geography (Benko 1995). An article by Helena Cordeiro (1993) entitled 'The "World City" of São Paulo and the Corporate Complex of its Metropolitan Centre' was included in a book edited by Milton Santos et al. (1993), drawing on the work of Sachar (1983), before Sassen became a reference on the topic.

Sassen's work became well-known in São Paulo and influential within academic circles mainly with the Brazilian edition of *Cities in a World Economy* (2018), the author's first work published in Brazil in 1998.[6] In this book, Sassen presents a longer list of cities that includes several others in addition to those considered in *The Global City*, as 'the most powerful of these new geographies of centrality at the global level bind the major international financial and business centres' (Sassen 2018: xv); Zurich, Amsterdam, Los Angeles, Sydney, and Hong Kong are some of them. She then adds that 'this geography now also includes cities such as Bangkok, Seoul, Taipei, São Paulo, Mexico City, and Buenos Aires' (Sassen 2018: xv).

According to Sassen, 'São Paulo has gained immense strength as a business and financial centre in Brazil overcoming Rio de Janeiro – once the capital and most important city in the country – and over the once-powerful axis represented by Rio and Brasilia, the current capital' (Sassen 2018: 8). This overtaking is presented by Sassen as one of the 'consequences of the formation of a globally integrated economic system' (Sassen 2018: 8), something that has been challenged since the economic power of São Paulo precedes globalisation.

Marques and Torres (2000) state that the idea of second-order global cities was present in the article by Friedmann (1986) and in articles included in the book by Knox and Taylor (1995) but that it gained strength with the advancement of other research. However, the application of an analysis of the attributes that would characterise a global city is more difficult when it comes to second-order cities. What makes them global is their role as intermediaries in the world city network. Their study should emphasise links with the network, but it runs into empirical difficulties. Analysing the available data, Marques and Torres maintain that the processes experienced by São Paulo 'confirm the importance of the city's role as a connection between the Brazilian economy and the world economy' but point out several specificities in the trajectories verified in each aspect analysed (Marques & Torres 2000: 167).

Ferreira acknowledges São Paulo's economic leadership role at the national and South American level (Véras 1999) but recalls that the gain in the economic importance of São Paulo greatly preceded the phenomenon of globalisation (Ferreira 2007: 29). For him, the notion of the global city is rather a myth or an ideology that confers 'false legitimacy' to activities of the real estate sector. According to the author, even if we accept the definition of the attributes generally used to characterise global cities, application to São Paulo would not allow us to classify it as such.

The global city paradigm appropriates some ideas from the economic geography debate about the new role of cities detached from the contexts in which they were formulated. Sometimes these ideas are reproduced as 'positive laws whose validity dispenses with temporal and historical mediations and relativisations, once they have been empirically proven' (Compans 1999: 97, my own translation). The diffusion of the global city paradigm functioned as an incentive for interurban competition and as a market for urban policy models offered by international consultants interested in disseminating supposedly successful experiences and demanded by municipal administrations interested in promoting local economic development by fulfilling a 'strategic agenda with which they can ensure the competitive insertion of their cities' (Compans 1999: 91, my own translation).

This was often associated with another influential article entitled 'Cities as Political Agents' (Borja & Castells 1996) published in a Brazilian journal, which was extracted from a report prepared by the authors for the Habitat II conference that took place in Istanbul and later incorporated in the book entitled *Local and Global* (Borja & Castells 1997). In the book, the authors present, rather than an analysis of proposals, 'real recipes for the application of the model' (Vainer 2000: 77): the strategic planning of cities. The importance of a serious and rigorous discussion of this urban planning model can hardly be overestimated given the commitment of agencies and multilateral institutions to its dissemination and basic concepts (Vainer 2000: 77). According to Vainer, the model has been disseminated through the combined action of various multilateral agencies and international consultants, especially Catalan ones led by Jordi Borja, whose aggressive marketing systematically promoted the success of Barcelona (Vainer 2000: 75).

Vainer's response is summarised in two articles published in a book edited with Otília Arantes and Ermínia Maricato, which has become one of the most important critical references for the model: *A cidade do pensamento único: desmanchando consensos* (Arantes et al. 2000). In the first article Vainer analyses the discursive strategy of the strategic urban planning model and in the second the strategic plan for the city of Rio de Janeiro carried out under the direction of a company chaired by Borja. Castells was already well-known within the Latin American debate circle since the publication of his classic book *La Question urbaine* (1972) introducing a structuralist Marxist theory on urbanisation, in addition to his connections with the research centre *Centro Brasileiro de Análise e Planejamento* (CEBRAP). He returned to Brazil in the 1990s, however, in a different political and economic context to participate in a debate on 'State Reform and Society' hosted in 1998 by the Council for State Reform and the Ministry of Administration and promoted by Bresser Pereira, then Minister of Federal Administration and State Reform (1995–1998). Thus, Castells participated in Brazil in the debate on a national scale about the role of the state in globalisation. On the other hand, Borja became known a bit later in the 1990s for the work he conducted in Barcelona.

Unlike what happened with Sassen's work, however, their ideas were immediately disseminated in the normative version by Borja and Castells themselves, taking Barcelona as a model to formulate and spread so-called 'Strategic Urban Planning'. A significant number of Latin American cities hired both as consultants, in particular Borja.

According to Borja, in order to become global, São Paulo should assume its 'leading role'. With 'some years of delay', in the 1990s, Latin American cities 'emerged' as protagonists thanks to a reaction motivated, among other reasons, by the economic opening of their countries (Borja & Castells 1996: 154). This opening mobilised economic agents who became 'aware of the need to have a competitive city, that is, attractive and functional' (Borja & Castells 1996: 157).

The diffusion of the texts increased with the presence of the authors on several occasions, particularly Borja, who acted as advisor for projects of urban revitalisation and as guest lecturer in urban planning conferences (Sandler 2007: 475), consulting for an urban redevelopment project in Santo André (a municipality in the São Paulo metropolitan area) and teaching a graduate class at the Faculty of Architecture and Urbanism of the University of São Paulo (FAUUSP) on megaprojects.

In *Local and Global*, Borja and Castells (1997) specify 'new roles of local governments'. The first of these is 'to build a strong and positive urban image to promote the city abroad' (Borja & Castells 1997: 160). This effort is part of what Saskia Sassen describes as the competition between local cities for branches and headquarters of transnational corporations. However, 'while Sassen identifies and critiques the process, Borja and Castells suggest how to succeed with it, putting a favourable spin on globalisation' (Sandler 2007: 476). The second function is to favour 'public–private partnerships' (PPPs) as a means to carry out foreign promotion and the works and services that 'the new urban demands and change in scale require' (Borja & Castells 1997: 160) In São Paulo, the ideology of PPPs was enhanced by the strategic urban planning but it was not introduced by it. Propositions for urban 'partnership' instruments began to be included in master plan proposals previous to this in the 1980s in the context of the fiscal crisis of the Brazilian state. For our purposes in this chapter, I emphasise that the instrument comprising the Urban Operation Consortium (OUC as per the Brazilian acronym), despite having a different origin and combining another set of references with regard to the strategic planning of cities, has much in common with the former. This convergence supports the reading that emerges from the aforementioned book *Cidade do pensamento único* ('City of the Single Thinking' in a free translation) (Arantes et al. 2000). The three authors aim at shattering the consensus and 'disrupting regressive unanimities, notably the alignments induced by the current hegemony of global capitalism' (Arantes et al. 2000: 7). Through their own pathway, these authors reached the conclusion that had been surrounding the same object for some time dressed up in various guises, which is found in the synthesis offered in the book's presentation. Otília Arantes emphasises the objective convergence of two models of production in a new urban configuration that is the *cultural-business-city,* one North American and the other European. In the text, she proves that the 'single thinking' regarding cities is not a mere fatality of global hegemony. Vainer, as we have seen, dedicates himself to showing how 'such fatalities are manufactured' (Vainer 2000: 8) by reconstituting the implementation of strategic urban planning in the city of Rio de Janeiro. A second point to mention is that the two main OUCs in São Paulo were implemented in an area usually associated with 'globalisation', so we will return to them in the fourth section.

Thus, the concept of the global city impacted the academic research and the imaginary of what São Paulo could become at the same time. However, this occurred in the case of São Paulo without coordinated and organised action around this concept. As an emblem, the global city was mobilised with varying emphases and interactions with other references. As a discourse, it presented 'elective affinities' with real estate interests, especially those that profit from the concentration of investments in a particular region of the city, as we will see in fourth section. In this case, the resulting urban landscape has a bearing on the perception of São Paulo as a global city through the designing of a part of the city as 'globalised'.

Thus, as the concept of the global city has taken on a life of its own, it has become detached from the 'invisible college' of world city researchers (Friedmann 1997: 28) to the point where its success (in terms of diffusion) has turned against it in the form of a simplified schema to be applied or criticised.

## GLOBALISATION AT STAKE

At the time that the term global city was gaining ground in debates about cities, the term globalisation was already widespread. A brief recapitulation of the critique of this term can help to identify the ideological and material bases on which the rapid assimilation of the concept of the global city took place, linking discourses to transformations in the world economy.

The adjective 'global' had appeared in the early 1980s in American business schools. The adjective was then popularised in the works of strategy and marketing consultants trained in these schools or in close contact with them (Chesnais 1996: 23) and spread by the economic and financial press. In the field of business administration, the term was aimed at large corporations to convey the message that obstacles to the expansion of activities had been overcome thanks to 'liberalisation and deregulation, and to advances in telecommunications' (Chesnais 1996: 23). Writings that made the case for globalisation presented this nascent world as 'borderless', as per the title of the 1990 book by K. Ohmae, a well-known consultant. These terms are therefore not neutral. On the contrary, they 'invaded everyday political and economic discourse so easily... [because they are] full of connotations' (Chesnais 1996: 24), mobilising the social imaginary.

At the time, globalisation was usually presented as a beneficial, necessary, and irreversible process to which society had to adapt. This was the key word. This adaptation presupposed carrying out liberalisation and deregulation so that companies enjoyed 'absolute freedom of movement' (Chesnais 1996: 25), and all fields of social life were subjected to the valorisation of private capital. Once the trap was cleared up, Chesnais went on to map out and discuss the actual transformations underway. In other words, it was not a matter of denying the existence of an important trend but of understanding it.

'There is no doubt that the word 'globalisation' was coined in the field of ideologies, later being transformed [into] a commonplace of enormous positive connotation, despite its visible conceptual imprecision' (Tavares & Fiori 1997: 7). This recognition was the starting point for the authors to advocate the importance of consistent critique of the word 'globalisation' as a way to contribute to the understanding of the transformations that capitalist economy had undergone since the crisis of the 1970s and the challenges posed for the future.

The project of a political economy of globalisation developed by Tavares and Fiori (1997) took as its starting point two articles by Conceição Tavares that offer 'an original view on the role of currency and American monetary policy'[7] and at the same time point to the emergence of a new regime of world accumulation in which the centre/periphery relationship is redrawn (Fiori 2000). The process of globalisation encompasses both core and peripheral countries, but the insertion of the former and the latter is quite different. From the point of view of markets, the relevant decisions regarding production are taken by a restricted set of companies and banks in central countries, whose strategy is effectively global, while the peripheral countries appear, in principle, as recipients of global consumption patterns diffused from the centre to the periphery and, depending on conjunctural macroeconomic conditions, as 'platforms for competitive expansion or auxiliary circuits of patrimonial and financial valorization – above all via privatisations and the rise of domestic interest rates – in which case they are classified as "emerging economies"' (Tavares & Fiori 1997: 89).

Chesnais argued that the globalisation of capital and the pretension of financial capital to dominate the movement of capital in its totality do not erase the existence of national states but accentuate the hierarchies between countries while redesigning their configuration. The gulf between the countries has widened even further (Chesnais 1996: 18). According to Chesnais, the weight of the United States increased not only due to the collapse of the Soviet Union and its unrivalled military power but also because of its position in the financial capital domain, which is superior to what it had in the industrial one (Chesnais 1996: 19).

The advance of neoliberalism found Brazil in a process of political redemocratisation after almost two decades of military rule (1964–1985), which culminated in the promulgation of the 1988 Constitution. Although with certain limits as the result of political battles, the Constitution was full of hopes, among them for democratic and popular urban reform. The 1988 Constitution included, after an intense process of struggle and social mobilisation, articles referring to the social function of property and to the right to housing as a social right, for instance. The regulation of these articles would be crystallised in the City Statute (Law 10.257/2011), a regulatory framework for urban policies in the country whose approval in 2001 owed much to the struggle of the National Forum of Urban Reform (Fórum Nacional de Reforma Urbana).

Although internationally recognised for its progressive dimension, the City Statute also endorsed public–private partnership instruments in the interests of the property market, a trait of 'urban entrepreneurship'. The administrations of the first two elected presidents after the end of the military dictatorship took place in this context of the advance of neoliberalism. Even if belatedly, in comparison with other countries, the Brazilian economy also opened to the global market under the justification that to adapt to the dictates of globalisation was the best – if not the only way – to develop. At that moment, the way the country found to escape the trap constituted by the high inflation of the binomial debt crisis[8] that marked the 1980s was the complete submission of its economic policy to the demands of creditors; in other words, the adoption of neoliberal discourse and practice (Paulani 2012: 91). The 1988 Constitution was 'totally incompatible with the goals of the rentier economy in this new stage' (Paulani 2008: 95). With the Union budget limited by countless mandatory bonds, the state had little freedom to promote policies that 'supposedly aimed to sustain the balance of public accounts' but aimed at 'opening space for its performance as a backer of the payment of public debt service' (Paulani 2008: 95). From that moment on, measures that followed prepared the country for its insertion in the international circuit of financial capital (Paulani 2008: 102).

Questions about globalisation and its effects on the population have also been raised by social movements and civil society organisations. One example is the World Social Forum (WSF), organised as a counterpoint to the World Economic Forum in Davos. The proposal for the WSF originated in large demonstrations such as the one in Seattle (USA) against the WTO Ministerial Conference of 1999. Not by chance, the first WSF was held in 2001 in Porto Alegre, a city that was a reference for its implementation of its participatory budget process.

At the same time, several multilateral organisations, such as the World Bank and the Inter-American Development Bank (IDB), advocated market management of housing policies with reduced state participation in housing finance as part of a needed 'urban adjustment' (Arantes 2006). The state should now take on the role of 'regulator' or 'inducer', creating the conditions for the private initiative. It was in this context that, 'ideologically weakened and disoriented' by the fall of socialist regimes and the welfare state, left-wing parties ended up convincing themselves that, in that globalised moment, it was 'up to capital to reassure and seduce' (Fiori 1995: 227–228).

## FINANCIAL FOUNDATIONS OF A MIRAGE

Architecture and urban form, while physically configuring space, provide us with our perception of the city. They are at once the materiality and the symbolic expression of a city (Zukin 1993). Corporate buildings, in their own way, project the image of a 'globalised' city in São Paulo and can help us better understand the process of which they are part.

The inauguration of the Brazilian unit of the World Trade Centre (WTC) in 1995 was a milestone in this landscape and was heralded as an icon of globalisation. So was the Centro Empresarial Nações Unidas (CENU), advertised as the largest of its kind in Latin America, inaugurated in the last years of the 1990s and located just beside the WTC tower (Fix 2007). What relationships can we thus identify between the changing links of the world economy and the new landscape of power? The urban image itself projects a set of illusions and I think we might learn from them.

Modest in size compared to the twin towers of the WTC in New York, the Brazilian version was a franchise of the brand and not a branch, as it seemed. The building was designed by a São Paulo architect, built by a Brazilian construction company (OAS), and financed by Brazilian pension funds. The CENU building complex consists of three office towers and a hotel interconnected on the ground floor by an austere and underutilised square and underground through a shopping centre that gives direct access to the WTC. The architectural ensemble is designed as a 'total space, a complete world, a kind of city in miniature', as per Jameson's definition of the Bonaventure Hotel in Los Angeles (Jameson 1996: 66).

For those passing by on the Marginal Pinheiros expressway, the effect of the ensemble is of a self-sufficient and internationalised 'new city', produced and financed by companies themselves – starting with the logos stamped on top of the buildings that can give the impression that the towers belong to foreign multinational companies when in fact they are occupied by tenants. A developer from the USA, Tishman Speyer Properties, participated in the venture, but its role was mainly as the administrator of the work carried out by Método Engenharia, a Brazilian construction company. Método in turn sought a large institutional investor, the Caixa Econômica Federal employees' pension fund Funcef. Funcef participated in the incorporation of the North Tower and became its main owner with 83.66% of the shares, functioning as a kind of substitute for real estate credit, without which the development would hardly have been viable. Among the first tenants of the North Tower new business centre were companies from the service and financial sectors, mainly telecommunications and information technology (like Compaq/HP and Microsoft), and companies that came to the country with the privatisation of Brazilian companies, like Duke Energy, which acquired some of the plants of the Companhia Energética de São Paulo (CESP, São Paulo Energy Company). Several companies were operating in the areas of fixed and mobile telephony, the Internet, and cable television. Among them was Turner Broadcasting System, at the time owner of television channels such as CNN, TNT, and Cartoon Network. The West Tower of CENU, in turn, had its floors occupied initially mainly by banks.

Most of the companies were from the USA and had recently entered the country, predominantly between 1995 and 1997 as part of the 'leap of privatisation' (Paulani 1998) and the denationalisation of Brazil's economy, which involved currency stabilisation at any cost, deindustrialisation, and the expansion of asset and financial appreciation, constituting the new macroeconomic model discussed in the previous section. During this period, foreign direct investment (FDI) grew strongly (Gonçalves 1999: 124). In 1998, on the eve of the inauguration of the North Tower, foreign-owned companies accounted for almost 60% of the capital raised from the privatisations of state-owned companies.

However, 'the depletion of state capital to be privatized and of domestic private capital to be acquired (the latter depreciated thanks to the unceremonious way of the economic opening process) made the hypothesis of continuity and regularity of FDI flows to Brazil unlikely at the time' (Paulani 2000). Denationalisation caused structural changes in the current account balance (with an increase in profit and dividend remittances) that could not be offset by FDI flows in the capital account. The fact that much of the foreign capital inflow was allocated to non-tradable sectors, with companies with a strong propensity to import, further accentuated vulnerability (Paulani 2000).

Shortly after, Faria Lima Avenue, part of the same business axis, reached a vacancy rate of around 70%. Many buildings were launched at the same time in a moment of great expectation. The depletion of FDI flows and the exhaustion of the privatisation cycle actually occurred, accompanied by the 1999 currency crisis, which was preceded by the crises in Mexico, Asia, and Russia.

A cable-stayed bridge inspired by foreign models, designed by engineer Santiago Calatrava albeit without the same formal refinement as usual, completed the spectacularisation of the landscape in 2008, becoming one of the city's main postcard images. Curiously, it was presented at the time of its construction as an attraction (a lure) for the property market rather than a solution for urban mobility. After all, how could a construction project of such cost, aimed only at cars, in one of the richest regions of the metropolis be justified? How would it be possible to explain to the residents of nearby favelas that the construction of that bridge would take precedence over the social housing to which they should have been entitled if the progressive Brazilian urban legislation conquered by their urban social struggle were applied? (See Figure 5.2) The answer lay in a supposedly progressive urban planning instrument that created the illusion that the improvement of the infrastructure of the region, including the bridge, would be financed with funds paid by real estate developers: the Urban Operation Consortium mentioned in section two.

The explanation offered by a public officer to the representative of the slum dwellers who had been struggling for years for social housing was that the more successful the execution of the works, the greater the interest of the real estate sector in the purchase of the Certificate of Additional Building Rights (CEPAC as per the Brazilian acronym), and, consequently, the greater the possibilities of obtaining funds for the completion of the works. The fate of favela dwellers becomes tied to the success of the real estate game.

The Urban Operation Consortium, in practice, allows the municipal government to authorise changes in the Land Use and Occupation Law to allow for additional building rights (increasing the floor area ratio) for a fee, within a certain perimeter of the city defined by the law. This payment is named the Additional Building Rights Levy. Since 2004, the municipality has issued bonds corresponding to these building rights certificates, linked to a specific OUC, and has marketed them in public auctions or used them to pay for infrastructure works carried out in the region. Like any financial asset, they can in principle be traded on the secondary market, which seldom happens (Fix 2011, Klink & Sroher 2017). According to the definition of Bovespa (the São Paulo Stock Exchange), CEPACs are variable income assets since their profitability is associated with the appreciation of urban spaces.

Paradoxically, as the municipality issues such certificates, it is considered reasonable for the government to seek to guarantee real estate gains with the means at its disposal, for example by concentrating investments in already favoured regions. The 'elitisation' of a neighbourhood comes to be seen as something positive, as registered in one of the prospects for the issuance of the CEPAC. The result is an incentive for the government to act as a real estate developer, putting oil in the gears of the 'growth machine'. Indirectly, this is an incentive to make the perimeters of urban operations more homogeneous in demographic terms (race and class) and, consequently, the city more unequal. Not by chance, the two main urban operations in São Paulo took place along this same business axis.

The OUC has become a central ingredient of urban policy since the mid-1990s. The dominant discourse was that the territory needed to be modernised to receive the towers required by international companies with their large open floor spaces. The appeal of the OUC was to supposedly make the beneficiaries pay for the infrastructure works by buying the additional building rights (CEPACs). However, my research on the subject has revealed that urban operations ended up justifying the greater importance given to non-priority works such as road works in already disproportionately privileged areas of the city and, in fact, were largely funded with public resources (Fix 2004, 2011). Thus, the self-sufficiency illusion the enclaves create is belied when we discover that they are heavily irrigated by public funds.

Before the opening of one of the region's largest business centres, hundreds of families living in the favelas were forcibly evicted from the area (Fix 2001). Many of them had been living in the area since the late 1970s in precarious settlements that became denser as people came to work on the construction sites of the office buildings, hotels, and shopping malls and later as cleaners, drivers, and gardeners. In a rapidly expanding metropolis, living close to work is increasingly important given the cost of transport and the time spent travelling. From the point of view of real estate interests, however, favelas were an obstacle to urban expansion and their 'removal' was seen as an opportunity to profit from the 'valorisation' that was being promoted by urban development.

The illegal status of the land was used as a justification for the use of violent methods of expulsion that disrespected the rights of the residents. The resistance struggle was permanent but faced all kinds of demobilisation attempts by municipal governments. With no real alternative, the vast majority of families moved to other favelas, many of them in environmental protection areas, water reservoirs of the city. To prevent a second wave of evictions, residents of some favelas organised public protests and filed appeals with the support of the Public Prosecution Service. The Jardim Edith housing estate is one such estate won by the resistance movement, built in one of the city's main business centres (see Figure 5.2).

*Source:* Mariana Fix.

*Figure 5.2  Land where the Jardim Edith favela was located in the São Paulo Central Business District soon after the eviction*

Paradoxically, in the quest to produce distinction, positioning the brand in the world market of iconic locations, the landscape became increasingly similar to others of its kind. The cable-stayed bridge was the missing piece in the effect that the new centrality produces. At the same time that it imposes over the reality the symbolism of its image, the bridge conceals the great desire to eliminate from the urban scene those who lived there, 'marking them with the indelible signs of difference as well as of indifference' (Santos 2002).

## CONCLUSIONS

The multiplication of real estate megaprojects, in my view a characteristic of the production of hosting bases in cities of the periphery of capitalism during globalisation (financial globalisation or financialisation), happened in São Paulo in a concentrated way in time and space: from 1990s onwards and in a particular stretch of the city. Its concentration has drawn a skyline that mimics the business hubs of central countries. After the liberalisation measures, trade and financial openness, flexibilisation of the labour market, economic and state reforms, and privatisations were implemented in Brazil over less than five years' time so the country was ready to function as 'platforms of international financial valorization' (Paulani 2008).

Companies from central countries that were turning transnational in the 1990s found in CENU and the other towers in the region bases to settle as renters, maintaining their mobility. The creation of this base set in motion a set of real estate agents who mobilised mainly national capital, applied in real estate investments and urban infrastructure. The creation of a hosting basis was possible by means of the concentration of resources that accentuated an already very uneven pattern of urbanisation. The new forms of production and reiteration of inequalities are based on the legacy of an unequal relationship between the centre and the periphery of capitalism. In São Paulo, they are based on the inheritance of an industrialisation process that, when completed, re-established the relationship of subordination and dependence with the central countries (Oliveira 1999).

This concentration finds some discursive support in the instruments of public–private partnerships, the prescription of strategic urban planning, and the stimuli for the aspiration to become global, throwing a smoke screen over the use and control of public funds and the despoiling character of several of the processes. A city resembling those of the central countries was recreated on a more modest scale. The eviction of hundreds of families living in the favelas of the surroundings made these areas more socially homogeneous, accentuating the class and racial segregation that characterises the metropolis of São Paulo (França 2022) and more generally Latin American cities, which have been racially structured from the outset (Silverio 2019: 28).

Faced with the 'increasing impossibility of becoming integrated as nations, and in a socially cohesive way' (Schwarz 1999: 160) into the capitalist world economy, Latin American cities have been hailed as 'political actors' (Borja & Castells 1996) who vie for space by competing with each other. When the 'myth of development' (Furtado 2020) seemed outdated due to the new obstacles in overcoming underdevelopment (Oliveira 2003), it was reborn, faded, in the form of the myth of global cities, competitive cities, and 'world-class' cities. Beyond its discursive dimension, I argue that this myth accompanies a real movement in the transformation of capitalism in its late stages and the world system that has one of its expressions in this global enclave.

## NOTES

1. This was the title, in Portuguese, of an article in a leading newspaper, echoing the speech of urban planner Jordi Borja at a seminar in São Paulo (Albanese 1994).
2. The book *The Global City* was published in 1991. The 2001 revised edition is taken here as the reference for quotations.
3. These transformations had a delay in Brazil when compared to the experiences in Chile under the Pinochet dictatorship, Mexico, and Argentina, and occurred in an accelerated manner. For a detailed analysis of the historical process of neoliberalisation in nine Latin American countries, see Cano (2000).
4. When interviewing a well-known developer in São Paulo, I was recommended the autobiography of one of the leading real estate developers of the 20th century, which was his bedside book (Zeckendorf & McCreary 1988). The developer recounts in detail the simplest operations

of buying and selling buildings, as well as more complex manoeuvres such as those that contributed to Wall Street's maintenance as the world's financial centre. Governors, the media, planners, and banks are all present in the accounts. The research carried out in São Paulo shows that coalitions of this kind can have a decisive influence on the urban configuration and should therefore be taken into account in analyses.

5. 'Where does the global function of major cities begin, and where does it end? How do we establish what segments of the thick and complex environment of cities are part of the global?' are some of the issues discussed by Sassen (2018: 3–4).
6. Originally published in 1994; the book is cited here in the fifth revised edition published in 2018 in digital format (Kindle). The book *Globalização e a estrutura urbana* (Schiffer 2004) also had an impact on the debate on global cities by including a Portuguese transcript of a conference given by Sassen in Brazil. Although also known in Brazil, *The Global City* (Sassen 1991) has not been translated into Portuguese.
7. In 'The Resumption of US Hegemony', published in the 1980s, in contradiction to the prevailing consensus, Tavares and Fiori argued that the ongoing movements of deregulation and financialisation of the international economy were not the fruit of a spontaneous and autonomous development of market forces. On the contrary, 'they were part of a successful strategic effort to restore US global hegemony, which had been put in check during the 1970s' (Tavares & Fiori 1997: 8).
8. The second oil shock and the interest rate shock, both triggered in 1979, opened a 15-year period of very high inflation. At the same time, unable to generate hard currency resources to cope with the new oil price hike and the rising value of external debt services, the country found itself entangled in the debt crisis (Paulani 2012: 91–92).

## REFERENCES

Albanese, R. (1994) SP tem vocação para ser 'cidade mundial'. *Estado de S. Paulo*, 24 October.
Arantes O.B.F. (2000) Uma estratégia fatal. In O.B.F. Arantes, E. Maricato & C. Vainer (eds.) *A Cidade do Pensamento Único: Desmanchando Consensos*. Petrópolis: Vozes, 11–74.
Arantes O.B.F., Maricato E. & Vainer C. (2000) *A Cidade do Pensamento Único: Desmanchando Consensos*. Petrópolis: Vozes.
Arantes, P.F. (2006) O ajuste urbano: as políticas do Banco Mundial e do BID para as cidades. *PosFAUUSP* 20: 60–75.
Benko, G (1995) *Economia, espaço e globalização na aurora do século XXI*. São Paulo: Hucitec.
Borja, J. & Castells, M. (1996) As cidades como atores políticos. *Novos Estudos Cebrap* 45: 152–66.
Borja, J. & Castells, M. (1997) *Local and Global: Management of Cities in the Information Age*. Abingdon: Routledge.
Brandão, C.A. & Siqueira, H. (2020) Underdevelopment in Brazil and its interpretations. *Oxford Research Encyclopedia of Latin American History*.
Braudel, F. (1977) *Afterthoughts on Material Civilization and Capitalism*. Baltimore and London: The Johns Hopkins University Press.
Brenner, N. & Keil, R. (eds.) (2006) *The Global Cities Reader*. London: Routledge.
Caldeira, T.P.R. (2000) *Cidade dos muros: crime, segregação e cidadania em São Paulo*. São Paulo: Edusp Editora 34.
Cano, W. (2000) *Soberania e política econômica na América Latina*. São Paulo: Editora Unesp.
Carvalho, M. (2000) Cidade global: anotações críticas sobre um conceito. *São Paulo em Perspectiva* 14(4): 70–82.
Castells, M. (1972) *La Question urbaine*. Paris: François Maspero.
Chesnais, F. (1996) *A mundialização do capital*. São Paulo: Xamã.
Chesnais, F. (1998) *A mundialização financeira*. São Paulo: Xamã.

Compans, R. (1999) O paradigma das global cities nas estratégias de desenvolvimento local. *Revista Brasileira de Estudos Urbanos e Regionais* 1: 91–114.
Compans, R. (2005) *Empreendedorismo urbano: entre o discurso e a prática*. São Paulo: Editora Unesp.
Cordeiro, H. (1993) A 'cidade mundial' de São Paulo e o complexo corporativo do seu centro metropolitano. In *O Novo Mapa do Mundo: Fim do Século e Globalização*. São Paulo: Hucitec/Anpur, 318–331.
Fainstein, S. (1994) *The City Builders: Property Development in New York and London, 1980–2000*. Oxford, UK and Cambridge, USA: University Press of Kansas.
Ferreira, J.S.W. (2007) *O mito da cidade-global: o papel da ideologia na produção do espaço*. Rio de Janeiro: Petrópolis and São Paulo: Vozes.
Fiori, J.L. (1995) A globalização e a 'novíssima dependência'. *Texto para discussão*, 343. Rio de Janeiro: Universidade Federal do Rio de Janeiro.
Fiori, J.L. (2000) Maria da Conceição Tavares e a hegemonia Americana. *Lua nova* 50: 207–242.
Fiori, J.L. (2023) Davos, Kiev e Brasília – o ocaso de um projeto. Retrieved from: https://aterraeredonda.com.br/davos-kiev-e-brasilia-o-ocaso-de-um-projeto/ (accessed 16 May 2023).
Fix, M. (2001) *Parceiros da Exclusão*. São Paulo: Boitempo.
Fix, M. (2004) A 'fórmula mágica' da parceria público-privada: Operações Urbanas em São Paulo. In *Urbanismo: Dossiê São Paulo–Rio de Janeiro*. Campinas: PUCCAMP/PROURB, 185–198.
Fix, M. (2007) *São Paulo, Cidade Global: Fundamentos financeiros de uma miragem*. São Paulo: Boitempo.
Fix, M. (2011) A bridge to speculation or the art of rent in the staging of a 'global city'. In C. Vanlença et al. (eds.) *Urban Developments in Brazil and Portugal*. Hauppauge, NY: Nova Science Publishers, 35–75.
França, D. (2022) *Segregação racial em São Paulo: residências, redes pessoais e trajetórias urbanas de negros e brancos no século XXI*. São Paulo: Blucher.
Friedmann, J. (1986) The world city hypothesis, *Development and Change* 17(1): 69–83.
Friedmann, J. (1997) Where we stand: A decade of world city research. In P. L. Knox and P. J. Taylor (eds.) *World Cities in a World-System*. Cambridge: Cambridge University Press, 21–47.
Furtado, C. (2020) *The Myth of Economic Development*. Medford, MA, USA and Cambridge, UK: Wiley.
Gonçalves, R. (1999) *Globalização e Desnacionalização*. São Paulo: Paz e Terra.
Hall, P. (1966) *Cities of Tomorrow: An Intellectual History of Urban Planning and Design in the Twentieth Century*. Oxford: Blackwell Publishing.
Harvey, D. (1985) *The Urbanization of Capital: Studies in the History and Theory of Capitalist Urbanization*. Baltimore: The Johns Hopkins University Press.
Harvey, D. (1989) *The Condition of Postmodernity: An Enquiry into the Origins of Cultural Change*. Oxford: Blackwell Publishing.
Jameson, F. (1996) *Pós modernismo: a lógica cultural do capitalismo tardio*. São Paulo: Ática.
Klink, J. & Stroher, L.E.M. (2017). The making of urban financialization? An exploration of Brazilian urban partnership operations with building certificates. *Land Use Policy* 69: 519–528.
Knox, P.L. & Taylor, P.J (1995) *World Cities in a World-System*. New York: Cambridge University Press.
Logan, J.R. & Molotch, H. (1987) *Urban Fortunes*. Berkeley: University of California Press.
Marcuse, P. & van Kempen, R. (2000) Conclusion: A changed special order. In P. Marcuse & R. van Kempen (eds.) *Globalizing Cities: A New Spatial Order?* Oxford: Blackwell Publishers, 249–275.
Maricato, E. (2000) As ideias fora do lugar, e o lugar fora das ideias. In O.B.F. Arantes, E. Maricato & C. Vainer (eds.) *Cidade do pensamento único*. Petrópolis: Vozes, 121–192.
Maricato, E. (2007) Prefácio. In J.S.W. Ferreira (ed.) *O mito da cidade-global: o papel da ideologia na produção do espaço*. Rio de Janeiro: Petrópolis, São Paulo: Vozes, 9–10.
Marques, E. & Torres, H. (2000) São Paulo no contexto do sistema mundial de cidades. *Novos Estudos* 56: 139–168.
Melbourne Centre for Cities (2022) The global city at 30: An anniversary roundtable.
Ohmae, K. (1990) *The Borderless World: Power and Strategy in the Interlinked Economy*. New York: Harper Business.
Oliveira, F. (1999) O atraso da vanguarda e a vanguarda do atraso. In M.C. Paoli & F. Oliveira (eds.) *Os sentidos da democracia*. Petrópolis: Vozes.

Oliveira, F. (2003) *Crítica à dualista/Ornitorrinco*. São Paulo: Boitempo.
Ortiz, C. (2022) Cardinal Subordination. In Y. Oren & N. Mammon (eds.) *TheoriSE, Debating the Southeastern Turn in Urban Theories*. Cape Town: African Centre for Cities, 53–59.
Paulani, L.M. (2000) Vulnerabilidade ampliada. *Jornal de Resenhas 62*.
Paulani, L.M. (2008) *Brasil delivery: servidão financeira e estado de emergência econômico*. São Paulo: Boitempo Editorial.
Paulani, L.M. (2012) A inserção da economia brasileira no cenário mundial: uma reflexão sobre a situação atual à luz da história. *Boletim de Economia e Política Internacional* 10: 89–102.
Paulani, L.M. (2021) Dependency 4.0: Theoretical considerations and the Brazilian case. *Latin American Perspectives* 49(2): 24–38.
Robinson, J. (2006) *Ordinary Cities: Between Modernity and Development*. New York: Routledge.
Sachar, A. (1983) A cidade mundial e sua articulação ao sistema econômico global. In B.K. Becker et al. (eds.) *Abordagens Políticas da Espacialização*. Rio de Janeiro: UFRJ, Departamento de Geografia, Programa de Pós-Graduação, 75–97.
Sampaio Jr, P.A. (2007) *Globalização e reversão neocolonial: o impasse brasileiro*. Buenos Aires: Clacso.
Sandler, D. (2007) Place and process: Culture, urban planning, and social exclusion in São Paulo. *Social Identities* 13(4): 471–493.
Santos, L.G. (2002) São Paulo não é mais uma cidade. In V. Pallamin (ed.) *Cidade e cultura*, São Paulo: Estação Liberdade, 111–118.
Santos, M. et al. (eds.) (1993) *Fim de Século e Globalização*. São Paulo: Hucitec-Anpur.
Sassen, S. (1991) *The Global City*. Princeton: Princeton University Press.
Sassen, S. (1998) *As cidades na economia mundial*. São Paulo: Nobel.
Sassen, S. (2001) *The Global City: New York, London, Tokyo (Revised)*. Princeton: Princeton University Press.
Sassen, S. (2005) The global city: Introducing a concept. *Brown Journal of World Affairs* XI(2): 27–43.
Sassen, S. (2018) [1994] *Cities in a World Economy*. Thousand Oaks: SAGE Publications.
Schiffer, S. (ed.) (2004) *Globalização e a estrutura urbana*. São Paulo: Editora Hucitec.
Schwarz, R. (1999) *Sequências brasileiras*. São Paulo: Cia das Letras.
Silverio, V. (2019) Uma releitura do 'lugar do negro' e dos 'lugares da gente negra' nas cidades. In A. Barone & F. Rios (eds.) *Negros nas Cidades Brasileiras*. São Paulo: Intermeios, 17–142.
Tavares, M.C. (1999) Império, território e dinheiro. In J.L. Fiori (ed.). *Estados e moedas no desenvolvimento das nações*. Petrópolis: Ed. Vozes, 449–489.
Tavares, M.C. & Fiori, J.L. (1997) *Poder e Dinheiro. Uma economia política da globalização*. Petrópolis: Vozes.
Vainer, C. (2000) Pátria, empresa e mercadoria. In O.B. Arantes, E. Maricato & C. Vainer (eds.) *Cidade do pensamento único*. Petrópolis: Vozes, 75–103.
Vainer, C. (2022) Some notes and seven propositions on the coloniality and decoloniality of urban thought and urban planning. In Y. Oren & N. Mammon (eds.) *TheoriSE, Debating the Southeastern Turn in Urban Theories*. Cape Town: African Centre for Cities, 53–59.
Véras, M. B. (1999) Enigmas da gestão da cidade-mundial de São Paulo: políticas urbanas entre o local e o global. In M. A. Souza et al. (eds.) *Metrópole e Globalização*. São Paulo: Cedesp, 197–217.
Villaça, F. (2007) Prefácio. In J.S.W. Ferreira (ed.). *O mito da cidade-global: o papel da ideologia na produção do espaço*. Rio de Janeiro: Petrópolis, São Paulo: Vozes, 11–13.
Zeckendorf, W. & McCreary, E. (1988) *Zeckendorf: An Autobiography of William Zeckendorf*. Chicago: Plaza Press.
Zukin, S. (1993) *Landscapes of Power: from Detroit to Disney World*. Berkeley: University of California Press.

# 6. Rentier and homeowner cities: a long-run comparative history of urban tenure

*Sebastian Kohl*

The second half of the 20th century has seen the transition of almost all societies from tenant to homeownership societies. With the curious exceptions of German-speaking countries, Greenland and Qatar (Kohl 2017), the majority of households in almost all countries currently live in owner-occupied housing and, in democratic countries, the median voter has become a homeowner even despite the recent rise of the so-called Generation Rent (Lund 2013).

What has gone slightly below the radar of these national-level accounts is the urban dimension of this large-scale shift to homeownership, which is where this chapter makes its contribution. Drawing on new data collection regarding urban homeownership rates in many countries globally since 1950 and on long-run city-level homeownership data going historically backwards as far as possible for cities of the Global North, this chapter therefore uncovers three stylised facts.

First, tenant cities have been the historical norm in Europe and beyond over the last centuries, with homeownership rates even decreasing throughout the 19th century's industrialisation. Since early modern times, European cities have housed tenant majorities and, at their troughs, homeownership rates in Paris, Amsterdam, Oslo or Berlin were below 5%. A small number of landlords received rents from the urban tenant populace in Europe's rentier cities until tenancy regulation, particularly strong in large cities (Kholodilin 2020), and homeownership rates started to rise in the early 20th century. Second, a large part of the rise in homeownership has been a rise in *urban homeownership*; i.e., cities have started to close the historical urban–rural homeownership gaps and through the simultaneous urbanisation it was cities that contributed most to total homeownership increases. This was made possible through suburbanisation of cities in owner-occupied single-family homes or through the use of shared ownership institutions (condos, cooperatives, etc.). Third, in the most recent decade (2010s), there has been a comeback of urban rental markets and new forms of urban rentierism, where landlords are not only other individual households living in the same city or even building but more diverse forms of institutional investors and financial vehicles.

The chapter proceeds as follows: a brief literature review describes how existing studies have traced and explained the rise of homeownership nationally but neglected its specifically urban dimension. The main empirical section then presents a long-run view of homeownership with a particular focus on the urban–rural dimension. The last section considers to what extent recent declines in urban homeownership could augur a comeback of rentier cities.

## THE RISE OF HOMEOWNERSHIP

The long-run rise of homeownership and homeownership societies has received much attention at the national level of analysis, but with few exceptions the spectacular rise of homeownership in cities has rarely been studied or even documented. The evolution towards societies of homeowners has been documented in several studies (Atterhög 2006, Doling 1997, Kohl 2017) and there are several theories explaining the rise of homeownership at the national level.

First, convergence theories of housing systems point to economic development as a common background condition, with higher GDP per capita levels allowing more homeownership for average citizens (Donnison & Ungerson 1982). Second, government subsidies with a homeownership bias have accompanied the rise of homeownership (Atterhög 2006, Kholodilin et al. 2023) and many country-specific studies tend to focus on the political support in favour of homeownership through state homeownership programs (Bengtsson et al. 2017, Norris 2016, Ronald 2008), in particular financial vehicles supporting homeowners (Schwartz 2009) and fiscal exemptions in favour of (indebted) homeowners (Pollard 2011). Next to the direct positive effect of policies for homeowners, overly stringent tenancy regulation may also have indirect positive effects on homeownership by making private rentals less attractive for landlords and creating rental shortages (Fetter 2013).

Demographic factors also play a role, with ageing societies more likely to live in owner-occupied homes (Andrews & Sánchez 2011), whereas the effect of urbanisation on homeownership at the national level is rather unclear: denser societies and city-dwelling may or may not be associated with more tenancy (Angel 2000). Existing studies of interregional homeownership differences have pointed to lower urbanisation, a warmer climate, higher rates of ethnic diversity, a larger population at property-buying age, easier credit availability, lower house prices and suburban locations, high inflation (expectations), low welfare expenditure, low construction and land prices as being among the correlates of higher homeownership rates (Angel 2000, Coulson 2002, Fisher & Jaffe 2003, Gwin & Ong 2004, Lauridsen et al. 2009, Lerbs & Oberst 2012).

Beyond these quantitative regional studies on homeownership, there are also individual-city studies. One case study of the high homeownership outlier city of Bremen in Germany, for instance, points to very specific and accessible mortgage institutions and building types making homeownership broadly accessible in that city (Albrecht 1988). Comparisons of tenement- and non-tenement cities in the US and Great Britain reveal that different legal institutions in leasehold and mortgage law can privilege certain building types or tenures over others (Daunton 1988) and studies of the Montreal–Toronto homeownership gap have also pointed to long-standing cultural differences as well as the extent of (unplanned) suburbanisation as a specifically urban explanation of homeownership differences (Choko & Harris 1990, Harris & Choko 1988). These case studies have been equally important in revealing long-term trends of single-city homeownership evolution.

The literature is divided on the question of whether having more homeowners in a city is a desired outcome or not. On the one hand, a number of studies find that homeowners make better citizens (Glaeser & DiPasquale 1998) in that they participate in local politics more often (André et al. 2017), support local democracy, are better community builders and take better care of their local environments (Yoder 2020). On the other hand, there are studies showing the potentially negative effect of local property owners and their associations: homeowners become risk-averse defenders of their local status quo, adopting a 'not-in-my-backyard' attitude (Fischel 2017) and becoming immobile in cases of employment shocks (Blanchflower & Oswald 2013), struggling against the urban growth machine that sets cities on the path of urban expansions (Molotch 1976). In this view, homeowners and their associations fight for club-like private cities built to protect house prices and maintain patterns of segregation. When house prices collapse, foreclosures can be an existential risk for homeowners but also entire neighbourhoods (Madden & Marcuse 2016). Whatever the take on homeowners' effects on cities, the literature has so far not offered a comprehensive long-run picture of homeownership development below the national level and for more than just single cities. This is the gap this chapter seeks to fill.

## URBAN HOMEOWNERSHIP – A LONG-RUN VIEW

There is only dispersed evidence on homeownership in cities before the 19th century, but tenant-populated cities have a long tradition in Europe, reaching back to early modern cities, which, by 1500, often had great majorities of tenants in larger cities and large shares of tenant households even in smaller cities (Kuhn 2007). Available sources point to high and increasing rates of tenancy in major European cities, with only 7% owner-occupiers or less in Milan, Venice, Turin and Paris between 1600 and 1800 (Lyon-Caen 2015). Smaller cities and the elites in large cities could also reach double-digit homeownership rates easily. Over these centuries, homeownership rates tended to decline in cities: Amsterdam still reported 31% homeowners at the end of the 16th century, which fell to 13% in 1806 and less than 5% in the 1900s (Van Tussenbroek 2019). Similarly, in German cities, homeowners had been the majority in the 15th and 16th centuries and this number fell to below 10% for large cities like in the extreme case of Berlin and to about 10–15% elsewhere by 1900 (Gransche & Rothenbacher 1985, Wischermann 1997: 368). Still, tenancy was not an invention of the industrial revolution but was widespread in early modern continental Europe.

In English-speaking Europe, this was not very different in Great Britain, the most urbanised country with an estimated ownership rate of 10% in the early 1900s, and in Scotland's major cities (Holmans 2005), where a tenement building tradition could be found alongside ownership rates of below 10% already in the 1850s (O'Carroll 1997). This was slightly different in the much younger cities in the 'New World' (formerly British or Spanish colonies) where homeownership levels were higher from the very beginning, with estimations of over 20% in Hamilton and Kingston and the suburbs of Toronto and Montreal (though lower in the central city) around 1850 (Harris 1984, Harris & Choko 1988). However, even in the cities of these young settler economies, including Philadelphia, the 'City of Homes' (Warner 1987), urban homeowners made up a minority and cities remained predominantly cities of tenants (Daunton 1988), often in single-family-home form.

In these historic cities, best studied through inheritance records in Paris (Postel-Vinay & Rosenthal 2014), a small share of up to 10% of the urban population could count on sufficient wealth, one third of which came from real estate, to live comfortable lives at above-average consumption levels. In these rentier cities, local property owners were not only an economic elite but also maintained tight political control, with active and passive voting rights being tied to property taxes. In the case of Prussia prior to 1918, even 50% and more of the city council had to belong to local property owners, often coinciding with taxpayers (Lenger 2009). The other side of the rentier cities was a large tenant population who spent large income shares on rent; the poorer the households, the higher the rental burden, which German statisticians of the 19th century observed as 'Schwabe's law' (Schwabe 1868). Many urban riots such as the Paris Commune or the pre-World War I living-cost protests were an integral part of this urban political economy (Harvey 2004).

The historically low percentage of households owning the housing units they occupied needs to be read with comparative caution as the household structure changed considerably over the centuries. First, the average size of households decreased over these centuries from five to six members to around three currently (Bradbury et al. 2014). Second, the number of non-household members in the household decreased to almost zero, as the 'whole house' kind of households including domestic and other employees as members disappeared. Third, the number of one-person households in cities has moved to extremes at over 50% of all households in the current day from centuries of historical lows that reached around 5% in the 19th century (Snell 2017). This implies that the historical population that lived in owner-occupied housing or rent-free arrangements might have been higher, but it also highlights that recent homeownership rate increases could occur *despite* a growing number of ever-smaller households.

Relative to these urban homeownership rates, ownership in rural areas was far more widespread, particularly with the end of feudal ownership arrangements that resulted in family farming becoming the norm in countries like Ireland and increasing in France and Belgium after the French Revolution, and especially given property-splitting inheritance laws (Swinnen 2002). Farm ownership probably underestimates rural households residing with homeownership as not all rural households farm and leasing farming households can still occupy a home of their own, but it nevertheless gives an approximation of how broadly farm ownership is distributed. Vanhanen's widely used measure of the share of acres under family farming, shown in Figure 6.1, considers family farms as those cultivating their own land, including owner-like possession, without large numbers of employees (Vanhanen 2004: 84). As it uses acres and not farm units as a measure, it most probably overestimates the real numbers.

While over time the family-farming rates went down or stagnated in the countries that reached early democratic property distributions in the 19th century (Swinnen 2002), the general trend across many countries has rather been a long-run increase in family farms in Europe, Asia and the Americas: about half of all farmed acres or more were in farm ownership in the Global North by 1950 (see Figure 6.1). The large-scale emigration from the countryside to growing cities therefore often implied leaving rural ownership for an urban tenancy arrangement and thus an increasing urban–rural homeownership gap.

In the 1950s, the UN started reporting countries' housing censuses using country-specific definitions for urban areas, consistent over time but differing by country, ranging from a few hundred inhabitants counting as a city (in Iceland) to four-figure numbers in many OECD countries and up to Japan's threshold of 50,000 inhabitants (United Nations 1983: xi). Based on these country-specific definitions, almost all countries still report a clear urban–rural homeownership gap, ranging between very few percentage points in countries like Australia to more than 30 percentage points in European and Asian countries (see Figure 6.2). Israel is exceptional with lower rural than urban homeownership rates since the 1980s, reflecting the relative poverty of rural areas (Hananel et al. 2021). The over-time trend for most countries and regions however is one of a narrowing urban–rural homeownership gap, as cities approach the levels of rural homeownership over the later 20th century, with increasing urbanisation also amplifying their share in total ownership.

A closer look at countries with available long-run data (Figure 6.3) shows that while the urban–rural divide in homeownership rates persists in a number of countries (often German- or English-speaking ones), it remains very low in Oceanic countries and even disappears in Southern and Eastern European countries, Latin American countries and Norway.

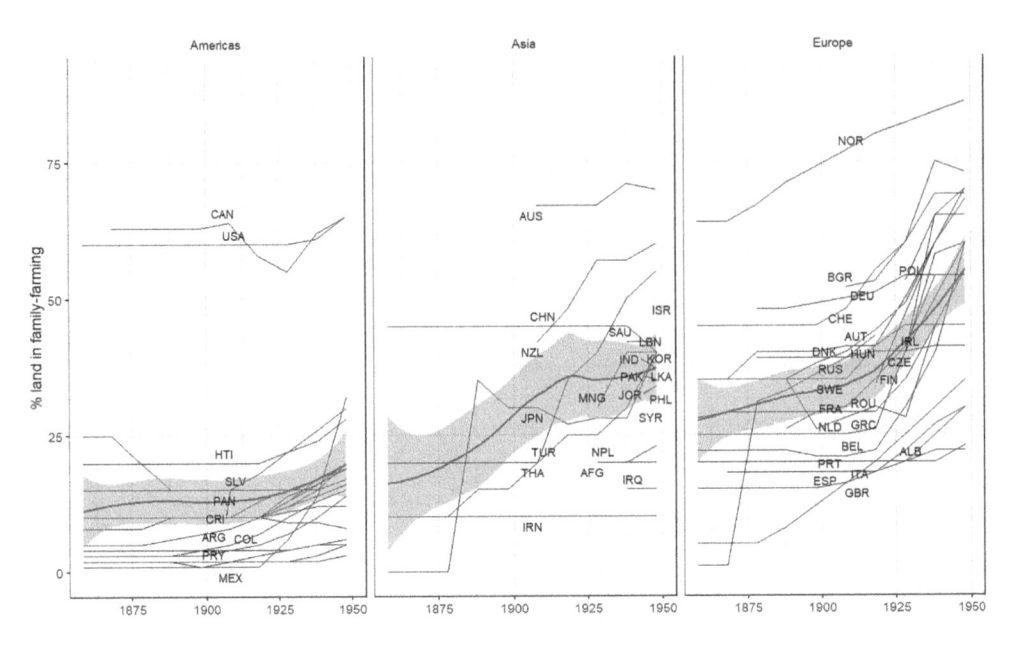

*Source:* Author's computation based on Vanhanen (2007).

*Figure 6.1    Percentage share of in-family farms*

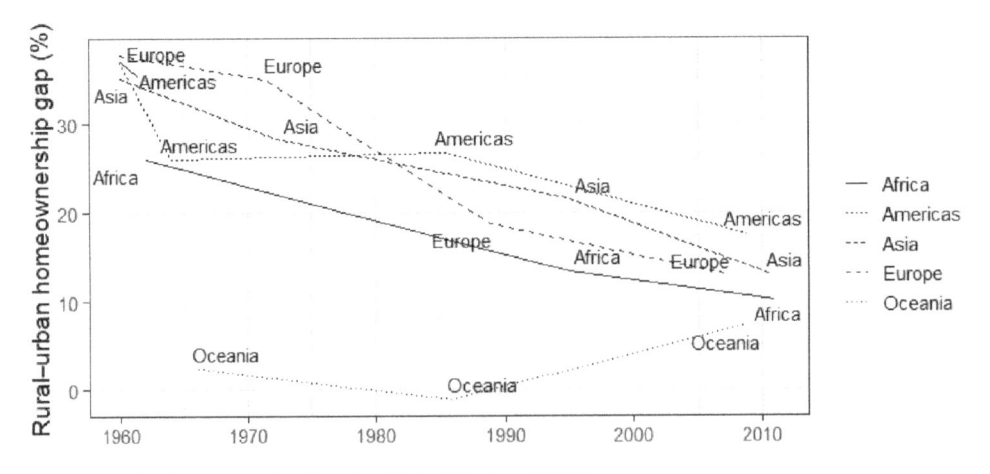

*Source:* Author's computation based on United Nations (1983).

*Figure 6.2    Rural–urban homeownership gap by continent and decennial non-weighted averages*

Figure 6.4 zooms in on the countries' major cities with a much longer historical perspective (i.e. capitals and cities with more than 100,000 inhabitants historically), thus excluding many smaller cities in the above UN definition. The selection was driven by long-run data availability. Some countries also have both an administrative city definition and a broader

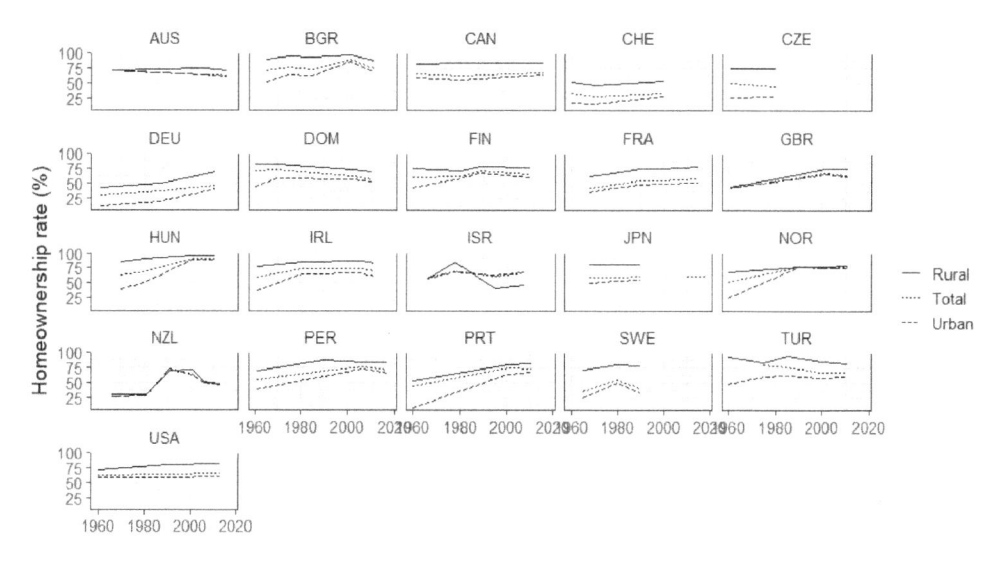

*Source:* Author's visualisation based on United Nations (1983).

*Figure 6.3    Urban, rural and total homeownership rates at countries' census dates (interpolated)*

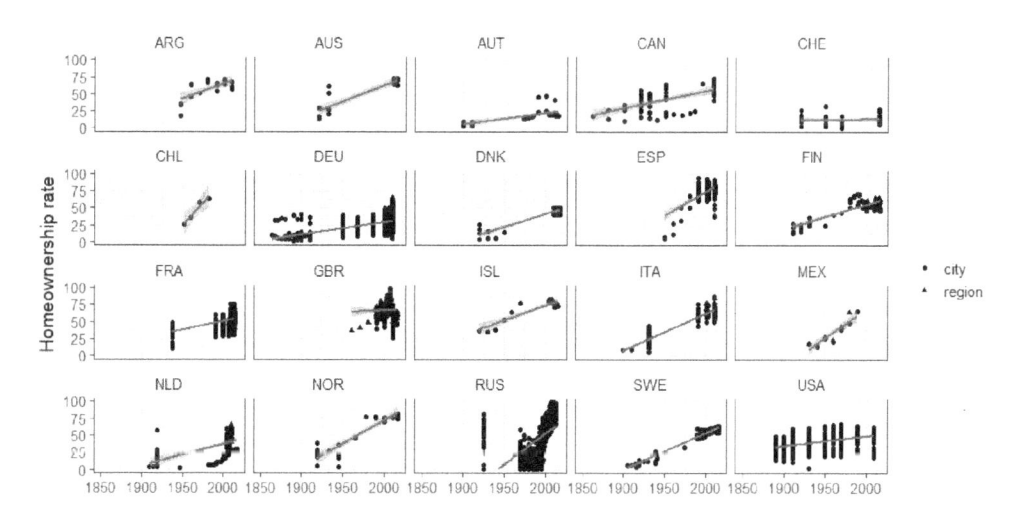

*Note:* Each dot is a homeownership rate for a given major city. For Scandinavia, German-speaking countries and Russia, see Kalyukin and Kohl (2019) and Kohl and Sørvoll (2021). See also the Canadian and US Census data from city data books, the European national housing counts for historical time periods and Eurostat's Urban Audit for recent years and Latin American countries' housing and population censuses.
*Source:*  Created by the author.

*Figure 6.4    Homeownership rates of major cities in selected countries in the long run*

regional definition (differently shaped dots in Figure 6.4). A closer look at countries' major cities reveals the extent to which homeownership rates have increased throughout: whereas the average urban homeownership rate was already high in many countries in the 1950s (displayed in Figure 6.3), the larger cities' homeownership rates shown in Figure 6.4 reveal the particularly strong increases the major population centres have undergone, albeit with different country trajectories.

The increases have been steeper for countries with a Roman law tradition (i.e., Southern Europe and Latin America), Scandinavia and post-Soviet cities. The Soviet trajectory also displays a unique communist U-shape. Increases have been comparatively moderate in cities of former British colonies because the initial homeownership rates were already high. They have also been more moderate in German-speaking countries because final homeownership rates have not risen to high levels. Finally, some statistical agencies define larger functional regions (Eurostat) or metropolitan areas in which homeownership rates are persistently higher, reflecting the suburbanisation of cities through more affordable housing, often in single-family-home form. Only recent years have seen a new decline in homeownership rates in major cities again.

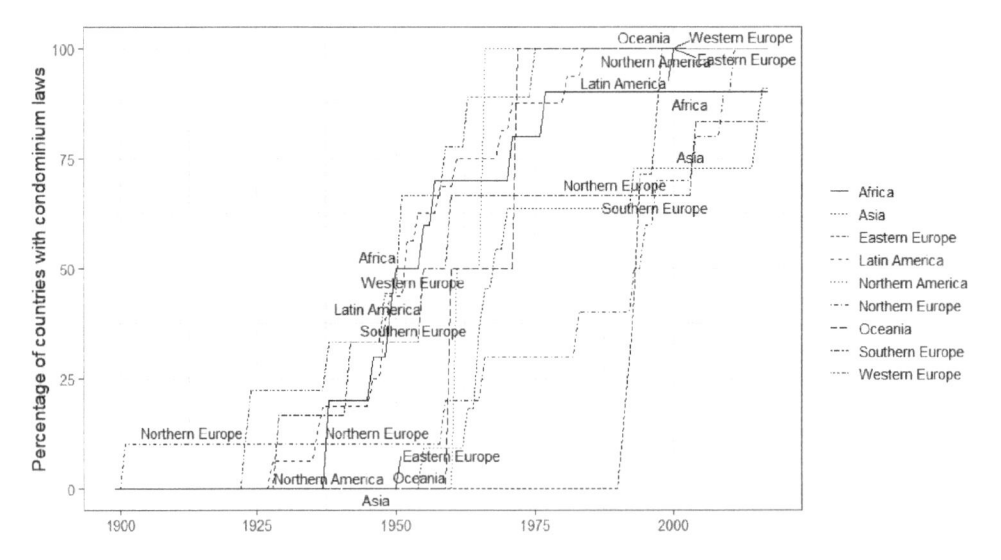

*Source:* Kholodilin and Kohl (2021a), author's graph.

*Figure 6.5*     *Average years of introduction of condominium ownership*

One important legal background condition for the spread of homeownership in cities was the introduction of modern forms of condominium ownership. Owning separate parts within a building on the same piece of land had always existed in some form but receded in light of the Roman '*superficies solo cedit*' doctrine (Thun 1997). With French Civil Law, owning flats separately in a building started to spread again as a legal institution, particularly and earlier in countries with a Roman law tradition, as Figure 6.5 on the average years of introduction of modern condominium ownership laws displays, which explains the particularly steep increase in those cities (Hoekstra 2005). In Scandinavian cities, it was rather tenant ownership cooperatives that acted as a functionally equivalent institution for flat ownership (Kohl & Sørvoll

2021), while post-Soviet countries moved particularly quickly to flat ownership institutions after 1990.

## CONCLUSION: BACK TOWARDS THE RENTIER CITY?

Since the Global Financial Crisis of 2008, homeownership rates have fallen in a large number of countries and this was again a predominantly urban phenomenon. The declines are considerable given the short amount of time but are obviously still far from reversing the course of a history of several decades of increases in homeownership. Yet in Europe the private rental share increased up to almost 20 percentage points in the case of Irish lower-income households and grew considerably throughout many other European countries (Figure 6.6).

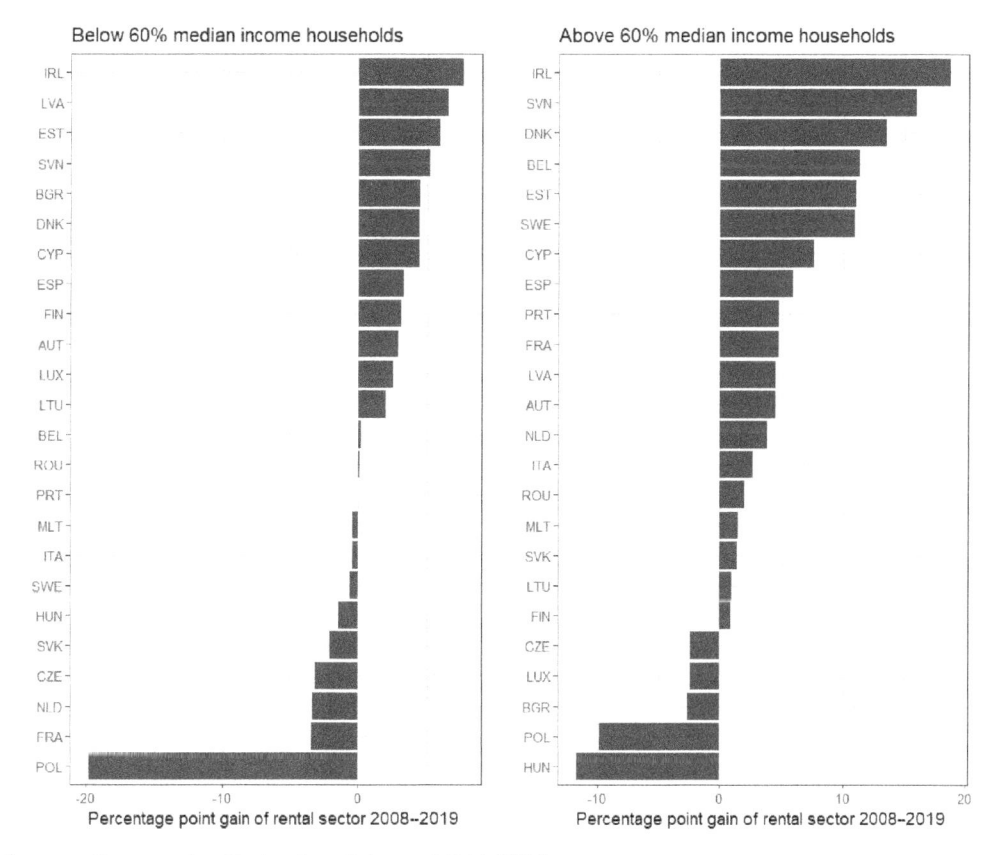

*Source:* Eurostat, visualisation from Gabor and Kohl (2022).

*Figure 6.6*  *Percentage point growth in the private rental sector among rich/poor households in Europe*

106  *Research handbook on urban sociology*

The recent increase in the private rental market segment has been accompanied by a certain comeback of the private landlord and rentierism (Aalbers et al. 2021, Christophers 2020), supported by policies such as 'buy-to-let' programs. Similar to the 19th century, current landlords in France (André et al. 2021) and Germany (Bartels & Schroeder 2020) continue to be a very selective group and income streams from renting are highly skewed towards the top-income strata of the population. The Luxembourg Income Study (LIS) allows a decomposition of rental revenue by household income quintiles for several countries of the last decade (see Figure 6.7). It shows that the top 20% have higher rental revenues than the poorer quintiles relative to their already much higher income: the absolute average rental income of the top 20% of households in Germany alone therefore easily exceeds the labour income of the bottom 20% in Germany (Bartels & Schroeder 2020).

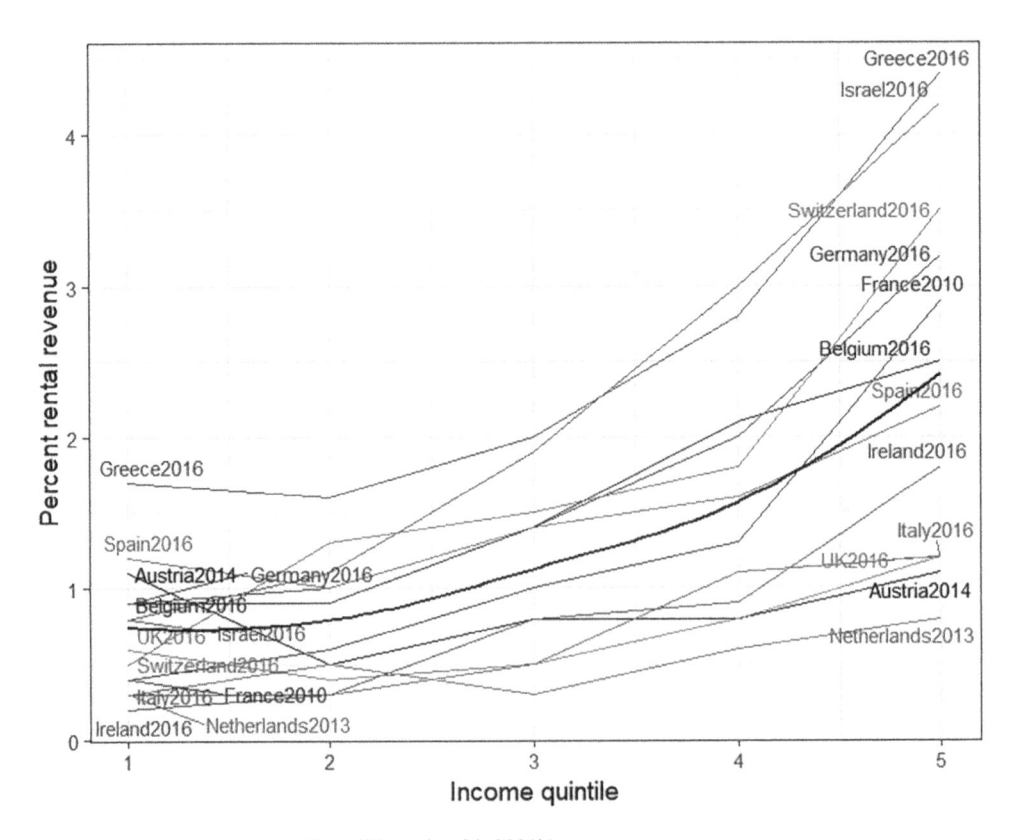

*Source:* LIS, computed from Kholodilin and Kohl (2021b).

*Figure 6.7*  *Share of revenue from rental income by household income quintile*

Against the background of several centuries of tenant cities, the modern 20th century rise of homeowner cities marks a fundamental change in urban residency, as this chapter has shown. Still, the historical layer of the rentier city built on private rental real estate owned by rich landlords and paid for by rents from poorer tenants is still persistent, even increasing in the recent decade. A particular feature of the recent increases is the variety of institutional forms landlordism can take in modern cities, where not only classical institutional investors such as insurance companies but also pension funds, real estate investment trusts (REITs) and other financial vehicles have signalled a new appetite for rental residential real estate among an investment class (Gabor & Kohl 2022). The rise of more institutionally owned real estate might change the way that the 'cities of tomorrow' and urban life look in the years to come.

Many studies referenced above suggest that tenure is not a socially or spatially neutral phenomenon. The dominant type of tenure in a given city may have considerable impact on individual urban life and metropolitan structures. Tenant cities have higher mobility and may face cost-of-living crises and corresponding protests more easily, whereas homeowner cities may be more immobile and face foreclosure crises and tax protests. The concentration of rental ownership among fewer landlords in turn reveals the monopolistic nature of urban markets much more clearly and also changes urban protest dynamics. All of this suggests that the slowly moving long-run trends towards cities with more institutional landlordism may not leave the urban fabric unchanged.

## REFERENCES

Aalbers, M., Hochstenbach, C., Bosma, J. & Fernandez, R. (2021) The Death and Life of Private Landlordism: How Financialized Homeownership Gave Birth to the Buy-To-Let Market. *Housing, Theory and Society* 38(5): 541–563.

Albrecht, G. (1988) Das Bremer Haus. Ein Sonderfall in der deutschen Baugeschichte um 1850. In A. Schildt & A. Sywottek (eds.) *Massenwohnung und Eigenheim. Wohnungsbau und Wohnen in der Großstadt seit dem Ersten Weltkrieg.* Frankfurt/New York: Campus Verlag, 233–251.

André, M., Arnold, C. & Meslin, O. (2021) 24 % des ménages détiennent 68 % des logements possédés par des particuliers. *Statistiques et études*, INSEE. Available at: https://www.insee.fr/fr/statistiques/5432517?sommaire=5435421.

André, S., Dewilde, C. & Luijkx, R. (2017) The Tenure Gap in Electoral Participation: Instrumental Motivation or Selection Bias? Comparing Homeowners and Tenants across Four Housing Regimes. *International Journal of Comparative Sociology* 58(3): 241–65.

Andrews, D. & Sánchez, A. (2011) The Evolution of Homeownership Rates in Selected OECD Countries: Demographic and Public Policy Influences. *OECD Journal: Economic Studies* 1.

Angel, S. (2000) *Housing Policy Matters. A Global Analysis.* Oxford: Oxford University Press.

Atterhög, M. (2006) The Effect of Government Policies on Home Ownership Rates: An International Survey and Analysis. In J. Doling & M. Elsinga (eds.) *Home Ownership: Getting In, Getting From, Getting Out.* Amsterdam: Ios Press, 7–34.

Bartels, C. & Schroeder, C. (2020) The Role of Rental Income, Real Estate and Rents for Inequality in Germany. *Forum New Economy Working Papers.*

Bengtsson, B., Ruonavaara, H. & Sørvoll, J. (2017) Home Ownership, Housing Policy and Path Dependence in Finland, Norway and Sweden. In R. Ronald & C. Dewilde (eds.) *Housing Wealth and Welfare.* Cheltenham, UK and Northampton, MA, USA: Edward Elgar Publishing, 60–84.

Blanchflower, D. & Oswald, A. (2013) Does High Home-Ownership Impair the Labor Market? National Bureau of Economic Research.

Bradbury, M., Peterson, M. & Liu, J. (2014) Long-term Dynamics of Household Size and their Environmental Implications. *Population and Environment* 36(1): 73–84.

Choko, M. & Harris, R. (1990) The Local Culture of Property: A Comparative History of Housing Tenure in Montreal and Toronto. *Annals of the Association of American Geographers* 80(1): 73–95.

Christophers, B. (2020) *Rentier Capitalism: Who Owns the Economy, and Who Pays for It?* London: Verso.

Coulson, E. (2002) Regional and State Variation in Homeownership Rates; or If California's Home Prices Were as Low as Pennsylvania's Would Its Homeownership Rate be as High? *Journal of Real Estate Finance and Economics* 24(3): 261–76.
Daunton, M. (1988) Cities of Homes and Cities of Tenements: British and American Comparisons 1870–1914. *Journal of Urban History* 14: 283–319.
Doling, J. (1997) *Comparative Housing Policy. Government and Housing in Advanced Industrialized Countries.* Basingstoke: Macmillan.
Donnison, D. & Ungerson, C. (1982) *Housing Policy.* Harmondsworth: Penguin.
Fetter, D. (2013) The Home Front: Rent Control and the Rapid Wartime Increase in Home Ownership. NBER Working Paper, No. 19604.
Fischel, W. (2017) The Rise of the Homevoters: How the Growth Machine Was Subverted by OPEC and Earth Day. Working Paper. Available at: https://sites.dartmouth.edu/wfischel/working-papers/.
Fisher, L. & Jaffe, A. (2003) Determinants of International Home Ownership Rates. *Housing Finance International* 18(1): 34–37.
Gabor, D. & Kohl, S. (2022) 'My Home is an Asset Class': The Financialization of Housing in Europe. Report for the Greens–European Free Alliance.
Glaeser, E. & DiPasquale, D. (1998) Incentives and Social Capital: Are Homeowners Better Citizens? NBER Working Paper, No. 6363.
Gransche, E. & Rothenbacher, F. (1985) *Langfristige Entwicklungstendenzen der Wohnverhältnisse in Deutschland 1861–1910.* Frankfurt/Mannheim: Mikroanalyt.
Gwin, C. & Ong, S. (2004) Do We Really Understand Home Ownership Rates? An International Study. Working Paper, Baylor Business School.
Hananel, R., Azary-Viesel, S. & Nachmany, H. (2021) Spatial Gaps – Narrowing or Widening? Changes in Spatial Dynamics in the New Millennium. *Land Use Policy* 109: 105693.
Harris, R. (1984) Class and Housing Tenure in Modern Canada. Research Paper, 153, Centre for Urban and Community Studies, University of Toronto.
Harris, R. & Choko, M. (1988) The Evolution of Housing Tenure in Montreal and Toronto since the Mid-Nineteenth Century. Research Paper, 166, Centre for Urban and Community Studies, University of Toronto.
Harvey, D. (2004) *Paris, Capital of Modernity.* London: Routledge.
Hoekstra, J. (2005) Is There a Connection between Welfare State Regime and Dwelling Type? An Exploratory Statistical Analysis. *Housing Studies* 20(3): 475–495.
Holmans, A. (2005) *Historical Statistics of Housing in Britain.* Department of Land Economy, University of Cambridge.
Kalyukin, A. & Kohl, S. (2019) Continuities and Discontinuities of Russian Urban Housing: The Soviet Housing Experiment in Historical Long-run Perspective. *Urban Studies* 57(8): 1768–1785.
Kholodilin, K. (2020) Long-Term, Multicountry Perspective on Rental Market Regulations. *Housing Policy Debate* 30(6): 994–1015.
Kholodilin, K. & Kohl, S. (2021a) Social Policy or Crowding-out? Tenant Protection in Comparative Long-run Perspective. *Housing Studies* 38(4): 1–24.
Kholodilin, K. & Kohl, S. (2021b) Rent Price Control – Yet Another Great Equalizer of Economic Inequalities? Evidence from a Century of Historical Data. DIW Discussion Paper.
Kholodilin, K., Kohl, S., Korzhenevych, A. & Pfeiffer, L. (2023) The Hidden Homeownership Welfare State: An International Long-term Perspective on the Tax Treatment of Homeowners. *Journal of Public Policy* 43(1): 86–114.
Kohl, S. (2017) *Homeownership, Renting and Society: Historical and Comparative Perspectives.* London: Routledge.
Kohl, S. & Sørvoll, J. (2021) Varieties of Social Democracy and Cooperativism: Explaining the Divergence between Housing Regimes in Nordic and German-speaking Countries. *Social Science History* 45(3): 561–587.
Kuhn, G. (2007) Citybildung und Dezentralisierung – urbane Wohnprojekte in der Weimarer Republik. In T. Harlander (ed.) *Stadtwohnen: Geschichte, Städtebau, Perspektiven.* Ludwigsburg: Wüstenrot Stiftung, 184–195.
Lauridsen, J., Nannerup, N. & Skak, M. (2009) Small Area Variation in Homeownership. *Housing Studies* 24(6): 793–808.

Lenger, F. (2009) *Stadtgeschichten. Deutschland, Europa und die USA seit 1800.* Frankfurt: Lang.
Lerbs, O. & Oberst, C. (2012) Explaining the Spatial Variation in Homeownership Rates: Results for German Regions. CESifo Working Paper.
Lund, B. (2013) A 'Property-Owning Democracy' or 'Generation Rent'? *The Political Quarterly* 84(1): 53–60.
Lyon-Caen, N. (2015) L'immobilier parisien au XVIIIe siècle. Un marché locative. *Histoire urbaine* 43(2): 55–70.
Madden, D. & Marcuse, P. (2016) *In Defense of Housing.* London: Verso.
Molotch, H. (1976) The City as a Growth Machine: Toward a Political Economy of Place. *The American Journal of Sociology* 82(2): 309–332.
Norris, M. (2016) *Property, Family and the Irish Welfare State.* London: Palgrave Macmillan.
O'Carroll, A. (1997) Tenement to Bungalows: Class and Growth of Home Ownership before 'World War II'. *Urban History* 24(2): 221–241.
Pollard, J. (2011) L'action publique par les niches fiscales – l'exemple du secteur du logement. In P. Bezes & A. Siné (eds.) *Gouverner (par) les finances publiques.* Paris: Sciences Po Les Presses, 263–97.
Postel-Vinay, G. & Rosenthal, J. (2014) Inherited vs Self-made Wealth: Theory and Evidence from a Rentier Society (Paris 1872–1937). *Explorations in Economic History* 51: 21–40.
Ronald, R. (2008) *The Ideology of Home Ownership. Homeowner Societes and the Role of Housing.* Basingstoke: Palgrave Macmillan.
Schwabe, H. (1868) Das Verhältnis von Miete und Einkommen in Berlin. Berlin und seine Entwicklung. *Gemeindekalender und städtisches Jahrbuch* 2: 264–267.
Schwartz, H. (2009) *Subprime Nation. American Power, Global Capital, and the Housing Bubble.* Ithaca: Cornell University Press.
Snell, K. (2017) The Rise of Living Alone and Loneliness in History. *Social History* 42(1): 2–28.
Swinnen, J. (2002) Political Reforms, Rural Crises, and Land Tenure in Western Europe. *Food Policy* 27(4): 371–394.
Thun, N. (1997) *Die rechtsgeschichtliche Entwicklung des Stockwerkseigentums. Ein Beitrag zur deutschen Privatrechtsgeschichte.* Hamburg: Lit.
United Nations (1983) *Compendium of Housing Statistics.* New York: United Nations.
Van Tussenbroek, G. (2019) The Great Rebuilding of Amsterdam (1521–1578). *Urban History* 46(3): 419–442.
Vanhanen, T. (2004) *Democratization: A Comparative Analysis of 170 Countries.* London: Routledge.
Vanhanen, T. (2007) Index of Power Resources (IPR) 2007 [dataset]. *Finnish Social Science Data Archive.* Available at: http://urn.fi/urn:nbn:fi:fsd:T-FSD2420.
Warner, S. (1987) *The Private City. Philadelphia in Three Periods of its Growth.* Philadelphia: University of Pennsylvania Press.
Wischermann, C. (1997) Mythen, Macht und Mängel: Der deutsche Wohnungsmarkt im Urbanisierungsprozeß. In J. Reulecke (ed.) *Geschichte des Wohnens. Band 3. 1800–1918. Das Bürgerliche Zeitalter.* Stuttgart: Deutsche Verlags-Anstalt, 333–502.
Yoder, J. (2020) Does Property Ownership Lead to Participation in Local Politics? Evidence from Property Records and Meeting Minutes. *American Political Science Review* 114(4): 1213–1229.

# 7. The flaws of urban financialization and rentierism: not distribution, but exploitation

*Ismael Yrigoy*

Few topics resonate more than financialization and rentierism in today's Marxist urban scholarship. Finance – mainly but not only through the keyword financialization – has become prominent 'in the [English-speaking] critical scholarly vocabulary and consciousness' (Christophers 2015: 184) since the 2000s. Land rents and rentierism have also become highly relevant concepts in urban scholarship following the influential work of authors such as Anne Haila, Thomas Piketty and Mariana Mazzucato, amongst others.

The deployment of the concepts of 'financialization' and 'rentierism' is supposed to reflect the increasing dominance of 'unearned' forms of surplus value appropriated through the built environment in the case of cities. The *problematic issue* of rentierism and financialization is, according to classical economists such as Ricardo, Smith and Keynes, that they disrupt the dynamics of capital accumulation as rentiers appropriate income that is produced elsewhere. This idea was first formulated by the French physiocratic school and has been adopted by virtually all political economists ever since.

In this chapter, I argue that the main *problematic* issue of rentierism and financialization *is not* about *who* appropriates the surplus value generated but that the very generation of surplus value embedded in the dynamics of rentierism and financialization generates labor *exploitation*. If financialization and rentierism should be problematized, it is not because of 'unearned income' that hampers accumulation but rather because this sort of income places a heavy toll on the labor force. There is an urgent need to dissect how the category of exploitation can be deployed to understand the social struggles embedded in financialization and rentierism.

The theoretical discussion on how exploitation occurs in the frame of financialization and rentierism proceeds as follows: section one provides a historical summary of how finance/financialization and rent/rentierism have historically been defined by political economists. Section two demonstrates how Marx rooted the main earnings of landowners (rents) and financial actors (interests) in the creation of surplus value. The third section discusses the difficulties in relating rentierism and financialization to exploitation. Here I make three interrelated arguments: (i) that financialization and rentierism entail exploitation in the production of value; (ii) that dwellers are forced to acquire the commodity form of housing to survive; and thus (iii) that financialization and rentierism not only easily realize the value of the commodity but create what I define here as a 'secondary' exploitation.

# THE PROBLEM WITH FINANCE AND RENT: AN UNJUST DISTRIBUTION OF SURPLUS VALUE

## Conceptualizing Rent as Unearned Income

Finance and rent became central categories in political economy in the 19th century through the works of Pierre-Joseph Proudhon, John Maynard Keynes, Karl Marx, Michal Kallecki, Rudolf Hilferding and Thorsten Veblen, amongst others (Dillard 1942, Foster 2007, Mader et al. 2020). In both the early 20th and 21st centuries, finance and rent have been studied in the frame of the *distribution* of surplus value between corporations on the one hand and rentiers/financiers on the other (Mader et al. 2020).

The first key concept used by classical political economists to address the issue of the distribution of surplus value – both in feudalism and capitalism – is the concept of *land rent*, also referred to as ground rent by Marx (1993). Land rents are the payments made for the use of land and the built environment that sits on land (Harvey 1982, Haila 1990). Corporate profits are the surplus value appropriated by a company that uses workers (Harvey 1982, Haila 1990). The very existence of rent has been heavily criticized as it is seen as an 'illegitimate' way of appropriating surplus value (Meek 1951, Haila 1990). Smith and Quesnay, as Marx did later on, distinguished between the surplus value required to maintain the productive activity (e.g., investments in maintaining machinery) and the rest of the surplus value, which is not immediately needed to maintain production. Within this latter sphere of surplus, the French physiocratic school assumed that 'the surplus took the form of land-rent and land-rent alone' (Meek 1951: 29). The problematization of the existence of land rent and of rentier actors was also developed by Adam Smith through his astounding critique of landlords: 'As soon as the land of any country has all become private property, the landlords, like all other men, love to reap where they never sowed, and demand a rent even for its natural produce' (Smith, 1977:76). David Ricardo and Thomas Malthus continued Smith's, Cantillon's and Quesnay's deep preoccupation with the distribution of surplus, seeing rent and rentierism as mere parasites in the production process. The distribution of surplus was thus seen as a problem for both capital accumulation and the labor force, as a share of the surplus that could be destined for corporate profits and/or labor wages was unfairly appropriated by a third agent external to the production process.

Proudhon essentially continued the same approach to distribution that Ricardo, Smith and Cantillon held in the 18th and 19th centuries. Proudhon, himself a moderate socialist defending private property, claimed that 'The abolition of unearned income, of so-called surplus-value, also called interest and economic rent, is the immediate economic aim of every socialistic movement' (Dillard 1942: 68). Yet here Proudhon was introducing a more complex outlook to the distribution issue: unearned income not only took the form of rent but also of interest. Such a distinction between two types of unearned income was later developed by Marx: a distinction between *interest* and the circulation of interest-bearing capital, closely linked with finance and financial actors, on the one hand, and *rent*, shaped by rentier actors, on the other. Indeed, Marx introduced a whole new discussion with deep interrelations with rent: the concept of finance.

In Volume III of *Capital*, Marx referred to different interrelated aspects that define what finance is: first, finance arises through a historical process by which money is consolidated as the main means of exchange (Marx 1993: 219). Second, Marx referred to finance as the management of money capital (e.g., accountants, investment advisors, etc.), which reduces the costs of capital circulation (Marx 1993). Third and more important, Marx distinguished the industrial capitalist who receives profits from the financial capitalist whose revenue arises in the form of interest (De Brunhoff 1976: 55, Marx 1993: 302). In short, the concept of finance means for Marx the irruption of sophisticated means of exchange, a new management function of the capitalist class and, most important, a fraction of the capitalist class that appropriates surplus in the form of interest. This third definition of finance as a fraction of capitalists (mainly banks) who appropriates surplus in the form of interest is the approach that has had more influence on political economy and not least on the idea of financialization itself. Note here that in this third definition of finance Marx is assuming that the relation between financial and industrial capitalist is antagonistic: there is a stark competition between two fractions of capital to appropriate surplus. In addition to the rent–profit distribution issue yet another distributive conflict arose: the problem of the distribution between rent and interest. The stance taken by Marx was similar to the approach historically taken by other political economists towards rentierism: financial capital is hoarding of the share of surplus value appropriated by corporations.

Marx's theorization of finance was further developed by Rudolf Hilferding (Harvey 1982). In his *Finance Capital*, Hilferding explained the history of what he regarded as the two large fractions of capital: financial and industrial capitalists. In the early 20th century Hilferding described the increasing dominance of financial capital over other fractions of capital, almost exactly the same process that has been defined as financialization in the 21st century. However, Hilferding also explained the logic by which industrial capital would be integrated into finance capital (Marois 2012). In a nutshell, Hilferding claimed that through lending to corporations, banks and their interests would become closely associated with the interests of corporations (Marois 2012: 154–156).

Yet in the early 20th century the distribution issue would increasingly be related both to finance and rent. Keynes saw interests as well as rent as non-functional, unearned income (Dillard 1984: 429). Whereas the analysis of finance and rent in Marx remained separate, in Keynes the concepts of rent and finance were almost used interchangeably. Keynes however believed that the dynamics of capital accumulation and the need to maximize profit would eventually end with the dominance of financiers and rentiers: 'Since interest compensates no genuine sacrifice any more than does land rent, the nonfunctional rentier-capitalist will gradually disappear, once a rational economic reform program is inaugurated' (Keynes quoted in Dillard 1942: 67). Interestingly, scholarly debates on rent and finance disappeared at the zenith of the Keynesian welfare state: the positivist turn in economics and social sciences made the political economists' problematization of the categories of rent and finance fade away.

## THE MARXIAN TURN AND THE CURRENT USE OF FINANCIALIZATION AND RENTIERISM: AN ANEMIC URBAN THEORIZATION

Following the Marxist turn in social sciences during the 1970s, Marxian concepts and theories acquired momentum, including the use of the concept of rent. Neil Smith's (1979) rent gap theory was key in the widespread use of the category of rent by Marxian sociologists and geographers. In fact, the rent gap thesis was the first theory in the English-speaking world that adapted the category of ground rent to the urban context. Shying away from the distribution discussion which had shaped the concepts of rent and finance, Smith (1979) linked urban renewal with the ability of capital to revalue and appreciate the built environment based on the cyclical process of devaluation and depreciation followed by investment, appreciation and revaluation.

The outset of the 2008 economic crisis went hand in hand with a renewed popularization of the categories of finance and rent (Ward & Aalbers 2016), with a twist in the way these categories were approached. Scholarship on finance and rent in the 2010s did not use as much the category of 'interest-bearing capital' as political economists did in the early 20th century, rather, the key concept for the former group became financialization. This concept links back to Epstein's (2005: 3) widely cited definition of financialization as 'the increasing role of financial motives, markets, actors and institutions in the operation of the domestic and international economies'. Following Gerald Epstein (2005), there was a popularization of the concept of financialization through political economists such as Engelbert Stockhammer (2004) and Greta Krippner (2005), who provided evidence of how surplus value was increasingly being generated by financial actors and using financial strategies. Financialization theorists drew upon world systems theorists and particularly Giovanni Arrighi (1994), who since the 1990s argued that there was a historical tendency towards the domination of finance. On the other hand, early financialization scholarship was inspired by authors who studied the role of finance in boosting and shrinking economic growth, particularly Hyman Minsky.

The notion of 'housing financialization', which refers to the increasing dominance of financial actors in housing markets, was popularized by Manuel Aalbers (2016) and quickly adopted by urban scholarship. It became mainstream in urban social sciences, with hundreds of works analyzing such phenomena across different countries in the Global North and Global South.

Shortly afterwards, the concept of land rents was displaced by *rentierism*, defined as the increasing prominence of the appropriation of surplus by rentier actors (Mazzucato 2018, Christophers 2020). While financialization emerged in the English-speaking sphere in the early 2000s, rentierism only came to the fore in the late 2010s. The ideas about rentierism started to be developed from 2014 onwards following key authors such as Thomas Piketty, Andrew Sayer, Guy Standing and Mariana Mazzucato, who focused yet again on the conflict between rentiers and productive capitalists. In short, the distribution problem as outlined since the 18th century remains the main question addressed by the key works on financialization and rentierism. As it had been for the main political economists of the late 19th and 20th centuries, the main issue with rentiers for these key authors was the appropriation by rentiers of a surplus produced by others. Even if Piketty (2014) carried out a path-breaking dissection of the social implications of rentierism, the key flaw of the literature is, as argued in the next section, the lack of theorization of the social implications of rentierism.

While empirical discussions on the strategies used to extract ground rents from the built environment and particularly from housing by financiers and rentiers have reinvigorated empirically the concepts of rent and finance, there is a need to theorize rentierism and financialization in relation to exploitation. Abellán (2023) however provides a Marxist-based epistemological critique of the concept of financialization and rentierism, arguing that there has been a 'mystification' of the social relations embedded in such concepts, which are ultimately based on the appropriation by capitalists of the socially necessary labor time embedded in the production of commodities.

## REVISITING RENT AND FINANCE IN MARX

Marx (1993) related the category of finance to the circulation of interest-bearing capital, whereas he related the category of rent to the payments for the right to use land and the built environment that sits on it. Rent therefore comes from a monopoly power over land property rights, whereas finance relies on monopoly power over money to be lent. Marx made two key arguments regarding the true nature of rent and finance. First, he claimed that the income from rentierism (land rents) and finance (interest and fee payments) ultimately comes from the same source, which is surplus value. Second, he showed how the apparently clear boundaries between financial income (in the form of interest) and rent become increasingly blurred precisely as both sources of income ultimately come from surplus value.

First, Marx clearly traced back the origins of rent and interest to surplus value. On the one hand, interest/fee payments (the main way by which finance creates income) and profits are just about the *form* that surplus value takes: 'One portion of the profit appears now as fruit due as such to capital in one form, as interest; the other portion appears as a specific fruit of capital in an opposite form, and thus as profit of enterprise' claims Marx (1993: 257). An intimate bond between profit and interest, Marx acknowledges, does exist. The rate of interest may not be related to the rate of profit in the short run, but in the long run interest can only exist if profits are created. On the other hand, Marx makes similar claims about the origin of land rents: 'profit of capital and ground-rent are no more than particular components of surplus value' (Marx 1993: 566). The source of surplus value is inevitably the same in interest payments and rents: labor. 'The distribution [of surplus value in the form of profits and rent] rather presupposes the existence of this substance, namely, the total value of the annual product which is nothing but materialised social labour' (Marx 1993: 567). The extraction of land rent is therefore ultimately based on the appropriation of socially necessary labor time by different agents, including rentiers.

Second, Marx (1993) dissected the key interrelations between finance-interest and rent. On the one hand, he argued that there are two forms of investment in land, which Marx labeled as interest-bearing, intertwined with ground rents. Marx (1993) refers to the investments that land users such as tenants or farmers make – via lending – to improve the value of land. Refurbishing a house or improving the productivity of land has in principle nothing to do, at least in the short run, with ground rent, 'which must be paid on stated dates annually for the use of land' (Marx 1993: 427). However, Marx points out that in the long run there is a relation between this type of interest-bearing capital and ground rent, insofar as when land lease contracts are renewed, the new contracts reflect the enhanced value of land and the built environment, an enhanced value that is often obtained via lending; that is, the circulation of interest-bearing capital. Moreover, the fact that for the productive land user the ground rent paid represents a deduction in future value created from that land is for Marx a form of interest-bearing capital in itself: 'If a capitalist buys land yielding a rent of £200 annually and pays £4000 for it, then he draws the average annual interest of 5% on his capital of £4000, just as if he had invested this capital in interest-bearing papers or loaned it at 5% interest' (Marx 1993: 427). On the other hand, Marx dissected how rents may be thrown back to the productive sphere. Indeed, revenues coming from rentierism can be directed towards capital circulation by boosting consumption, thus stimulating effective demand and helping to solve realization problems for capital (Harvey 1982: 365). Interestingly enough, one main way by which rents may be used again in production is through the reconversion of land rents into interest-bearing capital. This link, as Harvey

(1982: 366) pointed out, 'is easily observable and of great importance in capitalist history'. Revenues coming from land rents have indeed been commonly used by banks to lend money, which is used then to acquire and develop land. If rentierism and not least financialization may directly or indirectly boost the dynamics of accumulation, then there is a need to discuss the ways by which rentierism and financialization ultimately lead to exploitation.

## LABOR EXPLOITATION UNDERLYING RENT AND FINANCE IN URBAN SETTINGS

Financialization and rentierism are mechanisms by which capital undertakes exploitation, regardless of how such distribution of surplus takes place. Exploitation for Marx is embodied in the production of surplus value as the production of a commodity needs the use of labor to transform raw materials into commodities. Labor is, for Marx (1993), exploited in two interrelated ways. Exploitation occurs in the sense that labor needs to sell its capacity to work to capitalist agents in order to survive. However, it also occurs in the sense that it is labor that creates the value of the commodity, yet surplus value is distributed between capitalists and workers (and rentiers). Thus, as part of the value and therefore part of the effort exerted by workers is appropriated by third agents, exploitation is taking place (Marx 1993). Yet linking exploitation with the categories of rent and finance poses obvious theoretical complications.

First and foremost, the extraction of rents from non-developed land occurs before such land has been developed and thus value has been infused in that particular land. There is therefore an apparent contradiction 'between the law of value and the existence of rent on land' (Harvey 1982: 371). This apparent contradiction has provided the ground for a large number of authors to claim that rentierism and financialization are in fact detached from the sphere of production: for Lapavitsas (2014: 144) financial profit 'contains elements of surplus value but is, by construction, a broader category of profit that also includes other forms of monetary increments'. Lapavitsas (2014) argues that there is a zero-sum monetary exchange where financiers and rentiers extract rents through their intermediary role. This idea is also held for Piketty's (2014) $r > g$ hypothesis, which means that the rate of returns obtained by financial and rentier actors increases more than the rate of growth (in the productive sphere). The fact that rents in non-developed land are extracted before any productive activity takes place on that land reinforces Lapavitsas' and Piketty's perspectives.

Even though Marx claims that 'landed property has nothing to do with the process of production' and 'its role is confined to transferring a portion of the produced surplus-value from the pockets of capital to its own' (Marx 1993: 559), he did not elaborate in what sense and how the rent form can be extracted – and even be dependent on the production of surplus value – even if there is no production of surplus whatsoever. The key argument here is that land rents are an appropriation of a share of a surplus value that will be realized from that particular piece of non-developed land. In non-developed land, regardless of whether its potential productive use is realized or not, rent payments reflect the potential use that the land may have. Land rents embody potential exploitation of, in the case of housing, construction workers. The potential exploitation of workers is therefore captured by landowners in the form of land rents. Harvey (1982) treats land as a form of 'fictitious' capital insofar as the rent paid for this land is a claim on the *future* value that the land will have and thus the *future* labor exploitation. Christophers argues in this regard that the process of valorization of land and other assets is not only a process that stretches back in time (for instance throughout the 'dead labor' embodied in machinery) but also a 'process that stretches forward in time' (2016: 143). That is, the price that is paid for a piece of non-developed land is dependent on the value that the labor force will give to that land through its development. However, in the case of interest-bearing capital that is lent – for instance, to acquire land and to develop land – the money lent comes from surplus values based on past exploitation. For instance, the 'wall of money' (Fernandez & Aalbers, 2016) currently being used by key agents such as banks, hedge funds and real estate investment trusts in acquiring real estate assets across different urban settings around the globe (Yrigoy 2018, Christophers 2022) ultimately comes from corporate savings and/or laborers' wage-based savings; that is, it originally comes from past forms of exploitation. This surplus generated by past exploitation is the source of what is circulated in the form of interest-bearing capital.

The second complication is that the value of land as commodity is not only realized when it is sold after a process of valorization but in the case of dwellings that are sold or rented without any significant refurbishment rents are also extracted. In the case of real estate assets that have been produced in the past, the response by Marx is straightforward: capital fixes the product of labor in different forms and 'landed property' (Marx 1993: 560) fixes a portion 'in the form of rent'. The fact that rent is paid after the commodity is produced should not, according to Marx (1993), hide the fact that the substance of this rent ultimately comes from exploitation. One significant aspect that Marxian theory nonetheless needs to develop further is what occurs when appreciation takes place without significant revalorization. Rentierism is in this case, at least momentarily, not backed by any significant exploitation. Yet this appreciation without any significant increase in labor exploitation may be dependent on a demand that – especially in the case of housing – needs to acquire a commodity.

This links with a third element that needs to be taken into account: even if housing is sold as any other commodity, those who acquire the commodity of housing (either by acquiring or renting the house) are not doing so because they just want to consume but because a house (at least in the case of a primary house) is needed for social reproduction. The fact that acquiring a commodity is needed to survive denotes a *secondary* form of exploitation that does not take place in the production process but rather in the spaces of social reproduction; that is, in housing (Yrigoy 2021). By secondary form of exploitation, I understand here the share of dwellers' own wages that are destined to pay the necessary rents in order for them to be able to live in an accommodation. The extraction of land rents and interest-bearing capital is therefore not only based on primary but also on secondary forms of exploitation. As in the case of primary exploitation, the dialectical relation between past, present and future secondary exploitation is also important.

Last but not least, there are key interrelations between primary and secondary forms of exploitation. Note for instance the case of global corporate landlords, who are amongst the key land rentiers nowadays (Lima 2020). The investments being carried out by global corporate landlords ultimately originate in the idle money coming from sovereign funds from oil-producing countries such as Saudi Arabia or Norway and from pension funds from Germany, the United Kingdom and the United States, amongst others (Yrigoy 2021). The idle money comes, via different paths, from the productive sector; that is, from primary forms of exploitation. Whether from the corporate profits made directly or the wages saved by labor, the origins of such idle money are primary exploitation: exploitation that has been carried out in the past in the production process.

The fact that most of the 'wall of money' being fixed in housing does not come from corporate profits but from wages resulting from primary exploitation has massive political relevance for the understanding of the ultimate contradiction of capital embodied in urban forms. In other words, the idle money that is boosting the displacement of dwellers originates, in a very direct way, from labor exploitation: past wages (originating in primary exploitation) are being deployed in order to actually boost secondary forms of exploitation (wages being extracted in the form of land rents). This illustrates a dramatic contradiction arising within labor: the well-being of labor – through pension benefits – that was exploited in the past through primary forms of exploitation is dependent on current forms of secondary exploitation. If wages are not extracted in the form of land rents and interests for financial actors from a fraction of the labor force (e.g., tenants, new homeowners), there is no way by which the former workforce, exploited in the past, can have the minimum requirements to live.

This is in sum the problem of financialization and rentierism: it is not about which capitalist fraction is appropriating the surplus but rather the fact that financialization and rentierism are first of all mechanisms of capital circulation embedded in primary forms of exploitation that enforce secondary exploitation.

## CONCLUSIONS

If we are to understand the social and urban impacts of financialization and rentierism, we need to problematize what has been considered to be the problem of rentierism and financialization. If, following a long tradition of political economy studies, the focus is put on surplus distribution then the true implications of rentierism and financialization for the labor force will remain concealed. The ultimate problem of rentierism and financialization is not the distribution of surplus but the appropriation of the labor force.

Yet in order to fully grasp the dimensions of labor exploitation embedded in financialization there is a need to take into account two key dimensions of exploitation that are not usually considered: the variegated temporality and forms of exploitation. On the one hand, primary exploitation should not only be considered as the appropriation of social labor time in the exact moment that value is produced. Primary exploitation takes place in the process of producing a commodity and grabbing corporate profits. However, primary exploitation may not occur in the precise moment when land rents and interests are grabbed. This does not mean that primary exploitation is not a requirement in order for land rents and interests to be extracted. On the contrary, past and future exploitation is required in order for land rents to be extracted from the built environment, not least from housing.

On the other hand, the forms of exploitation suffered by the labor force are not only centered in the productive sphere but also in the sphere of social reproduction. Land rents and interests can be paid because of exploitation that has occurred/is occurring/will occur both in the productive sphere and in the sphere of social reproduction. Taking into account the secondary form of exploitation is necessary in order to unveil the ultimate contradiction of the fixation of idle money in housing: the present well-being of labor that was exploited in the past is ultimately dependent on the present exploitation of the workforce through the payment of rents to keep their own dwelling.

## REFERENCES

Aalbers, M. (2016) *Financialization of Housing: A Political Economy Approach*. London and New York: Routledge.

Abellán, J. (2023) *Alquiler, vivienda y mistificación del capital. Una crítica desde la escuela marxista a las teorías de la plusvalía inmobiliaria en la economía política urbana*. PhD thesis, Autonomous University of Madrid.

Arrighi, G. (1994) *The Long Twentieth Century: Money, Power, and the Origins of our Times*. London: Verso.

Christophers, B. (2015) The limits to financialization. *Dialogues in Human Geography* 5(2): 182–200.

Christophers, B. (2016) For real: Land as capital and commodity. *Transactions of the Institute of British Geographers* 41(2): 134–148.

Christophers, B. (2020) *Rentier Capitalism: Who Owns the Economy, and Who Pays for It?* London and New York: Verso Books.

Christophers, B. (2022) Mind the rent gap: Blackstone, housing investment and the reordering of urban rent surfaces. *Urban Studies* 59(4): 698–716.

De Brunhoff, S. (1976) *The State, Capital and Economic Policy*. London: Pluto Press.

Dillard, D. (1942) Keynes and Proudhon. *The Journal of Economic History* 2(1): 63–76.

Dillard, D. (1984) Keynes and Marx: A centennial appraisal. *Journal of Post Keynesian Economics* 6(3): 421–432.

Epstein, G. A. (ed.) (2005) *Financialization and the World Economy*. Cheltenham, UK and Northampton, MA, USA: Edward Elgar Publishing.

Fernandez, R. & Aalbers, M. B. (2016) Financialization and housing: Between globalization and varieties of capitalism. *Competition & Change* 20(2): 71–88.

Foster, J. B. (2007) The financialization of capitalism. *Monthly Review* 58(11): 1–12.

Haila, A. (1990) The theory of land rent at the crossroads. *Environment and Planning D: Society and Space* 8(3): 275–296.

Harvey, D. (1982) *The Limits to Capital*. London and New York: Verso Books.

Krippner, G. R. (2005) The financialization of the American economy. *Socio-economic Review* 3(2): 173–208.

Lapavitsas, C. (2014) *Profiting without Producing: How Finance Exploits Us All*. London and New York: Verso Books.

Lima, V. (2020) The financialization of rental housing: Evictions and rent regulation. *Cities* 105: 102787.

Mader, P., Mertens, D. & van der Zwan, N. (2020) Financialization: An introduction. In Mader, P., Mertens, D. & van der Zwan, N. (eds.) *The Routledge Handbook of Financialization*. Oxon and New York. Routledge, 1–16.

Marois, T. (2012) Finance, finance capital and financialization. In Fine, B., Saad Fliho, A. & Boffo, M. (eds.) *The Elgar Companion to Marxist Economics*. Cheltenham, UK and Northampton, MA, USA: Edward Elgar Publishing.

Marx, K. (1993) *Capital: A Critique of Political Economy. Volume III*. Penguin Books.

Mazzucato, M. (2018) *The Value of Everything: Making and Taking in the Global Economy*. London: Allen Lane.

Meek, R. L (1951) Physiocracy and classicism in Britain. *The Economic Journal* 61(241): 26–47.

Piketty, T. (2014) *Capital in the Twenty-first Century*. Cambridge, MA: Harvard University Press.

Smith, A. (1977) *An Inquiry into the Nature and Causes of the Wealth of Nations*. Chicago: University of Chicago Press.

Smith, N. (1979) Toward a theory of gentrification: A back to the city movement by capital, not people. *Journal of the American Planning Association* 45(4): 538–548.

Stockhammer, E. (2004) Financialisation and the slowdown of accumulation. *Cambridge Journal of Economics* 28(5): 719–741.

Ward, C. & Aalbers, M. B. (2016) 'The shitty rent business': What's the point of land rent theory? *Urban Studies* 53(9): 1760–1783.

Yrigoy, I. (2018) State-led financial regulation and representations of spatial fixity: The example of the Spanish real estate sector. *International Journal of Urban and Regional Research* 42(4): 594–611.

Yrigoy, I. (2021) The political economy of rental housing in Spain: The dialectics of exploitation(s) and regulations. *New Political Economy* 26(1): 186–202.

# PART II

# REVISITING DEBATES IN URBAN SOCIOLOGY

# 8. Renewing sociological research on the urban with Bourdieu

*Virgílio Borges Pereira*

Linked to research on the processes of social class formation, Pierre Bourdieu's sociology touched on a very wide range of themes and contexts. Crossing different social positions, the themes he dealt with were diverse, with the contexts involving a special attention to colonial Algeria and France, which he studied in different periods and with different methodologies, systematically under a relational mode of thought. The status of the relationship with physical space in Bourdieu's theoretical and methodological elaborations has been the subject of frequent discussion among sociologists and social scientists (Löw 2016, Reed-Danahay 2023). Equally important to this discussion is the status of state action itself. Revisiting the main themes of Bourdieu's sociological research, this chapter presents the way in which the French author's work integrated specific concerns with the understanding of the relations that social agents establish with physical space. Linking such relations with the social inscription of the agents, Bourdieu's proposals evolved and integrated themselves into the sociology of social space, being equally susceptible to articulation with the sociologies of the field of state action and of the economic field he promoted. Based on recent scholarship (Savage 2011, Wacquant 2018b), I argue that Bourdieu's sociological programme can be relevant for the constitution of a renewed sociological look at urban reality taking advantage of field analysis, the study of social spaces and their consequences in the analysis of relations with physical space. The city of Porto is an important urban context in Portuguese society, with dense social contrasts the conceptualisation of which gains consistency if informed by such a research programme. The sociological research that other scholars and I have conducted in the city of Porto illustrates the heuristic capacity associated with the mobilisation of Bourdieu's framework.

In this sense, and in short, I demonstrate at first that Bourdieu's concerns with the sociological conceptualisation of physical space are old. I stress in addition that such conceptualisations were progressively integrated into the theoretical programme, which led to the elaboration of concepts such as habitus, capital, and field gaining special salience when articulated with the concept of social space. The chapter goes on to demonstrate that the analytical coordinates deriving from these concepts have been stimulated in empirical research on differentiated urban contexts. It focuses specifically on the research potential involved in the use of this research programme for the sociological study of the city of Porto in Portugal.

## SOCIAL AND PHYSICAL SPACE

### The Ethnographic and Reflexive Genesis of a 'Total' Sociological Practice

Pierre Bourdieu's sociology developed from very early stages out of close attention to the study of the modes of (re)production of everyday practices and their inscription in the processes of social class formation. After studying philosophy at the École Normale Supérieure in Paris, Bourdieu arrived in Algeria in early 1956 to do part of his military service. On arrival in the country, he was confronted with a severe social transformation resulting from the war (which took place between 1954 and 1962) and the capitalist colonisation that the French state had been carrying out there since at least 1830. The experience of military service profoundly transformed Bourdieu's social and intellectual life, leading him from philosophy to anthropology and sociology (Bourdieu 2001 [1958], 2004, Addi 2002, Wacquant 2004, Yassine 2004, Martín-Criado 2008). Formatted in different ways and under the pretext of crisis situations, whether in colonial Algeria or soon afterwards in rural France, by the practice of engaged ethnographic observation (Pérez 2022a), the sociological work thus consummated intense dialogues with the philosophical thought that Bourdieu had cultivated in his academic training. Informed by the reading of G. Bachelard and the philosophers and historians of science, his training was defined by significant attention to phenomenology and to the study of the embodiment of temporal structures along the lines of the thought of E. Husserl and G. Canguilhem (Bourdieu 2004: 419). The analytical incursions at issue here include dense analyses of the processes of social class formation in which the relations with work, time, and space have their own value. With these concerns, Bourdieu's approach progressively summoned contributions coming from the research traditions inaugurated by Marx, Weber, Durkheim, and Cassirer (Wacquant 2018a).

In addition to a definition of life in the Arab city (Bourdieu 2001 [1958]: 54–59), the main results of the studies carried out by Bourdieu on urban Algeria began by highlighting the relevance of the division between proletariat and sub-proletariat and the impact on the latter of life defined around structural unemployment and uncertainty (Bourdieu 2021 [1963], 1977). Dedicated to the analysis of the crisis of Algerian traditional agriculture, *Le Déracinement* (*Uprooting*) (Bourdieu & Sayad 1964) in turn documented the process conducted by the French army between 1955 and 1962 of forced displacement and regrouping of peasant populations, with the aim of controlling nationalist resistance. At the beginning of the 1960s, more than two million Algerians were targeted by these processes (Bourdieu & Sayad 1964: 13), which hit the rural population particularly hard. Combined with the war, forced displacement accelerated the impoverishment of the rural inhabitants, who were transformed into 'dispeasanted peasants' (*paysans dépaysannés*) (Bourdieu & Sayad 1964: 115, 167). Based on fieldwork and surveys in the regions of Collo, Chélif, and Kabylia supported by the use of ethnographic photography (Bourdieu 2003a), this study documented the end of peasant agriculture. Regarding resettlements, Bourdieu and Sayad provided important contributions to the sociological analysis of the relationship between social morphology and physical space. By bringing differentiated groups together, the resettlement camp reveals itself to be a context of disruptive transformations of temporal rhythms, uses of space, and the peasant way of life (Bourdieu & Sayad 1964: 117–159).

First in Kabyle Algeria, then, and with the help of Sayad in his native Béarn in the south of France, Bourdieu definitively converted his gaze to sociology, entering it through one of its sub-disciplines more strongly concerned with the problem of space: rural sociology. In the first of the major studies on the subject, published in 1962, 'Célibat et condition paysanne' ['Celibacy and the Peasant Condition'] (Bourdieu 1962), and which, towards the end of his life, he would bring together in *Le Bal des célibataires* (*The Bachelors' Ball*) (Bourdieu 2002), Bourdieu tried to understand through ethnographic analysis, in-depth interviews, surveys, and the reconstitution of genealogies, and with the help of his close family (Heilbron & Issenhuth

2022), the crisis of the reproduction of the peasantry in France. Based on fieldwork carried out in 1959–1960, and already revealing many of the reflexive questions that would later define his sociology, Bourdieu attempted a dense portrait of the relationship between celibacy and the peasant condition. He deliberately appealed to his research experience in Algeria and drew at the same time the full consequences from a localised view of ethnographic research based on a 'total programme' of enquiry, as resulted from his reading of the influential ethnographic work of M. Maget (1962: XXXII, Pérez 2022b, Heilbron & Issenhuth 2022). To this end, Bourdieu defined the system of matrimonial exchanges in the past and identified the emergence of anomie in it. Marriage depended on a refined system of balances in which the late marriage and the reduction in the number of children was added to the celibacy of the youngest children and the regulation of the inheritance of land through dowry (Bourdieu 2002 [1962]: 26–40). After 1914, there was a progressive transformation of the peasant world in Béarn, which, by blocking the systems of traditional reproduction strategies, gave rise to a new profile of celibacy (Bourdieu 2002 [1962]: 44–54). The dynamics of marriage became dependent on other domains, such as lifestyles. The village society opened itself to the outside world, exposing the youngest, especially girls, to migration to the city. Marriage thus underwent a profound restructuring, the result of the extension of matrimonial areas to the town and of new divisions. Among them, Bourdieu highlighted the one that separated the inhabitants of the village (*bourg*), more exposed to urbanisation, from the peasant inhabitants of the dispersed cottages (*hameaux*). It became that those who lived in the cottages, and those who were older children, once heirs sought for marriage, had more difficulty in marrying. They were aged because they aged alone on the farms, they were the new bachelors (Bourdieu 2002 [1962]: 55–85). Bourdieu's impressive ethnographic objectivation of the Christmas ball in the village portrays 'a real clash of civilizations' in which those who have the objective and subjective conditions to dance are not peasants (Bourdieu 2002 [1962]: 113).

Written in 1963–1964, 'La maison kabyle' ('The Kabyle House') (Bourdieu 2019 [1969]) provides a refined framework of analysis for the relations between the social, the symbolic, and the physical space, becoming a milestone in Bourdieu's sociology. The relationship between the morphology of the physical space of the Kabyle peasant house and the social and symbolic operators invested in it by its inhabitants is presented. Bourdieu highlights the importance of significant spatial, social, and symbolic oppositions in the internal configuration of the house: 'The low, dark, nocturnal part of the house, place of damp, green or raw objects [...], place also of natural beings [...], of natural activities [...] and also of death, is opposed, like nature to culture, to the high, luminous, noble part, place of humans and in particular of the guest, of fire' (Bourdieu 2019 [1969]: 741, author's translation). In a complementary manner, this work makes it possible to explore the meaning of a theme dear to Bourdieu's relational mode of thought and underlines the relations of homology established between the oppositions constructed from the house, the female and male life worlds, and the outside world:

> [...] each of the parts of the house [...] is somehow qualified in two degrees, that is, firstly as feminine (nocturnal, dark, etc.) insofar as it participates in the universe of the house, and secondly as feminine or masculine insofar as it belongs to one or another of the divisions of this universe. [...] The house and, by extension, the village, [...] opposes under a certain aspect the empty fields of men [...] (Bourdieu 2019 [1969]: 749, author's translation)

Motivated by the experience of colonial domination in Algeria, the conversion of Bourdieu's gaze to sociology involved an original combination of civic and militant concerns that led him also to interrogate, almost simultaneously, his native peasant world in Béarn. Such a conversion, informed by in-depth readings of the anthropological literature on colonialism (Balandier 1951) and the sociological analysis of the rural world (Lefebvre 1963), above all involved embracing the programme of 'total' ethnographic analysis contained in the work of M. Maget (1962). With this, there occurred the progressive construction and renewal of analytical tools, such as the concept of 'habitus' (Pérez 2022a: 94, Heilbron & Issenhuth 2022: 105). Systematised theoretically in the writings that gave rise to the book *Esquisse d'une théorie de la pratique* [*Outline of a Theory of Practice*] (Bourdieu 1972), habitus is a mediating concept. By focusing on the body of the socialised individual, it accounts for the processes of 'interiorisation of exteriority' and 'exteriorisation of interiority'; it consists of socially constructed systems of dispositions that function as a matrix of perception, thought, and action and guide individuals in their responses to situations that occur in daily life (Wacquant 2005). The investigations around the peasant body or the relevance of photography in peasant daily life allowed Bourdieu to understand, as he advanced in the analysis of the localised expression of class inequalities, the specific meanings of the relation with physical space in these contexts.

**Socio-symbolic Topology, Place, and the State**

Continuously sensitive to the study of social classes, the domains of education and culture represented the most relevant areas of the sociological research conducted by Bourdieu throughout the 1960s. Associated with fundamental theoretical work, there were several analytical milestones in this process, some of them directly produced by Bourdieu, others more dependent on collective work in which he was influential. 'Différences et Distinctions' ('Differences and Distinctions') (Bourdieu 1966) was one such milestone. Here Bourdieu theorised the dynamics of the social, economic, and cultural transformations induced by France's post-war economic growth, focusing on the emergence of the middle classes, the contradictory demographic and social processes that underlay them, and the migrations from the countryside to the cities, along with what was implied in these in terms of peasant reconversion to urban life. The central argument of this work pointed out the relevance of distinctions through lifestyles and the processes of the respective class inscription.

Contemporary with this last work, J.-C. Chamboredon and M. Lemaire established decisive references for the sociological study of the city, giving special attention to the relationship between proximity in physical space and the constitution of social distances. 'Proximité spatiale et distance sociale: les grands ensembles et leur peuplement' ('Spatial Proximity and Social Distance: Large Housing Estates and their Settlement') (Chamboredon & Lemaire 1970) was the result of sociological research into the production of daily life in large social housing estates. Conceived and negotiated directly by Bourdieu with local authorities, the paper took as a reference the town of Antony in the southern suburbs of Paris, at the time the town where Bourdieu lived. According to Pasquali (2018), this research establishes a path markedly influenced by collective work around the social morphological legacy of M. Halbwachs (1938), the practice of ethnography as understood in the work of M. Maget (1962), and the reading of American interactionist sociology. As a result of French state interventions in the field of social housing, the high growth in the concentration of differentiated populations in these housing contexts called for specific renewed sociological perspectives on the relationships between social classes, space, and time: 'Within the same social class, social 'destiny' creates strongly opposed subcategories and the coexistence in space expresses the momentary meeting of very different social trajectories which spontaneous sociology confuses' (Chamboredon & Lemaire 1970: 10–11). To the homogenising ecological representation of the relations between physical spaces and social classes in social housing projects, Chamboredon and Lemaire's reading counterposed a portrait made of tensions arising from the coexistence in space of socially differentiated populations, an analysis of the crisis of neighbourhood solidarities, and the induction that this generates toward a greater demand on institutions. Moreover, the authors highlighted the emergence of stigmatisation processes that gave rise to different strategies for managing the 'self' in the daily life of these spaces (Pasquali 2018: 245–246).

Bourdieu's sociological research on culture and education developed throughout the second half of the 1960s and during the 1970s. In the process, Bourdieu deepened and transformed the sociological understanding of the processes of class formation (Wacquant 2013), inscribing the latter in a topological and relationally oriented perspective that made seminal analytical contributions in the paper 'Anatomie du goût' ('Anatomy of Taste') (Bourdieu & Saint-Martin 1976) and, above all, in *La Distinction* [*Distinction*] (Bourdieu 1979). In addition to the concept of habitus, this led him to stabilise other fundamental concepts of his sociology, such as those of 'capital' and 'field'. If habitus, as we have seen, refers to the systems of dispositions characteristic of the socialised body, capital concerns the resources, the 'energy of the social physics' (Bourdieu 1980: 209), generated in specific fields, which are in turn defined as historic spaces of social positions. The approach takes advantage of a theoretical and methodological framework, later fully conceived as 'participant objectivation' (Bourdieu 2003b), that combines questionnaire surveys and ethnographic analysis and uses sophisticated statistical analysis; in this case multiple correspondence analysis (MCA) (Rouanet et al. 2000). This research establishes coordinates for both the sociology of taste and the sociology of the social configurations in which the (re)production of taste is inscribed. Among the most significant implications associated with such an approach is the topological and relational conception of social and symbolic inequalities, and particularly the concept of 'social space'; equally relevant is the relationship of homology that is established between the latter and the spaces of lifestyles and position-taking (Bourdieu 1979: 140–141). In a more precise manner, at the heart of sociological reasoning is the understanding of social space based on a configuration structured around specific divisions – namely, divisions of the overall volume of the capital of social agents; of the structure/composition of the capitals of these agents, namely economic capital and cultural capital; and finally divisions in terms of the social trajectory of agents over time (past, present, and probable future). Such divisions are in turn homologous to those configured in terms of lifestyles: depending on the volume, structure, and trajectory of the agents' capitals there are significant relations with the sense of distinction, pretension, and necessity (Bourdieu 1979: 196). In each of the *regions* of the social space – namely bourgeois, petit bourgeois, and working class – significant shifts are marked out that are more sensitive to expressivity and to culture, more or less legitimised, and to the seniority of these shifts in the (dis)positions of social agents (Bourdieu 1979: 291–301, 391–398, 435–448). Analogous configurations are also identified in relation to politics (Bourdieu 1979: 526–541).

No less relevant is the sociological understanding of the relationship of homology that is thus established between the place occupied by agents in the social space and the physical space: '[…] the real social distance of a group to the goods must integrate the geographical distance that itself depends on the distribution of the group in space and, more precisely, on its distribution in relation to the economic and cultural 'core of values', that is, in relation to Paris or the great regional metropolises' (Bourdieu 1979: 136, 113, 552, author's translation).

Bourdieu had the opportunity to specify these analytical coordinates in some complementary texts, emphasising that: 'Social space tends to retranslate itself, in a more or less direct manner, into physical space in the form of a definite distributional arrangement of agents and properties. This means that all the distinctions proposed about physical space can be found in reified social space [...]' (Bourdieu 2018 [1991]: 107). Bourdieu also stressed that to the material aspects of the relation with the physical space, which are inscribed in the position occupied in the social space, one should also add the respective symbolic dimension. This is configured in the agents' practical dispositions and in their representations of the same physical space. Moreover, this argument is the central line of reasoning that he sustains in 'Effets de lieu' ('Site Effects'), one of his most relevant writings on the subject in *La Misère du monde* (*The Weight of the World*), the great collective work on social suffering that he coordinated and published in the early 1990s, when he states:

> The great social oppositions objectivated in physical space (e.g. capital/province) tend to be reproduced in minds and language in the form of oppositions that constitute a principle of vision and division, i.e. as categories of perception and appreciation or mental structures (Parisian/provincial, chic/non-chic, etc.). (Bourdieu 1993: 162, author's translation)

The prospect of sociological research that thus opens on the relationship between social space and physical space may also include complementary attention to the political action responsible for defining the configurations of physical space and its inscription in social space. Developed during the 1980s and 1990s, Bourdieu's research on state action and its relationship with the economic field in *Les Structures sociales de l'économie* (*The Social Structures of the Economy*) (Bourdieu 2000) made that analysis possible. It defined the social, economic, and political genesis of the decisions taken within the field of power, national and/or local, and the bureaucratic field regarding housing policy:

> It is in fact in the relations of force and struggle between, on the one hand, bureaucratic agents or institutions vested with different and often competing powers and endowed with sometimes antagonistic corporate interests and, on the other hand, institutions or agents (pressure groups, lobbies, etc.) who intervene to make their interests or those of their principals triumph that define, on the basis of antagonisms or alliances of interests and affinities of habitus, the regulations governing the world of real estate. (Bourdieu 2000: 116, author's translation)

Bourdieu, pursuing a sociology strongly engaged in ethnography and markedly topological from a social and symbolic point of view, did not immediately envisage himself as a sociologist of physical space. In any case, his incursions into rural contexts and the way in which he developed his theory and analysis of social space summoned him to specific readings of the relevance of the relations of homology between the divisions in social space and the divisions in socially produced and appropriated physical space. His developments in field theory, particularly in the fields of power, state action, and the economic field, also put into perspective the relevance of these fields in structuring the relations established by social agents with physical space.

## Using Bourdieu's Theory and Methods to Study the Urban

Even without being systematically put into perspective as such, the lines of analysis constructed by Bourdieu have the capacity to generate research programmes with promising results for the study of the relations between social space, symbolisation, and physical space.

Drawing consequences from the multidimensional and relational approach to inequalities promoted by Bourdieu's theory and method, several researchers have been fostering promising analyses from which research on the urban has benefited. For illustrative purposes, here are some significant milestones that intensify and extend Bourdieu's legacy in this domain. Rosenlund (2009), taking as a reference the case of the city of Stavanger in Norway, replicates the theory and method used by Bourdieu in *La Distinction* in one of the first empirically informed discussions of the approach, using data from a survey conducted in 1994. He studies social and symbolic divisions in the city, proving the relevance of overall volume and capital composition and divisions for understanding social space and the space of lifestyles (see also for an analysis of the Danish city of Aalborg Prieur et al. 2008). In addition to demonstrating the relevance of the sociological standpoint under analysis for understanding the city, this research has also opened a heuristic analytical perspective on the evolution of social space over time (Rosenlund 2019). Marom (2014) in turn has analysed the relationship between positions in the social space of Tel Aviv, Israel, and the logics of socio-spatial segregation according to dominant principles of distinction, also crossing the approach with a reading of the respective evolution over time. Laferté (2014), reassessing several decades of sociological research on French rural worlds but safeguarding the same significance for urban sociology, has highlighted the innovative capacity of sociological research on inequalities by referring to approaches grounded in localised social spaces.

With a more ethnographically inspired approach strongly linked to a collective and localised programme of research on social space, Cartier et al. (2016) explored the small trajectories of social mobility in a suburban context in northern Paris, deepening the knowledge of the residents' respective daily lives and the analysis of the social and symbolic tensions, objective and subjective, inscribed in the lives of these residents, almost always small owners of individual houses. Wacquant et al. (2014), drawing on the multi-sited and comparative ethnographic work developed by Wacquant (2008) in the hyperghetto of Chicago and in the antighetto of La Courneuve in the suburbs of Paris, combine the analysis of symbolic power proposed by Bourdieu with Goffman's analysis of 'deteriorated identity' to further the study of territorial stigmatisation and potentiate comparative research on the relationships between symbolisation, social space, and positioning in physical space in the most fragile urban regions. In seeking to capture the impact of territorial taint on the respective residents, the approach also focuses on street-level public bureaucracies and politicians (for an appraisal of this analytical framework, see Schultz Larsen & Delica 2019, 2021).

Extending this last line of analysis to research on political action in local contexts, Masclet (2003) developed a thick ethnographic work to document the social and symbolic recompositions that occurred in a large social housing estate in the Parisian red belt, analysing the declining relations with local politics here established. In a context historically dominated by the French Communist Party, the neighbourhood activists progressively lost space for representation and the possibility of encounters between them and most of the residents – workers, the poor, and often stigmatised individuals – within the local political and institutional contexts was lost.

At the heart of Bourdieu's sociology is an invitation to stimulate theoretically informed empirical research (Bourdieu & Wacquant 1992). The relevance of this invitation to the renewal of the study of the urban has been underlined in stimulating recent work. Slater (2021), drawing on an extensive research review, questions the place of ignorance and heteronomy in defining scientific and political portrayals of the unequal city; discussing gentrification, 'neighbourhood effects', the affordable housing crisis, and territorial stigmatisation, he takes up Bourdieu's work, among others, to assemble tools and arguments to dissolve the academic and political doxa on urban inequality. Deepening previous work (Wacquant 2008, 2018), Wacquant (2023) demonstrates, using an extensive review of the literature, the heuristic potential that can be associated with the mobilisation by urban research of the Bourdieusian concepts of habitus, social space, the bureaucratic field, and symbolic power, among others.

By discussing a research programme dedicated to the city of Porto in Portugal and its urban context, we show below some realisations of this potential.

## A BOURDIEU-INSPIRED RESEARCH PROGRAMME IN THE CITY OF PORTO

Having received Bourdieu's work early on, sociological research in Portugal developed in direct dialogue with his programme (Machado 2020, Madureira Pinto & Borges Pereira 2007). Documenting the socio-symbolic effects of the processes of the formation of the peasantry in the Portuguese northwest, the first two doctoral theses in sociology presented in Portuguese universities gave broad attention to the changing habitus of the peasant-workers of this region (Madureira Pinto 1985, Ferreira de Almeida 1986). Bourdieu's conception of sociological practice is here boosted from a relational reading of locally structured class inequalities. This framework was used for sociological research on other rural, industrial, and urban contexts in the transformation of the country (Borges Pereira 2011, Borges Pereira & Siblot 2017). In this sense, the city of Porto and its surroundings have been constituted as a ground for sociological objectivation, privileging specific domains of analysis. Sociability in the city, the social space of the city and its relationship with lifestyles, the evolution of the field of power (national and local) and its relationship with housing policy in the city, and the relationship between social housing policy, place, and territorial stigmatisation thus emerge as research themes benefiting from inspiration from Bourdieu's work.

**Sociability in the City Centre**

First, through the ethnography of intermediate space-times between work and family, such as those of cafés, combining the study of the respective practices of sociability with their inscription in the city centre (Borges Pereira 1995), and then with the deepening of the study of these practices in the parish of Vitória, in the historic centre of the city in several waves of research throughout the 1990s and 2000s, the studies on the city centre's sociability made it possible to document, in a context that saw its population ageing and the physical habitat under persistent degradation, a picture of poverty and social precariousness. This translated into a crisis of reproduction of the habitat, of significant segments of the present class fractions, specifically of routine employees and industrial workers, and of the respective lifestyles. This research identified the profound recompositions of the 'local matrix of habitus' that made possible the crisis of reproduction of the spaces and times of the urban 'popular cultures'. Preceding processes of gentrification and touristification (Queirós 2015), with these recompositions, patterns of social and symbolic relegation have emerged in the middle of the city's central and historic area (Borges Pereira & Madureira Pinto 2012).

**Social Space Formation and its Homologies**

Extending the same concerns and methodological orientations that underpinned the study of sociability practices in the historic city centre, a second domain of analysis combined the analysis of the processes of class formation with the study of the lifestyles of the residents (Borges Pereira 2005). Leveraging an approach using social space theory and the MCA methodology used by Bourdieu to develop the central arguments of *La Distinction*, the research made it possible to document the pertinence of Bourdieu's approach to the sociological understanding of the city and to corroborate the analytical propositions of his work on social space and lifestyles. Indeed, the research in Porto in the early 2000s, based on a questionnaire survey of household groups and ethnographic analysis in residential contexts, identified, through recourse to MCA, significant divisions in terms of the overall volume and structure of the capital of the city's residents (Borges Pereira 2018: 131–132). In addition to contributing to the definition of lifestyles likely to be read in terms of distinction, tension, and necessity (Borges Pereira 2016), the configuration of social space identified in the city revealed a significant relationship of homology with the physical space produced and appropriated by the respective residents (Borges Pereira 2018: 135). Ethnographic research on a neighbourhood scale reinforced the pertinence of these findings: the combination of the results of the ethnographic analysis with the study of the social trajectories and daily experiences of the residents, duly framed in the positions occupied by them in the local social spaces, made it possible to ascertain detailed sociological knowledge about the internal socio-economic hierarchies and symbolic boundaries of the different places in the city (Borges Pereira 2005).

**Field of Power and Housing Policy**

Based on the historical inscription of the city social space, a third research domain was dedicated to the study of the field of power and state action in the domain of housing in the city (Madureira Pinto 2019). Marked by significant housing problems that translated, for a good part of the 20th century, into housing absence, overcrowding, and dilapidated working-class accommodation, the city saw institutional responses to these problems emerge very slowly. Starting by targeting, in the first initiatives, social classes closer to the power of the state (Borges Pereira & Queirós 2013), and only much later targeting the most disadvantaged ones, the action of the central and local state in the city of Porto, although insufficient in quantity and social scope, gave rise to housing interventions that contributed to modifying the physical and social space of the city, revealing, in short, the city as a socio-political production. Reconstructing the genesis and the urban and social effects of the housing programmes carried out by the state during the 20th century in the city, this research made it possible to understand the ideological contradictions underlying the implementation of housing models (individual house vs collective housing; access through the promotion of property vs social renting) and the specific contributions that such policies made to the reconfiguration of the city social space (see Figure 8.1). With this, the state and the municipality became major housing owners and

*Source:* Miguel A. Martínez.

*Figure 8.1    Bouça cooperative housing in Porto (2006)*

the city of Porto a context, very original in the country, marked by a significant stock of social housing (Matos & Borges Pereira 2020, Borges Pereira & Queirós 2021, Machado 2012). This more socio-historical perspective was complemented by another dedicated to the understanding of how the capitalist urban rehabilitation market was more recently induced by the action of the state (Queirós et al. 2020). Similar perspectives to the latter were used to analyse the construction of the residential market in contexts adjacent to the city of Porto, revealing, once again and in different modalities and chronologies, the strong political imbrication to which the emergence and the action of the private housing market are subject and its relations with economic activity in the field of the construction industry (Coelho 2017, Lemos 2018, Borges Pereira et al. 2022).

**Place, Symbolisation, and Territorial Stigma**

The last strand of analysis was combined several times with localised analytical work on the relationships between the social and the symbolic. This research domain combined the study of the genesis of social housing policies with sociological analysis of the places to which they gave rise. In addition to reconstituting their political genesis and the respective social spaces, the analyses carried out privileged the study of the 'site effects' structured in these neighbourhoods (Borges Pereira 2017). It was also possible to document important processes of territorial stigmatisation in action (Wacquant et al., 2014) in the city combined with a dense world of neighbourhood relations. In sociological research conducted at the neighbourhood scale, which appealed to the methodological framework previously described, it was possible to launch between 2008 and 2010 a new wave of surveys and ethnographic work especially prepared for social housing estates produced and/or managed by the state. With this, the reconstitution of social spaces and spaces of residents' lifestyles revealed socially less homogeneous realities than commonly represented, as well as the existence of alternative strategies to face territorial stigma. It was possible to objectivate, among routine employees living in large social housing estates of the city's inner periphery, the emergence of 'subsistence sociability' and 'focused avoidance' as strategies for coping with the territorial stigma at work in and around these neighbourhoods while avoiding the high costs of exit and uncertain investment in collective action (Borges Pereira & Queirós 2014, Queirós, 2019). It was also possible to show that the social and political history of territorial stigma in the city was far from linear. Coinciding with the period after the April 1974 democratic revolution, specific social and political conditions enabled the paradoxical political mobilisation against extreme poverty, housing degradation, and stigmatisation of the inhabitants of the historic city centre. Although in their origin a remote possibility, the forms of contention (Tilly 1978) used by these residents realised, at least for a short period, a project of practical and symbolic improvement for their neighbourhood (Queirós & Borges Pereira 2018, Queirós 2015).

In short, Bourdieu's sociological theory and methods can be mobilised, with creativity and adaptations, to investigate urban reality. The city of Porto, in the light of this research framework, has been made the site of multidimensional and multi-level sociological research. Urban sociability analysed through the study of local matrices of habitus, the reading of socio-economic and cultural inequality using an analysis in terms of social space, the reconstitution of the action of the field of power in social housing in the city, and the study of symbolisation to understand, in detail and at the scale of the local neighbourhood, the effects of territorial stigmatisation are all analytical devices constructed with reference to Bourdieu's sociological work. The use of these devices in research on the city reveals its heuristic potential.

## CONCLUSIONS

Between the end of the 1950s and the beginning of the 1960s, because of the social, economic, cultural, and political shock represented by his experience of military service and life in colonial Algeria, Bourdieu faced an intellectual conversion and a reorientation of his intellectual path, taking him from philosophy, based on an intense experience of fieldwork, to anthropology and then to sociology. This fieldwork experience allowed him to impressively register the set of major social ruptures experienced by Algerians. The socio-spatial implications of such processes did not fail to be enshrined in his analyses and were combined with those he gradually began to develop for his native rural France. The progressive autonomisation of the central concepts of his praxeological sociological programme, in particular the concepts of habitus, capital, and field, involved a redefinition of the problem of social classes based on the concept of social space. In addition to the homological relationships between social space and the processes of symbolisation, Bourdieu, in individual and collective work, was able to draw consequences of the same nature in relation to socially produced and appropriated physical space. In the same way, he highlighted the importance of relations with the field of power and with the economic field itself in the production and reproduction of physical space. In their different aspects, the analytical strands contained in Bourdieu's research programme are being mobilised to promote innovative research on urban reality. The sociological research carried out in the city of Porto, exploring strands of analysis influenced by Bourdieu's research dedicated to sociability, social space, the evolution of housing policies, and the site effects and the meaning of territorial stigmatisation, allows us to identify analytical paths that can contribute to a renewal of the urban research agenda. At the heart of the approach is the production of empirical, theoretically informed research using the concept of social space, employed at different scales in the city and actively articulated with the analysis of the field of power and state action.

## REFERENCES

Addi, L. (2002) *Sociologie et anthropologie chez Pierre Bourdieu.* Paris, France: Éditions La Découverte.

Balandier, G. (1951) La situation coloniale: approche théorique. *Cahiers internationaux de sociologie* XI: 44–79.

Borges Pereira, V. (1995) Café com quê?!, uma análise sobre práticas semipúblicas de sociabilidade em espaços/ tempos intermediários da Baixa portuense. *Sociologia: revista da Faculdade de Letras da Universidade do Porto* 5: 151–176.

Borges Pereira, V. (2005) *Classes e Culturas de Classe das Famílias Portuenses: classes sociais e 'modalidades de estilização' da vida na cidade do Porto.* Porto, Portugal: Edições Afrontamento.

Borges Pereira, V. (2011) Experiencing unemployment: The roles of social and cultural capital in mediating economic crisis. *Poetics – Journal of Empirical Research on Culture, the Media and the Arts* 39: 469–490. https://doi.org:10.1016/j.poetic.2011.09.005.

Borges Pereira, V. (2016) The structuration of lifestyles in the city of Porto: A relational approach. In L. Hanquinet & M. Savage (eds.) *Routledge International Handbook of the Sociology of Art and Culture.* London, England: Routledge, 421–435.

Borges Pereira, V. (2017) Society, space and the effects of place: Theoretical notes and results of a sociological research on social housing in the city of Porto. In M. M. Mendes, T. Sá & J. Cabral (eds.) *Architecture and the Social Sciences: Inter- and Multidisciplinary Approaches between Society and Space.* Dordrecht, Germany: Springer, 99–120. https://doi.org/10.1007/978-3-319-53477-0_8.

Borges Pereira, V. (2018) Urban distinctions: Class, culture and sociability in the city of Porto. *International Journal of Urban and Regional Research* 42(1): 126–137. https://doi:10.1111/1468-2427.12532.

Borges Pereira, V. & Madureira Pinto, J. (2012) Espace, relations sociales et culture populaire dans le cœur ancien de la ville de Porto. *Sociétés contemporaines* 86: 113–133. https://doi.org/10.3917/soco.086.0113.

Borges Pereira V. & Queirós, J. (2013) Une maison pour le peuple portugais: Genèse et trajectoire d'un quartier du programme des «maisons économiques» à Porto (1938–1974), *Politix* 101: 49–78. https://doi.org/10.3917/pox.101.0049.

Borges Pereira, V. & Queirós, J. (2014) 'It's not a Bairro, is it?': Subsistence sociability and focused avoidance in a public housing estate. *Environment and Planning A: Economy and Space* 46(6): 1297–1316. https://doi.org/10.1068/a46300.

Borges Pereira, V. & Queirós, J. (2021) State, social housing and the changing city: Porto's 1956 improvement plan. In R. Garcia Ramos, V. Borges Pereira, M. Rocha & S. Dias da Silva (eds.) *Hidden in Plain Sight: Politics and Design in State-subsidized Residential Architecture.* Zürich, Switzerland: Park Books, 255–270.

Borges Pereira, V., Rodrigues, V., Coelho, M. I. & Lemos, T. (2022) Class formation and social reproduction strategies in the Portuguese construction industry. Elements for a relational sociological analysis. In C. Hugrée, É. Penissat, A. Spire & J. Hjelbrekke (eds.) *Class Boundaries in Europe. The Bourdieusian Approach in Perspective.* London and New York: Routledge, 116–136.

Borges Pereira V. & Siblot, Y. (2017) Comparer les classes populaires en France et au Portugal: Différences structurelles et histoires intellectuelles. *Actes de la recherche en sciences sociales* 219: 56–79. https://doi.org/10.3917/arss.219.0056.

Bourdieu, P. (1962) Célibat et condition paysanne. *Études rurales* 5–6: 32–135.
Bourdieu, P. (1966) Différences et Distinctions. In H. J. Darras (ed.) *Le Partage des bénéfices, expansions et inégalités en France*. Paris, France: Éditions de Minuit, 117–129.
Bourdieu, P. (1972) *Esquisse d'une théorie de la pratique: Précédé de «Trois études d'ethnologie kabyle»*. Geneva, Switzerland: Librairie Droz.
Bourdieu, P. (1977) *Algérie 60*. Paris, France: Éditions de Minuit.
Bourdieu, P. (1979) *La Distinction. Critique sociale du jugement*. Paris, France: Éditions de Minuit.
Bourdieu, P. (1980) *Le Sens pratique*. Paris, France: Éditions de Minuit.
Bourdieu, P. (1993) Effets de Lieu. In P. Bourdieu (ed.) *La Misère du Monde*. Paris, France: Éditions du Seuil, 159–167.
Bourdieu, P. (2000) *Les Structures sociales de l'économie*. Paris, France: Éditions du Seuil.
Bourdicu, P. (2001 [1958]) *Sociologie de l'Algérie*. Paris, France: Presses Universitaires de France.
Bourdieu, P. (2002) *Le Bal des célibataires*. Paris, France: Éditions du Seuil.
Bourdieu, P. (2003a) *Images d'Algérie: une affinité élective*. Paris, France: Éditions Actes Sud.
Bourdieu, P. (2003b) Participant objectivation. *Journal of the Royal Anthropological Institute* 9(2): 281–294. https://doi.org/10.1111/1467-9655.00150.
Bourdieu, P. (2004) Algerian landing. *Ethnography* 4: 415–443. shttps://doi.org/10.1177/1466138104 048826.
Bourdieu, P. (2018 [1991]) Social Space and the genesis of appropriated physical space. *International Journal of Urban and Regional Research* 42(1): 106–114. https://doi.org/10.1111/1468-2427.12534.
Bourdieu, P. (2019 [1969]) La maison Kabyle ou le monde renversé. In C. Lévi-Strauss, J. Pouillon & P. Maranda (eds.) *Échanges et communications, II: Mélanges offerts à Claude Lévi-Strauss à l'occasion de son 60ème anniversaire*. Berlin, Germany and Boston, USA: De Gruyter Mouton, 739–758. https://doi.org/10.1515/9783111698281-002.
Bourdieu, P. (2021 [1963]) *Travail et travailleurs en Algérie, édition revue et actualisée*. Paris, France: Éditions Raisons d'Agir.
Bourdieu, P. & Saint-Martin (1976) Anatomie du goût. *Actes de la recherche en sciences sociales* 5: 2–81.
Bourdieu, P. & Sayad, A. (1964) *Le Déracinement. La crise de l'agriculture traditionnelle en Algérie*. Paris, France: Éditions de Minuit.
Bourdieu, P. & Wacquant, L. (1992) *An Invitation to Reflexive Sociology*. Oxford, England: Polity Press.
Cartier, M., Coutant, I., Masclet, O. & Siblot, Y. (2016) *The France of the Little-Middles. A Suburban Housing Development in Greater Paris*. Oxford, England: Berghahn Books.
Chamboredon, J. C. & Lemaire, M. (1970) Proximité spatiale et distance sociale: les grandes ensembles et leur peuplement. *Revue française de sociologie* 11(1): 3–33.
Coelho, M. I. (2017) *Recomposição do Território e Estruturação do Quotidiano no Grande Porto. Sociologia de um lugar de Ermesinde: Gandra (1950–2014)*. Doctoral thesis, University of Porto.
Ferreira de Almeida, J. (1986) *Classes Sociais nos Campos. Camponeses parciais numa região do Noroeste*. Lisbon, Portugal: Instituto de Ciências Sociais.
Halbwachs, M. (1938) *La Morphologie sociale*. Paris, France: Armand Colin.
Heilbron, J. & Issenhuth, P. (2022) Une recherche anamnestique, le Béarn. In J. Duval, J. Heilbron & P. Issenhuth (eds.) *Pierre Bourdieu et l'art de l'invention scientifique. Enquêter au Centre de sociologie européenne (1959–1969)*. Paris, France: Classiques Garnier, 71–120.
Laferté, G. (2014) Des études rurales à l'analyse des espaces sociaux localisés. *Sociologie* 5: 423–439. https://doi.org/10.3917/socio.054.0423.
Lefebvre, H. (1963) *La Vallée de Campan. Étude de sociologie rurale*. Paris, France: Presses Universitaires de France.
Lemos, T. (2018) *L'Espace comme croyance. La formation du quartier de Matosinhos-Sul*. Doctoral thesis, PSL Research University.
Löw, M. (2016) *The Sociology of Space. Materiality, Social Structures, and Action*. Basingstoke, England: Palgrave Macmillan.
Machado, F. L. (2020) *Sociologia em Portugal. Da pré-história à institucionalização avançada*. Porto, Portugal: Edições Afrontamento.
Machado, I. (2012) *Lutas sociais, habitação e quotidiano: análise da génese e estruturação do Bairro da Bouça na cidade do Porto (do SAAL à solução cooperativa)*. Doctoral thesis, University of Porto.

Madureira Pinto, J. (1985) *Estruturas Sociais e Práticas Simbólico-Ideológicas nos Campos. Elementos de teoria e de pesquisa empírica*. Porto, Portugal: Edições Afrontamento.

Madureira Pinto, J. (2019) Institutions, dispositions et pratiques: le cas de la production du logement. In V. Borges Pereira & Y. Siblot (eds.) *Classes sociales et politique au Portugal. Pratiques du métier de sociologue*. Vulaines-sur-Seine, France: Éditions du Croquant, 63–97.

Madureira Pinto, J. & Borges Pereira, V. (eds.) (2007) *Pierre Bourdieu, a Teoria da Prática e a Construção da Sociologia em Portugal*. Porto, Portugal: Edições Afrontamento.

Maget, M. (1962) *Guide d'étude directe des comportements culturels*. Paris, France: CNRS.

Marom, N. (2014) Relating a city's history and geography with Bourdieu: One hundred years of spatial distinction in Tel Aviv. *International Journal of Urban and Regional Research* 38(4): 1344–1362. https://doi.org/10.1111/1468-2427.12027.

Martín-Criado, E. (2008) *Les Deux Algéries de Pierre Bourdieu*. Bellecombe-en-Bauges, France: Éditions du Croquant.

Masclet, O. (2003) *La Gaúche et les cités. Enquête sur un rendez-vous manqué*. Paris, France: Éditions La Découverte.

Matos, F. & Borges Pereira, V. (2020) Geografia social – Habitação: problemas e políticas. In J. A. Rio Fernandes (ed.) *Geografia do Porto*. Porto, Portugal: Book Cover, 130–143.

Pasquali, P. (2018) Une 'école de Chicago' en banlieue parisienne? Jean-Claude Chamboredon et la délinquance juvénile, de l'enquête à l'article. In G. Laferté, P. Pasquali & N. Renahy, *Le Laboratoire des Sciences Sociales. Histoires d'enquêtes et revisites*. Paris, France: Éditions Raisons d'Agir, 235–291.

Pérez, A. (2022a) *Combattre en sociologues. Pierre Bourdieu & Abdelmalek Sayad dans une guerre de liberation (Algérie, 1958-1964)*. Marseille, France: Agone.

Pérez, A. (2022b) Les révélations du terrain. Les premières experiences ethnographiques de Pierre Bourdieu et Abdelmalek Sayad. In J. Duval, J. Heilbron & P. Issenhuth (eds.) *Pierre Bourdieu et l'art de l'invention scientifique. Enquêter au Centre de sociologie européenne (1959–1969)*. Paris, France: Classiques Garnier, 41–69.

Prieur, A., Rosenlund, L. & Skjott-Larsen, J. (2008) Cultural capital today: A case study from Denmark. *Poetics – Journal of Empirical Research on Culture, the Media and the Arts* 36(1): 45–71. https://doi.org:10.1016/j.poetic.2008.02.008.

Queirós, J. (2015) *No Centro, à Margem: sociologia das intervenções urbanísticas e habitacionais do Estado no centro histórico do Porto*. Porto, Portugal: Edições Afrontamento.

Queirós, J. (2019) *Aleixo: génese, (des)estruturação e desaparecimento de um bairro do Porto (1969–2019)*. Porto, Portugal: Edições Afrontamento.

Queirós, J. & Borges Pereira, V. (2018) Voices in the revolution: Resisting territorial stigma and social relegation in Porto's historic centre (1974–1976). *The Sociological Review* 66(4): 857–876. https://doi.org/10.1177/0038026118777423.

Queirós, J., Rodrigues, V. & Borges Pereira, V. (2020) O Mercado da Reabilitação Urbana enquanto construção política: resultados de um percurso de pesquisa na cidade do Porto. In V. Borges Pereira (ed.) *Em (Re)Construção: elementos para uma sociologia da atividade na indústria da construção em Portugal*. Porto: University of Porto, 319–368.

Reed-Danahay, D. (2023) *Bourdieu and Social Space: Mobilities, Trajectories, Emplacements*. Oxford, England: Berghahn.

Rosenlund, L. (2009) *Exploring the City with Bourdieu: Applying Pierre Bourdieu's Theories and Methods to Study the Community*. Saarbrücken, Germany: VDM Verlag.

Rosenlund, L. (2019) The persistence of inequalities in an era of rapid social change. Comparisons in time of social spaces in Norway. *Poetics* 74: 101323. https://doi.org/10.1016/j.poetic.2018.09.004.

Rouanet, H., Ackermann, W. & Le Roux, B. (2000) The geometric analysis of questionnaires: The lesson of Bourdieu's *La Distinction*. *Bulletin of Sociological Methodology/Bulletin de Méthodologie Sociologique* 65(1): 5–18. https://doi.org/10.1177/0759106318795218.

Savage, M. (2011) The lost urban sociology of Pierre Bourdieu. In G. Bridge & S. Watson (eds.) *The New Blackwell Companion to the City*. London, England: Blackwell Publishing Ltd, 511–520.

Schultz Larsen, T. & Delica, K. (2019) The production of territorial stigmatisation. *City* 23: 540–563. https://doi.org/10.1080/13604813.2019.1682865.

Schultz Larsen, T. & Delica, K. N. (2021). Territorial destigmatisation in an era of policy schizophrenia. *International Journal of Urban and Regional Research* 45(3): 423–441. https://doi.org/10.1111/1468-2427.12994.

Slater, T. (2021) *Shaking Up the City. Ignorance, Inequality and the Urban Question*. Berkeley, USA: University of California Press.

Tilly, C. (1978) *From Mobilization to Revolution*. Harlow, England: Longman Higher Education.

Wacquant, L. (2004) Following Pierre Bourdieu into the field. *Ethnography* 5(4): 387–414. https://doi.org/10.1177/1466138104052259.

Wacquant, L. (2005) Habitus. In J. Beckert & M. Zafirowski (eds.) *International Encyclopedia of Economic Sociology*. London, England: Routledge, 317–320.

Wacquant, L. (2008) *Urban Outcasts: A Comparative Sociology of Advanced Marginality*. Oxford, England: Polity Press.

Wacquant, L. (2013) Symbolic power and group-making: On Pierre Bourdieu's reframing of class. *Journal of Classical Sociology* 13(2): 274–291. https://doi.org/10.1177/1468795X12468737.

Wacquant, L. (2018a) Four transversal principles for putting Bourdieu to work. *Anthropological Theory* 18(1): 3–17. https://doi.org/10.1177/1463499617746254.

Wacquant, L. (2018b) Bourdieu comes to town. Pertinence, principles, applications. *International Journal of Urban and Regional Research* 42(1): 90–105. https://doi.org/10.1111/1468-2427.12535.

Wacquant, L. (2023) *Bourdieu in the City. Challenging Urban Theory*. Oxford, England: Polity Press.

Wacquant, L., Slater, T. & Borges Pereira, V. (2014) Territorial stigmatization in action. *Environment and Planning A: Economy and Space* 46(6): 1270–1280. https://doi.org/10.1068/a4606ge.

Yassine, T. (2004) Pierre Bourdieu in Algeria at war. Notes on the birth of an engaged ethnosociology. *Ethnography* 4: 487–509. https://doi.org/10.1177/1466138104050703.

# 9. Urban social ecology and neighbourhood effects revisited

*Ngai-Ming Yip*

The neighbourhood has been, and still is, a hot topic in urban sociology. Since its inception over 100 years ago, the urban socio-ecological approach of the Chicago school of sociology has been the dominating perspective in this field. Using natural ecology, the survival of the fittest, as an analogy, the spatial distributions and composition of neighbourhoods are seen as the consequences of a series of competition and invasions by a succession of individuals and social groups across spatial boundaries. These invasions are driven by group functional imperatives, technical advancements, and population dynamics. Coupled with the rising popularity of the Chicago school of neo-classical economics in the 1950s and 1960s, 'by the 1960s, urban studies had crystallised into a hegemonic blend of the social and spatial theories of the Chicago school infused with the methods and assumptions of neo-classical economics' (Slater 2021: 120). It has been further boosted by both advancements in research methodology, like new statistical tools and sophisticated experimental designs, and the availability of finer empirical data through panel surveys and geographic information systems (GISs), urban ecological studies, social area analysis, and factor analysis.

According to the Chicago school of urban ecology, it is the ecological factors of the city that shape the neighbourhood. Even though the city plan 'imposes an orderly arrangement ... each separate part of the city is inevitably stained with the peculiar sentiment of its population ... a locality with sentiments, traditions, and a history of its own' (Park 1915: 579). Park also hinted at the concept of a 'neighbourhood effect' as '[the neighbourhood] exercises a decisive selective influence upon [the] city population and shows itself ultimately in a marked way in the characteristics of the inhabitants' (Park 1915: 583).

The idea that the 'naturalness' of competition, technical change, and collective adaptation within cities are the drivers of neighbourhood change was fiercely challenged by critical scholars of political economy and the 'new' urban sociology, which maintains that the domination and subordination of social groups across spatial boundaries comes from the proactive action or inaction of such groups in the pursuit of their particular social, economic, and political interests. In this respect, the neighbourhood has to be placed within the dynamic of social inequality, which is embedded in the political economy of the city and a hierarchical global system of competitive capitalism. This theoretical strand connects neighbourhood effects with the reproduction of class relations within the specific local processes and events in the neighbourhood and links up with a large volume of qualitative research on the neighbourhood that takes the neighbourhood as a place and examines specific social relations and interactions across a wide range of social phenomena, like bonding, cohesion, segregation, exclusion, etc.

Yet such scepticism did not have a great impact on urban sociologists' interest in neighbourhood effect research at the time. Instead, other aspects of such research grew exponentially in the 1990s and the early decades of the 21st century (Van Ham et al. 2012). One of the underlying forces pushing for the continuing popularity of the theory may be the policy initiatives regarding area-based intervention for social engineering, poverty alleviation, mitigation of social exclusion, and segregation. Apart from the convenience and cost efficiency approach that the scale of the neighbourhood is able to offer for urban sociology research, the findings coming from the neighbourhood effect research are also instrumental in policy lobbying, as well as in the assessment of state initiatives regarding area-based policies and programmes.

However, the abundance of research findings on neighbourhood effects does not seem to offer a great advancement of our knowledge about them. Recent empirical studies on labour markets and education outcomes, based on carefully designed methodologies and sophisticated statistical instruments, have found little or even no statistically significant contribution coming from neighbourhood effects (Galster 2012). Hence, there have been queries on whether neighbourhood effects as an 'unobserved' variable are really relevant to the understanding of the behavioural or health outcomes of an individual. There is a need to thoroughly rethink how we frame the relevant factors, the mechanisms, the processes, and other mediating and counteracting factors in the study of neighbourhood effects (Slater 2021).

It is not realistic to offer a comprehensive critical review of the Chicago school of urban ecology in a short chapter. Hence, this chapter seeks to engage in a critical review of the urban socio-ecological approach to the study of neighbourhood effects and the recent challenges from new (critical) urban sociology, as well as the issues the study of neighbourhood effects have to resolve. A re-examination of neighbourhood effects in such a context would help to shed light on the building of theories of neighbourhood effects, as well as on the policy discourse that relates to neighbourhood effects, like mixed neighbourhoods, social mixing policies, etc.

One point regarding nomenclature needs to be noted. Although we often refer to the ecological approach of the Chicago school of urban sociology as 'urban ecology' or 'urban social ecology', Park (1915) first used the term 'human ecology', which he borrowed from his colleagues H. Barrow (Abu-Lughod 1991) and R. McKenzie (1924), to describe it. The term 'urban ecology' first appeared in the paper by McKenzie (1925) titled 'The scope of urban ecology'. The term 'urban social ecology' began to be used in academic writing from the 1970s onwards. However, the Chicago school urban ecological approach is just one among the dozen or so disciplines that have incorporated elements of natural ecology or used an ecological analogy in their research (up to the early 1970s) (Young 1974). In recent years, a new multidisciplinary subject called 'urban ecology' has been promoted. Over 1000 articles from 2018 to early 2022 with urban ecology mentioned in their abstracts were found with a simple Google Scholar search. These articles cover issues across a wide variety of social science, technology, environmental, and policy disciplines, like land use, energy, urban design, greenhouse gas emission, sustainable development, smart cities, biodiversity, urban wild life, urban forestry, etc. In this chapter, the terms 'urban social ecology' and 'urban ecology' do not cover issues of such environmental or technology concerns. The terms 'urban social ecology' and 'urban ecology' are used interchangeably to denote the concept advocated by the Chicago school of sociology connected to the study of the neighbourhood.

# THE NEIGHBOURHOOD AND THE CHICAGO SCHOOL OF URBAN ECOLOGY

The Chicago school of urban ecology opened up a new front of empirical research on small spatial locations with the primary aim of studying social pathologies created by the complex interaction of urban institutions and human inhabitants in quickly expanding cities and their populations. The seminal work of Park (1915: 578) on the city concerns the impacts of the moral and physical organisation of the city, which 'mould and modify one other' and open up the 'crucial focus of human ecology ... that people create their city but then cities shape their lives' (Abu-Lughod 1991: 190).

Borrowing from the theoretical approach of natural ecology, the Chicago school of urban sociology attempted to study the city by making an analogy between the city and plants and animals, which need to adapt to the natural environment and compete for resources in a given location. As Hawley (1944: 403) explains, 'ecology is concerned with the elemental problem of how growing, multiplying beings maintain themselves in a constantly changing but ever restricted environment'. The human community possesses mechanisms, amidst the continual competition for resources, to regulate the behaviour of its members and to preserve the balance between resources and population (Park 1936). Such a balance will be maintained until the introduction of some innovation (e.g. new technology) that starts a new cycle of adjustment to a new equilibrium (McKenzie 1924). Like plants and animals in the natural ecosystem, invasion and succession are processes of group displacement in human society. In this respect, it is often 'a higher economic group [that] drives out the lower-income inhabitants, thus enacting a new cycle of the succession' (McKenzie 1926: 153).

However, in their ecological approach to studying changes in the social order of the city, early scholars of the Chicago school had more interest in pioneering tools to aid in the discovery of the patterns of urban change rather than the theories that would account for such patterns. This opened up a new academic tradition in the empirical study of the city involving the painstakingly tedious collection of quantitative data (e.g. Burgess 1925a) on the one hand and in-depth participant observations collecting ethnographic data around people and activities in specific locations (e.g. Zorbaugh 1929) on the other hand.

Although it was the city's spatial order that earlier scholars of the Chicago school sought to discover (e.g. the work of Park, Burgess, etc.), much of their empirical work had instead started with small locality-based neighbourhoods, not least because studying the whole city is resource-demanding and hence making detailed observations of small localities was more feasible. For Park (1915: 580), the neighbourhood is also one of the salient building blocks of a city besides other institutions like families, economic organisations, schools, and churches, so that neighbourhoods '[with their] proximity and neighbourly contact are the basis for the simplest and most elementary form of association with which we have to do in the organisation of city life'.

As urban ecology was built on the premise of 'natural order' in human society and as 'the product of orderly working of natural laws ... [it] is inevitable and hence predictable' (Alihan 1964: 50). Urban ecologists therefore believed in the existence of a 'natural area' in the city which 'comes into existence without design, and performs a function' (Park 1929: 9, cited in Alihan 1964). Such natural areas provide a community for the residents of the neighbourhood. Zorbaugh (1926: 223) defined these natural areas as 'a geographic area characterised both by a physical individuality and by the cultural characteristics of the people who lived in it'.

Hence, as the early social ecologists were also social reformists who aligned themselves with a liberal-democratic ethos, it would be more effective if their work could be done in these 'natural areas'. This also acted as an important driving force behind the intensive study of the neighbourhood in the 1920s and 1930s. It is also believed to be one rationale behind the development of census tracts (Schmid et al. 1958, cited in Abu-Lughod 1991). However, despite this intensive research effort, no coherently defined nor logically classified natural areas were discovered (Alihan 1964). Hence, the idea of the natural area was criticised for being only a construct of the researchers rather than something that actually exists (Abu-Lughod 1991). The study of natural areas thus gradually lost favour.

Notwithstanding the discontinuation of research that looked for the existence and underlying structure of natural areas, empirical studies of small areas continued to be an identified feature of the Chicago school of urban ecology. Burgess, inspired by mapping works in Europe, produced maps of social issues in Chicago together with his students that helped him to develop the insight for his seminal concentric zoning model of the growth of the city (Burgess 1925a), which connects the ecological factors involved in the competition of social groups that shape land use with the equilibrium of economic activities when the city expands. This mapping method, combined with the underlying concern for the geographic and social characteristics in the quest for natural areas, galvanised the development of social area analysis in the study of the city of Los Angeles (Shevky & Williams 1949) along the dimensions of class, family, and race to uncover 'social areas' that shared similar characteristics. Sociologists like Suzanne Keller and W. F. Whyte also employed the concept of natural areas in their research on the neighbourhood (Whyte 1943, Keller 1966). More recently, inspired by the mapping of Burgess, Davis (1998) produced a map of fear in Los Angeles in his analysis of the city in which the rich and the poor are segregated into 'gulag rims'. Likewise, Hannerz (1980), despite his criticism of the Chicago school approach to studying the city, adopted the premises of the Chicago school (particularly those of Wirth) to guide his network analysis of the life of the city.

A similar approach in studying small areas but in a reverse direction was pioneered by Bell (1955), who employed the method of factor analysis using a large number of social indicators to derive the underlying 'factors' without the need for pre-determined dimensions. Social area analysis and factorial ecology are examples of the quantitative analysis of the neighbourhood as they often use neighbourhood/census tracts as their unit of analysis. With the advancement of global positioning system (GPS) techniques and the availability of rich GIS data, social area analysis has been further enhanced, now with even wider applications.

## CRITIQUE OF THE URBAN ECOLOGICAL AND THE NEIGHBOURHOOD EFFECTS APPROACHES

Despite the popularity of the approach of the Chicago school of urban ecology, it has been criticised for building up concepts fundamental to the ecological analysis of the city and the neighbourhood that are confusing and internally inconsistent. Such inconsistency is not only found between different writers of the urban ecology school but also between writings of the same author. As Alihan (1964) notes, frequently interchanging usage of the concepts of society and community, the basic building blocks of the ecological analysis, has been employed without rigorous conceptualisation, causing confusion. Conceptual confusion also appears in the discussion of ecological organisation, economic organisation, and cultural and political organisations, all of which are at the heart of the subsequent neighbourhood effect discussion.

Likewise, Vasishth and Sloane (2002) identified flaws in the urban ecological approach in that it does not differentiate the influence of the community (neighbourhood effect) from the attributes of the residents who live in the neighbourhood. If the neighbourhood (community) is more than the sum of individuals, 'then community must be described at its own level of organization … community level patterns and processes as distinct from patterns and processes in populations of individuals' (Vasishth & Sloane (2002: 350). While the form and structure of the neighbourhood can be observed from its residents' attributes or behaviour, it would be problematic to infer such observations are the result of the underlying process of the neighbourhood, as it in turn influences the behaviour of the residents.

Perhaps the fiercest attack on the urban ecological approach started in the early 1970s. It was not directed against its conceptual clarity or consistency but against the ultimate premises of urban ecology and the ontological existence of neighbourhood effects per se. David Harvey, in his seminal work *Social Justice and the City*, challenged the basic assumptions of ecological determinism in which the ecological outcomes are generated by economic competition or cultural symbols (Park 1915). It is how real economic resources are distributed that shapes the urban form (Harvey 1973). While Park maintained that the urban ecology school interprets the spatial outcomes as a product of a 'moral order' and while it is a culturally derived form of social solidarity (Park 1915), it is morally unjust (Harvey 1973). As Harvey (1973: 132) comments, 'Park and Burgess did not pay a great deal of attention to the kind of social solidarity generated through the workings of the economic system nor to the social and economic relationship which derives from economic considerations'.

Harvey's work in the early 1970s signified a paradigm shift and the creation of a 'new' urban sociology and geography (Smith 1995, Gottdiener & Feagin 1988). The new urban sociology is a simultaneous attack on the mainstream urban sociology dominated by the urban ecology school combined with a critical perspective that connects the urban processes with the production and reproduction of capital accumulation and the complex relations between capital, state, and space (Gottdiener & Feagin 1988) within a hierarchical global system of competitive capitalism (Smith 1995). Particularly relevant to the critique of neighbourhood effects analyses is the thesis on the uneven development of capitalism (Harvey 1973) and the operations of the capitalist markets in land and real estate (Logan & Molotch 1987), as well as the social production of space (Lefebvre 1991).

The new urban sociology differs from the Chicago school of urban ecology with respect to the underlying processes and the driver of social change (and hence changes in the neighbourhood). Instead of being ruled by a set of the natural laws of human adaption, competition, technological innovation, and succession as the urban ecological approach claims, the outcomes of the neighbourhood (and the city) are products of a mode of production involving social organisation embedded in a class society and the uneven distribution of power among classes, the state, state machinery, regulations, and the specific process of reproduction and capital accumulation (Gottdiener & Feagin 1988). Hence the 'ecological patterns' that are observed are the results of the processes of production and reproduction of capital accumulation that produce socio-spatial patterns of inequality (Gottdiener & Feagin 1988), which are embedded in the secondary circuit of capital flows (Lefebvre 1991). It is real estate and the associated infrastructure underlying the push for urban development that are responsible for the generation of uneven development between the neighbourhoods (Harvey 1973).

For instance, Berry and Kasarda (1977) offer an ecological explanation of central-city restructuring arising from the need for the centralisation of the administrative and coordinating role of city government, which in turn is directly related to the size of the metropolitan hinterland. Yet such results, according to Gottdiener (1977), in fact signify the changing role of the city in the global economy, with city-centre restructuring being pushed by the emergence of multi-national capital as well as sweatshops in many downtown metropolitan areas that employ cheap migrant labour to feed the needs of the global production circuit (Gottdiener & Feagin, 1988). Likewise, suburbanisation is also not a direct consequence of innovative technology (e.g. the popularity of the automobile) pushing workers to migrate to the suburbs, as the ecological explanation puts it (Hawley 1950, cited in Gottdiener & Feagin 1988). Empirical research has instead found that the outmigration of manufacturing industries pre-dated the popular use of the automobile, and it was subsidised housing projects and the de-concentration of defence-related industries and later cycles of housing and real estate development that constituted the underlying driving force for suburbanisation (Gottdiener & Feagin 1988).

Hence, the creation of the neighbourhood for the so-called underclass, which attracts the bulk of neighbourhood effect research, is a direct result of the divestment created by the uneven development of capitalism (Slater 2021). As Smith (1982) vividly describes, it is 'the successive development, underdevelopment and redevelopment of given areas as capital jumps from one place to another, then back again, both creating and destroying its own opportunities for development' (Smith 1982: 151). If the problems of the neighbourhood are rooted in the wider social structure, it would be misleading only to focus on the attributes of the neighbourhood in understanding the root causes of the issue. It also misguides policy solutions for neighbourhood problems; as Andersson and Musterd (2005: 386) remark, 'problems in the neighbourhood are seldom problems of the neighbourhood ... an area focus cannot by itself tackle the broader structural problems, such as unemployment, that underlie the problems of small areas', so 'we need to measure heretofore unmeasured social level constructs and theorize the role of [the] neighbourhood context in influencing perceptions and interactions' (Sampson 2011: 245–246).

In fact, failing to locate the structural basis of neighbourhood problems would mean the neighbourhood effect 'has no place for any concern over what happens outside the very neighbourhoods under scrutiny' (Slater 2013: 124). The neighbourhood effect is only 'fixated on the idea of 'contained' or internal characteristics, almost as if neighbourhoods are islands unto themselves' (Sampson 2011: 234). Ecological determinism as practised by the urban ecology school according to the principle that 'where you live affects your life chance' stands only on shaky ground (Slater 2013) and '[tries] to reverse social and historical causation' (Slater 2021: 132). In this vein, neighbourhood effects only convey a 'falsely depoliticized vision of urban inequality' (Wacquant 2008: 284) and reflect deficiencies in public goods provision (Slater 2021) (see Figure 9.1).

## NEIGHBOURHOOD EFFECTS: COMPLICATION AND CONFUSION

Interestingly, the harsh criticism of the Chicago school of urban ecology coming from the 'new urban sociology' and the challenge to the validity of the concept of an 'independent' neighbourhood effect in the 1970s and early 1980s did not diminish the interest in neighbourhood effect research. In fact, research on the neighbourhood began to surge in the 1980s, probably as

*Source:* Miguel A. Martínez.

*Figure 9.1   Hong Kong (2014)*

the result of the growing attention paid to the area-based policy and projects that were popular in the UK and USA in the 1960s and 1970s. Van Ham et al. (2012) did a simple Google search using 'neighborhood/neighbourhood effect(s)' as the keywords and found 203,100 papers on this issue dating from 1987 to 2011. Academic interest in neighbourhood effects in fact grew steadily over this period with over 17,420 papers appearing in 2011 alone. Van Ham et al.

(2012) attributed this surge to the impact of the book *The Truly Disadvantaged* by Wilson (1987) on research on the neighbourhood effect, and particularly its relevance for disadvantaged groups, especially those disadvantaged on racial grounds. The total number of citations for Wilson (1987) reached 9,880 in early 2011 (Van Ham et al. 2012). In fact, the impact of Wilson (1987) has continued over the years following 2011 as, according to Google Scholar, the total number of citations reached 23,934 in late February 2022, a 2.5-fold increase over the last decade. Many of the recent research papers focus on the effect of the neighbourhood on specific policy areas like health (both physical and mental), crime, housing, and education.

With respect to the above, underpinning the revival of the interest in the neighbourhood effect is not only academic curiosity about how the neighbourhood (and society) works, but more importantly, it is also being driven by policy-related concerns. As Maclennan (2013: 272) notes,

> policy analysis is interested in how neighbourhoods are identified, ... defined, how they are chosen by different socio-economic groups, how they change over time and the consequences of neighbourhood outcomes not just for the individuals they contain but for the functioning of wider metropolitan areas. Pattern, choice, change and consequences are critical considerations in making policy. What stylised facts about neighbourhoods can guide place policy making?

Such a long list of questions seems to be not too different from what the urban ecologists were asking 100 years ago, albeit the conceptual and methodological language that is used nowadays is much more sophisticated.

Paradoxically, despite the tens of thousands of papers written on neighbourhood effects, it seems that our knowledge concerning neighbourhood effects has not advanced a lot (Galster 2012). Instead, more and more confusion has been revealed (Van Ham et al. 2012, Galster 2012). For instance, numerous qualitative research papers have produced consistent evidence of the neighbourhood effect from a rich supply of data on people's experiences and perceptions (Van Ham et al. 2012); however, the small number and limited coverage of the cases do not allow such research to be generalised. On the other hand, despite research using the quantitative approach in identifying generalisable causal neighbourhood effects with sophisticated modelling techniques and covering large samples not being in short supply, the impacts of the neighbourhood effects are, however, less clear in these pieces of research. In fact, the research results are mostly inconclusive or even contradictory (Galster 2012). Hence, how neighbourhood effects impact individual or collective behaviours remains a black box (Maclennan 2013). As most quantitative studies model neighbourhood effects with contextual information (e.g. income, socio-economic status, environmental factors, etc.), it is not always possible to identify the real underlying causal effects (Van Ham et al., 2012) or to avoid problems involving omitted variables, endogeneity, and the simultaneity of the independent variables (Durlauf 2004).

In addition the methodological issues involved in the study of the neighbourhood, one fundamental problem with the research on neighbourhood effects is how the neighbourhood is defined. This is not an incidental and trivial question as the choice of the scale of the spatial container (the neighbourhood) influences what effect we may be able to catch. If important information is missed, then the fine statistics and sophisticated modelling would be working on the wrong set of data (Maclennan 2013).

## Issues with Identifying the Boundaries of the Neighbourhood

After the unsuccessful attempt of the Chicago school urban ecologists to identify 'natural areas' in neighbourhood study, administratively defined locational units like the census tracts (Huckfeldt 1979) or postal codes and wards (Stafford et al. 2003) have been widely employed as boundaries of neighbourhoods. However, there are queries about whether such 'objectively' defined boundaries for the neighbourhood match the neighbourhood as conceived by its residents and hence are prone to bias regarding the analysis of any neighbourhood effect (Coulton et al. 2001). To overcome such potential bias, there have been attempts to explore whether neighbourhood boundaries can be built up from a collection of subjective mappings of residents of the neighbourhood using cognitive mapping techniques that have been developed since the 1950s; that is, by asking the residents *themselves* to draw the boundaries of their *own* neighbourhoods (Coulton et al. 2001). Yet it was found to be difficult to reach a consensus among residents living in close proximity to each other with respect to defining the spatial boundaries of their neighbourhood. Similar findings were reproduced in a larger study by Jenks and Dempsey (2007) in England designed to test whether objectively defined boundaries of a neighbourhood match resident-defined boundaries. However, the research found no consensus among the residents on what defined their neighbourhood despite, on the other hand, the result that 'they have less difficulty in identifying what is not considered part of their neighbourhood' (Jenks and Dempsey 2007: 163).

Spatial scale is another important concern. Recent research on the neighbourhood has raised concerns not just about how boundaries of a neighbourhood are defined but about the impacts of defining the unit of analysis at different spatial scales (Lewicka 2010). For instance Relph (1976) proposed a scale of seven different degrees of 'outsideness' and 'insideness' (which correspond to spatial units from one's home to the nation state) relevant to our understanding of sense of place and sense of belonging.

At the same time, a quantitative approach to exploring an objectively defined neighbourhood boundary was attempted by Galster (1986) using how people identify and map their externality spaces. The approach involves a complex assessment of groups of individuals around an array of externalities and the topology of the neighbourhood. Whilst such a definition is theoretically interesting, it is technically complicated and expensive to implement.

Hence, as it is difficult to arrive at a consensus on a resident-defined boundary of a neighbourhood, Coulton et al. (2001) still suggest, on pragmatic grounds for empirical research, drawing up objective boundaries of neighbourhoods for data collection, even if the risk of potential bias cannot be totally avoided. Thus, it is a pragmatic approach 'to capture the total area that residents consider to be their neighbourhood by employing objective delineation methods ... [and] census geography[, which] yield social measures that are similar to the neighbourhood reality for residents' (Coulton et al. 2001: 381). In such cases, adding a buffer zone (say 100 m, 200 m, etc.) may be needed 'to capture the diversity of residents' own definitions of their neighbourhoods' (Jenks & Dempsey 2007: 172–173).

## Issues of the Selection Effect

How to separate the neighbourhood effect and the selection effect is another fundamental issue in the research on neighbourhood effects. If households with certain characteristics would tend to choose a certain neighbourhood type, then the causal connection between neighbourhood attributes and residents' behavioural outcomes would just be reversed. It is the sorting process that creates the outcomes, but not the neighbourhood effects. Whilst residential choice is intensively researched, little is known about how households choose neighbourhoods (Hedman & Van Ham 2012). If households are able to acquire prior knowledge of a neighbourhood's externalities (i.e. some 'neighbourhood effects') before making the residential choice, it would make the separation of neighbourhood selection and the neighbourhood effect difficult (Maclennan 2013). The selection bias regarding neighbourhood effects would then be more than a statistical error (Hedman & Van Ham 2012) and there would be a high probability of there being collinearity between the neighbourhood effects and neighbourhood selection (Maclennan 2013).

To avoid selection bias in neighbourhood effect research it is necessary to target movers who do not have free residential choice. With such a goal in mind, Van Ham and Manley (2010) did research among residents in Scotland and found no neighbourhood effects on labour market outcomes among social tenants who did not have a choice of housing and neighbourhood, whereas selection bias was found among homeowners who had a free choice of their neighbourhood (Van Ham & Manley 2010). Similar findings were produced by Oreopoulos (2003) researching social tenants in Toronto. Both the two groups of authors argued that selection bias would be a problem only for those households that have free residential choice. Yet for most of the neighbourhood effect research that focuses on disadvantaged neighbourhoods, households seldom have any real choice, either because of their social housing allocation, which is largely done administratively, or owing to market failures that impede low-income renters from having a free choice of neighbourhood.

**The Problem with the Mechanisms Producing Neighbourhood Effects**

The neighbourhood is a complex and multifaceted construct. In his discussion of the nature of the neighbourhood, Burgess (1925b, cited in Alihan 1964) portrays natural areas (which create neighbourhoods) as an ecological, cultural, and political manifestation. More recently, Jenks and Dempsey (2007) described the neighbourhood as an entity with a layered frame of reference as well as an integration of different constructs: spatial, functional, and social. The spatial construct of the neighbourhood is based on its spatial attributes as well as its relation to the psycho-social-spatial concept of place, whereas the neighbourhood is also a functional construct as a venue where services supporting the needs of the residents, like housing, education, recreation, social development, etc., are provided. The social construct of the neighbourhood embraces not only norms and institutions, but also social relations and networks embedded in the place, as well as the meaning and identity of the place and the stigma that is associated with it.

Hence, neighbourhood effects may be generated in the complex interaction of factors in such constructs. A simple model of such effects on individual behaviour has been suggested by Friedrichs (2016) (Figure 9.2). While at the micro level, individual behaviour may be directly influenced by one's preferences and attitudes, such preferences and attitudes may in turn be shaped by both institutions like family and school at the meso level and also the conditions of the neighbourhood at the macro level. At the same time, neighbourhood conditions and residents' behaviour also jointly form the aggregated characteristics of the neighbourhood. Such a construction is in fact very close to the conception of the neighbourhood used by the Chicago school of urban ecology.

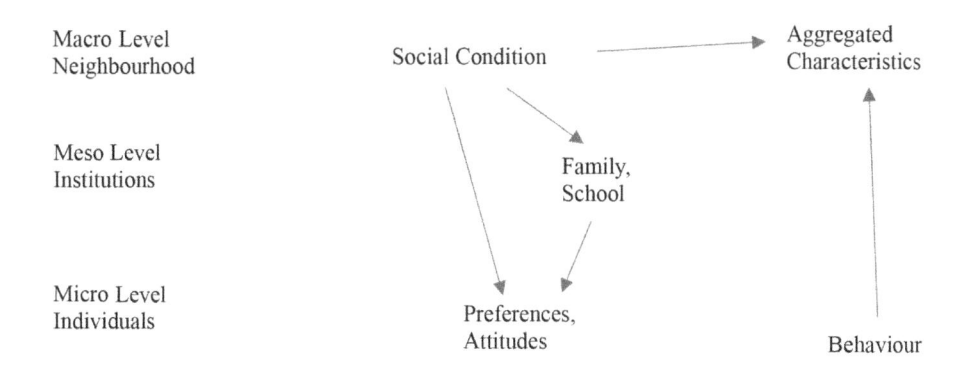

*Source:* Friedrichs 2016: 74.

*Figure 9.2   A macro–micro model of neighbourhood effects*

A recent comprehensive review of the mechanisms of neighbourhood effects was offered by Galster (2012), who identified, with an extensive review of the literature (mainly quantitative) on social and behavioural sciences, as well as epidemiological research, the potential pathways that link the neighbourhood context with individual behavioural and health outcomes. A broad range of mechanisms were identified that included nearly everything, such as the social-interactive mechanism at the individual level, mechanisms that relate to geographical factors of location and space, and institutional mechanisms that connect to social resources outside of the neighbourhood as well as the environmental mechanisms of nature or human-made attributes. A total of 15 distinctive linkages connected to such mechanisms were identified (Galster 2012: 25–27). This has instead further magnified the complexity of such mechanisms of neighbourhood effects. The possible interaction of these mechanisms with each other would also make the disentanglement of neighbourhood effects a daunting task.

There are still additional technical considerations for the relative contributions of different elements in neighbourhood effect modelling, even if the mechanisms generating neighbourhood effects have been identified. This is more than an issue of measurement and data collection. Galster (2012) uses the 'pharmacological metaphor' of 'dosage-response relationships' in investigating 'the dose of neighbourhood (effects)' that may 'cause' the observed individual (behavioural or health outcome) 'response'. Such considerations include the composition and administration of the dose and the frequency of administration, the duration, and the intensity of the dose, as well as other factors like threshold, timing, durability, etc. (Galster, 2012). However, it is not clear whether this 'dosage' analogy does any good with regards to clarifying the neighbourhood effects or whether it simply adds further complications to the already complex mechanisms of neighbourhood effects. On the one hand it requires high-precision measurement of the attributes involved, which is beyond what most social sciences measurement instruments are able to handle, while on the other hand the use of a pharmacological metaphor may already undermine agency factors in neighbourhood effects mechanisms.

## CONCLUSIONS

The urban ecological approach has been the mainstream perspective used by urban sociology since its creation in the 1920s and 1930s and has been dominating the research on the neighbourhoods. Inspired by the advancements in the theories of natural ecology, the Chicago school sociologists attempted to explore the relationships between the individual and the urban environments, the nature and meaning of progress, and the connection between structure, function, pattern, and process in cities and neighbourhoods via ecological analogies like adaptation, competition, invasion, and succession in an ever-changing environment.

Sub-population groups within the wider urban community compete for limited resources and opportunities for survival over a limited space and this sets up a mechanism to regulate the numbers and balance between them (Park 1936, Wirth 1938). The urban ecologists of the early 20th century focused their research on small and well-defined areas with distinct cultural characteristics (McKenzie 1924), which 'make the city a mosaic of little worlds which touch but do not interpenetrate' (Park 1915: 608). This directly links the ecological study of spatial communities with the modern-day concept of neighbourhood effects. Yet one main difference between the Chicago school of urban ecology and modern-day research on neighbourhood effects is that the former perspective is more interested, like biological ecology, in the aggregated outcomes of the population, whereas the latter is more concerned with the impacts of the neighbourhood on the individual.

The Chicago school of urban ecology was under serious attack in the 1970s and 1980s from the neo-Marxist and 'new' urban sociology scholars criticising the urban ecological perspective of extracting the neighbourhood from the wider political economic processes, which masks the root cause of poor neighbourhoods, depoliticises the problem, and justifies inequality. It is not some law of nature but the uneven development of the built environment driven by the capital accumulation imperative, enforced through the uneven distribution of political power, that produces such 'neighbourhood effects'.

Despite the challenge to the fundamental theoretical premises of the urban ecological approach and hence its usefulness for neighbourhood studies, studies on neighbourhood effects have continued to flourish since the 1980s. Apart from a small number of studies done from a critical perspective or with an ethnographic approach, the bulk of such research is quantitative. These quantitative studies often aim to identify factors, mechanisms, or processes that affect individual outcomes of concern, be they matters of individual behaviour, health conditions, or social or cultural attributes, which are beyond the attributes of the individuals but relate to the spatial, physical, social, or cultural attributes of the neighbourhood. Despite very few of such researchers packaging their approaches as urban ecological, what they are trying to look for is quite similar to what the urban ecological approach would have looked for, albeit modern-day neighbourhood effect research is more diversified in terms of disciplines and approaches, as well as more sophisticated in its methodology. Increasingly, more of the quantitative research done on neighbourhood effects employs econometric methods and the focus is more on health outcomes.

Despite the abundant supply of quantitative research on neighbourhood effects, Galster (2012) found only very weak conclusive evidence of neighbourhood effects from an extensive review of the relevant literature (at least up to the first decade of the 21st century). There is evidence for the environmental mechanism of the neighbourhood effects on health but not on neighbourhood decay, whereas for the geographic mechanism, the impacts of neighbourhood factors are divergent and non-conclusive. Perhaps this is because an overwhelming majority of such research is done in the United States where there are very different race and income profiles in neighbourhoods that would have produced very different neighbourhood effects (Galster 2012). On the other hand, the institutional mechanism has been found to make a big difference in the provision of public resources, but in the United States a deficiency in such provision may be compensated by resources from outside of the neighbourhood. Likewise, the welfare state efforts in European countries, as resources from outside of the neighbourhood, would also make the identification of the neighbourhood effect less straightforward (Galster 2012).

The urban ecological approach is perhaps a failed attempt at a grand theory or a unified conceptual approach to understanding changes at the neighbourhood level (though there was never a coherent framework in urban ecology). Like the creation of other grand theories, the more we know about social reality, the less such theories seem to be able to offer convincing accounts. The massive research on neighbourhood effects has so far still been unable to draw overarching theories for neighbourhood effects, and perhaps the best that has been done is a summary of the dimensions of such effects and the identification of a number of linkages that neighbourhood effects research can follow. The picture painted by Galster (2012) on the achievements of neighbourhood effect research is also less than optimistic. The conclusions most such research on neighbourhood effects are able to draw are either weak or the impacts observed are partial, and in many cases, the findings are in fact simply inconclusive. Despite such a weakness, insights of the Chicago school of urban ecology are still appealing to modern day sociologists. For instance, Ren (2019: 8) states that the 'reflective stance [of the Chicago school] towards systematic engaging with urban social inquiry ... [would help] to formulate a research agenda, and a comparative outlook [related to urbanisation in Chinese cities]'.

As policy intervention concerns are the driving force underlying most research on neighbourhood effects (MacLennan, 2013), it would not be surprising if future research on neighbourhood effects inevitably focuses on neighbourhood-level factors that produce the outcomes concerned, the detailed mechanisms for producing such impacts, the dosage and trajectories needed for the intervention, and mediating factors.

Yet there may be one consensus on the future of research on neighbourhood effects. It is that the neighbourhood is both dynamic and complex, and neighbourhood effects have to be understood within the context of a complex system embedded in an ever-changing social environment at different scales. Not only do we need the top-down view of neighbourhood effects that most existing research is currently using, a side-by-side or even a bottom-up view of neighbourhood effects may be necessary (Sampson 2011). In addition, notwithstanding the denouncement of the urban ecological premises advanced by the 'new' urban sociology, there are attempts to 'excavate' the old sociology of the Chicago school, aiming to discover a new direction for urban sociology by rediscovering the theoretical overlapping of the old and the new, as well as to advance the continuation of an established intellectual tradition (Smith 1995). As Vasishth and Sloane (2002: 348–349) note, 'many conventional critiques of the Chicago sociologists ignore the historical moment of their activity, and so underrate the transformative aspects of their ecological leanings ... [hence, the] ecology initiated by the Chicago urban theorists still provides a sound foundation for urban research'. Saunders also comments on some of criticisms of the Chicago school, where he specifically refers to Hawley's (1950) approach to human ecology and states that '[urban ecology is] one specialised area of study within the functionalist paradigm' (Sauders 1986: 82).

In this respect, perhaps a revised ecological framework for looking at neighbourhood effects integrating the old and the new is insightful. Ecological influences may be understood, as the critique of the critical school has suggested, within the political economic context of class, globalisation, and the state's role in the global capitalist system. Similarly, Vasishth and Sloane (2002: 360) suggest revising the ecological perspective into an ecosystem approach to consider 'a nested, scale-hierarchic arrangement of complex, self-organizing set of systems and subsystems nested within and around each other … within a wider suprasystem'. The impacts of neighbourhood factors on individual outcomes may also be focused on subjectivity and residential stress as well as neighbourhood dynamics and flow (Bailey et al. 2013).

## REFERENCES

Abu-Lughod, J. L. (1991) *Changing Cities: Urban Sociology.* New York: Harper Collins.
Alihan, M. A. (1964) *Social Ecology.* New York: Cooper Square Publishers.
Andersson, R. & Musterd, S. (2005) Area-Based Policies: A Critical Appraisal. *Tijd Voor Economic and Social Geography* 96(4): 377–389.
Bailey, N., Barnes, H., Livingston, M. & McLennan, D. (2013) Understanding Neighbourhood Population Dynamics for Neighbourhood Effects Research: A Review of Recent Evidence and Data Source Developments. In Van Ham, M., Manley, D., Bailey, N., Simpson, L. & MacLennan, D. (eds.) *Understanding Neighbourhood Dynamics: New Insights for Neighbourhood Effects Research.* Dordrecht, Heidelberg, London and New York: Springer.
Bell, W. (1955) Economic, Family, and Ethnic Status: An Empirical Test. *American Sociological Review*, 20(1): 45–52.
Berry, B. & Kasarda, J. (1977) *Contemporary Urban Ecology.* New York: Macmillan.
Burgess, E. W. (1925a) The Growth of the City. In Park, R. & Burgess, E. W. (eds.) *The City.* Chicago: University of Chicago Press.
Burgess, E. W. (1925b) Can Neighbourhood Work Have a Scientific Base. In Park, R. & Burgess, E. W. (eds.) *The City.* Chicago: University of Chicago Press.
Coulton, C., Korbin, J., Chan, T. & Su, M. (2001) Mapping Residents' Perceptions of Neighborhood Boundaries: A Methodological Note. *American Journal of Community Psychology* 29(2): 371–383.
Davis, M. (1998) *Ecology of Fear: Los Angeles and the Imagination of Disaster.* New York: Metropolitan Books.
Durlauf, S. N. (2004) Neighbourhood Effects. In Henderson, J. V. & Thisse, J. F. (eds.) *Handbook of Regional and Urban Economics. Volume 4 Cities and Geography.* Amsterdam: Elsevier.
Friedrichs, J. (2016) Neighbourhood Effects: Lost in Transition? *Analyse & Kritik: Journal of Philosophy and Social Theory* 38(1): 73–89.
Galster, G. C. (1986) What is Neighbourhood? An Externality-space Approach. *International Journal of Urban and Regional Research* 10(2): 243–263.
Galster, G. C. (2012) The Mechanism(s) of Neighbourhood Effects: Theory, Evidence, and Policy Implications. In Van Ham, M., Manley, D., Bailey, N., Simpson, L. & MacLennan, D. (eds.) *Neighbourhood Effects Research: New Perspectives.* Dordrecht, Heidelberg, London and New York: Springer.
Gottdiener, M. (1977) *Planned Sprawl: Private and Public Interests in Suburbia.* Beverly Hills: Sage.
Gottdiener, M. and Feagin, J. R. (1988) The Paradigm Shift in Urban Sociology. *Urban Affairs Quarterly* 24(2): 163–187.
Hannerz, U. (1980) *Exploring the City: Inquiries toward an Urban Anthropology.* New York: Columbia University Press.
Harvey, D. (1973) *Social Justice and the City.* London: Edward Arnold.
Hawley, A. H. (1944) Ecology and Human Ecology. *Social Forces* 22: 398–405.
Hawley, A. H. (1950) *Human Ecology: A Theory of Community Structure.* New York: The Ronald Press Company.

Hedman, L. & Van Ham, M. (2012) Understanding Neighbourhood Effects: Selection Bias and Residential Mobility. In Van Ham, M., Manley, D., Bailey, N., Simpson, L. R Maclennan, D. (eds.) *Neighbourhood Effects Research: New Perspectives.* Dordrecht, Heidelberg, London and New York: Springer.

Huckfeldt, R. (1979) Political Participation and the Neighborhood Social Context. *American Journal of Political Science* 23(3): 579–592.

Jenks, M. & Dempsey, N. (2007) Defining the Neighbourhood: Challenges for Empirical Research. *Town Planning Review* 78(2): 152–177.

Keller, S. (1966) Neighbourhood Concepts in Sociological Perspective. *Ekistics* 22(128): 67–76.

Lefebvre, H. (1991) *The Production of Space.* Oxford: Blackwell.

Lewicka, M. (2010) What Makes Neighborhood Different from Home and City? Effects of Place Scale on Place Attachment. *Journal of Environmental Psychology* 30(1): 35–51.

Logan, J. R. & Molotch, H. L. (1987) *Urban Fortunes: The Political Economy of Place.* Berkeley: University of California Press.

Maclennan, D. (2013) Neighbourhoods: Evolving Ideas, Evidence and Changing Policies. In Manley D., Van Ham, M., Bailey, N., Simpson, L. & MacLennan, D. (eds.) *Neighbourhood Effects or Neighbourhood Based Problems? A Policy Context.* Dordrecht, Heidelberg, London and New York: Springer.

McKenzie, R. D. (1924) The Ecological Approach to the Study of Human Community. *American Journal of Sociology* 30: 287–301.

McKenzie, R. D. (1925) The Scope of Urban Ecology. The Urban Community. *Selected Papers from the Proceedings of the American Sociological Society* 167–182.

McKenzie, R. D. (1926) The Scope of Urban Ecology. *American Journal of Sociology* 32: 141–154.

Minnery, J., Knight, J., Byrne, J. & Spencer, J. (2009) Bounding Neighbourhoods: How Do Residents Do It? *Planning Practice & Research* 24(4): 471–493.

Oreopoulos, P. (2003) The Long-run Consequences of Living in a Poor Neighbourhood. *Quarterly Journal of Economics* 118(4): 1533–1575.

Park, R. E. (1915) The City: Suggestions for the Investigation of Human Behavior in the City Environment. *American Journal of Sociology* 20: 577–612.

Park, R. E. (1929) City as Social Laboratory. In Smith, T.V. & White, L., D. (eds.) *Chicago: An Experiment in Social Science Research.* Chicago: University of Chicago Press.

Park, R. E. (1936) Human Ecology. *American Journal of Sociology* 42: 1–15.

Relph, E. (1976) *Place and Placelessness.* London: Pion.

Ren, X. (2019) Robert Park in China: From the Chicago School to Urban China Studies. In Forrest, R., Ren, J. & Wissink, B. (eds.) *The City in China.* Bristol: Policy Press, 1–16.

Sampson, R. J. (2011) Neighborhood Effects, Causal Mechanisms and the Social Structure of the City. In Demeulenaere, P. (ed.) *Analytical Sociology and Social Mechanisms.* Cambridge: Cambridge University Press.

Saunders, P. (1986) *Social Theory and the Urban Question* 2nd ed., London: Hutchinson Education.

Schmid, C. F., Camilleri, S. F. & Van Arsdol, M. D. (1958) The Ecology of the American City: Further Comparison and Validation of Generalizations. *American Sociological Review* 23: 392–401.

Shevky, E. & Williams, M. (1949) *The Social Areas of Los Angeles, Analysis and Typology.* John Randolph Haynes and Dora Haynes Foundation.

Slater, T. (2013) Capitalist Urbanization Affects Your Life Chances: Exorcising the Ghosts of 'Neighbourhood Effects'. In Manley, D., Van Ham, M., Bailey, N., Simpson, L. & MacLennan, D. (eds.) *Neighbourhood Effects or Neighbourhood Based Problems?* Dordrecht, Heidelberg, London and New York: Springer.

Slater, T. (2021) *Shaking Up the City: Ignorance, Inequality, and the Urban Question.* Berkeley: University of California Press.

Smith, D. (1995) The New Urban Sociology Meets the Old: Rereading Some Classical Human Ecology. *Urban Affairs Review* 30(3): 432–457.

Smith, N. (1982) Gentrification and Uneven Development. *Economic Geography* 58(2): 139–155.

Stafford, M., Bartley, M., Sacker, A., Marmot, M., Wilkinson, R., Boreham, R. & Thomas, R. (2003) Measuring the Social Environment: Social Cohesion and Material Deprivation in English and Scottish Neighbourhoods. *Environment and Planning A* 35(8): 1459–1475.

Van Ham, M. & Manley, D. (2010) The Effect of Neighbourhood Housing Tenure Mix on Labour Market Outcomes: A Longitudinal Investigation of Neighbourhood Effects, *Journal of Economic Geography* 10(2): 257–282.

Van Ham, M., Manley, D., Bailey, N., Simpson, L. & Maclennan, D. (2012) Neighbourhood Effects Research: New Perspectives. In Van Ham, M., Manley, D., Bailey, N., Simpson, L. & MacLennan, D. (eds.) *Neighbourhood Effects Research: New Perspectives.* Dordrecht, Heidelberg, London and New York: Springer.

Vasishth, A. & Sloane, D. (2002) Returning to Ecology: An Ecosystem Approach to Understanding the City. In Dear, M. J. (ed.) *From Chicago to L.A.: Making Sense of Urban Theory*. London: Sage Publications.

Wacquant, L. (2008) *Urban Outcasts: A Comparative Sociology of Advanced Marginality.* Cambridge: Polity.

Whyte, W. F. (1943) *Street Corner Society: The Social Structure of an Italian Slum.* Chicago: University of Chicago Press.

Wilson, W. J. (1987) *The Truly Disadvantaged: The Inner City, the Underclass and Public Policy.* Chicago: University of Chicago Press.

Wirth, L. (1938) Urbanism as a Way of Life. *American Journal of Sociology* 44: 1–24.

Young, G. L. (1974) Human Ecology as an Interdisciplinary Concept: A Critical Inquiry. *Advances in Ecological Research* 8: 1–105.

Zorbaugh, H. (1926) The Natural Areas of the City. In Burgess, E. W. (ed.) *Urban Community: Selected Papers from the Proceedings of the American Sociological Society*. Reprinted in Lin, J. & Mele, C. (eds.) (2005) *The Urban Sociology Reader*, 1st ed. Abingdon and New York: Routledge.

Zorbaugh, H. (1929) *Gold Coast and the Slum.* Chicago: Chicago University Press.

# 10. Questioning the foundations: the embedded racism in urban sociology theorization

*Miguel Montalva Barba*

Handbooks like this one are essential because they direct the discipline for about 20 years, and if they repeat the same patterns, then the discipline reinforces the mainstream (Slater 2021). Slater defines the 'mainstream' as 'an atheoretical, unquestioning embrace of the structural and institutional conditions (and concepts and categories) favored by city rules and the profiteering interests surrounding them' (2021: 8). Following Slater's definition, this chapter addresses how racism is embedded in urban theorization as scholars replicate the mainstream with atheoretical and unquestioning frames that have stagnated a complaisant urban sociology. By embedded racism, I mean how racism and White supremacy are hidden and included as a primarily unspoken norm or marker of normalcy in urban theorizing (Montalva Barba 2023: 2024).

Abrutyn and Lizardo's *Handbook of Classical Sociological Theory* (2021) includes a chapter by Clark and Wu that addresses urban theorization. Clark and Wu (2021) summarize more than a century of theorizing on the urban question. They develop four major theoretical themes to ground their analysis: human ecology (1890s), neo-Marxist political economy (1960s), world-system and global theory (1980s), and the cultural turn (1990s) (2021: 424). These major theoretical perspectives defined those eras, considering that some detail and specificities are lost when reducing wide breadths of knowledge and research. Nevertheless, synthesizing such a large amount of research into very tangible themes is commendable; those themes are used here to structure this argument.

The way racism and White supremacy embed themselves in urban theorizing most often occurs through colorblindness or colorblind urbanism (Montalva Barba 2023, Petersen 2022, Valle 2017, 2021). Ignoring that, White folks are also racialized and replicate those patterns, ideas and ideologies that are part of the dominant culture. By using these themes, I reveal how racism is embedded in urban theorizing, often appearing as colorblind, invisible, or unstated but always present and often hidden in the uncritical reproduction of research that follows the mainstream. Colorblind racism is so embedded in urban theorizing that even in Abrutyn and Lizardo's *Handbook,* which includes a chapter on Du Bois's erasure from sociology, no connection was included to engage his work. Like other forms of colorblindness, colorblind urbanism takes a presumed race-neutral approach that does not see color or only sees race when it relates to non-Whites in the city (Valle 2017). Race-neutrality always benefits White supremacy.

Urban theorizing rarely takes the role of racism, or more specifically the role of White supremacy, as a structural agent, especially regarding the socialization of White people (Montalva Barba 2021, 2023). When taking a structural (economy, state, institutions/family, government, education) approach to racism à la Critical Race Theory (CRT), scholars need to approach research knowing that racism and White supremacy are embedded in everything that Eurocentric notions touch – from the organization of the city to our interactions on the street.

Unless research questions are directly about White folks, their Whiteness is not discussed, ignored, assumed irrelevant, or reduced to class matters (Lipsitz 1998). Whiteness is a 'social, political, economic, and psychological standpoint of structural advantage that shapes the everyday' and essentially intersects skin color to power structures and access (Frankenberg 1997, Mills 2003, Montalva Barba 2021: 4). Thus, when scholars take on colorblindness, intentionally or not, their analysis perpetuates existing structural and ideological patterns that ignore the role of White supremacy in the mundane.

From the start, urban sociology set forth as a discipline aiming to understand 'urban problems' in the city – which mostly translated into understanding the large waves of (im)migrants, those considered non-White,[1] 'vice areas,' and any other population outside of those considered part of acceptable Whiteness (Baldwin 2004, Montalva Barba 2023, Yu 2001, Steinberg 2007). This was unique to US urban sociology and later disseminated to the rest of the world as international scholars came to US institutions for their graduate training. I use Clark and Wu's (2021) major theoretical perspectives to show how racism is embedded in the form of colorblind urbanism (Valle 2017), or 'race-neutral' or 'post-racial' urbanism, as race, racism, and White supremacy and how the power differentials or dynamics that (re)create it are hardly ever named. In the initial urban research, Whiteness is the standard from which the Other is measured and assessed (Baldwin 2004, Yu 2001). Moreover, 'race-neutral' research ignores a genuine engagement with discussions on racialized power relations and who benefits from exploiting those racialized minorities on the margins of society. The objective here is to redirect the academic gaze of urban sociologists to rethink our approach and research questions. In the following sections, I frame the conversation within the foundations of sociology and their relations to urban sociology. Next, I summarize each theoretical theme and show how racism is embedded in the four major waves. Finally, I offer a theoretical framework to guide future research and some suggestions to address this pervasive problem and conclude with suggestions to move forward.

## FOUR MAJOR THEORETICAL THEMES AND HOW RACISM IS EMBEDDED

### The Foundations and Progress Narratives

Sociology developed out of modernity following the Enlightenment. From sociology's inception, regardless of scale, the urban was at the heart of the discipline because founding theorists had as their central concern how the urban/rural dynamic was affecting the social. As urban sociology has evolved, progress narratives have primarily informed the discipline's development. Progress narratives, or master narratives, are forms of national ideology used to rationalize social structures and inequality. Progress narratives are rooted in global (in)differences as they justify state actors' social, political, economic, and place-based ideologies. They are also at the root of the classics, Marx, Du Bois, Weber, and Durkheim. Connell argues that progress narratives are at the center of the work of the classics mainly because they congregated around the 'difference between the civilization of the metropole, and an Other whose main feature was primitiveness' (1997: 1516–1517). While Connell's statement might seem to address anthropology's turbulent past, she addresses the work of early sociologists that focused on urban prosperity versus urban poverty. All foundational theorists include notions of progress in their theories used for empire-building (Connell 1997, Schwendinger & Schwendinger 1974).

As this chapter shows, the embedded racism in theories can be noticed by what is left unsaid but implied, ignoring Whiteness and White people as a racialized group or only speaking about race as something only non-White people have. For example, the human ecology approach (HEA) was too narrowly focused on the urban problems, mainly those racial and ethnic Others. This perspective informed the neo-Marxist political economy (MPE) theme, which missed the importance of racial ideology and its interrelatedness with structures. The next theme, world/global systems (WGS), reduced everything to macroeconomics and global forces, leaving local specificities and contexts behind. The cultural turn (CT) now combines several previous themes but still ignores foundational frames that created the fixation with 'diverse' cultures.

Except for Du Bois, the founders did not make their object of study the city directly, but it was indirectly part of their theorization (Saunders 2003 [1989]). Most often, it was noticed in their use of progress narratives or ideas about the social transformation that was taking place based on their social context (Saunders 2003 [1989]). For example, in Marx's work, progress narratives deal with the destructive consequences of capitalism and its effects on individuals as a multilayered and devastating alienation imposed by capitalist exploitation and class antagonism (Tucker 1978: 476). Like Marx, Tönnies was concerned with the transformation from the pre-modern to modern, outlined by the transition between *Gemeinschaft* and *Gesellschaft* (2002). *Gemeinschaft*, or community, for Tönnies is defined by close and personal social relations characterized by a shared sense of place. Contrastingly, *Gesellschaft* is characterized by impersonal, calculative, and self-driven social relationships. In *Gesellschaft*, social cohesion is maintained by developing contracts, laws, and formalized relations. Like Tönnies, Durkheim was also concerned with the continuum of transformation from 'mechanical' to 'organic' solidarity (1984). However, Durkheim rejected Tönnies' characterization of modernity as he understood that social cohesion in the modern period is maintained by an abstract collective consciousness developed through the interdependence of individuals and their belief in individuality overall. For Durkheim, such abstractness in the modern epoch facilitated more freedom for the individual than they exercised in mechanical solidarity, resulting in modern social ills; e.g., deviance, anomie, and unhappiness (Kasinitz 1995). Weber understood that individuals, through participation in the capitalist system, or the rationalization of life, would become calculative (1967). Weber's master metaphor, the iron cage, showed that individuals would become so immersed in capitalism that they cannot escape it as they become enmeshed within such a system of interdependency.

The work of the classics was part of a larger empire-building narrative (Connell 1997; Schwendinger & Schwending 1974), making the time and place of the development of sociology take a new definition:

> One of the major tasks of sociological research… was to gather up information yielded by the colonizing powers' encounter with the colonized world. *Sociology was formed within the culture of imperialism and embodies a cultural response to the colonized world.* This fact is crucial in understanding the content and method of sociology as well as the discipline's cultural significance. (Connell 1997: 1518–1519, emphasis added)

From the Chicago school's foundations onward, urban sociologists' theoretical themes broadly extended Eurocentric progress narratives in theories and research (Connell 1997). Like anthropology, sociology uses similar methods and logic to gather information about those 'social problems/people' in the US. The only difference is that sociology at large has not had to come to terms with this history like other disciplines. Progress narratives, although hardly stated, are at the center of urban theorizing. Scholars tend to focus on projecting onto cities their versions of what they believe cities, spaces, and places should strive to be, mainly imposing an ideology. Ideology always carries coercive powers, and those powers are always loaded with ideas, images, and ways of being. This becomes problematic as that ideology is often hidden or disguised behind objectivity/neutrality claims. For example, the ideology behind Park's research on race relations and Burgess's concentric circle model set into motion a system of theories and methods that relied heavily on an empire-building framework rooted in progress/origin narratives to explain the city (Baldwin 2004, Connell 1997, Go 2013, 2016, Jung 2009, Magubane 2014, Morris 2015, Schwendinger & Schwending 1974,). Not only does the name 'race relations' occlude power dynamics but, connecting with the concentric circle model, it gives a generational recipe for becoming assimilated into Whiteness (Baldwin 2004, Connell 1997, Steinberg 2007,) and thus reproducing White supremacy. The HEA, the first urban sociological theoretical theme, was rooted in explaining the cycle of order–disorder–order, and it exemplified the conveyer belt of civilization influenced by Thomas and Small (Baldwin 2004, Connell 1997). This order–disorder–order frame was primarily influenced by religious and bio-deterministic thought.

## HUMAN ECOLOGY APPROACH (1890s–1950s)

The Chicago school popularized the HEA. They emerged as the first sociological department focusing on the growing inequality in urban city centers at the turn of the 20th century (Abbott 1999, Anderson 1996, Hunter 2013, Kurtz 1984, Morris 2015, Sassen 2010, Yu 2001). As major US cities saw rapid urbanization, stark inequality, diverse waves of (im)migrants, and overpopulation, the city became the laboratory to explore these issues.

The Chicago school matured from Albion Small's desire to help influence the development of the 'kingdom of God on earth' (Greek 1992: 106). Coming from a theological background, Small merged the gospel with Darwinism to focus on social disorganization in the city based on the cultural traits of those groups/individuals present in Chicago (Montalva Barba 2023). Small's social disorganization (1916), along with Thomas's ethnic paradox, was merged with Burgess's concentric circles (1967) to create the HEA.

The HEA also incorporated Park's race relations cycle (1950) and Burgess's concentric zone theory (1967) to map the geographic order of the city, which became assimilation immigration theory.[2] Park and Burgess developed research that mirrored the natural sciences to solidify sociology with scientific legitimacy, focusing on what disrupts 'natural' homeostasis – invasive species or viruses. Thus, the studies produced focused on the spatially tied characteristics of the people occupying those spaces under study. For example, it was not just about Black people but about the Black people in the Black Belt, so their bodies became representative of those places and spaces. The focus extended to any group living within the city center that was outside the White middle- and upper-class standards. As such, the studies solidified homogeneous thinking about the bodies of those considered the Other. The HEA continues to be influential, even as it has been seen as deeply flawed (Lal 1987, Lyman 1968, Schwendinger & Schwendinger 1974). The Green Bible, *The City* (Park et al. 1967 [1925]), known for its original green color, is still considered a foundational text in urban sociology courses.

**Embedded Racism in the Human Ecology Frame**

Much has been written about this period and the Chicago school, but what is constantly left out of the conversation, with some exceptions, is that this timeframe was rooted in White supremacist thinking. By White supremacist thinking, I am referring to the spectrum of Whiteness that foregrounds the aesthetics, manners, comportment, and ways of being that support the nearly universal idea that Whiteness and White people are superior to those considered non-White/Other. In short, this theoretical theme completely missed, ignored, and occluded power differentials at the individual, local, state, national, and global levels. As the research of the Chicago school focused on what disrupts 'natural' homeostasis, those that were not part of Whiteness were seen as deficient or at some stagnated stage of civilization (Baldwin 2004). The structures that uphold racism and power dynamics that continually create spaces and places to exploit those on the margins were never included in the analysis. For example, these researchers focused on the Black Belts, ghettos, and areas of vice but ignored that Black folks were not allowed to live in other areas due to legal or de facto segregation (Drake & Cayton 2015 [1945], Du Bois 1968, 1920, Frazier 1997).

Further, many of those under study, like the Chinese, also had limited housing options due to racist thinking, behaviors, and policies. Studies created from this perspective instituted a pathologizing of the bodies of the Other, leaving the White majority as the standard. Urban scholars still need to contend with this legacy. When Black bodies are 'seen' as out of place if they are not in Black neighborhoods, when people perpetually think of Latine/Asian people as (im)migrants, inner city crime, Black on Black crime, the focus on neighborhood effects, and broken window theories, these are the pernicious effects of assigning a place to the bodies of the Others that have created great indifference. The embedded racism in HEA implicitly and explicitly used Whiteness as the standard. In the effort to study those 'little worlds,' a perpetual Othering was taking place wherein the construction of 'proper' Whiteness was being solidified and further cemented (Montalva Barba 2023).

From this period, the Chicago school also created another lasting problematic regarding scholars of color and their incorporation into sociology. The Chicago school only began to enroll students of color if they represented a sector of the population that was off limits to those White scholars (see Montalva Barba 2023, Yu 2001). Chinese and Black scholars, for example, were mainly accepted into the Chicago school if they were willing to study and represent their race and the communities they came from (Baldwin 2004, Yu 2001). Scholars of color had to be willing to learn what Zuberi and Bonilla-Silva (2008) call White logic and White methods. White logic, Zuberi and Bonilla-Silva state, 'refers to a context in which White supremacy has defined the techniques and processes of reasoning about social facts… assumes a historical posture that grants eternal objectivity to the views of elite Whites and condemns the views of non-Whites to perpetual subjectivity' (2008: 17). White methods are the tools 'to manufacture empirical data and analysis to support the racial stratification in society' (Zuberi & Bonilla-Silva 2008: 18). The non-White scholars selected were trained in White logic and White methods to study the communities they represented and to translate them to White academics. Yu argues that sociologists from that time produced knowledge not from exotic locals but from the bipolarity present in the city by training insiders to translate the knowledge 'of their little worlds' to outsiders; i.e., White professional men (Yu 2001). 'Chicago sociologists,' argues Yu, 'actively recruited insiders to translate their native knowledge into [White] sociological knowledge' (Yu 2001: 139). Like the anthropologists working abroad acquiring knowledge of foreign lands, sociologists at home worked to gain knowledge of the hobos, gangs, Catholics, Blacks, Asians, (im)migrants, and any other category that might have been unfamiliar to referential Whiteness, translating the knowledge gained from native informants into institutionalized White knowledge.

**Marxist Political Economy (1960s–)**

Reacting to the social, cultural, revolutionary, and decolonial movements across the globe, especially in the Global South, of the 1950s and 1960s, neo-Marxists began to reject the limited scope that urban theorizing had taken (Clark & Wu 2021, Gottdiener et al. 2018, Harding & Blokland 2014). For example, the HEA was too narrow in focus, centered on the neighborhood level, and too specific to problems that disconnected the analysis from more significant dynamics: capitalism and global forces (Castells 2007, Molotch 1976, Smith 1996).

The alternative presented was to think of the urban via MPE terms. The political economy approach to urban theorizing stayed connected to Marxist thinking by analyzing the city as a product of class antagonism created to benefit the interests of those that control the means of production. Henri Lefebvre's contribution was vital as it utilized Marxist concepts to study and analyze the city (Gottdiener et al. 2018, Lefebvre 2014). In short, Lefebvre made the case that city development was a creation of the capitalist system. By focusing on the city's role within a Marxist frame, Lefebvre added part of what was present in Marx and Engels but not fully developed. Harvey (1975, 1985, 2006) embraced what Lefebvre had started and developed an urban development analysis that defines the city as a spatial node that concentrates and circulates capital where class conflict is enacted (Gottdiener et al. 2018).

The other leading idea of the time was thinking of the city as a 'growth-machine' (Logan & Molotch 2007, Molotch 1976, 1990). In this theoretical frame, growth and development are necessary for the survival and persistence of cities, creating the conditions for the city, state, and capitalists (Harding & Blokland 2014). Therefore, competition between cities for resources and services is vital to move forward. Private and state actors have a role in attracting corporations and government funding to make each city more competitive than the next. Although most of the work that developed primarily centered on reducing everything to capitalism and competition, some scholars extended their analysis to other oppressive structures like race, age, and gender, but the central focus was always on capitalism and class conflict. The MPE follows the linear progress narrative thinking, as scholars emphasize urban development. It made urban theorization concentrate on capital accumulation as the city's driver of change, and this is where the racism is embedded.

**Embedded Racism in Political Economy**

Like traditional Marxist theorizing, MPE dismisses the importance of space-specific history and cultural dimensions, focusing more on capital conditions rather than the roles that place, space, and actual people play in and through the lived environment. Reducing the analysis to economic terms and arrangements ignores how socio-spatial patterns impact, reflect, and (re)create those economic structures. This dismissal is where the embedded racism hides. In places like the US, Europe, Latin America, and Africa, a global White supremacy is enmeshed in cultural and ideological systems (hooks 1999). Reducing our understanding of cities and urban life to the processes of capital accumulation through class struggles, consumption patterns, or market terms hides the role of gendered, racial, sexual, and ableist structures maintaining oppressive systems.

As has been argued in Harris's 'Whiteness as Property' (1993), within the US and other states that base their property law around liberal principles that extend from the Enlightenment period, private property is synonymous with Whiteness. The racial identity of Whiteness developed to protect the interests of White propertied men supported by US law (Haney López 1996, Harris 1993). The MPE theme where capital investments, rentiers, land value, land use, and exchange value are key factors (Harvey 1973, Logan & Molotch 2007), not paying attention to the role of White supremacy and Whiteness in the capitalist system, further mystifies the role of racism and the structuring of urban economies.[3]

This theoretical theme is characterized by its Eurocentrism and uneven application of theories (Harding & Blokland 2014). As MPE focuses on property and capitalism, the analysis embeds a White supremacist notion of private property and property law (Bhambra 2020, Bhandar 2018, Harris 1993, Nichols 2020, Saito 2020), using a Eurocentric notion of the work that does not acclimate well to other parts of the world. This leaves White supremacy unacknowledged as a structural agent.

**World-systems and Global Theory (1980s–)**

WGS theory grew out of the developments of MPE. From a particular perspective, political economy began exploring the connection between global forces and capitalist accumulation (Gottdiener et al. 2018). WGS theory aimed to bring together distinct phenomena that had been separated, due to discipline boundaries limiting their engagement (Friedmann & Wolff 1982, Hall 2001, Wallerstein 2004). As meta-theories or all-encompassing theories, they understood the city as a product of global forces based on nation-state conditions (Clark & Wu 2021). WGS theory analyzes urban processes based on the unequal distribution of wealth globally: while some countries benefit, others are exploited and are affected by the unjust and unequal distribution of resources. Therefore, the Global North, the 'core,' extracts most of the world's goods and resources, while the countries of the Global South, the 'semi-periphery and periphery,' are underdeveloped based on the unjust historical patterns of global exploitation, imperialism, and (neo)colonialism. WGS theory expanded and invigorated the limitations of MPE by extending the analysis outside each locality, focusing on global connection and interdependence (Clark & Wu 2021, Sassen 2001, 2004a), but much was left unquestioned. For example, Sassen's global city (2001, 2004a, 2004b) highlights the importance of financial capital and the bureaucratic arrangements needed to make a global economy possible where globalization is produced.

**Embedded Racism in World-systems and Global Theory**

In foregrounding the interconnectivity and interdependence of the world's economy, considerably less weight is placed on other elements, or they are missed entirely. Thus, WGS theory has a limited explanatory capacity as it has difficulty addressing the state's role (Ren 2018, Sassen 2001) and the individual's agency (Slater 2021, Wallerstein 2011, 2004). WGS theory focuses on the experience, history, factors, and logics of the Global North as the drivers of all 'progress' and, indirectly, history, reducing all form of inequality to capitalist production (Clark & Wu 2021, Ren 2018). The Global South, the 'less developed' periphery localities, is positioned as a reactionary place and space in relation to processes occurring in the Global North.

Further, centering the analysis on global capitalism ignores human agency and the inseparability of White supremacy and capitalism. When the analysis centers on the experience of the Global North, those on the periphery become only dependent actors in relation to those in the Global North. Aligning the human experience with the Global North and treating the rest of the world as passing or supporting characters maintains systemic inequality (Bhandar 2018, Nandy 1983). Overall, this theoretical theme continues the legacy of urban sociology as a theory of Western progress, where those at the center are the typical players or the focus is on a few places (Clark & Wu 2021). Ignoring global White supremacy's role in driving capitalism concretizes colorblind urbanism, and as shown above, the notions of capital, property, and economic accumulation are based on propertied Whiteness.

**Urban Cultural Turn Approach (1990s–)**

The CT is the most recent and, in some ways, brings us back to the Chicago school (Musil 2004). Storper argues that the CT produces 'theory and research based on the notion that the key to understanding contemporary society and transforming it lies in the ways that culture orients our behavior and shapes what we are able to know about the world' (Storper 2001: 161). Postmodernism partly informs this perspective; like culture, language is both a structuring and structural agent, not just a byproduct of political economy. As such, much of what this research has shown is a documentation of the difference found in cities, places, and spaces (Musil 2004). At the middle of the CT is consumption. Stated differently, Musil argues that urban cultural sociology has changed '…into a kind of institutional and economical analysis of cities' (2004: 289). The city, its localities, and bodies are available goods for consumption. Cities become amenities available to the highest bidder for consumption as the cultures seem to be the driver of growth and progress (Florida 2002, Hutton 2019, Lloyd 2010, Musil 2004, Ward & Hubbard 2019, Zukin 2011). With deindustrialization and the disappearance of factory and production centers, the CT claims that street art, art, the food industry, tourism, and other cultural components have become significant forces in urban centers (Hutton 2019). Zukin's *The Cultures of Cities* (1996) shows how ethnicity, aesthetics, and marketing – 'culture' – shape and reshape urban spaces and places. As there are many of these aspects of urban cultures, the public and private sectors use them to revitalize such spaces and amenities. Thus, the spaces, places, and cultures embedded in those localities become amenities available to investors, which reduces everything to its consumptive value (Zukin 1998). Private and public investors and revitalizers use the cultures of places and spaces to attract urban newcomers, causing social and economic inequality – the displacement and emplacement around gentrification.

**Embedded Racism in the Urban Cultural Turn Approach**

The CT embeds racism as it lacks conversations about power differentials, treats culture as a stand-in for race and ethnicity, avoids questioning Whiteness and White supremacy, and replicates early Chicago school ideas (Musil 2004) with the help of new technology. In this form, culture stands for race, ethnicity, and other intersecting identities infused into place and space. Unfortunately, much of the research done within this theoretical approach misses that places and spaces with a cultural, economic value, like Black, Indigenous, Asian, Latine, Queer, or marginalized spaces, were created and kept because of power differentials. Thus, research that is merely descriptive, devoid of theory (Venkatesh 2008, Wacquant 2002), essentially works to translate those 'little worlds' into White logic and White methods (Zuberi & Bonilla-Silva 2008).

In a larger sense, the CT becomes what bell hooks called 'eating of the other' (hooks 1999), where the bodies, spaces, and culture of the Other(s) are there to be enjoyed and played with to spice up the bland White pallet. As consumption is crucial and global White supremacy has a fascination with the 'primitive,' this creates an obsession with the Other as a form of White entertainment and a ritualistic form of self-transformation and revitalization (hooks 2000). Looking at a progressive White community, I have shown that a sense of community and diversity are in direct opposition, as the label 'diverse' hides inequality (Montalva Barba 2021). I also argue that progressive White residents replicate settler colonial narratives, like frontier myths, to rationalize inequality in their neighborhood (Montalva Barba 2021; 2024). Here, settler colonialism narratives are understood as frames or stock stories that rationalize 'the ongoing process where colonizers settle in someone else's land, creating social, political, legal, and economic institutions solely for their benefit' (Montalva Barba 2021: 3, Saito 2020).

In the end, this examination of the distinct periods of urban theorizing and how they embed racism shows that urban sociology has moved in conjunction with sociology at large in prioritizing progress narratives. Race and racism in each theme protect, embed, and occlude from sight White privilege and White supremacy. The HEA was too narrowly focused on the urban problem, mainly racial Others (Montalva Barba 2023). This perspective determined how MPE missed the importance of ideology and its interrelatedness with structures, followed by WGS, which reduced everything to macro-economics and global forces, leaving behind the local specificities, and leading to the CT, which brings together several of the previous themes but ignores foundational frames that have created these 'diverse' cultures. There have been calls from different prominent scholars to critically understand the role that race, racism, White supremacy, settler colonialism, and empire have on the social and the urban (Bonilla-Silva 2006, 2015, Fenelon 2016, Glenn 2015, Go 2016, Itzigsohn & Brown 2020 Rios 2015, Slater 2021, Veracini 2010).

## ADDRESSING EMBEDDED RACISM IN URBAN THEORIZING

To address the embedded racism in urban theorizing, I offer several ways of thinking about race, racism, White supremacy, and settler colonialism. First, to recalibrate urban sociology's gaze, critical race and global critical race and racism (GCRR) theorizing suggest some cultural changes to the discipline (Christian 2019). A GCRR perspective brings together world-systems and global theorizing, political economy, and urban cultural studies, in conjunction with a race critical perspective. A GCRR perspective reconnects and builds on Du Boisian sociology, which is profoundly urban and centered on a global interconnectivity that urban sociologists must embrace (Itzigsohn & Brown 2020).

## Critical Race and Global Critical Race and Racism

The concept of race only tells us that racism persists as its creation is rooted in domination and exploitation, justifying all forms of inequality. Most of the time, when speaking about race, people are genuinely talking about racism, White supremacy, and inequality. Racism and White supremacy are active structures that work with other structures to justify global inequality (Banerjee-Dube 2014, Du Bois 1920, Fields & Fields 2014, Grosfoguel 2011, Mills 2003, Mullings 2005, Pierre 2012). Whiteness, like all dominant categories, hides in urban research (Montalva Barba 2023) as scholars often ignore the role that it serves as an (in)visible category present in the city (Clarke & Garner 2010). Whiteness as a social, historical, and political category is inseparable from conceptions of the city, social problems, and the characterization of the Other (powell 1997). Gotanda states that the US Constitution was written in a colorblind manner that enables White racial domination (1995: 257). Gotanda presents four ways the US Constitution uses race for domination: status-race, formal-race, historical-race, and cultural-race (Gotanda 1995). Status-race is the traditional way of understanding race as a social category, while formal-race is the normative interpretation of race that lacks imposed meanings and characteristics (Gotanda 1995). Historical-race, however, includes those proposed meanings and characteristics assigned to race – historical and contemporary racial subordination (Gotanda 1995). Cultural-race uses codes to signify specific characteristics; e.g., Blackness as the equivalent of African American lifestyle, culture, consciousness, and diaspora (Gotanda 1995). While this is rooted in a US context, the implication of thinking about race, as Gotanda articulates, can help urban scholars see past limitations and provide scholars with a frame to move forward. The HEA mainly used a cultural-race frame, which is invested in infusing racial categories into space, places, and bodies, while the CT tends to use both the cultural- and status-race approaches. Approaches based on capital accumulation and class antagonism, such as WGS theory, rely on a status- or a formal-race approach that actively de-emphasizes the complexity of racism and White supremacy as a structuring mechanism.

By taking Gotanda's race theorizing seriously, urban scholars can begin to see alternative ways to focus on a more historical understanding of race and racism. A historical-race perspective will influence scholars to consider how racism and racial categories have changed in different locations. Gotanda states that formal definitions of race do not consider the historical and social implications and largely leave race as a neutral identity qualifier (Gotanda 1995) or something that only non-White folks have. CRT proposes that racism is a global project that takes shape differently in specific localities but is ultimately rooted in global White supremacy (Bonilla-Silva 2001, Christian 2019; Christian et al. 2019, Jung 2020).

Christian proposes a 'GCRR framework that assumes the following: the racial structure is global and worldwide, national histories shape contemporary racial practices and mechanisms, materiality is the foundation, racism is defined structurally and ideologically, and global White supremacy is produced and rearticulated in new deeply rooted and malleable forms' (2019: 172). As Christian argues, this framework is undergirded by the idea that race and racism are malleable and have changed over time, and as such, 'we can identify how racism transforms depending on historical, political, and geographic boundaries marked by critical juncture events and path-dependent processes spotlighting both the *relational* and *interconnective* character between countries but still rooted in the foundation of global white supremacy' (2019: 172). A GCRR framework is built by the world system of global White supremacy and racializes zones and localities based on historical (empire, colonial modes) and global (racial neoliberalism, the War on Terror) processes (Christian 2019). Such processes engage with racist structures (state, economy, and institutions) and ideologies (discourses and representation) that create and maintain a national racial system, order, and inequality (Bonilla-Silva 2006, Christian 2019).

Due to globalization, empire, colonization, and settler colonialism, global White supremacy operates worldwide (Mills 2003). As Nandy states, 'The West is now everywhere, within the West and outside; in structures and in minds' (1983: 9). Some scholars will hesitate to embrace the premise that a racial structure is operating globally; I challenge such scholars to take an inventory of how Whiteness and White supremacy might operate in relation to their research, theoretical standpoints, and statuses in academia. As legal scholar Mary Matsuda (1990) points out, one should ask the other question when addressing intersectional coalition building. By this provocation, Matsuda challenges often taken-for-granted positionalities or standpoints to arrive at a more inclusive alliance that addresses how a global White supremacist structure operates. Matsuda states,

> The way that I try to understand the interconnection of all forms of subordination is through a method I call 'ask the other question.' When I see something that looks racist, I ask, 'where is the patriarchy in this?' When I see something that looks sexist, I ask 'Where is the heterosexism in this?' When I see something that looks homophobic, I ask 'Where is the class interest in this?' (1990: 1189)

While Matsuda is speaking about intersectional coalition building, the same questions can be valid for research agendas, positionalities, and statuses in academia. Global racial politics have been and will continue to be important because of globalization and global interconnectivity, which have been at the forefront since even before formal colonization.

## CONCLUSIONS

The role that embedded racism plays in urban sociology must be reconsidered, and our theorizing and research must account for urban sociology's foundation. Challenging embedded racism in urban theorizing must consider whom we cite and what we teach. The insights offered by GCRR and CRT should provide scholars with starting points to exploring what Shaw calls 'White Cities' (2007) and 'White institutional spaces' (Moore 2008). Historical-race perspectives that consider a robust and contemporary understanding of racism and race are needed. Research agendas that work to make the settler colonial visible in the city (Montalva Barba 2021, 2023) are needed along with work that questions White upper and middle-class parents (Hagerman 2018), how Whiteness operates in localities (Ramos-Zayas 2020), and how White supremacy takes place in spaces and places (Lipsitz 1998, 2011, 2019) and rethinks old terms like 'inner city' (Ansfield 2018, Wacquant 2002).

Urban sociologists need to come to terms with the legacies of the discipline to undo what has been and continues to be done. Slater calls for critical urban scholars to guard 'against the subordination of scholarly to policy agendas and challenge the rise of policy-driven research at the expense of research-driven agendas' (2021: 185). From the onset of urban sociology, funding from governmental agencies and non-profits has driven the urban question (Baldwin 2004, Montalva Barba 2023, Yu 2001). The early Chicago school's partnership with the city and the Rockefeller Foundation drove HEA research agendas, and this has only accelerated as the field has evolved. Leading to the question 'what has changed?' urban scholars must stand with their insights and forms of seeing the urban and not be limited by funding agencies or institutions. Who has the power when grants and state agencies lead this field forward?

## NOTES

1. I use 'non-White' to reference that in the US, whiteness has been constructed by the courts and has shifted over time; at different points, non-Whites included Italians, Polish, and Jewish people (see Haney López 1996).
2. Park's immigration and migrant assimilation theory was based on the work produced to understand the city. As populations become assimilated, they would 'naturally' move away from the city center and lose their differences. Park showcased the way White populations would become assimilated, not those marked with non-White racial difference (see Lipsitz 2011, Lyman 1968, Steinberg 2007).
3. See Robinson (1993, 2019) for his contributions to racial capitalism.

## REFERENCES

Abbott, A. (1999) *Department and discipline: Chicago sociology at one hundred*. Chicago: University of Chicago Press.
Abrutyn, S., & Lizardo, O. (2021) *Handbook of classical sociological theory*. Cham: Springer Nature.
Anderson, E. (1996) Introduction to *The Philadelphia Negro*. In *The Philadelphia Negro: A social study by W. E. B. Du Bois*. Philadelphia: University of Pennsylvania Press.
Ansfield, B. (2018) Unsettling 'inner city': Liberal protestantism and the postwar origins of a keyword in urban studies. *Antipode* 50(5): 1166–1185.
Baldwin, D. L. (2004) Black belts and ivory towers: The place of race in US social thought, 1892–1948. In Pfohl, S. et al. (eds.) *Culture, power, and history: Studies in critical sociology*. Leiden: Brill Publishers, 325–378.
Banerjee-Dube, I. (2014) Caste, race and difference: The limits of knowledge and resistance. *Current Sociology* 62(4): 512–530.
Bhambra, G. K. (2020) Colonial global economy: Towards a theoretical reorientation of political economy. *Review of International Political Economy* 28(2): 307–322.
Bhandar, B. (2018) *Colonial lives of property: Law, land, and racial regimes of ownership*. Durham: Duke University Press.
Bonilla-Silva, E. (2001) *White supremacy and racism in the post-civil rights era*. Boulder: Lynne Rienner Publishers.
Bonilla-Silva, E. (2006 [2003]). *Racism without racists: Color-blind racism and the persistence of racial inequality in the United States*. Durham: Rowman & Littlefield Publisher.
Bonilla-Silva, E. (2015) More than prejudice: Restatement, reflections, and new directions in critical race theory. *Sociology of Race and Ethnicity* 1(1): 73–87.
Burgess, E. W. (1967 [1925]) The growth of the city: An introduction to a research project. In Park, R. et al. (eds.) *The city: Suggestions for investigation of human behavior in urban environments*. Chicago: University of Chicago Press, 47–62.
Castells, M. (2007 [1968/1976]) Is there an urban sociology? In Pickvance, C. (ed.) *Urban sociology: Critical essays*. Abingdon: Routledge, 33–59.
Christian, M. (2019) A global critical race and racism framework: Racial entanglements and deep and malleable whiteness. *Sociology of Race and Ethnicity* 5(2): 169–185.
Christian, M., Seamster, L. & Ray, V. (2019) New directions in critical race theory and sociology: Racism, white supremacy, and resistance. *American Behavioral Scientist* 63(13): 1731–1740.
Clark, T. N., & Wu, C. (2021) Urban theorizing. In Abrutyn, S. & Lizardo, O. (eds.) *Handbook of classical sociological theory*. Cham: Springer Nature.

Clarke, S. & Garner, S. (2010) *White identities: A critical sociological approach*. Boston: Pluto Press.
Connell, R. W. (1997) Why is classical theory classical? *American Journal of Sociology* 102(6): 1511–1557.
Drake, S. C. & Cayton, H. R. (2015 [1945]) *Black metropolis: A study of negro life in a northern city*. Chicago: University of Chicago Press.
Du Bois, W. E. B. (1920) *Darkwater: Voices from within the veil*. Mineola: Dover Publications.
Du Bois, W. E. B. (1968) *Dusk of dawn: An essay towards and autobiography of a race concept*. New York: Oxford University Press.
Durkheim, E. (1984) *The division of labor in society* (2nd ed.). Basingstoke: Macmillian.
Fenelon, J. V. (2016) Critique of Glenn on settler colonialism and Bonilla-Silva on critical race analysis from indigenous perspectives. *Sociology of Race and Ethnicity* 2(2): 237–242.
Fields, K. E., & Fields, B. J. (2014) *Racecraft: The soul of inequality in American life*. London: Verso Books.
Florida, R. (2002) *The rise of the creative class* (Vol. 9). New York: Basic books.
Frankenberg, R. (1997) Introduction: Local whiteness, localizing whiteness. In Frankenberg, R. (ed.) *Displacing whiteness: Essays in social and cultural criticism*. Durham: Duke University Press, 1–33.
Frazier, E. (1997 [1957]) *Black bourgeoisie*. New York: Simon and Schuster.
Friedmann, J., & Wolff, G. (1982) World city formation: An agenda for research and action. *International Journal of Urban and Regional Research* 6(3): 309–344.
Glenn, E. N. (2015) Settler colonialism as structure: A framework for comparative studies of US race and gender formation. *Sociology of Race and Ethnicity* 1(1): 54–74.
Go, J. (2013) For a postcolonial sociology. *Theory and Society* 42(1): 25–55.
Go, J. (2016) *Postcolonial thought and social theory*. Oxford: Oxford University Press.
Gotanda, N. (1995) A critique of 'our constitution is color-blind'. In Crenshaw, K. et al. (eds.) *Critical race theory: The key writings that formed the movement*. New York: The New Press, 257–275.
Gottdiener, M., Hutchison, R., & Ryan, M. (2018) *The new urban sociology*. New York: Routledge.
Greek, C. E. (1992) *The religious roots of American sociology*. New York: Garland Publishing Inc.
Grosfoguel, R. (2011) Decolonizing post-colonial studies and paradigms of political-economy: Transmodernity, decolonial thinking, and global coloniality. *Transmodernity: Journal of Peripheral Cultural Production of the Luso-Hispanic World* 1(1).
Hagerman, M. A. (2018) *White kids*. New York: New York University Press.
Hall, P. (2001) Global city-regions in the twenty-first century. In Scott, A. (ed.) *Global city-regions: Trends, theory, policy*. Oxford: Oxford University Press, 59–77.
Haney López, I. (1996) *White by law: The legal construction of race*. New York: New York
Harding, A., & Blokland, T. (2014) *Urban theory*. London: Sage.
Harris, C. I. (1993) Whiteness as property. *Harvard Law Review* 106(8): 1707–1791.
Harvey, D. (1973) *Social justice and the city*. London: Edward Arnold.
Harvey, D, (1975) Class structure in a capitalist society and the theory of residential differentiation. In Peel, R. et al. (eds.) *Process in physical and human geography: Bristol essays*. London: Heinemann Educational Books.
Harvey, D. (1985) The geopolitics of capitalism. In Gregory, D., & Urry, J. (eds.) *Social relations and spatial structures*. London: Palgrave, 128–163.
Harvey, D. (2006) *Spaces of global capitalism*. New York: Verso.
hooks, b. (1999) *Black looks: Race and representation*. Boston: South End Press.
hooks, b. (2000) *Feminism is for everyone*. Boston: South End Press.
Hunter, M. A. (2013) *Black citymakers: How The Philadelphia Negro changed urban America*. New York: Oxford University Press.
Hutton, T. (2019) The cultural economy in cities. In Schwanen, T. & Van Kempen, R. (eds.) *Handbook of urban geography*. Cheltenham, UK and Northampton, MA, USA: Edward Elgar Publishing.
Itzigsohn, J. & Brown, K. L. (2020) *The sociology of W. E. B. Du Bois*. New York: New York University Press.
Jung, M. K. (2009) The racial unconscious of assimilation theory. *Du Bois Review: Social Science Research on Race* 6(2): 375–395.
Jung, M. K. (2020) *Beneath the surface of white supremacy*. Palo Alto: Stanford University Press.

Kasinitz, P. (1995) *Metropolis: Center and symbol of our times* (Vol. 3). New York: New York University Press.
Kurtz, L. R. (1984) *Evaluating Chicago sociology: A guide to the literature, with an annotated bibliography*. Chicago: The University of Chicago Press.
Lal, B. (1987) Black and blue in Chicago: Robert E. Park's perspective on race relations in urban America, 1914–44. *The British Journal of Sociology* 38(4): 546–566,
Lefebvre, H. (2014 [1991]) The production of space. In Gieseking, J. et al. (eds.) *The people, place, and space reader*. New York: Routledge.
Lipsitz, G. (1998) *The possessive investment in whiteness: How white people profit from identity politics*. Philadelphia: Temple University Press.
Lipsitz, G. (2011) *How racism takes place*. Philadelphia: Temple University Press.
Lipsitz, G. (2019) The sounds of silence: How race neutrality preserves white supremacy. In Crenshaw, K. (ed.) *Seeing race again: Countering colorblindness across the disciplines*. Los Angeles: University of California Press, 23–51.
Lloyd, R. (2010) *Neo-bohemia: Art and commerce in the postindustrial city*. Routledge: New York.
Logan, J., & Molotch, H. (2007 [1987]) *Urban fortunes: The political economy of place*. Berkeley: University of California Press.
Lyman, S. M. (1968) The race relations cycle of Robert E. Park. *The Pacific Sociological Review* 11(1): 16–22.
Magubane, Z. (2014) Science, reform, and the 'science of reform': Booker T. Washington, Robert Park, and the making of a 'science of society'. *Current Sociology* 62(4): 568–583.
Matsuda, M. J. (1990) Beside my sister, facing the enemy: Legal theory out of coalition. *Stanford Law Review* 43: 1183.
Mills, C. W. (2003) *The racial contract*. New York: Cornell University Press.
Molotch, H. (1976) The city as a growth machine: Toward a political economy of place. *American Journal of Sociology* 82(2): 309–332.
Molotch, H. (1990). Urban deals in comparative perspective. In Logan, J.R. & Swanstrom, T. (eds.) *Beyond the city limits: Urban policy and economic restructuring in comparative perspective*. Philadelphia: Temple University Press, 175–198.
Molotch, H., & Logan, J. (1990) The space for urban action: Urban fortunes; a rejoinder. *Political Geography Quarterly* 9(1): 85–92.
Montalva Barba, M. (2021) (Re)enacting settler colonialism via white resident utterances. *Critical Sociolog*, 47(7–8): 1267–1281.
Montalva Barba, M. (2023) To move forward, we must look back: White supremacy at the base of urban studies. *Urban Studies* 60(5): 791–810.
Montalva Barba, M. (2024) *White supremacy and racism in progressive America: Race, place, and space*. Bristol: Bristol University Press.
Moore, W. L. (2008) *Reproducing racism: White space, elite law schools, and racial inequality*. Lanham: Rowman & Littlefield.
Morris, A. (2015) *Scholar denied: W. E. B. Du Bois and the birth of modern sociology*. Los Angeles: University of California Press.
Mullings, L. (2005) Interrogating racism: Toward an antiracist anthropology. *Annual Review Anthropology*, 34, 667–693.
Musil, J. (2004) Fifty years of urban sociology. In Genove, N. (ed.) *Advances in Sociological Knowledge*. Cham: Springer Science, 269–298.
Nandy, A. (1983) *The intimate enemy: Loss and recovery of self under colonisation*. Chapel Hill: University of North Carolina Press.
Nichols, R. (2020) *Theft is property! Dispossession and critical theory*. Durham: Duke University Press.
Park, R. E. (1950 [1918]) The collected papers of Robert Ezra Park. In Everett, C. H. et al. (eds.) *Vol. 1: Race and Culture*. Glencoe: Free Press.
Park, R. E., Burgess, E., & McKenzie, R. D. (1967 [1925]) *The city: Suggestions for investigation of human behavior in urban environments*. Chicago: University of Chicago Press.
Petersen, C. (2022) Capitalizing on heritage: St. Augustine, Florida, and the landscape of American racial ideology. *City & Community* 21(3): 193–213.
Pierre, J. (2012) *The predicament of blackness*. Chicago: University of Chicago Press.

powell, j. (1997) The 'racing' of American society: Race functioning as a verb before signifying as a noun. *Law and Inequality* 15(99): 99–125.

Ramos-Zayas, A. Y. (2020) *Parenting empires: Class, whiteness, and the moral economy of privilege in Latin America*. Durham: Duke University Press.

Ren, X. (2018) From Chicago to China and India: Studying the city in the twenty-first century. *Annual Review of Sociology* 44: 497–513.

Rios, V. M. (2015) Decolonizing the white space in urban ethnography. *City & Community* 14(3): 258–261.

Robinson, C. J. (1993) *Black Marxism: The making of a Black radical tradition*. Chapel Hill: The University of North Carolina Press.

Robinson, C. J. (2019) *An anthropology of Marxism*. Chapel Hill: UNC Press Books.

Saito, N. T. (2020) *Settler colonialism, race, and the law*. New York: New York University Press.

Sassen, S. (2001 [1991]) *The global city: New York, London, Tokyo*. Princeton: Princeton University Press.

Sassen, S. (2004a) New frontiers facing urban sociology at the millennium. *British Journal of Sociology* 51(1): 143–159.

Sassen, S. (2004b) The global city: Introducing a concept. *Brown Journal of World Affairs* 11: 27.

Sassen, S. (2010) The city: Its return as a lens for social theory. *City, Culture, and Society* 1: 3–10.

Saunders, P. (2003 [1989]) *Social theory and the urban question*. Los Angeles: Routledge.

Schwendinger, H., & Schwendinger, J.R. (1974) *The sociologists of the chair: A radical analysis of the formative years of North American sociology (1883–1922)*. New York: Basic Books.

Shaw, W. S. (2007) *Cities of whiteness*. Malden: Blackwell Publishing.

Slater, T. (2021) *Shaking up the city*. Oakland: University of California Press.

Small, A. W. (1916) Fifty years of sociology in the United States (1865–1915). *American Journal of Sociology* 21(6): 721–864.

Smith, N. (1996) *The new urban frontier: Gentrification and the revanchist city*. London: Routledge.

Steinberg, S. (2007) *Race relations: A critique*. Stanford: Stanford University Press.

Storper, M. (2001) The poverty of radical theory today: From the false promises of Marxism to the mirage of the cultural turn. *International Journal of Urban and Regional Research* 25(1): 155–179.

Tönnies, F. (2002 [1887]) *Community and society*. Mineola: Dover Publications Inc.

Tucker, R. (1978) *The Marx-Engels reader*. New York: W. W. Norton & Company.

Valle, M. M. (2017) Revealing the ruse: Shifting the narrative of colorblind urbanism. *International Journal of Urban and Regional Research*. Available at: https://www.ijurr.org/spotlight-on/race-justice-and-the-city/revealing-the-ruse-shifting-the-narrative-of-colorblind-urbanism/.

Valle, M. M. (2021) Globalizing the sociology of gentrification. *City & Community* 20(1): 59–70.

Venkatesh, S. A. (2008) *Gang leader for a day: A rogue sociologist takes to the streets*. New York: Penguin Press.

Veracini, L. (2010) *Settler colonialism: A theoretical overview*. New York: Palgrave Macmillan.

Wacquant, L. (1995 [1989]) The ghetto, the state and the new capitalist economy. In Kasinitz, P. (ed.) *Metropolis: Center and symbol of our times*. New York: NYU Press, 413–449.

Wacquant, L. (2002) Scrutinizing the street: Poverty, morality, and the pitfalls of urban ethnography. *American Journal of Sociology* 107(6): 1468–1532.

Wallerstein, I. (2004) *World-systems analysis*. Durham: Duke University Press.

Wallerstein, I. (2011 [1974]) *The modern world-system I: Capitalist agriculture and the origins of the European world-economy in the sixteenth century* (Vol. 1). Los Angeles: University of California Press.

Ward, J., & Hubbard, P. (2019) Urban regeneration through culture. In Schwenen, T. and Kempen, R. (eds.) *Handbook of urban geography*. Cheltenham, UK and Northampton, MA, USA: Edward Elgar Publishing.

Weber, M. (1967 [1930]) *The protestant ethic and the spirit of capitalism*. New York: Charles Scribner's Sons.

Weber, M. (1978 [1921]) The city (non-legitimate domination). In Roth, G., and Wittich, C. (eds.) *Economy and society*. Berkeley: University of California Press.

Yu, H. (2001) *Thinking orientals: Migration, contact, and exoticism in modern America*. New York: Oxford University Press.

Zuberi, T. & Bonilla-Silva, E. (2008) *White logic, white methods: Racism and methodology.* New York: Rowman & Littlefield Publishers, Inc.

Zukin, S. (1996) *The cultures of cities.* New York: Wiley-Blackwell.

Zukin, S. (1998) Urban lifestyles: Diversity and standardization in spaces of consumption. *Urban Studies* 35(5–6): 825–839.

Zukin, S. (2011) Is there an urban sociology? Questions on a field and a vision. *Sociologica* 3: 1–17.

# 11. Sociology of gentrification
*Andrej Holm*

In German newspapers, the term 'gentrification' was explained for years as a foreign-language technical term with the addition 'sociologists call the process...'. Now long-established in the linguistic mainstream, the question still arises as to what sociologists actually mean by the buzz word 'gentrification', as it is not clear since German journalists associate gentrification with a field of sociological research.

In fact, in the almost 60 years since Ruth Glass first used the term, research on gentrification has established itself in many academic fields and has become an interdisciplinary research topic: geographers analyze the spatial processes of gentrification and displacement; economists examine the influence of land rents and management practices on real estate markets; cultural scholars direct their research towards questions of symbolic gentrification, cultural use, and the changing representation of urban spaces; urban planners examine the role of state programs and state actors in urban development processes; and political scientists ask about the institutional contexts of gentrification.

However, what are sociologists actually interested in when they study gentrification? Is there a specifically sociological approach to the research field and if so what does it consist of?

A sociological perspective in general focuses on the social dimensions of societies and asks about the significance of social groups, social relations, and social processes. Sociological theorists are always concerned with 'understanding or explaining social processes in terms of their causes, manifestations and effects, and interpreting them in terms of their social and cultural consequences' (Rosa et al. 2007: 15). From a sociological perspective, three questions are at stake: what holds the society together? What keeps society changing, what forces it to change? How can social development be (politically) controlled or even guided?

In the broad field of sociological theories and research approaches, differences are visible across two dimensions: a) in the level of observation (micro, macro, meso) and b) in the perspective of the explanatory approaches (theories of agency and structure). A look at theory formation and research practice shows that sociology can focus on social conditions, relationships, and practices for individual relationships, as well as interaction in and between groups and institutions, and for societies as a whole. A central aspect of the sociological perspective is to consider individual and collective action and behavior in their entanglements and their relation to broader societal processes.

Regardless of the manifold further developments of sociological theories, two basic explanatory approaches can be identified. First, structural theory approaches attempt to explain individual intentions and actions from the prevailing social-structural conditions. In this perspective, the development and transformation of these structural conditions also result from their own regularities and are therefore to be explained from the structural conditions themselves. In contrast, agency-based theoretical approaches focus on the social actions of individuals or groups in interaction processes and try to identify structural patterns and social mechanisms in them. In this perspective, changes in structural conditions result from the sum of individual behavior and social interactions.

Whether and how these sociological perspectives are used in gentrification research and what specific contribution sociology can offer to the understanding of gentrification processes will be clarified in this chapter. In the first sections of the text, the common definitions of gentrification as well as the explanations and assumptions about gentrification processes established in urban research are presented. This is followed by a section on current research debates and conceptual questions for gentrification research. The chapter then discusses whether an explicitly sociological perspective can make an independent contribution to understanding gentrification processes. Basic categories of sociological research (social groups, social ties, social relations, and social order) are placed in the context of gentrification. A concluding section discusses in summary what contribution a sociological perspective can make to gentrification research and what its limitations are.

## DEFINITION

A first clue for the definition of gentrification can be found in a retrospective look at the gentrification research of the last 60 years. The term was first mentioned in London in 1964. The British sociologist and urban planner Ruth Glass summarized the changes she observed in the London district of Islington as follows:

> One by one, many of the working class quarters of London have been invaded by the middle classes – upper and lower. Shabby, modest mews and cottages – two rooms up, two down – have been taken over, when their leases have expired, and have become elegant, expensive residences. Larger Victorian houses, downgraded in an earlier or recent period – which were used as lodging houses or were otherwise in multiple occupation – have been upgraded once again. [...] Once this process of 'gentrification' starts in a district, it goes on rapidly until all or most of the original working class occupiers are displaced, and the whole social character of the district has changed. (Glass 1964: 18)

The main features of this early description of gentrification are a) the economic valorization of real estate, b) the physical upgrading of buildings, c) a population exchange through the displacement of lower classes, and d) a change in the social character of the neighborhood. The spatial reference unit of gentrification in Ruth Glass's definition is the neighborhood; it is neither an individual building nor the whole city.

In addition to these general criteria, in her London case study she names location-specific and time-specific characteristics of gentrification. With the description of the 'great Victorian houses', Ruth Glass refers to an architectural-historical precondition of gentrification processes and places them in a life-cycle evolution of buildings with the description of structural decay.

Since the Islington study, a respectable branch of research in geography and urban sociology has developed around the term, which arose from an analogy with the return of the 'gentry'; i.e. the lower nobles from the countryside in the 18th century. Well over 1000 internationally published articles, books, and anthologies stand for the establishment and topicality of an independent field of research. The conceptual and analytical apparatus of gentrification research has in particular produced approaches and instruments for investigating the economic and social dimensions of urban restructuring.

Most gentrification studies assume an interrelation between economic interests and urban changes and the early conceptions especially focus on the process of rehabilitation in the sense of renewal and modernization of already existing residential buildings:

> By gentrification I mean the process by which working class residential neighborhoods are rehabilitated by middle class homebuyers, landlords and professional developers. I make the theoretical distinction between gentrification and redevelopment. Redevelopment involves not rehabilitation of old structures but the construction of new buildings on previously developed land. (Smith 1982: 139)

Despite the relatively narrow scope of the object of investigation, a controversial understanding of gentrification has emerged in academic and public debates. Even after decades of debate about the causes, typical course, and consequences of gentrification processes, there is still no clear definition of the object of study in terms of precise models and hypotheses. However, this 'chaos of gentrification', as Robert Beauregard put it in the late 1980s, is less an expression of academic arbitrariness than a tribute to the complexity of urban processes (Beauregard 1986). In gentrification processes, structural and infrastructural changes in the neighborhoods overlap with real estate value creation, changed resident structures, new forms of urban policy, and symbolic revaluations of residential neighborhoods. In particular, attempts to elevate singular aspects of gentrification processes to a core definition have always been criticized for neglecting other important aspects.

The proposals for a 'minimal consensus' on the description of gentrification, are mostly justified by including only the dependent variable in the definition, without including the explanatory factors. Typical of such attempts at a definition that only includes the effects is that offered by Kennedy and Leonard:

> [Gentrification is] the process by which higher income households displace lower income residents of a neighborhood, changing the essential character and flavor of that neighborhood. (Kennedy & Leonard 2001: 6)

However, the majority of gentrification research assumes a multi-dimensional understanding of gentrification, including architectural and physical changes (Barry 1985), increases in property values (Clark 1987, 1991, Smith 1979, 1986), and changes in the character of the neighborhood understood as a new composition of local facilities and shops, changed moods on the street, and a new image of the neighborhood (Patch 2008, Zukin 2010).

Regardless of the discussions about the different elements that should be included in the definition of gentrification, many researchers have insisted that displacement constitutes the essence of gentrification processes (Hartmann 1982, Marcuse 1992). In his work on New York, Peter Marcuse specified the concept of displacement and systematized various forms and facets: he distinguished between (1) last-resident displacement, (2) direct-chain displacement, (3) exclusionary displacement, and (4) displacement pressure. He considered direct displacement through both rising housing costs ('economic displacement') and unacceptable housing conditions ('physical displacement'), as well as indirect displacement through neighborhood changes ('displacement pressure') and rising costs in the allocation of housing ('exclusionary displacement') (Marcuse 1986: 156f.).

In recent years, a multiplication of gentrification research has become established. Some of the research work is increasingly focusing on the subjective aspects of gentrification and places questions of identity and authenticity at the center of the analyses (Brown-Saracino

2019, Zukin 2010). In doing so, the perspectives of gentrifiers and middle-class members are increasingly taken up and they are asked how they incorporate the changes in the neighborhoods into their distinction-oriented lifestyles and give gentrification a performative character in their way of life (Schlichtman et al. 2017).

Another perspective, more strongly influenced by political economy, has in recent years focused on the political conditions in which gentrification processes unfold. These contributions point to the crucial role of urban policy, which, with its regulatory instruments, promotes or accelerates gentrification or even makes it possible in the first place (Bernt 2022). Some authors, such as Loretta Lees, even assume that there has been no gentrification without an urban policy impulse (Lees 1994a, 1994b, Lees et al. 2008). The latter two arguments in particular give an idea of why gentrification has developed from an academic analytical approach to a concept that is often disputed in urban policy. In particular, the emphasis on socially negative effects (displacement) and the involvement of the political administrative system in gentrification raise the question of political responsibility. As displacement describes a proactive process of (re)production of social inequalities, the notion of gentrification has become a contested concept, especially in political and public debates: 'Precisely because the language of gentrification tells the truth about the class shift involved in "regeneration" of the city, it has become a dirty word to developers, politicians, and financiers' (Smith 2002: 445).

# EXPLANATION

Gentrification research in urban studies should not limit itself to the observation, description, and measurement of phenomena but is faced with the task of offering explanations for the observed developments. Three central explanatory approaches have emerged in gentrification research.

(1) Demand-side explanations of gentrification research attribute the upgrading of inner-city districts to changing lifestyles, new occupational demands, and a demographic change in society. In addition to the new attractiveness of inner cities as places of residence for the middle classes (Ley 1996), changed labor relations in the transition to a service economy, forms of a new gendered division of labor, and the establishment of distinction-oriented lifestyles are cited (Häußermann & Siebel 1987). The central argument of these explanatory approaches attributes gentrification to changing economic conditions and a re-composition of social structures throughout society, which is reflected in a change in demand. Gentrification takes place because the middle classes are increasingly drawn to the inner cities.

(2) Production-oriented explanatory approaches place the economic framework conditions of urban upgrading at the center of their analyses. The central question is when and under what conditions investors are willing to invest money in the modernization of old residential buildings. In this perspective, upgrading processes do not appear as the effect of a change in demand but as the consequence of a change in supply (Smith 1979). Essential aspects of this argumentation are a macroeconomic explanation for the cyclically recurring attractiveness of investing in the real-estate sector, the microeconomic rationality of so-called rent gaps, and the transitions from a rentier economy to a profit economy. The rentier economy in the context of the housing market can be understood

as long-term and regular interest income derived from the ownership and control of land or other assets. The profit economy, on the other hand, describes income and often short-term profits derived from entrepreneurial investments and a targeted strategy of value extraction. This can include, for example, speculation on land, upgrading through modernization measures, or even the conversion of rental housing into owner-occupied property. The central argument of this explanation is the general economic conditions of capital accumulation and locally specific investment decisions that result in changing housing supply and expected economic returns. Gentrification occurs because commercial interests of owners, developers, and landlords are realized in previously undervalued neighborhoods.

(3) Urban policy explanatory approaches have established themselves in international gentrification research as a third explanatory pattern alongside demand- and production-oriented approaches. The particularities of local gentrification processes that have become apparent in international comparisons have been attributed to different strategies and instruments of urban policy. Funding programs, heritage protection laws, and planning law, but also the different goals of state revitalization strategies and the entrepreneurial orientation of urban policy, are seen as important framework conditions for the different courses of gentrification (Hochstenbach 2017, Lees 2003a, López-Morales 2019). A number of studies, especially on cities in Latin America (Gaffney 2016, López-Morales et al. 2021, Sánchez & Broudehoux 2013) and Southeast Asia (He 2019, La Grange & Pretorius 2015, Shin & Kim 2016), show how public urban development programs and state-owned enterprises play a central role in gentrification. The central argument of this explanatory approach emphasizes the active role of state programs, instruments, and institutions in enabling and implementing gentrification. Gentrification takes place because state actors have an interest in gentrification and have the means to realize these interests.

For many years, gentrification research was characterized by a dispute about the 'right' explanatory approach. Especially in empirical case studies, it regularly became clear that in almost all cases gentrification in the studied neighborhoods could only be adequately described by a combination of different causes. Without middle-class households seeking to move into the gentrified inner-city areas: no gentrification; without owners and developers buying properties and investing in the building stock: no gentrification; and without a local government that allows or even promotes the respective developments: no gentrification. However, the scope of theoretical explanations should not be judged by whether their elements can be empirically represented, but by whether they have an analytical added value that contributes to a deeper understanding of the observed processes.

For an understanding of gentrification that focuses on the displacement processes, demand-side theories offer only limited explanatory value because the expansion of the changed housing preferences of the middle classes alone cannot explain why the displacement of the lower classes from the respective areas occurs. Economic and political explanations are more useful in this respect because they target mechanisms and intentions that are directly linked to the question of displacement. The production-side theoretical approaches essentially describe an economic logic of valorization through displacement. Precisely because low-income households in run-down residential areas with a lack of facilities mainly live with low rents after decades of disinvestment, displacement becomes a necessary precondition for the business model of gentrification. When Peter Marcuse states that 'displacement is the essence of gentrification and not an unintended side effect' (Marcuse 1992: 80), this is not just an empirical observation but a logical conclusion from the economic explanatory model. Closing the rent gap – as elaborated by Neil Smith (1979) – requires a change in land-use patterns. At its core, the concept of the rent gap states that the currently capitalized ground rent is obtained under conditions that do not correspond to the best and highest uses. It is only through a change in land use and the subsequent displacement of previous users and residents that it is possible to realize the potential ground rent.

In a very similar way, policy explanations also offer a direct link between state intervention and displacement in gentrification areas. In many cases, the state and local authorities shape the conditions for investment or have a direct interest in gentrification and actively implement displacement processes. Gentrification can be understood from the perspective of political economy explanatory approaches as a neighborhood-related upgrading process in which real estate economic valorization strategies and/or political strategies of upgrading require the exchange of populations for their success.

Critical urban scholars in particular have expended a great deal of energy establishing and defending the political and economic explanations (Calbet & Elias 2018, Shaw 2008, Slater 2006, 2009, Smith 2002). This is not so much a matter of academic arrogance ('my explanation is better than yours') but of insisting on a view of urban development, gentrification, and displacement as expressions and arenas of social contestation rather than as a necessary 'natural process'.

## NEW QUESTIONS IN GENTRIFICATION RESEARCH

Many contributions to the international debate emphasize that gentrification is not a rigid concept. Thus, both gentrification dynamics and research approaches have changed and been modified over the last 40 years. Neil Smith and Jason Hackworth (2001) attempted to describe the phenomena of gentrification with larger historical cycles of gentrification dynamics. They located a first wave in the late 1960s and early 1970s (in Western Europe and US cities) as sporadic, highly localized, and state-sponsored gentrification in disinvested residential inner-city areas to counteract the decline of these neighborhoods (Hackworth & Smith 2001: 466).

A consolidation and intensification of gentrification in the late 1970s after the recession is referred to as the second wave. This phase was characterized by an expansion of spatial arenas to neighborhoods and cities 'that had not previously experienced gentrification' and laissez-faire policies aimed at promoting the private market in general rather than directly subsidizing gentrification. Moreover, gentrification dynamics in this period were more integrated into national and global economic and cultural processes and no longer exclusively due to location-specific conditions (Hackworth & Smith 2001: 466f.).

A third wave of gentrification following the economic crises of the late 1980s began in the mid-1990s and was 'characterized by interventionist government working with private sector to facilitate gentrification' (Shaw 2004: 183). Gentrification was more closely linked to large-scale capital than in the past and was characterized by an increased presence of larger corporations rather than small landlords. In contrast to the culturally mediated gentrification of the previous phase, developments were only very marginally determined by economic forces (Hackworh & Smith 2001: 468).

Loretta Lees, Tom Slater, and Elvyn Wyly argued that a fourth wave of gentrification in the years following the recession at the turn of the millennium can be identified, as 'intensified financialization of housing combined with the consolidation of pro-gentrification politics and polarized urban policies' (Lees et al. 2008: 179).

In his research, Manuel Aalbers observed a further shift in the interplay between the economy and the state, describing a fifth wave of gentrification as the 'materialisation of financialised or finance-driven capitalism'. In particular, he reflected on observations in the years following the financial crisis of 2007/08 of a partial cooling and reluctance of the state to directly promote gentrification and an increasingly leading role for finance. He pointed to the importance of institutional investors, corporate landlords, and conversions from rental to short-term rental housing in the shadow of the emerging platform capitalism. In contrast to earlier waves, 'the prominent role of the state' in enforcing gentrification 'is now being complemented by finance' (Aalbers 2019: 5). (See Figure 11.1)

*Source:* Miguel A. Martínez.

*Figure 11.1    Construction site in Berlin (2019)*

## MULTIPLE SPATIAL MANIFESTATIONS OF GENTRIFICATION

The dynamics of gentrification processes in recent decades have contributed to an expansion of urban manifestations of gentrification. Unlike in the days of Ruth Glass, gentrification processes are no longer limited to small inner-city islands of upgrading. If we take the research of recent years as a reference, gentrification is discussed in almost all spatial contexts, is seen as a global phenomenon and is analyzed as a process that is never actually complete.

(1) Gentrification is everywhere. As examples in New York and London show, gentrification processes are no longer limited to individual neighborhoods, but have developed from an exceptional situation into a new urban mainstream (Wyly & Hammel 1999). Comparable cascades of upgrading could also be described for developments in Berlin (Holm 2013). Beyond this spread within the cities, several studies in recent years have identified gentrification processes – as a first spatial modification – outside the large metropolises. Examples include cities such as Bristol (Bridge 2003), Portland, Maine (Lees 2006), and Leeds (Dutton 2003, 2005), but also the approaches to investigating rural gentrification (Darling 2005, Ghose 2007, Hjort 2009, Phillips 2005). A second spatial modification of gentrification refers to the structural contexts of upgrading processes. For example, a number of authors draw on the concept of gentrification in their studies of the regeneration of former industrial and port sites (Davidson & Lees 2005, Rérat et al. 2009, Visser & Kotze 2008). Tim Butler and Loretta Lees refer to the displacement dimension of so-called 'new-build gentrification' when neighborhood and citywide contexts are included in the upgrading analysis of new construction projects (Butler & Lees 2006: 469). Examples from Newcastle (Cameron 2003) and London also show that the newly built luxury housing developments have an impact on the land prices of the surrounding area and trigger revaluation processes there. Loretta Lees and Mark Davidson use the metaphor of 'tentacles of gentrification' for these effects (Davidson & Lees 2005: 1186).

(2) Gentrification is global. Rowland Atkinson describes gentrification as a 'new urban colonialism' and refers to a double globalization effect. First, gentrification processes are no longer limited to Western European and North American metropolises but have long since reached a global scale (Atkinson & Bridge 2005, Lees et al. 2015, 2016). Thus, the international gentrification debate has been enriched in recent years by numerous examples from beyond the previous research landscapes. These include studies on gentrification processes in Eastern European cities (Badyna & Golubchikov 2005, Feldmann 2000, Kovács 1998, Ruoppila & Kärik 2003, Sykora 2005), as well as examples from Japan (Fujitsuka 2005, Namba 2000), Turkey (Ergun 2004, Islam 2010, Uzun 2003), and Brazil (Rubino 2005). On the other hand, internationally active investment firms and globally operating project developers are increasingly identified as central actors in the upgrading process (Hackworth & Smith 2001: 468). Neil Smith interprets gentrification under these conditions as a 'global urban strategy' and argues for an integrated analysis of the connections between globalization, neoliberal urban policy, and gentrification (Smith 2002).

(3) Gentrification has no end. Recent studies use the term 'super-gentrification' to describe extended cycles of upgrading in already gentrified neighborhoods and make clear that urban development processes have no end point. Loretta Lees described her observations in New York's Brooklyn Highs as a 'transformation of already gentrified, prosperous and solidly upper-middle-class neighborhoods into much more exclusive and expansive enclaves' (Lees 2003b: 2487). She locates these processes of 'intensified re-gentrification' in a few selected areas of global cities like London and New York, driven by a new generation of super-rich bankers from the booming financial sector. Just as the tertiarization of the 1980s with the newly emerging inner-city jobs of the service economy forced the inner-city housing demand of well-educated middle-class people, the third wave of gentrification is forming on the basis of a globalized financial economy

(Hackworth & Smith 2001: 469). Using the example of Barnsbury in London, Loretta Lees and Tim Butler describe 'super-gentrification' as a social change characterized by the influx of new, more elite and globally connected gentrifiers who are different from both traditional gentrifiers and the traditional urban upper classes (Butler & Lees 2006: 467). Compared to earlier waves of gentrification, processes of 'super-gentrification' are associated with higher financial and economic investment in the neighborhood (Lees et al. 2008: 149).

The three described expansions and modifications of gentrification are not only reflected in a plethora of studies and publications but also pose new challenges for the research concept itself. In particular, the analyses of the political involvement and promotion of gentrification processes, the investigation of international financial and investment flows, and the description of the new appropriation strategies of the urban middle classes will not be possible with the traditional instruments of gentrification research (quantitative studies on population exchange).

With the geographic expansion of gentrification research and the multiplication of the studied manifestations of urban upgrading and displacement processes, the limitations of gentrification conceptions become clear. As more and more phenomena were studied as gentrification that differed from the processes originally studied in inner-city poor neighborhoods of London or New York, gentrification definitions became increasingly abstract. In the context of their studies of new construction gentrification in London, Mark Davidson and Loretta Lees (2005) solved the difficulties of applying the classical definition to the so-called 'gentrification mutations' by modifying the definition of gentrification to fit their research.

The desire 'to keep gentrification general enough to facilitate universality' (Lees et al. 2016: 203) increases the danger of losing the focus on the specific contexts of urban development. In many studies, gentrification thus becomes a kind of academic checklist in which a series of characteristics are checked in order to present a gentrification diagnosis and to identify the particularities of the case under investigation as contextual conditions. Such studies are not expected to provide any deeper understanding of gentrification.

On the one hand, this abstract definition makes it possible to subsume a multitude of different manifestations under the headword 'gentrification'; on the other hand, the definition loses its clarity to embrace specific developments. While early gentrification studies viewed gentrification as 'islands of renewal in a sea of decay' (Barry 1985) and sought to use the concept to explain exceptional phenomena in urban development, the dynamics of gentrification and displacement have long since become mainstream in many cities and have lost their neighborhood-specific reference. When areas with very different characteristics can become subject to gentrification, it becomes clear that the focus on individual neighborhoods loses its explanatory reach. This becomes clearer in the political communication of initiatives and social mobilizations in the field of housing policy than in academic discussions. In cities like Berlin, housing policy protests were organized for many years as neighborhood initiatives and used the term gentrification for their analyses and justification of their demands. In the meantime, buzzwords such as 'housing crisis' and 'rent madness' have replaced the G-word, and demands also increasingly refer to city-wide and cross-cutting instruments. While neighborhood initiatives in the 1990s and 2000s demanded rent caps for modernizations in urban renewal areas and effective protection against displacement, the current agenda includes a city-wide rent cap law, the strengthening of municipal housing construction, and the expropriation of large housing corporations (Holm 2021).

The broadening of contexts in current gentrification research entails such complexity that recent research contributions have fundamentally questioned the explanatory power of gentrification analyses. Already in the 1980s gentrification was considered a 'chaotic concept' from an epistemological point of view (Rose 1984), as no causal processes of change could be derived in the complex arrangement of different factors. With the current multiplications of gentrification phenomena, this challenge seems to have become even more pronounced. Asher Ghertner argues that the classic Anglo-American concept of gentrification does not adequately take into account the economic and political characteristics of radical transformations in metropolises of the Global South (Ghertner 2015: 552ff.). At its core, this postcolonial critique of gentrification research is directed against the omission of the extra-economic drivers of urban development and thus the country- and city-specific contexts. However, with a consistent context specification, the academic concept of gentrification calls itself into question. Matthias Bernt has formulated an important attempt to systematically include the various local and political contexts in gentrification research with his reflections on commodification gaps. His proposal to focus on the specific conditions in each case that provide an incentive for investment in the housing stock ('commodification gap') at least makes it possible to look at very different initial conditions, processes, and actors (Bernt 2022).

## THE ROLE OF SOCIOLOGY IN GENTRIFICATION RESEARCH

The contributions of sociology up to now operate within the classical gentrification concepts and are used in particular for a) empirical description of upgrading and displacement processes, b) analyzing the diversity and internal differentiation of actor groups, or c) investigating the connection between position in the gentrification process, attitudes, and lifestyles.

The studies of the first group especially, which understand displacement processes as an exchange of different social groups, are limited to a methodological contribution to gentrification. With the routinized categorizations of social classes, social status, or lifestyle affiliation, almost all gentrification descriptions fall back on the mindset and typifying of classical empirical social research (Blasius et al. 2016). Challenges here are in the definition of the social groups involved in gentrification. Categorizing characteristics (e.g., age, education, income, household type) not only differ across countries and cities but change over time. Moreover, social structural changes in studied neighborhoods may have broader origins that are not exclusively attributable to area-specific dynamics of change. For example, studies on London point to the fact that a working class defined by occupational groups is disappearing not only in gentrification areas but throughout the city (Hamnett 2003). The analytical added value of these empirical studies is usually low because the strong fixation on original residents, pioneer gentrifiers, and late gentrifiers almost always refers to demand-side explanatory models and conceptually hardly goes beyond the standard economic models of supply and demand. These limitations also apply to studies that take up race and gender relations for their analyses if they are not used to provide a specific explanation for the origin and course of gentrification processes. The sociological perspective, which is mainly oriented towards the analysis of the groups involved in gentrification, conceptually hardly goes beyond the socio-ecological models of the Chicago school and mainly contributes to the understanding that displacement and gentrification can have different manifestations (Blasius et al. 2016, Blasius & Friedrichs 2019).

A second group of sociologically informed gentrification studies strengthens the critique of the limitations of demand-side gentrification explanations through an increasingly nuanced analysis of the social groups involved. Feminist studies, for example, have pointed to the contradictory role of women in gentrification processes as 'both the agents and the victims of gentrification' (Bondi 1991: 196). Studies on the role of gay and lesbian communities in gentrification processes (Knopp 1995, Doan 2018) or on the relationship between gentrification and black communities (Boyd 2008, Freeman 2009, Huse 2018, Moore 2009) also show that the complex realities in an intersectional perspective are beyond a simple categorization of individual groups as gentrifiers or victims of displacement. In the overlapping power relations and hierarchies, clear indicators for identifying the displaced and the displacing are increasingly difficult to find and all the more elusive for a universalist approach to gentrification research. Rather, these studies show that not only can gentrification have different faces but also the groups involved. In most cases, the studies on the contradictory interactions between specific communities or social groups provide more insights into the groups and power relations studied than they contribute to a deeper understanding of gentrification.

The third group of sociological gentrification studies is concerned with the connections of positioning in the gentrification process with different attitudes, motives for action, and lifestyles of different social groups. While earlier demand-side explanations describing a social proliferation of 'conspicuous consumption' and changing housing preferences were central to gentrification (Beauregard 1986), recent sociological studies are increasingly concerned with the mechanisms of self-justification of gentrifiers and the contradictory motivations and patterns of action of middle-class people in gentrifying areas. For example, recent studies analyze different strategies of placemaking by different social groups in gentrification areas and show how narratives of spatial imaginaries not only reflect the processes of upgrading and displacement but are also used by the gentrifiers to justify them (Blokland 2009, Moran & Berbary 2021). Other studies highlight the tense friction between structure and agency in gentrification processes and, based on interviews, describe a picture of well-meaning gentrifiers and involuntary displacement without falling into the trap of moralizing (Schlichtman et al. 2017: 13ff.). Similarly, Tim Butler's and his colleagues' studies of neighborhood relations in London gentrifying areas primarily expose contradictions and point to a large gap between diversity-seeking attitudes and exclusionary structures of middle-class households' lifestyles (Butler & Robson 2003, Butler 2003, Jackson & Butler 2015). From a more spatial perspective, Sharon Zukin also analyzes the strategies used to justify gentrification processes and uses the example of different neighborhoods to show how the assertion of authenticity is used as a tool to legitimize gentrification and displacement (Zukin 2010). The contribution to the understanding of gentrification processes is limited to the in-depth analysis of the inner worlds of gentrifiers and the individual and collective strategies of justification. An explicit sociological reference point in many of these studies is the work of Bourdieu on the importance of social and symbolic capital in the reproduction of social inequalities and his question about the function of spatial dimensions for social trajectories of distinction and positioning in the social field (Bourdieu 1985, 2018).

# WHAT CONTRIBUTION CAN SOCIOLOGY OFFER TO THE FUTURE OF GENTRIFICATION RESEARCH?

Most sociological approaches to gentrification research offer an established methodological toolkit for empirical investigation and findings from a low level of abstraction. Sociology may not know '50 words for snow' but has countless differentiations for gentrification trajectories, gentrifiers, and displacement types. Unfortunately, with this great delight in increasingly fine-grained typification of observed phenomena related to gentrification processes, sociology contributes little to a deeper understanding of gentrification.

A more consistent search for connections between everyday experiences in gentrification areas, the structural framework, and its institutionalized embeddedness could remedy this situation. Related to the three basic sociological questions (what holds society together? How do societies change? How can this change be shaped and controlled?), a sociological contribution to gentrification research could consist of the following elements: a) an analysis of the social order that becomes visible in gentrification processes; b) an analysis of the agency of individual, collective, and institutional actors; and c) an analysis of state interventions and social movements in gentrification processes.

**Analysis of Social Order in Gentrification Processes**

A central theme of classical sociology was the analysis of basic principles of social order. With this work, the structural theoretical approaches of sociology aimed to contribute to understanding the observable everyday realities in a social context and to explain their social mechanisms. Sociologists countered an apparently natural or divine predetermination of events and developments with explanations that saw individual and collective behavior, positioning in social rankings, and even inner convictions as the result of social structures and social interactions. The analysis of concrete observations was intended to analyze the social mechanisms and social structures behind concrete actions. Émile Durkheim describes the regularities of everyday life, which are perceived as objective, as social facts and assumes that they are institutionally condensed and thus a social order is internalized in the sense of a set of rules of society that are no longer or only rarely questioned (Durkheim 1995). Accordingly, the task of sociological research would be to ask which fundamental social mechanisms become visible in the recurring and seemingly inevitable gentrification dynamics and how they reproduce themselves in gentrification processes.

In classical sociological theories, the fields of politics, law, and economics are assumed to be typical areas in which social orders are condensed and transformed into unquestioned frameworks of social action. Accordingly, the program of an explicitly sociological analysis in the field of gentrification research could consist of examining the logics and basic principles of investment decisions in gentrification processes (economics), uncovering the power and domination relations between different interests and groups in displacement processes (politics), and examining the normative ideas and their codification that become visible in urban gentrification processes and make them possible in the first place (law). In their work on the political economy of the housing question, Manuel Aalbers and Brett Christophers have named three features of the capitalist economic system – the logic of property, the logic of accumulation, and the logic of growth (Aalbers & Christopher 2014: 375) – which also unfold their effectiveness in gentrification processes and are suitable for systematically analyzing the basic economic principles of our social order using the example of gentrification processes. Economic historian Thomas Piketty describes societies as systems of inequality and assumes that each society produces its own ideological narrative to justify these inequalities (Piketty 2020: 17ff.). Sociological gentrification research in search of the patterns and mechanisms of the social order could find what it is looking for in the analysis of the legitimation narratives for gentrification processes and formulate conclusions about the social conditions in which gentrification takes place.

**Analysis of Agency in Gentrification Processes**

A more agency-theoretical strand of sociology places individual, collective, and institutional actions themselves at the center of analyses. Central elements of a sociological theory of agency are the subject of action, the type of action, the modality of action, and the context of action. The goal of such analyses is, on the one hand, to explain the agency itself and, on the other hand, to identify the effects of the actions on the collective or social structures. Exemplary for this approach is rational choice theory, which assumes that every social action is based on a decision that is made in a goal- and purpose-determined manner (Coleman 1991, 2015). Max Weber, for example, differentiates the motivation for action into purpose-rational, value-rational, affective, and traditional action (Weber 1973: 13f.). The action itself is seen as a sequence of a logic of situation (perception and evaluation of a specific constellation that gives rise to an action), a logic of selection (choice between several options for action), and a logic of aggregation (effects of the various individual actions on the system of action under investigation) (Coleman 1990: 10ff.).

Even if sociological theories of action are called 'methodological individualism' (Schumpeter 1909: 231) and likely to be ridiculed, especially by critical research approaches, action-theoretical approaches can contribute to a better understanding of gentrification processes. Thus, decisions to move in and out of a neighborhood, decisions to invest or disinvest by property owners, or even decisions by state institutions and administrations for or against social protection mechanisms or instruments of investment incentive in gentrification areas could be studied. An analysis of patterns of action and interactions in gentrification processes can help to better understand the scope, limits, and consequences of individual action phenomena in a social context.

Some research aims at tracing the decisions for residential moves and investigates the specific expectations, motives, and options of middle-class households in gentrification processes. For example, research in Parisian suburbs has shown that the motives of middle-class households moving in have changed over time and influenced their place-making strategies (Bacqué et al. 2014). Other studies point to the close connection between occupational group-specific subjectivities and their residential place-making decisions (Dorschel 2022) or to the impact of economically rational decisions to purchase second homes on the neighborhoods concerned (Paris 2009). In contrast to the economic studies on consumer sovereignty, the sociological considerations do not stop at the fact that relocation decisions are made but analyze them in their social contexts. The task of sociological gentrification research is not to reproduce the demand-side explanatory models but rather to fathom the social and societal contexts in which these decisions are made and to analyze the framework conditions that favor or also impede the implementation of these decisions.

While some studies are already available on the relocation motives and expectations of early and late gentrifiers with all their differentiations (Butler & Robson 2003, Schlichtman et al. 2017), there are only a few studies on the concrete investment and disinvestment decisions of owners and landlords, most of which date back a long time (Marcuse 1986, McCrone & Elliott 1989, Sternlieb 1966). There have been few studies on the rationality of the actions and decisions of political and bureaucratic actors in the context of gentrification processes. Analyses of local political regimes or interest blocs (Jessop 1997, Logan & Molotch 1987) could help here to explore the recurring coalitions between local politics and the real estate industry. Sociological analyses in these areas could help shed light on the black box of individual, collective, and institutional decisions in gentrification processes and help develop approaches and proposals for concrete interventions.

**Analysis of Statehood and Collective Actors**

The third guiding question of sociology is directed at the controllability of social change and is addressed in, among other areas, sociological and socio-historical theories of the state and collective actors. In addition to political economy approaches to state theory, which explain structures and functions of state action from their relationship to and dependence on the capitalist mode of production (Becker & Jäger 2012, Boyer 2018, Jäger 2003), and analyses of the welfare state (Esping-Andersen 1990, Kemeny 1992, Stephens 2016), explicitly sociological approaches to the efficacy and scope of protests and social movements (Castells 1983, Thompson 1963) provide important clues as to how economic and social processes of social change are influenced.

Since gentrification processes are always to be located in specific institutional contexts, a systematic analysis of the concrete local political arrangements in which property titles are granted and secured and in which commodification gaps and investment conditions are shaped is useful (Bernt 2022). The instruments with which protection rights and participation opportunities of residents in upgrading areas are ensured also go back essentially to the political framework conditions. Theories of state action and also the analysis of welfare regimes can help to analyze the character of state intervention, its scope, and its limits. On the one hand, the study of gentrification can thus contribute to a deeper understanding of the modalities of state action. On the other hand, explicit recourse to theoretical concepts of state action analysis can help explain the specific course, pace, and social consequences of gentrification and displacement in each case.

Theories of collective actors and social movements provide a second avenue for analyzing the ways in which gentrification dynamics can be influenced and controlled. For example, theories of moral economy as a driver and motivation for social protest (Susser 2018, Thompson 1971) might help explain why organized protests against gentrification occur in some neighborhoods and not in others. The concepts of social movement analysis in the early writings of Manuel Castells can also be used to draw overarching insights from the study of gentrification processes (Castells 1983, 2012). Instead of explaining developments in cities exclusively with a logic of derivation from the main contradictions of capitalism, he examines movements and protest as acting subjects of urban development and as active agents of social change (Castells 1983: 305). Social movements are thereby understood as expressions of new social contradictions that can be used as the empirical basis of a fundamental analysis of society (Castells 2012: 38f.).

A number of studies and publications on gentrification research focus on protests and resistance in their analyses. In her work, Sandra Annunziata has clearly emphasized that the occasions, strategies, and demands for anti-gentrification protests differ significantly between neighborhoods, cities, and countries and are each integrated into specific political and administrative contexts (Annunziata & Lees 2016, Annunziata & Rivas-Alonso 2018). Other studies also examine the concrete local conditions for urban movements against gentrification (Karaman 2014), their historically evolved strategies (Holm 2021), or the reasons why protest movements do not emerge (Sakızlıoğlu & Uitermark 2014). Especially because of the place- and time-specific nature of protests, these analyses are well-suited to understanding the various contextual conditions of urban social movements and to identifying the concrete conditions for the successful implementation of alternative strategies.

## CONCLUSIONS

Multidimensional processes such as gentrification quite rightly require an interdisciplinary research strategy in which different perspectives can be taken and different aspects examined. Particularly in the international field of gentrification research, the focal points and debates are primarily structured thematically and examine the manifestations, causes, and consequences, as well as the political and economic framework conditions, of gentrification processes. This research, interdisciplinary in the best sense of the word, has contributed to a broad understanding of gentrification processes.

The aim of this chapter was to make visible the specifically sociological perspective in gentrification research and to ask about the potential of an explicitly sociological contribution to gentrification research.

Looking back at the gentrification research of the last decades, three aspects were identified that can be seen as sociological contributions: a) a more methodological contribution to the scientific description of gentrification and displacement processes, b) an empirical contribution that has especially strengthened the understanding of the growing diversity and also contradictions of the actors involved in gentrification processes, and c) a more conceptual contribution that has established the connections between gentrification processes, lifestyles, and place-making strategies in gentrification research.

In the context of sociological perspectives in gentrification research, I speak very deliberately of sociologically informed research strategies because the methods and concepts of urban sociology are not only reserved for scholars from sociology departments but have also been taken up and used in practice by researchers from geography, urban studies, and other research fields.

Beyond this status quo of the sociological contribution to gentrification research, sociology could provide even stronger theoretical-conceptual impulses in the future if classical sociological questions were translated into the field of gentrification research. I am not advocating a what-would-Georg-Simmel-say-about-it strategy at this point, but I am suggesting that some typical sociological perspectives be more explicitly incorporated into gentrification research. For example, studies analyzing the social order could examine the interactions between orientations, resources, and the social norms in the context of gentrification processes, and in particular deconstruct the various elements of legitimation narratives that accompany many gentrification processes. An analysis of agency in gentrification processes places the actors and their modes of action as well as the contexts of action at the center of the investigations. For gentrification research, the motives and action orientations of the social groups involved could in particular be deciphered in order to go beyond the observable practice of individual groups of actors and decipher the social causes of stigmatization, distinction practices, and attempts at concealment by middle-class households. The third contribution of sociology could be approaches to the analysis of institutions and collective actors. The sociological perspective is expected to provide insights into the conditions for a collective articulation of problems and demands, which are particularly important for the analysis of protests and grass-roots mobilizations against gentrification processes. There is already empirical research on all the topics proposed here, but so far it has rarely been linked back to the sociological theories on which it is based.

In short, sociology has more to offer for gentrification than the empirical tools for a social structure analysis. In sum, sociological approaches will not turn gentrification research on its head, but a self-conscious use of sociological theories and concepts can help both to better understand gentrification phenomena and to draw socio-political conclusions from gentrification research. The aim of urban sociology is not only to describe the phenomena of urban developments but to explain them causally and thus to better understand social power relations and structures as a whole and (in the best case) to outline ways of overcoming them.

## REFERENCES

Aalbers, M. B. (2019) Introduction to the forum: From third- to fifth-wave gentrification. *Tijdschrift voor economische en sociale geografie* 110(1): 1–11.

Aalbers, M. B. & Christophers, B. (2014) Centring housing in political economy. *Housing, Theory and Society* 31(4): 373–394.

Annunziata, S. & Lees, L. (2016) Resisting 'austerity gentrification' and displacement in Southern Europe. *Sociological Research Online* 21(3): 148–155.

Annunziata, S. & Rivas-Alonso, C. (2018) Resisting gentrification. In Lees, L. & Phillips, M. (eds.) *Handbook of Gentrification Studies*. Cheltenham, UK and Northampton, MA, USA: Edward Elgar Publishing, 393–412.

Atkinson, R. & Bridge, G. (2005) *Gentrification in a Global Context. The New Urban Colonialism*. London: Routledge.

Bacqué, M. et al. (2014) The middle class 'at home among the poor' – How social mix is lived in Parisian suburbs: Between local attachment and metropolitan practices. *International Journal of Urban and Regional Research* 38(4): 1211–1233.

Badyna, A. & Golubchikov, O. (2005) Gentrification in central Moscow. A market process or a deliberate policy? Money, power and people in housing regeneration in Ostozhenka. *Geografiska Annaler B* 87(2): 113–129.

Barry, B. (1985) Islands of renewal in seas of decay. In Paul, E. P. (ed.) *The New Urban Reality*. Washington, DC: Brookings Institute, 69–96.

Beauregard, R. (1986) The chaos and complexity of gentrification. In Smith, P. & Williams, P. (eds.) *Gentrification of the City*. Boston: Allen & Unwin, 35–55.

Becker, J. & Jäger, J. (2012) Integration in crisis: A regulationist perspective on the interaction of European varieties of capitalism. *Competition & Change* 16(3): 169–187.

Bernt, M. (2016) How post-socialist is gentrification? Observations in East Berlin and Saint Petersburg. *Eurasian Geography and Economics* 57(4–5): 565–587.

Bernt, M. (2021) Die Grenzen der rent-gap Theorie. In Glatter, J. & Mießner, M. (eds.) *Gentrifizierung und Verdrängung: Aktuelle theoretische, methodische und politische Herausforderungen*. Bielefeld: transcript, 91–106.

Bernt, M. (2022) *Commodification Gap. Gentrification and Public Policy in London, Berlin and St. Petersburg*. Oxford: Wiley.

Blasius, J. et al. (2016) Pioneers and gentrifiers in the process of gentrification. *International Journal of Housing Policy* 16(1): 50–70.

Blasius, J. & Friedrichs, J. (2019) Changes of lifestyles in the social space: The case of gentrification. In Blasius, J. et al. (eds.) *Empirical Investigations of Social Space.* Cham, Switzerland: Springer, 61–79.

Blokland, T. (2009) Celebrating local histories and defining neighbourhood communities: Place-making in a gentrified neighbourhood. *Urban Studies* 46(8): 1593–1610.

Bondi, L. (1991) Gender divisions and gentrification: Towards a framework for analysis. *Transactions of the Institute of British Geographers* 16: 190–198.

Bourdieu, P. (1985) The social space and the genesis of groups. *Social Science Information* 24(2): 195–220.

Bourdieu, P. (2018) Social space and the genesis of appropriated physical space. *International Journal of Urban and Regional Research* 42(1): 106–114.

Boyd, M. (2008) Defensive development: The role of racial conflict in gentrification. *Urban Affairs Review* 43(6): 751–776.

Boyer, R. (2018) Marx's legacy, regulation theory and contemporary capitalism. *Review of Political Economy* 30(3): 284–316.

Bridge, G. (2003) Time-space trajectories in provincial gentrification. *Urban Studies* 40(12): 2545–2556.

Brown-Saracino, J. (2019) *A Neighborhood that Never Changes: Gentrification, Social Preservation, and the Search for Authenticity*. Chicago: University of Chicago Press.

Butler, T. (1997) *Gentrification and the Middle Classes*. Ashgate: Aldershot.

Butler, T. (2003) Living in the bubble: Gentrification and its 'others' in London. *Urban Studies* 40(12): 2469–86.

Butler, T. & Lees, L. (2006) Super-gentrification in Barnsbury, London: Globalisation and gentrifying global elites at the neighbourhood level. *Transactions of the Institute of British Geographers* 31(4): 467–487.

Butler, T. & Robson, G. (2003) *London Calling: The Middle Classes and the Remaking of Inner London*. Oxford: Berg.

Calbet, I. & Elias, L. (2018) Financialised rent gaps and the public interest in Berlin's housing crisis: Reflections on N. Smith's 'generalized gentrification'. In Albet, A. & Benach, N. (eds.) *Gentrification as a Global Strategy: Neil Smith and Beyond*. London: Routledge, 165–176.

Cameron, S. (2003) Gentrification, housing redifferentiation and urban regeneration: 'Going for growth' in Newcastle upon Tyne. *Urban Studies* 40(12): 2367–2382.

Castells, M. (1983) *The City and the Grassroots. A Cross-Cultural Theory of Urban Social Movements*. Berkeley and Los Angeles: University of California Press.

Castells, M. (2012) [1975] *Kampf in den Städten. Gesellschaftliche Widersprüche und politische Macht*. Hamburg: VSA.

Clark, E. (1987) *The Rent Gap and Urban Change: Case Studies in Malmö 1860–1985*. Lund: Lund University Press.

Clark, E. (1991) Rent gaps and value gaps: Complementary or contradictory? In Van Weesep, J. & Musterd, S. (eds.) *Urban Housing for the Better-off: Gentrification in Europe*. Utrecht: Stedelijke Netwerken, 17–29.

Coleman, J. S. (1990) *Foundations of Social Theory*. Cambridge, MA and London: The Belknap Press.

Coleman, J. S. (1991) Rational action, social networks, and the emergence of norms. In Calhoun, C. et al. (eds.) *Structures of Power and Constraint. Essays in Honor of Peter M. Blau*. Cambridge: Cambridge University Press, 91–112.

Coleman, J. S. (2015) Social capital and the creation of human capital (1988). In Edles, L. & Appelrouth, S. (eds.) *Sociological Theory in the Classical Era. Text and Readings*. Los Angeles: Sage, 222–232.

Darling, E. (2005) The city in the country: Wilderness gentrification and the rent gap. *Environment and Planning A* 37(6): 1015–1032.

Davidson, M. & Lees, L. (2005) New-build 'gentrification' and London's riverside renaissance. *Environment and Planning A* 37(7): 1165–1190.

Doan, P. (2018) Non-normative sexualities and gentrification. In Lees, L. & Phillips, M. (eds.) *Handbook of Gentrification Studies*. Cheltenham, UK and Northampton, MA, USA: Edward Elgar Publishing, 155–169.

Dorschel, R. (2022) A new middle-class fraction with a distinct subjectivity: Tech workers and the transformation of the entrepreneurial self. *The Sociological Review* 70(6): 1302–1320.

Durkheim, E. (1995) [1895] *Die Regeln der soziologischen Methode*. Frankfurt: Suhrkamp.

Dutton, P. (2003) Leeds calling: The influence of London on the gentrification of regional cities. *Urban Studies* 40(12): 2557–2572.

Dutton, P. (2005) Outside the metropole: Gentrification in provincial cities or provincial gentrification? In Atkinson, R. & Bridge, G. (eds.) *Gentrification in a Global Context. The New Urban Colonialism*. London: Routledge, 209–224.

Ergun, N. (2004) Gentrification in Istanbul. *Cities* 21(5): 391–405.

Esping-Andersen, G. (1990) *The Three Worlds of Welfare Capitalism*. Princeton: Princeton University Press.

Feldmann, M. (2000) Gentrification and social stratification in Tallinn: Strategies for local governance. SOCO Project Paper No. 86. Vienna: Institute for Human Science.

Freeman, L. (2009) Neighbourhood diversity, metropolitan segregation and gentrification: What are the links in the US? *Urban Studies* 46(10): 2079–2101.

Fujitsuka, Y. (2005) Gentrification and neighborhood dynamics in Japan: The case of Kyoto. In Atkinson, R. & Bridge, G. (eds.) *Gentrification in a Global Context. The New Urban Colonialism*. London: Routledge, 137–150.

Gaffney, C. (2016) Gentrifications in pre-Olympic Rio de Janeiro. *Urban Geography* 37(8): 1132–1153.

Ghertner, D. A. (2015) Why gentrification theory fails in 'much of the world'. *City* 19(4): 552–563.

Ghose, R. (2007) Big sky or big sprawl? Rural gentrification and the changing cultural landscape of Missoula, Montana. *Urban Geography* 25(6), 528–549.

Glass, R. (1964) Introduction: Aspects of change. In Centre for Urban Studies (ed.) *Aspects of Change*. London: McGibbon and Kee, xviii–xix.

Hackworth, J. & Smith, N. (2001) The changing state of gentrification. *Tijdschrift voor Economische en Sociale Geografie* 92(4): 464–477.

Hamnett, C. (2003) Gentrification and the middle-class remaking of inner London 1961-2001. *Urban Studies* 40(12): 2401–2426.

Hartmann, C. (ed.) (1982) *Displacement: How to Fight It*. Berkeley: National Housing Law Project.

Häußermann, H. & Siebel, W. (1987) *Neue Urbanität*. Frankfurt: Suhrkamp.

He, S. (2019) Three waves of state-led gentrification in China. *Tijdschrift Voor Economische En Sociale Geografie* 110(1): 26–34.

Hjort, S. (2009) Rural gentrification as a migration process: Evidence from Sweden. *Migration Letters* 9(1): 91–100.

Hochstenbach, C. (2017) State-led gentrification and the changing geography of market-oriented housing policies. *Housing, Theory and Society* 34(4): 399–419.

Holm, A. (2013) Berlin's gentrification mainstream. In Holm et al. (eds.) *The Berlin Reader. A Compendium on Urban Change and Activism*. Bielefeld: transcript, 171–187.

Holm, A. (2021) From protest to program: Berlin's anti-gentrification-movement since reunification. In Fregolent, L. & Nel-lo, O. (eds.) *Social Movements and Public Policies in Southern European Cities*. Cham: Springer, 33–52.

Huse, T. (2018) Gentrification and ethnicity. In Lees, L. & Phillips, M. (eds.) *Handbook of Gentrification Studies*. Cheltenham, UK and Northampton, MA, USA: Edward Elgar Publishing, 186–204.

Islam, T. (2010) Current urban discourse, urban transformation and gentrification in Istanbul. *Architectural Design* 80(1): 58–63.

Jackson, E. & Butler, T. (2015) Revisiting 'social tectonics': The middle classes and social mix in gentrifying neighbourhoods. *Urban Studies*, 52(13): 2349–2365.

Jäger, J. (2003) Urban land rent theory: A regulationist perspective. *International Journal of Urban and Regional Research* 27(2): 233–249.

Jessop, B. (1997) A neo-Gramscian approach to the regulation of urban regimes: Accumulation strategies, hegemonic projects, and governance. In Lauria, M. (ed.) *Reconstructing Urban Regime Theory: Regulating Urban Politics in a Global Economy*. Thousand Oaks: Sage, 1–74.
Karaman, O. (2014) Resisting urban renewal in Istanbul. *Urban Geography* 35(2): 290–310.
Kemeny, J. (1992) *Housing and Social Theory*. London: Routledge.
Kennedy, M. & Leonard, P. (2001) *Dealing with Neighbourhood Change: A Primer on Gentrification and Policy Choices*. Washington, DC: The Brookings Institution Center on Urban and Metropolitan Policy, PolicyLink.
Knopp, L. (1995) Sexuality and urban space: a framework for analysis. In Bell, D. & Valentine, G. (eds.) *Mapping Desire. Geographies of Sexualities*. London: Routledge, 149–161.
Kovács, Z. (1998) Ghettoization or gentrification? Post-socialist scenarios for Budapest. *Journal of Housing and the Built Environment* 13(1): 63–81.
La Grange, A. & Pretorius, F. (2015) State-led gentrification in Hong Kong. *Urban Studies* 53(3): 506–523.
Lees, L. (1994a) Gentrification in London and New York: An Atlantic gap? *Housing Studies* 9(2): 199–217.
Lees, L. (1994b) Rethinking gentrification: Beyond the positions of economics and culture. *Progress in Human Geography* 18(2): 137–150.
Lees, L. (2003a) Policy (re)turns: Urban policy and gentrification, gentrification and urban policy. *Environment and Planning A* 35(4): 571–574.
Lees, L. (2003b) Super-gentrification: The case of Brooklyn Heights, New York City. *Urban Studies* 40(12): 2487–2509.
Lees, L. (2006) Gentrifying down the urban hierarchy: 'The cascade effect' in Portland, Maine, USA. In Bell, D. & Jayne, M. (eds.) *Small Cities: Urban Experience beyond the Metropolis*. London: Routledge, 91–104.
Lees, L. et al. (2008) *Gentrification*. New York: Routledge.
Lees, L. et al. (eds.) (2015) *Global Gentrifications: Uneven Development and Displacement*. Bristol: Policy Press.
Lees, L. et al. (2016) *Planetary Gentrification*. Cambridge, UK, and Malden, MA: Polity.
Ley, D. (1996) *The New Middle Class and the Remaking of the Central City*. Oxford: Oxford University Press.
Logan, J. R. & Molotch, H. L. (1987) *Urban Fortunes: The Political Economy of Place*. Berkeley: The University of California Press.
López-Morales, E. (2019) State-led gentrification. *The Wiley Blackwell Encyclopedia of Urban and Regional Studies*, 1–6. https://doi.org/10.1002/9781118568446.eurs0321
López-Morales, E. et al. (2021) State-led gentrification in three Latin American cities. *Journal of Urban Affairs* 45(8): 1397–1417.
Marcińczak, S., Gentile, M. & Stępniak, M. (2013) Paradoxes of (post) socialist segregation: Metropolitan sociospatial divisions under socialism and after in Poland. *Urban Geography* 34(3): 327–352.
Marcuse, P. (1986) Abandonment, gentrification, and displacement: The linkages in New York City. In Smith, N. & Williams, P. (eds.) *Gentrification of the City*. Boston: Allen & Unwin, 153–177.
Marcuse, P. (1992) Gentrification und die wirtschaftliche Umstrukturierung New Yorks. In Helms, H. G. (ed.) *Die Stadt als Gabentisch. Beobachtungen zwischen Manhattan und Berlin-Marzahn*. Leipzig: Reclam Verlag, 80–90.
McCrone, D. & Elliott, B. (1989) *Property and Power in the City. The Sociological Significance of Landlordism*. Houndsmill and London: MacMillan.
Moore, K. (2009) Gentrification in black face? The return of the black middle class to urban neighborhoods. *Urban Geography* 30(2): 118–142.
Moran, R. & Berbary, L. A. (2021) Placemaking as unmaking: Settler colonialism, gentrification, and the myth of 'revitalized' urban spaces. *Leisure Sciences* 43(6): 644–660.
Namba, T. (2000) Gentrification of prewar inner city housing. *Bulletin of Nagoya College*, 38.
Paris, C. (2009) Re-positioning second homes within housing studies: Household investment, gentrification, multiple residence, mobility and hyper-consumption. *Housing, Theory and Society* 26(4): 292–310.

Patch, J. (2008) Ladies and gentrification: New stores, residents and relationships in neighborhood change. In DeSena, J. (ed.) *Gender in an Urban World*. Bingley: Emerald, 103–126.
Phillips, M. (2005) Differential productions of rural gentrification: Illustrations from North and South Norfolk. *Geoforum* 36(4): 477–494.
Piketty, T. (2020) *Capital and Ideology*. Harvard: Harvard University Press.
Rérat, P. et al. (2009) From urban wastelands to new-build gentrification: The case of Swiss cities. *Population, Space and Place* (Special Issue Paper), http://www3.interscience.wiley.com/cgi-bin/fulltext/122617447/PDFSTART.
Rosa, H. et. al. (2007) *Soziologische Theorien*. Konstanz: UVK.
Rose, D. (1984) Rethinking gentrification: Beyond the uneven development of Marxist urban theory. *Environment and Planning D: Society and Space* 2(1): 47–74.
Rothenberg, T. (1995) 'And she told two friends': Lesbians creating urban social space. In Bell, D. & Valentine, G. (eds.) *Mapping Desire*. London: Routledge, 165–81.
Rubino, S. (2005) A curious bled? City revitalisation, gentrification and commodification in Brazil. In Atkinson, R. & Bridge, G. (eds.) *Gentrification in a Global Context. The New Urban Colonialism*. London: Routledge, 225–239.
Ruoppila, S. & Kärik, A. (2003) Socio-economic residential differentiation in post-socialist Tallin. *Journal of Housing and the Built Environment* 18(1): 49–73.
Sakızlıoğlu, B. & Uitermark, J. (2014) The symbolic politics of gentrification: The restructuring of stigmatized neighborhoods in Amsterdam and Istanbul. *Environment and Planning A* 46(6): 1369–1385.
Sánchez, F. & Broudehoux, A.-M. (2013) Mega-events and urban regeneration in Rio de Janeiro: Planning in a state of emergency. *International Journal of Urban Sustainable Development* 5(2): 132–153.
Schlichtman, J. J., Patch, L. & Hill, M. L. (2017) *Gentrifier*. Toronto: University of Toronto Press.
Schumpeter, J. (1909) On the concept of social value. *The Quarterly Journal of Economics* 23(2): 213–232.
Shaw, K. (2004) Local limits to gentrification. In Atkinson, R. & Bridge, G. (eds.) *Gentrification in a Global Context*. London: Routledge, 168–184.
Shaw, K. (2008) A response to 'the eviction of critical perspectives from gentrification research'. *International Journal of Urban and Regional Research* 32(1): 192–94.
Shin, H. B. & Kim, S.-H. (2016) The developmental state, speculative urbanisation and the politics of displacement in gentrifying Seoul. *Urban Studies* 53(3): 540–559.
Slater, T. (2006) The eviction of critical perspectives from gentrification research. *International Journal of Urban and Regional Research* 30(4): 737–757.
Slater, T. (2009) Missing Marcuse: On gentrification and displacement. *City* 13(2–3): 278–311.
Smith, N. (1979) Toward a theory of gentrification: A back to the city movement by capital, not by people. *Journal of American Planning Association* 45(4): 538–548.
Smith, N. (1982) Gentrification and uneven development. *Economic Geography* 58(1): 139–155.
Smith, N. (1986) Gentrification, the frontier, and the restructuring of urban space. In Neil, S. & Williams, P. (eds.) *Gentrification of the City*. Boston: Allen & Unwin, 15–33.
Smith, N. (2002) New globalism, new urbanism: Gentrification as global urban strategy. *Antipode* 34(3): 427–450.
Stephens, M. (2016) The use of Esping-Andersen and Kemeny's welfare and housing regimes in housing research. *Critical Housing Analysis* 3(1): 19.
Sternlieb, G. (1966) *The Tenement Landlord*. New Brunswick: Rutgers.
Susser, I. (2018) The contemporary significance of the moral economy: Is housing a home or an asset? *Critique of Anthropology* 38(2): 236–241.
Sykora, L. (2005) Gentrification in post-communist cities. In Atkinson, R. & Bridge, G. (eds.) *Gentrification in a Global Context. The New Urban Colonialism*. London: Routledge, 90–105.
Thompson, E. P. (1963) *The Making of the English Working Class*. London: Victor Gollancz.
Thompson, E. P. (1971) The moral economy of the English crowd in the eighteenth century. *Past and Present* 50: 76–136.
Uzun, N. C. (2003) The impact of urban renewal and gentrification on urban fabric: Three cases in Turkey. *Tijdschrift voor Economische en Sociale Geografie* 94(3): 363–375.

Visser, G. & Kotze, N. (2008) The state and new-build gentrification in central Cape Town, South Africa. *Urban Studies* 45(12): 2565–2593.

Weber, M. (1973) [1921] *Wirtschaft und Gesellschaft. Grundriss der verstehenden Soziologie*. Tübingen: J. C. B. Mohr.

Wyly, E. & Hammel, D. (1999) Islands of decay in seas of renewal: Housing policy and the resurgence of gentrification. *Housing Policy Debate* 10(4): 711–771.

Zukin, S. (2010) *Naked City: The Death and Life of Authentic Urban Places*. Cambridge: Oxford University Press.

# 12. Feminist urban sociology and social reproduction
*Bahar Sakızlıoğlu*

Gender plays a crucial role in how we construct, experience, understand, and investigate cities in relation to other categories of social differentiation. The production of urban space and inequalities is heavily influenced by gender norms, roles, and power dynamics. Likewise, the nature of the inquiries posed by urban sociologists regarding urban matters, as well as the methodologies employed to study cities, are shaped by gendered perspectives.

Feminist urban theory starts from the experiences and perspectives of marginalized groups, including but not restricted to women, people of color, low-income groups, and queer people, who are often marginalized from decision-making processes and are more vulnerable to urban dispossessions. By doing so, a feminist urban perspective can powerfully scrutinize the production of intersectional urban dispossessions by urban processes and policies (Peake 2016).

This chapter aims to showcase how adopting a feminist urban perspective can provide insights into the production of urban inequalities and dispossessions in cities with a focus on the contemporary feminist urban theory of social reproduction. To support this argument, the chapter draws on examples from the field of gentrification studies.

The next section poses the question of what constitutes feminist urban sociology. Does it entail conducting more research on women and disadvantaged groups or does it solely focus on gender issues? Should we refer to feminist urban sociology or feminist urban sociologies? Are there specific methodologies that must be employed for sociological inquiry to be considered feminist? To shed light on these questions, the next section aims to outline some fundamental principles of feminist sociology.

After establishing these principles, the next section focuses on the social reproduction lens as one crucial 'feminist urban theory of our times' (Peake et al. 2021). In this section, I will critically analyze the literature on gentrification through a social reproduction lens, linking gentrification to the crisis of social reproduction. Using gentrification as an example, my aim is to demonstrate that the social reproduction lens provides a powerful analytical tool to expose intersecting dispossessions and inequalities inherent in gentrification. Such an approach not only connects capitalist production and social reproduction within cities but also ties the social reproduction of human and more than human life in gentrifying neighborhoods. In this section, I will draw examples from my own research in Tarlabaşı, Istanbul, which is a longitudinal study of gentrification.[1] The last section provides the conclusions of the chapter.

## WHAT CONSTITUTES FEMINIST URBAN SOCIOLOGY?

Starting from 1960s and 1970s, feminist scholars underlined the malestream bias in sociology, which was born as a male discipline (Abbot et al. 2005). Scholars have critiqued malestream urban sociology for neglecting to acknowledge the gendered nature of the production of urban space and the inequalities that arise from it (Massey 1994, Obberhauser et al. 2018). Malestream urban sociology typically conceives of urban spatial and social relations in terms of hierarchical binaries, such as public/private, home/work, and paid/unpaid labor. This binary perspective often renders invisible disadvantaged groups, including women and the spaces they occupy, and perpetuates the existing gendered division of labor (Jarvis et al. 2009, Obberhauser et al. 2018). Malestream sociology, with its assertion of objective and universal knowledge, tends to disregard or diminish alternative modes of knowing and diverse experiences of different groups in various contexts. This approach creates hierarchies regarding what knowledge is produced, who produces it, and how (Abbot et al. 2005, Littlewood 2014). In contrast, feminist urban sociologists have worked to dismantle these hierarchies and highlight the gendered, classed, and racialized nature of knowledge production. The aim is to promote more inclusive and diverse ways of producing knowledge (Jarvis et al. 2009, Obberhauser et al. 2018).

Feminist scholars have advocated for the re-conceptualization of sociological concepts and categories. They have pursued the exploration of alternative ways of theorizing and diverse forms of knowledge in urban sociological inquiry. Additionally, they have posed new inquiries that center on the everyday experiences of marginalized groups, thus opening new areas of study within sociology (Abbot et al. 2005, Littlewood 2014). For instance, feminist urban scholars have investigated the intersection of gender, race, and class in relation to housing, domestic work, urban economic change, etc. (Doshi 2013, Massey 1994, McDowell 1999, 2003, Peake and Rieker 2013, Skeggs 1997).

Feminist urban sociology is based on a critique of malestream urban sociology regarding what we can know (ontology), how we can know (epistemology), how we conduct research (methodology), and why we want to know (the link between theory and practice). These critiques can be thought to constitute the working principles of feminist urban inquiry.

Feminist ontology challenges the binary, hierarchical, and oppositional understanding of Cartesian thought that underpins Western knowledge. Feminist scholars emphasize the relational and co-constructive nature of what Cartesian ontology portrays as dualisms, such as body/mind, culture/nature, public/private, self/other, emotions/reason, etc. (Jarvis et al. 2009). Moreover, feminist urban scholars have scrutinized the category of 'women' by adopting an ontology of gender. They have moved away from treating gender as an isolated category and have embraced an intersectional understanding of gender. This approach acknowledges how gender intersects with other social differences, such as class, age, physical ability, sexual orientation, and race (Abbott et al. 2005, Crenshaw 1991). In addition to the intersectional understanding, gender is now perceived as a continuum rather than a binary construct.

Feminist epistemology acknowledges the partiality, situatedness, and relational nature of knowledge production. It challenges the traditional positivist claim to objective and universal knowledge, instead emphasizing the partiality of socially 'situated knowledges' as conceptualized by Haraway (1988). According to this perspective, all knowledge is partial as it is shaped by the lived experiences of both the researcher and the researched (Hesse-Biber 2014). Furthermore, all knowledge is relational because it is produced through everyday social relations. Feminist scholars recognize that knowledge is not value-free, as it is influenced by the values of individuals in their daily lives and during the knowledge production process (Abbot et al. 2005, Hesse-Biber 2014). Additionally, feminist epistemology is attuned to historical and geographical differences (Katz 2001).

Feminist research does not have a fixed set of methods but rather a feminist approach to methodology (Hesse-Biber 2014). This approach is characterized by positionality, reflexivity, and a feminist ethics of care. Positionality and reflexivity require the researcher to consider how their social position influences their research questions, data collection, interpretation, and overall knowledge production. Feminist scholars engage in reflexive thinking in order to be accountable for their own positionality and its effects on their research process. Additionally, feminist researchers emphasize the importance of ethics in research, specifically responsibility, empathy, and care (ibid.). A feminist ethics of care underlines mutual support and care in the ways we make, understand, and change everyday life.

As for the link between feminist theory and practice, feminist theory has emerged from and is grounded in feminist movements. According to bell hooks (1984), feminist theory is not done for the sake of producing knowledge about sexist oppressions but to end these oppressions through practice backed by theory: feminist praxis. Feminist praxis engages in collaborative, collective, and reflexive production of knowledge, contesting exploitative and hierarchical knowledge production.

It is important to recognize the multiplicity of feminist perspectives within urban sociology. Just as there is no singular feminism but rather multiple feminisms, there is no single feminist urban sociology. Instead, there are multiple feminist perspectives situated within different branches of urban sociology, including post-colonial feminist urban sociology, ecological feminist urban sociology, queer urban sociology, and many others. In the next section, I will focus on a feminist lens of social reproduction.

## SOCIAL REPRODUCTION AS 'A FEMINIST URBAN THEORY FOR OUR TIME'[2]

Several decades ago, feminist urban scholars began emphasizing the need to incorporate the lens of social reproduction into the study of cities. Social reproduction refers to the tangible and intangible processes involved in maintaining and sustaining human and more than human life, both daily and across generations (Katz 2001: 709, Strauss & Meehan 2015: 13). By employing a social reproduction lens, one can gain a more profound understanding of the complexities of urban life (Peake et al. 2021).

The urgency of this approach is further underscored by the increasing prevalence of urban neoliberalization and austerity measures, which lead to heightened levels of dispossession and insecurity in contemporary cities. These conditions have a direct impact on the ability to maintain social reproduction, creating a challenging environment that affects both the material and emotional aspects of daily life (ibid.). For instance, reduced public access to resources coupled with increasing economic insecurity in job markets can take a toll on the mental and physical health of the disadvantaged, who struggle with strained living conditions.

Peake et al. (2021) claim that 'critical urban scholarship continuously fails to recognize both the analytical interdependence between relations of social reproduction and production and how this interdependence shapes social relations and urban futures' (2). They build on the critical work of Marxist feminist scholars that contest the understanding of economic production and social reproduction as separate processes and social relations (see Figure 12.1). They emphasize the role and relations of social reproduction shaping the everyday urban life in relation to capitalist production in and of the cities. What makes social reproduction a crucial lens to understand the everyday production of the neoliberal city is that it underlines the centrality of intersecting systems of oppression regarding how processes and relations of production and social reproduction are shaped and contested. By doing so, it glues together anti-racism, feminism, anti-capitalism, and environmental justice, which helps discern the complexity of everyday urban life (ibid.).

*Source:* Miguel A. Martínez.

*Figure 12.1* *First of May demonstration in Stockholm (2017)*

Social reproduction is not limited to human life but also encompasses more than human life, including animals, plants, and microorganisms in nature (Marks 2015, Strauss & Meehan 2015). The social reproduction of more than human life involves material and social practices that sustain these living organisms. Social reproduction of human and more than human life is mutually dependent. The social reproduction perspective has the potential to embody the post-human feminist challenge to anthropocentric theory building, which overlooks the role of more than humans in the production of urban environments. Embracing the social reproduction lens has the potential to bridge different epistemologies and offer a comprehensive perspective on the urban that acknowledges the interdependence of human and more than human life (Strauss & Meehan 2015).

The next section contributes to the growing feminist endeavor to approach the urban from a social reproduction perspective by critically engaging with the gentrification literature through a social reproduction lens.

## CRITICAL ENGAGEMENT WITH THE GENTRIFICATION LITERATURE THROUGH A SOCIAL REPRODUCTION LENS

Research on gentrification has overwhelmingly focused on how gentrification can be explained based on production and consumption theories. Much less attention has been focused on the relation between gentrification and social reproduction. Some 35 years ago, Rose underlined the nexus of social reproduction and gentrification (Rose 1984: 53).

Rose (1984, 2010) discussed how the changing needs and relations of social reproduction are crucial in shaping processes of gentrification. She suggested that gentrification can be seen as a spatial solution to social problems faced by lower-middle- and middle-class households (Rose 2010). Gentrification rather offers a convenient socio-spatial constellation to manage households' time-space budgets with commodified services for housing, food, health, care, and entertainment, as well as amenities – i.e., proximity to the city center, security, walkability – that makes it possible to meet the social, economic, and cultural needs of middle-class households. Gentrifying neighborhoods at the same time host gender non-confirming groups such as the LGBTQI+ community and single mothers, thus creating spaces for the social reproduction of these non-traditional households (ibid.).

This spatial solution, however, often brings about the displacement of lower-class residents (Rose 1984). It cuts their access to the city center and disperses their supportive social networks. In other words, a process that facilitates the social reproduction of the middle classes makes the social reproduction of the lower classes difficult, if not impossible.

As Rose (2010) suggested, social reproduction cannot be viewed as taking place through the consumption and/or 'lifestyle choices' of 'non-traditional households' involved in gentrification. A mere focus on consumption and lifestyles renders invisible gendered reproductive work, domestic labor, and the struggles of gender non-conforming groups in gentrifying neighborhoods (Rose 2010: 400).

Scholars have contributed to the literature on gentrification and social reproduction from various perspectives (Boterman & Bridge 2015, Karsten 2003, 2007, Kern 2013, Luke & Kaika 2019). The literature can be mapped across two domains: 1) the human domain, which focuses on communities and households, and 2) the more than human domain.

To start with the human domain, the expanding literature on family gentrification underlines the importance of changing relations of gender and social reproduction in explaining gentrification. Karsten (2003, 2007), for instance, showed how young urban professional parents (YUPPs) tried to combine childbearing and career-making by choosing to live in central neighborhoods where they could enjoy the convenience of living in proximity not only to work but also to infrastructures of social reproduction. Both Karsten (2003, 2007) and Boterman and Bridge (2015) underline that family gentrifiers can afford a rather equitable gendered division of labor at home partly due to gentrification offering spatial solutions in terms of managing household time-space budgets.

While gentrification can facilitate the social reproduction of middle-class households, it often threatens the social reproduction of low-income households. Scholars have highlighted the emotional burden of displacement, with feelings of loss and grief being common among lower-class residents who experience displacement (Desmond 2012, Fullilove 2004, Grier & Grier 1980). Some scholars describe the experience of those who remain in gentrifying neighborhoods as the 'slow violence of gentrification' (Kern 2016 or 'everyday displacement', resulting in the ongoing loss of security, agency, and the freedom to 'make place' (Stabrowski 2014: 787). Other scholars have also underscored the emotional toll of displacement (Curran 2019, Huse 2014, Kern 2015, 2021, Paton 2014, Sakızlıoğlu 2014).

Many scholars have investigated the impacts of gentrification on the social reproduction of working-class communities. While Luke and Kaika (2019) found that gentrification can disrupt the social networks and infrastructures necessary for working-class communities, other scholars have noted that the pursuit of social reproduction during gentrification and displacement is a gendered process (Doshi 2013, Paton 2014, Sakızlıoğlu 2020). For instance, in her ethnography of gentrification, Paton (2014) discussed how working-class women increased their respectability through caring roles, actively participating in the social reproduction of their gentrifying neighborhood. However, it became a heavier burden due to declining welfare services, aging, drug addiction, and psychological problems.

As for the more than human domain, a growing literature on environmental/ecological or green gentrification discusses how the appropriation of urban ecologies works to create more space for affluent urban citizens while displacing and degrading the 'dirty', 'unhealthy' bodies and practices of often working-class people (Kern 2015) and more than human actors (Patrick 2014). Ecological gentrification involves cleaning up industrial areas or selectively greening the city for higher-income groups for the sake of so-called sustainable futures. These processes, however, decrease the affordability of housing, access to public services, and green space for those with lower incomes (Kern 2015), creating social and environmental injustice (Anguelovski et al. 2019). Other scholars discuss how gentrification displaces more than humans (Hubbard & Brooks 2021, Hunold 2020, Patrick 2014) to make space for further development of the urban spaces of luxury.

Feminist scholars have raised important questions about how gentrification appropriates and transforms more than human life, and how such transformations serve (or do not serve) the social reproduction of different groups. They have begun to link the social reproduction of households and communities (of human life) to the social reproduction of more than human life in the context of gentrification, connecting the crisis of social reproduction to the ecological crisis.

Recently, I discussed elsewhere the importance of approaching gentrification as a part and parcel of the contemporary 'crisis of social reproduction' (Sakızlıoğlu, in review). Such an approach links gentrification to the systemic dynamics and pressures that enable or decrease the capacities of different households and communities, as well as of more than human life forms, to reproduce themselves (Sakızlıoğlu, in review). In the following discussion, I will revisit the connection between gentrification and the systemic crisis of social reproduction. To illustrate this connection, I will draw on a case study of state-led gentrification in Tarlabaşı, which I conducted between 2015 and 2019. Throughout this discussion, I will provide examples to support my arguments.

## LINKING GENTRIFICATION TO THE SYSTEMIC CRISIS OF SOCIAL REPRODUCTION

Fraser (2017) defines the 'crisis of social reproduction' as an intensified contradiction between economic production and social reproduction in the context of financialized capitalism, characterized by the neoliberal restructuring of the welfare state and the individualization of responsibility for care, among other factors. This erosion of support for the care of individuals and communities exacerbates the care gap (ibid.).

Gentrification can be viewed as a manifestation of the crisis of social reproduction. It also perpetuates this crisis. The state's retraction from social provisioning in the context of financialized capitalism externalizes the responsibility of social reproduction onto households and communities. On the other hand, diminishing public provision, women's increasing participation in labor, and increasing care demands of aging populations decrease the capacities of households to perform reproductive work, thus widening the care gap (Fraser 2017). The middle classes fill this gap by moving to central areas where they economize on time-space budgets and/or through transferring care work to others, often migrants from more disadvantaged countries or regions within a country living in disadvantaged neighborhoods. Lower-class, often racial-minority and female care workers take on the care responsibilities of more privileged households, while doubling their reproductive duties, both as paid and unpaid work. Alternatively, they transfer their unpaid care work to other female family members – often daughters – or to more disadvantaged women in their home country or region. Fraser argues that 'far from filling the "care gap", the net effect is to displace it – from richer to poorer families, from the Global North to Global South' (2017: 34).

Katz (2001, 2011) has criticized the lack of attention to social reproduction in Marxist work, arguing that capitalism disposes of certain populations, such as sex workers, refugees, and drug addicts, both discursively and materially, making their social reproduction impossible. Direct displacement from gentrifying areas and zero-tolerance policies are examples of this dispossession. Katz (2011) emphasizes the importance of examining the scale of everyday life to understand the struggles for continuing social reproduction as a means of contesting accumulation by dispossession. As she puts it, 'The scale of dispossession is witnessed not just in uneven geographical developments like colonialism, gentrification, suburbanization, or "urban renewal," but also at the intimate scales of everyday life. Foreclosure takes place—quite literally—at the very heart of people's existence' (Katz 2011: 49–50).

Gentrification involves a discursive and material reorganization of space that displaces certain groups, rendering their social reproduction in certain areas impossible (Wright 2013). The changes brought on by gentrification affect access to housing, the labor market, public spaces, services, and social networks for different class, race, ethnicity, and gender groups, directly impacting households' and communities' ability to secure their livelihoods. Pursuing social reproduction in gentrifying neighborhoods and after displacement can be seen as a contestation of accumulation by dispossession (Katz 2001).

Inspired by Katz's and Fraser's work, I argued elsewhere that gentrification has an important function regarding the production and displacement of the crisis of social reproduction (Sakızlıoğlu 2020). Linking gentrification to the systemic crisis of social reproduction is like using a magnifying glass that enables us to better understand the production of urban inequalities and dispossession through urban transformation (Sakızlıoğlu 2020).

The lens of social reproduction enables us to understand urban dispossessions involved in gentrification in four important ways.

**Moving beyond Dualisms**

Approaching gentrification as a symptom and producer of the crisis of social reproduction helps us see this process beyond a local urban transformation and rather as a process rooted in broader social, political, and economic structures. It enables us to move beyond the consumption versus production explanations for gentrification and highlight the complexity and relational connectedness of capitalist production and social reproduction in and of the city. It allows us to approach the capitalist production of the city, of which gentrification is a manifestation, and social reproduction within the city as interdependent processes.

Zooming in on the very micro and intimate scales of the body, the everyday, and the more than human, the social reproduction lens helps scrutinize the differentiated dispossessions that the very macro processes of capitalist production and accumulation by dispossession bring about for individuals and communities Such a lens provides a more holistic understanding of gentrification, which goes beyond the dualisms of production versus social reproduction and micro versus macro scales.

As an example of this, I can refer to my research on the state-led gentrification of Tarlabaşı in Istanbul, where the neighborhood was reconstructed to cater to higher-middle-class residents who could afford to live in the renewed historical center. However, this capitalist transformation of the neighborhood resulted in displacement for many residents, while others in adjacent areas faced ongoing displacement pressures for years. Even those who were not physically displaced, particularly women, experienced 'everyday displacement' characterized by a gradual loss of security, agency, and freedom to 'make place' (Stabrowski 2014: 787). Sıdıka, a long-term resident, was one such example of someone who felt threatened by the changes in her neighborhood. She frequently encountered young people making fires in front of her door at night. She warned them, but they did not take her seriously. They would use drugs and alcohol. This scared her from reporting them to the police. Her daughter worked late nights at a hair salon, leaving Sıdıka anxiously waiting for her behind a thick curtain every night. She felt trapped and unable to afford to move out of the neighborhood. In addition, Sıdıka had to constantly repaint the front facade of her building due to the smoke from fires made by young people. It was crucial for her to keep her home decent and clean. Her physical labor, combined with the emotional stress of displacement, took a toll on her, resulting in acute shoulder pain.

Sıdıka's acute shoulder pain is an embodied form of displacement and dispossession brought about by state-led gentrification. The feminist perspective on social reproduction sheds light on the experiences and struggles of women, linking the capitalist production in Istanbul with the declining infrastructures of social reproduction that disproportionately affect disadvantaged groups. It also recognizes the intersection of the micro-level aspects of daily life, including the body and intimate relationships, with the macro-level dynamics of global gentrification and accumulation by dispossession (Katz 2001, 2011, Mountz & Hyndman 2006). With the social reproduction perspective, it is plausible to connect Sıdıka's shoulder pain with the neoliberal urban restructuring in Istanbul, which fosters gentrification and puts many at risk of displacement, leading to their struggle for survival.

### Relational Perspective on Dispossessions across Different Geographies and Groups

Connecting gentrification to the systemic crisis of social reproduction illuminates the interrelated politics of scale that impact efforts to pursue social reproduction. The daily challenges of sustaining social reproduction in gentrifying neighborhoods not only affect but also are shaped by power struggles over social reproduction in other scales and locations (Peake and Rieker 2013). Adopting this relational perspective enables a comprehensive and nuanced examination of dispossessions across various geographies. Adopting a relational perspective also allows for an exploration of the ways in which social boundaries are constructed among the dispossessed, based on factors such as gender, race, and sexuality.

The urban renewal project in Tarlabaşı serves as a good example. Increasing disinvestment in the area brought about deteriorating housing and social conditions as well as a rising number of vacant homes before and during the project. That is why Tarlabaşı became a temporary refuge for various marginalized groups, such as Syrian Kurds and Doms, who were displaced due to the devastating effects of war in their home country. Many long-term Kurdish residents, especially women, complained about the gender norms and relations among the newcomers, which were different from their own. For instance, the Syrian newcomers were more likely to practice polygamy, which some Kurdish women perceived as a threat. Some Kurdish men even used this gender norm to assert their dominance and reinforce traditional masculinity, as Gulizar, a married Kurdish woman, experienced firsthand when her partner told her during an argument, 'look there are many [Syrian women] out there and they are free'.

This created a division between Kurdish and Syrian women, with accusations of 'low morality' and being 'undeserving' and 'irresponsible' mothers, which obscured the underlying power dynamics and abuse involved. The struggle for social reproduction in Tarlabaşı was already challenging for Kurdish women facing the threat of displacement. With the arrival of the newcomers, they also had to bear the emotional burden of reinforced masculinity triggered by the gender norms of the newcomers. This mutual constitution of gendered and racialized dispossession in a gentrifying neighborhood illustrates how crises of social reproduction in different geographies intersect and reinforce one another.

### Unpacking the Dismantling of Marginalized Spaces and Lives

The social reproduction perspective sheds light on how gentrification disrupts the lives of marginalized communities in gentrifying neighborhoods. Examining the dismantling of neighborhoods and the dispossession of their inhabitants allows us to explore the material and social infrastructures that enabled the existence of these neighborhoods as a home for marginalized and non-gender-conforming groups and facilitated their social reproduction.

As an example, I can draw on my research in Tarlabaşı, which shows how the urban renewal project in that area resulted in the displacement of sex workers, predominantly transgender women, who lived and worked within the designated renewal area (Sakızlıoğlu 2020). Some sex workers were forced to relocate to nearby districts, while others who could not afford to leave remained in Tarlabaşı. The closure of their workplaces was detrimental, leading some to work in the streets or in vacant buildings in or near the renewal area, increasing their exposure to violence. The loss of their communal living and working spaces also canceled the material and emotional benefits of being together. Those who moved away became targets of homophobic attacks in their new neighborhoods, and the displaced faced the heavy burden of finding a new safe place to work and live.

Displacement made it impossible for gender non-conforming individuals to continue their social reproduction in Tarlabaşı and beyond. It also disrupted the relationship between these individuals and Tarlabaşı residents who adhered to traditional gender norms. As the conditions and visibility of sex work changed, social boundaries between the gender non-conforming residents and others were redrawn, harming the possibility for intersectional solidarities.

The process of place un-making and extensive dispossession underscores the critical role of queer spaces in marginalized neighborhoods for the social reproduction of gender non-conforming groups. The social reproduction perspective prompts us to ask new questions about the everyday sociology of queerness and emancipation as experienced and lived in disadvantaged neighborhoods. This perspective is especially valuable in a context where gentrification is redefining emancipation and queerness in market terms (Curran 2019, Kern 2016).

**Bridging Different Epistemologies**

Finally, the social reproduction perspective has the potential to bridge different epistemologies in the gentrification literature, including both more than human and human (anthropogenic) perspectives. Gentrification is a complex process that is both fueled by and feeds into the ecological crisis, as highlighted in prior research (Curran & Hamilton 2012, Kern 2015, Patrick 2014). Gentrification not only harms urban ecologies but also re-appropriates and commodifies environmentalist claims, pushing aside redistributive and justice claims (Curran 2019). The social reproduction lens provides a framework for understanding the interrelatedness of human and more than human life in gentrifying areas, allowing us to move beyond a purely anthropocentric analysis and embrace a post-human sociology of gentrification. The social reproduction lens is crucial in fully grasping the complex linkages between the displacement of human and more than human life in gentrifying areas.

As an illustration of this point, I can refer to my research, which shows that the displacement of disadvantaged groups due to gentrification is often accompanied by the displacement of more than human inhabitants, such as street animals, plants, and trees, in the renewal area. The state-led gentrification process in Tarlabaşı had a significant impact on the social reproduction of more than human inhabitants in the area. Street cats and dogs were a common sight on the streets of Tarlabaşı before the renewal project. Residents would often provide them with food and shelter. However, as evictions increased, street animals started seeking refuge in vacant houses. With fewer people remaining in the project area, only a few adjacent residents continued to provide food for the animals.

According to Yildirim, after the completion of the Tarlabaşı urban renewal project, the number of dogs with chips provided by the Beyoglu Municipality increased in the Kurtkoy forest area (Yildirim cited in Ozguner 2019). This suggests that these animals were removed from the streets of Tarlabaşı before the construction began and were subsequently relocated to isolated forest areas in Istanbul without any shelter or food. Similarly, residents of adjacent areas complained about the dust during the construction process that killed their balcony plants, which were highly valued by residents in a neighborhood with almost no green areas.

In contrast, the Tarlabaşı urban renewal project was awarded a certificate[3] for Leadership in Energy and Environmental Design (LEED), a certificate that is awarded to green buildings, promising sustainable living and working conditions for new residents with energy-efficient green buildings and recycling facilities. The new sustainable and green living in Tarlabaşı will, however, be exclusive to the new residents who can afford it.

## CONCLUSIONS

This chapter has discussed the significance of adopting a feminist perspective when studying the intersectional production of urban inequalities and dispossessions in everyday life, as well as its applicability in comprehending broader urban transformations. The chapter highlights the crucial role of feminist urban perspectives that center on social reproduction as a contemporary feminist theory, with supporting examples and evidence drawn from the field of gentrification studies.

The growing precariousness of urban life has brought feminist perspectives on social reproduction to the forefront (Peake et al. 2021), emphasizing diverse ways of understanding the urban that can inspire new political interventions to address the inequalities inherent in the production and reproduction of urban space and life, both human and more than human.

Building on the works of many feminist scholars who focused on the nexus of gentrification and social reproduction, I have underlined the role of gentrification in the production and displacement of the crisis of social reproduction (Sakızlıoğlu 2020). Drawing a connection between gentrification and the systemic crisis of social reproduction allows us to gain a clearer understanding of how urban inequalities and dispossessions are produced and reproduced through urban transformations.

Drawing examples from my research in Istanbul, I discussed how the lens of social reproduction allows us to understand urban dispossessions involved in gentrification in four significant ways. First, approaching gentrification as a symptom of the crisis of social reproduction enables us to move beyond the consumption versus production explanations for gentrification, underlining the relational connectedness of capitalist production and social reproduction in and of the city. It helps connect the micro to the macro scales, underlining the embodied, affective dispossessions. Secondly, I argued that linking gentrification to the systematic crisis of social reproduction helps us understand the mutual constitution of urban dispossessions across different scales and geographies in relation to each other.

Regarding the third argument, examining the dismantling of marginalized spaces and lives allows us to gain a better understanding of the material and social conditions that facilitated the social reproduction of marginalized groups in these neighborhoods. This approach can inform interventions aimed at improving the lives of these groups by identifying the factors that enabled their existence in these spaces.

Lastly, I discussed how the perspective of social reproduction has the potential to bridge different epistemologies within the literature on gentrification, encompassing both post-human and anthropogenic (human) perspectives. By understanding gentrification as a component of the systemic 'crisis of social reproduction' for both human and more than human lives, rather than as merely another spatial process that affects social reproduction and environmental degradation, we gain a more comprehensive understanding of how gentrification deeply impacts people's everyday lives and urban ecologies.

In conclusion, social reproduction theory as a feminist perspective on urban studies can enrich our comprehension of urban dispossessions and urban transformations at large. Just as the invisibility of social reproduction labor is a clear manifestation of patriarchy, the scarcity of attention paid to social reproduction in the gentrification literature and in urban sociology reflects the prevalence of masculine perspectives that shape research agendas in these fields. It is crucial to recognize the significance of social reproduction and to center feminist and intersectional perspectives in urban studies to better address the intersecting inequalities and power dynamics at play.

## NOTES

1. This longitudinal study took place from 2005 to 2019 in the scope of different research projects, including my master's, doctoral, and post-doctoral research. The latter was funded by an H2020 Marie Curie Individual Fellowship scheme (EC-658875).
2. Here I refer to title of the book by Peake et al. (2021): *A Feminist Urban Theory for Our Time: Rethinking Social Reproduction and the Urban*.
3. LEED is a rating system for green building certification.

## REFERENCES

Abbott, P., Tyler, M. & Wallace, C. (2005) *An Introduction to Sociology: Feminist Perspectives*. New York: Routledge.

Anguelovski, I., Connolly, J. J. & Garcia-Lamarca, M. (2019) New scholarly pathways on green gentrification: What does the urban 'green turn' mean and where is it going? *Progress in Human Geography* 43(6): 1064–1086.

Boterman, W. R. & Bridge, G. (2015) Gender, class and space in the field of parenthood: Comparing middle-class fractions in Amsterdam and London. *Transactions of the Institute of British Geographers* 40(2): 249–261.

Crenshaw, K. (1991) Mapping the margins: Intersectionality, identity politics, and violence against women of color. *Stanford Law Review* 43(6): 1241–1299.

Curran, W. (2019) *Gentrification and Gender*. New York: Routledge.

Curran, W. & Hamilton, T. (2012) Just green enough: Contesting environmental gentrification in Greenpoint, Brooklyn. *Local Environment: The International Journal of Justice and Sustainability* 17(9): 1027–1042.

Desmond, M. (2012) Eviction and reproduction of urban poverty. *American Journal of Sociology* 118(1): 88–133.

Doshi, S. (2013) The politics of the evicted: Redevelopment, subjectivity, and difference in Mumbai's slum frontier. *Antipode* 45: 844–865.

Fraser, N. (2017) Crisis of care? On the social-reproductive contradictions of contemporary capitalism. In Bhattacharya, T. (ed.) *Social Reproduction Theory: Remapping Class, Recentering Oppression*. London: Pluto Press, 21–36.

Fullilove, M. T. (2004) *Root Shock: How Tearing Up City Neighborhoods Hurts America, and What We Can Do About It*. New York: Ballantine Books.

Grier, G. & Grier, E. (1980) Urban displacement: A reconnaissance. In Laska, S. & Spain, D. (eds.) *Back to the City: Issues in Neighborhood Renovation*. Oxford: Pergamon Press, 252–261.

Haraway, D. (1988) Situated knowledges: The science question in feminism and the privilege of partial perspective. *Feminist Studies* 14(3): 575–599.

Hesse-Biber, S. N. (2014) A re-invitation to feminist research. In Hesse-Biber, S. N. & Leavy, P. L. (eds.) *Feminist Research Practice*. Los Angeles: Sage Publications, 1–13.

hooks, b. (1984) *Feminist Theory: From Margin to Center*. Boston: South End Press.

Hubbard, P. & Brooks, A. (2021) Animals and urban gentrification: Displacement and injustice in the trans-species city. *Progress in Human Geography* 45(6): 1490–1511. https://doi.org/10.1177/0309132520986221.

Hunold, C. (2020) Urban greening and human-wildlife relations in Philadelphia: From animal control to multispecies coexistence? *Environmental Values* 29(1): 67–87.
Huse, T. (2014) *Everyday Life in the Gentrifying City: On Displacement, Ethnic Privileging and the Right to Stay Put*. Farnham: Ashgate.
Jarvis, H., Cloke, J. & Kantor, P. (2009) *Cities and Gender*. New York: Routledge.
Karsten, L. (2003) Family gentrifiers: Challenging the city as a place simultaneously to build a career and to raise children. *Urban Studies* 40(12): 2573–2584.
Karsten, L. (2007) Housing as a way of life: Towards an understanding of middle-class families' preference for an urban residential location. *Housing Studies* 22(1): 83–98.
Katz, C. (2001) Vagabond capitalism and the necessity of social reproduction. *Antipode* 33: 709–728.
Katz, C. (2011) Accumulation, excess, childhood: Toward a countertopography of risk and waste. *Documents d'Anàlisi Geogràfica* 57: 47–60.
Kern, L. (2013) All aboard? Women working the spaces of gentrification in Toronto's junction. *Gender, Place, and Culture* 20(4): 510–527.
Kern, L. (2015) From toxic wreck to crunchy chic: Environmental gentrification through the body. *Environment and Planning D: Society and Space* 33: 67–83.
Kern, L. (2016) Rhythms of gentrification: Eventfulness and slow violence in a happening neighbourhood. *Cultural Geographies* 23: 441–457.
Kern, L. (2021) *Feminist City. Claiming Space in a Man-made World*. London: Verso.
Lees, L., Slater, T. & Wyly, E. (2008) *Gentrification*. New York: Routledge.
Littlewood, B. (2014) *Feminist Perspectives on Sociology*. New York: Routledge.
Luke, N. & Kaika, M. (2019) Ripping the heart out of Ancoats: Collective action to defend infrastructures of social reproduction against gentrification. *Antipode* 51(2): 579–600.
Marks, B. (2015) Making shrimps and unmaking shrimpers in the Mississippi and Mekong Deltas. In Meehan, K. & Strauss, K. (eds.) *Precarious Worlds: Contested Geographies of Social Reproduction*. Athens, Georgia: University of Georgia Press, 156–173.
Massey, D. (1994) *Space, Place and Gender*. Minneapolis: University of Minnesota Press.
McDowell, L. (1999) *Gender, Identity and Place: Understanding Feminist Geographies*. Minneapolis: University of Minnesota Press.
McDowell, L. (2003) *Redundant Masculinities: Employment Change and White Working-Class Youth*. Oxford: Blackwell.
Mountz, A. & Hyndman, J. (2006) Feminist approaches to the global intimate. *Women's Studies Quarterly* 34(1/2): 446–463.
Obberhauser, A., Fluri, J., Whitson, R. & Mollett, S. (2018) *Feminist Spaces: Gender and Geography in a Global Context*. New York: Routledge.
Ozguner, B. (2019) Ekolojik Yıkım Ve Kentleşme Kıskacında Görülmeyenler: Hayvanlar! Sivil Sayfalar, Kuzey Ormanlari, 16 March, http://www.burakozguner.com/ekolojik-yikim-ve-kentlesme-kiskacinda-gorulmeyenler-hayvanlar/ (accessed 20 June 2023)
Paton, K. (2014) *Gentrification: A Working-Class Perspective*. London: Routledge.
Patrick, D. J. (2014) The matter of displacement: A queer urban ecology of New York City's High Line. *Social & Cultural Geography* 15(8): 920–941.
Peake, L. (2016) The twenty-first century quest for feminism and the global urban. *International Journal of Regional and Urban Studies* 40(1): 219–227.
Peake, L. & Rieker, M. (2013) Rethinking feminist interventions into the urban. In Peake, L., & Rieker, M. (eds.) *Rethinking Feminist Interventions into the Urban*. New York: Routledge, 1–22.
Peake, L., Koleth, E., Tanyildiz, G. S., Reddy R. N. & Patrick, D. (2021) *A Feminist Urban Theory for Our Time: Rethinking Social Reproduction and the Urban*. New Jersey: Wiley & Sons and Series Antipode Books.
Rose, D. (1984) Rethinking gentrification: Beyond the uneven development of Marxist urban theory. *Environment and Planning D: Society and Space* 1: 47–74.
Rose, D. (2010) Refractions and recombinations of the 'economic' and the 'social': A personalized reflection on challenges by – and to – feminist urban geographies. *The Canadian Geographer/Le Géographe canadien* 54: 391–409.
Sakızlıoğlu, B. (2014) Inserting temporality into the analysis of displacement: Living under the threat of displacement. *Tijdschrift Voor Economische En Sociale Geografie* 105(2): 206–220.

Sakızlıoğlu, B. (2020) Soylulastirma, Cinsiyet and Yeniden Uretim: Tarlabaşı Ornek Olayi. *Praksis*, Ankara.

Sakızlıoğlu, B. (in review) A feminist ethnography of gendered dispossessions in gentrifying Tarlabaşı, Istanbul. *International Journal of Urban and Regional Studies*.

Skeggs, B. (1997) *Formation of Class and Gender: Becoming Respectable*. London: Sage.

Stabrowski, F. (2014) New-build gentrification and the everyday displacement of Polish immigrant tenants in Greenpoint Brooklyn. *Antipode* 46(3): 794–815.

Strauss, K. & Meehan, K. (2015) Introduction: New frontiers in life's work. In Meehan, K. & Strauss, K. (eds.) *Precarious Worlds: Contested Geographies of Social Reproduction.* Athens, Georgia: University of Georgia Press, 1–24.

Wright, M. W. (2013) Feminicidio, narcoviolence, and gentrification in Ciudad Juárez: The feminist fight. *Environment and Planning D: Society and Space* 31(5): 830–845.

# 13. Who cares? The moral architecture of urban conflict

*Tino Buchholz and Jere Kuzmanić*

Understanding social conflict is to understand what people care for, what they esteem, respect, and love. Approaching the other on eye level – as autonomous equals – and recognizing their lifeworlds, politics, and experiences is different from shared knowledge in the sphere of education. It also differs from imagination. Shared experience in shared space is key to intimate affection and immediate care. The relationship between social and spatial distance then introduces complexity and poses difficulties for organic solidarity with strangers, as Durkheim and Simmel already observed (Horgan 2017, 2012). Touching upon the ontological dimension of social self, community, and institutional formations with inner, emotional obligations and outer, socio-spatial constraints, we here revisit and update urban sociology's conceptual foundations of solidarity and mutual care.

Investigating the question of mutual care from inside (personal, inner nature) and outside (political, social nature), the chapter outlines pioneer sociological contributions around the epistemological questions of who cares for what, for whom, and why care in the first place. Defining the field of social ties around social norms, forms, and scale, in the first part we discuss inner obligations and outer constraints of social care as ontological arguments of social will formation – that is, Tönnies's (2017) 'essential will' of organic communities versus the 'arbitrary will' of mechanic society. Asking where individual and social motivations to care for others come from, in the first part we treat spatial relations implicitly. The urban experience nevertheless informs early concepts of social will formations, as Simmel (2020) looks at metropolitan experiences not as the 'lost unity' of organic communities but rather the 'lost control' of small-town obligations and the family. With a metropolitan view on modern society, Simmel (Berlin) and Durkheim (Paris) looked rather optimistically towards social formations in large cities, which are characterized by anonymity and alienation, on the one hand, and provide for an idea of social freedom, on the other. This picture is contrasted by small-town-resident Ferdinand Tönnies, who was more pessimist about the modern urban constellation and the loss of immediate social drives to care (i.e. shared experiences in shared space). Spatial relations thus significantly inform our analysis of these classic contributions.

With Axel Honneth we then go one step further to investigate the moral grammar of social conflicts. Honneth's (1995, 2011) work mobilizes social philosophy, sociology, and social psychology in order to craft a critical theory of conflict, justice, and social freedom that relies on emotional, legal, and social struggles for recognition. On ontological grounds he systematically links the subject's inner moral motivation to care to ethical, social struggles for mutual recognition (Petherbridge 2011). Restoring individual self-confidence through mobilizations of collective support and solidarity – beyond Foucault – his analysis comes with consequences for political idealism and ideology, delivering a powerful explanation for the formation of social movements deeply rooted in subjective experiences of social disrespect (Honneth 1993, 1995). The outcome is a philosophy of justice that revives subjective morality and what we want from life: recognition of who we are or want to be as human beings (i.e. love, rights, solidarity) – to be at home in the other, as Honneth's Hegelian formula goes.

Social and spatial movements impart complexity to local struggles regarding whether one finds minimum recognition in local communities of shared values and when to resign, resist, or relocate (Buchholz 2016). The simultaneity of multiple, competing meanings, where, for example, homes are at least two things at once (i.e. economic privilege, achievement, and investment vs social need, good, and right), pose difficulties in terms of not losing oneself in alienated 'relations of relationlessness' (Jaeggi 2014). Moral explorations into individual and social expectations of a meaningful life thus pose questions regarding everyday, local community and imagined communities (i.e. national state and propertied society), which are also crucial for the planners' community when intervening into the lifeworld of others in the name of property or the greater good.

Addressing the self-confidence and self-limitations of planners, the chapter then discusses the moral architecture of urban conflict, and planning ethics, to present self-critical insights into personal, political, and institutional formations around propertied order. Urban planners are crucial agents for conflict and urban change when acting upon and within urban struggles but usually remain distant, neutral mediators. This is problematic for an understanding of polyrational conflict and mutual care (Inch et al. 2017, Davy et al. 2023). The legitimacy of planning interventions cannot be simply based upon legality but stems from an understanding of legitimacy, how planners ethically relate to normative values, struggles, and lifeworlds of distant others. Planners' distance from urban struggles and their normative, emotional reservations thus come with damage for ethical institutions such as urban planning (Baum 2015). Hence, we address political subjectivity, social autonomy, and emotional rationality as crucial concepts for self-critical planning ethics, bringing Habermasian, insurgent, and anarchist planning scholars into conversation.

## FROM COMMUNITY TO SOCIETY: LOST UNITY AND LOST CONTROL

From the outset of sociology, common ground of what is shared between individual members of society and what shared space has to do with this have been contested from the start (Dahme & Rammstedt 1984). Delegating the theoretical, normative challenges of the societal contract to philosophy, the founding fathers keep distant from society as object, or subject, of their studies. They rather speak of sociation (Simmel), social action (Weber), non-logical action (Pareto), or collective consciousness (Durkheim). Ferdinand Tönnies, whose pioneer work *Community and Society* (2017) explicitly targets the two grand categories for sociology, speaks of a system of social exchange as bottom line.

As a member of his time, Tönnies looked at sociology as a mix of social biology, social anthropology, and social psychology, although in a dialectical manner. In his seminal study *Community and Society*, first published in 1887, community life is organic and society is rather mechanic. For Tönnies (2017), organic community life does not rely on the reflective thought of a societal contract: it is spontaneous, immediate, emotional, and naturally pre-given. As such he emphasizes the family and the home as origin of the organic community: 'the study of home is to the study of community what the study of organic cells is to the study of social life' (Tönnies 2017: 47, authors' translation, see also Wirth 1926).

In the conventional modern family, social ties come about naturally, where the mother expresses ultimate care, crafting a common language, while it is the father who first introduces notions of powerful authority to the organic community. Siblings establish the most organic ties, which consist of *shared memory*, *custom*, and therefore equality – care – when growing up together (Tönnies 2017: 27). Beyond the family, Tönnies highlights the neighborhood for a sense of shared identity through routine customs of everyday encounters. Friendship is not associated with the immediate intimacy of the home or the routine encounter of the neighborhood. Friendship does not have a place-specific shared aspect. Friendship, in other words, departs from the organic community of the nuclear family and its self-made friends; friendship is normatively chosen.

The constitutive elements of organic community formation for Tönnies thus strongly rely on shared history and shared space, where lived encounters of shared habits, customs, and memories shape inner obligations of mutual care to form the 'essential will' of the community (Cahnman 1976, Marcucci 2017). Bodily ties further lead him to speak of villages and cities as a social body and living organism, an ensemble of cooperatives and families, whose language, customs, soil, and architecture reveal continuity and change (Tönnies 2017: 60ff.).

Differentiating between the 'essential will' of organic communities and the 'arbitrary will' of state-led societies, Tönnies traces forms of lost social unity, harmony and the limits of social cohesion – contested by modernity and industrial urbanization – through social will formation (Marcucci 2017). While organic community life brings means and ends together through interpersonal ties of immediate affection as essential will, the modern social contract of societies comes with artificial ties and rational thought alone. Hobbes's 'war of all against all' guides his social analysis of evolutionary development, while his critique of state-led society anticipates what Anderson (2006) has called 'imagined communities'. Tönnies is not naive however. Humankind can take the form of social and asocial characters, and both momentums depend on specific contexts and complement one another: 'Yet … the organic view, he means to say, precedes the rationalistic view logically and historically' (Cahnman 1976: 843).

Tönnies' reading of historical social relations thus quasi-ontologically investigates *social will* as defining element of local social ties. For the arbitrary moment of societal will formation various scholars struggle with the confusion inherent to the German publication since Tönnies originally used *Willkür*, which indeed translates as the *arbitrariness* of societal will, but changed his terminology for the third edition of the book into the softer notion of *Kürwille* (Lichtblau 2012: 11). *Kürwille* is a neologism that is unique to Tönnies' sociology, which still bears the *artificial* connotation but which also links to the *art* of making society. Scholars further debate why Durkheim, in contrast, came up with a reverse conceptualization of mechanic and organic solidarity, framing pre-modern solidarity among equals as mechanic solidarity, while modern solidarity between privileged and underprivileged strangers serves as a desirable standard of organic solidarity (Aldous et al. 1972, Horgan 2017, Marcucci 2017). This organic standard of solidarity was neither realized during Durkheim's lifetime nor is human society anywhere close to organic solidarity on a global scale today.

## FROM SOCIAL WILL TO SOCIAL FORM

The Parisian Durkheim and Berlin-born Simmel both looked at modern social relations with more optimism than Tönnies. Giving weight to the role of the individual in community and society, Simmel (2020) focuses less on the loss of social unity but rather on social diversity in urban processes of sociation. Emphasizing social forms over norms, his normative reservations express the positivist spirit and socialist controversies around 1900 (Levine 1984). Simmel's major motivation was to shift sociology away from naturalistic explanations when focusing on the project of modernity; that is, the formation of individualization, sociation, and reification are placed at its core. He shared the non-organicistic interest with economic historian Max Weber, who only later turned to sociology. With Weber he also shared the claim of value-free non-normativity as a sociological lens of analysis. In contrast to Weber's positivist take on objectivity, Simmel sought to objectify subjective needs as sociation process, looking at 'norms in their forms' (1910: 377), rather than promoting objectivity as a social research outcome (Adorno et al. 1993, Rammstedt 1988).

In his essay 'How is Society Possible?' Simmel (1910) keeps a distance from positivist accounts of what members of society necessarily share. He highlights a variety of social forms and the role of the individual therein: 'The matter in question is the processes of reciprocation which signify for the individual the fact of being associated' (Simmel 1910: 378). Addressing the fragments of individual performance and societal abstraction, Simmel thus brings together norms, forms, and scales of socialization processes, addressing a concept of reciprocity that reveals the pitfalls of individual action and social reality: 'a single life ... is lived from two sides' (Simmel 1910: 382).

Social abstraction from individual performance – at a greater scale – makes Simmel insist on particular constellations and speak of 'imagined completeness' while 'each element of a group is not a societary part, but beyond something else' (Simmel 1910: 381). Social abstraction, in other words, informs functional, political judgments of various sorts: are all sinners evil, all teenagers foolish, all planners technocrats, all cops bastards? Specific moments and places may certainly provide the political context for polarized, normative judgment. Without such a context, however, for Simmel (1910) the individual is always something extra: a product of society and a member thereof. The singular crucially informs the social constellation, and the other way around (Aronowitz 1994). Differentiating forms of socialization, Simmel thus includes norms in forms but excludes morality from his sociological analysis of social formations.

For Durkheim, by contrast, social life is nothing else than the moral milieu that surrounds the individual (Levine 1984: 322). For Durkheim morality is an outer social phenomenon that is imposed on the individual by the church, state, and society (Cahnman 1976). Even the most intimate act of individual defeat – suicide – Durkheim (2014) explains as social consequence. Although an early source of inspiration, Simmel remained too vague for Durkheim's interest in social facts, and he was not alone in this, as Aronowitz (1994: 412) notes:

> Whereas, Lukacs, Ernst Bloch and others ... saw the [revolutionary] fulfillment of the new Life in the Bolshevist forms, Simmel's tragic imagination, which was anything but utopic, held him back. Despite his own insistence that history is the working out of the contradiction between life and form ... he could only see the chaos immanent in a revolution that appeared to be directed against form itself.

As Aronowitz further observes, Lukacs later revised his revolutionary enthusiasm when embracing the limits of revolutionary class consciousness in history and everyday life: 'Thus, while much of contemporary sociology considers conflict an exceptional event to be resolved by formal reconciliation, for Simmel and Lukacs 'becoming' and its presupposition, 'dissonance', is the essence of life' (Aronowitz 1994: 405).

## A STAGE FOR CONFLICT: EMOTIONAL, LEGAL, AND SOCIAL SELF-REALIZATION

Investigating *the moral grammar of social conflicts*, Axel Honneth's (1995) philosophical anthropology takes together sociological explorations into the (inner) emotional obligations and (outer) social constraints discussed above, delivering a systematic threefold explanation of social conflict around social, legal, and emotional *struggles for recognition*. Following sociology's interest in the relationship between autonomous subjects and community formation with Hegel's philosophy and G. H. Mead's social psychology, his interest targets the nature of social interaction with mutual recognition relations that rely on subjective, moral expectations of the good life and ethical relations-to-self that reveal a reflexive idea of social autonomy and social freedom (Deranty 2009, Honneth 2011). For Frankfurt school scholars, subjectivity has a central role to play for a critical theory of society, which is always reflexively social and political (Scherr 2005). Taking up political subjectivity, social autonomy and the making of self-confidence as starting point for care and conflict, Honneth outlines his critical theory of justice (Buchholz 2021).

Although Tönnies and Durkheim both approached the empirical project of sociology with their lens of diagnosing the limits of morality, solidarity, and law in the modern social contract (Aldous et al. 1972, Cahnman 1976, Marcucci 2017), 'neither of them give the phenomenon of social confrontation a systematic role in their basic concepts', as Honneth (1995: 160) states. Simmel's sociology certainly started to give weight to the individual motivation and socializing function of conflict, as he considered forms of social difference and hostility as sources of conflict, 'but he does so little to trace this dimension of personal and collective identity back to intersubjective preconditions associated with recognition that it is impossible for moral experiences of disrespect to come into view as the occasions for social conflict' (Honneth 1995: 161).

Honneth explicitly points to the limits of academic sociology – giving priority to interests instead of needs – underrating subjective moral experiences of disrespect for the emergence of conflict and social movements (Honneth 1995). Capturing the personal victims' perspective, Honneth deeply embraces the subjective dimension of social suffering and social struggle, where harms to subjective morality form the start of any conflict, protest, and resistance. 'For the victims of disrespect … engaging in political action has the direct function of tearing them out of the crippling situation of passively endured humiliation and helping them in turn, on their way to a new, positive relation-to-self' (Honneth 1995: 164). Through protest and resistance, disrespected individuals thus restore their self-confidence, self-respect, and self-esteem, which are central elements to the structure of recognition relations.

For social psychology Honneth (2012) follows Mead and Winnicott, where individual needs for mutual recognition take the form of lifelong struggles that start at birth. Here, the innocent child depends on primary caretakers – the mother or other –, *internalizing* the need for emotional care and social ties through intersubjective gestures and rituals. Winnicott goes as far as to state that even adults never lose the experience of this initial impulse when later experiencing growing individual autonomy: searching for emotional care of others throughout

*Table 13.1    Structure of recognition relations*

| Modes of recognition | Emotional support | Cognitive respect | Social esteem |
|---|---|---|---|
| Dimension of personality | Needs and emotions | Moral responsibility | Traits, abilities, and achievements |
| Forms of recognition | Primary relationships (love, friendship) | Legal relations (rights) | Community of value (solidarity) |
| Relation-to-self | Self-confidence | Self-respect | Self-esteem |
| Forms of disrespect | Abuse and rape | Denial of rights, exclusion | Denigration, insult |
| Threatened component of personality | Physical integrity | Social integrity | 'Honor', dignity |

*Source:*   Honneth (1995: 129), edited by the authors.

the course of social life, the individual frequently falls back to the initial need for *intense fusion* the human subject has once experienced, that is, love (Honneth 2012: 210). Rooting one's need for emotional care in early childhood, Honneth (2012) ontologically outlines the formation of *the I in We* throughout lifelong struggles for intersubjective self-realization in the spheres of emotional, social, and legal recognition (i.e. friends and family, community and society, the market and the state) (see Table 13.1). The internalization of moral values thus starts in childhood and is later experienced in the other social constellations of school and everyday life, where the state, church, society, and property market challenge the legitimacy of *homemade* moral achievements and a just social order. For the legitimacy of legality, Honneth argues that unconditional love and context-specific solidarity compete with historical, legal conventions, while legal recognition historically follows social recognition as a 'parasite' (Honneth 2011: 221).

Although not free from ambivalence (Butler 2021) Honneth's philosophical anthropology thus touches upon the inner nature and interpersonal social outplay of identity formations. His point should not be confused with identity politics, as Nancy Fraser puts it, but rather associated with identity formation, as when he states: 'The reproduction of social life is governed by the imperative mutual recognition, because one can develop a practical relation-to-self only when one has learned to view oneself, from the normative perspective of one's partners in interaction, as their social addressee' (Honneth 1995: 92). Against Fraser he argues that identity formation is a social process that relies on the intersubjective moment of recognition – or disrespect – between at least two subjects, who provide one another with the mutual recognition that is needed for self-confidence, self-respect, and self-esteem. Normative struggles of social self-formation and political order precede distributional justice (Fraser & Honneth 2003). Whoever seeks to escape the narcissistic trap of *atomistic self-formation* thus requires a social idea of human interaction and the social response of others. One cannot do this alone (Ehrenberg 2015). In contrast to egocentric, atomistic self-formation, which is characteristic of neoliberal ideas of self-realization, Honneth's moral starting point of social engagement thus concerns the *quality* and *mutuality* of social relations within three spheres of mutual recognition: social esteem, legal respect, and emotional care (see Table 13.1).

## POWER AND SCALES OF STRUGGLES FOR RECOGNITION

While subjective moral expectations highlight normative values one cares for emotionally, respects legally, and esteems socially, these inner moral expectations then enter the social arena of interpersonal ethical relations at different social, legal, and spatial scales. Honneth (1997: 37) makes clear that *normativity* and *scale* both impact the forms of recognition significantly. Scale is crucial to normative limits of shared identity (see Figure 13.1). Beyond the interpersonal dimension of social interaction and conflict, he is moreover aware of historical and ideological group formations, where *intra*-subjective moral values (e.g. father, teacher, leader, god) inform powerful *inter*-subjective ethical struggles. When challenged to differentiate between recognition and power, Honneth argues that powerful recognition relations are interpersonal in the end and 'practices of recognition don't empower persons, but subject them' (2007: 323). Like his Frankfurt colleagues and Foucault, Honneth is skeptical about an alienated perspective on power relations, as if they were not human-made or socially approved: recognition can take the form of ideology (i.e. nationalist, classist, racist, sexist, and so on). Historicizing moral progress with normative reservations and emphasis on human agency for self-critical judgment, he states: 'Because we live in an era that regards itself as being *morally superior* to past ages, we are certain that the esteem enjoyed by the virtuous slave, the good house-wife, and the heroic soldier was of purely ideological character' (Honneth 2007: 326, emphasis added).

What sounds provocative at first sight is due to critical theory's reliance on *immanent critique* (Stahl 2013): not to judge political constellations from an outer standpoint but to aim for normative reconstruction of the legitimating moral infrastructure situated at moments and places. Following Deranty (2009), Honneth's *Critique of Power* (1993) reads like an explicit critique of Habermas when making the notions of interpersonal power and infinite struggle strong:

> As Honneth writes, the institutions of the economy and the state are never just embodiments of purely objective, instrumentally rational considerations; they are framed within 'political-practical principles', which themselves depend upon (distorted) communicative processes. The same can be said of economic and administrative institutions. What falls out of view, in the end, is the centrality of *struggle* in the organisation of society. (Deranty 2009: 97, emphasis added)

The value of Honneth's self-critical theoretical turn, therefore, is to realize the normativity of moral values individuals consider just or good, which implies historical constellations and situated practices of qualitative recognition for social hierarchies, power relations, and uneven developments that do not necessarily lead to open, public conflict but are internalized and articulated in different forms. This comes with consequences for scales of common human ties (i.e. global solidarity) and postcolonial critique, the historical limits of moral progress, and the abandonment of a social telos in the name of modernity (Allen 2016) on the right side of history: 'We must ask, therefore, whether we can continue to speak of a "moral grammar" or ascribe an emancipatory meaning to the struggle for recognition once we have realised that recognition as such implies neither freedom from domination nor the absence of power' (Honneth 2007: 350). Feminist critique contributes to this line of reason, as social justice has deep roots in feminist urban anthropology and sociology (Mann & Huffman 2005, Tristan 1840, Weber & Bermingham 2003) focused on gender inequality in suburban, heteronormative lifestyles, and emotional labor (Hochschild 1983, Komarovsky 1940). Iris Marion Young (2007) explicitly targets 'love's labor' in Honneth's feminism and welcomes his overall argument.

## THE MORAL ARCHITECTURE OF URBAN CONFLICT

Spatial relations complicate the picture for political analysis of urban conflict once *people move* towards or away from local conflict – voluntarily or forced – for the sake of normative ideals of a better life or to stay alive. Beyond the limits of chance and choice in moving freely, the question remains: what touches, what moves the subject socially, legally, and emotionally? Spatial relations of social formations reveal *simultaneous* social orders in the form of territorial b/orders, propertied order, gendered practices, and cultural qualities of social life at different places, which do not only involve one single conflict or one history but many (España 2021, Massey 2005). The multitude of simultaneous local conflicts also raises questions of socio-spatial complexity: ideas of spatial un/consciousness, spatial autonomy, and polyrationalities of the good life in place (Davy et al. 2023, Pohl 2019). Such complex urban constellations made Edward Soja (2010: 71) claim: 'We are spatial beings'.

For moral geography, David M. Smith (1994, 2000) has stressed common human needs, while respecting differences, explicitly referring to ethical, mutual recognition relations with Kant and Habermas: 'We should not be prepared to do to distant others what we would not do to ourselves and our own kind' (Smith 1994: 294). Considering a variety of intellectual routes to normative justice, he argues that relativist and relational spatial explanations benefit from a universal idea of social relations. For this matter also Walzer (2019) makes a distinction between thin universal morality and a thick, particular, local morality, which connects to Honneth's argument on strong ethical relations and a weak idea of the moral good (Fraser & Honneth 2003: 262).

Localizing struggles for recognition in history and geography is to link *normative* ideas of social self-realization to *forms* of struggle and the *scale* of the greater good (see Figure 13.1). Individuals, in this sense, seek mutual recognition (of who they are or want to be) and communities of shared values – be they the traditional or chosen family (friends) or other social constellations of solidarity – where they find minimum recognition in social space (Horgan 2017). In case of local disrespect, they may suffer and 'resign' (i.e. lower expectations of an urban experience and the good life while remaining in place), 'resist' the ruling social order (i.e. restore self-confidence when opposing ideological recognition in place), or 'relocate' after time (i.e. struggle for the good life elsewhere). Possibilities of relocation primarily respond to one's energy to struggle (i.e. local commitment to values and place), chances for resistance, and the quality of resignation at a certain moment and place. Relocation further responds to education and imagination (i.e. the good life elsewhere) and fundamentally requires freedom of movement and other resources (i.e. purchase power, property, citizenship, solidarity), which are limited (Buchholz 2016).

For possibilities of relocation, it is important to be aware of both territorial and intellectual relocation; that is, to leave the site of struggle physically and consciously for good or rather unconsciously and temporarily. Beyond territorial movements, intellectual relocation comes with imagination, illusion, and fantasy (Pohl 2019, 2023). Relocating one's consciousness with the help of literature, film, music, technology, drugs, or gods, the subject nevertheless remains in place. Modern cynicism complements the picture of inner struggle (i.e. inner resistance

210  *Research handbook on urban sociology*

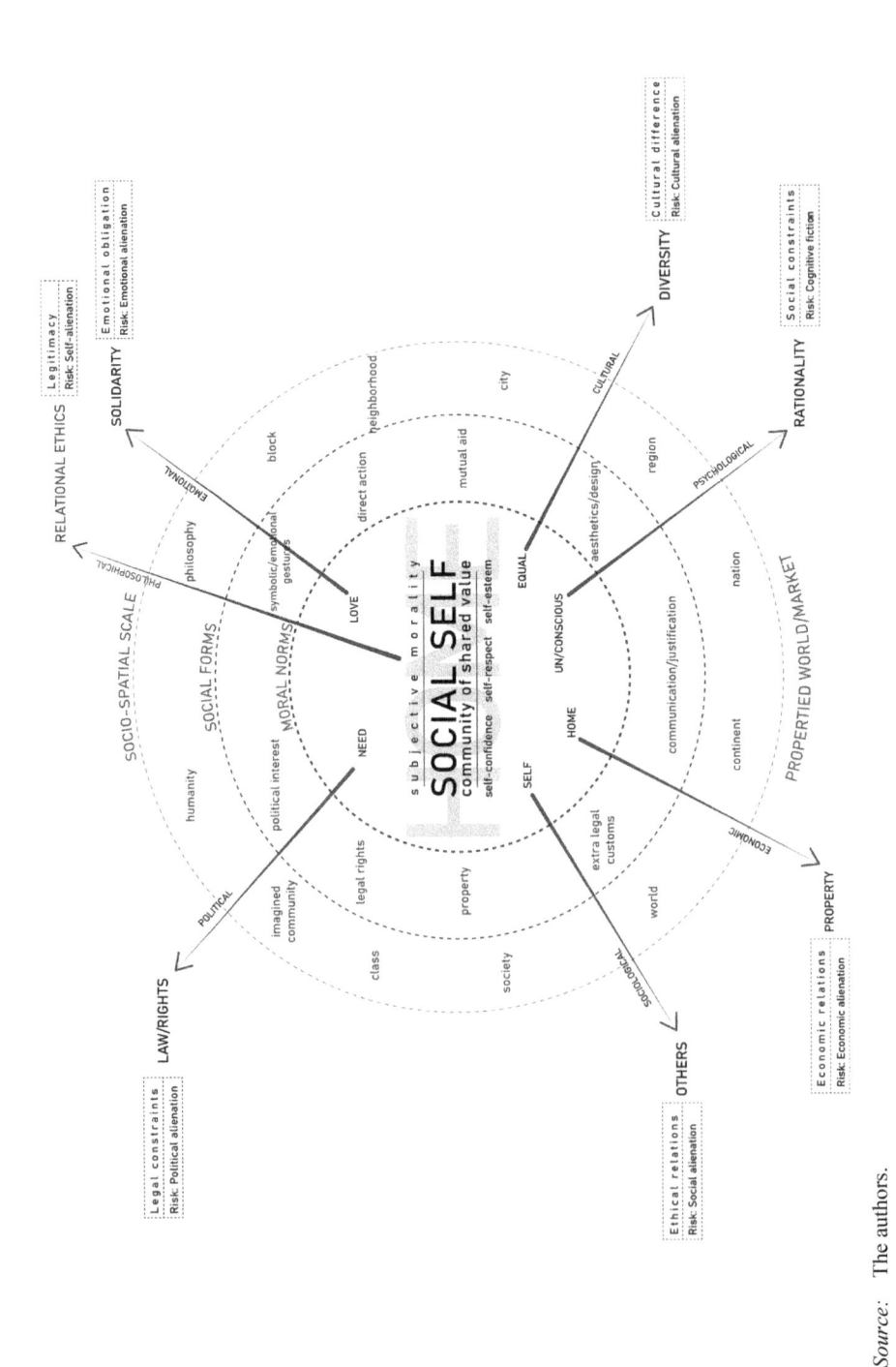

*Source:* The authors.

*Figure 13.1  Socio-spatial comfort zones of care and conflict. Norms, forms, and scales of the social self and community formation*

vis-à-vis inner resignation) when disengaging from morality with intellectual moves of *moral relocation*. Investigating morality and cynicism, Vice (2011) differentiates the aloof from the affected cynic, where the former comes with superior knowledge while the latter has experienced the damage of idealism and ideology. Both types are characterized by disengagement from ideals in social life: 'Rage or despair are just as possible and why the cynic adopts cynicism rather than gives in to these emotions will often depend on idiosyncratic, pragmatic, or aesthetic considerations' (Vice 2011: 174).

## SELF-CRITICAL PLANNING ETHICS AND INSURGENT SELF-CONFIDENCE

Planners are not free from cynicism. As organizers of (local) struggles for (local) recognition and places called home, urban planners have been designated modern 'demigods' (Lefebvre 2003: 131) who serve as 'architects of social inequality' (Marshall cited in Davy 2019: 290). Some may think of the historical phenomenon of Western modernity, while others are skeptical about prevailing economic imperatives and technocratic procedures, where post-political techno-politics and techno-planning go hand in hand (Buchholz 2022, Gualini et al. 2015). Determining what is good for others, planners, by the very nature of their profession, intervene into the lifeworld of others in the name of the greater good. Maintaining cognitive distance from subjectivity and emotionality has led Howell Baum (2015) to pose the question of *planning with half a mind*. Deriving from the discussion above, the philosophy of recognition offers novel pathways to embrace inner tension and resistance – emotionally – and rethink superior arguments of cognition with recognition relations that link personal to political self-confidence for insurgent, institutional change (Jaeggi 2011).

Habermasian planning scholars have done a good deal to tackle functionalist reason and embrace intersubjectivity for social, communicative rationality (Bond 2011). They even show sensitivity to the emotional dimension of communicative practices but always hold onto collective subjectivity (Forester 1993, 2013, Healey 1992). They never go all the social anthropological way. Embracing the planner as a rational, neutral, and somewhat invisible agent, the communicative planner is hardly ever emotionally affected by the urban intervention at hand but takes a distant, pragmatic, privileged perspective. The victim's perspective is hardly ever taken into account, as planning theorists claim: 'sympathy is not an option' (Inch et al. 2017: 474). The communicative pragmatic planner listens, learns, and tells stories but hardly ever his or her own. Such a perspective on alienated planners is deeply problematic for social rationalities and planning ethics (Pløger 2004, 2018). Why do they not share experiences of disrespect, exclusion, or marginalization? Who are these planners listening to and learning from different lifeworlds, different to their own?

These questions put self-critical ethical relations at the forefront of analysis so as to see planners as being involved and committed co-creators of ethical procedures and just outcomes. Lived experience makes a difference to ethical encounters of housing insecurity, homelessness, and subsequent forms of self-help and direct action (Lutz 2018,; Martínez 2020). If the planner can personally relate to the struggle at hand and still endorses an urban intervention in the name of the greater, public good, such critical relations-to-self introduce a robust understanding of self-critical planning ethics, if not a cynical one. The *problematique* thus involves privileges with respect to education, socialization, and the imagination of desirable urban futures that likely divide middle-class planners (with access to higher education and likely property) from underprivileged residents in problematic neighborhoods who have limited chances, limited choices, and thus limited means to lead a meaningful life. Here, political subjectivity and emotional rationality are crucial to organic solidarity with underprivileged strangers.

Ideological links to propertied order are an easy response for the privileged planner. Thick universal values conveyed in ideology confine their scope and relieve planners from emotional obligations with the contrasting lifeworlds of precarious communities. The risk is a form of naivety, preventing (self-)confident civil servants from experiencing, feeling, and negotiating these lifeworlds and struggles outside of the scope of the ideology they may adhere to. The alternative is to accept parallel worlds when working with the legal, propertied order and simultaneously departing from personal ideals of morality and the good. Such abstraction, disengagement, or self-alienation from one's own lifeworld is not only pragmatic but similarly cynical (Vice 2011). John Forester (2013) is clear on the two dangers of naivety and cynicism, which follow from idealism, ideology, and pragmatism. Their tension is crucial as it nourishes alienation.

Alienation is admittedly an old analytical category, which has suffered from essentialist dangers and inflationary use. The concept has been revived by Rahel Jaeggi (2014) as 'relation of relationlessness', which above all stresses the simultaneous multitude of competing meanings, where a house is always two things at once (i.e. social and economic good), confronting complexity and threatening *self-control* over one's life. Aiming to find a way through multiple justifications, Forester (1993: 5) prominently highlights the Habermasian benefits for planning theory of clarifying 'what' is the problem and 'how' can it be solved. With Honneth, however, the deeper question for social rationality and communicative practice is *why* to engage in the first place and *who* exactly cares. Political subjectivity and ethical relations-to-self are key to (self-)critical analysis of planning interventions and competing rights to the city (i.e. propertied vs urban citizenship) while the legitimacy of propertied citizenship is in question.

Looking at propertied order and the hegemonic achievement principle, the ethical ties of achievement and property have long been broken, as inherited property significantly distorts the liberal achievement principle because the individual's work effort is lacking (Piketty 2014). Property is shot through with moral expectations regarding achievement and use (Heins 2009), while ethical relations-to-self highlight self-achievement and self-use. For inherited property and multiple ownership this is not the case. What is perceived as ethical violation in everyday gentrification processes, for instance, is the confrontation of low-income tenants with affluent new neighbors, who have jumped the queue when buying themselves in. They are aliens to their neighbors on political, economic, social, and cultural grounds. Hence, political subjectivity and ethical relations-to-self are vital to justify competing claims of propertied vs urban citizenship, which involves personal performance to mobilize self-confidence for shared obligations in community and social institutions for just cities.

## INSURGENCIES AND ANARCHIST PLANNING

Insurgent planners come close to an emotional framework of planning and resistance, conflict and care, when stressing personal commitment to local struggles, which runs counter to the picture of neutral planners, distant mediators, or aloof cynics (Porter et al. 2012). Insurgent planners intuitively embrace political subjectivity when expressing struggles of discrimination, marginalization, and invisibilization (Huq 2020, Miraftab 2009). As such, however, they fall short of substantial debate and tend to romanticize insurgent movements as necessarily progressive. A closer look at normativity and the politics of conservative, regressive alt-right movements does not allow for universal abstraction or optimism (Davy 2019). Interested in visibility, inclusion, and desirable social change, insurgent planners can benefit from recognition-theoretical analysis, as invisibility is one foundational argument related to mutual recognition (Honneth 2001): not to look through underprivileged others (caretakers, cleaners, neighbors, migrants, homeless people, etc.) because one does not equally recognize their status or very existence (Herzog 2018). The making of insurgent self-confidence thus connects the personal-political performance for propertied critique and visible change.

Interstitial, insurgent change is central to anarchist planning, embracing political subjectivity and ethical reciprocity, when propagating mutual aid, direct action, and altruism (*'Vivre pour autrui'*) as the basis for (inter-)action towards social justice. While anarchist influence on urban planning can be traced back to the early days of the discipline (Hall 1988, Oyón & Kuzmanić 2022), its general ideas progressed in theory and practice mostly in the Cold War decades, seeking the third path away from the market–state dichotomy through direct action in housing and grassroots planning via social action (De Carlo 1948, Doglio 1970, Proli 2017, Turner 1976, Ward 1989). Although less attentive to (mutual) recognition relations, as discussed above, anarchist planners are decisive on eliminating the divide between political subjectivities, putting all pressure on the dwellers, planners included, as autonomous subjects in the provision of better lives. Going as far as declaring that urban planning can become revolutionary 'if we succeed in rescuing it from the blind monopoly of authority and in making it a communal organ of research and investigation into the real problems of social life' (De Carlo 1948), anarchist planners propose a radical shift in what planning does for the final user. Dismantling the professional attire, Colin Ward (1989) thus proposes that planning be handed to citizens. 'Well-organized, well-briefed and well-motivated local people are', in his words, capable of 'giving places and spaces social meaning through the endeavour of social management' (1989: 102). However this form of radicality (or naivety) comes with a price for a larger scale of social recognition.

Notions of permanent temporality, immanent conflict, or 'the spirit of revolt' (Springer 2016) are strongly present in anarchist tradition and the history of urban life. Unlike Marxist explanations, anarchist thought has been deeply marked by the geographical imagination from the start (Kropotkin 1902). Spatial dedication to social change goes as far as declaring that 'anarchist theory *is* geographical theory' (Peet 1975: 43), a claim fiercely defended by a range of more recent anarchist geographers (Breitbart 2009, Ince 2012, Springer 2016). All of them build on Kropotkin's (1902) model of society that emerges from territorial dependencies of social subjects based on historical evidence of mutual aid as lived practice. Anarchists thus developed an early idea of social self-realization, which comes at the price of one's comfort zone and embraces the altruistic moment of mutual aid (Spoerri & Stenglein 2021).

Throughout the scale of time and the complexity of social formations, anarchist authors give weight to acts of mutual aid by means of political anthropology, social philosophy, the history of urban planning, and architecture. What they share can be read as two threads of mutual aid: 1) the insurgent moment, where immediate care and solidarity are weapons of the underprivileged against the status quo of the ruling class, capitalist injustice, and propertied urban space; and 2) as part of the power of everyday life, where acts of neighbors, companions, and strangers in a community of shared values in *shared* space condense into collective incremental efforts towards a different, better life. Springer et al.'s *The Practice of Freedom* set out to explore the political potential of everyday change here and now, as the authors envision 'revolution as a politics of the everyday, a product of immanence ... [and an] ongoing enactment of our actual daily performances [through which] freedom itself is called into being' (Springer et al. 2016: 2). This calls for practices that are equally concerned with 'challenging our imaginary (what is possible and desirable?) and our action (what is practical and enactable?)' (ibid.).

In contrast to the Marxist primacy of a state-leaning solution to social struggles, which comes with waiting for the revolutionary moment in the waiting room of history (Harvey 2017, Springer 2017), anarchist practice has never engaged with the telos of final solution(s) in history, ending injustice, oppression, and poverty at once and for good. Focused on means, Castoriadis (1997: 151) goes as far as presenting means and ends as a mere linguistic trap as struggles for autonomy, freedom, and the good life are mere beginnings. This recreates the political project of the future as continuous and unresolved, but certainly in the hands of those who care. Social freedom requires struggle; individual freedom is not an end in itself. Emphasizing means over ends with respect to gradual, social change, Ward then optimistically points to pluralist shifts in everyday, interstitial change, which smoothly resonates with the bottom line of Frankfurt school critical theory: '[O]nce you begin to look at human society from an anarchist point of view you discover that the alternatives are already there, in the interstices of the dominant power structure. If you want to build a free society, *the parts are all at hand*' (Ward 1973: 14, emphasis added).

## CONCLUSIONS

Recalling Tönnies's lost social unity, Simmel's lost social control, and Durkheim's search for solidarity among strangers, we have outlined the mutual moment of social, legal, and emotional recognition relations in Honneth's philosophical anthropology. Admittedly, we have addressed the normative question of what the good life can be all about in a rather abstract manner. We have done so to allow for theoretical openness, political subjectivity, and social autonomy. Employing a thin universal morality, any issue at hand is thickened through situated, ethical practice. For the housing question, for example, a moral discourse on a place called home clearly implies normative commitment to such a place. Which form it takes – be it administrative, spatial, or aesthetic form – follows from the desired norm. Emotional need and social esteem are the first to define this desired (minimum) standard, which may then take the form of legal recognition and connect to scale; that is, housing as a legal right for all. The moral architecture of urban conflict thus brings together emotional need and social esteem for social *and* emotional rationality, while legal respect would need to follow.

In any case, the controversy of conflict and care responds to norms, forms, and scales of recognition vis-à-vis disrespect, which implies normativity at the moral core – what we love – and multiple forms of tenderness in cities to come about (España 2021, Gabauer et al. 2022). The philosophy of recognition provides the above discussed schools of thought with a robust foundation of emotional care and social conflict, deeply rooted in political subjectivity and historical struggles. As such it paves the way for self-critique, emotional rationality, and insurgent practices (Baum 2015, Porter et al. 2012 Schubert 2014), where the restoration of damaged self-confidence is crucial to community, movement, and institutional formations for political justice and desirable urban change.

## REFERENCES

Adorno, T. W., Albert, H., Dahrendorf, R., Habermas, J., Pilot, H. & Popper, K. R. (eds.) (1993) *Der Positivismusstreit in der deutschen Soziologie*. Munich: DTV Wissenschaft.

Aldous, J., Durkheim, E. & Tönnies, F. (1972) An exchange between Durkheim and Tönnies on the nature of social relations with an introduction by Joan Aldous. *American Journal of Sociology* 77(6): 1191–1200.

Allen, A. (2016) *The End of Progress: Decolonizing the Normative Foundations of Critical Theory*. New York: Columbia University Press.

Anderson, B. (2006) *Imagined Communities: Reflections on the Origin and Spread of Nationalism*. London: Verso.

Aronowitz, S. (1994) The Simmel revival: A challenge to American social science. *The Sociological Quarterly* 35(3): 397–414.

Baum, H. (2015) Planning with half a mind: Why planners resist emotion. *Planning Theory & Practice* 16(4): 498–516.

Bond, S. (2011) Negotiating a 'democratic ethos': Moving beyond the agonistic–communicative divide. *Planning Theory* 10(2): 161–186.

Breitbart, M. M. (2009) Anarchism/anarchist geography. In Kitchin, R. & Thrift, N. (eds.) *International Encyclopedia of Human Geography*. Oxford: Elsevier, 108–115.

Buchholz, T. (2016) *Struggling for Recognition and Affordable Housing in Amsterdam and Hamburg: Resignation, Resistance, Relocation*. Groningen: University of Groningen.

Buchholz, T. (2021) New directions in Frankfurt critical theory for critical urban theory. In Orum, A., Ruiz-Tagle, J. & Vicari, S. (eds.) *Companion to Wiley-Blackwell Encyclopedia of Urban and Regional Studies*. Hoboken: Wiley-Blackwell, 155–175.

Buchholz, T. (2022) Technoplanung und die Internationale Bauausstellung in der kritischen Phase der Urbanisierung: Was kann IBA? *Derive* 89(4): 43–48.

Butler, J. (2021) Recognition and the social bond: A response to Axel Honneth. In Ikäheimo, H., Lepold, K. & Stahl, T. (eds.) *Recognition and Ambivalence*. New York: Columbia University Press, 31–55.

Cahnman, W. J. (1976) Tönnies, Durkheim and Weber. *Social Science Information* 15(6): 839–853.

Castoriadis, C. (1997) Marxism and revolutionary theory. In Curtis, D. A. (ed.) *Cornelius Castoriadis: The Castoriadis Reader*. Oxford: Blackwell, 139–195.

Dahme, H. J. & Rammstedt O. (1984) Die zeitlose Modernität der soziologischen Klassiker. Überlegungen zur Theoriekonstruktion von Emile Durkheim, Ferdinand Tönnies, Max Weber und besonders Georg Simmel. In Dahme, H. J. & Rammstedt, O. (eds.) *Georg Simmel und die Moderne*. Frankfurt: Suhrkamp, 449–478.

Davy, B. (2019) Evil insurgency. A comment on the interface 'strengthening planning's effectiveness in a hyper-polarized world'. *Planning Theory & Practice* 20(2): 290–297.

Davy, B., Levin-Keitel, M. & Sielker F. (2023) Plural planning theories: Cherishing the diversity of planning. *European Planning Studies* 31(11): 2267–2276.

De Carlo, G. (1948) Planning & anarchism. *Freedom Journal* 9(12): 2.

Deranty, J. P. (2009) *Beyond Communication: A Critical Study of Axel Honneth's Social Philosophy*. Leiden: Brill.

Doglio, C. (1970) Il piano armonico (la pianificazione della libertà). *Anarchismo '70. Materiali per un dibattito* 6: 29–33.

Durkheim, E. (2014 [1897]) *Der Selbstmord*. Berlin: Suhrkamp.

Ehrenberg, A. (2015) *Das erschöpfte Selbst – Depression und Gesellschaft in der Gegenwart*. Frankfurt: Campus.

España, K. (2021) *Die Sanfte Stadt*. Vienna: Transversal.

Forester, J. (1993) *Critical Theory, Public Policy, and Planning Practice – Toward a Critical Pragmatism*. Albany: State University of New York Press.

Forester, J. (2013) On the theory and practice of critical pragmatism: Deliberative practice and creative negotiations. *Planning Theory* 12(1): 5–22.
Fraser, N. & Honneth, A. (2003) *Redistribution or Recognition: A Political-philosophical Exchange.* London: Verso.
Gabauer, A., Knierbein, S., Cohen, N., Lebuhn, H., Trogal, K., Viderman, T. & Haas, T. (eds.) (2022) *Care and the City – Encounters with Urban Studies.* London: Routledge.
Gualini, E., Mourato, J. M. & Allegra, M. (eds.) (2015) *Conflict in the City – Contested Urban Spaces and Local Democracy.* Berlin: Jovis.
Hall, P. (1988) *Cities of Tomorrow: An Intellectual History of Urban Planning and Design in the Twentieth Century.* New York: Blackwell.
Harvey, D. (2017) 'Listen anarchist!' A personal response to Simon Springer's 'Why a radical geography must be anarchist'. *Dialogues in Human Geography* 7(3): 233–250.
Healey, P. (1992) Planning through debate: The communicative turn in planning theory. *The Town Planning Review* 63(2): 143–162.
Heins, V. (2009) The place of property in the politics of recognition. *Constellations* 16(4): 579–592.
Herzog, B. (2018) Invisibilization and silencing as an ethical and sociological challenge. *Sociological Epistemology* 32(1): 13–23.
Hochschild, A. R. (1983) *The Managed Heart: Commercialization of Human Feeling.* Berkeley: University of California Press.
Honneth, A. (1993) *The Critique of Power.* Cambridge: The MIT Press.
Honneth, A. (1995) *The Struggle for Recognition – The moral grammar of social conflicts.* Cambridge: Polity Press.
Honneth, A. (1997) Anerkennung und moralische Verpflichtung. *Zeitschrift für philosophische Forschung* 51(1): 25–41.
Honneth, A. (2001) Invisibility – on the epistemology of 'recognition'. *Aristotelian Society* 75(1): 111–126.
Honneth, A. (2007) Recognition as ideology. In Brink, H. H. A. van den & Owen, D. (eds.) *Recognition and Power. Axel Honneth and the Tradition of Critical Social Theory.* New York: Cambridge University Press, 323–371.
Honneth, A. (2011) *Das Recht der Freiheit.* Berlin: Suhrkamp.
Honneth, A. (2012) *The I in We – Studies in the Theory of Recognition.* Cambridge: Polity Press.
Horgan, M. (2012) Strangers and strangership. *Journal of Intercultural Studies* 33(6): 607–622.
Horgan, M. (2017) Interaction, indifference, injustice: Elements of a normative theory of urban solidarity. In Kurasawa, F. (ed.) *Interrogating the Social – A Critical Sociology of the 21st Century.* London: Palgrave Macmillan, 61–93.
Huq, E. (2020) Seeing the insurgent in transformative planning practices. *Planning Theory* 19(4): 371–91.
Ince, A. (2012) In the shell of the old: anarchist geographies of territorialisation. *Antipode* 44(5): 1645–1666.
Inch, A., Laurian, L., Mouat, C., Davies, R., Davy, B., Legacy, C. & Symonds, C. (2017) Planning in the face of immovable subjects: A dialogue about resistance to development forces. *Planning Theory & Practice* 18(3): 469–488.
Jaeggi, R. (2011) Was ist eine (gute) Institution? In Forst, R., Hartmann, M., Jaeggi, R. & Saar, M. (eds.) *Sozialphilosophie und Kritik.* Berlin: Suhrkamp.
Jaeggi, R. (2014) *Alienation.* New York: Columbia University Press.
Komarovsky, M. (1940) *The Unemployed Man and His Family; The Effect of Unemployment upon the Status of the Man in Fifty-nine Families.* Dryden Press.
Kropotkin, P. (1902) *Mutual Aid: A Factor of Evolution.* London: Heinemann
Lefebvre, H. (2003) *Die Revolution der Städte.* Dresden: Postplatz.
Levine, D. (1984) Ambivalente Begegnungen: 'Negationen' Simmels durch Durkheim, Weber, Lukács, Park und Parsons. In Dahme, H. J. & Rammstedt, O. (eds.) *Georg Simmel und die Moderne.* Frankfurt: Suhrkamp, 318–388.
Lichtblau, K. (2012) Einleitung. In Lichtblau, K. (ed.) *Ferdinand Tönnies – Studien zu Gemeinschaft und Gesellschaft.* Wiesbaden: Springer, 7–27.

Lutz, M. (2018) *Governing Poor Spaces. Homeless Encampments and the New Management of Housing Insecurity in the US*. PhD dissertation, Freie Universität Berlin.
Mann, S. & D. Huffman (2005) The decentering of second wave feminism and the rise of the third wave. *Science & Society* 69(1): 56–91.
Marcucci, N. (2017) Between facts and wills: Tönnies, Durkheim, and the sociological critique of modern obligation. *Journal of Classical Sociology* 17(4): 276–292.
Martínez, M. (2020) *Squatters in the Capitalist City – Housing, Justice, and Urban Politics*. London: Routledge.
Massey, D. (2005) *For Space*. London: Sage.
Miraftab, F. (2009) Insurgent planning: Situating radical planning in the global south. *Planning Theory* 8(1): 32–50.
Oyón, J. L. & Kuzmanić, J. (2022) The anarchist strain of planning history: Pursuing Peter Hall's 'Cities of Tomorrow' thesis through the Geddes connection, 1866–1976. In Welch, M., Abarkan, A., Castrillo, M. A. & Pekár, M. (eds.) *European Planning History in the 20th Century: A Continent of Urban Planning*. New York: Routledge: 213–221.
Peet, R. (1975) For Kropotkin. *Antipode* 7: 42–43.
Petherbridge, D. (ed.) (2011) *Axel Honneth: Critical Essays. With a Reply by Axel Honneth*. Leiden: Brill.
Piketty, T. (2014) *Capital: In the Twenty-First Century*. Cambridge: Belknap Press.
Pløger, J. (2004) Strife: Urban planning and agonism. *Planning Theory* 3(1): 71–92.
Pløger, J. (2018) Conflict and agonism. In Gunder, M., Madanipour, A. & Watson, V. (eds.) *The Handbook of Planning Theory*. London and New York: Routledge, 264–275
Pohl, L. (2019) Das urbane Unbewusste: Psychoanalyse und kritische Stadtforschung. *Sub\urban. Zeitschrift für kritische stadtforschung* 7(3): 47–64.
Pohl, L. (2023) Psychoanalytic geographies. In Lees, L. & Demeritt, D. (eds.) *Concise Encyclopedia of Human Geography*. Cheltenham, UK and Northampton, MA, USA: Edward Elgar Publishing, 307–311.
Porter, L., Sandercock, L. & Umemoto, K. (2012) What's love got to do with it? Illuminations on loving attachment in planning. *Planning Theory & Practice* 13(4): 593–627.
Proli, S. (2017) Carlo Doglio (1914–1995): The theory and practice of slingshot planning. *Planning Perspectives* 32(4): 533–556.
Rammstedt, O. (1988) Wertfreiheit und die Konstitution der Soziologie in Deutschland. *Zeitschrift für Soziologie* 17(4): 264–71.
Scherr, A. (2005) Social subjectivity and mutual recognition as basic terms of a critical theory of education. In Fischman, G. et al. (eds.) *Critical Theories, Radical Pedagogies, and Global Conflicts*. Lanham: Rowman & Littlefield, 145–153.
Schubert, A. (2014) Emotionale Rationalität und Planung: Planungsansätze einer 3. Generation. *Sub/urban. Zeitschrift für kritische stadtforschung* 2(1): 71–94.
Simmel, G. (1910) How is society possible? *American Journal of Sociology* 16(3): 372–391.
Simmel, G. (2020 [1903]) *Die Großstädte und das Geistesleben*. Berlin: Suhrkamp.
Smith, D. M. (1994) *Geography and Social Justice*. Oxford: Blackwell.
Smith, D. M. (2000) *Moral Geographies. Ethics in a World of Difference*. Edinburgh: Edinburgh University Press.
Soja, E. (2010) *Seeking Spatial Justice*. Minneapolis: University of Minnesota Press.
Spoerri, G. & Stenglein, F. (eds.) (2021) *Anarchistische Geographien*. Münster: Westfälisches Dampfboot.
Springer, S. (2016) *The Anarchist Roots of Geography. Towards Spatial Emancipation*. Minneapolis: University of Minnesota Press.
Springer, S. (2017) The limits to Marx: David Harvey and the condition of postfraternity. *Dialogues in Human Geography* 7(3): 280–294.
Springer, S., White, R. & Lopes de Souza, M. (eds.) (2016) *The Practice of Freedom: Anarchism, Geography and the Spirit of Revolt*. New York: Rowman & Littlefield.
Stahl, T. (2013) What is immanent critique? SSRN working paper. doi: 10.2139/ssrn.2357957.
Tönnies, F. (2017 [1935]) *Gemeinschaft und Gesellschaft*. 8th edition. Munich: Profil Verlag.
Tristan, F. (1840) *Promenades ans Londres*. Paris: Biblioteque Marguerite Durand.

Turner, J. F. C. (1976) *Housing by People: Towards Autonomy in Building Environments*. London: Marion Boyars.
Vice, S. (2011) Cynicism and morality. *Ethical Theory and Moral Practice* 14(2): 169–184.
Walzer, M. (2019) *Thick and Thin – Moral Argument at Home and Abroad.* Notre Dame: University of Notre Dame Press.
Ward, C. (1973) *Anarchy in Action*. London: Allen & Unwin.
Ward, C. (1989) *Welcome, Thinner City: Urban Survival in the 1990s.* London: Bedford Square Press.
Weber, M. & Bermingham, C. R. (2003) Authority and autonomy in marriage. *Sociological Theory* 21(2): 85–102.
Wirth, L. (1926) The sociology of Ferdinand Tönnies. *American Journal of Sociology* 32(3): 412–422.
Young, I. M. (2007) Recognition of love's labor: Considering Axel Honneth's feminism. In Brink, H. H. A. van den & Owen, D. (eds.) *Recognition and Power: Axel Honneth and the Tradition of Critical Social Theory*. Cambridge: Cambridge University Press, 189–212.

# 14. Planetary urbanisation reloaded: a radical theory for the burning issues of our time
*Max Rousseau*

During the long heatwave in the summer of 2022, devastating fires in the Landes region destroyed more than 20,000 hectares of forest. France has now joined a growing list of countries that have to face up to the burning issue of megafires. The phenomenon of gigantic wildfires was formerly limited to the southern hemisphere (Amazonia, Australia, the Congo Basin) before it spread to North America (California, Canada) and Southern Europe (Spain, Portugal, and then France). These extremely intense megafires are directly and indirectly sparked by human activity; for example, when land is burnt for the purposes of agriculture and resource extraction and when measures to suppress wildfires near housing and economic infrastructure in areas where natural fires occur actually intensify combustion when fires do break out (Dalby 2018). Megafires are driven by the climate crisis. In turn, they release large amounts of $CO_2$ into the atmosphere, which accelerates it. They are a feature of the 'capitalocene', a concept according to which capitalism, not humanity as a whole, is responsible for the current environmental crisis (Malm 2016, Moore 2015).

It should come as no surprise that Landes was the outpost of megafires in France. The region is a massive industrial tree plantation that was created in the mid-19th century to produce resin for the nascent chemical industry, as well as wood for shipbuilding and export to England. To grasp the full implications of the situation, it is important to understand that the Landes forest should not be considered as a natural area but as the product of 'planetary urbanisation'. Henri Lefebvre, a French Marxist sociologist, described the phenomenon of planetary urbanisation half a century ago. He used the term to refer to a process in which what he called the 'urban fabric' is constantly expanding and, thus, causing degradation in apparently preserved spaces: forests, cultivated fields, deserts, mountains, oceans, ice floes, and even the atmosphere. If we adopt this view, Landes could be considered as an urban district rather than a natural forest (Rousseau 2022): it has uniform plots of the same-sized trees, which are not dissimilar to alignments of buildings governed by urban planning regulations; the practice of clear-felling, where every tree is felled to make way for monoculture tree plantations with a calibrated lifespan, echoes urban renewal, when buildings deemed obsolete are razed to the ground to make way for more lucrative developments; even the straight firebreaks, designed to slow the spread of fires, are comparable to the monotonous road networks typically found in housing estates.

As the example of Landes demonstrates, planetary urbanisation is a powerful tool, which can help dismantle boundaries often taken for granted, such as the urban/rural, anthropic/wild, or North/South. Thus, it is increasingly accepted by critical urban scholars as a key theory for spatialising global capitalism. Its theoretical roots go back to the tumultuous 1960s. Today, Lefebvre is widely recognised as the first proponent of planetary urbanisation. At the same time, similar issues were raised by scholars from the Global South who were influenced by dependency theory. For example, Vegliò (2021) observed that as early as 1967 the Peruvian sociologist Quijano argued that before 'the urbanization of the economy' began in Latin America, 'the urban and the rural were fairly independent and substantially isolated from each other: any change that occurred on one side was essentially irrelevant to the other – although the urban tended to change much more rapidly and noticeably' (Quijano, cited in Vegliò 2021). Quijano also observed that 'this situation seems to be completely changing: that isolation was 'mostly destroyed' and the rural was 'increasingly placed in a position of dependency … in such a way that each of the processes that happens on an urban level necessarily affects, directly or indirectly, slowly or quickly, rural life' (Quijano, cited in Vegliò 2021).

The revised theory of planetary urbanisation draws on Lefebvre's insight. It goes further than the original theory, which makes it an even more potent intellectual tool. As mentioned above, Lefebvre was a sociologist and philosopher. He was born in 1901 and raised in the Landes region, a century after Germany developed scientific silviculture (Scott 1998) and half a century after Napoleon III launched what would be known as the 'Haussmannisation' of Paris. This involved the demolition of the city's old working-class neighbourhoods to make way for boulevards for the enjoyment of the burgeoning middle classes. Paris became the 'capital of modernity' (Harvey 2003). An imperial decree was issued at the same time, putting an end to the traditional agro-pastoral system in Landes. As a result, the Landes region was turned into Western Europe's largest industrial forest. Lefebvre started reflecting on planetary urbanisation partly due to the accelerating modernisation in post-war France and partly because of his intellectual and geographical background.

Once a prominent intellectual in the powerful post-war French Communist Party, Lefebvre left the Communist Party in the late 1950s. He denounced Stalinism and developed a heterodox Marxism that would inspire students who took part in the May 1968 uprising. Lefebvre developed the Hegelian existentialist side of Marxism in the 1950s and 1960s with the philosopher Sartre. This shift came before the structuralist reaction, led by Althusser (Poster 1975) in the field of philosophy and his PhD student Castells in the field of critical urban studies (Merrifield 2002). In parallel, Lefebvre conducted research in rural sociology before focusing on urban issues in the 1960s. Thus, he was well-placed to observe the modernisation of the French countryside and the virtual disappearance of the peasantry during the Fordist era (Ross 1995). His background explains why his critique of the 'generalised urban' is also indefectibly a denunciation of the 'colonization of everyday life' (Lefebvre 1961). In the late 1950s, he conducted a major sociological study on daily life in Mourenx, a new town built for the purpose of exploiting the gas and oil fields in southwestern France. He argued that boredom was the 'new public enemy' engendered by modernity (Lefebvre 1960: 201). Lefebvre clearly contradicted the French Communist Party's then-official interpretation of Marxism by suggesting that alienation does not stop at the factory exit but that the whole modern city itself becomes alienating.

In his book *La Révolution urbaine* (Lefebvre 1970b; published in English under the title *The Urban Revolution* in 2003), Lefebvre suggests that the global triumph of 'urban society' is transforming all practices, including social and political relations, as well as cultural and artistic representations. He argues that this major transformation is driven by the 'complete urbanisation' of society, which invades the countryside to subordinate it further. Urbanisation is the result of a double movement: the dispersal of populations to the urban fringes (suburban housing estates, 'large housing estates') and greater centrality. Exchange value replaces use value, and segregation (social, ethnic, generational), which is both 'spontaneous' (the 'rich' and 'poor' 'ghettos') and 'programmed' (the urban planning 'zones'), separates populations and fragments the city (understood as a common good). Therefore, the new urban society is profoundly inegalitarian. The masses are pushed out to the periphery and dispossessed, in terms of space and time (with a huge rise in travel time). According to Lefebvre, this process is a global phenomenon. In industrialised countries, cities are endlessly divided, with the rejection of working-class populations, who are forced to move to large housing estates or remote new towns. In parallel, agrarian societies are imploding and shantytowns in so-called 'underdeveloped' countries are exploding. All around the planet, the generalised colonisation of space by decision-making hubs blurs the border between urban and rural. As Lefebvre explains:

> Whether contemporary society can be described as 'urban society' characterizing both its reality and its tendency – that we are entitled to prefer this name to others that have been or are being proposed (industrial society, consumer society, leisure society, etc.) –, we take it for granted. This is because economic growth and industrialization extend their effects to all national and regional territories; they are eliminating the traditional grouping of peasant life specific to the village, absorbing and reabsorbing it into larger units integrated into industrial production. The concentration of population goes hand in hand with the concentration of means of production. Small and medium-sized agglomerations are caught up in the proliferating urban fabric except, in large industrialized countries, stagnant or dying areas. For agricultural producers, the agrocity ['*l'agroville*'] is on the horizon. A hypothesis and a possibility as a starting point for reflection: one hundred percent urbanization. This defines urban society. (Lefebvre 1970a: 243)

From the outset, Lefebvre's proposal is a radical critique of what he refers to as 'urbanism'. He calls for a shift in the focus of urban sociology. Despite his theory's apparent pessimism, Lefebvre remains a libertarian Marxist. Thus, planetary urbanisation is also a normative theory with a strong emancipatory content. Lefebvre's aim is, first and foremost, to launch a programme that involves research and then political action. The ultimate goal is to enable communities to regain control of their everyday lives. Fifty years on, we can fairly say that the goal has never been achieved in France. Since the late 1970s, the French school of critical urban social sciences has lost momentum. At the same time, the field of international critical urban studies has developed, drawing on Lefebvre's theories on spatial issues, as well as on other key thinkers. This chapter argues that neo-Lefebvrian planetary urbanisation, or reloaded planetary urbanisation, can be applied as a theoretical, epistemological, and analytical tool that can be combined with other theories.

The chapter is organised in three parts. In the first part, I introduce the reloaded planetary urbanisation theory and describe its controversial reception in the field of critical urban studies. In the second part, I review some recent research that analyses processes of extended urbanisation, mostly in the Global South. My objective here is to show how the neo-Lefebvrian paradigm can be applied to a relational multi-scale analysis of how processes (seemingly) shape non-city spaces. In the third part, I demonstrate how reloaded planetary urbanisation is relevant for analysing issues on a global scale, using the example of pandemics. Here, I draw on original, real-time research conducted during the global spread of Covid-19 in early 2020 (Charmes & Rousseau 2020, 2022).

## THE CONTROVERSIAL LAUNCH OF 'RELOADED' PLANETARY URBANISATION

A decade ago, Lefebvre's almost forgotten programme was revived in the field of critical urban theory under the influence of Brenner and Schmid (Brenner & Schmid 2012, 2015, 2018, Brenner 2014, Schmid et al. 2015). Both scholars identified four processes, which have dramatically accelerated since Lefebvre's pioneering thinking on 'the complete urbanization of society' (Lefebvre 1970b): 1) 'the creation of new scales of urbanisation'; 2) 'the blurring and re-articulation of urban territories'; 3) 'the disintegration of the "hinterland"'; and 4) 'the end of the "wilderness"' (Brenner & Schmid 2012: 11–13). All four processes are driven by processes of urbanisation, which go beyond 'the city' limits and have become 'planetary'. To fully grasp these shifts, it is time to reload the planetary urbanisation theory:

> Adopting a global orientation means first of all decentring the centre of analysis, looking from an ex-centric position, which looks from the periphery and asks where to find the 'urban'. Such an orientation allows the researcher to detect a wide variety of expressions of the urban that have traditionally been excluded from analytical consideration because they are located outside ... the large agglomerations and metropolitan regions and their immediate hinterlands ... It traces the effects of the various relationships and mutual interactions between centralities and peripheries. (Schmid 2018: 592)

More specifically, critical urban studies should abandon their idea of 'the city' as a bounded spatial unit. In fact, all existing urban typology needs to be revised. 'The urban' should be redefined as 'a multiscalar *process* of sociospatial transformation' (Brenner & Schmid 2015). Reloaded planetary urbanisation has three features, which interact continuously to produce specific forms of socio-spatial organisation and uneven development: 1) concentrated urbanisation, which is an agglomeration of firms, workers, and infrastructure in space; 2) extended urbanisation, whereby the 'non-city' is no longer an outside space but a terrain that is integral to urbanisation, since extra-local 'operational landscapes' provide goods and services (e.g. food, water, energy, and construction materials are extracted to support the agglomeration); and 3) differentiated urbanisation, which refers to the creative destruction and uneven development of agglomerations and their 'operational landscapes', driven by capitalist forces (Brenner & Schmid 2015). In other words, according to Merrifield, who studied Lefebvre in detail and was a key proponent of planetary urbanisation, 'within this conceptualization, it's possible to conceive planetary urbanization not as simply bricks and mortar, as high-rise buildings and autoroutes, but as a process that produces skyscrapers as well as unpaved streets, highways as well as back roads, by-waters and marginal zones that feel the wrath of the world market – both its absence and its presence' (Merrifield 2014: 5). By advocating 'an urban theory without an outside' (Brenner 2014), reloaded planetary urbanisation proposes no less than a total epistemological shift in critical urban studies.

It is hardly surprising that reloaded planetary urbanisation was initially met with scepticism. Criticisms disputed its universal claims, accusing it of being inadequate on an empirical level. Some argued that the theory was too abstract for practical applications (Storper and Scott 2016). Other critics, particularly those advocating feminist, postcolonial, and 'relational' approaches to urban studies, argued that planetary urbanisation ignored 'difference' (Peake et al. 2018). For example, it does not consider issues of gender, sexuality, and race. Thus critics argue that it could end up forgetting the city itself and denying the differences between different contexts, particularly between the South and the North. Lastly, they suggest it may overlook the fact that the city is made by its inhabitants and, as a result, social movements could be denied the possibility of changing the course of urbanisation (Angelo and Goh 2020). While Brenner and Schmid's initial proposal was clearly very ambitious, it lacked sufficient empirical evidence (Giroud 2015). Another set of critics focused on epistemological issues. This time, the approach was accused of being gendered, North-centric, masculinised, or even neo-colonial: an attempt to impose a meta-theory, which may conceal the desire to universalise the opinion of a small group of white, predominantly male, Euro-Americans who hold powerful positions in academic circles (Angelo & Goh 2020).

However, adopting a multi-scale view does not mean that the processes of urbanisation are similar, regardless of place. In recent years, many articles have developed specific elements of reloaded planetary urbanisation. Indeed, it is essential to go beyond 'rural studies' and 'urban studies' (which Lefebvre advocated during his career) in order to shed light on extended urbanisation in the Global South. Indeed, in the South, the urbanisation process is often linked to 'accumulation by dispossession' (Harvey 2004), especially in the case of predatory land appropriation. Kanai (2014), for example, shows how attempts to globalise Manaus led to territorial restructuring and socio-spatial change that went far beyond the city's boundaries. There is now not only greater inequality in the area where urbanisation is concentrated but the financial and symbolic appropriation of standing rainforests (by metropolitan conservationism) is also marginalising remote communities. In the Global North, recent studies focusing on the destruction of wilderness show how the latter is integrated into an urban system – without necessarily referring to planetary urbanisation. For example, Farrell (2020) shows how the wealthy and ultra-rich, aware that they are morally corrupt or perceived as such, are increasing their investments in nature. Teton County, the wealthiest county in the United States, the richest country in the world, is a case in point. The rich newcomers remain rooted in dense urban areas but develop a world of their own, by appropriating the mountain (for private ski slopes, chalets, and ranches at prices ranging from a few million to tens of millions of US dollars).

Recently, research on mineral extraction has also been influenced by the reloaded planetary urbanisation framework. The social, economic, and environmental impact of extraction in a seemingly desert region goes way beyond the site of the mine itself. This is because mining operations are often controlled from a metropolitan area in a different county. The reloaded planetary urbanisation framework provides a fluid relational approach, which allows us to rethink the uneven geographical development in an era of supply chain capitalism. For example, Arboleda (2020) uses it to analyse how mines in Chile's Atacama Desert – the driest in the world – are linked to an expanding constellation of megacities, ports, banks, and factories across East Asia. Similarly, other research has shown that despite its conceptual nature, reloaded planetary urbanisation could shed light on social differences in everyday life in empirical research. For example, Angelo and Goh (2020) show how it can be combined with the traditional 'small and concrete' approach. Thus, they focus on social, spatial, and environmental marginalisation to improve their analysis of the development of grassroots movements in informal settlements in Jakarta, Indonesia. Here, a non-city-centric view

> illuminates the ways in which these movements, although developed in response to historically specific, place-based, social and spatial marginalization, are also responding to biophysical, environmental threats that are linked to both very localized geospatial and political conditions as well as *larger* spatial-scale environmental planning modes and to more generalized *abstract* development patterns. (Angelo & Goh 2020)

To fully grasp this idea, let us go back to the French hinterland. Sainte-Soline is a small village in Poitou, in southwest France. The region was traditionally used to cultivate maize, a water-intensive crop largely grown for livestock feed and export. In terms of planetary urbanisation, the region is clearly an operational landscape. In April 2023, less than a year after the megafire that devastated huge tracts of the Landes forest 200 km to the south, 30,000 people converged to protest against the construction of a new 'mega reservoir' ('*mégabassine*') in a region increasingly concerned by water shortages. These reservoirs are intended to store water for agricultural use. They are filled in the winter by pumping groundwater, and the water is then used for irrigation in the summer, when pumping groundwater is prohibited. The demonstration in Sainte-Soline was motivated by political, social, as well as environmental concerns; for example, the huge costs of maintaining the reservoirs are paid for with public money, the water is monopolised by a few farmers alone, the evaporation rate is likely to be high, and water-hungry crop production practices should not be encouraged to the detriment of a model based on agro-ecology.

In the 2010s, there were numerous conflicts surrounding 'areas to be defended' ('*Zones à Défendre*') involving protests against new projects of extended urbanisation, such as landfill sites for nuclear waste, airports, motorways, and logistic and commercial zones (Subra 2016). Thus, protestors who had taken part in various French and European demonstrations converged in the hinterland of Sainte-Soline. However, this time, things were different. The demonstration and planned sabotage did not target extended urbanisation per se, but a project designed to 'adapt' the 'operational hinterland' to climate change (Malm 2023). Measures to adapt to climate change should involve a democratic debate, with discussions about a new social, economic, and environmental configuration for the area. This is particularly the case in Sainte-Soline, which has been dependent on planetary urbanisation for years. However, that did not happen. The protestors were met with a violent police response involving dozens of trucks, two armoured vehicles, motocross bikes, and explosive ammunition. Some 4,000 grenades were used by police in just two hours, leaving two demonstrators in a coma (Libération 2023).

Although a violent police response had been expected, protestors still gathered together to chat and walk towards the huge reservoir in Sainte-Soline. The situation did not prevent what Merrifield qualifies as the 'politics of the encounter': when the urban fabric stretches across space, destroying it but unifying people at the same time. What will happen now after the widely covered events in Sainte-Soline? The recent past might hold the clue: many activists involved in the *Zones à Défendre*, which bloomed in the French hinterland in the 2010s, ultimately went back to dense settlements. In so doing, they also exported the social bonds, ideas, and tactics developed collectively in areas of extended urbanisation and introduced them in areas of concentrated urbanisation. This process partly explains why 'new municipalism' – a movement calling for direct democracy at a local level, which originally emanated from villages in the mid-2010s – shook the French local elections in 2020. The movement denounces neoliberal urbanism and is calling for urban commons (Béal et al. 2023).

## SEEING EXTENDED URBANISATION FROM THE GLOBAL SOUTH

As we will see, the pandemic appears to confirm the observation made by Harvey after the onset of the 2008 financial crisis: 'We are ... in the midst of a huge crisis – ecological, social, and political – of planetary urbanization without, it seems, knowing or even marking it' (Harvey 2014: 29). Yet for years the planetary urbanisation crisis appeared to be limited to the South, where megacities were struggling to provide basic services and infrastructure and to resolve social conflicts (Simone 2006). To address these tensions, new concepts have been developed in research. They focus on the agency of people faced with congested or collapsing institutional structures, who are overwhelmed by the planetary urbanisation crisis. These notions, such as 'subaltern urbanism' (Roy 2011), highlight processes that the Global South has known about for years: the agency of inhabitants, their capacity to organise themselves when outdated systems of governance refuse or simply cannot provide basic goods and services (Belarbi & Rousseau 2019, Zérah 2020). These concepts are no longer reserved for the South alone: recent research applies them to the inner-cities in the American Rustbelt, which imploded as a result of deindustrialisation and the financial crisis following the collapse of subprime loans (Schindler 2014, Rousseau & Béal 2021).

Postcolonial studies question the universal scope of planetary urbanisation, particularly because applying the theory to Southern countries, where pre-industrial, industrial, and post-industrial forms of production co-exist, does not seem that simple. Postcolonial studies suggest that planetary urbanisation should be contextualised in the light of detailed knowledge of local situations in the Global South (Robinson 2016, Robinson & Roy 2016). Today, the perspective offered by reloaded planetary urbanisation is actually proving to be more pertinent in the Global South. Brenner and Schmid's conceptualisation of the 'operationalization of places, territories and landscapes' is a response to 'the most basic socio-metabolic imperatives associated with urban growth' (Brenner & Schmid 2018). The idea of 'operational landscapes' is part of an emerging field of research, which has been particularly developed in the Brazilian Amazon (Castriota & Tonucci 2018).

Over the last decade, research has focused on the emergence of urban corridors, which are intrinsically linked to globalisation in the Global South (Africa, South Asia, South America). These corridors are embedded in complex international investments and national regulations (Kanai & Schindler 2019). In India, increasingly complex half-urban, half-rural continua have emerged from the hybridisation that has occurred between political-economic dynamics and the rationale of subaltern urbanism. By focusing on agrarian histories, Balakrishnan (2019) shows how India's new economic corridors are creating new processes of urbanisation, which reflect the specific, caste-ridden history of western Maharashtra, a region shaped by colonial and postcolonial agrarian modernisation. These corridors push 'the urban' way beyond the forms traditionally associated with it. As Kanai and Schindler (2019) explain, these new urban spaces may not provide the full benefits of centrality (jobs, services, infrastructure) but they are affected by the extension of the urban fabric nonetheless: increased traffic, waste and pollution, new forms of dispossession, and violence.

New methods of analysis are required to represent planetary urbanisation and the differentiated flows resulting from it. One method reveals the *process* of urbanisation, by following the flow of raw materials used in building construction. Choplin (2020), for example, follows the flow of cement between different production and distribution sites along the Accra–Lagos corridor. By working with the OpenStreetMap Benin community, Choplin was able to use drones to identify the cement resale points along the corridor. By mapping the production chain (from the owner of the cement factory to the street vendor), she reveals the phenomenon of 'urbanization without a city', where there are 'urban markers', such as the omnipresence of hardware stores, which sell construction materials and attract the cement giants. In this example, the urban form is no longer concentric but scattered, 'unfinished'. The Accra–Lagos corridor looks like a long, interstitial, rather informal construction site. Urbanisation is concentrated in several areas that are far apart and extends beyond these corridors. As a result, there is increasing competition for the control of the hinterland.

Similar urbanisation processes are now visible in Africa with the continued exploitation of the subsoils, an increase in agricultural land grabbing (by foreign firms or states), and the dispossession of peri-urban populations; for example, the former miners in Zambia's Copperbelt (Potts 2005), and peri-urban farmers in Rabat and Casablanca in Morocco (Rousseau et al. 2021). Over the last decade, the reloaded planetary urbanisation framework has made it possible to re-examine processes of extended urbanisation in the Global South. As I will demonstrate, the paradigm also sheds a different light on processes taking place on a global scale, such as the spread of pandemics.

## COVID-19: A VIRUS AT THE HEART OF PLANETARY URBANISATION

Lefebvre's theory on the triumph of urban society is rooted in a radical critique of capitalism and in what the author sees as its main lever for developing space in its own image: technocracy or, in Lefebvre's terms, 'urbanism'. Half a century later, the reloaded planetary urbanisation framework is also based on a critique of the technocratic vision of the 'urban'. The difference being that criticism now targets proponents of the 'urban age'. According to this paradigm, which is very influential in major international organisations, over half of the world's population lives in cities. Therefore, problems that were once 'urban' must now be considered 'global'. Brenner and Schmid (2014) suggest that this paradigm is little more than the latest variation in the tendency in urban studies to consider the city as a limited space. The concept of 'urban age', which is static and descriptive, fails to explain what drives urbanisation. In contrast, a heuristic approach to urbanisation, which considers dynamic interconnected processes, could reveal how governments failed to prevent the spread of new pandemics. As we have demonstrated (Charmes & Rousseau, 2020, 2022), this type of approach reveals the fact that health policies are incapable of taking urban developments into account when it comes to the prevention of infectious diseases. Planetary urbanisation proposes a starting point that helps to explain why the recommendations made by international organisations (e.g. the World Health Organisation) and national government action failed to tackle the rapid spread of the Covid-19 pandemic. Italy was the first country to be affected in Europe. Initially, the government imposed a lockdown in the province of Lodi in mid-February 2020 (50,000 people). Two weeks later, the measure was extended across the north of the country (16 million people), and a national lockdown was announced (60 million people) the following day. The rest of Europe followed in quick succession, as national lockdowns were imposed and national border functions were reactivated.

The pandemic abruptly ended the rationale of European integration, which had prevailed since World War II. How can this be explained? With the blurring of urban perimeters, the extensive networks formed by the nuclei of urbanisation and the intense flows along the networks, isolating individual households or cities proved to be impossible. The only sanitary cordons that could be put in place were the traditional national borders. A series of more or less authoritarian lockdown measures followed, involving restrictions on movement, business closures, curfews, etc., interspersed with brief periods of 'business as usual', when people were allowed to move freely. How can the emergence and spread of the pandemic be understood using the tools applied in planetary urbanisation?

One of the key features of the reloaded planetary urbanisation framework is the destruction of wilderness caused by extended urbanisation. Epidemiologists consider this to be one of the main reasons for the emergence of new pandemics (Wallace 2020). In all regions of the world, areas considered to be wild are being destroyed by planetary urbanisation for mining, planting rubber, or building new towns. This disrupts ecosystems and brings fauna and flora into contact with humans. Human diseases of animal origin, including zoonoses, account for 60% of infectious diseases worldwide and three quarters of the new pathogens detected in recent decades. Geographers who have conducted research on recent pandemics (from SARS to Ebola) have shown how extended urbanisation increases vulnerability to infectious disease spread (Ali & Keil, 2006, Connolly et al. 2021). It is no coincidence that the recent major viruses have emerged in areas with the fastest urbanisation rate. For example, in China, West Africa, and the Middle East, there has been a rise in the number of new contacts between human societies and the remaining wilderness (Treffers et al. 2021). This advancing urbanisation is a feature of new intensive farming systems. As Wallace (2020), a radical epidemiologist, explains: the expansion of industrial agriculture involves deforestation. With deforestation, the natural barriers between viruses and human communities are broken. Simultaneously, genetic monocultures, combined with overcrowding, create favourable conditions allowing 'pathogens … [to] quickly evolve around the commonplace host-immune genotype' (Wallace 2020: 51). Moreover, while some species are threatened with extinction, the species that survive and thrive – rats and bats, for instance – are more likely to host potentially dangerous pathogens capable of making the species jump to humans (Tollefson 2020). As Brenner and Ghosh (2022: 20) conclude,

> the socio-ecological supports and impacts of the intensively infrastructuralized landscapes crystallize far beyond such landscapes to encompass variegated, more-than-human territories and political ecologies across the planet. In this sense, emergeous infectious diseases must be understood as plagues of the capitalocene, and indeed, of planetary urbanization: they are produced within the unevenly extended spatial matrix of the capitalist urban fabric and its volatile, churning metabolism.

Another key aspect of the reloaded planetary urbanisation theory is the emergence of 'urban galaxies', whose components interact almost simultaneously with the entire globe. The Covid-19 virus is an indicator of the significance of the planetary scale. Epidemiological research carried out in France suggested that the first cases would appear as early as the end of 2019, despite the fact that the Chinese government was still investigating the potential transmission of the virus between humans. The rate of disease spread highlights the scale of the human flows. In the first three critical months, between December 2019 and February 2020, 750,000 passengers entered the US from China. The human flows, coupled with the virus' ability to spread without symptoms, can explain why it was impossible to contain the outbreaks. Governments clearly failed to grasp the dynamics of planetary urbanisation and how they have continued to accelerate since the 1970s.

Eight centuries ago, the Great Plague took about 15 years to travel the Silk Road to Europe (Schmid et al. 2015). Recent major epidemics have spread more rapidly but not as fast as Covid-19. In 2003, four months after the appearance of SARS-COV, there were 1,600 cases of infection worldwide. In comparison, four months after SARS-COV-2 emerged, there were almost 900,000 cases; i.e. 500 times more (Charmes & Rousseau 2020). At the time, globalisation was nothing like what it is today: in 2018, the number of air passengers was estimated at 4.2 billion, almost three times higher than in 2003. The airport in Wuhan, one of China's main hubs, played a key role. As a result, the virus spread outside China at a speed that few had really anticipated.

A third key element of planetary urbanisation is to redefine the metropolis, which can no longer be reduced to the notion of a dense, vertical city. Brenner and Schmidt (2012) refer to a continuous process of 'implosions/explosions', where islands of density are floating in the middle of irregular trails of diffuse urbanisation. This phenomenon has been widely observed in urban geography and was singularly confirmed by the location of Covid-19 outbreaks (Connolly et al. 2021), which often revealed unexpected interconnections. In France, the first outbreaks occurred in Méry-sur-Oise (a commune on the outskirts of Paris with a population of 10,000), Les Contamines-Montjoie (an Alpine ski resort), La Balme-de-Sillingy (a village on the outskirts of Annecy), and an evangelical church in Mulhouse (Charmes & Rousseau 2020). These sites are kilometres away from the heart of major French metropolises. In Italy, the first outbreaks were also reported in villages or small towns (Codogno or Vo') rather than the central districts of Milan or Venice.

With these first European outbreaks, the virus revealed the role of the hinterland in the globalisation of industrial value chains. Indeed, the flows along different networks do not only concern the business districts in big cities: they connect production sites. The intense links between the textile factories in Val Seriana and China explain why a peri-urban area northeast of Bergamo became one of the first Italian hotbeds of Covid-19 (Cremaschi 2020). In Germany, the infection was first reported in Starnberg, a community with a population of 20,000 located about 20 kilometres from Munich and connected to the rest of the world through its automobile equipment factory. It was only later that the centres of large cities became the main epicentres of the epidemic.

## A PANDEMIC THAT REVEALS THE URBANISATION OF INEQUALITIES

Another element that characterises planetary urbanisation is the spatial reconfiguration of social inequalities. This feature has not really been developed by the advocates of reloaded planetary urbanisation in the last decade. Of course, the urbanisation of inequalities is not new. Urbanisation depends on the extraction of an agricultural surplus to feed a class freed from the constraints of food production (Childe 1950) to the detriment of peasant self-sufficiency. Europe's medieval cities had fairly clear limits, organised around a well-defined central square or market. According to Weber (1958), this allowed the emergence of a social class, the bourgeoisie, which then engaged in a process of capital accumulation. By pushing back feudal or religious boundaries and by integrating an increasingly remote hinterland into the urban economy, this accumulation laid the foundations for capitalism. One example is the privatisation of the commons. As the urban fabric encroached on the English countryside, land was privatised and the bourgeoisie and the City of London became more powerful. With the enclosures, millions of landless peasants became a source of cheap labour. They were forced to move to cities, like London and Manchester, to find work, which fuelled capitalist industrialisation (Sevilla-Buitrago 2022).

Urbanisation then gradually took over from industrialisation as the main engine of capitalism (Lefebvre 1970b, Soederberg & Walks 2018). Therefore, the planetary spread of urbanisation is the ultimate phase in the rise of extreme inequality, which is a feature of the urban fabric. In fact, the emergence of 'planetary gentrification' is one of the most striking features of planetary urbanisation (Lees et al. 2016). These inequalities play a major role with regard to the impact of Covid-19 on our societies. Indeed, pandemics tend to occur at times when social disparities increase. Turchin (2007) observes a historical correlation between the level of inequality, the intensity of links between distant territories, and the virulence of pandemics. The richer a class becomes, the more conspicuous their consumption of exotic luxury goods. However, viruses travel primarily with long-distance trade. It is striking to note that the chronology of the different outbreaks of Covid-19 around the world reveals the major role played by places frequented by the upper classes (Charmes & Rousseau 2022). Unlike tuberculosis or cholera, whose victims tend to live in slums or poor countries, the new epidemic did not hit dense working-class neighbourhoods to start with: it spread first as a result of the mobility and sociability of the groups that benefit most from global urbanisation (Charmes & Rousseau 2022).

In a second phase, the virus spread more widely, both spatially and socially. Here again planetary urbanisation helps explain how. First, globalisation operates at the grassroots level as well (Choplin & Pliez 2018). For example, in Singapore, the virus was also carried by working-class migrants rather than expatriates, albeit more slowly. The migrants' poor living conditions were conducive to the spread of infection, which was harder to control in overcrowded dormitories than in condominiums in affluent districts. Generally, social distancing is more difficult in shantytowns. Indeed, a significant share of the population in major African, Latin American, and Asian metropolises live in shantytowns (Davis 2006), which are an important feature of global urbanisation.

The virus also spread through the networks that constitute urban constellations. The migration that preceded the public announcement of lockdowns revealed the extent and diversity of this interdependence, which extends well beyond the suburbs and peri-urban rings. In India and in several African countries, it revealed the precarity of huge numbers of migrants in the heart of large metropolises, for whom going back to the countryside was a matter of survival (Dahdah et al. 2020). In rich countries, where lockdown measures were fairly permissive, such as the United States or France, many students went back to their parents' homes if they could. The more affluent left the metropolitan areas to live in more comfortable places. In the days before the first national lockdown in France was announced, the highly selective nature of mobility became apparent. Similarly, the ongoing processes of explosion and implosion, which characterise planetary urbanisation, became more visible.

For example in France, many people were appalled when wealthy city dwellers, who spent lockdown in their second homes, published their 'lockdown diaries'. Eleven percent of residents left Paris before lockdown (Acs & Mosny 2020). This revealed the inequality of 'extended urbanisation', bringing to light the stark contrast between those with second homes in the countryside and those in working-class neighbourhoods, who were confined in dense urban areas. During lockdown, it was primarily the residents in working-class neighbourhoods who had to continue commuting to work. This mobility, combined with greater dependence on public transport, explains why there were more cases and more deaths in working-class areas. Ultimately, Covid-19 reveals the extreme inequalities associated with planetary urbanisation with the wealthy nomadic classes, who travel for leisure or work and who carried the virus to all four corners of the Earth, on the one hand; and the far more sedentary working classes, who serve the former, on the other. The working classes were the hardest hit by the pandemic. This was exacerbated by the fact that the vaccines were distributed unequally between the South and the North and within the North (where the number of unvaccinated people is higher in working-class and isolated rural areas). For example, in the working-class suburban department of Seine-Saint-Denis, in the north of the Parisian agglomeration, men's life expectancy decreased by two years between 2019 and 2021 (Institut Paris Région & Observatoire Régional de Santé 2023). This new manifestation of inequality further demonstrates the vulnerability of an urbanised planet: Covid-19 variants emerge in areas with no access to vaccines before spreading rapidly across the world.

However, lockdown opened an interstice, albeit a temporary one. In cities that were emptied and where urban services stopped (schools, maintenance of roads, and green spaces), forms of ruralisation emerged during lockdown. New and less frenetic social practices flourished in cities numbed by lockdown; wildlife came back (rewilding in public gardens, for example). It remains to be seen whether what people experienced in cities under lockdown will help slow down planetary urbanisation. In France, the wealthiest people left the city for their second homes, which may have given hope to local politicians in shrinking cities and declining areas in the hinterland. The so-called 'losers' of 'differentiated urbanisation' may have been led to believe in the miracle of an 'urban exodus', which might be capable of redeveloping the places left behind by planetary urbanisation (Pike et al. 2023). However, the property transactions observed since March 2020 are rarely followed by migrations. Massive amounts of money from areas of concentrated urbanisation (mostly the Parisian agglomeration) are being invested in the French hinterland (especially Brittany). 'Extended urbanisation' is accelerating, but it appears to be more to do with land grabbing, a process usually associated with Africa (Zoomers et al. 2017), than redressing the balance that characterises differentiated urbanisation (Delage & Rousseau 2022). Added to the growing impact of the climate crisis on the hinterland, the process of extended urbanisation ultimately explains why there is increasing conflict in 'non-city' areas. This is clearly illustrated by the Yellow Vests movement, which emerged in low-density areas, and by protests against new developments that aim to transform the hinterland into an operational landscape to serve the city.

## CONCLUSIONS

Five decades after Lefebvre's intuitive theory about the continuous 'urbanization of society', the idea that the urban fabric transforms the planet still holds. In fact, it is thought to be causing ever greater destruction (Ruddick 2015). As shown by the example of the Landes forest, discussed at the beginning of this chapter, non-city spaces are increasingly linked to areas of concentrated urbanisation. Various socio-ecological processes are involved (Brenner & Schmid 2015, Lefebvre 1970b). The process of planetary urbanisation intensifies land uses, thickens infrastructure connectivity, and accelerates socio-ecological transformations to increase global capitalist accumulation (Jain & Korzhenevych 2022). In the 21st century, it has impacted even the most remote areas. This raises serious issues about the Earth's limits, given the rate of climate change and biodiversity loss. Planetary urbanisation is considered to be a key component of the capitalocene. Yet the latter is jeopardising the former by severely damaging areas of concentrated urbanisation, which are now increasingly vulnerable to devastating floods, heatwaves, and hurricanes (Dawson 2017). Similarly, areas of extended urbanisation are also being affected, for example, with the spread of megafires.

In a context where pandemics and megafires are raging, planetary urbanisation is an extremely useful tool, but it does not give much cause for optimism. A decade after Brenner and Schmid launched their controversial theory and half a century after Lefebvre's intuitive thinking about society's complete urbanisation, planetary urbanisation reloaded has flourished. The theory successfully overcame initial criticisms thanks to the growing number of case studies, particularly on extended urbanisation in the Global South. It is now widely regarded as one of the most dynamic approaches in the field of critical urban studies. As this chapter has demonstrated, planetary urbanisation is a relevant frame for analysing both micro and macro processes (e.g. the outbreak and spread of pandemics). Last but not least, planetary urbanisation is also a radical theory, which holds a political capability for addressing the challenges posed by the capitalocene.

Nonetheless, this may be where neo-Lefebvrian critical urban studies comes up against a new limit. Lefebvre's gradual integration into the international (i.e. English-speaking) academic world has been complicated by the piecemeal translation of his numerous books. This could explain why the field of critical urban studies generally proposes a structuralist interpretation of his theories (Revol 2012). Indeed, structuralist interpretations have prevailed in the ten years since the advent of reloaded planetary urbanisation. Although Lefebvre hoped that a renewed understanding of space would spread and enhance the idea of the right to the city, he had a change of heart shortly before he died:

> The more the city extends, the more social relations deteriorate. The city has experienced extraordinary growth in most developed countries since the end of the last century, raising many hopes. But in reality, city life has not given rise to entirely new social relations. It is as if the expansion of old cities and the creation of new ones have served as a shelter and refuge for relationships of dependence, domination, exclusion and exploitation. (Lefebvre 1989: 17)

In line with the late Lefebvre, the 'hinterlands of the capitalocene' (Brenner & Katsikis 2020) have become even more of a burning issue, with land grabbing, new extractive practices, the commodification of nature for the middle-classes, the privatisation of nature for the exclusive use of the elite, and the relegation of undesirable infrastructures and populations (Neel 2018). Despite this pessimistic view, it is important to note that the acceleration of extended urbanisation over the last decade has been accompanied by a rise in powerful social movements. As a philosopher, Lefebvre was instrumental in bringing existentialism to rigid French Marxist circles (Poster 1975). As a sociologist, he argued that space was a political product, as well as a possible instrument of change (Busquet 2012). However, this aspect has been less integrated into the nascent international approach to planetary urbanisation (for exceptions, see Kipfer (2018) and Lesutis (2021)). Merrifield recalls the humanist version of Marxism advocated by Lefebvre throughout: since urbanisation relates to the creation of social interactions, bringing people together in a public space, planetary urbanisation is, therefore, also necessarily a deeply political process that extends the 'politics of the encounter' into non-city spaces (Merrifield 2013, 2014). Critical urban studies may have an important role to play here by focusing on the contradictions identified by Henri Lefebvre between the globalisation of the urban and his idea of a non-alienated global urban society (Millington 2016). Planetary urbanisation is a key component of the capitalocene. Yet it has the capacity to create opportunities for large-scale emancipatory change.

# REFERENCES

Acs, M. & Mosny, E. (2020) 208 000 résidents parisiens en moins dans la capitale pendant le premier confinement. *INSEE Flash Ile-de-France*, 57. Retrieved from https://www.insee.fr/fr/statistiques/4996530 (accessed 1 May 2023).

Ali, H. & Keil, R. (2006) Global cities and the spread of infectious disease: The case of severe acute respiratory syndrome (SARS) in Toronto, Canada. *Urban Studies* 43(3): 491–509.

Angelo, H. & Goh, K. (2020) Out in space: Difference and abstraction in planetary urbanization. *International Journal of Urban and Regional Research* 54: 732–744.

Arboleda, M. (2020) *Planetary Mine: Territories of Extraction under Late Capitalism*. London and New York: Verso Books.

Balakrishnan, S. (2019) *Shareholder Cities: Land Transformations along Urban Corridors in India*. Philadelphia: University of Pennsylvania Press.

Béal, V., Maisetti, N., Pinson, G. & Rousseau, M. (2023) When Bookchin faces Bourdieu. French 'weak' municipalism, legitimation crisis and zombie political parties. *Urban Studies* 60(11): 2195–2213.

Belarbi, W. & Rousseau, M. (2019) Morocco's 'pirate suburbs' from punishment to controlled integration: Neoliberalizing the regulation of Casablanca's 'Chechnya'. In M. Güney, R. Keil & M. Üçoğlu (eds.) *Massive Subarbanisms. (Re)Building the Global Periphery*. Toronto: University of Toronto Press, 223–240.

Brenner, N. (ed.) (2014) *Implosions/Explosions. Towards a Study of Planetary Urbanization*. Berlin: Jovis.

Brenner, N. & Ghosh, S. (2022) Between the colossal and the catastrophic: Planetary urbanization and the political ecologies of emergent infectious disease. *Environment and Planning A: Economy and Space* 54(5): 867–910.

Brenner, N. & Katsikis, N. (2020) Operational landscapes: Hinterlands of the capitalocene. *Architectural Design* 90: 22–31.

Brenner, N. & Schmid, C. (2012) Planetary urbanization. In M. Gandy (ed.) *Urban Constellations*. Berlin: Jovis, 10–13.

Brenner, N. & Schmid, C. (2014) The 'urban age' in question. *International Journal of Urban and Regional Research* 38: 731–55.

Brenner, N. & Schmid, C. (2015) Towards a new epistemology of the urban? *City* 19(2–3): 151–182.

Brenner, N. & Schmid, C. (2018) Elements for a new epistemology of the urban. In S. Hall & R. Burdett (eds.) *The Sage Handbook of the Contemporary City*. London: Sage, 47–68.

Busquet, G. (2012) L'espace politique chez Henri Lefebvre : l'idéologie et l'utopie. *Justice Spatiale/Spatial Justice* 5. Retrieved from http://www.jssj.org/ (accessed 1 May 2023).

Castriota, R. & Tonucci, J. (2018) Extended urbanization in and from Brazil. *Environment and Planning D: Society and Space* 36 (3): 512–28.

Charmes, E. & Rousseau, M. (2020) La mondialisation du confinement. Une faille dans la planétarisation de l'urbain ? *La Vie des idées*. Retrieved from https://laviedesidees.fr/La-mondialisation-du-confinement.html (accessed 4 May 2023).

Charmes, E. & Rousseau, M. (2022) It's the geography stupid! Planetary urbanization revealed. In T. J. Sugrue & C. Zaloom (eds.) *The Long Year. A 2020 Reader*. New York: Columbia University Press, 23–40.

Childe, V. G. (1950) The urban revolution. *The Town Planning Review* 21(1): 3–17.

Choplin, A. (2020) *Matière grise de l'urbain. La vie du ciment en Afrique*. Geneva: Metis Presses.

Choplin, A. & Pliez, O. (2018) *La mondialisation des pauvres*. Paris: Seuil.
Connolly, C., Keil, R. & Ali, H. (2021) Extended urbanisation and the spatialities of infectious disease: Demographic change, infrastructure and governance. *Urban Studies* 58(2): 245–63.
Cremaschi, M. (2020) Pourquoi Bergame ? Le virus au bout du territoire. *Métropolitiques*. Retrieved from https://metropolitiques.eu/Pourquoi-Bergame-Le-virus-au-bout-du-territoire-1521-1521.html (accessed 3 May 2023).
Dahdah, M. A., Ferry, M., Guérin, I. & Venkatasubramanian, G. (2020), L'Inde face à la crise du Covid-19. Une tragédie humanitaire à venir. *La Vie des idées*. Retrieved from https://laviedesidees.fr/L-Inde-face-a-la-crise-du-Covid-19 (accessed 2 May 2023).
Dalby, S. (2018) Firepower: Geopolitical cultures in the Anthropocene, *Geopolitics* 23(3): 718–742.
Davis, M. (2006) *Planet of Slums*. London: Verso Books.
Dawson, A. (2017) *Extreme Cities. The Peril and Promise of Urban Life in the Age of Climate Change*. London: Verso Books.
Delage, A. & Rousseau, M. (2022) L''exode urbain', extension du domaine de la rente. *Métropolitiques*. Retrieved from https://metropolitiques.eu/L-exode-urbain-extension-du-domaine-de-la-rente.html (accessed 4 May 2023).
Farrell, J. (2020) *Billionaire Wilderness: The Ultra-Wealthy and the Remaking of the American West*. Princeton: Princeton University Press.
Giroud, M. (2015) Au-delà de 'l'urbanisation planétaire': refonder la recherche urbaine contemporaine. *Métropolitiques*. Retrieved from http://www.metropolitiques.eu/Au-delade-l-urbanisation.html (accessed 4 May 2023).
Harvey, D. (2003) *Paris, Capital of Modernity*. New York and London: Routledge.
Harvey, D. (2004) The 'new' imperialism: Accumulation by dispossession. *Socialist Register* 40: 63–87.
Harvey, D. (2014) The crisis of planetary urbanization. In M. Gadanho (ed.) *Uneven Growth. Tactical Urbanisms for Expanding Megacities*. New York: MoMA, 26–31.
Institut Paris Région & Observatoire Régional de Santé (2023) La santé des Franciliens. March. Retrieved from https://www.ors-idf.org/nos-travaux/publications/la-sante-des-franciliens-2/ (accessed 10 May 2023).
Jain, M. & Korzhenevych, A. (2022) The concept of planetary urbanization applied to India's rural to urban transformation. *Habitat International* 129: 102671.
Kanai, J. M. (2014) On the peripheries of planetary urbanization: Globalizing Manaus and its expanding impact. *Environment and Planning D: Society and Space* 32(6): 1071–1087.
Kanai, J. M. & Schindler, S. (2019) Peri-urban promises of connectivity: Linking project-led polycentrism to the infrastructure scramble. *Environment and Planning A: Economy and Space* 51(2): 302–322.
Kipfer, S. (2018) Pushing the limits of urban research: Urbanization, pipelines and counter-colonial projects. *Environment and Planning D: Society and Space* 36(3): 474–493.
Lees, L. H. B. S. & López-Morales, E. (2016) *Planetary Gentrification*. London: Polity Press.
Lefebvre, H. (1960) Les nouveaux ensembles urbains. Un cas concret : Lacq-Mourenx et les problèmes urbains de la nouvelle classe ouvrière. *Revue française de sociologie* 1–2: 186–201.
Lefebvre, H. (1961) *Critique de la vie quotidienne. Tome II: Fondements d'une sociologie de la quotidienneté*. Paris: L'Arche.
Lefebvre, H. (1970a) *Du rural à l'urbain*. Paris: Anthropos.
Lefebvre, H. (1970b) *La révolution urbaine*. Paris: Gallimard.
Lefebvre, H. (1989) Quand la ville se perd dans une métamorphose planétaire. *Le Monde Diplomatique*.
Lesutis, G. (2021) Planetary urbanization and the 'right against the urbicidal city'. *Urban Geography* 42(8): 1195–1213.
Libération (2023) Violences policières à Sainte-Soline : 'Leurs grenades équivalent à des armes à feu'. *Libération*, 27 March. Retrieved from https://www.liberation.fr/ (accessed 2 May 2023).
Malm, A. (2016) *Fossil Capital: The Rise of Steam Power and the Roots of Global Warming*. London: Verso Books.
Malm, A. (2023) Sainte-Soline est une lutte avant-gardiste. *Mediapart*. Retrieved from https://www.mediapart.fr/ (accessed 01 May 2023).
Merrifield, A. (2002) *Metromarxism: A Marxist Tale of the City*. London and New York: Routledge.

Merrifield, A. (2013) The urban question under planetary urbanization. *International Journal of Urban and Regional Research* 37(3): 909–922.
Merrifield, A. (2014) *The New Urban Question*. London: Pluto Press.
Millington, G. (2016) The cosmopolitan contradictions of planetary urbanization. *British Journal of Sociology* 67(3): 476–496.
Moore, J. W. (2015) *Capitalism in the Web of Life: Ecology and the Accumulation of Capital*. London: Verso Books.
Neel, P. (2018) *Hinterland: America's New Landscape of Class and Conflict*. London: Reaktion Books.
Peake, L., Patrick, D., Reddy, R. N., Sarp Tanyildiz, G., Ruddick, S. & Tchoukaleyska, R. (2018) Placing planetary urbanization in other fields of vision. *Environment and Planning D: Society and Space* 36(3): 374–386.
Pike, A., Béal, V., Cauchi-Duval, N., Franklin, R., Kinossian, N., T. Lang, T., T. Leibert, T., D. MacKinnon, D., Rousseau, M., Royer, J., Servillo, L., Tomaney, J. & Velthuis, S. (2023) 'Left behind places': A geographical etymology. *Regional Studies*. DOI: 10.1080/00343404.2023.2167972.
Poster, M. (1975) *Existential Marxism in Postwar France: From Sartre to Althusser Princeton*. NJ: Princeton University Press.
Potts, D. (2005) Counter-urbanisation on the Zambian Copperbelt? Interpretations and Implications. *Urban Studies* 42: 583–609.
Revol, C. (2012) Le succès de Lefebvre dans les urban studies anglo-saxonnes et les conditions de sa redécouverte en France. *L'Homme & la Société* 186(3–4): 105–118.
Robinson, J. (2016) Comparative urbanism: New geographies and cultures of theorizing the urban. *International Journal of Urban and Regional Research* 40(1): 187–199.
Robinson, J. & Roy A. (2016) Debate on global urbanisms and the nature of urban theory. *International Journal of Urban and Regional Research* 40(1): 181–186.
Ross, K. (1995) *Fast Cars, Clean Bodies: Decolonization and the Reordering of French Culture*. Cambridge: MIT Press.
Rousseau, M. (2022) Sortons la forêt de l'urbanisation planétaire. *Libération*, 19 July. Retrieved from https://www.liberation.fr/ (accessed 1 May 2023).
Rousseau, M., Amarouche, M. & Salik, K. (2021) Requiem for a rural hinterland. The contradictions of laissez-faire regulation and the urbanisation of grey areas in Rabat (Morocco). *DisP* 57(3): 68–82.
Rousseau, M. & Béal, V. (2021) *Plus vite que le cœur d'un mortel. Désurbanisation et résistances dans l'Amérique abandonnée*. Caen: Grevis.
Roy, A. (2011) Slumdog cities: Rethinking subaltern urbanism. *International Journal of Urban and Regional Research* 35(2): 223–38.
Ruddick, S. (2015) Situating the anthropocene: Planetary urbanization and the anthropological machine. *Urban Geography* 36(8): 1113–1130.
Schindler, S. (2014) Understanding urban processes in Flint, Michigan: Approaching 'subaltern urbanism' inductively. *International Journal of Urban and Regional Research* 38(3): 791–804.
Schmid, B. V., Büntgen, U., Easterday, W. R., Ginzler, C., L. Walløe, L., Bramanti, B. & Stenseth, N. C. (2015) Climate-driven introduction of the Black Death and successive plague reintroductions into Europe. *Proceedings of the National Academy of Sciences* 112(10): 3020–3025.
Schmid, C. (2018) Journeys through planetary urbanization: Decentering perspectives on the urban. *Environment and Planning D: Society and Space* 36(3): 791–804.
Scott, J. C. (1998), *Seeing Like a State: How Certain Schemes to Improve the Human Condition Have Failed*. Yale: Yale University Press.
Sevilla-Buitrago, A. (2022) *Against the Commons. A Radical History of Urban Planning*. Minneapolis: University of Minnesota Press.
Simone, A. (2006) Pirate towns: Reworking social and symbolic infrastructures in Johannesburg and Douala. *Urban Studies* 43(2): 357–370.
Soederberg, S. & Walks, A. (2018) Producing and governing inequalities under planetary urbanization. From urban age to urban revolution? *Geoforum* 89: 107–113.
Storper, M. & Scott, A. (2016) Current debates in urban theory: A critical assessment. *Urban Studies* 53(6): 1114–1136.
Subra, P. (2016) *Zones à Défendre, de Sivens à Notre-Dame-des-Landes*. La Tour d'Aigues: Editions de l'Aube.

Tollefson, J. (2020) Why deforestation and extinctions make pandemics more likely. *Nature* 584: 175–176.
Treffers, S., Ali, S. H., Keil, R. & Fallah, M. (2021) Extending the boundaries of 'urban society': The urban political ecologies and pathologies of Ebola Virus Disease in West Africa. *Environment and Planning E: Nature and Space* 5(4): 2011–2032.
Turchin, P. (2007) Modeling periodic waves of integration in the Afro-Eurasian world-system. In G. Modelski, T. Devezas & W. R. Thompson (eds.) *Globalization as Evolutionary Process*. London: Routledge, 163–191.
Vegliò, S. (2021) Postcolonizing planetary urbanization: Aníbal Quijano and an alternative genealogy of the urban. *International Journal of Urban and Regional Research* 45(4): 663–678
Wallace, R. (2020) *Dead Epidemiologists: On the Origins of COVID-19*. New York: Monthly Review Press.
Weber, M. (1958) [1924] *The City*. New York: The Free Press.
Zérah, M.-H. (2020) *Quand l'Inde s'urbanise. Services essentiels et paradoxes d'un urbanisme bricolé*. Paris: Éditions de l'Aube.
Zoomers, A., Noorloos, F., Otsuki, K. & Westen, G. S. (2017) The rush for land in an urbanizing world: From land grabbing toward developing safe, resilient, and sustainable cities and landscapes. *World Development* 92: 242–52.

# 15. Inhabiting the right to the city
*Margherita Grazioli*

In 1968's 'Le Droit à la ville', Henri Lefebvre coined the ground-breaking concept of the 'right to the city' to frame the 'demand... [for] a transformed and renewed access to urban life' (Lefebvre 1996: 158). This seemingly loose definition was intended to prioritise the spatial character of the panoply of cries for social justice that were agitating the French urban working class and that would later infuse the uprisings in different countries at least until the end of the 1970s. Since its introduction, the right to the city has become a staple in the grammar of urban social movements worldwide, whilst leading transnational institutions like the United Nations have tried to co-opt and operationalise it. For instance, the UN-Habitat has defined the right to the city as 'the right of all inhabitants present and future, to occupy, use and produce just, inclusive and sustainable cities, defined as a common good essential to the quality of life' (United Nations 2017: 26) and identified its pillars for a new global urban agenda focused on environmental, socioeconomic, and spatial sustainability (ibid.). These goals yet are at odds with the reality of global cities ravaged by the situated ramifications of neoliberal urbanisation (Mayer 2013), compounded by the 'polycrisis' context that involves climate change and environmental depletion, pandemic outbreaks, wars, the dismantlement of the social welfare, austerity politics, the hyper-financialisation of housing (Aalbers 2016), and urban shrinkage vs the uncontrolled expansion of cities, just to mention some facets (Lesutis 2021, Rossi 2022).

Within this scenario, the advancement of housing vulnerability as a global phenomenon has furthered what I define as the 'habitability crisis' that involves the diverse geographies involved in planetary neoliberal urbanisation (Brenner & Schmid 2014, 2015). When looking at cities, AbdouMaliq Simone argues that 'curated unaffordability, disinvestment, overt erasure, expulsion, segregation, and social disentanglement have long been the familiar tools for making space uninhabitable' (Simone 2019: 23). The 'curated' uninhabitability of the urban fabric hence undermines the ontological security of the individuals, and communities that are subjected to housing precarity, segregation, and deprivation (Desmond 2012, Madden & Marcuse 2016). Authors like Lesutis (2021) and Rossi (2022) also advance that these patterns of neoliberal urbanisation are overtly 'urbicidal', whereby the growing uninhabitability of cities threatens their own meaning and existence.

On the other hand, the manifold facets of the 'habitability crisis' are certainly not uncontested, with urban social movements all over the word protesting against its localised and trans-scalar effects by means of contentious political actions, that, in their claims, aim at reappropriating the right to the city that poor, precarious, disenfranchised urban dwellers have been stripped of (Della Porta & Mattoni 2014, Enright & Rossi 2018 Tilly & Tarrow, 2015). Among them, squatting emerged as a prominent way of reappropriating, self-managing, and transforming the urban fabric against dispossessing patterns of planetary neoliberal urbanisation (Martínez 2020, Squatting Europe Kollective 2013, 2014, Vasudevan 2017).

Against this backdrop, in the chapter I make a case for the persisting importance of the right to the city as an analytical lens and a political token for contemporary urban social movements, despite the limitations it presents as a fuzzy concept that is thus hard to politically 'operationalise' or even ready to be mobilised by those urban actors that understand the right to the city as the right to private ownership and liveability for the affluent. To this purpose, I propose a review of the transdisciplinary debates and concerns around Lefebvre's concepts across different historical periods and geographical contexts. I then situate the *problematique* of the actualisation and enactment of the right to the city within the empirical framework offered by the housing rights movements (Movimento per il Diritto all'Abitare) of Rome. The analysis dwells upon the reflections and observations I have developed through my engagement as an activist-researcher in the Blocchi Precari Metropolitani (Precarious Metropolitan Block) collective (Grazioli 2021). The latter together with the Coordinamento Cittadino di Lotta per la Casa (Urban Network of the Housing Struggle) form Rome's Movimento per il Diritto all'Abitare (Movement for the Right to Habitation) (Grazioli & Caciagli 2018, Nur & Sethman 2017).

From 2015 to 2020 I lived inside two different housing squats on Via Tiburtina; since 2020, I have continued my activism inside the Blocchi Precari Metropolitani even though I have moved out to a different accommodation. During this (ongoing) period, I have been using different 'activist-ethnographic' (Graeber 2009, Juris & Kasnabish 2013) data elicitation methods that include: participatory action research; self-ethnography through fieldwork diaries and notes; discursive analysis of semi-structured, recorded interviews and informal interactions involving different subjects concerned in the housing crisis with different roles and perspectives (fellow activists and housing squatters, housing and human rights advocates, local residents and activists, frontline social workers, municipal administrators); visual analysis; and archival research.

Hence, the chapter argues that the everydayness, and contentious politics, of Rome's Movement for the Right to Habitation's reflect three tenets of Lefebvre's theorisations about the right to the city (1996), the production of space (Lefebvre 1991a, 1996), and urban everyday life (Lefebvre 1991b, 2004, 2008):

- The transformational potential of grassroots self-management and collective deliberation over the urban fabric's spaces;
- The non-formal status of the urban *citadins* (citizens) who realise the right to the city;
- The importance of everyday life for transformational urban politics.

This case study hence shows how the right to the city represents a political tool of urban social movements concerned with tackling what makes the city uninhabitable while offering a nuanced theoretical perspective for interpreting their actions and claims.

## IS THE RIGHT TO THE CITY STILL IN TOWN?

It is widely acknowledged that Henri Lefebvre did not use to pay great attention to housing as a strategic point of contention of the right to the city or as an oeuvre for observing the dominant societal paradigm at work within the urban fabric. This obliteration of housing occurred irrespective of Lefebvre's consideration that the capitalist paradigm of dwelling had suppressed the communal, homemaking aspects of habitation to impose a family based paradigm reduced to 'minimal living-space, as quantified in terms of modular units and speed of access; likewise minimal facilities and a programmed environment' (Lefebvre 1991a: 318). By the same token, Lefebvre did not mention in his books the squatting movements that were emerging in Europe at the time of writing 'Le Droit à la ville' nor acknowledge their 'pleas for a post-capitalist city or urban society' in the making (Martínez 2020: 49), regardless of the attention paid to everyday life (Lefebvre 1991b, 2008) and to self-management as a tool for realising the coveted 'Urban Revolution' (2003).

According to Manuel Castells (1979), this lack of translation of urban struggles into Lefebvre's theory was due to the indeterminacy of the right to the city, which does not offer an outline of any 'concrete process[es] of constructing new social relations through the revolutionary transformation of different political, economic, ideological agencies by means of class struggle' (Castells 1979: 89). Its indeterminacy as a bundle of multiple aspirations emerging as well as more established rights even impairs the activation of the right to the city, including by possibly well-intentioned structures of governance in favour of subaltern urban dwellers (Simone 2005).

On the other hand, the fuzziness of 'the right to the city' has made it possible for governmental agents and even corporate actors to mobilise the Lefebvrian concept to create new sources of legitimisation of the spatial and societal models they pursue. In *The New Urban Question*, Merrifield (2014) shows how the 1948 United Nations' Declaration of Human Rights on the one hand vaguely consecrates a generic definition of decent dwelling standards that individuals shall be entitled to (Article 17) while it details the individual and collective right to property as inalienable (Article 25). Put this way, the right to the city can be used as a proxy to defend ownership against dispossessed, subaltern urban dwellers. An example of this kind of application of the right to the city is shown by authors like Dewaele (2017) and Morange and Spire (2019), who discuss from a Global South perspective how the right to the city has been invoked by the residents of affluent neighbourhoods and gated communities to remove undesirable subjects like street vendors and homeless people from the areas where they live and own residential properties.

A similar example of the institutional conflation between the right to the city and the right to preserving private property was also evident in two recent judgments of the European Court of Human Rights. In 2018 and 2020, the Court ruled in favour of corporate actors that had opened lawsuits respectively against the Italian and Greek states because they did not carry out the evictions of two properties (a former private clinic and a hotel) squatted in Rome and Athens for housing purposes. The judgments claimed that this inaction had violated the legal owners' right to private property, as sanctioned by Article 1 of the 1952 European Convention of Human Rights (Protection of Property).[1]

Put this way, it seems like the reciprocal resonance between Lefebvre's right to the city and urban social movements (especially squatting ones) can be seen only in a retrospective view (Martínez 2020: 48) and that Lefebvre's concept definitely 'does not suffice to capture the socio-spatial practices and structures of constraints (and opportunities)' (Martínez 2020: 55) at stake in struggles like squatting for housing purposes. However, and while taking stock of all these conundrums, manifold scholars from diverse disciplines have tried to grapple the contemporary potentialities and limitations of the right to the city, especially in the light of the fact that a 'general tagline of the right to the city' (Merrifield 2014: xvii) is still practically and tactically effective for articulating the place-based contentious politics of urban social movements concerned with opposing the plural spatialised manifestations of urban injustice (Grazioli 2017, Merrifield 2011, 2014, Purcell 2002) that make the habitability crisis.

Regarding the conceptualisation of centrality entrenched in Lefebvre's understanding of the urban, the openness of the right to the city disrupts the dichotomy between urban centrality and what is (considered) peripheral, interstitial, and *non-urban*, as Lesutis (2021) notices. On the one hand, Lefebvre retained the understanding of the city centre as the privileged site for the agglomeration of material wealth and the production of symbolic and political power (Harvey 1989, 2012, Lefebvre 2003). On the other hand, Lefebvre himself argued that, through the transformational, prefigurative power exerted by revolutionary *citadins*, potentially every urban liminality and interstice could 'become a home, a place of convergence, a privileged site, to the extent that every urban space bears within it this possible-impossible, its own negation' (Lefebvre 2003: 39).

This point is crucial considering that 'planetary urbanisation' is largely happening in non-urban geographies, thus making cities only one of the several forms of contemporary neoliberal urbanisation (Brenner & Schmid, 2014, 2015, Lesutis 2021). The fuzziness of the 'right to the city (Attoh 2011) can thus be strategic for opening to new conceptualisations of the urban and habitation within the specific political, social, economic, geographical contexts where urban social movements act (Mayer 2012) and scaling up their actions to contest multi-level policies, policing, and property regimes (Mitchell 2003).

Furthermore, the emergent character of the right to the city, alongside more established rights (such as those designated by social welfare (Martínez 2020)), can foster a radical rethinking of the notion of 'rights' and citizenship, starting with the identification of the *citadins* (Lefebvre 1996: 34) who claim and practice 'the right to the city' as those who live 'out the routines of everyday life in the space of the city' (Purcell 2002: 102), irrespective of their formal or informal status.

Lastly, Lefebvre's emphasis on self-management and collective deliberation as the transformative forces that realise the right to the city, and the critical attention paid to the realm of everyday life, reflect the daily experience of those militants-activists who are increasingly called to put all of their everyday life in order to realise transformative urban politics (Martínez 2020:151). Squatting movements point towards restoring that collective value of habitation that Lefebvre saw dilapidated by capitalist housing, whereby the segregation between private life and public space has to be strategically disrupted in order to support communal habitation (Caciagli 2022, Grazioli 2017, 2021, Martínez 2020). Moreover, the processes of homemaking and living in common activated out of necessity by the dispossessed urban inhabitants inside neglected spaces, interstices, and vacancies confirm Lefebvre's intuition that every urban space is potentially transformable into a viable home and societal model where the right to the city can be affirmed and realised (Dadusc et al. 2019, Stavrides 2016, 2021).

Against this backdrop, the example of Rome's Movement for the Right to Habitation situates the *problematique* of the right to the city within the daily struggles of those who organise in the first place to address their basic need for habitation and then to envision in their everyday life a new model of urban habitation based on mutual aid, solidarity, and commoning outside of (and against) the commodification of housing and social reproduction.

## SITUATING THE *PROBLEMATIQUE*: ROME'S MOVIMENTO PER IL DIRITTO ALL'ABITARE

The conceptualisation and practice of the right to the city as the right of the urban working class to stay put and inhabit with dignity the urban fabric is certainly not novel in those global cities where diverse forms of contention (and contestation) of housing insecurity can be observed, although with differential intensities and persistence. In Southern European cities, the post-Second World War consolidation of urban social movements around the fight for housing through squatting actions was triggered by the weaponisation of the urban, industrial real estate development of cities against the poor, the migrants, and the socially marginalised urban dwellers attacked by both dictatorial and formally democratic regimes (Di Feliciantonio 2017, Leontidou 1990, 2010, Stavrides 2016).

In the city of Rome, the twentieth century's housing question was initiated by the choice made by the fascist local government to forcibly remove and displace to remote areas the inhabitants of the centre to restore urban decor and hygiene alongside the 'imperial magnificence' of central areas. At the same time, the local government was also the first one to remove rent caps and forbid internal migrants to move in the city during the 1930s through the so-called laws 'against urbanism'. Last but not least, the forcibly displaced populations of the city centre and the undesired internal migrants who kept coming to the city were channelled into the urban shantytowns and poorly built popular neighbourhoods (the so-called *borgate*) that were created in previously rural, uninhabited areas of the urban fabric.

The unbearable living conditions of those who lived in these areas, and the failed promise of mass-scale prosperity, underpinned the prominent role of the housing struggles within the urban social movements that during the 1960s and 1970s revolted against the post-war capitalist, fundamentally patriarchal paradigm of society. That period of struggles achieved important results, such as new regulatory plans and the massive allocation of public houses to those who were living in the shantytowns (Di Feliciantonio 2017, Vasudevan 2017). However, the resolution of Rome's housing crisis was only temporary due to global and local circumstances.

Looking from a multi-scalar perspective, Rome's housing patterns followed the global commodification of housing into a prevalently owned asset as one of the pivots of the post-war political economy. By the same token, the state and its local articulations were not passive recipients of the shift to more market operations; they were the primary drivers and sponsors of housing financialisation, the dismantlement of social welfare systems, and austerity as they reoriented policy processes, planning, and regulatory procedures (Aalbers 2016, Tulumello et al. 2021). The restricted access to safe, decent, affordable housing was also part of the enforcement of differentially inclusive border regimes that aimed at extracting surplus by all the temporalities of migration and mobility (from the first reception to long-term settlement) (Dadusc et al. 2019, Dadusc & Mudu 2022, Mezzadra & Neilson 2013, 2019).

Going to the urban scale, these global trends precipitated into a metropolis where the forcible sprawl of the urban fabric initiated by the fascist mass displacement had already disrupted the sociospatial coherence, intimacy, and cohesion of the city (Merrifield 2011, Mezzadra & Neilson 2019). Well before the 2008 financial crisis, the vast majority of Rome's population was concentrated in what are still labelled as 'peripheries', with an accent on their sociospatial marginalisation in comparison to an affluent and money-value city centre. Moreover, the expansion of gentrification and touristification processes towards former peripheries had already begun before the 2008 crisis (Mudu 2006), whereby the historical city centre was already saturated by hyper-financialisation processes (Annunziata & Lees 2016, Gainsforth 2019).

Lastly, the hyper-financialisation of housing in Rome became conflated with the differential access to housing determined by border regimes that strategically excluded migrants from the access to public affordable houses. Along these lines, refugees, asylum seekers, and Roma people were forcibly channelled into camps and infrastructures of the 'humanitarian complex system' (Dadusc & Mudu 2022, Maestri 2019), such as reception centres and temporary shelters, whilst others were abandoned to the spikes of the private rental market (Mudu 2006, Nur & Sethman 2017). Against this backdrop, and following the 2008 financial crash, Rome's housing rights movements were confronted with the necessity of adjusting their historical repertoires of organisational forms and confrontational politics to the new dynamics, and intersectionality, of the housing crisis.

In Rome, this shift was epitomised by the reconfiguration and renaming of the traditional housing struggle ('*La lotta per la Casa*') into a more comprehensive fight for the 'right to habitation' ('*Diritto all'Abitare*'), intended as the ensemble of material, immaterial, and relational resources needed to move, and settle, with dignity inside the city (Grazioli & Caciagli 2018). These include safe, decent, affordable housing as well as access to a salary/income that can support the household's livelihoods, robust social welfare systems, and mobility rights. Once again, squatting practices are at the core of the contentious politics developed by the Movement for the Right to Habitation (Grazioli & Caciagli 2018) that has resurfaced since the 2000s.

The Movimento is formed by two main groups: the Blocchi Precari Metropolitani and the Coordinamento Cittadino di Lotta per la Casa. The latter was created in the 1980s, consolidating the housing solidarity actions carried out by the Autonomia Operaia (Worker's Autonomy) movement in support of the inhabitants of Rome's shantytowns who were massively occupying vacant public houses (Vasudevan 2017). While they mainly used to occupy vacant public houses, the Coordinamento in the early 2000s changed their strategy by choosing to squat non-residential public vacancies that could be repurposed for habitation. This was for instance the case with the former military barracks of Porto Fluviale located in the highly gentrified (and central) area of Ostiense, occupied in 2003 and reconverted by the squatters into houses and self-made infrastructures such as tea rooms, theatre halls, biking areas, and jewellery laboratories (Annunziata & Lees 2016).

On the other hand, the Blocchi Precari Metropolitani appeared for the first time during a strike called in 2007 by grassroots trade unions. On that occasion, the new group of activists blocked the main streets of the city and occupied a building built by a real estate developer with public funding yet left vacant and unused (Grazioli 2021). In March 2009, the Blocchi Precari Metropolitani occupied with dozens of families of various ethnic and national groups an abandoned salami factory, progressively transforming it into a housing space for 60 households and a self-managed museum (Grazioli 2021, Salvatori 2021).

The largely migrant composition of early 2000s squats anticipated what could later be observed during the 2012–2013 Tsunami Tours. The latter were simultaneous rounds of squatting of vacant buildings that were realised in December 2012 and April 2013 in different areas of Rome by various housing solidarity groups and tenants' unions together with thousands of housing-deprived, precarious people, resulting in over 25 new housing squats inside the city (Caciagli 2022, Di Noto 2020, Nur & Sethman 2017, Squatting Europe Kollective 2013, 2014). The consolidation and diversity of the new 'Squatted City' (see Figure 15.1) (Vasudevan 2015, 2017), which self-defines as *meticcia* ('mestiza') (Grazioli & Caciagli 2018, Grazioli 2021), has required the adaptation of the housing rights movements' consolidated repertoire of organisational practices, tactics, and strategies in order to harmonise the daily lives of the housing squatters while coping with the multilevel housing governance within a neoliberal urbanism scenario. In the following sections, I analyse how the everyday life and politics of those who inhabit the housing squats that are part of the Movement for the

Right to Habitation actualise Lefebvre's approach to the right to the city as a transformative force of urban space and everydayness while confirming its relevance as a tagline for the urban politics of reappropriation.

*Source:* Margherita Grazioli.

*Figure 15.1* Squatting action in Rome (2023)

**Reappropriating the Right to Centrality**

As briefly outlined, the Movement for the Right to Habitation in Rome represents, on the one hand, the historical memory of the grassroots, confrontational, and collective actions for 'the right to stay put in the city' (Grazioli & Caciagli 2018) that were enacted by the 'historical' urban proletariat, made mostly of post-Second World War displaced urban dwellers and Italian migrants coming from remote and inner areas and regions. However, the shift in the types, and location, of urban vacancies targeted by squatting attempts represents the ambivalence of what urban centrality is, alongside the change in the composition of the housing crisis (addressed in the following section). Regarding the urban fabric's spatial configuration, the distribution of housing squats in central as well as peripheral areas reflects the polycentricity of the urban fabric. The ambition to make the city centre (where wealth, activities, construction, and valorisation are accumulated) affordable and habitable again even for non-affluent urban dwellers is harmonised with the pragmatic support for the habitability of those supposedly peripheral areas where most of the population still lives. On the one hand, the choice to repurpose urban vacancies and interstices that are seemingly unused (and useless) reflects Lefebvre's idea that the transformative character of the right to the city can potentially make every urban liminality and interstice into a place where new processes of homemaking, living, and deliberating in common can be re-activated. On the other hand, the Movement for the Right to Habitation also regularly takes to the streets of the city centre where different level of governance (from the national to the local level) are represented with diverse forms of direct action that include squatting, rallies, marches, flash mobs, and protest camps. This tactical and strategic approach to centrality thus aligns with Lefebvre's understanding of the 'right to centrality' regarding the possibility of having a direct say in urban politics and decisions and also creates new political, spatial arenas where collective deliberation and self-management can be practiced. By this token, if the enactment of the right to the city creates new spatialities and forms of urban life, it also configures new centralities (and the right to them) that have nothing to do with the hierarchical, profit-driven dichotomy between centre and periphery, nor with the formal boundaries of the urban fabric and citizenship, as the next section articulates.

## From Citizens to *Citadins*

The previous section addressed how Rome's Movement for the Right to Habitation has situated the *problematique* of urban centrality mainly through the reappropriation of urban vacancies and interstices for habitation purposes. In this section, I focus on how the Movement's confrontational politics reflects Henri Lefebvre's tension towards the problematisation of citizenship as a formally sanctioned status. The latter is epitomised by Lefebvre's identification of the *citadins* (Lefebvre 1996: 34) as the subjects entitled to exert a transformative force on the urban fabric by the fact of 'living out the routines of everyday life in the space of the city' (Purcell 2002: 102), irrespective of their legal enfranchisement to do so.

The Movement for the Right to Habitation's analysis of the housing crisis' intersectionality since the 1990s when migration movements became more apparent and debated has led them to frame and pursue 'the right to the city' as the satisfaction of 'established' as well as new rights and needs connected to settlement and mobility that formal citizenship or residential statuses do not frame or sanction (Lecoq & Waine 2020, Mezzadra & Neilson 2013). While some of these rights (like the access to local social welfare) can be claimed on a municipal or even neighbourhood level, others involve scaling up political action to the level of regional, national, and even transnational governmental assemblages where racialised regimes of mobility, settlement, labour, and property are strategised (Dadusc & Mudu 2022, Mitchell 2003, Montagna & Grazioli 2019).

The trans-scalar, contested value of urban citizenship is epitomised by the Italian government's choice to weaponise the formal recognition of the status of 'resident' against those who cannot afford to own, purchase, or monetise a house. With law n. 80/2014 (23rd May), the national government decided to introduce what has been popularised as 'Article 5' with the purpose of discouraging the post-Tsunami Tours spike in squatting for housing purposes as part of a renewed strategy of (de)regulation in the management and selling of the public estates.

'Article 5' denies the urban squatters the right to register their home address in the place where they live for proof of residency, electoral lists, welfare service access, tax purposes, and electricity, gas, and water use. For those whose residency is tied to a visa, this means an active form of invisibilisation and hence an increased threat of deportability (De Genova 2010). Moreover, housing squatters are also excluded from the general lists of public housing for five years as a form of punishment for their illegal reappropriation of housing, irrespective of their homeless or housing-deprived status (Grazioli 2022, Gargiulo 2020).

As underlined by the Italian sociologist Enrico Gargiulo (2020), this law presents on the one hand a sheer continuity with the fascist laws 'against urbanism', which aimed at curtailing mobility from Italian rural and inner areas to the cities by forbidding the new residents to move or declare their legal address in urban areas. Moreover, Gargiulo notices that it aligns with the post-1990s effort made by different Italian municipalities to differentiate the degree (and possibility) of accessing local welfare services for the purpose of selecting desirable/undesirable populations, with particular reference to extra-EU migrants, homeless people, and Roma descendants (Maestri 2019).

Since its entrance into force, Article 5's application and consequences have been put under scrutiny by a large coalition composed by the Movement for the Right to Habitation, other housing rights organisations, tenants' unions, associations, legal aid teams, and NGOs. The same actors have been mobilised in local, regional, and national campaigns demanding the abolition of the law or at least local waivers in its application (Grazioli 2022).

One of the points protested by these diverse actors is how the law punishes housing vulnerability and then compounds pre-existing patterns of sociospatial exclusion, all the while without addressing the roots of the housing crisis. Furthermore, Article 5 has been pinpointed by the Italian antiracist movements as the epitome of how formal citizenship operates as a device of differential inclusion and thus cannot be reformed as such (Isin 2009, Mezzadra & Neilson 2013, Papadopoulos & Tsianos 2013). By this token, these social movements, as well as the Movement for the Right to Habitation, prefigure through their direct actions and political elaborations a radically alternative paradigm of urban citizenship that is enacted through the grassroots (re)distribution and/or creation of all the material and immaterial infrastructures that are needed to settle, move, and live the daily routines inside the city with dignity.

In this perspective, the intersectional, self-defined 'mestiza' (*meticcia*) composition of the urban squatters who occupy and repurpose seemingly unproductive urban vacancies for dwelling purposes represent the quintessence of Lefebvre's *citadins* both in reference to the questioning of the formal rules that inform the attribution and fruition of urban citizenship and the transformative action they exert over the urban fabric. By mutually recognising their commonality as housing-deprived people irrespective (and because) of their class, educational, and migratory status, Rome's urban squatters craft their collective identity and purpose through the bodily, emotional, and intellectual experience of living in common out of necessity (Dadusc et al. 2019, Lancione & Simone 2021, Stavrides 2021). Hence, they enact what Subirats calls the 'political co-production of citizenship' that 'can no longer be a simple receptacle or container of recognized rights, but must become a permanent exercise of joint responsibility and social solidarity in the face of shared problems' (Subirats 2011: 86). Within this process, collective identities and the sense of legitimacy and pride (Nicholls 2016) are not forged through exclusion or differential inclusion (Isin 2009, Mezzadra and Neilson 2013). These new identities also become the grounds for fighting against institutional discriminations such as the ones introduced by Article 5 while recognising their differential impact on different people. If Article 5 indiscriminately denies access to basic social welfare to all the people who inhabit a housing squat, it in fact compounds the effects of racialising, differentially inclusive border regimes. The reciprocity and mutual support deployed in these circumstances thus make the Movement for the Right to Habitation's material and immaterial infrastructures 'places in themselves' where 'localised solidarities and relational attributes are viewed as a means of nourishing and feeding larger scale political struggles' (Nicholls 2009: 80) and whose endurance is pursued through the organisational rites described in the next section.

## Organisational Rites and Everyday Life

One pioneering aspect of Lefebvre's theoretical elaboration is the definition of the driven as well as compelling rites (profane, religious, and political) and rhythms that articulate the city's everyday life and social reproduction (Lefebvre 1991b, 1996, 2004, 2008). Participatory observation of everyday life inside housing squats makes it possible to identify a fourth category of urban rites: 'organisational rites' (Grazioli 2021). The latter differ from all the aforementioned types of rites categorised by Lefebvre as they dwell upon the political collective knowledge that was transmitted through the accomplishments and failures of the 1970s *lotta per la casa* (struggle for housing) to enable the new housing squatters to live and struggle collectively. The organisational rites that articulate the ordinary as well as 'exceptional' times of the housing squats that are part of the Movement for the Right to Habitation are: 1) the communal care and distribution of habitation and defence infrastructure; 2) the assembly as the site and methodology of plural decision-making; and 3) the commoning of everyday social reproduction and care work (Grazioli 2021).

From the moment of breaking into a place, the assembly is established as the time and space of collective decision-making. In the beginning, the first deliberations usually pertain to how to mount and guard collectively the barricading infrastructures that are supposed to help the squatters resist an immediate attempt at eviction. Moreover, the assembly structures the process through which the activists help the squatters to map the space and figure out how to repurpose the existing infrastructures (which, as mentioned before, are often not intended for residential uses) into spaces for common use (especially the assembly room) and dwelling units that can be designed and distributed according to equitable principles (Caciagli 2022: 230).

Once the housing squat is 'stabilised', the assembly is confirmed as the moment when the activists-squatters meet on a regular basis, share information about the state of the art of the housing struggle in the city (and beyond), and make decisions about their communal life through an entirely self-designed methodology of collective deliberation. By this token, the assembly room becomes the spatial core of the squatters' life in common, where different sets of events (from birthday parties to political meetings) take place. It is important to highlight that the housing squats that have more sophisticated configurations can have additional assemblies that include also the 'external' members (i.e. non-activists, non-squatters) involved in the creation of new autonomous infrastructures (as in the case of Metropoliz's Museum of the Other and the Elsewhere (see Figure 15.2) or Porto Fluviale's ensemble of laboratories) (Annunziata & Lees 2016, Di Noto 2020, Grazioli 2021).

The entanglement between the communal care of spaces and the ritualisation of the assembly epitomises the new way of intending 'housing' as a comprehensive modality of habitation that is finally made visible by the commoning of everyday life. In fact, inside housing squats, aspects like childcare, gendered relations, and healthcare are not private matters handled by the single households behind closed doors. They become part of the collective social reproduction activities that forge new spaces, awareness and needs (e.g. putting reproductive and care work in common) and new collective identities, solidarities, and desires from a factual condition of necessity (Nicholls 2009).

Even this brief account shows how the Movement for the Right to Habitation's organisational rites are well-framed by Lefebvre's theories in two main ways. On a general level, organisational rites show both the driven and compelling character of the urban rites that

*Source:* Margherita Grazioli.

*Figure 15.2  Metropoliz squatted social centre and houses in Rome (2023)*

articulate (or disrupt) urban eurhythmia (Lefebvre 2004). They also give reason to Lefebvre's extensive attention to (and critique of) everyday life (Lefebvre 1991b, 2008), given that its definition (or radical change) bridges the gap between imagining transformational politics and actually enacting them. Secondly, they embody Lefebvre's understanding that collective self-management and deliberation represent the scaffolding of the spatially transformative politics that should realise the urban revolution (Lefebvre 2003) and hence materialise the right to the city (Lefebvre 1996).

Regarding the specific character of the Movement for the Right to Habitation's organisational rites, the overlap between 'activists' and 'squatters' means that almost the whole of everyday life is put on the line of the struggle and that 'private life and communal living demands as much effort as public life and urban struggles' (Martínez 2020: 151–152). Since 'domestic tasks, gender relations, and the emotional dimensions of activism are regularly tackled' (Martínez 2020: 152), it is necessary to frame the way in which people can transform their approach to these questions daily at the same time as they transform the city and affirm their right to stay put in a highly saturated, conflicted environment like Rome's (Bresnihan & Byrne 2014, Huron 2015).

When these challenges are overcome, the adaptability of the Movement for the Right to Habitation's organisational rites to the housing squats' everyday life and situated composition resembles what Stavrides describes as a 'collective reflex' towards commoning (Stavrides

2021: 303). The latter stems from the housing squatters' recognition of the benefits of mutual cooperation and reciprocity for their everyday survival, which could not be explained otherwise. However, it is undeniable that living in common out of necessity is an extremely challenging process, the harmonisation of which can be easily disrupted if organisational rites are not taken care of and embedded into the exceptional and ordinary temporalities of communal living. Hence, the daily replication (or lack thereof) of the organisational rites inside housing squats is what determines the difference between the housing squat's capacity to stay put in the city and keep their transformational potential vis-à-vis their degradation into disjointed forms of dwelling that can easily be disrupted by forcible evictions or internal conflicts (Grazioli 2017, 2021).

## CONCLUSIONS

Decades after the first appearance of the right to the city in 'Le Droit à la ville' in 1968, Lefebvre's ground-breaking concept still represents a point of reflection and contention for scholars and activists engaged with reading (and supporting) the grassroots actions and social movements that try to counter what makes cities uninhabitable. The chapter thus contributes to the interdisciplinary scholarly debates about whether or not Lefebvre's concept is still a useful tactical and practical tool for urban social movements or an empty token that every urban actor can co-opt and divert from its original meaning. On the one hand, the literature review primarily raised the question of the indeterminacy of 'the right to the city' as the main cause for the challenges in implementing it within radical, as well as in more 'moderate', progressive political frameworks. Furthermore, the fuzziness of the right to the city is seen as a proxy for its mobilisation by urban actors interested in finding additional sources of legitimisation for ownership-based neoliberal urbanisation patterns.

These issues are even more pressing for housing rights and squatting movements. Lefebvre paid little attention to housing and emerging squatting movements as strategic points of realisation of the right to the city as a transformative force in the urban fabric. Hence, the right to the city would seem poorly appropriate to frame their practices, opportunities, and constraints. While taking stock of these important theoretical, practical, and political issues, the chapter argues that Lefebvre's concept still represents tactical and practical guidance for urban social movements. The latter strategically fill the indeterminacy of the right to the city with place-specific meanings and actions to affirm their radical opposition to the localised ramifications of neoliberal planetary urbanisation.

Furthermore, Lefebvre's work is also a promising analytical kaleidoscope for reading the everyday politics and social reproduction of contemporary urban social movements through three distinctive features: the relationship between the right to the city and the transformation of the urban fabric, the emphasis on everyday life routines and rites, and the importance of self-management and collective deliberation for the affirmation and consolidation of the revolutionary potential of the right to the city.

Zooming into these features through the perspective offered by the case study of Rome's Movement for the Right to Habitation, the chapter proposes one possible way for situating the *problematique* of Lefebvre's right to the city in the materialities of the urban social movements that claim it. The ways in which they interpret (and mobilise) the right to centrality, the understanding of urban squatters as *citadins*, and the housing squats' organisational rites suggest that the right to the city is and will be a tagline for the radical politics that intend to affirm a just, 'habitable' paradigm of urbanism and cities within and beyond the definition initially formulated by Henri Lefebvre in 1968.

## NOTE

1. The Italian case 'Casa di Cura Valle Fiorita S.r.l. v. Italy' was decided on December 13, 2018 (case file no. 67944/13), whilst the Greek one 'Papachela and Amazon v. Greece' was decided on December 3, 2020 (case file no. 12929/18).

## REFERENCES

Aalbers, M. (2016) *The Financialization of Housing. A Political Economy Approach*. New York: Routledge.
Annunziata, S. & Lees, L. (2016) Resisting 'Austerity Gentrification' and Displacement in Southern Europe. *Sociological Research Online* 21(3): 148–155.
Attoh, K. A. (2011) What Kind of Right Is the Right to the City? *Human Geography* 35(5): 669–685.
Brenner, N. & Schmid, C. (2014) Planetary Urbanization. In N. Brenner (ed.) *Implosions/Explosions: Towards a Study of Planetary Urbanization*. Berlin: Jovis Verlag, 160–163.
Brenner, N. & Schmid, C. (2015) Towards a New Epistemology of the Urban? *City* 19(2–3): 151–182.
Bresnihan, P. & Byrne, M. (2014) Escape into the City: Everyday Practices of Commoning and the Production of Urban Space in Dublin. *Antipode* 47(1): 36–54.
Caciagli, C. (2022) *Housing Movements in Rome. Resistance and Class*. Singapore: Palgrave Macmillan.
Castells, M. (1979) *The Urban Question. A Marxist Approach*. London: Edward Arnold Publishers.
Dadusc D., Grazioli, M. & Martínez M. A. (2019) Introduction: Citizenship as Inhabitance? Migrant Housing Squats versus Institutional Accommodation. *Citizenship Studies* 23(6): 521–539.
Dadusc, D. & Mudu P. (2022) Care without Control: The Humanitarian Industrial Complex and the Criminalisation of Solidarity. *Geopolitics* 2(4): 1205–1230.
De Genova, N. (2010) The Queer Politics of Migration: Reflections on 'Illegality' and Incorrigibility. *Studies in Social Justice* 4(2): 101–126.
Della Porta, D. & Mattoni, A. (eds.) (2014) *Spreading Protest. Social Movements in Times of Crisis*. Colchester: ECPR Press.
Desmond, M. (2012) Disposable Ties and the Urban Poor. *American Journal of Sociology* 117(5): 1295–1335.
Dewaele, A. (2017) Comparative Analysis of the Building of a Right to the City by Middle Classes in Three Indian New Towns (Gurgaon, Navi Mumbai, Salt Lake). Communication during the international conference 'Droit à la ville au Sud, expériences citadines et rationalités de gouvernement'. 15–17 November, Paris Diderot University.
Di Feliciantonio, C. (2017) Spaces of the Expelled as Spaces of the Urban Commons? Analysing the Re-emergence of Squatting Initiatives in Rome. *International Journal of Urban and Regional Research* 41(5): 708–725.
Di Noto, I. (2020) La Città Pubblica (R)Esiste! *Crítica Urbana* III(12): 8–12.
Enright, T. & Rossi, U. (2018) *The Urban Political: Ambivalent Spaces of Late Neoliberalism*. Basingstoke: Palgrave Macmillan.
Gainsforth, S. (2019) *Airbnb Città Merce: Storie di Resistenza alla Gentrificazione Digitale*. Roma: DeriveApprodi.
Gargiulo, E. (2020) *Invisible Borders: Administrative Barriers and Citizenship in the Italian Municipalities*. Cham: Palgrave Macmillan.
Graeber, D. (2009) *Direct Action: An Ethnography*. Chico: AK Press.
Grazioli, M. (2017) From Citizens to *Citadins*: Rethinking Right to the City inside Housing Squats in Rome, Italy. *Citizenship Studies* 21(4): 393–408.

Grazioli, M. (2021) *Housing, Urban Commons and the Right to the City in Post-Crisis Rome: Metropoliz, The Squatted Città Meticcia*. Cham: Palgrave Macmillan.
Grazioli, M. (2022) Batti il 5! Grassroots Strategies against the Administrative Invisibilisation of Rome's Housing Squatters before and during the Pandemic. *Radical Housing Journal* 4(1): 31–50.
Grazioli, M. & Caciagli, C. (2018) Resisting the Neoliberal Urban Fabric: Housing Rights Movements and the Re-appropriation of the 'Right to the City' in Rome, Italy. *VOLUNTAS: International Journal of Voluntary and Nonprofit Organizations* 29(4): 697–711.
Harvey, D. (1989) From Managerialism to Entrepreneurialism: The Transformation in Urban Governance in Late Capitalism. *Geografiska Annaler B* 71(1): 3–17.
Harvey, D. (2012) *Rebel Cities. From the Right to the City to the Urban Revolution*. London and New York: Verso.
Huron, A. (2015) Working with Strangers in Saturated Space: Reclaiming and Maintaining the Urban Commons. *Antipode* 47(4): 963–979.
Isin, E. F. (2009) Citizenship in Flux: The Figure of the Activist Citizen. *Subjectivity* 29: 367–388.
Juris, J. S. & Khasnabish, A. (eds.) (2013) *Insurgent Encounters. Transnational Activism, Ethnography and the Political*. Durham and London: Duke University Press.
Lancione, M. & Simone, A. (2021) Dwelling in Liminalities, Thinking Beyond Inhabitation. *Environment and Planning D: Society and Space* 39(6): 969–975.
Lecoq, M. & Waine, O. (2020) The Right to the City: An Emancipating Concept? *Metropolitics*, July 3. Retrieved from https://metropolitics.org/The-Right-to-the-City-An-Emancipating-Concept.html (accessed 4 December 2022).
Lefebvre, H. (1991a [1974]) *The Production of Space*. Oxford and Malden, MA: Blackwell Publishers.
Lefebvre, H. (1991b [1947]) *Critique of Everyday Life Volume 1. Introduction*. London: Verso.
Lefebvre, H. (1996) *Writing on Cities*. Oxford and Malden, MA: Blackwell Publishers.
Lefebvre, H. (2003 [1970]) *The Urban Revolution*. Minneapolis: University of Minnesota Press.
Lefebvre, H. (2004 [1992]) *Rhythmanalysis: Space, Time and Everyday Life*. London and New York: Continuum.
Lefebvre, H. (2008 [1961]) *Critique of Everyday Life Volume II. Foundations for a Sociology of the Everyday*. London and New York: Verso.
Leontidou, L. (1990) *The Mediterranean City in Transition: Social Change and Urban Development*. Cambridge: Cambridge University Press.
Leontidou, L. (2010) Urban Social Movements in 'Weak' Civil Societies: The Right to the City and Cosmopolitan Activism in Southern Europe. *Urban Studies* 47(6): 1179–1203.
Lesutis, G. (2021) Planetary Urbanization and the 'Right Against the Urbicidal City'. *Urban Geography* 42(8): 1195–1213.
Madden, D. & Marcuse, P. (2016) *In Defense of Housing: The Politics of Crisis*. London: Verso.
Maestri, G. (2019) *Temporary Camps, Enduring Segregation: The Contentious Politics of Roma and Migrant Housing*. Basingstoke: Palgrave Macmillan,
Martínez M. A. (2020) *Squatters in the Capitalist City. Housing, Justice, and Urban Politics*. London and New York: Routledge.
Mayer, M. (2012) The 'Right to the City' in Urban Social Movements. In N. Brenner et al. (eds.) *Cities for People, Not for Profit. Critical Urban Theory and the Right to the City*. Abingdon: Routledge, 63–85.
Mayer, M. (2013) First World Urban Activism. *City* 17(1): 5–19.
Merrifield, A. (2011) The Right to The City and Beyond. *City* 15(3–4): 473–481.
Merrifield, A. (2014) *The New Urban Question*. London: Pluto Press.
Mezzadra, S. & Neilson, B. (2013) *Border as Method, or, the Multiplication of Labor*. Durham and London: Duke University Press.
Mezzadra, S. & Neilson, B. (2019) *The Politics of Operations: Excavating Contemporary Capitalism*. Durham and London: Duke University Press.
Mitchell, D. (2003) *The Right to the City. Social Justice and the Fight for Public Space*. New York: The Guilford Press.
Montagna, N. & Grazioli M. (2019) Urban Commons and Freedom of Movement: The Housing Struggles of Recently Arrived Migrants in Rome. *Citizenship Studies* 23(6): 577–592.

Morange, M & Spire, A. (2019) The Right to the City in the Global South. Perspective from Africa. *Cybergeo: European Journal of Geography* 895(May): 1–20.
Mudu, P. (2006) Patterns of Segregation in Contemporary Rome. *Urban Geography* 27(5): 422–440.
Nicholls, W. (2009) Place, Network, Space: Theorising the Geographies of Social Movements. *Transactions of the Institute of British Geographers* 34(1): 78–93.
Nicholls, W. (2016) Politicizing Undocumented Immigrants One Corner at a Time: How Day Laborers Became a Politically Contentious Group. *International Journal of Urban and Regional Research* 40(2): 299–320.
Nur, N. & Sethman, A. (2017) Migration and Mobilization for the Right to Housing in Rome: New Urban Frontiers? In P. Mudu & S. Chattopadhyay (eds.) *Migration, Squatting and Radical Autonomy: Resistance and Destabilization*. London and New York: Routledge, 78–92.
Papadopoulos, D. & Tsianos, V. (2013) After Citizenship: Autonomy of Migration, Organisational Ontology and Mobile Commons. *Citizenship Studies* 17(2): 178–196.
Purcell, M. (2002) Excavating Lefebvre: The Right to the City and its Urban Politics of the Inhabitant. *GeoJournal* 58: 99–108.
Rossi, U. (2022) The Existential Threat of Urban Social Extractivism: Urban Revival and the Extinction Crisis in the European South. *Antipode* 54(3): 892–913.
Salvatori, G. (2021) *Metropoliz o il Tempo del Sogno. Discorsi, Relazioni e Pratiche in un'Occupazione Abitativa Romana*. Rome: Sapienza Università Editrice.
Simone, A. (2005) The Right to the City. *Interventions* 7(3): 321–325.
Simone, A. (2019) *Improvised Lives: Rhythms of Endurance in an Urban South*. Cambridge: Polity Press.
Squatting Europe Kollective (ed.) (2013) *Squatting in Europe. Radical Spaces, Urban Struggles*. Wivenhoe, New York and Port Watson: Minor Compositions.
Squatting Europe Kollective (ed.) (2014) *The Squatters' Movement in Europe. Commons and Autonomy as Alternatives to Capitalism*. London: Pluto Press.
Stavrides, S. (2016) *Common Space. The City as Commons*. London: Zed Books.
Stavrides, S. (2021) Commoning as Collective Reflex: Emerging Creative Practices, Reinhabiting Public Spaces, Resisting Carceral Societies. *Radical Housing Journal* 3(1): 301–306.
Subirats, J. (2011) *Otra sociedad ¿otra política?: De 'No Nos Representan' a la Democracia de lo Común*. Barcelona: Icaria Asaco.
Tilly, C. & Tarrow, S. (2015) *Contentious Politics*. 2nd Edition. New York: Oxford University Press.
Tulumello, S., Dagkouli Kyriakoglou, M. & Colombo A. (2021) Financialization of Housing in Southern Europe – The Role of the State. Regional Studies Associations. Retrieved from https://regions.regionalstudies.org/ezine/article/financialization-of-housing-in-southern-europe-the-role-of-the-state/?doi=10.1080/13673882.2020.00001074 (accessed 4 December 2022).
United Nations (2017) *Habitat III Policy Papers: Policy Paper 1 The Right to the City and Cities for All*. New York: United Nations.
Vasudevan, A. (2015) The Makeshift City: Towards a Global Geography of Squatting. *Progress in Human Geography* 39(3): 338–359.
Vasudevan, A. (2017) *The Autonomous City. A History of Urban Squatting*. London and New York: Verso.

# PART III

# SOCIO-SPATIAL SEGREGATIONS

# 16. Social mix and its critics: reflections on housing policies

*Marie-Hélène Bacqué and Éric Charmes*

The notion of social mix represents an important objective for urban policies but also an object of controversy in urban studies and between researchers and actors. Several studies have highlighted the ambiguity of the issues that so-called social mix policies claim to address and have questioned their results. In the speeches of political leaders and planners, the problems raised by social segregation are frequently associated with the prescriptive ideal of social mix, and social mix policies are often considered to be antidotes to segregation. In order to combat urban segregation, the aim is to bring the middle classes into poor neighbourhoods, to demolish social housing, and to disperse poor populations.

Of course, there is little doubt about the negative effects of segregation and the need for public policies to counterbalance their impact on the lowest income groups and minority populations (Brun & Rhein 1994, Massey & Denton 1995, Sampson 2012). Yet, at the same time, for decades research has also shown that extreme caution is required when it comes to the idea that social mix would represent a cure for the ills of segregation and should be an inviolable policy goal. As this chapter demonstrates, many scientific studies have highlighted the limitations and even the perverse effects of social mix policies.

First of all, the notion of social mix lacks conceptual clarity (Charmes & Bacqué 2016). Admittedly, many indices of segregation and dissimilarity exist, which sometimes involve quite sophisticated mathematical tools (Jones et al. 2015, Reardon & Sullivan 2004). However, evaluating social mix raises problems that go beyond questions of measurement. Social mix can be evaluated according to many criteria, like social position, geographic origin, age, or gender. It also depends on the scale of analysis, like stairwell, block, neighbourhood, or city. Normative issues are also at stake: does a mixed neighbourhood or a mixed housing project have to reflect the national or metropolitan reality in terms of average statistics? Is social mix desirable in any situation and at any scale? These questions make it difficult to assess social mix.

These issues may be dealt with by focusing on a specific criterion and a specific scale, as many countries do when assimilating social mix with a share of social housing at the municipal scale. Indeed, social mix has for a long time been a major aim of public housing policies in very different contexts (for a recent global panorama, including the so-called Global South, see Levin et al. 2022). This chapter thus examines how the ideal of social mix is used in housing policies. It does so through a focus on public policies and research conducted in France and the United States. In both countries, the idea of social mix has helped shape public policies, while many scientific studies have contested it. Such a comparison is instructive because France and the United States are two very different countries, with their own distinct political and philosophical approaches to the diversity of geographic and ethno-racial origins. In contrast to the socio-political structure of the United States, the French so-called 'Republican model' hardly recognises the existence of communities and gives the state a central role. If in both contexts racial segregation remains obvious, the opportunity to frame policies in racial terms is the subject of important discussions in France. Contrasting public policies and debates in those two countries thus helps to identify the issues that go beyond national specificities. Conversely, it highlights the importance of local contexts.

The first part of this chapter presents the main criticisms or reservations expressed by the social sciences with regard to social mix and the policies implemented in its name. It does so by focusing on two seminal papers discussing the relevance of social mix at the neighbourhood scale. The second part presents some explanations and proposes some hypotheses on why academic critics have not prevented housing policies from continuing to refer to social mix. It insists on the normative and philosophical reasons that make social mix a desirable goal, regardless of its limitations in housing policies.

## SOCIAL SCIENCES AND SOCIAL MIX: A VIEW FROM THE 1960s

Research on social mix at the scale of neighbourhoods or residential estates is plethoric. This chapter does not attempt to summarise this huge literature (Arthurson 2012, Bolt & Van Kempen 2013, Charmes & Bacqué 2016, Epstein & Kirzbaum 2003, Galster & Friedrich 2015, Goetz 2003, Lelévrier 2010, Levin et al. 2022, Van Kempen & Bolt 2009). Rather it focuses on two seminal articles. The first one, published by the American sociologist Herbert Gans in 1961 is a theoretical discussion about the virtues of a 'balanced community'. The second one, published three years later by the French sociologists Jean-Claude Chamboredon and Madeleine Lemaire (1970), is a discussion about the effects of social mix policies based on in-depth quantitative and qualitative empirical research. From two contrasting contexts, these two articles converge and complement each other in their criticisms. Both opened a discussion that has been enriched over the years and continues today.

**The Balanced Community in Question**

The virtues of social mix have long been a subject of debate among researchers. In the United States, the notion of social mix was discussed in the 1960s by Gans after his research work on a suburb developed and built by the company Levitt and Sons (Gans 1967). His work actually set out to answer the criticisms of the suburbs that were popularised, among others, by Whyte (1956). The critics highlighted the extreme uniformity of the suburban populations and fuelled Jacobs' belief in and well-known apologia of the diversity and social mix in her neighbourhood, Greenwich Village in New York (Jacobs 1961). Before Gans published his work on Levittown and in the same year that Jane Jacobs published *Death and Life of Great American Cities* (1961), he published an article in which he disputed four arguments in favour of social mix, or what he called the 'balanced community' (Gans 1961). Some of his arguments are still discussed nowadays, which confirms the relevance of his overall criticisms in sociology, geography, psychology, and political science.

(1) In response to the idea that social mix may represent a social resource while suburban uniformity might for example deprive young households with children of the resources that the elderly can offer, Gans argues that differences can be a source of conflict, hindering mutually beneficial exchanges and the development of social capital. This obser-

vation was taken up by Putnam in relation to racial issues. In an article that received considerable attention, Putnam (2007) argued that in a neighbourhood, racial diversity could reduce trust between neighbours. When the other is perceived negatively in terms of racial stereotypes, co-presence rarely generates trust but rather, according to Putnam, inward-looking attitudes and anomie (in contrast to what Gans highlighted, i.e. conflict). The method used by Robert Putnam has been contested (Dawkins 2008, Wessel 2009), but the findings make sense: social psychology studies on inter-group contact show that simple co-presence is not enough to establish communication or contact, let alone trust (Pettigrew & Tropp 2006). Other conditions are often required, such as the support of dedicated institutional programmes. In addition, the capacity to benefit from the contact with people who are different is often unequal. Indeed, the experience of urban diversity praised in the literature on the creative classes primarily benefits the more affluent (Slater 2006).

(2) Social mix is also presented as a source of social and cultural tolerance. Of course, a significant number of studies have shown that the coexistence of different groups and people can help develop skills such as civility (Tonnelat 2016, Wessel 2009). However, such skills and competences may be more easily acquired in urban public spaces where being a stranger is the norm rather than in one's neighbourhood. Moreover, it is one thing to coexist peacefully, to be civil with one's neighbours; it is quite another, as Valentine shows, to regard other people's behaviour and opinions as acceptable, let alone legitimate (Valentine 2008). In his article, Gans argues specifically that in a neighbourhood the clash between conflicting interests and points of view, for example about school, can hinder democratic debate by preventing dialogue and discussion. In other words, when important issues are at stake (which is more often the case in one's neighbourhood than in urban public spaces), co-presence does not necessarily lead to tolerant positions. Last but not least, valuing tolerance and belittling conflicts tends to conceal power relations. Valentine indeed points out that the dominant groups make the best out of the norm of tolerance.

(3) More specifically, against the idea that heterogeneity could have an educational value for children by making them more tolerant with regard to social, racial, and generational diversity, Gans argues that visual contact does not automatically produce a relationship. He states that tolerance is based on other forms of learning, especially the behaviour and values transmitted by parents. While children from city centres cross more different people every day than children from suburbs like Levittown, observations show that they are not automatically more tolerant. Their socialisation with their parents, their friends, or their teachers is more important than what they see. Generally, over and above the question of children's education, the experience of social mix is framed by dominant representations. For Gans, as long as unequal racial representations and the structural jurisdictions of inequality continue, there is little chance that race relations will change. Thus, in the United States, research has shown that while social mix in a neighbourhood can be associated with whites being less hostile towards Hispanics or Asians, it is not the case for neighbourhoods where whites and blacks mix because of the powerful racial prejudices that blacks are victims of (Dixon 2006).

(4) Lastly, Gans discusses the idea that diversity can promote education by example and middle-class supervision of social life. This idea refers to the notion of role models and still provides a reference for social action today, especially in France (Gilbert 2009). If

Gans accepts that the middle classes traditionally played a supervisory role in community centres and neighbourhood facilities, he recalls that these institutions have never attracted a significant working-class clientele, apart from children and the most socially mobile. This was already demonstrated by Foot Whyte's *Street Corner Society* (1943).

These four arguments discussed by Gans in his paper resonate with the extensive literature on 'neighbourhood effects', which assesses how the characteristics of a neighbourhood impact the fate of its inhabitants. Many studies have examined the impact of poverty concentration in a neighbourhood by analysing different registers: the behaviour of individuals at different periods of life, with a focus on delinquent behaviour; the state of health; children's level of 'development' and success at school; and access to employment and professional insertion for young people and adults. Several syntheses (Brooks-Gunn et al. 1993, Ellen & Turner 1997, Marpsat 1999, Sampson 2012) have drawn mixed results with no clear conclusion. The neighbourhood's social environment seems to play a role in socialisation, individual 'success', and social insertion. However, it is still difficult to identify which of these effects are specifically linked to the neighbourhood and which stem from the social characteristics of individuals and families (for a severe critic of the 'neighbourhood effect' literature, see Slater 2021).

## Spatial Proximity and Social Distance

Gans' purpose was not to evaluate social mix policies. Yet numerous studies on social mix are linked to the evaluation of such policies, be it through pro-active development of socially mixed neighbourhoods, urban renovation projects, or policies supporting gentrification of low-income neighbourhoods. For that matter, the French policy of *grands ensembles* deserves special attention. The *grands ensembles* are vast housing estates realised between the mid-1950s and early 1970s with the aim of quickly mass-producing housing in the context of a deep crisis after the second world war. These *grands ensembles* were built according to modern town planning guidelines, as advocated by the International Congress of Modern Architecture (CIAM). Their construction had a huge impact on the country by constituting entire neighbourhoods on the city fringes. These large complexes were largely composed of social housing, but also of so-called intermediate rental housing or privately owned apartments which, in the early years, welcomed the middle and upper classes. Many of them did not stay for long, and many *grands ensembles* ended up with a high concentration of social problems and became the focus of local special remedial policies (see below the comments on *la politique de la ville*). Yet from the outset to today's current renewals, social mix has been and remains central to the discourses justifying state actions (Avenel 2005).

The critics of these policies go back a long way, just like in the United States. In France, the publication by Jean-Claude Chamboredon and Madeleine Lemaire of an article entitled 'Proximité spatiale et distance sociale' ('Spatial Proximity and Social Distance') greatly opened up the debate (Chamboredon & Lemaire 1970). In this article, which became one of the most commonly quoted in French sociology, the two researchers, who were close to Pierre Bourdieu, presented the findings of a survey conducted in 1968 on a *grand ensemble* located in a Parisian southern suburb. The starting point for the analysis was a critique of authors like the humanist sociologist Chombard de Lauwe (1965), as well as the earlier work of the Marxist philosopher Lefebvre (1960), who stated that the new housing conditions provided by the *grands ensembles* heralded the emergence of a new society where traditional social divisions had been erased.

Chamboredon and Lemaire began by showing that the way populations were gathered in *grands ensembles* actually induced the coexistence of extremely heterogeneous subgroups. However, as the title of their article suggests, spatial proximity tends to foster social distance rather than closeness. Being gathered in a neighbourhood does not eradicate social disparities, it may even worsen them by masking class conflicts with a curtain of moral issues. In the *grand ensemble* they studied, social heterogeneity resulted in moral tensions, especially about questions of education, which involve different norms and put social reproduction at stake. What used to be perceived as relations of class between different social groups became moral and behavioural antagonism in a process that demeans working class norms. One of the major effects of social diversity policies undoubtedly lies in the fostering of the representation 'of a society of degrees' instead of a society of conflicting classes. This led Chamboredon and Lemaire to question whether the mixing of various population in *grands ensembles* could not induce a 'rupture of class solidarity'. The second part of this chapter will come back to this.

This criticism opened the door to other studies on the coexistence of various social groups. In the early 1980s, the sociologist Michel Pinçon studied a social housing operation developed in the Nantes suburbs that was explicitly designed as a social mix project (Pinçon 1982). Pinçon described the contradictions that divided the social groups, especially with regard to the management of socio-cultural facilities. He concluded that the spatial proximity promotes middle-class cultural hegemony and that the experience of cohabitation for the working-class categories is tantamount to losing their identity, unless they organise and protect their own independent expression.

This research has not prevented social mix from becoming a key element in the *politique de la ville*, a policy centred on so-called *difficiles* (socially troubled) neighbourhoods, mainly *grands ensembles*, which developed in the early 1980s (Tissot 2007). This policy aimed to contain the 'ghettoisation' of *grands ensembles* based on research analysing the social problems affecting these areas and their populations in terms of exclusion or disadvantages, which thus concealed broader unequal processes (Donzelot 1999, Dubet & Lapeyronnie 1992, Estèbe 2005). If the neighbourhoods are ailing, those researchers claimed, it is because they have high poverty rates. Therefore, the population should be diversified.

Increasingly, race and geographic origins became key in the definition of diversity. Initially, to identify the neighbourhoods in need of specific social action, a statistical analysis was conducted involving different social criteria, such as age, unemployment rate, the share of single-parent families, health status, and education. Although these criteria included the proportion of foreigners, the population's ethno-racial composition was not explicitly considered because ethno-racial statistics are not authorised in France. Widely euphemised, this question was nonetheless very significant since the targeted neighbourhoods concentred recent immigrants. In the last decade, it has become a more open feature of public debates, when a rhetoric blaming certain communities for not respecting republican values became increasingly common in France, particularly after the attacks claimed by ISIS in Paris in 2015 (Lorcerie & Moignard 2017).

The situation appears very different in the United States. First, the racial question has been central to discussions since the Chicago school's initial work on the logic of urban segregation. Moreover, housing policies are generally based on the market rather than public action. Social housing barely represents 2% of the US housing stock compared to 17% in France.

Yet the question of social mix remains central. In particular, 30 years after the publication of Gans' article, the issue gained momentum in conjunction with three different concerns: racial, social, and urban. As an extension of the civil rights movement and the fight against racial segregation, experiments were launched with the aim of giving poor black families access to more affluent, mainly white neighbourhoods (Briggs de Souza 1997). In parallel, the existence of public social housing, however marginal, was also called into question. Its demolition was politically justified by the need to eradicate pockets of poverty where a culture of dependency could develop (Galster & Zobel 1998, Goetz 2003). Lastly, a new urban planning model emerged, the so-called 'New Urbanism', promoting the return to more 'traditional' urban forms and a functional as well as social mix (Talen 1999). This conjuncture of different concerns linked to social mix echoed what was happening in other countries, including France.

**Limited Benefits for Low-income Groups**

Social mix policies are thus still promoted in the United States as well as in France. Yet subsequent research on those policies reached similar conclusions as those of Gans and Chamboredon and Lemaire. More specifically, numerous assessments clearly question their relevance for low-income households (Bacqué & Fol 2007). This is shown, in particular, by the Yonkers and Gautreaux experiments in Chicago (the latter named after a civil rights activist who filed a suit). These initiatives encouraged black families living in ghettoised neighbourhoods to move to affluent neighbourhoods (Rosenbaum 1995). These experiments served as a model for a federal experiment, Moving to Opportunity, launched in 1992 by the Department of Housing and Urban Development (HUD). It began in 1994 in five cities (Baltimore, Boston, Chicago, New York, and Los Angeles) and made it possible to rehouse 4,500 families living in social housing (known as *public housing* in the United States) in areas where at least 40% of the population was below the federal poverty line (Goering & Feins 2003). Although moving to middle-class or affluent neighbourhoods allowed these families to escape insecurity, improve their state of health, and provide better schooling for their children, the results in terms of professional and social insertion were disappointing (Galster & Santiago 2006). Moving to an affluent neighbourhood (which often means a white neighbourhood) sometimes caused new problems and social isolation. This was exacerbated by the loss of social ties and support networks, since the cohabitation with wealthier households generated a feeling of social distance (Briggs de Souza 2005). Sharing the same neighbourhood or the same building did not really encourage the different social groups to establish social relations. In addition, in affluent neighbourhoods, access to social services is often harder and poverty is more 'hidden'. Lastly, local social networks seem to work essentially between members of the same social group (Galster & Santiago 2006). Therefore, the poorest are hardly able to take advantage of the resources that a middle-class neighbourhood can offer. Thus, some households went back to live in their old neighbourhood (Comey et al. 2008) or let their children stay at their old schools.

The search for diversity is just as ambivalent when it comes to restructuring existing housing. The HOPE VI programmes were launched in 1994 by the Clinton administration to encourage income-based diversity and reduce the high poverty rates in social housing projects. They advocated the partial demolition of such projects. The programmes also aimed to make the neighbourhoods more attractive. By improving their image and developing services, the programmes sought to transform the population using a tenant screening policy and by diversifying the available accommodation to house the middle classes. Methods of social control were also set up. Like the desegregation operations, the HOPE VI programmes were assessed and criticised on several counts. The first criticism focuses on the possibility of creating community ties in a neighbourhood that artificially brings together populations with different incomes, i.e. low and average (Popkin et al. 2000). This echoes Gans' earlier statement that the principle of the role model, for example, does not operate automatically (Schill 1997). The second criticism focuses on the screening of residents organised by the public housing authorities, which drove the most vulnerable tenants to other equally or even more deprived neighbourhoods (Goetz 2010). On top of that, the HOPE VI programmes actually reduced the supply of affordable housing.

In France, similar policies led to similar results. Many urban renewal projects supported by the state via the National Urban Renewal Agency (ANRU), created in 2003, are primarily geared to the demolition of the most dilapidated social rental housing units to replace them with buildings for first-time buyers (Epstein 2013, Lelévrier 2010). The evaluations of these projects reveal the same limitations as in the United States. On both sides of the Atlantic, there are winners and losers in operations conducted in the name of social mix. These operations regularly fall short of the stated goals and often reduce access to housing for working classes, the poor, and racial minorities.

The same applies to urban renaissance or gentrification policies, where there are constant references to social mixing (Lees 2008, Slater 2006). The discourses draw on some of the arguments discussed above, particularly the advantages for the poor, who can benefit from a more affluent neighbourhood, and the personal gains of experiencing difference. The reality is less enchanting. Some studies have focused on the experience of people affected by gentrification rather than its promoters. They describe the relations of power and domination associated with the processes of social and urban transformation (Giroud 2016, Manzo 2012). Obviously, some people affected by gentrification, especially property owners, may temporarily rejoice in seeing their neighbourhood move upmarket and their capital assets grow. Nonetheless, modest owners are often forced to leave their neighbourhood because of the rise in taxes, adjusted to property values, or because their new neighbours vote for embellishment that they cannot afford financially. They are then following tenants forced out by rent increases and by the transformation of the shops, with more and more expensive products (Zukin et al. 2009). Some policies (like tenants' protection) may mitigate the displacement (Ghaffari et al. 2017), but, generally, gentrification does not bode well for the low-income households. In many cases, they are forced to move to the suburbs. Discourses praising social mixing in gentrifying neighbourhoods thus appear as euphemisms for a mechanism through which poor or low-income populations are replaced with other better-qualified or better-paid populations (Bridge et al. 2012, Chabrol et al. 2016, Van Criekingen 2012). By giving a positive connotation to the settlement of relatively affluent households in a working-class neighbourhood, the reference to social mixing hides relations of domination that are a feature of these residential dynamics. Here again, social mix serves as a justification rhetoric for policies and urban dynamics that, using Henri Lefebvre's words, reduce the right to the city (Lefebvre 1972); that is, the right of city dwellers to access all urban amenities, to choose where they live, and to be able to decide on the transformation of their city and their neighbourhood.

# CRITICISMS THAT FAIL TO CALL PUBLIC POLICIES INTO QUESTION

Numerous studies on social mix and its policies thus converge on their limited or even negative effects. This convergence goes beyond the differences in national contexts and has stood the test of decades. However, the notion of social mix is still used to legitimise many urban policies. Not only that, it is taken up by social movements in the name of the right to the city or the fight against discrimination.

This persistence can be explained by various political and normative factors. The following pages insist on some of the most prevalent ones. On the political side, for social movements or progressive policies, social mix is a good argument for justifying certain actions of solidarity for the poor, like the production of social housing. From another perspective, policies implemented in the name of social mix make poverty less visible and prevent the formation of local bases for political mobilisation. On the normative side, social mix reflects ethical and moral standards and ideals that prevail over the findings revealed by social science.

**Social Mix as a Political Stake**

In France, social mix is regularly mobilised to endorse the production of social housing. It is in the name of social diversity that the law obliges urban municipalities to have at least 20% social housing in their overall housing stock (in 2013, the rate was increased to 25% in large cities). Some American cities, like Boston, use the same argument to impose a quota of affordable housing in new real estate operations. Yet two other important arguments could be used in this way without referring to social mix: the right to housing and economic performance. Regarding the former, most of its definitions do not refer to social mix but rather to access to housing for all throughout a city. Regarding economic performance, the production of social housing can be justified by the need to limit pressure on salaries by containing rents (Singapore is a well-known example of this (Haila 2015)). It is also functional for large metropolitan centres to provide affordable housing to 'key workers' (service personnel, carers, teachers, etc.), who are essential for social and economic life (Launay 2011).

Having said that, in the major cities, where competition for housing is high and where even the middle classes are struggling (Bacqué et al. 2015, Vermeersch et al. 2018), the right to housing generally involves constructing social housing in middle-class neighbourhoods. When it comes to building social housing in an upmarket neighbourhood (not to mention when it comes to building a refugee reception centre), residents do not hesitate to express their opposition. Many arguments are put forward to challenge projects, like when the residents in Yonkers (Briggs de Souza 1997) or those in the upper-class neighbourhoods of Paris claim their 'peacefulness' is threatened (Launay 2011) or when some French mayors shamelessly refuse to increase the share of social housing in their municipality, preferring to pay penalties, in order to defend the desire of the privileged to stay among themselves.

In the face of such local resistances, the reference to social mix is a way to delegitimise the opponents, by dismissing them as egoistic and Nimbys (Scally & Tighe 2015). In fact, in France, in national debates, social mix is undoubtedly the most consensual argument in favour of the production of social housing. It is rarely called into question by national political bodies, regardless of whether they are left-wing (and thus determined by the right to housing) or right-wing (and therefore more determined by economic performance). The laws that impose social housing quotas on municipalities in the name of social mix were enacted by left-wing governments, but they were only marginally called into question when the government changed side. It is mostly at a local level in very affluent suburbs that these quotas can be challenged and their application can be refused.

In the United States, where racial segregation remains acute, social mix is less consensual and therefore less efficient as a political argument. Moreover, as already mentioned, the production of social housing is not a key political issue, unlike in France. Nonetheless, social mix is still promoted as a means to establish civic rights. Like the value of tolerance (Valentine 2008), it may be considered politically correct in elite progressive spheres. Thus, the presence of low-income groups can be defended in neighbourhoods that are being gentrified. Here again however, the social mix argument is ambivalent. It is actually interwoven in the logic of power, as in Boston's South End, where the upper classes use social mix to legitimise acute forms of social control (Tissot 2015).

However, political uses of social mix are not limited to housing policies. The intensification of the social mix rhetoric corresponds to a shift in social issues in recent decades, notably the way working-class neighbourhoods have been progressively reduced to problem neighbourhoods. With this shift, dispersing low-income populations in the name of social mix appears to be the best way to oblige the different municipalities of a metropolitan area to share the fiscal and economic 'burden' such populations are commonly considered to be. Further research is required to disentangle the factors at issue. However, a scissor effect has emerged: on the one side, policies supporting individual initiatives are valorised to the detriment of territorial redistribution policies; and on the other, resources specific to working class neighbourhoods are devalued.

For the Social Democrats or the Social Liberal parties, the central political issue has gradually evolved from redistributing resources between social groups to promoting capabilities and improving individuals' chances of success. On both sides of the Atlantic, discourses have emerged about the need to make poor populations accountable for extricating themselves from a culture of poverty or dependency (e.g. the so-called 'third way' theorised by Giddens (1998)). Such discourses insist on individual responsibilities while bracketing structural issues. There has then been a gradual shift away from the question of territorial wealth distribution, a focus that has been embodied in France by the *banlieues rouges* (red suburbs) run by the Communist Party. Rather, social mix came to be advocated to give everyone access to an environment that is equally conducive to the development of their individual 'potential' (Biggeri & Ferrannini 2014).

This change can be linked to the deep transformations in the sociological base of liberal and progressive political movements, which began in the late the 20th century. A liberal elite has emerged, which Thomas Piketty describes as the 'Brahmin left' (Piketty 2020), defined by its level of qualifications. This elite more readily adheres to ideals like social mix (namely, the idea that the experience of social mix is enriching) than to redistributive fiscal policies that may significantly weight on their income.

This ideological shift was supplemented by the growth of a more conservative discourse, which considers areas with a high poverty rate as a social and political threat. This is old rhetoric (in the case of France, see Magri (1993)), but it has gained ground in recent decades. In addition, for a growing number of politicians and opinion leaders, sociological explanations that highlight the impact of structural social factors have become 'excuses' for deviant behaviour (Lahire 2016).

These conservative discourses are fuelled by structural changes. Several decades of economic crisis, the deconstruction of productive industrial apparatuses, growing insecurity for workers, and the dismantling of the social state have eroded the cornerstones that made working-class neighbourhoods places of strong social and political identities (Bacqué & Sintomer 2001). More than ever, they are characterised by social hardship. In the United States, they are commonly described using the notion of the underclass while in France the notion of exclusion is often used. The theory of 'neighbourhood effects' developed in the United States and later imported to France has supported, albeit against the intentions of some of its proponents, this idea (Slater 2021). A discourse highlighting the negative impacts of segregation can slip into a discourse denouncing the harmful effects of life in poor neighbourhoods. From there, one can jump to the conclusion that dispersing the households living in such neighbourhoods is a necessity. Thus, the idea that social mix is required to fight urban segregation effects came to be supplemented by the idea that the existence of working-class neighbourhoods is a problem in itself. This obliterated the fact that the right to the city could be based on the redistribution of resources and on the choice of city dwellers rather than on constraint and on the dispersal of the poorest.

This is how more and more working-class neighbourhoods have been designated for destruction rather than development. The policy implemented with the ANRU in France and the HOPE VI programmes in the United States clearly illustrate this vision and its impact on public policies. These programmes are presented as a way of channelling investments to help 'fragile' neighbourhoods. However, rather than helping working-class neighbourhoods, they aim to transform them into 'normal' neighbourhoods by making their populations more like those in neighbourhoods dominated by the middle classes. Thus, operations are based on large-scale destruction and major population displacement. Practically and symbolically, this is extremely violent for the inhabitants of working-class neighbourhoods, who are the only ones bearing the costs and consequences of displacement policies.

This dominant trend may be tempered by community development policies that seek to mobilise collective local resources in working-class communities, particularly in Great Britain and the United States. However, these policies raise a number of questions. In a context of state and public authority withdrawal, residents end up shouldering the burden of policies that were previously executed by public agencies (Bacqué & Biewener 2013). In addition, the residents are primarily encouraged to develop businesses that will appeal to middle-class households. In France, local businesses are thus often dismissed as 'communitarian' and discouraged in favour of supposedly more mainstream businesses (Zouari & Charmes 2020).

From that perspective, calling for social mix prevents empowerment, defined as the political mobilisation of people living in working-class neighbourhoods (Bacqué & Biewener 2013, Balazard 2015). Considering such neighbourhoods as ghettoes that must be eradicated represents a deliberate failure to recognise their residents as legitimate political actors; it is a refusal to draw on the social and political dynamics that shape these territories. It also obscures the fact that working-class neighbourhoods can be political bases. Yet the *banlieues rouges* in France participated in the birth and development of the Communist Party, a political force for half a century. The historian Annie Fourcaut uses the notion of 'parochial communism' to show how municipalities invested by the dominated classes were able to play a major political role (Fourcaut 1986). Joining together with peers can actually help build a common discourse and a common experience. It can improve the visibility of minorities in the public political arena (Imbroscio 2010). As Fraser suggests (2003), the existence of subaltern public spaces is a prerequisite for the functioning of a large public space that welcomes and recognises the diversity of social groups and does not obscure conflict, which is an intrinsic part of democracy (Squires 2002).

**Social Mix as an Ideal**

Incidentally, the reference to social mix is not simply a hypocritical veneer that serves hidden interests. Many actors acknowledge the pertinence of the criticisms developed above, yet they remain philosophically attached to the social mix goal. In their view, the difficulties that challenge the ideal do not actually call it into question. The limits of social mix policies do not obliterate the normative power of the arguments in favour of social mix. Hence, we end this chapter by reviewing the philosophical background of some of the arguments discussed at the start with Gans' seminal paper.

For many researchers, academics, and politicians, the intermingling of various populations is central to the very concept of a city. Unlike rural and village society, urban and city society is defined by the contact it fosters between very diverse populations that are strangers to each other. This is considered a key constituent of the city for many reasons, of which three are particularly important.

(1) First, the mixing of populations that characterises cities helps to address an essential philosophical question: how can different people dwell together in a common polity? Such questioning has for a long time been at the heart of the philosophical debates about city life (Simon 2021). However, it remains to be established whether, from a practical point of view, social mix should happen primarily at the city level, with public spaces being places where mixing occurs, or at the neighbourhood level. Iris Young was cautious on this point and defended the first option by proposing an ideal of 'together-in-difference' (Young 1990). However, some scholars think that, since the neighbourhood is a determining space for everyday experiences, mixing should be encouraged at this level. They do not ignore the possible costs of such an aim but consider that steps can be taken to limit their burden, especially for low-income people (like with social housing). This constitutes the philosophical background in much of the critical literature on the middle-class tendency to live among people like themselves. The studies that assimilate gated communities to enclavism are a good illustration of this (Atkinson & Blandy 2005). Indeed, in such cases, groups of like-minded people tend to see themselves as outside the common polity, thus undermining what the city should be (Marcuse 2005). From this point of view, housing policies should promote social mix to prevent the upper and middle classes from living in social and political bubbles.

(2) In an approach that is close to liberalism, social mix is generally considered to be a necessary source of creativity and enrichment, not just intellectual and moral but economic as well. Richard Florida (2005), the guru of 'creativity', and the economist Edward Glaeser (2011) suggest that mixing is a source of inspiration and new ideas and that being confronted with differences helps to challenge assumptions that are too easily taken for granted. By stimulating the imagination of city dwellers, mixing enhances city creativity and economic dynamics. Of course, as stated above, social mix has not always been favourable to the exchange of ideas. However, that does not prevent exchange from being a possibility, nor does it prevent initiatives to promote such exchange. Here

again, it remains to be seen whether social mix should be defended in all places and at every level. What is the best way to guarantee the existence of vibrant public spaces? Defending the presence of working-class neighbourhoods in city centres may support this vibrancy. Inversely, defending social mix on a neighbourhood level may encourage the gentrification of working-class neighbourhoods in city centres and therefore the homogenisation of the cities.

(3) Social mix is also defended because it nurtures the learning of civility, a skill that makes it easier to coexist peacefully with others. Even if co-presence does not always lead to a respect for difference, civility cannot be acquired without the experience of difference. In such a view, the big city, where experiences of difference and alterity are multiplied, is the best place to learn how to live under what Elijah Anderson calls the 'cosmopolitan canopy' (Anderson 2011). From a philosophical point of view, the reasoning often goes even further: civility is a determining factor for social cohesion, at least when it comes to tolerating the existence of the other. Further than that, civility may be one of the foundations of the democratic debate because it is a prerequisite for accepting and respecting the expression of different points of view (Boyd 2006, Ferry 2001). Here again the question is to know where and how civility can be learnt. Despite the abovementioned critics, the idea that the neighbourhood level can be determinant remains very strong. This theory is for example supported by *The Big Sort*, a popular book by Bill Bishop, which suggests that clusterings of like-minded people generally exacerbate intolerance toward people with different opinions, up to the point that it becomes difficult to coexist with them (Bishop 2009). This theory was later qualified with in-depth statistical analyses (Martin & Webster 2020), but the success of Bill Bishop's work is revealing. To many, maintaining population diversity at a neighbourhood level is necessary to fight the political Balkanisation of urban societies.

All those arguments have a normative bias in favour of the large city. This can be illustrated by the fact that some advocates of social mix are opposed to the big city. Going back to the origins of the ideal of social mix in town planning in Great Britain and the United States, Wendy Sarkissian (1976) suggests that it takes roots in the mid-19th century. At that time, the image of the village where harmony and social mix prevailed emerged in critics of the city. This image was borne by an anti-urban reaction, which unlike the opinions presented above sees the development of cities as destructive of solidarity and moral values. As a cure to the ills of the big city, these discourses recommend a return to the village community, with its social diversity tempered by community bonds. Such ideas are quite uncommon in urban studies, but they are still influential, particularly in the United States. In fact, they were widely used by some proponents of the 'New Urbanism', especially its 'neo-traditional' branch (Fulton 1996). More recently, they were revived by the growth of environmental movements promoting localism (at both the right and left of the political spectrum).

However, the world is urban and the moral and ethical defence of the social milieu associated with the city is widely shared. Thus, the findings drawn from empirical studies sometimes appear insufficient and even irrelevant for calling into question social mix policies. From a philosophical point of view, obstacles may challenge a goal without necessarily calling it into question. This is particularly true for social mix. Indeed, if the research presented in the first part of the chapter shows that the effects of social mix policies are complex and ambivalent, they also show that positive effects can be expected in certain conditions (especially those on prejudice discussed in the literature on contact theory) and for some audiences. Undoubtedly, the genuine question is how to reconcile the social mix goal with others, especially recognition, equality, and the right to the city. Often, this question goes down to how social mix can be beneficial to the working classes and marginalised groups; for example, by mitigating displacement, as mentioned above (Ghaffari et al. 2017).

## CONCLUSIONS

Politicians and a number of social movements are thus advocating social mix as an essential goal for housing policies, despite the many reservations formulated by the social sciences. The reference to social mix is successful in large part because it is a plastic ideal that can justify widely different policies: in the name of social mix, a municipality can construct social housing in attractive neighbourhoods but it can also decide to demolish a social housing estate and attempt to disperse its unwanted population; it can also accelerate gentrification of a former working-class neighbourhood for the benefit of the middle classes. The right to housing can even be undermined in the name of social mix, as in France, where recent measures limit access to social housing for most vulnerable households in neighbourhoods that are labelled as the *politique de la ville*.

As a plastic ideal, social mix also allows the manufacture of consensus. It can be considered as the seed of social cohesion and solidarity; as an essential element for the vitality of life in a neighbourhood; or even as a key ingredient to make a large city attractive to the creative classes. Above all, calling for social mix can mobilise the left (in the name of the fight against ghettoes and the right to the city), liberals (in the name of the existential value of the experiences of diversity), and conservatives (calling for social mix may be another name for defending peaceful coexistence in a hierarchical society).

For those reasons, despite the empirically based criticism, social mix remains sufficiently valued to put into brackets the means used to achieve it. Yet, as this chapter reminds us, the path toward social mix is far from neutral. It may have a cost that weighs very heavily on the poor and on low-income groups. It is often only the lower classes that are asked to contribute to the ideal of social diversity, which further reduces their residential choice. Moreover, social mix can distract from policies that would be more effective at promoting the right to the city and tackling the issues raised by socio-spatial segregation. The constant reference to social mix limits the scope of redistribution policies or denatures them. For that matter, one of the often-forgotten advantages of social mix is that it has less impact on public budgets. Focusing on social mix is also a way to sideline the structural, economic, and social factors linked to the negative effects of segregation.

In the end, beyond the various evaluations carried out by researchers, the notion of social mixing is too often based on an abstract ideal of a city of mixture and harmony, which make social, racial, and gender inequalities invisible. This ideal also comes up against the reality of social practices, and the increased competition for access to city resources. Again, this does not mean that social mix should be discarded as an ideal. Far from that, in many circumstances, the case for social mixing is robust and convincing. However, the desirability of this ideal depends on contextual issues. To be used as a prescriptive reference guiding action, this ideal needs to be specified and qualified. The weight social mix policies put on the lower classes must be taken into consideration and action has to be taken to reduce it. Moreover, social mix is not an absolute good. Its value has to be weighed against other normative issues, like sustaining a territorial base for the dominated classes. This chapter demonstrated all this about housing policies, but the same analysis could have been done with other policies, like those regarding schooling (see for example Lipman (2009)).

## REFERENCES

Anderson, E. (2011) *The Cosmopolitan Canopy: Race and Civility in Everyday Life*. New York: W.W. Norton.
Arthurson, K. (2012) *Social Mix and the City: Challenging the Mixed Communities Consensus in Housing and Urban Planning Policies*. Collingwood: CSIRO Publishing.
Atkinson, R. & Blandy, S. (2005) Introduction: International perspectives on the new enclavism and the rise of gated communities. *Housing Studies* 20(2): 177–186.
Avenel, C. (2005) La mixité dans la ville et dans les grands ensembles. *Informations sociales* 5: 62–71.
Bacqué, M.-H. & Sintomer, Y. (2001) Affiliations et désaffiliations en banlieue: réflexions à partir d'exemples de Saint-Denis et d'Aubervilliers. *Revue française de sociologie* 42(2): 217–249.
Bacqué, M.-H. & Fol, S. (2007) Effets de quartier: enjeux scientifiques et politiques de l'importation d'une controverse. In J. Y. Authier, M.-H. Bacqué & F. Guérin-Pace (eds.) *Le quartier. Enjeux scientifiques, actions politiques et pratiques sociales*. Paris: La Découverte.
Bacqué, M.-H. & Biewener, C. (2013) *L'empowerment, une pratique émancipatrice?* Paris: La Découverte.
Bacqué, M.-H, Bridge, G., Benson, M., Butler, T., Charmes, E., Jackson, E., Launay, L. & Fijalkow, Y. (2015) *The Middle Classes and the City*. London: Palgrave Macmillan.
Balazard, H. (2015) *Agir en démocratie*. Ivry-sur-Seine: Editions de l'atelier.
Biggeri, M. & Ferrannini, A. (2014) *Sustainable Human Development: A New Territorial and People-centred Perspective*. Springer.
Bishop, B. (2009) *The Big Sort: Why the Clustering of Like-Minded America Is Tearing Us Apart*. Boston: Mariner Books.
Bolt, G. & Van Kempen, R. (2013) Mixing neighbourhoods: Success or failure? *Cities* 35: 391–396.
Boyd, R. (2006) The value of civility? *Urban Studies* 43(5–6): 863–878.
Bridge, G. Butler, T. & Lees, L. (eds.) (2012) *Mixed Communities: Gentrification By Stealth?* Bristol: Policy Press.
Briggs de Souza, X. (1997) Moving up versus moving out: Neighbourhood effects in housing mobility programs. *Housing Policy Debate* 8(1): 77–220.
Briggs de Souza, X. (2005) *The Geography of Opportunity: Race and Housing Choice in Metropolitan America*. Washington, DC: Brookings Institution Press.
Brooks-Gunn, J., Duncan, G. J., Klebanov, P. K. & Sealand, N. (1993) Do neighborhoods influence child and adolescent development? *The American Journal of Sociology* 99(2): 353–395.
Brun, J. & Rhein, C. (1994) *La ségrégation dans la ville*. Paris: L'Harmattan.
Chabrol, M., Collet, A., Giroud, M., Launay, L., Rousseau, M. & Minassian, H. (2016) *Gentrifications*. Paris: Editions Amsterdam.
Chamboredon, J.-C. & Lemaire, M. (1970) Proximité spatiale et distance sociale. *Revue française de sociologie* XI: 3–33.
Charmes, E. & Bacqué, M.-H. (eds.) (2016) *Mixité sociale et après?* Paris: Presses Universitaires de France.
Chombard de Lauwe, P. H. (1965) *Des hommes et des villes*. Paris: Payot.
Comey, J., Briggs, X. & Weissmann, G. (2008) Struggling to stay out high-poverty neighborhoods: Lessons from the Moving to Opportunity Experiment. Urban Metropolitan Housing and Communities Center, brief no. 6. Washington, DC: Urban Institute.
Dawkins, C. J. (2008) Reflections on diversity and social capital: A critique of Robert D. Putnam's 'E Pluribus Unum: Diversity and community in the twenty-first century. The 2006 Johan Skytte prize lecture'. *Housing Policy Debate* 19(1): 207–217.

Dixon, J. C. (2006) The ties that bind and those that don't: Toward reconciling group threat and contact theories of prejudice. *Social Forces* 84(4): 2179–2204.
Donzelot, J. (1999) La nouvelle question urbaine. *Esprit* 258: 87–114.
Dubet, F. & Lapeyronnie, D. (1992) *Les quartiers d'exil*. Paris: Editions du Seuil.
Ellen, I. E. & Turner, M. A. (1997) Does neighborhood matter? Assessing recent evidence. *Housing Policy Debate* 8(4): 833–866.
Epstein, R. & Kirzbaum, T. (2003) L'enjeu de la mixité sociale dans les politiques urbaines. *Regards sur l'actualité* 292: 63–74.
Epstein, R. (2013) *La Rénovation urbaine: Démolition-reconstruction de l'État*. Paris: Presses de Sciences Po.
Estèbe, P. (2005) Les quartiers, une affaire d'État, un instrument territorial. In P. Lascoumes & P. Le Galès (eds.) *Gouverner par les instruments*. Paris: Presses de Sciences Po, 49–50.
Ferry, J.-M. (2001) *De la civilisation. Civilité, légalité, publicité*. Paris: Éditions du Cerf.
Florida, R. (2005) *Cities and the Creative Class*. New York: Routledge.
Fourcaut, A. (1986) *Bobigny, banlieue rouge*. Paris: Les Éditions Ouvrières and Presses de la FNSP.
Fraser, N. (2003) Repenser l'espace public: une contribution à la critique de la démocratie réellement existante. In E. Renault (ed.) *Où en est la théorie critique?* Paris: La Découverte, 103–134.
Fulton, W. (1996) *The New Urbanism*. Cambridge: Lincoln Institute of Land Policy.
Galster, G. & Zobel, A. (1998) Will dispersed housing programs reduce social problems in the US? *Housing Studies* 13(5): 605–622.
Galster, G. & Santiago, A. (2006) What's the 'hood got to do with it? Parental perceptions about how neighborhood mechanisms affect their children. *Journal of Urban Affairs* 38(3): 201–226.
Galster, G. & Friedrich, J. (2015) The dialectic of neighborhood social mix: Editors' introduction to the special issue. *Housing Studies* 30(2): 175–191.
Gans, H. (1961) The balanced community: Homogeneity or heterogeneity in residential areas? *Journal of the American Institute of Planners* XXVII(3): 176–184.
Gans, H. (1967) *The Levittowners: Ways of Life and Politics in a New Suburban Community*. Pantheon Books.
Ghaffari, L., Klein, J-L. & Angulo Baudin, W. (2017) Toward a socially acceptable gentrification: A review of strategies and practices against displacement. *Geography Compass* 12(2): e12355.
Giddens, A. (1998) *The Third Way: The Renewal of Social Democracy*. John Wiley & Sons.
Gilbert, P. (2009) Social stakes of urban renewal: Recent French housing policy. *Building Research & Information* 37(5–6): 638–648.
Giroud, M. (2016) Mixité, contrôle social et gentrification. In E. Charmes & M.-H. Bacqué (eds.) *Mixité sociale et après?* Paris: Presses universitaires de France.
Glaeser, E. (2011) *Triumph of the City: How Our Greatest Invention Makes Us Richer, Smarter, Greener, Healthier, and Happier*. New York: Penguin Press.
Goering, J. & Feins, J. D. (eds.) (2003) *Choosing a Better Life? Evaluating the Moving to Opportunity Social Experiment*. Washington, DC: Urban Institute Press.
Goetz, E. G. (2003) *Clearing the Way: Deconcentrating the Poor in Urban America*. Washington, DC: Urban Institute Press.
Goetz, E. G. (2010) Better neighborhoods, better outcomes? Explaining relocation outcomes in HOPE VI. *Cityscape* 5–31.
Haila, A. (2015) *Urban Land Rent: Singapore as a Property State*. John Wiley & Sons.
Imbroscio, D. (2010) *Urban America Reconsidered. Alternatives for Governance and Policy*. Ithaca: Cornell University Press.
Jacobs, J. (1961) *The Death and Life of Great American Cities*. New York: Random House.
Jones, K., Johnston, R., Manley, D. et al. (2015) Ethnic residential segregation: A multilevel, multigroup, multiscale approach exemplified by London in 2011. *Demography* 52(6): 1995–2019.
Lahire, B. (2016) *Pour la sociologie: et pour en finir avec une prétendue 'culture de l'excuse'*. Paris: La Découverte.
Launay, L. (2011) *Les politiques de mixité par l'habitat à l'épreuve des rapports résidentiels. Quartiers populaires et beaux quartiers à Paris et à Londres*. PhD thesis, Université de Paris Ouest Nanterre La Défense.

Lees, L. (2008) Gentrification and social mixing: Towards an inclusive urban renaissance? *Urban Studies* 45(12): 2449–2470.
Lefebvre, H. (1960) Les nouveaux ensembles urbains. *Revue française de Sociologie* 1(2): 186–201.
Lefebvre, H. (1972) [1968] *Le Droit à la ville: suivi de Espace et politique*. Paris: Anthropos.
Lelévrier, C. (2010) La mixité dans la rénovation urbaine: dispersion ou re-concentration? *Espaces et sociétés* 140–141: 59–74.
Levin, I., Santiago, A. M. & Arthurson, K. (2022) Creating mixed communities through housing policies: Global perspectives. *Journal of Urban Affairs* 44(3): 291–304.
Lipman, P. (2009) The cultural politics of mixed-income schools and housing: A racialized discourse of displacement, exclusion, and control. *Anthropology & Education Quarterly* 40(3): 215–236.
Lorcerie, F. & Moignard, B. (2017) L'école, la laïcité et le virage sécuritaire post-attentats: un tableau contrasté. *Sociologie* 8(4): 439–446.
Magri, S. (1993) Villes, quartiers: proximités et distances sociales dans l'espace urbain. *Genèses* 13(1): 151–165.
Manzo, L. (2012) On people in changing neighborhoods. Gentrification and social mix: Boundaries and resistance. *Cidades, Comunidades e Territórios* 24: 1–29.
Marcuse, P. (2005) Enclaves yes, ghettos no. In D. Varady (ed.) *Desegregating the City: Ghettos, Enclaves, and Inequality*. New York: SUNY Press, 15–30.
Marpsat, M. (1999) La modélisation des 'effets de quartier' aux États-Unis, une revue des travaux récents. *Population* 54(2): 177–204.
Martin, G. & Webster, S. (2020) Does residential sorting explain geographic polarization? *Political Science Research and Methods* 8(2): 215–231
Massey, D. & Denton, N. (1995) [1993] *American Apartheid*. Paris: Descartes & Cie.
Pettigrew, T. F. & Tropp, L. R. (2006) A meta-analytic test of intergroup contact theory. *Journal of Personality and Social Psychology* 90(5): 751–783.
Piketty, T. (2020) *Capital and Ideology*. Cambridge: Harvard University Press.
Pinçon, M. (1982) *Cohabiter, groupes sociaux et modes de vie dans une cité HLM*. Paris: Ministère de l'urbanisme et du logement.
Popkin, S. J., Buron, L. F., Levy, D. K. et al. (2000) The Gautreaux legacy: What might mixed-income and dispersal strategies mean for the poorest public housing tenants? *Housing Policy Debate* 11(4): 911–942.
Putnam, R. D. (2007) E Pluribus Unum: Diversity and community in the twenty-first century. *Scandinavian Political Studies* 30(2): 137–174.
Reardon, S. F. & O'Sullivan, D. (2004) Measures of spatial segregation. *Sociological Methodology* 34(1): 121–162.
Rosenbaum, J. (1995) Changing the geography of opportunity by expanding residential choice: Lessons from the Gautreaux Program. *Housing Policy Debate* 6(1): 231–269.
Sampson, R. (2012) *Great American City: Chicago and the Enduring Neighborhood Effect*. Chicago: University of Chicago Press.
Sarkissian, W. (1976) The idea of social mix in town planning: An historical review. *Urban Studies* 13(3): 231–46.
Scally, C. P. & Tighe, J. R. (2015) Democracy in action?: NIMBY as impediment to equitable affordable housing siting. *Housing Studies* 30(5): 749–769.
Schill, M. (1997) Chicago's mixed-income new communities strategy: The future face of public housing? *Urban Affairs Annual Review* 46: 135–157.
Simon, J. (2021) Introduction: Introducing philosophy of the city. *Topoi* 40: 387–398.
Slater, T. (2006) The eviction of critical perspectives from gentrification research. *International Journal of Urban and Regional Research* 30(4): 737–757.
Slater, T. (2021) *Shaking Up the City. Ignorance, Inequality, and the Urban Question*. Oakland: University of California Press.
Squires, C. R. (2002) Rethinking the black public sphere: An alternative vocabulary for multiple public spheres. *Communication Theory* 12(4): 446–468.
Talen, E. (1999) Sense of community and neighborhood form: An assessment of the social doctrine of new urbanism. *Urban Studies* 36(8): 1361–1379.
Tissot, S. (2007) *L'Etat et les quartiers. Genèse d'une catégorie de l'action publique*. Paris: Seuil.

Tissot, S. (2015) *Good Neighbors: Gentrifying Diversity in Boston's South End*. London: Verso Books.
Tonnelat, S. (2016) Espace public, urbanité et démocratie. In E. Charmes & M.-H. Bacqué (eds.) *Mixité sociale et après?* Paris: Presses Universitaires de France.
Valentine, G. (2008) Living with difference: Reflections on geographies of encounter. *Progress in Human Geography* 32(3): 323–37
Van Criekingen, M. (2012) Meanings, politics and realities of social mix and gentrification – A view from Brussels. In G. Bridge, T. Butler & L. Lees (eds.) *Mixed Communities: Gentrification by Stealth?* Bristol: Policy Press, 169–184.
Van Kempen, R. & Bolt, G. (2009) Social cohesion, social mix, and urban policies in the Netherlands. *Journal of Housing and the Built Environment* 24(4): 457–475.
Vermeersch, S., Launay, L., Charmes, E. & Bacqué, M.-H. (2018) *Habiter Paris. Les classes moyennes entre périphéries et centres*. Grâne: Créaphis.
Wessel, T. (2009) Does diversity in urban space enhance intergroup contact and tolerance? *Geografiska Annaler: Series B, Human Geography* 91(1): 5–17.
Whyte W. F. (1943) *Street Corner Society: The Social Structure of an Italian Slum*. Chicago: University of Chicago Press.
Whyte W. F. (1956) *The Organization Man*. New York: Simon & Schuster.
Young, I. M. (1990) Residential segregation and differentiated citizenship. *Citizenship Studies* 3(2): 237–252.
Zouari, N. & Charmes, E. (2020) Entre fermeture et ouverture. La légitimité d'une centralité populaire de banlieue en question. In A. Fleury, M. Delage, L. Endelstein, H. Dubucs & S. Weber (eds.) *Le petit commerce dans la ville monde*. Paris: L'oeil d'or, 203–216.
Zukin, S., Trujillo, V., Frase P., Jackson, D., Recuber, T. & Walker, A. (2009) New retail capital and neighborhood change: Boutiques and gentrification in New York City. *City & Community* 8(1): 47–64.

# 17. Producing and closing rent gaps: political and social dimensions

*Defne Kadıoğlu*

Rent gap theory is arguably late Marxist human geographer Neil Smith's most discussed and best-known legacy in the wider field of urban studies (1979, 1987). Rent gaps signify the difference between capitalised and potential ground rent; i.e., the income realised from the ownership of a given land and the potential maximum income that could be made if that land were put to its 'highest and best use' (Smith 1979: 543). Smith mobilised rent gap theory to explain the underlying mechanism behind gentrification, the social upgrading of a – typically inner city – neighbourhood through the replacement of the sitting working-class population with middle- and/or upper-class residents. According to Smith, it is this difference between the current and the potential income that triggers the gentrification process. While Smith's focus was on the movement of capital along cycles of dis- and reinvestment, he was also clear that the realisation (or closing) of rent gaps indicates displacement, in that it is the better-off residents who can actualise the maximum rent, by being able to pay higher rents and by attracting other, better-off residents. Accordingly, from Smith's perspective, the closing of rent gaps and the related gentrification processes are always inherently violent.

It is the grand ambition that underlies rent gap theory, namely, to explain not one but *the* underlying cause of gentrification, that has made it so contentious among urban scholars: since its inception, it has been celebrated for its 'ingenious simplicity' (Ley 1996: 42), its 'normative thrust' (Slater 2017b: 119), and its ability to make us 'ask illuminating questions of reality' (Yung & King 1998: 540) on the one hand and has been berated as 'reductionist' (Bernt 2016: 641), 'economistic and deterministic' (Hamnett 1991: 180), and 'purely theoretical' (Ley 1987: 466) on the other. The question that underlies much of these debates is how much room rent gap theory allows for a discussion of institutional configurations, social relations, political power, and struggle. Put differently: where is rent gap theory located in the larger discussion around agency and structure as well as politics, culture, and capital within the social sciences? In this chapter, alongside empirical examples from Berlin and Stockholm, I embark on discussing this underlying question by pondering the political and social dimensions of rent gaps. Relying on existing studies and theoretical explorations of the rent gap, as well as my own field work, I contend that debates around rent gap theory should consider three related aspects.

*Conceptual finetuning:* To weave political and social factors into rent gap theory there is merit in deconstructing how rent gaps are produced, widened, and finally closed. It is particularly the closure of rent gaps that is not evident and can differ enormously in different contexts. For example, legal frameworks might prevent developers and investors from realising the value of a property (Krijnen 2018, Christophers 2021). This conceptual finetuning of rent gap theory, as I will suggest, does not negate its main function as centrepiece for explaining gentrification and uneven urban development in general but rather opens the opportunity for theoretical and empirical enrichment.

*Conceptual extension:* Rent gap theory will necessarily have to be complemented by a discussion of the role of the state, wider social structures, and political configurations. This is not precluded by Smith and is in fact encouraged by other concepts he has coined or critically re-appropriated, such as state-led gentrification, the urban frontier, and urban revanchism (Hackworth & Smith 2001, Smith 1996). As I will discuss further, related sociological concepts such as territorial and/or racial stigmatisation (Slater 2017a, 2017b) are similarly equipped to enhance rent gap theory and account for the role of symbolic structures in conjunction with the rent gap (Kallin 2017).

*Conceptual distinction*: This is, perhaps, the most controversial aspect but I suggest that rent gap theory can explain processes that go beyond a sociological understanding of gentrification – i.e. as a process in which the working-class population are replaced in several waves, first by 'pioneers' with low economic but high social and cultural capital and then by middle- and upper-class residents and investors. In fact, rent gap theory can be applied to cases where no replacement of working-class residents is happening, but land rents (or regular rents and prices, often used as a proxy for land rent) are increasing nevertheless. This can, for example, be the case in neighbourhoods where tenants have little moving alternatives, leading to other consequences such as overcrowding and diminished quality of life (August & Walks 2018). Whether some of these processes can then be referred to as gentrification might be of secondary relevance.

I am using two case studies to illustrate the need for the conceptual extension, finetuning, and distinction of rent gap theory. In Berlin I consider an inner-city working-class neighbourhood that had long been considered 'too bad for gentrification' (Smith 2007) but has advanced to one of the most popular areas for hipsters and financial investors alike. In Stockholm I discuss the case of a suburban housing estate that has been bought off by a transnationally operating financialised housing company and in which tenants are 'squeezed' (August & Walks 2018) out of revenues through renovations as well as under- or delayed maintenance. I suggest that these two cases are illustrative of rent gap theory's versatile applicability. The chapter commences with an overview about the main fault lines – past and present – around rent gap theory and reviews its contemporary applications. I then present the case studies in brief and with respect to the three aspects highlighted above. I end the chapter by summarising the main arguments and by pointing to the ongoing relevance of rent gap for theory and practice.

## HOW IT STARTED: THE RENT GAP BETWEEN CONSUMPTION AND PRODUCTION

In 1979, in a seminal piece in the *Journal of the American Planning Association*, Smith shared the rent gap with the world. The ideas had been developed from his unpublished undergraduate thesis titled 'The Return from the Suburbs and the Structuring of Urban Space: State Involvement in Society Hill, Philadelphia'. As gentrification was gaining in speed and geographical scope throughout the 1980s, the scholarly community engaged in a decades-long debate around the accuracy of Smith's theory. I will briefly review the debate around consumption- versus production-centred explanations of gentrification and its current bearing.

Scholars such as David Ley (1980, 1987), Damaris Rose (1984), and Chris Hamnett (1991) have conceptualised gentrifying neighbourhoods as emergent geographies of the post-industrial society. They have suggested that the economic shifts that occurred after the

1970s have been accompanied by an expansion and fragmentation of the middle class. These new factions became gentrifiers by virtue of their tastes and needs that could no longer be satisfied in the suburbs, such as proximity to urban amenities and diversity, which could be found in the often disinvested, minority-heavy, and working-class urban cores. Gentrifiers are thus produced by changed labour conditions and conditions of labour reproduction. While first movers (so-called pioneers) were typically characterised by low economic and high cultural capital, wealthier newcomers were likely to follow them, further contributing to a rise in rents and changes in local infrastructure. Consumption-side explanations have been highly influential, often focusing on the behaviour of these different groups of newcomers. Rose (1984), for example, has found that transformed gender relations after the sexual revolution of the 1960s and 1970s are closely linked to gentrification. Mobilising the notion of 'marginal gentrifiers', she connected the influx of women and sexual minorities into the inner city to a lack of amenities in the suburbs catering to their differential needs, such as child-friendly activities, community centres, or cafes in walking distance.

It is also within the circle of proponents of consumption-side explanations that we will find more benevolent views of gentrification: Jon Caulfield (1989) has, for example, argued that gentrification is in fact an emancipatory practice of the middle class, opening the opportunity for interaction between different classes and social groups in a heterogeneous inner-city environment. Gentrification is here seen as a win-win situation in which the 'creative class' (Florida 2005) is lured into the inner city by cultural diversity and the residents of the gentrifying area benefit from socio-economic upheaval. Others have integrated consumption-side explanations into a more critical perspective. Sharon Zukin has written about the distinctive infrastructure emerging in gentrifying neighbourhoods. The today stereotypical farmers' markets or 'ethnic' food shops, so she suggests, give gentrifiers the opportunity to 'perform difference from mainstream norms' (Zukin 2008: 724) without structurally including those through whom this difference is performed, such as racial minorities. The result is that gentrifying neighbourhoods are not only characterised by rent increase or the occasional cupcake shop, but by displacement that frequently materialises along racial lines (Drew 2012).

It is often insinuated that consumption-side explanations are cultural and position lifestyle changes as the root cause for gentrification. However, as Smith (1992: 112) himself points out, Ley and others centralise class and class composition in their analysis by suggesting that the increased and changed demand for inner-city living from parts of the middle class hails from the changed relationship between capital and labour (Hamnett 1991). Their explanations are thus as 'economic' as Smith's. The decisive issue is not so much whether we opt for culture, politics, or economics – as if these were mutually exclusive – but where scholars chose to place their 'theoretical priority' (Hamnett 1991: 186): the rent gap's gist is that it challenges the idea that it is primarily demand and choices of urban consumers that shape the physical and social geography of the city. As Bourassa (1993: 178) in his own disparagement of the rent gap writes, Smith 'completely reversed' the 'explanatory emphasis' by positing that the main gentrifiers are the real estate sector, investors, developers, and the state. The main point of contention is thus not whether it matters where young urbanites want to live – which Smith agreed is an important factor in shaping the landscapes of gentrification – but whether this is the *underlying cause* of gentrification:

Although it is of secondary importance in initiating the actual process, [...] consumer preference and demand are of primary importance in *determining the final form and character of revitalized areas.* (Smith 1979: 540, author's emphasis)

Following Smith, one can thus argue that consumption-side theories are helpful in providing a nuanced picture of the gentrification process, generating concepts that allow researchers to deconstruct how gentrification is occurring and what the distinct effects of gentrification, as opposed to other forms of urban transformation, are in terms of issues such as gender and race. Rent gap theory on the other hand is most useful when addressing the 'why' of gentrification rather than the 'how'. It may be considered as a necessary but not sufficient explanation for gentrification: '[a]reas with a large rent gap *might not* gentrify, but areas without a rent gap *cannot* gentrify' (Krijnen 2018: 438).

Testing the rent gap, however, has proven difficult given that in available datasets there is usually nothing that would allow researchers to cleanly distinguish and operationalise capitalised versus potential rent. Accordingly, there are only a few studies that have embarked on this journey, some of them providing strong evidence in favour of the rent gap (Badcock 1989, Clark 1988, Hammel 1999, O'Sullivan 2002, Sýkora 1993). What seems to unite these studies is the agreement that the rent gap needs to be enmeshed within a 'wider conceptual framework' (Millard-Ball 2000: 1689) to account for changes in the urban political economy as well as for politico-economic contexts. Some of the more recent works employing the rent gap are reviewed in the next section.

## HOW IT'S GOING: FINETUNING, EXTENDING, AND DISTINGUISHING THE RENT GAP

Despite the decades that have passed since its inception, the rent gap is still subject to a vivid scholarly debate. Some scholars have doubled down on Smith's notion of rent gap-induced and state-led gentrification as a 'global urban strategy' by introducing the concepts of 'planetary gentrification' (Lees et al. 2016) and subsequently 'planetary rent gaps' (Calbet i Elias 2017, Slater 2017b). The argument is that the existence of different forms of gentrification across the world (or 'gentrifications' (Shin 2019)) does not negate its planetary scope since the underlying logic – closing the gap between the currently realised and the potentially-to-be-made rent – stands. Others, particularly scholars of postcoloniality, have, in turn, maintained that rent gap theory does not account for what Asher Ghertner (2015) calls 'extra economic forces' or the 'more-than-economic'. Ghertner suggests that rent gap theory 'fails' outside the Global North, chiefly because it assumes the existence of clearly circumscribed private and public property relations. In countries such as India, most displacements and urban transformations are not market-induced but moulded by state power in the form of regulatory and legal changes that allow for the commodification of hitherto public or semi-private land and housing. Matthias Bernt has made a similar argument, positing that 'rent-gap theories only allow general statements' and 'downplay non-economic instances' which he finds to be 'deeply embedded within the reductionist conceptual architecture of the rent-gap' (Bernt 2016: 641–642). He, however, has also maintained that, despite its shortcomings, the rent gap can serve well as a 'starting point' if conceptually developed (Bernt 2022: 31). While I suggest that the rent gap can be more than a starting point in that it serves to make sense of gentrification, and possibly other forms of uneven development, I agree with Bernt that conceptual development is necessary. I draw on three related aspects: the conceptual distinction, finetuning, and extension of the rent gap.

First, while rent gap theory is a theory of gentrification, Smith refused to see consumer preference as the main cause behind gentrification and had a broader conception of the process as being related to cycles of investment. I here suggest that even if a narrower understanding of gentrification is applied, rent gap theory can still be useful to explain other forms of urban change, regardless of what we may choose to call them. Put differently, the question of what gentrification exactly is and in which ways it is related to cultural changes is secondary to the question of whether rent gap theory is useful. This can also be inferred from the fact that in many current studies on rent gaps, gentrification only plays a subordinate role and/or is conceptualised very broadly as denoting various forms of uneven urban development. For example, Brett Christophers (2021) and Laura Calbet i Elias (2017) write on the development of financialised rent gaps, i.e., the production of rent gaps under the impact of global investment vehicles such as asset managers or real estate investment trusts. They show how rent gaps globalise, allowing, for example, US American private equity giant Blackstone to apply similar investment strategies across borders. Whether these strategies to exploit rent gaps then lead to gentrification in conjunction with the class and cultural change David Ley and others describe is, essentially, secondary to their argument. In that sense the question of whether gentrification is planetary may be analytically distinguishable from the question of whether rent gaps are.

Second, there is merit in emphasising the processual and temporal aspect of rent gap development and closure: not every neighbourhood with a rent gap is gentrifying or experiencing reinvestment. However, rather than seeing this as proof that rent gap theory is wrong, there lies a chance to deconstruct and finetune the rent gap by distinguishing between the production of a rent gap, its widening, and its closure. For rent gaps to exist, they must have been produced by some prior process, such as suburbanisation fuelled by urban redevelopment outside the city centres or material neglect of the inner city. Accordingly, rent gaps do not just 'emerge' but are a result of prior decisions that pull capital into different directions. The sheer existence of a rent gap, however, does not necessarily draw in the necessary investment. As Smith contends, gaps need to be wide enough (Smith 1979: 545) for developers to buy or build cheaply and sell/rent with a profit. Accordingly, rent gaps need to be widened, which may be achieved through additional incentives, such as subsidies or through the symbolic denigration of the to-be-gentrified area (Kallin 2017, Wright 2014). Marieke Krijnen (2018) draws attention to this question by suggesting that introducing this processual and temporal deconstruction of the rent gap allows us to better grasp local variations. She describes for the case of Beirut how not only legislation and policy but also informal property relations, corruption, and clientelism affect not only how rent gaps are formed but if and how they are closed. Christophers (2021), as referenced above, in a case study of Blackstone's investment strategies in Denmark, Sweden, and Germany has shown that though rent gaps existed in all contexts they did not close in the same way and along the same timeline in all locations. Local or national regulations such as rent regulations, selling freezes, or limitations on renovation can effectively delay, narrow, or possibly even forestall the realisation of profit from the rent gap. The role of the state is pivotal, and the rent gap is a necessary but not sufficient condition for gentrification to happen. Ben Teresa (2019) and David Wachsmuth and Alexander Weisler (2018) in turn respectively describe how the financialisation of housing markets and the related and technology-fuelled introduction of new players, such as Airbnb, lead to new forms of rent gap production. In their cases the logic is not so much that capital flows into a previously disinvested neighbourhood but that rent gaps are *reopened* in spaces where they had previously been closed, or at least considerably narrowed. This can lead to processes previously described as 'super-gentrification' (Lees 2003). What all these studies show is that for rent gap theory to be applicable in different contexts, a careful dissection of the moment(s) of emergence/production, widening, and closure is necessary and enriching.

Third, to grapple further with the 'extra-economic', a conceptual extension is necessary: Tom Slater (2016, 2017a, 2017b) has been at the forefront of this attempt. He has suggested that rent gap theory is a theory of state involvement in producing uneven urban development (see Smith 1996, Hackworth & Smith 2001). He has also maintained that the sociological concept of territorial stigma (Wacquant 1996) can help to resolve a puzzle around gentrification; namely, why it typically does not start from the most distraught neighbourhoods. Hammel (1999: 1290), who discussed the role of scale, and in specific the scale of the neighbourhood in conjunction with the rent gap, reasoned as follows:

> Inner city areas have many sites with a potential for development that could return high levels of rent. That development never occurs, however, because the perception of an impoverished neighbourhood prevents large amounts of capital being applied to the land.

The role of an often-deep seated taint attached to certain places in the city in the gentrification process has consequently been explored in various empirical studies. What can be seen from these studies is that there is a contradictory effect, with stigma being at once enabling and disabling for the effective rent gap closure and thus gentrification. Andrea Mösgen et al., for example, drawing on the case of Frankfurt, Germany, have shown that stigma can inhibit or at least significantly delay the effective capture and closure of rent gaps because a negative image can lead to an 'inertia' (Mösgen et al. 2019: 428) among investors who still perceive it as too risky to sink their capital into a neighbourhood that is very tainted in the public eye. Melissa Wright (2014) makes a similar argument by showing how the municipality of a Mexican–US American border city first recognised the existence of a rent gap and then deliberately tried to widen it by normalising the violence and forced disappearance of female sex workers in the city. The (local) state is thus often actively involved in creating the symbolic structures that allow for the material exploitation of neighbourhoods and residents by producing, intensifying, and finally lifting stigma. Inspiration can also be found in Smith's (1996) usage of the concept of the urban frontier and revanchism. Thörn and Holgersson (2016: 663) suggest that Smith's frontier mythology stands in an immediate relation with capital movement and directly affects 'how and where rent gaps are created'. Relating the rent gap to questions of stigma, racialisation, and the punitive state is fruitful because it allows us to grasp more fully the different trajectories the production, widening, and closure of rent gaps can take.

Finally, thinking about the specific circumstances that allow rent gaps to be produced, widened, and/or closed also opens about more space for considering the role of social struggles (Cowen et al. 2012). Struggles can slow down or even circumvent the closure of rent gaps, as it has been the case in some of the above discussed studies: Blackstone could not efficiently close the rent gap in its Danish housing stock because individual tenants and the tenants' union mobilised to pressure the government to intervene in their 'buy low-renovate-displace-sell' strategy. The government then issued a law that curbed Blackstone's and similar companies' ability to renovate and raise the rent (Christophers 2021). Understanding how capital circulates and finds new opportunities to invest and reinvest is thus crucial in pushing national and local states to reinstate use value for urban communities by eliminating the mechanisms that produce, widen, and allow for the closure of rent gaps (Clark 2014, Harvey 1973: 137).

## CASE STUDIES

I discuss the conceptual distinction, extension, and finetuning of the rent gap alongside two cases: a gentrifying district in Berlin that has advanced from a heavily stigmatised area to one of the most popular spots in the city with rapid rent increases, and a suburban neighbourhood in Stockholm that has been targeted by a series of national and international housing investors leading to a series of disadvantages for tenants, including but not limited to displacement. Field work for the Berlin case was conducted in different periods: first in 2012 and 2013, when gentrification was still at a relatively early stage and I mostly interviewed residents; and second in 2019 and 2020, when I mostly interviewed activists (some of whom were residents too) who had been involved in the struggle against gentrification. Fieldwork in Stockholm was conducted in 2020 and 2021 together with Ilhan Kellecioğlu (2021) who, as a tenant himself, conducted most of the interviews with tenants. The empirical discussion of these two cases below serves to illustrate how conceptual extension and finetuning of rent gap theory allows for its enmeshment with political and social dimensions.

**Neukölln (Berlin)**

Neukölln is a district with a population of about 300,000 in the south of Berlin, alongside the former western side of the wall. The subject of this case study is particularly the northern parts of Neukölln, which are the ones that are gentrifying, working class, and immigrant-dense (ca. 50 percent), housing around 160,000 people. Almost a third of the population is at risk of poverty, meaning that their disposable income constitutes less than 60 percent of the average income in Germany (Amt für Statistik Berlin-Brandenburg 2019).

While other parts of the German capital went through gentrification processes shortly after reunification (Holm 2006, 2013), Neukölln, even after the turn of the century, was considered to be among the 'losers' (Krätke 2004: 61) of the wider economic growth of Berlin. Attested to have 'a most spectacular concentration of social problems' (ibid.), a study in the late 2000s suggested that the poor from other, already gentrifying, inner-city districts were displaced to north Neukölln (Häußermann et al. 2008). In theory, the northern parts of Neukölln were not that much different in their characteristics than the already more popular southern parts of Kreuzberg: housing stock hailing from the mid-19th century (pretty to look at from the outside, basic quality from the inside), a working-class, immigrant-dense population, and a relatively fragmented ownership structure with north Neukölln having mostly individual private landlords who had frequently inherited buildings from their families. However, while both areas have long histories of territorial and racial stigmatisation and are still often invoked as Germany's prime 'ghettos' (Eksner 2013), Kreuzberg's edgy history as home to artists, misfits, and squatters made it an attractive destination for newcomers and tourists after reunification, while Neukölln remained 'too bad for gentrification' (Smith 2007: 10) in the public imagination for long after.

Throughout the 2000s and early 2010s the district government tried to incentivise newcomers and investors through neighbourhood-level interventions such as brokering vacant spaces to artists and other creative workers who were supposed to function as so-called 'urban pioneers'; i.e., first movers who would contribute to Neukölln's de-stigmatisation and drive demand. Given the exploding rent prices in Kreuzberg, this worked well, as a young café owner who had moved to Neukölln in 2007 recalled:

> I wanted to move to Kreuzberg, and the apartment was advertised as Kreuzberg. Then I didn't care, I took it. Directly at Maybachufer, opposite of Kreuzberg, then I took it. At the beginning I was laughed at 'oo Neukölln blablabla' and yes, now I can soon not even afford my own apartment. (Interview with male resident, December 2012)

At the same time 'the right hand of the state' (Bourdieu et al. 2008) was working its magic: throughout the 1990s and 2000s policing increased in all of Berlin, with Neukölln and other immigrant-heavy spaces being heavily targeted (Eick 2012). Accordingly, the local state engaged in strategies that, on the one hand, further stigmatised the area in conjunction with certain social groups and, on the other, intended to de-stigmatise it by articulating the possibility for change (Kadıoğlu 2022). This is, as Kallin (2017) and others suggest, directly related to cycles of dis- and reinvestment: places are framed and reframed in line with actual and wished-for capital movements.

In 2009 the district also initiated a regeneration project on the area's main shopping street, which included the marketing of vacant buildings, such as former department stores and the old postal office, to investors. While rents in North Neukölln – in line with the general spread of gentrification throughout the German capital – had already started to rise significantly in the early 2010s, land value remained low to moderate (Immoeinfach 2020). In other words, the rent gap remained open:

> Why would anyone buy the empty C&A building [department store chain] here, only because some hip boutiques have now settled here in some side streets? That has changed the perception about Neukölln, but it does not amount to anything if the big buildings remain empty. I must deliver him [the investor] a picture of Neukölln that is more representable towards the outside, I must show him the strength that Neukölln has, namely relatively moderate land price, a purchasing power that is a little lower but, for that, a relative high rent level. So, for that, you must also promote the soft skills […] (Interview with project leader, January 2013)

While not reducible to one reason, I suggest that Neukölln's 'sticky stigma' (Pinkster et al. 2020, Schultz Larsen & Delica 2021) contributed to the delayed and incomplete closure of the rent gap in the North of the district. Though by the early 2010s, as exemplified in the two interview quotes, the public perception of Neukölln was already changing, the district had to fuel, articulate, and highlight its potential (the potential inherent in the rent gap) to investors by encouraging the influx of middle-class newcomers and capital and discouraging the presence and practices of stigmatised populations. Kallin's (2017) concept of the 'reputational gap' – a gap between the perceived status quo of a neighbourhood or a city and its 'promised' future and a conceptual complement of the rent gap – serves to elucidate what was happening in Neukölln in the early 2010s: 'soft skills' here in particular translate into a reimagination of the district without or with less of its current residents and with more of what the district government in its own monthly magazine referred to as the 'new Neuköllners', described as a 'young, creative and smart target group' (Broadway Neukölln 2017).

Understanding the rent gap as an 'injection of a broader, global logic into a specific local political context' (Thörn & Holgersson 2016: 680) rather than as universalising and complete theory also means accounting for the 'semiotic side of gentrification' (ibid.: 72). While this was not Smith's primary concern in his original piece of 1979, it is clear from his subsequent writings on gentrification and the rent gap that he was very aware that it is not only the existence but the subsequent recognition and seizure of the rent gap that is of pivotal importance. During a visit in Berlin, Smith was, for example, asked whether an area like North Neukölln could in fact be considered 'too bad for gentrification'. His reply was telling:

> The question whether a particular neighbourhood will or will not gentrify depends on the depth of the rent gap and the particulars of local policy, but it also depends on many other local issues, neighbourhood characteristics and so on. If the rent gap is deep enough, I don't think any neighbourhood is 'too bad' for gentrification, but at the same time there is no guarantee that a particular neighbourhood will in fact be gentrified. (Smith 2007: 10)

All in all, the case of North Neukölln illustrates how local characteristics, such as a long history of stigmatisation, but also the existence of a strong community or low tenant turnover, can affect *how and when* rent gaps are widened and closed. In North Neukölln rental prices have increased around 1.5-fold since the late 2000s (Kluge 2019). Ground rents in the whole district, while being mostly stagnant between 2007 and 2015, more than doubled between 2015 and 2019 (Immoeinfach 2020). Whether this means that the rent gap in Neukölln is closed and sealed is difficult to predict – currently ground rents in the whole city are falling due to global inflation and crisis (though rents are still rising) (Bünger 2023). Whether a new rent gap trajectory will emerge after the current economic decline remains to be seen.

**Husby (Stockholm)**

Husby is a suburb in the northwest of Stockholm with approximately 11,500 inhabitants located in the borough of Rinkeby-Kista. Around 90 percent of residents have a minority background (as opposed to 33 percent in Stockholm) and income is around 40 percent below the Stockholm average and unemployment twice as high, making the neighbourhood one of the most ethnically segregated and disadvantaged in Sweden (Stockholms stad 2020). The area was built as part of Sweden's ambitious Million Homes program of the 1960s and 1970s, under which over a million affordable dwellings were constructed within a decade (see Figure 17.1).

As Christophers (2021) describes, together with the global economic crisis of the 1970s and curbed migration, vacancies in Stockholm's suburbs, such as Husby, rose, with no rent gap in sight. At the same time, a lack of investment into rental housing units of the Million Homes program era built up renovation needs (Baeten et al. 2017). Financial pressure and legal changes in the 1990s led public housing companies to sell to private investors. Moreover, in 2011, prompted by EU legislation, the Swedish government issued a law that mandated that public housing companies also had to become profitable (Grander 2019), further increasing the pressure to sell the slowly degrading housing stock and bringing them much closer to the conduct of private housing companies. The simultaneous move of selling combined with the changed rule of conduct for public housing companies sparked a wave of privatisation in the 2000s and 2010s, especially in Stockholm (Westerdahl 2021, Gustafsson 2021a: 98). In the 2000s internal and external migration started to rise again, prompting heightened demand.

Decades of under-construction fed into a shortage and, consequently, a crisis of affordable housing in all of Sweden's major cities. The specific way the rent gap opened in the – mostly underprivileged – suburbs of Sweden was thus related to the history of housing in the country, with a universalist, social-democratic approach in the post-war era that step-by-step was steered into a neoliberal direction (Grundström & Molina 2016).

*Source:* Miguel A. Martínez.

*Figure 17.1   Husby neighbourhood, Stockholm (2019)*

Both sharply rising demand and the renovation build-up made the housing stock in neighbourhoods like Husby, once it was up for sale, attractive to private investors. Since the late 1990s, the privatised rental in Husby (about 35 percent of the total stock in the area) has changed hands in rapid succession. Each of these owners – eight in total within 25 years, the first one being a Swedish private housing company, the current one being Vonovia, a German transnationally operating stock-listed housing giant that is currently Europe's biggest landlord – came out with a profit; however, none of them closed the rent gap completely during their ownership. As Christophers (2021: 6) describes for the Million Homes areas, previous companies only renovated a fraction of the apartments before they sold again. He ponders several reasons, such as high demand that makes housing profitable even without renovation, availability of capital, as well as regulatory frameworks that slow down such interventions.

What happened in neighbourhoods such as Husby in the last years is that companies engaged in so-called 'concept renovations', meaning they renovated each apartment individually once it was (for whatever reason) vacated. This allowed them to conduct renovation work without encountering much resistance. These renovations then included 'standard-raising' elements, such as floor heating or a kitchen renewal, that allowed the owners to increase rent substantially (around 40 to 50 percent) (Olsén & Björkvald 2019). Given the large number of units and the need to vacate the apartment, companies must ensure a relatively quick turnover rate, which leads to quick renovation work:

> It takes a month for them to renovate an apartment, a month! It should not be able to go so fast, it shows how badly and carelessly they renovate. (Interview with tenant, 2020)

This sort of quick concept renovation that includes rent-raising interventions that tenants often described as 'cosmetic' is a particular way of exploiting the rent gap: it increases the profit that can be made from closing the gap for each apartment. However, renovations do not stand alone as 'investment strategy' (Gustafsson 2021b) when it comes to producing and closing rent gaps. Tenants in Husby simultaneously experience delayed and poor maintenance, as well as multiple nuisances due to renovation work in neighbouring units. This can have several effects: first the renovation process might speed up because tenants become worn out and come under displacement pressure (Baeten et al. 2017, Polanska & Richard 2019, Pull & Richard 2021). This is also supported by the fact that the current landlord offers tenants deals to move into renovated apartments in the neighbourhoods, such as living in a renovated apartment with the old rent for six months. This can lead to quicker displacement and mobility-induced closure of the rent gap. Second, in the longer term, the rent gap can be further widened through this strategy (renovation and poor maintenance) if tenants agree to partial renovation works in their apartments that also raise the rent but do not (yet) amount to a full 'concept renovation':

> The toilet bowl has broken but they do not want to change it, they only want to renovate. I don't want to get a bad renovation and get a higher rent, then the toilet bowl stays. It's not right, they want 1000 kr extra a month to renovate the toilet. (Interview with tenant, 2020)

The case of Husby is exemplary for the role of the state in not only producing or articulating rent gaps but in preparing the legal ground on which rent gaps can be closed. The step-by-step deregulation of the Swedish housing market through weakened rental protections and changed rules of conduct for public housing companies that allowed private, often financialised, landlords to step in and seize the rent gap that had been produced by heightened demand, disinvestment, and financial pressure illustrates this. It is also a case that shows that economic actors can close rent gaps in different ways, generating different levels of profit along the way by, for example, putting pressure on tenants or incentivising them to move within the neighbourhood. Moreover, as Christophers (2021) has discussed, the developments in the Million Homes areas in Sweden over the last decades show that just because a rent gap is open and recognised it does not necessarily mean that it will be immediately seized. A lack of opportunity or incentive on the side of the investors/owners can delay the closure or drag it out over time, which, in turn, can lead to a distribution of the profit over several actors. In Husby, it was exactly because none of the owners had quickly engaged in a wholesome renewal that would close the rent gap that further selling was possible. Each of them, however, profited, even without a full closure. Shares for the acquisition of the housing stock in Husby more than doubled within three years from 2016 (when the stock was sold to a private-equity firm) and 2019 (when it was sold to the current owner). It is thus the non-closure of the gap that has made the housing stock attractive for each subsequent owner. Tenants are then not only confronted with rent-increase or maintenance issues but also with rapid ownership changes that exacerbate problems with communications with the landlord and increase tenants' precarity (Kadıoğlu et al. 2022).

The case of Husby also shows how rent gap theory can be applied to cases where gentrification-induced displacement is not (yet) visible. Reasons are multifold: first, neither Husby's location nor its modernist housing stock are particularly conducive to attracting pioneers or gentrifiers. Second, the current state of the Swedish housing market produces 'lock-in effects': tenants with secure contracts do not typically experience high rent increases if no renovation is conducted. These tenants then are unlikely to move simply because they will not be able to find another, affordable, rental in the city. Thus, they either endure problems around maintenance and communication, possibly accept smaller renovations with more incremental rent increases, or move within the neighbourhood (switching contracts with other tenants). All of this, however, does not mean that gentrification will never happen: in Husby's neighbouring area of Kista, Europe's largest technology park is growing, attracting 'expat' populations. If and when this might lead to gentrification along the way remains to be seen.

## CONCLUSIONS

Enmeshing social and political dimensions with the rent gap model entails complicating the rent gap model and accounting for the multiscalarity of the gentrification process (Teresa 2019: 1404). In this chapter I have suggested that three related conceptual moves can help to enhance rent gap theory and its applicability to specific instances of gentrification or other forms of reinvestment: distinction, extension, and finetuning.

By distinction I mean that the rent gap can be a useful analytical frame even in cases where no gentrification has (yet) occurred, at least not in the form of a comprehensive class transformation. Following scholars such as Brett Christophers, Ben Teresa, and Laura Calbet i Elias, I contended that this is particularly the case when financialised landlords invest into hitherto undiscovered (and from a gentrification standpoint unattractive) affordable housing stock.

By extension I mean that other concepts, for instance from sociology, political science, or anthropology, can be integrated into rent gap theory so as to understand why and along which specific pathway a neighbourhood is gentrifying (or not). Following scholars such as Tom Slater and Hamish Kallin, I have here discussed the role of territorial stigma in not only normalising gentrification but as an important symbolic structure that has the potential for widening rent gaps as well as enabling or forestalling their closure.

Finetuning then is another way rent gap theory can be more attuned to account for different empirical instances. Introducing temporality by divorcing the process of the production and existence of a rent gap from its closure is not only analytically fruitful but also opens a whole new set of possibilities for conceptual enrichment. Rather than assuming that rent gap theory is not true simply because gentrification does not follow it in some cases, one can now ask which factors – be it neighbourhood characteristics, histories of stigmatisation, national or metropolitan regulations, or developments on the global market – may inhibit the realisation of an identified rent gap. It is on researchers to find out why and how a rent gap closes in a specific case (or, precisely, not). The cases discussed here show that rent gap theory is not a predictor theory but a centrepiece in the explanation of gentrification and uneven urban development that can be fruitfully enriched with other concepts.

To sum up, rent gap theory is not an overpowering, all-encompassing law of nature but, on the contrary, a theory that allows us to identify and expose class interests in the gentrification process (Slater 2017a: 88), which is often efficiently disguised behind a thick veil of trickle-down economics (Holgersen & Baeten 2016), 'healthy' social mixing (Lees 2008), or 'false choice urbanism' (Slater 2014).

# REFERENCES

Amt für Statistik Berlin-Brandenburg (2019) Regionaler Sozialbericht Berlin und Brandenburg. Berlin. Retrieved from https://www.statistik-berlin-brandenburg.de/produkte/pdf/SP_Sozialbericht-000-000_DE_2019_BBB.pdf (accessed 3 September 2020).

August, M. & Walks, A. (2018) Gentrification, suburban decline, and the financialization of multi-family rental housing: The case of Toronto. *Geoforum* 89: 124–136.

Badcock, B. (1989) An Australian view of the rent gap hypothesis. *Annals of the Association of American Geographers* 79(1): 125–145.

Baeten, G., Westin, S., Pull, E. & Molina, I. (2017) Pressure and violence: Housing renovation and displacement in Sweden. *Environment and Planning A: Economy and Space* 49(3): 631–651.

Bernt, M. (2016) Very particular, or rather universal? Gentrification through the lenses of Ghertner and López-Morales. *City* 20(4): 637–644.

Bernt, M. (2022) *The Commodification Gap: Gentrification and Public Policy in London, Berlin and St. Petersburg*. London: Wiley.

Bourassa, S. C. (1993) The rent gap debunked. *Urban Studies* 30(10): 1731–1744.

Bourdieu, P., Droit, R. P. & Ferenczi, T. (2008) The left hand and the right hand of the state. *Variant* 32: 3–4.

Broadway Neukölln (2017) 101 Neukölln-Neustart im Kaufhaus. *Broadway*, No. 8 – 2016/2017. Retrieved from https://www.kms-sonne.de/broadway-8/101-neukoelln (accessed 3 September 2020).

Bünger, R. (2023) Breite Analyse des Marktes: Nun fallen auch in Berlin die Immobilienpreise. *Der Tagesspiegel*, 27 February. Retrieved from https://www.tagesspiegel.de/wirtschaft/immobilien/breite-analyse-des-immobilienmarktes-nun-fallen-auch-in-berlin-die-preise-9422264.html (accessed 27 February 2023).

Calbet i Elias, L. (2017) Financialised rent gaps and the public interest in Berlin's housing crisis: Reflections on N. Smith's 'generalised gentrification'. In Albet, A. & Banach, N. (eds.) *Gentrification as a Global Strategy. Neil Smith and Beyond*. New York: Routledge, 165–176.

Caulfield, J. (1989) 'Gentrification' and desire. *Canadian Review of Sociology/Revue canadienne de sociologie* 26(4): 617–632.

Christophers, B. (2021) Mind the rent gap: Blackstone, housing investment and the reordering of urban rent surfaces. *Urban Studies* 59(4): 698–716.

Clark, E. (1988) The rent gap and transformation of the built environment: Case studies in Malmö 1860–1985. *Geografiska Annaler: Series B, Human Geography* 70(2): 241–254.

Clark, E. (2014) Good urban governance: Making rent gap theory not true. *Geografiska Annaler: Series B, Human Geography* 96(4): 392–395.

Cowen, D., Harvey, D., Haraway, D., Rameau, M., Bacon, N., Bissen, M., ... & Miller, J. (2012) Neil Smith: A critical geographer. *Environment and Planning D: Society and Space* 30(6): 947–962.

Drew, E. M. (2012) 'Listening through white ears': Cross-racial dialogues as a strategy to address the racial effects of gentrification. *Journal of Urban Affairs* 34(1): 99–115.

Eick, V. (2012) The co-production of purified space: Hybrid policing in German Business Improvement Districts. *European Urban and Regional Studies* 19(2): 121–136.

Eksner, H. J. (2013) Revisiting the 'ghetto' in the New Berlin Republic: Immigrant youths, territorial stigmatisation and the devaluation of local educational capital, 1999–2010. *Social Anthropology* 21(3): 336–355.

Florida, R. L. (2005) *Cities and the Creative Class*. New York and London: Routledge.

Ghertner, D. A. (2015) Why gentrification theory fails in 'much of the world'. *City* 19(4): 552–563.

Grander, M. (2019) Off the beaten track? Selectivity, discretion and path-shaping in Swedish public housing. *Housing, Theory and Society* 36(4), 385–400.

Grundström, K. & Molina, I. (2016) From Folkhem to lifestyle housing in Sweden: Segregation and urban form, 1930s–2010s. *International Journal of Housing Policy* 16(3): 316–336.

Gustafsson, J. (2021a) Spatial, financial and ideological trajectories of public housing in Malmö, Sweden. *Housing, Theory and Society* 38(1): 95–114. https://doi.org/10.1080/02673037.2021.1982872.

Gustafsson, J. (2021b) Renovations as an investment strategy: Circumscribing the right to housing in Sweden. *Housing Studies*, 1–22. https://doi.org/10.1080/02673037.2021.1982872

Hackworth, J. & Smith, N. (2001) The changing state of gentrification. *Tijdschrift voor economische en sociale geografie* 92(4): 464–477.

Hammel, D. J. (1999) Re-establishing the rent gap: An alternative view of capitalised land rent. *Urban Studies* 36(8): 1283–1293.

Hamnett, C. (1991) The blind men and the elephant: The explanation of gentrification. *Transactions of the Institute of British Geographers* 16(2): 173–189.

Harvey, D. (1973) *Social Justice and the City*. London: Edward Arnold.

Häußermann, H., Dohnke, J. & Förste, D. (2008) *Trendanalyse der Entwicklung von Neukölln und Neukölln-Nord im Vergleich zu Berlin insgesamt und zu anderen Teilgebieten in Berlin*. Berlin: res urbana.

Holgersen, S. & Baeten, G. (2016) Beyond a liberal critique of 'trickle down': Urban planning in the City of Malmö. *International Journal of Urban and Regional Research* 40(6): 1170–1185.

Holm, A. (2006). Urban renewal and the end of social housing: The roll out of neoliberalism in East Berlin's Prenzlauer Berg. *Social Justice* 33(3): 114–128.

Holm, A. (2013). Berlin's gentrification mainstream. In Bernt, M., Grell, B. & Holm, A. (eds.) *The Berlin Reader. A Compendium of Urban Change and Activism*. Berlin: transcript, 171–188.

Immoeinfach (2020) Immobilienpreise Berlin Neukölln 2020. Retrieved from https://immoeinfach.de/immobilienpreise/berlin/neukoelln/ (accessed 24 April 2023).

Kadıoğlu, D. (2022) Producing gentrifiable neighborhoods: Race, stigma and struggle in Berlin-Neukölln. *Housing Studies*, 1–23. https://doi.org/10.1080/02673037.2022.2042494

Kadıoğlu, D., Kellecioğlu, I. & Listerborn, C (2022) Transnationella bostadsbolag, ägarbyten och lokal organisering bland hyresgäster. In Bengtsson, B., Holdo, M. & Holmqvist, E. (eds.) *Allas Rätt till Bostad*. Gothenburg: Daidalos, 275–291.

Kallin, H. (2017) Opening the reputational gap. In Kirkness, P. & Tije-Dra, A. (eds.) *Negative Neighbourhood Reputation and Place Attachment*. London: Routledge, 102–118.

Kellecioğlu, I. (2021) *Rapport inifrån 'Hemblahelvetet'. Röster från Hemblas bostäder i Husby*. Malmö: Malmö University.

Kluge, C. (2019) Mieten in Neukölln in zehn Jahren um 146 Prozent gestiegen. *Der Tagesspiegel*, 5 May. Retrieved from https://www.tagesspiegel.de/berlin/langzeitstudie-zum-berliner-mietenmarkt-mieten-in-neukoelln-in-zehn-jahren-um-146-prozent-gestiegen/24312280.html (accessed 14 October 2022).

Krätke, S. (2004) Economic restructuring and the making of a financial crisis: Berlin's socio-economic development path 1989 to 2004. *disP – The Planning Review* 40(156): 58–63.

Krijnen, M. (2018) Gentrification and the creation and formation of rent gaps: Opening up gentrification theory to global forces of urban change. *City* 22(3): 437–446.

Lees, L. (2003) Super-gentrification: The case of Brooklyn Heights, New York City. *Urban Studies* 40(12): 2487–2509.

Lees, L. (2008) Gentrification and social mixing: Towards an inclusive urban renaissance? *Urban Studies* 45(12): 2449–2470.

Lees, L., Shin, H. B. & López-Morales, E. (2016) *Planetary Gentrification*. Cambridge: Polity.

Ley, D. (1980) Liberal ideology and the postindustrial city. *Annals of the Association of American Geographers* 70(2): 238–258.

Ley, D. (1987) Reply: The rent gap revisited. *Annals of the Association of American Geography* 77(3): 465–468.

Ley, D. (1996) *The New Middle Class and the Remaking of the Central City*. Oxford: Oxford University Press.

Millard-Ball, A. (2000) Moving beyond the gentrification gaps: Social change, tenure change and gap theories in Stockholm. *Urban Studies* 37(9): 1673–1693.

Mösgen, A., Rosol, M. & Schipper, S. (2019) State-led gentrification in previously 'un-gentrifiable' areas: Examples from Vancouver/Canada and Frankfurt/Germany. *European Urban and Regional Studies* 26(4): 419–433.

Olsén P. & Björkvald M. (2019) *Konceptrenoveringens konsekvenser. Ekonomiska och socioekonomiska effekter*. Stockholm: Hyresgästföreningen.

O'Sullivan, D. (2002) Toward micro-scale spatial modeling of gentrification. *Journal of Geographical Systems* 4(3): 251–274.

Pinkster, F. M., Ferier, M. S. & Hoekstra, M. S. (2020) On the stickiness of territorial stigma: Diverging experiences in Amsterdam's most notorious neighbourhood. *Antipode* 52(2): 522–541.

Polanska, D. & Richard, Å. (2019) Narratives of a fractured trust in the Swedish model: Tenants' emotions of renovation. *Culture Unbound. Journal of Current Cultural Research* 11(1): 141–164.

Pull, E. & Richard, Å. (2021) Domicide: Displacement and dispossessions in Uppsala, Sweden. *Social & Cultural Geography* 22(4): 545–564.

Rose, D. (1984) Rethinking gentrification: Beyond the uneven development of Marxist urban theory. *Environment and Planning D: Society and Space* 2(1): 47–74.

Schultz Larsen, T. & Delica, K. N. (2021) Territorial destigmatization in an era of policy schizophrenia. *International Journal of Urban and Regional Research* 45(3): 423–441.

Shin, H. B. (2019) Planetary gentrification: What it is and why it matters. *Space, Society and Geographical Thought* 22: 127–137.

Slater, T. (2014) Unravelling false choice urbanism. *City* 18(4–5): 517–524.

Slater, T. (2016) Revanchism, stigma, and the production of ignorance: Housing struggles in austerity Britain. In Soederberg, S. (ed.) *Risking Capitalism*. Bingley: Emerald Group Publishing Limited, 23–48.

Slater, T. (2017a) Clarifying Neil Smith's rent gap theory of gentrification. *Tracce urbane. Rivista italiana transdisciplinare di studi urbani* 1: 83–101.

Slater, T. (2017b) Planetary rent gaps. *Antipode* 49: 114–137.

Smith, N. (1979) Toward a theory of gentrification: A back to the city movement by capital, not people. *Journal of the American Planning Association* 45(4): 538–548.

Smith, N. (1987) Gentrification and the rent gap. *Annals of the Association of American Geographers* 77(3): 462–465.

Smith, N. (1992) Blind man's buff, or Hamnett's philosophical individualism in search of gentrification. *Transactions of the Institute of British Geographers* 17(1): 110–115.

Smith, N. (1996) *The New Urban Frontier: Gentrification and the Revanchist City*. New York and London: Routledge.

Smith, N. (2007) Interview mit Prof. Dr. Neil Smith von der City University New York. *MieterEcho* 324: 9–12. Berliner Mietergemeinschaft. Retrieved from https://www.bmgev.de/mieterecho/324/06-gentrifizierung-neukoelln-ah.html (accessed 15 December 2021).

Stockholms stad (2020) *Områdesfakta Husby Stadsdel*. Retrieved from https://start.stockholm/globalassets/start/om-stockholms-stad/utredningar-statistik-och-fakta/statistik/omradesfakta/vasterort/rinkeby-kista/husby.pdf (accessed 15 December 2021).

Sýkora, L. (1993) City in transition: The role of rent gaps in Prague's revitalization. *Tijdschrift voor economische en sociale geografie* 84(4): 281–293.

Teresa, B. F. (2019) New dynamics of rent gap formation in New York City rent-regulated housing: Privatization, financialization, and uneven development. *Urban Geography* 40(10): 1399–1421.

Thörn, C. & Holgersson, H. (2016) Revisiting the urban frontier through the case of New Kvillebäcken, Gothenburg. *City* 20(5): 663–684.

Wachsmuth, D. & Weisler, A. (2018) Airbnb and the rent gap: Gentrification through the sharing economy. *Environment and Planning A: Economy and Space* 50(6): 1147–1170.

Wacquant, L. J. (1996) The rise of advanced marginality: Notes on its nature and implications. *Acta sociologica* 39(2): 121–139.

Westerdahl, S. (2021) *Det självspelande pianot: Kalkylerna och kapitalet som skapar Sveriges bostadskris.* Stockholm: Dokument Press.

Wright, M. W. (2014) The gender, place and culture Jan Monk distinguished annual lecture: Gentrification, assassination and forgetting in Mexico: A feminist Marxist tale. *Gender, Place & Culture* 21(1): 1–16.

Yung, C. F. & King, R. J. (1998) Some tests for the rent gap theory. *Environment and Planning A* 30(3): 523–542.

Zukin, S. (2008) Consuming authenticity: From outposts of difference to means of exclusion. *Cultural Studies* 22(5): 724–748.

# 18. School choices and gentrification in late capitalist cities: the neighborhood as a distinction strategy of the middle class[1]
*Carlotta Caciagli*

Gentrification is one of the most characteristic processes of late capitalist Western cities. It has multiple and widespread effects on urban transformation, determining many socio-economic inequalities. The process has been widely analyzed from many points of view and nowadays we have a rich inventory of its main drivers. Nevertheless, gentrification still appears as a chaotic and conflictual process in many aspects (Beauregard 2013). This is in part because, across time and space, gentrification develops toward different forms and dynamics. Indeed, as neoliberalism it intersects differently and heterogeneously with national and urban regimes (Brenner et al. 2010). In part its obscurity is related to the variegated impact of this urban transformation in different subsets of population.

To make things easier, we can say that studies on gentrification can be grouped in two branches: those concentrating on the supply side and those looking at the demand side. The first strand of research focuses on the material side of gentrification, underling the objective conditions that allow the process to nurture. Scholars inquiring in this direction argue that gentrification occurs mainly because of the rent gap; that is "the disparity between the potential ground level and the actual rent capitalized under the present land use" (Smith 1979: 545). When the gap is wide enough, landlords, builders, and many other professional developers start investing in the area and profiting from urban rehabilitation. According to this perspective, the necessary condition for gentrification is the presence of a geographical area with the structural and architectural potentialities to be renewed.

A second analytical approach looks at gentrification by focusing on the demand side. Scholars assuming this perspective argue that to trigger gentrification it is not enough to have new capital investments in an area, we also need "potential gentrifiers" (Beauregard 2013), social groups attracted by living in inner city environments (Hamnett 1991) and for whom the life in the area works as a mechanism of class distinction (Jager 1986). These social groups, considered to correspond to certain subsets of middle classes, pave the way for new demand for housing, leisure, and retail. The demand-side has been and still is a crucial perspective for inquiring about gentrification. Not by chance, tastes and values of middle and upper classes are also named as the main vectors by Ruth Glass, who first coined the notion of gentrification. She wrote that:

> One by one many of the working class quarters of London have been invaded by the middle classes—upper and lower… Once this process of 'gentrification' starts in a district it goes on rapidly until all or most of the original working class occupiers are displaced and the whole social character of the district is changed. (Glass 1964: 18–19)

On the base of her pioneering studies, scholars paid increasing attention to the interconnection between real estate (supply-side) changes and the development of middle-class choices, tastes, and preferences. However, while the studies on the supply side can be grouped in a homogeneous body of literature, the research on the demand side has been much more fragmented. Indeed, to set the boundaries of the social group or groups responsible for gentrification is challenging.

Some scholars identified in the "creative class" the typical gentrifiers. The creative class could be defined as those people who add value from their creativity (Florida 2004: 165). Part of this group are artists, engineers, intellectuals, and other similar professionals. Nevertheless, these subjects are far away from constituting a homogeneous social group. They differ largely in income, social, and political background. Moreover, scholars have pointed out that different gentrifiers contribute to change the neighborhood through diverse dynamics because they are attracted by different features of the same areas. Young people pave the way for gentrification by looking for trendy bars and underground culture. On the other hand, adults are more likely to look for agreeable public spaces, specific housing features, and the presence of a certain type of school for their children. Despite this heterogeneity, most of the studies fail to unpack the broad universe in which the middle class and gentrification enmesh with one another. That is why we nowadays are aware of the broad mechanisms linking urban transformation and the middle class but we do not know how exactly this process is reproduced by different types of people and also in different periods of their lives. The research at the base of this chapter hopes to contribute to partially filling these gaps by exploring a specific subset of the middle class in a specific moment of their lives to understand deeply a small piece in the chain of choices and preferences that are at the base of gentrification.

Most notably, this chapter accounts for the school choices of middle-class parents. In particular, I base the analysis on a specific portion of middle-class families: the highly educated, professional parents characterized by high cultural capital and not necessarily by high economical capital. As we will see in the forthcoming sections, the literature on school choices and inequalities focuses largely on what could be called "intellectual" parents (Van Zanten 2009), debating their values and priorities but recognizing their main role in reproducing school inequalities. In my research I acknowledge this role and I want to inquire into it deeply, exploring the social construction beyond school choices and preferences. Two main points emerge. Firstly, the territory plays a crucial role in decision-making processes around the school. Indeed, the relationship with the neighborhood is revealed to be a distinguishing value for this social group. Secondly, this approach to the neighborhood, alongside other factors already pointed out by the literature, contributes to the creation of school inequalities by polarizing a group of pupils in some schools, so constructing homogeneous classes in a socially mixed area. By accounting for this process, I aim at providing new instruments to understand the complexity of gentrification in contemporary cities.

The chapter is organized as follows. In the next section I explore the theoretical debate on the middle class, school choices, and socio-spatial inequalities. The following section illustrates and discusses the results of the two-year ethnographic research that I conducted in Affori, a neighborhood of Milan (Italy). In the last section I provide some conclusions that highlight the potentialities of continuing to work around middle-class school choices to understand the multiple paths and effects of gentrification in contemporary cities.

## THE MIDDLE CLASS AND SCHOOL CHOICES: A THEORETICAL LENS TO UNDERSTAND GENTRIFICATION PATHS

The analytical perspective on the demand side of gentrification is crucial and puzzling at the same time. Setting the boundaries of the middle class has always being challenging for sociologists. However, following in the footsteps of Bourdieu, scholars agree in highlighting, on top of the economic dimension, the peculiarity of the middle-class roots in the continuous attempt to distinguish themselves from other social groups (Devine & Savage 2000, Savage et al. 2015) through choices, lifestyles, and attitudes. Thus, they agree in saying that the core of the middle class has to be retraced in distinction-seeking practices and aspirations.

The socially mixed and ethnically diverse environment that such neighborhoods under requalification offer fits well with the multi-cultural attitudes and aesthetic taste of the middle class. In particular, the literature points out that in post-Foridist societies great attention should be paid to lifestyle choices in constructing social groups. Indeed, with the increasing precarization of the labor market, professional knowledge workers have also emerged and increased, people not gathered together by working in the same workplace but by the fact of having high social and cultural capital. At the same time and contrary to what used to be in Fordist times, high cultural and educational resources no more go hand in hand with high income and economic resources. Many studies have explored the correlation between these structural changes in society and the real essence of gentrification (see Gourzis et al. 2022).

Contrary to the elitism of the upper classes, the characteristic of the middle class that fits and triggers gentrification is their "omnivore" attitude (Peterson & Kern 1996). The middle class's aim to distinguish themselves from the lower classes does not pass through highbrow taste or places to live but through the attempt to adopt and live in mainstream and popular places while giving them a new meaning. As Janna Michael pointed out, the search for "authenticity" drives the habits and lifestyles of the urban middle class in post-industrial and contemporary times (Michael 2013), working as a social group recognition mechanism. These reflections match with what some authors said about post-Fordism. They have identified this era as featuring a symbolic economy that produces culture for consumption as well as spaces (Drew 2011: 103). Thus, the distinction of different social groups develops over the living spaces in daily life. In this sense, space becomes a dimension to accumulate symbolic capital (Valli 2021). Put in other terms, there is a struggle around place-making in the way a space is commodified, used, and lived. This happens not just through the displacement of lower classes (Marcuse 1986) but also through the construction of a local environment that follows and reproduces interests and possibilities of specific social groups. Despite this awareness, the relationship between the middle class and space-making is still underexplored.

First of all, existing studies concentrate mainly on the housing dimension and the displacement mechanisms that middle-class gentrifiers put in place. In this sense, the analysis of housing trajectories represents the main field explored to understand how middle classes design the local space and reproduce their social group. Secondly, existing studies have focused principally on the consumption dimension, leaving aside an analysis of how the cultural dimension connects with places. For example, education, which is considered a mark of cultural capital, has been approached as a part of consumption practices. Nevertheless, education is a pivot mechanism around which many choices, habits, and processes are triggered. This has been assumed by the literature on school segregation, which has shown well how choices around education go beyond the educational field. They reproduce many socio-economic inequalities, so they are also a matter of urban transformation. For these reasons I consider it to be worthy to create a more in-depth dialogue between the literature on the demand side of gentrification and that on school choices and segregation.

From the culturalist turn, the idea that the school realm touches broader aspects than those related just to culture itself has been consolidated. School reflects and exacerbates socio-economic differences, working also as a social reproduction device for the upper classes (Bourdieu 1979). Thus, the sociological interest in school goes beyond the sociology of education. Indeed, a branch of urban sociology has inquired extensively into this issue, exploring the patterns of socio-spatial segregation nurtured by education. School segregation can be defined as the uneven distribution across schools of pupils on the basis of inequalities in terms of socio-economic, ethnic, or other social characteristics (Ball 2003, Boterman et al. 2019). Scholars have identified three main drivers of school segregation: the educational system; the residential distribution of the population, which is linked to the unequal access to housing; and parents' agency.

The educational system varies across countries: in some countries there is no possibility of choice and pupils are forced to attend the neighboring school, or better said, the one for their catchment area. In other countries there is a market (or quasi-market) system, in which the schools can be selected across the whole city (or in which the priority is given to proximal pupils but you can ask to attend a school that is not in your catchment area). In the first case, school segregation is more likely to reproduce residential and housing segregation; in the second case, the two forms of segregation are enmeshed in a more complex way. To better understand inequalities within the second type of system, which is in force in Italy, scholars have focused extensively on parents' behavior, preferences, and expectations. This opens the field to parents' agency analysis.

A fruitful field of studies concentrates on the school choices and preferences of parents when selecting the educational paths of their children (Reay & Ball 1997, Van Zanten 2009, Vincent & Ball 2006, 2007). Among scholars, the idea that parental behavior regarding schools is very composite and often does not follow a rational choice mechanism has been corroborated. Modes of preference formation differ according to social classes, race, and household habits, resulting in different parental styles. According to many scholars, middle-class parents invest more in children's education while the working class, because of their lack of economic and cultural resources, are less engaged in their children's curriculum and extra-curricular activities (Haylett 2003, Lareau 2003). Thanks to the increasing studies on the topic this assumption has been problematized and a richer and variegated picture emerged.

Ball and Vincent (1998) suggest that the polarization between well-informed middle-class parents and badly informed working-class parents, even when it exists, is socially constructed, related to the difficulties for low-skilled people of dealing with the school institution, which is constructed on the basis of middle-class competences and resources. Many studies also corroborate the idea that middle-class parents refer to a system of values that is different from the working class, giving importance to academic curricula more than practical tasks, but these two systems of values should not be put on a hierarchical ladder. This simply means that they look for different information for decision-making (Hastings et al. 2007).

Some scholars directly put into relation school choice and space. In particular, they have made the impact of school choices on housing market dynamics emerge (Wilson & Bridge 2019). Indeed, middle-class families often decide where to live on the basis of the school they want their children to attend. To this extent, school choices explain, at least partially, the housing patterns in contemporary cities. Other studies, much more focused on a long-term perspective, have demonstrated the role played by the presence of schools with a high reputation in increasing the housing costs of inner-city neighborhoods. In this sense, schooling mechanisms have been recognized as one of the drivers fostering gentrification through housing markets changes.

While the relationship between school choices and socio-spatial inequalities has been largely recognized, it has also been overlooked. This is in part due to the empirical difficulties of disentangling the relationship at the neighborhood level, distinguishing individual behaviors and social patterns (Maloutas et al. 2013). Thus, scholars succeed in explaining the impact of choice on the territory but not the impact of the territory in forging the choice. This is weird because sociology always recognizes the spatial dimension of any social phenomenon (Castells 1983, Sassen 2012, Smith 2002). Additionally, when scholars analyze different patterns of choice, they divide them into two clusters – middle class and working class – assuming people act differently between them but homogeneously within them. This has led many studies to take for granted the working class as not-choosing actors who stay in the proximal schools because of practical reasons. In contrast, in recent decades some studies have shown how choosing local schools could also be part of the distinguishing values of the middle class, as well as the racial diversity (Raveaud & Van Zanten 2007). However, few studies have explored this deeply within the middle class (Cordini 2019), and a coherent analysis of the different approaches to local schools of different profiles of middle-class families is still missing.

These gaps in the analyses are in part due to the fact that scholars have dealt with parental choices by considering them mainly as something made by parents for the future of their children, thus considering choices as strategies to maintain or increase class privileges and positions. This approach risks neglecting the broad realm that school takes into account. School is a complex institution that involves the active participation of adults, whether they are teachers, deans, or parents. Thus, school choices cannot only be looked as functional for the future of the children but should be analyzed in a broader sense as sets of decisions that are rooted in the present and have impact on adults' relationships and social group formation.

The research discussed in this chapter hopes to partially contribute to filling these gaps by focusing on a specific profile of middle-class families and inscribing the school choices in a more composite picture that takes together pupils and parents.

## SCHOOL CHOICES AND GENTRIFICATION IN MILAN (ITALY)

The data at the base of this chapter come from a two-year ethnographical study I conducted during 2020 and 2022 in Milan (Italy) on the topic of school segregation and parental choices for primary school. The research represents an in-depth study of Affori, a neighborhood in the northern part of Milan that is going through a gentrification process. The spatial features of this neighborhood make it a very desirable place to live. First of all, it is a quite peripheral area but extremely well-connected to the city center and also to surrounding towns. Indeed, there are two metro stations of the underground that bring passengers directly to the central station in less than twenty minutes; moreover, there is a train station from which many trains depart to the surrounding metropolitan cities. Secondly, its architectural and infrastructural features make it a very pleasant zone (see Figure 18.1). Affori has working-class origins but the bourgeoisie always lived in some areas of the neighborhood. Differently from the nearby industrial areas that were configured as factory neighborhoods, the urban development of Affori followed a different path. Indeed, even if it was part of an industrial district, there were no big factories or warehouses. Therefore, working-class people living here were employed in nearby neighborhoods. People I interviewed talked about a double soul of Affori: on the one side inhabited by immigrants and on the other side by the aristocracy and upper classes for a long time.

Due to the many green areas, pedestrian zones, and enjoyable houses, Affori has been progressively targeted by young, middle-class people as a good place for families. This was confirmed by the association members and local activists I interviewed. As I could witness and reconstruct, gentrification is not occurring through massive changes in retail or through the targeting of this area for nightlife for young people (which is also because of the distance to the main universities of Milan) but rather through changes in the housing market. Many adults with children decide to move here and those who are from this neighborhood decide to stay put because the life here is considered to be sustainable. Additionally, Affori's educational offers for primary school are quite rich. Besides many nursery schools, there are three public schools and two private ones. Moreover, schools are close to one another and can be easily reached from any part of Affori by walking or by bicycle, as indeed many parents do.

The Italian school regime is a quasi-market one: even if pupils are assigned to a catchment area, parents can decide to enroll them in a different school. Due to the autonomy of every school, principals can decide the criteria to accept children: usually the priority is given to those of the catchment area but places are also reserved for pupils residing in other areas. Looking at Affori schools, the data show that in 2020 and 2021 many pupils moved from the school of the catchment area to another one. Most of them selected another school in the same neighborhood. Due to this, the three public schools have different user profiles despite the social mix that features in Affori. This is not an uncommon phenomenon; indeed, the social mix of the neighborhood does not necessarily represent an improvement for the underprivileged pupils (Kadıoğlu 2021). The school Don Orione is placed at the very core of the neighborhood, at 4 Via Fabriano. Among the three schools it is the one with the higher profile and with the lowest number of migrant pupils. The school Caracciolo, on Via Iseo in the most external area of the neighborhood, is a more mixed one. Lastly, the school on Via Scialoia named Italo Calvino is the most segregated one. Indeed, it has the highest number of foreign pupils and a large part of the parents, looking at data about income and education, can be described as part of the working class.[2] The polarization of pupils makes this neighborhood a good case to explore the reasons for and effects of middle-class school choices.

In this ethnographic study I collected 25 interviews with parents of children attending one of the three local and public schools. In this chapter, excerpts of eight interviews are quoted. I targeted parents ascribable to the category of intellectuals as already explored by Agnes Van Zanten (2009) but with some specificities. I defined the category of intellectuals as people with high cultural and educational capital working in creative or intellectual sectors. Indeed, the families I describe here were composed of at least one person with a master's degree (in most families both parents held a university degree). In many cases the two parents had high-skilled jobs. In two cases just one member of the family did not work but he/she had a university qualification. In three cases they were mixed-race families.

I decided to inquire into this subset of the middle class because they have been recognized by the existing literature as the most responsible for school inequalities in market and quasi-market regimes. As I touched on in the introduction, many authors have stressed the fact that high-skilled parents are more inclined to make an exit choice and send their children to high-performance schools with specific academic curricula and high popularity (Allen & Burgess 2013). For example, Gomez et al. (2012) demonstrated how the importance given to test scores increases with family income. According to these studies, this occurs because middle-class families tend to have higher cultural capital that pushes them to consider this dimension more important than others. These types of parents are also responsible for so-called "white flight" (Cordini et al. 2019, Pacchi & Ranci 2017), which is the tendency of the white middle class to avoid local schools in mixed neighborhoods in order to attend more homogeneous, even if not proximal, schools. According to these studies, the fact of staying put in a neighborhood should be interpreted like the approach of passive parents, who have been mainly identified with working-class parents (Reay & Ball 1997).

Nevertheless, other studies that specifically stressed the link between school choices and gentrified neighborhoods highlighted an opposite trend. For example, according to some authors, low-income families are much more likely to consider academic factors, maybe because they aim at improving their social position through their children becoming pupils, while high-income families are instead attracted by the racial mixture of schools, considering cosmopolitanism a distinguishing value of their class (Kleitz et al. 2000, Olson Beal & Munro Hendry 2012). Therefore, to stay put in the local school can become a choice for a subset of the middle class (Raveaud & Van Zanten 2007). The research I conducted in Milan helps to deepen the understanding of the choices of local schools by middle-class families, as well as the reasons for and effects of these choices. The research presented here adds some important nuances of meanings to the already existing knowledge on this topic. In particular, the relationship with the neighborhood is revealed to be a core asset around which the decision-making process develops, prioritized over other aspects of the school experience.

First of all, in all the interviews the presence of immigrants was framed as an added value because it represents a "significant pedagogical experience" for children. The academic dimension was almost never mentioned as the main criterion parents looked at. In some cases, when I asked them, interviewees demonstrated that they were prepared about the academic differences between schools, telling me that they took different curricula into account, but it was not a determining factor for the final decision. In contrast, the good mix between natives and immigrants was considered a determining factor and this was reported to me even without asking. As these interviewees testified:

> I'm absolutely not concerned about the presence of immigrants, not at all. I want to be in the public school because of this: I don't want to make my son grow up in a bubble. The world is not like the one you have in a private school and I don't think I do the best for my son if I decide to cut him off from the diversity that exists in the world. (Int. 1, social media manager, February 9, 2021)

> My daughters' best friends are immigrants, but can I really name them 'immigrants'? I don't think so. They speak Italian better than me. So, I don't care. It makes no sense to look at the color of children to evaluate a school. (Int. 2, manager of a sport society, March 15, 2021)

Most of the parents think that, quoting an interviewee, the "humanity lesson" is even more important than the eventually problematic learning processes when a class is heterogeneous. This does not mean that interviewees were not concerned about the pedagogical goals; indeed, most of them put the ethnic composition of the class in relation to the possibility of having a learning gap. Nevertheless, most of them told me that they were ready to fill the gaps with private lessons. For example, many of them stated that their children attended private

English classes and in their free time parents themselves stimulated pupils with cultural experiences, such as working labs for children or organizing museum visits. To this extent, this decision-making process was shown to have a class connotation. Indeed, the decision to give priority to human lessons over learning notions was based on the cultural and educational capital that families could dispose of.

*Source:* Carlotta Caciagli.

*Figure 18.1  Square in a gentrified area of Milan, next to Affori neighborhood (2021)*

Despite the positive approach of parents to immigrants, we can witness a polarization of children in the three schools. Most of the Italians living in this catchment area decided to enroll children in one of the other schools, mainly the one on Via Fabriano, which is the nearest one. In the school on Via Scialoia we found few parents with a bachelor's degree and the income per family was lower than in the other two schools. The numbers and the interviews corroborated what was already pointed out by Boterman (2013): that the presence of immigrants is welcome as long as the numbers are kept under control; i.e. low. When I asked parents about this point, the reasons they put forward were interesting.

Parents explained the desire not to have too many migrants because a high number could prevent a good relationship among the local parents with whom they felt they could construct a relationship. So, to decide whether to exit or not from the catchment area, they looked mainly at who the users were, meaning the parents. These excerpts of interviews are paradigmatic:

> I took into account at least three schools but then I selected the one on Via Iseo because of the users. I carefully watched the faces of parents waiting in front of the school and I figured out the typologies. The school on Via Iseo seemed to me to have a better profile. (Int. 3, employee in communication enterprise, May 4, 2021).

> I finally selected Via Fabriano because of the parents attending the other school of the catchment area. I had a terrible experience with my first daughter because of the parents. They were not collaborative, they didn't participate in school activities. They were not immigrants, they were Italians but with fewer instruments than us, less educated. It has been hard to construct a community because of them. So for my son I selected another school that was advised by another mom who is also a friend of mine. (Int. 4, employee in a publishing company, February 26, 2021)

> I think that when you find good vibes with the other parents everything is gonna be all right for you and your children. It is normal… you need to be lucky and find parents like you. (Int. 5, engineer, March 17, 2021)

This deliberative process seemed to be applied not just to those perceived to be part of the lower classes or immigrants but also to upper-class people. Indeed, families who had the economic possibility of letting their children attend the private schools decided not to do so. Their trust in the public school was stated as the main reason, as well as the parents, who were, however, considered different to them, even with a different perspective:

> It is exactly the same thing: I have nothing in common with the bumpkin of Via Iseo, and I have nothing in common with these upper-class schools which consider immigrants to be a problem. I'm far away from both. I would never bring my children to a school in which social inclusion is not a value because I would not have any type of relationship with the parents and it would be problematic for the growth of my children too. (Int. 4, employee in a publishing company, February 26, 2021)

What is also interesting to note is that the perception of a school attended by "people like us" varied largely among parents. Indeed, parents recognized similar users in different schools. Parents who were in the catchment area of Via Iseo, for example, considered the school on Via Iseo as their best option, often choosing to not change school. At the same time, those living in the catchment area of Via Scialoia or of Via Iseo but in a more central position in the neighborhood perceived Via Fabriano as better than the other two.

My daily presence in the field made me establish a connection with the different surrounding spaces in which the schools are inserted. The school on Via Iseo is placed in the north part of the neighborhood, and the two proximal neighborhoods are inhabited by many immigrants and low-income families. Middle-class families living near Via Iseo compared this school to other ones placed in popular neighborhoods. Looking at the mix of people, they perceived Via Iseo as the most "white" and "middle-class" one. At the same time, many of the parents in the catchment area of Via Iseo but in the more central part compared the users of Via Iseo with those of Via Fabriano and they perceived the latter as the best option. In a nutshell, depending on where families live and the part of the neighborhood they frequent, the same school can be considered a good or a bad option. This also means that the parents' perception is highly shaped by the very immediate daily life spaces. As this interviewee points out:

> My catchment area was the one on Via Fabriano but I decided to move my child to the school on Via Iseo. We are exactly in between the two schools, so it is not a matter of home-to-school distance. However, I prefer the other part of the neighborhood: my children go to the swimming pool that is near there, our friends live near there... Via Iseo is our corner in the neighborhood. (Int. 6, employee in an insurance company, April 1, 2021)

Few words more need to be spent on this point. Studies in the literature have already pointed out that the process of preference formation does not follow a rational path but is informed by beliefs and prejudices that are shaped beside the so-called "hot grapevine" (Ball & Vincent 1998). Parents, in particular the middle-class ones, largely rely on the comments and judgments of people of their social circuits. This research goes a step further, indicating that this mechanism is extremely related to space. Parents said that in order to make a decision they go directly in front of the schools, but they also look for advice from people they associate with in their daily life in the neighborhood. A lot of parents said that they ended up with a decision mainly by asking moms they met at the park. This excerpt of an interview is an example:

> Well, I'm not so confident about the open days or the website information. Of course you will never find in the school website somebody who tells you, 'oh, this school is not good'. That is why I preferred to ask parents I know. I wanted the other mothers at the park to tell me, 'you can go there, it has been a great experience for us'. (Int. 7, housewife, June 18, 2021)

A large part of the studies around education and class consider the school realm as the occasion for the middle and upper classes to pass down and increase their class privileges in the future (Bourdieu & Passeron 1970). Thus, school decisions have been analyzed as made *by* parents *for* their sons and daughters. From this ethnographic study we can see how school decisions are about the parents' relationships in the present and their attempts to be part of a social group. As we have seen, the reasons at the base of school selection cannot be ascribed only to practical concerns. Indeed, in Affori the schools are very close to one another and in many cases the parents are placed halfway between at least two schools.

Even when parents decide to exit from the catchment area, they stay put in the neighborhood. This happens despite the presence in the surrounding area of two other public schools placed in the proximal neighborhood of Niguarda, which in recent years became very popular among middle- and upper-class families because of the innovative approach they have. Most of the parents I talked to told me they had considered these other schools but in the end opted for the local ones. The explanations are related from different angles to their relationship with the neighborhood. These excerpts of interviews demonstrate this point:

> Yes, I know very well the school in Niguarda and I'm sure it is a wonderful school. Nevertheless, I start from the assumption that I stay put in the neighborhood. Maybe if my daughters had special needs, I would have made another choice. But they have no problems so why should I select another school and uproot them from their environment? They live here and they have to relate to what they find here. Furthermore, here it is not Bronx! (Int. 8, educator, May 20, 2021)

Some other parents explicitly prioritized the relationship with the neighborhood over the alternative approach of the schools:

> Well, I think that the relationship with the neighborhood is even more important than the best program in the world. It is important for him [the son] after school to meet his peers at the park. Imagine: for

the birthday party nobody from the school would come because his friends would not be around. (Int. 1, social media manager, February 9, 2021)

School is considered not just for the learning process but for the broad universe of relationships gravitating around it. This is perceived to be important as well as the scholastic notions:

> What happens surrounding the school is as important as what happens in the school. I like him to feel part of a community. If not, it is like me: I work near the station and it is my workplace but not my home, it is not a place I know and am part of. I don't want my child to be like that. (Int. 4, employee in a publishing company, February 26, 2021)

The need to decide in favor of school performance or in favor of the relationship with the neighborhood can also be a dilemma for parents. Nevertheless, they often privileged the latter:

> This [to give priority to school performance or to stay put in the neighborhood] is a big dilemma. When I was young, I changed home and school many times and I always attended private schools. But, at the end, I was alone. On the one side, I want to prepare my daughter through the best schools; on the other side, I want her to be a happy kid, full of friends and well-integrated in her environment. (Int. 1, social media manager, February 9, 2021)

What parents hope for their children they hope for themselves too. Parents perceive the importance of local schools for themselves to construct a fruitful parental school experience:

> The importance of attending the local school is not just for them, but also for me, because I can meet the other moms, we can chat while they are in the park, this is important for me and my son. It is crucial that you can say 'hello' to people you meet in the street, that we can meet in the park without making a date and that you find however friendly faces there. I think this opportunity matters at least as much as attending a better school. (Int. 7, housewife, June 18 2021)

In these and in many other interviews, parents addressed the neighborhood and the school realm as the fields in which their children's and also their own social lives mostly occur. That is why decision-making processes about the school go beyond the school proposals, programs, and official goals and refer to broader social mechanisms that have to do with the role played, or aimed to be played, in society. To this extent, the school has to do with a way of living in the daily spaces of middle-class families.

The input coming from this research introduces a new perspective to interpret the process through which school inequalities are reproduced in contemporary cities. Among the many factors that scholars have considered to understand how middle-class choices produce school inequalities and segregation, the decision to stay put in the neighborhood has been largely underestimated. A lot of importance has been given to the different resources in accessing information that would allow middle-class parents to have a broader range of options (Fossey 1994). These parents are also more likely to be inserted in highly educated social networks from which they gain input and suggestions. It has been largely taken for granted that with these resources middle-class parents are more inclined to take a long-term perspective and to exit from the catchment area to enroll their children in the best-performing schools. In contrast, this study shows that middle-class choices do not necessarily give priority to academic factors and that this can end up with the decision to stay put in the neighborhood. This parental approach's impacts on school segregation and the effects need to be inquired into as well.

This mechanism opens reflections about the patterns of inequalities that can be reproduced when the decision-making process takes into account the relationship with neighborhoods. As we have seen, choosing a local school does not mean not exiting from the catchment areas; indeed, many parents try to find a compromise between what is perceived to be the school with "people like us" and the desire to live their daily life in the neighborhood. That is why for example they choose schools placed in the same neighborhood but in a different catchment area. This means that it is not just the access to information or the attempt to look for high-quality information that drives the polarization of children in highly mixed neighborhoods; the relationship with the territory when it is lived as a distinguishing value also becomes a driver of segregation or at least of polarization. To this extent, inequalities can be deeply linked to bottom-up processes and considered spatially dependent. Instead of giving up the neighborhood to improve quality, we can observe a sort of "colonization" approach among highly educated parents, for whom the neighborhood life is a priority. Therefore, it is worth looking not just at the choice of middle-class parents to move as a driver of school inequalities but also at the choice to stay put.

## CONCLUSIONS

This chapter aimed to shed light on the decision-making processes around school of a subset of middle-class people: the highly educated parents of children attending primary school. In selecting the profile of parents to focus on I decided to privilege the educational dimension because it is one of the main assets through which the middle class distinguishes and reproduces itself. The socio-spatial dimension emerges explicitly as a value that orients preference formation. Indeed, along with the desire to reproduce a social position in the future, school choices also have to do with the desire of parents to participate and let their children participate in a very local scale. In the context of the economic and social fragmentation of the middle class, the neighborhood turns out to be a dimension in which it is possible to recognize "people like us" and to be part of social groups. To this extent, this study aimed at going beyond the micro-scale analysis of a neighborhood and hopes to contribute to defining the characteristics of contemporary gentrifiers besides housing and consumption habits by taking an educational approach. The chapter also highlighted that the process of school decision-making can reproduce segregation even in ways not yet deeply studied by urban scholars. Indeed, along with exit choices, inequalities can also be reproduced by choosing to stay put in the neighborhood and colonizing through a middle-class approach local schools in socially mixed areas.

The chapter presents an in-depth study of a single neighborhood of Milan in which a process of gentrification is ongoing. Therefore, the results cannot be generalized. However, the research paves the way for the development of further studies. New research should explore what happens in different inner-city neighborhoods, inquiring into the extent to which the relationship with the neighborhood is dependent on the specific spatial features of the neighborhood itself or whether it is related to the middle class, no matter the spaces in which schools are located. This would also represent a step further in the analysis of the urban middle class beyond schooling and the educational dimension. The chapter suggests that, because of the centrality of the territorial dimension in middle-class choices, the relationship with space should be better integrated into the analysis of the class formation process. Indeed, while spatial variables have deeply entered the analysis of modes of capitalist reproduction, they are missing in the explanation of class structure formation and stratification. Insights coming from this study suggest that it is fruitful to systematically introduce this perspective in class studies.

## NOTES

1. The research here presented was conducted thanks to a research fellowship founded by the excellence department (l. 232/2016) "Territorial Fragility". I wish to thank Professor Costanzo Ranci who supervised this work with professors and researchers of the *Dastu* department of the Polytechnic University of Milan who gave me stimulating comments and insights. Additionally, my gratitude goes to the research group of the Laboratory of Social Policies for sharing with me their knowledge about the topic and the reflections from data collected in previous studies. However, I bear the sole responsibilities for any shortcomings.
2. Data on this point come from a database constructed for the Erasmus Plus Project ECASS (European Cities against school segregation) in which I have been partially involved. Data were furnished by the Municipality of Milan and by the Invalsi database and involve all the schools in the country.

## REFERENCES

Allen, R. & Burgess, S. (2013) Evaluating the provision of school performance information for school choice. *Economics of Education Review* 34: 175–190.
Ball, S.J. (2003) *Class Strategies and the Education Market: The Middle Classes and Social Advantage*. New York: Routledge.
Ball, S.J. & Vincent, C. (1998) I heard it on the grapevine: Hot knowledge and school choice. *British Journal of Sociology of Education* 19(3): 377–400.
Beauregard, R.A. (2013) [1986] The chaos and complexity of gentrification. In N. Smith & P. Williams (eds.) *Gentrification of the City*. London: Routledge, 12–23.
Boterman, W.R. (2013) Dealing with diversity: Middle-class family household and the issue of "black" and "white" schools in Amsterdam. *Urban Studies* 50(6): 1130–1147.
Boterman, W.R., Musterd, S., Pacchi, C. & Ranci, C. (2019) School segregation in contemporary cities: Socio-spatial dynamics, institutional context and urban outcomes. *Urban Studies* 56(15): 3055–3073.
Bourdieu, P. (1979) *Distinction: A Social Critique of the Judgement of Taste*. Cambridge: Harvard University Press.
Bourdieu, P. & Passeron, J.C. (1970) *La reproduction. Eléments pour une théorie du système d'enseignment*. Paris: Les Éditions de Minuit.
Brenner, N., Peck, J. & Theodore, N. (2010) Variegated neoliberalization: Geographies, modalities, pathways. *Global Networks* 10(2): 182–222.
Castells, M. (1983) *The City and the Grassroots*. London: Arnold.
Cordini, M. (2019) School segregation: Institutional rules, spatial constraints and households' agency. *International Review of Sociology* 29(2): 279–296.
Cordini, M., Parma, A. & Ranci, C. (2019) White flight in Milan: School segregation as a result of home-to-school mobility. *Urban Studies* 56(15): 3216–3233.
Devine, F. & Savage, M. (2000) Conclusions: Renewing class analysis. In R. Crompton et al. (eds.) *Renewing Class Analysis*. Oxford: Blackwell, 184–199.
Drew, E.M. (2011) "Listening through white ears": Cross-racial dialogues as a strategy to address the racial effects of gentrification. *Journal of Urban Affairs* 34(1): 99–115.
Florida, R. (2004) *Cities and the Creative Class*. New York and London: Routledge.
Fossey, R. (1994) Open enrolment in Massachusetts: Why families choose. *Educational Evaluation and Policy Analysis* 16(3): 320–334.
Glass, R. (1964) *London: Aspects of Change*. London: MacGibbon and Kee.

Gomez, D., Chumacero, R.A. & Paredes, R.D. (2012) School choice and information. *Estudios de Economía* 39(2): 143–157.

Gourzis, K., Herod, A., Chorianopolous, I. & Gialis, S. (2022) On the recursive relationship between gentrification and labour market precarization: Evidence from two neighbourhoods in Athens, Greece. *Urban Studies* 59(12): 2545–2564.

Hamnett, C. (1991) The blind men and the elephant: The explanation of gentrification. *Transactions of the Institute of British Geographers* 16(2): 173–189.

Hastings, J.S., Van Weelden, R. & Weinstein, J. (2007) Preferences, information, and parental choice behaviour in public school choice. NBER Working Paper 12995, National Bureau of Economic Research, Inc.

Haylett, C. (2003) Culture, class and urban policy: Reconsidering equality. *Antipode* 35(1): 55–73.

Jager, M. (1986) Class definition and the aesthetic of gentrification: Victoriana in Melbourne. In N. Smith & P. Williams (eds.) *Gentrification of the City*. London: Routledge, 78–90.

Kadıoğlu, D. (2021) The role of schools in the de- and revalorization of stigmatized neighbourhoods: The case of Berlin-Neukölln. *Journal of Race, Ethnicity and the City* 2(2): 135–15.

Kleitz, B., Weiher, G.R., Tedin, K. & Matland, R. (2000) Choices, charter schools and household preferences. *Social Science Quarterly* 81(3): 846–854.

Lareau, A. (2003) *Unequal Childhoods: Class, Race, and Family Life*. Berkeley and Los Angeles: University of California Press.

Maloutas, T., Hadjiyanni. A., Kapella, A., Spyrellis, S.N. & Valassi, D. (2013) Education and social reproduction: The impact of social origin, school segregation and residential segregation on educational performances in Athens. Paper presented at the conference RC21 "Resourceful Cities", Berlin, August 23–31.

Marcuse, P. (1986) Abandonment, gentrification and displacement. The linkages in New York City. In N. Smith & P. Williams (eds.) *Gentrification of the City*. London: Routledge, 333–347.

Michael, J. (2013) It's really not hip to be a hipster: Negotiating trends and authenticity in the cultural field. *Journal of Consumer Culture* 15(2): 163–183.

Olson Beal, H. & Munro Hendry, P. (2012) The ironies of school choice: Empowering parents and reconceptualizing public education. *American Journal of Education* 118(4): 521–550.

Pacchi, C. & Ranci, C. (eds.) (2017) *White Flight a Milano. La segregazione sociale ed etnica nelle scuole dell'obbligo*. Milan: Franco Angeli.

Peterson, R.A. & Kern, R.M. (1996) Changing highbrow taste: From snob to omnivore. *American Sociological Review* 61(5): 900–907.

Raveaud, M. & Van Zanten, A. (2007) Choosing the local school: Middle class parents' values and social and ethnic mix in London and Paris. *Journal of Educational Policy* 22(1): 107–124.

Reay, D. & Ball, S.J. (1997) "Split for choice": The working class and educational markets. *Oxford Review of Education* 23(1): 89–101.

Sassen, S. (2012) Urban capabilities: An essay on our challenges and differences. *Journal of International Affairs* 65(2): 85–95.

Savage, M., Cunningham, N., Devine, F., Friedman, S., Laurison, D., McKenzie, L., Miles, A., Snee, H. & Wakeling, P. (2015) *Social Class in the 21st Century*. London: Pelican Books.

Smith, M.P. (2002) Power in place: Retheorizing the local and the global. In J. Eade & C. Mele (eds.) *Understanding the City: Contemporary and Future Perspectives*. Oxford: Blackwell, 109–130.

Smith, N. (1979) Toward a theory of gentrification. A back to the city movement by capital, not people. *Journal of the American Planning Association* 45(4): 538–548.

Valli, C. (2021) Artistic careers in the cyclicality of art scenes and gentrification: Symbolic capital accumulation through space in Bushwick, NYC. *Urban Geography* 43(8): 1176–1198.

Van Zanten, A. (2009) Competitive arenas and schools' logics of action: A European comparison. *Compare: A Journal of Comparative and International Education* 39(1): 85–98.

Vincent, C. & Ball, S.J. (2006) *Childcare, Choice and Class Practices: Middle-Class Parents and Their Children*. London and New York: Routledge.

Vincent, C. & Ball, S.J. (2007) "Making up" the middle-class child: Families, activities and class dispositions. *Sociology* 41(6): 1061–1077.

Wilson, D. & Bridge, G. (2019) School choice and the city: Geography of allocation and segregation. *Urban Studies* 56(15): 3198–3215.

# 19. Use and abuse of the ghetto concept in Chilean urban sociology

*Nicolás Angelcos*

The return to democracy in 1990 faced one of its most significant challenges in the housing deficit, inherited after 17 years of military dictatorship (1973–1989).[1] To address illegal land occupations, the government developed a policy of social housing construction on a mass scale, which completely transformed the urban landscape of Chile's major cities. In the mid-1980s nearly half the population of the Metropolitan Region lived in informal settlements (Tironi 2003). By 2002, more than 97% of the urban poor lived in legally recognized housing (Murphy 2013).

Initially, this policy was well-received, to the extent that it was exported to other countries of the Global South, such as Brazil, Costa Rica, Colombia, and South Africa (Gilbert 2004). However, in the early 2000s, Chilean urban sociology began to denounce the negative effects of the segregation experienced by the urban poor in the periphery of the city. Unlike the informal settlements described by Castells (1973)—characterized by a high level of organization and connection to left-wing political parties—the neighborhoods built by the state are characterized by the presence of various social pathologies, such as crime, drug addiction, alcoholism, teenage pregnancy, and the presence of young people who neither work nor study (Sabatini et al. 2013c).

To frame these so-called pathologies, urban sociologists imported the concept of the ghetto that Wilson (1987) had employed to describe the new urban poverty in the United States. From this perspective, housing policies developed by the state, focused on lower-income families, socially isolate the poor, resulting in a series of behaviors that deviate from middle-class norms and values. Although this school of sociology recognizes the existence of community organization in some neighborhoods, it tends to describe it as a vanishing subculture, increasingly displaced by 'ghettoized poverty' and drug trafficking (Salcedo & Rasse 2010; Sabatini et al. 2013c).

This negative view of low-income neighborhoods, synthesized in the ghetto notion, has become a widely disseminated label in the media, to the degree that it is currently used descriptively to refer to low-income neighborhoods, especially social housing complexes built by the state during the 1990s. In a report entitled *Guetos en Chile* (Atisba 2010), they are defined based on four criteria: 1) high social homogeneity, 2) high density, 3) low service coverage, and 4) low connectivity with the rest of the city. Approximately 10% of the population of the country resides in 64 areas identified as ghettos.

In this chapter, we explore how the concept of the ghetto represents an epistemological obstacle, not only because it associates urban poverty with disorganization (Wacquant 1997) but also because it limits the understanding of the forms of collective action that contribute to the production of low-income neighborhoods (Martinez 2019). As Kokoreff (2009) points out, regarding the use of the concept of the ghetto in France, it creates a homogeneous image of the urban periphery with almost no acknowledgment of any positive forms of relating to one another or of collective resistance to the social and political exclusion that characterizes it. Consequently, it 'assumes that marginalization and depoliticization go hand in hand' (Kokoreff 2009: 570). As we will explore in this chapter, the residents of low-income neighborhoods that national urban sociology describes as ghettos have deployed various collective actions to denounce the poor quality of housing and the insecurity in which they live stemming from drug trafficking and crime; in some cases, they have managed to organize at a national level to demand that the state recognize their right to the city (Angelcos & Pérez 2023, Pérez 2022).[2]

To support this argument, first I will reconstruct the history of the concept of the ghetto in American urban sociology; second, I will analyze its use in Latin American and, especially, Chilean sociology; third, I will show the way in which neighborhoods described as ghettos by Chilean urban sociology have developed various forms of organization and protest; and, finally, I will describe the resurgence of the *pobladores*[3] movement, which constitutes the most organized expression of politics in low-income neighborhoods.

## THE CONCEPT OF THE GHETTO IN AMERICAN URBAN SOCIOLOGY

The word 'ghetto' appears in 1516 in connection with the confinement of the Jewish community on an island in Venice that took its name from a copper foundry or *geto* (Duneier 2016). While the concept had appeared previously in sociological studies by Zeublin (1895), it was popularized by Wirth (1927), who used it to describe the life of Jewish immigrants in the Chicago ghetto. The author described how Jews voluntarily chose to live within the ghetto, which functioned as a refuge from an openly anti-Semitic social environment. Therefore, while acting as a space of control and isolation, it also allowed the community to flourish culturally.

This concept was later adapted to describe African-American communities. In their classic study, Drake and Cayton (1945), unlike Wirth, emphasize that the 'black ghetto' is not an area of voluntary confinement but the result of the racist attitudes of the white middle class who, through residential restrictive covenants, limit their mobility within the city. Likewise, Clark (1965) highlights the 'black ghetto' as the product of racial segregation and subordination to external political and economic forces, resulting in a series of pathological behaviors, including drug addiction. Along the same lines as Wirth, Wacquant (2005: 12) defines the community ghetto as a two-faced institution: 'for the dominant category, its rationale is to *confine and control* [...] [for the subordinate category], however, it is a *protective and integrative device* [...]. Enforced isolation from the outside leads to the intensification of social exchange and cultural sharing inside.'

Contemporary use of the ghetto concept can be traced to the work of Wilson (1987). According to this author, by the mid-1970s, a series of behaviors could be observed within the black ghetto that differed significantly from those of society at large. In contrast to the community ghetto, with its high level of organization, sense of community, and emotional attachment to the neighborhood, contemporary ghettos are associated with high 'rates of crime, drug addiction, out-of-wedlock births, female-headed families, and welfare dependency' (Wilson 1987: 20). From that perspective, these problems cannot be explained only as the result of racial discrimination. Important socio-demographic changes must also be taken into account (migration of the African-American population from the South to the North, declining age) and structural transformations of the labor market (shifting from an industrial to a service economy). The latter is of special significance, since it represented a major change in the social composition of the ghetto. While previous decades saw the coexistence of different social classes, a significant number of middle-class African-Americans migrated to the suburbs in the 1970s, resulting in a concentration of low-status families in the ghetto. This process would have negative effects on the African-American community, as middle-class families had previously served as role models for low-income families, reinforcing a positive perception of education, stable work, and the nuclear family. In this sense, the key concept to explain the anomic behavior of low-income families is social isolation resulting from the migration of the middle class and part of the working class to the suburbs.

This association between poverty concentration and social disorganization has been strongly criticized by Small (2004). Based on the study of a Puerto Rican community in Boston, he points out that the weakening of participation in social organizations is not the result of an absence of middle-class families' cultural influence in the day-to-day life of low-status families, but of the way in which new generations interpret life in their neighborhood. He therefore proposes a different understanding of the relationship between culture and poverty that does not directly associate the behavior of low-income families with a form of social deviance but rather recognizes the capacity of individuals and collectives to imbue the place where they live with meaning (Small 2004).

The series of urban riots that took place in France, England, and the United States in the early 1990s helped revive the discussion of the ghetto concept in sociology. According to Wacquant (1997), the American debate on racial division and urban poverty simply uses the ghetto concept to designate an urban area that concentrates high rates of poverty and to point out the supposed disorganization that characterizes it. Consequently, it is used descriptively and not analytically, which prevents us from seeing the structural forces that would explain the riots. From Wacquant's perspective, these protest events, primarily carried out by young people, would constitute a response to the structural violence emanating from the economic and political transformations observed since the mid-1970s throughout major industrial centers. This violence has three main components: 1) mass unemployment, 2) the relegation of low-income families to poor neighborhoods, and 3) territorial stigmatization (Wacquant 2007). To emphasize the negative effects of this violence, Wacquant proposes the concept of the 'hyperghetto', which highlights the exclusionary dimension historically ascribed to the ghetto over its capacity for integration.

While agreeing with Wacquant's association between structural violence and the material and symbolic deterioration of ghettos in the United States, we posit, in light of Small's (2007) assessment, that the characteristics Wacquant associates with the hyperghetto do not apply to the majority of poor neighborhoods. Consequently, it acts as a stereotype that conceals the heterogeneity of this type of neighborhood, which possesses varied levels of social organization, and where not all residents feel involuntarily segregated. Moreover, as Caldeira (2009) points out, his approach promotes a nostalgic vision of the Fordist model that prevents us from observing the new political identities and forms of collective action that occur in working-class neighborhoods. According to Wacquant (2007: 30), the residents of the hyperghetto cannot access the organizational resources to forge their own identity or voice collective demands in the public sphere. Thus, urban revolts constitute an *infra-political protest*, expressed in a language incomprehensible to the state.

In opposition to Wilson's association between residential segregation and social disorganization and Wacquant's nostalgic approach to 20th century popular politics, I will explore the way in which, despite the Chilean state's housing policy resulting in the creation of highly homogeneous and stigmatized low-income areas, various forms of collective action and (in the case of the housing conflict) a significant urban movement have managed to emerge. According to Martínez (2019: 26), 'urban movements may be defined as sustained collective actions of claim-making in the production, governance and change of cities, according to specific societal contexts.' In this regard, Chilean urban sociology's use of the ghetto concept acts as an epistemological obstacle to understanding contemporary popular politics.

In the following section, I explore the highly controversial use of the concept of the ghetto in Latin America. In particular, a considerable part of Chilean urban sociology has employed it to analyze the social and political behavior of low-income families, especially those relocated by the state to the periphery of metropolitan areas.

## THE USE OF THE CONCEPT OF THE GHETTO IN LATIN AMERICAN AND CHILEAN URBAN SOCIOLOGY

Beginning in the 1930s, Latin America experienced a mass migration of people from the countryside to the main urban centers, who increasingly ended up settling on the outskirts of the city proper. Two main theories were developed to interpret the behavior of these new groups: marginality theory and the theory of urban social movements.

Within marginality theory, Vekemans and Silva (1976) use the concept of the ghetto, understood as a subculture of poverty, but do not develop it further. In contrast to the standard use of the concept in the United States, marginal populations are characterized by the 'internal disintegration' of the nuclear family and of local community networks. Consistent with the work of Lewis (1964) in Mexico, the marginalized are characterized by their 'resignation, abulia, and apathy' (Vekemans & Venegas 1966). Therefore, they are incapable of self-liberation and require the guidance of external agents, the state and the Catholic Church in particular.

In contrast to this approach, Castells (1974) developed the theory of urban social movements. Unlike marginality theory, Castells (1973) emphasizes the heterogeneity of Chilean *poblaciones callampas*,[4] which, contrary to the hegemonic opinion of the elite, contain not only a concentration of the 'lumpenproletariat' but an important part of the industrial working class as well. Likewise, their behavior is not characterized by a tendency towards deviance or delinquency but rather by the existence of various forms of social consciousness, associated with the diverse positions that their residents occupy in the productive structure. From this perspective, the housing crisis allowed for the formation of a vigorous urban social movement— the *pobladores* movement—which played a key role in the process of transition to socialism that was taking place in the country at that time.

As we can see, the concept of the ghetto is limited to a descriptive role in the two classic approaches used by Latin American urban sociology to interpret the social and political behavior of the urban poor. Gilbert (2012) posits that this is due to several reasons, including the following: 1) the low presence of Jews in the region; 2) the high presence of Afro-American people in regions like Brazil and the Caribbean, which precludes them from being described as a minority and inhabiting racially homogeneous spaces; 3) in most countries in the region, the low-income population does not constitute a small proportion of the population; and 4) despite being a very unequal region, residential segregation is, in some cases, less extreme than in many cities in the United States.

Despite the acknowledged difficulties in applying the ghetto concept in a Latin American context (Auyero 2001, Gilbert 2012, Wacquant 2005), in the early 2000s, Chilean urban sociology began using it to describe the 'new urban poverty'. After the return to democracy in 1990, faced with the threat of potential illegal land occupations, the state developed a policy of mass social housing construction. Based on targeted social spending, that is, on the selection of low-income families, the urban poor were relocated to the periphery of the Metropolitan Region. This resulted in the formation of highly homogeneous urban spaces, without access to protected jobs, health centers, or quality schools and with a strong presence of criminal gangs and drug traffickers (Sabatini et al. 2001).

In the estimation of national urban sociology, this relocation of the poor to the periphery of the city had the effect of increasing school dropout rates, unemployment, crime, and drug addiction (Tironi 2003). This perspective also emphasized that the neighborhoods built by the state during the 1990s experienced a process of 'ghettoization', characterized by a series of deviant or anomic attitudes, such as 'the perception of abandonment by the state, the acceptance or legitimization of illegality, the absence of opportunities in the area—beyond those afforded by drugs and crime—and the acceptance of violence and stigma' (Sabatini et al. 2013a: 230). Even while insisting that most of the residents of these neighborhoods do not undertake illegal actions, they continue to be described as the victims of youths and gangs that consume and sell drugs (Lunecke 2016), thus emphasizing the idea that the vast majority of those who live in this type of neighborhood wish to leave them (Sabatini & Wormald 2013).

To explain this behavior, these authors criticize the vision that Wacquant has of the ghetto. From their perspective, Wacquant explains the 'new marginality' in a deterministic way, as a necessary consequence of capitalist restructuring and the retreat of the welfare state (Sabatini et al. 2013b). In contrast to this vision, they propose to instead center the analysis on the segregation of low-income families in the periphery of major cities. Following Wilson's (1987) argument, they point out that the concentration of low-income people in certain areas of the city has an effect of 'social disintegration'. Living near people of higher status, on the other hand, allows low-income families to adopt a middle-class identity, internalizing the value of consumption, education, and social mobility (Sabatini et al. 2013a). Therefore, rather than speaking of a ghetto, they speak of the ghettoization of the new urban poverty.

This theoretical approach—centered on the concept of the ghetto—also has important consequences when observing the political behavior of the urban poor. Throughout the 1980s, Chilean sociologists conducted numerous studies aimed at understanding the participation of *pobladores* in the demonstrations against the dictatorship[5] as well as in community organizations. Although no consensus was reached, several researchers keyed into a sense that fluctuated between survival and political action (Campero 1987). However, for this new urban sociology we have described, the development of urban ghettos is detrimental to the organization and struggle for rights. Unlike in previous decades, these researchers do not ascribe a political dimension to community organization: in highly segregated neighborhoods, it is described as a form of resistance to territorial stigma (Sabatini et al. 2013b); in others, better integrated into the urban tapestry, it is seen as a rational strategy to access greater resources in the geography of opportunities (Sabatini & Brain 2008).

The use of the ghetto concept in the analysis of the new urban poverty in Chile has been criticized by some contemporary studies for a variety of reasons: first, it has been argued that it creates a homogeneous representation that stigmatizes its residents (Cociña 2018); second, the association between concentrated poverty and pathological behaviors has been questioned, as it obscures the action of institutions external to the neighborhood in the production of said behaviors (Ruiz-Tagle et al. 2016); third, Salcedo et al. (2017), while using the ghetto notion themselves, criticize how it prevents the observation of strategies employed by members of the community to resist the occupation of public spaces by criminal gangs. Finally, with the aim of further developing the relationship between urban poverty and ghetto culture, Salcedo and Rasse (2010) propose the existence of five distinct subcultures that regulate the behavior of families. Although this proposal explicitly criticizes the concept of the ghetto and recognizes the heterogeneity within low-income communities, it proposes a limited vision for understanding the political behavior of the residents of low-income neighborhoods since it draws a clear line between those who are politically involved ('organized poverty') and those who are not. It also describes them as a subculture in retreat in the face of the growing hegemony of 'street culture' and drug trafficking.

To summarize, despite the controversial nature of the use of the concept of the ghetto in Latin America, the majority of Chilean urban sociologists have used it to analyze the behavior of the urban poor in the 21st century. In general, they use urban ghettos to describe highly segregated low-income neighborhoods whose social isolation leads to social disintegration, without accounting for the racial dimension that is at the core of US theories. Thus, this demonstrates the difficulty of importing a concept created to describe the evolution of urban poverty in different socio-spatial contexts. For the purposes of this chapter, the main problem we identify is that it does not allow for the analysis of popular mobilization in these types of neighborhoods, as I explore in the following section.

## POPULAR MOBILIZATION BEYOND THE GHETTO

On October 18, 2019, the most important urban uprising in contemporary Chilean history took place. Initially driven by secondary students protesting the increase in the price of public transportation in the capital, it quickly spread to the whole country, eventually leading to a series of heterogeneous social demands (Angelcos & Sembler 2020). Like other uprisings in Latin America, middle classes and low-income sectors participated in different forms of organization and protest (Silva & Rossi 2018). In many neighborhoods, territorial assemblies and councils spontaneously emerged, seeking to promote democratic deliberation beyond the existing institutionality. In other sectors, especially urban downtown and peripheral areas, various expressions of violence took place, such as direct confrontations with police, attacks on police stations, and looting of large retail stores, to name a few (Somma 2021). In response to the pressure created by the movement, on November 15 of the same year, the main political authorities in the government and the opposition signed an 'Agreement for Social Peace and the New Constitution', which established that a plebiscite would be held to change the 1980 Constitution, the main legacy of the military dictatorship (1973–1989).

In December 2019, along with a research team,[6] we began conducting in-depth interviews with residents of various low-income neighborhoods that had taken part in the uprising. In particular, we focused our attention on Bajos de Mena in Puente Alto, a district of Santiago located in the southwest sector of the city. Since the early 1990s, 49 social housing complexes (totaling 25,466 housing units) have been built there. Eighteen of them are made up of three-

and four-story apartment buildings (Cociña 2016). Most of the residents are homeowners who have gained access to these housing units—some of them entering into debt with banking institutions as well—thanks to a subsidy from the state. With a population of around 130,000 people and very limited access to services and urban equipment and designated by the state as a 'critical neighborhood' due to its high levels of violence and drug trafficking, Bajos de Mena has been labeled as 'the largest ghetto in Chile' (Atisba 2010) and has been the subject of numerous investigations and interventions.

During the uprising of 2019, various demonstrations took place in the area, from pot-banging protests, neighborhood councils, and territorial assemblies to barricades and attacks on the police station. Figure 19.1 captures some of the graffiti painted by residents.

*Source:* Nicolás Angelcos.

*Figure 19.1* *Graffiti in Villa Estaciones Ferroviarias, Santiago de Chile (2019)*

Later, in the wake of the Covid-19 pandemic and the associated economic crisis, the residents banded together to organize communal kitchens at various locations, some self-managed and some supported by municipal authorities.

Among the neighbors we interviewed, especially among adult women with low cultural capital, participation in the revolt was not their first experience with mobilization. As an article that appeared in the mid-2000s showed, the neighbors of Bajos de Mena have employed a range of strategies to bring their demands to the public debate: 1) they have organized demonstrations outside the neighborhood, for example, at the offices of the Housing and Urbanism Service; 2) they have invited political authorities to visit the neighborhood; and 3) they have put up barricades in the area (Salcedo et al. 2017).

In order to delve more deeply into these strategies, we conducted 22 in-depth interviews and an analysis of stories in the media between 2001 and 2020. The latter was carried out online, analyzing the record of demonstrations associated with Bajos de Mena in various media outlets, including several independent ones. Based on the information gathered, we were able to identify four major conflicts: the oldest one in the sector is promoted by several associations of housing debtors, who, through various actions (barricades, vigils, hunger strikes, among others), have sought to lobby the state to cancel the debt they have with the banks. The Coordinadora de Pobladores en Lucha (COPOL) and the Asociación Nacional de Deudores Habitacionales (Andha Chile) emerged from this dispute.

Andha Chile was to play an important role through the early 2000s in several districts of the metropolitan periphery. The organization was composed primarily of low-income families who had achieved home ownership through a state subsidy and a bank loan. Their main demand was debt forgiveness and, to this end, they deployed a wide range of actions, which tended to favor direct action over negotiation (Guzmán 2015).

In Bajos de Mena, most of the women leaders we met had first become politically active through this organization. Although Andha Chile was originally highly critical of the neoliberal model and liberal democracy, after several internal disputes, some of its main leaders, who no longer belong to the organization, now maintain clientelistic relations with the municipality of Puente Alto, which has been governed by the right wing for over 20 years.

A second major conflict stems from the explosion of an underground chamber in 2003, which released a significant amount of toxic gas, the result of the construction of 25,000 housing units on the site of a former garbage dump. In the wake of this event, a well-known neighborhood leader, who had also been a member of Andha Chile, joined with her neighbors to form the Puente Alto Popular Assembly. In direct opposition to the clientelistic strategy adopted by other leaders, her organization favors direct action. During our interview, she expressed her total rejection of institutional political mediation, to the extent that she completely distrusted the constitutional process underway at the time. In a demonstration at UNICEF offices in 2011, the Assembly denounced both the state 'for the criminal decision to settle thousands of people in a landfill' and the mayor of Puente Alto for his 'attacks and scare tactics' (Pobladores de Puente Alto 2011).

A third conflict, less widely known but which persists in the memory of its inhabitants, revolves around a fire in one of the 49 social housing complexes in the area, which took the lives of a young mother and her two children on June 10, 2012. In connection with this incident, the neighbors set up barricades and organized marches in Bajos de Mena to denounce the precarious living conditions in the tenements: 'This is the armpit of the city, we don't even have a place to charge a Bip card!'[7] a neighbor told La Cuarta, a national newspaper. Regarding these events, the mayor of Puente Alto at the time declared: 'The case of Bajos de Mena is the direst in Chile, these poverty-stricken ghettos must be torn down' (González 2012).

Finally, in connection with these statements, we identified a fourth conflict. It stems from the 'solution' proposed by the government during the first administration of Sebastián Piñera[8] for the situation in Bajos de Mena. In light of the problems of construction and daily violence experienced in the area, the government decided that the best option was to provide the neighborhood's residents with a 'Second Chance'. This entailed tearing down some of the social housing complexes while offering their current residents a new subsidy to buy a house elsewhere in the city (Cociña 2018). This created a true political schism within Bajos de Mena, between those who supported the program proposed by the government and those opposed to it. Among the people we interviewed, one of the leaders who maintains clientelistic relations with the municipality fully endorsed the government's proposal since she regarded it as a good response to the demands promoted by the neighbors. However, the leader associated with the environmental dispute rejected it, since, from her perspective, it did nothing to address their demands for a solution to the contamination issue (Angelcos et al. 2023).

As we can see, the residents of Bajos de Mena have adopted diverse strategies to denounce the precarious conditions of their daily lives, along with the responsibility of the state in providing a solution. Therefore, the fact that this type of neighborhood has been labeled as a ghetto does not imply an absence of organization or political participation. From this analysis, we identified a number of characteristics of the politics observed in this type of neighborhood:

(1) The majority of organizations are led by women. Women's participation in community organizations has been widely documented, especially in response to the economic crisis that affected the country during the military dictatorship in the early 1980s. At that time, it has been argued that men prefer union participation or militancy in political parties, while women associate community work with their role as mothers (FLACSO 1987). Compared to 20th century popular politics, the main difference is that local organizations interacted with national-level politics through political parties or even the Catholic Church; nowadays, however, women leaders themselves seek political recognition, either through clientelistic ties with local politicians or through direct action.

(2) These organizations have difficulties in staying active and coordinating among themselves. Unlike urban movements (Martínez 2019), these organizations are highly dependent on the activism exercised by their leaders and the strategies they design to influence local or national politics. These organizations' autonomy from political parties, although highly valued by the participants and leaders themselves, also makes it difficult for them to coordinate and obtain resources to keep them active. In the following section, we explore the most systematic effort to coordinate the various collective actions observed in low-income neighborhoods.

## THE RESURGENCE OF THE *POBLADORES* MOVEMENT

The case of Bajos de Mena, along with those of other state-sponsored housing projects since the 1990s, has served as a cautionary tale not only for their own residents but also for thousands of families who aspire to a dignified life through home ownership. On November 11, 2019, less than a month after the uprising, some 300 families attempted to occupy a plot of land in the Lo Hermida[9] sector of southeast Santiago. In a statement signed by various organizations, they called on 'all the *pobladores* of Chile to stand up, join the righteous struggle for dignified housing, and to take a leading role in the process of social change that our country is undergoing. Chile has awakened. this is not a time to wait for solutions, it is a time to conquer them' (Romero 2019).

This call directed at the *pobladores* echoes the movement for housing demands that emerged in Chile in the second half of the 20th century, which rose to prominence at the end of the 1960s and during the government of Salvador Allende (1970–1973). In that period, political parties, especially the Communist Party, sought to integrate illegal land occupations into the process of transition to socialism.

The military dictatorship (1973–1989) and the policy of mass social housing construction adopted by the state during the 1990s ultimately caused the movement to demobilize. However, since 2010, it has shown signs of reactivation (Angelcos & Pérez 2017). Unlike the movement described by Castells (1973), current housing mobilizations are not led by traditional political parties but by autonomous organizations that explicitly criticize capitalism and the type of democracy that was set up after the end of the military dictatorship.

Although numerous illegal land occupations did take place during the uprising, the main feature of the contemporary *pobladores* movement is the formation of housing committees which, through a wide range of actions, look to put pressure on the state to provide housing for the poorest. Faced with the fear of being relocated to the outskirts of the city, cut off from family and local networks, the *pobladores* demand that their housing be built in the neighborhoods or districts where they currently live. Therefore, they seek to include the demand for housing within the broader framework of the right to the city (Angelcos & Pérez 2017, Pérez 2022).

These new organizations have replaced traditional political parties at the forefront of the debate around housing demand. The framework they have built is meant to strengthen the participation of *pobladores* through the housing committees they organize and to boost the positive values that are part of a working-class identity (hard work and sacrifice), inserting the demand for housing into a larger struggle for dignity (Angelcos & Rodríguez 2023).

In contrast to the interpretation generated by the urban sociology we have analyzed, the demand for 'dignity' is not just a byproduct of the desire for better access to services and urban equipment: it derives from the construction of autonomous spaces through which to advance in the 'democratization of the city' (Rodríguez 2020). As a leader of the Movimiento de Pobladores en Lucha points out: 'we want to build neighborhoods, we are builders, not beneficiaries. Being habitat builders, we want to build our houses, our neighborhoods, and we do not want them to tell us where and how to live' (Becerra 2016).

In the wake of the 2019 uprising, the word dignity was placed at the center of critical discourse towards the neoliberal model. For the *pobladores* movement, this word has a major historical significance. For much of the 20th century, *pobladores* used the word 'dignity' to argue with the state over the definition of the minimum conditions to guarantee not only survival but a decent life. The housing battle has been a key part of this struggle. Until the 1980s, the struggle for a dignified life meant leaving the *población callampa* to build homes and communities that the State could legally recognize (Murphy 2015).

Today, that struggle is no longer defined by access to home ownership. As the conflict in Bajos de Mena shows, the life to which the urban poor aspire entails the construction of a community with access to quality urban services and equipment: a 'quiet' neighborhood, free of crime and drug trafficking. Contemporary *pobladores* organizations try to frame these expectations within an anti-capitalist political discourse, attempting to show, as in the past, that the chance of achieving a 'dignified life' requires a radical transformation of the social, economic, and political model (Angelcos & Rodríguez 2023).

To achieve these goals, many organizations have developed an institutional strategy of gaining access to political power. In 2010, the main housing debtor organization—the aforementioned Andha Chile—together with other *pobladores* organizations founded the Partido Igualdad (Equality Party). While identifying with radical leftist tradition, it seeks to generate a new discourse that places the people at the center of its political project (Angelcos et al. 2019). One of the first milestones of this new party was the 2013 presidential campaign of Roxana Miranda, one of Andha Chile's leaders, in which she obtained 1.37% of the vote. Their main focus, however, remains on local government, where they have gone from having 1 municipal council member in 2012 to 27 in 2021 (SERVEL 2023). As Rodríguez (2020) points out, this strategy allows the movement not only to seek representation in their local municipal councils but also to create spaces of greater autonomy for the *pobladores*.

The 2019 uprising represented a political opportunity for a wide range of social actors, including the *pobladores* movement. First, as we mentioned previously, illegal land occupations have increased by 20.8% since October of 2019 (Techo et al. 2021). While these events cannot be attributed exclusively to actions by the movement, they have contributed to bringing the housing crisis to the forefront of public debate. Second, the movement sought to take part in the process to draft a new constitution, nominating candidates to the Constitutional Assembly, with a focus on the sections of the document that would guarantee the right to housing. Even though this draft of the new constitution was rejected in a plebiscite held in September 2022, the constitutional guarantee of housing rights continues to be a relevant issue on the political agenda.

As we can see, despite undergoing significant demobilization after the return to democracy, the *pobladores* movement has been reorganizing since 2010. Unlike in the past, it is not led by traditional political parties, but by autonomous organizations that are making important efforts to integrate the demand for housing—at the local level—with a process of national transformation. These organizations form the basis of a major urban movement (Martínez 2019) that questions the capitalist production of the city and the exclusion of the people from the political field.

## CONCLUSIONS

The concept of the ghetto was first used in urban sociology to explain the situation in which the Jewish community found itself in the United States. Beginning in the mid-1940s, it was adapted to describe the racial segregation affecting African-American communities living in the major industrial centers of the country. Since the late 1980s, however, it has been a key concept in the analysis of the new urban poverty in the US. From a culturalist perspective, Wilson (1987) associated the concentration of low-income people with a series of pathological behaviors that separated them from society at large. Wacquant (2007), for his part, attempted to demonstrate that underlying these behaviors were structural forces inherent to the post-industrial capitalism that had taken root in major urban centers since the mid-1970s.

Although it did not have its own history in Latin America, Chilean urban sociology employed the concept of the ghetto to describe the new poverty that emerged after the return to democracy in 1990. Unlike in previous decades, the poor no longer lived in informal, largely undeveloped settlements but in social housing complexes built by the state. What was initially perceived as a successful housing policy (Ducci 1997) later came under criticism, since the focus of state action on low-income families resulted in the urban poor being relocated to the periphery of the main metropolitan areas, without access to protected jobs, health services, quality education, and safety. From a culturalist perspective, Chilean urban sociology tried to use the ghetto concept to demonstrate how residential segregation, as in the North American case, resulted in social disintegration (Sabatini et al. 2013c).

This analysis has been criticized in the field of urban studies, not only internationally but also in Chile. It is generally observed that the ghetto concept creates a homogeneous image of low-income neighborhoods that tends to highlight their negative features and, therefore, contributes to their stigmatization (Cociña 2018). Likewise, as Wacquant posits, pathological behavior is not an effect of the concentration of low-status families but of the actions of external institutions that are part of the structural violence that affects these neighborhoods (Ruiz-Tagle et al. 2016). In this chapter, I explored how the concept of the ghetto constitutes an epistemological obstacle to the analysis of popular politics. While it is true that, as is the case in Europe and the United States (Wacquant 2007), the crisis of the labor movement and of major left-wing parties had a negative impact on working-class movements in Latin America (especially in Chile), this does not mean that other forms of mobilization and new political languages have not emerged within these neighborhoods. As Caldeira (2009) points out, this was the case in Brazil.

As in other countries in Latin America and the Global South, the neoliberal economic model and representative democracy have been strongly questioned by a wide range of social actors, including residents of low-income neighborhoods (Martínez 2019). Even within highly segregated social housing complexes, numerous attempts at organization that fail to be publicly recognized, in many cases due to lack of resources, continue to occur. This is not to say that drug trafficking and day-to-day violence, as described by national urban sociology, are not a reality, but they coexist with the actions of organizations fighting for a safer environment. At the same time, in various parts of the country, new generations of *pobladores* have revived the movement, demanding through both disruptive and institutional actions that the state recognize the right to housing and the city.

From this perspective, the concept of the ghetto, while useful for denouncing the material and symbolic deterioration of low-income neighborhoods, acts as an epistemological obstacle that prevents the observation of numerous collective actions that unfold in the territories and that, in some cases, have managed to bring the housing problem to the forefront of national political discussion. It is therefore more appropriate to inductively reconstruct popular politics at the neighborhood level without resorting to an imported concept intended to describe a very different reality than the one found in Chile and throughout Latin America in general.

## NOTES

1. In 1991, the deficit affected 800,000 families (Ducci 1997). It steadily decreased until it reached 391,546 housing units in 2015. According to the latest available data, the deficit has increased to 541,295 housing units (Centro UC Políticas Públicas & Déficit Cero 2022).
2. This analysis is based on research conducted since 2010. From December 2019 to October 2022, together with a research team, we carried out research in two low-income neighborhoods in southwest Santiago. This project received funding from the National Fund for Science and Technology (ANID/FONDECYT/11190211) and the Center for the Study of Conflict and Social Cohesion (ANID/FONDAP/15130009).
3. '*Pobladores*' is a term used in Chile to refer to low-income families who gained access to home ownership through illegal land occupations. The *pobladores* movement was a major social movement in the late 1960s and early 1970s.
4. '*Poblaciones callampas*' refers to informal squatters' settlements. Their name comes from the fact that they originally appeared along the banks of rivers, like mushrooms (callampas) in damp areas.
5. Between 1983 and 1986, massive protests against the military dictatorship took place, led, among others, by the young residents of low-income neighborhoods.
6. This team included Andrea Roca and Valentina Abufhele. Additionally, several of the interviews conducted in Bajos de Mena were conducted by Carolina Frías.

7. The Bip! card is the official payment method used for the public transport system in Santiago.
8. Sebastián Piñera was president of Chile in two different periods: 2010–2014 and 2018–2022.
9. This sector was the result of an illegal land occupation in 1970 by the Movimiento de Izquierda Revolucionario (Revolutionary Left Movement).

## REFERENCES

Angelcos, N. & Pérez, M. (2017) De la 'desaparición' a la reemergencia: Continuidades y rupturas del movimiento de pobladores en Chile. *Latin American Research Review* 52(1): 94–109.

Angelcos, N. & Pérez, M. (eds.) (2023) *Vivir con dignidad: Transformaciones sociales y políticas de los sectores populares en Chile*. Santiago de Chile: Fondo de Cultura Económica.

Angelcos, N. & Rodríguez, J. P. (2023) Amplifying dignity in the neoliberal city: The Pobladores movement in Chile. *Social Movement Studies*. DOI: 10.1080/14742837.2023.2171383.

Angelcos, N. & Sembler, C. (2020) 'No son 30 pesos, son 30 años.' Análisis crítico de la movilización social. *Análisis del año 2019*, 135–148.

Angelcos, N., Jordana, C. & Sandoval, C. (2019) *Sólo en el pueblo confiamos*: la estructura moral del discurso político radical de los pobladores en el Partido Igualdad. *Izquierdas* 46: 22–46.

Angelcos, N., Roca, A. & Abufhele, V. (2023) 'Bajos de Mena despertó.' Mujeres populares, reconocimiento y revuelta. In N. Angelcos et al. (eds.) *Vivir con dignidad: Transformaciones sociales y políticas de los sectores populares en Chile.* Santiago de Chile: Fondo de Cultura Económica, 130–148.

Atisba (2010) *Guetos en Chile*. Santiago de Chile: Atisba Estudios y Proyectos Urbanos Ltda.

Auyero, J. (2001) *La política de los pobres: las prácticas clientelistas del peronismo*. Buenos Aires: Manantial.

Becerra, A. (2016) Pobladores denuncian lucro en proyecto habitacional del Serviu. *Diario Uchile*, 21 September. Retrieved from https://radio.uchile.cl/2016/09/21/pobladores-de-penalolen-denuncian-lucro-en-proyecto-habitacional-del-serviu/ (accessed 12 April 2023).

Caldeira, T. (2009) Marginality, again?! *International Journal of Urban and Regional Research* 33(3): 848–852.

Campero, G. (1987) *Entre la sobrevivencia y la acción política: las organizaciones de pobladores en Santiago*. Santiago de Chile: Estudios ILET.

Castells, M. (1973) Movimiento de pobladores y lucha de clases en Chile. *EURE* 3(7): 9–35.

Castells, M. (1974) *Movimientos sociales urbanos*. Madrid: Siglo XXI Editores.

Centro UC Políticas Públicas & Déficit Cero (2022) Déficit habitacional: ¿cuántas familias necesitan una vivienda y en qué territorio? Boletín 1: estimación y caracterización del déficit habitacional en Chile. Retrieved from https://deficitcero.cl/pdf/Minuta_EstimaciondelDeficit.pdf (accessed 12 April 2023).

Clark, K. (1965) *Dark ghetto. Dilemmas of social power*. New York: Harper & Row.

Cociña, C. (2016) Habitar desigualdades: Políticas urbanas y el despliegue de la vida en Bajos de Mena. United Nations Development Programme Working Paper, 5: 1–21.

Cociña, C. (2018) Housing as urbanism: The role of housing policies in reducing inequalities. Lessons from Puente Alto, Chile. *Housing Studies*. DOI: 10.1080/02673037.2018.1543797.

Drake, S. C. & Cayton, H. (1945) *Black metropolis*. Chicago: Chicago University Press.

Ducci, M. E. (1997) Chile: el lado obscuro de una política de vivienda exitosa. *EURE* 23(69): 99–115.

Duneier, M. (2016) *Ghetto. The invention of a place, the history of an idea*. New York: Farrar, Straus & Giroux.

FLACSO (1987) *Espacio y poder: Los pobladores*. Santiago de Chile: Facultad Latinoamericana de Ciencias Sociales.

Gilbert, A. (2004) Learning from others: The spread of capital housing subsidies. *International Planning Studies* 9(2–3): 197–216.

Gilbert, A. (2012) On the absence of ghettos in Latin American Cities. In R. Hutchinson et al. (eds.) *The ghetto. Contemporary global issues and controversies.* Boulder: Westview Press, 191–224.

González, C. (2012) El infierno en Bajos de Mena. *La Cuarta*, 10 June. Retrieved from https://www.lacuarta.com/cronica/noticia/el-infierno-en-bajos-de-mena/122492/ (accessed 12 April 2023).

Guzmán, S. (2015) 'Should I trust the bank or the social movement?' Motivated reasoning and debtor's work to accept misinformation. *Sociological Forum* 30(4): 900–924.

Kokoreff, M. (2009) Ghettos et marginalité urbaine. Lectures croisées de Didier Lapeyronnie et Loïc Wacquant. *Revue française de sociologie* 50(3): 553–572.

Lewis, O. (1964) *Los hijos de Sánchez*. Ciudad de México: Fondo de Cultura Económica.

Lunecke, A. (2016) Inseguridad ciudadana y diferenciación social en el nivel microbarrial: el caso del sector Santo Tomás, Santiago de Chile. *EURE* 42(125): 109–129.

Martínez, M. (2019) Framing urban movements, contesting global capitalism and liberal democracy. In N. M. Yip et al. (eds.) *Contested cities and urban activism*. Singapore: Palgrave, 25–45.

Murphy, E. (2013) Between housing and home: Property titling and the dilemmas of citizenship in Santiago, Chile. In E. Murphy et al. (eds.) *The housing question: Tensions, continuities and contingencies in the modern city*. London: Ashgate, 199–218.

Murphy, E. (2015) *For a proper home: Housing rights in the margins of urban Chile, 1960–2010*. Pittsburgh: University of Pittsburgh Press.

Pérez, M. (2022) *The right to dignity: Housing struggles, city making, and citizenship in urban Chile*. Stanford: Stanford University Press.

Pobladores de Puente Alto (2011) Pobladores mantienen tomada la Oficina Central de UNICEF en Santiago. *Piensa Chile*, 27 July. Retrieved from https://piensachile.com/2011/07/27/pobladores-mantienen-tomada-la-oficina-central-de-unicef-en-santiago/ (accessed 12 April 2023).

Rodríguez, J. P. (2020) *Resisting neoliberal capitalism in Chile. The possibility of social critique*. Cham: Palgrave Macmillan.

Romero, N. (2019) Peñalolén : Se toman Viña Cousiño Macul en ejercicio del poder constituyente. *Revista De Frente*, 11 November. Retrieved from https://www.revistadefrente.cl/penalolen-se-toman-vina-cousino-macul-en-ejercicio-del-poder-constituyente/ (accessed 12 April 2023).

Ruiz-Tagle, J., Labbé, G., Álvarez, M., Montes, M. & Aninat, M. (2016) Una teoría del espacio institucional de barrios marginales: herramientas conceptuales desde una investigación en curso en Santiago de Chile. *Congreso Internacional Contested Cities, eje 1: teoría urbana. Serie (IV-1B)*. Retrieved from http://contested-cities.net/working-papers/2016/una-teoria-del-espacio-institucional-de-barrios-marginales-herramientas-conceptuales-desde-una-investigacion-en-curso-en-santiago-de-chile/.

Sabatini, F. & Brain, I. (2008) La segregación, los guetos y la integración social urbana: mitos y claves. *EURE* 34(103): 5–26.

Sabatini, F. & Wormald, G. (2013) Segregación de la vivienda social: reducción de oportunidades, pérdida de cohesión. In F. Sabatini et al. (eds.) *Segregación de la vivienda social: ocho conjuntos en Santiago, Concepción y Talca*. Santiago de Chile: Colección Estudios Urbanos UC, 11–32.

Sabatini, F., Cáceres, G. & Cerda, J. (2001) Segregación residencial en las principales ciudades chilenas: tendencias de las tres últimas décadas y posibles cursos de acción. *EURE* 27(82): 21–42.

Sabatini, F., Cáceres, G. & Rasse, A. (2013a) Bifurcación de senderos: entre la segregación que 'guetiza' los barrios populares y la gentrificación que ayuda a su 'moyenización.' In F. Sabatini, G. Wormald & A. Rasse (eds.) *Segregación de la vivienda social: ocho conjuntos en Santiago, Concepción y Talca*. Santiago de Chile: Colección Estudios Urbanos UC, 221–242.

Sabatini, F., Salcedo, R., Gómez, J., Silva, R. & Trebilcock, M. P. (2013b) Microgeografías de la segregación: estigma, xenofobia y adolescencia urbana. In F. Sabatini, G. Wormald & A. Rasse (eds.) *Segregación de la vivienda social: ocho conjuntos en Santiago, Concepción y Talca*. Santiago de Chile: Colección Estudios Urbanos UC, 37–66.

Sabatini, F., Wormald, G. & Rasse, A. (eds.) (2013c) *Segregación de la vivienda social: ocho conjuntos en Santiago, Concepción y Talca*. Santiago de Chile: Colección Estudios Urbanos UC.

Salcedo, R. & Rasse, A. (2010) The heterogeneous nature of urban poor families. *City & Community* 11(1): 94–118.

Salcedo, R., Hermansen, P. & Rasse, A. (2017) Habitando el gueto. Estrategias para sobrevivir un espacio público deteriorado: el caso de Bajos de Mena en Santiago, Chile. In T. Errázuriz et al. (eds.) *Salcedo*. Santiago de Chile: Bifurcaciones, 175–192.

SERVEL (2023) Elección de Concejales 2021. Retrieved from https://historico.servel.cl/servel/app/index.php?r=EleccionesGenerico&id=227 (accessed 11 April 2023).

Silva, E. & Rossi, F. (eds.) (2018) *Reshaping the political arena in Latin America. From resisting neoliberalism to the second incorporation*. Pittsburgh: University of Pittsburgh Press.
Small, M. (2004) *Villa Victoria. The transformation of social capital in a Boston barrio*. Chicago: Chicago University Press.
Small, M. (2007) Is there such a thing as 'the ghetto?' *City: Analysis of Urban Trends, Culture, Theory, Policy, Action* 11(3): 413–421.
Somma, N. (2021) Power cages and the October 2019 uprising in Chile. *Social Identities* 27(5): 579–592.
Techo, Fundación Vivienda & CES (2021) *Catastro nacional de campamentos 2020–2021*. Santiago de Chile: TECHO-Chile y Fundación Vivienda.
Tironi, M. (2003) *Nueva pobreza urbana. Vivienda y capital social en Santiago de Chile, 1985–2001*. Santiago de Chile: Predes/RIL Editores.
Vekemans, R. & Silva, I. (1976) *Marginalidad, promoción popular y neomarxismo*. Bogotá: CEDIAL.
Vekemans, R. & Venegas, R. (1966) Marginalidad y promoción popular. *Revista mensaje* 15(149): 218–222.
Wacquant, L. (1997) Three pernicious premises in the study of the American ghetto. *International Journal of Urban and Regional Research* 20(2): 341–53.
Wacquant, L. (2005) Les deux visages du ghetto. Construire un concept sociologique. *Actes de la recherche en sciences sociales* 160: 4–21.
Wacquant, L. (2007) *Urban outcasts: A comparative sociology of advanced marginality*. Cambridge: Polity Press.
Wilson, W. J. (1987) *The truly disadvantaged: The inner city, the underclass, and public policy*. Chicago: University of Chicago Press.
Wirth, L. (1927) The ghetto. *American Journal of Sociology* 33(1): 57–71.
Zeublin, C. (1895) The Chicago ghetto. In Addams, J. (ed.) *Hull House maps and papers: A presentation of nationalities and wages in a congested district of Chicago, together with comments and essays on problems growing out of the social conditions*. Chicago: Hull House Association.

# 20. Processes of urban hyper-marginalisation under climate change: examples from Angola and Mozambique

*Cristina Udelsmann Rodrigues*

The Global South in general faces a set of challenges when it comes to addressing climate change and particularly its effects in cities (Gottdiener et al. 2019). Not only are the mitigation and adaptation systems overdue regarding what would be desirable, but also most countries are lagging behind in crucial competences and resources to deal with climate change and technical and knowledge capacities to handle the negative effects, and consequently deal with the impacts, which are, in particular, deeper social inequalities and marginalisation.

As climate change impacts are increasingly evident, the 'new urban sociology' (Gottdiener et al. 2019) will more recurrently integrate climate change preoccupations and specifically research about how they relate to urban inequalities and climate change-induced hyper-marginalisation. While the advancements in environmental sociology have been significant, there is an emphasis on the need to further mainstream the disciplinary approach (Lockie 2022) to address the preoccupations with climate change – the shifts in temperatures and weather patterns. According to Castells, the 'work necessary to research and understand the new relationships between space and society' involves systematic integrations of new concepts (Castells 2002: 17). The conceptual frameworks for climate-related urban issues are somehow still under early consideration if compared to the beginning of the 2000s when they were practically absent. However, climate change urban effects and impacts have entered the scientific literature with a steady progression. Other 'novel' topics will follow, like, for instance, the disproportionate exposure of the urban poor to the Covid-19 pandemic, which keeps them marginalised (Matamanda et al. 2022).

Despite the progresses in the introduction of climate concerns in the urban sociological analysis, its effects are not normally listed as one of the areas propelling forward the study of inequality, urban social problems, and where the urban form will lead to (Prener 2020: 5). Exploring urban spatial inequalities, while requiring investigations on how they intersect with social identities or hierarchies or with issues such as labour markets, is rarely equated with variable vulnerabilities regarding climate effects (Tickamyer 2000). Inequality, segregation, and marginalisation, further impacted by climate-related effects on the lives of the urban poor, call for a revision of the conditions that maintain and aggravate marginalisation.

While engaging in the sociological discussions about hyper-segregation, this chapter explores marginalisation and the vulnerability of populations living in what are already segregated and marginalised places and the cumulative consequences climate change has for amplified precarity, poverty, and inequalities. The discussion of hyper-marginalisation is illustrated with empirical research conducted in Luanda (Angola) and Maputo (Mozambique) in risk-prone neighbourhoods of the capitals. This research has been part of comparative research projects and data produced in this context are used here as case-study evidence (Udelsmann

Rodrigues 2019, 2021). In the absence of sufficient technical data or studies about socioeconomic impacts of climate change, the sociological approach in such contexts must focus on qualitative research and straddle international comparisons and local realities. The cases from the Global South can contribute to renewed perspectives in urban theory, both focussed on the Global South and in general cases. At the same time, case studies provide the tools for urban policy in the continent (Magrath 2010).

The chapter starts with a revision of the main concepts and discussions on the relations between urban precarity and climate change and then moves to the analysis of hyper-marginalisation in the Global South countries and poor areas of cities globally and in Luanda and Maputo specifically. The discussion that follows focuses on the cumulative and juxtaposed 'segregations' and 'marginalisations' of the urban poor in Global South countries to show how climate change is part of the conditions that concur with what can be considered in the same sense as hyper-marginalisation.

## URBAN PRECARITY AND CLIMATE CHANGE: AN OVERVIEW WITH PARTICULAR ATTENTION TO THE GLOBAL SOUTH

This chapter discusses climate change and marginalisation around the simple argument that effects of climate change contribute to increased and aggravated forms of marginalisation, precarity, and poorer urban living for those already in the margins. It defends the idea that climate change effects in Global South cities are adding to existing precarity, inequality, and marginalisation. This is an important consideration to define global and local understandings of and strategies to deal with climate change, which require such a comprehensive approach. Pointing out and describing possible ways of analysing the urban social effects of climate change in the Global South is an entry point and contribution to the engagements of urban sociology with crucial world transformations.

Urban effects of climate change broadly refer to housing and infrastructure, livelihoods, or access to services (like health or education). The consequences of climate change for already existing inequalities are expected and, on many occasions, already there, with the already marginalised urban populations predictably having their conditions of living aggravated in the coming years. This will be further developed below.

More than 80% of the world population that will inhabit urban areas by 2050 will be concentrated in the Global South and in low-income countries (United Nations Population Division 2019), where informal precarious settlements – and most notoriously slums – are the predominant urban forms (Bai et al. 2018, Dodman et al. 2019). In these areas, urban infrastructure and services are generally absent, insufficient, or of very bad quality: 'landfills are overflowing and unsanitary, and the provision of waste services has been highly uneven, with wealthier and central city commercial areas receiving more effective services than poorer areas' (Myers 2019: 2). The analysis of inequalities of urban living and of marginalised urban dwellers develops from a perspective that understands 'urban margins' not as essences or entities but as forms of relations between urban dwellers shaped by processes of political, economic, spatial, and social marginalisation (Aceska et al. 2019: 1).

The literature on marginalisation further develops the 'ways in which urban dwellers make the city from the margins' and the 'entanglements with spaces of power and resources' (Aceska et al. 2019: 9). Marginalisation implies less power and socioeconomic advantage for certain urban residents and has been frequently studied in the field of urban studies (Bernt 2013). It is both a condition and a process in which economically and socially disadvantaged groups remain or are conduced into the margins of the society and the economy. In sociology broadly, there are three main perspectives to consider: cultural, social, and structural (social, political, and economic) marginality (Billson 2005), the latter generating a greater consensus (Bernt 2013). Spatially, the main focus of the discussions about urban marginality is that it refers to 'stigmatized neighbourhoods situated at the very bottom of the hierarchical system of places that compose the metropolis' (Wacquant 2008: 1), as seen all over the world. Marginal urban life, however, encompasses more than the location of marginal households in urban peripheries (Pieterse 2018); it involves social, cultural, and economic life and disadvantaged positions in terms of resources, power, or information. African cities are among those where marginal urban living has been analysed in detail (Pieterse 2018, Satterthwaite 2007), including in Angola and Mozambique (Udelsmann Rodrigues 2019, 2021).

**Segregation and Hyper-marginalisation**

When it comes to issues beyond separations of types of urban dwellers and social strata (segregation), marginalisation, as discussed, is a more comprehensive concept. Segregation implies keeping people of, for instance, different sexes, races, or religions apart, socially and/or physically, while marginalisation encompasses both these separations and the mentioned cultural and economic dimensions (access to resources, power, or information), with the many combinations.

Based on the sociological discussions about hyper-segregation (Horne 2008, Massey & Denton 1993), it is possible to develop the argument that the marginalisation and vulnerability of populations living in what are already segregated countries and cities are increasingly bearing the cumulative consequences of climate change, which leads to amplified poverty, precarity, and inequalities.

Hyper-segregation has been traditionally associated with issues of racial inequalities that add to other segregation factors, with many examples coming from apartheid South Africa. However, theoretical debates have expanded the emphasis to issues beyond race and increasingly recognise the importance of social and economic conditions to explain spatial and socioeconomic separations between different groups. Hyper-segregation is defined as 'an extreme case of spatial segregation and institutional or business isolation' (Gottdiener et al. 2019: 4). Departing from the analysis of South Africa's context, recent studies have characterised hyper-segregation as 'indirect racial and economic segregation of poor neighbourhoods' and both hyper-segregation and class-based segregation as 'economic in nature, not [fully] racial' (Geyer & Mohammed 2015: 35). While segregation is less useful to explain the inequalities and imbalances as it focuses on general aspects of social and economic conditions of individuals and groups, marginalisation can better encompass issues of spatial, social, and economic separations and distinctions.

Looking at amplified situations of marginality, the concept of hyper-marginalisation has rarely been mobilised, at occasions being used to refer to indigenous minorities (Bessire 2014). When adding to existing marginalisation and other pressures from society or the environment, it becomes clear that people already segregated and socially and economically marginalised who at the same time are isolated by public institutions suffer more acutely the effects of, for instance, climate-related phenomena. The example of the consequences of Hurricane Katrina in New Orleans in 2005 illustrates the vulnerability of the urban poor and the higher impacts of negative climate effects on them (Geyer & Mohammed 2015).

Like in other parts of the Global South in particular, in Luanda and Maputo populations living in natural disaster risk-prone areas are also less covered than others by urban planning, urban infrastructure and services, and mitigation procedures that can institutionally reduce the already existing levels of segregation and marginalisation than those who inhabit other areas.

**Climate Change Exacerbating Marginalisation**

Hyper-marginalisation will then be the circumstance of those already marginalised who are subject to additional factors affecting their exclusion; namely, climate-related effects. Climate change further entrenches structural inequalities and marginalisation (Porter et al. 2020). It is therefore a more useful concept to analyse and discuss climate change and urban inequalities in cities of the Global South.

While precarious urban conditions of living are characterised by structural socioeconomic, spatial, or cultural disadvantages and exclusions, exposure to climate change-related effects further increases the vulnerability and marginalisation of urban slum-dwellers (Parnell & Walawege 2011, Winsemius et al. 2015). Global South cities face harder conditions for urban living, with much higher proportions of populations living in precarious areas. Examples are those inhabiting precarious peripheries with no infrastructure or services, where urban planning is either absent or never applied.

The emphasis on marginal situations is related to the growing need for urban studies to 'critically understand the wider societal and material implications of strategic responses to the pressures of climate change' (Hodson & Marvin 2010). On the other hand, social justice, economic justice, and environmental justice intersect across different experiences of marginality, whether related to gender, ethnicity, income, or residence (Swyngedouw & Heynen 2003). The contributions to urban policy in the Global South are crucial: 'historical-geographical insights into these ever-changing urban configurations are necessary for the sake of considering the future of radical political-ecological urban strategies' (Swyngedouw & Heynen 2003: 898).

The production and reproduction of urban segregation and marginalisation in the Global South have their own dynamics resulting from specific socioeconomic and political arrangements, from historical paths that have drawn many of the features of cities in the Global South (Myers 2019) and that can explain the existing clearly marked inequalities and the subjection of the poorer cohorts to worse living. This involves four key interconnected dimensions: 1) vast disparities in causal responsibility for greenhouse gas emissions between countries/cities; 2) climate impacts are unevenly distributed; 3) vulnerability to these impacts results from pre-existing patterns of privilege and marginalisation (again, as an example, the effects of Hurricane Katrina); 4) finally, those who have benefited from emissions and those who are most harmed are segregated from each other by social or physical distance and time (Klinsky & Mavrogianni 2020: 413–414).

As a result, urban disaster governance is in essence a matter of 'justice for and power of marginalised urban people' (Meriläinen et al. 2019: 187). In some analyses, climate justice is explained and explored in relation to how decisions about the built environment in the climate context 'intersect with human wellbeing' (Klinsky & Mavrogianni 2020: 412). The recognition that climate change effects concur with the exacerbation of worse living among the urban poor and lead to more marginalisation is therefore key for better urban planning and management.

This discussion will be illustrated with data collected in Luanda and Maputo in risk-prone neighbourhoods during empirical research conducted between 2017 and 2019. In this research, qualitative information collected through over 50 interviews in six neighbourhoods in Luanda and Maputo – three in each city – led to the analysis of the mutual implications of climate and natural events in the lives of urban residents in the margins (Udelsmann Rodrigues 2019, 2021). These data are here mobilised to provide a sense of some of the issues at stake, in particular those related to deteriorating living conditions and positionalities because of climate change-related effects. In-depth interviews were conducted with a variety of local actors – urban management authorities at the central and local levels, specialists in environmental issues, families, and urban residents of the six neighbourhoods selected: Bairro dos Pescadores, Polana Caniço II, and Bairro Luís Cabral (Maputo) and Bairro dos Pescadores/ Cacuaco, Comandante Bula, and Viana (Luanda). Figure 20.1 shows one example of flooding found in one of the neighbourhoods. The purposive selection of these neighbourhoods aimed at collecting accounts of a varied set of climate change-impacted neighbourhoods relating to rising sea levels (the two Bairros dos Pescadores) and flooding (the other four).

*Source:* Cristina Udelsmann Rodrigues.

*Figure 20.1* *Flooded neighbourhood in Luanda (2019)*

# HYPER-MARGINALISATION PRODUCED BY CLIMATE CHANGE

Poverty, precarity, and marginalisation are already by themselves characteristics that place residents of cities of the Global South in disadvantaged positions. They are caused by social and economic inequalities and by unequal access to urban infrastructure and services and recurrently result in spatial inequalities and separations. The analysis of these urban features along with the increasing effects of climate change in urban settings points to worsening situations and to hyper-marginalisation. This is evident in the analysis of trends related to poverty in cities of the Global South and most critically in the accounts of urban dwellers when called to refer to the implications of climate for urban life.

## Hyper-marginalisation in Poor Areas of Global South Cities

While the estimates for the continent's urban population are some of the lowest compared to other world regions, the percentage of the population living in slums in Sub-Saharan Africa was the highest in the world in 2018, above 50%, which corresponds to 237,840,000 people (UN-Habitat 2020: 26). The percentage of the population in the region living in multidimensional poverty in urban areas was 31% in 2018 (UN-Habitat 2020), which normally translates into precarious living conditions. Notwithstanding the negative indicators for poverty and inequality in the context of Global South countries, 'Sub-Saharan Africa has the world's second highest level of income inequality after Latin America' (UN-Habitat 2020: 23), with high Gini coefficients, and among cities on the continent, South African cities are the most unequal. While the indicators confirm the generalised precarious conditions of the urban population living in the margins, the portion of the population living in cities – of all sizes – in Africa will tend to increase in the coming years: the percentage of the urban population living in urban areas will increase from 43.5% in 2020 to 50.9% in 2035 (UN-Habitat 2020).

Urban impacts of climate change-related hazards are varied, with droughts affecting water supply; hurricanes, floods, and landslides destroying or damaging houses; and extreme temperatures making living in poor housing more difficult. Coastal cities like Luanda and Maputo are increasingly prone to the effects of rising sea levels. The urban poor in Africa face growing problems of severe flooding. Increased storm frequency and intensity related to climate change are exacerbated by local factors such as the growing occupation of floodplains, increased run-off from hard surfaces, inadequate waste management, and silted-up drainage (Douglas et al. 2008). In 2020, many cities around the world experienced extreme temperatures 'not seen for years' (World Economic Forum 2022: 8). The examples of how climate change is impacting cities in Africa are varied and abundant (Douglas et al. 2008, Kareem et al. 2020), but there is not yet a comprehensive set of data allowing a follow-up of the progression of natural hazards related to climate change. However, the consequences are unquestionable, not only in terms of the physical living conditions but also of livelihoods and access to infrastructure and services, especially among the urban dwellers already in the margins.

Beyond the accounts of cases and episodes throughout the world related to the urban impacts of climate change (Kareem et al. 2020), both the development technical literature – international reports and action-oriented analyses – and academic research progressively provide evidence of the causal interrelations. Specific references to the particular effects on the urban poor and those in marginal positions are also growing. For the development instances, the nature and location of urban informal precarious settlements 'means that they are often exposed to a range of climate-related hazards' (UN-Habitat 2018: 8). Here, the majority of housing is of poor quality, often lacking, among other things, tenure security, basic infrastructure and service provision, access to food and water, financial services, and urban planning. These deficiencies expose residents to climate hazards more than in other places.

Examples of increased effects of climate-related hazards on already-poor urban populations can be seen in many parts of the world but most notably in the Global South (Baker 2012, Hallegatte 2016, Satterthwaite 2007, Tacoli 2009, Vairavamoorthy et al. 2008, Winsemius et al. 2015). Sociological research on environmental inequality – and justice – has in turn revealed that there are differences between those who are less and more affected across social class, gender, and ethnic lines, among others, with the 'less powerful' being the more affected (Zehr 2015: 138). While generally the most marginalised are more heavily hit (Porter et al. 2020), age and gender add to the vulnerabilities, with children, the elderly, and women being more prone to suffer from the adversities of climate change associated with poverty (Zehr 2015). The 'intersectional experiences of climate vulnerability' concur with the greater marginalisation of the already marginalised urban dwellers throughout the world (Anguelovski & Pellow 2020: 308). Lacking the means, data, and infrastructural conditions to mitigate climate change-related effects, 'the urban poor become acutely exposed,' continuously subject to poverty and marginalisation 'in even more pronounced ways' (Henrique & Tschakert 2020: 8).

While it is apparently easy to establish a correlation between negative effects and the social cohorts more vulnerable to them, it is important to examine in more detail the changing realities on the ground in as many and as varied as possible urban cases, and thus contribute to the revision of the conceptualisations on marginalisation and its components through evidence about nuances, differences, and local perceptions.

**Hyper-marginalisation in Angolan and Mozambican Cities**

In both Luanda and Maputo, the dynamics of urban growth are strongly related to migration from rural areas originating from displacements caused by long-lasting armed civil conflicts in the period of 1975–2002 in Angola and 1975–1996 in Mozambique. Both the forced migrations and the continued rural migration motivated by the search for better living conditions led to massive settlement in some of the most environmentally risky areas of the cities and to unplanned settlements without infrastructure (Cain 2018, Jenkins 2001, Udelsmann Rodrigues 2019). The result is that today in Maputo the most populated areas, where slum dwellers are concentrated, are most at risk (UN-Habitat 2014: 229) and in Luanda low-income poor settlements tend to be the most vulnerable to climate effects (Cain 2017: 8).

The population of both countries is in general vulnerable to climate-related negative effects (Table 20.1) but in the urban areas, where living conditions are precarious, these effects tend to be more acute. While disaggregated urban and rural figures are scarce, both flooding and drought affect large numbers of the population in Angola and in Mozambique, as shown in Table 20.1. United Nations estimates for the future are, in all cases, even higher, with the only exception being the number of people affected by flooding in Angola in the coming years.

*Table 20.1   Population in Angola and Mozambique affected by flooding and drought*

|  | Angola 2018 | Angola future (projected period 2051–2100) | Mozambique 2010 | Mozambique future (projected period 2051–2100) |
|---|---|---|---|---|
| Flooding: annual average number of affected people | 115,000/year | 71,000/year | 600,000 | 1,500,000 |
| Drought: annual average number of affected people | 900,000/year | 8,500,000/year | 200,000 | 250,000 |

*Source:*   CIMA & UNISDR (2018), World Bank (2020).

Climate change directly affects local economies and livelihoods and consequently all types of residents. However, in specific cases, as a resident of the Bairro Costa do Sol in Maputo indicated (OM, 60 years old, male, Maputo, January 2019), 'many live on the fishing activities here at the coast; while farming land is reducing because the land becomes brackish from year to year.' Weaker urban capacities to deal with the effects of climate change affect all urban residents. As a resident of the Bairro Costa do Sol in Maputo emphasised, 'unfortunately, the development of the neighbourhood has not been proportionated to the needs of the residents, as there are still problems with sanitation, water drainage problems, roads, and water problems.' Paradoxically, these problems affect everyone, the 'rich' and the 'poor.' However, besides the references from the literature, urban dwellers in Luanda and in Maputo are recurrently clear about the worsening conditions of those who are already poor and live in the more precarious areas of the cities when climate-related events take place. As OM added, 'those who have money pay to elevate the land around their houses to escape the rain; when it rains, the water is retained in the houses of the poorer.' For many residents, especially the poorer, moving to other neighbourhoods is not an option, first because of the resources needed to build or buy another house but also, in many cases, because residents depend on economic activities located nearby. A 39-year-old fisherman in Cacuaco (Angola) noted that 'some families do not have a place to stay when it is the rainy season and their houses are flooded; those are the most in danger' (DAM, Bairro dos Pescadores, Luanda, May 2019).

As OM emphasised, 'the most affected are the fishermen that have small boats; that is combined with the reduction of water resources over the years.' Socioeconomic vulnerability is amplified by climate-related phenomena, as mentioned by a 47-year-old resident: 'the worse cases are women that do not have husbands to help them rebuild the houses [when there are galcs]' (LM, female resident, Bairro da Costa do Sol, January 2019) Moreover, a location at certain parts of neighbourhoods can make the difference in terms of vulnerability, as referred to by a 46-year-old female resident of Bairro Costa do Sol: 'those who live in the lower parts of the *bairro* are the most affected by flooding and when the sea comes up' (GS, resident since 1995, February 2019). Long-term savings or even lifetime savings can be destroyed, making families return to 'square zero' after years of progression, as a 59-year-old female resident illustrated: '[with the flooding] I had damages in my freezer; I had a wardrobe that came from South Africa, made of white wood. When it inundated, everything was ruined' (PS, Bairro Luís Cabral, February 2019).

In other cases, 'there has been a serious problem, because those who have money have raised the soils to be able to escape the waters, and when it rains the water is retained in the homes of the less favoured causing floods in the low areas' (OM, male, 52, January 2019). The poor are the ones who suffer more according to the majority of the accounts collected. In Luanda too, the combination of living in poor precarious areas and the lack of resources to deal with climate-related effects places urban dwellers in more disadvantaged positions: 'Those who do not have money or jobs, even when their houses have water coming from the ground, they do not go out [of the houses, of the neighbourhood]; they have nowhere to go' (MM, male, 50, coordinator of the Bairro Mateba, Luanda, May 2019). As another resident in Luanda of Bairro Comandante Bula puts it, 'low-income families are unable to leave their homes [when flooding occurs] due to lack of financial resources' (FB, male, 49, coordinator of the Bairro).

As climate change affects all urban residents, namely all of those in the already risk-prone neighbourhoods of the two distinct countries analysed, the consequences most notably affect domestic economies and assets, with those in the more disadvantaged positions – due to their location or their inability to move, even if temporarily, or due to having less family support – being more exposed to them.

## CONCLUSIONS

While the indications of worsening conditions for the urban poor in the face of climate-related effects are relatively abundant, particularly in the Global South, accurate updated data as well as specific research on trends and comparisons over time are limited. Moreover, investigations of the juxtapositions and accumulations of marginalising conditions of the urban poor are often passed over by focused analyses, whether in terms of infrastructural and housing inequalities in cities or, for instance, access to health differentials among urban socioeconomic groups. Accounts from residents in Luanda and Maputo show that this accumulation of negative conditions is clearly perceived.

The interest of looking at urban vulnerabilities concerning climate change that, combined with other factors, concur with hyper-marginalisation relates not only to the fact that the topic is still not sufficiently explored and assessed but also the evaluation of trends. Hyper-marginalisation may lead to more pronounced socioeconomic polarisations in the near future given that climate effects are tending to become exacerbated. On the other hand, assessing the features and conditions for hyper-marginalisation helps in prioritising urban management and planning, namely in what concerns the physical living environment in cities – housing and infrastructure – and the ways of aiming at better distribution. Moreover, it helps in better identifying the sectors of urban economies (more) affected by this increased marginalisation and consequently in addressing urban livelihoods with a more inclusive perspective. The same is true regarding the distribution and conditions of access to services such as health or education in urban milieus.

In conclusion, climate change effects intensify the trends toward hyper-marginalisation in cities of the Global South countries but there is not been sufficient reflection on how this leads to increased polarisation of urban societies and economies. Further residential and spatial inequalities are tendentially produced in urban spaces due to climate change effects, with sociopolitical implications. Sociological reflections need to incorporate such factors more actively into the disciplinary analytical frameworks, as set forward by the new urban sociology. Climate change effects notably impact the economies and assets of urban residents, with those in the more disadvantaged positions – in different neighbourhood areas, with less capacity to move, even if temporarily, when the weather events take place, or with less family support – being more exposed to them. In this sense, the urban socioeconomic analysis of changing urban livelihoods also needs to increasingly address and equate climate change-related factors. Suggestions for future research agendas include case studies that can provide accounts and figures for deteriorating urban lives and livelihoods and increased marginalisation resulting from the effects of climate change. Comparative research is also welcome, most crucially to assess global, inter-country, and inter-region imbalances in terms of climate change effects on cities and processes of marginalisation. By incorporating hyper-marginalisation in the sociological urban analysis, as a concept that considers the additional factors and conditions for increased marginalisation, particularly in the Global South, urban studies can provide better input to both knowledge and policy on poverty and precarity. Further understanding vulnerabilities and the conditions that amplify them not only helps in strengthening the role of the social sciences in urban research but also, among other contributions, puts in dialogue preoccupations that concern a variety of areas of knowledge and research.

# REFERENCES

Aceska, A., Heer, B. & Kaiser-Grolimund, A. (2019) Doing the city from the margins: Critical perspectives on urban marginality. *Anthropological Forum* 29(1): 1–11.

Anguelovski, I. & Pellow, D. N. (2020) Towards an emancipatory urban climate justice through adaptation? *Planning Theory & Practice*, 21(2): 308–313.

Bai, X., Dawson, R. J., Ürge-Vorsatz, D., Delgado, G. C., Salisu Barau, A., Dhakal, S., Dodman, D., Leonardsen, L., Masson-Delmotte, V., Roberts, D. C. & Schultz, S. (2018) Six research priorities for cities and climate change. *Nature* 555(7694): 23–25.

Baker, J. L. (2012) *Climate change, disaster risk, and the urban poor: Cities building resilience for a changing world*. Washington, DC: World Bank Publications.

Bernt, M. & Laura, C. (2013) *Exclusion, marginalization and peripheralization: Conceptual concerns in the study of urban inequalities*. Working Paper 49. Erkner: Leibniz-Institut für Regionalentwicklung und Strukturplanung (IRS).

Bessire, L. (2014) The rise of indigenous hypermarginality. *Current Anthropology* 55(3): 276–295.

Billson, J. M. (2005) No owner of soil: Redefining the concept of marginality. In R. M. Dennis (ed.) *Marginality, power and social structure: Issues in race, class, and gender analysis*. Oxford: Routledge, 29–47.

Cain, A. (2017) *Water Resource management under a changing climate in Angola's coastal settlements*. London: IIED.

Cain, A. (2018) Informal water markets and community management in peri-urban Luanda, Angola. *Water International* 43(2): 205–216.

Castells, M. (2002) Urban sociology in the twenty-first century. *Cidades Comunidades e Territórios* 5: 9–19.

CIMA & UNISDR (2018) Angola disaster risk profile. https://www.undrr.org/publication/disaster-risk-profile-angola

Dodman, D., Archer, D. & Satterthwaite, D. (2019) Editorial: Responding to climate change in contexts of urban poverty and informality. *Environment and Urbanization* 31(1): 3–12.

Douglas, I., Alam, K., Maghenda, M., McDonnell, Y., McLean, L. & Campbell, J. (2008) Unjust waters: Climate change, flooding and the urban poor in Africa. *Environment and Urbanization* 20(1): 187–205.

Geyer, H. S. & Mohammed, F. (2015) Hypersegregation and class-based segregation processes in Cape Town 2001–2011. *Urban Forum* 27(1): 35–58.

Gottdiener, M., Hohle, R. & King, C. (2019) *The new urban sociology*. New York: Routledge.

Hallegatte, S. (2016) *Shock waves: Managing the impacts of climate change on poverty*. Washington, DC: The World Bank.
Henrique, K. P. & Tschakert, P. (2020) Pathways to urban transformation: From dispossession to climate justice. *Progress in Human Geography* 45(5): 1169–1191.
Hodson, M. & Marvin, S. (2010) Urbanism in the anthropocene: Ecological urbanism or premium ecological enclaves? *City* 14(3): 298–313.
Horne, J. (2008) *Breach of faith: Hurricane Katrina and the near death of a great American city*. New York: Random House.
Jenkins, P. (2001) Strengthening access to land for housing for the poor in Maputo, Mozambique. *International Journal of Urban and Regional Research* 25(3): 629–648.
Kareem, B., Lwasa, S., Tugume, D., Mukwaya, P., Walubwa, J., Owuor, S., Kasaija, P., Sseviiri, H., Nsangi, G. & Byarugaba, D. (2020) Pathways for resilience to climate change in African cities. *Environmental Research Letters* 15(7).
Klinsky, S. & Mavrogianni, A. (2020) Climate justice and the built environment. *Buildings and Cities* 1(1): 412–428.
Lockie, S. (2022) Mainstreaming climate change sociology. *Environmental Sociology* 8(1): 1–6.
Magrath, J. (2010) The injustice of climate change: Voices from Africa. *Local Environment* 15(9–10): 891–901.
Massey, D. & Denton, N. A. (1993) *American apartheid: Segregation and the making of the underclass*. Cambridge: Harvard University Press.
Matamanda, A. R., Dunn, M. & Nel, V. (2022) Broken bridges over troubled waters: COVID-19 and the urban poor residing in Dinaweng informal settlement, Bloemfontein, South Africa. *South African Geographical Journal* 104(3): 309–327.
Meriläinen, E. S., Fougère, M. & Piotrowicz, W. (2019) Refocusing urban disaster governance on marginalised urban people through right to the city. *Environmental Hazards* 19(2): 187–208.
Myers, G. (2019) Environmental issues in Africa's cities. In A. M. Orum (ed.) *The Wiley Blackwell encyclopedia of urban and regional studies*. London: John Wiley & Sons, 1–9.
Parnell, S. & Walawege, R. (2011) Sub-Saharan African urbanisation and global environmental change. *Global Environmental Change* 21: S12–S20.
Pieterse, M. (2018) Where is the periphery even? Capturing urban marginality in South African human rights law. *Urban Studies* 56(6): 1182–1197.
Porter, L., Rickards, L., Verlie, B., Bosomworth, K., Moloney, S., Lay, B., Latham, B., Anguelovski, A. & Pellow, D. (2020) Climate justice in a climate changed world. *Planning Theory & Practice* 21(2): 293–321.
Prener, C. G. (2020) Finding the city in sociology: Broadening and deepening the geographic scope of the urban and inequality literatures. *Sociology Compass* 14(2): e12756.
Satterthwaite, D. (2007) *Adapting to climate change in urban areas: The possibilities and constraints in low- and middle-income nations*. London: IIED.
Storper, M. & Scott, A. (2016) Current debates in urban theory: A critical assessment. *Urban Studies* 53(6): 1114–1136.
Swyngedouw, E. & Heynen, N. (2003) Urban political ecology, justice and the politics of scale. *Antipode* 35(5): 898–918.
Tacoli, C. (2009) Crisis or adaptation? Migration and climate change in a context of high mobility. *Environment and Urbanization* 21(2): 513–525.
Tickamyer, A. R. (2000) Space matters! Spatial inequality in future sociology. *Contemporary Sociology* 29(6): 805–813.
Udelsmann Rodrigues, C. (2019) Climate change and DIY urbanism in Luanda and Maputo: New urban strategies? *International Journal of Urban Sustainable Development* 11(3): 319–331.
Udelsmann Rodrigues, C. (2021) Where is the state missing? Addressing urban climate change at the margins in Luanda and Maputo. *Urban Forum* 33(1): 1–15.
UN-Habitat (2014) *The state of African cities: Re-imagining sustainable urban transitions*. Nairobi: UN-Habitat.
UN-Habitat (2018) *Addressing the most vulnerable first: Pro-poor climate action in informal settlements*. Nairobi: UN-Habitat.
UN-Habitat (2020) *World cities report 2020*. Nairobi: UN-Habitat.

United Nations Population Division (2019) World urbanization prospects: The 2018 revision.

Vairavamoorthy, K., Gorantiwar, S. D. & Pathirana, A. (2008) Managing urban water supplies in developing countries – Climate change and water scarcity scenarios. *Physics and Chemistry of the Earth, Parts A/B/C* 33(5): 330–339.

Wacquant, L. (2008) *Urban outcasts: A comparative sociology of advanced marginality*. London: Wiley.

Winsemius, H. C., Brende, J., Veldkamp, T. I. E., Hallegatte, S., Bangalore, M. & Ward, P. (2015) *Disaster risk, climate change, and poverty: Assessing the global exposure of poor people to floods and droughts*. Washington, DC: The World Bank.

World Bank (2020) Disaster risk profile – Mozambique. https://drmims.sadc.int/sites/default/files/document/2020-03/2019_MozambiqueRiskProfile.pdf.

World Economic Forum (2022) The global risks report 2022. https://www.weforum.org/reports/global-risks-report-2022/.

Zehr, S. (2015) The sociology of global climate change. *Wiley Interdisciplinary Reviews: Climate Change* 6(2): 129–150.

# 21. Crime, policing, and youth orientations towards urban futures

*Naomi van Stapele and Samuel Kiriro*

On Sunday 26th December 2021, at 5 o'clock in the evening, a group of 24 youths, both young men and women around 20 years old, robbed all people and businesses they passed on their way from one end of Mathare (a large low-income urban settlement in Nairobi (Huchzermeyer 2011)) to the other (Muungano Support Trust 2012). The people they robbed at knifepoint were their friends, neighbours, and fellow residents trying to make ends meet in one of Nairobi's poorest settlements, locally dubbed ghettos. The following morning, we drank tea at a local *kibanda* (Swahili for a makeshift eatery on the roadside) and listening to an agitated debate among the other tea-drinkers and the cook on the incident. The young female cook frowned, her hands elbow deep in chapati dough pounding away as she said to us: 'This is not normal. They just came with knives, *pangas*, 24 of them, and robbed everybody, we know them, you know them.' She pointed at us with doughy fingers. The shock was palpable among all customers. How was this possible? The ten or so Mathare residents gathered at the *kibanda*, sitting and standing while drinking tea and debating, all agreed that this had not happened since the 1990s. 'Yes,' one customer spoke in a voice dripping with doom, 'crime is there, but such a large group of youth? And from people they know? No! This reveals we have a deeper problem, what do you think now will happen next year during elections? If already now they can do this?' Some customers merely looked bewildered, not knowing how to make sense of what had happened, while others were speculating what would happen next. 'You know the groups from Mlango [a neighbourhood in Mathare] will revenge, and then they need to retaliate again, and so on until New Year's Eve.'

Indeed, the next day we learned that youth from Mlango had stolen a motorbike from one of the 24 suspects. We received this news when we were on our way to Rowland camp where youth from Ghetto Foundation were having their annual camp at a scouting site in a forest near Kibera on the other side of Nairobi. Ghetto Foundation is a social justice centre in Mathare founded by the second author of this chapter. The first author has conducted research with the second author and with other social justice activists since 1998. Driving into the forest where they were camping, we deliberated whether the 22 youth members from Ghetto Foundation, called Ghetto Youth, should stay at the campsite until 1st January 2022 for safety purposes. As soon as we sat down for lunch with the youth group, under a circle of majestic trees at the campsite and surrounded by massive baboons trying to steal food from our plates, one of the youth leaders confirmed our premonition. When discussing the tensions at home, one of the youth leaders called Shafi said:

> If we go home now, our friends [the 24 suspected robbers] will ask us to help them defend our part of the neighbourhood. We can't refuse, we must protect each other, even if we don't agree with what they have done. We are one community, one ghetto. A police bullet may hit one of us, or we may be killed by a *panga*. We are reforming, we can't go back now.

And so they stayed at the campsite until 1st January. All expected peace to return after the New Year celebrations given their conviction that the 24 violent young street muggers had been driven by a desire to get money to party on the 31st. Crime rates normally go up in Mathare and other low-income urban settlements during the month of December, which is often explained locally by alluding to the pressure youth feel to offer family, friends, and themselves a nice holiday (which includes dressing up and going out to drink and eat). Nevertheless, the sheer organisation, size, and brazenness of this group kept everyone in disbelief, including the members of Ghetto Youth, who tried so hard to escape a life in crime.

Crime and policing are common threads of everyday life in Mathare and have been extensively explored by anthropologists, sociologists, urban geographers, and other types of scholars (Diphoorn et al. 2019, Jones et al. 2017, Kimari 2021, Médard 2010, Price et al. 2016, Rasmussen & Van Stapele 2020, Thieme 2017). Equally, ample studies have explored crime prevention and rehabilitation of children and youth engaged in crime in violent urban settings in African cities (Segalo & Sihlobo 2021, Cheruiyot & Wainaina 2020) and elsewhere (Weegels 2018). This chapter adds to these and other studies on youth in African cities (Mabala 2011, Rasmussen & Van Stapele 2020, Sommers 2012, 2011) and cities worldwide (Jeffrey & Dyson 2009) by exploring the dimension of time (Thieme 2021) in addition to socio-spatial analyses of urban youths' organising and social navigations (Vigh 2006, 2009). Social navigation is useful to study choice-making and analyse people's movements (including making decisions and acting on them) within constantly shifting temporal and spatial contexts such as is the case in Mathare (Abend 2018). This notion highlights the social and bodily praxis aimed at improving social possibilities by evaluating 'the immediate and the imagined' (Vigh 2006: 13, 136) and taking action (including 'inaction') accordingly.

In this chapter, we set out to explore the decision by Shafi and other youth from Ghetto Foundation to reform in the context of these interconnecting types of violence. What does it mean to reform in their view? What kind of orientations to the future does reform entail? What do their orientations tell us about the everyday life of youth in highly marginalised neighbourhoods in African cities? The way Shafi and his peers conceptualise reform connects to the importance of choice-making in desisting from crime (Farral 2002). Choice-making among youth has been explored abundantly in relationship to crime, but mostly from an interventionist perspective (Bugnon 2020, Werth & Ballestero 2017). Shafi's notion of reform is closer to Foucault's notion of 'technology of the self' (Foucault et al. 1988), which brings out choice-making as a resource for subjectivation that allows new relations to self and world to emerge. These new relations make new futures possible. Orientations as a conceptual lens bring into view choice-making within specific 'urban life worlds' (Hahn 2010) of young people in Mathare by drawing our attention to the way futures shape presents (Bryant & Knight 2019: 2). Building on Bryant and Knight (2019), we understand orientations as future-oriented vistas that to a large measure shape our actions in the present. As such, we heed their call for research that takes a fuller account of the teleologies of individual and group actions in the present and how these pertain to making (new) urban futures possible. Among the myriad ways the future may orient individuals and groups and vice versa, we focus mostly on two that are most pertinent for our interlocutors: anticipation and aspiration (Appadurai 2004, 2013: 285–286). These two orientations emerge from the same socio-spatial reality of Mathare, but they produce vastly different urban futures for its youth. While such orientations are often entangled, as will become clear below, foregrounding one or the other, Shafi shared with us, means 'the difference between life and death for us' (27 December 2021, Nairobi).

Shafi and his peers aspired to a future free from crime and being policed while simultaneously anticipating being sucked into both — especially during the dangerous month of December. Anticipation moves beyond expectation as both crime and being policed are considered inevitable, thus prompting an embodied readiness (*kukaa rada* in Sheng, an urban version of the creolising language Swahili (Githinji 2006, Githora 2018)) among youth. Their aspirations tell of futures in which they are not only alive but in which they have the capacity to build meaningful lives. Aspirations are bound up with ideas of 'a good life' and can thus be considered as desired futures (ends) as well as moral compasses for action in the present moment (means), which reveals the co-constitutive nature of 'ends' and 'means' and the potentiality of temporal shifts and even conflation between them (Frye 2012: 1572).

Anticipations and aspirations are moulded within urban contexts while also defining such material conditions and dynamics; hence, this chapter does not look at the individual youths or at social contexts but at the interactions between them. The urban conditions underlying the youths' orientations to their futures, and to which they give rise, constitute the city as a 'multiplicity' rather than a 'whole' (Farías 2011). This draws our attention not just to spatial and scalar configurations of the urban but also to its temporal dimensions, which are inspired by and productive of the wide variety of urban lived experiences and materialities. Accordingly, we depart from youth perspectives to study relationalities and possibilities between and across not only space and scale (Muller 2015: 29) but also times, with a specific emphasis on future time, to advance critical urban sociology (Beckert & Suckert 2021, Brenner et al. 2011, Pieterse & Simone 2013, Roy 2011, Simone & Pieterse 2017). A focus on urban life worlds through the prism of future time in relation to space and multiscalar power configurations enables a re-engagement with the notion of 'the social' (Glick Schiller & Schmidt 2016) as the interface between social vistas and choice-making. Significantly, interrogating future time as part of urban life worlds across space, power, and scale and from the perspectives of youth brings into view time as affect (Johnsen et al. 2019). Critical urban sociology stands to gain from a more comprehensive integration of perceptions of the future into its empirical investigations. This includes expectations, aspirations, and beliefs about the future. An in-depth approach to incorporating these factors could enhance the discipline's ability to provide nuanced insights into urban phenomena and their underlying social processes (Beckert & Suckert 2021). Orientations toward the future occur through ongoing everyday struggles for urban futures in which socio-spatial and temporal multiplicities link at various scales and shift according to ever-unfolding actualities, processes, and events (Anderson & McFarlane 2011). By taking the city as an entanglement of such multiplicities, and not as a coherent map, urban life worlds of youths and how these are defined by and in turn define urban futures are brought in view.

## POLICING YOUNG AND POOR MEN IN MATHARE

The anticipation of Shafi and fellow members of Ghetto Youth regarding violent policing in Mathare in December 2021 highlights the quotidian entrenchment of a specific form of police violence in urban Kenya. Policing of neighbourhoods such as Mathare, as in many other low-income African urban settlements, is often organised through complex, localised, and shifting arrangements between the official police service, community-based organisations, gangs, individual citizens, and private corporations (Buur & Jensen 2004, Colona & Diphoorn

2017, Diphoorn & Van Stapele 2019, Diphoorn et al. 2019, Kyed & Albrecht 2014). In Kenya, such arrangements are mostly geared towards eradicating crime but also entail a wide variety of other economic and political objectives (Cooper-Knock & Owen 2015), including criminal ones (Van Stapele 2020, 2021).

Police killings of crime suspects in Mathare is an equally complex issue, where what is considered illegal or criminal police violence by law may, in some instances, be seen as entirely legitimate by some residents of Mathare. Police officers' use of illegal – but to some legitimate – lethal force is the result of negotiating 'permissive spaces' (Cooper-Knock 2018, LeBas 2013) with Mathare citizens for such violence. The rampant killing of young male crime suspects by the police in this and other similar neighbourhoods in Nairobi (Jones et al. 2017, MSJC 2017) is the outcome of tense collaborations between police units and the residents of such neighbourhoods (Van Stapele 2020). Identifying citizens who collaborate with police in police killings is not always clear-cut. In some of the more than 200 cases we have investigated since 2017 as part of our work for the social justice movement in Kenya, we found that most of these citizens were professional informants who were paid by the police to provide information, such as pictures of local crime suspects. However, in other instances, they were rival gang members who wanted to eliminate their competition. In yet other cases, community members who had repeatedly warned the youths against stealing from them but to no avail reported them to the police out of exasperation.

Most police officers operating in Mathare are not from the neighbourhood or even from the city. Consequently, they rely on local citizens for information about Mathare. Low-income urban settlements like Mathare are often formally unplanned neighbourhoods with iron-sheet houses, rickety tenement buildings, or low-rise houses made from crumbling stone or mud (Huchzermeyer 2011). Mathare has approximately 200,000 residents but no indoor plumbing and a broken sewer system. It has a high population density and high unemployment rate and lacks basic services such as garbage collection and proper sanitation. All this has led residents to organise various forms of 'shared self-provisioning' (Kinder 2016), including the local provision of security, which sometimes includes collaborations with police. Such collaborations between residents and police are inevitably characterised by tensions because citizens from Mathare also frequently and violently close ranks against the police; for instance, when the police escort the electricity company to cut all illegal connections.

Police killing of young male crime suspects in Mathare, and elsewhere in Kenya, is facilitated by an extralegal space created by a widespread demand for 'immediate justice' (Hornberger 2013: 12). The link between the call for 'vigilante justice' (Buur & Jensen 2004, Cooper-Knock 2018, Moser & Rodgers 2005, Pratten & Sen 2007, Pratten 2008, Rodgers 2008) and 'police vigilantism' (Jauregui 2016) is mainly due to a deep-seated lack of trust in the judiciary (Mbote & Akech 2011). This yearning for safety from theft, combined with distrust of the justice system, has led to a readiness among some Mathare residents to accept illegal police violence against crime suspects in public spaces (Ruteere & Pommerolle 2003).

A critical urban sociological perspective thus complicates the prevailing notion that violent policing is mostly directed against marginalised communities by highlighting that it may also be a consequence of shifting arrangements between police officers and members of such communities. Hence, the use of excessive force by police in Mathare erodes trust not only between law enforcement and communities but also between community members themselves. Understanding this complexity is essential for comprehending the socially fractured environment in which young individuals like Shafi are reconfiguring their urban life worlds by imagining alternative futures. Shafi and his peers were apprehensive of being labelled as criminals and facing dire consequences. They also feared severing ties with friends, despite some of them being involved in crime. Additionally, they were anxious about being victimised by crime, as local criminals increasingly teamed up with associates from outside Mathare. However, similar to policing, the concept of crime in Mathare is not immediately clear or obvious.

## CRIME IN MATHARE

The concept of crime is generally considered as contingent on a particular convergence of historical, political, cultural, etc., dynamics and can carry varying connotations and interpretations for different communities (Kamal Ahamed 2021). Depending on such a convergence in a specific time and place, some communities do not view official legal norms as legitimate and often construe social notions of crime and legality based on what is locally considered crime. The local here is a low-income urban settlement. Taking inspiration from the recent thesis on 'planetary urbanisation' (Brenner & Schimd 2015), it is hard to determine solid boundaries between the urban and the rural, given that the globalising process of capitalist urbanisation currently spans the globe. Building on Roy (2016), we take urban areas as sites of intensified encounters, and low-income urban settlements in particular are localities where people from many different backgrounds come together and interact in a context of scarcity and uncertainty. Social structures in such areas tend to be highly complex, with a great diversity of people and shifting social roles. The specific socio-spatial relations and processes at play in this locality give rise to particular meanings of what is locally considered crime (Tyner & Inwood 2014: 771).

Local definitions of crime in Mathare often deviate from dominant notions in Kenya. For example, selling heroin is widely perceived as a criminal act in Kenya but in Mathare this is not considered a crime. Selling heroin and other types of drugs is frowned upon and drug bosses and dealers manoeuvre mostly out of the limelight, as do brokers of stolen goods. Nevertheless, these activities are not considered crimes locally, even if they are deemed immoral and/or illegal. Without fail, when Mathare residents are asked to differentiate between crime and illicit ways to generate income, all reply that stealing inside their neighbourhood is a crime and all other dominantly considered criminal ways to generate income, often including stealing outside their neighbourhood, are merely considered forms of hustling (interviews with 20 older (>35) and 20 younger (<35) residents in November and December 2020; Fagan & Freeman 1999, Hagedorn 2001, 2007, Nordstrom 2004, Roitman 2006, Thieme et al. 2021).

As one of the authors (Samuel) recalls, during the early 1990s it was not uncommon for youth to go to nearby neighbourhoods or to the city centre to steal from pedestrians (mostly through pickpocketing or scams), but stealing inside Mathare was met with immediate violence from passers-by and rarely occurred. Samuel's co-worker at Ghetto Foundation, Daniel, who like Samuel grew up in Mathare, recounted on 29th December 2021 that:

> Something changed since the 1990s, police killings went up and it is now too dangerous to steal outside Mathare. Though, still many go outside, but others stay inside and steal from residents along Juja road or going to the bridge [connecting one side of Mathare to the other side].

When discussing why some youth steal, Daniel shared:

Even us we did, when we were young. [...] No, not inside Mathare, that would be hard. That time, our neighbours were also our parents, they would beat us. Nowadays, people are more on their own, not like before. Now you can't beat your neighbour's child. And pressures are so high for youth, now with social media they see how rich people live, just on their phones, we did not have this.

Most youth we worked with over the past two decades had engaged in stealing at one point in their young lives, often driven by desperation in the face of food shortages, rent arrears, or mounting hospital and funeral bills combined with social pressures to 'show success' (Newell 2012, Van Stapele 2021).

Previously, stealing inside Mathare was mostly dealt with by residents themselves, sometimes with death as a result (interviews with 20 older (>35) Mathare residents in November 2020). When crime rates increased in Mathare from late 2009 onwards, local informers began to collaborate more intensively with police and a violent spiral ensued (interviews with 20 younger (<35) Mathare residents in December 2020). Crime incidents surged in Mathare following a complex history of successive gangs and a sudden power vacuum during the last months of 2009 (Van Stapele 2015: 267) while at the same time going outside the neighbourhood to steal became increasingly dangerous. Moreover, recent residents (i.e., not born or raised in Mathare, locally dubbed *watu wakukam* – 'migrants' in Sheng) seemed more likely than 'native' residents of Mathare (locally dubbed *wazaliwa* – 'natives' in Swahili) to collaborate with police to put crime suspects on police death lists (Van Stapele 2020). This shows that local migration patterns and other histories are crucial to understand shifting social structures in Mathare from which both crime and policing emerge.

In response to surging crime rates, police killings also went up, especially by what are locally dubbed 'killer cops' (interviews with 20 younger (>35) Mathare residents in December 2020). Killer cops are police officers, known by name and face, who have been witnessed to execute young male crime suspects (Van Stapele 2020). Though such killer cops have been roaming these neighbourhoods at night since as early as the 1990s, the most recent decade did see both an intensification and spread of such police officers in low-income settlements in Nairobi who, despite ample evidence, get off scot-free. In response, youth engaged in stealing outside shifted to stealing inside Mathare because outside became too dangerous. This trend has led to an increase in the involvement of police officers in Mathare with the assistance of local residents to apprehend suspected criminals, resulting in a deadly cycle. This has escalated further during the COVID-19 pandemic due to lockdown measures and rising living costs. As more youths have dropped out of school and turned to theft within Mathare, there has been a surge in police killings.

In this light, the street muggings by the 24 youths on 26th December 2021 were even more astounding to the tea-drinking customers. One said 'What now? Informers will tell on them, send their pictures to the police, and we will see police killings go up again. Other groups will seek revenge. Why do these youth take that risk? We know them, all of them are from here.' The tea-drinkers shared with us that the 24 youths came from different *bazes* in Mathare and, to their surprise, also included young women. *Baze* is a Sheng term that refers to a rather fluid network of friends – generally male age-mates who live in the same part of a neighbourhood – and to the particular site where they mostly hang out (Githinji 2006). This can be a public toilet managed by some of them, a waterpoint, or another central place near where they live and where some of their members earn a living. At the *baze* they chat, smoke, drink, chew *khat* (a stimulant comparable to coca leaves), gamble (using cards), and organise work (which may include a vast array of legal and illegal and/or criminal income-generating activities) – and each *baze* has a particular name, such as Gaza or Uprising.

Working with many different *bazes* for over ten years now, we learned where, when, and how they imagined borders of *bazes* and of their neighbourhoods and how these borders shifted between day and night and in response to the constant fear of police killings. Borders also changed in accordance with events such as elections and strife between *bazes*. Though mostly imagined as masculine spaces, *bazes* have always also included young women. The surprise acclaimed by the tea-drinkers regarding the presence of young women was more prompted by their visibly violent role – that is, carrying knives and stealing from people themselves – rather than the fact that young women too were part of this group. Commonly, women (young and old) are imagined as having a more supportive role during violent junctures; for example, by gathering stones for young men to throw at the police during riots (personal observations by both authors during days of clashes between Mathare residents and police in August 2019).

All this brings out that for Shafi and his fellow youth-group members one of the main questions guiding their everyday social navigation (Vigh 2006, 2009) concerned their desire to escape these entangling types of urban violence and build meaningful lives outside crime by imagining new urban futures.

## ANTICIPATING URBAN FUTURES IN MATHARE

Orientations towards new urban futures lead us to think of the teleological affect of time and how exploring the future through anticipations helps us to understand urban life worlds from the perspectives of individuals and collectives. Such teleologies are by nature indeterminate and open-ended, though they are firmly grounded in urban materialities. Hence, looking at these helps us to comprehend the role of future time in understanding individual and collective actions (Miyazaki 2004, 2006, Strathern 2005) in specific urban settings and how this produces particular urban socialities. Bryant and Knight argue that 'the concept of 'orientations' is intended to help us gain an ethnographic hold on the relationship between the future and action, including the act of imagining the future' (Bryant & Knight 2019:16). Orientations may invoke a linear notion of time, which in the case of the youth in focus here seems to some extent accurate regarding their everyday lives; however, the ends anticipated by them are plural and inform multiple social navigation trajectories (Vigh 2006, 2009). The collective decision by Shafi and his peers to stay away from Mathare until 1st January 2022 was first and foremost informed by their anticipation of violence and the inevitability of their involvement if they returned too soon, in one way or the other. Anticipation projects the present into the future and attempts to shape the future in the present by taking precautions. Heidegger calls the way in which anticipation shapes present-day actions 'anticipatory resoluteness' (1962: 370, cited in Bryant & Knight 2019: 25) while Schatzki emphasises the interface between anticipating urban futures and human activity (such as decision-making) in the present as key to understanding the creation and (re-)arrangement of urban sites and of particular social orders (Schatzki 2002: 92–95, 204–210, cited in Bryant & Knight 2019: 33).

The anticipation of violence infuses everyday life with the threat of violence and hence with the anxiety of uncertainty (Vigh 2011). Staying away from Mathare during this juncture of anticipated violence allowed the youth to contribute to altering their immediate futures and imbued their everyday life with a momentary feeling of certainty, even if only for a few days.

Upon return, Shafi shared that staying away had been easy, but coming back to Mathare had been hard. The forest surroundings of the scouting camp, being sure of three meals a day, and a sense of physical safety all contributed to a feeling of blissful suspension of the everyday reality back home, marred by violence and uncertainty. Shafi expounded:

> It was easy to stay away. Our friends at home kept us informed but did not push for us to come back. They thought we had planned to stay away for the entire period [until 1st January], so they did not ask questions why we did not come back to support them. Coming back was difficult.

Shafi and other youth explained to us during a debrief meeting on 8th January 2022 that the convergence of the simmering conflict between groups inside Mathare (following the robbing spree on 26th December 2021) and the escalation of electoral campaigns in the run up to the 2022 general elections had reinforced their anticipation of ongoing violence. In contrast to their previous expectations that violence would subside after 1st January 2022, the enduring tensions and growing political turmoil forced the youth to drastically reconfigure their orientations towards their futures from expectation to anticipation of violence. Here it is important to consider the difference between anticipation and expectation. Bryant and Knight aptly differentiate between these two orientations towards the future by defining expectation 'as a conservative teleology, one that gives thickness to the present through its reliance on the past' (Bryant & Knight 2019: 22). They posit that, with expectations, past experiences inform current expectation about the future, while anticipation denotes 'the act of looking forward', which pulls one 'in the direction of the future and prepares the groundwork for that future to occur' (Bryant & Knight 2019: 28). In the case of expectation of violence, past experiences of how particular social phenomena, processes, and events converge may give substance to the idea that violence is near, but it may or may not take place. With the anticipation of violence, violence is certain to occur.

A few days after this meeting, their anticipation was actualised, and violence once again exploded in Mathare. On 12th January 2022, the opposition candidate William Ruto visited Eastlands, Nairobi, and after leaving Mathare his convoy left a trail of violence. Some groups of youth (including several of the suspects of the 26th December 2021 incident) responded to the campaign visit by again robbing from by-passers while looting from and destroying roadside businesses, including the *kibanda* from the initial vignette. Shafi and his peers again did not participate. Daniel from Ghetto Foundation tried to make sense of this later during our own reflection meeting on the 13th January 2022:

> Many youth dropped out of school, because of COVID, and their parents also lost their jobs. Business is down, but prices are up, like gas, milk, sugar, and flour. Other youth, who are still in school, they only have maybe one week holiday now. The terms are different now and the calendar is confusing, putting a lot of pressures on students. They see no hope. That is why you also see school burnings. There is a lot of frustration, hunger, and anger. So this election year will see a lot of violence. Not so much because of political instigation but because our youth are fed up, they are tired and do not believe in government anymore.

As expected, the mounting violence by youth in Mathare was met by growing surveillance and more extra-judicial killings by police. During such times of chronic anticipation of crime and police killings, how did Shafi and his peers maintain their aspiration to reform? In the midst of the increasingly dangerous intersection of crime and policing, exacerbated by political provocation, these youths faced constant pressure to join their peers in criminal activities while keeping their desire to reform in front of their minds. This illustrates the complex interplay of different outlooks on urban futures and their impact on daily social interactions. It also underscores the significance of understanding these dynamics from the youths' perspectives and how this informed their daily praxes.

## ASPIRING URBAN FUTURES IN MATHARE

Anticipation cannot be decoupled from aspiration when analysing how orientations towards urban futures shape the unfolding of urban life worlds and vice versa. Had Shafi and his peers envisioned a future urban landscape where they could serve as defenders of their community and take charge of their neighbourhood, they would have swiftly returned to Mathare upon receiving news of their friends' situation during the December 2021 camp. Moreover, Shafi and some of his fellow youth members would perhaps have joined in the looting spree on 12th January. Instead, Shafi and the other youth imagined themselves as reformed, which to them denoted that they aspired to a different future from most of their friends, a future they dubbed as 'crime-free' and 'peaceful.' This inspired their decision to 'stay away' (*kukaa mbali* in Swahili) in the anticipation of (ongoing) violence. Obviously, staying away from escalating violence while their friends were implicated was decidedly easier when the youth were at camp as opposed to on 12th January. On that Wednesday, criminal violence by their friends happened outside their houses and near their hangouts, and all Ghetto Youth members were physically present and under pressure to take part. So why and how were they able to continue to 'stay away' while being back in Mathare?

On 15th January, Ghetto Youth had their weekly meeting, and their main point of discussion was their anticipation of ongoing violence that involved youth, informers, and police. Shafi kicked their discussion off as follows:

> Reform is a decision, right? We help each other to reform. Yes, when your friend is attacked you help him, but you don't have to go out and do what he does. How do we keep each other safe? And how do we support our friends but also protect ourselves? These are our questions we need to help each other to reform.

Shafi's story highlights the prominent and collective daily praxis of choosing to reform, indicating that this was not a one-time or occasional decision but a continuous one made by these young individuals together. Following a four-hour discussion held in the cramped office of Ghetto Foundation at the entrance of the ghetto, the youth members had not yet concluded their deliberations and decided to take a break and grab some tea at the newly fixed *kibanda*, still loudly enthralled in their debate. None of the youth members had been part of the two junctures of violence, nor in their aftermaths. To Shafi, this illustrated the determination of the entire group of in total 58 members and the importance of their collective decision-making to reform, a decision, he explained to us later, they needed to reiterate regularly together to keep it 'alive'. They kept their decision alive by reminding each other of their aspirations.

Schatzki draws our attention to 'the temporality of activity' to bring out how 'acting towards an end' is indicative of 'what motivates' (Schatzki 2010: 1053 cited in Bryant & Knight 2019: 25). Anticipating criminal and police violence in a 'vernacular time' of crisis (Ringel 2020), the aspiration of the 58 Ghetto Youth members to reform prompted their everyday decision to realise reform, which in turn shaped their anticipatory responses. This praxis of decision-making was a daily effort, thus bringing to the fore the importance of a continuing and collective recap of their aspiration to reform. The youth engaged in this praxis not only during their weekly meetings but also in their daily conversations, when they hung out together and on WhatsApp. Their everyday anticipatory responses were entangled with their aspirations and as such projected into their collective urban future a particular temporality that marked their future as a threshold and made their present ever liminal. Crossing the thresholds into their projected future led to a constant radical reorientation of present and past. Their particular modes of responding to their anticipation of violence in their neighbourhood – that is, by staying away in more than one sense – became a collective way of stepping into their aspired-for future and thus towards its actualisation. Their aspired-for futures became integrated into their daily urban lives through the small and large decisions they made on a daily basis (Abend 2018). Not engaging in crime, not buying a stolen phone, and not hanging out at the *baze* but with their fellow youth members were all daily actions through which they sought to make new futures possible. These praxes reflected a desire to create new possibilities for themselves and their community driven by a complex mix of hope and fear for what lay ahead. Ultimately, this illustrates how their perception of future time influenced their current decisions and behaviours.

The praxes Shafi and his friends developed can be described as 'technologies of the self', a concept developed by Foucault in his work on self-care and self-discipline (Foucault et al. 1988). Understanding these technologies in their local context is important from a critical urban sociological perspective because it not only lays bare the inequalities and other social structures that produce crime and police violence but also highlights the agency of youth to make choices 'against the grain' (Abend 2018). This brings in view how these youth navigate and challenge social structures and expectations and open up possibilities for new urban futures to manifest. To this end, it is important to grasp reform in their local language and collective praxes.

'Reform' is a term many Kenyan urban youths use in English to denote a process of cultivating new dispositions that take seriously the possibility of having crime-free and peaceful urban futures. The possible local connotations of this term are brought out by the often-used slogan groups like Ghetto Youth take on to underscore their desired change from gang members to recognised youth group members: '*Form ni KuReform!*' (which loosely translate to 'our plan is to reform'). In their vernacular uses, the term 'form', mostly uttered as a question ('*form?*'), has come to replace the more traditional '*habari?*' (meaning 'news' in Swahili) in their everyday speak. '*Form?*' may be used to ask after another's current state and/or their plans for the day, which potentially, and often hopefully, include the person who is asking this question. While '*habari?*' is often replied with a perfunctory '*nzuri*' (meaning 'good' in Swahili), when asked '*form?*' one is expected to reply in one of the following three ways: 1) *niko tu* (indicating one 'is in place' and does not have a plan 'to make money'); 2) *poa* (signifying that one's current state is cool – in the popular sense of this English term), or 3) *roundi tu* (connoting a more general plan to be 'on the move' – with the aim of making money). The greeting '*form?*' in their local uses may thus allude to both (variations between and qualities of) movement and rest, and the underlying ideas that shape these bodily states. Reform may then be taken as a (desired) shift in ideas and bodily practices and, subsequently, in their qualitative states of movement and rest. Indeed, the group's decision to reform demarcates a conscious and continuous reflection on the quality of movement as compared to rest in situations that expect otherwise from them.

Despite the volatile circumstances in which these young people live, it is remarkable that Shafi and his peers hold aspirations for a future free of crime and characterised by peace, where they can create purposeful and fulfilling lives. Coming together as a group and reminding each other of their aspiration to reform reveals aspirations as a means to open up a space of contemplation and reflection on the present, allowing them to think about what might be but what is not yet. The situated and relational meanings these young people ascribed to aspirations reflect how much control they felt over their future (Bernard et al. 2008: 10) and how much they needed each other to enact their decisions as individuals and collectives. This accentuates that individual desires should not be considered in the social isolation of feeling in control in relationship to other people, institutions, and ideas. Given that aspirations are socially determined, understanding how aspirations are contingently formed and collectively solidified and how these change in space and over time requires a careful analysis of urban life worlds and cultures from both individual and collective perspectives. Aspirations as navigational capacities involve particular understandings of how one can navigate the 'dense combination of nodes and pathways' (Appadurai 2004: 69) that lies between 'the present and an imagined future' (Vigh 2006: 136, 2009). Appadurai is not alone in his call for an 'ethnography of the future', as it has been termed elsewhere (Clammer 2012: 129).

In contexts where many young individuals fear an early death, the question of how urban futures are envisioned and negotiated, as well as why, becomes increasingly pressing. Long- and short-term aspirations are reconfigured accordingly (Frye 2012: 1573). Bryant and Knight contend 'that hope as a futural orientation bridges the gap between potentiality and actuality' (2019: 136). However, we add here that Shafi and his peers at Ghetto Youth make an acute distinction between aspiration and hope. During the youth meeting on Saturday 15th January 2022, one youth member called Fatuma explained it as follows: 'We decide together that we are reforming. This means we need to do something different every day to see that change happens to us. We hope for a better future, yes, but we can also make change happen now.' Fatuma brings out here that aspirations can translate into something one does and as such can be considered more agentive, whereas hope is something one wishes but over which one may not feel much control. 'Hope is for God,' another youth member called Tema acclaimed.

## CONCLUSIONS

Whether Shafi and his peers succeed in realising crime-free and peaceful urban futures for themselves and other youth in Mathare remains to be seen in the coming years. At issue here is what they did achieve through their persistent everyday praxes; namely, making new urban life worlds possible in the present by aspiring to new futures amidst anticipations of crime and police violence.

This chapter has explored the importance of considering the future as constitutive of the complex and dynamic nature of urban life worlds in critical urban sociological investigations. Through a case study of a youth group in a low-income neighbourhood in an African city, we have demonstrated the value of examining different orientations toward urban futures as a means of gaining insights into how present-day actions are shaped by future imaginaries and as such make new urban life worlds possible. Specifically, by examining their anticipations of crime and police violence and their aspirations for reform on an experiential level, we have gained a deeper understanding of how everyday urban life worlds connect with urban socio-spatial materialities marred by crime and police violence and temporal vistas envisaged by individuals and collectives.

Our analysis highlighted the significance of exploring how urban futures are lived today to offer an analytical framework for investigating micro-politics of change within specific urban contexts. By taking into account the youths' perspectives in this chapter, this approach suggests a more nuanced and textured understanding of not only how future imaginaries shape present-day actions to actualise aspired futures but also how such orientations toward urban futures engender specific urban life worlds in the now, in the present moment. In Mathare, the youth group opened up such possibilities for other youths as well, which in time may also contribute to realising such futures.

Urban critical sociology could benefit from more systematic integration of orientations toward the future into its empirical investigations of urban life worlds, especially in volatile urban settings where young people's futures are deeply uncertain. This includes considering actor anticipations, aspirations, and other future beliefs in present-day decision-making to gain a view of how futures are lived today and make new ways of urban living possible. Our analysis underscores the importance of recognising the significance of understanding how urban futures are brought into being as an integral part of the everyday lives of the people we study. By examining the ways in which urban futures are imagined, experienced, and acted upon, we can gain a more comprehensive understanding of the complex and dynamic nature of urban life worlds in the making.

# REFERENCES

Abend, G. (2018) Outline of a Sociology of Decisionism. *The British Journal of Sociology* 69(2): 237–264.

Anderson, B. & McFarlane, C. (2011) Assemblage and Geography. *Area* 43(2): 124–127.

Appadurai, A. (2004) The Capacity to Aspire: Culture and the Terms of Recognition. In V. Rao & M. Walton (eds.) *Culture and Public Action*. Redwoon City: Stanford University Press, 59–84.

Appadurai, A. (2013) *The Future as a Cultural Fact: Essays on the Global Condition*. London: Verso.

Baron, R. & A. C. Cara, A. C. (eds.) (2011) *Creolization as Cultural Creativity*. Jackson: University Press of Mississippi.

Beckert, J. & Suckert, L. (2021) The Future as a Social Fact. The Analysis of Perceptions of the Future in Sociology. *Poetics* 84: 101499.

Bernard, T., A.S. Taffesse, A. S. & Dercon, S. (2008) Aspirations Failure and Well-Being Outcomes In Ethiopia: Towards An Empirical Exploration. Retrieved from https://www.iig.ox.ac.uk/output/presentations/ pdfs/E13-Aspirations-and-WellBeing-Outcomes-in-Ethiopia.pdf (Accessed on 15 July 2023).

Brenner, N., Madden, D. & Wachsmuth, D. (2011) Assemblage Urbanism and the Challenges of Critical Urban Theory. *City* 15(2): 225–240.

Brenner, N. & Schmid, C. (2015) Combat, Caricature and Critique in the Study of Planetary Urbanization. Working Paper. Urban Theory Lab (Harvard GSD) and Contemporary City Institute (ETH Zurich). Retrieved from: http://urbantheorylab.net/uploads/Brenner_ Schmid_Richard%20Walker_2015.pdf (accessed on 15 July 2023).

Bryant, R. & D. M. Knight, D. M. (2019) *The Anthropology of the Future*. Cambridge: Cambridge University Press.

Bugnon, G. (2020) *Governing Delinquency Through Freedom: Control, Rehabilitation and Desistance*. Taylor & Francis.

Buur, L. & Jensen, S. (2004) Introduction: Vigilantism and the Policing of Everyday Life in South Africa. *African Studies* 63(2): 139–152.

Cheruiyot, G. B. & Wainaina, L. (2020) Effect of Crime Deterrence Strategies on the Control of Juvenile Gang Crime in Mombasa County, Kenya. *International Academic Journal of Social Sciences and Education* 2: 270–293.

Clammer, J. (2012) *Culture, Development and Social Theory: Towards an Integrated Social Development.* London: Zed Books.

Colona, F. & Diphoorn, T. (2017) Eyes, Ears and Wheels: Policing Partnerships in Nairobi, Kenya. *Conflict and Society* 3: 8–23.

Cooper-Knock, S. J. (2018) Beyond Agamben: Sovereignty, Policing and 'Permissive Space' in South Africa, and Beyond. *Theoretical Criminology* 22(1): 22–41.

Cooper-Knock, S. J. & Owen, O. (2015) Between Vigilantism and Bureaucracy: Improving our Understanding of Police Work in Nigeria and South Africa. *Theoretical Criminology* 19(3): 355–375.

Diphoorn, T. & Van Stapele, N. (2019) 'Ready to Shoot!' vs. 'Ready to Loot!': The Violent Potentialities of Demonstrations in Kenya. In M. Ruteere & P. Mutahi (eds.) *Enhancing Democratic Policing of Public Gatherings and Demonstrations in Kenya*. Nairobi: CHRIPS.

Diphoorn, T., Van Stapele, N. & Kimari, W. (2019) Policing for the Community? The Mismatch between Reform and Everyday Policing in Nairobi, Kenya. In S. Howell (ed.) *Policing the Urban Periphery in Africa*. Cape Town: APCOF.

Fagan, J. & R. B. Freeman, R. B. (1999) Crime and Work. *Crime and Justice* 25: 225–290.

Farías, I. (2011) The Politics of Urban Assemblages. *City* 15: 365–374.

Farrall, S. (2002) *Rethinking What Works with Offenders: Probation, Social Context and Desistance from Crime*. Cullompton: Willan Publishing.

Foucault, M., Martin, L. H., Gutman, H. & Hutton, P. H. (eds.) (1988). *Technologies of the Self: A Seminar with Michel Foucault.* Amherst: University of Massachusetts Press.

Frye, M. (2012) Bright Futures in Malawi's New Dawn: Educational Aspirations as Assertions of Identity. *American Journal of Sociology* 117(6): 1565–1624.

Githinji, P. (2006) Bazes and Their Shibboleths: Variation and Sheng Speakers. Identity in Nairobi. *Lexical Nordic Journal of African Studies* 15(4): 443–472.

Githora, C. (2018) *Sheng: Rise of a Kenyan Swahili Vernacular*. Suffolk: James Currey.

Glick Schiller, N. & Schmidt, G. (2016) Envisioning Place: Urban Sociabilities within Time, Space and Multiscalar Power. *Identities* 23(1): 1–16.

Hagedorn, J. M. (2001) Gangs and the Informal Economy. In R. C. Huff (ed.) *Gangs in America III*. Beverly Hills: Sage, 101–120.

Hagedorn, J. M. (2007) Gangs, Institutions, Race and Space: The Chicago School Revisited. In J. M. Hagedorn (ed.) *Gangs in the Global City: Alternatives to Traditional Criminology*. Chicago: University of Illinois Press, 13–133.

Hahn, H. P. (2010) Urban Life-Worlds in Motion: In Africa and Beyond. *Africa Spectrum* 45(3): 115–129.

Heidegger, M. (1962) *Being and Time*. Translated by J. Macquarrie and E. Robinson. New York: Harper Collins.

Hornberger J (2013) From General to Commissioner to General – On the Popular State of Policing in South Africa. *Law & Social Inquiry* 38(3): 598–614.

Huchzermeyer, M. (2011) *Tenement Cities: From 19th Century Berlin to 21st Century Nairobi*. London: Africa World Press.

Jauregui, B. (2016) *Provisional Authority. Police, Order, and Security in India*. Chicago: University of Chicago Press.

Jeffrey, C. & Dyson, J. (2009) *Telling Young Lives: Portraits of Global Youth*. Philadelphia: Temple University Press.

Johnsen, R., Johansen, C. B. & Toyoki, S. (2019) Serving Time: Organization and the Affective Dimension of Time. *Organization* 26(1): 3–19.

Jones, P., Kimari, W. & Ramakrishnan, K. (2017) Only the People Can Defend This Struggle: The Politics of the Everyday, Extrajudicial Executions and Civil Society in Mathare, Kenya. *Review of African Political Economy* 44(154): 559–576.

Kamal Ahamed, V. (2021) Defining the Concept of Crime: A Sociological Perspective. *SSRN*. http://dx.doi.org/10.2139/ssrn.3864739.

Kimari, W. (2021) The Story of a Pump: Life, Death and Afterlives within an Urban Planning of 'Divide and Rule' in Nairobi, Kenya. *Urban Geography* 42: 141–160.

Kinder, K. (2016) *DIY Detroit: Making Do in a City without Services*. Minneapolis: Minnesota University Press.

Kyed, H. M. & Albrecht, P. (2014) Introduction: Policing and the Politics of Order-making on the Urban Margins. In P. Albrecht & H. M. Kyed (eds.) *Policing and the Politics of Order-Making*. Oxon: Routledge, 1–23.

LeBas, A. (2013) Violence and Urban Order in Nairobi, Kenya and Lagos, Nigeria. *Studies in Comparative International Development* 48: 240–262.

Mabala, R. (2011) Youth and 'the Hood': Livelihoods and Neighbourhoods. *Environment and Urbanization* 23(1): 157–181.

Mbote, P. K. & Kech, A. M. (2011) Kenya Justice Sector and the Rule of Law. AfriMAP and the Open Society Initiative for Eastern Africa. Retrieved from: https://www.opensocietyfoundations.org/sites/default/files/kenya-justice-law-20110315.pdf (Accessed on 29 January 2022).

Médard, C. (2010) City Planning in Nairobi: The Stakes, the People, the Sidetracking. In H. Charton-Bigot & D. Rodriguez-Torres (eds.) *Nairobi Today: The Paradox of a Fragmented City*. Nairobi: IFRA, 25–60.

Miyazaki, H. (2004) *The Method of Hope: Anthropology, Philosophy and Fijian Knowledge*. Stanford: Stanford University Press.

Miyazaki, H. (2006) Economy of Dreams: Hope in Global Capitalism and Its Critiques. *Cultural Anthropology* 21(2): 147–172.

Moser, C. & Rodgers, D. (2005) Change, Violence and Insecurity in Non-conflict Situations. Working Paper 245. London: Overseas Development Institute.

MSJC (2017). A Participatory Actions Research Report Against the Normalization of Extrajudicial Executions in Mathare. Nairobi: MSJC.

Muller, M. (2015) Assemblages and Actor-Networks: Rethinking Socio-material Power, Politics and Space. *Geography Compass* 9(1): 27–41.

Muungano Support Trust (2012) Mathare Zonal Plan. Nairobi/Kenya: Collaborative Plan for Informal Settlement Upgrading. Nairobi and Berkeley: University of Nairobi and University of California.

Newell, S. (2012) *The Modernity Bluff: Crime, Consumption, and Citizenship in Côte d'Ivoire*. Chicago: University of Chicago Press.

Nordstrom, C. (2004) *Shadows of War: Violence, Power, and International Profiteering in the Twenty-first Century*. Oakland: University of California Press.

Pieterse, E. & Simone, A. (eds.) (2013) *Rogue Urbanism: Emergent African Cities*. Auckland Park: Jacana Media.

Pratten, D. (2008) Introduction to the Politics of Protection: Perspectives on Vigilantism in Nigeria. *Africa* 78(1): 1–15.

Pratten, D. & Sen, A. (2007) Global Vigilantes: Perspectives on Justice and Violence. In D. Pratten & A. Sen (eds.) *Global Vigilantes*. New York: Colombia University Press, 1–24.

Price, M., Albrecht, P., Colona, F., Denney, L. & Kimari, W. (2016) *Hustling for Security: Managing Plural Security in Nairobi's Poor Urban Settlements*. The Hague: Clingendael Conflict Research Unit.

Rasmussen, J. & Van Stapele, N. (2020) 'Our Time to Recover': Young Men and Political Mobilisation during the 2017 General Elections in Nairobi. *Journal of Eastern African Studies* 14(4): 724–742.

Ringel, F. (2020) Analytics for the Future. *Etnofoor* 32(2): 123–128.

Rodgers, D. (2008) When Vigilantes Turn Bad. In D. Pratten & A. Sen (eds.) *Global Vigilantes*. New York: Columbia University Press, 349–370.

Roitman, J. (2006) The Ethics of Illegality in the Chad Basin. In J. Comaroff & J. L. Comaroff (eds.) *Law and Disorder in the Post-colony*. Chicago: University of Chicago Press, 247–270.

Roy, A. (2011) Slumdog Cities: Rethinking Subaltern Urbanism. *International Journal of Urban and Regional Research* 35(2): 223–238.

Roy, A. (2016) What is Urban about Critical Urban Theory? *Urban Geography* 37(6): 810–823.

Ruteere, M. & Pommerolle, M. (2003) Democratizing Security or Decentralizing Repression? The Ambiguities of Community Policing in Kenya. *African Affairs* 102: 587–604.

Schatzki, T. R. (2002) *The Site of the Social: A Philosophical Account of the Constitution of Social Life and Change*. University Park: Pennsylvania State University Press.

Schatzki, T. R. (2010) *The Timespace of Human Activity: On Performance, Society, and History as Indeterminate Teleological Events*. Lanham: Lexington Books.
Segalo, L. & Sihlobo, M. (2021) Rehabilitation of Inmate Young Offenders and the Education System: Offenders' Perspective in South Africa. *FWU Journal of Social Sciences* 15(3): 45–59.
Simone, A. & Pieterse, E. (2017) *New Urban Worlds: Inhabiting Dissonant Times*. Cambridge, Polity Press.
Sommers, M. (2011) Governance, Security and Culture: Assessing Africa's Youth Bulge. *International Journal of Conflict and Violence* 5(2): 292–303.
Sommers, M. (2012) *Stuck: Rwandan Youth and The Struggle For Adulthood*. Athens: University of Georgia Press.
Strathern, M. (2005) *Kinship, Law and the Unexpected: Relatives Are Always a Surprise*. Cambridge: Cambridge University Press.
Thieme, T. A. (2017) The Hustle Economy: Informality, Uncertainty, and the Geographies of Getting By. *Progress in Human Geography* 42(4): 529–548.
Thieme T. A. (2021) 'Youth Are Redrawing the Map': Temporalities and Terrains of the Hustle Economy in Mathare, Nairobi. *Africa* 91(1): 35–56.
Thieme, T. A., Ference, M. & Van Stapele, N. (2021) Harnessing the 'Hustle': Struggle, Solidarities and Narratives of Work in Nairobi and Beyond. Introduction. *Africa* 91(1): 1–15.
Tyner, J. A. & Inwood, J. (2014) Violence as Fetish: Geography, Marxism, and Dialectics. *Progress in Human Geography* 38(6): 771–784.
Van Stapele, N. (2015) 'Respectable Illegality': Gangs, Masculinities and Belonging in a Nairobi Ghetto. Dissertation, Amsterdam University.
Van Stapele, N. (2020) Police Killings and the Vicissitudes of Borders and Bounding Orders in Mathare, Nairobi. *Environment and Planning D Society and Space* 38(3): 417–435.
Van Stapele, N. (2021) Providing to Belong – Masculinities, Hustling and Economic Uncertainty in a Nairobi Ghetto. *Africa* 91(1): 57–76.
Vigh, H. (2006) *Navigating Terrains of War: Youth and Soldiering in Guinea-Bissau*. New York: Berghahn.
Vigh, H. (2009) Motion Squared: A Second Look at the Concept of Social Navigation. *Anthropological Theory* 9: 419–438.
Vigh, H. (2011) Vigilance: On Conflict, Social Invisibility, and Negative Potentiality. *Social Analysis* 55(3): 93–114.
Weegels, J. (2018) 'The Terror and Scourge of the Barrio': Representations of Youth Crime and Policing on Nicaraguan Television News. *Journal of Latin American Studies* 50(4): 861–887.
Werth, R. & Ballestero, A. (2017) Ethnography and the Governance of Il/Legality: Some Methodological and Analytical Reflections. *Social Justice: A Journal of Crime, Conflict and World Order* 44(1): 10–26.

## 22. Feminist urban planning: women transforming territories through participatory action methods

*Blanca Valdivia and Sara Ortiz Escalante*

Feminist urbanism is based on the assumption that cities are not neutral spaces but a social and cultural production and, as such, urban planning reflects hegemonic values, making the diversity of experiences invisible and perpetuating structural inequalities. Although historically urban planning has been considered a neutral matter, it has caused great social inequalities and damage to certain groups of the population; in particular, women, the LGBTI+ population, ethnic minorities, racialized people, indigenous people, etc. (Sandercock 1998). The space is organized according to male needs and interests, making it hierarchical and powerful (Corpas Reina & García 1999).

Since the 1970s, a number of authors have analyzed women's lives in the city and their relationship with the urban configuration (Bofill Levi 2008, Bondi & Rose 2003 Greed 1997, Sandercock 1998). These works provide evidence of the differences linked to gender relations and roles in areas such as the perception of safety (Falú 2009, Michaud 2002, Wekerle & Whitzman 1995), mobility (Beall 1996, Jirón 2007, Miralles-Guasch 2010), public spaces (Segovia & Oviedo 2000, Green 1998), and facilities (England 1991, Horelli 2006, Walker et al. 2013), concluding that urban planning responds to a patriarchal social system that prioritizes male experiences and needs (García Ramón 1989, Karsten & Meertens 1992, McDowell 1999).

The origin of the differences affecting space and gender can be traced to the public–private space dichotomy. Modern cities have been planned on the basis of the sexual division of labor, a reflection of the naturalization of the patriarchal order and the public–private dichotomy. According to Durán (1998), with the sexual division of labor, framed within the family, men are in charge of productive tasks, those related to the market, which take place in the public sphere, while women are in charge of reproductive tasks, which take place in the domestic sphere. This division led to a delimitation of male and female spatial spheres through which a series of values and ideologies have reinforced the cultural construction of the categories of men and women (Fernández Moreno 1995). Furthermore, this division has also strengthened gender-oppressive structures and the social construction of the devaluation of domestic and care work that accompanied the development of mercantile production (Carrasco et al. 2011).

The public–private dichotomy has not been a historical constant but rather is a consequence of the sexual division of labor, which in turn occurred during the growth and expansion of capitalism after the Industrial Revolution (Valdivia 2021). Silvia Federici (2011) points out the relationship between capitalism and patriarchy when she states that the expansion and consolidation of the capitalist system was possible thanks to the patriarchal order, since the capitalist system is sustained by the sexual division of labor that was made possible by a series of strategies of moral criminalization that curtailed the freedom of women in the European context. Capitalism thus depends on the work of social reproduction performed, in large part, free of charge by women (Fraser 2015, Mies 2019).

Urban sociology has made great contributions linking the relationship between the shaping of cities and capitalism and its effects. However, it has forgotten that the patriarchal system is universal and influences all spheres of society and also the production of space. As Darke (1998) points out, patriarchy takes many forms and changes over time. It coexists with most economic systems, including capitalism, and in many settings: in the family, in the workplace, in government, etc. It is so deeply embedded in social relations that many people do not identify it and regard male domination as natural.

Although the public–private dichotomy is the socio-spatial basis on which modern cities have been configured, many feminist historians, geographers, and urban planners have shown that this duality is a fallacy and a deeply Eurocentric and classist notion based on the experience of the cities of the Global North, since working-class women have always been involved to a greater or lesser extent in the public sphere, working in factories, in the countryside, as merchants, artisans, etc. (Fernández Moreno 1995, Murillo 1996, Nash 1995, Segura 2006). On the other hand, based on this dualism, activities related to reproduction and care have been restricted to the domestic sphere, despite the fact that there are many reproductive activities that are carried out in the public sphere too: shopping, taking children to school, accompanying a sick person to the doctor, etc. However, the fact that urban spaces have been thought from such a rigid conception means that currently our cities are not designed to support and accompany the development of reproductive tasks and people's complex everyday lives (Col·lectiu Punt 6 2019, Valdivia 2021).

The androcentric logic that stems from the public–private dualism has led to certain activities being considered socially more important. This is materialized in cities that prioritize some uses over others, giving them more space and better locations and connectivity. Priority is given to tasks related to production, adapting space and time to serve capital, and the rest of the activities we carry out in our daily lives—care, affective, personal, and community activities—are relegated to the background. For instance, public transportation schedules and routes prioritize workers reaching their workplaces, but transportation planning does not take into account that people have to get to schools and hospitals, among other everyday facilities, with the same ease.

The hierarchies and priorities of space according to the social organization of the patriarchal system are reinforced by the neoliberalism of the current capitalist phase (Fraser 2015). Neoliberal policies, which weaken an already precarious welfare state, take the form of cuts in public spending and services, cause great social imbalances that are materialized territorially in phenomena such as the commodification of public space, speculation, gentrification, and touristification, all of which affect women in particular (Bondi 1991, Sakızlıoğlu 2018).

In recent years, urban planning from a gender perspective has gained prominence and this has materialized in an increase in publications and projects developed with this approach (Kern 2021; Sarmiento et al. 2022). However, in the context of a global crisis of care (according to Oxfam data (2020) women and girls undertake more than three quarters of unpaid care work in the world and make up two thirds of the paid care workforce), feminization of poverty (UN Women (2022) estimated that globally 388 million women and girls would be living in extreme poverty in 2022 compared to 372 million men and boys), and everyday violence against women (according to the Gender Data Portal of the World Bank (2022), 30% of women have experienced intimate partner violence or non-partner sexual violence), it is not enough to develop partial actions. It is therefore essential to develop a paradigm shift that puts the sustainability of life/lives in the center and questions the privileges of a small part of the population.

In this chapter we present the approach developed by Col·lectiu Punt 6 (2019) as a critique of androcentric and capitalist urban planning. The latter is understood as a science of specialists that does not recognize the knowledge and experience of neighbors and, at the same time, is distant from the everyday life of the territory and standardizes needs from an ideal of a universal subject type, which is a white middle-class male without any dependency. This is why Col·lectiu Punt 6, in response to predatory models of urban planning, goes beyond gender analysis. We engage with feminist urban planning that seeks to place the lives of everyday people at the center of urban decisions, understanding people's diversity and analyzing how gender roles and intersectionality have a direct impact on the right to the city.

Through this perspective, we work to rethink community, public and domestic spaces, and mobility networks from an intersectional feminist perspective. As Hill Collins and Bilge explain, intersectionality considers 'that the main axes of social divisions in a given society and at a given time, for example, race, class, gender, sexuality, dis/ability and age, do not function as independent and mutually exclusive entities, but build on each other and act together… They are also categories that acquire meaning from the power relations of racism, sexism, heterosexism, and class exploitation' (Hill Collins & Bilge 2019: 16, 18). This approach seeks to make visible the fact that self-identified women are not a homogeneous social group but one crossed by different axes of oppression and privileges. Accordingly, in the next section we introduce the main goals of the feminist urban planning we advocate for, and in the following section we discuss our participatory-action methodology with an intersectional lens for the radical transformation of everyday life spaces.

## GOALS OF FEMINIST URBAN PLANNING

Feminist urban planning is not a subject or a field of knowledge. It is a complex perspective on our territories aiming to understand how capitalism and patriarchy interact and generate inequalities and injustices in our daily living spaces. This approach has its own theoretical genealogy and methodology. This perspective allows one to address the different variables that are worked on in urbanism (public space, facilities, mobility, land use planning, housing, etc.).

Feminist urban planning places people's daily lives at the center of urban decisions, taking into account the diversity of experiences and analyzing how gender roles influence and have direct implications on the uses, perceptions, and needs of our cities and towns. Likewise, feminist urban planning also acknowledges that women have always participated in both the public and reproductive spheres, that reproductive and care tasks not only occur within the home but also in public space, and that they should not be the exclusively responsibility of women but a social and public responsibility. Hence, this perspective provides us with criteria, strategies, and tools to make a radical change that puts people's lives at the center.

Finally, from our point of view, feminist urban planning must have a transformative aspiration to build spaces that contribute to eliminating social inequalities, without discrimination in the use of and access to urban spaces. Accordingly, we work towards three goals for feminist urban planning, as presented below.

### Changing Priorities to Place People's Lives and Care at the Center of Urban Decisions

Feminist economist Amaia Pérez Orozco (2014) states that feminism claims to center the sustainability of life, which is the possibility of achieving a life worth living and the generation of an embodied and daily well-being under the whole gear of paid and unpaid work, of mercantile and non-mercantile policies and processes that go from the macro (international, state) to the micro (individual), crossing the meso (local, regional) level. Just as Pérez Orozco and other feminist economists (Carrasco 2001, Ezquerra 2018) speak of placing life at the center when referring to the economy, when we speak of 'feminist urban planning' at Col·lectiu Punt 6 we refer to this simple but radical idea of putting people's lives at the center of urban decisions. Placing people's everyday lives at the center means valuing all the needs derived from everyday activities, making visible and recognizing the importance of reproductive and care tasks.

Through our work, we try to intervene in urban planning processes by responding to the complexity and diverse needs that exist in a neighborhood or community. In order to promote more just territories in social and environmental terms, it is essential to integrate care into urban planning on the basis that vulnerability is an innate characteristic of people, which places us in a relationship of interdependence with other people and the natural environment.

The patriarchal system naturalizes reproductive tasks and makes them invisible, which means that they are also forgotten when it comes to territorial planning and public policies. The urban space has not been conceived as a space where care is carried out, and this has led to the city not being thought of as a physical support that facilitates the performance of care tasks (Valdivia 2018, 2021, 2022).

The role of cities is to provide adequate social and physical support to satisfy the complex network of care that is necessary to sustain life. This support can be materialized in public or community structures and infrastructures that provide material and immaterial conditions for the development of care, supporting the autonomy of dependent persons and supporting caregivers (Mogollón & Fernández 2016, Segovia & Rico 2017, Jarvis 2011), such as the following (Valdivia 2023):

- Facilities (libraries, childcare centers, elder care centers, youth centers, etc.);
- Services and programs (home support services, leisure time services for caregivers, personal mobility devices, etc.);
- Urban elements (benches, public toilets, playgrounds, fountains, handrailings in steep streets, accessible pavement, etc.);
- Assistance for the organization and community management of care (provision of spaces, organization of time banks).

Feminist urban planning also integrates ecofeminism in its practice. Ecofeminism, on the one hand, criticizes the model of production and consumption that lives with its back to natural balance and human welfare and, on the other hand, challenges the patriarchal system that subordinates the freedom and rights of women, who are half of humanity (Herrero 2013, Puleo 2002). In the face of the environmental crisis (climate crisis, energy crisis, problems of water access, artificial chemical substances with unknown effects on human beings) and the crisis of care (which exceeds the material limits of human time, especially women's time), the capitalist and patriarchal system is identified as a producer of unsustainability and injustice and as the cause of the deterioration of the quality of life (Grupo de Ecofeminismo, Ecologistas en Acción 2011). In this sense, Herrero et al. (2018) emphasize that human life develops in a natural environment on which we depend to exist and reproduce and which has physical limits and self-organizes in natural cycles and trophic chains in order to survive and resist.

Feminist urban planning thus follows the need to promote a radical change in the urban model that includes eco-dependence and natural limits in aspects such as mobility, residential underutilization, waste management, and the provision of energy services, as well as promoting spaces that prioritize people and not only productive logics. This is why placing people at the center of urban decisions means working towards the 'City of Care' that takes into account the diversity of experiences, needs, and desires. We define a caring city as a city that cares for you, lets you care for yourself, allows you to care for others, and cares for the environment (Col·lectiu Punt 6 2019, Valdivia 2021).

## Making Spaces and Cities Safe for All

The second goal of feminist urban planning consists of making spaces and cities safe for all, free from violence against women and other hate crimes, such as racism, homophobia, and ableism. Urban safety continues to focus mainly on addressing crime against private property, excluding gender violence from its analysis, and does not take into account that the perception of safety is also different between women and men (Sweet & Ortiz Escalante 2010, Wekerle & Whitzman 1995). Most governmental crime prevention and control measures come from the field of justice and criminology, focusing on restrictive strategies such as increasing policing and controlling access to public spaces. Urban planning has often worked on the issue of safety but always closely related to everything that is considered a crime by the legal code (Col·lectiu Punt 6 2018). However, other types of violence, such as sexual harassment suffered by many women in public spaces or institutional violence, are not taken into account.

The perception of safety conditions people's movements, especially women (Falú 2011, Sweet & Ortiz Escalante 2010). To feel safe is to have autonomy and freedom to use public spaces. Often people, especially women, restrict their everyday movements because they perceive certain spaces as unsafe. This perception is closely related to the socialization process women undergo, in which they are constantly victimized and treated as fragile subjects in a constant situation of vulnerability, especially at night.

The work that has been done in relation to safety from a feminist perspective always seeks to go beyond what is understood by crime. From a feminist approach safety is analyzed by differentiating and complexifying what is understood by gender-based violence, safety, or perception of safety. As Michaud (2002) argues, if there is a street where 100% of the people who live there are women and one of them is raped, the consequences are not only for 1% of the population (the raped woman) but for 100% of the women, since this fact will increase the perception of fear of the women who live there because they feel that it could happen to them as well.

The perception of safety is conditioned by the difference that exists between the types of violence that people can experience depending on their gender, age, origin, etc. As Del Valle (2006) says, fear, like safety, has different referents and meanings for men and women. Women's fear or perception of fear is marked by the violence exercised on their sexual bodies and determines to a large extent how they live in different spaces, whether domestic, community, or public spaces. As Falú (2009) points out, the violence exercised both in public spaces and behind closed doors subjugates women's bodies. Women's bodies are the territory at stake, to be occupied, conceived as appropriable merchandise, perceived as available by men;

but they are also a political category, a place for women to exercise rights and resist violence: the body as resistance (Falú 2009).

Fear can be defined as the emotional and practical responses of people and communities to violence (Pain 2001). Fear and the perception of safety affect women's daily lives and mobility, how they use the city, and their participation in their everyday surroundings (Pain 1991). These restrictions increase when it gets dark (Lynch & Atkins 1988, Whitzman et al. 2013). Furthermore, including women's perception of safety and fear also means going beyond the physical characteristics of the public space and considering social roles in a society that discriminates against women (Kallus & Churchman 2004). In this sense, although there is much work to be done from a social point of view, there are some physical characteristics that can improve the perception of spaces, which have been classified as the six principles of safety from a feminist perspective: 1) know where you are and where you are going; 2) see and be seen; 3) hear and be heard; 4) be able to escape and get help; 5) live in a clean and welcoming environment; and 6) act collectively (Michaud 2002). They can be translated into six correspondent qualities that spaces should have: vital, signalized, equipped, visible, surveyed, and communitarian (Col·lectiu Punt 6 2011, 2018).

**Increasing Community Participation and People's Diverse Everyday Life Experiences**

The third goal of our approach aims at increasing community participation and people's diverse everyday life experiences by recognizing the experiences and knowledge of women and non-hegemonic subjects and making them visible. As a consequence, the intersectional feminist perspective applied to urban planning can only be approached from the everyday life experience and, therefore, from an analysis at a scale close to the community and the neighborhood that allows for an interscalar analytical reading (city, region). The experience of a territory can only be gathered through the active participation of people who inhabit a community or neighborhood since they are the greatest experts in these territories (see Figure 22.1). Moreover, it is these people who will be directly affected by the transformation (Col·lectiu Punt 6 2019). This means that urban planning is not an exclusive field of planners and architects but a field where different social and technical disciplines converge. However, it should also be a discipline that breaks gender hierarches and increases women's participation in urban planning teams.

Based on specific practices of community participation, critical reflections, and self-evaluations, Col·lectiu Punt 6 proposes three strategies to change cities from the grassroots and beyond institutions. These consist of de-hierarchizing, de-patriarchalizing, and territorializing planning.

(1) De-hierarchizing planning processes by giving value to the situated and embodied knowledge that neighbors have of their territories and breaking the boundaries of urban planning as a hermetic discipline. It is necessary to break with the hierarchy between professionals, political and economic powerholders, and neighbors since it is the people who inhabit a territory who have a greater knowledge of the dynamics that occur and what their needs are, while also recognizing that these needs are heterogeneous and changing. In this sense, we suggest restricting the power of institutions and economic lobbies in decision-making in the city and that the issues on the urban agenda should not

*Source:* Col·lectiu Punt 6.

*Figure 22.1   Feminist urban workshop*

be marked by partisan or economic interests but configured on the basis of the needs of people who inhabit the territories.

(2) De-patriarchalizing urban planning by making the role of women in the construction of cities visible, both in professional practice and in social movements, since both have been highly male-dominated with a prevalence of patriarchal dynamics. To this end, feminist demands must be incorporated into urban struggles and actions in a cross-cutting manner, making women and non-normative groups visible as leading political agents for social transformation while valuing social reproduction and sustainability of life.

(3) Territorializing feminism by integrating the spatial and territorial factor in feminist struggles. The differences between contexts and scales (urban–rural, center–periphery) are essential to understand the different social phenomena and how they materialize in space, while all the issues addressed by feminism—economics, health, ecology, violence—have a territorial component. Moreover, the struggle for land itself has to be a cross-cutting feminist demand.

## FEMINIST PARTICIPATORY METHODS

Our proposed change of model in urban planning also requires a methodological transformation in the way cities and urban areas are planned, integrating diverse disciplines that interweave the different scales of analysis. Feminist epistemology began to develop in the 1970s and, according to Blázquez (2010), the work from this time has two points in common: they consider gender as a key social organizer of social life and they stress the need for action to contribute to building a fairer world.

Feminist methodologies are both practices and different forms of reflection. Feminists produce knowledge from very different starting points and theoretical and social frameworks (Esteban 2014). Harding (1987) argues that the techniques themselves are not feminist but the way they are used and that the feminist method alludes to who can be the subject of knowledge. Therefore, there is no specific methodology for applying a feminist perspective to research, although qualitative and participatory methodologies are usually more valued to identify particularities of people's everyday lives. The methodologies used from this approach are a counterpoint to others that seek objectivity as a result, since the former establish perspectives that propose new categories of analysis.

The positivist paradigm, from a position of intellectual superiority, presents itself as the champion of objectivity. However, the neutrality of science has been questioned for decades and multiple authors have made visible the androcentric bias present in most publications and research. According to Arranz Lozano (2015), knowledge is deployed in a structuring exercise on the development of the social relations of men and women, and the epistemic non-questioning of this knowledge device implies the reproduction of the male hegemonic order. This device has as regulatory principles of knowledge, on the one hand, neutrality, which assumes that an observer can remain oblivious to the fact of being a sexualized being and, on the other hand, universality, which transfers the particular male values to universal values (Arranz Lozano 2015).

Feminist epistemology (Baylina 1997, Biglia & Bonet-Martí 2009, Blázquez 2010, Haraway 1995) assumes that neutrality is impossible and that our personal experiences shape and influence our way of perceiving and analyzing the world. Haraway (1995) defends the existence of situated knowledge linked to the context and the subjectivity of the person who looks at it: embodied objectivity, materialized in partial, located, and critical knowledge. This situated knowledge makes possible unexpected connections and openings.

The feminist perspective is thus used as an analytical tool with the goal of understanding how gender relations and roles determine people's interaction and their position in the world and how these intersect across all areas of people's lives, from their relationship with the labor market to their health to the way individuals communicate.

This theory of knowledge from a feminist perspective rejects the premise of universal subjects and criticizes the principles of objectivity and neutrality defended by positivist science. Feminist epistemology also questions the creation of knowledge based on dichotomous logics, whereby meaning is given to one phenomenon in opposition to another (nature–culture, masculine–feminine, public–private), and the tendency to conceptualize people outside their social context and disconnected from the environment, which results in the homogenization of subjects and realities.

Using a feminist epistemology, feminist urban planning takes everyday life as a source of analysis and transformation through active and transformative participation of the community—and, in particular, of women in their diversity (Smith 1990). Feminist epistemologies value women's knowledge and life experiences in urban planning and consider women as experts of their communities and neighborhoods because of the knowledge accumulated through the complexity of carrying out paid work, unpaid domestic responsibilities, and community work (Dyck 2005, Gilroy & Booth 1999, Lykogianni 2008).

**Participatory Planning from an Intersectional Feminist Perspective**

Neighbors have a great deal of knowledge of their neighborhood or city that comes from their daily experience. This situated and embodied knowledge should be included in urban planning interventions. In addition, participation increases the feeling of belonging and the level of satisfaction of residents and it is also an opportunity to give decision-making power to people and groups that have historically been excluded, particularly women.

Hence, participation should be integrated in the different parts of the urban project: assessment, proposal of actions and recommendations, project design, and evaluation once the interventions have been implemented. Community participation can be applied to multiple projects and processes, such as the transformation of a square or public space, the reduction of traffic on an avenue, the development of a five-year urban plan, the evaluation of an urban planning transformation or project, and the design of safer transportation infrastructures, among many others.

A participatory process does not guarantee per se that participation will be horizontal or that within the group involved there will be people with diverse socioeconomic characteristics and varied experiences and realities. In this sense, in mixed participatory processes in European contexts, it is more common to find certain types of people: middle-aged, European, middle-class men with economic interests (landlords, traders, investors). If a feminist perspective is not applied to participation, participatory processes may contribute to reinforcing the power relations that exist inside a community. Most times the material and immaterial conditions of participation promote the involvement of certain types of people and not others. For example, often the space in which participation takes place, the format and content of the participation, or its dissemination channels do not break with the predominant structures that perpetuate power roles and, as a consequence, other types of subjectivities feel excluded.

The incorporation of an intersectional feminist perspective in participatory planning makes it possible to integrate different individuals with diverse needs and experiences, in addition to making visible decisive factors in people's everyday lives: the importance of the care sphere; the conditioning factors of having a gendered body in relation to the use of space; the relationships between women, men, and non-binary subjects; how masculinity and femininity are constructed; and the implications of gender in the roles and attitudes of individuals.

These elements have a great impact on urban configuration; for example, which services are prioritized, how mobility systems are structured, and people's perception of safety in public space. Therefore, including an intersectional feminist perspective in community participation is fundamental in order to take into account such factors in urban planning and design.

Often, participatory processes try to address the needs related to the productive sphere (salaried work, private transport, flow of goods, etc.), making invisible all the needs derived from reproductive and care work without which the development of life is not possible (Ortiz Escalante & Valdivia 2015). At other times, participatory processes seek to elaborate proposals related to leisure, recreation, or festivities in which reproductive tasks are still not taken into account.

This is why we encourage making care work visible in participatory processes and highlighting the essential role it plays in the maintenance of any society. This leads to the awareness that working on the basis of everyday life means including all the activities that take place on a daily basis and how these different tasks, times, and spaces relate to each other, in the same way that people interact in different spheres of life.

In order to plan while including women, it is therefore necessary to reconceptualize their role in society. Although the gender perspective makes the reproductive sphere visible and women continue to be the ones who mostly perform these tasks, the reconceptualization is better achieved by developing participatory dynamics from a transforming position that reflects the needs of women according to their realities, but without constraining women in their role as caregivers and without perpetuating gender stereotypes.

Based on the above, a participatory process that truly aims to integrate the diversity of existing voices and realities must consciously incorporate different mechanisms and strategies to integrate people who are normally excluded from decision-making because if a standard call for participation is made, they will not feel involved. The traditional male domination of urban planning makes many women, especially those who are older or from rural environments, feel that this is an area 'for specialists' about which they must have certain knowledge and in which they have nothing to contribute. In this sense, as Beall (1996: 9) argues, 'new forms of urban participation are needed to develop participatory processes that include women and men in all phases of urban development'.

Using feminist urban planning to de-hierarchize planning research and practice entails de-patriarchalizing and decolonizing planning through the practice of cultural humility as 'a practice of and ongoing commitment to self-evaluation and self-critique by professionals for the purpose of rebalancing power inequities' (Sweet 2018: 4). A feminist participatory process entails reflexivity, reciprocity, and accountability, which can allow a more sustained and continued engagement with residents/co-researchers, who are the experts of their everyday/everynight lives (Ortiz Escalante 2019). From this perspective, 'trained' planners should take the role of facilitators, accompanying communities in analyzing their everyday/everynight life needs and designing policies, projects, and programs that better respond to these needs.

Therefore, a feminist participatory process has to be conducted in a way that breaks down the privileges and dynamics by which heteronormative white men monopolize the debate and minimize or ridicule other contributions (mansplaining). It must also facilitate a space where the plurality of voices of women and other historically excluded groups (such as youth, non-white people, people with disabilities, etc.) are central. To this end, it is essential that the facilitating team has experience in feminist urban planning, uses data collection and analytical tools adapted to the diverse groups, and adapts to the experiences and participation needs of each group.

In the practical work of Col·lectiu Punt 6, methodologies and tools are adapted depending on the duration, aims, and context of the project. One of the strategies we use in our processes is to work with groups of different identities, first through a separate group task—to identify the specific and diverse needs of each group's daily network—and then by sharing the results to become aware of these diversities. Therefore, when we carry out participatory assessment, and after analyzing the context of each place, we propose workshops by groups and with adapted methods because people, according to their identity and socialization process, have different ways of participating. For example, elderly women are more involved in small, non-mixed groups than in open discussion groups. In the different participatory processes, we have worked separately with children, young people, teenagers, people with (dis)abilities, migrants, transgender people, elderly people, neighborhood associations, young women, and elderly women, among others. This provides us with a wealth of knowledge and shows us the complexity in the use and access to everyday spaces depending on the intersectional identity of each person.

After carrying out the assessment part with different groups of people, joint work is undertaken in which groups are mixed and the differentiated and intersectional analysis of daily life is shared. This leads to an awareness of collective needs, not only those of the group to which they belong but also those of other groups. Therefore, this process has the potential to assess needs as a whole, recognizing diversity and complexity and proposing responses and transformations that will include this richness.

There are also numerous projects in which we only work with women, such as processes linked to urban safety. The participation of women to share their experiences and perceptions of safety implies generating non-mixed spaces, with conditions of confidence and trust—for example, exploratory walks, a methodology developed by feminist urbanists in Canada, which have been used in multiple contexts to work on safety from daily experience and with a communitarian and non-victimizing vision (Col·lectiu Punt 6 2011). In Catalonia since 2017, Col·lectiu Punt 6 has led more than 100 exploratory marches (see Figure 22.2) that have made it possible to collect a wide range of information on the perception of safety among women and other groups.

Working with a wide diversity of groups means using methods and tools that are accessible to people with different levels of education, socioeconomic status, national origins, or ages, avoiding formal or technical language that may be exclusive and ensuring that all voices are incorporated. The activities' structure and methodologies must favor the participation of all people and be flexible and creative but without losing depth and an integral analysis of the different spatial scales of everyday life (neighborhood, municipality, territory). They also entail guaranteeing adequate spaces and schedules that are compatible with care tasks. Participatory activities should include the diversity of realities in different aspects, such as location, temporality, schedule, accessibility, compatibility with other tasks, and channels of dissemination.

In our approach, participatory urban processes must transgress heteropatriarchal gender roles in order to respond to women's demands and promote the capacity to question these roles and stereotypes. In this way we can ensure that participatory processes, as Kabeer (2005) argues, are gender-transformative; that is, transformers of gender relations.

In turn, becoming actively involved in the community or neighborhood often entails for women the addition of an extra working day to the double working day, paid and unpaid, with

*Source:* Col·lectiu Punt 6.

*Figure 22.2    Feminist urban night walk*

which they are already burdened. The objective of participatory processes with an intersectional feminist perspective should not imply an overload of work but rather finding the necessary space and time so that women can participate and be present in the decision-making and transformation processes. To this end, society must be made jointly responsible for domestic and care tasks so that they are not the exclusive responsibility of women.

From this point of view, we have been considering for some time how the involvement of people, particularly women, in participatory processes should not be abandoned to voluntarism but should be socially valued in some way and should apply an ethics of care (Edwards & Mauthner 2002, Engster 2004, Gilligan 1982, Robinson 1997, Tronto 2020) in the sense of taking care of the participatory process and all those involved, taking the concrete needs of community participants as the starting point for what must be done (Tronto 2020).

On the other hand, the voluntary nature of participation has also led, in some contexts, to fatigue and saturation among the members of the organizations that are always invited to intervene, as is currently happening in the case of Barcelona, where a lot of participatory processes are opened by the City Council but there is not always a return or compliance commitment from the institution. To avoid this, we suggest that community participation should also be socially or economically compensated.

There are examples of participatory action-research processes in which participants are compensated monetarily, not as a way of guaranteeing their involvement but as a way of making it visible that this is also community work to which time and space must be dedicated (Col·lectiu Punt 6 & Ortiz 2017).

## CONCLUSIONS

Engaging the everyday users of cities and spaces, particularly women, in planning analysis is essential to incorporate grounded knowledge, which is often absent in institutional urban planning policies. Planning research and practice should integrate feminist participatory action methods to be complete. Feminist participation should be a central form or method for planning research and practice. This entails working towards breaking hierarchical power structures within the discipline of planning and challenging the divide between the 'experts' and the 'residents', the 'researcher' and the 'participants'.

Through time, feminist urban planning has achieved a collective empowerment of women in multiple territorial scales: local, state, and international. At the present time, both at the community and institutional levels, the need to include women's knowledge in the processes of urban transformation and improvement is increasingly recognized. We have succeeded in making women's knowledge and contributions to the construction of the city visible, promoting activism, and advancing women's right to inhabit it. In the Spanish and Latin American context, feminist urbanism is increasingly being discussed and different cities (such as Santa Coloma de Gramenet, Montevideo, Mexico City, and Barcelona) have promoted feminist urban planning projects. International organizations and multilateral agencies are incorporating the discourse of urban planning from a gender perspective too, for example in the New Urban Agenda of UN-Habitat, UN Women, and the World Bank.

As a result, more and more participatory processes are being promoted in which women are the main agents, especially when it comes to women's urban safety. However, there are also other examples in other areas of urban planning: from projects of the Catalan Neighborhood Law—implemented in different municipalities—to more recent processes in which there has been active participation by women. However, women are still far from being a central decision-making part of the transformation processes. Cities that approve measures to incorporate the gender perspective in urban planning do not do it systematically and transversally in all their projects. It continues to be a battle for the feminists who, from inside or outside the institutions, continue to advocate for this paradigm shift. We continue to encounter barriers, both political and technical, when it comes to advancing towards a feminist transformation of the city.

Urban sociology has approached the analysis of urban phenomena from a critical perspective, linking the relationship between the economy and social relations with urban life. However, in most work, the gender perspective is absent, making invisible how gender relations and roles influence both the conformation of urban space itself as well as the uses and experiences in the city. In this sense, feminist urbanism can contribute to fill these gaps.

Urban sociology evidences the role of capitalism in shaping cities and also its determining role in urban phenomena where the economic logics of private profit determine the social conditions of city dwellers. However, many of these analyses forget the relationship between capitalism and patriarchy as two systems that feed back into each other. They underestimate the fact that the social reproduction of labor continues to be sustained mainly by women throughout the world. The still current sexual division of labor has an impact on the distribution of spaces, itineraries, and times in cities, a reality that should not be ignored in sociological analyses.

Feminist urbanism also highlights the importance of gender as a category that generates asymmetrical material and immaterial conditions (feminization of poverty, care that is mainly the responsibility of women, and perceptions and experiences of non-hegemonic bodies, such as harassment and daily violence). Power relations and roles affect participation in social movements and neighborhood organizations, collectives in which women are co-protagonists and where women's participation represents the majority, such as struggles for housing, but where the places of public visibility are still mostly dominated by men.

In this sense, urban sociology has also been a pioneer in introducing research-action-participation processes, but these processes have often made internal community inequalities invisible. The lesson that can be drawn from feminist urbanism is that participation is also not neutral and that community processes can reinforce power relations and roles.

Finally, urban sociology legitimizes the academy as the only space for knowledge generation. Feminism in general, and feminist urbanism in particular, claims that knowledge can be drawn from multiple places. We thus advocate conducting militant urban sociology, even beyond the constrained structures of academia.

Nowadays more and more institutions are considering the incorporation of the gender perspective in participation linked to urban, territorial, or mobility planning, something that can be an opportunity for change and consolidation or, at the same time, a strategy to instrumentalize and extract political credit from feminism. However, on the other hand, we are experiencing a global rise of fascist, misogynist, racist, and LGBTphobic ideologies, which find a voice in the media and parliamentary representation through the extreme neoliberal right-wing parties. Therefore, these are turbulent times in which the search for social justice for all must be the way and the end.

## REFERENCES

Arranz Lozano, Fátima (2015) Meta-análisis de las investigaciones sobre la violencia de género: el estado produciendo conocimiento. *Athenea digital: revista de pensamiento e investigación social* 15(1): 171–203.

Baylina, Mireia (1997) Metodología cualitativa y estudios de geografía y género. *Documents d'anàlisi geogràfica* 30: 123–138.

Beall, Jo (1996) Participation in the city in the city: Where do women fit in? *Gender & Development* 4(1): 9–16.

Biglia, Barbara and Bonet-Martí, Jordi (2009) La construcción de narrativas como método de investigación psicosocial. Prácticas de escritura compartida. *Forum Qualitative Sozialforschung/Forum: Qualitative Social Research* 10(1): 25–35. http://nbnresolving.de/urn:nbn:de:0114-fqs090183.

Blázquez, Norma (2010) Epistemología feminista: temas centrales In Blázquez, Norma, Flores Palacios, Fátima and Ríos Everardo, Maribel (eds.) *Investigación feminista. Epistemología, metodología y representaciones sociales*. Universidad Nacional Autónoma de México, 21–38.

Bofill Levi, Anna (2008) *Guia per al planejament urbanístic i l'ordenació urbanística amb la incorporació de criteris de gènere*. Barcelona: Generalitat de Catalunya, Institut Català de les Dones.

Bondi, Liz (1991) Gender divisions and gentrification: A critique. *Transactions of the Institute of British Geographers* 16(2): 190198. doi: 10.2307/622613.

Bondi, Liz and Rose, Damaris (2003) Constructing gender, constructing the urban: A review of Anglo-American feminist urban geography. *Gender, Place & Culture: A Journal of Feminist Geography* 10(3): 229–245.

Carrasco, Cristina (2001) La sostenibilidad de la vida humana: ¿un asunto de mujeres? *Mientras Tanto* 82: 43–70.

Carrasco, Cristina, Borderías, Cristina and Torns, Teresa (2011) Introducción. El trabajo de cuidados: antecedentes históricos y debates actuales. In Carrasco, Cristina, Borderías, Cristina and Torns, Teresa (eds.) *El trabajo de cuidados: historia, teoría y políticas.* Madrid: Catarata.

Col·lectiu Punt 6 (2011) Construyendo entornos seguros desde la perspectiva de género. In Freixanet, María (ed.) *No surtis sola Espais públics segurs amb perspectiva de gènere.* Barcelona: Institut de Ciències Polítiques i Socials, Universitat Autònoma de Barcelona, 145–231.

Col·lectiu Punt 6 (2018) *Entornos Habitables. Auditoría de Seguridad Urbana con perspectiva de género en la vivienda y el entorno.* Barcelona: Col·lectiu Punt 6. http://www.punt6.org/wp-content/uploads/2016/08/Entornos_habitables_CAST_FINAL.pdf.

Col·lectiu Punt 6 (2019) *Urbanismo Feminista. Por una transformación radical de nuestros espacios de vida.* Barcelona: Virus Editorial.

Col·lectiu Punt 6 and Ortiz, Sara (2017) *Nocturnas. La vida cotidiana de las mujeres que trabajan de noche en el Área Metropolitana de Barcelona.* Barcelona: Col·lectiu Punt 6.

Corpas Reina, Ma and García, José Diego (1999) *La ciudad y el urbanismo desde una perspectiva de género: el uso del espacio y el tiempo.* Universidad de Córdoba.

Darke, Jane (1998) La ciudad, espacio de propiedad patriarcal. In Booth, Chris, Darke, J. and Yeandl, Susan (eds.) *La vida de las mujeres en las ciudades: la ciudad, un espacio para el cambio.* Madrid: Narcea, 122–126.

Del Valle, Teresa (2006) Seguridad y convivencia: Hacia nuevas formas de transitar y de habitar. In *Urbanismo y género. Una visión necesaria para todos.* Barcelona: Diputación de Barcelona, 275–292.

Durán, María Ángeles (1998) *La ciudad compartida. Conocimiento, afecto y uso.* Madrid: Consejo Superior de los colegios de arquitectos de España.

Dyck, Isabel (2005) Feminist geography, the 'everyday', and local–global relations: Hidden spaces of place-making. *Canadian Geographer/Le Géographe Canadien* 49(3): 233–243. doi: 10.1111/j.0008-3658.2005.00092.x.

Edwards, Rosalind and Mauthner, Melanie (2002) Ethics and feminist research: Theory and practice. *Ethics in Qualitative Research 2:* 14–31.

England, Kim V.L. (1991) Gender relations and the spatial structure of the city. *Geoforum* 22(2): 135–147.

Engster, Daniel (2004) Care ethics and natural law theory: Toward an institutional political theory of caring. *The Journal of Politics* 66(1): 113–135.

Esteban, Mari Luz (2014) El feminismo vasco y los circuitos de conocimiento: el movimiento, la universidad y la casa de las mujeres In Mendia, Irantzu et al. (eds.) *Otras formas de (re)conocer. Reflexiones, herramientas y aplicaciones desde la investigación feminista.* Universidad del País Vasco-Simref, 61–76.

Ezquerra, Sandra (2018) ¿Qué hacer con los cuidados?: De la Economía Feminista a la democratización de los cuidados. *Viento sur: Por una izquierda alternativa,* 156: 39–47.

Falú, Ana (2009) Violencia y discriminaciones en las ciudades. In Falú, Ana (ed.) *Mujeres en la Ciudad. De Violencias y Derechos.* Santiago de Chile: Red Mujer, Hábitat de América Latina, and Ediciones Sur: 15–38.

Falú, Ana (2011) Restricciones ciudadanas: las violencias de género en el espacio público. In Largarde, Marcela and Valcárcel, Amelia (eds.) *Feminismo, género e igualdad.* Pensamiento Iberoamericano 9: 127–146.

Federici, Silvia (2011) *Calibán y la bruja. Mujeres, cuerpo y acumulación originaria.* Madrid: Traficantes de sueños.

Fernández Moreno, Nuria (1995) Una aproximación antropológica al origen de los espacios segregados. In Bisquert Santiago, Adriana (ed.) *Actas de curso: Urbanismo y mujer. Nuevas visiones del espacio público y privado, Málaga 1993–Toledo 1994.* Madrid: Seminario permanente Ciudad y Mujer, 99–106.

Fraser, Nancy (2015) Las contradicciones del capital y los cuidados *New Left Review* 100: 111–132.

García Ramón, Maria Dolors (1989) Para no excluir del estudio a la mitad del género humano. Un desafío pendiente en geografía humana. *Boletín de la Asociación de Geógrafos españoles* 9: 27–48.
Gilligan, Carol (1982) *In a Different Voice*. Cambridge: Harvard University Press.
Gilroy, Rose and Booth, Chris (1999) Building an infrastructure for everyday lives. *European Planning Studies* 7: 307–324. doi:10.1080/09654319908720520.
Greed, Clara (1997) Género y planificación del territorio ¿Un mismo tema? *Fòrum Internacional de planificación del territorio desde una perspectiva de género*. Barcelona: Fundació Maria Aurèlia Capmany, 2–26.
Green, Eileen (1998) Las mujeres y el ocio en la vida urbana. In Booth, Chris, Darke, Jane and Yeandle, Susan (eds.) *La vida de las mujeres en las ciudades. La ciudad, un espacio para el cambio*. Madrid: Narcea, 167–182.
Grupo de Ecofeminismo, Ecologistas en Acción (2011) *Menos para vivir major. Ecofeminismos, anticapitalismo y mundo urbano*. Madrid: Ecologistas en Acción.
Haraway, Donna (1995) *Ciencia, cyborgs y mujeres. La reinvención de la naturaleza*. Madrid: Cátedra.
Harding, Sandra G. (ed.) (1987) *Feminism and Methodology: Social Science Issues*. Bloomington: Indiana University Press.
Herrero, Yayo (2013) Pautas ecofeministas para repensar el mundo. In Vicent, Lucía, Castro, Carmen, Agenjo, Astrid and Herrero, Yayo (eds.) *El desigual impacto de la crisis sobre las mujeres*. Madrid: Dossier Fuhem Ecosocial, 29–37.
Herrero, Yayo, González Reyes, María, Pascual, Marta, and Gascó, Emma (2018) *La vida en el centro. Voces y relatos ecofeministas*. Madrid: Libros en acción (Ecologistas en Acción).
Hill Collins, Patricia and Bilge, Sirma (2019) *Interseccionalidad*. Madrid: Editorial Morata.
Horelli, Liisa (2006) Environmental human-friendliness as a contextual determinant for quality of life. *European Review of Applied Psychology* 56(1): 15–22.
Jarvis, Helen (2011) Saving space, sharing time: Integrated infrastructures of daily life in cohousing. *Environment and Planning A* 43(3): 560–577.
Jirón, Paola (2007) Implicaciones de género en las experiencias de movilidad cotidiana urbana en Santiago de Chile. *Revista Venezolana de Estudios de la Mujer* 12(29): 173–197.
Kabeer, Naila (2005) Gender equality and women's empowerment: A critical analysis of the third millennium development goal 1. *Gender & Development* 13(1): 13–24.
Kallus, Rachel, and Churchman, Arza (2004) Women's struggle for urban safety. The Canadian experience and its applicability to the Israeli context. *Planning Theory & Practice* 5(2): 197–215.
Karsten, Lia and Meertens, Donny (1992) La geografía del género: sobre visibilidad, identidad y relaciones de poder. *Documents d'anàlisi geogràfica* 19–20: 181–193.
Kern, Leslie (2021) *Ciudad feminista: La lucha por el espacio en un mundo diseñado por hombres*. Barcelona: Ediciones Bellaterra.
Lykogianni, Rouli (2008) Tracing multicultural cities from the perspective of women's everyday lives. *European Urban and Regional Studies* 15: 133–43. doi: 10.1177/0969776407087546.
Lynch, Gary and Atkins, Susan (1988) The influence of personal security fears on women's travel patterns. *Transportation* 15: 257–277.
McDowell, Linda (1999) *Género, identidad y lugar*. Madrid: Ediciones Cátedra Universidad de Valencia Instituto de la Mujer.
Michaud, Anne (2002) *Guide d'aménagement pour un environnement urbain sécuritaire*. Montreal: Femmes et Ville de la Ville de Montréal. http://ville.montreal.qc.ca/pls/portal/docs/page/femmes_ville_fr/media/documents/Guide_amenagement_environnement_urbain_securitaire.pdf.
Mies, Maria (2019) *Patriarcado y acumulación a escala mundial*. Traficantes de sueños.
Miralles-Guasch, Carme (2010) *Dones, mobilitat, temps i ciutats*. Col·lecció Quaderns de l'Institut 14, Perspectives des del feminisme. Barcelona: Institut Català de les Dones.
Mogollón, Irati and Fernández, Ana (2016) *Arquitecturas del cuidado. Viviendas colaborativas para personas mayores. Un acercamiento al contexto vasco y las realidades europeas*. Emakunde-Instituto Vasco de la Mujer.
Murillo, Soledad (1996) *El mito de la vida privada*. Madrid: Siglo XXI.
Nash, Mary (1995) Identitat cultural de gènere, discurs de la domesticitat i definició del treball de les dones a l'Espanya del segle XIX. *Documents d'anàlisi geogràfica* 26, 135–146.

Ortiz Escalante, Sara (2019) *Planning the Everyday/Everynight: A Feminist Participatory Action Research with Women Nightshift Workers*. University of British Columbia. https://open.library.ubc.ca/soa/cIRcle/collections/ubctheses/24/items/1.0379046.

Ortiz Escalante, Sara and Valdivia, Blanca G. (2015) Planning from below : Using feminist participatory methods to increase women's participation in urban planning. *Gender & Development* 23 (1): 113–26. doi: 10.1080/13552074.2015.1014206.

Oxfam (2020) Time to care. Unpaid and underpaid care work and the global inequality crisis. https://www.oxfam.org/en/research/time-care (accessed 14 December 2023).

Pain, Rachel (1991) Space, sexual violence and social control: Integrating geographical and feminist analyses of women's fear of crime. *Progress in Human Geography* 15(4), 415–431.

Pain, Rachel (2001) Gender, race, age and fear in the city. *Urban Studies* 38(5–6): 899–913.

Pérez Fernández, Irene (2009) *Espacio, identidad y género*. Sevilla: ArCiBel.

Pérez Orozco, Amaia (2014) *Subversión feminista de la economía. Aportes para un debate sobre el conflicto capital-vida*. Madrid: Traficantes de sueños.

Puleo, Alicia H. (2002) Feminismo y ecología. Un repaso a las diversas corrientes del ecofeminismo. *El Ecologista* 31: 36–39.

Robinson, Fiona (1997) Globalizing care: Ethics, feminist theory, and international relations. *Alternatives* 22: 113–33. doi: 10.4324/9780429500183.

Sakızlıoğlu, Bahar (2018) Rethinking the gender–gentrification nexus. In Lees, Loretta and Phillips, Martin (eds.) *Handbook on Gentrification Studies*. Cheltenham, UK and Northampton, MA, USA: Edward Elgar Publishing.

Sandercock, Leonie (ed.) (1998) *Making the Invisible Visible. A Multicultural Planning History*. Oakland: University of California Press.

Sarmiento, María Laura, Tavares, Rossana Brandão and Novas Ferradás, María Novas (2022) *Gestión feminista del hábitat: reflexiones desde la piel doméstica al desafío de la existencia*. Córdoba: Centro de Investigaciones y Estudios sobre Cultura y Sociedad.

Segovia, Olga and Oviedo, Enrique (2000) Espacios públicos en la ciudad y el barrio. In Segovia, Olga and Dascal, Guillermo (eds.) *Espacio público, participación y ciudadanía*. Santiago de Chile: Ediciones Sur, 54–69. http://www.sitiosur.cl/r.php.

Segovia, Olga and Rico, María Nieves (2017) ¿Cómo vivimos la ciudad? Hacia un nuevo paradigma urbano para la igualdad de género. In Rico, María Nieves and Segovia, Olga (eds.) *¿Quién cuida en la ciudad? Aportes para políticas urbanas de Igualdad*. Santiago de Chile: Naciones Unidas—Comisión Económica para América Latina y el Caribe (cepal), 41–69.

Segura, Isabel (2006) La memoria, una forma de arquitectura. In Diputació de Barcelona, Àrea d'Infraestructures (ed.) *Urbanisme i gènere. Una visió necessària per a tothom*. Barcelona: Diputació de Barcelona, Xarxa de municipis, 195–198.

Smith, Dorothy E. (1990) *The Conceptual Practices of Power: A Feminist Sociology of Knowledge*. Toronto: University of Toronto Press.

Sweet, Elizabeth L. (2018) Cultural humility: An open door for planners to locate themselves and decolonize planning theory, education, and practice. *EJournal of Public Affairs* 7(2): 1–17. http://www.ejournalofpublicaffairs.org/cultural-humility/.

Sweet, Elizabeth L. and Ortiz Escalante, Sara (2010) Planning responds to gender violence: Evidence from Spain, Mexico and the United States. *Urban Studies* 47(10): 2129–2147. http://usj.sagepub.com/cgi/doi/10.1177/0042098009357353.

Tronto, Joan C. (2020) *Moral Boundaries: A Political Argument for an Ethic of Care*. London: Routledge.

UN Women (2022) UN Women Data. Research highlight: Gender and Covid-19. https://data.unwomen.org/features/poverty-deepens-women-and-girls-according-latest-projections (accessed 14 December 2023).

Valdivia, Blanca (2018) Del urbanismo androcéntrico a la ciudad cuidadora. *Habitat y sociedad* 11: 65–84.

Valdivia, Blanca (2021) *La ciudad cuidadora. Calidad de vida urbana desde una perspectiva feminista*. Universitat Politécnica de Catalunya. www.tesisenred.net/handle/10803/671506.

Valdivia, Blanca (2022) La Ciudad Cuidadora: por un espacio urbano que ponga la vida en el centro. In Gil Junquero, Mónica and Jubeto Ruiz, Yolanda (eds.) *Quaderns Feministes*. Valencia: Tirant Editorial.

Valdivia, Blanca (2023) *Ecosistema Urbà de suport a les cures als municipis de Barcelona*. Barcelona: Diputació de Barcelona.

Walker, Julian, Frediani, Alexandre Apsan and Trani, Jean-François (2013) Gender, difference and urban change: Implications for the promotion of well-being. *Environment and Urbanization* 25(1): 111–124.

Wekerle, Gerda R. and Whitzman, Carolyn (1995) *Safe Cities: Guidelines for Planning, Design, and Management*. New York: Van Nostrand Reinhold.

Whitzman, Carolyn, Legacy, Crystal, Andrew, Caroline, Klodawsky, Fran, Shaw, Margaret and Viswanath, Kalpana (2013) *Building Inclusive Cities: Women's Safety and the Right to the City*. London: Routledge.

World Bank (2022) Gender Data Portal. https://genderdata.worldbank.org/ (accessed 14 December 2023).

# PART IV

# THE HOUSING QUESTION

# 23. Financialization and the rescaling of large developers: the built environment and national business groups

*Ivana Socoloff*

This chapter departs from the premise that in recent years a 'distinctive investor class' has emerged, such as hedge and private equity funds capable of centralizing capital (Harvey 2020), whose investment decisions have had an effect not only on the actions of national and local states but also of all economic agents, including traditional real estate developers. Capital accumulation has transformed the scale, size, and power of firms involved in space production. This rescaling of capital undoubtedly challenges urban sociologists who intend to critically analyze cities' built environment.

Within this framework, studies on real estate financialization have shown that various financial mechanisms drive the capital centralization that is poured into the built environment (Aalbers 2019, Aalbers et al. 2020). For scholarship in the field, financialization promotes the repetition of certain urban patterns (like large-scale urban projects, 'modern' iconic high-rise office towers, big multifamily apartment complexes, and shopping malls, among others) while transforming developers' rationalities, strategies, and capacity for action. These trends undoubtedly put any debate on 'local power' in cities into question. Nevertheless, the modes in which financialization shapes cities are diverse and variegated (Aalbers 2017), giving rise to enormous heterogeneity in firms' trajectories, product specializations, articulations, and relationships.

The study of these dynamics has proliferated over the years. If works in the past focused more on local governance and large urban developments, more contemporary studies have put developers back into the center (Ball 2008, Guy & Henneberry 2002, Weber 2015), making them key agents of a global 'real estate financial complex' (Aalbers 2013). In fact, a recent comparative study has analyzed the social relationships established by real estate developers to carry out their projects. By focusing on the 'work of developers', researchers were able to identify the contradictory interests, the heterogeneous motivations, and their changing alliances to discuss the processes of interest formation in real estate production (Ballard & Butcher 2020).

However, this emphasis on local governance complexities and developers' network-building strategies, while offering a welcome nuanced look at the action of developers, obscures more structural elements linked precisely to the rescaling, concentration of capital, and growing corporate empowerment of real estate developers observed by various studies. An analysis from the perspective of the firms makes it instead possible to show their growth, territorial expansion, and articulation with international funds.

Moreover, as this study focuses on Buenos Aires, one of Latin America's largest cities, it is important to note that the concentration and centralization of capital takes the form of diversified business groups in the region (Fernández Pérez et al. 2015). While diversified groups are not exclusive to Latin America (Colpan & Hikino 2018), their role is critical in understanding the region's political and economic dynamics (Schneider 2013). These groups have participated in the real estate business, as we will demonstrate later, and they continue to hold significant local and national power in generating and mobilizing surplus value.

Thus, attention will be given to the articulation between the developer, its business group, and the financing strategies, which requires a careful look at different geographical scales. As will be presented later, diversified national groups – the target of foreign investments and the key players of financialization – have played a significant role in local real estate development, and real estate investments have played an important part in the groups' strategies.

The chapter is organized as follows. In the first part, I review the rescaling of governance debate and contributions from financialization studies to describe the effects identified on local governments and firms. Second, I show how these global processes have been analyzed in the light of the Latin American urban sociology debate, bringing to light the importance of looking not only at the traditional mechanisms of capital centralization carried out by banks or capital markets but also at the role of business groups as traditional spaces for organizing the national economy. Next, I present empirical evidence that shows their heterogeneous trajectories despite the homogeneity in the products, their recent collective empowerment, and a link between these large developers and business groups. Afterwards, the chapter asserts that the city remains the target of accumulation for traditional national groups and comprehending this phenomenon necessitates examining the rescaling of developers. Hence, it demands urban sociologists appeal to multi-scalar research techniques and understand the language of finance.

## THE RESCALING OF DEVELOPERS: FROM COALITIONS TO MULTISPATIAL METAGOVERNANCE

The purpose of this section is to present classical and current debates on the role of developers at the local level, as well as the contributions made by financialization studies in better understanding the ongoing radical transformations of firms and their impacts on local governance.

An initial examination of this topic directs our attention to the seminal works of French sociologist Christian Topalov, who explored the increasing interconnection between real estate developers, major banks, and finance capital in France in his early works. For the French Marxist, 'state monopoly capitalism' was traversed by greater participation of finance capital oriented towards urban production, in which private banks were increasingly able to centralize the savings of the middle classes and finance housing through mortgage loans (Topalov 1974). In the Anglo-Saxon world, a similar interest in finance and urban transformations was shared by David Harvey (1982), although much of the literature tended to focus on studying developers' growth coalitions and political regimes (Fainstein 1994, Feagin & Parker 1990, Logan & Molotch 1987, Stone 1989). They analyzed, for example, the formation of more or less stable urban agendas in times where the central state was cutting funding to local governments. The emphasis, in this case, was placed on the processes of building alliances or on the 'internal dynamics' (Stone 2015) that showed that real estate developers worked with political and social support in the expansion of cities.

However, by the end of the 80s, some critical academic productions began to uncover the role of global capital in transforming cities (Castells 1991, Harvey 1989, Sassen 1991). For them, international capital's pressure was able to gear local politics to a more entrepreneurial direction or, in today's words, a neoliberal one. That is why the authors of the 1990s began to question localism, arguing that we were witnessing a process of 'rescaling of urban governance' (Brenner 1999, Swyngedouw 1992), making this local arrangement more diffuse. Stone himself recently stated that:

> Priority setting is now rarely a matter of fixing a strategic direction backed by a stable circle of top leaders; it seems more often a matter of ad hoc initiatives based on opportunistic assemblages of resources [...] For many cities, with collective business leadership now largely in remission, long-term strategic planning by the business sector has given way to piecemeal, short-term pursuits of profit. (Stone 2015: 111)

In what Rossi calls the 'third stage of urban entrepreneurialism' (2017: 53–58), we see a ramification of agents, models, and networks, with the involvement of a myriad of public and private actors, along with international agencies and economic players. Furthermore, global funding sources and institutions that spread 'best practices' impose global urban development models, giving rise to what could be called 'multispatial metagovernance' (Jessop 2016).

To shed light on the topic, it is important to highlight how extra-local economic agents and international financing logics, together with the economic dynamics of the real estate and construction sectors, shape urban policy and developers' strategies. As the economy becomes financialized, that is, dominated by predatory and speculative credit practices as a response to overaccumulation and crisis (Harvey 2003, 2018), extra-local agents can exert a 'direct influence on urban policy decisions' (Kirkpatrick & Smith 2011). This extra-urban discipline is tied to more or less visible mechanisms that operate on local politics (such as bondholder value, credit rating, systemic public-sector austerity), guiding the decisions of local authorities (Peck & Whiteside 2016).

Now, the current centralization of capital and great global liquidity configure what some have called the 'wall of money' (Fernandez & Aalbers 2016) looking for profit 'outlets', a process that has intensified after the crisis of 2008 (Harvey 2018). In this context, the built environment is seen as a 'safe' investment allocation insofar as it can offer a good return-to-risk ratio (Aalbers et al. 2020). Thus, land, real estate, or infrastructure, among other factors, emerge as privileged areas for the reproduction of financial capital (Aalbers 2019, O'Brien et al. 2019, Whiteside 2019). All of this shapes local governments' policies and economic agents' strategies; but how have the transformations of capitalism and financialization impacted developers' corporate structures?

While the answer is not mechanical, under neoliberalism, decision-making authority among entrepreneurs was the outcome of urban policies geared towards creating a favorable business climate and hastening the 'creative destruction' of the built environment. However, the financialization of the economy amplified these mechanisms and intensified debt, leading to a quicker turnover of capital in construction and a proliferation of financial gains. Within this process, some observed trends having to do with real estate being designed progressively more towards satisfying investors' interests than users' needs (Lizieri 2009, Weber 2015). Other trends include real estate services' internationalization under pressure from institutional investors – observed early in the commercial segment – which helps incorporate local real estate markets into international real estate investment networks (Magalhães 2001). As a result, the real estate community has become more complex (Weber 2015) and rationalities that guide the action of developers are transformed, including mechanisms of anticipation of what will be valued by the financial community (Guironnet & Halbert 2014), 'filtering risks' (Halbert

& Rouanet 2014, Searle 2016), and promoting new development or imposing aesthetics and ways of living (Weber 2015), deepening, as a consequence, the spatial selectivity of financial capital (Sanfelici & Halbert 2018).

On the investor side, we observe a growing heterogeneity that exceeds the classifications of 'global and local' and 'institutional or particular' (Özogul & Tasan-Kok 2020: 476). All of this has been expanded by innovative trans-local capital pooling strategies based on financial deregulation and the emergence of new financial instruments.

In this regard, Manuel Aalbers et al. (2020) have shown, for example, an even deeper passage in housing financialization that points to the spread of real estate funds in the form of real estate investment trusts (REITs) from a predominance in the commercial segment to a larger influence in single-family rental housing. As they argue, although none of those trends are new per se, their diffusion and global expansion reshape real estate markets around the world. In short, the *rescaling* to which I refer occurs in various ways, among which we see:

- Access to new sources of financing through financial innovation and growing cross-border investments. These sources can include either large international institutional investors – such as pension funds or insurance companies – or small family savers who, through the capital market, have access to securities – a negotiable financial instrument – that indirectly invest in real estate.
- Corporate restructuring, which includes complex transnational organizational structures designed in many cases for tax avoidance. For example, the passage from regular firms to real estate funds with tax incentives.
- Mergers, acquisitions, and the diffusion of franchises. Plus, mechanisms of oligopolization through either hyper-specialization processes, diversification, or integration of the entire production chain are observed. These mergers involve territorial expansion, jumps in scale, etc.
- Dissemination of valuation, rankings, and certification practices designed in think tanks with global impact.

Therefore, although capital takes various forms, when analyzing the trajectories of the leading developers in a given city in the global North or South, we will probably find that they are traversed by one or more of these processes. Now, one interesting dimension to highlight in this work is the importance of including the analysis of business groups when examining so-called peripheral countries (Maxfield & Schneider 1997, Schneider 2013). This is because although these groups may not necessarily explain the greater volume of housing production, they often constitute the most 'innovative' agents that impact the rest of the market by imposing scales, prices, and logics (Rufino & Pereira 2011). In addition, while in many developed countries equity markets and private banks have been the sources of long-term productive investment, in Latin America, family-controlled business groups and global corporations have always been the primary private institutions responsible for mobilizing capital for investment with strong support from the state (Lluch et al. 2021, Schneider 2013).

# LARGE DEVELOPERS IN LATIN AMERICA: BUSINESS GROUPS, ELITES, AND THE PRODUCTION OF THE BUILT ENVIRONMENT

**Developers and the Real Estate Financialization Debate in Latin America**

Following the discussion on business groups, this section presents some empirical results and theoretical reflections on the role of developers in Latin America in light of what might be termed the 'financial subordination' of non-core economies (Alami et al. 2021).

Without reifying current conditions, real estate studies in non-central cities generally observe some prevailing trends that are, however, not exclusively presented there. The first thing observed is that urban planning codes are often diffuse, promoting more land disputes than in core cities, a certain degree of regulatory and constructive flexibility, or even flagrant violations of basic standards (Shatkin 2017). In these contexts, information on real estate transactions circulates in more restricted social groups (Deal & Rosso 2001), making the markets 'less transparent', according to global consultants (JLL 2022).

Second, the channeling of capital might not necessarily take the form of 'private' capital or the conventional 'development' firm, especially in cities where the role of the state cannot be thought of as merely a 'facilitator' since it visibly adopts tasks more typically assumed by 'private' capital (Çelik 2021, Shatkin 2017). Third, and perhaps due to the survival of more compact elites due to greater social inequality, family businesses have greater importance (Fernández Pérez et al. 2015), which translates into real estate business.

Finally, as a result of cities' competition for investments (Harvey 1989), real estate developers in peripheral cities are forced to offer higher rates of return to attract global capital, guaranteeing extraordinary earnings, often supported by states.

In Latin America, one of the most urbanized developing regions in the world, self-building and building commissioning have been the predominant forms of housing production (Jaramillo 1977, Schteingart 1989). However, over the past two decades speculative real estate development has become dominant due to its effects on the rest of the production chain by progressively guiding investments, impacting supplier strategies, and determining location (Rufino & Pereira 2011).[1] It was at the turn of the century that the real estate cycle showed a boom linked to commodities' international prices, followed by a series of publicly funded responses to the international crisis and, finally, a new cycle of crisis from 2014–2015, which has only been aggravated with the Covid-19 pandemic (Mioto 2022).

In the context of the boom, research in the region has emphasized the political empowerment of the leading real estate developers (Kornbluth Camblor 2021, Oliveira & Rufino 2022, Rufino 2012, 2020, Sanfelici 2013a, Socoloff 2018) vis à vis the centralization of real estate capital through fusions and acquisitions by business groups (Lencioni 2014, Rufino 2012, Rufino et al. 2021a). This political empowerment is also largely explained by enabling urban policies (Jaramillo 2021) and by growing access to funding through the capital market (Kornbluth Camblor 2021, Sanfelici 2017).

Among the financial instruments that have contributed to deepening developers' access to financial capital in Latin America, it is possible to observe: 1) the diffusion of development firms' initial public offerings, that is, the first offering of shares to the public through new stock issuance (Rufino 2012, Sanfelici 2013b, Sanfelici & Halbert 2015); 2) the proliferation of increasingly specialized real estate funds such as REITs (Cattaneo Pineda 2011, Daher 2013, Gasca Zamora & Castro Martínez 2021, Magnani & Sanfelici 2022, Sanfelici & Halbert

2018, Socoloff 2021, Vergara-Perucich 2021); 3) the centralization of capital through public funds that poured resources into the real estate sector (Hernández 2021, Royer 2009); 4) the development of mortgage loan securitization instruments (Faustino & Royer 2022, Rolnik 2018, Torres et al. 2022); and 5) the diffusion of real estate financing platforms (Kalinoski & Procopiuck 2022).

Local and national governments clearly contributed to these ongoing processes through the dissemination of financialized urban planning schemes, present mainly in the Brazilian case, such as: a) public–private partnerships for large urban projects (Rufino et al. 2021b); b) urban operations (Fix 2007, Mosciaro 2021, Stroher 2017); and c) 'special axes' and 'special areas' of urban renovation. Additionally, governments have promoted housing policies that directly stimulate the financialization process, such as: a) massive housing programs aimed at the acquisition of units in large-scale projects; b) the implementation of public–private partnership models of residential rental (Rolnik et al. 2021); and c) the spread of inflation-indexed housing mortgage loans to protect investors (Socoloff 2020).

Within this context, inquiry into financialization's effects on traditional powerful agents becomes necessary. In this regard, some Latin American researchers have begun to investigate business groups' participation in this process of real estate financialization. Recent attempts (Kornbluth Camblor 2021, Rufino et al. 2020, Socoloff 2018) have been added to some initial and general works (David 2013, Fix 2007, Rufino 2012, Socoloff 2013), but much is still under scrutiny. For example, in a case that might remind us of Pirelli's Bicocca (Kaika & Ruggiero 2016), Rufino's work on Votorantim's diversified group reveals how the traditional group used its brownfield land from the industrialization period and its bank to promote large-scale developments. They did so by integrating the entire production and financing chain and thanks to the group's national political influence and power (Rufino 2019).

Another example might be that of IRSA-Cresud group in Argentina, which was rapidly able to alter the real estate market in Buenos Aires thanks to its access to international funding (provided by George Soros's fund in its interest to enter the Argentinean market), gain control of high-quality assets and political influence at the local and national levels, dominate in a few years the shopping center segment, acquire systemic importance in commercial buildings, and take control of the privatized Banco Hipotecario Nacional (National Mortgage Bank), as well as other second-rank financial entities (Socoloff 2013). So far, the questions refer mainly to understanding what role the traditional elites have played in the construction booms and busts, what investment channels they have privileged, and the effect of international capital on their strategies. With this in mind, the next section explores Argentina's leading development firms.

**The Top Ten Developers in Argentina: Groups, Elites, and the City**

Here I present the results of analyzing the ten most active real estate development firms in the aftermath of the global 2007–2008 crisis in Argentina. There are multiple reasons for choosing this approach. Firstly, the universe of real estate development companies is inaccessible due to the diversity of legal forms that encompass the activity and the lack of statistical data. Even the local government is not aware of all the agents involved (see Figure 23.1). Secondly, information about companies that do not trade publicly is limited, even among the top ten most active firms. Finally, considering only publicly traded companies would introduce bias with respect to their financing mechanisms, which often involve large investors or families who do not necessarily rely on the capital markets to allocate their resources. In contrast, focusing on

*Source:* Miguel A. Martínez.

*Figure 23.1  Buenos Aires (2018)*

the most active firms in this chapter allows me to concentrate on those with greater visibility and for which there are a variety of verifiable sources.[2]

Four indicators were considered in this analysis: 1) Who are the controlling business groups and what is the trajectory of their main representative? 2) What are their main funding strategies? Does the group have access to national and/or international capital markets? 3) How do firms' leaders participate in the political sphere (for example, through an association as members or leaders and/or direct or indirect participation in public positions, either local or national)? 4) Finally, what is the firms investments' geographical scope? Do they invest outside of Buenos Aires or in other countries?

Based on the firms' financial information as well as press and legal data, we see evidence of the concentration and centralization of capital and a clear link between the leading firms and the wealthy traditional national elites that control the most dynamic sectors of the economy and, hence, the most important business groups. The increasing prominence of business groups in the real estate sector and of the real estate sector within the business groups' strategies shows not only that the process of internationalization has had an effect on the real estate firms but also that their access to financial capital is mediated by the groups themselves.

As evidence of the connection between real estate development in Buenos Aires, national business groups, and the national elite, we observe that four out of the 40 wealthiest families in Argentina (as ranked by Forbes) built their fortunes by founding real estate companies (Jorge Pérez, now living and developing in Miami; Eduardo Elsztain; Moisés Khafif; and David Sutton). Plus, at least half of these families' groups have openly ventured into real estate development at some point or another of their trajectory. In addition, like their counterparts around the globe, the elite in Argentina also tend to favor real estate as an investment outlet. As per declared tax data, the wealthiest 10,000 individual taxpayers (who comprise only the top 0.025% of the population) rank real estate as their third investment choice, with a particular emphasis on properties located outside the country (AFIP 2021).

If we consider now the ten companies that developed the largest amounts of real estate in Argentina in square meters between 2009 and 2015, a pattern emerges: seven of these firms belong or are tied to the 40 wealthiest families in the country. Moreover, these companies are part of diversified holdings: nine are affiliated with business groups, six of which originally emerged from the real estate or construction sectors but have since expanded their investments to include areas such as banking, agribusiness, mining, and energy (see Table 23.1). Therefore, these firms now constitute an additional line of business for many of the top business groups in Argentina, which have diversified their portfolios by keeping investments in land.

Another crucial point is the transfer of the groups' assets to foreign hands and the participation of foreign capital in these real estate ventures. In this respect, it should be noted that obtaining accurate information or establishing the boundary between national and foreign is difficult, especially considering that the leaders of these organizations and the firms themselves are politically recognized as representatives of a 'national bourgeoisie', and researchers place these groups as part of 'national capital' (Gaggero & Schorr 2017).[3] However, all in all, it is possible to see the participation of global hedge funds (as bond investors, shareholders, or project partners), as well as international banks pouring resources into these firms despite Argentina being considered a 'risky market' for global capital.

The examples of the IRSA-Cresud and Pampa groups are illustrative in this regard. The firms' financial statements reveal the association between JP Morgan, Goldman Sachs, and IRSA in the shopping mall segment, as well as Blackrock's and British investor Joe Lewis's stock ownership in Pampa.[4] Two other examples linked to the previous ones are also worth noting: TGLT-GCDI, in which IRSA-Cresud owns a 27% share, and Creaurban, founded by the father of the former president Macri, in which Pampa has a share. Both TGLT and Pampa are connected to the hedge fund PointState Capital, run by Zachary Jared Schreiber, through a fund called PointArgentum Master Fund LP.[5] PointArgentum holds 41.73% of the stocks in TGLT and an undisclosed amount of Pampa's stocks. The tricky part in these cases is understanding the role of the Caputo and Macri groups, owned by two families who have been business partners and friends for decades. Both families had to sell their real estate and construction businesses due to their ties to the national and local government and their infrastructure deals with the state. Strikingly, both families sold to the same buyer without disclosing whether they participated in the Cayman Islands funds that ultimately held the stocks managed in New York, as was hinted by the press (Revista Noticias 2018).

This topic leads us to the *empowerment* dimension of our analysis. Throughout the 2000s, nine out of these ten companies became part of the Chamber of Urban Development Entrepreneurs (Cámara Empresaria del Desarrolladores Urbanos in Spanish) (See Table 23.1). This chamber – created in 2001 – went from being an unknown entity on the political scene to becoming a relevant actor at the national level, mainly from 2009 onwards, when it became an active advocate of indexed mortgage loans in times of crisis (Socoloff 2020). In 2015, the CEDU began to lead first the National Construction Board, despite not having construction companies as members, and then the National Housing Board, both publicly convened spaces for lobbying. In this regard, it is important to highlight that these entities scaled from being local informal public–private meetings to being institutionalized national entities designed for receiving policy proposals from the chambers.

Furthermore, in the case of the top companies, we see a ramification of their political power and influence through different public or private institutions. Specifically, the leaders of these firms or individuals associated with them have held positions of power in national and local government. In fact, of the twelve groups' CEOs – one development firm changed hands two times in the period – we see that six of them were linked to ministerial-level officials at the national level or high-ranking officials in the City of Buenos Aires. We already mentioned the case of Creaurban, previously owned by former president and former head of government in Buenos Aires, Mauricio Macri. However, we can also highlight the TGLT-GCDI case, which merged with the Caputo construction firm partially owned by Macri's personal friend Nicolas Caputo, who was appointed as Consul in Singapore during his government, and also the cousin of the former chief of finance and director of the central bank (Luis Caputo). For its part, IRSA-Cresud has also gained enough power to appoint a national minister of economics and local authorities in Buenos Aires (Socoloff 2013) while former national deputy Francisco De Narváez controls Ribera.

The *geographical expansion* of these developers into different regions is another important aspect to consider. While there is a more heterogeneous panorama in terms of the specific paths taken by each firm, the overall trend indicates that during the real estate boom and after the global crisis there was a movement from Buenos Aires to other cities within Argentina, as well as towards other countries. This expansion was primarily driven by the desire to hedge against the instability of the Argentine economy. Thus, as shown in Table 23.1, most firms carried out developments outside Argentina, either in Uruguay – which functions as a kind of tax haven for the Argentine elite – or in the USA, especially in Miami in the post-crisis period, where the Argentines were some of the city's recovery protagonists.[6]

Furthermore, while observing an expansion outside Buenos Aires, we also see a common orientation of their investments to the luxury segment – due to different economic and policy conditions – particularly in a renowned large-scale real estate development in Buenos Aires called Puerto Madero. Today, this recently developed neighborhood has the most expensive

Financialization and the rescaling of large developers    369

Table 23.1    Top ten developers in Argentina and their business groups (2009–2015)*

| Developer | Real estate segment/s | Square meters developed (in thousands) | Type of developer | Year founded | Geographical scope | Listed | Developer's chamber member | Group | Group segments | Group's owner, CEO, or person in charge | Forbes top 40 (2012) | Forbes top 50 (2018) | First business endeavors |
|---|---|---|---|---|---|---|---|---|---|---|---|---|---|
| 1 Consultatio | Residential/office | 3786 | Developer – new holding | 1994 | Argentina USA Uruguay | Yes (Argentina) | Yes | Consultatio | Real estate/financial | Eduardo Costantini | 25 | 12 | Finance |
| 2 Ribera | Residential/mix | 3670 | Developer – fund | 2005 | Mainly Buenos Aires | Yes (Argentina – REIT) | No | Grupo De Narváez | Diversified | De Narváez | No | No | Retail |
| 3 TGLT-GCDI | Residential/office | 837.7 | Developer – newcomer | 2005 | Argentina Brazil Uruguay | Yes (Argentina and Brazil – delisted) | Yes | Caputo | Construction | Nicolás Caputo | No | 30 | Construction |
| 4 Raghsa | Residential/office | 357.6 | Developer – historical | 1969 | Argentina Uruguay** | Yes (Argentina) | Yes | Raghsa | Real estate | Moisés Khafif | 33 | 30 | Real estate |
| 5 IRSA | Office/shopping malls/hotels | 328.1 | Developer – new holding | 1943/1989 | Argentina USA Latin America and Israel | Yes (Argentina and NYSE; Nasdaq through the group) | Yes | CRESUD | Real estate/rural land/financial | Eduardo Elsztain | 37 | No | Real estate |

| Developer | Real estate segment/s | Square meters developed (in thousands) | Type of developer | Year founded | Geographical scope | Listed | Developer's chamber member | Group | Group segments | Group's owner, CEO, or person in charge | Forbes top 40 (2012) | Forbes top 50 (2018) | First business endeavors |
|---|---|---|---|---|---|---|---|---|---|---|---|---|---|
| 6 Newside/ Ginevra International Realty | Residential/ shopping malls | 300 | Developer – historical | 1973 | Mainly Buenos Aires Uruguay | No | No | GNV Group | Real estate/ construction/ linked to a bankrupt bank in the 1990s | Jorge Ginevra (passed away) and Alejandro Ginevra | No | No | Broker |
| 7 Vizora | Residential/ mix | 299.4 | Developer – newcomer | 2005 | Mainly Buenos Aires | Yes (Argentina and NYSE through the group) | Yes | Grupo Macro | Financial/ agro/real estate | Jorge Brito | 24 | 10 | Finance |
| 8 Fernández Prieto y Asociados | Residential/ office | 250 | Construction – traditional | 1975 | Argentina USA Uruguay | No | Yes | Fernández Prieto y Asociados | Construction/ real estate | Alberto Fernández Prieto | No | No | Construction |

*Financialization and the rescaling of large developers* 371

| Developer | Real estate segment/s | Square meters developed (in thousands) | Type of developer | Year founded | Geographical scope | Listed | Developer's chamber member | Group | Group segments | Group's owner, CEO, or person in charge | Forbes top 40 (2012) | Forbes top 50 (2018) | First business endeavors |
|---|---|---|---|---|---|---|---|---|---|---|---|---|---|
| 9 Creaurban | Residential/ office | 240 | Construction – traditional | 1995 | Argentina Uruguay | Yes (Argentina and NYSE through group) | Yes | Grupo Macri | Construction/ infrastructure | Franco Macri (passed away) and family, including Argentina's former President Mauricio Macri | 30 | 28 | Construction |
|  |  |  |  |  |  |  |  | Grupo ODS | Construction/ energy/real estate | Angelo Calcaterra | No | No | Construction |
|  |  |  |  |  |  |  |  | Pampa Energia | Energy | Marcelo Midlin | No | 26 | Real estate |
| 10 Alvear | Residential/ hotel | 146.5 | Developer – historical | 1983 | Argentina | No | No | Grupo Sutton | Luxury/ hotels/ perfumes/real estate | David Sutton | 40 | No | Luxury – perfume |

*Notes:*
\* The selected firms come from Forbes Argentina Developers Ranking (Forbes Argentina 2015). The firm Qualis was excluded from this ranking because it was dissolved in 2015.
\*\* In 2017 they started investing in New York.
*Source:* Authors' elaboration based on secondary data.

square meters in Latin America (Properati 2021), and all of the leading firms in the sample except for Ribera-Grupo De Narváez took part in this development through either one or more projects. In this respect, and without a doubt, the firms' capacity to pool larger sums of money is at the basis of their ability to access Puerto Madero's exclusive land.

Let us now discuss the last dimension considered: the *financing and financialization* of these firms. The first indicator of a process of financialization of real estate production has to do with the listing of companies in the capital market. Capital markets allow any firm – at least in theory – not only to have access to a greater diversity of investors but also to raise a greater volume of capital, for example, to progressively create a larger portfolio of rented units (commercial, offices, or houses). This also stimulates the firm to orient its practices towards satisfying investors' demands and searching for financial gains.

Even though the process is incipient and fragmentary in the Argentine case (Socoloff 2021), what we see is that there is growing participation in the national capital market. Of this sample, four are directly listed on the stock exchange, and three more are listed only indirectly (two through their controlling group and one through a real estate fund). In this scenario, the case of IRSA once again stands out. IRSA was one of the first active listed real estate companies and in the 1990s became listed on the NYSE and Nasdaq through its holding company Cresud, which allowed IRSA to access international funding conditions. Vizora and Creaurban are also listed in the USA but through their holding companies. TGLT also stands out since this company was listed and delisted on the Sao Paulo Stock Exchange after the 2008 international crisis.

In this respect, it is important to mention that this international funding does not simply constitute an 'alternative access to capital at a lower cost' to carry out 'industrial activities' such as housing construction. Instead, the access of non-financial companies to global markets, through their business groups, can potentially turn them into 'surrogate intermediaries' in peripheral countries (Shin & Zhao 2013). This means that they could become channels for the transmission of international liquidity and global economic cycles into the national economy, as was the case during the period of flexible monetary policies aimed at increasing liquidity, also known as quantitative easing policies (Fernandez et al. 2018). In particular, some large corporations in Latin America have followed this track and functioned as pseudo-financial companies based on their ability to borrow in international foreign currency markets and retain liquid assets, carrying out carry-trade or speculative operations and thus counteracting the efforts of national authorities to control national liquidity (Zeolla 2021). This has been the case with Pampa Energía, IRSA-Cresud, and Grupo Macro.

Likewise, Argentina's slow but growing financing strategy through REITs can be observed as a possible indication of a 'financialization 2.0' (Aalbers et al. 2020), which allows firms numerous tax advantages and access to institutional investors. However, as I have analyzed in another work, this access is fragmentary, and the evolution toward dominance of the REIT form is neither clear nor linear in Argentina. This is due to the fluctuating economic conditions as well as some internal real estate dynamics, such as clashing timings, currencies, and rules between the functioning of the capital market and how real estate developers manage risk outside regulated markets (Socoloff 2021).

More can be said about these firms' corporate structure and about their 'formation of external assets' (or capital flight strategies) that support the circulation of capital across borders. By analyzing these ten companies, it is possible to verify that at least eight of them have related firms abroad, mainly in Uruguay, and, therefore, serve as a platform to access other tax havens.[7] Likewise, 10 of the 12 leading CEOs in our sample appear in at least one of the four investigation reports on capital flight and possession of undeclared assets in tax havens carried out by Argentina's authorities and/or the global press (the Panama Papers, Pandora Papers, and others) (Bona 2018). As a result, one could say that both their international corporate structure and their access to tax heavens are supporting Buenos Aires's real estate-related gains to cross the border either to promote developments in other cities or to simply inflate their non-declared accounts abroad.

In summary, large developers in Argentina and (trans)national elites are closely connected through family-run economic groups that invest in real estate, often as part of a wider business conglomerate. These developers have expanded their investments beyond Buenos Aires and even beyond Argentina, creating a network of associated firms, some of which are located in tax havens. Many of these firms are listed on national and international capital markets, linking their activities to global funds interested in diversification and enabling them to engage in speculative financial trades. Moreover, these firms and their leaders are politically organized at the national level, not only through a specific chamber but also through various initiatives that further empower developers and their collective action.

## CONCLUSIONS

The growing concentration and centralization of capital and the financialization of the economy have posed new and renewed challenges for analyzing local urban policy. By analyzing financial data and specialized press information and conducting a study of their leaders' trajectories, this research has demonstrated the intertwined relationship between large developers, (trans)national elites, financialization, and the expanding web of associated firms that operate across borders. Moreover, this study has also shown that the city continues to be the object of accumulation of traditional elites but that it has also been the target of new agents and flows of capital. Understanding this process requires, in my view, an analysis of the developer's rescaling.

These findings therefore have implications for our understanding of urban governance and economic development. The rise of global and diffuse powers operating at the local level and the increasing investment of international funds in real estate have transformed the character of land disputes and construction activity in cities around the world.

To truly understand these transformations, it is essential that we develop multi-scalar methodological strategies and insights from other disciplines. Among many possible tools available, financial anthropology has developed techniques like 'multi-sited ethnography' to study global value chains in the construction sector and ethnographies in financial institutions to comprehend the rationalities around financial devices (Ho 2009). Likewise, critical financial geographers have taught us ways to 'follow the money' and 'follow the firm' to apprehend how urban developments are financed and how variable the modes in which state agencies commit public resources and assume risks are (Brill & Özogul 2021, Hughes-McLure 2022). Plus, geographical studies have emphasized the importance of understanding spatial variegation, territories' hierarchization, and flows and circuits of investments for these phenomena.

This chapter has emphasized the urgent need for sociologists to develop an understanding of financial instruments, reports, corporate structures, consultant reports, risk-rating agencies' statements, and other related aspects. In other words, I firmly believe that speaking the language of finance in a financialized economy is crucial in today's world to 'tell how fortunes are made' (Logan & Molotch 1987: 248).

However, in light of these findings, it is clear that there is a pressing need for policymakers, grassroots organizations, and scholars alike to confront the challenges posed by the financialization of the economy and its impact on urban development. As we continue to grapple with these issues, we must remain vigilant in our efforts to understand the complex relationships between local and global actors and the ways in which they shape the built environment. Only through sustained engagement and interdisciplinary collaboration can we hope to build more just and equitable cities for all.

## NOTES

1. In the case of Sao Paulo, the authors explain how speculative, for-profit real estate development has expanded from the city center to the poorer periphery, becoming spatially dominant in that sense.
2. For other works with different approaches to the topic, see Socoloff (2018, 2020, 2021).
3. Another element that makes this inquiry difficult is the enormous ownership dynamics since firms change hands very rapidly. Plus, none of the reports on investment recommendations in Argentina mention real estate as a dynamic sector or as having potential in the economy (Deloitte 2021, PWC 2018, Santander 2021).
4. Given that its corporate structure leads to organizations incorporated in tax havens, it is impossible to determine the actual role of international investors.
5. The fund is run by an Argentinean based in the USA called Dario Lizzano and bought its TGLT shares, in turn, from the Brazilian-based real estate company PDG Realty S.A. and another private equity fund located in the Cayman Islands controlled by New York-based fund manager Bienville Capital Management.
6. Regarding the significance of international operations compared to national ones, it is worth mentioning a key point about the directly listed firms. While IRSA is strongly internationalized, its real estate activities are primarily concentrated in Argentina. Raghsa, TGLT, and Consultatio have made limited investments in Uruguay compared to their investments in Argentina, along with a few ventures in the USA (Raghsa has one development and Consultatio has completed two). For the three indirectly listed firms, Vizora, Ribera, and Creaurban, foreign investments are either marginal or nonexistent, as in the case of Creaurban with one venture in Uruguay. Finally, it is essential to note that measuring the impact of international investments for the remaining non-listed firms (Alvear, Fernandez Prieto, GNV) is difficult because of the lack of complete information about their assets beyond what is reported in the specialized press.
7. Uruguay has been included in the past, though it was recently excluded, from what is known as the 'Grey List' (in the Stay of Play section of the report) of Non-Cooperative Jurisdictions for Tax Purpose, according to the European Union (EU 2023). Through the years, Uruguay's investment attraction policies have facilitated the settlement of Argentine capital and citizens.

## REFERENCES

Aalbers, M. B. (2013) The real estate/financial complex. *Cities in Crisis 3: Financialization.* Society for Advancement of Socio-Economics (SASE) Annual Conference, Milan.

Aalbers, M. B. (2017) The variegated financialization of housing. *International Journal of Urban and Regional Research* 41(4): 542–554. doi: 10.1111/1468-2427.12522.
Aalbers, M. B. (2019) Financial geography II: Financial geographies of housing and real estate. *Progress in Human Geography* 43(2): 376–387. doi: 10.1177/0309132518819503
Aalbers, M. B., Fernandez, R. & Wijburg, G. (2020) The financialization of real estate. In P. Mader, D. Mertens & N. Van der Zwan (eds.) *The Routledge International Handbook of Financialization*. London: Routledge.
AFIP (2021) *Aporte Solidario Extraordinario*. Buenos Aires: Agencia Federal de Ingresos Públicos.
Alami, I., Alves, C., Bonizzi, B., Kaltenbrunner, A., Kodddenbrock, K., Kvangraven, I. & Powell, J. (2021) International financial subordination: A critical research agenda. Greenwich Papers in Political Economy, No. 33233. University of Greenwich, Greenwich Political Economy Research Centre. Retrieved from https://ideas.repec.org/p/gpe/wpaper/33233.html.
Ball, M. (2008) Markets and institutions in real estate and construction. Retrieved from https://nbn-resolving.org/urn:nbn:de:101:1-201410257479.
Ballard, R., & Butcher, S. (2020) Comparing the relational work of developers. *Environment and Planning A: Economy and Space* 52(2): 266–276. doi: 10.1177/0308518X19893684.
Bona, L. (2018) *La fuga de capitales en la Argentina: Sus transformaciones, alcances y protagonistas desde 1976*. Buenos Aires: Facultad Latinoamericana de Ciencias Sociales (FLACSO). Retrieved from https://flacso.org.ar/wp-content/uploads/2018/12/Bona_La-fuga-de-capitales-en-la-Argentina_DT24_Area_economia.pdf.
Brenner, N. (1999) Globalisation as reterritorialisation: The re-scaling of urban governance in the European Union. *Urban Studies* 36(3): 431–451. doi: 10.1080/0042098993466.
Brill, F. & Özogul, S. (2021) Follow the firm: Analyzing the international ascendance of build to rent. *Economic Geography* 97(3): 235–256. doi: 10.1080/00130095.2021.1931108.
Castells, M. (1991) *The Informational City: Information Technology, Economic Restructuring, and the Urban-regional Process*. Oxford: Blackwell.
Cattaneo Pineda, R. (2011) Los fondos de inversión inmobiliaria y la producción privada de vivienda en Santiago de Chile: ¿Un nuevo paso hacia la financiarización de la ciudad? *Revista de Estudios Urbano Regionales* 37: 112–115.
Çelik, Ö. (2021) The roles of the state in the financialisation of housing in Turkey. *Housing Studies* 38(6): 1006–1026. doi: 10.1080/02673037.2021.1928003.
Colpan, A. M. & Hikino, T. (eds.) (2018) *Business Groups in the West* (Vol. 1). Oxford: Oxford University Press. doi: 10.1093/oso/9780198717973.001.0001.
Daher, A. (2013) Fondos inmobiliarios y riesgo urbano. *Revista de Urbanismo* 15(29). doi: 10.5354/0717-5051.2013.30303.
David, L. (2013) La production urbaine de Mexico: Entre financiarisation et construction territoriale. Une analyse de l'insertion du réseau financier transnational dans les marchés d'immobilier d'entreprise. PhD thesis, Université Paris-Est. Retrieved from https://tel.archives-ouvertes.fr/tel-00971515/document.
Deal, M. & Rosso, C. (2001) Foreign investment in Latin American real estate: A comparison of Argentina, Brazil and Mexico. Master's thesis, Massachusetts Institute of Technology.
Deloitte (2021) Doing business in Argentina. Retrieved from https://www2.deloitte.com/ar/es/pages/impuestos/articles/doing-business-argentina-2021.html.
EU (2023) Taxation: British Virgin Islands, Costa Rica, Marshall Islands and Russia added to EU list of non-cooperative jurisdictions for tax purposes. Council of the EU press release. Retrieved from https://www.consilium.europa.eu/en/press/press-releases/2023/02/14/taxation-british-virgin-islands-costa-rica-marshall-islands-and-russia-added-to-eu-list-of-non-cooperative-jurisdictions-for-tax-purposes/.
Fainstein, S. S. (1994) *The City Builders: Property, Politics, and Planning in London and New York*. Oxford and Cambridge: Blackwell.
Faustino, R. B. & Royer, L. de O. (2022) O setor imobiliário habitacional pós-2015: Crise ou acomodação? *Cadernos Metrópole* 24(53): 147–172. doi: 10.1590/2236-9996.2022-5306.
Feagin, J. R. & Parker, R. (1990) *Building American cities: The Urban Real Estate Game* (2nd ed.). Englewood Cliffs, NJ: Prentice Hall.

Fernandez, R. & Aalbers, M. B. (2016) Financialization and housing: Between globalization and varieties of capitalism. *Competition & Change* 20(2): 71–88. doi: 10.1177/1024529415623916.

Fernandez, R., Bortz, P. & Zeolla, N. (2018) The politics of quantitative easing. A critical assessment of the harmful impact of European monetary policy on developing countries. SOMO. Retrieved from https://www.somo.nl/wp-content/uploads/2018/06/Report-Quantitive-Easing-web.pdf.

Fernández Pérez, P., Lluch, A. & Barbero, M. I. (eds.) (2015) *Familias empresarias y grandes empresas familiares en América Latina y España: Una visión de largo plazo* (1st ed.). Bilbao: Fundación BBVA.

Fix, M. (2007) *Sao Paulo cidade global: Fundamentos financeiros de uma miragem*. Sao Paulo: Boitempo Editorial Anpur.

Forbes Argentina (2015) Contra Viento y Marea. Retrieved from: http://forbesargentina.infonews.com:80/contra-viento-y-marea/

Gaggero, A. & Schorr, M. (2017) Las grandes empresas nacionales de la Argentina bajo los gobiernos del kirchnerismo. *H-industri@: Revista de historia de la industria, los servicios y las empresas en América Latina* 21: 54–75.

Gasca Zamora, J. & Castro Martínez, E. de J. (2021) Financiarización inmobiliaria en México: Una mirada desde los Fideicomisos de Inversión en Bienes Raíces (FIBRAS). *Revista INVI* 36(103): 112–136. doi: 10.4067/S0718-83582021000300112.

Guironnet, A. & Halbert, L. (2014) The financialization of urban development projects: Concepts, processes, and implications. Retrieved from https://hal-enpc.archives-ouvertes.fr/hal-01097192.

Guy, S. & Henneberry, J. (eds.) (2002) *Development and Developers: Perspectives on Property*. Oxford and Malden, MA: Blackwell Science.

Halbert, L. & Rouanet, H. (2014) Filtering risk away: Global finance capital, transcalar territorial networks and the (un)making of city-regions: An analysis of business property development in Bangalore, India. *Regional Studies* 48(3): 471–484. doi: 10.1080/00343404.2013.779658.

Harvey, D. (1982) *The Limits to Capital*. Chicago: University of Chicago Press.

Harvey, D. (1989) From managerialism to entrepreneurialism: The transformation in urban governance in late capitalism. *Geografiska Annaler. Series B, Human Geography* 71(1): 3–17. doi: 10.2307/490503.

Harvey, D. (2003) *The New Imperialism*. New York, NY: Oxford University Press.

Harvey, D. (2018) *Marx, Capital and the Madness of Economic Reason*. New York, NY: Oxford University Press.

Harvey, D. (2020) *The Anti-capitalist Chronicles* (edited by J. T. Camp & C. Caruso). London: Pluto Press.

Hernández Trejo, F. D. J. (2021) Financiarización y crisis del mercado hipotecario de viviendas nuevas para los trabajadores en México. *Scripta Nova. Revista Electrónica de Geografía y Ciencias Sociales* 25(1). doi: 10.1344/sn2021.25.32232.

Ho, K. Z. (2009) *Liquidated: An Ethnography of Wall Street*. Durham: Duke University Press.

Hughes-McLure, S. (2022) Follow the money. *Environment and Planning A: Economy and Space* 54(7): 1299–1322. doi: 10.1177/0308518X221103267.

Jaramillo, S. (1977) *Hacia una teoría de la renta del suelo urbano*. Centro de Estudios sobre Desarrollo Económico, Universidad de los Andes.

Jaramillo, S. (2021) Reorientación del gran capital hacia lo inmobiliario. *Punto Sur* 4: 26–46. doi: 10.34096/ps.n4.10401.

Jessop, B. (2016) Territory, politics, governance and multispatial metagovernance. *Territory, Politics, Governance* 4(1): 8–32. doi: 10.1080/21622671.2015.1123173.

JLL (2022) Global real estate transparency index, 2022. Jones Lang Lasalle. Retrieved from https://www.us.jll.com/en/trends-and-insights/research/global-real-estate-transparency-index.

Kaika, M. & Ruggiero, L. (2016) Land financialization as a 'lived' process: The transformation of Milan's Bicocca by Pirelli. *European Urban and Regional Studies* 23(1): 3–22. doi: 10.1177/0969776413484166.

Kalinoski, R. & Procopiuck, M. (2022) Financeirização imobiliária em dois momentos: Da produção à ocupação via proptechs. *Cadernos Metrópole* 24(53): 119–146. doi: 10.1590/2236-9996.2022-5305.

Kirkpatrick, L. O. & Smith, M. P. (2011) The infrastructural limits to growth: Rethinking the urban growth machine in times of fiscal crisis. *International Journal of Urban and Regional Research* 35(3): 477–503. doi: 10.1111/j.1468-2427.2011.01058.x.

Kornbluth Camblor, D. L. (2021) El diseño político del proceso de financiarización de la vivienda y la infraestructura en Chile. *Revista INVI* 36(103): 54–84. doi: 10.4067/S0718-83582021000300054.

Lencioni, S. (2014) Reestruturação imobiliária: Uma análise dos processos de concentração e centralização do capital no setor imobiliário. *EURE* 40(120): 29–47. doi: 10.4067/S0250-71612014000200002.

Lizieri, C. (2009) *Towers of Capital: Office Markets and International Financial Services*. Chichester and Ames, IA: Wiley-Blackwell.

Lluch, A., Monsalve Zanatti, M. & Bucheli, M. (eds.) (2021) *Historia empresarial en América Latina: Temas, debates y problemas*. Lima and Bogotá: Universidad del Pacífico and Universidad de los Andes.

Logan, J. R. & Molotch, H. L. (1987) *Urban Fortunes: The Political Economy of Place*. Berkeley: University of California Press.

Magalhães, C. S. D. (2001) International property consultants and the transformation of local markets. *Journal of Property Research* 18(2): 99–121. doi: 10.1080/09599910110014156.

Magnani, M. & Sanfelici, D. (2022) O e-commerce e os fundos imobiliários logísticos: Estratégias de captura de rendas imobiliárias. *Cadernos Metrópole* 24(53): 173–198. doi: 10.1590/2236-9996.2022-5307.

Maxfield, S. & Schneider, B. R. (eds.) (1997) *Business and the State in Developing Countries*. Ithaca: Cornell University Press.

Mioto, B. T. (2022) Dinâmica econômica e imobiliária: Periodização dos macrodeterminantes dos anos 2000 e 2010. *Cadernos Metrópole* 24(53): 15–32. doi: 10.1590/2236-9996.2022-5301.

Mosciaro, M. (2021) O complexo imobiliário/financeiro no Brasil e na Itália: Ferramentas para a produção financeirizada do espaço urbano. *Scripta Nova. Revista Electrónica de Geografía y Ciencias Sociales* 25(1). doi: 10.1344/sn2021.25.32249.

O'Brien, P., O'Neill, P. & Pike, A. (2019) Funding, financing and governing urban infrastructures. *Urban Studies* 56(7): 1291–1303. doi: 10.1177/0042098018824014.

Oliveira, I. F. B. de & Rufino, B. (2022) As grandes incorporadoras, o segmento econômico e a desconstrução da promoção pública habitacional. *Cadernos Metrópole* 24(53): 93–118. doi: 10.1590/2236-9996.2022-5304.

Özogul, S. & Tasan-Kok, T. (2020) One and the same? A systematic literature review of residential property investor types. *Journal of Planning Literature* 35(4): 475–494. doi: 10.1177/0885412220944919.

Peck, J. & Whiteside, H. (2016) Financializing Detroit. *Economic Geography* 92(3): 235–268. doi: 10.1080/00130095.2015.1116369.

Properati (2021) Los barrios más caros de Argentina y Latinoamérica. Retrieved from https://blog.properati.com.ar/los-barrios-mas-caros-de-argentina-y-latinoamerica-version-2021/ (accessed on 12 January 2021).

PWC (2018) Doing business in Argentina. Retrieved from https://www.pwc.com.ar/es/doing-business/assets/doing-business-in-argentina-2018.pdf.

Revista Noticias (2018) Quién es Darío Lizzano, el socio tapado del nuevo poder. Retrieved from https://noticias.perfil.com/noticias/politica/2018-02-01-quien-es-dario-lizzano-el-socio-tapado-del-nuevo-poder.phtml.

Rolnik, R. (2018) *La guerra de los lugares: La colonización de la tierra y la vivienda en la era de las finanzas* (translated by A. L. Granero). Barcelona: Descontrol.

Rolnik, R., Guerreiro, I. de A. & Marín-Toro, A. (2021) El arriendo – formal e informal – como nueva frontera de la financiarización de la vivienda en América Latina. *Revista INVI* 36(103): 19–53. doi: 10.4067/S0718-83582021000300019.

Rossi, U. (2017) *Cities in Global Capitalism*. Cambridge and Malden, MA: Polity Press.

Royer, L. de O. (2009) Financeirização da política habitacional: Limites e perspectivas. Thesis, Universidade de São Paulo. doi: 10.11606/T.16.2009.tde-19032010-114007.

Rufino, B. (2012) A incorporação da metrópole: Centralização do capital no imobiliário e nova produção do espaço em Fortaleza. Thesis, Universidade de São Paulo. doi: 10.11606/T.16.2012.tde-22062012-143019.

Rufino, B. (2019) Grandes grupos econômicos na produção do espaço: Um olhar sobre atuação imobiliária do Grupo Votorantim. In F. J. G. de Oliveira, L. D. de Oliveira, R. H. Tunes & R. M. Pessanha (eds.) *Espaço e economia: Geografia econômica e a economia política*. Consequência, 367–398. Retrieved from http://journals.openedition.org/espacoeconomia/7927.

Rufino, B. (2020) União de gigantes da construção: A Associação Brasileira de Incorporadoras (ABRAINC) como ator político na financeirização da produção imobiliária. In S. Freitas & C. E. S. Pinho (eds.) *Empresariado e poder político no Brasil: Uma perspectiva multidimensional*. São Paulo: Alameda, 361–401.

Rufino, B. & Pereira, P. C. X. (2011) Segregação e produção imobiliária na metrópole latinoamericana: Um olhar a partir da cidade de São Paulo. *Transformações sócio-territoriais nas metrópoles de Buenos Aires, São Paulo e Santiago*. Retrieved from https://repositorio.usp.br/item/002186938.

Rufino, B., Wehba, C. & Magalhães, A.-L. (2020) Cuando los contratistas se vuelven promotores: Una mirada sobre las articulaciones entre la producción inmobiliaria y de infraestructuras en la ciudad de São Paulo del siglo XXI. *EURE* 47(140). doi: 10.7764/EURE.47.140.08.

Rufino, B., Da Silva, R., Paulani Paschoa, A. T. & Lima, H. (2021a) Centralização do capital e metropolização do espaço: A atuação das grandes incorporadoras de São Paulo no contexto de expansão e crise imobiliária. In A. Cardoso & C. D'Ottaviano (eds.) *Habitação e Direito à Cidade: Desafios para as metrópoles em tempos de crise*. Rio de Janeiro: Letra Capital Editora LTDA – Observatorio das Metrópoles.

Rufino, B., Faustino, R. & Wehba, C. (2021b) *Infraestrutura na reestruturação do capital e do espaço: Análises em uma perspectiva crítica*. Sao Paulo: Letra Capital Editora LTDA.

Rufino, M. B. & Pereira, P. C. X. (2011) Segregação e produção imobiliária na metrópole latinoamericana: Um olhar a partir da cidade de São Paulo. *Transformações sócio-territoriais nas metrópoles de Buenos Aires, São Paulo e Santiago*. Retrieved from https://repositorio.usp.br/item/002186938

Sanfelici, D. (2013a) *A metrópole sob o ritmo das finanças: Implicações socioespaciais da expansão imobiliária no Brasil*. Thesis, Universidade de São Paulo. doi: 10.11606/T.8.2013.tde-07012014-093205.

Sanfelici, D. (2013b) Financeirização e a produção do espaço urbano no Brasil: Uma contribuição ao debate. *EURE* 39(118).

Sanfelici, D. (2017) La industria financiera y los fondos inmobiliarios en Brasil: Lógicas de inversión y dinámicas territoriales. *Economía Sociedad y Territorio* 367–397. doi: 10.22136/est002017685.

Sanfelici, D., & Halbert, L. (2015) Financial markets, developers and the geographies of housing in Brazil: A supply-side account. *Urban Studies* 53(7): 1465–1485. doi: 10.1177/0042098015590981.

Sanfelici, D. & Halbert, L. (2018) Financial market actors as urban policy-makers: The case of real estate investment trusts in Brazil. *Urban Geography* 40(1): 83–103. doi: 10.1080/02723638.2018.1500246.

Santander (2021) Argentina: Inversión extranjera. Retrieved from https://santandertrade.com/es/portal/establecerse-extranjero/argentina/inversion-extranjera.

Sassen, S. (1991) *The Global City: New York, London, Tokyo*. Princeton, NJ: Princeton University Press.

Schneider, B. R. (2013) *Hierarchical Capitalism in Latin America: Business, Labor, and the Challenges of Equitable Development*. Cambridge: Cambridge University Press. doi: 10.1017/CBO9781107300446.

Schteingart, M. (1989) *Los productores del espacio habitable: Estado, empresa y sociedad en la ciudad de México* (1st ed.). El Colegio de México, Centro de Estudios Demográficos y de Desarrollo Urbano.

Searle, L. G. (2016) *Landscapes of Accumulation: Real Estate and the Neoliberal Imagination in Contemporary India*. London: University of Chicago Press.

Shatkin, G. (2017) *Cities for Profit: The Real Estate Turn in Asia's Urban Politics*. Ithaca: Cornell University Press.

Shin, H. S. & Zhao, L. Y. (2013) Firms as surrogate intermediaries: Evidence from emerging economies. Retrieved from http://econweb.umd.edu/~zhao/files/paper_surrogate.pdf.

Socoloff, I. (2013) *Reflexiones en torno a las relaciones entre empresa, Estado Y ciudad: Un estudio a partir del caso IRSA en. Buenos Aires (1991–2012)*. Universidad de Buenos Aires.

Socoloff, I. (2018) Grandes desarrolladores inmobiliarios: Hacia una tipología de sus estrategias de inversión y financiamiento entre 2002 y 2015. In L. Menazzi & I. Socoloff (eds.) *Jornadas Empresas, empresarios y burocracias estatales en la producción del espacio urbano a través de la historia*. Buenos Aires: IIGG (FSOC – UBA) IEALC (FSOC – UBA).

Socoloff, I. (2020) Subordinate financialization and housing finance: The case of indexed mortgage loans' coalition in Argentina. *Housing Policy Debate* 30(4): 585–605. doi: 10.1080/10511482.2019.1676810.

Socoloff, I. (2021) Fondos inmobiliarios cotizados y financiarización de la vivienda en Argentina. *Revista INVI* 36(103): 85–111. doi: 10.4067/S0718-83582021000300085.

Stone, C. N. (1989) *Regime Politics: Governing Atlanta, 1946–1988*. Lawrence, KS: University Press of Kansas.

Stone, C. N. (2015) Reflections on regime politics: From governing coalition to urban political order. *Urban Affairs Review* 51(1): 101–137. doi: 10.1177/1078087414558948.

Stroher, L. E. M. (2017) Operações urbanas consorciadas com Cepac: Uma face da constituição do complexo imobiliário-financeiro no Brasil? *Cadernos Metrópole* 19(39): 455–477. doi: 10.1590/2236-9996.2017-3905.

Swyngedouw, E. (1992) The Mammon quest: 'Glocalization', interspatial competition and the monetary order: The construction of new scales. In M. Dunford & G. Kafkalis (eds.) *Cities and Regions in the New Europe. The Global-Local Interplay and Spatial Development Strategies*. Jackson, MS: Belhaven Press, 39–67. Retrieved from https://www.research.manchester.ac.uk/portal/en/publications/the-mammon-quest-glocalization-interspatial-competition-and-the-monetary-order-the-construction-of-new-scales(6f994225-65ab-435f-bf1b-d02b9f5e7c92)/export.html.

Topalov, C. (1974) *Les promoteurs inmoviliers: Contribution à l'analyse de la production capitaliste du logement en France*. Paris: Mouton.

Torres, R. da S., Tonucci Filho, J. B. M. & Almeida, R. P. (2022) Financeirização do imobiliário no Brasil: Uma análise dos Certificados de Recebíveis Imobiliários (2005–2020). *Cadernos Metrópole* 24(53): 35–62. doi: 10.1590/2236-9996.2022-5302.

Vergara-Perucich, J. F. (2021) Precios y financiarización: Evidencia empírica en mercado de la vivienda del Gran Santiago. *Revista INVI* 36(103): 137–166. doi: 10.4067/S0718-83582021000300137.

Weber, R. (2015) *From Boom to Bubble: How Finance Built the New Chicago*. Chicago: University of Chicago Press.

Whiteside, H. (2019) Advanced perspectives on financialised urban infrastructures. *Urban Studies* 56(7): 1477–1484. doi: 10.1177/0042098019826022.

Zeolla, N. (2021) *Dimensión nacional e internacional de la financiarización en América Latina: Un estudio en base a Estados Contables de Grandes Empresas No Financieras de 2000 a 2015*. PhD thesis, Universidad de Buenos Aires.

# 24. How Airbnb and short-term rentals push the frontier of financialisation through housing assetisation

*Javier Gil*

Airbnb was born in 2007 in the city of San Francisco. Brian Chesky and Joe Gebbia, two young designers, were about to lose their apartment the day their landlord informed them that the rent was going up. Taking advantage of the fact that a designers' conference was to be held in San Francisco, that all the hotels were fully booked and that they had three inflatable mattresses, they decided to offer accommodation in their living room to three people coming to the conference. Their lodging offer included sleeping on the inflatable mattresses, breakfast, a transportation card, and loose change to give to the city's homeless. The idea worked and during the days of the congress three people stayed at their place paying USD 80 a day.

Airbnb was born from the need to make extra money in order to pay raising rents. Its founders thought that what had happened to them was not something exceptional and that there were many other people in a similar situation. The benefit for both parties was clear: the hosts could earn extra income to pay rent, and visitors could stay with local individuals at a lower price than hotels.

At first, turning this idea into a business was a complete failure. The company did not get off the ground until Sequoia Capital (one of the most important venture capital funds in Silicon Valley that has financed companies such as Google, Apple, Oracle, PayPal, YouTube, Instagram, Yahoo!, Dropbox and WhatsApp) invested in it. The fund was not interested in the idea of peer-to-peer (p2p) hosting but rather knew that the tourist accommodation economy represented a very important business. Since then, the company has changed some of its most important fundamentals. The most relevant change was that they allowed hosts to rent homes on Airbnb while they were not at home. This change is crucial in the history of Airbnb because it ushered in Airbnb to lead a new speculative market.

Airbnb has reached over seven million accommodations and has more lodgings internationally than the five largest hotel chains in the world combined. It is present in over 100,000 cities and more than 220 countries and accumulates more than 300 million bookings per year. It manages more than one billion guest arrivals at all times, and every night more than two million people stay on average in an Airbnb. In 2021, the company was valued at USD 113 billion, up from 75 billion the previous year.

This chapter takes an alternative view of Airbnb in particular and short-term rentals (STRs) in general. From a political economy perspective, it suggests that STRs have become a new medium for the assetisation of housing, which promotes housing financialisation. This facilitates capital switching from other sectors and markets into housing units that are converted into STRs. As a result, in many regions of the world (mainly in the Global North), thousands of homes are being taken out of the housing rental market and rented out as STRs. However, this process is at the expense of local tenants, who are massively displaced and increasingly face unaffordable housing markets. It is therefore suggested that STRs constitute a new urban process of accumulation through dispossession.

The chapter is divided into five sections. The next section analyses the context in which STRs emerge, introducing the concepts of financialisation, the asset economy and rentier capitalism. The third section explains, theoretically and through a review of the literature on STRs, how STRs contribute to housing assetisation. The fourth section reviews the principles of the 'sharing economy' and how Airbnb and STRs do not represent a type of sharing economy but a tool that fosters housing assetisation. The fifth section examines how Covid-19 reinforced the role of STRs as a means of housing assetisation. Finally, the sixth section analyses the social impact of STRs and suggests that they constitute a process of urban accumulation through dispossession since capital accumulation through STRs is only possible by displacing tenants and worsening housing conditions.

## HOUSING FINANCIALISATION AND RENTIER CAPITALISM

Housing financialisation is a key concept to understand the urban transformations that STRs produce. In order to explore how STRs contribute to housing financialisation, it is necessary to analyse STRs in relation to the economic context in which STRs have emerged, since STRs are part of greater economic changes associated with the transformations of neoliberalism. In this sense, numerous authors have recently pointed out the need to analyse STRs in relation to the real estate complex this market has prompted (Clancy 2022, Jover & Cocola-Gant 2022).

Neoliberal restructuring since the 1970s and the extension of financialisation as its hegemonic economic form have given rise to what can be framed as rentier capitalism (Christophers 2022). Rentier capitalism is characterised by a system where productivity increases do not lead to sustainable profits; therefore, capital is switched from the sphere of production to the tertiary circuits of capital investment, such as services and finances (Aalbers 2008, Harvey 2001). This accumulation regime is mainly articulated and stabilised through asset price inflation (Adkins et al. 2020). In this regime, the dominant form is not the commodity anymore but the asset, which now replaces the commodity 'as the primary basis of contemporary capitalism' (Birch & Muniesa 2020: 2). Asset-based income becomes associated with the extraction rather than creation of value (Christophers 2022), giving birth to economic schemes of 'profiting without producing' (Lapavitsas 2014). A main feature of this regime is that assets are owned and controlled not for the sake of production but in order 'to get a durable economic rent from them' (Birch & Muniesa 2020: 2). The objective is to extract rent out of ownership and control of an asset, and the actor who receives the payment – 'purely by virtue of controlling something valuable' (Christophers 2022: 19) – is the rentier. In this way, asset revaluation and rents accumulation via asset control become main characteristics of contemporary capitalism. This constitutes 'a mode of economic organization in which success is based principally on what you control, not what you do' (Christophers 2022: 21). Asset ownership now becomes more important than employment or salaries as a determinant of class position, and class positions become asset-based (Adkins et al. 2020). Within rentier capitalism, there are multiple core asset types from which to extract rents, such as financial and intellectual property, natural resource reserves, or digital platforms (Birch & Muniesa 2020, Christophers 2022). For this research, the focus will be put on housing as a core asset in contemporary rentier capitalism.

Housing in contemporary societies has a dual function (Madden & Marcuse 2016): a social function, in relation to the use value of the dwelling as a home, as a place to live; but also an economic function, in relation to its exchange value, housing as an asset, as a means of making profits. All dwellings fulfil both functions simultaneously but to different degrees. Ryan-Collins & Murray have developed the concept of housing market 'rentierization' to describe 'the shift in the treatment of housing away from its use as a consumption good to an asset from which economic rent can be extracted' (Ryan-Collins & Murray 2021: 23). Over the last decades, housing has increasingly become a source of economic rent extraction rather than a source of (affordable) shelter and security, and 'those patterns of (speculative) investment rather than home ownership seem to be a key driver of price formation in housing markets' (Ryan-Collins & Murray 2021: 2). Housing financialisation took off from the 1980s onwards in the context of capital switching to its secondary and quaternary circuits (Aalbers 2008). This process was articulated through the extension of homeownership, credit/mortgage loans for homes and the unprecedented growth of private indebtedness. Growing numbers of homeowners started to think of their property increasingly in terms of an investment in order to fund their retirement and as a means of accessing wealth, giving rise to asset-based welfare regimes (Regan & Paxton 2001). The 'homeownership ideology' spread worldwide (Aalbers & Christophers 2014) and homeowners increasingly behave like real estate speculators (Wainwright 2012), giving rise to a mode of accumulation known as 'asset price Keynesianism' (Brenner 2006), 'house price Keynesianism' (Watson 2010: 20) or 'privatized Keynesianism' (Crouch 2011).

Over the last decades, housing has increasingly been restructured into a commodified asset, along with the development of financial instruments (Beswick et al. 2016, Byrne 2016, Christophers 2010, Gotham 2009). In the housing financialisation period from the 1990s to 2008, instruments such as mortgage securitisation were crucial for this purpose and for the extension of homeownership (Aalbers 2019, Forrest & Hirayama 2015). After 2008, capital was globally and massively switched into the built environment as a response to the Great Financial Crisis (GFC) (Fields 2018, Gil & Martínez 2023). This process reinforced the condition of housing as a safe-haven asset. The excess of liquidity in capital markets produced by historically low negative interest rates and monetary policies such as 'quantitative easing' created a 'wall of money', a global pool of liquid assets, avid for investment opportunities (Fernandez et al. 2016). New instruments were deployed in order to facilitate the recovery of housing markets, such as the promotion of bad banks, the introduction of REITs, and the creation of Golden Visas (Beswick et al. 2016, Byrne 2016, Gabor & Kohl 2022, Gil & Martínez 2023, Jover & Cocola-Gant 2022). The effects of the GFC in the 'homeownership society' produced a shift in housing trajectories, expanding the private rental sector and its tenants' social base (Fields 2017, Forrest & Hirayama 2015). Massive flows of housing investment were directed into the private rental sector. This process was dual, since it was carried out by institutional investors that acquired massive portfolios of housing and non-performing loans and configured themselves as global corporate landlords (Beswick et al. 2016) but also by wealthy households through buy-to-let housing investment schemes, extending private landlordism and producing a 'generation landlord' (Aalbers et al. 2020, Ronald & Kadi 2018). This process has increasingly converted rental housing into a new asset class (Gabor & Kohl 2022, Aalbers et al. 2020, Fields 2017, 2018), and rental housing has become the new frontier of financialisation (Fields 2017).

Recently, new lines of research on platform capitalism have demonstrated how digital platforms have pushed housing financialisation even further (Dagkouli-Kyriakoglou et al. 2022, Dal Maso et al. 2021, Fields 2022, Fields & Rogers 2021, Gil et al. 2023, Sadowski 2020, Shaw 2020). The term 'automated landlord' has been used in reference to how the management of tenants and real estate properties is increasingly governed by digital platforms, infrastructures and devices that reaffirm housing as a liquid asset (Fields 2022). Sadowski (2020) uses the concept of the 'internet of landlords' in reference to how technology is materially essential for 'new sources of rent, new infrastructures of rentier relations, and new mechanisms of extraction and enclosure' (Sadowski 2020: 564). Shaw (2020) introduced the term 'real estate platforms' to describe how recent innovations in digital technology are abruptly transforming urban real estate markets. For Fields and Rogers (2021), real estate platforms are mainly developed to enhance the exchange value of housing and therefore reshape the geographies of real estate investment and flows of finance capital. These platforms reshape the relationships between property owners, investors, real estate professionals, tenants, and residents, which facilitates the dynamics of capitalist production and exploitation and reshapes the power relations within housing markets. A key aspect of interest to us is how the system of real estate platforms secures capital turnover, eliminating resistance and making capital circulation as frictionless as possible (Dal Maso et al. 2021, Fields & Rogers 2021). These studies demonstrate how digital platforms foster new mechanisms of rent extraction, reshape relationships between property owners and residents, create new opportunities for real estate investment and facilitate the circulation of capital through real estate, enhancing the exchange value of housing and reaffirming housing as a liquid asset. This is the economic, real-estate and financial context in which STRs and platforms such as Airbnb have massively expanded.

## CONVERTING HOUSES INTO ASSETS THROUGH SHORT-TERM RENTALS

In this context, STRs become a mechanism to foster housing assetisation, pushing the frontier of the financialisation of housing. This is due to two particularities of STRs. Firstly, STRs increase the flexibility of housing as an asset (Dagkouli-Kyriakoglou et al. 2022, Sequera et al. 2022). STRs allow landlords to obtain rents without having to comply with tenants' protection laws that limit the economic profit of landlords through the uses they can make of their properties (Cocola-Gant & Gago 2019, Dagkouli-Kyriakoglou et al. 2022, Gil et al. 2023, Gil & Martínez 2023, Kemp 2020). As Kempt puts it: 'for landlords, rental housing is a much more 'liquid' investment where tenants have weak security of tenure than where they have strong tenancy protection' (Kemp 2020: 145–146). Tulumello and Cocola-Gant argue that STRs have the potential to produce revenue for property owners without needing tenants but at the same time give owners control to sell the property or abandon the market when they wish, without been constrained by tenant's laws. For the authors, this 'hyper-flexible nature is key to understanding the success of STR digital platforms among property owners and investors' (Dagkouli-Kyriakoglou et al. 2022: 3). Gil et al. (2023) demonstrated how the Covid-19 pandemic fostered the emergence of digital polyplatform rentierism. Digital platforms increasingly blur the boundaries between short-, medium- and long-term rentals and between tourist and residential use. They increasingly become platforms for the transformation of property use and the hybridisation of rental markets, depending on the markets' opportunity for rent extraction. For property owners, it is 'easier to extract housing from the residential market and put it to other uses to increase the rents they generate. This process amplifies the exchange value of housing and the owners' future profit expectations, enhancing the opportunities and means for the financialisation of housing' (Gil et al. 2023: 9).

Secondly, STRs allow higher amounts of rent to be extracted from the property. The fact is that a property rented for short periods to tourists through Airbnb generates higher rents than a property rented in the residential market. Multiple studies have resorted to Smith's (1996) rent gap theory precisely to explain how STRs allow higher amounts of real estate surplus value to be appropriated (Amore et al. 2020, Bosma & van Doorn 2022, Cheung & Yiu 2022, Wachsmuth & Weisler 2018, Yrigoy 2018). STRs increase the 'potential rent' of housing since, under a more 'efficient' use of housing that increases its yield, the owner capitalises a higher rent. The difference between the 'actual ground rent' of the dwelling in the residential market and the 'potential ground rent' that its owner could obtain by renting it as an STR determines the Airbnb-induced rent gap. Therefore, the larger the rent gap, the greater the motivation for property multi-owners to convert their homes into STRs and the greater the incentive for investors to direct capital flows into residential real estate (Amore et al. 2020, Wachsmuth & Weisler 2018, Yrigoy 2018).

Professional and corporate actors have seized the opportunities STRs create to increase real estate rents and manage properties with more flexibility as relative liquid assets. STR markets are mainly controlled by professional actors specialised in the STR business, which debunks the misleading image that this is a peer-to-peer activity mainly performed by residents in their primary residence (Cocola-Gant et al. 2021, Cocola-Gant & Gago 2019, Cox & Haar 2020, Gil & Sequera 2022, Katsinas 2021). Their business consists of extracting housing units from the residential market, converting them into STRs and renting them throughout the year on platforms such as Airbnb (Cocola-Gant & Gago 2019, Cox & Haar 2020, Gil et al. 2023, Jover & Cocola-Gant 2022, Sequera et al. 2022). In Greece, investors have outcompeted amateur hosts and contributed to the professionalisation of STRs and the concentration of revenues (Katsinas 2021). In Portugal, the expansion of the STR markets has also consolidated the transition from a sharing economy activity to a professional industry, with property management passing from individual hosts to highly professionalised 'corporate hosts' (Cocola-Gant et al. 2021). Recently, the concept of *platform-scale rent gaps* has been introduced to explain the economic logic that drives Airbnb to professionalise its hosts (Bosma & van Doorn 2022). All this produces an infrastructure that makes it easier for investors and capital to be switched into real estate properties that are converted into STRs (Cocola-Gant et al. 2021, Dagkouli-Kyriakoglou et al. 2022, Gil et al. 2023, Sequera et al. 2022).

## SHARING ECONOMY OR ASSET ECONOMY?

The emergence of the so-called 'sharing economy' after 2008 was accompanied by a whole series of enthusiastic discourses announcing how it was going to positively change our world. It was going to *disrupt* all spheres of life through integral economic, social and environmental transformations. Among these, it was pointed out that they develop very efficient economic processes; make more efficient use of resources; contribute to employment, competitiveness, and growth; boost innovation; increase economic activity; generate new services; reduce the price of products; increase the consumption capacity of the population; and make it easier for individuals to offer services and recover the purchasing power lost in the crisis (Botsman & Rogers 2010, European Commission 2016, Sundararajan 2016). All these effects supposedly derive from a necessary condition that any activity of the sharing economy must meet: the idle capacity of the resource that is introduced into the market. In other words, a necessary principle that any activity in the sharing economy must comply with is that the resource that is used to offer the service is temporarily disused (Benkler 2008, Botsman & Rogers 2010, Frenken 2017, Horton 2015, Oskam & Boswijk 2016, Rifkin 2014, Stors & Kagermeier 2017, Sundararajan 2016, Zervas et al. 2014, Schor & Attwood-Charles 2017). That is, it must be a 'temporarily idle good' whose use value is not being taken advantage of. People acquire resources for their use and consumption (a house, a vehicle, a drill). There are always times when these goods are not used and therefore from the perspective of the sharing economy they become idle. Contemporary platforms, by reducing transaction costs, make it possible to introduce these temporarily-in-disuse goods into the sharing economy market so that someone else takes advantage of the use value of the good while the owner obtains a profit for it (Benkler 2008, Botsman & Rogers 2010, Rifkin 2014, Sundararajan 2016).

Airbnb originally emerged as a sharing economy hosting platform and is based on the same principle, on the idea that housing also serves the function of a temporarily underutilised and idle resource (Botsman & Rogers 2010, Horton 2015, Oskam & Boswijk 2016, Schor & Attwood-Charles 2017, Stors & Kagermeier 2017, Sundararajan 2016, Zervas et al. 2014). If a person goes on vacation for a week and their home remains empty, from the perspective of the sharing economy the home will be an underutilised asset during those seven days: it is empty and someone else can consume its use value. The positive effects of introducing housing in Airbnb are clear: the tenant gets some extra income to pay for his or her vacation, the guest consumes a lodging at a lower price, no more hotels have to be built to cover the tourist demand, etc.

From a political economy perspective, the situation is very different. Platforms such as Airbnb are not platforms for mobilising underutilised resources but for converting consumption goods into assets. More than creating a 'sharing economy', they are extending the 'asset economy'. The great transformation brought about by these platforms is that they broaden the profile of participants in these economies. That is, it is not a market restricted to large capital players and the barriers to entry are very low. Gago (2017) stresses how neoliberalism is propelled not just from above by international finance, corporations and governments but also by the most impoverished and precarious populations 'from below'. In this way, I propose that through these platforms new forms of rentierism from below emerge.

Although digital platforms broaden the profile of people who may participate in the asset economy, this does not produce an economic democratisation. Not everyone participates in the same way, on equal terms, nor do they obtain the same amount of profits. In the case of Airbnb it has been widely demonstrated that even if precarious people can participate in it, the market is controlled by highly professionalised actors who accumulate large amounts of capital and obtain most of the rents produced by the platform (Cocola-Gant & Gago 2019, Gil 2023, Wachsmuth & Weisler 2018). It is therefore important to ask: how does housing become an asset through STR digital platforms?

At least five ways in which properties are converted into assets by converting dwellings into STRs have been identified. As will be seen, the effects and conditions vary considerably between one type and another.

## Housing as a Temporarily Idle Resource

These are the cases in which the principle of housing as a 'temporarily idle resource' is best fulfilled: situations in which a person does not sporadically use the dwelling where they live and temporarily converts it into an STR so a stranger can take advantage of its use value; for example, when the person goes on holidays.

The low-frequency rent rate and the fact that the use value of the home is mainly taken advantage of by its tenant/owner do not allow hosts to earn an important amount of money this way. As a result, this activity does not significantly increase the exchange value of the asset and the impact on the rental market is minimum or non-existent. The most remarkable thing about this activity is that it expands the possibilities for rent extraction through housing. It allows a person who uses a property for its use value – a place to live – to simultaneously exploit its exchange value.

In this way, those who extend rentier capitalism are not agents or financial institutions. They are precarious people and the middle classes who, from their everyday lives, extend the boundaries of housing financialisation and the rentier society, configuring new forms of rentierism from below.

## Housing as a Generally Idle Resource

This category refers to secondary residences that are rented as STRs. Secondary residences are used by their owners throughout the year during specific periods and remain empty the rest of the time. Most of the time, the use value of the dwelling is not enjoyed since the resource itself spends more time underutilised than in use.

When these properties are temporarily converted to STRs, the 'temporarily idle resource' principle is met. However, this situation is problematic. A second residence is an unproductive consumption good that does not produce a constant income flow for the owner but normally in the long run increases the owners' wealth through the appreciation of the asset price. When rented as an STR, the property can temporarily be transformed into an investment asset. Since the property is empty most of the time, the essence and value of the property for its owner are transformed, and the property ceases to be exclusively a consumption good. Now it will only be a consumption good during the days per year that the owner uses it as a second residence, but the rest of the time it will be an investment asset that produces fluent rents.

Houses used as STRs disrupt second homes markets by increasing their profitability as assets. Traditionally, people who had a secondary home had enough wealth to own a property that was only temporary used. Under the STR model, the second home market ceases to be unproductive and becomes a very productive market. The logic is reversed as STRs create new opportunities to invest in second homes: people no longer own a second home for occasional use but can now acquire a second home to rent it throughout the year as an STR and incidentally take advantage of it for occasional use. In this case, the principle of a temporarily underutilised asset is fulfilled, but the logic of the process is reversed: the property is not acquired for its use value but for its exchange value, although the owner can temporally take advantage of its use value.

This activity increases the exchange value of dwellings because: i) these are properties that previously could not generate constant income flows and now do; and ii) the absolute profits they generate are high because the property is unused by the owner most of the time, so it can potentially be rented throughout the year. In fact, the biggest impact of this activity is that it makes it much more profitable to invest in and own second homes. This activity has a strong impact on the residential rental market as it facilitates the conversion of dwellings into second homes rented out as STRs.

In this way, STRs are completely transforming the second home property market by creating new opportunities for property investment through this type of housing. These investments are not led by real estate companies but by individuals, as they are based on the idea that housing is not only used for economic purposes but is also used by the owner at certain times of the year. The middle and upper-middle classes are the main drivers of this type of investment. Overall, it is observed that STRs create new opportunities for them to participate in real estate markets.

## Generation of an Artificial Situation of Housing as a Temporarily Idle Resource

These are cases in which the situation of housing as a 'temporarily idle resource' does not naturally exist and is artificially created. This occurs when the dwelling is not going to be vacant but the person rents it as an STR, having to look for another place to live during that time.

In this situation, the host stops taking advantage of the home's use value in order to produce a service – an accommodation offer – that allows another person to temporarily take advantage of the dwelling's use value. Therefore, the situation of housing as a temporarily idle resource is artificially produced. This practice inverts the logic of the 'temporarily idle resource'. It is no longer a question of producing services and increasing the service supply over a given series of social relations and practices but of altering and transforming a series of social relations and practices in order to produce a service. In the case of housing, it is no longer a matter of introducing in the market the dwelling when it is not being used but abandoning ones' own residence in order to be able to rent it as an STR and obtain rents. In these cases, the property is not temporarily idle but the condition of an idle resource is artificially created.

These cases involve very precarious people who are financially insecure or have an extra expense but no income to pay for it (for example, because they have lost their job and urgently need the income to pay the rent). In order to convert their dwelling into an STR, they temporarily become homeless and move in with their partner or their parents or to a friend's couch for a few days. This activity tends to take place during weekends, since it is when the demand for STRs is higher. Therefore, the person only takes advantage of the use value of the dwelling from Sunday to Thursday, since from Friday to Sunday it is rented on Airbnb. In fact, these people can be considered as Airbnb urban nomads since they become temporarily nomad on a regular basis in order to be able to rent their dwelling on Airbnb. In this manner, from an economic and material point of view, housing can be considered as an idle good. From a socio-cultural perspective, it is not based on a culture of making use of society's under-utilised social and material capacities but on the culture of modifying one's life and everyday life in order to convert personal resources into assets.

The rents obtained from this activity are low (since the rental time is short) and the impact on the rental market is also low (although it enables tenants to pay high rents due to the income made through this particular form of subletting). What is most novel is how it extends the possibilities of rent extraction, as it allows rent to be extracted from a property that is actually being used by the person at the cost of the person being temporarily displaced or homeless. It is a situation of extreme precariousness that enables the process of rent extraction and extends the boundaries of housing financialisation and of rentier capitalism. As in the first case of the typology, this is a form of rentierism from below.

**Housing as a Permanently Idle Resource**

Housing as a 'permanently idle resource' occurs when the property is kept vacant and the use value of the dwelling is not being taken advantage of by anyone. The owner of the property does not live in it, rent it on the residential market or occasionally use it. These are homeowners who are not willing to rent properties on the residential housing market as long-term rentals – even if it is at the cost of keeping them empty and not obtaining rents – but are willing to rent them on Airbnb as STRs.

The main reason for keeping the home vacant is that the owners do not need to take advantage of its use value at the moment but want to be able to have access to its use value in the future (for example, because they expect to have a family member using it in the future). This occurs in areas where tenant laws are very strict (for example, where rental contracts are open-ended), and once the home is rented, the landlord loses their access to the use value of the home in the long term.

For these home owners, Airbnb generates a new rental market with new rules. This market allows owners to profit out of their dwelling while also having control of the future access to the use value of the property. In this case, it is not only the rent gap what causes the residential conversion from long-term rental to STR but the legal framework. Under these circumstances, owners can extract rents out of their property without losing control of their property (without tenancy acts limiting their control over the property). As with second homes, it can also trigger speculative movements, since it makes this type of housing investment more profitable.

**Housing Never Fulfils the Function of a Temporarily Idle Resource**

These are cases in which the only function of the property is to be rented on the long-term residential market. These homes never fulfil the function of a 'temporarily idle resource' since there are tenants living in the property. For these homeowners, housing fulfils the function of an investment good, given that they do not own the home to live in it but to profit and increase their wealth. They do not benefit from the use value of the property as a home but rather from the exchange value of the property and the income flows it produces.

As the STR market develops, these landlords decide not to renew the tenants' contracts in order to rent the property as a STR. However, the use value of the property as a home had never ceased to be absorbed: there were people living in the property so the dwelling was not idle nor temporarily underused at any time. This process changes the function of the dwelling – from long-term rental to STR – and the type of person who takes advantage of the use value of the dwelling – from local citizens who live in the city to travellers who temporally visit the city. However, in both cases the property fulfils the same function as an asset, although by switching its use and market. The flexibility of housing as an economic asset and the rents produced by the asset both increase.

This type of hosting does not comply with the principle of the 'temporarily idle resource' so it constitutes a form of traditional real estate economy that develops through a digital platform. This has been the main form in which the Airbnb supply has expanded globally, and concepts such as the professionalisation of STRs, the tourist-led rentier (Gil et al. 2023) or corporate hosts (Cocola-Gant et al. 2021) mainly capture this form of converting housing into a new asset class through STRs.

## FROM ABSOLUTE CRISIS TO THE EXPANSION OF THE ASSET ECONOMY: COVID-19 EFFECTS ON SHORT-TERM RENTALS[1]

The Covid-19 pandemic brought much uncertainty to the future of STRs between 2020 and 2022. Prior to the pandemic, converting residential housing into STRs had become a very profitable business, and Airbnb's international growth is based on this process. The pandemic all of a sudden halted this process. People were not allowed to travel and lockdowns were declared worldwide. Governments approved the suspension of the opening to the public of hotels and similar tourist accommodation. Over the next few days, there was an avalanche of cancellations on Airbnb from prospective guests and hosts experienced an 'economic nightmare'. They faced 'total ruin', as they described: 'I've put all 15 apartments on the traditional rental markets, to see if I can recover some money, even though they pay less. I don't think I can rent any of them out' (Airbnb multi-ownership in the face of the Covid-19 crisis) (Otto 2020). Their stories express a sense of economic decline: 'It was like an axe or a guillotine blow'; 'It was like a chain reaction – bookings collapsed and everyone started to cancel'; 'March came and all the bookings, but one, disappeared' (Gil et al. 2023). We began to study how hosts were reacting to the pandemic and what was happening to all those properties that had been converted to STRs (Gil et al. 2023). Were they going to return to the residential market, increasing the supply of rental housing, bringing prices down and putting an end to the unaffordable housing crises they had driven in many cities?

Our research in the city of Madrid shows that STRs started to be massively listed on residential rental platforms. It first seemed as if properties were going to return to the residential market. However, our research showed that STRs were not returning to the residential market and were not being rented under Tenancy Act contracts, even though they were advertised on residential rental platforms. The strategy of these rentiers was to avoid the residential market at all costs but at the same time try to ride out the storm by switching their real estate from STR platforms to long-term rental market platforms in a way that bordered on breaking the law. They advertised their properties with a new type of 'short-term', 'month-to-month' or 'temporary' contract. The hosts' objective was to rent out the STRs as residential rentals but under seasonal contracts until the crisis was over, when they would be able to switch their properties back to the more lucrative tourist market. In order to do so, they had to avoid renting their properties to tenants under contracts regulated by the Spanish Tenancy Act (which imposes a minimum duration of five years). In reality, they were renting out the homes as residences but under seasonal contracts. These dwellings became temporary residential housing for people who were unable to access stable residential homes. Tenants would even take out one seasonal contract after another for the same dwelling, which constitutes an infringement of the Tenancy Act by the landlords but is de facto tolerated since no inspections or sanctions are enforced by the authorities. Since housing liquidity varies depending on state actions and the legal and regulatory frameworks that support the exchange value of housing (Gotham 2009), by failing to prosecute these fraudulent activities the state indirectly fosters markets that increase housing liquidity.

The pandemic fostered what we termed 'digital polyplatform rentierism' (Gil et al. 2023). These platforms blur the boundaries between short-, medium- and long-term rentals or between tourist and residential use. They increasingly become platforms for the transformation of property use and the hybridisation of rental markets, depending on the opportunity for rent extraction. Platforms make it easier to detect, at what time and under what circumstances, if it is possible to offer the property use that maximises its economic performance. These dwellings constitute a form of floating residential housing supply. One week a property might serve as a tourist apartment but then be used as a temporary home for a student visiting the city for two semesters and then for a digital nomad who stays for two months, for a businesswoman who comes to the city for a week or even for a local resident who cannot find an apartment and uses the property as their main residence for a certain period of time. This leads to a decrease in specialisation, as rental platforms adapt their functions and create new products. As a result, an infrastructure is created to facilitate the continuous transformation of housing uses. Owners transfer their properties between markets, leading to market and platform hybridisation. The main effect is that they find it easier to extract housing from the residential market and put it to other uses to increase the rents they generate. This process amplifies the exchange value of housing and the owners' future profit expectations, enhancing the opportunities and means for housing financialisation.

The study of STRs/real estate platforms during the pandemic demonstrates that, in light of the new opportunities that digital polyplatform rentierism and tourism create for urban accumulation, the Tenancy Act and tenants themselves become a barrier for accumulation. Renting a property to a tenant fixes capital in a property for a given period of time, reducing its liquidity. It increases turnover times, interferes with the circulation of capital and reduces properties' exchange value. In this context, the residential rental market becomes the 'lowest and worst use', and the objective of capital is to flee from the 'prison' (Gotham 2009) that the Tenancy Act and tenants themselves constitute. As a result, switching capital into rental housing, which until recently was considered the new frontier of financialisation (Fields 2017), becomes the worst available option for accumulation. From the capitalist perspective of economic efficiency, taking advantage of all the possibilities offered by digital polyplatform rentierism can significantly increase the city's overall value, as measured in the value of its real estate assets. Therefore, it can be suggested that when the economy increasingly depends on the value of its assets (Adkins et al. 2020), the future of the neoliberal city is increasingly subordinated to the implementation of digital polyplatform rentierism in order to maximise the rent extracted from the urban built environment. In our research, we estimated that the process of listing STRs on the real estate platform during the pandemic may have reduced the real estate rents obtained through STRs by between EUR 40 and 110 million per year, but it would have been much greater without the hybridisation of the markets and the application of digital polyplatforms.

For tenants, the consolidation of digital polyplatform rentierism and the hybridisation of platform-based rental markets produces a neoliberal tenant dystopia. If properties can be more easily switched from one use and market to another, there are more opportunities for landlords to keep their properties removed from the residential market. This reduces the supply of rental housing but also influences the power dynamic between landlords and tenants – empowering the former and weakening the latter. Dagkouli-Kyriakoglou et al. argued that the STR/digital platform nexus creates a neoliberal utopia of a perfectly flexible market (Dagkouli-Kyriakoglou et al. 2022). Following our study, we suggested that this argument could be stretched even further since the hybridisation of rental markets is producing a new neoliberal tenant dystopia. In the same way that dwellings constitute a form of floating residential housing supply, in a context organised exclusively by market forces and the absence of tenant protection measures, tenants themselves increasingly become a floating population. The residential rental housing stock decreases and becomes more flexible, so tenants now compete not only with other tenants for housing but also with tourists, digital nomads and international students. This produces a dystopian scenario where the market is the only factor that determines property use and allocation. Housing displacements become the norm of a regime whose only rule is for-profit economic rationality. The housing stability guaranteed by tenancy laws is replaced by flexibility and market forces. The more affluent residents benefit from this model, since housing flexibility increases housing supply for them, even if they pay higher prices. On the other hand, the most vulnerable residents find themselves unprotected and competing with people with greater purchasing power – such as tourists or digital nomads – for the same housing, which increases their housing precarity. Consequently without stricter public policy to protect the right to housing and the right to live in the city, the platformisation of housing will result in less stable and less affordable rental prices, thereby fostering housing precarity and tenants' impoverishment.

## THE SOCIAL IMPACT OF THE IRRUPTION OF SHORT-TERM RENTALS: DISPOSSESSION AND DISPLACEMENTS

In the previous sections it has been seen how digital platforms such as Airbnb make it possible to convert housing into assets by converting their uses and switching them into the STR market. This process is at the expense of tenants, who are displaced from their homes, facing housing unaffordability and housing precarity, and certain areas of the city become unliveable for them. This is why STRs' expansion not only constitutes a process of urban accumulation but also of urban dispossession.

Displacements are always the effects of multiple urban transformations. This has led scholars to classify displacements in different types in order to understand how diverse urban processes lead to different forms of displacement. Marcuse's well-referenced typology described four types of displacements caused by the simultaneous forces of gentrification and abandonment: direct last-resident displacement, direct chain displacement, exclusionary displacement, and displacement pressure (Marcuse 1985). This typology has subsequently been adapted and reduced to three types in order to explain the effects of STRs on displacement (Cocola-Gant 2016). These three types of displacement can be defined as follows:

(1) *Direct displacement*: tenants who are displaced when their rental lease is not renewed and the landlord converts the property into an STR.
(2) *Exclusionary displacement*: converting rental properties into STRs reduces the supply of residential rental housing and increases rental prices. As a result, tenants in the area are displaced since they cannot pay the new rental price, even if their dwelling is not converted into an STR, and housing becomes increasingly unaffordable in this area.
(3) *Displacement pressure*: displacement caused by the transformation of urban spaces into unliveable places for residents, where the coexistence of residents among tourists is increasingly impossible. These are the same displacement issues produced by traditional forms of touristification. In addition, STRs add more problems than the traditional

tourist industry through the deterioration of community life when residents coexist with STRs in the same building.

The interrelation within these displacement forces is also particular. Generally, full impact displacement occurs due to all forces of displacement operating simultaneously (Cocola-Gant 2016, Marcuse 1985). With the approach adopted in this chapter, it is considered that a distinction should be made within this typology in relation to STRs. Every time a tenant's lease is not renewed in order to convert the property into an STR, someone directly suffers direct displacement. In contrast, for exclusionary displacement to occur, the process of converting properties into STRs has to materialise at a larger scale so it has enough power to aggregately affect housing supply and rental prices in the area. In the case of displacement pressure, the aggregate effect must be even greater so STRs can produce transformations in the neighbourhood (in commerce, public space, community liveability, etc.). With regard to displacement pressure, STRs usually do not produce it by themselves. In most cities, STRs concentrate in already touristified areas (Ardura et al. 2020, Combs et al. 2019, Crommelin et al. 2018, Dudás et al. 2017, Elíasson & Ragnarsson 2018, Gil & Sequera 2020, Gurran & Phibbs 2017, Lee 2016, Schäfer & Braun 2016, Wachsmuth & Weisler 2018, Yrigoy 2018), so STRs produce displacement pressure by adding extra pressure in areas where the traditional tourist industry is already producing it.

Can situations arise in which residents resist the forces of direct and exclusionary displacement but are displaced due to displacement pressure? In the case of STR housing assetisation displacements, the interrelation within the different displacement forces varies depending on whether the resident is a tenant or a homeowner. In the case of tenants, it is unlikely. Tenants are very vulnerable against the STR forces of economic displacement, especially in those places with soft tenancy legislation that do not guarantee the tenants' right to 'stay put'. Therefore, it is likely that tenants will suffer the force of economic displacement sooner than displacement due to urban transformations in the neighbourhood. It is different in the case of homeowners. These are residents not affected by direct economic displacement. On the contrary, in economic terms, they benefit with the expansion of STRs, since STRs normally increase the value of properties in a given area. In these cases, homeowners may decide to leave due to displacement pressure but with their property revalued, so it is a particular type of displacement where homeowners are forced to leave with a substantial economic compensation. In fact, they might move to another area and convert their property into a STR (Cocola-Gant & Gago 2019), obtaining economic benefits from being displaced. These differences are important since they reflect the fact that the effects of STRs on displacements vary in relation to whether residents are tenants or homeowners, which also influences whether STRs can be interpreted within a class relation frame.

This leads to differentiation between gentrification, touristification and STR housing assetisation from a class perspective. Through gentrification, the lower-income population is replaced by higher status classes, and through touristification, a cross-class displacement occurs (Sequera & Noffre 2018). This is why the urban change produced by the expansion of urban tourism does 'not necessarily mean class antagonism to upscale a certain neighbourhood of the city' (Sequera & Noffre 2018: 9). In contrast, this cannot be affirmed with respect to STR housing assetisation. It is mainly investors and landlords directly displacing tenants (normally a population with worse economic conditions than homeowners). Investors and landlords use housing as an asset to increase their capital, as opposed to tenants who use housing as a home to live in. This conflictual relationship transcends the field of touristification and should be framed as part of the new expressions of class antagonism around housing in contemporary societies due to housing financialisation (Madden & Marcuse 2016) as a conflict between those actors that need housing for its exchange value and those that need it for its use value. Previous research on rental housing financialisation has underlined 'how the divergence between the exchange value of housing-backed financial assets and the use value of housing itself exposes the working poor to violence that contradicts their ability to carry out their everyday existence' (Fields 2017: 589). STR housing assetisation also reproduces these relations, since tenants are displaced from their homes, facing housing unaffordability and housing precarity, and certain areas of the city become unliveable for them, while investors and landlords profit and increase their wealth from this situation.

From this perspective, the rise of STRs must be seen in the context of the rise of new instruments, actors, policies and processes that push the frontier of financialisation, such as REITs, Golden Visas, global corporate landlords and buy-to-let investments (Beswick et al. 2016, Byrne 2016, Gabor & Kohl 2022, Gil & Martínez 2023, Jover & Cocola-Gant 2022). It can be stated that urban conflicts produced by STRs are primarily not conflicts produced by tourism but by housing financialisation, and those displacing the residents are not the tourists but real estate investors and landlords. Housing struggles against STRs are commonly framed as struggles against touristification. To better grasp the causes and effects of these accumulation and dispossession strategies, they can be better framed as struggles against housing financialisation. This is a complicated issue since in many cases even the discourses around this conflict are analysed in terms of touristification and not in terms of housing financialisation (for example, when neighbours who are homeowners only complain about coexistence problems such as noise in the building but not about the housing problems STRs create, such as tenants' displacement).

This distinction has significant implications, for example, from a public policy approach. From the STR housing assetisation perspective, STRs' negative impacts ultimately should be ultimately approached through housing policies, since policies that focus on tourism are insufficient. In fact, during the pandemic, when the tourist markets stopped due to mobility restrictions and lockdowns without an effective tourist demand to maintain the business, STRs did not return to the residential market (Gil et al. 2023). In this case, the displacement forces created by the STRs were maintained even if tourism had halted, which demonstrates the need to address them from a housing policy perspective.

In fact, from this perspective, housing policies constitute the main barrier for the development of STRs. This is mainly because, under strict housing regulation, STR-induced rent gaps cannot emerge, so STRs do not produce opportunities to convert properties or switch capital to STRs. Without this business opportunity, there is no market for professional actors to emerge, and therefore the urban transformations observed in this study would not occur. On the other hand, as long as regulations allow for the development of STR-induced rent gaps, investors and landlords will massively convert properties and switch capital to STRs, leading to the dispossession and displacement of the most vulnerable residents.

## CONCLUSIONS

This chapter has analysed the emergence and development of Airbnb and STRs and their impact on housing and urban processes. It has shown that the platform emerged in a context where technological innovations created new opportunities for people to share spaces and resources, the so-called 'sharing economy'. However, from a political economy perspective, this chapter has shown that this economy has little to do with *sharing*. On the contrary, it has been argued that it is better understood within the framework of the *asset economy* since it is based on the transformation of consumer goods into assets that generate a constant flow of income; in other words, a process that promotes the financialisation of housing by increasing its exchange value, its liquidity and its function as an asset class. This means that the conversion of housing into STRs has become a very lucrative business, and over the last decade thousands of homes have been converted into STRs (mainly in cities of the Global North). As a result, STRs constitute a new frontier for housing assetisation.

This process is at the expense of local tenants, who are displaced from their homes, face housing unaffordability and housing precarity and find certain areas of the city uninhabitable. For this reason, some of the core contemporary urban conflicts are about the social impact of STRs. These conflicts arise from the fact that investors and landlords use housing as an asset to increase their capital, as opposed to tenants who use housing as a home in which to live. This is a conflict between those actors who seek housing for its exchange value and those who need it for its use value, a conflict that can only be resolved through housing policies that do not allow housing to become STRs: policies that enhance the social function of housing as a place to live and impede housing assetisation.

## NOTE

1. This section is based on research I conducted with Pablo Martínez and Jorge Sequera on the impact of Covid-19 on Airbnb in the city of Madrid (Gil et al. 2023).

## REFERENCES

Aalbers, M. B. (2008) The financialization of home and the mortgage market crisis. *Competition & Change* 12(2): 148–166.
Aalbers, M. B. (2019) Financial geography II: Financial geographies of housing and real estate. *Progress in Human Geography* 43(2): 376–387.
Aalbers, M. B. & Christophers, B. (2014) Centring housing in political economy. *Housing, Theory and Society* 31(4): 373–394.
Aalbers, M. B., Hochstenbach, C., Bosma, J. & Fernandez, R. (2020) The death and life of private landlordism: How financialized homeownership gave birth to the buy-to-let market. *Housing, Theory and Society* 38(5): 541–563.
Adkins, L., Cooper, M. & Konings, M. (2020) *The asset economy*. John Wiley & Sons.
Amore, A., de Bernardi, C. & Arvanitis, P. (2020) The impacts of Airbnb in Athens, Lisbon and Milan: A rent gap theory perspective. *Current Issues in Tourism* 23(4): 1–14.
Ardura, A., Lorente-Riverola, I. & Ruiz, J. (2020) Platform-mediated short-term rentals and gentrification in Madrid. *Urban Studies* 57(15): 3095–115. https://doi.org/10.1177/0042098020918154.
Benkler, Y. (2008) *The wealth of networks*. Yale University Press.

Beswick, J., Alexandri, G., Byrne, M., Vives-Miró, S., Fields, D., Hodkinson, S. & Janoschka, M. (2016) Speculating on London's housing future: The rise of global corporate landlords in 'post-crisis' urban landscapes. *City* 20(2): 321–341.

Birch, K. & Muniesa, F. (2020) Introduction: Assetization and technoscientific capitalism. In K. Birch & F. Muniesa (eds.) *Assetization: Turning Things into Assets in Technoscientific Capitalism*. MIT Press.

Bosma, J. R. & van Doorn, N. (2022) The gentrification of Airbnb: Closing rent gaps through the professionalization of hosting. *Space and Culture*. https://doi.org/10.1177/12063312221090606.

Botsman, R. & Rogers, R. (2010) *What's mine is yours: How collaborative consumption is changing the way we live.* Collins and LFT.

Brenner, R. (2006) *The economics of global turbulence: The advanced capitalist economies from long boom to long downturn, 1945–2005.* Verso.

Byrne, M. (2016) Bouncing back: The political economy of crisis and recovery at the intersection of commercial real estate and global finance. *Irish Geography* 48(2): 78–98.

Cheung, K. S. & Yiu, C. Y. (2022) Touristification, Airbnb and the tourism-led rent gap: Evidence from a revealed preference approach. *Tourism Management* 92: 104567.

Christophers, B. (2010) On voodoo economics: Theorising relations of property, value and contemporary capitalism. *Transactions of the Institute of British Geographers* 35(1): 94–108.

Christophers, B. (2022) *Rentier capitalism: Who owns the economy, and who pays for it?* Verso.

Clancy, M. (2022) Tourism, financialization, and short-term rentals: The political economy of Dublin's housing crisis. *Current Issues in Tourism* 25(20): 3363–3380.

Cocola-Gant, A. (2016) Holiday rentals: The new gentrification battlefront. *Sociological Research Online* 21(3): 112–120. https://doi.org/10.5153/sro.4071

Cocola-Gant, A. & Gago, A. (2019) Airbnb, buy-to-let investment and tourism-driven displacement: A case study in Lisbon. *Environment and Planning A: Economy and Space* 53(7): 1671–1688.

Cocola-Gant, A., Jover, J., Carvalho, L. & Chamusca, P. (2021) Corporate hosts: The rise of professional management in the short-term rental industry. *Tourism Management Perspectives* 40: 100879.

Combs, J., Kerrigan, D. & Wachsmuth, D. (2019) Short-term rentals in Canada: Uneven growth, uneven impacts. *Canadian Journal of Urban Research* 29(1): 119–34.

Cox, M. & Haar, K. (2020) Platform failures. How short-term rental platforms like Airbnb fail to cooperate with cities and the need for strong regulations to protect housing. GUE/NGL group, European Parliament.

Crommelin, L., Troy, L., Martin, C. & Pettit, C. (2018) Is Airbnb a sharing economy superstar? Evidence from five global cities. *Urban Policy and Research* 36(4): 429–444.

Crouch, C. (2011) *The strange non-death of neo-liberalism*. Polity.

Dagkouli-Kyriakoglou, M., Tulumello, S., Cocola-Gant, A., Iacovone, C. & Pettas, D. (2022) Digital mediated short-term rentals in the (post-) pandemic city. *Digital Geography and Society* 3: 100028.

Dal Maso, G., Robertson, S. & Rogers, D. (2021) Cultural platform capitalism: Extracting value from cultural asymmetries in RealTech. *Social & Cultural Geography* 22(4): 565–580.

Dudás, G., Vida, G., Kovalcsik, T. & Boros, L. (2017) A socio-economic analysis of Airbnb in New York City. *Regional Statistics* 7(1): 135–151.

Elíasson, L. & Ragnarsson, Ö. P. (2018) *Short-term renting of residential apartments: Effects of Airbnb in the Icelandic housing market*. Economics and Monetary Policy Department of the Central Bank of Iceland.

European Commission (2016) Communication from the Commission to the European Parliament, the Council, the European Economic and Social Committee and the Committee of the Regions. European Commission.

Fernandez, R., Hofman, A. & Aalbers, M. B. (2016) London and New York as a safe deposit box for the transnational wealth elite. *Environment and Planning A: Economy and Space* 48(12): 2443–2461.

Fields, D. (2017). Unwilling subjects of financialization. *International Journal of Urban and Regional Research*, 41(4), 588–603.

Fields, D. (2018) Constructing a new asset class: Property-led financial accumulation after the crisis. *Economic Geography* 94(2): 118–140.

Fields, D. (2022) Automated landlord: Digital technologies and post-crisis financial accumulation. *Environment and Planning A: Economy and Space* 54(1): 160–181.

Fields, D. & Rogers, D. (2021) Towards a critical housing studies research agenda on platform real estate. *Housing, Theory and Society* 38(1): 72–94.
Forrest, R. & Hirayama, Y. (2015) The financialisation of the social project: Embedded liberalism, neoliberalism and home ownership. *Urban Studies* 52(2): 233–244. https://doi.org/10.1177/0042098014528394.
Frenken, K. (2017) Political economies and environmental futures for the sharing economy. *Philosophical Transactions of the Royal Society* 375. https://royalsocietypublishing.org/doi/full/10.1098/rsta.2016.0367.
Gabor, D. & Kohl, S. (2022) *The financialization of housing in Europe: My home is an asset class.* The Greens/EFA, European Parliament.
Gago, V. (2017) *Neoliberalism from below: Popular pragmatics and baroque economies.* Duke University Press.
Gil, J. (2023) Not gentrification, not touristification. Short-term rentals as a housing assetization strategy. *Journal of Urban Affairs.* https://doi.org/10.1080/07352166.2023.2242532.
Gil, J., & Martínez, M. A. (2023) State-led actions reigniting the financialization of housing in Spain. *Housing, Theory and Society* 40(1): 1–21. https://doi.org/10.1080/14036096.2021.2013316.
Gil, J., Martínez, P. & Sequera, J. (2023) The neoliberal tenant dystopia: Digital polyplatform rentierism, the hybridization of platform-based rental markets and financialization of housing. *Cities* 137. https://doi.org/10.1016/j.cities.2023.104245.
Gil, J., & Sequera, J. (2022) The professionalization of Airbnb in Madrid: Far from a collaborative economy. *Current Issues in Tourism* 20: 3343–3362.
Gotham, K. F. (2009) Creating liquidity out of spatial fixity: The secondary circuit of capital and the subprime mortgage crisis. *International Journal of Urban and Regional Research* 33(2): 355–371.
Gurran, N. & Phibbs, P. (2017) When tourists move in: How should urban planners respond to Airbnb? *Journal of the American Planning Association* 83(1): 80–92. https://doi.org/10.1080/01944363.2016.1249011.
Harvey, D. (2001) Globalization and the 'spatial fix'. *Geographische Revue* 2(3): 23–31.
Horton, J. J. (2015) The tragedy of your upstairs neighbors: Is the Airbnb negative externality internalized? arXiv preprint, 1611.05688.
Jover, J. & Cocola-Gant, A. (2022) The political economy of housing investment in the short-term rental market: Insights from urban Portugal. *Antipode* 55(1): 134–155.
Jover, J. & Díaz-Parra, I. (2020) Gentrification, transnational gentrification and touristification in Seville, Spain. *Urban Studies* 57(15): 3044–3059.
Katsinas, P. (2021) Professionalisation of short-term rentals and emergent tourism gentrification in post-crisis Thessaloniki. *Environment and Planning A: Economy and Space* 53(7): 1652–1670.
Kemp, P. A. (2020) Commentary on multiple property ownership. *International Journal of Housing Policy* 20(1): 144–155.
Lapavitsas, C. (2014) *Profiting without producing: How finance exploits us all.* Verso.
Lee, D. (2016) How Airbnb short-term rentals exacerbate Los Angeles's affordable housing crisis: Analysis and policy recommendations. *Harvard Law & Policy Review* 10: 229.
Madden, D., & Marcuse, P. (2016) *In defense of housing. The politics of crisis.* Verso.
Marcuse, P. (1985) Gentrification, abandonment, and displacement: Connections, causes, and policy responses in New York City. *Journal of Urban & Contemporary Law* 28: 195–240.
Oskam, J. & Boswijk, A. (2016) Airbnb: The future of networked hospitality businesses. *Journal of Tourism Futures* 2(1): 22–42.
Otto, C. (2020) El covid-19 acorrala los pisos de Airbnb: "Ganaba 3.700€ al mes y ahora pierdo 1.000". El Confidencial, 29 April. https://www.elconfidencial.com/tecnologia/2020-04-29/coronavirus-covid-airbnb-pisos-idealista_2554019/.
Regan, S. & Paxton, W. (2001) *Asset-based welfare: International experiences.* Institute for Public Policy Research.
Rifkin, J. (2014) *The zero marginal cost society: The internet of things, the collaborative commons, and the eclipse of capitalism.* St. Martin's Press.
Ronald, R. & Kadi, J. (2018) The revival of private landlords in Britain's post-homeownership society. *New Political Economy* 23(6): 786–803. https://doi.org/10.1080/13563467.2017.1401055.

Ryan-Collins, J. & Murray, C. (2021) When homes earn more than jobs: The rentierization of the Australian housing market. *Housing Studies* 38(10): 1888–1917. https://doi.org/10.1080/02673037.2021.2004091.

Sadowski, J. (2020) The internet of landlords: Digital platforms and new mechanisms of rentier capitalism. *Antipode* 52(2): 562–580.

Schäfer, P. & Braun, N. (2016) Misuse through short-term rentals on the Berlin housing market. *International Journal of Housing Markets and Analysis* 9(2): 287–311.

Schor, J. B. & Attwood-Charles, W. (2017). The sharing economy: Labor, inequality and sociability on for-profit platforms. *Sociology Compass* 11(8): e12493.

Sequera, J. & Nofre, J. (2018) Shaken, not stirred: New debates on touristification and the limits of gentrification. *City* 22(5–6): 843–855.

Sequera, J., Nofre, J., Díaz-Parra, I., Gil, J., Yrigoy, I., Mansilla, J. & Sánchez, S. (2022) The impact of COVID-19 on the short-term rental market in Spain: Towards flexibilization? *Cities* 130: 103912.

Shaw, J. (2020) Platform real estate: Theory and practice of new urban real estate markets. *Urban Geography* 41(8): 1037–1064.

Smith, N. (1996) *The new urban frontier: Gentrification and the revanchist city*. London and New York: Routledge.

Stors, N. & Kagermeier, A. (2017) The sharing economy and its role in metropolitan tourism. In M. Gravari-Barbas & S. Guinand (eds.) *Tourism and gentrification in contemporary metropolises. International perspectives*. Routledge, 181–206.

Sundararajan, A. (2016) *The sharing economy: The end of employment and the rise of crowd-based capitalism*. MIT Press.

Wachsmuth, D. & Weisler, A. (2018) Airbnb and the rent gap: Gentrification through the sharing economy. *Environment and Planning A: Economy and Space* 50(6): 1147–1170.

Wainwright, T. (2012) Transferring securitization, bond-rating, and a crisis from the US to the UK. In M. B. Aalbers (ed.) *Subprime cities: The political economy of mortgage markets*. Wiley-Blackwell, 54–97.

Watson, M. (2010) House price Keynesianism and the contradictions of the modern investor subject. *Housing Studies* 25(3): 413–426.

Yrigoy, I. (2018) Rent gap reloaded: Airbnb and the shift from residential to touristic rental housing in the Palma Old Quarter in Mallorca, Spain. *Urban Studies* 56(13): 2709–2726.

Zervas, G., Proserpio, D. & Byers, J. W. (2014) The rise of the sharing economy: Estimating the impact of Airbnb on the hotel industry. *Journal of Marketing Research* 54(5): 687–705. http://journals.ama.org/doi/abs/10.1509/jmr.15.0204.

# 25. From social housing to upscale regeneration: the pitfalls of residents' participation in Dublin
*Valesca Lima*

In recent years, many cities have set up urban regeneration projects in run-down or depressed areas through a range of policy initiatives. Urban regeneration schemes are initiatives that combine urban planning and the resolution of social, economic, and environmental issues to create new, vibrant urban spaces while still preserving the unique spatial characteristics of the area. Lately, these schemes usually involve the creation of favourable conditions to attract private investment as part of a strategic plan to draw wealth to a particular urban area (Boyle et al. 2018). In the process, rents and property values escalate, changes are made to the character and culture of particular neighbourhoods, and communities are displaced to give way to development (Kearns & Mason 2013, Marco et al. 2020). While this is a description of what has been termed 'gentrification' – often used negatively to describe the displacement of local, poor communities – dramatic changes in the urban landscape bring new challenges to scholars and local activists trying to understand and interfere in the processes and impacts of urban regeneration. The experience in Dublin is illustrative of a rich assortment of regeneration initiatives and it poses the classic question: urban redevelopment for whom? (Fox 2001). Particularly in the inner-city central areas, urban regeneration projects, in combination with rapid changes and a prolonged economic crisis, have contributed to the removal and dispersal of working-class communities, permanently dismantling original social structures (Hearne et al. 2014, MacLaren & Kelly 2014). Community participation has been an often overlooked element in those regeneration projects, a fact that has attracted criticism from urban planners, residents, and campaigners.

I here focus on a case of decision-making for affordable housing: the property-led regeneration of a social housing complex in Dublin, O'Devaney Gardens. In my interpretation, while the rhetoric of community participation has become an integral element of urban planning, competing perceptions are hindering the realisation and implementation of the long struggle for affordable housing in Dublin. Community participation has often been undermined by the state, as shown in the highly neoliberal land use and developments that have been part of the Irish government's agenda since the 2000s, and this has been forced on vulnerable, poor, working-class inner-city communities over the years (MacLaran et al. 2007, MacLaren & Kelly 2014). The O'Devaney Gardens estate has been at the centre of a heated debate about the use of public land for private development while Ireland is in the midst of a serious homeless and housing crisis. This chapter provides insights into the complex relations between urban development contradictions and the interactions between private capital, the state, and local residents. Supported by the emergent literature on urban and housing regeneration, this work contributes with critical insights into market-led urban regeneration, decision-making, and the implementation of urban regeneration in social housing scholarship (Della Spina et al. 2020, Hearne & Redmond 2014, Watt 2021). Empirically, this study provides evidence on the conflict around valuable land being used for urban housing developments, given how Dublin, a vibrant and attractive European city, is the setting for a host of conflicts in contemporary urban planning, such as liveability problems, growth management issues, the lack of affordable housing, and gentrification (Norris & Hearne 2016, Punch 2009).

The analysis presented in this chapter draws on content analysis, a method of qualitative data analysis that involves the examination and coding of textual data for patterns and themes. As a research tool, content analysis is useful to identify patterns and understand underlying themes in the collected dataset, allowing the author to draw conclusions about the data and also providing a structure to the data that can be used to identify relationships and trends (Bengtsson 2016). The data consist of publicly available policy documents, media reports, policy statements, and previous scholarship on urban regeneration that has engaged with the original residents of O'Devaney Gardens. In particular, the study uses reports obtained from the Dublin City Council (DCC) Housing Land Initiative Programme database, where documents regarding the urban regeneration of O'Devaney Gardens can be accessed. They comprise feasibility studies, maps, agreements, background information reports, manuals, and letters.

This text is organised as follows. In the next section, I present a critical overview of the literature on inclusive urban regeneration. Next, I focus on the study's methodology and provide some background information on Dublin's history of urban development and the impact of the public–private partnership (PPP) redevelopment model on regeneration projects, which scattered the O'Devaney Gardens community. I then move to an analysis of policy documents in order to shed light on the regeneration plans and the process of community disintegration under such plans, showing how the opportunities for affordable housing change or decrease during the different phases of the development. In the discussion, I examine urban regeneration in Dublin in terms of economic growth concerns and the opportunities for sustainable and inclusive regeneration in the city. In the conclusion, I reflect on my findings and consider avenues for further research.

## URBAN REGENERATION AND COLLABORATIVE DECISION-MAKING

Public participation in urban regeneration encompasses strong interaction between the state and civil society. The literature on urban regeneration has highlighted several processes of socio-spatial change as part of larger urban transformation processes. Urban regeneration is a multidisciplinary research area, covering fields such as policy-making and practice, city planning, urban design, sustainable housing, transportation, economics, and community development (Leary & McCarthy 2013). An urban area targeted for intervention is often considered by planners in an integrated manner: the physical connections among city areas (transportation, access), the management of funds from different sources (i.e. the private sector), and integration between the policies of different policy area departments and between levels of local and national administration (Mendes 2014).

Regardless of its degree or intensity, urban regeneration is associated not just with improvements but also with functional development and deliberate attempts to counteract the forces and factors that are the cause of urban degeneration (Mendes 2013). In the classic definition of Roberts and Sykes (1999: 17), urban regeneration is a comprehensive and integrated vision and action that leads to the resolution of urban problems, seeking to bring about lasting improvements in the economic, physical, social, and environmental condition of an area that has been subject to change. The authors refer to regeneration as a proactive response to urban problems in light of the need to plan the built environment and also economic, social, and environmental factors. This chapter uses this definition as the point of departure for understanding the regeneration process.

As one of the main strategies to address inner-city decline and deprivation, urban regeneration involves attempts to reverse that decline by improving both the physical structure and, more importantly and elusively, the economy of those areas (Weaver 2001). As noted by Jones and Evans (2013), urban planning is often viewed as one of the incentives of economic growth, and while the valorisation of economic prosperity can be a powerful tool to improve social well-being and the recovery of the physical conditions of the cities, economic interests can override social ones. Regeneration projects often include the integration of social and environmental factors, often through partnerships between different public and private organisations. However, while gentrification is not an automatic result of regeneration, the literature has highlighted that regeneration often attracts private capital as a strategic factor in the redevelopment of the cities, which increases property values, contributing to urban fragmentation and the segregation of the urban space (Albet & Benach 2018, Della Lucia et al. 2016, Mendes 2014, Pérez et al. 2018). Godschalk (2004) refers to gentrification as a conflict between competing views on how to preserve poorer neighbourhoods, which results in new or renovated buildings for those on higher incomes, thus exacerbating the inequality and social exclusion that the regeneration was supposed to address.

**Consultation and Participation in the Regeneration of Social Housing Estates**

Community consultation and public participation are vital to ensure open and transparent housing development decisions in residential neighbourhoods (Kenna & O'Sullivan 2014), so collaborative decision-making is another significant aspect of urban regeneration. The involvement of multiple stakeholders and multi-spatial needs adds a layer of complexity to decision-making and implementation (Wang et al. 2014, Zheng et al. 2015). The involvement of a multitude of actors often requires that decisions be negotiated and modified to provide sufficient incentives for action by participants whose objectives differ and one way to handle this is via collaborative decision-making and a shared responsibility for implementation (Rhodes & Murray 2007: 79).

The literature has shown that the political complexity of urban regeneration can be addressed by a participatory planning approach but, without substantive knowledge and engagement, participatory decision-making is annulled (Mayer et al. 2016). Superficial participatory planning – which will be further discussed in this study – often degenerates into a one-sided, superficial venting of frustration, as communities are frequently included when planning is already at an advanced stage or when important decisions are actually made elsewhere (Wyman & Shulman 2002). Administrators and developers are inclined to avoid the hassle of participatory decision-making processes and these often seem an 'obligatory ritual' (Mayer et al. 2016). This is one of the reasons why collaborative decision-making is frequently not present in final projects, especially when participatory processes are disconnected from central decision-making processes (Vergara et al. 2019). As suggested by Cortese et al. (2019: 140), urban regeneration requires innovative ways of governing that include the voices of all the stakeholders affected, in line with the complexity of social problems and in combination with transparency.

Over the past few decades in Ireland, community participation in urban regeneration has dramatically increased. In Ireland, participatory practices first emerged in the early 2000s, when the government started to focus on bringing together citizens, local government, and non-governmental organisations to create a more inclusive process of urban development. These processes are often characterised by attempts to generate public engagement, civic dialogue, and collective decision-making (Whyte 2014), even if they are frequently implemented to comply with legal requirements (e.g. statutory consultations) (Shannon & O'Leary 2020). Notable projects include the regeneration of the Fatima Mansions complex in Rialto (Dublin), the Dublin Docklands regeneration programme, and the Cork City Northwest Quarter Regeneration Plan.

Social housing has been an important part of Irish urbanism since the early 1900s. It underwent several changes throughout the 20th century, from the building of local authority housing in the 1920s and 1930s to the introduction of housing associations and the housing action plan in the 1980s and 1990s. In recent decades, the ideology driving social housing interventions has shifted to a more neoliberal approach, with an emphasis on privatisation, marketisation, and reduction of investments in social housing (Lima 2021, Lima et al. 2022). Conflicts over valuable land for urban housing developments are often observed in PPPs that plan to offer mixed-tenure housing (social housing and private sector housing). This shift has been further influenced by external forces, such as the global financial crisis of 2008, which led to a decrease in public spending and the widespread introduction of market-based approaches to urban regeneration (Hearne 2020, Norris & Redmond 2005).

Taken together, the studies examined support the notion that the processes of urban regeneration are complex and involve a myriad of stakeholders. A way to cope with so many conflicting interests is through collaborative decision-making, but this often takes place superficially. In addition, the conflicts over the use of urban land and the gentrification process further influence the processes of urban change. In the next section, I examine urban regeneration within Ireland's urban policy, with emphasis on the process of urban regeneration under PPPs in the case of O'Devaney Gardens, and I demonstrate how the lack of collaborative participation in decision-making and conflicts over the best use of public land have made the area a new political battleground in the dispute on affordable housing.

## BACKGROUND FOR THE RESEARCH AND CASE STUDY

The story of O'Devaney Gardens and the PPP exemplifies the cycle of investment and disinvestment in Ireland. Constructed in 1956 in the Stoneybatter area of Dublin's north inner city, O'Devaney Gardens was a public housing development with 278 apartments, constructed, managed, and owned by Dublin City Council (DCC), the municipal local authority. The neighbourhood is originally one of the most disadvantaged inner-city areas and was largely mono-ethnic (white, Irish) but the districts surrounding the apartment complex contain a mix of housing tenures, commercial and residential development, and (particularly in recent years) higher-income and more ethnic groups (Norris & Hearne 2016). Stoneybatter has seen many transformations over the years. Initially a largely working-class neighbourhood in which residents were mainly employed by the adjacent Guinness Brewery factory and Jameson's

Distillery (Kearns 1996), today the area has attracted many new property developments, sleek restaurants and themed bars and shops, due to its mixed-income, ethnically diverse population, varied services, and close proximity with the Phoenix Park and Dublin's city centre.

Dublin's inner-city areas were heavily affected by unemployment in the 1970s after a period of deindustrialisation and economic downfall and further undermined in the 1980s (MacLaren & Kelly 2014). In this period, a heroin crisis was concentrated in Dublin's inner-city areas and outer estates where poverty, multi-generational unemployment, high population density (particularly of young adults), and abandonment of public services and structural building decay were the most present (O'Gorman 1998, Punch 2005). As a response to these issues in disadvantaged urban neighbourhoods, the Irish state carried out improvement schemes from the mid-1980s on to promote socio-economic regeneration and improvements to dwellings and public spaces in run-down estates. Targeting in particular estates built during the 1960s and 1970s, DCC's Remedial Works Scheme and the Area Regeneration Programme were implemented to redevelop deprived inner-city areas from the mid-1990s onwards (Norris & Redmond 2005). These programmes had some positive impact in inner-city neighbourhoods, such as Fatima Mansions and Dolphin House, but have been criticised because of the many separate funding streams and difficulties in raising money for multifaceted urban redevelopment schemes (Norris & Hearne 2016, Punch 2009).

In the mid-2000s, O'Devaney Gardens and another seven inner-city housing estates were earmarked for demolition and rebuilding, to be funded by PPPs. In a PPP, the state contracts a private company to design, build, and sometimes finance and/or maintain a public service or infrastructure. The local government invited private developers to regenerate neighbourhoods as mixed-tenure estates. In this scheme, a private developer would receive free public land to build and sell properties on the private market while also providing new social housing units on the same site (Hearne 2009). O'Devaney Gardens' residents demanded to be involved in the plan for the site. A forum for discussion was created and talks about regeneration began, with the community rejecting being at the will of private developers. However, their interaction with DCC and developers was largely one-sided, with little space for meaningful citizen engagement. The plans for regeneration started in 2003 and the process of regeneration has been criticised by residents' representatives and community workers as lacking any significant community participation, with the mechanisms of the redevelopment process making it difficult for the community to influence the process (Russell & Redmond 2009).

In the late 1990s, residents of O'Devaney Gardens in Dublin started a campaign to improve their neighbourhood by providing better community facilities. However, in 2003, DCC revealed plans to redevelop the area under a PPP, which included demolition and rebuild, in disaccord with what residents had been lobbying for. Residents quickly mobilised and tried to lobby to influence the plans, but the developer withdrew in 2008 due to a lack of economic viability, causing the plans to be abandoned. This led to the break-up of the community, in contrast to the successful PPP redevelopment of Fatima Mansions (Norris & Hearne 2016).

With the collapse of the property market in 2008, which had serious consequences for Ireland, including an IMF financial rescue package, urban regeneration projects were suspended, and thus funding for social housing, together with the hopes and expectations of the community, quickly vanished (Norris & Hearne 2016). The project remained in limbo until a series of feasibility studies were released and developers were invited to tender, once the economic crisis subsided in the mid-2010s. In 2017, in the context of the post-crisis situation and the economic recovery, talks about the urban regeneration of O'Devaney Gardens were reinitiated, but with several changes to the original plan. The main stumbling block to the new regeneration plan was that some local councillors wanted the redeveloped O'Devaney Gardens to be a public rent-only estate, whereas DCC wanted the proposed 479 planned units to be a mixture of social and private housing (Sirr 2016). The tendering process for a new regeneration project started in 2015, as Dublin councillors moved to revive the regeneration effort as part of the Housing Land Initiative. Most of the buildings on the site were torn down in 2016, and when the last residents were re-housed in 2018, the remaining apartment blocks were demolished.

A motion was put forward in 2016 by the Workers' Party councillor Éilis Ryan stating that the redeveloped site should be 100% public mixed-income housing, including 50% homes for people on the housing waiting list and the other 50% for those struggling to pay rent in the private sector. The motion was approved but later rescinded because councillors were afraid this model would concentrate poverty and the area would become a 'ghetto'. After that a new local election took place in 2018 and new councillors were elected, and a new regeneration proposal emerged. The new plan includes 30% social housing, 20% affordable housing, and 50% private-purchase housing, while the total number of new homes has increased to 824 units. Former residents and housing activists were not involved in the discussion of the new plan, which has reignited an intense public debate about the best use of public land. In late 2019, progressive-leaning councillors attempted to rescind a EUR 7 million deal with the developer Bartra,[1] alleging the 20/30/50 project was approved based on misleading information, such as 1) the price tag for the affordable homes (the upper bracket for the affordable homes was EUR 420,000); 2) the poor use of state land, with developers making a large profit from public land (around EUR 67 million while the site was sold to developer Bartra Capital for EUR 7 million); and 3) the low amount of social housing (192 units). In November 2019, the newly elected councillors wanted to vote to alter the deal with Bartra, alleging it was a bad deal. The deal was approved anyway by 61.5% of the councillors, so a sideline informal deal was achieved with the developer, who agreed to lower the price of the affordable homes and offer 30% of the private homes for sale to an Approved Housing Body (housing association) for a cost-rental scheme. The housing minister Eoghan Murphy, however, later stated that this informal deal was invalid and that there was no funding for acquiring extra social housing units.

## RESEARCH FINDINGS – URBAN REGENERATION AND COMMUNITY DISINTEGRATION

### Weakened Community Structures

The contradictions between the vision for the city held by planners, developers, and residents and local needs and values initially fed into the emergent patterns of community organisation and collective action (Punch 2009). Most of the communities earmarked for redevelopment cooperated with the PPP in Dublin but neighbourhoods differed significantly in terms of their strength and lobbying capacity to shape PPPs (Norris & Hearne 2016). While some communities such as Fatima Mansions demonstrated a very strong capacity to resist top-down regeneration and shaped the process, others had weaker organisational structures. O'Devaney Gardens residents failed to influence the DCC plans for the redevelopment of their area due to a lack of engagement between the residents and the DCC. Despite the residents' attempts to engage with the Council, they were unable to effectively communicate their needs and concerns to the Council. Consequently, the Council failed to adequately consult with and engage the residents on the plans for the redevelopment of the area. As a result, the Council was not able to take into account the views of the local residents and the plans for the redevelopment of O'Devaney Gardens did not reflect the local community's needs and preferences. Thus, when the PPP collapsed as a result of the economic crisis between 2007 and 2008, the community was left 'devastated' (Norris & Hearne 2016: 41), considering many residents were already relocated and some of the buildings made vacant and boarded. With all of the residents dispersed, there were even less opportunities for them to participate and influence the redevelopment strategy supposedly created for their benefit.

Notwithstanding the serious deprivation and social issues in the estates assigned for regeneration (O'Gorman 1998, Punch 2005), most of the communities affected shared a strong connection and pride, with varying potential for community organisation and resistance (Bisset 2008). Even with a weaker tradition of community mobilisation, previous scholarship has presented evidence of the emergence of new organising agents with objectives relating to the regeneration and improvement of O'Devaney Gardens. The existence of community representatives is due to the establishment of the regeneration project (Hearne 2009, Rhodes & Murray 2007). Residents' representative groups were created specifically in response to the possibility of regeneration so as to better position themselves in relation to the city council. As described by Norris and Hearne (2016), O'Devaney residents began organising for improvements to their neighbourhood in the late 1990s when an ad hoc group was created to campaign for the provision of better community facilities and the redevelopment of the area without the need for demolitions. The story took a further twist with the state's engagement with urban regeneration via PPPs, the most overt expression to date of the infection of urban policies by neoliberal ideologies, as the residents' representatives were informed that PPP funds were to be used to finance and deliver the redevelopment of public housing stock and the revitalisation of the area (Punch 2009).

As a reaction to the new regeneration plans, the community hurried to appoint their own representatives and pushed for a process of greater consultation and communication with people to let them know a redevelopment was going to happen. During the discussion phase of the PPP in 2003, the DCC attempted to transfer the maintenance and management of the housing stock to the private and charity sector. Residents opposed the possibility of a large part of the site being given over to high-density private apartments, and an agreement between DCC and community representatives was achieved in which the initial level of public housing units was to be maintained and they were to remain city council tenants (Hearne 2009). Work on implementing the PPP moved quickly, and despite descriptions of community consultation in policy documents,[2] there is very little evidence that the consultations and community participation were meaningful (Hearne 2009, Indymedia Ireland 2005, Norris & Hearne 2016). Without a clear indication of when the redevelopment would start, a significant number of people wanted to leave between 2007 and 2008. The area had deteriorated substantially, and residents were frustrated with the conditions on the estate, the delays in the project, and their lack of involvement in the ongoing negotiations over the future of the project (Hearne 2009).

## The Fragmentation of the Consultation Process

An examination of policy documents shows that consultations with statutory environmental authorities, other interested parties, and the public through the statutory planning application should take place, as established in the guideline 'Quality Housing in Sustainable Communities – Best Practice Guidelines for Delivering Homes, Sustaining Communities'.[3] A policy context report informs us that the O'Devaney Gardens community 'has actively engaged in the formulation of the development proposals through a range of community-based activities and initiatives co-ordinated by Dublin City Council',[4] while other reports state that feasibility studies were prepared in consultation with residents of the complex (Environmental Impact Statement Section 2). Some community feedback and consultation indeed took place in the first PPP attempt (2003–2008). According to reports, some work had been done by local community regeneration boards (involving development workers, residents, and DCC officials). This is confirmed in the detailed work by Hearne (2009), which presents an account of a model of social and physical regeneration that allowed residents and stakeholders to pressure the state into accepting significant resident participation in the regeneration, with residents participating in consultation and receiving technical support. Policy documents state that local residents were active participants in the elaboration of the original master plan for O'Devaney Gardens (Environmental Impact Statement Section 2) but the extent to which the spaces of direct participation for influencing the design of the project really empowered residents is unclear. Similar research in other inner-city Dublin estates has shown that consultation and resident participation did not help residents to assert their agenda or to meet the minimum necessary EU guidelines in relation to resident consultation (Hearne 2009).

The redevelopment of O'Devaney through the PPP regeneration scheme was susceptible to failure because it was substantially contingent on the property market. During the 2008 economic downturn, the PPP project for the regeneration of the flats complex collapsed. Even though the preferred bidder in the PPP for O'Devaney had signed the contract, the developer Bernard McNamara withdrew from its commitment and later declared bankruptcy. Once an estate has been earmarked for regeneration, de-tenanting is likely to occur over a period of time, resulting in vacancy, boarded housing units, and dereliction. Deserted and filled with expectations, residents continued to suffer from vandalism and became the fated losers in the process. Residents were angered at the injustice of their estate being allowed to fall into disrepair while banks received a huge financial bailout from the Irish government (Hardiman & Metinsoy 2019), indicating much about the character, values, and priorities of the state when it came to urban redevelopment. Only the PPP in Fatima Mansions was completed. Abandoned communities in O'Devaney Gardens, and also in St Michael's Estate, reacted with great anger and frustration, resulting in a series of protests in front of the city council offices to draw attention to the human cost of the collapse of five PPP regeneration deals (Russell & Redmond 2009). The collective outpouring of anger evolved not just because of the significant time and expectations invested in the regeneration project but also because of their vulnerable situation, behind which lay long years of struggles, achievements, and losses (Punch 2009).

## Focus on Relocating Residents Rather Than Keeping the Community in Place

Third, there was an overemphasis on the relocation of residents and demolition instead of focusing on sustaining the living conditions for existing communities. To enable the first phase of the rebuilding, the partial demolition of the complex took place before the collapse of the PPP. DCC moved out some 100 tenants (out of 278) from residential blocks to the north of the estate to facilitate the redevelopment, leaving 93 units occupied (Planning Reg. Ref 3607/10).[5] Long-term residents and community leaders left as vacant dwellings were being used for anti-social activity and little maintenance was being carried out. The remaining residents requested to be transferred to other social housing and were relocated elsewhere. In 2012, DCC announced that the redevelopment plans were being cancelled due to a lack of funding after 15 years of discussion and planning (Bohan 2012). The process of de-tenanting and selective transfer was used by DCC to wipe the community clean and start afresh, without any opposition (Hearne 2009). This ultimately led to the devastation of this community (Norris & Hearne 2016).

In the next section I examine the opacity around the new redevelopment plans and the lack of inclusion of the community's voice in the new proposal for O'Devaney Gardens.

## PARTICIPATION IN URBAN REDEVELOPMENT AND LAND USE CONFLICTS: A DISCUSSION

In urban regeneration planning, citizen participation is a key element for successful regeneration projects. The experience of urban regeneration initiatives in O'Devaney Gardens shows that the redevelopment strategy had very negative consequences for residents. Even with attempts to influence the shape of the redevelopment in its early stages, their weak mobilisation structures meant that they were not able to resist and shape the regeneration project imposed on them. The result is that local social networks are now weak. Demolition and clearance did not solve the underlying problems that caused the decline of the community, and gentrification and private housing make physical renewal more challenging (Rohe 2009).

The principle that citizens should take part in collaborative decision-making in urban planning has gained acceptance since the 2000s, a fact now reflected in Irish legislation, which commonly includes area-based community participation in planning efforts. However, the ability to have an effective influence on the general public when it comes to urban planning has been diminished with the increased reliance on joint ventures between the state and private capital (PPPs), a strategic alliance forged between urban planning, the economic boosterism lobby, and the property-development sector to reinvent the image of the city (MacLaren & Kelly 2014: 30). As noted by MacLaran et al. (2007), in the Irish political environment the collaborative participation of citizens is an official requirement, but critical attention must be focused on the formal structures of inclusive participation and on the manner in which the commitment has been realised. MacLaran et al. (2007) were referring to community participation before the economic crisis in their writing. However, as the years have passed, the nature of the government's commitment to community participation in planning remains questionable.

In the face of rhetorical commitments to community participation in the project plan for O'Devaney Gardens, the role of local residents and stakeholders is limited to consultation. Policy decisions are taken elsewhere, a policy practice in which participation is undermined by the state. As previously mentioned, the current redevelopment project references community participation as having 'an active say in how the community is developed'.[6] This participation structure included, in the first phase of the project (2003–2008), a Regeneration Board composed of resident representatives, DCC officials, elected local councillors, and other key stakeholders. It was a forum that met on a quarterly or bi-monthly basis to discuss the master plan in the first phase of the project, according to the policy documents.[7] These documents do not state when the meetings took place and what they discussed or decided. In the current revised redevelopment scheme (2017–), the Land Initiative Regeneration report establishes that the 'new O'Devaney Gardens Regeneration Consultative Forum'[8] will meet every two months, which involves an independent person acting as chair, one DCC official, two city councillors, six residents from the relevant local estates, and two community groups. A DCC Monthly Management Report from June 2019 states that a consultative forum and meeting has been set up[9] but, in practice, there is little to no information about who is taking part in the O'Devaney Community Consultative Forum, how often they meet, or what is discussed at meetings. The few members identified by media sources complained about the vagueness of the plans and the lack of community voice (Finnan 2018). A report from 2018 states that the forum met on five occasions in 2017 but no further details were available.

The first known public consultation event occurred in October 2018, hosted by DCC – the Next for O'Devaney workshop – involving citizens, municipal administration representatives, and architects in interactive activities. According to its final report, the aim of the workshop was to gather local residents, interested parties, community groups, and key stakeholders in order to explore the community's 'view for the development'. It was supposed to be the 'final round of consultations with the local community' to inform them about 'the brief for the developers to be appointed for O'Devaney Gardens'.[10] Attendees watched presentations and shared their hopes and expectations in a one-off event. The consultative forum, however, has no statutory power, just like the previous Regeneration Board. In order to ensure the economic viability of the regeneration project and profits for private developers in the PPP regeneration, there is no guarantee that communities' needs and wishes will be 'briefed' to those tendering. The key word is 'consultative', which has often served to effectively marginalise the views of dissenting residents and to depoliticise a highly political agenda (MacLaren & Kelly 2014). Previous research has highlighted how PPP 'consultation' processes involved prompting residents on the necessity to reduce their aspirations in relation to the quantity of social housing and community gain provided in the regeneration plans (Hearne 2009).

In a period of rising house prices, housing shortages, and increasing homelessness, the market-based approach of using the increased value of land to regenerate old social housing in the inner city through PPPs demonstrates the particularly strong role of the private sector as the main housing provider. The policy practices discussed in this study have sustained and legitimated the process of gentrification and working-class displacement in Dublin. Neoliberal ideas of 'regeneration' in the current conflict about the use of state land have to be viewed in light of a long-established process of defining regeneration solely in terms of economic growth concerns (Jones & Evans 2013, Mendes 2014, Pérez et al. 2018). Addressing the conflicts among the various stakeholders in the process of land-use allocation requires time and commitment, and with the short time between awarding the tender to developers and the commencement of construction it is unlikely that a more engaged public consultation will take place. For a community now detached and scattered, the rocketing value of inner-city land affects the continuation of social housing in these areas. A highly political neoliberal land-use and development agenda has been forced on vulnerable, poor, working-class inner-city communities (MacLaren & Kelly 2014) and, in the case of O'Devaney Gardens, the majority of the original residents are no longer present to demand social housing.

## CONCLUSIONS

This research examined the complex relations between competing views on urban regeneration and the interactions between private capital, the state, and local residents, with the story of the redevelopment of O'Devaney Gardens as a case study. This study has shown that the Irish central government and DCC remain committed to PPPs as the preferred mechanism to deliver urban regeneration. With the economy starting to show signs of recovery, PPPs are again a key component of urban regeneration as controversial plans to build a mix of social and private housing are again on the table. The research has identified the key issues in urban regeneration and community disintegration: the weak community structures, the fragmentation of the consultation process, and the focus on the relocation of residents rather than sustaining the community. Together these findings reflect the market-driven approaches to social regeneration, which have given way to a land-use conflict over the best use of publicly owned sites with high potential for housing development. While these developments are much needed, the revised version of the O'Devaney regeneration imposes higher residential density without relevant public consultation, as the project is once again dominated by a private housing scheme in an area that used to be a social housing estate.

The opportunity for affordable housing changed or decreased during the different phases of the development. In the early 2000s, funding was available and some level of engagement with the government took place. The O'Devaney Gardens community's needs however were not fully attended to and by the post-2008 period the PPPs collapsed. With the economic recovery around 2015, a new wave of plans ensued, with even less community engagement since many of the original residents had already left and a much stronger role for private developers and for-profit housing construction was included.

A meaningful process of citizen participation and collaborative decision-making could promote the cooperation of multiple stakeholders and reduce the conflict around land use and housing tenure allocation. The PPP model is still heavily based on the cyclical market approach, and the regeneration programme proposed for O'Devaney Gardens failed to capture the long history, rich culture, and social networks of the inner city in order to promote social regeneration and sustainability, as the regeneration consultation process itself disempowered residents. Instead, the rich diversity of these communities was used to facilitate the process of gentrification and displacement. Considering Ireland's success with direct participation in the Citizen's Assembly, people in Ireland have played an important role in the political framework of the country and the results have promoted a series of social changes, including new legislation in several areas, such as reproductive rights and same-sex marriage. However, this success does not yet apply to the area of urban planning.

Furthermore, this research sheds light on current strategies of urban regeneration taking place in other contexts. The analysis presented, although limited to a case study, allows for a reflection on the enormous financial commitments and private sector interest in urban regeneration, which raises several issues in relation to both social and spatial justice, legitimacy of decisions, and impacts on local communities. The participatory dimension in the perspective of urban regeneration, although present in form of consultation, is commonly held hostage by being undervalued in relation to economic growth opportunities, in which participation in collaborative decision-making as an urban and housing policy component has effectively remained a residual practice. In addition to the participatory element, one of the major issues is how redevelopment affects the opportunities for affordable housing.

This work contributes to the literature on urban regeneration and collaborative decision-making by adding to the understanding of the underlying dynamics of urban regeneration and how different actors interact in the urban policy context. These findings could be of interest to scholars and policy-makers interested in how contemporary decision-making approaches and policy-making processes need to be more inclusive to allow for the advancement and encouragement of a sustainable and fair process of regeneration. As a result of this study, further research might be conducted on the specific roles and agendas of private developers in redeveloping inner-city areas.

## NOTES

1. Bartra is an Irish property group that is heavily involved in the development of social housing in Ireland. Due to delays in planning permissions, renegotiation of contracts with the Dublin City Council, and deferral of the start date for the new development construction, Bartra has been criticised and threatened to have the contract taken away (see: https://dublininquirer.com/2022/12/21/as-developer-still-has-not-built-homes-at-o-devaney-gardens-councillors-call-to-take-back-the-land). The latest update at the time of the writing is that construction was set to commence in February 2023 (see: https://www.irishtimes.com/ireland/2023/02/10/odevaney-gardens-redevelopment-to-start-this-month/).
2. O'Devaney Gardens Environmental Impact Statement Section 2, Characteristics of the Proposed Development.
3. O'Devaney Gardens Environmental Impact Statement Section 3, Planning Policy Context.
4. O'Devaney Gardens Environmental Impact Statement Section 3, Planning Policy Context (page 8).
5. O'Devaney Gardens Environmental Impact Statement Chapter 1.
6. O'Devaney Gardens Environmental Impact Statement Section 4: Human Beings (page 4).
7. O'Devaney Gardens Environmental Impact Statement Section 2: Characteristics of the Proposed Development (page 11).
8. O'Devaney Gardens Land Initiative Regeneration Project report (page 24).
9. Report No. 209/2018. Members of Dublin City Council Report of the Chief Executive Monthly Management.
10. Next for O'Devaney report (2018, page 4).

## REFERENCES

Albet, A. & Benach, N. (2018) *Gentrification as a Global Strategy: Neil Smith and Beyond*. Oxford: Routledge.

Bengtsson, M. (2016) How to plan and perform a qualitative study using content analysis. *NursingPlus Open* 2: 8–14.

Bissett, J. (2008) *Regeneration: Public Good or Private Profit?* Dublin: TASC.

Bohan, C. (2012) After more than 15 years, plans for O'Devaney Gardens officially scrapped. *TheJournal.ie*. Available at: https://www.thejournal.ie/o-devaney-gardens-scrapped-694646-Dec2012/ (Accessed: 23 April 2020).

Boyle, L., Michell, K. & Viruly, F. (2018) A critique of the application of neighborhood sustainability assessment tools in urban regeneration. *Sustainability* 10(4): 1005.

Cortese, T.T.P. et al. (2019) Tecnologias e sustentabilidade nas cidades. *Estudos Avançados* 33(97): 137–150.

Della Lucia, M., Trunfio, M. & Frank, M.G. (2016) Heritage and urban regeneration: Towards creative tourism. In Bellini, N. (ed.) *Tourism in the City: Towards an Integrative Agenda on Urban Tourism.* Cham: Springer.

Della Spina, L., Calabrò, F. & Rugolo, A. (2020) Social housing: An appraisal model of the economic benefits in urban regeneration programs. *Sustainability* 12(2): 609.

Finnan, S. (2018) Stoneybatter residents want more say in plans for O'Devaney Gardens. *Dublin Inquirer.* Available at: https://www.dublininquirer.com/2018/10/24/stoneybatter-residents-want-more-say-in-plans-for-o-devaney-gardens (Accessed: 21 April 2020).

Fox, K.G. (2001) Redevelopment for whom and for what purpose? A research agenda for urban redevelopment in the twenty first century. In K.G. Fox (ed.) *Critical Perspectives on Urban Redevelopment.* Bingley: Emerald Publishing, 429–452.

Godschalk, D. (2004) Land use planning challenges: Coping with conflicts in visions of sustainable development and livable communities. *Journal of the American Planning Association* 70(1): 5–13.

Grebler, L. (1962) Urban renewal in European countries. *Journal of the American Institute of Planners* 28(4): 229–238.

Hardiman, N. & Metinsoy, S. (2019) Power, ideas, and national preferences: Ireland and the FTT. *Journal of European Public Policy* 26(11): 1600–1619.

Hearne, R. (2009) *Origins, Development and Outcomes of Public Private Partnerships in Ireland: The Case of PPPs in Social Housing Regeneration.* Combat Poverty Agency.

Hearne, R. (2020) *Housing Shock: The Irish Housing Crisis and How to Solve It.* Bristol: Policy Press.

Hearne, R., Kitchin, R. & O'Callaghan, C. (2014) Spatial justice and housing in Ireland. In Kearns, G., Meredith, D. & Morrissey, J. (eds.) *Spatial Justice and the Irish Crisis.* Dublin: RIA, 57–77.

Hearne, R. & Redmond, D. (2014) The collapse of PPPs: Prospects for social housing regeneration after the crash. In MacLaran, A. & Kelly, S. (eds.) *Neoliberal Urban Policy and the Transformation of the City: Reshaping Dublin.* London: Palgrave Macmillan, 219–232.

Indymedia Ireland (2005) O'Devaney gardening: Sowing the seeds of regeneration in an inner city community. Available at: https://www.indymedia.ie/article/71921?condense_comments=true&userlanguage=ga&save_prefs=true (Accessed: 23 April 2020).

Jones, P. & Evans, J. (2013) *Urban Regeneration in the UK: Boom, Bust and Recovery.* Los Angeles: SAGE.

Kearns, A. & Mason, P. (2013) Defining and measuring displacement: Is relocation from restructured neighbourhoods always unwelcome and disruptive? *Housing Studies* 28(2): 177–204.

Kearns, K. (1996) *Stoneybatter: Dublin's Inner-urban Village.* Dublin: Gill & Macmillan.

Kenna, T. & O'Sullivan, M. (2014) Imposing tenure mix on residential neighbourhoods: A review of actions to address unfinished housing estates in the Republic of Ireland. *Critical Housing Analysis* 1(2): 1–23.

Leary, M.E. & McCarthy, J. (2013) Introduction: Urban regeneration, a global phenomenon. In Leary, M.E. & McCarthy, J. (eds.) *The Routledge Companion to Urban Regeneration.* Abingdon: Routledge.

Lima, V. (2021) Urban austerity and activism: Direct action against neoliberal housing policies. *Housing Studies* 36(2): 258–277.

Lima, V., Hearne, R. & Murphy, M.P. (2022) Housing financialisation and the creation of homelessness in Ireland. *Housing Studies* 38(9): 1695–1718.

MacLaran, A., Clayton, V. & Brudell, P. (2007) *Empowering Communities in Disadvantaged Urban Areas: Towards Greater Community Participation in Irish Urban Planning?* Combat Poverty Agency.

MacLaren, A. & Kelly, S. (eds.) (2014) *Neoliberal Urban Policy and the Transformation of the City: Reshaping Dublin.* London: Palgrave Macmillan.

Marco, C.M.D., Santos, P.J.T. dos & Möller, G.S. (2020) Gentrificação no Brasil e no contexto latino como expressão do colonialismo urbano: o direito à cidade como proposta decolonizadora. *Urbe. Revista Brasileira de Gestão Urbana* 12.

Mayer, I.S. et al. (2016) Collaborative decisionmaking for sustainable urban renewal projects: A simulation – gaming approach. *Environment and Planning B: Planning and Design* 32(3): 403–423.

Mendes, L. (2013) A regeneração urbana na política de cidades: inflexão entre o fordismo e o pós-fordismo. *Urbe. Revista Brasileira de Gestão Urbana* 5(1): 33–45.

Mendes, L. (2014) Gentrification and urban regeneration policies in Portugal: A critical analysis in light of Neil Smith's rent gap thesis. *Cadernos Metrópole* 16(32): 487–511.

Norris, M. & Hearne, R. (2016) Privatizing public housing redevelopment: Grassroots resistance, co-operation and devastation in three Dublin neighbourhoods. *Cities* 57: 40–46.

Norris, M. & Redmond, D. (2005) *Housing Contemporary Ireland: Policy, Society and Shelter*. Institute of Public Administration.

O'Gorman, A. (1998) Illicit drug use in Ireland: An overview of the problem and policy responses. *Journal of Drug Issues* 28(1): 155–166.

Pérez, M.G.R., Laprise, M. & Rey, E. (2018) Fostering sustainable urban renewal at the neighbourhood scale with a spatial decision support system. *Sustainable Cities and Society* 38: 440–451.

Punch, M. (2005) Problem drug use and the political economy of urban restructuring: Heroin, class and governance in Dublin. *Antipode* 37(4): 754–774.

Punch, M. (2009) Contested urban environments: Perspectives on the place and meaning of community action in central Dublin, Ireland. *Interface* 1(2): 83–107.

Rhodes, M.L. & Murray, J. (2007) Collaborative decision making in urban regeneration: A complex adaptive systems perspective. *International Public Management Journal* 10(1): 79–101.

Roberts, P. & Sykes, H. (1999) *Urban Regeneration: A Handbook*. Los Angeles: SAGE.

Rohe, W.M. (2009) From local to global: One hundred years of neighborhood planning. *Journal of the American Planning Association* 75(2): 209–230.

Russell, P. & Redmond, D. (2009) Social housing regeneration in Dublin: Market-based regeneration and the creation of sustainable communities. *Local Environment* 14(7): 635–650.

Shannon, L. & O'Leary, F. (2020) *Local Government: Engaging and Empowering Local Communities*. Dublin: Institute of Public Administration.

Sirr, L. (2016) Stumbling block of social housing stalls O'Devaney Gardens. *The Sunday Times*, 1 September. Available at: https://arrow.tudublin.ie/beschrecmed/35.

Vergara, L.M. et al. (2019) *Housing and Urban Regeneration of Deprived Neighborhoods in Santiago: North-South Perspectives about Collaborative Processes*. Delft: TU Delft Open.

Wang, H. et al. (2014) A framework of decision-making factors and supporting information for facilitating sustainable site planning in urban renewal projects. *Cities* 40: 44–55.

Watt, P. (2021) *Estate Regeneration and Its Discontents: Public Housing, Place and Inequality in London*. London: Bristol University Press.

Weaver, M. (2001) Urban regeneration – the issue explained. *The Guardian*, 19 March.

Whyte, J. (2014) From spark to flame: Community participation in the regeneration of Fatima Mansions. In Readdick, A. (ed.) *Irish Families and Globalization: Conversations about Belonging and Identity across Space and Time*. Michigan: Michigan Publishing, 1–23.

Wyman, M. & Shulman, D. (2002) *From Venting to Inventing: Dispatches from the Frontiers of Participation in Canada*. Citizens and Governance Programme.

Zheng, H.W. et al. (2015) Simulating land use change in urban renewal areas: A case study in Hong Kong, *Habitat International* 46: 23–34.

# 26. Resisting the destruction of home: un-homing and homemaking in the formation of political subjectivities

*Dominika V. Polanska*

Having a safe place to call home is a basic human need. Although not all nuances of home and home life are always positive for all members of a society, home is an important foundation of safety and privacy among its members. The topic of home has in the first two decades of the 21st century been the focus of a significant number of studies that have concentrated on how it is given meaning and how it can be conceptualized (Fox O'Mahony 2007, Fox O'Mahony & Sweeney 2016, Mallett 2004, Miller 2001). The subject of home and its meanings however aroused interest long before (Fried 1966, Hayward 1975). The notion of home is multifaceted and complex and 'transcends quantitative, measurable dimensions' (Lawrence 1995), including dimensions of material and immaterial character. Quantitative, measurable, and technical dimensions are often used when referring to housing; home is something more than the materiality of dwelling. Fox O'Mahony (2007) has in her conceptualization of home distinguished several material and immaterial dimensions: financial, practical, emotional, psychological, social, and cultural. She argued that when the home's multifaceted and complex meaning cannot be translated into measurable or quantifiable data, it often becomes trivialized (Fox O'Mahony 2007: 24).

The meanings of home can vary. In the Global North homes' durability and permanency is often conditioned by people's financial ability and tenancy security in a specific housing regime. Müller (2021) points to the connection of home as a place for political engagement and urban security, where homes are spaces to be defended against external threats. In urban studies the focus has often been on how space is produced, not only in physical terms but also how space is given meaning and (re)presented (Harvey 2006, Lefebvre 1991). The processes creating disturbances and ruptures that generate uncertainty in people's place-attachment and making of a home, such as forced relocation or local changes that create alienation, have in urban studies been called *displacement* (Davidson 2009, Marcuse 1986, Porteous & Smith 2001) and *gentrification* (Lees 2000, Marcuse 1986, Slater 2006). In this study, the forced relocation of residents, displacement, and its effects on how home is given meaning stand in focus. Displacement is a result of what Harvey (2003) called *accumulation by dispossession*, a process including appropriation, exploitation, privatization, commodification, and the conversion of property rights to protect private property owners and private ownership in the capitalist system. Massive dispossessions have followed the process of financialization of homes, turning housing into a 'mechanism of rent extraction, financial gain and wealth accumulation' (Rolnik 2019: 5), resulting in urban marginality, increased segregation in cities, and growing housing inequalities. Housing financialization on a global scale (Aalbers 2008, 2017, Rolnik 2019, Fuller 2021) together with neoliberal austerity and the dismantling of the welfare state in the Global North have opened up massive dispossessions and growing inequalities by promoting market-based logics and de- and re-regulation. One such dispossession materializes when people are forced to leave their homes against their will or live with displacement pressure (Marcuse 1986). Those most affected are the poorest communities, who live in a constant housing crisis (Madden and Marcuse 2016).

The aim of this chapter is to analyze the process of home destruction and how home is given meaning and politicized by those experiencing displacement through renovation. The objective is to conceptualize the processes of the destruction but also the creation and re-creation of home, homemaking, and to understand the role homemaking plays in citizens' negotiation of their place and position in society, their political engagement, and agency. Sociologists and other social scientists interested in social movements, class formation, or the functioning of local communities have all been, in some way, concerned with the formation of political subjectivities and the subject formation of actors fighting for social change. The perspective guiding this work is that the processes causing the destruction of home are encountered by active subjects resisting and organizing collectively to protest and amend the harmful forces of neoliberal urbanism inherent in late capitalism. Furthermore, I place the processes of un-homing and homemaking as pivotal for the development of political subjectivity amongst the affected tenants.

Sweden will serve as an example of a post-welfare context where the 'post' refers to a shift, not a definite break, in welfare state policies, where decentralization of welfare provision along with market-oriented policies are central (Baeten et al. 2015, Rannila 2021). In Sweden neoliberal urban policy is mixed with elements of regulation, contributing to the growth of urban inequality (Christophers 2013) – increasing housing wealth and tenure inequality (Christophers 2021) – and the financialization of housing (Gustafsson 2022), and political subjects are opposing these processes in resisting the destruction of home. In this light, the concept of *renoviction* (a composition of two words (renovation and eviction) referring to the displacement of tenants following extensive renovations) sheds light on the current material and immaterial/symbolic displacement processes going on in the country. The systemic perspective is here grounded in the individual and collective experiences of tenants facing the risk of displacement in the form of forced relocation due to renovation and what in the international research has been referred to as *displacement pressure* (Marcuse 1986), *loss of place* (Davidson 2009), and *symbolic displacement* (Atkinson 2015) – experiences of living with displacement.

The work presented builds on interviews with tenants who organized to resist renovations in their neighborhoods. The material includes 60 semi-structured interviews conducted between 2018 and 2021 with tenants living in nine neighborhoods in two Swedish cities engaged in tenants' organizations of different kinds. Interview questions revolved around tenants' experiences of housing renovation, communication with housing companies, and collective mobilization and resistance, along with individual experiences of resistance to renovation plans and the meaning of home in the process. The interviews have been pseudonymized, transcribed, and thematically coded. All interviewees were granted anonymity and asked to give signed informed consent. They were, moreover, informed on how interview data would be handled and stored and their right to withdraw. When citing I am restrictive in mentioning any sensitive information (city, district, housing company, name of association, name of person, personal characteristics, etc.) that could be associated with the interviewees and the cited interviews are numbered in the text.

The chapter starts with a review of the displacement research analyzing the destruction of home from the perspective of residents and then describes the specificity of the Swedish case, where renovations can cause material and immaterial displacement among tenants. The impact of these processes on tenants is presented along with the still scarce number of studies focusing on tenants' mobilizations in the country. Next, the process of the formation of political subjectivity among tenants facing renovation is analyzed, distinguishing between the social, political, spatial, and material dimensions, including the destruction of home but also the creation and re-creation of home, in the understanding of the development of tenants' political subjectivity.

## DISPLACEMENT AND THE DESTRUCTION OF HOMES IN THE INTERNATIONAL LITERATURE

Displacement refers to the violent process of forced moves (Davidson 2009) and can be experienced by individual households and local communities due to its psychological, social, and material consequences. It is a material experience that can be embodied directly in forced relocation and indirectly through the symbolic pressure it creates (Marcuse 1986). From the literature on displacement terms like *domicide* or *displacement pressure* have emerged to describe how homes are destroyed in material and immaterial terms. This process has also been called *un-homing* (Atkinson 2015) and analyzed in terms of how the connection between people and place is ruptured (Elliott-Cooper et al. 2020). Displacement as an affective, emotional, and material rupture has been conceptualized in the work of Brickell et al. (2017) and its traumatic nature has been described in the work of Fullilove (2005) and Pain (2019). *Domicide* was coined by Porteous and Smith (2001) to refer to the destruction of home as expressed in different ways of depriving people of their home, while *displacement pressure* was introduced by Marcuse (1986) to describe the risk of displacement that economically vulnerable residents often experience, but the term also covers the pressure created for those who remain put in an area that has been gentrified or displaced and where housing costs have increased. A similar dimension of the displacement process has been captured in the notions of *loss of place*, coined by Davidson (2009) to refer to the alienation residents experience when facing neighborhood gentrification, and *symbolic displacement*, introduced by Atkinson (2015) to describe the experiences of those who stay put in a neighborhood under social and physical change. According to Madden and Marcuse (2016: 3) the global scale of displacement caused by construction and urban development in recent decades is comparable to the scale of displacement caused by disasters and armed conflicts.

There are numerous studies on the quantifiable aspects of displacement (Easton et al. 2020, Freeman 2005, Ramiller 2022) and the discussion on how to measure displacement is lively. It is, however, the focus of this chapter to study how displacement has been responded to by the residents. Even though research on displacement has focused on the responses of residents to the risk of being displaced and losing one's home in material and immaterial terms (Atkinson 2015, Davidson 2009, Marcuse 1986), the focus has prevalently been on the destructive side of the process, emphasizing the trauma and ruptures it causes (Elliott-Cooper et al. 2020, Marcuse 1986, Porteous & Smith 2001) and giving less attention to the constructive side of residents' responses to displacement, the positive effects that collective action can spur, and with it the politicization of home in this process. This focus on the destructive side of displacement in the literature has to a lesser degree stressed the capacity of local communities to overcome helplessness and resist traumatic experiences in building solidarity, emotional ties, and new collective memories along with redefinitions of the space they inhabit (Oliver-Smith 2010, Pain 2019, Polanska & Richard 2019). The contribution of this chapter lies in uncovering this capacity without neglecting the severity of the effects of the displacement process on residents' experiences and the ruptures it creates.

## THE SPECIFICITY OF THE SWEDISH CASE: DISPLACEMENT THROUGH RENOVATION

The Swedish rental housing stock is aging and national investigations have pointed to the urgent need for renovation and a 'renovation deficit' in Sweden (Swedish Government Offices 2019). In the past decade over half a million dwellings out of 1.5 million (SCB 2022) have been renovated, and 155,000 still awaited renovation in 2019 (Industrifakta 2011, Trä och Möbelföretagen 2019). In 2016 the average rent increase following renovations in the rental sector was calculated to be 37 percent (TV4 2016) and researchers have shown an increase in housing allowances and financial assistance among those staying in an area after renovation (Lind et al. 2016). The National Audit Office has reported on the tendency to 'over-renovate'; that is, the inclination among landlords to renovate apartments unnecessarily extensively to maximize the profit (Swedish Riksdag 2020) and this inclination has also been recorded in research (Baeten et al. 2017, Gustafsson 2021, Polanska & Richard 2019, Westin 2011), while rental housing has gained a central role in this process in the Swedish context (Grander 2017, Gustafsson 2021, Westerdahl 2021).

The term *renoviction* has been used among Swedish scholars to refer to the displacement caused by extensive renovations in the country in the last decade (Baeten et al. 2017, Polanska & Richard 2019, 2021, Westin 2011). Studies have shown that the voices of the residents are silenced and made invisible in this process through different governing practices employed by housing companies (Gustafsson 2021, Polanska & Richard 2019, 2021), seemingly democratic procedures of consultation (Bengtsson & Bohman 2020, Stenberg 2018, Thörn & Polanska 2023), legal practice (Polanska 2023), or the politics of responsibility, shifting the responsibility for the renovations from the public sphere to the private (Thörn & Polanska 2023). Swedish tenants have, however, during this period increasingly mobilized to make their voices heard and politicize the issue of renovations (Gustafsson et al. 2019, Listerborn et al. 2020, Polanska & Richard 2019, 2021, Pull & Richard 2019, Thörn 2020, Thörn & Polanska 2023).

The slow, subtle, and discreet form of housing violence, in a housing context where the welfare state has played an important role in levelling economic inequalities, has been picked up by Rannila (2021) in her study of the privatization of a Swedish suburb where housing renovation was central in the transformation of the area. It has been shown that previous long-term neglect of the maintenance of rental housing built over a half decade ago and located in the outskirts of the cities (Gustafsson 2021, Pull & Richard 2019, Rannila 2021) has contributed to the displacement of tenants in 'social renovations that could be implemented in the guise of physical renovations' (Rannila, 2021: 3) in a context where the rental stock amounts to less than 30 percent of the total housing stock in Sweden (SCB 2019) and poorer households tend to be represented among the tenants (Baeten et al. 2017, Grundström & Molina 2016, Polanska & Richard 2019, Westin 2011).

The mix of regulation and market-based elements in Swedish housing (Christophers 2013) gives rise to poisonous solutions affecting tenants whose homes are being renovated. The Swedish rent-setting system is neither market rent nor rent control; it is based on negotiations and the use value of the apartments, allowing, however, for rent increases when the standard of the apartment is raised. Grander (2018: 116) points to this 'loophole' in the Swedish 'use-value system', which was originally created to protect tenants from drastic rent increases but allows renovations with increased standards and thus increased use value followed by 40–50 percent rent increases. In these cases, tenants who cannot afford the new rent tend to move out (Boverket 2014, Bergenstråle & Palmstierna 2016, Pull 2020) and they experience alienation and displacement pressure (Baeten et al. 2017, Polanska & Richard 2019, Pull & Richard 2019).

Tenants facing extensive renovation and the threat of displacement have increasingly engaged in protesting and mobilizing against renovation schemes in Swedish cities. There has been an intensification in this kind of protest in the last decade that can be traced to: 1) the changed legislation regarding the running of public housing companies in 2011 affecting rent-setting in the country and the role of public housing companies (Grander 2018); 2) the general intensification in renovation programs in this time period (Baeten et al. 2017, Listerborn et al. 2020, Polanska & Richard 2021); and 3) the increase in economic inequalities, residential segregation, and stigmatization of poor urban areas (Christophers 2021, Grundström & Molina 2016, Hedin et al. 2012) accompanied by area-based urban development programs directed at marginalized urban areas (Thörn & Polanska 2023), where renovation is central. What is still understudied is the constructive effects of how this kind of collective action affects the politicization of home and political subjectivity formation among tenants.

## THEORETICAL FRAMEWORK: POLITICAL SUBJECTIVITY FORMATION AND THE MEANINGS OF HOME

Displacement through development or renovation is to be seen as a process characterized by invisible slow violence inherent in capitalism (Baeten et al. 2017, Polanska and Richard 2019, Rannila 2021) and a somewhat different temporality than other traumatic and catastrophic urban events argues Pain (2019), emphasizing the healing and rebuilding potential in collective responses to slow violence. Drawing on feminist and postcolonial theory devictimizing residents and giving precedence to their experience of slow violence, Pain (2019: 394) stresses the collective, spatial, and material dimensions of the experience, arguing that trauma can be overcome and rebuilt into resistance and solidarity. Here, the literature on the strategies (collective and individual) of poor communities to state and interpersonal violence stressing the creativity and resilient nature of these responses (Deckard & Auyero 2022) can be helpful in grasping the agency of tenants. Unsurprisingly, the most developed accounts of common strategies among poor people have been covered by ethnographic work, uncovering the importance of neighborhood ties, informal institutions, and collective action (Deckard & Auyero 2022: 22).

Resistance among tenants to renovictions has in the Swedish context previously been conceptualized as everyday, individual, and collective acts of defiance to the threats posed to tenants' homes (Polanska & Richard 2021) or as claims for *dignity* regarding equality, housing standards, neighborhood security, continuous maintenance, and the right to stay put

(Listerborn et al. 2020). In the resistance against extensive renovations tenants are engaged through the direct threat to their homes, but their collective resistance with neighbors often transforms to include broader issues. Like social movement studies, these interpretations of the tenants' responses stress collective action and interaction (Melucci 1995) as central to the formation of collective identity. Moreover, the emotional ties created through collective action and interaction keep collective actors together even under hostile conditions (Flesher Fominaya 2010, Hunt & Benford 2004, Jasper 1997). The contribution of this chapter is situated between the slow violence of displacement through renovation and resistance through collective action and the formation of tenants as political subjects.

I follow Blackman et al.'s (2008: 7) call to conceptualize the relationship between political agency and power and consider the complexity of subjectivity formation, especially in contexts and situations that conventionally have not stood in the focus of political analysis or did not classify in the narrow definition of the 'political' (see also the emerging body of literature on the post-socialist experience of political becoming; for instance, Baca 2017, Jacobsson 2015, Polanska 2017). As Häkli and Kallio (2018: 58) emphasize, in the recent developments in the scholarship on the subject and the reconceptualization of what the concept of the political entails, it has 'expanded to denote a broad spectrum of issues, events, sites and ways of acting, affecting and impacting'. Here, the understanding of the political is inspired by feminist theory connecting the intimate with the collective experiences of the workings of power (Pain 2019). *Political subjectivity* is here conceptualized as agency based on subjective and shared multi-scalar understandings of oneself as a tenant and as part of a collective of tenants, a multi-dimensional process characterized by social, political, material, and spatial dimensions in its formation. It is the process of how tenants become active subjects in a complex of power relations that stands at the fore here (Häkli & Kallio 2013, 2018), acknowledging 'that subjectivity is at once deeply personal and fundamentally social, and that political subjectivities emerge through relational dynamics and exceed determination by power structures' (Häkli & Kallio 2018: 58).

Tenants' political subjectivity forms intersubjectively in the interaction with other subjects and through collective action, with the tenants positioning themselves within a system of power and acting upon that position by contesting, altering, or accepting it. This political subjectivity is forming in the defense of a space, the home, carrying many different meanings ranging from financial, practical, emotional, psychological, and social to cultural meanings (Fox O'Mahony 2007). Since home and homemaking acquire so many different meanings, the formation of subjectivity around the issue of home is complex and multi-scalar and ranges from the very personal experience of the dwelling, a home situated in space, through the neighborhood and neighbors with the understanding of oneself as a tenant and part of the collective of tenants to the positioning of oneself in society in political terms.

This chapter stresses that the process of political subjectivity formation in relation to the home is multi-layered and multi-dimensional, encompassing social/collective, political, material, and spatial dimensions that are intimately interconnected. It emerges from the personal experience through the collective and relational dynamic to the political, where power structures are identified and politicized.

## THE SOCIAL, POLITICAL, MATERIAL, AND SPATIAL DIMENSION OF POLITICAL BECOMING

**Social Dimension**

When tenants recalled how they were initially engaged in the issue of renovation, the social dimension was crucial. They would recall that after receiving information about the renovation, the topic of renovation was frequently discussed among neighbors previously known and unknown. The topic dominated interaction with neighbors while walking the stairs, taking the elevator, or walking the dog. Most of the interviewed tenants were concerned and worried about how the renovation would impact their neighbors. Often the perceived immorality of forced relocation, where the housing company or different representatives of the state were held responsible for displacement, was discussed when tenants realized that some of their neighbors needed to move. One of the tenants asked rhetorically: 'Where are you pushing all these people? You take all low-income earners to an area again, where parents do not have time with their children. How many of them are single parents? What will happen to those children when they are bored?' (1, 2019, man, private rental).

Interaction and socialization with other tenants played an important role in the formation of the political subjectivity of tenants and solidarity with neighbors: 'As political agents we exist intersubjectively, share our experiences intuitively or deliberately, enact and debate norms and moralities collectively, and articulate our concerns in socially meaningful ways' (Häkli & Kallio 2018: 64). Some tenants created contacts and shared experiences outside of their immediate environment, with other tenants in the same city or in other cities, thus placing their shared experience in relation to each other. One of the tenants recalled that a group of tenants from another city visited them to share their experiences and the groups of tenants, despite their disparate backgrounds, started to act collectively and formed a 'we':

> We were a very diverse group. What did we do? First, we handed out information to all the stairwells that you did not have to sign the approval [of the renovation] and then there were many who had already signed on, I think. And then we got help from the Tenants' Union and at the first meeting they came, *Everyone should be able to stay*, who have been involved in Gothenburg, at Pennygången. So, then we received information: First, the tenants who were present and, then, we disseminated the information in the stairwells. And then we organized a demonstration. (2, 2019, woman, private rental)

When recalling how they were informed about the planned renovation, tenants talked about strong emotional reactions to the plans and, interestingly, about intensified contacts between neighbors that followed. One described the meeting with their neighbors in the following way: 'Yes, we have to do something, I was very excited and thought it was fun that neighbors also felt the same way' (3, 2019, man, private rental). The individual reaction that information about the renovation set off was altered when tenants met their neighbors and talked about the issue. In their description of the process the feeling of loneliness was transformed into a sense of collective loneliness and solidarity, realizing that the threat of being displaced was shared among neighbors. The realization often transformed into political agency. One of the tenants said:

> It felt like this: 'Are we crazy? Are we the only ones protesting? Why do not more people care about this? Why can people not understand the difference between getting a rent increase of a couple of hundred bucks and getting new strains and getting a... real environmental technology experiment from the EU?' People did not seem to see that there was any difference between the two things. And it felt very, very... You felt very alone in it. (4, 2019, woman, public rental)

It was by relating to others that solidarity with those in the same situation or those yet unaware that was built, that tenants' subjectivity was formed. The relational dynamic included above all neighbors who shared the same concern, but also other tenants who were facing extensive renovations elsewhere. Tenants' subordinate position was contrasted to the responsible housing company, local politicians, and sometimes even to the Tenants' Union, who were perceived as powerful and influential but unaware of the economic situation of tenants. The social dimension in this process carried a clear aspect of solidarity with others in the situation where homes and neighborhoods were threatened by displacement: material and immaterial. One tenant analyzed the situation from the point of view of incomes in the area:

> They [the housing company] know our median income is 14,000 SEK, they know we cannot pay it. It's just to kick us out. I will be able to afford it. I will get a job when I get well, I am a [profession] and will earn well, but my neighbors do not. The pensioners who live here do not or... you know, a mother and her child who live alone, they will not be able to live... yes, they will be able to live, but they will live like... request money from the state and end up in a financial situation that is totally useless and so on, and it eats away at the psyche. (1, 2019, man, private rental)

The solidarity with neighbors in a strained financial situation was often expressed by those who could afford the new rent and they expressed concern about how future housing costs would impact their closest neighbors and the neighborhood, mentioning a possible change in the social composition and existing social ties in the area. Those involved in collective organizations protesting renovation witnessed that the collective action with their neighbors, caused by the threat of steep rent increases, strengthened their place attachment, neighborhood ties, and local identity. One tenant summarized it in the following way: 'You know your neighbors a little more. In any case, they have been talked to' (2, 2019, woman, private rental). It was not uncommon that tenants expressed frustration that all the strong ties they created together with their neighbors in the process of protesting the renovation soon would be destroyed when renovation forced them to move, some temporarily (evacuated during the renovation) and some permanently. Others, organized for longer periods of time, argued that the networks and the sense of community built in resistance to renovations and municipal plans were recurrently used to widen the engagement in the area and engage intergenerationally and in other protests against issues threatening the local community:

> And we got to know each other and built trust locally, and so, for each other. A kind of local community. And those contacts and those networks were the precondition for us to be able to mobilize in the way we did, against closures and such. (5, 2019, man, owner-occupied)

Mobilization that started as a protest against extensive renovation and rent increases of around 70 percent transformed over time and with initial successes and was activated with new threats to the local community (like closures of public facilities, privatization, neglect of maintenance, and so on) (see for instance Figure 26.1 showing a demonstration against privatization of rental housing in Stockholm in 2019). Across the country, tenants' mobilizations have broadened their focus over time and grassroots tenants' groups have built coalitions and networks spinning between different Swedish cities. Along with resistance to extensive renovations resulting in steep rent increases, Swedish tenants have in the last decade engaged in protesting against conversions of public housing, privatization of public property, poor maintenance/ disinvestment in rental housing, and most recently proposals to introduce market rents in new construction and rent increases through the reorganization of the model for rent setting (Gustafsson et al. 2019, Listerborn et al. 2020, Polanska & Richard 2021). An important role in gathering housing activists across the country has been the annual conference of *Bostadsvrålet* (The Housing Roar) held since 2014. Tenants have been involved in re-responsibilizing housing companies and municipal governments and this has been done through collective action (Thörn & Polanska 2023), a development closely related to the political dimension of tenants' subjectivity formation.

*Source:* Dominika V. Polanska.

*Figure 26.1   Demonstration against the privatization of rental housing, Stockholm (2019)*

**Political Dimension**

The social dimension of subjectivity formation is difficult to separate from the political dimension. The political dimension in tenants' formation as political subjects was articulated when they realized that their individual situation was not unique but inscribed in a larger system of power relations and housing inequality and policy favoring ownership. The political is an investigation of the workings of power and a search for alternatives to the current situation.

One of the tenants described the position of tenants in relation to the legislation and practice in the rent tribunals where the landlords tend to win the approval to renovate (Bengtsson & Bohman 2020, Polanska 2023):

> We have no power. Even if we want information or we say 'no', if we want to go to the rent tribunal, 3 out of a 100 wins against the landlord in the rent tribunal, with the current laws. 'Have you raised the use value of the property? Is it a little too expensive for the tenant? Let them move'. So that's how it looks. (6, 2019, woman, public housing)

The hopelessness of the situation was placed in a context of power relations and thus exceeded 'determination by power structures' (Häkli & Kallio 2018: 58) by proposing alternatives and imagining a different future. The future orientation was central in the politicization of the situation and the political agency that tenants expressed. It could take various forms, and as Polanska and Richard (2019) have emphasized, was not necessarily always collective or explicitly active and could thus take the form of an act of passivity or what the authors called 'disengagement politics'.

The political subjectivity of tenants was formed in a process that was informed by knowledge on the prevailing housing policy, the practice of rent tribunals, housing inequalities, tenure inequalities, and the politics of un-homing. That knowledge was gained primarily through social interaction (gossip) with other concerned tenants and through reading, investigating on the Internet, contacting experts (engineers, architects, and researchers), and understanding the situation in relation to urban and housing policies and the current housing situation. The configurations of power in housing and the position of tenants were central to this understanding. The personal troubles that according to the neoliberal logic are ascribed to individual shortcomings became, in the sociologist C. Wright Mills' (1959) words, public issues that were politicized and related to structural issues in society. It was evident that the defense of homes set off a negotiation of tenants' place and position in society that could be analyzed in line with Müller's (2021: 1030) understanding of how the intimate and private sphere of the home 'can shape the ways citizens negotiate their place in urban politics'. Studying tenants' mobilization in reaction to an extensive renovation in an area in Gothenburg, Thörn (2020) demonstrated that the threat of losing one's home mobilized tenants to act collectively and to analyze their individual situation from a structural and societal point of view, politicizing the issue of housing and pointing to flaws in current housing policy affecting tenants.

The political dimension became more explicit when tenants acted together. A group of tenants presented a housing policy program that the tenants' collective was involved in creating, raising issues that they could identify locally and proposing law amendments, changes in the tax policy, and other ways to strengthen the rights of tenants in the future. The future and the past as time dimensions played an important role in the politicization of the situation. For instance, the issue of a maintenance debt was raised, where tenants would argue that the housing company was responsible for covering the cost of the modernization due to a debt caused by negligence in maintenance in the past. The issue was framed by one of the tenants: 'First of all, we have paid rent for lots of years, where that rent should include that you take care of the maintenance of this house. We should not have to have rent increases like this' (3, 2019, man, private rental). Likewise, the future was important in imagining alternatives and improvements to the current situation of tenants.

In the politicization of the home and the formation of tenants' subjectivity the role and responsibility of the established Tenants' Union were recurrently questioned by tenants.

Several of the interviewed tenants mobilized outside or parallel to the Tenants' Union, criticizing it for not being able to act upon the situation they and their neighbors were in. One said: 'They do not have much power, they have... they know the rules, they know the laws, but it is we who live there who have to do things, totally unexpected' (1, 2019, man, private rental).

They felt surprised that the organization, despite its large size and position, could do little to affect their situation, and sometimes they blamed the Union for not doing enough to stop the rent increases that followed renovations. The lack of power and support from the Union was surprising to the tenants, who then argued that grassroots organizing could push the issue forward. Thörn and Polanska (2023) argued that the role of the Tenants' Union is ambivalent, as the Union is both involved in negotiating the rent after renovation and in protecting the tenants against steep rent increases. Listerborn et al. (2020: 126) described the Tenants' Union as being 'perceived as part of the establishment' by the housing activists due to its institutionalization and professionalization. Grassroots organizations formed by tenants in protest to the risk of renoviction and other pressing issues have been, however, forcing the Union to redefine its priorities lately (Listerborn et al. 2020: 127) and political subjectivities formed in this process have played a central role.

Moreover, the structural critique and the politicization of the home and the issue of renovations contributed to the removal of individual blame and shame in a situation where the tenants lacked control over their homes. By politicizing the issue, tenants, at least discursively, regained control in a situation where their homes belonged to someone else. The realization that ownership determines the right to decide upon a renovation was shocking and has been captured in previous research conducted by Ekström in the 1990s: 'The place where one had created one's home was someone else's, a landlord's with whose ownership went the right of determination. What previously had been taken for granted was now gone' (Ekström 1994: 382). In politicizing this, tenants could question the rights of owners and in the process pinpoint the absurdity of the Swedish term for 'tenants', which is '*hyresgäster*', translating to 'rental guests', and their position as 'guests' in their homes. Tenants raised the issue of the rights of owners as unquestioned in society and frequently referred to the usual practice in the rent tribunals when discussing the power asymmetry between tenants and landlords.

**The Material and Spatial Dimensions**

The material dimension and spatial dimension in the formation of political subjectivity revolved around the home as a material reality in need of protection and its multiple spatial scales stretching from the dwelling to the neighborhood, the local district, and the city, depending on the situation and how agency was understood based on the subjective and shared multi-scalar understanding of oneself as a tenant and part of a tenants' collective. Home was described as a dwelling, situated in space and embedded in social relations that transgressed the boundaries of the dwelling and privately owned material property within the dwelling (Polanska & Richard 2019, 2021). The materiality of this process was also expressed in the material practices of homemaking that became the site of negotiation and politicization, when the personal and private become public and political.

When tenants politicized home, not only did this politicization include their dwellings but also the notion of a neighborhood and the local community that was under threat and defined as parts of the home. The home was defined in spatial and social terms as a space and as a family, a notion that was extended to the people living in the same area: 'They are welcome to build as many condominiums as they like, but you should not touch my home. Just like that. The people here are very familiar, so: Do not touch my family, do not touch my house. Do not touch my people' (7, 2019, woman, owner-occupied).

In a district that has recurrently, over a period of two decades, been the subject of government-led urban renewal programs, including renovations, the local place-based identity among the residents grew strong. Mobilization was described as a reaction of the local community to the external threats repeatedly directed to the district (Deckard & Auyero 2022). One of the tenants described the transformation of the local associational life into more grassroots organizing during the period, engaging new subjects:

> There has always been a lively local community here in [district] throughout history. In the first years, it was mostly these ordinary associations. Yes, a lot of strong local associations. The political… Social Democrats were strong here and PRO [National Organization for Pensioners] was also here. But during this more turbulent period [referring to the period when the urban renewal plan was introduced] and when we, where this organization from below got started, it was in response to [the name of the urban renewal plan]. (8, 2019, man, public rental)

The threats of un-homing created a stronger sense of home and community in this district and extended the networks, so tenants were ready to defend it collectively. The spatially based collective identity of tenants was in the above case built during a long period of time in reaction to repeated state violence directed against homes, the local community, and the neighborhood. Networks of tenants and previous experiences of acting together and sharing a common vision were decisive when repeatedly meeting threats and calling upon the notion of tenants as political subjects. The presence of physical spaces where tenants could meet in the residential area was raised by tenants as crucial for their mobilization. These spaces were often mentioned when tenants talked about their engagement, their community, and its development. They served as spaces for reimagining the future of the local community and for healing (Pain 2019). I subscribe to Baca's (2017: 1127) argument that the spatial and social dimensions are interwoven in the formation of political subjectivity in 'how counter-hegemonic spaces of alterity transform socio-spatial power arrangements by democratizing and legitimizing, in and through space, the voice of hitherto invisible political actors'. The centrality of these spaces cannot be undermined when studying political subjectivity formation.

## CONCLUSIONS

Displacement and neoliberal urbanism are posing serious threats to peoples' homes and a large body of research discussed here has been focused on the processes of un-homing and the destruction of homes across the Global North (Atkinson 2015, Davidson 2009, Elliott-Cooper et al. 2020, Marcuse 1986, Porteous & Smith 2001). Those who do not own their homes are particularly precarious and exposed to the violence of displacement when financialization of housing goes hand in hand with privatization and the dismantling of public housing policies and public funding (Rolnik 2019: 19).

The body of literature devoted to displacement tends to unanimously focus on the destructive side of displacement, on its harmful effects on individuals, local communities, and cities. The objective of this chapter was not to underestimate the destructive power of displacement but to stress its potential in rebuilding and uniting communities of residents involved in collective action resisting this process. It has been argued in this chapter that the experience of the threat of being displaced among the tenants studied here was accompanied by the strengthening of the social and collective dimension of tenants' subjectivity, a process pivotal for the politicization of home and the political becoming of tenants. In other words, the threat of tenants losing their homes called on social, spatial, and material dimensions of the experience and was transformed into solidarity and politicization of individual situations.

The conclusions of this work are somewhat paradoxical, contributing to demonstrating the many complexities of the formation of subjectivity. At the same time that tenants facing renovation are experiencing the trauma of slow violence, the rupture in routines and the destruction of home and social networks, they are also involved, especially when interacting with their neighbors, in the re-creation and politicization of the home and the revival of the social and spatial relations in which the home is embedded. The politicization of home encompasses collective identification of personal problems that are politicized, residents becoming political subjects as tenants and their actions turning into political agency. Additionally, the politicization of the issue removes individual blame and shame and strengthens the individuals' claims to the right to their homes. Finally, it questions the primacy of ownership in a society that favors homeownership and where rental housing conditions are increasingly becoming more precarious.

## REFERENCES

Aalbers, M. (2008) The financialization of home and the mortgage market crisis. *Competition & Change* 12(2): 148–166.
Aalbers, M. (2017) *The Financialization of Housing*. London: Routledge.
Atkinson, R. (2015) Losing one's place. Narratives of neighbourhood change, market injustice and symbolic displacement. *Housing, Theory and Society* 32(4): 373–388.
Baca, B. (2017) The student's two bodies: Civic engagement and political becoming in the post-socialist space. *Antipode* 49(5): 1125–1144.
Baeten, G., L.D. Berg & A. Lund Hansen (2015) Introduction: Neoliberalism and post-welfare Nordic states in transition. *Geografiska Annaler: Series B, Human Geography* 97(3): 209–212.
Baeten, G., S. Westin, E. Pull & I. Molina (2017) Pressure and violence. Housing renovation and displacement in Sweden. *Environment and Planning A* 49(3): 631–651.
Bengtsson, B. & H. Bohman. (2020) Tenant voice – As strong as it gets. Exit, voice and loyalty in housing renovation. *Housing, Theory, and Society* 38(3): 365–380.
Bergenstråle, S. & P. Palmstierna (2016) *Var tredje kan tvingas flytta – En rapport om effekterna av hyreshöjningar i samband med standardhöjande åtgärder i Göteborg* [Every third person may be forced to move – A report on the effects of rent increases in connection with standard-raising measures in Gothenburg]. Hyresgästföreningen, Göteborg.
Blackman, L., J. Cromby, D. Hook, D. Papadopoulos & V. Walkerdine (2008) Creating subjectivities. *Subjectivity* 22(1): 1–27.
Boverket (2014) *Flyttmönster till följd av omfattande renoveringar* [Moving pattern due to extensive renovations].
Brickell, K., M.F. Arrigoitia & A. Vasudevan (2017) Geographies of forced eviction: Dispossession, violence, resistance. In Brickell, K., M.F. Arrigoitia & A. Vasudevan (eds.) *Geographies of Forced Eviction*. London: Palgrave Macmillan, 1–23.
Christophers, B. (2013) A monstrous hybrid: The political economy of housing in early twenty-first century Sweden. *New Political Economy* 18(6): 885–911.
Christophers, B. (2021) A tale of two inequalities: Housing-wealth inequality and tenure inequality. *Economy and Space* 53(3): 573–594.

Davidson, M. (2009) Displacement, space and dwelling. Placing gentrification debate. *Ethics, Place and Environment* 12 (2): 219–234.
Deckard, F.M. & J. Auyero (2022) Poor people's survival strategies: Two decades of research in the Americas. *Annual Review of Sociology* 48(1): 373–395.
Easton S., L. Lees, P. Hubbard et al. (2020) Measuring and mapping displacement: The problem of quantification in the battle against gentrification. *Urban Studies* 57(2): 286–306.
Ekström, M. (1994) Elderly people's experiences of housing renewal and forced relocation. Social theories and contextual analysis in explanations of emotional experiences. *Housing Studies* 9(3): 369–391.
Elliott-Cooper, P. Hubbard & L. Lees (2020) Moving beyond Marcuse: Gentrification, displacement and the violence of un-homing. *Progress in Human Geography* 44(3): 492–509.
Flesher Fominaya, C. (2010) Collective identity in social movements: Central concepts and debates. *Sociology Compass* 4: 393–404.
Freeman, L. (2005) Displacement or succession? Residential mobility in gentrifying neighborhoods. *Urban Affairs Review* 40 (4): 463–491.
Fried, M. (1966) Grieving for a lost home. In J. Wilson (ed.) *Urban Renewal: The Record and the Controversy*. Cambridge: MIT Press, 229–248.
Fox O'Mahony, L. (2007) *Conceptualising Home: Theories, Laws and Policies*. Oxford: Hart Publishing.
Fox O'Mahony, L. & J.A. Sweeney (2016) *The Idea of Home in Law: Displacement and Dispossession*. London and New York: Routledge.
Fuller, G. (2021) The financialization of rented homes: Continuity and change in housing financialization. *Review of Evolutionary Political Economy* 2(3): 551–570.
Fullilove, M.T. (2005) *Root Shock: How Tearing Up City Neighborhoods Hurts America, and What We Can Do About It*. New York: One World.
Grander, M. (2017) New public housing: A selective model disguised as universal? Implications of the market adaptation of Swedish public housing. *International Journal of Housing Policy* 17(3): 335–352.
Grander, M. (2018) *For the Benefit of Everyone? Explaining the Significance of Swedish Public Housing for Urban Housing Inequality*. Malmö: Malmö University.
Grundström, K. & I. Molina (2016) From Folkhem to lifestyle housing in Sweden: Segregation and urban form, 1930s–2010s. *International Journal of Housing Policy* 16(3): 316–336.
Gustafsson, J. (2021) Renovations as an investment strategy: Circumscribing the right to housing in Sweden. *Housing Studies*. doi: 10.1080/02673037.2021.1982872.
Gustafsson, J. (2022) *The State of Tenancy. Rental Housing and Municipal Statecraft in Malmö, Sweden*. Stockholm: Stockholm University.
Gustafsson, J., E. Hellström, Å. Richard & S. Springfeldt, (2019) The right to stay put: Resistance and organizing in the wake of changing housing policies in Sweden. *Radical Housing Journal* 1(2): 191–200.
Häkli, J. & K.P. Kallio (2013) Subject, action and polis: Theorizing political agency. *Progress in Human Geography* 38(2): 181–200.
Häkli, J. & K.P. Kallio (2018) On becoming political: The political in subjectivity. *Subjectivity* 11: 57–73.
Harvey, D. (2003) *The New Imperialism*. Oxford and New York: Oxford University.
Harvey, D. (2006) *Spaces of Global Capitalism*. London: Verso.
Hayward, G. (1975) Home as an environmental and psychological concept. *Landscape* 20(26): 2–9.
Hedin, K., E. Clark, E. Lundholm & G. Malmberg (2012) Neoliberalization of housing in Sweden: Gentrification, filtering, and social polarization. *Annals of the Association of American Geographers* 102(2): 443–463.
Hunt, S. & R. Benford (2004) Collective identity, solidarity, and commitment. In Snow, D., S. Soule & H. Kriesi (eds.) *The Blackwell Companion to Social Movements*. Oxford: Blackwell, 466–457.
Industrifakta (2011) Behov och prioriteringar i rekordårens flerbostadshus. En intervjubaserad lägesanalys av åtgärdsbehov och väntad utveckling 2011 2015 [Needs and priorities in the apartment buildings of the record year. An interview-based situation analysis of the need for action and expected development 2011–2015].
Jacobsson K. (ed.) (2015) *Urban Grassroots Movements in Central and Eastern Europe*. Farnham: Ashgate.

Jasper, J. (1997) *The Art of Moral Protest*. Chicago: University of Chicago Press.
Lawrence, R. (1995) Deciphering home: An integrative historical perspective. In Benjamin, D. & D. Stea (eds.) *The Home: Words, Interpretations, Meanings and Environments*. Avebury: Aldershot.
Lees, L. (2000) A reappraisal of gentrification. Towards a 'geography of gentrification'. *Progress in Human Geography* 24(3): 389–408.
Lees, L., H. Bang Shin & E. López Morales (2016) *Planetary Gentrification*. Cambridge: Polity Press.
Lefebvre, H. (1991 [1974]) *The Production of Space*. Oxford: Blackwell.
Lind, H., K. Annadotter, F. Björk, L. Högberg & T. Af Klintberg (2016) Sustainable renovation strategy in the Swedish Million Homes Programme: A case study. *Sustainability* 8(4): 1–12.
Listerborn, C, I. Molina & Å. Richard (2020) Claiming the right to dignity: New organizations for housing justice in neoliberal Sweden. *Radical Housing Journal* 2(1): 119–137.
Madden, D. & P. Marcuse (2016) *In Defense of Housing*. London: Verso.
Mallett, S. (2004) Understanding home: A critical review of the literature. *Sociological Review* 52: 62–89.
Marcuse, P. (1986) Gentrification, abandonment, and displacement: Connections, causes, and policy responses in New York City. *Washington University Journal of Urban and Contemporary Law* 28: 195–248.
Melucci, A. (1995) The process of collective identity. In Johnston, H. & B. Klandermans (eds.) *Social Movements and Culture*. Minneapolis: University of Minnesota Press, 41–63.
Miller, D. (2001) *Home Possessions: Material Culture Behind Closed Doors*. Oxford and New York: Berg.
Mills, C. Wright (1959) *The Sociological Imagination*. Oxford: Oxford University Press.
Müller, F. (2021) Home matters: The material culture of urban security. *International Journal of Urban and Regional Research*. doi: 10.1111/1468-2427.12879.
Oliver-Smith, A. (2010) *Defying Displacement*. Austin: Texas Press.
Pain, R. (2019) Chronic urban trauma: The slow violence of housing dispossession. *Urban Studies* 56(2): 385–400.
Polanska, D.V. (2017) Marginalizing discourses and activists' strategies in collective identity formation: The case of Polish tenants' movement. In Jacobsson, K. & E. Korolczuk (eds.) *Civil Society Revisited: Lessons from Poland*. New York: Berghahn Books, 176–199.
Polanska, D.V. (2023) Legal geographies of displacement through renovation: Legal interpretative practices in Sweden. *Antipode* 55(6): 1877–1897.
Polanska, D.V. & Å. Richard (2019) Narratives of a fractured trust in the Swedish model: Tenants' emotions of renovation. *Culture Unbound* 11(1): 141–164.
Polanska, D. V. & Å. Richard (2021) Resisting renovictions: Tenants organizing against housing companies' renewal practices in Sweden. *Radical Housing Journal* 3(1): 187–205.
Porteous, J. D. & S. E. Smith (2001) *Domicide: The Global Destruction of Home*. Montréal: MQUP.
Pull, E. (2020) The original sin – On displacement through renoviction in Sweden. PhD dissertation, Roskilde University.
Pull, E. & Å. Richard (2019) Domicide: Displacement and dispossessions in Uppsala, Sweden. *Social and Cultural Geography* 22(4): 545–564.
Ramiller, A. (2022) Displacement through development? Property turnover and eviction risk in Seattle. *Urban Studies* 59(6): 1148–1166.
Rannila, P. (2021) Housing violence in the post-welfare context, *Housing, Theory and Society*. doi: 10.1080/14036096.2021.1925340.
Rolnik, R. (2019) *Urban Warfare: Housing under the Empire of Finance*. London: Verso.
SCB (2019) Boende i Sverige [Housing in Sweden]. Available at: https://www.scb.se/hitta-statistik/sverige-i-siffror/manniskorna-i-sverige/boende-i-sverige/ (accessed 10 July 2022).
SCB (2022) Nästan 5,1 miljoner bostäder i landet [Almost 5.1 million homes in the country]. Available at: https://www.scb.se/hitta-statistik/statistik-efter-amne/boende-byggande-och-bebyggelse/bostadsbyggande-och-ombyggnad/bostadsbestand/pong/statistiknyhet/bostadsbestandet-31-december-2021/ (accessed 10 December 2022).
Slater, T. (2006) The eviction of critical perspectives from gentrification research. *International Journal of Urban and Regional Research* 30(4): 737–757.

Stenberg, J. (2018) Dilemmas associated with tenant participation in renovation of housing in marginalized areas may lead to system change. *Cogent Social Sciences* 4(1): 1528710.

Swedish Government Offices (2019) Sveriges tredje nationella strategi för energieffektiviserande renovering. Available at: https://www.regeringen.se/495d4b/contentassets/b6499271ac374526b9aa6f5e944b0472/sveriges-tredje-nationella-strategi-for-energieffektiviserande-renovering.pdf (accessed 2 July 2021).

Swedish Riksdag (2020) Riksrevisionens rapport om stöd till renovering och energieffektivisering. Available at: https://www.riksdagen.se/sv/dokument-lagar/dokument/skrivelse/riksrevisionens-rapport-om-stod-till-renovering_H70371 (accessed 2 July 2021).

Thörn, C. (2020) 'We're not moving': Solidarity and collective housing struggle in a changing Sweden. In Krase, J. & J. DeSena (eds.) *Gentrification around the World, Volume I.* Cham: Palgrave Macmillan, 175–195.

Thörn, H. & D.V. Polanska (2023) Responsibilizing renovation: Governing strategies and resistance in the context of the transformation of Swedish housing policy. *City* 27(1–2): 209–231.

Trä och Möbelföretagen (2019) Renoveringsbehov i Miljonprogrammet [The need of renovation in the Million Program]. https://www.mynewsdesk.com/se/tra-_och_mobelforetagen/documents/renoveringsbehov-i-miljonprogrammet-2019-90882 (accessed 10 September 2022).

TV4 (2016) Nya chockhyror oroar [New shocking rents cause concern]. https://www.tv4.se/klipp/va/3282854/nya-chockhyrororoar (accessed 8 September 2022).

Westerdahl, S. (2021) *Det självspelande pianot. Kalkylerna och kapitalet som skapar Sveriges bostadskris* [The self-playing piano. The calculations and capital that create Sweden's housing crisis]. Stockholm: Dokument Press.

Westin S. (2011) '*…men vart ska ni då ta vägen?' Ombyggnation ur hyresgästernas perspektiv* ['…but where are you going to go then?' Renovation from the tenants' perspective]. Uppsala: Uppsala University.

# 27. Migrants, markets, movements: immigrants and housing as commodity and right in Madrid

*Sophie Gonick*

In Madrid in the mid-2000s, Maria Eugenia wanted to buy an apartment. An immigrant from Ecuador, she saw others in her milieu purchasing homes in the city's explosive real estate market. She pooled together her savings, a mortgage, and a personal loan in order to buy a modest apartment at the very edge of the city. She found herself far from friends and the amenities she had enjoyed when she lived in San Blas, a neighborhood with a burgeoning South American population. When the financial crisis began in 2008, she also found she could not make her monthly mortgage payment. Isolated from her community, mired in debt, Maria Eugenia felt alienated and adrift in her adopted city. She soon faced foreclosure and subsequent eviction.

When I met Maria Eugenia, however, she was leading a workshop training other people struggling to keep their homes—both immigrants and native Spaniards—to address and contest their mortgage problems. In the cool basement of a community center in a working-class neighborhood of the capital city, she carefully led participants through the various steps they could take to stave off foreclosure. Part of the Plataforma de Afectados por la Hipoteca (PAH—Platform for People Affected by Mortgages), she had first sought out their help to avoid eviction and cancel her enormous housing debt.[1] The collective, however, insists on a model of solidarity against welfarism. Without work, Maria Eugenia quickly became more active in the PAH, establishing both authority over her mortgage problem and blossoming friendships with other activists.

Maria Eugenia's experience, alongside numerous others, prompts me to ask how working-class migrants navigate homeownership societies. Her story offers a window into the role of homeownership in shaping immigrant urban worlds. In this intervention, I examine the relation between migrant populations and housing markets using the case of Madrid. Rather than capture a snapshot in time, I look instead across a key period, namely the Spanish boom and subsequent bust (2002–2013), to draw out how propertied housing markets shape immigrant urban worlds, modes of integration, and forms of contestation.

In this chapter, I argue that homeownership—and the hegemony of private property more generally—profoundly affects how immigrants experience the city. Its influence derives not only from its capacity to exclude; rather, *inclusion* into the homeownership regime also produces inequalities and forms of dispossession. In a moment of increased precarity and rising living costs, however, it also provides new avenues for contestation, novel claim-making, and empowerment. As such, property regimes create competing pathways of incorporation into the city. In the case of Madrid, at distinct moments homeownership provided modes of participation: during the boom, it was a means of participating in an effervescent economy, albeit fleetingly, while in the crisis it provided a potent target for social movement resistance and empowerment against forms of exclusion. Methodologically, then, immigrant homeownership must be taken as a starting point for analysis rather than assumed to be the endpoint of settlement in the city. Further, as I demonstrate herein, ethnography is a key method of research that can illuminate fine-grained processes of settlement, incorporation, and the formation of dissent.

## THE MIGRATION–HOUSING NEXUS

In many cities throughout the globe, the primacy of private property markets on one hand and increased mobility and migration on the other have provoked profound transformation. Yet despite this reality, little qualitative work has attended to the intersection between housing and immigration as it shapes and is shaped by the city. In particular, critical attention has yet to be paid to the specificities of privately owned housing as it affects immigrant urban worlds. In this section, I consider why and how this empirical gap has developed.

### Housing, Homeownership, and Ethnography

We are currently in the midst of a global housing crisis, tied in large part to the dominance of property markets within the economy (Potts 2020, Rolnik 2019). How might sociology engage critically with these markets as they structure everyday urban life and experiences of housing? In a seminal piece, Mary Pattillo argues that housing has been relatively hidden within the sociological tradition, while related disciplines have been more attuned to its role in structuring urban worlds.[2] She writes:

> Sociologists are frequently more interested in the functioning of households inside of homes, the markets in which housing is bought and sold, the distribution of various social groups across collections of houses in neighborhoods, and the local, national, and supranational policy regimes that define responsibilities (or lack thereof) to provide housing. Sociologists are more likely to study housing as and in context than to study it as a commodity or a right. (Pattillo 2013)

Similarly, Atkinson and Jacobs write that it is 'surprising that the study of housing has not been a central focus in the social sciences' (Atkinson & Jacobs 2017:1–2). A 'new sociology of housing' (Martin 2017), however, has drawn out the ways in which housing systems are integral to the production of urban inequality. In particular, Matthew Desmond's *Evicted* and Eva Rosen's *The Voucher Promise* demonstrate the role of housing and its insecurities in keeping poor people mired in poverty (Desmond 2016, Rosen 2020). These texts also allow us to apprehend both the production of inequality and how it is lived and reproduced on a daily basis in discrete urban locales. Their ethnographic detail also demonstrates various bureaucratic mechanisms and government spaces, seemingly neutral and stolid, to be generative of unequal outcomes. Through interviews, observation, and immersion, these scholars show private rental housing to be intimately connected to myriad areas of life, conjoining aspiration, economic disadvantage, statecraft, and social reproduction. What flickers on the edge of these accounts, but which neither Desmond nor Rosen fully explore, is the hegemony of private property within contemporary urban systems of shelter.

We encounter property most frequently and explicitly within the guise of owner occupation, or homeownership. Sociology and related disciplines have articulated the paradoxes, demands, inequities, and promises of this habitational system. A small but robust line of sociological inquiry has examined its role in structuring the economy and producing capitalist subjects who must constantly toil to afford their homes (Bourdieu 2014), some of its myths and false promises (Kemeny 1981, McCabe 2016), and circulating ideologies that buttress this system of shelter (Ronald 2008). Through largely archival work, for example, McCabe analyzes how rhetoric around civic harmony and engagement animates homeownership even while its realities perpetuate exclusions and can preclude community. This strand of sociological inquiry, however, does not really attend to the relation between homeownership and the city per se. As such, we do not get a broader sense of the influence of private property upon urban space, its sociality, and its myriad inequities.

At the same time, historical work across the social sciences and humanities has demonstrated the integral role of property and ownership in producing the city and its registers of belonging and abjection. This line of inquiry has demonstrated homeownership to be fundamental in producing (sub)urbanism, thus influencing the look and feel of our everyday built environments (Boyer 1986, Jackson 1985, Sugrue 2014, Wright 2012). It has also attended to the registers of difference homeownership produces, reifying gender norms and racialized notions of worth (Hayden 1984, Taylor 2019). Rather than take this system of housing tenure as either neutral arbiter of good or engine of inequality, homeownership instead apportions rights and responsibilities while also furthering racialized inequity and producing class status (Connolly 2014). More than just a means by which we shelter ourselves, homeownership thus brings together an array of actors, implicates moral and juridical obligations, and produces both the city and its trajectories of incorporation. Yet homeownership rarely receives the same kind of ethnographic analysis that Desmond and Rosen, for example, bring to the private rental market. Nor does this critical strand of urban research attend to the particularities of the immigrant experience. How its inequities, promises, and exclusions are lived and perpetuated contemporarily, particularly among newly arrived populations, remains largely unexplored.

Pattillo outlines two competing paradigms for the study of housing, as both commodity and right. Ethnographic attention to homeownership can illuminate those paradigms and how they structure everyday life. Here I am concerned with how everyday urban denizens navigate a system that remains both highly differentiated and no less hegemonic culturally, socially, politically, and economically. Indeed, rather than relegate its vagrancies to the confines of history, homeownership has become ever more precarious. It is often extended on unequal terms to populations marginalized on the basis of race, class, age, gender, or migratory origin and status (García-Lamarca 2022, Taylor 2019, Wyly et al. 2012, Wyly & Ponder 2011). This reality is a global one, as homeownership and its attendant markets influence policy, lending practices, planning, and housing provision in a number of places across the world (Aalbers 2012, Ghertner 2015). Yet despite disjunctures in who and how homeownership includes, it is central to development programs, poverty alleviation schemes, and popular imaginaries of the good life (Kwak 2015, Manturuk et al. 2017, Ronald 2008, Soto 2000). It continues to be regarded as 'an important rite of passage through life' (Atkinson & Jacobs 2017:2). Thus, we can identify a gap between homeownership's inequalities and its animating fantasies. As I demonstrate in this chapter, that gap is a fruitful site for ethnographic inquiry that might illuminate competing propertied paradigms, in addition to providing a space of analysis to interrogate the production of dissent to the propertied order.

## Immigrants, Housing, and Homeownership

At the same time that our cities are shaped by propertied regimes of shelter, they are also sites of diversity brought about through migration (Barber 2017, Çaglar & Schiller 2018, Castañeda 2018, Sandoval-Strausz 2019). How might we understand immigrants within this panorama of housing, home, and property? The idea of homeownership as rite of passage, as a stolid system promoting incorporation, remains dominant in sociological examinations of immigration. Here homeownership is often the endpoint of an immigrant's settlement, a fruitful conclusion to a difficult and lengthy process of dislocation, migration, and incorporation (Alba & Logan 1992, Clark 2003, Kauppinen et al. 2015, Kurz 2004, McConnell & Marcelli 2007). It suggests permanence, stability, and successful entry into the mainstream against forms of economic marginalization, racialization and discrimination (Telles & Ortiz 2008). Here it offers proof of integration—economic, social, cultural, and political. Homeownership is thus a normative goal rather than a complex system of social relations that produces both value and disadvantage. In this analytic, becoming a homeowner means one has both gained full access and can thus reap its rewards, including the accrual of equity and the guise of permanence. Here, emphasis, while subtle, is on housing as a commodity that becomes more valuable over time, and participation within civic life is often predicated on defending the monetary value of one's home (McCabe 2016). Yet, as I demonstrate later, homeownership as a tool of economic incorporation only works at certain moments with certain conditions. Its precarity and loss can lead to novel political openings that paradoxically provide other avenues for empowerment. Indeed, that observation dovetails with an emergent strand of scholarship looking to migrant participation within housing movements. Analysis has revealed how housing struggles are novel arenas for cooperation and exchange against the vagrancies of the market (Martínez 2017, Montagna & Grazioli 2019, Mudu & Chattopadhyay 2017, Suárez 2017). If homeownership is thought to empower economic independence and political action based on one's identification as a homeowner, here I demonstrate that housing struggles evince a different horizon of possibility and a politics of empowerment independent from the market.

The disjuncture between homeownership as a complex system of social relations and as normative goal plays out within immigrant urban worlds. Ideas of permanence, inclusion and incorporation, and financial reward lubricate immigrants' entry into homeownership, even while it is then experienced on differential terms (Gonick 2021). Yet critical urban sociology has not been very attuned to the political economy and/or materiality of housing as it relates to, produces, and confines the immigrant experience of the city (Baiocchi 2023, Gonick 2021). The discipline has been acutely concerned with immigration and its effects on demography, integration, and inclusion (Bloemraad 2006, Castañeda 2018, Sassen 1999).[3] Seminal work on urban immigration, however, has privileged dynamics of segregation and inequality rather than the material conditions, everyday experiences, and sociality of migrants as they navigate unequal housing systems (Portes & Shafer 2007, Portes & Stepick 1993). Meso-level analyses offer great insight into patterns of disadvantage and opportunity across neighborhoods and urban landscapes. However, they rarely delve into the specific demands of housing, the financial stress it might provoke, and the daily experiences of shelter. In this chapter, therefore, I take homeownership as a starting point from which to analyze immigrant lifeworlds rather than as an end in itself. Attending to homeownership through ethnographic analysis allows me to draw out how it is lived, often with unequal outcomes. Fine-grained attention to its daily dynamics and demands can illuminate homeownership's multiple meanings and outcomes in ways other methods of inquiry cannot. I provide a means to trace the production of aspiration, inequality, and subsequent contestation and empowerment. Immigrant homeownership thus becomes a site of urban dreams, disadvantage, and dissent.

## THE SPANISH DREAM

Spain provides a unique case in which to examine the relation between immigrants and housing, particularly in the form of homeownership. Owner occupation is the overwhelming norm across Spanish housing landscapes, peaking at over 80% during the boom. Generations of policy under the Franco dictatorship (1939–1975) and subsequent democratic era (1975–) have privileged homeownership (Gonick 2021). As a result, the rental market has until recently been small, poorly regulated, and seen as an option of last resort.

While the country has long been defined by its culture of homeownership, it has only much more recently become one of immigrant arrival and settlement (Agrela 2002, Bruquetas-Callejo 2008, Calavita 2005). Over the course of the boom, the foreign-born population exploded from under a million people in 1998 to almost 6 million ten years later. Immigrants arrived in a place experiencing multiple transformations. Entry into the European Union, changing banking laws and an influx of foreign capital, and the liberalization of land use meant that Spain was building at a frantic speed and scope (López & Rodríguez 2011). Madrid was the crucible for many of these changes, starting in the Franco era with efforts to concentrate power and urbanization in the capital. Many years later, it would also be home to a burgeoning Ecuadorian population, as almost half a million people had left behind the 1998 financial crisis and subsequent structural adjustment in search of better opportunity in the former metropole. Easy access to credit meant many immigrants, only a few years after arrival, could purchase housing and take part in the 'Spanish dream' of homeownership. This was nowhere more true than amongst the South American community where close-knit ties, cultural associations, and the proliferation of financial institutions aimed at and staffed by immigrants spread mortgage debt easily.

Yet for many immigrants, homeownership was short-lived. The onset of the Great Financial Crisis in 2008 caused interest rates on mortgages to rise and employment to fall. Many immigrants found they were soon out of work. If they owned homes, foreclosure and subsequent eviction followed shortly behind. This intense period of boom, bust, and urban and demographic transformation thus offers a key window to examine the relation between homeownership and immigration. Following immigrants into subsequent housing mobilizations, moreover, allows me to demonstrate how social movements provide forms of belonging that homeownership cannot.

**Methods**

This chapter draws upon extensive archival and ethnographic work in Madrid. From late 2012 to early 2014, I worked with the PAH and related housing mobilizations in the city. Drawn to the PAH because of the outsized presence of immigrants, I was particularly attuned to emergent solidarities within the Spanish struggle over shelter. In a moment of financial crisis and subsequent popular outrage, the housing movement was the one area of contestation in which numerous immigrants were taking part. I set out to find out why. In so doing, I attended protests, counseling sessions, weekly assemblies, and actions in the banks and courts. As I became well-versed in Spanish mortgage law and techniques to stave off foreclosure and eviction, I started to advise people on their mortgage problems during thrice-weekly PAH meetings. I interviewed activists, mortgage debtors and defaulters both native and foreign-born, lawyers, academics, and social workers. Alongside ethnographic data, I amassed archival materials from historical planning records, policy debates, popular media and immigrant press, and architectural and urban design periodicals.

In this chapter, I focus on Maria Eugenia's trajectory because it is particularly illustrative of the kinds of choices, dispossessions, and struggles many Ecuadorian mortgagers experienced over the boom and bust. Only through extended immersion, close observation, and relational analysis am I able to alight on a single narrative as synecdoche for more generalized experiences of acquisition, inequity, and political action. Attention to one protagonist, moreover, might illuminate 'migrant stories' that shape not only larger processes of demographic transformation but also political subjectification (Lawson 2000). It is also a decision that responds to work that uses biography as a key device to unravel broader processes of loss and dissent (Auyero 2003).

*Source:* Miguel A. Martínez.

*Figure 27.1*     *Meeting of the PAH, Madrid (2020)*

## THE PROMISE OF HOMEOWNERSHIP

Let me return to Maria Eugenia. In the mid-2000s, like many other immigrants across Spain, she decided to buy a house. Since her arrival in Madrid, she had rented: first a shared room and then a shared flat. Renting was difficult. Without housing assistance, and with or without papers, low-income immigrants confront fractured and expensive rental landscapes. Prior to the crisis in Madrid, the rental market was small and offered no protections against discrimination. As immigrant homeowners described to me, the newly arrived relied on social networks for housing, finding themselves sharing flats and even rooms with other family members or even strangers. One middle-aged Ecuadorian man told of his first housing situation in Madrid, which 'made me terribly outraged… four people in a family reduced to one bedroom when [the baby] was still nursing… 30 people lived in the rest of the house, where they charge each one of us water, electricity, this, that, and the other thing.' Out on the open market, which many explore once settled for a bit, immigrants face discrimination and high prices. Landlords charge exorbitant security deposits or refuse rental contracts altogether. The absence of anti-discrimination laws and rent regulations means immigrants face steep hurdles in finding safe and secure housing. As I have written about elsewhere, the predations of the market make homeownership an attractive option, where many can escape landlord abuses and uncertainty (Gonick 2021). Buying would allow Maria Eugenia to escape the whims of landlords and their sometimes-usurious demands.

As in many ownership societies, the Spanish rental market is an afterthought, deliberately left outside the careful regulation of the state. In Spain, as in the United States and other places that privilege the owner-occupation model, the government had long worked to make homeownership attractive through state subsidies and tax breaks to developers and favorable incentives to homebuyers. The Franco dictatorship very explicitly sought to transform proletarians into propertied bourgeois subjects in order to both eradicate any communist sympathy and stimulate the economy through the construction of housing. It froze urban rents in the 1950s, condemning rental housing stock to decay. Once unfrozen in the 1980s, rents remained poorly regulated, at the complete discretion of the landlord. Urban legends around renting abounded, convincing owners not to rent their empty units for fear of uncouth occupants who might destroy their patrimony. Those who did let out units might, as a precaution against such perfidy, ask for huge security deposits of six months or a year's worth of rent. Everyday Spaniards also eschewed renting; it was akin to 'throwing one's money down a hole' as many interlocutors reported. Parental emancipation, which might take place well into adulthood, would only occur upon being able to purchase a home.

In the early 2000s, the dream of homeownership was suddenly in reach for many. The democratic era in Spain had seen several waves of legislation to modernize mortgage markets. In the late 1970s, immediately following the death of Franco and the inauguration of democracy, for example, the country changed home loans so that they would only require 20% down payments with the remaining amount to be amortized over 30 years, in keeping with standard mortgage terms in other developed countries. In the late 1990s and early 2000s, the country then passed a series of laws related to securitization, allowing for the introduction of new, much more insecure forms of credit. Spain pursued these kinds of changes to make its markets more legible to foreign investment and further integrate its economy within global systems of money and finance. Here we see housing privileged in the guise of commodity to be bought and sold on the open, international market. Deregulation meant everyone could be brought into this commodity market: new financial products flooded the market, allowing people who couldn't afford traditional down payments to take out loans for all or even more than the purchase price of a house. Maria Eugenia was part of a wave of buyers deemed 'subprime' by financial and real estate markets across many spaces across the globe (Chakravartty & Silva 2013). In Madrid, young people, single people, immigrants, and members of the traditional working class could suddenly access the Spanish dream of homeownership.

When she went to buy her house, the real estate agent showed her a number of properties in Carabanchel and Latina. These areas were far removed from where she had previously lived in San Blas, which had become an Ecuadorian enclave. However, prices in that neighborhood had risen precipitously. What were left for her and her modest budget were old flats at the outskirts of the city. As she related to me several years later, you did not really have much of a choice in what agents showed you—you basically had to follow along as they dictated what and where you could buy. The real estate agent encouraged her to act quickly. Prices, he implied, might rise from one day to the next; these units might soon be outside her budget.

Social ties are what encouraged Maria Eugenia to buy in the first place. As another immigrant homeowner put it, the 'contagion' of the mortgage traveled through immigrant circles, as people observed their friends and families buying homes. The chatter at work sites, in bars and restaurants, and across *futbol* fields on weekends all extolled the virtue of homeownership. Its virtuousness was also splashed across the pages of immigrant publications. The newspaper *Latino*, with circulation in the hundreds of thousands, portrayed aspirational domestic scenes to its readers. There cozy families enjoyed the warmth of cozy homes, a distinct contrast to the substandard living conditions many immigrants endured upon first arrival in Madrid. Several friends and acquaintances offered to introduce Maria Eugenia to real estate agents who might show her potential homes. Little did she know that many of these people actually got minor commissions for referrals. Financial firms were smart—they knew how to financialize the close-knit ties of the Ecuadorian community in order to spread the mantra of homeownership and thus mortgage credit. Buying a home for Maria Eugenia also meant showing to herself and her community that she was savvy.

During the short-lived Spanish boom, becoming a homeowner was a mode of integration into the city.[4] Immigration law required adequate and secure housing in order to bring family members over or gain permanent residence. If rental housing was difficult and expensive to come by, buying a house was suddenly in easy reach. As housing prices spiraled upwards and everyone seemed to get rich, buying into the market was also a means of reaping economic rewards, or at least that is how it seemed. In a country of owners, what, too, could be more Spanish that buying a home? The frantic increase in housing costs, meanwhile, induced one to try to act immediately for fear of missing out. Here we see the allure of housing as a commodity, one that might appreciate handsomely in value.

## THE AGONY OF HOMEOWNERSHIP

However, this mode of integration was in many ways deeply fraught. The reality of homeownership was not one of comfort and economic advancement. Bourdieu, writing on the single family home market in France, argued that homebuyers are always induced to spend just a little bit more than they can afford (Bourdieu 2014). The house, then, becomes a haven from the world, yes, but also a burden. Its expensiveness and the work to make ends meet constantly remind the inhabitant of her own place in society. She must scrimp and save, perhaps even taking on extra work. The privately owned house can thus confine her to her social status rather than providing promised upward mobility.

For immigrants in millennial Madrid, homeownership proved in many ways a burden even before the onset of financial crisis. Remittance money sent back to Ecuador or Peru now went towards mortgage payments; the idea was that an eventual sale of the house would provide much greater wealth for a return home. Still, the reduced flow of cash had an impact on household budgets in countries of origin. Thus, homeownership was constantly about calculations of risk and reward, weighing extended social relations in the here and now against imagined futures.

However, where and then how immigrants bought also frayed more immediate networks. Maria Eugenia chose an aging apartment in a housing block in Carabanchel. She was far from the nearest subway station, about a 20 minute walk. There was little street life on her block, but around the corner from her building there was a small clutch of businesses that mostly catered to the local Chinese population. The grocery store carried products that were strange to her; in her old neighborhood several South American outlets offered beloved items from back home. The flat was also far from her work; it required three subway lines to reach her job making waffles for tourists near the Real Madrid stadium. Her commute was much longer than before, cutting into her ability to socialize with friends. Many of those friends still lived in her old neighborhood and were reluctant to traverse the city to see her in her new place. They had children and spouses who required attention, help with homework, and meals to be prepared.

This area of town was also degraded and shabby. Erected during the late years of the Franco era, many housing units lacked good insulation and heating. Maria Eugenia lived in a fifth floor walkup. Her building, like many around it, had been constructed through the sweat equity of native working class Spaniards in the late 1960s and 1970s. Few of these squat concrete buildings had elevators; adding one would be costly and disruptive. Only a few years earlier, many units had lacked proper bathrooms and much of the housing stock in the area was considered substandard by the municipal government. To bring it up to code, however, would take a huge influx of cash from either the city or residents themselves. As the neighborhood became increasingly immigrant, household economies could only stretch so far. Many of the native residents of the area had left, purchasing units in newly built estates that had cropped up at the edge of the city. As they left, older working class neighborhoods experienced what Wacquant labeled 'territorial stigma,' now being associated with crime and deviancy (Wacquant 2008). The city spent less money of basic services such as trash retrieval and street lighting, while social services became overwhelmed with need even before the start of crisis.

Once crisis hit in 2008, the collapse of the property market fractured social relations. Maria Eugenia saw her monthly mortgage payment shoot up to a rate she could no longer afford. Her work had reduced her hourly wage and soon also made cuts to her schedule. Far less money was flowing into her accounts than just mere months earlier. Even by greatly reducing her expenses she could not make her mortgage payments. She had always thought that she would just sell the place and maybe even make some money if she could not make payments. However, with hundreds of thousands of households in positions similar to her own, there were no buyers. She also saw the value of her property suddenly plummet; commodities, after all, can also depreciate. She soon found herself on a credit blacklist that prohibited a number of different economic tasks integral for daily survival. She also had over 100,000 euros in unpaid mortgage debt.

The specter of debt first caused her to seek out extra work wherever she could find it. She worked odd jobs at odd hours, sometimes late into the night or first thing in the morning. What might once have been considered leisure time was now dedicated to sleep or to job searching. Secondly, her mounting debts made her ashamed. She had considered herself fairly savvy, worked hard, and listened to the advice of bankers and real estate agents. Her inability to pay, to find enough work, must certainly be the result of her own moral failing. The demands of precarious work and the burden of debt's mortification conspired to wrest her from urban sociality.[5] Gone were laughter and gossip with friends and idle weekend afternoons spent strolling the Retiro park or window shopping along Gran Vía.

Homeownership in Madrid, rather than offering great riches and reward, instead increased differentiation for many immigrants. The housing they were able to afford was degraded and far from the center. As such it was isolating and exposed them to territorial stigma. Its poor conditions could also provoke health problems and required extra cash for maintenance and unforeseen repairs. When crisis set in, how they bought also condemned them to a lifetime of debt, in addition to spreading ruin throughout immigrant communities. Finally, it affected transnational communities by disrupting the flow of remittances.

## FROM EXCLUSION TO EMPOWERMENT

If homeownership can prove to diminish immigrant urban worlds and exacerbate vulnerability, what might be the antidote? In this final section, I reveal how social movement organizing provides a potent venue for empowerment and inclusion against the vagrancies of the market. Housing as a right to be demanded and enacted allows for processes that housing as a commodity can preclude.

Saddled to her unpayable mortgage, adrift in a city wrecked by crisis, Maria Eugenia chanced upon a flyer for a housing rights group in her neighborhood. She was apprehensive about attending and walked past the meeting several times before venturing inside. She had little to lose at that point. Standing on the sideline of a room packed with people, she began to hear stories that echoed her own: overdue payments, the harassment of bankers, isolation, and shame. There were numerous immigrants in the room, but also native Spaniards. The woman leading the meeting was Ecuadorian, like Maria, but spoke with authority and rage about her mortgage problem. She incited the crowd to understand the problem of their mortgage not as their own failing but instead as the result of massive, state-sponsored fraud.

Maria returned to the meetings several times before she gained the courage to speak publicly. After attending for about a month, she ventured to the front of the room, where the meeting's moderator, this time a native Spanish man in his late 50s, encouraged her to share her story. She took a deep breath and began narrating. At first she was uncertain, but by the end of the intervention she found herself full of anger and passion. Others in the audience clamored to support her (see Figure 27.1).

A year later, when I met Maria as part of my fieldwork with the PAH, she had become a committed activist. She had successfully negotiated with the bank in order for them to forgive her loan after being evicted from her home. She was still angry about the years of toil that had seemingly been flushed away with the folly of her mortgage. She now lived with a sister in Vallecas, which was convenient because it was close to PAH meetings. Despite the challenges of recent years, she took solace in housing activism. There, she had found new friends and new purpose. She accompanied others on trips to the bank and the courthouse, helped file petitions, and occasionally even led meetings. When she first got involved, mostly immigrants came for help. Now, increasingly it was Spanish families who sought out the support of the PAH. Many were embarrassed, seeing the problem of a mortgage as one of immigrants. She taught them differently. She also realized that as an immigrant, someone subjected to the casual racism and minor cruelties on a daily basis, she could enunciate the hypocrisies of the propertied order in ways that were alien to many of her native counterparts.

The PAH, of course, has been the subject of a wealth of critical housing and social movement scholarship (Feliciantonio 2017, Fominaya 2015, Fominaya & Montañes 2014, García-Lamarca 2017). One thread of this literature has been particularly attuned to the role of empowerment in transforming people mired in crisis into activists who have enacted radical forms of claim-making and urban citizenship. Within Maria Eugenia's journey, for example, she experienced the city differently upon joining the PAH. Rather than bow to the pressure of banks and the demands of the unequal propertied order, she instead articulates her own demands and exerts authority through her testimony, her activism, and her identification as an *afectada* (someone *affected* by mortgages). She has transformed her dispossession into a political critique that has empowered her against the inequities of the Spanish housing system. Foreclosure meant not just the potential loss of the home but also the loss of the self as it became unmoored from previous social worlds and mired in financial distress. In the space of the assembly, Maria Eugenia, however, could serve as an expert witness to her own financial downfall and subsequent rebirth as an activist. In so doing, she led others in similar situations through their own processes of empowerment.

Housing movements such as the PAH are thus potent venues for the reclamation of the self and its sociality. Homeownership is a system that relies on notions of self-realization and independence and the production of harmonious communities (McCabe 2016, Ronald 2008). Yet in the case of immigrants in Madrid, it often serves to increase vulnerability and unmoor the immigrant from her understanding of herself in the world. Paradoxically, housing movements that take on the inequities of this system of urban habitation can be rich terrain in which to reclaim the self through processes of empowerment. Within the space of the PAH, Maria Eugenia found her voice and authority, claiming a place for herself against loss and dispossession.

## CONCLUSIONS

As I have shown throughout this chapter, the demands and insecurities of privately owned housing structure immigrant worlds. Its inequities and precarity calcify otherness and exclusion, heightening territorial stigma. In Madrid, post-crisis housing landscapes have become increasingly insecure, despite potent demands and organizing for just shelter. As the city was mired in economic distress, the central government passed a new law to stimulate the rental market. Rather than incentivize renting or pass new regulations that might empower tenants, the law accorded landlords more rights. Standard rental contracts would be shortened from five to three years, and eviction for non-payment would be easier to carry out. Here again we see the shoring up of property rights for the elite and the primacy of the owner. In the same moment, landlords throughout many metropolitan areas in Spain turned to Airbnb in order to make money; the security of prepaid online clientele mitigated against fears of nonpayment.

Thousands of units were removed from the open market. The historical currents that had long denigrated renting and renters conspired to make it even more difficult and uncertain to find a decent place to live. Rent has only skyrocketed, sending people farther afield to live, often in overcrowded conditions.

The influence of unequal housing systems on immigrant urban life was brought to bear in the depths of the pandemic. Madrid was at one point the global epicenter of COVID-19, and the government put in place some of the strictest lockdown measures. As Madrid faced its second wave in late summer of 2020, the President of the Madrid regional government, Isabel Ayuso, stated rising case numbers were because of 'the lifestyle of our immigrant population in Madrid' and 'their density in *those* neighborhoods and towns' (Viejo & Mateo 2020). She mandated harsh lockdowns and restrictions, but only for certain neighborhoods with high case numbers—and immigrant populations—such as Vallecas (Anon 2020). Residents' movements were strictly circumscribed. They could, however, leave their zones in order to go to work in wealthier neighborhoods, where no such lockdowns were in place. Even as residents of these zones went to work, they worried they might lose their employment because of 'stigmatization' as 'they [had been] converted into *apestados* [disease carriers]' (Ferrero et al. 2020). Once again the reality of housing under the tyranny of the market only furthered immigrant abjection.

The dynamics of private housing markets—substandard conditions, overcrowding, and their relation to money and debt—provoke and exacerbate vulnerability for immigrants. As such, the hegemony of private property undergirds the exclusion of immigrants from urban life, both physically and socially. We often think of migrant abjection as produced at the border, in the camp or detention center, along the sea crossing. However, housing is one more practice where borders emerge, proliferate, and harden into common sense.

Against these forms of predation and exclusion, housing struggles—that is, struggles against the dominant terms of habitation—can serve to fight against and even abolish such vagrancies and differences. They are key venues in which people experience empowerment to contest the contemporary housing crisis. Indeed, as the pandemic marched on, mutual aid groups emerged to contest the punishing logics of lockdowns. While not chiefly concerned with housing per se, these clusters of empowered citizens helped to mitigate its role in differentiating populations on the basis of residency and national origin. As cities emerge from the pandemic and a wealth of locales confront crises of both migration and shelter, housing struggles are important sites for the transformation of the self and the creation of community.

Finally, I want to return again to the question of methods and methodology. Immigrant homeownership, I have shown, is something to be examined across time rather than within one static moment. In so doing, we can apprehend the multiple meanings and realities of ownership as it structures everyday life. As a dominant and proliferating system in many places throughout the world, homeownership deserves scrutiny, in part because its promises can be greatly removed from the demands it makes on modest actors as they navigate urban worlds. Ethnographic attention to this system of shelter, meanwhile, can illuminate its multivalent meanings and experiences.

It is precisely among marginalized groups that we can apprehend homeownership to be a double-edged sword, at once promising great riches and serving as an engine of extraction for elite interest. As the case of Maria Eugenia demonstrates, homeownership's demands can activate aspiration against the tyranny of predation and othering, but also, because contemporary housing systems are enmeshed with racialized logics, produce greater abjection (Fields

& Raymond 2021). Yet at the same time, drawing once again on Pattillo's seminal formation, the intersection of immigration and homeownership might allow us to see how a commodity can become a right. Immigrant housing struggles—both as challenge to find adequate housing amidst the ravages of the market and as collective contestation against those ravages—reveal that a commodity's false promises can transform it into a potent target for radical politics. Indeed, Maria Eugenia's story reveals that housing is *both* commodity and right depending on socio-economic conditions and emergent collective politics. To do understand this double nature, we must locate housing within a broader terrain of economic extraction and social contestation. Here accounting for time in addition to space might illuminate how marginalized communities channel their dispossession to transform a commodity into a right.

## NOTES

1. In Spain, once a house in repossessed, the mortgager is left with the outstanding debt. That debt cannot be discharged through bankruptcy and will pass on to any next of kin in the event of death.
2. Sociology, for example, has long privileged the scale of the neighborhood, provoking much discussion about 'neighborhood effects' as primary motors of urban inequality.
3. The sociological literature on immigration is vast. I have provided citations for a few notable works on the subject, but to do this subfield justice would demand an entire other chapter, if not a proper book-length treatment.
4. Integration is a concept fraught with competing ideologies, academic discussion, and political debates. It is often a normative project of the state (Nicholls & Uitermark 2017). Here I use it to mean a process by which immigrants are induced to participate in dominant socio-economic, political, and/or cultural systems. In this case, it implies statecraft but also actually existing daily practice.
5. Both mortgage and mortification derive from '*mort*' or death. Mortgage means 'dead pledge,' while mortification comes from old French meaning 'destroy, overwhelm, punish' or quite literally to kill. In writing about mortgage debtors in Spain, I deploy the concept of 'civil death'—often used by PAH activists—as an affective and embodied condition produced through debt that provokes myriad forms of socio-spatial exclusion.

## REFERENCES

Aalbers, Manuel (2012) *Subprime Cities: The Political Economy of Mortgage Markets*. Chichester and Malden: Wiley-Blackwell.

Agrela, Belén (2002) Spain as a Recent Country of Immigration: How Immigration Became a Symbolic, Political, and Cultural Problem in the 'New Spain'. Center for Comparative Immigration Studies.

Alba, Richard D. & John R. Logan (1992) Assimilation and Stratification in the Homeownership Patterns of Racial and Ethnic Groups. *International Migration Review* 26(4): 1314–41. doi: 10.1177/019791839202600411.

Anon. (2020) Las zonas de Madrid que proponía confinar Ayuso para evitar el estado de alarma. *El País*. Retrieved January 18, 2022 (https://elpais.com/espana/madrid/2020-10-09/las-zonas-de-la-comunidad-que-proponia-confinar-ayuso-para-evitar-el-estado-de-alarma.html).

Atkinson, Rowland & Keith Jacobs (2017) *House, Home and Society*. London: Bloomsbury Publishing.

Auyero, Javier (2003) *Contentious Lives: Two Argentine Women, Two Protests, and the Quest for Recognition*. Durham: Duke University Press.

Baiocchi, Gianpaolo (2023) Personal correspondence.

Barber, Llana (2017) *Latino City: Immigration and Urban Crisis in Lawrence, Massachusetts, 1945–2000*. Chapel Hill: UNC Press Books.

Bloemraad, Irene (2006) *Becoming a Citizen: Incorporating Immigrants and Refugees in the United States and Canada*. Berkeley: University of California Press.

Bourdieu, Pierre (2014) *The Social Structures of the Economy*. Chichester: John Wiley & Sons.

Boyer, M. Christine (1986) *Dreaming the Rational City: The Myth of American City Planning*. Cambridge: MIT Press.

Bruquetas-Callejo, M. (2008) Immigration and Integration Policymaking in Spain. IMISCOE Working Paper, 21.

Çaglar, Ayse, & Nina Glick Schiller (2018) *Migrants and City-Making: Dispossession, Displacement, and Urban Regeneration*. Durham: Duke University Press.

Calavita, Kitty (2005) *Immigrants at the Margins*. Cambridge: Cambridge University Press.

Castañeda, Ernesto (2018) *A Place to Call Home: Immigrant Exclusion and Urban Belonging in New York, Paris, and Barcelona*. Stanford: Stanford University Press.

Chakravartty, Paula & Denise Ferreira da Silva (2013) *Race, Empire, and the Crisis of the Subprime*. Baltimore: Johns Hopkins University Press.

Clark, William A. V. (2003) *Immigrants and the American Dream: Remaking the Middle Class*. New York: Guilford Press.

Connolly, N. D. B. (2014) *A World More Concrete: Real Estate and the Remaking of Jim Crow South Florida*. Chicago: University of Chicago Press.

Desmond, Matthew (2016) *Evicted: Poverty and Profit in the American City*. New York: Crown Publishers.

Feliciantonio, Cesare Di (2017) Social Movements and Alternative Housing Models: Practicing the 'Politics of Possibilities' in Spain. *Housing, Theory and Society* 34(1): 38–56. doi: 10.1080/14036096.2016.1220421.

Ferrero, Berta, Fernando Peinado & Nicholas Dale Leal (2020) Miedo a perder el trabajo y rabia por la 'segregación' de Ayuso en los barrios de Madrid. *El País*. Retrieved January 18, 2022 (https://elpais.com/espana/madrid/2020-09-18/miedo-a-perder-el-trabajo-y-rabia-por-la-segregacion-de-ayuso-en-los-barrios-de-madrid.html).

Fields, D. & E. L. Raymond (2021) Racialized Geographies of Housing Financialization. *Progress in Human Geography* 45(6): 1625–1645.

Fominaya, Cristina Flesher (2015) Redefining the Crisis/Redefining Democracy: Mobilising for the Right to Housing in Spain's PAH Movement. *South European Society and Politics* 20(4): 465–85. doi: 10.1080/13608746.2015.1058216.

Fominaya, Cristina Flesher & Antonio Montañes Jimenéz (2014) Transnational Diffusion across Time: The Adoption of the Argentinian Dirty War 'Escrache' in the Context of Spain's Housing Crisis. In Atak, K., O. Císař, P. Daphi et al. (eds.) *Spreading Protest: Social Movements in Times of Crisis*. Colchester: ECPR Press, 19–42.

García-Lamarca, Melissa (2017) From Occupying Plazas to Recuperating Housing: Insurgent Practices in Spain. *International Journal of Urban and Regional Research* 41(1): 37–53. doi: 10.1111/1468-2427.12386.

García-Lamarca, Melissa (2022) *Non-Performing Loans, Non-Performing People: Life and Struggle with Mortgage Debt in Spain*. Athens: University of Georgia Press.

Ghertner, D. Asher (2015) *Rule by Aesthetics: World-Class City Making in Delhi*. New York and Oxford: Oxford University Press.

Gonick, Sophie L. (2021) *Dispossession and Dissent: Immigrants and the Struggle for Housing in Madrid*. Stanford: Stanford University Press.

Hayden, Dolores (1984) *Redesigning the American Dream: The Future of Housing, Work, and Family Life*. New York: W.W. Norton.

Jackson, Kenneth T. (1985) *Crabgrass Frontier: The Suburbanization of the United States*. New York: Oxford University Press.

Kauppinen, Timo M., Hans Skifter Andersen & Lina Hedman (2015) Determinants of Immigrants' Entry to Homeownership in Three Nordic Capital City Regions. *Geografiska Annaler: Series B, Human Geography* 97(4): 343–62. doi: 10.1111/geob.12085.

Kemeny, Jim (1981) *The Myth of Home-Ownership: Private versus Public Choices in Housing Tenure.* Milton Park: Routledge & Kegan Paul.
Kurz, Karin (2004) *Home Ownership and Social Inequality in a Comparative Perspective.* Stanford: Stanford University Press.
Kwak, Nancy H. (2015) *A World of Homeowners: American Power and the Politics of Housing Aid.* Chicago: University of Chicago Press.
Lawson, Victoria A. (2000) Arguments within Geographies of Movement: The Theoretical Potential of Migrants' Stories. *Progress in Human Geography* 24(2): 173–89. doi: 10.1191/030913200672491184.
López, Isidro & Emmanuel Rodríguez (2011) The Spanish Model. *New Left Review* (69): 5–29.
Manturuk, Kim R., Mark R. Lindblad & Roberto G. Quercia (2017) *A Place Called Home: The Social Dimensions of Homeownership.* New York and Oxford: Oxford University Press.
Martin, Isaac William (2017) New Sociology of Housing. *Contemporary Sociology* 46(4): 392–96. doi: 10.1177/0094306117714499a.
Martínez, Miguel A. (2017) Squatters and Migrants in Madrid: Interactions, Contexts and Cycles. *Urban Studies* 54(11): 2472–89.
McCabe, Brian J. (2016) *No Place Like Home.* New York and Oxford: Oxford University Press.
McConnell, Eileen Diaz & Enrico A. Marcelli (2007) Buying into the American Dream? Mexican Immigrants, Legal Status, and Homeownership in Los Angeles County. *Social Science Quarterly* 88(1): 199–221. doi: 10.1111/j.1540-6237.2007.00454.x.
Montagna, Nicola & Margherita Grazioli (2019) Urban Commons and Freedom of Movement: The Housing Struggles of Recently Arrived Migrants in Rome. *Citizenship Studies* 23(6): 577–92. doi: 10.1080/13621025.2019.1634375.
Mudu, Pierpaolo & Sutapa Chattopadhyay (eds.) (2017) *Migration, Squatting and Radical Autonomy: Resistance and Destabilization of Racist Regulatory Policies and B/Ordering Mechanisms.* Milton Park: Routledge.
Nicholls, Walter & Justus Uitermark (2017) *Cities and Social Movements: Immigrant Rights Activism in the United States, France, and the Netherlands, 1970–2015.* Chichester: John Wiley & Sons.
Pattillo, Mary (2013) Housing: Commodity versus Right. *Annual Review of Sociology* 39(1): 509–31. doi: 10.1146/annurev-soc-071312-145611.
Portes, Alejandro & Steven Shafer (2007) Revisiting the Enclave Hypothesis: Miami Twenty-Five Years Later. In Ruef, M. & M. Lounsbury (eds.) *The Sociology of Entrepreneurship.* Bingley, UK: Emerald Group Publishing, 157–190.
Portes, Alejandro & Alex Stepick (1993) *City on the Edge: The Transformation of Miami.* Berkeley: University of California Press.
Potts, Deborah (2020) *Broken Cities: Inside the Global Housing Crisis.* London: Zed Books.
Rolnik, Raquel (2019) *Urban Warfare.* London and New York: Verso Books.
Ronald, Richard (2008) *The Ideology of Home Ownership: Homeowner Societies and the Role of Housing.* New York: Springer.
Rosen, Eva (2020) *The Voucher Promise: 'Section 8' and the Fate of an American Neighborhood.* Princeton: Princeton University Press.
Sandoval-Strausz, A. K. (2019) *Barrio America: How Latino Immigrants Saved the American City.* New York: Basic Books.
Sassen, Saskia (1999) *Guests and Aliens.* New York: New Press.
Soto, Hernando de (2000) *The Mystery of Capital: Why Capitalism Triumphs in the West and Fails Everywhere Else.* New York: Basic Books.
Suárez, Maka (2017) Debt Revolts: Ecuadorian Foreclosed Families at the PAH in Barcelona. *Dialectical Anthropology* 41(3): 263–77.
Sugrue, Thomas J. (2014) *The Origins of the Urban Crisis: Race and Inequality in Postwar Detroit.* Princeton: Princeton University Press.
Taylor, Keeanga-Yamahtta (2019) *Race for Profit: How Banks and the Real Estate Industry Undermined Black Homeownership.* Chapel Hill: UNC Press Books.
Telles, Edward M. & Vilma Ortiz (2008) *Generations of Exclusion: Mexican-Americans, Assimilation, and Race.* New York: Russell Sage Foundation.
Viejo, Manuel & Juan José Mateo (2020) Ayuso señala que algunos contagios de Madrid se producen por el modo de vida de los inmigrantes. *El País.* Retrieved January 16, 2022 (https://elpais.com/espana/

madrid/2020-09-15/ayuso-senala-que-algunos-contagios-de-madrid-se-producen-por-el-modo-de-vida-de-los-inmigrantes.html).
Wacquant, Loïc (2008) *Urban Outcasts: A Comparative Sociology of Advanced Marginality*. Cambridge and Malden: Polity.
Wright, Gwendolyn (2012) *Building the Dream*. New York: Knopf Doubleday Publishing Group.
Wyly, Elvin & C. S. Ponder (2011) Gender, Age, and Race in Subprime America. *Housing Policy Debate* 21(4): 529–64. doi: 10.1080/10511482.2011.615850.
Wyly, Elvin, C. S. Ponder, Pierson Nettling, Bosco Ho, Sophie Ellen Fung, Zachary Liebowitz & Dan Hammel (2012) New Racial Meanings of Housing in America. *American Quarterly* 64(3): 571–604. doi: 10.1353/aq.2012.0036.

# 28. Socially and culturally produced boundaries in housing access in relation to sexuality

*Myrto Dagkouli-Kyriakoglou*

Like snails born with their shell, Greek children are born with the social imaginary that family should provide them with a housing solution at some point in their adult – if not already in their late teenage – life. The high degree of familism in many life aspects, like housing provision, has deep foundations in Greece. For many decades, the state acted only as an enabler while family was the main welfare agent. During recent decades, after the 2008 global financial crisis (GFC), this self-evident housing pathway assisted by family support has become crooked but it seems like the family housing strategies are being adjusted once again to offer support to members. However, the hegemony of family as a provider also charges it with great power to impose rules on the beneficiaries. In particular, the prevalence of the asymmetrical heteropatriarchal imaginary for how family should be in accordance with gender roles and relations can constitute a fertile ground for discrimination against those who do not comply with these roles that can lead to complications regarding housing support. This chapter, by focusing on the experiences of LGBTQ+ beneficiaries of family housing support in Athens, Greece, in 2017, aims to map the socially and culturally produced boundaries in housing access in relation to sexuality.

Housing policies in Greece have mainly consisted of indirect economic indicators that aim to promote certain housing coping practices, especially the self-regulation of housing needs through the support of the family and kin, with a focus on homeownership (Allen et al. 2004, Leontidou 1990, Mantouvalou 1985). In the Greek context, family is 'a social institution […] a stable network of relationships between (socially defined) roles, a summary of customized roles of personal and/or collective action' (Mousourou 1993: 14), and it usually refers to the extended and not just the nuclear family. The preference towards homeownership still prevailing today was promoted intensively by both the state and the market. The support for homeownership and the imposed imaginary of a 'regular' life path are evident in the fiscal state support for newlyweds in order to acquire a house (Allen et al. 2004). Indicatively, there exist incentives for homeownership for young couples with tax exemptions when they acquire their primary residence. In Greece this legislation is based on a law from 1980, updated in 2009 (currently the law also includes single people as long as they live in Greece). Specifically, according to Article 21 of the Constitution, family and marriage are under the protection of the state and therefore 'married people are entitled to tax exemption from the property transfer taxation for the acquisition of the family house' (Council of the State (2008). The housing policies highlight a preferable, prefabricated heteronormative life trajectory that is in accordance with the preservation of the institution of the traditional family and kinship and the related welfare that acts as a persistent pillar in Greek society.

At the same time, according to the International Lesbian, Gay, Bisexual, Trans and Intersex Association (ILGA) annual review for 2016, Greece offers protection only for 'sexual orientation, gender identity and gender expression' (International Lesbian, Gay, Bisexual, Trans and Intersex Association 2017: 109) in the labour market and it does not guarantee any other protection from other forms of discrimination or in other fields related to sexual and gender identity. This means that, concerning housing, LGBTQ+ people are not protected against discriminatory behaviours.

While the issue of LGBTQ+ homelessness has been highlighted only recently in Greece (Geltis 2019), LGBTQ+ organisations stress that because of the absolute lack of institutional alternatives for LGBTQ+, the threat of homelessness is high (Pettas et al. 2022). Indicatively, in Europe and the USA, 40% of homeless people self-identify as LGBTQ+ while in the general population the respective percentage is smaller (Abramovich 2013, Geltis 2019). Societies that acknowledge this problem attempt to offer adequate welfare services for these people, who face homelessness, abusive behaviours from their families and others, and financial problems (Hunter 2008). Moreover, the available communal and family resources are more restricted for LGBTQ+ people according to Human Rights Watch (2010). In Greece, citizens rely heavily on family-based assistance: the danger of homelessness or forced displacement is impacted mainly by the ability of a family to support its members and the will of LGBTQ+ people to hide or suppress their identity and life plans in order not to lose support if the family disapproves of them (Dagkouli-Kyriakoglou 2021a, Pettas et al. 2022). Thus, it seems that the cultural/religious characteristics of Greek society force a related coming-out approach on its LGBTQ+ citizens.

At the same time, as crisis was evolving, austerity reinforced gender binaries, heteronormative attitudes, and conservatism in social life in Greece (Eleftheriadis 2015). Golden Dawn, the Greek neo-Nazi party that was part of the parliament between 2012 and 2019, promoted sexist and homophobic discourses and behaviours while praising heteronormativity and aggressive masculinity (Avdela & Psarra 2012, Eleftheriadis 2015). Furthermore, three different extreme right and conservative political parties have achieved numerous parliamentary seats during the 2023 general elections, which were won by the main right-wing party. Their ideas and aggressive behaviours found fertile ground among Greek citizens (Vaiou 2014b). Women, according to Golden Dawn's discourse, should 'stay at home', look after the family, and stop taking men's jobs (Athanasiou 2012, Vaiou 2014a). This is another expression of the regained power of the heteropatriarchal family as the main welfare agent, which can be responsible for reproducing certain heteronormative gender roles – such as the patriarchal provider. During this climate of financial insecurity and social backwardness, we should observe and highlight how people dependent on family welfare for one of their basic needs and rights (housing) who do not fit into the heteropatriarchal imaginary are impacted.

Here I investigate the multiple dimensions of sexual identity's impact on family housing support through empirical material that was collected in 2017. Sixteen in-depth, semi-biographical interviews were conducted with people who self-identified as LGBTQ+ living in Athens at that time. The recruitment of the research partners was achieved primarily through my social networks and then with snowball sampling from multiple initial contacts. The main theoretical approach was the 'housing pathway' perspective as it enabled me to explore, demonstrate, and analyse the housing changes affecting individuals as part of a household and its interactions (Clapham 2002). In order to investigate the different dimensions of housing practices and family support, the method of double biographies was used. The aim was to construct double or triple biographies contextualising any change in housing practices and relating them to the person's experience in other arenas (Forrest & Murie 1995, Mayer & Tuma 1987, May 2000). The life stories of the research partners were collected with housing as a primary focus and the coming-out process as a secondary one. 'Coming out' in this work is defined as the process of disclosure of one's sexual orientation, moving away from the heteronormative expression of sexuality. During the interviews, timelines were created for the interviewees' housing pathways. Research partners' process of 'coming out' to family – if it had occurred – was discussed and situated in their housing pathways. One major question explored was the direct impact, if any, of the disclosure of their sexual orientation on their housing pathways. Moreover, precautions were employed by changing any identifying information that was provided, such as names and places, for the sake of anonymity and confidentiality. Therefore, pseudonyms are used and concerning geographical attributes there is reference only to the size of places (e.g. towns, villages), except for Athens, which was the field of this research.

The chapter is structured in four more sections. The first one analyses the Greek welfare regime and how this is linked to the cultural, economic, political, and religious dimensions of Greek society. The second section focuses on the queer geographies of Athens and the current housing situation. The third one presents the empirical results showing the boundaries in housing and beyond for LGBTQ+ people in Greece. In the concluding section, I briefly discuss the broader debates on the housing access boundaries produced by a familistic welfare regime in relation to sexual orientation.

## THE GREEK TRIPTYCH

The Southern European welfare regime that Greece enjoys is characterised by the underdevelopment of the welfare state (Gough 1996, Leibfried 1992), an informal but strong culture of micro-solidarities inspired by religious and cultural values (Castles 1993), and the family as the main resilient shock absorber of socioeconomic turbulence (Martin 2015, Moreno & Marí-Klose 2013, Naldini & Jurado 2013). The responsibility for providing the care and inter-generational support is assigned mainly to the family but the institution is not supported by state policies, resulting in a situation of 'unsupported familialism' (Saraceno 1994). Moreover, there exists a dual system both in labour and in housing where insiders are protected and outsiders are not. In the labour market the dualism is between public employees and those with a permanent contract versus precarious workers and freelancers, while in the housing market the dualism is between owner-occupiers and renters (Arundel & Lennartz 2018). The 'strong family ties, emphasis on pensions, secure jobs during active life, high intra-family transfers in crucial phases of the life cycle' and high percentages of homeownership constitute a rigid system in Greece (Ferrera 2010: 171). At least before the 2008 GFC, this system depended on the traditionally male breadwinner who benefited from good job opportunities during his active years and significant pensions afterwards with which he could support family and kin (Naldini & Jurado 2013). This scheme exacerbated the position of women in comparison to men, creating additional social discrimination and a female family dependency (Minguez 2005, Kourachanis 2018). Even this unequal support however concerns only the citizens entitled to it: the 'insiders' argument. Other outsiders such as migrants and refugees are even more subject to the above constraints.

Concerning housing in particular, the lack of an effective housing and social policy together with the factors mentioned above leads to the social reproduction of the patriarchal family (Ferrera 1999, Marí-Klose & Moreno-Fuentes 2013). The role of the family has deep historical roots and citizens tend to follow familistic housing strategies such as late emancipation from the parental home, intergenerational co-residence, and residential spatial proximity to members of the same extended family (Allen et al. 2004, Clogg 1983, Ferrera 2010). The scarcity and precariousness of employment opportunities for young people in combination with the absence of support from the state renders them insecure in moving on from their transitional life stage and realising their personal housing pathways (Bricocoli & Sabatinelli 2016, Micheli & Rosina 2010, Serracant 2015).

A triptych that is unfortunately commonplace in the public discourse but still represents the essence of Greek society is 'nation, religion, family' (*patris, thriskia, oikogenia*) (Carastathis 2018). These three institutions still reproduce the heteronormative imaginary while also being dependent on it.

The Greek state needs people focused on their microcosm – family – and willing to protect the rest of the family members, their belongings, and thus their territory by replacing the welfare state. Family, the main welfare provider of care, housing, and social protection, is put under extreme pressure to cover the needs of its members, moving the obligation and the cost away from employers and the state (Papadopoulos & Roumpakis 2013). Other forms of family outside of the heteropatriarchal model could harm this prosperous state strategy. Religion, the Greek Orthodox church in particular, is still linked administratively, financially, and ideologically with the state and retains a highly conservative stance against any form of lifestyle except for the heteropatriarchal one. Indicatively, according to Article 21 of the Constitution of the Republic of Greece (Hellenic Parliament 2008) (In the name of the Holy and Consubstantial and Indivisible Trinity): 'The family, being the cornerstone of the preservation and the advancement of the Nation, as well as marriage, motherhood and childhood, shall be under the protection of the State'. This phrase could testify to how important family is not just in terms of the state but also to the church, which supports this institution insofar as it reinforces its power. The three institutions are all based on specific gender roles and power imbalances and built upon patriarchal, racist, and discriminatory structures and a rhetoric aiming to reproduce them.

Family in Greek culture is associated with the concept of home, as the home is where a family is formed and maintained (Mallett 2004). The family home is where individuals' identities and collective family identities are expressed; therefore, there is continuous renegotiation through the successive generations about them (Valentine et al. 2003). The family home cannot be considered as merely a safe shelter or a hostile place per se (Mallett 2004), as both good and bad experiences, pain and happiness, create a stained glass of emotions and affirmations that can be embodied, in particular, by LGBTQ+ subjectivities. Family homes in particular act as sites for the imposition of ideals, rules, and primary societal behaviours; indeed, even when younger people move out, their childhood home remains a reference point for their personality and identity and defines their housing biographies. At home, people create their identities under the umbrella of prevailing social and power relations (Gorman-Murray 2008b). Conversely, the family home also constitutes a key site to challenge hegemonic social identities and develop unique identities (Gorman-Murray 2008a). In the context of Southern Europe, the family home is the base of the asymmetrical heteropatriarchal family, which has certain heterosexual and gendered relations. Therefore, LGBTQ+ members may have to suppress, in some cases, their non-normative sexuality and lifelong plans while they are still dependent on their families. In other words, the contemporary heterosexual family home formed in Greece may 'exclude' LGBTQ+ members because of the socio-sexual power relations that are dominant (ibid.). Although Greece is one of the first states in the European Union supposed to implement ideal modernised social reforms, domestic factors and especially the economy and religion have impacted in a conservative way the policy reforms that Greece undertook (Ayoub 2015). In particular, the Orthodox Church has been aggressively opposed to the EU regulations concerning rights for non-normative sexual preferences (Ayoub 2015).

The Orthodox Church sustains a great influence in Greek society and promotes, like the dominant political ideology, the heterosexual family as the core structure of the society (Allen et al. 2004). According to the ILGA report about Greece, there are incidents where the church is against LGBTQ+ rights and human rights in general. Indicatively, Amvrosios, the archbishop of Kalavryta, has stated that homosexuality is a deviation from the laws of nature and predicts that 'within a few years, the way things are headed, normal, physiological people will run and hide whereas the abnormal will double and control with their heinous pride' (Carastathis 2018, International Lesbian, Gay, Bisexual, Trans and Intersex Association 2017: 111, Pettas et al. 2022). One of the research partners, Olga, who self-identifies as lesbian and has not come out to her family, narrates her experience with the Orthodox Church's rhetoric and strategies:

> You can't imagine what propaganda exists from the Greek Orthodox Church [...] Christ said that the worst crime in the world is to be homosexual, to love the same sex [she points out ironically]. The church is giving them [the religious people] leaflets which say that worse than homicide is homosexuality. We are talking about this kind of hate being preached from the orthodox indoctrination. Unbelievable [...] I am insisting on this because this kind of brochure reaches me sometimes. My mother brings them and she makes me read them, so I see my enemy [...] I can't believe how outrageous they are.

The social progress that the Syriza–ANEL government tried to promote during their mandate – by trying to please the Church at the same time – faced religious hindrances that were only partly overcome. In particular, during the 2017 political debate about legal sex identity recognition based on self-determination the bishop Ieronymos exclaimed: 'All of these discussions are games. The Church has its own stance. Our *country* has its traditions, has the *family*. All the rest are invented to waste our time' (TVXS 2017). At the same time, LGBTQ+ community in Greece always challenged the heteronormative boundaries and this is evident especially in the history of queer geographies in Athens.

## ATHENS' QUEER GEOGRAPHIES AND HOUSING PROBLEM

The very first testimonies that queer geographies exist in Athens stem from the 1920s and liken Athens to the large European metropolises (Papanikolaou 2014). Until the 1970s, homoerotic public activities were natural and occurred without any taboos or discrimination, creating diffused homosexual geographies in Athens inside cinemas, buses, public baths, and parks with non-specific geographical margins, even though some streets were more appropriated than others in the centre of Athens (e.g. Patission street) (Aggelides 2009). In the 1970s, there were specific places catering to a more homosexually orientated clientele, especially in the Plaka area (Papanikolaou 2014). Later, during the 1980s and around the first outbreak of HIV, the city tried to control homoerotic expression by 'sanitising' the gay urban spots in order to attract tourism (Aggelides 2009, Papanikolaou 2014). Thereafter, the 'gay-friendly' places became more hidden and isolated in order to protect their clientele.

By the end of the 20th century, the commercialisation of homosexuality became apparent in the city, creating specific places and promoting gay culture as progressive and trendy (Marnelakis 2014). As a result, since the 2000s, Athens has offered gay and lesbian bars and restaurants, saunas, cafés, and even community centres in certain central areas such as Gazi, Psyrri, Metaxourgeio, and Kerameikos, creating an LGBTQ+ consumerist hub (Papanikolaou 2014). All in all, Athens has never had a clear-cut homosexual topography but it has contained urban islets of freedom that have changed over time and became more restricted as the decades went on. Thus Athens was a haven for Greek (and expat) LGBTQ+ individuals with dynamic homosexual geographies (Papanikolaou 2014: 166), but during the financial crisis, the geographies of homosexuality seemed even more tangled as a result of the economic downturn and the fascisisation of Greek society.

Nowadays, Athens is experiencing rapid commodification of its housing market and especially its accumulation through international funds (Alexandri & Janoschka 2018). The previous Greek financial crisis in connection with the Global Financial Crisis of 2008 was signed off by the sovereign debt crisis, which brought about the implementation of austerity policies with strict, mainly indirect budgetary cuts that affected housing and threatened the local and already 'fragile social fabric' (Matthijs 2014: 105). Specifically, the indirect cuts and drops in public expenditure impacted the formation of households and the related housing practices that families adopted in order to face the challenges (Naldini & Jurado 2013, Pinto & Guerra 2013, Serracant 2015).

The housing scenario of 'post-crisis' Greece is exposing another housing problem: the absence of construction activity for more than a decade in connection with the absence of housing loans from banks and the indebtedness of households because of the recent crisis and austerity. Since 2009, the bank loans for acquiring property stopped with the result that there has been a dramatic decrease in construction activity to zero (Pelevani 2020). Every year 15,000–20,000 households seek housing and the first choice is homeownership, but the absence of available and affordable options has turned more and more people toward the rental market (Pelevani 2020). This choice was not culturally popular in the years of prosperity before the crisis (until around 2009) as homeownership was always an aspiration for Greek families, which employed strategies in order to achieve this for their members.

In research by Eurostat, it was found that tenants in Greece spend more than 40% of their income on housing. Young people aged 20–30 in Greece will not be able to achieve homeownership as income is rising at a much slower pace than housing prices. In particular, Greece experienced a prolonged recession that lasted until 2017 and increasingly led housing prices down (42.5% from 2007 to 2017) (Delmendo 2022). Since 2018 the housing market seems to be recovering. By 2021 the property prices had risen by 20% (Wulandari 2022). The Covid-19 pandemic and the enhanced remote working positions in combination with the increase in savings brought about an amplified demand for properties, leading to an increase in housing prices. Moreover, disruptive housing trends, like digitally mediated short-term rentals (STRs) and real estate investments from international funds, exacerbated the housing problems in combination with the absence of any housing policy that could protect people. The bank-owned houses caused by foreclosures and the fact that property taxation led many people to sell their properties in previous years (Pelevani 2020) facilitated the success of STRs and the Golden Visa scheme, which offers permanent residency to non-EU citizens who invest EUR 250,000 in properties – the cheapest in Europe as it was proclaimed. This led to a situation of 'transnational gentrification', as Sigler and Wachsmuth (2016) suggested, where rent gaps are globally scaled without large new capital investments as it is just the existing housing reserves that are being taken advantage of, and this can cause crisis for the local residents who face housing prices set mainly by global rather than local demand. Therefore, there is evidence of housing unaffordability and displacement through the reduction in housing availability for long-term residents and increasing rents and housing prices (Gourzis et al. 2019). The displacement therefore is twofold, 'direct' and 'exclusionary', following Marcuse's (1985) distinction regarding gentrification's impact. In the first scenario, tenants are directly evicted by the landlords in order to raise rents, while in the second, the gentrification impacts on housing prices render them unaffordable for the local population (Wachsmuth & Weisler 2018).

So, more than ever now, inhabitants of Greece have to face multiple challenges related to social, economic, political, and cultural elements of the Greek housing system and LGBTQ+ people may face even bigger obstacles because of the related discrimination. This is also testified to by the housing movements that have been rising up during recent years after 2017 in urban centres.

## BOUNDARIES INSIDE THE HOME AND BEYOND

Research partners strove to navigate the available housing solutions in connection with their financial, social, and sexual statuses in the cultural context of the Greek family.

To grasp the imaginary of the daughter in the assemblage of inter-generational housing support, I here quote Alexandra (bisexual, 29), who faces the typical prospects for a daughter where her mother aspires to providing a future house for her in extreme proximity to the maternal one. However, Alexandra has not come out to her mother as a bisexual woman and faces multiple pressures to fit into the 'typical daughter' imaginary. Alexandra states:

> In general, my mother has imprinted the attitude: 'I'm not living away from my parents; I am with my parents and if I go, they will be very devastated'. […] My mother wanted to be with her mother and her father. I always wanted to leave. I liked very much living alone. […] She had thrown at me that, 'When you get married…'. 'Mum, I can't, I don't even have a job that could support me and my child and my family in general'. 'Don't you worry, we are here! It is OK, just 'make grandchildren for me', I will give you the house downstairs [which is her property] to live underneath my house and [I will provide you with] any food you need. We will be here, we will be together!' […] and I tell her, 'I don't like this thought, I don't support something like that, I don't like it, I wouldn't like to live like this'. […] Today I told her that, 'When I come back in the evening I want to talk to you' […] and she told me, 'Ouch, I understand that […] you are going to cohabitate. This is not positive for me. You are going to abandon Mummy'.

In the case of Alexandra, in addition to the naturalisation of heteronormativity, the dimension of gender highlights the inter-generational obligations that facilitate care reciprocity according to gender roles (Dagkouli-Kyriakoglou 2021b). Gender, ethnicity, class, and sexuality significantly mark one's rapport with the home (Mallett 2004). Therefore, even though she already feels the pressure to fulfil the imaginary of the daughter, she is also expected by her mother to stay close as long as she is single. Things become even more complicated when her coupledom cannot be disclosed because of the gender of her partner, keeping the single status for longer and reproducing these familial gender stereotypes:

> What I am afraid of is that when I tell her that I am moving in with X [a female friend] now, she is going to ask—'Is there something going on with X? Why do you want to move in with X? Why don't you find a man to move in with?' […] I am really afraid of that talk. […] In order to calm her down, I will tell her that one of us will be sleeping in the living room and the other one in the room.

In a similar note, Alex (27, sexuality disclosed) expressed the boundaries that are imposed in everyday life for LGBTQ+ people as long as they are supported in housing by the family:

> For example, I could meet a guy, and he would tell me, e.g. 'I live with my parents'. […] Then, because, obviously, we live in this era and this country, I cannot go to his home and watch a movie while hugging, and this is an important issue for the progress of a relationship. This situation occurred with my ex. […] He stayed in his paternal house, […] but because his parents were there, it was a burden for the whole relationship. […] In the beginning, I was thinking that it did not bother me, and nothing bad happened, but as time went on, you want to see the other person's place a bit, because I think that is how you get to know a person.

As it has been mentioned, inside the home there is a profound naturalisation of heteronormativity that accordingly imposes certain heterosexual and gendered relations (Valentine 1993). As Gaboury (2018) explains, queerness is marked by failure just because it is not considered useful – and even considered harmful – to a given society. Within capitalism, a clear connection between family, sex, desire, and consumption is demanded (Hocquenghem 1993) that for many decades was synonymous only with heterosexual reproduction. This happens in combination with the Greek welfare system, which is based on the existence of the nuclear family in order to free the state from its welfare obligations because it 'cannot afford' to lose the heteropatriarchal version of the family. Therefore, LGBTQ+ family members who 'come out' can face hostility reaching up to physical assault as a way for their parents to exercise their 'legitimate' power and retain the control of private space, i.e. the family home (Carastathis 2018). The local society and even the family may impose forced translocations on LGBTQ+ people, excluding them from areas – especially in the countryside – where non-heteronormative identity is highly stigmatised (ibid.). This attitude was encountered by Alex (27), whose mum expressed reluctance towards his attempt to come out in a specific geographical context, which was a small town:

> When I told her, 'What if […] I introduce you to a boy for my partner?' She said, 'OK, it is not my favourite option, but […] if it were in a bigger city like Athens, it would not bother me so much, because here in X [small Greek town], you know how the situation is…'.

'Home' is not a defined space per se, its boundaries are subjective and do not concern only the space that the dwelling occupies (Blunt 2005, Mallet 2004), but it can expand in areas and territories that one is able to control and appropriate. Therefore, in the queer literature there are also indications that LGBTQ+ people stretch home to the public space, blurring the actual boundaries and facilitating the affirmation and unhindered performance of non-heteronormative sexual and gender identities in everyday life with high 'public-private interaction' (Gorman-Murray 2006: 56). Correspondingly, there also exist geographical boundaries for the freedom to express oneself, and in Greece this concerns in particular the countryside. The countryside can suppress the freedom of LGBTQ+ people, whereas larger urban centres are regarded as more progressive places (Di Feliciantonio & Gadelha 2016, Guaracino 2007).

The countryside is not, at least presently, a welcoming place where LGBTQ+ people can live their personal lives, especially when there are family connections with these places. Most participants were at pains to emphasise that they could indeed go to their parents' hometowns as vacation destinations, but they had to conceal the identities of their partners if they wished to bring them there as well:

> I would bring him [the partner] there comfortably, but I wouldn't say to my dad, 'Dad, I am going with my boyfriend to X [the village]'. The same way I am going with my friends, I would also go with my boyfriend. (Aris, 30, closeted)

In most of the cases encountered in my fieldwork, people found ways to conceal or negotiate their rights to their personal lives without losing all their families' housing support. However, this was possible – at least at the beginning – only by 'play[ing] with their identities to gain normative heterosexual privileges' (Rodó-de-Zárate 2013: 8).

In a way, with this strategy, they succeeded in 'queering the family home' but suffered the cost of concealing their personal lives. The imposed boundaries for LGBTQ+ people in living their personal lives out in the open may harm their emotional and psychological well-being or, at least, lead to them losing intimate personal and family moments that every person has the right to experience. Therefore, it can be argued that the Greek household can become an 'unconscious queer shelter and site of blind-eye treatment' instead of the powerful image of a 'site of resistance to heterosexism and support for the ongoing development of gay, lesbian, bisexual identities' (Gorman-Murray 2008c: 32).

## CONCLUSIONS

The state, in connection with the family, the school, and the Church, supports the dominance of patriarchy, and this is also established through the state choice not to address housing needs through policy and to rely on family welfare. Moreover, during critical moments, people face boundaries on their housing possibilities from both the socioeconomic and political reality and the context of a familistic society that faces the weakening of the already inadequate welfare state and the rise of financial insecurity, which tend to lead to higher dependence on family for material and emotional support (Hughes & Valentine 2011). This can lead back to obedience to conservative, traditional social patterns (Serracant 2015). In contemporary Greece, there are still boundaries in relation to sexuality regarding who can enjoy housing and where. These boundaries are socially and culturally produced but also stem from the politics at stake.

As argued by housing scholars, family may also function as a decommodification mechanism (Papadopoulos & Roumpakis 2013: 207, Petmesidou 2013: 600). However, in an era of growing financialisation coupled with the neoliberalisation of the already weak welfare state, both family welfare and the housing dependent on it are at risk. Moreover, the new crisis related to Covid-19 highlighted the need for adequate and safe housing, which coincided with the reality of rapid commodification of housing in Greece. The more marginalised social groups will undoubtedly be more affected as they lack formal and informal support. In this vein, the LGBTQ+ community in Greece may have to deal with multiple obstacles to ensure housing. At the same time, during the pandemic (2020–2021), people were confined for many months in their homes in a domestic environment that was potentially hostile for women and queer people (Chatzifotiou & Andreadou 2021). It is important to investigate how LGBTQ+

people living with conservative, heteronormative families or dependent on them negotiated the new challenges.

There is a profound interconnection between the social and the economic, political, and cultural dimensions that exist in Greece and reproduce the family housing support patterns. The families that retain urban properties ensure an asset for the next generation and a form of financial security that reproduces social stratification through the years. This intergenerational provision of access to housing in a context of neoliberal urbanism and growing housing financialisation penalises those who belong to the more marginalised groups, exacerbating existing inequalities. The current housing problems in Greece are the worst that people have faced in the post-war period (1949 onwards). Now, as the main asset of family welfare is being attacked, people may have to struggle for their housing rights in the public arena and not just inside the family. Now that the shock-absorber (the family) has been weakened and housing problems are rising unprecedentedly in Greece, there may be an opportunity for a wider population to consider trusting alternative welfare agents and kinships, as well as housing arrangements. Refusing the confines of the successful normative life and housing pathway pushed by neoliberalism, patriarchy, and religion might offer new ways of being and homemaking.

# REFERENCES

Abramovich, A. (2013) No fixed address: Young, queer, and restless. In S. Gaetz et al. (eds.) *Youth Homelessness in Canada: Implications for Policy and Practice*. Toronto: Canadian Homelessness Research Network Press, 387–403.

Aggelides, D. (2009) Gay chronocapsoula [interview about gay life in 1970s in Athens]. 10%, 26. Retrieved from: http://www.10percent.gr/periodiko/teyxos26/12032009-06-19-09-14-03.html (in Greek).

Alexandri, G & Janoschka, M. (2018) Who loses and who wins in a housing crisis? Lessons from Spain and Greece for a nuanced understanding of dispossession. *Housing Policy Debate* 28(1): 117–134.

Allen, J., Barlow, J., Leal, J., Maloutas, T. & Padovani, L. (2004) *Housing and Welfare in Southern Europe*. Oxford: Blackwell Publishing/RICS Foundation.

Athanasiou, A. (2012) *Crisis as 'State of Emergency': Critiques and Resistances*. Athens: Savvalas (in Greek).

Arundel, R. & Lennartz, C. (2018) Dualization in labour markets and housing outcomes: Insiders versus outsiders. HOUWEL Working Paper Series, 12, 26.

Avdela, E. & Psarra, A. (2012) Secret aspects of the black vote. *Synchrona Themata* 117: 4–5 (in Greek).

Ayoub, P. M. (2015) Contested norms in new-adopter states: International determinants of LGBT rights legislation. *European Journal of International Relations* 21(2): 293–322.

Blunt, A. (2005) Cultural geography: cultural geographies of home. *Progress in Human Geography* 29(4): 505–515.

Bricocoli, M. & Sabatinelli, S. (2016) House sharing amongst young adults in the context of Mediterranean welfare: The case of Milan. *International Journal of Housing Policy* 16(2): 184–200.

Carastathis, A. (2018) 'Gender is the first terrorist': Homophobic and transphobic violence in Greece. *Frontiers: A Journal of Women Studies* 39(2): 265–296.

Castles, F. (1993) *Family of Nations. Patterns of Public Policy in Western Democracies*. Aldershot: Hants.

Chatzifotiou, S. & Andreadou, D. (2021) Domestic violence during the time of the COVID-19 pandemic: Experiences and coping behaviour of women from northern Greece. *International Perspectives in Psychology: Research, Practice, Consultation* 10(3): 180.

Clapham, D. (2002) Housing pathways: A post modern analytical framework. *Housing, Theory and Society* 19(2): 57–68.

Clogg, R. (ed.) (1983) *Greece in the 1980s*. London: Palgrave MacMillan.

Council of the State (2008) Council of the state 3003/2008. Exemption of first residence from real estate transfer tax. *Taxheaven*. Retrieved from: https://www.taxheaven.gr/circulars/11064/stc-3003-2008 (Accessed 12 November 2022).

Dagkouli-Kyriakoglou, M. (2021a) 'When housing is provided, but you have only the closet'. Sexual orientation and family housing support in Athens, Greece. *Social & Cultural Geography* 23(9): 1257–1274.

Dagkouli-Kyriakoglou, M. (2021b) 'Keeping the children close and the daughters closer'. Is family housing support in Greece gendered? *European Journal of Women's Studies* 29(2): 266–281.

Delmendo, L. (2022) Economic growth increasing. *Global Property Guide*, 11 March. Retrieved from: https://www.globalpropertyguide.com/Europe/Greece (accessed 20 May 2022).

Di Feliciantonio, C. & Gadelha, K. B. (2016) Situating queer migration within (national) welfare regimes. *Geoforum* 68: 1–9.

Eleftheriadis, K. (2015) Queer responses to austerity: Insights from the Greece of crisis. *ACME: An International Journal for Critical Geographies* 14(4): 1032–1057. Retrieved from: https://www.acme-journal.org/index.php/acme/article/view/1159.

Ferrera, M. (1999) Reconstructing the welfare state in Southern Europe. In M. Matsaganis (ed.) *Prospects of the Welfare State in Southern Europe*. Athens: Ellinika Grammata, 33–66 (in Greek).

Ferrera, M. (2010) The South European countries. In F. G. Castel, S. Leibfried, J. Lewis & C. Pierson (eds.) *The Oxford Handbook of the Welfare State*. Oxford: Oxford University Press, 616–629.

Forrest, R. & Murie, A. (eds.) (1995) *Housing and Family Wealth: Comparative International Perspectives*. London: Routledge.

Gaboury, J. (2018) Becoming NULL: Queer relations in the excluded middle. *Women & Performance: A Journal of Feminist Theory* 28(2): 143–158.

Geltis, T. (2019) LGBTQ homeless and networks of housing support. In N. Kourachanis (ed.) *Housing and Society: Problems, Policies and Social Movements*. Athens: Dionikos Publications, 423–446 (in Greek).

Gorman-Murray, A. (2006) Homeboys: Uses of home by gay Australian men. *Social & Cultural Geography* 7(1): 53–69.

Gorman-Murray, A. (2008a) Reconciling self: Gay men and lesbians using domestic materiality for identity management. *Social and Cultural Geography* 9(3): 283–301.

Gorman-Murray, A. (2008b) Masculinity and the home: A critical review and conceptual framework. *Australian Geographer* 39(3): 367–379.

Gorman-Murray, A. (2008c) Queering the family home: Narratives from gay, lesbian and bisexual youth coming out in supportive family homes in Australia. *Gender, Place and Culture* 15: 31–44.

Gough, I. (1996) Social assistance in Southern Europe. *South European Society and Politics* 1(1): 1–23.

Gourzis, K., Alexandridis, G., Gialis, S. & Caridakis, G. (2019) Studying the spatialities of short-term rentals' sprawl in the urban fabric: The case of Airbnb in Athens, Greece. *IFIP International Conference on Artificial Intelligence Applications and Innovations*. Cham: Springer, 196–207.

Guaracino, J. (2007) *Gay and Lesbian Tourism: The Essential Guide for Marketing*. Amsterdam: Butterworth-Heinemann.

Hellenic Parliament (2008) The constitution of Greece. Retrieved from: https://www.hellenicparliament.gr/UserFiles/f3c70a23-7696-49db-9148-f24dce6a27c8/001-156%20aggliko.pdf (Accessed 10 May 2022).

Hocquenghem, G. (1993 [1972]) *Homosexual Desire*. Durham, NC: Duke University Press.

Hughes, K. & Valentine, G. (2011) Practices of display: The framing and changing of internet gambling behaviours in families. In E. Dermott & J. Seymour (eds.) *Displaying Families, A New Concept for the Sociology of Family Life*. Basingstoke: Palgrave Macmillan, 125–144.

Human Rights Watch (2010) *My So-Called Emancipation: From Foster Care to Homelessness for California Youth*. New York, NY: Human Rights Watch.

Hunter, E. (2008) What's good for the gays is good for the gander: Making homeless youth housing safer for lesbian, gay, bisexual, and transgender youth. *Family Court Review* 46(3): 543–557.

International Lesbian, Gay, Bisexual, Trans and Intersex Association (2017) Annual review for Greece. Retrieved from: https://www.ilga-europe.org/sites/default/files/2017/greece.pdf.

Kourachanis, N. (2018) Forms of social exclusion in familistic welfare capitalism: Family homelessness in Athens. *Journal of Social Research & Policy* 9(1): 69–80.

Leibfried, S. (1992) Towards a European welfare state. In S. Ferge & J. Kolberg (eds.) *Social Policy in a Changing Europe*. Boulder: Westview Press, 245–279.

Leontidou, L. (1990) *The Mediterranean City in Transition: Social Change and Urban Development*. Cambridge: Cambridge University Press.

Mallett, S. (2004) Understanding home: A critical review of the literature. *The Sociological Review* 52(1): 62–89.

Mantouvalou, M. (1985) Building in Athens after the war: Economic and social views of an opportunistic development, Athens as it (does not) look. Report of the Hellenic Ministry of Culture, Education and Religious Affairs 1940–1985. Retrieved from: http://courses.arch.ntua.gr (in Greek).

Marcuse, P. (1985) Gentrification, abandonment, and displacement: Connections, causes, and policy responses in New York City. *Journal of Urban and Contemporary Law* 28: 195–240.

Marí-Klose, P. & Moreno-Fuentes, F. J. (2013) The Southern European welfare state model in the post-industrial order. Still a distinctive cluster? *European Societies* 15(4): 475–492.

Marnelakis, G. (2014) *Close Contacts of Gender, Sexuality and Space*. Athens: Futura (in Greek).

Martin, C. (2015) Southern welfare states: Configuration of the welfare balance between state and the family. In M. Baumeister & R. Sala (eds.) *Southern Europe? Italy, Spain, Portugal & Greece from the 1950s until the present day*. New York, NY and Frankfurt: Campus, 77–100.

Matthijs, M. (2014) Mediterranean blues: The crisis in Southern Europe. *Journal of Democracy* 25(1): 101–115.

May, J. (2000) Housing histories and homeless careers: A biographical approach. *Housing Studies* 15(4): 613–638.

Mayer, K. & Tuma, N. (eds.) (1987) *Application of Event History Analysis in Life Course Research*. Berlin: Max Planck Institute for Human Development.

Micheli, G. A., & Rosina, A. (2010) The vulnerability of young adults on leaving the parental home. In C. Ranci (ed.) *Social Vulnerability in Europe: The New Configuration of Social Risks*. Basingstoke: Palgrave Macmillan, 189–218.

Minguez, A. M. (2005) The persistence of male breadwinner model in Southern European countries in a compared perspective: Familism, employment and family policies. *MCFA Annals* IV.

Moreno, L. & Marí-Klose, P. (2013) Youth, family change and welfare arrangements: Is the South still so different? *European Societies* 15(4): 493–513.

Mousourou, M. L. (1993) *Sociology of Modern Family*. Athens: Gutenberg (in Greek).

Naldini, M. & Jurado, T. (2013) Family and welfare state reorientation in Spain and inertia in Italy from a European perspective. *Population Review* 52(1): 43–61.

Papadopoulos, T. & Roumpakis, A. (2013) Familistic welfare capitalism in crisis: Social reproduction and anti-social policy in Greece. *Journal of International and Comparative Social Policy* 29(3): 204–224.

Papanikolaou, D. (2014) Mapping/unmapping: The making of queer Athens. In M. Cook & J. V. Evans (eds.) *Queer Cities, Queer Cultures: Europe since 1945*. Bloomsbury, 151–170. https://doi.org/10.5040/9781474210898.ch-008.

Pinto, T. C., & Guerra, I. (2013) Some structural and emergent trends in social housing in Portugal. Rethinking housing policies in times of crisis. *Cidades, Comunidades e Territórios*, 27: 1–21.

Pelevani, M. (2020) Why did the rent prices rise? [Γιατί εκτοξεύτηκαν οι τιμές των ενοικίων]. *tvxs.gr*, 18 February. Retrieved from: https://tvxs.gr/news/ellada/giati-ektokseytikan-oi-times-ton-enoikion (accessed 10 March 2021) (in Greek).

Petmesidou, M. (2013) Is social protection in Greece at a crossroads? *European Societies* 15(4): 597–616.

Pettas, D., Arampatzi, A., & Dagkouli-Kyriakoglou, M. (2022). LGBTQ+ housing vulnerability in Greece: Intersectionality, coping strategies and, the role of solidarity networks. *Housing Studies*, doi: 10.1080/02673037.2022.2092600.

Rodó-de-zárate, M. (2013) Young lesbians negotiating public space: An intersectional approach through places. *Children's Geographies* 13(4): 413–434.

Saraceno, C. (1994) The ambivalent familism of the Italian welfare state. *Social Politics* 1(1): 60–82.

Sigler, T. & Wachsmuth, D. (2016) Transnational gentrification: Globalisation and neighbourhood change in Panama's Casco Antiguo. *Urban Studies* 53(4): 705–722.

Serracant, P. (2015) The impact of the economic crisis on youth trajectories: A case study from Southern Europe. *Young* 23(1): 39–58.
TVXS (2017) Ieronymos for gender identity: Greece has traditions, all the rest is invented. *TVXS*, 2 October. Retrieved from: http://tvxs.gr/news/ellada/ieronymos-gia-taytotita-fyloy-iellada-exei-paradoseis-ola-ta-alla-einai-efeyrimata (in Greek).
Vaiou, D. (2014a) Tracing aspects of the Greek crisis in Athens: Putting women in the picture. *European Urban and Regional Studies* 23(3): 220–230.
Vaiou, D. (2014b) Is the crisis in Athens (also) gendered?: Facets of access and (in) visibility in everyday public spaces. *City* 18(4–5): 533–537.
Valentine, G. (1993) (Hetero)sexing space: Lesbian perceptions and experiences of everyday spaces. *Environment and Planning D: Society and Space* 11(4): 395–413.
Valentine, G., Skelton, T. & Butler, R. (2003) Coming out and outcomes: Negotiating lesbian and gay identities with, and in, the family. *Environment and Planning D: Society and Space* 21(5): 479–99.
Wachsmuth, D. & Weisler, A. (2018) Airbnb and the rent gap: Gentrification through the sharing economy. *Environment and Planning A: Economy and Space* 50(6): 1147–1170.
Wulandari, F. (2022) Greece house price crash: Are an overheated economy and high inflation setting the scene for another property price bubble? *Capital.com*, 15 December. Retrieved from: https://capital.com/greece-house-price-crash (accessed 4 July 2022).

# 29. Urban squatting movements, the right to the city and solidarity networks: the case of the metropolitan region of Belo Horizonte, Brazil

*Clarissa Cordeiro de Campos*

This chapter assumes that most struggles over power in urban space by social movements, such as squatting, are forms of daily anti-hegemonic resistance against contemporary neoliberal policies and their effects. Neoliberal political and economic doctrine suggests that individual entrepreneurial freedoms, strong private property rights, free markets, and free trade are key to promoting human well-being (Harvey 2005). Neoliberal policies therefore relate to the role of the state in promoting the necessary institutional framework to guarantee the effective operation of that logic. Some of their effects, however, are rampant income inequality, drastically reduced social protections by the state, and market-oriented urban planning that overwhelmingly excludes low-income populations (Harvey 2005).

In this sense, the proposed analysis draws upon several authors who have historically considered space as at the same time a product and a conditioner of social relations (Lefebvre 1991, 2016, Soja 2000, Souza 2006). In other words, space, traditionally controlled by heteronomous urban planning imposed by external agents without participation from local communities, or by institutionalised participation, is not merely the physical and inert base on which one acts. On the contrary, in its articulations, openings and closures, circulations, interruptions, and locations, space becomes a crucial resource for the way one lives and acts and thus for the configuration of power relations (Foucault 1995). In the latter, the interests of the ruling classes are usually imposed to the detriment of the dominated social groups (which in Brazil are predominantly black and poor people). For this reason, I argue for the necessity of connecting social struggles to the social processes of the production of space.

Insurgent spatial practices—that is, those practices that are fundamentally rooted in the appropriation, transformation, and use of space, more often by subaltern social groups, in opposition to long-naturalised, homogenised, heteronomous, and oppressive socio-spatial relations (Souza 2010)—express, experiment with, and even prefigure other possibilities for life and society. A significant example of such practices is the unauthorised occupation of land and buildings, commonly referred to in English as squatting. There is currently a rich literature on the topic. Nonetheless, in large part publications refer to cases in the Global North. These include views on squats as alternatives to capitalism and vectors of autonomous practices and struggles for housing and the right to the city; squatting and its connections with art and culture and gender and ethnic issues; the interfaces between squatting and mainstream and alternative media; institutionalisation, criminalisation, and repression of squatting; historical aspects of squatting; and many other topics (Cattaneo et al. 2014, Martínez 2002, 2018, 2020, Moore & Smart 2015, Polanska 2019, Squatting Europe Kollective 2013, Squatting Everywhere Kollective 2018, Vasudevan 2017).

In Brazil, the expression *sem-teto* (roof-less) has historically been used to refer to the street population, especially among the mainstream media. However, activists of *sem-teto* movements participating in occupations are, in reality, a specific type of squatters, usually poor people, informal workers in hyper-precarious situations, and generally quite politicised (Souza 2006). They have grown in relevance, especially since the 1990s (Souza 2006), and deeply relate to the lack of decent housing and land for the poor, including both urban and rural dimensions. One of their primary forms of action is taking power over space, squatting abandoned buildings and/or unproductive rural and urban lands belonging to the state or reserved for real estate speculation (Bastos et al. 2017, Campos 2020, Franzoni 2018, Moreira 2017).

In the specific context of the *Região Metropolitana de Belo Horizonte* (RMBH, Metropolitan Region of Belo Horizonte), the third-largest urban agglomeration in Brazil, there are studies that have investigated several aspects of squatting, including both land and building occupations; interfaces and interconnections between squatting, other social movements, and supportive collectives; legal issues, repression, evictions, and displacements; squats as spaces of autonomy and as urban commons and their contradictions; and squats in relation to theories of space (Bastos et al. 2017, Campos 2020, Franzoni 2018, Lelis 2016, Lourenço 2014, Moreira 2017, Nascimento & Libânio 2016, Nogueira 2019, Tonucci Filho 2017). Even though the vast majority of squatters in the RMBH are poor families who occupy due to housing needs, there have been some novel developments, especially in the last ten years. Among these are a pronounced tendency to form solidarity networks and a sustained expansion of struggles in the direction of the right to the city (Lefebvre 2016, Mayer 2012), which are this chapter's main focus of interest.

This chapter contends that these are significant features of squatting practices in the RMBH and suggests that they can be understood as a specific type of urban social movement instead of isolated forms of direct action. Even though other authors have argued that squatting can be understood as an urban social movement in other countries (Babic 2015, Martínez 2020, Owens 2013, Padrones Gil 2017) and even in Brazil (Souza 2010), in the RMBH it is broadly seen as a form of direct action strategically organised by other social movements, not as a social movement in itself.

In this regard, Souza (2006) makes an accurate differentiation between the concepts of *social activism* and *social movement*. For this author, social activism should be considered as a more comprehensive concept, constituted by different forms of organised, essentially public and collective actions, which may include local activist groups that operate more or less as mere pressure groups 'in order to preserve certain privileges or obtain some gains in the general framework of the economic and political status quo, and without criticising status quo as such' (Souza 2006: 340). On the other hand, social movements would be special forms of social activism, particularly ambitious and critical, 'at the same time embedded in place-specific experiences and committed to more general, "universal" ethical values and broader political goals' (Souza 2006: 340). In this sense, while every movement can be considered a form of activism, the opposite is not true (Souza 2001).[1]

This chapter partially presents the results of the author's doctoral research (Campos 2020).[2] It was based on participant observation and semi-structured interviews with activists, researchers, participants, and residents in urban squats across the RMBH. Participant observation fieldwork covered land occupations for housing/self-construction and squats in abandoned buildings both for housing and for other political and cultural uses. In total, nine field visits to occupations were conducted, and 15 people agreed to participate in interviews, either individually or as a group. Additionally, the author currently coordinates a counter-mapping project (Kollectiv Orangotango 2018, Peluso 1995) in cooperation with other researchers, activists, and squatters in the RMBH, which also contributed to formulating some of the ideas presented in this chapter.

The following sections present a brief theoretical overview of squatting in different parts of the globe and, more specifically, in the RMBH. Afterwards, the empirical data concerning squatters' struggles for the right to the city and the relevance of their solidarity networks are critically assessed, followed by concluding remarks.

## URBAN SQUATTING IN THE 'GLOBAL NORTH AND SOUTH': DIFFERENCES AND POSSIBLE APPROXIMATIONS

The differentiation between the Global North and South, given its clear power-imposing intentions (political, economic, intellectual) and its oversimplifying and generalising logic, is not sufficient to systematise and critically analyse social phenomena from an international point of view. On the other hand, precisely because it reflects existing power relations and domination interests so well, it is also quite hard to escape its use. Thus, it is with caution that I apply these terms.

Comparative research in urban studies also presents technical obstacles. For example, language barriers and geographical distances (Grashoff & Yang 2020), or even possible incommensurability when contexts are just too different (Robinson 2011), may limit any such efforts. If carefully conducted, however, comparative research can promote different insights and innovative thinking by contributing to testing theoretical propositions and to identifying limitations or omissions in existing accounts (McFarlane 2010, Robinson 2016).

While squatting is an inherently local phenomenon, squatters frequently seek broader solutions or alternatives to wide-ranging political issues. As a result, even though squatters' actions and achievements vary according to particular frameworks of opportunities and constraints (Martínez 2020), some of their methods and strategies, and many of their ideological points of view, coincide.

The literature review and fieldwork activities I conducted (Campos 2020) allowed the identification of diverse common features between squatting movements in different parts of the globe, both in the North and the South. For instance, squatters usually aim at becoming autonomous in terms of housing and frequently experiment with new forms of dwelling instead of simply submitting to the bureaucratic regulation of housing by the state and the market (Nascimento & Libânio 2016, Pruijt 2013, Vasudevan 2015). In doing so, they contest unjust norms of private property rights, such as long and time-consuming waiting lists, expensive rental rates, housing shortages, real estate speculation, and false civil participation (Bastos et al. 2017, Franzoni 2018, Martínez 2013, Pruijt 2013).

In all the addressed contexts, squatting also implied intense processes of political socialisation that work as pedagogical tools for the collective exercise of civil rights, self-organisation, and self-expression (Lourenço 2014, Martínez 2013). At the same time as squatters are intensely politicised, their ideological views are diversified and they include anarchists, communists, anti-imperialists, anti-fascists, animalists (respect for and protection of the rights of all animals), feminists, queers, and others (Fucolti 2015, Lledin 2015, Moore & Smart 2015). Such autonomous principles also contribute to the definition of self-management methods, which usually include assembly-oriented decision-making processes (Bastos et al. 2017, Martínez 2013, Tonucci Filho 2017).

When we turn to local specificities instead of general principles, however, particularities tend to surface. Even though squatting movements are historically and deeply related to struggles for decent housing, in many European cities there is a pronounced presence of squats that are not specifically for housing (at least in terms of how they publicly present themselves) but rather engage with other social, political, and cultural concerns (Squatting Europe Kollective 2013, Squatting Everywhere Kollective 2018). In Brazilian cities, on the other hand, as is the case in the RMBH, although urban squatting movements encompass a broad range of political, economic, and social issues, they are mainly targeted at providing housing for those in need (Campos 2020, Campos & Martínez 2020, Lelis 2016).

Moreover, while land occupations for housing in peripheral areas represent the majority of cases in Brazil and the RMBH, these might be only occasional elsewhere. In Spain, for instance, while there are cases of unauthorised occupations of empty land within the boundaries of consolidated cities, these are mostly used for setting up community gardens and meeting places, while land occupations for housing only occasionally appear in peripheral areas of the main cities (Campos & Martínez 2020).

Singularities such as these justify testing wide-ranging theoretical assumptions, especially those conceived in distinct contexts from those under study. While the right to the city seems a plausible theoretical lens to study squatting movements in general (Mayer 2012), in their practices and discourses squatters appropriate, actualise, and create new meanings for what a right to the city should be to meet their demands (Campos 2020). Thus, it is not a matter of simply checking whether or not squatting fits into this notion, as if it were a paradigm that needs to be met. Rather, it concerns the possibility of expanding our understanding of what the right to the city implies in different contexts and struggles.

In a correlated manner, squatters' aptitude and capability to form networks at different scales is a key dimension of their daily social lives and mobilisations (Cattaneo 2013, Fucolti 2015, Padrones Gil 2017, Tonucci Filho 2017). Unlike the stiffness of institutionalised networks, squatters' networks are usually flexible, permeable, and changeable, formed by more or less stable bonds based mainly on affinity, exchange, solidarity, and mutual aid. Nonetheless, while networking seems to be widely perceived as desirable and beneficial (Campos 2020), squatters' concerns about interactions with other actors and correlated issues differ in each case.

In this sense, although similarities contribute to a sense of shared identity across the various manifestations of squatting, it is rather the differences in contexts and practices that truly reveal the complexity and rich diversity of squatting movements, hence the need to avoid a universalising theoretical practice and instead commit to thinking through a diversity of urban outcomes (Robinson 2016). With this in mind, the next sections present some of the specific features of the squatting movement in the RMBH.

## SOCIOECONOMIC SHIFTS IN BRAZIL AND THEIR IMPLICATIONS FOR URBAN SQUATTING IN THE RMBH

Urban neoliberalism and its effects have been historically contested by squatting practices and movements in Brazil, mainly since the 1990s (Souza 2006). Although Brazil has important and consolidated constitutional regulations, such as the social function of private property (implying that the right to private property is necessarily tied to its use according to the general interest) and the right to adequate housing, housing injustice remains a key driver of unauthorised occupations.

In practice, even if an important part of the existing legislation aims at combating the perpetuation of real estate speculation—which is basically the constitution of a stock of empty and unused properties by a wealthy minority in the expectation that their market value will increase in the future—instruments available to curb this type of practice are hardly ever employed or are insufficiently applied, demonstrating a clear prioritisation of the right to private property over the guarantee of its social function. Similarly, housing policies have not been sufficient to overcome the issue of housing provision for the least privileged populational groups, resulting in significant housing deficits. Thus, although considered illegal, the unauthorised occupation of unused land and buildings might be seen as a 'tool in the hands of lay citizens to meet the constitutional dispositions' (Campos & Martínez 2020: 117)—which is also frequently a part of squatters' arguments to justify their actions.

The global financial crisis that started in 2008 also had important consequences in Brazil. While in the first moment the most severe impacts were felt by countries in the Global North, economic growth rates in most of Latin and South America were still rising. According to Cardoso (2018), in the years 2000–2016 some of the countries in South America could reduce social vulnerability by establishing socioeconomic policies addressing social inclusion, recovering the role of the state, and setting foreign policies with relative independence. With this strategy, some countries, including Brazil, did not immediately suffer as much from the impacts of the global crisis and were even able to continue expanding domestic consumer markets (Cardoso 2018). As an example, a recent report demonstrates that between 2002 and 2014 there was a consistent reduction in socioeconomic inequality in Brazil, which reached its lowest level in 2010 compared to the previous 50 years. This was the result of investments in education and social programs, as well as the economic stability promoted by the *Plano Real* (Real Plan).[3]

At the same time, however, Latin American countries have historically invested in economic policies mainly oriented to the export of agricultural and mineral raw materials to the detriment of regional economic integration and productive diversification. The decline in exports and the market value of raw materials from 2013 represented an essential factor for the current undermining of Latin American economies (Katz 2016). Brazil is no exception: since 2014, the socio-political and economic scenario in the country has drastically changed. Processes of privatisation and scrapping of state-owned companies became rampant, food security policies became at risk of being dismantled, the income of workers fell, unemployment rates turned increasingly high, and domestic markets in turn shrunk (Cardoso 2018). In this scenario, although still profoundly motivated by housing injustice, urban squatting movements in the country have presented a broader spectrum of struggles for socio-spatial justice, especially in the last decade.

Depending on local specificities, these may include struggles for urban infrastructure; access to public transportation, services, and facilities; leisure and job opportunities; cultural, political, and other neighbourhood-oriented projects; and many others. In some cases, the remarkable spatial struggles to appropriate the city centre also indicate that, as suggested by Campos and Martínez (2020), the fulfilment of the right to housing is not complete unless accompanied by adequate living conditions, social visibility, and political recognition, pointing to a broader dispute for the right to the city (Lefebvre 2016).

It is, however, important to note that land occupations for housing in peripheral urban areas are still the majority of cases in the RMBH (of which Belo Horizonte is the main city). These are basically constituted by poor people, frequently unemployed or employed under precarious and informal work conditions. They can include tens to thousands of families in areas that do not offer adequate access to quality urban infrastructure, public services, cultural venues, leisure areas, job opportunities, and other amenities. In squatting large portions of neglected land, the squatters' primary objective is to stay put and consolidate their communities while at the same time struggling for adequate living conditions.[4]

Building occupations, on the other hand, are in most cases for housing, even though some of the most recent cases also include cultural uses, support for women in situations of violence, and other political purposes, such as safe spaces to hold meetings for different collectives and the organisation of talks, debates, campaigns, protests, parties, cultural events, and other activities. Equally important, not only do the squatters desire to access the many benefits of being located in central areas but in many cases they also aim to provide collectively built reference spaces, open to the local neighbourhoods and the city. Similar to land occupations for housing, people who live in building occupations are most frequently poor, in many cases unemployed or informal workers of various ages.

## STRUGGLES FOR THE RIGHT TO THE CITY

The notion of the right to the city has been extensively discussed and to some extent (even if tentatively or debatably) applied over the years from South to North by many actors, be they representatives of the state or private interests, academics, members of social movements, or activists. Not only has this resulted in fruitful theoretical proposals and developments related to Lefebvre's work (Marcuse 2012, Martínez 2020, Mayer 2012, Merrifield 2011, Mitchell 2003), but elements of the right to the city framework have also figured as part of recent urban policies (albeit more often in a reductionist and limited fashion) and served as recurring slogans of certain urban social movements.

Nonetheless, while this notion has been somewhat incorporated into laws, governmental agendas, and policies, it is striking how frequently the demands of grassroots initiatives are contrary to the results of these same policies, which supposedly share with them the same democratic principles. As an example, Brazilian Law no. 10,257/2001—the City Statute—regulates and complements the urban policy instruments provided for in Articles 182 and 183 of the country's Federal Constitution of 1988. The City Statute has as one of its general guidelines the guaranteeing of the right to sustainable cities (Article 2), understood as the right to urban land, housing, environmental sanitation, urban infrastructure, transportation and public services, work, and leisure for present and future generations. Furthermore, in its text, the City Statute reaffirms the democratic and participative management of urban projects and policies (especially Articles 2, 4, 40, 43, 44, and 45) and the fulfilment of the social function of properties while regulating instruments aimed at avoiding real estate speculation (see for example Articles 2, 4, 5, 6, 7, 8, and 39).

As can be noted, some of the constitutive elements of the right to the city as defended by Lefebvre (2016) are to a certain point present throughout the text of this law, as is the case regarding the capacity to access different parts of the city with quality transportation and within a reasonable time, the right to be provided with adequate public spaces and services, the right to have access to dignified housing and work, and the possibility of participating in the processes of producing the city—even though participation is still understood as a heteronomous process. Nonetheless, as Mayer (2012) suggests, institutionally enumerated rights, even if fully realised (which is usually not the case), target particular aspects of the current city as it exists instead of aiming to transform the existing city. As much as certain components of the right to the city may be listed in laws and regulations, it remains something to be fought for. As obvious as it might seem, a real change is not in the plans of those who assure their privileges by maintaining the status quo.

More in tune with the Lefebvrian notion, Mayer (2012) observes, the right to the city that urban social movements refer to is an oppositional demand that challenges the claims of the rich and powerful, and as such it exceeds the juridical scope. For example, the Movimento de Luta nos Bairros, Vilas e Favelas (MLB, Movement of Struggles in Neighbourhoods, Villages, and Favelas) is a national social movement in Brazil that considers squatting a fundamental strategy of struggle and anti-capitalist resistance.[5] The MLB was founded in 1999 and currently has outstanding participation in the squatting movement in the RMBH. In a recent publication, the MLB stated that, among other aspects:

> the city is the place of diversity, of meeting, of collective coexistence, of democratic life. That is why all people should have the right to the city, understood as the right to land, means of subsistence, housing, environmental sanitation, health, education, public transportation, food, work, leisure, and information. The right to the city is also the right to say in which city we want to live, the right to change the city, to recreate it, to democratise it. (Movimento de Luta nos Bairros, Vilas e Favelas 2019)

For Martínez (2020), in turn, the notion of the right to the city as proposed by Lefebvre, as broad as it may be, does not suffice to cover all the kinds of claims, socio-spatial practices, opportunities, and challenges that most squatters' struggles encompass. The author contends:

> that the right to the city approach illuminates the theoretical interpretation of squatting movements as far as: (1) these activists perform concrete appropriations of urban spaces; (2) squatted spaces are centrally located in relation to other urban facilities and social networks; and (3) beyond occupying empty properties for dwelling, squatters develop deep practices of self-management, self-help, direct democracy, the empowerment of the dispossessed and oppressed by capitalism, non-commercial services, social encounters, and infrastructures for political mobilisation. (Martínez 2020: 56)

This chapter suggests that the notion of centrality, a vital aspect of the right to the city as proposed by Lefebvre, should be looked at with caution. As Merrifield (2017) suggests, Lefebvre linked the right to the city with a geographical right to the centre of the city (one that was overpriced and becoming gentrified and turned into a tourist spectacle). There are indeed several squats in central economic and political areas of cities, including in the RMBH, their locations intentionally chosen to allow as much access as possible to a whole, complete, inclusive urban life. Other examples, however, show us that centrality may have different meanings for different people—or, as Lefebvre (1991: 332) himself suggests, 'centrality is movable' and permanence in the city centre might, in some cases, even be contested by squatters.

As the fieldwork conducted in the RMBH substantiates, while land occupations for housing represent 68% of the total occupations identified in this Metropolitan Region, most of which

464  *Research handbook on urban sociology*

are located in peripheral neighbourhoods of Belo Horizonte, occupations of abandoned buildings, the vast majority also for housing, account for an important share of 32%. Differently from land occupations, with very few exceptions building occupations are in central and economically privileged areas of the city. In general, the choice to squat the city centre is related, among other things, to better conditions of urban infrastructure, public transportation, job opportunities, and greater access to public services, such as healthcare facilities, schools, and recreational areas—as well as to an expectation that occupying buildings is less costly (in terms of time, money, and other factors) since, although it certainly involves maintenance work, it does not imply self-construction of houses and urban infrastructure.

Over ten years of systematically occupying the city centre,[6] on the other hand, has allowed squatters, social movements, and collectives to better understand and reflect on its positive aspects and the important challenges that could only be experienced through practice. Firstly, some of the agreements that have been negotiated with the local government partially refer squatters back to more peripheral locations rather than contributing to their further integration in the city centre. However, it is of great importance to note that, at least in part, this shift back to self-construction out of central areas also reflects a preference expressed by some of the squatters after experiencing living in the city centre.

Although this was not consensual among interviewees, examples of issues that arose from their experiences of squatting long-abandoned buildings in central areas were: 1) time- and resource-demanding maintenance processes, which also implied physical and psychological distress for residents, to the point that some squatters gave up staying in the buildings; 2)

*Source:* Clarissa Cordeiro de Campos.

*Figure 29.1*   *Paulo Freire occupation in the Metropolitan Region of Belo Horizonte (2019)*

difficulties in identifying suitable buildings with sufficient area to adequately house the large numbers of homeless families; 3) a sometimes overwhelming collectiviation of life within the limited area of the buildings, which, according to the interviewees, may be much more intense than in lands for self-construction, leading eventually to conflictive situations.

In this sense, as much as struggles for the right to the city may be linked to critically squatting central areas of the cities, the experiences in land occupations for self-construction in the RMBH should not be disregarded as such (see Figure 29.1). These large portions of disused peripheral land with no urban infrastructure sometimes house thousands of families. They represent massive squatting actions, which, if at first responding to the primary need for survival, are followed by a profound aspiration to a full social life. They encompass the creation of new spaces, the demand for services and infrastructure, and the claim to be heard and seen as producers of culture, knowledge, and alternative forms of work. This chapter thus contends that in such cases the right to the city is often related to coming out of the shadows of invisibility, to ceasing to inhabit a non-space, ceasing to be non-citizens, and to being recognised as political beings: a right to the city that is also a right to produce and integrate the city.

## NETWORKING AS A FUNDAMENTAL ASPECT OF SQUATTING

Squats in the RMBH exist in relation to all other socio-spatial aspects of cities and therefore they should not be looked at in isolation. On the contrary, squatters' aptitude and capability to form networks at different scales are inherent in their everyday lives. More than a simple will to interact, networking is vital for squatters as a means of solidarity and of exchanging knowledge or seeking legitimation and support (from the surrounding neighbourhood, the media, or even local governments). It is also strategic, functioning as a tool for strengthening initiatives, diversifying mobility possibilities (e.g. in cases of eviction), and amplifying their range of action.

Networking can also reflect shifting scales and different levels of action, such as between different squats, squats and their neighbourhoods, squatters and other activists, and other groupings, which can happen all at the same time. Finally, there is an essentially heterogeneous character to squatters' networks that reflects their different interests, practices, discourses, and demands. These are sometimes related to political and ideological views such as feminism and combating racism, homophobia, and state violence. In other cases, networks are triggered by the need for greater access to urban infrastructure, services, culture, leisure, workplaces, and other amenities.

The concern with further integration with local communities is an important feature in both land and building occupations in the RMBH. Even in the case of occupations mainly geared at providing housing as a primary and urgent need, forging ties with people from the immediate vicinity and the city and planning open activities are part of their agenda. As an interviewee from Dandara (a land occupation for housing in the RMBH) observed, their struggles would bring improvements to other neighbourhoods nearby as well, and this was why, in her opinion, it was important to have unity. As she explained, when they demand improvements—say, the construction of a school, a healthcare centre, street paving, and appropriate sewage systems— these are not exclusively for the people in Dandara. On the contrary, they inevitably include other underserved districts nearby.

Organising activities that promote integration with people from the 'outside' also presents important opportunities and contributes to strengthening and legitimising squatters' demands. When people living nearby participate in the activities organised in squats or even propose and organise new activities, they contribute to giving meaning to and to putting into practice the idea of having open spaces for the community and the city. They show support for the squatters' demands and initiatives to create self-managed spaces, alternative cultural venues, housing spaces, and other spaces; they contribute to giving visibility to grassroots initiatives and social struggles; they may become more familiarised with the arguments, models of organisation, and modes of action of squatting (and other social) movements; and sometimes they may even become activists themselves.

There are many ways to integrate with others. Examples cited during the interviews in the RMBH included movie sessions, concerts, theatre groups and presentations, parties, workshops, discussions, classes, popular pre-ENEM[7] courses, book launches, communal kitchens and daycare, production of a newspaper and other publications, fairs, and carnival block rehearsals. Interactions between different squats and other actors are also significant. Some squatters are (or become) members of other social movements and collectives, and there are several initiatives that support them.

As examples, there are collectives and groups that give legal advice, such as the Coletivo Margarida Alves (Margarida Alves Collective); offer advice and support in architecture and urbanism, such as the project Arquitetura na Periferia (Architecture in the Periphery); promote collective and sustainable agriculture, such as the Agroecologia na Periferia (Agroecology in the Periphery) initiative; and many others. There is also a notable presence of universities, represented by research and outreach groups, faculty, and students who propose and participate in several activities, mainly when demanded. Interactions with leftist political parties also occur. Eventually, this contributed to the emergence of different types of squats geared toward culture, political standing, support for women victims of violence, work, and other issues.

Notably, there is also an important presence of religious entities, especially in land occupations for housing in the RMBH. As pointed out by Moreira (2017), the religious aspect of these struggles, depending on how it is experienced, may or may not be an obstacle to human emancipation, as more progressive groups but also some of the conservative branches of the Pentecostal and Neo-Pentecostal churches are present. It is not rare for the latter, members of which are present in large numbers in Brazil, to aim at profit and accumulating capital, abusing the trust of faithful masses, who, for their part, do not see their actions as spoliation (Moreira 2017). On the other hand, certain groups of the church (although in smaller numbers) are strongly committed to the emancipatory causes of the less favoured classes, with a critical, protesting, and subversive approach (Moreira 2017). An outstanding example of the latter, the Comissão Pastoral da Terra (Pastoral Land Commission), has important involvement in the struggles for housing and land in the RMBH.

Moreover, undeniable interference from drug-trafficking agents was referred to on more than one occasion by interviewees in the RMBH. Although they should not be disregarded, it is important to note that such agents were considered harmful or undesirable whenever mentioned. In some cases, it was possible to control or avoid their presence in occupations as a result of efforts by the squatters themselves. However, on the other hand, it is not possible to determine how enduring the absence of—or, better said, the distancing from—narcotrafficking agents is. After all, drug trafficking is a widespread, intricate, highly structured phenomenon involving actors from very diverse origins, not to mention remarkably powerful and violent ones.

Remarkably, feminist struggles are also an essential aspect of squatters' networks in the RMBH. Firstly, principles such as equality of rights and women's empowerment and emancipation, contrary to oppressive and naturalised patriarchal models and violence against women, are frequently present in discussions in squats and reflected in their internal norms and discourses. Most leadership figures in squats for housing are women—in some cases, all of them (Franzoni 2018). The possibility of having a place to live, even if in an occupation, brings with it (minimum) physical and financial security, as also reflected in the possibility of better nutrition for the family, rupture with abusive relationships, and independence in relation to men (Franzoni 2018). As stated by two of the interviewees:

> One thing we joke about is that every occupation generates divorce and children. And it is true, you know? Because it is a very liberating process for women.

> The whole struggle in Dandara was made up of women… On the marches, it was the women with their children who were there. To do the *mutirões*,[8] the women with their children, too.

Finally, the formation of squatters' networks in the RMBH can present variations in intensity, levels of activity and engagement, and types and numbers of participants. Often, supportive actors are called upon when a specific demand arises without necessarily permanently participating in a squat. In unexpected or urgent matters, such as eviction threats/orders/actions or cases of police violence, or when it is necessary to pressure local governments to meet certain demands, squatters are very frequently able to swiftly activate a broader network to undertake collective actions, ranging from joint publications in social media and demonstrations to attempts to resist and remain in their spaces.

Nonetheless, there are no specific initiatives geared toward forming and organising a network of all squats. Squatters' networks in the RMBH are flexible, permeable, and changeable, formed by more or less stable bonds based mainly on affinity, exchange, solidarity, and mutual aid. Even though different modes of interaction do not come unchallenged by important contradictions, as exemplified above, networking is widely perceived as desirable and beneficial.

## CONCLUSIONS

Following what Souza (2006) proposes when he affirms that every movement is a form of activism but the opposite is not true, squatters' movements are, at the same time that they are formed by site-specific experiences, particularly ambitious and critical, committed to more general, universal ethical values and broader political goals. Nonetheless, important contextual differences and other particularities, as illustrated in the course of the present chapter, add to marked variation in terms of integration at different scales, indicating that if we can talk about squatting movements, it would be inaccurate to consider squatting as a single movement on a global scale.

Squatting in the RMBH should be regarded as a social movement in itself and not as an isolated form of insurgent spatial practice within broader social movements, although it has rarely been recognised as such. Even though urban squats in this Metropolitan Region are frequently related to immediate or urgent needs and usually committed to site-specific projects and concerns, in reality they represent localised but integrated focuses of resistance that insist, some due to necessity, others due to conviction, and very often due to both, on fighting head-on against naturalised power structures and demonstrating that other forms of social relations are possible. In other words, at the same time as they are formed by site-specific experiences, squatters are committed to more general, universal ethical values and broader political goals.

At the same time that squatters in the RMBH oppose different forms of housing injustice (such as homelessness and precarious housing conditions), housing as an extreme necessity is deeply connected to a desire to have a durable basis from which to fight for other rights and a fulfilling life. Thus, squatters' struggles constitute a dispute for the right to the city.

Together with their ability to form alliances and networks, this contributes to a sense of cohesiveness and shared identity—although more often than not in a loose and non-formalised way—making it possible to talk about a squatting movement. While individual squats may not endure, networking practices can contribute to the transmission of past experiences over time and to the survival of unfulfilled ideals for the future.

In their quotidian insurgent spatial practices, these actors put housing injustice, the capitalist mode of production, and other forms of oppression to the test. In the spaces they produce and adapt, squatters demonstrate that a different life, one that is not based on profit rates, private property, and repressive social control, is a tangible possibility.

In a broader sense, in the spaces they produce, and also by overcoming their physical limits, reaching the streets of the cities and other forums of political debate, by publicising their actions and in many other ways, squatting movements carry potential to influence and reverberate in different spheres, scales, and times. Whether short- or long-lived, squatters' actions may secure the collective use of spaces instead of their private exploitation; help avoid unjust evictions of people in need of shelter; provide housing for large numbers of people; contribute to the strengthening of various social movements, collectives, and initiatives; and engage with networks of mutual care. Combined, their actions may draw attention to the need to curb real estate speculation, unfair processes of displacement, and many other forms of socio-spatial injustices at the same time as they propose fairer and more inclusive ways of living in cities.

## NOTES

1. Outstanding examples in Brazil are the Movimento dos Trabalhadores Rurais sem Terra (MST, Landless Rural Workers' Movement), founded in 1984, including about 350,000 families and currently organised in 24 Brazilian states, and the Movimento dos Trabalhadores Sem Teto (MTST, Roofless Workers' Movement), created within the MST in 1997 and geared toward struggles for housing and decent living conditions in several Brazilian cities. Both these social movements have squatting as one of their most important forms of action. See http://www.mst.org.br/ and https://mtst.org/ (accessed on 21 December 2021).
2. This research was partially funded by a scholarship granted by the Capes Foundation, Brazil, process number 88881.189843/2018-01.
3. The report from the Fundação Getúlio Vargas (Getúlio Vargas Foundation) is entitled 'Qual foi o impacto da crise sobre a pobreza e a distribuição de renda?' ('What was the impact of the crisis on poverty and income distribution?'). It analyses data from before the Plano Real (Real Plan, a government program that had as one of its main objectives the stabilisation of the Brazilian economy and which implemented the Real as the new national currency) in 1994 to

the end of President Temer's administration in 2018. See https://bit.ly/3bt5nRl (accessed on 21 December 2021).
4. Although this is an important feature of squatting in the RMBH, it is not generalisable for the country as a whole. The way in which occupations are organised and their goals, processes of self-management, forms of negotiation, and other aspects may vary significantly in different cities and regions of Brazil. To cite one example, while in Belo Horizonte when a group of people decides to squat their intention is usually to stay where they are, in São Paulo it is usual to also have temporary, provisional camps as part of a negotiation strategy for the inclusion of the occupants in public housing programs.
5. Retrieved from https://www.mlbbrasil.org on 21 December 2021.
6. I identified a total of 66 land and building occupations in the RMBH started at different moments since the 1920s but in particular from the 1990s onwards. Strikingly, 67% of all building occupations started after the year 2010 and were located (with very few exceptions) in central and economically privileged areas of Belo Horizonte (Campos 2020).
7. The Exame Nacional do Ensino Médio (ENEM, National Secondary Education Exam) is currently the main form of evaluation for access to higher education in Brazilian public universities.
8. A term in Portuguese that refers to collective self-construction work by the local community and its supporters to build urban infrastructure, housing, and other structures.

# REFERENCES

Babic, J. (2015) Metelkova, mon amour: Reflections on the (non-) culture of squatting. In A. W. Moore & A. Smart (eds.) *Making room: Cultural production in occupied spaces.* Barcelona: Other Forms and The Journal of Aesthetics and Protest, 298–311.

Bastos, C. D., Magalhães, F. N. C., Miranda, G. M., Silva, H., Tonucci Filho, J. B. M., Cruz, M. D. M., & Velloso, R. D. C. L. (2017) Entre o espaço abstrato e o espaço diferencial: Ocupações urbanas em Belo Horizonte. *Revista Brasileira de Estudos Urbanos e Regionais* 19(2): 251–266.

Campos, C. (2020) *Squatting for more than housing: Alternative spaces and struggles for the right to the city in three urban areas in Brazil, Spain, and the Basque Country.* PhD dissertation. Belo Horizonte: Universidade Federal de Minas Gerais.

Campos, C., & Martínez, M. A. (2020) Squatting activism in Brazil and Spain: Articulations between the right to housing and the right to the city. In U. Grashoff (ed.) *Comparative approaches to informal housing around the globe.* London: UCL Press, 110–129.

Cardoso, J. Á. de L. (2018) A América do Sul diante das crises cambiais. *Outras Palavras.* Retrieved from https://bit.ly/2QPNdS1 (accessed 6 January 2022).

Cattaneo, C. (2013) Urban squatting, rural squatting and the ecological-economic perspective. In Squatting Europe Kollective (ed.) *Squatting in Europe: Radical spaces, urban struggles.* Wivenhoe: Minor Compositions, 139–160.

Cattaneo, C., & Martínez, M. A. (eds.) (2014) *The squatters' movement in Europe: Commons and autonomy as alternatives to capitalism.* London: Pluto Press.

Foucault, M. (1995) *Discipline and punish: The birth of the prison* (translated by A. Sheridan). New York: Vintage Books.

Franzoni, J. Á. (2018) *O direito & o direito: Estórias da Izidora contadas por uma fabulação jurídico-espacial.* PhD dissertation. Belo Horizonte: Universidade Federal de Minas Gerais.

Fucolti, E. (2015) Centri sociali (social centres) in Italy. In A. W. Moore & A. Smart (eds.) *Making room: Cultural production in occupied spaces.* Barcelona: Other Forms and The Journal of Aesthetics and Protest, 196–199.

Grashoff, U., & Yang, F. (2020) Towards critique and differentiation: Comparative research on informal housing. In U. Grashoff (ed.) *Comparative approaches to informal housing around the globe.* London: UCL Press, 1–21.

Harvey, D. (2005) *A brief history of neoliberalism.* Oxford: Oxford University Press.

Katz, C. (2016) Is South America's 'progressive cycle' at an end? *SP The Bullet*, 4 March. Retrieved from https://socialistproject.ca/2016/03/b1229/ (accessed 6 January 2022).
Kollectiv Orangotango (eds.) (2018) *This is not an atlas: A global collection of counter-cartographies*. Bielefeld: Transcript.
Lefebvre, H. (1991) *The production of space* (translated by D. Nicholson Smith). Malden: Blackwell.
Lefebvre, H. (2016) *O direito à cidade [The right to the city]* (translated by C. Oliveira). Iapevi: Nebli.
Lelis, N. (2016) Ocupações urbanas: A poética territorial da política. *Revista Brasileira de Estudos Urbanos e Regionais* 18(3): 428.
Lledin, J. (2015) Managing the image: Squats and alternative media in Madrid (2000–2013). In A. W. Moore & A. Smart (eds.) *Making room: Cultural production in occupied spaces*. Barcelona: Other Forms and The Journal of Aesthetics and Protest, 260–263.
Lourenço, T. C. B. (2014) *Cidade Ocupada*. Master's dissertation. Belo Horizonte: Universidade Federal de Minas Gerais.
Marcuse, P. (2012) Whose right(s) to what city? In N. Brenner, P. Marcuse, & M. Mayer (eds.) *Cities for people, not for profit: Critical urban theory and the right to the city*. London: Routledge, 24–41.
Martínez, M. A. (2002) *Okupaciones de viviendas y de centros sociales: Autogestión, contracultura y conflictos urbanos*. Barcelona: Lallevir S.L./VIRUS editorial.
Martínez, M. A. (2013) The squatters' movement in Spain: A local and global cycle of urban protests. In Squatting Europe Kollective (ed.) *Squatting in Europe: Radical spaces, urban struggles*. Wivenhoe: Minor Compositions, 113–138.
Martínez, M. A. (ed.) (2018) *The urban politics of squatters' movements*. New York: Palgrave Macmillan.
Martínez, M. A. (2020) *Squatters in the capitalist city: Housing, justice, and urban politics*. New York: Routledge.
Mayer, M. (2012) The 'right to the city' in urban social movements. In N. Brenner, P. Marcuse, & M. Mayer (eds.) *Cities for people, not for profit: Critical urban theory and the right to the city*. London: Routledge, 24–41.
McFarlane, C. (2010) The comparative city: Knowledge, learning, urbanism. *International Journal of Urban and Regional Research* 34(4): 725–742.
Merrifield, A. (2011) The right to the city and beyond: Notes on a Lefebvrian re-conceptualisation. *City* 15(3–4): 473–481.
Merrifield, A. (2017) Fifty years on: The right to the city. In Verso Books (ed.) *The Right to the City: A Verso Report*. New York: Verso Books.
Mitchell, D. (2003) *The right to the city: Social justice and the fight for public space*. New York: Guilford Press.
Moore, A. W., & Smart, A. (eds.) (2015) *Making room: Cultural production in occupied spaces*. Barcelona: Other Forms and The Journal of Aesthetics and Protest.
Moreira, G. L. (2017) *A luta pela terra em contexto de injustiça agrária: Pedagogia de emancipação humana? Experiências de luta da CPT e do MST*. PhD dissertation. Belo Horizonte: Universidade Federal de Minas Gerais.
Movimento de Luta nos Bairros, Vilas e Favelas (2019) *Cadernos de Formação Política: As propostas do MLB para a reforma urbana*. Setorial Nacional de Formação do MLB.
Nascimento, D. M., & Libânio, C. (eds.) (2016) *Ocupações urbanas na Região Metropolitana de Belo Horizonte*. Belo Horizonte: Favela é isso Aí.
Nogueira, M. (2019) Displacing informality: Rights and legitimacy in Belo Horizonte, Brazil. *International Journal of Urban and Regional Research* 43(3): 517–534.
Owens, L. (2013) Have squat, will travel: How squatter mobility mobilises squatting. In Squatting Europe Kollective (ed.) *Squatting in Europe: Radical spaces, urban struggles*. Wivenhoe: Minor Compositions, 185–207.
Padrones Gil, S. (2017) *El Movimiento de Okupación como Proceso Emancipador: El caso de Donostialdea*. PhD dissertation. Alicante: Universidad Miguel Hernández de Elche.
Peluso, N. L. (1995) Whose woods are these? Counter-mapping forest territories in Kalimantan, Indonesia. *Antipode* 27(4): 383–406.
Polanska, D. V. (2019) *Contentious politics and the welfare state: Squatting in Sweden*. Abingdon: Routledge.

Pruijt, H. (2013) Squatting in Europe. In Squatting Europe Kollective (ed.) *Squatting in Europe: Radical spaces, urban struggles.* Wivenhoe: Minor Compositions, 17–60.

Robinson, J. (2011) Cities in a world of cities: The comparative gesture. *International Journal of Urban and Regional Research* 35(1): 1–23.

Robinson, J. (2016) Comparative urbanism: New geographies and cultures of theorizing the urban. *International Journal of Urban and Regional Research* 40(1): 187–199.

Soja, E. W. (2000) *Postmetropolis: Critical studies of cities and regions.* Malden: Blackwell.

Souza, M. L. de (2001) *Mudar a cidade: Uma introdução crítica ao planejamento e à gestão urbanos.* Rio de Janeiro: Bertrand Brasil.

Souza, M. L. de (2006) Together with the state, despite the state, against the state: Social movements as 'critical urban planning' agents. *City* 10(3): 327–342.

Souza, M. L. de (2010) Com o Estado, apesar do Estado, contra o Estado: Os movimentos urbanos e suas práticas espaciais, entre luta institucional e ação direta. *Cidades: Revista científica* 7(11): 13–47.

Squatting Europe Kollective (ed.) (2013) *Squatting in Europe: Radical spaces, urban struggles.* Wivenhoe: Minor Compositions.

Squatting Everywhere Kollective (ed.) (2018) *Fighting for spaces, fighting for our lives: Squatting movements today.* Münster: Edition Assemblage.

Tonucci Filho, J. B. M. (2017) *Comum urbano: A cidade além do público e do privado.* PhD dissertation. Belo Horizonte: Universidade Federal de Minas Gerais.

Vasudevan, A. (2015) The autonomous city: Towards a critical geography of occupation. *Progress in Human Geography* 39(3): 316–337.

Vasudevan, A. (2017) *The autonomous city: A history of urban squatting.* New York: Verso.

# 30. Urban commons in practice: housing cooperativism and city-making
*Lorenzo Vidal*

Urban commons encompass a series of collective social practices as well as a political principle that has re-emerged out of the struggles against neoliberal capitalism (Dardot & Laval 2019). They have become a lens through which to conceptualise social processes of collective (re)appropriation of urban resources. Engaging with the commons from an urban sociological perspective implies being attentive to the social groups that are involved in these processes and how they transform and are transformed by their urban context. Housing cooperativism can be understood as a form of urban commoning and has received renewed attention as one of the responses to the 'return of the housing question' (Hodkinson 2012). This chapter explores the potential, limits and contradictions of the cooperative route to urban housing commons in light of the experiences of three cities: Barcelona, Copenhagen and Montevideo. How can housing cooperativism provide a collective and non-commodified housing alternative and for whom?

During the fallout from the 2007–8 global financial crisis, Barcelona was a city teeming with practices of urban commoning. The spirit of the Plaça Catalunya occupation during the *indignados* uprisings of 2011 spilled over to decentralised assemblies engaged in collectively appropriating their neighbourhoods through social centres, urban gardens and squatted housing, as well as anti-eviction pickets. Public services such as healthcare, education and transportation were being revalued and reclaimed by *mareas* (tides) of workers and users in response to austerity and budget cuts. A new generation of production and consumption cooperativism also took off in the face of precarity and unemployment. In 2015, moreover, local elections were won by a new municipalist platform called Barcelona En Comú (Barcelona in Common), signalling an affinity to the notion of the commons. This social and political momentum was channelled in different directions and has taken diverse organisational and institutional forms. This chapter will hone into the debates and decisions driving a new generation of user housing cooperatives in the city. It is a story embedded in local history and movements, but also heavily influenced by practices and policy mobilities from other cities, particularly Copenhagen and Montevideo.

As made explicit on the website of La Borda, one of Barcelona's pioneer user housing cooperatives, the cooperative housing models in Uruguay and Denmark have served as a 'direct reference' for local praxis (La Borda, no date). Their collective property and limited-equity character embody an alternative to the entrenched local imaginaries of individual homeownership. Copenhagen is as an example of just how significant such housing alternatives can become. More than 30% of the city's housing stock belongs to 'private housing cooperatives' (*privat andelsboligforening*) and another 20% to 'common housing' (*almene boliger*), a sector of non-profit rental housing associations with roots in the country's cooperative housing history and governed through a system of 'tenant democracy' (See Table 30.1). The latter sector comprises 550 housing associations with 7000 residential estates (BL 2015). In Uruguay, cooperative housing represents approximately 3% of the national housing stock and

*Table 30.1    Housing sectors rooted in housing cooperativism*

|  | Copenhagen |  | Montevideo | Barcelona |
|---|---|---|---|---|
| Sector | Common housing | Private housing cooperatives | User cooperatives | User cooperatives |
| Tenure | Indefinite leases | Limited-equity shares | Limited-equity shares | Limited-equity shares |
| Access | Queues | Queues, inheritance or transactions (variations) | Queues, inheritance or transactions (variations) | Queues, inheritance (variations) |
| Governance | Housing association boards and estate-level boards and assemblies | Cooperative boards and assemblies | Cooperative boards and assemblies | Cooperative boards and assemblies |

*Source:*   Author's elaboration.

almost half of these cooperatives are located in Montevideo (Barenstein et al. 2023: 10). What has stood out most in this case is the activism of the Uruguayan Federation of Mutual-Aid Housing Cooperatives (FUCVAM in Spanish). This umbrella organisation is an inspirational example of how housing cooperativism can develop into an important social movement pushing for housing solutions. In Catalonia, the user cooperative housing sector is still emerging and taking shape. At the end of 2021 there were 30 user cooperatives in either the development or living phase, 17 of which were located in Barcelona (La Dinamo Fundació 2021).

The history of housing cooperativism in Uruguay and Denmark has its lights and shadows when viewed from an urban commons perspective. These have informed discussions in Catalonia's nascent cooperative housing sector, which is eager to become an affordable and accessible alternative in a context of housing crisis. This chapter will address some of the key issues that have centred such discussions: the affordability and accessibility of cooperative housing, its scalability, its resilience to enclosure and commodification pressures and its role in broader urban processes in a context of the 'generalisation of gentrification as a global urban strategy' (Smith 2002). Before analysing these concrete issues, the notion of the urban commons and the efforts to put it into practice through cooperativism will be introduced. How community, class and capital can be conceptualised in relation to cooperative housing will also be discussed in order to theoretically frame the empirical analysis.

I argue that housing cooperatives can be a vehicle for urban commoning and are best equipped to confront recurring dynamics of enclosure when nested in multi-scalar and multi-stakeholder institutional and organisational structures. These structures must harness the redistributive capacities of the state whilst simultaneously defending their autonomy from both the state and the market. The geographies of (to different degrees) collectively self-governed and inter-linked cooperative housing communities can potentially provide the groundwork for such possibilities. These spaces, however, interact with broader urban processes that are beyond their reach. This constitutes both a limiting factor as well as the point of engagement with other practices and movements reclaiming the commons. These insights are of interest to urban sociologists concerned with the political-economy enablers and constraints for urban change and the class dimensions of both cooperative housing and urban commons.

The chapter draws from research fieldwork in Copenhagen (2015) and Montevideo (2016) in the context of my doctoral studies, as well as from direct personal involvement in the cooperative housing sector in Barcelona since the year 2017. Fieldwork in Copenhagen and Montevideo included 60 semi-structured interviews with policymakers, practitioners, activists and cooperative housing members, as well as documentary analysis of extensive grey literature. This material is referenced indirectly here through previous publications (Vidal 2018, 2019a, 2019b). In Barcelona, I am a member of a housing cooperative, a delegate in the sector-wide coordination space and part of the advisory board of La Dinamo, a foundation dedicated to the promotion of cooperative housing. Inputs from this personal experience have not been systematically recorded, yet they have nevertheless informed my knowledge on the subject.

## URBAN COMMONING THROUGH COOPERATIVISM

The notion of the commons has been gaining popularity in the past three decades. A broad and diverse body of work in the social sciences has engaged with this concept and two main approaches can arguably be discerned: the institutionalist and the neo-Marxist. The institutionalist approach emerges largely as a response to Hardin's (1968) well-known essay on the 'tragedy of the commons'. Hardin argued that shared resources that were subtractable and difficult to exclude people from tended to be overexploited due to the 'rationally' self-serving behaviour of their users. His paradigmatic hypothetical example of this was grazing ground for cattle. The only solution, in his view, was either privatisation or state control over the resource. The institutionalists, notably Ostrom (1990), contend instead that 'common-property regimes' based on user-centred collective institutions designed around a key set of principles can and have provided a sustainable alternative. Although initially centred on natural 'common-pool resources', this literature has since applied this analysis to a number of contexts, from the digital space of the internet (Hess & Ostrom 2007) to the urban space of the city (Foster & Iaione 2019), including housing cooperatives (Vogel et al. 2016).

Rather than addressing a 'tragedy' derived from a thought experiment, the starting point for the neo-Marxist approach is the historical process of enclosure of the commons during capitalism's 'primitive accumulation' (Marx 1995); that is, the proletarianisation of rural communities as they were stripped of their common rights to access and use local land, pastures, forests and other natural resources that were essential to their livelihoods. These resources then became the exclusive property of private owners or of the modern state. The Midnight Notes Collective (1990) first argued that this process does not only belong to the pre-history of capitalism but that there are persistent 'new enclosures' that separate the population from their means of subsistence. As neoliberal globalisation pushed forward, they were referring to a diverse range of processes: from the displacement of indigenous peoples from their lands to the privatisation of public assets. For Holloway (2010), moreover, this separation is never a finished process but is constantly active and at issue. A dialectical interplay between enclosures and commons then ensues, as the forms of producing and managing the means of subsistence are continuously contested.

From the neo-Marxist perspective then the commons refers to a collective and non-commodified social relation between a community and its 'actually existing or yet-to-be-created social or physical environment deemed crucial to its life and livelihood', as

Harvey (2012: 73) puts it. It is a practice, commoning (Linebaugh 2008), consisting of enacting and/or claiming this type of social relation 'in, against and beyond' capitalism (Caffentzis & Federici 2014, Cumbers 2015, Holloway 2010). This practice is often pre-figurative and imperfect, generating 'restricted commons', as Martínez (2020) puts it. The neo-Marxist approach has informed a burgeoning literature on cooperative housing in different ways (Aernouts & Ryckewaert 2018, Balmer & Bernet 2015, Card 2020, Huron 2018, Nonini 2017, Noterman 2016, Thompson 2020b, Vidal 2019b). The present chapter positions itself within this literature, which still draws key insights from institutionalist approaches. The collective and (partially) decommodified dimensions of cooperative housing, collective property and non- or limited equity, are features that can be conceptualised through the lens of the commons.

Urban commoning involves recreating communities anew and providing collective means for their social reproduction in built-up landscapes already parcelled out into private and state property. There are specific 'urban challenges' to the commons (Kip 2015) and certain elements that make urban commons 'materially distinct' (Huron 2017, 2018). These can be summarised as (1) population density, transience and diversity – the coming together of strangers with different backgrounds, worldviews and material conditions; (2) the coupling of urbanisation and capital accumulation, operating in a context shaped by its centrality to the circulation of commodities and capital, the storage of surplus value and the extraction of rents; and (3) the state's regulation of the latter, existing under the close gaze and presence of state authority and power. Due to the centrality of urban areas for capital accumulation and state power and their more heterogeneous and mobile populations, the urban commons' communities and boundaries are often characterised by somewhat more contestation and porosity than rural commons. There is also a 'scale problem' (Harvey 2012) when it comes to the urban commons. Urban life is sustained by large-scale and complex intersecting processes and infrastructures than cannot be managed by local communities alone. Urban communities cannot even fathom the possibility of self-sustenance through the collective appropriation of their local environment. Urban commoning must thus develop multi-scalar understandings of community and collective institutionality.

The urban proletariat engaged early on in mutualism and cooperativism to secure some relative autonomy from their dependence on the market. The cooperative association can be seen to provide an 'organizational shell' (Barenstein et al. 2023) and a new set of norms for the commons in contexts where traditional rural customs no longer hold. The 'Rochdale principles' are an example of a modern ethical code of values, as well as an organising guideline. The cooperative society provides a legal framework for a collective form of organisation that is inscribed in the modern system of laws and property rights. Commoning under this guise operates through the collective ownership of the cooperative, rather than through customary use. Belonging to the community is gained through membership rather than through social ties to place. The cooperative is an association that arises out of the common pooling of resources, but the urban proletariat has little to pool together beyond its own labour power, wages and savings. Cooperatives have often scaled-up through federalist structures, yet without a broader social change in property rights, cooperatives can only expand by drawing on the surpluses of their activity or by capturing resources from the state. The former option is limited by their non-profit status, unless they abandon their non-commodified character. The latter establishes a complex nexus between the member-based community of the cooperative and the abstract citizen-based community of the state.

The 'public–cooperative nexus' (Ferreri & Vidal 2021) underpins many experiences of urban commoning. Housing cooperatives often appropriate extra financial as well as physical resources, such as land and buildings, from the state. The state's legal apparatus and redistributive functions provide opportunities for scaling the cooperative housing sector and making it more affordable. Yet the state is 'a form of social relations, a way of doing things', as Holloway (2010: 58) insists, that is part of the process of separation of 'the common affairs of the community from the community itself', a separation enforced by a hierarchical state bureaucracy. The nexus between cooperatives and the state thus involves the interaction of diverse and contravening logics. The balance between housing cooperatives' embeddedness in the state and their autonomy is a precarious one, in which the cooperatives can grow but also run the risk of losing their independence (Ganapati 2010). Making a similar but broader argument, De Angelis (2017) argues that the commons runs the risk of being co-opted by the state and the market. However, the opposite is also true. The commons can strategically use the complexity of these systems for their own development.

Municipal public administrations have a central role in articulating the 'public–cooperative nexus' when it comes to cooperative housing. This is due to the urban and local dimension of housing but also the fact that the electoral successes of social-democratic and left-wing parties often start and endure relatively longer at the municipal scale. This has been the case in Copenhagen, Montevideo and Barcelona. In the latter case, winning municipal elections was initially conceived of as a 'strategic entry point' for commons-oriented social change (Russell 2019). The hypothesis was that municipal public administrations lay closest to the level at which relations of proximity take place, the everyday practices in which communities are formed (Observatorio Metropolitano 2014: 148). They are thus best positioned to promote communities engaged in urban commoning, as well as to include them in processes of co-production of urban policies (Blanco & Gomà 2019). As Thompson (2020c: 336) poses, 'the political promise of municipalism is the bridge it builds between alternative economic spaces that prefigure post-capitalist futures and the institutional supports at the municipal or city-regional scale required to nurture and sustain them'. Cooperatives and the social and solidarity economy more generally have been conceived of as key non-state actors within this approach (Miró 2017, 2018). Relations between left-leaning parties and cooperative organisations have not always been close and complicit, yet the municipal scale has proved central to the public–cooperative nexus developed in all three cities.

## COMMUNITY, CLASS AND CAPITAL IN COOPERATIVE HOUSING COMMONS

Urban land and housing present a series of peculiarities that require closer consideration when appropriated as commons through housing cooperativism. Urban housing is composed of individual residential buildings, each with its own community of residents. The sum of these buildings, as well as of the plots of land available for future residential use, amounts to the residential infrastructure of cities and towns upon which urban dwellers as a whole depend. Yet housing is necessarily an excludable good: its use by current residents prevents others from using it. Since it is such an essential infrastructure for urban life, however, how it is managed concerns the wider community of current and future urban dwellers, more so when considering that land for residential use is limited and non-reproducible. On the other hand, housing is part of the 'secondary circuit of capital' (Harvey 2006), where capital is stored and ground rents are extracted. As such, urban land and housing are traversed by diverse uses and interests, overlapping boundaries of community and class dynamics.

Housing cooperativism involves communities that are bounded by membership in the cooperative association. This association is often restricted to current residents, although housing estates can also be nested within larger structures. This is the case of Sostre Cívic in Catalonia, for example, a cooperative that integrates a number of different housing projects. Danish common housing associations also have a multi-scalar organisational structure, bringing together different housing estates organised around both local as well as association-wide assemblies and boards. These structures sustain multi-scalar forms of community, yet can still only represent current residents in the cooperative housing stock. As such, they can still become 'inward facing' (Thompson 2020a) and develop only 'internal solidarity' (Sørvoll & Bengtsson 2020) amongst members. Membership, however, can also be open to non-resident collaborators and stakeholders. This is the case for many user cooperatives in Catalonia, for example, where collaborating non-resident members also have (minority) representation in the governing board. Another example is the many Danish common housing associations that have municipalities and other external actors represented in their governing boards. These multi-stakeholder organisational frameworks broaden the boundaries of the community involved in cooperative housing.

Commons often involve 'layered or nested rights' (Bruun 2015) and 'multiple claimants' (Amin & Howell 2016) that go beyond a strictly predefined community and a narrow definition of insiders and outsiders. As Stavrides insists, openness and porosity should be important characteristics of urban commons within their 'anti-enclosure dynamic' (2016: 113). The right to exclude, on which the privacy and security of the home is grounded, must be balanced by outsiders' 'right not to be excluded' (Blomley 2020) from the cooperative housing stock. How this balance is struck is complex. Dardot and Laval (2019) argue that the commons do not entail a passive entitlement but an active and practical one. Communities are constituted through the practice of producing and using the commons and co-producing their terms and rules of use. For non-residents to be actively involved in cooperative housing, specific mechanisms must be put in place. Multi-stakeholder organisational frameworks, such as those mentioned above, are one possibility. The public–cooperative nexus through legal and policy instruments is another. The state can act as a channel for wider social claims to the commons, albeit in highly mediated, indirect and contradictory ways. Housing cooperatives can also be embedded in a more diffuse 'moral economy' in which residents are considered local stewards and caretakers of a resource that ultimately belongs to society as a whole (Bruun 2015).

How the *right not to be excluded*, as distinguished from *a right to be included*, is materialised is largely dependent on the ways in which access to the cooperative housing stock is mediated. Using a *Bourdieusian* framework (Bourdieu 1986), the endowments of economic, social and cultural capital are key mediating dimensions to take into account. The affordability of cooperative housing determines the extent to which the endowment of economic capital and capacity to pay is a factor of exclusion. The extent to which the endowment of cultural and educational resources and/or participation in certain social networks and spaces, as well as knowledge of the norms, values and attitudes that regulate them, are implicitly required to gain membership in a housing cooperative are also factors of exclusion. It is through the operation of these often less explicit forms of capital that housing cooperatives can become inaccessible to socially disadvantaged and excluded groups. Lack of transparency in many private housing cooperative waiting lists in Copenhagen, for example, has often meant that one must 'know somebody' to get in, which has produced a local and middle-class selection bias (Boterman 2011). In Barcelona, the self-management dynamics of housing cooperative groups have disproportionately favoured (precarious) middle-class activists with more available time and collective self-management skills. Specific organisational mechanisms, such as transparent queues and technical and external support, for example, can make such cases more inclusive.

From a Marxist perspective, the class character of cooperative housing can be gauged from the enclosure–commons dialectic. Cooperative housing can be conceived of as part of the commons that has been reclaimed and recreated by the 'commoners without a commons', as Linebaugh (2014: 202) defines the urban proletariat. The stronger tenure security provided by housing cooperatives can partially deproletarianise the condition of their members, as they reconnect to land and home in a more stable way. This security, in turn, can provide a relatively stronger position from which to negotiate conditions in the labour market. Since Engels' take on the 'housing question', however, Marxists have worried that approximations to homeownership can embourgoise the working classes and create shared interests with the propertied (Hodkinson 2012). Dweller control over cooperatives, in fact, has in many cases been used to commodify housing for individual gain or to enact tenure changes to individual homeownership. In this sense, Sørvoll (2013) formulates a 'fragility hypothesis' in relation to cooperative housing. He considers that its strong element of user ownership makes it susceptible to deregulation and vulnerable to market-oriented reforms. Housing, after all, is a significant asset that can be capitalised upon, mobilised to extract rents and leveraged to access credit. The temptation to tap into their housing's equity can drive cooperative members to share the interests of property owners in maximising the exchange value of their assets. As such, only insofar as the cooperative housing stock maintains its collective and decommodified characteristics can it function as a common resource for the urban proletariat.

## ACCESSING AND SCALING THE COOPERATIVE HOUSING SECTOR

For cooperative housing to develop into a significant alternative to dominant forms of housing provision, it must become a broadly available option that is affordable and accessible to urban dwellers. This depends on its capacity to reduce the profit, ground rent and interest components that bourgeon housing costs and/or to leverage state resources for a progressive socialisation of these costs. Housing cooperativism involves fewer intermediaries in the promotion, development and management of housing and thus fewer opportunities for fee-based revenues and profit margins. Furthermore, non- or limited-equity cooperatives reduce the ground rent component of housing costs in the cooperative housing stock in the long run. Through legal and policy tools, the state can facilitate access to credit, land and buildings and direct subsidies towards covering construction costs as well as the monthly payments of residents. Beyond the creation and maintenance of new cooperative housing stock, the norms and mechanisms regulating access to its housing units also determine what population can opt to become residents. After the first wave of pilot projects in Barcelona, how to scale the sector and make it more affordable have centred local discussions and campaigns. This section analyses the trajectories of cooperative housing in Denmark and Uruguay in this regard, as well as outlining the first steps taken in this direction in Barcelona.

Cooperative housing has expanded in Denmark and Uruguay in the context of an enabling legal framework and policy mix. In Denmark, the first housing cooperatives emerged at the end of the 19th century as self-help initiatives of workers organised in their workplaces and trade unions (Greve 1971). This form of housing broadened its population base as public subsidies were directed towards cooperatives in the inter-war years and subsequently became a central part of post-Second World War reconstruction (Bro 2009, Jensen 2013). These policies reflected a compromise between the social democratic party, keen on promoting public housing, and liberal and conservative parties, which were weary of state ownership. Through state involvement, cooperatives and non-profit associations and foundations were gradually brought together into what is today known as the common housing sector (Larsen & Lund Hansen 2015, Richman 1995, Vidal 2019b). Through this process, cooperatives lost part of their autonomy. Today, public authorities participate in the sector's common fund (*Landsbygefonden*, LBF) and new-build developments require prior approval from municipalities. New-build developments in this sector do receive an initial grant from municipal public authorities equivalent to 14% of the total cost and mortgage payments are partially subsidised by the central state (Gibb et al. 2013: 37, Nielsen 2010b: 208). Tenants are also eligible for rental payment subsidies. After going through a process of residualisation due to middle-class flight towards property ownership opportunities, it has become the sector that today houses the population with the lowest average income in the country.

In Uruguay, housing cooperativism took off after the National Housing Law of 1968, which provided the basic legal and institutional framework for its development. The only antecedents were three pilot projects developed two years prior by the Uruguayan Cooperativist Centre (Centro Cooperativista Uruguayo 2016). The inclusion of a chapter on housing cooperatives was inspired by Nordic European experiences and was initially a peripheral aspect of the law. Cooperatives soon became a popular option, however, for groups that formed in workplaces and trade union centres. The law defined the basic characteristics of housing cooperatives and created a National Housing Fund for the provision of mortgage credit. Public land was available for purchase under market rates for cooperatives, a mechanism that was later systematised following the institutional progression of the left-wing Frente Amplio party, first through a Municipal Land Portfolio in Montevideo in 1991 and then a National Land Portfolio in 2008. Throughout its history, FUCVAM has been pushing for public resources for the sector through political lobbying, demonstrations and land occupations (González 2013, Nahoum 2013). Cooperative groups today can present their projects for public land or buildings and mortgage credit in regular open calls by the Ministry of Housing. In the majority of cooperatives, no initial down payment is required in exchange for a commitment to 20 hours of weekly work per household during the construction phase. In addition, low-income members are eligible for monthly payment subsidies. Finally, there are income ceilings for beneficiaries of these schemes. In all, housing cooperatives have become an affordable option for the middle- to lower-middle-income population.

Tenure change in existing residential stock has been another key avenue for the expansion of cooperative housing. Copenhagen stands out as a prime example. It is through this route that private housing cooperatives have taken over more than one third of the city's housing stock in less than three decades. This housing model, in which members own a share in the collective property of the cooperative, was instituted in the mid-1970s with the backing of a broad political coalition, including the left-wing People's Socialist Party and the Conservative Party (Richman 1995: 154). Tenants in rental housing buildings were granted a right of first refusal if at least 60% of them organised into a private housing cooperative association when their landlords put up their homes for sale. The prior prohibition of the horizontal division of urban properties and strict rent controls made landlordism an unattractive business in aging tenements, prompting cheap sales to sitting tenants-cum-cooperativists. Furthermore, most municipally owned rental housing in Copenhagen was sold off via this formula in the mid-1990s (Velfærdsministeriet 2008). Cooperative housing communities in this case were formed by the tenants residing in the buildings at the moment of purchase and reflected the socio-economic composition of tenants in the local area or neighbourhood. As cooperative membership implied losing eligibility for rent subsidies, however, many low-income and vulnerable tenants opted out of the tenure change and continued as renters with the cooperative as their new landlord (Larsen & Lund Hansen 2008, Vidal 2019a). Today, the average income of residents in private housing cooperatives is higher than in both the private rental and common housing sectors but lower than that of the individual homeowners.

Beyond direct economic determinants, access to cooperative housing is also shaped by other processes in the formation of cooperative groups and the transfer of housing units. During the creation of new housing cooperatives, how groups are formed and organised has important socio-economic implications. Groups that are self-selected are often formed around established social networks and favour those with more social and cultural capital. Collective self-management also requires time and skills that are often out of reach for those with heavier workloads and care responsibilities. In Uruguay, FUCVAM works to put individuals in contact to form new groups and the law regulates the Technical Assistance Institutes that support groups during the different stages of the promotion process. These institutes are non-profit companies with multi-disciplinary staff, from architects and accountants to social workers, whose services are price-regulated and covered by the public loan that cooperatives are eligible for. Once cooperative housing is built and inhabited, how housing units are transferred is another key determinant of accessibility. Whereas in Danish common housing units cannot be inherited, both the shares and the housing units in Danish private cooperatives and Uruguayan user cooperatives can. As such, they constitute a family resource that is less available to society as a whole. The former stock is further accessed through open and transparent waiting lists, whereas the functioning of queues in the latter two models varies from cooperative to cooperative.

In Barcelona, growing and opening up the emerging cooperative housing sector has centred efforts in the context of a pressing social need for housing. A key challenge has been not to fall into a form of 'municipalist vanguardism' (Thompson 2020c: 336) that threatens the 'ability to include, mobilise or represent the material interests of less empowered, disenfranchised social groups'. Economic costs for cooperatives have been reduced by leasing municipally owned land and buildings for 75 to 99 years at a symbolic price. Cooperatives have also received mortgage credit from the Catalan public credit institution and subsidies for construction from the Barcelona municipal housing institute and Spanish state housing plans. Land and subsidies, in turn, are conditioned with income ceilings for cooperative members. A campaign for further public support to guarantee affordability has become a strategic axis for the sector (Sectorial 2021). Regulation of the inheritability of shares and housing units though varies from cooperative to cooperative, and in terms of unit transfers, many have opted for open and transparent queues. In all, the sector is undergoing an active and uneven process of expansion and configuration.

## RESILIENCE TO ENCLOSURE AND COMMODIFICATION PRESSURES

Cooperative housing operates in urban landscapes shaped by state and market logics. The collective and decommodified dimensions of cooperatives are subject to both latent and direct pressures by these more dominant forms of social relations. In this context, cooperative housing commons can be subject to enclosures enacted by the state and by cooperative members themselves navigating the market. This section analyses how these dynamics have played out in the Danish and Uruguayan cases and how they are currently being addressed in Barcelona. Resident-based collective ownership characterises the housing models analysed in all three cases and (partial) decommodification operates through cost-priced rents in Danish common housing and membership share equity limitations in the rest. The resilience of these collective and non-market characteristics depends to a large extent on the organisational and institutional configuration of these housing sectors.

Autonomy from the state has been crucial for cooperative housing in the face of privatisation policies promoted by neoliberal governments. In Uruguay, the cooperative housing sector confronted two privatisation attempts in the mid-1980s. During the last stages of the dictatorship, a Horizontal Property Law in 1983 aimed to forcefully convert all cooperative housing into owner-occupied units. FUCVAM reacted by collecting signatures to call for a referendum against the law and by intensifying its participation in the mobilisations against the regime. The dictatorship soon came to the end and, rather than abolishing the law, the newly elected conservative government forced a vote in all cooperatives for each to decide on the matter. In a context of high mobilisation and politicisation, voting results overwhelmingly backed the user cooperative model (González 2013: 113). In Denmark, the liberal-conservative government during the 2000s sought to privatise common housing by implementing a 'right to buy' scheme for sitting tenants. The common housing associations, grouped together in their national federation Boligselskabernes Landsforening (BL), mobilised against the measure claiming it amounted to an unconstitutional expropriation of their properties (BL 2003). The Supreme Court's final decision (Højesteret 2007) fell mid-way between the government's original intention and the sector's position by granting local tenant assemblies, rather than the associations, the prerogative to decide on sales in their estates. For a sale to occur, however, the final scheme further required a 2/3 majority vote, the backing of either the local municipality and/or the 'parent' housing association and that the association could not prove that the sale would result in significant negative net proceeds. The effect of the scheme was negligible (LBF 2016: 105).

How autonomy from the state has been articulated has proven an equally crucial factor in the face of commodification pressures. Nesting dweller control within broader collective processes and multi-scalar and multi-stakeholder organisational structures has made cooperative housing more resilient to enclosure. Members of user cooperatives in Uruguay voted not to become property owners in the context of wider social mobilisations against neoliberal measures and an active sector-wide federation. Tenants in Danish common housing did not buy out units after years of sector-wide campaigns and the conditioning of this decision to the approval of other stakeholders. The evolution of Danish private housing cooperatives provides a contrasting example. The price of shares in these cooperatives are capped to the valuation of the property as rental housing. Yet in the year 2004 the liberal-conservative government lifted a ban on the use of cooperative shares as collateral for personal credit. As a result, cooperative dwellings were allowed to start functioning similarly to a private mortgageable commodity (Larsen & Lund Hansen 2015). In the context of rental market liberalisations, cheap credit and a housing boom, property valuations rose dramatically. Cooperative assemblies had the option of keeping share prices down or following the valuation hikes and overwhelmingly voted for the latter (Bruun 2018, Vidal 2019a). The decentralised and atomised nature of the sector meant that there was no sector-wide space in which such transcendental decisions could be discussed and coordinated. Moreover, the decision was exclusively in the hands of cooperative shareholders. A broader appropriation of cooperatives as commons has proven important in pre-empting such enclosures from within.

This broader appropriation also has to do with the ways in which access to cooperative housing is mediated and units are transferred. In the case of Danish private housing cooperatives, the delegitimation of its non-market transfer mechanism based on queues laid the groundwork for its subsequent substitution by market exchanges. The lack of transparency in the queuing system, practices of nepotism and 'money under the table' in the buying and selling of shares, often amplified by the media, damaged social perceptions of the sector. In this context, market exchange gained legitimacy as a more 'objective' and 'just' alternative for outsiders. This social climate underpinned the legal changes and cooperative decisions that have led to the decline of the queuing system. Private exchanges at new quasi-market prices are increasingly taking its place. Uruguay's user cooperatives have not undergone comparable transformations, yet the absence of a rigorous queuing system has also proved problematic in some cases. In housing cooperatives located in revalorised coastal neighbourhoods of Montevideo, for example, there are accounts of shares having been irregularly sold at above regulated prices (Solanas 2016: 269–321). Although a relatively marginal phenomenon, it re-emphasises the idea that robust non-market mechanisms are necessary to prevent market mediations from creeping into the functioning of cooperative housing.

In building autonomy from both the state and the market, the use of state resources becomes a contradictory but necessary element. State funding cutbacks have been fought by cooperative housing federations in order to keep affordability and a supporting crutch against market dynamics. In 2002, the Danish liberal-conservative government sought to increase the self-financing of the common housing sector by using the sector's own common fund (LBF) in financing new-build projects. The sector campaigned against this measure and argued that the construction of new common housing was society's task, to be paid via progressive taxation, rather than via a 'Robin Hood in reverse' 'special tax' on the sector itself (Nielsen 2010a). In Uruguay, FUCVAM has also mobilised for public subsidies to cover monthly payments of low-income members so as to guarantee the 'right of permanence' in cooperative housing and protection from fluctuating conditions in the labour market (FUCVAM 2016). The federation has also engaged in mortgage strikes to renegotiate their public debts and achieve substantial debt reductions (Vidal 2018). As these examples illustrate, resources funnelled from the state can help build up the size and clout of cooperative housing sectors, planting the seeds of a counter-power to the state in certain historical contexts. As such, although state involvement can in some aspects curtail the cooperative sector's autonomy, in others it can contribute to building it up vis-à-vis both the market and the state itself.

In Barcelona, the emerging cooperative housing sector is currently pushing for measures to entrench its decommodified character, primarily by aiming to modify the Catalan cooperative law to legally ground and delimit its collective property and limited-equity characteristics. Yet, as laws can be eventually changed and modified, robust non-state institution-building is an equally important and pending task. In terms of the organisational structure of the sector itself, sector-wide coordination provides a space for deliberation but does not have any concrete powers in the governing organs of housing cooperatives. Only Sostre Cívic, as mentioned beforehand, centralises key economic and strategic decisions of the different housing projects under its organisational umbrella. For those projects leasing municipally owned plots, housing equity is restricted in any case by the absence of ownership over the land. However, a change in municipal policies once the leases expire is a possibility and a risk. The creation of a community land trust (CLT) model of land stewardship, based on a tripartite ownership structure including public authorities, social entities and residents, is a future development that is being considered (Cabré 2020). This type of multi-stakeholder control of the land upon which cooperatives are built would further entangle the sector in multiple and layered rights, which would make it difficult for any actor to unilaterally appropriate and enclose a part of the sector's stock.

## HOUSING COOPERATIVES IN THE MAKING AND REMAKING OF THE CITY

Housing cooperatives can be considered 'enclaves' (Bruun 2011) or 'islands' (Vidal 2019a) within the capitalist city. How cooperatives interact with their surrounding environment and are inserted within broader urban processes is important in gauging their role in wider urban commoning strategies. The true significance of where cooperatives are located, what activities they host and what kind of relations they build with surrounding neighbours and other urban actors can only be fully understood in the broader urban context – in particular, in relation to urbanisation processes and the valorisation and devalorisation of space that characterise the uneven geographical development of capital (Slater 2017, Smith 1982). This section analyses some of the key dimensions to be considered in this regard in the Uruguayan and Danish cases and centres on the role of cooperatives in the more recent context of the 'generalisation of gentrification as a global urban strategy' (Smith 2002) or 'planetary gentrification' (Lees et al. 2016). In revalorising urban environments, cooperatives' collective and decommodified characteristics are strained and 'put to test', allowing for a more focused analysis of their strengths, weaknesses and contradictions. Lessons learned are of interest to Barcelona and beyond.

Cooperative housing has often been constructed in the fringes of the city where land prices are lower. This has been mostly the case for housing cooperatives in Montevideo, which have been extending the city and its urban infrastructures. Cooperativists have not only engaged in housing construction but have also laid energy, water and sewage groundwork and constructed social and community infrastructure from libraries to crèches to sports facilities. Many of these infrastructures have been shared, on a permanent or temporal basis, with surrounding urban developments and neighbours. In this case, commoning by members has spilled beyond the boundaries of the cooperative community and provided spaces for broader social encounters. Yet this openness is fragile and often vulnerable to the harsh dynamics of urban life, as well as to the broader social climate generated by urban conflicts and inequalities. In response to heightened perceptions of urban insecurity and crime, many cooperatives have gradually built walls and fences around their estates in the past years. This stricter differentiation between cooperative and public space has undermined the broader appropriation of housing cooperatives as commons.

*Source:* Miguel A. Martínez.

*Figure 30.1    FUCVAM estates in the historical centre of Montevideo (2018)*

Cooperatives have also participated in the urban renewal of city centres. In the early 1990s, FUCVAM took a strategic decision to go beyond building in the periphery of Montevideo and set an agenda for urban reform and the right of the popular classes to inhabit the central city (FUCVAM 1997). Housing cooperative initiatives were started in central areas, particularly in the historic Ciudad Vieja district, on municipal plots or through the renovation of publicly owned derelict buildings (see Figure 30.1). The first housing cooperative in the neighbourhood, COVICIVI, came together under the slogan of the 'right of neighbours to live in their neighbourhood', in the midst of an embryonic urban regeneration process that had triggered displacements of low-income and marginalised residents (Abin 2014, Díaz Parra & Pozuelo Rabasco 2013). In the context of liberalised urban land rent regulations and the earmarking of the district for cultural and touristic activities, housing cooperatives have had an ambiguous effect in undoing the renewa–gentrification coupling: firstly because despite housing low-income neighbours, they have not been able to integrate the local marginalised population living in informal accommodation and lacking the required economic, social and cultural capital to participate as members and secondly because their participation in the improvement of the built environment has been capitalised upon by surrounding landlords in the form of rising property values and rents. As a result, cooperatives have partially functioned as pioneers in the neighbourhood's uneven gentrification processes (Martinet 2015, Vidal 2019a).

Private housing cooperatives in the central areas of Copenhagen have also participated in urban transformations entangled in gentrification processes. The neighbourhood of Vesterbro, once the city's infamous 'red-light district', is an illustrative case in point. A comprehensive and far-reaching policy of urban renewal was initiated in the neighbourhood in the 1990s, set on integrally refurbishing its mostly rental and private cooperative buildings and incorporating the area into Copenhagen's 'creative city' strategy (Bayliss 2007, Lund Hansen et al. 2001). In the process of refurbishment, many cooperatives were pushed to merge small flats and renovation investments translated into higher monthly payments. Rental-to-cooperative tenure conversions were also facilitated during this time and many low-income and vulnerable tenants incapable of becoming members opted to be rehoused elsewhere. Despite these dynamics, many of the district's low- and middle-income tenants still managed to remain in the neighbourhood's newly refurbished buildings as cooperative members. However, once cooperative assemblies followed the valuation hikes in the 2000s mentioned in the previous section, membership share prices skyrocketed to more closely reflect the market appraisal of their new building quality and central location. As such, whereas the increase in membership share prices has enriched long-time residents of cooperative housing, equivalent low-income groups can no longer afford to move into the neighbourhood. As Larsen and Lund Hansen (2008) argue, housing cooperatives in Vesterbro have in this sense generated 'exclusionary displacement' (Marcuse 1986).

As these cases illustrate, the wider urban regulations and processes in which housing cooperatives are immersed strongly mark their impact and trajectory. Cooperatives participate in, and are vulnerable to, urban transformations that operate across multiple scales. Commoning in its collective properties might produce contradictory and perverse effects in its interaction with its commodified urban environment. Thus, exercising broader powers over the process of urbanisation also requires engaging with state policies and regulations that influence the socio-spatial configuration of the city. The municipalist movement seeks to capture local governments to align commoning logics within and outside the state but faces serious difficulties in steering the state away from governing for capital. The Barcelona experience points to the advances that can be achieved in this sense but also to its limits. The new wave of user cooperatives in the city could not have expanded without favourable municipal policies, but cooperative projects continue to be just a drop in the ocean. In Montevideo and Copenhagen, municipal public authorities have promoted housing cooperativism, yet also enacted policies enabling capital-driven urbanisation and gentrification processes. In all three cases, moreover, key legal and policy competencies that shape urban space are in the hands of supra-municipal authorities. In all, housing cooperativism within urban commoning strategies implies being attentive to the interaction between housing cooperatives and their surrounding urban environment, as well as to their position within multi-scalar strategies to appropriate the city itself as commons.

## CONCLUSIONS

This chapter has discussed theoretical and practical challenges involved in urban commoning, with specific reference to cooperative housing. The main theoretical challenges have concerned situating urban commoning within the dynamics of capitalism and defining the communities involved in these commoning practices. I have placed the commons in a dialectical interplay with enclosures and argued for a broad and practically instituted notion of community. The practical challenges have concerned the specific organisational and institutional configuration of the commons and its development in concrete historical and geographical contexts. I argue that cooperatives can create the organisational space for commoning in modern urban settings within institutional frameworks that are also shaped by the state and the market. The cases of Barcelona, Copenhagen and Montevideo provided the empirical material for an analysis of the concrete development and trajectories of housing cooperatives. With references to these cases, the chapter has focused on how cooperative housing can be scaled to become a significant alternative to dominant forms of housing provision, the evolution of cooperative housing in the face of recurrent dynamics of enclosure and the interaction between housing cooperatives and broader urban processes.

Multi-scalar and multi-stakeholder organisational and institutional frameworks have been identified as key to the scaling-up of cooperative housing and to its resilience to enclosure and commodification. It is through the public–cooperative nexus (Ferreri & Vidal 2021) that the cooperative sector can become more affordable and grow in size and in relative autonomy from the market. However, it is by keeping a strong foothold outside of the state that it can confront state-led enclosures. The interlinking of (to different degrees) self-governed urban communities through sector-wide federations can create a significant counter-power to the state in certain historical contexts. A broader social appropriation of cooperative housing, however, is also important in preventing enclosures from within by residents themselves. This broader appropriation is tied to wider social claims over cooperative housing as commons that the rest of society has a *right not to be excluded* from (Blomley 2020, Bruun 2015), as well as to specific institutional mechanisms that allow for the participation and inclusion of non-residents. The latter include equity limitations to maintain affordability and housing transfer regulations that keep the sector relatively open and accessible. The direct participation of non-residents within the governing bodies of the cooperative housing sector is another key mechanism present in the Catalan and Danish cases. In all, commoning in, against and beyond the state and the market requires building a robust institutional and organisational framework that obstructs enclosures.

The limits of housing cooperatives as a vehicle for urban commoning are brought to relief when situated against the backdrop of capitalist urbanisation processes. Housing cooperatives participate in, and are vulnerable to, broader urban dynamics that are largely beyond their reach. The interaction of housing cooperatives with their surrounding urban environment can produce contradictory and perverse effects. The participation of housing cooperatives in gentrification processes has been used as an extreme and illustrative example of this. This example is useful in signalling the importance of broader alliances to amplify urban commoning and exercise social control over the process of urbanisation. Municipalism underscores the strategic position of municipal governments and urban-based social movements and organisations in articulating these broader strategies, yet has its own set of limits and contradictions and problems of scale. It does contribute, however, to broadening the terrain of action beyond more traditional alliances, such as between the cooperative movement, trade unions and social-democratic parties, that have been influential in Nordic countries like Denmark and beyond. As the three cases show, the role of cooperatives within these broader alliances is not a given but is contingent on concrete historical processes.

Finally, urban sociology has much to contribute to the literature on the urban commons and cooperative housing, particularly in understanding the interplay between structure and agency that shapes these experiences. In this sense, the chapter has underscored the importance of analysing their social composition, the organisational structures that they develop and the state and market constraints and enablers with which they operate. Much is still to be investigated regarding the role of housing cooperatives and other urban commoning experiences within broader social transformation strategies. Social theories on social structures and movements can provide key analytical tools for such enquires. Empirically, further research on the socio-economic and class composition of urban commoners can also provide important insights, particularly regarding the prefigurative potential and practical impact of urban commoning.

## REFERENCES

Abin, E. (2014) Por el derecho de los vecinos a vivir en su barrio. *Trama* 5: 61–75.
Aernouts, N. & Ryckewaert, M. (2018) Reproducing housing commons. Government involvement and differential commoning in a housing cooperative. *Housing Studies* 34(1): 92–110.
Amin, A. & Howell, P. (2016) Thinking the commons. In Amin, A. & Howell, P. (eds.) *Releasing the Commons: Rethinking the Futures of the Commons*. New York: Routledge.
Balmer, I. & Bernet, T. (2015) Housing as a common resource? Decommodification and self-organization in housing – Examples from Germany and Switzerland. In Dellenbaugh, M. et al. (eds.) *Urban Commons: Moving Beyond State and Market*. Basel: Bauwelt Fu.
Barenstein, J. D. et al. (2023) Struggles for the decommodification of housing: The politics of housing cooperatives in Uruguay and Switzerland. *Housing Studies* 37(6): 955–974.
Bayliss, D. (2007) The rise of the creative city: Culture and creativity in Copenhagen. *European Planning Studies* 15(7): 889–903.
BL (2003) *BL's høringssvar på – rapporten fra regeringens udvalg om salg af almene boliger*. Copenhagen. Available at: http://www.bytbolig.dk/media/73983/BLhoringssvar.pdf.
BL (2015) *The Danish Social Housing Sector*. Available at: https://bl.dk/in-english/ (Accessed: 28 July 2015).
Blanco, I. & Gomà, R. (2019) New municipalism. In Kitchin, R. and Thrift, N. (eds.) *International Encyclopedia of Human Geography*. 2nd edition. Amsterdam: Elsevier.
Blomley, N. (2020) Urban commoning and the right not to be excluded. In Özkan, D. & Büyüksaraç, G. B. (eds.) *Commoning the City*. London: Routledge.
Boterman, W. R. (2011) Deconstructing coincidence: How middle-class households use various forms of capital to find a home. *Housing, Theory and Society* 29(3): 321–338.
Bourdieu, P. (1986) The forms of capital. In Richardson, J. (ed.) *Handbook of Theory and Research for the Sociology of Education*. New York: Greenwood, 241–258.
Bro, H. (2009) Housing: From night watchman state to welfare state. *Scandinavian Journal of History* 34(1): 2–28.
Bruun, M. H. (2011) Egalitarianism and community in Danish Housing cooperatives. *Social Analysis* 55(2): 62–83.
Bruun, M. H. (2015) Communities and the commons: Open access and community ownership of the urban commons. In Borch, C. & Kornberger, M. (eds.) *Urban Commons: Rethinking the City*. London: Routledge, 153–170.
Bruun, M. H. (2018) The financialization of Danish cooperatives and the debasement of a collective housing good. *Critique of Anthropology* 38(2): 140–155.
Cabré, E. (2020) Barcelona launches its first CLT-inspired housing initiative. *Housing Europe*. Available at: https://www.housingeurope.eu/blog-1485/barcelona-launches-its-first-clt-inspired-housing-initiative (Accessed: 26 November 2021).
Caffentzis, G. & Federici, S. (2014) Commons against and beyond capitalism. *Community Development Journal* 49(1): 92–105.
Card, K. (2020) Contradictions of housing commons: Between middle-class and anarchist models in Berlin. In Özkan, D. & Büyüksaraç, G. B. (eds.) *Commoning the City*. London: Routledge, 159–176.

Centro Cooperativista Uruguayo (2016) El comienzo. *Dinámica Cooperativa* 126. Available at: http://www.chasque.net/vecinet/CCU_Dina.pdf.
Cumbers, A. (2015) Constructing a global commons in, against and beyond the state. *Space and Polity* 19(1): 62–75.
Dardot, P. & Laval, C. (2019) *Common*. London: Bloomsbury.
De Angelis, M. (2017) *Omnia Sunt Communia*. London: Zed Books.
Díaz Parra, I. & Pozuelo Rabasco, P. (2013) ¿Revitalización sin gentrificación? Cooperativas de vivienda por ayuda mutua en los centros de Buenos Aires y Montevideo. *Cuadernos Geográficos* 52(2): 99–118.
Ferreri, M. & Vidal, L. (2021) Public-cooperative policy mechanisms for housing commons. *International Journal of Housing Policy* 22(2): 149–173.
Foster, S. R. & Iaione, C. (2019) Ostrom in the city. In Hudson, B. Rosenbloom, J. & Cole, D. (eds.) *Routledge Handbook of the Study of the Commons*. Routledge, 235–255.
FUCVAM (1997) Conclusión del Encuentro por Reforma Urbana. *El Solidario* 4.
FUCVAM (2016) Subsidio a la Quota: Derecho a la Permanencia. *Enforma*. Available at: http://www.fucvam.org.uy/wp-content/uploads/2017/03/ENFORMA-Subsidio-a-la-cuota-Derecho-a-la-permanencia-2016.pdf.
Ganapati, S. (2010) Enabling housing cooperatives: Policy lessons from Sweden, India and the United States. *International Journal of Urban and Regional Research* 34(2): 365–380.
Gibb, K., Maclennan, D. & Stephens, M. (2013) *Innovative Financing of Affordable Housing: International and UK Perspectives*. York: Joseph Rowntree Foundation. Available at: https://www.jrf.org.uk/sites/default/files/jrf/migrated/files/affordable-housing-finance-full.pdf.
González, G. (2013) *Una historia de Fucvam*. Montevideo: Trilce.
Greve, J. (1971) *Voluntary Housing in Scandinavia: A Study of Denmark, Norway and Sweeden*. Birmingham: Centre for Urban and Regional Studies, University of Birmingham.
Hardin, G. (1968) The tragedy of the commons. *Science* 162(3859): 1243–1248.
Harvey, D. (2006) *The Limits to Capital*. London: Verso.
Harvey, D. (2012) *Rebel Cities*. London: Verso.
Hess, C. & Ostrom, E. (eds.) (2007) *Understanding Knowledge as a Commons*. Cambridge, MA: MIT Press.
Hodkinson, S. (2012) The return of the housing question. *Ephemera* 12(4): 423–444.
Højesteret (2007) *Salg af almene familieboliger til lejere var ikke i strid med grundlovens § 73*. Copenhagen. Available at: http://www.hoejesteret.dk/hoejesteret/nyheder/pressemeddelelser/Pages/Sag5092006.aspx.
Holloway, J. (2010) *Crack Capitalism*. London: Pluto Press.
Huron, A. (2017) Theorising the urban commons: New thoughts, tensions and paths forward. *Urban Studies* 54(4): 1062–1069.
Huron, A. (2018) *Carving out the Commons*. Minneapolis: University of Minnesota Press.
Jensen, L. (2013) Danmark – Lokal Boendedemokrati och Nationell Korporatism. In Bengston, B. et al. (eds.) *Varför så olika?* Malmö: Égalité: 49–118.
Kip, M. (2015) Moving beyond the city: Conceptualizing urban commons from a critical urban studies perspective. In Dellenbaugh, M. et al. (eds.) *Urban Commons: Moving Beyond State and Market*. Boston: Birkhauser: 42–59.
La Borda (no date) Grant of use. Available at: http://www.laborda.coop/en/project/grant-of-use/ (Accessed: 30 December 2021).
La Dinamo Fundació (2021) *Assequibilitat econòmica de l'habitatge cooperatiu en cessió d'ús: diagnosi, reptes i propostes*. Barcelona. Available at: https://ladinamofundacio.org/wp-content/uploads/2021/11/Assequibilitat-economica_habitatge-cooperatiu_informe-1.pdf.
Larsen, H. G. & Lund Hansen, A. (2008) Gentrification – Gentle or traumatic? Urban renewal policies and socioeconomic transformations in Copenhagen. *Urban Studies* 45(12): 2429–2448.
Larsen, H. G. & Lund Hansen, A. (2015) Commodifying Danish housing commons. *Geografiska Annaler B* 97(3): 263–274.
LBF (2016) Årsberetning 2016. Copenhagen. Available at: https://www.lbf.dk/media/1465838/lbf-aarsberetning_2016_310317.pdf.

Lees, L., Shin, H. B. & López Morales, E. (2016) *Planetary Gentrification*. Cambridge: Polity Press.
Linebaugh, P. (2008) *The Magna Carta Manifesto: Liberties and Commons for All*. Berkley, CA: University of California Press.
Linebaugh, P. (2014) *Stop, Thief! The Commons, Enclosures and Resistance*. Oakland, CA: PM Press.
Lund Hansen, A., Andersen, H. T. & Clark, E. (2001) Creative Copenhagen: Globalization, urban governance and social change. *European Planning Studies* 9(7): 851–869.
Marcuse, P. (1986) Abandonment, gentrification and displacement. In Smith, N. & Williams, P. (eds.) *Gentrification of the City*. Boston, MA: Routledge, 153–177.
Martinet, G. (2015) *Conquérir la Ciudad Vieja*. Dissertation, Sorbonne Nouvelle University.
Martínez, M. A. (2020) Urban commons from an anti-capitalist approach. *Partecipazione e Conflitto* 13(3): 1390–1410.
Marx, K. (1995) *Capital, Volume I*. Marx/Engels Internet Archive. Available at: https://www.marxists.org/archive/marx/works/1867-c1/ch26.htm (Accessed: 21 December 2021).
Midnight Notes Collective (1990) Introduction to the new enclosures. *Midnight Notes* 10: 1–9. Available at: http://www.midnightnotes.org/pdfnewenc1.pdf (Accessed: 15 December 2017).
Miró, I. (2017) Common & coops. In Xarxa d'Economía Solidaria de Catalunya (ed.) *Esmolem les Eïnes*. Barcelona: Pol·len Edicions, 59–102.
Miró, I. (2018) *Ciutats cooperatives*. Barcelona: Icaria.
Nahoum, B. (2013) Forty years of self-management in popular housing in Uruguay. In *Cooperatives and Socialism: A View from Cuba*. London: Palgrave Macmillan, 190–211.
Nielsen, B. G. (2010a) Is breaking up still hard to do? – Policy retrenchment and housing policy change in a path dependent context. *Housing, Theory and Society* 27(3): 241–257.
Nielsen, B. G. (2010b) *The Hidden Politics of a Haunted Sector*. Copenhagen: University of Copenhagen.
Nonini, D. (2017) Theorizing the urban housing commons. *Focaal* 79: 23–38.
Noterman, E. (2016) Beyond tragedy: Differential commoning in a manufactured housing cooperative. *Antipode* 48(2): 433–452.
Observatorio Metropolitano (2014) *La apuesta municipalista*. Madrid: Traficantes de sueños.
Ostrom, E. (1990) *Governing the Commons*. New York, NY: Cambridge University Press.
Richman, N. (1995) From worker cooperatives to social housing: The transformation of the third sector in Denmark. In Heskin, A. D. & Leavitt, J. (eds.) *The Hidden History of the Cooperative*. Davis, CA: Cooperative Centre University of California, 143–162.
Russell, B. (2019) Beyond the local trap: New municipalism and the rise of the fearless cities. *Antipode* 51(3): 989–1010.
Sectorial (2021) *Fem assequible l'habitatge cooperatiu*. Available at: https://xes.cat/comissions/habitatge/ (Accessed: 15 October 2021).
Slater, T. (2017) Planetary rent gaps. *Antipode* 49: 114–137.
Smith, N. (1982) Gentrification and uneven development. *Economic Geography* 58(2): 139–155.
Smith, N. (2002) New globalism, new urbanism: Gentrification as global urban strategy. *Antipode* 34(3): 427–450.
Solanas, M. (2016) *Las cooperativas de vivienda uruguayas como sistema de producción social del hábitat y autogestión de barrios*. Seville: Universidad Pablo de Olavide.
Sørvoll, J. (2013) *The Politics of Cooperative Housing in Norway and Sweden 1960–1990 (1945–2013)*. Oslo: University of Oslo.
Sørvoll, J. & Bengtsson, B. (2020) Mechanisms of solidarity in collaborative housing – The case of co-operative housing in Denmark 1980–2017. *Housing, Theory and Society* 37(1): 65–81.
Stavrides, S. (2016) *Common Space*. London: Zed Books.
Thompson, M. (2020a) From co-ops to community land trusts: Tracing the historical evolution and policy mobilities of collaborative housing movements. *Housing, Theory and Society* 37(1): 82–100.
Thompson, M. (2020b) *Reconstructing Public Housing*. Liverpool: Liverpool University Press.
Thompson, M. (2020c) What's so new about new municipalism? *Progress in Human Geography* 45(2): 317–342.
Velfærdsministeriet (2008) Notat om erfaringerne med Københavns Kommune salg af beboelsesejendomme gennem Ejendomsselskabet TOR I/S. Available at: http://www.ft.dk/samling/20072/lovforslag/l176/bilag/12/573198.pdf.

Vidal, L. (2018) The politics of creditor–debtor relations and mortgage payment strikes: The case of the Uruguayan Federation of Mutual-Aid Housing Cooperatives. *Environment and Planning A* 50(6): 1189–1208.

Vidal, L. (2019a) Cooperative islands in capitalist waters: Limited-equity housing cooperatives, urban renewal and gentrification. *International Journal of Urban and Regional Research* 43(1): 157–178.

Vidal, L. (2019b) Securing social gains in, against and beyond the state: The case of Denmark's 'common housing'. *Housing, Theory and Society* 36(4): 448–468.

Vogel, J. A., Lind, H. & Lundqvist, P. (2016) Who is governing the commons: Studying Swedish housing cooperatives. *Housing, Theory and Society* 33(4): 424–444.

# PART V

# SOCIALLY SHAPED CITIES

# 31. Structures and agents: re-scaling citizen participation in urban regeneration

*Luca Sára Bródy*

Citizen participation has always been a popular theme of contemporary urban studies. It is usually translated as a process of seeking consensus- or conflict-based solutions to social problems at the urban level. However, the present chapter proposes to interpret citizen participation as an outcome of broader processes. In reality, existing participation is fixed in time and space and relates to interdependent phenomena that shape societies. Thus, citizen participation is also a complex and volatile matter.

The urban sociology of citizen participation is embedded in two major intertwined traditions: one focuses on understanding the structural conditions of contemporary societies, while the other looks at narratives and the ideological grounding of agency. For some, the development of conceptual tools has proven to be useful in understanding how political economic conditions affect urban settings, and how urban settings affect everyday lives of people, their thinking, and their ways of interaction. Meanwhile, others have been interested in how these conditions can be reinforced or challenged by counter-narratives (Flanagan 1993).

However, the urban question is less targeted when proving the dominance of structure over agency, or vice versa. Instead, most analyses concentrate on the precise ways in which these two major aspects of social life come together. Those scholars who intend to stress the role of structure in their analytical framework often utilise grand theoretical frames concerning how societal structures exert a powerful force on agents. Agency, on the other hand, is perceived as the active dimension of society, the ability of individuals or groups—neighbourhood groups, movements, economic or political allies—to facilitate change amidst given conditions. Rather than deciding whether the logic of structure (political economic conditions) or agency (the role of local actors in shaping these political economic conditions) matters most, the main inquiry should be how and when these logics matter in the negotiations over urban transformation. Disregarding both overly structuralist and interpretive approaches of contemporary urban sociological theory, this chapter deals with middle-range theories that emphasise the importance of both dimensions.

Thus, the aim of this chapter is to disentangle the diverse meanings attached to citizen participation through the deployment of contemporary approaches and paradigms. What is common in these theoretical attempts is that ultimately they share the silent agreement that the shape of social action is first of all an outcome of the kind of structure that reigns while also accounting seriously for the agency attached to the promotion of and resistance to the actual social order. To honour that, a cultural political economy approach to citizen participation is proposed.

In the following, to illuminate major shifts in theorisations about scale, political economic forces, agents, and varying local contexts, the chapter proceeds with a theoretical review of how the structure–agency debate informed the analysis of citizen participation in urban regeneration. In the remainder of the chapter, the empirical section focuses on citizen participation practices in Budapest, Hungary. Divided into three periods, the sections reveal how the complexity of political economic conditions, narratives of citizen participation, types of coalitions, and urban contestations shaped the practice and meaning of citizen participation. Finally, in conclusion, the chapter draws on the implications of the presented empirical analysis and identifies lessons on the structure–agency debate, as well as suggesting future research.

## EMBEDDING CITIZEN PARTICIPATION IN THE STRUCTURE–AGENCY DEBATE

This section provides an overview of contemporary approaches and their sociological roots, centring arguments around citizen participation in urban transformations. By definition, 'citizen participation' encompasses citizen rights as a range of diverse activities, from participatory democracy (holding public authorities accountable) to representative democracy (such as voting) and participation in community life, including political participation. Accordingly, the questions to organise this section's overview are: 1) How do economic conditions of state restructuring affect the urban governance of cities? 2) How does state restructuring affect communities and the self? 3) What interests drive social groups to sustain or challenge urban governance? 4) How do social groups resist and contest urban transformations? Essentially, the main challenge in answering these questions is to find a way in which all these dimensions can be articulated together.

### Economic Conditions and the Politics of Scale

Urban sociologists employed analytic models for a long time to stress the change in cities. Inspired by the Chicago school of urban ecology, empirical approaches explored the effects of urbanisation and urban life in the 1940s (Whyte 1943, Wirth 1938). The emergence of the political economy paradigm in the 1970s overturned the dominance of empirical endeavours, privileging the influence of globalised capitalism on social structures. This paradigm shift also brought attention to the broadening of analysis to the regional and global level. International capitalism as the fundamental source of change provided the necessary vantage point to understand what was going on at the local level. Consequently, political economy looked at economic restructuring and its sociological consequences, analysing whose interest was served by these profound changes.

The attention given to cities under advanced capitalism is represented by the Marxist approach of new urban sociology and the seminal works of Harvey (1987) and Castells (1977 in English, original in 1972). While Harvey was interested in the interaction of capital accumulation and class struggle, focusing on the city's role in the production of capital (investment flows, mediating financial institutions, and credit mechanisms), Castells was more interested in the reproduction of the means of production, the segregation of social classes, and grassroots political movements (Zukin 1980). Little attention had previously been paid to the politics of scale (Smith 1992), which problematised the reterritorialisation of the state to multiple spatial scales, understood as a process of 'glocalisation', a term coined by Swyngedouw (1992)—as well as Peck and Tickell (1994)—to acknowledge that the understanding of urban-level phenomena had to be amended by the complex interplay of local, regional, and global scales.

This tradition provides a fruitful lens to analyse the relationship between urban restructuring and the role of urban regeneration in cities (i.e. the transforming nature of tackling urban problems). Present-day cities have become targets of various neoliberal experimentations, which primarily pursue the transformation of public urban spaces for the accommodation of economic growth and increased consumption practices (Peck & Tickell 2002), resulting in new governing arrangements beyond the state (Swyngedouw 2005). Along with that, the operation of cities has come under double pressure: on the one hand, the attraction of foreign capital has become the main driver of the economy, while cities have also become mitigators of emerging and growing inequalities (Brenner 1998). In the European Union (EU) this meant that urban policies envisioned the role of cities as that of both creators of local sustainability and, at the same time, engines of international competitiveness (Jessop 2002). As part of that, participatory mechanisms served the mandate of bringing people closer to EU institutions through institutional settings of consultation assemblies or practices such as participatory budgeting, countering concerns of EU integration leading to a hollowed out democratic accountability (Polletta 2016).

**Governmentality, Responsibilisation, and the Soul of the Citizen**

As we move closer to the micro level of urban policies, fewer explanatory factors stem from the re-scaling literature in clarifying the everyday rationalities of individuals. Some scholars have stressed that although the literature has very much been focused on scalar changes and their effects on nation states and regions, the level of individuals has remained unexplored, suggesting that the 'microphysics of governmentality' and 'questions around subjectivity' have stayed out of the orbit of former attempts (MacLeod 2001: 822). In a Weberian tradition, this focus emphasises that the city, being a site of political practices, provides a lens to analyse different representations of groups and interests (May et al. 2005), and the political and cultural conditions that constitute capitalism.

In a similar vein, Michel Foucault, in his lectures in 1978–9, began to study the exercise of power at the scale of society at large, proposing the notion of 'governmental rationality' (Gordon 1987). He denied the Marxist notion that capitalism has one universal form. Alternatively, he invoked Weber to argue that 'the history of capitalism can only be an economic-institutional history' (Foucault 2008: 164). In *The Birth of Biopolitics*, his interest in governmental rationalities builds deeply on the thought of Weber (1978) on how different regimes shape national forms of capitalist economies and how social and economic institutions shape the individual (Flew 2015). Among the many aspects that allow the work of Max Weber and Michel Foucault to be compared, the studies on domination and techniques of discipline are the most visible commonalities (Gordon 1987). The governmentality perspective is widely acknowledged in later scholarly works (Rose 1999) aiming to understand links between political power, expertise, and the self. These undertakings resemble a kind of political economy that aspires to take account of the mutations of welfare institutions in contemporary societies and how neoliberal governance affects individual life, not only in a narrow economic sense. In the era of globalisation, 'community has become a new spatialization of government' (Rose 1996: 327), which links the various identities of individuals together through the management of expert authority. In this context, urban policy seeks to activate citizens in certain ways, to take greater responsibility for their own well-being (Raco & Imrie 2000).

In deploying communities as a government tool for urban transformation, authors pointed out the mechanisms of neoliberalising cities: shrinking social welfare services in which the participation of citizens receives a prominent role while advocating for the re-representation of the city through entrepreneurial discourses. Critics highlighted that underlying power relations in neoliberalising cities strip citizens of their most important strength: to be able to mobilise against marginalisation (Beaumont & Nicholls 2008, Ghose 2005, Purcell 2009).

**Urban Development Coalitions**

In the end, public policy instruments are always about who gets excluded and which clientele receive resources (Le Galès 2018). Drawing on Bourdieu's theory, urban regeneration can be perceived as a field in which different stakeholders struggle to achieve their goals and wish to dominate (Bourdieu 1984). He analysed the salience of symbolic power in explaining inequities in the distribution of public services with the deployment of the notion of the 'field'. The concept refers to social arenas in which battles take place to gain desired resources and power (Bourdieu & Wacquant 1992). One of the strengths of Bourdieu's framework is the ability to link different analytical scales—macro structures of power (state) and meso-level institutions (a professional field) with the everyday interactions of individuals (Wacquant 2018). In the urban sociological tradition of the analysis of the city, 'urban regime analysis' (DiGaetano 1989, Stoker 1989) and urban 'growth machines' or 'growth coalitions' (Harding 1994, Logan & Molotch 1987, Molotch 1976) have been two influential approaches that resemble Bourdieu's understanding of different groups aiming for hegemony in a field. The goal of these approaches has been to unravel how various public officials and business elites cooperate to deliver resources and negotiate which actors have access to them.

Democratisation processes led to a myriad of experimentation at the urban level. Participation in public policy-making and the various modes of governance almost always serves the aim of countering particular powerful, well-established interest groups (Le Galès 2018). Alongside the spread of participatory practices, a whole new infrastructure for organising, implementing, and evaluating these practices emerged in areas of urban planning and design, consultation firms, and participatory design specialists. As a consequence, scholarship on citizen participation also started to change and address new concerns. For instance, the redirection of citizen participation by various urban coalitions enforced the responsibilisation of citizens (Rose 1999) with the transfer of welfare duties to the voluntary sector, as is well-illustrated in neo-communitarian strategies (Fyfe 2005). Many argued that participation had lost its radical edge and been turned into a depoliticised addition to the development world (Cooke & Kothari 2001, Ferguson 1994) or a third-way politics for neoliberal experimentation that utilises the communitarian spirit and the voluntarism of the third sector (Marinetto 2003, Mohan 2012). Others called for the return to politics of participatory development (Williams 2004), while Silver et al. stressed that the democratisation of governance through participation is often presented 'as an unalloyed good, countering concern about declining social capital, heavy-handed bureaucracy, government inefficiency and social exclusion' (2010: 453).

**Urban Contestations**

As Le Galès notes, 'governing is a two-way process. A lot depends upon the population which is governed' (2018: 217). Castells probably would strongly agree. In his early work he analysed social movements in Paris (Pickvance 1976), and during the development of his research he ended up abandoning structural Marxism for the aim of analysing popular movements as key agents in urban change. In his seminal work *The City and the Grassroots* (Castells 1983), he renounces his views on class struggle, reducing it merely to just one basis of urban coalitions. This turn highlights the shift of focus towards ordinary individuals and communities and how they experience advanced capitalism in the city. The focus on agency and how discourses take part in the promotion of urban strategies has contributed to urban sociological research by highlighting the mechanisms of shared representations, collective identity, and the social construction of hegemonic concepts, which act upon and change institutions and norms (Shields 1999). Overall, the emphasis on agency is useful to address the historic failure of the urban development world in fixing underdevelopment, and how it was challenged to renew its discourse and practice (Leal 2007). Participation was key to this process.

Movements in advanced capitalism are often exploited by authorities to solve 'fiscal as well as legitimation problems, and the movements shifted their strategies "from protest to program" in order to put their alternative practice onto a more stable footing' (Mayer 2009: 364). In the context of recurring crises, as Mayer (2013) observed after the 2008 Great Financial Crisis (GFC), the fragmentation of movements stems from a particular intensifying trend. Polarisation and displacement are already quite disruptive within cities, but this does not affect only the previously disadvantaged.

Youth, students, and middle-class segments have also been burdened by neoliberal measures, which results in diverse social groupings of autonomous leftist or right-wing organisations, middle-class urbanites, precarious groups, artists and creative professionals, local environmental groups, and also the rarely present marginalised people of colour, who all occupy very different positions in the neoliberal city (Della Porta et al. 2022, Eizaguirre et al. 2017, Florea et al. 2018, Mayer 2013). Hence, these diverse groups have been divided between those being absorbed into creative and smart city policies, wherein responsibilisation is emphasised above political empowerment, and on the other side, urban outcasts, who are completely locked out of neoliberal crisis management.

## A CULTURAL POLITICAL ECONOMY OF CITIZEN PARTICIPATION IN URBAN REGENERATION

It is both desired and challenging to combine global and local phenomena. Most powerful theories emphasise not only the historically specific geographies of social relations but also the contextual and historical variation (Jessop et al. 2008). Nonetheless, there is 'the quietly growing acceptance of the global context of capitalism as the ultimate unit of analysis, the context in which all change has to be understood: localities, elites, citizen coalitions, ordinary individuals and their agendas and challenges' (Flanagan 1993: 11). Therefore, the lack of middle-range theories between the grand narrative of advanced capitalism and the detailed analysis of local varieties needs to be confronted with a more nuanced approach.

Cultural political economy makes it possible to analyse complex relationships between multiple actors and their broader environment. Going beyond the type of analysis that provides a snapshot view of contexts and social dynamics, the current analysis shows how long-term processes generate conditions, group formations of agents, and struggles over time. This chapter argues that neoliberalisation does not explain it all, even if it is undoubtedly part of the equation. Globalisation does not generate 'a single set of pressures' (Jessop 2010: 42) that affect urban policies equally, and there is no common response by all states. Even if scalar arrangements become fixed, this always remains temporary, being the subject of a political project (Purcell 2003). Jessop and Sum highlight similar concerns: in their quest for a theory that explores individual-level experiences of state re-scaling, they state that 'political economy has an impoverished notion of how subjects and subjectivities are formed and how different modes of calculation emerge and become institutionalised' and call for an approach that 'articulates the micro-foundations of political economy with its macro-structuring principles in an overall material–discursive analysis' (Jessop & Sum 2001: 97).

The Marxist tradition of urban political economy did not leave much space for the analysis of 'culture' in its broad meaning (Le Galès 1999), and urban scholars argued for the shortcomings of political economic perspectives, saying that 'cities change for many reasons, neoliberalism being only one of them' (Le Galès 2016: 4). To capture the finer weight of agency, political economic theories have to be amended with the inclusion of topics on discourse and meaning-making (Jessop & Oosterlynck 2008, Jessop 2004, Sayer 2001, Sum & Jessop 2013) to understand how structural conditions and local translations of these conditions relate to each other. Thus, not are only structural constraints and opportunities and their effect on the individual crucial but also how various political economic coalitions and elite groups aim to become hegemonic in a specific field. Moreover, how the particular field is subject to resistance and contestations by citizens is also important.

Therefore, to grasp the mechanisms that link the restructuration of urban regeneration to practices of citizen participation, in the following, this chapter argues that to be able to understand the complexity of the local context, the analysis of the relationship between 1) political economic conditions, 2) the competing narratives over these conditions, 3) experts and their role in shaping citizen participation practices, and 4) the contestation of these conditions by civic groups is necessary.

The empirical analysis is guided by four dimensions. The first dimension of analysis deals with how political economic junctures shape normative and institutional frames of citizen participation in urban regeneration. Second, brought about by restructuring, how do these longer-term processes deliver new narratives? How are former approaches invalidated or shaped? Do other aspects gain importance? Third, what is the impact of changing political economic structures on the role of municipal employees and experts in the field? Do these changes broaden or narrow their room to manoeuvre? What is the relationship between the political and technical realm? How does the position of key players change? Fourth, do these changes help to mobilise resources? Do they bring consensus or polarisation of agents? How do urban transformations affect contestations?

The empirical section is based on two major types of material. First, it includes written resources (such as national legislation, reports produced and published by state institutions, and the academic literature) on citizen participation in urban regeneration in Hungary. The second type of material stems from 24 in-depth interviews conducted between 2017 and 2018 in Budapest with organisers and participants of citizen groups, NGOs, acknowledged experts in the field, and municipal employees working on participatory mechanisms. The main citizen groups that the interviews focused on consisted of initiatives dealing with housing and cityscape protection, groups focusing on community development or inequalities arising from urban development, and local neighbourhood organisations. Interviews were conducted with municipal employees and acknowledged experts in the field who had been working directly on participatory projects and aimed at nurturing participatory mechanisms, along with NGOs addressing the same issues.

Taking the example of Budapest, the empirical discussion reveals complex relationships stretching over a period from the 1990s to the 2010s. The subsequent sections discuss the shifts in dominant approaches towards the implementation of citizen participation in urban regeneration by highlighting three different eras. Overall, the empirical sections aim to trace connections between structural transformations and their narrative framing, and the related coalitions and resistance that address or are linked to these changes.

# THE METAMORPHOSIS OF CITIZEN PARTICIPATION IN BUDAPEST

**The Contours of Urban Regeneration in the 1990s**

The years following the regime change were marked by mass privatisation and market liberalisation. During the decentralisation of state power to local governments in the 1990s, local governments sought market-based urban regeneration programmes, which resulted in underinvested poor areas on the one hand, and state-funded programmes promoting investment and partnership on the other (Czirfusz et al. 2015). Significant development had begun in the appreciating inner district areas of Budapest: downtown areas were enriched with new business districts, shopping centres, and residential areas while depreciating, degraded, and difficult-to-sell dwellings remained in municipal ownership. The condition of privatised residential buildings also deteriorated in many cases, as residents were unable to raise the funds needed for the inherited renovation tasks (Kovács & Wiessner 2004, Somogyi et al. 2007). To counter the process of rapid polarisation, in 1993 the Municipality of Budapest created the so-called Urban Rehabilitation Fund to cover the regeneration of the municipal rental stock, as a state ordinance in the same year made it mandatory for local governments to sell their housing stock to current tenants unless they had an urban regeneration plan in place. The Urban Rehabilitation Fund was allocated on a separate municipal account and the fund consisted of the inflowing payments of district municipalities, which they realised through the privatisation of their public assets. Throughout the coming years, urban regeneration majorly targeted the physical renovation of buildings.

The foundations of urban policy-making already started to take shape during the 1980s (Jelinek 2021), and the most important task of the early transition years was to counter the drastic decline in public housing construction and the housing and social tensions caused by privatisation. Initial interventions imagined large housing blocks instead of narrow streets and small, closed courtyards, with a shared park inside the blocks. These regeneration plans were mainly typical in the ninth district of Budapest. In another inner area of the city, the eighth district, in place of the buildings condemned for demolition, condominiums were built with private investment. The displacement of residents during these regeneration programmes was not given much attention. During the 1990s and early 2000s, a sharp professional distinction between the concept of 'gentrification' and 'urban development' did not exist (Keresztély & Scott 2012). Gentrification was often used as an analogue of desirable neighbourhood development: 'I wish the area where I live would gentrify even a bit, and not just continue to sink downwards on the social slope' (Schneller 2006). Moreover, as the architect of an inner district municipal development company expressed, gentrification was an inevitable step: 'it could not have been done otherwise', as he insisted.

It was a frequently used procedure to coordinate and manage the regeneration activities of local governments by creating independent municipal companies. Alongside asset management organisations and private investors, these companies served as think tanks deciding on the principles of implementing regeneration plans. Overall, experts working in these companies agreed during the first decade of the transition that the strategy of footloose private capital handling urban regeneration was the solution to restructure the state socialist institutional heritage. As Jelinek showed (2019), this meant that social aspects were secondary considerations amidst the growing number of evictions and looming gentrification.

Civic mobilisation responded to the processes of deepening capitalism and the market economy (Beluszky 1992). Protests targeted specific locations and mobilised small crowds in relation to urban development. Precarious housing and the protection of the cityscape were the main drivers of the formation of various groupings. In the field of housing, the Tenants' Association founded in 1991 countered the large-scale sale of municipal rental housing, and several organisations have been set up to protect the poor, Roma, the homeless, and displaced residents in need of adequate housing (Sebály 2021). Furthermore, the intensity of foreign capital investment following economic restructuring gained much more momentum in the inner districts (Földi & Van Weesep 2007, Kovács 2009), where non-residential investments mixed with the destruction of monuments. In addition to the spread of 'ruin pubs' (Lugosi et al. 2010), privately funded cultural and entertainment venues gained importance (Csizmady & Olt 2014), while buildings were gradually replaced with hotels and office spaces. The main area of civic intervention concentrated on these changes. The Budapest City Protection Association (BCPA)—which was informally already active on a national level in the 1980s but was only established formally in 1990—openly criticised the value-destroying practice of contemporary urban policy decisions (Szívós 2018). The role of the association in the 1990s was followed by the formation of several non-governmental organisations in the early 2000s, including groups that are still active today.

**Applying Participatory Practices in the Mid-2000s**

From a political economic viewpoint, growing budget deficits and government debt preceded the EU accession of 2004. Preparations for EU membership were considered as another neoliberal 'shock therapy' that characterised Hungary's early 1990s transformation to a market economy (Sokol 2001, Varró 2010). Budapest already absorbed around half of all the incoming foreign investments (Kovács 2009), which only increased after the accession. In the mid-2000s, the transformation of the inner districts of Budapest continued rapidly. Urban regeneration turned into a common policy tool, benefitting from the significant inflows of EU funds, while the amount spent on state-funded urban regeneration began to shrink. Consequently, Western European examples of integrated urban development strongly steered the domestic design and implementation of projects. The Hungarian version has been named by experts as 'social urban rehabilitation' to counter the formerly mere physical renovation of buildings and squares. The 'social' element referred to the fact that the participation of affected residents has been incorporated into urban regeneration programmes aside from the original focus on physical interventions.

Thus, during the second half of the decade, institutionalised forms of citizen participation gained ground in local development plans, as a condition of receiving EU funds. Experimentation and high expectations of pilot participatory processes marked this era. Probably the most well-known, the Magdolna Quarter Programme in the eighth district became a widely recognised but also controversial example for the inclusion of residents in neighbourhood regeneration. Even though the sensitive side of urban regeneration developed in these years, there was also an emerging 'project class' (Kovách 2007), which consisted of a growing number of lucrative occupations that managed the complex and bureaucratic maze of EU projects in the field of urban development. The project-based management of public tasks has created a divided society with high-income professionals being responsible for the administration and allocation of EU funds on the one hand, and on the other, a community for whom the opaque logic and bureaucracy of projects represented by professionals did not provide a real basis for solving their everyday grievances (Gille 2010). Increasingly, such state-driven flagship projects started to become exclusionary towards the poor and Roma communities (Czirfusz et al. 2015). By the mid-2010s, a rapid population change took place in many inner district areas, where original residents were replaced by better-off ones.

Nevertheless, professional circles were—and many still are today—in denial about the failures and controversies attached to 'social urban rehabilitation' projects. As an architect interviewee recalls, the mid-2000s were a 'pioneer era' for the profession: 'that's when we first saw "regeneration" abroad… They dealt with people, jobs, education, cohesion, and a lot of other stuff', he described. While the uneven nature of urban development has not changed much in the city, the effects of gentrification and the situation of vulnerable groups had a more important weight in the way experts thought or expressed themselves about urban regeneration. A sociologist interviewee working for a private consultant firm illustrated the (wishful) milieu of this period:

> As a sociologist, I see it differently… A planner has social responsibility. You need to be aware that there is no best solution, and there are certain political economic conditions, and you should always be a little socially committed. If something increases inequality, segregation, violation of the right to the city, I will deny executing such a plan. This attitude of a planner would be important, but it is not taught anywhere. How to help those who do not see the [negative] consequences [of urban regeneration], how to communicate their will. And that doesn't mean you have to be an activist. We should take action against policies that prevent a fairer city.

Taking a look at civic participation, the experimentation with participatory projects provided an opportunity for informal civic organisations to develop a more cooperative and contractual, long-term partnership with district governments. It mostly meant that civic organisations had better communication channels with district governments to advocate for residents who were (temporarily or persistently) forced out of the neighbourhood because of demolitions. Moreover, civic interventions—led by environmental and housing activists or a group of active residents—aimed to empower locals to become involved in the transformation of downtown areas. However, the implementation and the logic of the projects have often failed to protect citizens or to meet their needs. The conditional elements of qualifying for EU tenders were by no means a traditional part of Hungarian urban regeneration (Földi 2009). The idealistic world of designers often did not fit the real conditions and could not become inclusive as it was originally imagined. The integration of Roma and non-Roma was partial in the case of various projects. Despite the professional commitment associated with the innovative nature of 'social urban rehabilitation', a high proportion of lower-status residents were evicted, segregation was increasing, and preventing population change was not fully achieved (György 2012, Horváth 2019).

**Phasing Out Solidarity in the Authoritarian Turn of the 2010s**

As the touristification of the city advanced, the focus shifted from neighbourhood regeneration towards public space development and the commercialisation of culture (see Figure 31.1). A series of key government investments aimed at the spectacularisation and hygienisation of public spaces, serving the needs of the middle class and tourists over locals or vulnerable groups. In the management of public spaces, regulation, cleanness, and the security of spaces received a prominent role in order to boost the pace of tourism and real estate development. Moreover, the visibility of poverty and homelessness in public spaces was curtailed or directly punished, preventing for example food distribution in larger public spaces but also implementing the recurrent criminalisation of homelessness (Udvarhelyi 2013), which rose to a national level for the first time in 2013.

The public perception of civil society has been radically manipulated from 2014–15 onwards by central government rhetoric, led by the supermajority of the right-wing Fidesz party since 2010. A forced political divide was created between state- and foreign-funded NGOs, contrasting the 'nation' with international funders of NGOs as 'foreign agents' (Gagyi 2016). Consequently, participatory practices became compromised, and experts working in municipal development companies and technical staff found it difficult to convince the political sphere about the importance of carrying out participatory projects. Even though civil society organisations were seen as possible political opponents by local politicians, instrumentalising participatory processes through the Urban Rehabilitation Fund for city marketing thrived in this period. Experts and municipal employees working in the urban development department of the city reported that the suspicion over civic organisations was overcome by the exertion of political power over projects, while the process of participation was subordinated to large-scale development projects that intended to improve the city image for tourism and investment. Instrumentalising participatory practices even became a necessity during the culmination of the crisis in 2010. It created a situation where vacant downtown spaces could not be filled from the market, residential and real estate investment stagnated, and local governments had to seek an alternative to boost the economy.

Many positions and branches at the district governments of Budapest were created in this period to hire professionals in city marketing strategies. However, former technical staff and experts experienced a loss of autonomy over decision-making in the field, feeling a considerable amount of pressure from big politics. As an architect involved in 'social urban rehabilitation' projects of the previous period summarised, 'politicians have also realised what a "fancy" urban marketing tool participatory planning is'. Thus, instead of aiming to plan together with communities through participation, citizen involvement has been deployed to legitimise urban transformation goals. According to a technical employee in the Municipality of Budapest, public space renewals served as the 'business card of the city' and the 'field of innovation'. The involvement of civic groups was considered by city branding experts as a remedy for the economic downturn of the Great Financial Crisis of 2008: 'people had the will to do something for the city, and creatives have an eye for that. We wanted to act on it, everything is better than doing nothing. It seemed our problems will be solved if Budapest becomes a cool place',

502  *Research handbook on urban sociology*

*Source:* Miguel A. Martínez.

*Figure 31.1  Construction workers at Bálna cultural and commercial centre, a large-scale investment by the Hungarian Tourism Agency in inner Budapest (2013)*

said an interviewee working on smart city strategies. Citizen participation was therefore transformed into an instrument of reimagining and reinventing the function of public spaces and public buildings. The new wave of participatory designers filling municipal positions was described sourly by a former employee of a public development company:

My obsession with community involvement is decision-making, so community involvement should go into the broad spectrum between representative and direct democracy. Community involvement is now at the point where it is very cool, it is trying to rationalise representative democracy… In my reading, it should serve the promotion of direct democracy, so decision-making levels should be as low as possible. But that's not about it at all. Even the coolest community designs are all about making 'cool stuff' in the end.

Those civic groups who were not explicitly political in their action could stay involved in the city's participatory projects; however, party politics strongly steered the direction of these project-based collaborations—varying from the planning of a community garden to planning leisure activities in a public space to advocating for greener public spaces. Therefore, participation as a method has not receded, but the subjects and goals of municipal civic cooperation have shifted significantly. Meanwhile, the attention of grassroots organisations had turned to those living in deep poverty and segregation by the end of the 2010s (Sebály 2021), especially in the field of housing, building coalitions with various oppositional and marginal groups.

# CONCLUSIONS

As we have seen through the case of Budapest, participatory practices were represented by diverse civic action, holding a blurry definition, while their success remained hard to measure (Mayer 2020). Thus, what have we learnt about theorising citizen participation? Given its ambiguous character, the study sought to answer the question of how the interplay of societal dynamics and different interests of relevant actors define its purpose and usefulness for public interest.

This chapter serves as a contribution to better unpacking how the structural and political economic conditions of urban regeneration are entangled with the agency of various interest groups in different periods, influencing the way and mode of how citizens react. We have seen that structure can be both enabling and constraining for citizen participation. In addition to that, the narrative power of structures also plays a key role in determining what is possible to think. There are times when organised systems of governance and collective action are strengthened, allowing for autonomy, the decrease of inequality, or an improvement in the quality of life for residents. However, participatory practices are frequently employed to safeguard political advantages, elites, and the wealth and power of particular groups. Overall, it is not an either/or question whether structure or agency drives the other, but an issue of being able to manage the complexity of research through deploying both lenses. Accordingly, the empirical research in Budapest offers three main lessons.

First, the main insight regarding citizen participation is that the type of participation was a reaction to structural changes: to emerging inequalities in deepening capitalism, the widening of institutional opportunities during EU integration, and re-centralisation of state power in the authoritarian turn. Participation was further steered by the changing extent of consensus and polarisation between expert and civic groups that depended much on the political realm. The case study stretching over a long period of time showed how ephemeral these coalitions can actually be.

Second, that said, the example of citizen participation showed that transformation processes need to be considered in the long term. Past features such as scalar changes, institutional legacy, and power relations between social groups remain a central feature of participatory practices and the tension between those who govern and those who are governed (Le Galès 2018). The changing narratives over the position of citizens in urban regeneration had been represented by different expert groups who have had more power in designing urban interventions that aligned with the narrative of that time.

Finally, citizen participation remains persistent, in governance techniques as much as in informal practices. The initial protests of the 1990s took a more stable turn during the institutionalisation of the 2000s, but as opportunities were curbed in the 2010s, informality regained strength in articulating demands beyond institutional settings. Given the structural pressures of neoliberalising cities, we need to take a closer look at the conditions under which these practices unfold, and even more so, at the strategies with which contestations can thrive better. Whether citizen participation can become transversal or co-opted to serve urban development goals depends not just on the formal settings of these practices but also on how much pressure can be accumulated outside of institutional settings. Future studies should therefore concentrate on the dynamics of mobilisations and how demands can be made more far-reaching.

## REFERENCES

Beaumont J. & Nicholls W. (2008) Plural governance, participation and democracy in cities. *International Journal of Urban and Regional Research* 32(1): 87–94.
Beluszky P. (1992) Budapest és a modernizáció kihívásai [Budapest and the challenges of modernisation]. *Tér és Társadalom* 6(3–4): 15–54.
Bourdieu P. (1984) *Distinction: A social critique of the judgement of taste*. Cambridge: Harvard University Press.
Bourdieu P. & Wacquant L. (1992) *An invitation to reflexive sociology*. Chicago: University of Chicago Press.
Brenner N. (1998) Between fixity and motion: Accumulation, territorial organization and the historical geography of spatial scales. *Environment and Planning D: Society and Space* 16(4): 459–481.
Castells M. (1977) *The urban question: A Marxist approach*. London: Edward Arnold.
Castells M. (1983) *The city and the grassroots: A cross-cultural theory of urban social movements*. Berkeley and Los Angeles: University of California Press.
Cooke B. & Kothari U. (eds.) (2001) *Participation: The new tyranny?* London and New York: Zed Books.
Csizmady A. & Olt G. (2014) Kreatív miliő egy átalakuló negyedben – a romkocsmák belső-erzsébetvárosi világa. *Kultúra és Közösség* 5(2): 27–42.
Czirfusz M., Horváth V., Jelinek C., Pósfai Z. & Szabó L. (2015) Gentrification and rescaling urban governance in Budapest-Józsefváros. *Intersections. East European Journal of Society and Politics* 1(4): 55–77.
Della Porta D., Bertuzzi N., Chironi D., Milan C., Portos M. & Zamponi L. (2022) Bringing grievances back in? Socio-economic inequalities and the political participation of protesters. In C. Milan, N. Bertuzzi, L. Zamponi, M. Portos, D. Chironi & D. Della Porta (eds.) *Resisting the backlash: Street protest in Italy*. London and New York: Routledge, 27–55.
DiGaetano A. (1989) Urban political regime formation: A study in contrast. *Journal of Urban Affairs* 11(3): 261–281.
Eizaguirre S., Pradel-Miquel M. & García M. (2017) Citizenship practices and democratic governance: 'Barcelona en Comú' as an urban citizenship confluence promoting a new policy agenda. *Citizenship Studies* 21(4): 425–439.
Ferguson J. (1994) *The anti-politics machine. 'Development,' depoliticization, and bureaucratic power in Lesotho*. Minneapolis and London: University of Minnesota Press.
Flanagan W.G. (1993) *Contemporary urban sociology*. New York: Cambridge University Press.
Flew T. (2015) Foucault, Weber, neoliberalism and the politics of governmentality. *Theory, Culture & Society* 32(7–8): 317–326.

Florea I., Gagyi Á. & Jacobsson K. (2018) A field of contention: Evidence from housing struggles in Bucharest and Budapest. *Voluntas* 29(4): 712–724.

Földi Z. (2009) A társadalmi részvétel szerepe a városfejlesztés gyakorlatában – európai és hazai tapasztalatok. *Tér és Társadalom* 23(3): 27–43.

Földi Z. & Van Weesep J. (2007) Impacts of globalisation at the neighbourhood level in Budapest. *Journal of Housing and the Built Environment* 22(1): 33–50.

Foucault M. (2008) *The birth of biopolitics: Lectures at the Collège de France, 1978–1979*. Edited by A.I. Davidson & M. Senellart. New York: Palgrave Macmillan.

Fyfe N.R. (2005) Making space for "neo-communitarianism"? The third sector, state and civil society in the UK. *Antipode* 37(3): 536–557.

Gagyi Á. (2016) 'Coloniality of power' in East Central Europe: External penetration as internal force in post-socialist Hungarian politics. *Journal of World-Systems Research* 22(2): 349–372.

Ghose R. (2005) The complexities of citizen participation through collaborative governance. *Space and Polity* 9(1): 61–75.

Gille Z. (2010) Is there a global postsocialist condition? *Global Society* 24(1): 9–30.

González S. & Healey P. (2005) A sociological institutionalist approach to the study of innovation in governance capacity. *Urban Studies* 42(11): 2055–2069.

Gordon C. (1987) The soul of the citizen: Max Weber and Michel Foucault on rationality and government. In S. Whimster & S. Lash (eds.) *Max Weber, rationality and modernity*. London and New York: Routledge, 293–316.

György E. (2012) *A Nyolcker a rendszerváltás után – egy városnegyed identitásának meghatározása*. Doctoral dissertation. Budapest: Eötvös Loránd Tudományegyetem.

Harding A. (1994) Urban regimes and growth machines toward a cross-national research agenda. *Urban Affairs Quarterly* 29(3): 356–382.

Harvey D. (1987) Flexible accumulation through urbanization reflections on 'post-modernism' in the American city. *Antipode* 19: 260–286.

Horváth D. (2019) A városrehabilitáció társadalmi sokszínűségre gyakorolt hatásainak térbeli-társadalmi vizsgálata Józsefvárosban. *Területi Statisztika* 59(6): 606–643.

Jelinek C. (2019) A városrehabilitáció korszakai Magyarországon: Az állam szerepe marginális városi terek (újra)termelésében. *Tér és Társadalom* 33(4): 17–37.

Jelinek C. (2021) Turning a 'socialist' policy into a 'capitalist' one: Urban rehabilitation in Hungary during the long transformation of 1989. *Journal of Urban History* 47(3): 511–525.

Jessop B. (2002) Liberalism, neoliberalism, and urban governance: A state–theoretical perspective. *Antipode* 34(3): 452–472.

Jessop B. (2004) Critical semiotic analysis and cultural political economy. *Critical Discourse Studies* 1(2): 159–174.

Jessop B. (2010) Cultural political economy and critical policy studies. *Critical Policy Studies* 3(3–4): 336–356.

Jessop B. & Oosterlynck S. (2008) Cultural political economy: On making the cultural turn without falling into soft economic sociology. *Geoforum* 39(3): 1155–1169.

Jessop B. & Sum N.-L. (2001) Pre-disciplinary and post-disciplinary perspectives. *New Political Economy* 6(1): 89–101.

Jessop B., Brenner N. & Jones M. (2008) Theorizing sociospatial relations. *Environment and Planning D: Society and Space* 26(3): 389–401.

Keresztély K. & Scott J.W. (2012) Urban regeneration in the post-socialist context: Budapest and the search for a social dimension. *European Planning Studies* 20(7): 1111–1134.

Kovách I. (2007) A fejlesztéspolitika projektesítése és a projekt osztály – Hozzászólás a projektesítés következményei vitához. *Szociológiai Szemle* 3–4: 214–222.

Kovács Z. (2009) Social and economic transformation of historical neighbourhoods in Budapest. *Tijdschrift voor economische en sociale geografie* 100(4): 399–416.

Kovács Z. & Wiessner R. (2004) Budapest. Restructuring a European metropolis. *Europa Regional* 12(1): 22–31.

Le Galès P. (1999) Is political economy still relevant to study the culturalization of cities? *European Urban and Regional Studies* 6(4): 293–302.

Le Galès P. (2016) Neoliberalism and urban change: Stretching a good idea too far? *Territory, Politics, Governance* 4(2): 154–172.
Le Galès P. (2018) The political sociology of cities and urbanisation processes: Social movements, inequalities and governance. In S. Hall & R. Burdett (eds.) *The SAGE handbook of the 21st century city*. London: Sage, 215–235.
Leal P.A. (2007) Participation: The ascendancy of a buzzword in the neo-liberal era. *Development in Practice* 17(4–5): 539–548.
Logan J. & Molotch H. (1987) *Urban fortunes*. Berkeley: University of California Press.
Lugosi P., Bell D. & Lugosi K. (2010) Hospitality, culture and regeneration: Urban decay, entrepreneurship and the 'ruin' bars of Budapest. *Urban Studies* 47(14): 3079–3101.
MacLeod G. (2001) New regionalism reconsidered: globalization and the remaking of political economic space. *International Journal of Urban and Regional Research* 25(4): 804–829.
Marinetto M. (2003) Who wants to be an active citizen? The politics and practice of community involvement. *Sociology* 37(1): 103–120.
May T., Perry B., Le Galès P., Sassen S. & Savage M. (2005) The future of urban sociology. *Sociology* 39(2): 343–370.
Mayer M. (2009) The 'right to the city' in the context of shifting mottos of urban social movements. *City* 13(2–3): 362–374.
Mayer M. (2013) First world urban activism: Beyond austerity urbanism and creative city politics. *City* 17(1): 5–19.
Mayer M. (2020) The promise and limits of participatory discourses and practices. In M. do Mar Castro Valera & B. Ülker (eds.) *Doing tolerance: Urban interventions and forms of participation*. Berlin: Verlag Barbara Budrich, 72–94.
Mohan J. (2012) Geographical foundations of the big society. *Environment and Planning A* 44(5): 1121–1129.
Molotch H. (1976) The city as a growth machine: Toward a political economy of place. *American Journal of Sociology* 82(2): 309–332.
Peck J. & Tickell A. (1994) Searching for a new institutional fix: The after-Fordist crisis and the global-local disorder. In A. Amin (ed.) *Post-Fordism: A reader*. Oxford: Blackwell Publishers, 280–315.
Peck J. & Tickell A. (2002) Neoliberalizing space. *Antipode* 34(3): 380–404.
Pickvance C.G. (ed.) (1976) *Urban sociology*. London and New York: Routledge.
Polletta F. (2016) Participatory enthusiasms: A recent history of citizen engagement initiatives. *Journal of Civil Society* 12(3): 231–246.
Purcell M. (2003) Citizenship and the right to the global city: Reimagining the capitalist world order. *International Journal of Urban and Regional Research* 27(3): 564–590.
Purcell M. (2009) Resisting neoliberalization: Communicative planning or counter-hegemonic movements? *Planning Theory* 8(2): 140–165.
Raco M. & Imrie R. (2000) Governmentality and rights and responsibilities in urban policy. *Environment and Planning A: Economy and Space* 32(12): 2187–2204.
Rose N. (1996) The death of the social? Re-figuring the territory of government. *International Journal of Human Resource Management* 25(3): 327–356.
Rose N. (1999) *Governing the soul: The shaping of the private self*. 2nd ed. London: Free Association Books.
Sayer A. (2001) For a critical cultural political economy. *Antipode* 33(4): 687–708.
Schneller I. (2006) A városrehabilitáció helyzete Budapesten. *Tér és Társadalom* 20(3): 151–154.
Sebály B. (2021) „Lakni kell!" A magyar lakhatási mozgalom elmúlt 30 éve – alulnézetből. In L. Vankó (ed.) *Éves Jelentés a Lakhatási Szegénységről 2021*. Budapest: Habitat for Humanity Magyarország.
Shields R. (1999) Culture and the economy of cities. *European Urban and Regional Studies* 6(4): 303–311.
Silver H., Scott A. & Kazepov Y. (2010) Participation in urban contention and deliberation. *International Journal of Urban and Regional Research* 34(3): 453–477.
Smith N. (1992) Geography, difference and the politics of scale. In J. Doherty, E. Graham, & M. Malek (eds.) *Postmodernism and the Social Sciences*. London: Palgrave Macmillan, 57–79.
Sokol M. (2001) Central and Eastern Europe a decade after the fall of state-socialism: Regional dimensions of transition processes. *Regional Studies* 35(7): 645–655.

Somogyi E., Szemző H. & Tosics I. (2007) Városrehabilitáció kétszintű önkormányzati rendszerben: budapesti sikerek és problémák (1994–2006). In G. Enyedi (ed.) *A Történelmi Városközpontok Átalakulásának Társadalmi Hatásai*. Budapest: MTA Társadalomkutató Központ, 69–92.

Stoker R.P. (1989) A regime framework for implementation analysis: Cooperation and reconciliation of federalist imperatives. *Review of Policy Research* 9(1): 29–49.

Sum N.-L. & Jessop B. (2013) *Towards a cultural political economy: Putting culture in its place in political economy*. Cheltenham, UK and Northampton, MA, USA: Edward Elgar Publishing.

Swyngedouw E. (1992) The Mammon quest. 'Glocalisation', interspatial competition and the monetary order: The construction of new scales. In M. Dunford & G. Kafkalas (eds.) *Cities and regions in the new Europe*. London: Belhaven Press, 39–67.

Swyngedouw E. (2005) Governance innovation and the citizen: The Janus face of governance-beyond-the-state. *Urban Studies* 42(11): 1991–2006.

Szívós E. (2018) Tűrt és támogatott határán: a Budapesti Városszépítő Egyesület mint misszió és civil mozgalom az 1980-as években. *Korall* 19(74): 150–178.

Udvarhelyi T.É. (2013) 'If we don't push homeless people out, we will end up being pushed out by them': The criminalization of homelessness as state strategy in Hungary. *Antipode* 46(3): 816–834.

Varró K. (2010) Re-politicising the analysis of 'new state spaces' in Hungary and beyond: Towards an effective engagement with 'actually existing neoliberalism'. *Antipode* 42(5): 1253–1278.

Wacquant L. (2018) Bourdieu comes to town: Pertinence, principles, applications. *International Journal of Urban and Regional Research* 42(1): 90–105.

Weber M. (1978) *Economy and society: An outline of interpretive sociology*. G. Roth & C. Wittich (eds.) Berkeley, Los Angeles, and London: University of California Press.

Whyte W.F. (1943) *Street corner society*. Chicago: University of Chicago Press.

Williams G. (2004) Towards a re-politicisation of participatory development: Political capabilities and spaces of empowerment. In S. Hickey & G. Mohan (eds.) *From tyranny to transformation? Exploring new approaches to participation*. London: Zed Books.

Wirth L. (1938) Urbanism as a way of life. *American Journal of Sociology* 44(1): 1–24.

Zukin S. (1980) A decade of the new urban sociology. *Theory and Society* 9(4): 575–601.

# 32. Temporalities and everyday lives of Filipina domestic workers in Hong Kong

*Maren K. Boersma*

Time is a key dimension for understanding social life and social processes in cities. Cities produce various temporalities to regulate social life, for instance, in the shape of opening hours of shops and services or the timetables of public transportation. Furthermore, global processes produce distinctive spatialities and temporalities, which locate in cities, where they are implemented through local and national measures (Sassen 2000). In this way, the temporalities of global processes become tangible and leave their mark in cities, as they are implemented via regulations and infrastructures, embedded in the arrangement of physical space, or even materialize as social events, rhythms of absence or presence. These various temporalities are embedded in policies of citizenship, employment, unemployment services, or school times that become part of people's temporal experiences (Besedovsky et al. 2019) and inform their social practices (Davies 2001).

How temporalities are interwoven with the production of social life and urban space in cities has hardly been addressed in urban sociological research. Despite insightful theoretical works on the relation between time, space, and urban daily life (Crang 2001, Lefebvre 2004 [1992]), studies that bring together time and urban social life tend to conceive of time as a quality of linearity (historical) (Chacko & Price 2020) or purely describe the rhythms (Wunderlich 2013) or the comings and goings of people (Tan 2020) around a certain place. Other studies show that the temporal experiences of citizens are affected by, but do not parallel, the temporalities of urban redevelopment (Koster 2020), or how ethnic groups use temporal experiences as a means to appropriate or negotiate 'white' urban space (Kidman et al. 2020). Only a few studies address temporality as intertwined with the production of social processes in an urban context. Recent work on 'temporal infrastructures' (Besedovsky et al. 2019) shows that temporalities of urban planning and financialization processes 'pre-structure' social and spatial processes in cities (Grafe & Hilbrandt 2019) and that the time of marginalized groups loses out to economic interests entangled with time in urban development (Bond 2019). Other research shows that local governments use temporal regulations as a means to govern the presence of specific ethnic groups for political purposes (Baumann 2019). These works bear resemblance to time research on the unequal nature of temporalities (Sharma 2014). Nevertheless, the urban literature makes little reference to social theory on time and fails to explain how temporalities interact with urban space in the production of urban daily life.

On the other hand, social research that sees time as a key constituent of social processes (Adam 2004, Bryson 2007) has not recognized the city as a major site where these processes take place. This is surprising given that cities are considered major nodes in today's globalizing world (Castells 2000) and that they form the habitat for the majority of the world population. Research on the cultural politics of time observes that under global, neoliberal forms of capitalism, temporalities are differentially and unequally constructed for different social groups (Sharma 2014). Social groups are positioned in distinct ways in global economic processes that entail the global economy (Massey 1991). Additionally, individuals and social groups are engaged in structural dependency relations of time, as the time use of one group enables or constrains the time use of others (Bryson 2007). Dominated by capitalist temporalities, these dependency relations produce temporal inequalities, wherein non-capitalist orderings and meanings of time are deemed irrelevant (Adam 2008). In this context, time is recognized as a structuring order in which power relations are reproduced and come into expression (Bryson 2007). In some cases, temporalities not only constrain social groups in their movements and access to discretionary time but also disempower them (Boersma 2018). Temporalities thus contribute to the (re-)production of structural and unequal relations.

This chapter is concerned with this interrelation between time and the social processes that take place and are produced in cities. It provides insight into the way temporalities contribute to the structuring of everyday lives of social groups in the city and illustrates how this contributes to the (re-)production of structural unequal relations. With this aim, the chapter focuses on the concept of temporality (Adam 2008) to understand *how* time is organized in social processes and how this contributes to urban social life. The chapter draws on social theory of time and temporalities, which is complemented by an analysis of temporalities in the everyday lives of Filipina domestic workers in Hong Kong (Boersma 2016). This group has a distinct relation to time, as they release their employers from the temporal constraints of caregiving and domestic work, while as temporary migrants, they are subject to stringent employment and migration regimes encompassing various temporalities aimed to regulate their labour and temporary stay in Hong Kong.

The global city Hong Kong has been described as a model of the free market economy (Peck et al. 2023). As a major financial centre in Asia and worldwide, the city is dominated by the service economy, attracting both high-income workers and low-income service-sector workers from across the globe. Moreover, the city is characterized by stark social inequalities, as economic growth and the rise of a global elite paralleled an increase in social groups in poverty (Goodstadt 2013). Not least, due to its high urban density and a highly speculative market, housing prices in Hong Kong are among the highest in the world and pose a challenge for the majority of the population, especially for the lowest income groups who end up in subdivided, windowless apartments (Inclan-Valadez et al. 2011). The city is characterized by laissez faire governance (Peck et al. 2023) including a lack of standardized working hours (Society for Human Resource Management 2018). This allows for high flexibilization of the labour force. The average working week in Hong Kong is 44 hours, with one in five employees working 55 hours or more (Census and Statistics Department Hong Kong SAR 2021). On top of this, many residents have substantial daily commutes, as they travel from the outer districts to central areas of Hong Kong where many jobs are located (Lau 2010).

The next section covers the theoretical framework, including an overview of key scholarly work on differentiated temporalities under global capitalism and how to empirically investigate temporalities in everyday life. It then discusses existing research from urban and migration studies, before moving on to the analysis of temporalities in the everyday lives of Filipina domestic workers in Hong Kong. The final section reflects on these insights and discusses the merit of investigating temporalities as co-contributors of social and spatial processes in cities.

## DIFFERENTIATED AND UNEQUAL TEMPORALITIES UNDER GLOBAL CAPITALISM

To comprehend how temporalities contribute to urban social life, it is key to understand time as multiple and relational. A relational understanding of time and space (Harvey 2007, Murdoch 2006) conceives of time and space not as abstract containers but as interrelated time-space, constituted in and constitutive of social practices and processes. Social practices take place across and connect different spaces and temporalities, depending on the nature of networks and the actors involved (Harvey 2007). This implies an understanding of space and time as multiple, connecting different locales – local, regional, global – *and* temporalities – past, present, future, cyclical, or commodified time. Social theory of time (Adam 2008) provides a useful addition to this understanding of relational time-space, as it clarifies the nature of time as produced in and intertwined with various distinctive, social processes. Particularly insightful is the conceptualization of time as *temporality*, referring to *how* time is entangled with social processes. This includes how time is organized or ordered, how it runs or flows and in which direction, and how it is operationalized (Adam 2008). Thereby, temporalities should be understood as interrelated with space and materiality, though foregrounding the temporal to draw attention to the role of time in social processes (Adam 2008, Wajcman & Dodd 2017).

Similarly, in relational terms, cities can be understood as materializing compositions of various social processes, each encompassing distinctive spatio-temporalities and drawing together various actors in urban space. While locating in urban space, these spatio-temporalities also contribute to social processes. Foregrounding the temporal in urban sociological inquiry means investigating these temporalities at play in an urban setting, whilst acknowledging that they relate to urban spatialities and are 'grounded' in urban space through physical materialities. Urban space thus not only hosts social processes but also functions as an 'active presence' (Murdoch 2006: 15) co-constitutive of the temporalities intertwined with various social processes in cities. Due to the importance of cities in the global economy, (spatio-) temporalities of global capitalism are key to understanding temporalities in cities. Existing scholarly work from human geography, sociology, culture, and media studies has extensively demonstrated how time is unequally produced and ordered under global capitalism. The remainder of this section attempts to identify temporalities that are relevant for understanding everyday urban life. It discusses how temporalities of capitalism are embedded in social processes and how these contribute to the (re-)production of structural unequal relations in people's everyday lives.

In neoliberal societies, global capitalism plays a dominant role in the production of time. Under neoliberal capitalism, time is conceived as abstract, quantifiable time and a major resource that can be manipulated to earn profits and be competitive (Harvey 1989). Time-space compression, whereby space is compressed by technological affordances 'to manipulate and control time' (Harvey 1989: 240), has become inherent to the organization of the global economy and neoliberal societies. The notion that 'time is money' and speed is a means to make profits predominates in social and economic processes (Hassan 2009, Tomlinson 2007). Institutionalized in social structures, such as organizations, culture, consumption, and administrative processes, speed, instantaneity, and the intensification of activities are embedded in people's everyday lives, most prominently at work (Castells 2000, Gregg 2018).

The literature on time in society emphasizes that groups are differentially and unequally affected by the temporalities produced by global neoliberal capitalism (Adam 2002, Bryson

2007, Sharma 2014). With the concept of power-geometry, Massey (1991) argues that different social groups and individuals are positioned in the global economy in distinct ways and that how they are placed in time-space compression is 'highly complicated and extremely varied' (Massey 1991: 28). Moreover, the mobility and control of some groups can occur at the cost of the mobility and control of others and weaken the power of disadvantaged groups. Some groups benefit from the affordances of time-space compression, while others are 'effectively imprisoned by it' (Massey 1991: 28). Sharma (2014) shows that various groups of labourers differentially experience the dominant discourse of speedup and that their time maintenance is unequally accommodated in societies in 'temporal infrastructures'. Temporal infrastructures provide groups of the political economy with tools, resources, and imperatives to remain productive and comprise 'technologies, commodities, policies, plans, programs and the labour of others' (Sharma 2014: 139). For example, business travellers working '24/7' at a high pace can rely on extensive temporal infrastructures. However, formal or institutionalized temporal infrastructures hardly exist for taxi drivers, who rely on sub-alternative architectures of time maintenance and self-regulating technologies (Sharma 2014: 76).

Adam (2002) argues that inequalities under globalization are inextricably bound up with the gendered politics of time. This draws attention to other perspectives on time that are important for understanding social inequalities. Time, as constituted in global capitalism, is interwoven with and dependent on other forms of time (Adam 2004). These include natural, cyclical, and task-oriented time, such as seasonal rhythms, the rhythms of day and night, bodily rhythms and cycles, and social practices of domestic work or care that are often unpredictable and open-ended and define their own time. Going beyond abstract time means acknowledging that people do not just live in the moment but through actions, plans, hopes and fears, memories, and expectations that also link the present to the past and the future.

Unable to be incorporated into the logic of clock time, concrete forms of time are generally undervalued in the global market (Adam 2002). Similarly, forms of social organizing that do not fit the logic of capitalism are often invisible or rendered irrelevant. As many of those activities, such as agriculture and domestic and care work, are performed by women, they are easily marginalized and devaluated – while at the same time their invisible labour in large numbers makes the functioning of the global economy possible (Adam 2002). Under neoliberal forms of capitalism, such dependency relations are expressed as the global transfer of care. This refers to the process in which low-income migrant workers from poorer regions provide care time to high-income workers who experience care deficits (Ehrenreich & Hochschild 2004). In turn, low-income workers have to arrange their own 'maid' or caretaker, often as informal care provided by family members, thus transferring a more severe time deficit to their home communities (Parreñas 2001). However, while analyses of time tend to foreground economic relations in an attempt to criticize capitalism, the linkages to the people and communities who create and give meaning to time are often neglected (Adam 2004).

**Empirical Investigations of Temporalities in Everyday Life**

Rhythmanalysis (Lefebvre 2004) offers an approach to empirically investigate the multiplicity of time in everyday life. A basic principle of rhythmanalysis is that urban life is polyrhythmic, consisting of multiple rhythms that structure everyday life in cities. The embodied experience of time – *lived time* – is a key instrument for distinguishing different temporalities at play in urban space. Resembling Lefebvre's 'lived space', lived time goes beyond the generalizing understanding of time as linear, abstract clock time reigning over urban social life. Instead, it distinguishes multiple rhythms at play that may overlap, but can also conflict with, contradict, or support one another. As argued by sociologists and feminists, these overlapping temporalities are implicated with social relations (Davies 2001) and power relations (Adam 2004) that inform people's use and experience of time. Social relations include the needs of significant others and involvement in various social institutions (Davies 2001), such as the household, family, community, work, government offices, or daycare. These institutions involve power and dependency relations and have their own spatial and temporal characteristics (Burkitt 2004). Furthermore, they carry norms and regulations that affect what people (can) do, when, and how; for example, through timetables or proper timings, such as what age to get married, or the idea that employees should use their working time efficiently (Burkitt 2004).

The normalizing, prescribing, and ordering temporalities of social institutions that people interact with in everyday life furthermore contribute to the pursuit of their desired goals and outcomes that they plan to achieve in the long run (Crang 2001). This is also how daily activities get meaning, as they simultaneously reach forward into the future and back into the past (Crang 2001). Similarly, Knowles (2011) emphasizes that thinking of interconnected spatialities and temporalities helps to understand the unfolding of biographies that give meaning to daily social practices. The temporalities people encounter in everyday life are inscribed with meanings and reproduced or negotiated in social practices. By interrogating lived time we can distinguish multiple temporalities at play and identify how these contribute to the structuration of people's everyday lives.

An example of how temporalities affect people's everyday lives comes from Baumann (2019), who gives elaborate insight into how temporal measures impact the daily lives of Palestinian workers. The state regulation of the daily mobility of Palestinian workers in East Jerusalem showcases temporal regimes that are designed to deliberately deregulate Palestinian time through checkpoints for Palestinians, entailing long queues and waiting times. Baumann (2019) shows that this results in unpredictable commutes and spatio-temporalities in the daily lives of these workers. The daily lives of Palestinians get so disturbed that they are unable to maintain their ties to and plan for a future in the city – unless they apply for Israeli citizenship. Moreover, the incorporation of the Palestinian transportation system into Israeli structures and timekeeping contributes to the synchronization of Palestinian and Israeli rhythms. While racial questions are undoubtedly implicated in this example, Baumann (2019) shows how temporal regulations operate in tandem to reinforce social and political normalization processes.

Temporal measures also prominently feature in the governance of temporary migrants and other citizens with precarious status. The residential status of such groups is often temporary, their lives curtailed by specific temporal regimes in state or local policies that have a constraining or disciplining character (Chacko & Price 2020). In Bergamo, Italy, temporalities of housing and employment programs for refugees cause precarious housing conditions (Dotsey & Lumley-Sapanski 2021). Merla and Smit (2023) show that temporalities of migration regimes conflict with the daily and biographical time of high-skilled migrant workers, who struggle to achieve permanent residency and pursue their life projects. Scholars further problematize the use of temporary measures in labour import by nations and cities that provide limited rights and deny migrants permanent residency (Chacko & Price 2020). For low-paid migrants, temporal restrictions often limit social participation in the host society. Additionally, low wages and harsh working conditions impose further temporal restrictions, as they put pressure on discretionary time (Boersma 2018). In this respect, stark differences exist between low-paid migrant workers and high-paid workers (Hugo 2009), who often benefit from considerable freedom of movement, a high salary, and relocation allowances (Elliot & Urry 2010). The temporalities imbued with migration regimes thus not only inform the course of migration trajectories but can also support or constrain migrants in their daily lives, depending on their status in the global division of labour.

## LIVED TIME OF FILIPINA DOMESTIC WORKERS

The presence of large numbers of migrant domestic workers in Hong Kong is an expression of structural interdependencies of time that must be understood in the context of the global transfer of care. Hong Kong is residence to around 370,000 domestic workers from the Philippines (55.5%), Indonesia (42.2%), and other countries (2.3%), such as Thailand and Myanmar (Hong Kong Immigration Department 2021b). This number has increased substantially since the 1970s when Hong Kong allowed for the massive in-migration of domestic workers driven by the demand of working-class families' needs for family care (He & Wu 2019). Since then, female labour market participation in Hong Kong has risen steadily (Wee & Sim 2005). The cost of hiring a domestic worker is relatively low (HK$ 4,730/month in 2023). The minimum monthly household income required is HK$ 15,000 for every domestic worker that is hired (Hong Kong Immigration Department 2021a). Hiring a domestic worker is thus not only for the privileged but also accessible to the lower-middle class (He & Wu 2019).

Hong Kong's migration regime reflects the position of migrant domestic workers as part of the flexible labour force under the global division of labour. The domestic workers are employed on standardized two-year contracts. Domestic workers in Hong Kong do not have the prospect of gaining permanent residency and are not allowed to bring their families – a right that is granted to other non-Chinese citizens after spending a continuous seven years in Hong Kong (Wee & Sim 2005). The working hours of domestic workers are unregulated, except for the right to one rest day of 24 hours a week. Moreover, they are obliged to live in with their employers. This allows employers considerable power over their domestic workers (Yeoh & Huang 2010) and gives rise to different forms of abuse and violation of their rights (Agarwal 2022, Ullah 2015). Besides this, gender and race issues contribute to the structural undervaluation of the job of domestic worker (Constable 2010), which is mostly done by women from developing countries. Despite their vulnerable position in Hong Kong, domestic workers depend on their jobs to provide income for their extended families.

## TEMPORALITIES AND SPATIALITIES OF EVERYDAY LIFE

The employment of Filipina domestic workers is subject to various spatial and temporal regulations. Employers need to provide 'suitable and furnished accommodation' with 'reasonable privacy' (Hong Kong Immigration Department 2021a). However, accommodation is a challenge in Hong Kong where houses are cramped. Many residences have separate and decent 'maid quarters', but some of these do not even fit a mattress and often maid rooms are used for other purposes. Mission for Migrant Workers (Mission for Migrant Workers 2021) has shown that domestic workers suffer from a wide variety of inadequate or inhumane accommodation conditions, such as lack of privacy, camera surveillance, sleeping in bathrooms or next to a refrigerator, and wet laundry. Some employers ask their domestic workers illegally to 'live out', in shared houses, as they prefer that they do not live in. However, this is risky as the domestic workers would be banned from working in Hong Kong if it came out.

The live-in rule implies that during their working days domestic workers spend most of their time at their employer's house, where they work and sleep. In combination with the lack of regulation of working hours, the live-in rule gives employers considerable '24/7' control over their domestic workers. This flexibility allows domestic workers to synchronize with the schedules of the different household members and cater to the various, conflicting rhythms of, for instance, dual-income workers who do not have time to attend to their children. Many work more than 12 or even 16 hours a day and have little time and space to attend to their personal needs. It is not uncommon for the family's time deficit to literally manifest in the domestic worker, who may experience a lack of sleep herself.

The intersection of the temporal and spatial regulations (restrictions) of the domestic workers' employment gives employers substantial control over their domestic workers' time. The practical organization of the domestic worker's employment, working and living in close distance within the intimacy of the employer's house, involves complex power relations. Within the invisible and informal setting of the employer's residence in which a domestic helper's job is shaped, employers are free to decide what constitutes a domestic helper's job. Some employers demand intensive cleaning routines or keep their domestic workers busy under the premise that 'their time is already paid for'. Hong Kong's laissez faire approach towards working time regulations gives employers considerable power over the time of domestic workers. It clears the ground for maltreatment and abusive behaviour. Domestic workers report disrespect, malnutrition, bullying, illegal work, and severe working conditions, such as working under continuous supervision or long, anti-social hours. At the same time, some domestic workers are treated with dignity and respect and are more or less assigned the role of household manager. They have substantial autonomy and some also have free time to engage in personal activities during the week.

The weekly rest day of most domestic workers – for most of them on Sunday – starkly contrasts with the spatial and temporal constraints of their working days. Every Sunday, Hong Kong's public spaces are crowded with migrant domestic workers. We get a glimpse of the impact of temporalities under global capitalism, as Filipino, Indonesian, Thai, and domestic workers of other nationalities gather and socialize with their fellow migrants. The rest day is a special day for the domestic workers in Hong Kong. They get to do social activities and experience freedom after being confined to the domestic space of their employer's household during the rest of the week. As Diana explains, on Sunday, 'We're like a bird! Freed from the cage'.

The presence of domestic workers substantially impacts the social dynamics in the city of Hong Kong on Sundays. On this day they claim public space and use it for private time and social activities. They meet their friends in parks, squares, walkways, or shopping malls, where they settle on sheets or cardboard boxes and rest, chat, laugh and eat together, polish their nails, or make a (video) call back home. They run errands and remit money in the World Wide House, which caters specifically to Hong Kong's low-paid migrant workers. They organize social events, such as religious services and beauty pageants, or go hiking or cycling in the natural scenery of Hong Kong. Others are active in migrant organizations, based in various offices in the city, or engage in other political activities. Especially in the more central parts of Hong Kong, public spaces are not designed to cater for the large inflow of domestic workers.

However, their presence in these large numbers is tolerated and regulated by the Hong Kong government. With Hong Kong Central as one of the major sites, the government even reserves part of Chater Road, a busy road during workdays, for domestic workers on Sundays (see Figure 32.1). Moreover, their weekly presence is accompanied by a local, temporal infrastructure (Sharma 2014): an informal economy in the shape of hawkers selling cardboard boxes, clothes, or mobile phone cards, and domestic workers selling rice or other prepared foods. Away from the sometimes busy and stressful working environment, these Sunday places and activities enable domestic workers to relax and get peace of mind.

Yet it is important to realize that this flight of domestic workers into Hong Kong's public spaces is not entirely voluntary. Domestic workers feel forced because staying at home with their employers' family makes them feel awkward or results in them being put back to work. Moreover, many domestic workers are required to work on their rest day, before they leave the house or when they come back at night.

*Source.* Marcel K. Boersma.

*Figure 32.1*    *Domestic workers practicing a dance on Chater Road in Hong Kong Central on a Sunday*

**Uncertain Migration Trajectories and Temporal Dis-orientation**

The temporal arrangement of the employment of domestic workers in temporary two-year contracts contributes to indeterminate migration trajectories. Hong Kong's migration policies for domestic helpers allow them to renew their contract as often as they want – as long as they are deemed fit to work. Many domestic workers make use of this possibility and renew their contract, with the same or a different employer, multiple times. It also happens that women return to their home country after their first contract, to later return to Hong Kong or another destination. Some migrant domestic workers even travel to multiple destinations (Paul 2017). Of the Filipina domestic workers in this study, ten had stayed in Hong Kong between 4 and 8 years, nine had stayed between 10 and 18 years, and three women had stayed more than 20 years. Some of these women had worked in other destinations before they came to Hong Kong.

Domestic workers are often the major breadwinner of the family and need to take care of expenses for a long period. With their earnings, they support multiple family members: siblings, parents, their children but also nieces and nephews who use the money for necessities such as food, shelter, clothing, education, and medical care. Some women need to pay off loans or illegal agency fees, which may take several months or years (Hugo 2009). Domestic workers cherish their job as it offers a relatively stable income that is hard to come by in the Philippines. Experiences of lived time of the Filipina domestic workers reveal how the overlapping and intersecting temporalities of the migration regime, the domestic worker's family, and her life course produce indeterminate migration trajectories.

Particularly, the intersecting, open-ended time frames of earning money and care give rise to unpredictable and long-lasting migration trajectories (Amrith 2021: 256). Earning money is an unpredictable process complicated by the fact that the financial and care needs of relatives are ongoing and change over time. With their extended families depending on them, it is difficult to determine when they have made enough money so that they can return to the Philippines. Most domestic workers plan to stay in Hong Kong until they have earned enough, but when asked, many are unsure when that moment will arrive. Domestic workers explained that earning money is difficult and takes time, as with their children growing up, expenses rise. Sometimes, plans suddenly change due to unexpected events back home, which forces domestic workers to delay their plans for return.

These unpredictable migration trajectories give rise to strong feelings of uncertainty about how long domestic workers plan to stay in Hong Kong. This was apparent both among women who had been working as domestic workers for a shorter period, as well as with those who had been working as domestic workers in Hong Kong for over 10 years. Those who had recently started their jobs were sometimes optimistic, but usually did not know how long they would stay. The vast majority found it difficult to anticipate a possible return migration and the optimism that some of them had at the beginning of their employment did not last. Domestic workers who had been in Hong Kong for more than 10 years expressed that they had not expected to stay as long as they did. Vicky (52) talked about her long-term stay as a succession of contracts in which she evaluated her financial situation every two years:

> maybe before I thought only like that, oh I will just stay two years or four years, then I will go back. But when I finished the two years, no money, another sign [she makes a signing gesture with her hand], finished four years, no money, another sign…! So that's why I stayed longer… Ha-ha-ha…!

Vicky's explanation is illustrative of the unfolding of the migration trajectories of Filipina domestic workers. Their trajectories unfold in an unpredictable manner and they have little control over the course of their migration. At the time of the interview, Vicky was still uncertain about when she would return to the Philippines. Other women also still experienced uncertainty about their migration trajectories after an already long-term employment career in

Hong Kong, such as Bernice (41) and Elma (45), who had worked abroad for 12 and 25 years, respectively.

Thus, the organization of the employment of domestic workers in temporary, two-year contracts gives them an uncertain future outlook. The two-year contract provides the stable income that they desire and multiple contracts may eventually lead to a more permanent job, but that is only true in retrospect. In the meantime, they reside in Hong Kong by temporary arrangement and are uncertain of how their migration trajectories will evolve – and how long they can cater to the financial needs of their extended families. This lasting temporariness is burdensome for those domestic workers who get caught between the hope that they can go home in the foreseeable future, when their current contract expires, and the presumption that they will probably need to stay. These domestic workers actively experience this situation of 'permanent temporariness' (Bailey et al. 2002) that they have to bear in their daily lives.

The unpredictability of migration trajectories and continuous re-orienting of time horizons according to the possible succession of contracts is also confusing. The juxtaposition of the temporariness of their stay and longevity of employment leaves the domestic workers in Hong Kong in a state of *temporal dis-orientation*. While their job as domestic workers enables them to contribute to various life projects, ensuring that their children and other relatives stay out of poverty, saving money for retirement, or building incremental housing, the unpredictability of their migration trajectories hinders them from actually looking forward, anticipating, and navigating towards their desired futures. When Bernice (41), who had been working abroad for more than 13 years, was asked if she thinks of going back to the Philippines, she responded utterly seriously: 'By now? I don't think so, because I have to earn money so that I have to control myself'. Later she said: '…maybe after I finish my contract in 2016'. Then she again expressed uncertainty: 'Still working… ai! I don't know until when!'.

**The Disciplining Effect of Temporalities**

The temporalities of Hong Kong's migration regime for domestic workers potentially amplify dependency relations between domestic workers and their employers. Domestic workers (and their relatives) are so dependent on their job that many of them would not dare to risk losing it. Many domestic workers fear having their jobs prematurely terminated by their employers. This fear is amplified by the temporal restrictions that come into play in the case of premature termination. In this case, domestic workers have only two weeks to find a new employer, or their visa expires. If they do not succeed they have to leave Hong Kong. Back in the Philippines, the women may apply again to become domestic workers in Hong Kong, but this comes with expenses, such as plane tickets and 'administrative' fees for a psychological test and medical check-ups when applying through an employment agency in the Philippines. Premature termination comes with the risk of losing the relatively stable income they use to support their extended families or to accumulate savings for their return. As Cleo (32) states: '[once] we lose our job, we lose our future also'.

Both employers and domestic workers can terminate the contract prematurely, with one month's notice. Under special circumstances, contracts can be terminated with immediate effect by paying one month of salary in lieu of notice (Hong Kong Immigration Department 2021a); for instance, if a domestic worker is guilty of misconduct, fraud, or dishonesty; disobedient or habitually neglects domestic duties; or fears physical danger, experiences ill-treatment, or is declared permanently unfit for the job. It can happen that domestic workers are terminated for unjust reasons or dismissed without one month's notice or payment of outstanding wages or other entitlements. If the premature termination of a domestic worker's contract has been handled incorrectly or unjustly or if a domestic worker wants to terminate the contract herself, she can approach the Hong Kong Labour Department to process a claim against her employer.

The temporal regulations of the employment contract have a disciplining effect (Chacko & Price 2020) on domestic workers, who are reluctant to speak up and negotiate with their employer in their daily lives. The fear that they might instantly lose their jobs disciplines them into obedient workers. In some instances, domestic workers' contracts are terminated unexpectedly even if they have a good employment relationship or have worked for the same employer for multiple contracts. Most domestic workers have heard stories of co-migrants who were released prematurely and suddenly had to move back to the Philippines. The fear of job loss stops domestic workers from speaking up for themselves in their daily lives, even when this means that their rights are violated. For example, although they knew that were entitled to a full 24-hour rest day, different women explained that if their employer asked them to work they did not dare to say no because they did not want to risk premature termination. Employers are aware that domestic workers fear termination and some use it as a means of power to exploit their domestic workers. Casey (32) suffers from maltreatment. She sleeps in a shack on the roof of her employer's house made out of corrugated sheets. She gets little food, works non-stop under her employer's supervision, and is required to work illegally in her employer's office. When Casey does not get breakfast for a couple of days, she confronts her employer and asks for her food allowance. In response, her employer threatens to terminate the contract and requires her to illegally work in her son's house. Casey chooses to be obedient even though her employer is breaching the contract:

> From Wednesday until Saturday, I don't have breakfast anymore. So… so, I argue, I'm asking for my food allowance. Then she [my employer] told me that she will break the contract already, she will terminate me, just because of the food… Then she said, 'OK if you want to work again, if you want to continue, I ask you to work for my son in Kowloon'. Because her daughter-in-law got pregnant, so she asked me to go there and work. Since that she wants to terminate me, that's why I have to go there and work.

Domestic workers can report contract breaches to the Immigration or Labour Department in Hong Kong, but processing a legal case is also circumscribed by strict temporal regulations that work to disadvantage domestic workers. A major obstacle is that during a legal case, domestic workers are not allowed to work. This means that during this time they need to find food and shelter and do not obtain an income. This could lead to financial problems. Moreover, they are not certain that they will receive any financial compensation for the days that they are unable to work. A board member at Mission for Migrant Workers said that when it comes to processing a legal case, time is often a problem for the domestic workers: 'Because they don't have it' (Father Dwight). He explained that legal cases take a longer time to process and that domestic workers often settle for financial compensation below the amount that they could obtain because they cannot afford to be jobless. Time poverty excludes them from engaging in legal processes. They do not have the time to wait for the best possible outcome and cannot fully claim their rights. Their time is regulated in such a way that it severely limits their agency. Furthermore, some domestic workers refrain from terminating their contract or starting a legal case altogether because this comes with the uncertainty of being jobless for an undecided period. Their strong dependency on their job makes them vulnerable and places them in a disadvantaged position as they are not able to use their time for other purposes.

## CONCLUSIONS

If we conceive of cities as places where global processes locate and where spatialities and temporalities are implemented in various ways, we can start to understand how temporalities contribute to social life in cities. Foregrounding temporalities in social urban analysis embraces the underlying dynamics of social processes that come into expression in urban space. Multiple, overlapping temporalities interact as a dynamic whole, thereby contributing to the unfolding of urban social life. Cities are compositions of social processes each defining their own spatial and temporal frameworks, or, as Crang (2001) argues, spaces of becoming. A key merit of focusing on temporalities, then, is that this helps to understand how the everyday lives of people living in cities are affected by processes that connect their past, present and future, thus acknowledging that everyday life itself is a process. Cities play an important role in this because these are the places where the majority of the world's population reside and where they are exposed to social processes that are reproduced in everyday social practices.

As I have shown, the temporalities bound up with global social and economic processes evidently affect the daily lives of the Filipino domestic workers, as they are subject to various temporal and spatial regulations imposed on them by the local government. Global temporalities – how time is entangled in the division of labour, the global transfer of care, and operationalized under global capitalism – are reproduced in everyday life in cities. This is visible in the daily lives of the Filipina domestic workers in Hong Kong, whose space and time are literally compressed. Strongly bound to employers' homes due to the live-in rule, employers have considerable authority over their domestic workers' time, which is unregulated except for a 24-hour rest day. Hong Kong's cramped housing and the lack of private space that domestic workers experience contribute to excessively long working hours among domestic workers, who take over the time deficit of their employers and in the worst cases experience maltreatment or abusive situations. Paralleling their disadvantaged position in the global labour market, the temporal and spatial regulations and space itself reflect Massey's (1991) observation that some groups are effectively imprisoned by time-space compression.

Furthermore, temporalities of Hong Kong's employment and migration policies together discipline the domestic workers to be obedient. However, this time discipline bears no resemblance to the disciplining of the clock of factory workers at the beginning of the 19th century (Thompson 1967). Instead, it is through orderings of time and their interaction with other temporalities in the lives of the domestic workers that time gets its disciplining effect. The two-week rule and the employer's ability to terminate the contract on short notice clash with the long-lasting dependency of domestic workers on their temporary jobs, which enable them to support their families and pursue their own life projects, thus going beyond discipline by abstract clock time to discipline through relational time-spaces. At the same time and seemingly paradoxically, the domestic workers' severe time poverty constrains them, in various ways, from claiming their rights. Due to its dominance under neoliberal capitalism, abstract time remains an important resource for people to maintain their daily life but may also work to exclude those whose time is drastically undervalued.

Linking everyday temporalities to long-term life projects exemplifies how Hong Kong's migration regime substantially contributes to the unfolding of the life paths of many domestic workers. Nevertheless, while these migrants make a long-term contribution to Hong Kong's economy, what they get in return seems disproportionate to the time and effort they put into it. Subject to various measures of temporal control, the spatialities and temporalities of the labour and migration regimes of Hong Kong reflect how they are only marginally institutionally embedded and literally do not gain much ground in the city. Above and beyond this, the disciplining temporalities of labour and migration regimes, grounded in and amplified by urban space, thus contribute to the reproduction of structural unequal relations between social groups in the city and beyond.

This chapter has shown that temporalities get embedded as local, social, and physical 'temporal infrastructures' in urban space and that spatialities moreover help to enforce temporal measures. Thinking through temporal infrastructures (Sharma 2014) helps to identify how temporalities differently affect social groups in their daily lives. The notion of temporal infrastructures, involving tools, technologies, space, and the labour of others, thus also constitutes a starting point for further urban sociological inquiry as a means to critically analyze the disposition of disadvantaged groups with tools to maintain their time. Hence, I suggest linking these temporal infrastructures in everyday life to the unfolding of people's biographies and various forms of time that give meaning to life.

## REFERENCES

Adam, B. (2002) The gendered time politics of globalization: Of shadowlands and elusive justice. *Feminist Review* 70: 3–29.
Adam, B. (2004) *Time*. Cambridge: Polity.
Adam, B. (2008) Of timescapes, futurescapes and timeprints. Paper presented at Lüneburg University.
Agarwal, A. (2022) Hong Kong's foreign domestic workers: End our abuse. Retrieved from: https://www.fairplanet.org/story/hong-kongs-foreign-domestic-workers-end-our-abuse/ (accessed 13 May 2023).
Amrith, M. (2021) Ageing bodies, precarious futures: The (im)mobilities of 'temporary' migrant domestic workers over time. *Mobilities* 16(2): 249–261.
Bailey, A. J., Wright, R. A., Mountz, A. & Miyares, I. M. (2002) (Re)producing Salvadoran transnational geographies. *Annals of the Association of American Geographers* 92(1): 125–144.
Baumann, H. (2019) Disrupting movements, synchronizing schedules: Time as an infrastructure of control in East Jerusalem. *City* 23(4–5): 589–605.
Besedovsky, N., Grafe, F.-J., Hilbrandt, H. & Langguth, H. (2019) Time as infrastructure: For an analysis of contemporary urbanization. *City* 23(4–5): 580–588.
Boersma, M. K. (2016) A maid's time? The everyday lives of Filipina domestic workers in Hong Kong. Doctoral thesis. Retrieved from: https://scholars.cityu.edu.hk/en/theses/theses(f1398ea5-56cb-4502-a079-594249e3ad07).html.
Boersma, M. (2018) Filipina domestic workers in Hong Kong: Between permanence and temporariness in everyday life. *Current Sociology* 67(2): 273–293.
Bond, P. (2019) Contradictory time horizons of Durban energy piping in an era of looming climate chaos. *City* 23(4–5): 631–645.
Bryson, V. (2007) The politics of time. *Soundings: A Journal of Politics and Culture* 36: 100–110.
Burkitt, I. (2004) The time and space of everyday life. *Cultural Studies* 18(2–3): 211–227.
Castells, M. (2000) *The Rise of the Network Society* (2nd ed.). Oxford: Blackwell Publishers.
Census and Statistics Department Hong Kong SAR (2021) Women and men in Hong Kong. 2021 edition. Retrieved from: https://www.censtatd.gov.hk/en/data/stat_report/product/B1130303/att/B11303032021AN21B0100.pdf (accessed 16 May 2023).

Chacko, E. & Price, M. (2020) (Un)settled sojourners in cities: The scalar and temporal dimensions of migrant precarity. *Journal of Ethnic and Migration Studies.* https://doi.org/10.1080/1369183X.2020.1731060.

Constable, N. (2010) *Maid to Order in Hong Kong: Stories of Filipina Workers* (2nd ed.). Ithaca: Cornell University Press.

Crang, M. (2001) Rhythms of the city: Temporalised space and motion. In J. May & N. Thrift (eds.) *Timespace: Geographies of Temporality.* London: Routledge, 187–207.

Davies, K. (2001) Responsibility and daily life: Reflections over timespace. In J. May & N. Thrift (eds.) *Timespace: Geographies of Temporality.* London: Routledge, 133–148.

Dotsey, S. & A. Lumley-Sapanski (2021) Temporality, refugees, and housing: The effects of temporary assistance on refugee housing outcomes in Italy. *Cities.* https://doi.org/10.1016/j.cities.2020.103100.

Ehrenreich, B. & Hochschild, A. R. (eds.) (2004) *Global Woman: Nannies, Maids, and Sex Workers in the New Economy.* New York: Holt Paperbacks.

Elliott, A. & Urry, J. (2010) *Mobile Lives.* New York: Routledge.

Goodstadt, L.F. (2013) *Poverty in the Midst of Affluence.* Hong Kong: The University of Hong Kong.

Grafe, F.-J. & Hilbrandt, H. (2019) The temporalities of financialization: Infrastructures, dominations and openings in the Thames Tideway Tunnel. *City* 23(4–5): 606–618.

Gregg, M. (2018) *Counterproductive: Time Management in the Knowledge Economy.* Durham and London: Duke University Press.

Harvey, D. (1989) *The Condition of Postmodernity: An Enquiry into the Origins of Cultural Change.* Oxford: Blackwell.

Harvey, D. (2007) Space as keyword. In N. Castree & D. Gregory (eds.) *David Harvey: A Critical Reader.* Oxford: Wiley-Blackwell, 270–293.

Hassan, R. (2009) *Empires of speed: Time and the Acceleration of Politics and Society.* Leiden and Boston: Brill.

He, G. & Wu, X. (2019) Foreign domestic helpers hiring and women's labor supply in Hong Kong. *Chinese Sociological Review* 51(4): 397–420.

Hong Kong Immigration Department (2021a) Employment contract for a domestic helper recruited from outside Hong Kong – English version. Retrieved from: https://www.immd.gov.hk/eng/forms/forms/id407.html (accessed 30 December 2021).

Hong Kong Immigration Department (2021b) Statistics on the number of foreign domestic helpers in Hong Kong (English). Retrieved from: https://data.gov.hk/en-data/dataset/hk-immd-set4-statistics-fdh/resource/063e1929-107b-47ae-a6ac-b4b1ed460ac3 (accessed 30 December 2021).

Hugo, G. (2009) Best practice in temporary labour migration for development: A perspective from Asia and the Pacific. *International Migration* 47(5): 23–74.

Inclan-Valadez, L., Taylor, M., Yip, P. S. F., Leung, P. & Chak, S. G. (2011) Living at density: Voices of Hong Kong residents. *LSE Cities.* London: London School of Economics and Political Science.

Kidman, J., MacDonald, L., Funaki, H., Ormond, A., Southon, P. & Tomlins-Jahnke, H. (2020) 'Native time' in the white city: Indigenous youth temporalities in settler-colonial space. *Children's Geographies* 19(1): 24–36.

Knowles, C. (2011) Cities on the move: Navigating urban life. *City* 15(2): 135–153.

Koster, M. (2020) An ethnographic perspective on urban planning in Brazil: Temporality, diversity and critical urban theory. *International Journal for Urban and Regional Research* 44, 185–199.

Lau, J. C. Y. (2010) The influence of suburbanization on the access to employment of workers in the new towns: A case study of Tin Shui Wai, Hong Kong. *Habitat International* 34: 38–45.

Lefebvre, H. (2004 [1992]) *Rhythmanalysis: Space, Time and Everyday Life.* London: Bloomsbury Academic.

Massey, D. (1991) A global sense of place. *Marxism Today* 38: 24–29.

Merla, L. & S. Smit (2023) Enforced temporariness and skilled migrants' family plans: examining the friction between institutional, biographical and daily timescales. *Journal of Ethnic and Migration Studies* 49(1): 371–388. https://doi.org/10.1080/1369183X.2020.1857228.

Mission For Migrant Workers (2021) Between a toilet bowl and a wall: The continuing problem of unsuitable accommodation for migrant domestic workers under mandatory live-in arrangements. Retrieved from: https://www.migrants.net/researches (accessed 13 May 2023).

Murdoch, J. (2006) *Post-structuralist Geography.* London and Thousand Oaks: Sage.

Parreñas, R. S. (2001) *Servants of Globalization: Women, Migration and Domestic Work*. Stanford: Stanford University Press.
Paul, A. M. (2017) *Multinational Maids: Stepwise Migration in a Global Labor Market*. New York: Cambridge University Press.
Peck, J., Bok, R. & Zhang, J. (2023) Hong Kong – a model on the rocks? *Territory, Politics, Governance*. https://doi.org/10.1080/21622671.2020.1837221.
Sassen, S. (2000) Spatialities and temporalities of the global: Elements for a theorization. *Public Culture* 12(1): 215–232.
Sharma, S. (2014) *In the Meantime: Temporality and Cultural Politics*. Durham and London: Duke University Press.
Society for Human Resource Management (2018) Comply with work-hours rules in China, Hong Kong and Singapore. Retrieved from: https://www.shrm.org/resourcesandtools/legal-and-compliance/employment-law/pages/global-china-hong-kong-singapore-work-hours.aspx (accessed 28 October 2022).
Tan, Y. (2020) Temporary migrants and public space: A case study of Dongguan, China. *Journal of Ethnic and Migration Studies*. https://doi.org/10.1080/1369183X.2020.1732615.
Thompson, E. P. (1967) Time, work-discipline, and industrial capitalism. *Past & Present* 38: 56–97.
Tomlinson, J. (2007) *The Culture of Speed: The Coming of Immediacy* (1st ed.). Los Angeles and London: Sage.
Ullah, A. A. (2015) Abuse and violence against foreign domestic workers. A case from Hong Kong. *International Journal of Area Studies* 10(2): 221–238.
Wajcman, J. & Dodd, N. (2017) Introduction: The powerful are fast, the powerless are slow. In J. Wajcman & N. Dodd (eds.) *The Sociology of Speed: Digital, Organizational, and Social Temporalities*. Oxford: Oxford University Press, 1–10.
Wee, V., & Sim, A. (2005) Hong Kong as a destination for migrant domestic workers. In S. Huang, B. S. A. Yeoh & N. Abdul Rahman (eds.) *Asian Women as Transnational Domestic Workers*. Singapore: Marshall Cavendish Academic, 175–209.
Wunderlich, F. M. (2013) Place-temporality and urban place-rhythms in urban analysis and design: An aesthetic akin to music. *Journal of Urban Design* 18(3): 383–408.
Yeoh, B. S. A., & Huang, S. (2010) Transnational domestic workers and the negotiation of mobility and work practices in Singapore's home-spaces. *Mobilities* 5(20): 219–236.

# 33. Urban public space and biopolitical social control
*Jorge Sequera*

Urban public space refers to physically open spaces in urban geographies that are constantly changing (Massey 1994) and through which objects, bodies, practices, norms, and sounds pass (Di Masso et al. 2017: 62). It is defined by Gehl (2001) as the life between buildings, establishing a typology of activities that occur in public space based on defining events: necessary activities, such as going to school or work; optional activities, such as going to the park or taking a walk; and social activities, which require intentional interaction between people. Kilian (1988) describes public space as a place of contact and a place of representation. Malone (2002), on the other hand, speaks of open and closed spaces to define them in terms of acceptance of difference and diversity: open spaces have loosely defined boundaries and higher levels of social mixing and diversity, while closed spaces have more defined boundaries and selectively exclude people who do not conform. De Backer et al. (2016) refer to public space as a place of constant negotiation, conflict, and surveillance, where the physical environment shapes and is shaped by everyday social interaction.

Returning to Lefebvre's reading of the city (2020 [1974]), public space is an open and representational space. Thus, from a socio-spatial perspective, the triad proposed by Lefebvre between perceived space, lived space, and conceived space helps us to understand the struggle for meaning within urban public space. Perceived space, which corresponds to spatial practice, is the closest to everyday life. In the context of a city, spatial practice refers to what happens in the streets and squares. Lived space is understood as a space of representation, of the symbolic systems that encode it in images and imaginaries – both the codes imposed by public and private powers and the forms of public insurrection in which the struggle can take place. The conceived space ultimately depends on power relations and the production of a certain public order, the aim of which is to hegemonise perceived and experienced spaces. This understanding of the urban considers the importance of class structure, gender, and ethnicity in the urban structure, as well as collective consumption and the social determinants of inequality – particularly in access to housing, urban amenities, and universal access to urban public space.

In *The Urban Question*, Castells (1982) defines urbanisation as the spatial concentration of population and the diffusion of values, attitudes, and behaviours that shape 'urban culture'. Castells argues that a society's spatial form is directly related to the processes of urban creation and transformation, expressing the struggles and conflicts between social actors. Castells, in his early days, questioned what is understood by the city and the urban. Henri Lefebvre (1983) proposed an end to the use of the term 'city', to be replaced by 'urban society'. Decades before, Louis Wirth (1928) of the Chicago school of sociology had argued that the urban is not a bounded physical entity but a way of life with its own rules. Richard Sennett (2018) refers to the 'ville' as the built environment and place of cohabitation of thousands of people, whereas the 'cité' is the complex materialisation of the social environment of collective life, with each influencing the other. Therefore, the city is only one attribute of the urban, as argued by Andy Merrifield (2014), who claims that the urban is not a transitive attribute of society but its immanent substance.

Throughout this chapter, I use a concept of urban public space that excludes other spaces referred to as 'third spaces' (Carmona 2010): cafés, bookstores, libraries, social centres, and other semi-public, semi-private, or semi-communal places that are important for understanding public life. The idea of 'third places' proposed by Oldenburg (1999) and others refers to spaces of public and informal life, such as hairdressers, shopping centres, gyms, libraries, shops, and other leisure spaces, as well as other small private places that are fundamental in mediating between the individual and society. Instead, I here only refer to physical public spaces such as the interstitial and interbuilding spaces that make up the city – the streets, squares, parks, etc. (Low 2010). The reason for excluding 'third spaces' is that, although they are undoubtedly spaces of public life, they have significant limitations, since access is determined by the private ownership of the place. I also exclude the use of digital space in the form of public space, i.e. the cinema as a form of entertainment, which has been replaced by Netflix; newspapers purchased from kiosks, which are now read online via subscription; shopping, which is now ordered through Amazon; and other activities that used to take place in the urban space and are now increasingly carried out in the domestic space and through the digital space. Likewise with public communication, which has evolved within the home, from physical commuting to various forms of communication via online chat, Zoom, TikTok, WhatsApp, etc.

In this chapter, I first review some of the main currents in social studies of urban public space, focusing on 1) its romanticisation, 2) critical views, and 3) the privatisation and managerial organisation of public space. In the second part of the chapter, I present how public space is managed in risk societies from a Foucauldian perspective; that is, from a spatial reading of securitarian policies governing the public space. In this sense, I interpret that there is a revanchist element in the contemporary management and control of public spaces (Mitchell 2020, Smith 2001), given that the strategies adopted by urban policies to address real or perceived problems in public space confirm that the political, the urban-planning, and architectural techniques that have an impact on it favour a hyper-regulated use, displacing other possible uses or punishing them instead of complying with them, respecting them, or resolving them in a collective and democratic manner in the event of conflict. I therefore explore the securitarian policies of these urban spaces, focusing on the mechanisms that legitimise a firm hand against certain behaviours through a) dissuasive actions (video surveillance), b) punitive actions (bylaws), and c) preventive actions (geoprevention and defensive spaces).

## THE ROMANTIC CONCEPT OF PUBLIC SPACE

There is a current of thought within urban studies that signals the end of public space from an idealised and romantic perspective, such as Sennet's perspective in the 1970s. The latter heralded the death of public space, based on the predominance of the cultural production of intimacy and privacy in social relations in post-Fordist cities. Sennett (1977) argued that the decline of public life is caused mainly by the growing emphasis on private relationships and families. As a consequence, he understood that there has been a retreat into the domestic space, while places of public life have increasingly been replaced by one's own home in the suburbs or by gated communities. In addition, access to and diffusion of new technologies and private places of exchange have made the public sphere seem less necessary, and such events have moved into private space.

From this pessimistic and romanticised reading of urban public space comes the idea of the loss of that very space, based on an idealised view of an a-historical past, a time imagined as a place of peaceful democratic exchange. According to Di Masso et al. (2017), these optimistic theses that propose optimal criteria for intervention in public space – such as the right of presence, appropriation, modification, and disposition, as well as opportunities to eat, sit, watch and enjoy, along with accessibility and direct participation in its use and management – are paradoxically accompanied by discourses of risk, prevention, and punishment in the face of perceived insecurity and uncivic behaviour in public space. This portrays a territory at permanent risk of anomie (Cohen 2002), where both postulates – insecurity and harmony in public space – trace a unifying nexus from an idea of functional coexistence based on management and constant surveillance.

This is accentuated by ideas of gated urbanism from the 1990s, including gated communities. According to this perspective, public spaces become places of passage rather than places where people stay, resulting in a reconversion of public spaces into empty or semi-empty spaces only adequate for circulation or consumption. These ideas operate primarily in North American cities and have a strong influence on the private and personal life of suburban communities, where car travel and major motorways are a predominant feature, with public policies exported to the Latin American urban model. Authors such as Brill (1989) point out that it is not public space that is being lost, but rather neighbourhood spaces or community social life that are disintegrating. It is precisely for this reason that the idea of a genuine public space is at odds with a public space that has always been a place of conflict and struggle and proposes a critical urban sociology that goes beyond these postulates.

Jacobs (1961) explains that the city is defined by the fact that it is full of strangers and emphasises public space as an ever-changing, evolving place that allows interaction between these more or less anonymous people, as well as the creation of diverse communities. This is an idea that originated with the German sociologist Georg Simmel and was later incorporated into the Chicago school of sociology. Simmel, who was mainly concerned with the effect of urban life on the formation of personality, conceived of the city as a whole, separate from the rural space, in which it was important to understand the lifestyles that tended to be produced as a result of the way in which urban life was organised or structured. In his 1903 work 'The Metropolis and Mental Life', he argued that the metropolis was a social space in contrast to the village and the rural environment (Simmel 1950). Rural relations were associated with populations predominantly devoted to agriculture, and were essentially face-to-face. Simmel's contemporary, Ferdinand Tönnies, from an admittedly nostalgic perspective, would define these relations as essentially *communal*, based on custom and tradition, as opposed to the *associative* relations typical of the city, understood as elusive relations. Urban relations, Simmel said, therefore tend to be associative, based on particular interests and linked to experiences that converge on specific issues and where spaces are anonymous.

As it is known today, the city is not about anonymity in the strict sense – far from it. It is about recognisable strangers: strangers in public space are recognisable by their socio-economic identity, which includes their habitus, their dress, their aesthetics, and the places they regularly frequent within the city. This interaction is recurrent and essential in public space, allowing knowledge to be not anonymous, but personal and in some cases intimate, thus fostering broad communities that are close to each other (see Figure 33.1). Blokland (2017) points out how city dwellers interact in public spaces, explaining that those who are disconnected from each other but have sustained encounters can generate familiarity, while repeated encounters with strangers in public spaces can generate social capital. The importance of the street and of local life is thus emphasised, according to Jane Jacobs' works, based on their ability to generate bonds and trust in the community life of residents and in organised responses to inequalities.

*Source:* Miguel A. Martínez.

*Figure 33.1  Public space in the historical centre of Lisbon (2014)*

## CRITICAL VIEWS OF PUBLIC SPACE

In the 1970s and 1980s, Tibbalds (2001) criticised public space from a conservative stance as a polluted, congested, and unsafe place populated by homeless people and beggars. Others, such as Trancik (1986), used the term 'lost space' to refer to places in need of redevelopment, such as squares, abandoned car parks, and dilapidated parks, as well as marginal public housing projects. Others have spoken of 'in-between spaces' or 'liminal spaces' such as border crossings and meeting places that can facilitate valuable exchanges and connections between activities and people (Sennett 1990, Zukin 1995). This logic also includes '24-hour spaces' where interactions between nightlife users, local businesses, and residents are negotiated. These urban landscapes became models of urban and neighbourhood regeneration in the 1990s, driven by mixing and youth activities (Chatterton & Hollands 2003. In this case, it is not so much that the spaces have been abandoned, but that market forces and public administration have been left to regulate the place and its counterparts (Carmona 2010).

Authors such as Gehl and Gemzøe (2011) speak of 'invaded spaces', where the impact of the car has changed the concept of public space, usurping the pedestrian space of streets and squares, generating noise and visual pollution. As a result, these urban public spaces lose their social function and are characterised as an archipelago of intermediate enclaves that go unnoticed as individuals pass by at high speed in their motorised vehicles, remain empty of social activity, and are perceived as impoverished (Lofland 1998). According to these interpretations, when public spaces are no longer used for social, cultural, political, or economic activities, they can fall into a vicious circle of decay, according to Jan Gehl or Jane Jacobs, which has led to a fragmentation of public space associated with the risk society, where fear, suspicion, and conflicts between different social groups have led to a hyper-regulation of public space (Lofland 1998). Lofland already refers to these forms of spatial segregation in terms of class, ethnicity, race, age, and occupation type as spaces appropriated by certain specific groups so that those who pass through them may feel like strangers or guests, depending on the fit or urban enclave. In the same vein, Loukaitou-Sideris (1996) describes public space users as being suspicious of strangers, which has led to a strong segregation between different types of spaces and users. Nowadays, there are exclusionary public spaces that are only for certain age groups, such as children's playgrounds, skate parks, or gyms for the elderly. In short, public spaces have undergone changes and fragmentation in their conception and use over time, in a process influenced by social, economic, and cultural factors.

In large cities, for example, parents are reluctant to allow their children to play in the street or to walk to school. Children are perceived as a threat to public order because of the dominant presence of the car in contemporary urban developments. Other groups, such as the poor, the homeless, and young people, are actively excluded from public space, as I will discuss later in this chapter. This may be due to their inability to consume or because their entertainment is considered antisocial, due to conflict with other age groups, or even due to alleged damage to street furniture, as in the case of skateboarders and the constant campaign of criminalisation to which they are subjected. Today, authors such as Fainstein (2001) point out how urban public spaces are increasingly contested by these different spatial identities. One solution that seems to be spreading is the homogenisation of public space to avoid these disputes. This idea also highlights the importance of a space feeling or being interpreted as safe. Over-management of public space and surveillance therefore become key elements. This is why zoning is increasingly advocated, where specific spaces are designated for activities such as skateboarding, football, bar terraces, children's areas, pet areas, etc. Instead of the space being shared, its uses are encapsulated, which could create problems of social integration, cohesion, and the right to freedom of movement.

The dominant idea is to segment these public spaces instead of sharing them, which prevents equitable use by different groups without harming others. Crime is consequently used as an argument for the (often pre-emptive) installation of fences or the removal of certain practices or economies in public space to the outskirts. Even vulnerable people, such as undocumented migrants, feel safer in their own homes than in public space, where they are constantly exposed to possible police controls. Mike Davis (1992) refers to this notion of security as the militarisation of public space, where devices of control and punishment such as walls, fences, and video surveillance cameras increase.

According to Di Masso et al.'s (2017: 60) explanation of these 'conflict-based theses', public space has always been based on some form of social exclusion. The condition of exclusion, or the struggle of excluded sectors to be included and accepted as legitimate publics, is the structural condition of public space itself. Thus, public space is the natural territory for the expression of the right to the city also through conflict, where street contestation in public space is the very engine of urban life. Demonstrations, actions, protests, and rallies (reclaiming the street) fight for the right to have a place, to physically fit in, to not be persecuted, segregated, or excluded, but also to be recognised or accepted as a legitimate inhabitant of public space (Barnes et al. 2004).

## PRIVATISATION AND MANAGERIALISM IN URBAN PUBLIC SPACE

On the other hand, especially in the Anglo-Saxon world, debates about the management of public space highlight concerns about privatisation and security issues. Low and Smith (2013) already speak of the rise of prohibition and surveillance in public spaces. They also point to links with the privatisation of public space for commercial interests involving the closure, redesign, and policing of public parks and squares, as well as the direct transfer of rights to public space for the construction of corporate plazas or permanent events by various companies. This private management begins to control the use and consumption of public space.

From this perspective, the idea is not to see the city as real, but to create hyper-real environments composed of and fragmented by secure elements where there are no political, social, and cultural intrusions that might be feared by the establishment. Today, it is the city government that acts as a facilitator of these processes rather than a provider of these uses, so that privatised public spaces are no longer even managed by the police, but by private security. This is a transfer of power over public space from the state to capital (Minton 2006). The Business Improvement Districts (BIDs) approved in England are one example of these environments. These are privatised public spaces where private management oversees the public space. Following close behind are the projects recently launched and in the approval phase in Madrid's financial sector in 2023, where the public space is ceded to companies that will regenerate it for 40 years and where the concessionary company will charge the City Council for the costs of maintaining the area (electricity, repairs, security, gardening, cleaning, etc.) (Casado 2022). Meanwhile, in other countries, public space is considered an inalienable asset, but its management can be privatised. This also happens in nightlife venues, where security is managed by private nightclubs, which even manage entire streets, as is the case on Pink Street in Lisbon (Nofre et al. 2019).

Sorkin (1992) argues that the new corporate city heralds the end of traditional public space, transforming spaces into global spaces for consumption only. These spaces are heavily managed by security measures and are only connected to their historical past through simulations of heritage. I refer to a market of experiences and a postmodern search for authenticity in urban capitalism, as described by Zukin (2009). In some cases, financial or economic exclusion can also occur when entrance fees are charged, as is the case in some urban public parks such as Park Güell in Barcelona or in the recurring musical or festive events organised and managed by private entities (music festivals, circuses and immersive exhibitions, beer festivals, Christmas markets, etc.).

The idea of an invented space is also taken into account, as a place built according to a formula that imitates one city after another, such as the Chinatowns or the Sohos; the streets that imitate other streets in other cities; or the theme parks in the docks or ports – all of which

*Source:* Miguel A. Martínez.

*Figure 33.2  Santa Ana Square in the historical centre of Madrid (2023)*

respond to a logic of place marketing. This idea of Disneyland and public space is explored by Zukin (1995), who refers to it as the fabrication of places; it occurs in a wide range of contexts, from the total invention of specific places to the regeneration of historic urban spaces. It is a constant search for authentic experiences in public space, and it does not matter so much whether the place is invented, recreated, or pre-existing but rather that it serves to impose certain constant and recurring uses of public space.

Finally, it is also necessary to consider spaces of fear (De Souza 2014, Tulumello 2015), which represent a difficult power relationship between access and exclusion. Kilian (1988) speaks of residents as controllers, visitors as controlled, and outsiders as undesirables, i.e. those who have no right of access and are by definition excluded. It is often the fear of crime, together with subjective insecurity, that drives initiatives to privatise public space and segregate different street uses and communities. Mitchell (1995) explains in 'The End of Public Space' that the perception of crime is linked to the presence of different groups sharing the same space, creating mutual suspicion between them. Elsewhere (Mitchell 2003) he refers to public space as a normative ideal, i.e. as an ideal representation in the social imaginary, as a category with an aspect of harmony and social coexistence. He himself criticises this as completely unrealistic and far removed from a hyper-regulated reality.

In this sense, Minton (2006) refers to 'hot spots' of affluence, those places with clean and safe policies that displace social problems, and 'cold spots', those places where social outcasts are found who are not welcome in the hot spots (see Figure 33.2). The result is a polarisation of urban public spaces and their sociability. This often leads to polarised public spaces, where those considered undesirable in central areas are left out and pushed to the periphery, where problems are exacerbated rather than solved. In addition, use-by-zoning follows the city's socio-spatial distribution, and its class and ethnic segregation.

## BIOPOLITICS IN PUBLIC SPACE STUDIES

By biopolitics I refer to the idea according to which life itself is subsumed to capital, and capital valuation is produced by a whole society integrated into work, including all social and vital relationships. In other words, it is an intervention over living conditions with the intention of modifying or normalising them (Foucault 2009a). I am referring to a biopower that must be understood according to two mechanisms: 1) political techniques employed by governments to take care of the population, and 2) technologies of the self, the subjectivation process by which the individual's identity is linked with their self-awareness, though motivated by an external power (Foucault 1990). Returning to the concept of power introduced by Foucault (1977) to understand the interventions in urban space and the different strategic relationships involving the subject, power – for this author – is not possessed but rather exercised, i.e., it is a strategy. In this way, it approaches what he called the 'microphysics of power', which goes beyond power understood only as the repressive and omnipresent capacity of the state. Power transpires through all bodies; it is not just part of the superstructure (the state, the productive role model, the institution) but appears everywhere, though it is expressed differently. These axioms break away from the imaginary of power as something merely negative, which hides or impedes, and start regarding it as something that produces or normalises. The result of power relationships is, according to this approach, to create public spaces made by productive subjects, by consumerist bodies.

Thus, when production is no longer separated from daily life, the whole city becomes a living production machine; a work object and subject; the raw material and finished product all at once. As Domínguez states (2008: 8), 'in post-Fordist society, the social spaces that escape capitalist exploitation and domination have been noticeably reduced'. This happens following the implementation of a whole series of *dispositifs* (also referred to in the literature as devices, apparatuses, and dispositives) that turn planned urban restructurings into a useful mechanism for disciplining the users of urban space (Delgado 2007: 54). In fact, urban managers, architects, and city planners regulate this in their urban strategies, which unfold to create an 'other space' (Dehaene & De Cauter 2008, Foucault & Miskowiec 1986), apparently perfect, precise, and tidy; one that clashes strongly with the one that actually exists.

Accordingly, the main goal of the public administration (through architects, urban planners, politicians, and different space controllers) and capital interventions is therefore to manage and control the way cities work, allowing and securing different ways for people, goods, etc. to circulate around it through constant surveillance and inspection in a relentless search for the ideal city, keeping risks for the population within the acceptable limits for the city to function.

Understood as the relationship between government, population, and political economy (Lazzarato 2002) by means of urban space, biopolitics becomes the object of the mechanism by which subjects and public subjectivities are produced in the city. The regulation that is established in neoliberalism, as understood by the French school (Dardot & Laval 2019, Laval & Dardot 2013) and based on the Foucauldian perspective (Foucault 2009a, 2009b), is constructed around a kind of governmental rationality whose objective is the administration of society and subjects according to forms of self-government of the subject itself. However, self-governance (Lorey 2008: 63–64), which appears here under an apparent free judgement, is simultaneously self-discipline in the sense addressed by Elias (1982), displayed as self-coercion that strengthens inner fears and as coercion demonstrated by the individuals themselves during rationalisation processes. As a result, it confronts a paradox in which the subjects who are (figuratively) sovereigns of themselves are who that are governed: in the end, the individual is the *subject* over whom the power is exercised.

As described by Rose (1999) when he refers to 'psy-technologies', agents, subjectivities, and forms of knowledge are being generated that restrict possible relationship scenarios in urban spaces. As a consequence, this neoliberal art of government understands society as 'a group of energies and initiatives to be facilitated and strengthened' (Vázquez 2009: 14), as a new relationship between government and knowledge, which implements a depoliticisation of the public space, based on apparent non-ideological technical criteria (Ong 2006, Sequera & Mateos 2015, Stavrides 2010).

In this context, the 'government' is understood as a technique that orders and connects the triangular *dispositif* of *security–population–government*. The art of good government, Foucault would say, is in the sense of taking on the population, leading them down a given route by supporting and driving them. The arts of good government in modern societies are therefore not about implementing repressive actions but about extending self-control, a constant search for the perfect neoliberal civility. This power play is inscribed within a series of *dispositifs* (Deleuze 1992, Foucault 1991) or machines (Deleuze & Guattari 1988), as mechanisms of visibility, society reading, and power-knowledge.

In this way, *dispositifs* such as architecture, urban planning, public facilities, or institutions interact with each other, weaving a power network that shapes the meaning of a public place in which the subject is exposed. In conclusion, this subject is defined from a perspective of governmentality based on a rational planning model that attempts to produce and guide political subjectivities and, in order to do so, interpellates the space as a generator of spatial and ambient causalities (Huxley 2007: 199). These are the technologies and power strategies that must be analysed in urban social processes because they deploy the rhetoric of biopolitics as a form of government. In neoliberalism, this remains confined to a subjugation of social practices – in our case, about public space – to tolerable margins for the contemporary capitalist city. In the following sections I therefore examine three securitarian policies of urban public space by means of a) dissuasive measures (video surveillance), b) punitive measures (bylaws), and c) preventive measures (geoprevention and defensive spaces).

**Dissuasive Actions: Video Surveillance**

The use of video surveillance cameras is constantly increasing in urban public spaces (Firmino & Duarte 2016, controlling and indiscriminately recording daily practices (whether these are unlawful or not), acting as a refinement of governments' knowledge-power strategies over the population. Increasingly sophisticated technologies are being implemented, including surveillance using high-accuracy cameras from helicopters during demonstrations or other forms of protest, biometric technology (Muller 2008), automated facial recognition, iris or fingerprint scanners, and the idea of installing radio-frequency identification (RFID) chips beneath the skin of citizens. These are used to guard, punish, and normalise places. Paradoxically, these control *dispositifs* are used both to generate an arguable feeling of safety and to recreate a feeling of distrust, panic, or fear (Aramayona & Nofre 2021, Tulumello 2015). As Foucault (1990) reminds us, it is not about the individual being punished, but about ensuring that he/she never behaves badly, since then he/she is subject to an almost omnipresent visibility (luckily, not yet omnipotent) in the public space. To achieve this, as one of the main protagonists of urban planning (Davis 1992), police forces obtain a technological prosthesis that awards them the detailed legibility of the public space, a knowledge-power device. Among the reasons that can be glimpsed for the strengthening of these urban control technologies, Davis proposes that this extensive surveillance creates a virtual *scanscape*, a space of protective visibility that increasingly defines the area in which office workers and middle-class tourists feel safe downtown.

A paradigmatic case is that of the United Kingdom, which has four million cameras (Sorrel 2009), where systems for detecting suspicious behaviours (speeding vehicles, mobs, suspicious objects in public spaces, etc.) have been deployed and are also capable of distinguishing people already *known* to the police. The use and effectiveness of these systems were put to the test during the August 2011 riots, with the use of thousands of video cameras installed all over London to aid the 'search and seizure' of *looters* (Domínguez & Ezquiaga 2012: 131), in the most genuinely *Western* way (The Guardian 2011). However, many of them are useless (The Independent 2009) and are simply part of the subjective security and risk monitoring game or, similarly, of the subjectivation of certain forms of security and of the risk of being monitored. What one generation may perceive as repressive and illegitimate, the next will accept as natural.

**Punitive Actions: Bureau Repression**

In a complementary way, there is a propagation of laws that regulate the public space and that affect precisely the people who make more use of and express themselves in open places through the banning of certain activities such as begging and alcohol consumption (Jayne et al. 2006) or the criminalisation of traditional cultural practices in public spaces. In short, these policies attack vulnerable subjects, prioritising hegemonic social practices and restricting spaces to achieve social cleansing (Oliver & Urda 2015). By using preventive strategies, certain practices are legislated against as offences in an attempt to establish norms and to naturalise this reconstruction of 'the public' as the 'civic', effectively sterilising the place. Under a disciplinary power that develops a government technology to distribute activities and individuals across the urban space, encouragement is given to citizen role models that are typical of the social panopticon. In fact, this increase in public space regulations through civil bylaws and a greater physical police presence – with the latter becoming one of the main protagonists of inner city planning (Davis 1992) – calls to mind the governmental system or dispositive of bureau repression. This is a form of repression based on indiscriminate administrative sanctions against individuals for exercising their fundamental rights (Oliver et al. 2013). It means control and dissuasion through administrative (non-criminal) lawsuits that are brought against vulnerable or excluded groups. The concept of public space is redefined in order to introduce a wide range of measures and bureau-repressive fines against the presence in certain spaces of social groups excluded from the formal economy and from other privatised and commodified spaces (García & Ávila 2015: 2021).

Indeed, these securitarian *dispositifs* entail a persistent stigmatisation of strategic areas and social sectors in the neighbourhood. The results include selective identity checks, which are characterised as systematic checks based on xenophobic, racist, and classist criteria. These are conducted in commuting and transport hubs, making it impossible for citizens to travel freely and to perform their normal activities. In some cases, 'preventive arrests' are made, riskily leading to the futurist concept of 'pre-delinquence'. As Ávila and Malo remind us (2008: 511), 'nowadays it is possible to live in a place and not have any rights there; to live in a place and not feel part of it; to have rights only halfway in the place where people live and feel only halfway part of it; to share a space with people that have different rights from us and for whom, as a result, a different destiny awaits'.

**Preventive Actions: Geoprevention and Defensive Spaces**

The above two *dispositifs* – video surveillance and bureau repression – are accompanied in the neoliberal city by 'crime prevention through environmental design' (CPTED), which falls within the geoprevention paradigm as an attempt to reduce the probability of delinquent acts. This takes place through natural access control, natural surveillance, public space maintenance, or territorial reinforcement. This trend nuances the concept of security based on a multifaceted reality: as a legal, normative, political, and social value. A distinction can be made between civic security and public security as a key question for these sorts of geopreventive policies. Public security is regulated by the services provided by the different police forces and justice courts (state-monopolistic concept), in order to eradicate and control violent and criminal behaviours within a society. Civic security, on the other hand, involves other social actors (citizens, neighbourhood organisations, etc.). I am referring to mutual surveillance programmes, organised through neighbourhood associations, as well as new forms of private or self-managed prevention. One such example is the Neighbourhood Watch, an Anglo-Saxon initiative based on providing civil society with certain powers and responsibilities and featuring those technologies of the self that are typical of neoliberal governmentality. These kinds of policies, based on spatial prevention, claim to rely on the complicity of citizens and the fact that they are incorporated into institutional policy.

In this regard, Jacobs (1961), an author cited by opposing theoretical fields of social sciences, already gave meaning to 'informal' social control in the name of crime prevention. On that subject, she asserted that, in order to build safer cities, it was necessary to diversify the uses of urban land, increasing activity in the streets and promoting surveillance options in urban spaces, thereby overlapping normal neighbourhood activity with observation options. Subsequently, Newman (1972) developed these concepts, but linking delinquency with urban design to generate the key concept of 'defensible space'. His proposal seeks to restructure urban design based on community, allowing neighbours to control their immediate surroundings. This scientific stream argues that the physical and social urban environment tends to create opportunities for committing crimes, and that these can be reduced by modifying certain environmental parameters (access control, surveillance, territorial reinforcement, public space maintenance and community involvement, and situational prevention).

As I mentioned above, contemporary trends include the construction of gated communities, reflecting the desire of affluent groups to separate themselves from the rest of society, to limit the ways in which the city is physically constructed, and to turn public space into private space. In so doing, they turn their backs on public space as it was previously understood under the idea of hyper-fortification (Davis 1992) and fortified private residential enclosures, as in the idea of defensible spaces. Thus, in recent years, the presence of defensive architecture and discriminatory urban planning – such as metal spikes in strategic areas to prevent the homeless from spending the night, the partitioning or removal of benches in public spaces (to prevent these from being used as beds and shelters by vulnerable groups), or installing individual chairs instead of benches – is increasing. It is even suggested that neighbourhood management be handed over to private companies and that new bylaws and laws be allowed that prevent the right to assembly and the historically protest-based use assigned to these spaces, resulting in what we could consider an urban 'state of exception' (Vainer 2015).

## CONCLUSIONS

While streets and squares are meeting places, and spaces for dialogue and sociability in the romanticised version of public space, actual public spaces draw a line between social groups, establishing relations of domination and discriminatory processes of subjectivation and privatised management and managerialism, according to critical perspectives. Public spaces – the result of discourses, struggles, and power strategies – that are constructed in an unequal and contested way, through their specific appropriation by social groups with different capitals (cultural, economic, symbolic), give rise to displacement and segregation.

In terms of the biopolitical approach, I have suggested that public space is a device that, through various technologies of governance (such as different forms of control architecture, video surveillance, bureaucratic repression, or preventive urbanism), tends to intensify surveillance, administrative punishment, and the regulation of procedures such as the distribution of individuals in space or geoprevention as a form of anticipatory control over activities that have not yet occurred. This fosters mistrust, panic, fear, and paranoia in public urban spaces, which in turn reify the need for social control measures. These rising trends indicate that it is not only a question of punishing individuals but of preventing them from doing anything wrong in the first place, to the extent that the population feels submerged, immersed in a total field of vision in which the opinion, gaze, and discourse of the other prevent them from doing anything wrong or harmful.

## REFERENCES

Aramayona, B. & Nofre, J. (2021) The city of (dis-) trust: Balconies, the biopoliticised self, and the new everyday governmentality of the public space in Madrid in times of COVID-19. *Town Planning Review* 92(2): 257–262.
Ávila, D. & Malo, M. (2008) ¿Quién puede habitar la ciudad? Fronteras, gobierno y transnacionalidad en los barrios de Lavapiés y San Cristóbal. In Observatorio Metropolitano (ed.) *Madrid, ¿la suma de todos? Globalización, territorio, desigualdad*. Madrid: Traficantes de sueños, 505–632.
Barnes, R., Auburn, T. & Lea, S. (2004) Citizenship in practice. *British Journal of Social Psychology* 43(2): 187–206.
Blokland, T. (2017) The public life of social capital. In Hall, S. & Burdett, R. (eds.) *The SAGE handbook of the 21st century city*. London: Sage, 552–566.
Brill, M. (1989) Transformation, nostalgia, and illusion in public life and public place. In Altman, I. & Zube, E. (eds.) *Public places and spaces*. Boston, MA: Springer, 7–29.
Carmona, M. (2010) Contemporary public space: Critique and classification, part one: Critique. *Journal of Urban Design* 15(1): 123–148.
Casado, D. (2022) El Ayuntamiento de Madrid defiende privatizar AZCA durante 40 años. *Eldiario.es*, September. Available at: https://www.eldiario.es/madrid/somos/tetuan/ayuntamiento-madrid-defiende-privatizar-azca-durante-40-anos-oportunidad-no-pasar_1_9571763.html.
Castells, M. (1982) *La cuestión urbana*. Mexico: Siglo XXI.
Chatterton, P. & Hollands, R. (2003) *Urban nightscapes. Youth cultures, pleasure spaces and corporate power*. New York: Routledge.
Cohen, S. (2002) *Folk devils and moral panics*. London: Routledge.
Dardot, P. & Laval, C. (2019) Neoliberalism and the alternative of the common. In Howe, K., Boal, J. & Soeiro, J. (eds.) *The Routledge companion to theatre of the oppressed*. London: Routledge, 203–210.
Davis, M. (1992) Beyond blade runner: Urban control, the ecology of fear. *Open Media* 23.
De Backer, M., Melgaço, L., Varna, G. & Menichelli, F. (eds.) (2016) *Order and conflict in public space*. Routledge.
Dehaene, M. & De Cauter, L. (eds.) (2008) *Heterotopia and the city: Public space in a postcivil society*. London & New York: Routledge.
Deleuze, G. (1992) What is a dispositif. In Armstrong, T. J. (ed.) *Michel Foucault: Philosopher*. Hemel Hempstead: Harvester Wheatsheaf, 159–168.
Deleuze, G. & Guattari, F. (1988) *A thousand plateaus: Capitalism and schizophrenia*. London: Bloomsbury Publishing.
Delgado, M. (2007) *La ciudad mentirosa. Fraude y miseria del 'Modelo Barcelona'*. Madrid: La Catarata.
De Souza, M. L. (2014) Phobopolis: Violence, fear and sociopolitical fragmentation of the space in Rio de Janeiro, Brazil. In Kraas, F., Aggarwal, S., Coy, M. & Mertins, G. (eds.) *Megacities: Our global urban future*. New York: Springer, 151–164.
Di Masso, A., Berroeta, H. & Vidal i Moranta, T. (2017) El espacio público en conflicto: Coordenadas conceptuales y tensiones ideológicas. *Athenea Digital: Revista de Pensamiento e Investigación Social* 17(3): 53–92.
Domínguez, M. (2008) Trabajo material e inmaterial. Polémicas y conceptos inestables, marco teórico y estado de la cuestión. *Youkali, Revista Crítica de las Artes y el Pensamiento, Madrid*. Available at: http://www.youkali.net/5a1-YOUKALI-Dominguez-Sanchez-Pinilla.pdf.
Domínguez Sánchez-Pinilla, M. & Ezquiaga Fernández, M. (2012) Cuando la rabia prende. *Teknokultura. Revista de Cultura Digital y Movimientos Sociales* 9(1): 123–147.
Elias, N. & Jephcott, E. (1982) *The civilizing process (vol. 2)*. New York: Pantheon Books.
Fainstein, S. S. (2001) *The city builders: Property development in New York and London, 1980–2000*. Kansas: University Press of Kansas.

Firmino, R. & Duarte, F. (2016) Private video monitoring of public spaces: The construction of new invisible territories. *Urban Studies* 53(4): 741–754.
Foucault, M. (1977) *Microphysique du pouvoir*. Turin: Einaudi.
Foucault, M. (1990) *Tecnologías del yo y otros textos afines*. Barcelona: Paidós.
Foucault, M. (1991) Governmentality. In Burchell, G., Gordon, C. & Miller, P. (eds.) *The Foucault effect: Studies in governmentality*. Chicago: University of Chicago Press, 87–104.
Foucault, M. (2009a) *Security, territory, population: Lectures at the Collège de France 1977–1978*. London: Macmillan.
Foucault, M. (2009b) *Nacimiento de la biopolítica: curso del Collège de France (1978–1979)*. Madrid: Akal.
Foucault, M. & Miskowiec, J. (1986) Of other spaces. *Diacritics* 16(1): 22–27.
García, S. & Ávila, D. (eds.) (2015) *Enclaves de riesgo. Gobierno neoliberal, desigualdad y control social*. Madrid: Traficantes de Sueños.
Gehl, J. (2001) *Life between buildings*. Copenhagen: The Danish Architectural Press.
Gehl, J. & Gemzøe, L. (2001) *New city spaces*. Copenhagen: The Danish Architectural Press.
Huxley, M. (2007) Geographies of governmentality. In Crampton, J. & Elden, S. (eds.) *Space, knowledge and power: Foucault and geography*. Aldershot: Ashgate, 185–204.
Jacobs, J. (1961) *The death and life of great American cities*. New York: Vintage Books.
Jayne, M., Holloway, S. L. & Gill, V. (2006) Drunk and disorderly: Alcohol, urban life and public space. *Progress in Human Geography* 30: 451–468.
Kilian, T. (1998) Public and private power and space. In Light, A. & J.M. Smith, J. M. (eds.) *Philosophy and geography II: The production of public space*. Lanham: Rowman and Littlefield, 115–134.
Laval, C. & Dardot, P. (2013) *La nueva razón del mundo*. Gedisa.
Lazzarato, M. (2002) From biopower to biopolitics. *Pli: The Warwick Journal of Philosophy* 13(8): 1–6.
Lefebvre, H. (1983) *La revolución urbana*. El libro de bolsillo.
Lefebvre, H. (2020 [1974]) *La producción del espacio*. Capitán Swing Libros
Lofland, L. (1998) *The public realm: Exploring the city's quintessential social territory*. New Jersey: Aldine Transaction.
Lorey, I. (2008) Gubernamentalidad y precarización de sí. Sobre la normalización de los productores y las productoras culturales. In Transform (ed.) *Producción cultural y prácticas instituyentes. Líneas de ruptura en la crítica institucional*. Traficantes de Sueños, 57–78.
Loukaitou-Sideris, A. (1996) Cracks in the city: Addressing the constraints and potentials of urban design. *Journal of Urban Design* 1(1): 91–103.
Low, S. M. (2010) *On the plaza: The politics of public space and culture*. Austin: University of Texas Press.
Low, S. M. & Smith, N. (eds.) (2013) *The politics of public space*. New York: Routledge.
Malone, K. (2002) Street life: Youth, culture and competing uses of public space. *Environment and Urbanization* 14(2): 157–168.
Massey, D. (1994) *Space, place and gender*. Cambridge: Polity Press.
Merrifield, A. (2014) *The new urban question*. London: Pluto Press.
Minton, A. (2006) *What kind of world are we building? The privatisation of public space*. London: RICS.
Mitchell, D. (1995) The end of public space? People's Park, definitions of the public, and democracy. *Annals of the Association of American Geographers* 85(1): 108–133.
Mitchell, D. (2003) *The right to the city: Social justice and the fight for public space*. New York: Guilford Press.
Mitchell, D. (2020) *Mean streets: Homelessness, public space, and the limits of capital*. New York: University of Georgia Press.
Muller, B. J. (2008) Securing the political imagination: Popular culture, the security dispositif and the biometric state. *Security Dialogue* 39(2–3): 199–220.
Newman, O. (1972) *Defensible space*. New York: Macmillan.
Nofre, J., Martins, J. C., Vaz, D., Fina, R., Sequera, J. & Vale, P. (2019) The 'Pink Street' in Cais do Sodré: Urban change and liminal governance in a nightlife district of Lisbon. *Urban Research & Practice* 12(4): 322–340.
Oldenburg, R. (1999) *The great good place: Cafes, coffee shops, bookstores, bars, hair salons, and other hangouts at the heart of a community*. Cambridge: Da Capo Press.

Oliver, P. (ed.) (2013) *Burorrepresión. Sanción administrativa y control social.* Madrid: Bomarzo.
Oliver, P. & Urda, J. C. (2015) Bureau-repression: Administrative sanction and social control in modern Spain. *Oñati Socio-legal Series* 5(5): 1309–1328. Available at: http://ssrn.com/abstract=2574670.
Ong, A. (2006) *Neoliberalism as exception: Mutations in citizenship and sovereignty.* Durham: Duke University Press.
Rose, N. (1999) *Powers of freedom: Reframing political thought.* Cambridge: Cambridge University Press.
Sennett, R. (1977) *The fall of public man.* New York: Knopf.
Sennett, R. (1990) *The Conscience of the eye. The design and social life of cities.* New York: Alfred Knopf.
Sennett, R. (2018) *Building and dwelling: Ethics for the city.* New York: Farrar, Straus and Giroux.
Sequera, J. & Mateos, E. (2015) Contested taming spatialities. In Allen, A., Lampis, A. & Swilling, M. (eds.) *Untamed urbanisms.* Routledge, 244–256.
Simmel, G. (1950) *The sociology of Georg Simmel.* New York: Simon and Schuster.
Smith, N. (2001) Global social cleansing: Postliberal revanchism and the export of zero tolerance. *Social Justice* 28(3): 68–74.
Sorkin, M. (1992) *Variations on a theme park: The new American city and the end of public space.* New York: Macmillan.
Sorrel, C. (2009) Britain to put CCTV cameras inside private homes. Available at: http://www.wired.com/gadgetlab/2009/08/britain-to-put-cctv-cameras-inside-private-homes/ (accessed on: 8/8/2011).
Stavrides, S. (2010) *Towards the city of thresholds.* Trento: Professional dreamers.
The Guardian (2011) Reading the riots. Available at: http://www.theguardian.com/uk/series/reading-the-riots.
The Independent (2009) CCTV in the spotlight: One crime solved for every 1,000 cameras. 25 August. Available at: http://www.independent.co.uk/news/uk/crime/cctv-in-the-spotlight-one-crime-solved-for-every-1000-cameras-1776774.html (accessed on: 5/7/2011).
Tibbalds, F. (2001) *Making people friendly towns: Improving the public environment in towns and cities.* London: Spon Press.
Trancik, R. (1986) *Finding lost space: Theories of urban design.* New York: Van Nostrand Reinhold.
Tulumello, S. (2015) From 'spaces of fear' to 'fearscapes' mapping for reframing theories about the spatialization of fear in urban space. *Space and Culture* 18(3): 257–272.
Vainer, C. (2015) Mega-events and the city of exception. In Gruneau, R. & Horne, J. (eds.) *Mega-events and globalization: Capital and spectacle in a changing world order.* London and New York: Routledge, 1–28.
Vázquez García, F. (2009) *La invención del racismo. Nacimiento de la biopolítica en España.* Madrid: Akal.
Wirth, L. (1928) *The ghetto.* Chicago: University of Chicago Press.
Zukin, S. (1995) *The cultures of cities.* Oxford: Blackwell.
Zukin, S. (2009) *Naked city: The death and life of authentic urban places.* Oxford: Oxford University Press.

# 34. The logic of informality in shaping urban collective action in the Global South

*Sonia Roitman and Peter Walters*

Urban informality is the paradigmatic and fastest growing form or mode of social and economic organisation in many cities in the Global South, where the informal economy and informal settlements (slums) are the predominant form of social organisation (despite its conceptual simplification, here we use slums and informal settlements as synonymous (UN-Habitat 2003, UN-Habitat 2016)). Broadly defined, urban informality refers to a largely organic mode of urbanisation that takes place in the absence or ignorance of formal regulation, fiscal policy and urban planning regimes (Kudva 2009, Roy 2005) and can be applied in the realms of housing, other land uses, service and infrastructure provision, livelihoods and governance. However, as we shall demonstrate in this chapter, the nature, dynamics and normative understandings of informality are contested, creating a range of different ontological perspectives, the best of them moving beyond the simple binaries between 'regulated and unregulated' that characterised much of the early literature. Urban informality, if it has not already gained this status, deserves its place as the most important paradigm in urban sociology for the 21st century because it is here that the great urban sociological questions and policy challenges will arise in the context of economic, environmental, social and political justice. As we shall also demonstrate, it is thinkers from the Global South who are leading the vanguard for a form of theorisation that sets itself apart from the dominant themes established by the traditional thought leaders of urban sociology in the North.

While informality exists in both the Global North and South (Devlin 2019), in this chapter we limit our discussion to informality in the South, where poverty, rural-to-urban migration, the legacy of colonialism and the inequalities wrought by neoliberalism mean informality in all its forms is a dominant mode of existence in the city. Normatively, we will balance what is often presented as a deficit model of informality to provide a deeper texture that respects the agency, culture and resilience of mostly informal residents and the essential role they play in the everyday life of cities in the Global South. Although informality in urban planning processes and livelihoods is well spread across socio-economic strata in most urban areas in the South, we focus our discussion here primarily on informality as it affects poor and disadvantaged social groups.

Following a conceptual discussion on informality including its main features as a social phenomenon, we move to an examination of the 'social logic' of informality to illustrate the distinctiveness of informal social organisation and its contribution to urban sociology. We draw on examples from our own research working with informal settlements in Indonesia and Bangladesh and additional cases provided by the literature to give a richer insight into the diversity of informal practices. We end this discussion with a reflection on the role of informality in a broader discussion on urban sociology.

## CONCEPTUALISING INFORMALITY

In its most general usage, informality is characterised as an economic phenomenon where pervasive poverty and precarious self-employment are the norm, and a form of spatiality where shelter and service provision are improvised or organic (Kudva 2009). This stands in opposition to those parts of urban space and organisation that are institutionally planned, regulated and taxed. Boudreau and Davis (2017: 155) understand informality 'through the lens of flexibility, negotiation, or situational spontaneity that push back against established state regulations and the constraints of the law'.

Informality in the Global South has become a normalised condition due to its prevalence and scale, whereas it is an 'exemption' or less-developed condition in the Global North. The informality of the conditions in which the majority of the residents in the Global South work and live clashes with the supposed formality of the planning system that governments try to impose, creating a 'conflict of rationalities' (Watson 2009). It is the same regulatory system that produces informality that establishes what is good or bad according to the system's rules (Roy 2005). Other authors also refer to the notion of an 'alternative' when defining informality as informality 'serves primarily as an alternative to the constraints of the formal structures' (Bayat 1997: 60).

While academic work can be guilty of 'othering' those in the informal realm, the uneasy relationship between formal institutions and informal economies, settlements and their occupants in cities in the Global South results in the stigmatisation of the informal. Roy (2005: 149) argues 'informality must be understood not as the object of state regulation but rather as produced by the state itself'; however, the state is also complicit in an active project of 'othering' informal citizens (Fattah & Walters 2020).

From a postcolonial perspective, many cities in the Global South have inherited both a colonial spatial logic and the remnants of an associated colonial planning system. Colonists, particularly the British, but also the French and other Europeans in Africa, established cities that were sharply divided between formal planned spaces for the elite and a periphery where the impoverished were ignored and cut off from the services and amenity afforded to the elite (Fattah & Walters 2020). This pattern of occupation and spatial division has been perpetuated by elites in the postcolonial era, with the urban poor often remaining in their subaltern state. Urban planning in the Global South often fails to address the realities of contemporary Southern cities as these inherited colonial planning systems continue to be adapted from Northern planning models (Watson 2009).

Urban informality often has its roots in rural poverty, as the result of mass migration to cities in search of opportunity (Bayat 1997) where social and cultural life in informal settlements adapts and adjusts from traditional rural life in the context of urban survival. In the city, poverty is maintained and reproduced by systems of urban governance that serve to limit opportunity and reproduce intergenerational poverty with few opportunities to access education, secure work, or secure housing tenure (Lemanski & Marx 2015, World Bank 2019).

There is a strong relationship between neoliberalism and the rapid contemporary growth in informality in Southern cities. The hypermobility of global capital has created a demand for cheap, expendable industrial labour in the Global South that has further expanded the role of informality. While many of the modes of work and economic activity that are now categorised as informal predate capitalism, the need for this categorisation and its othering in relation to formal regulation and governance is a product of urban postcolonial modernity and the rapid pace of economic liberalisation in the neoliberal era (McFarlane 2012). Capitalism forces those groups that are marginalised or excluded from the system to find their own alternatives within capitalist markets (Sheppard et al. 2020).

## DOMAINS OF INFORMALITY

There are different 'domains' of informality, including the informal economy, informal access to infrastructure and services and informal land and housing. There is significant overlap among these domains. We review them here to provide an overview of the magnitude and diversity that this social phenomenon can present, but we concentrate our analysis on the domain of informality and its social organisation in relation to land and housing.

Economic informality refers to 'businesses that either do not enjoy legal status or whose "relations of production" are characterised by low levels of systematisation' (Phelps 2021: 2).

In the Global South in cities such as Dhaka, Jakarta, Lagos and Mumbai, informality is often the dominant form of economic activity and keeps the city functioning, with a vital role in sectors such as transport, food distribution and retailing, local domestic sanitation and domestic and construction labour serving the needs of large business and the elite. In sub-Saharan African cities, around 75 percent of basic everyday consumption is provided by the informal economy (World Bank 2020). According to Yiftachel (2009: 89), economic informality can 'characterize a vast number of metropolitan regimes' where most of the population can be regarded as either working in the unregulated economic sector or living in informal settlements or 'squatting' without formal tenure.

Informality does not necessarily equate to poverty, although poverty is usually to be found in informality. In long-established slums in cities such as Rio de Janeiro, Mexico City and Mumbai, informal economic life is inextricably linked to the formal sector in an environment of mutual dependence. Informal labour provides a vital, cheap and expendable resource. Longstanding communities living in informal settlements have complex social and economic hierarchies. A degree of political power and strong social organisation at the grassroots level are seen as a means to cope with poverty and improve everyday life (Roitman 2019a, Murwani et al. 2023). However, in some cases where extreme poverty exists, the capacity for strong community networks and cultures of reciprocity can diminish as individuals and families atomise and struggle to survive from day to day (Walters 2018).

Informal residents occupy a paradoxical position in the life of the Southern city. Although informality is organic and responsive, it is subject to the needs and threats of institutional forces in the city including the state and abstract capital and often exists despite the desire of these two institutions to either eradicate the informal economy and those who rely on it or to bring it under effective control.

The second domain of informality refers to the informal provision of services and infrastructure in cities. Poor and marginalised urban areas, including informal settlements, often lack basic services and infrastructure and residents resort to informal and often illegal practices to obtain electricity, drinking water and basic sanitation. This is an everyday, established (and mostly accepted) practice common in Global South cities (Bayat 1997). In the informal settlements of Dhaka, for those urban residents with no secure land tenure, the government is unwilling to provide formal access to water so residents rely on a network of informal water vendors, as documented by Sultana et al. (2016) in relation to Korail, one of the largest informal settlements in Dhaka. Similarly, using nine case studies in the Global South, Allen et al. (2006: 15) describe how peri-urban growth has led the residents of these emerging areas to develop 'a wide spectrum of informal practices to access water and sanitation which often remain "invisible" to policy-makers and lie outside formal support strategies and mechanisms'. In Cairo, the Zabbaleen, or 'garbage collectors', informally collect and manage the solid waste of one third of the city and have become not only visible but vital for the effective management of the whole city (Fahmi & Sutton 2006).

The third domain is the informality of land and housing, or spatial informality, which has an important spatial character and where the formal-informal divide is used as a 'spatial categorisation' (McFarlane 2012). Residents in informal settlements have no formal or legal land tenure, which can lead to a degraded identity. Governments have grounds to treat those who live outside of the formally recognised residential address system as outsiders or non-citizens who struggle to claim the same rights and privileges as the 'formal' city. However, there are multiple situations in which the government contradicts itself, not recognising these settlements on the one hand but providing infrastructure (such as paving streets) in the same settlements on the other hand.

Spatial informality is a characteristic of city-making and how cities are produced in four different ways: first, through informal makeshift housing built by poor residents who cannot access housing provided by the public or private sectors; second, through private developers who work outside of formal rules and regulations, as it is more profitable to do so, or where formal processes result in slow progress for the supply of urban infrastructure and services; third, through the state in tolerating informality because the scale of informality is overwhelming and it plays an essential role in the urban economy; fourth, through the state creating regulations that arbitrarily establish what is formal and informal in the city, thus justifying the neglect of these informal areas as outside their competency.

Informal housing, where it occupies land owned by the state or private sector, can either be concentrated in a particular zone or spread opportunistically through the city. Most urban residents rely on informal practices to claim a space in the city, a tenuous 'right to reside' (Sheppard et al. 2020) or 'right to stay' (Roitman 2019b). Land occupation is a result of individual and collective actions that can be spontaneous or organised, responding to an economic 'logic of necessity' in highly stratified societies where there is polarisation of wealth (Abramo 2012). Roy (2005: 149) describes a 'complex continuum of legality and illegality, where squatter settlements formed through land invasion and self-help housing can exist alongside upscale informal subdivisions formed through legal ownership and market transaction but also in violation of land use regulations'. Both forms of housing are informal but are very different manifestations of legitimacy (Roy 2005). Abramo (2012) argues that although the informal land market is outside legal frameworks, it has its own institutional structure that guarantees the reproduction of hierarchies of ownership in the practices of buying, selling and renting land or buildings. The planning and legal apparatus of the state has the power to determine what is formal and what is not, and which forms of informality thrive and which disappear (Roy 2005).

Although many informal settlements are quasi-permanent due to their longevity and apparent embeddedness in the life of a city and its politics, they are still, by their nature, never fully settled, remaining in a state of legal and tenure limbo (Lombard 2015). This is the result of the dynamic influence of changing needs and a lack of formal planning constraints, as well as the constant threat of the state and capital reappropriating land at any time for profit, beautification, social planning or sometimes just redistribution. One of the more famous examples of this is the Dharavi slum in central Mumbai, which is over 100 years old with approximately 900,000 inhabitants and an estimated economy of USD 1 billion (Saglio-Yatzimirsky 2021). Dharavi, despite its claims to permanence and cultural importance in the city of Mumbai, is under constant and increasing threat of demolition and relocation as real estate developers promote grandiose plans to transform the slum, which occupies some of the most expensive real estate in the world (Boano et al. 2011, Weinstein 2014).

While residents from informal settlements play an essential role in the functioning of the city in economic sectors such as transport, food supply chains, unskilled and domestic labour and manufacturing, the presence of informal settlements is often resented by city elites, and informal settlements are a convenient scapegoat for the failure of the state to manage disease, crime, vice, congestion and aesthetic blight (Fattah & Walters 2020). The state retains the power to determine what is informal, illegal or tolerated.

Informality can then be understood as a 'governmental tool' or 'organisational device' (McFarlane 2012) that implies forms of intervention in relation to service provision and resource allocation. Thus, 'gray spaces' (Yiftachel 2009) become a common element of the city: 'In the urban policy sphere, including planning, gray spaces are usually tolerated quietly, even encouraged, while being encaged within discourses of "contamination", "criminality" and "public danger" to the desired "order of things"' (Yiftachel 2009: 89). Urban spatial planning becomes a potentially powerful governing tool with which to shape people's lives and subjectivities: 'Planning (or lack of it) provides the authorities with a set of technologies with which they can legalize, criminalize, incorporate or evict. Planning categories and mechanisms allow the loci of power to construct or destroy, "whiten" or "blacken" urban development and populations. The negotiation of gray space, either locally or regionally, has become in many cities the stuff of urban politics itself' (Yiftachel 2009: 96).

## CHALLENGING BINARIES

There is a tendency by some authors to see the formal and informal as a simple binary or urban dialectic. Recio et al. (2017) explain that in relation to informal economic activities, there are two streams: one that clearly distinguishes between formal and informal economic activities (e.g. Hanser 2016, Rukmana 2011) and a second one that recognises that formality and informality are one interlocking and mutually dependent system (Boudreau & Davis 2017, Sanyal & Bhattacharyya 2009).

A more useful perspective is to recognise the boundaries between formal and informal as porous and contingent through time and space. The whole city has a relationship as participant, client or opponent of informality depending on need and interest. Urban informality is 'an organizing logic, a system of norms that governs the process of urban transformation itself' (Roy 2005: 148). Informality is not a separate sector or realm but rather 'a series of transactions that connect different economies and spaces to one another… informality is a mode rather than a sector' (Roy 2005: 148). Boudreau and Davis (2017: 160) identify a similar phenomenon by arguing 'people living in cities think beyond rigid categories of the formal and the informal and the power relations involved in these uses and abuses of categories'. This binary distinction emerged from 'a set of power-relations centred on strengthening the positions of social and political elites – including planners and designers' (Doherty & Silva 2011: 32).

The meaning and extent of formality and informality is continually negotiated in the city. Thus, it is important to consider whether formality and informality are 'mutually enabling or delimiting, or increasingly asymmetrical and non-antonymic' (McFarlane 2012: 90). Acuto et al. (2019: 477) argue for the need to transcend 'the othering of informality for the benefit of a more inclusive urban theory contribution' that recognises and develops the theory required to understand the Southern city as a set of mutually constitutive elements. Binary thinking about informality situates it as something that requires either correction or eradication (Acuto et al. 2019). 'Correction' is sought by those who impose the rules for how formality (or the lack thereof) is defined, such as the state.

The simple binary of 'planned and unplanned' can be misleading. The often chaotic manner in which land use is partly planned, authorised, seized and re-allocated and rules are broken in cities in the Global South (Bhan 2013, Gururani 2013) defeats any attempt to draw clear lines of distinction between the entitled and un-entitled when it comes to land use. A degraded spatial identity can result in an inability to access the normal range of services and recognition granted to those in the more accepted formal realm of the city who have addresses, recognised employment and access to education (Fattah & Walters 2020, Perlman 2010).

## THE SOCIAL CONFIGURATIONS OF INFORMALITY

While the terms 'slum' or 'squatters' are used both in a general and derogatory sense for informal settlements, they are the sites of a rich set of social dynamics and hierarchies that give the southern city much of its vitality and will be discussed in more detail below. In 2003, UN-Habitat (2003: 9), following the ideas of Eckstein (1990), famously asked whether it was appropriate to talk about 'slums for hope' or 'slums for despair'. The former were considered '"progressing" settlements, which are characterized by new, normally self-built structures, usually illegal (e.g. squatters) that are in, or have recently been through, a process of development, consolidation and improvement', while the latter were viewed as '"declining" neighbourhoods, in which environmental conditions and domestic services are undergoing a process of degeneration'. This was the start of a challenge to the deficit conception of international agencies. Later this progressed into a 'continuum of land rights', acknowledging the diversity of land tenure situations (UN-Habitat 2008), followed by the recognition of 'the plurality of tenure types' in the New Urban Agenda (United Nations 2017).

An overly pessimistic rendering of slum life works to rob people living in these settlements of the agency that characterises everyday life and the adaptations people make to create secure lives and communities. Alongside the literature of deficit, exploitation and existential threat is a smaller literature that highlights the ingenuity, resourcefulness and entrepreneurship of the informal economy and its members. These qualities should not be romanticised – informality, particularly slum life, implies an absence of some of the most basic human rights to adequate shelter, services and ontological security. However, as a dominant and enduring quality of many cities, the ability of those living in informality to adapt, organise and improvise should also be acknowledged and theorised.

How does cohesion arise from a haphazard collection of roots, aspirations and livelihoods (Simone 2001)? The organisational and spatial logic of informal settlements that allows residents to function effectively for their own survival is a fundamental part of the functioning of the wider urban environment. In the next section we turn our analysis to the 'value' arising from informality in relation to the urban poor. We discuss this below in a range of social responses and adaptations to conditions of informality.

**Responsive Adaptation to Necessity**

Tonkiss describes informality as:

> flexible, responding to environmental conditions and limits, organized around habitual patterns of movement, and expressive of social solidarities, often around family or kinship networks. One of the key defences for informal modes of settlement is their adaptive quality, their capacity (usually born of necessity) to support different uses, as well as the physical flexibility that allows for extension and conversion. (Tonkiss 2014: 102)

As Bayat (1997) describes, when men and women find themselves in a city without the basics of life, they occupy what land they can and then organise to demand the provision of utilities. If these are not forthcoming, they resort to 'do it yourself mechanisms of acquiring them illegally' (Bayat 1997: 54). They establish roads to link a network of makeshift housing that is gradually improved over time. Residents organise garbage collection and hygiene in public areas. They establish small businesses catering to either an internal demand or demand from the wider city. They establish places of worship and rudimentary education and healthcare facilities. These improvements may be supported or facilitated by the state or NGOs. According to Carrero et al. (2019: 254), 'informal social networks consist of unofficial, non-institutional ties between individuals that stem from personal relations; ordinary socialising in an individual's living environment or in working and voluntary environments, neighbour-to-neighbour or peer-to-peer, respectively'. Sheppard et al. see the organising ability of informality as 'a survival strategy whereby the monetarily poor can compensate for their lack of income through commoning' (2020: 1). Their responsive capacity and adaptation are used as tools to overcome necessity.

Nijman (2010: 14), using Mumbai as an example, argues that it is the more organically created informal parts of the city that best reflect the 'sensual and rhythmic diversity' of urban space in the city, incorporating kinship and religious and artisanal traditions imported from the rural hinterland and adapted and sustained for urban life. It is these networks and webs of social capital that form the basis for reciprocity and resilience where it exists in informal urban settlements. Informal spaces 'make possible more-than-capitalist political norms, sociability, and informal exchange that exceed those of possessive individualism and capitalist markets' (Sheppard et al. 2020: 4). Sanyal and Bhattacharyya (2009: 38) make a similar argument when they describe a 'needs economy' as opposed to the accumulation economy; a space where the labour of the informal poor is closer to the 'moral economy of the peasant' serving the survival needs of communities, beyond the everyday exploitation of wage labour markets. These qualities of informality reflect a more socially embedded economic life than is possible under advanced neoliberalism and allow for communal responses to threats, as we continue to discuss below.

**Creativity and Innovation**

Although there is an extensive literature that addresses the deficiencies, exploitation and marginalisation of the informal, there is also a literature that is more positive and hopeful about informality as an important economic and social generator for cities in the Global South. Much of this literature focuses on the inherent creativity, adaptability and flexibility of informal economies and their participants (Phelps 2021). In Indonesia, where *kampung* is the term mostly used for urban informal settlements, the 'creative *kampung*' has recently been praised as a location where the 'creative economy' and innovation can be fostered. For example, in Solo (Surakarta) many *kampungs* take their name based on their main activity: Kampung Laweyan (*lawe*- means thread, referring to fabrics and *batik*) and Kampung Kemlayan (where *gamelan* makers live) (Rifai et al. 2023). In addition to the social and cultural elements embedded in the notion of *kampung*, the 'creative *kampung*' concept acknowledges the contribution of these locales to the economy of the city and further asserts their place in the urban fabric and popular imagination.

Following this logic, in Malang, Indonesia, two informal settlements have been recently transformed from invisible neighbourhoods to popular tourism destinations, visited and supported by local politicians (Sutikno 2023). In 2016, a group of students from a local university, in collaboration with a paint company, proposed to the residents of an informal settlement to paint the roofs of houses in an informal settlement with different colours as a marketing strategy. This was adopted by the community, which at this stage was just the recipient of the initiative. When the process was complete, the local mayor attended an 'opening ceremony'. The local community then initiated a process of 'slum tourism', where people come and visit the settlement by paying a small fee. Following this success, the community of a second settlement decided to create 3D photographic spots in their neighbourhood with the support of local students. This was later supported by the mayor who, using informal channels, requested the paint company to also support these residents to paint their roofs. Both settlements have now become very popular local tourist destinations. They use the funding from the entrance and the parking fees to support the needs of the community members, such as financial hardships or sickness. This example shows not only the entrepreneurship and creativity of both students and residents of informal settlements but also how the formal/informal binary fails to explain these more complex processes in which, despite being informal and therefore not really part of city planning, these locales become visible and even formally supported by city authorities.

## Resistance

The logic of informality is formed by tacit rules and cultural norms, social conventions, routine practices and the requirement for various forms of resistance to the depredations and abandonment of the rest of the city. It does not only follow a logic of survival or subsistence but in many cases the need for survival translates into insurgency and transgression (Fattah & Walters 2020). While this can be initially seen as a survival response, it can also become a more subtle but complex response opposing the dominant systems and groups and encouraging a different logic of everyday practices (Bayat 1997). Insurgency, while often in the pursuit of basic survival, can be used to counterbalance the hegemony of dominant groups, including the state and formal urban planning.

Insurgency also allows informal settlers to establish how inclusion is defined, challenging the idea that participation merely refers to incorporating civil society and the public in decision-making processes (Miraftab 2009). Insurgency helps to establish a conversation on how and when grassroots organisations want to become involved in the processes established by formal power. Informal workers and residents who develop insurgent practices 'invent' their spaces for action (Miraftab 2009).

Informal settlements and the logic of necessity produce citizens, particularly local leaders who become hardened and adept at negotiating with the formal structures their world intersects, including local politicians, law enforcement, landowners and other gatekeepers (Appadurai 2001). These leaders often form the core of, or are supported by, networks of grassroots NGOs who not only work to fill the gap between the entitlements of ordinary citizens and the deficits experienced by those who live in a state of partial citizenship and that selective recognition creates for those who live in informal settlements. As an example of this, Fattah and Walters (2023) describe an effective protest in 2012 against a state-initiated slum clearance in the interests of private developers by local leaders of an informal settlement in Dhaka, Bangladesh. In what they describe as a 'contrary mobilisation', in a deliberately peaceful demonstration coordinated by community leaders and grassroots NGOs, thousands of the urban poor halted the earthmoving equipment sent in to demolish their homes and created a gridlock in the city. This very public and visible demonstration of resistance caused the demolition to be postponed for long enough for local leaders, with legal assistance from NGOs, to mount a high court case to have their homes protected, setting a fragile precedent for future slum clearances.

The invention of new spaces for collective action by informal settlers requires constant adaptability to the external conditions that constrain or enable their actions. It also requires the creation of alliances with similar collectives to gain wider visibility and thus become 'invited' actors who receive legitimation from dominant actors (Miraftab 2009). There is a constant and fluid relationship of interaction and mutual constitution between invited and invented spaces for action (Miraftab 2009). A recent example of this is the case of Kampung Akuarium in Jakarta, Indonesia where residents, using their collective voice and with the involvement of local NGOs, survived a planned eviction and demolition and managed to become part of the decision-making process for an in situ upgrading of their housing (Sarih et al. 2023).

**Informal Space and Social Organisation**

Neuwirth (2011) refers to the power of informal community organisation as 'system D', borrowed from the French '*l'economie de la débrouille*' (the ingenuity economy):

> ...the ingenuity economy, the economy of improvisation and self-reliance, the do-it-yourself, or DIY, economy... It is a product of intelligence, resilience, self-organization, and group solidarity, and it follows a number of well-worn though unwritten rules. It is, in that sense, a system. (Neuwirth 2011: 20)

The will-to-community requires local leadership, which either emerges organically or through existing cultural, religious or kinship structures. It is this ability to organise and respond that constitutes one of the key 'assets' of poor communities. In some cases, this leadership is shared and distributed democratically; for example, in Yogyakarta, Indonesia, Kalijawi, a female collective of informal settlers with whom we have been working for several years, has a formal leadership structure (Roitman 2019a). However, roles usually rotate annually, as decided in the annual meeting of the organisation when the action plan for the following year is discussed. The activities by Kalijawi to provide financial support to their members reflect this relationship between invented and invited, formal and informal, as mutually constituted conditions. The organisation has formed savings groups in 16 informal settlements (230 members in total) to provide financial assistance to residents who do not have access to formal banking institutions. Members of the savings groups can borrow money for individual or community projects and pay back the loans with low interest rates. The continuation and success of the group is based on the trust of the members and the collective support. The savings collected since 2014 have formed a Community Development Fund with nearly USD 50,000. In 2020, the members of the savings groups decided to form a social enterprise, which is registered as a business unit by the government (Murwani et al. 2023). This has provided legitimacy to Kalijawi and the savings group members. These informal savings groups become part of this formal organisation (cooperative) shifting from informal to formal, showing that they are informal (savings groups) and formal (cooperative) at the same time.

**Responsive Adaptation to Disasters and Crises**

Disasters, including floods, fires, earthquakes, volcanic eruptions and droughts and health crises, such as the Covid-19 pandemic, all of which have become more frequent, often have a greater impact on poor residents, and especially those living in informal settlements. Informal responses to disasters are a very important element of the recovery of many communities and cities in the Global South. Residents from informal settlements are obliged to deal with threats to their existence without the resources enjoyed in more affluent neighbourhoods. For this reason, urban informal residents are required to demonstrate an endogenous resilience to threats and disasters, rather than rely upon any support provided by wider metropolitan institutions or norms of support (Padawangi & Douglass 2015, Walters 2015).

When Mumbai was flooded in 2005, slum dwellers, who were the worst affected by the disaster, provided spontaneous help not only to fellow slum residents but also to other city residents, rescuing people stranded in cars or buses and offering tea, water and food (McFarlane 2012). Thus, slum residents 'were seen to demonstrate an infrastructure of generosity and hospitality in the face of severe and multiple network infrastructure collapse' (McFarlane 2012: 96).

Analysing the responses to an earthquake in Nepal, Carrero et al. (2019: 563) discuss the significance of the informal networks of actors that 'emerge comparatively quickly to cater for the un-met needs', calling them 'tacit networks' that provide crucial care. These relations happen outside formal organisations but are in constant dialogue with the formal planning system. Therefore, there is a need for the formal system to recognise the value and significance of the contribution of informal responses to disaster recovery.

In Arua, Uganda, a region which faces regular dry seasons, water is very scarce. Residents of informal settlements need to travel at least 30 minutes to get access to water. This has a significant impact on women and girls, who are usually responsible for providing water to households, who might drop school to attend household chores, including water collection, and are exposed to sexual harassment while walking great distances to find water. The communities living in some districts of Arua have organised themselves to first conduct a settlement survey to collect data on the needs of these neighbourhoods. Self-surveying (known as 'enumeration') as a means of governmentality from below provides more than abstract shape and texture to slum communities, in comparison to formal governments who do not bother to collect such data (Appadurai 2001). After the survey, supported by the National Slum Dwellers Federation of Uganda, Arua region branch, water shortage was identified as the most pressing need to be addressed. With the support of the Federation, six water units were installed in 2012. Residents pay a small fee for the jerry cans to cover the costs of these works (ACTogether 2021). These responses from below show how communities at a micro level of the neighbourhood manage to provide solutions to structural problems (climate change and disasters and lack of government support).

## CONCLUSIONS

Urban sociology as a discipline is incomplete without the recognition that it is the cities of the Global South that will provide the most pressing challenges and opportunities for scholarship in the 21st century. Old notions of urban political economy, post-industrialisation and suburbanisation are now questions that require reframing in light of the growth and dynamism of cities in Asia, Africa and Latin America. It is also important to understand that urban sociology cannot continue to characterise Southern cities as just a function of a colonial past. While Southern economies continue to suffer the effects of developmentalism and structural readjustment imposed by the North, global cities in the South have their own socio-spatial and economic logics. Binaries that divide the city into formal and informal will do little to help urban sociologists to understand the ways that global challenges like climate change are affecting the cities' most vulnerable groups and how dense networks of mutual dependency across whole cities should respond and adapt.

The positive construction of informal social life that emphasises self-organisation, entrepreneurship and creativity must be tempered by the constraints of political oppression, neglect and neoliberal exploitation that characterise the conditions of slum life (Roy 2011). Informal places are constantly at risk of existential obliteration, ontological disappearance or 'domicide' (Porteous et al. 2001) and so the meaning created by attachment to place is invested with existential anxiety.

An undeniable reality for informal settlements is precariousness, poverty and stigmatisation. In response to these deficits, much of the literature on informality focuses on poverty and poverty alleviation, with a development focus. There is less focus on the nature of social organisation in informal populations and its importance in underwriting the resilience of informal communities and indeed the wider social and economic functioning of the city. To ignore the politics and social organisation of everyday life, or 'slum habitus', is to 'ignore the urbanism that is the life and livelihood of much of the world's humanity' (Roy 2011: 228). As an integral part of the functioning of the city, informal settlements and economic networks in most cases operate remarkably efficiently within the constraints imposed on them by poverty, oppression and stigmatisation.

The practices of informal settlers at the community and neighbourhood levels seek to respond and adapt creatively to the negative effects that stigmatisation and formal neglect bring. The analysis of the social logic of informality contributes to urban sociology by demonstrating how the agency and resilience of the residents in informal settlements is in constant interaction with structural effects.

To properly understand the way that informality works in poor cities requires a 'decolonisation' of approaches to everyday social life in these places (Robinson 2002). The decolonisation of research allows researchers to take on the perspective of the informal subject and observe the important place of informality in the life and economies in cities of the Global South. This is not to say that the North should abandon its efforts to improve conditions of life in the

Global South, but a less colonising perspective on research (Robinson 2002), particularly one that recognises the rich theorisation of Southern authors and activists, may better inform development institutions and donors of where their resources are best devoted. Rather than treating cities just as places with a deficit of development, urban scholarship needs to incorporate the level and quality of theorisation that is devoted to cities in wealthier contexts. There are myriad possibilities to extend and deepen the corpus of explanatory devices for poor cities, where the vast weight of urban growth will be focused in the 21st century.

## REFERENCES

Abramo, P. (2012) La ciudad informal com-fusa: El mercado y la producción de la territorialidad urbana popular. In Salazar, C. (ed.) *Irregular. Suelo y mercado en América Latina*. Mexico: El Colegio de Mexico, 85–124.

ACTogether (2021) Together we can do more. ACTogether Uganda Blog. Available at https://actogetheruganda959867238.wordpress.com/2021/07/28/together-we-can-do-more/ (accessed 31 January 2022).

Acuto, M., Dinardi, C. & Marx, C. (2019) Transcending (inf)formal urbanism. *Urban Studies* 56(3): 475–487.

Allen, A. et al. (2006) *Governance of Water and Sanitation Services for the Peri-urban Poor. A Framework for Understanding and Action in Metropolitan Regions*. London: DPU.

Appadurai, A. (2001) Deep democracy: Urban governmentality and the horizon of politics. *Environment and Urbanization* 13(2): 23–43.

Bayat, A. (1997) Un-civil society: The politics of the 'informal people'. *Third World Quarterly* 18(1): 53–72.

Bhan, G. (2013) Planned illegalities: Housing and the 'failure' of planning in Delhi: 1947–2010. *Economic and Political Weekly* 48(24): 58–70.

Boano, C., Lamarca, M. G. & Hunter, W. (2011) The frontlines of contested urbanism mega-projects and mega-resistances in Dharavi. *Journal of Developing Societies* 27(3–4): 295–326.

Boudreau, J.-A. & Davis, D. E. (2017) Introduction: A processual approach to informalization. *Current Sociology* 65(2): 151–166.

Carrero, R., Acuto, M., Tzachor, A., Subedi, N., Campbell, B. & To, L. S. (2019) Tacit networks, crucial care: Informal networks and disaster response in Nepal's 2015 Gorkha earthquake. *Urban Studies* 56(3): 561–577.

Devlin, R. T. (2019) A focus on needs: Toward a more nuanced understanding of inequality and urban informality in the Global North. *Journal of Cultural Geography* 36(2), 121–143.

Doherty, G. & Silva, L. (2011) Formally informal: Daily life and the shock of order in a Brazilian favela. *Built Environment* 37(1): 30–41.

Eckstein, S. (1990) Urbanization revisited: Inner-city slum of hope and squatter settlement of despair. *World Development* 18(2): 165–181.

Fahmi, W. S. & Sutton, K. (2006) Cairo's zabaleen garbage recyclers: Multi-nationals' take over and state relocation plans. *Habitat International* 30: 809–837.

Fattah, K. N. & Walters, P. (2020) 'A good place for the poor!' Counternarratives to territorial stigmatisation from two informal settlements in Dhaka. *Social Inclusion* 8(1): 55–65.

Fattah, K. & Walters, P. (2023) Locating agency at the urban grassroots: Resistance and reworking in the everyday politics of informal settlements. *Geoforum* 141: 103703.

Gururani, S. (2013) Flexible planning: The making of India's 'millennium city', Gurgaon. In Rademacher, A. & Sivaramakrishnan, K. (eds.) *Ecologies of Urbanism in India*. Hong Kong: Hong Kong University Press, 119–143.

Hanser, A. (2016) Street politics: Street vendors and urban governance in China. *The China Quarterly* 226: 1–20.

Kudva, N. (2009) The everyday and the episodic: The spatial and political impacts of urban informality. *Environment and Planning A* 41(7): 1614–1628.

Lemanski, C. & Marx, C. (2015) Introduction. In Lemanski, C. & Marx, C. (eds.) *The City in Urban Poverty*. Basingstoke: Palgrave Macmillan, 1–12.
Lombard, M. (2015) Constructing informality and ordinary places: A place-making approach to urban informal settlements. In Lemanski, C. & Marx, C. (eds.) *The City in Urban Poverty.* Basingstoke: Palgrave Macmillan, 85–110.
McFarlane, C. (2012) Rethinking informality: Politics, crisis, and the city. *Planning Theory & Practice* 13(1): 89–108.
Miraftab, F. (2009) Insurgent planning: Situating radical planning in the Global South. *Planning Theory* 8(1): 32–50.
Murwani, A., Rochayati, A., Surati, Utami, W., Susilah, Cahyanti, E., Sujiyanti, Mulia, J. & Roitman, S. (2023) Community organisation and neighbourhood improvement through collective action and bottom-up gender planning in Yogyakarta. In Roitman, S. & Rukmana, D. (eds.) *The Routledge Handbook of Urban Indonesia*. Routledge: New York and Abingdon: 102–116.
Neuwirth, R. (2011) *Stealth of Nations: The Global Rise of the Informal Economy*. New York: Anchor.
Nijman, J. (2010) A study of space in Mumbai's slums. *Tijdschrift voor economische en sociale geografie* 101(1): 4–17.
Padawangi, R. & Douglas, M. (2015) Water, water everywhere: Towards participatory solutions to chronic urban flooding in Jakarta. *Pacific Affairs* 88(3): 517–550.
Perlman, J. (2010) *Favela: Four Decades of Living on the Edge in Rio de Janeiro*. Oxford: Oxford University Press.
Phelps, N. A. (2021). The inventiveness of informality: An introduction. *International Development Planning Review* 43(1): 1–12.
Porteous, J. D. & Smith, S. E. (2001) *Domicide: The Global Destruction of Home*. Montreal: McGill-Queen's University Press.
Recio, R., Mateo-Babiano, D. & Roitman, S. (2017) Revisiting policy epistemologies on urban informality: Towards a post-dualist view. *Cities* 61: 136–143.
Rifai, A., Asterina, N., Hidayani, R. & Phelps, N. (2023) The creativity of the *Kampung*. In Roitman, S. & Rukmana, D. (eds.) *The Routledge Handbook of Urban Indonesia*. New York and Abingdon: Routledge, 248–260.
Robinson, J. (2002) Global and world cities: A view from off the map. *International Journal of Urban and Regional Research* 26(3): 531–554.
Roitman, S. (2019a) Slum dwellers strategies and tactics in Yogyakarta, Indonesia. In Rocco, R., & Van Ballegoijen, J. (eds.) *The Routledge Handbook on Informal Urbanisation*. Abingdon: Routledge, 281–292.
Roitman, S. (2019b) Urban activism in Yogyakarta, Indonesia: Deprived and discontented citizens demanding a more just city. In Yip, N., Martínez, M. & Sun, X. (eds.) *Contested Cities and Urban Activism – East and West, North and South*. Singapore: Springer Singapore, 147–174.
Roy, A. (2005) Urban informality: Toward an epistemology of planning. *JAPA* 71(2): 147–158.
Roy, A. (2011) Slumdog cities: Rethinking subaltern urbanism. *International Journal of Urban and Regional Research* 35(2): 223–238.
Rukmana, D. (2011) Street vendors and planning in Indonesian cities. *Planning Theory & Practice* 12(1): 138–144.
Saglio-Yatzimirsky, M.-C. (2021) *Dharavi: From Mega-slum to Urban Paradigm*. London: Routledge.
Sanyal, K. & Bhattacharyya, R. (2009) Beyond the factory: Globalisation, informalisation of production and the new locations of labour. *Economic and Political Weekly* 44(22): 35–44.
Sarih, A., Hermintomo, A., Irawaty, D. & Tanny, V. (2023), Participation within the insurgent planning practices: A case of Kampung Susun Akuarium, Jakarta. In Roitman, S. & Rukmana, D. (eds.) *The Routledge Handbook of Urban Indonesia*. New York and Abingdon: Routledge, 58–72.
Sheppard, E., Sparks, T. & Leitner, H. (2020) World class aspirations, urban informality, and poverty politics: A North-South comparison. *Antipode* 52(2): 393–407.
Simone, A. (2001) Straddling the divides: Remaking associational life in the informal African city. *International Journal of Urban and Regional Research* 25(1): 102–117.
Sultana, F., Mohanty, C. & Miraglia, S. (2016) Gender equity, citizenship and public water in Bangladesh. In McDonald, D. (ed.) *Making Public in a Privatized World*. London: Zed Books, 149–164.

Sutikno, F. (2023) Community action and legibility of the state: The case of Malang. In Roitman, S. & Rukmana, D. (eds.) *The Routledge Handbook of Urban Indonesia*. New York and Abingdon: Routledge, 88–101.

Tonkiss, F. (2014) *Cities by Design: The Social Life of Urban Form*. Cambridge: Polity.

UN-Habitat (2003) *The Challenge of Slums. Global Report on Human Settlements 2003*. London: Earthscan.

UN-Habitat (2008) *Secure Land Rights for All: Global Land Tools Network*. Nairobi: UN-Habitat.

UN-Habitat (2016). *Slum Almanac 2015–2016*. UN-Habitat. https://unhabitat.org/slum-almanac-2015-2016-0.

United Nations (2017) *New Urban Agenda*. Document including index. New York: Habitat III Secretariat.

Walters, P. (2015) The problem of community resilience in two flooded cities: Dhaka 1998 and Brisbane 2011. *Habitat International* 50: 51–56.

Walters, P. (2018) The limits to participation: Urban poverty and community driven development in Rajshahi City, Bangladesh. *Community Development* 49(5): 539–555.

Watson, V. (2009) Seeing from the South: Refocusing urban planning on the globe's central urban issues. *Urban Studies* 46(11): 2259–2275.

Weinstein, L. (2014) *The Durable Slum: Dharavi and the Right to Stay Put in Globalizing Mumbai*. Minnesota: University of Minnesota Press.

World Bank (2019). *The Long Shadow of Informality*. World Bank. https://thedocs.worldbank.org/en/doc/37511318c092e6fd4ca3c60f0af0bea3-0350012021/related/Informal-economy-Chapter-1.pdf.

World Bank (2020) Supporting Africa's urban informal sector: Coordinated policies with social protection at the core. Retrieved from https://blogs.worldbank.org/africacan/supporting-africas-urban-informal-sector-coordinated-policies-social-protection-core (accessed 7 July 2023).

Yiftachel, R. (2009) Critical theory and 'gray space': Mobilization of the colonized. *City* 13(2): 246–263.

# Rethinking China's urbanisation through informal politics

Yunpeng Zhang

Since its opening up to the global capitalist market in 1978, the world has witnessed drastic social, economic, and spatial reconfigurations in China. Although statistical measurement of rural-to-urban migration is critiqued for the bounded view of cities (Brenner & Schmid 2014), it still provides a useful snapshot of the breathtaking speed and scale of urbanisation in China. Whereas around 26 per cent of the Chinese population lived in cities in 1990 (an increase of less than 9 per cent from the number in 1978), the urban population surpassed the rural population for the first time in 2010 and accounted for 60 per cent of the total population as of 2019 (China Statistics Bureau 2021). Despite mounting challenges from rapid urbanisation within a short span of three decades, continuous urbanisation remains an uncompromising goal of the Chinese state for the years to come (The State Council 2014).

China's urbanisation trajectory has inspired considerable urban studies scholarship. As explained in the next section, the bulk of the existing literature revolves around the state–capital nexus, which has offered great insights into *why* cities were built so fast in China. This chapter enriches the existing literature by focussing on the question of *how* cities were made. Specifically, it zooms into the informal, illicit practices of state actors, developers, and denizens involved in turning rural settlements into a modernist, master-planned new city in Yangzhou in eastern China. The intent is not to downplay the importance of formal, licit practices. Rather, as urban development is subject to proliferating regulations in post-reform China, the interest is to render more visible the prevalence of under-researched informal and illicit city-making activities in China (Zhu 2012). In line with recent discussions on informality (Goodfellow 2020, Smart 2018), this chapter will show that informal and illicit practices are not exceptional but integral to the planning and construction of a new city, testifying to what Chiodelli and Gentili (2021) call the many shades of grey in urban development and governance.

Although informal settlements and labour practices are important to note (Swider 2015, Wu 2022a), they are not the focus of this chapter. Practices under study here are related to coalition-building, city-making, and land-taking activities. They are explored in two sections. The first of these looks from the side of the ad hoc project-based pro-growth coalition of state agents and developers. Theories of the urban growth machine and urban regime have been applied, with adjustment, to explain urban expansion and urban development in China (Chien & Woodworth 2018, Jiang et al. 2016, Zhang 2002). This chapter shows that this alliance was not formed automatically nor simply from formal, licit channels and arrangements. Instead, it was facilitated by informal and illicit practices, such as under-the-table agreements, circulation of favours, or outright corruption. Informality and illicitness were not the result of the absence of state recognition but were actively used by state agents in urban development and productive of formal state practices (Roy 2005).

The next section turns the lens to affected residents. As discussed in the literature, affected residents in China have not been passive but have deployed a wide range of discursive and material and individual and collective tactics to defend their rights in the process of land-taking and property dispossession (Hsing 2010). Similarly, in the urbanisation project in Yangzhou discussed below, residents fought back. It is notable that most residents resorted to informal bargaining, personal networks, and some illicit activities to negotiate for a better deal. At times, they did so under the tolerance or even with the help of the township officials and village cadres who were deployed to the frontline of displacements. However, although residents used informal tactics to bargain for better terms of compensation, one should avoid romanticising informal practices (Banks et al. 2020). Whilst providing residents a means to squeeze more compensation out of the pro-growth coalition, they were not capable of stopping the bulldozers' wheels or shaping the planning or construction of the new city in a meaningful way. Importantly, residents had to take advantage of the ambiguity afforded by informal practices because of various constraints whilst the tolerance of denizens' informal practices remained arbitrarily controlled by agents of the state.

## THEORISING CHINA'S URBANISATION

### Beyond the Capital/State Dichotomy

Before China's market-oriented reforms began in 1978, a sharp rural–urban divide existed. This was created by the *hukou* system, which categorised the Chinese people into two classes—the rural population and the urban population. In the countryside, People's Communes organised rural production and rural households were exploited to support industrialisation. Urban economies on the other hand were organised by work units, or *danwei* in Chinese, which provided welfare to urbanites. Planned to serve industrial production, cities under the planned economy lacked investments in collective consumption, such as housing and urban infrastructures. Functioning like an internal passport system (Chan 2009), the *hukou* system strictly restricted population movements between rural and urban areas. The market-oriented reforms transformed socio-economic organisations of China. Although *hukou*-induced inequalities and exclusion still persist in China, after several reforms, *hukou* no longer limits population movements, thus clearing the barriers to urbanisation.

Urbanisation is a multidimensional process entailing changes in material landscapes, regulatory frames, and lived experiences (Brenner & Schmid 2015). It is notoriously challenging to accurately measure China's urbanisation rate. One reason is the lack of consistent census data. Different criteria have been used to determine who counts as urbanites. The other reason is related to the adjustment of jurisdictional boundaries, which at times can create cities through merging or annexing territorial units (Liu & Fan 2015). The consensus of the existing literature is that urbanisation of land has been occurring at a much faster speed than that of the population since the 1990s (Sorace & Hurst 2016). What this means is that more land is consumed for urban expansion yet many people, despite living in cities, remain excluded from decent urban lives. Ghost cities and the exclusion of renters' children from accessing quality education are telling examples in this regard (Shepard 2015, Wu et al. 2018).

A large body of literature has been generated to unravel the mechanisms of urbanisation in China. Most of this literature revolves around the state–capital nexus, contributing to bringing

...ilarities of China's urbanisation experiences (Wang 2020, Wu 2018). The
lens extends Harvey's geographical political economy approach (Harvey 1978)
...rbanisation, as spaces of capital accumulation, to China's evolving accumulation
...In his theories of urbanisation of capital, Harvey distinguishes three circuits of
...ie primary circuit of industrial production, the secondary circuit of built environment
...ion, and the tertiary circuit of expenditures in sciences, technology, and labour power
...duction (Harvey 1978). In times of accumulation crises, capital may be switched between
...its or places, thereby temporarily resolving crises. Seen in this light, urbanisation as built
...vironment production provides a spatial fix (Harvey 2001) to capitalist accumulation crises.

Extending this perspective to China, China's opening up in the late 1970s and subsequent shift to urbanisation as built environment production provides an outlet for both domestic and international surplus capital to restore profitability. Revenues generated in the process in turn have enabled the Chinese state to finance public goods and spend on social expenditures (e.g., expanding social welfare networks; namely, the tertiary circuit) (Andreas & Zhan 2016). They have also allowed many local governments to subsidise costs of land acquisitions for building industrial facilities and of labour reproduction, thereby supporting capital accumulation in the primary circuit (Huang 2011). Therefore, in China, capital accumulation via the secondary circuit is occurring in tandem with capital accumulation in the primary circuit and contributes, at least partially, to labour welfare. This is distinct from the property boom underpinned by large flows of surplus capital to real estate development in many European and North American cities in the past two decades (Christophers 2011, Coq-Huelva 2013). It is also different from urbanisation experiences in many Southern cities which, according to Schindler (2017), feature the primacy of capital investments in real estate and infrastructure development and a disconnect between capital and labour as the formal economic sectors are unable to absorb wage labourers.

The different patterns of capital circulations in China may be partially explained by the roles played by the Chinese state. From a state-centric perspective, the extant literature has explored regulatory changes and resulting effects on accumulation strategies, the built environment, and intra-state relations (Hsing 2010, Pan et al. 2016, Rithmire 2015). As revealed in this branch of the literature, reforms of land management in the late 1980s cleared the barriers to land commodification whereas fiscal and tax reforms in the 1990s strengthened the central government's control of local budgets and took away the majority of several important taxes from local governments. Until very recently, career evaluation and progression of leading state agents depended on GDP growth (Zhang et al. 2022). These changes created an incentive structure for local governments to shift from rural industrialisation to extract landed revenues from urbanisation (Lin 2014). China's state-dominated land management system—state monopoly of the conversion of collectively owned rural land into state ownership for urban development—makes this shift possible.

Against this backdrop, as Hsing (2010) astutely observed, land has replaced tax to become a key object of political bargaining since the 1990s. Battles for land control have been waged from both within and outside the state. Many rural settlements in former urban fringes were demolished, often involving excessive violence, to give way to urban expansion. Those in remote rural areas have also been absorbed into urban-centric accumulation through instruments like development rights transfer (Zhang 2018). Development rights transfer is often used by local governments to circumvent rigid land use planning, which determines fixed amounts of land available to local governments for developments within a planned period.

By demolishing rural settlements in remote areas where land values are low, development rights transfer schemes allow local governments to acquire additional developable land quotas cheaply to accommodate urban expansion in peri-urban areas where land values are high. In so doing, local governments can capture differential rents and make a profit. However, local governments' pursuit of capital accumulation via the built environment production does not always square well with the central government's interest in socio-economic stability and environment protection (Zhang 2018). In response, the central government periodically tightens its grip on local governments (He 2019). The more recent literature on urban development since the 2010s points to a shift in development rationalities beyond growth (Wu et al. 2021).

Operating on an abstract level, both capital-centric and state-centric approaches offer great insights into the driving forces and state politics underlying China's urbanisation. They also chart out, in broad strokes, macro changes in Chinese politics, economy, and society. However, both approaches weakly capture the embodied experiences of city-making. The debates on growth coalitions and informal politics, as discussed next, offer useful conceptual tools for intervention.

**City-making Coalitions, Political Informality, and *Biantong***

Both urban growth machine theory and urban regime theory have a strong appeal to students of China's urbanisation for the explication of relations of power and interests underpinning China's urbanisation. Derived from observation of urban politics in the USA, both theories share an interest in the coalition of state agents and a place-bounded rentier class. The growth machine theory looks at the relations of property and attributes the formation of a growth-oriented coalition to the shared landed interests of business communities, public officials, financial institutions, property-owning classes, and other similar groups (Molotch 1976). This shared interest motivates their pursuit of strategies to commodify places and maximise land's exchange values. Urban regime theory on the other hand has a more expansive focus that goes beyond growth (Stone 1993). It holds that resources required to govern cities are fragmented, hence the need for public agencies to form networks with other local actors, especially business elites. However, participants drawn into a coalition may be driven by various agendas (e.g., environment protection, affordable housing), reflective of the social, political, and economic conditions. Thus, the patterns and outcomes of urban regimes vary in times and places.

In extending these theories to China, many urban China studies have rightly cautioned against overly stretching both theories to conceive the politics of urban development in China. To qualify a coalition as a regime, it needs to be more enduring and revolve around an explicit agenda. In China, by contrast, many coalitions are more ad hoc and project-based (Ren 2011). Whilst urban regimes are often considered to be city-level coalitions, the national government has a more significant influence in urban governance and development in China, especially in large-scale urban projects (Wu 2018, Zhang & Wu 2008). In addition to growth, socialist ideologies and redistributive goals have also been found to be important agendas for actors involved in development coalitions (Rithmire 2015). This is perhaps most evident when state-owned enterprises are involved. Unlike private businesses which are driven by their interest in profits, state-owned enterprises are believed to often-times prioritise extra-economic goals (Tsai & Naughton 2015).

However, this literature inadequately explains how the urban coalition comes into existence in the first place. Renewed debates on informality provide an entry point. This may appear counter-intuitive as debates on informality conventionally focus on the poor. Informality is seen as a sign of exclusion and marginalisation, resulting from unplanned or unregulated activities (Banks et al. 2020). Conversely, it has been celebrated as a form of resistance by those excluded or marginalised to claim their rights (Varley 2013). Moreover, existing research has called into question the blurring boundaries of formal/informal and licit/illicit (Lund 2006, Roy 2005) and the tendency to reinforce the normative hierarchy rendering those classified as informal inferior to those deemed to be formal (Banks et al. 2020, Bromley & Wilson 2018).

These conceptual challenges notwithstanding, as Banks et al. (2020) argue, informality remains a useful lens to unravel enduring patterns and practices in urban development. Focussing on informality may also help to bring analyses of pro-growth coalitions in China closer to Stone's (1989: 6) conceptualisation of the constitution of a regime through 'the informal arrangements.' To this end, Banks et al. (2020) advocate for a critical analysis of the evolving positions of the state in informality and the state–society interactions, since informality is often defined as the suspension or circumvention of state regulations. Relatedly, as Banks et al. (2020) suggest, research ought to broaden its scope and investigate the subjectivities and agency of a more diverse group of social actors, including the more resourceful economic or political elites. Just as the poor may take advantage of informality to improve their conditions, those already in privileged positions may exploit informality to consolidate their advantage and dominance.

For instance, against the Foucauldian understanding of knowledge as an instrument of the state to control populations and territories, Roy (2009) demonstrates how confusion about land ownership, strategically created by the Indian state, enables it to maintain flexibility in territorial organisation and speculative land development. Similarly, in response to the strange neglect of political informality in Western Europe, a growing body of literature problematises how informality, often framed as 'innovation' to improve urban interventions and governance, is increasingly tolerated by the state for the benefits of businesses (Jaffe & Koster 2019, Ward 2022). Stressing criminality and its connection with housing informality in urban development, Weinstein's (2008) work on India shows how large mafias, supported by political and other local elites, emerged as dominant land players and profiteered from real estate developments. The study by Chiodelli (2019) similarly underscores the roles of organised crime in incentivising informal, illicit housing construction by, in most cases, people who have economic resources and political connections. These studies show that informality can contribute to reproducing social inequality.

Within the literature on Chinese politics, there is a plethora of studies on political informality, especially in relation to state actors. Focussing on the everyday state, Sun (2004) demonstrates that flexibilisation of formal rules, policies, or regulations—or *biantong* in Chinese—by subnational state units is one of the defining features of China's market-oriented reforms. Sun (2004) identifies various *biantong* practices, which can be broadly grouped into: 1) 'entrepreneurial' interpretation and adaptation of existing regulations and policies; 2) strategic prioritisation or partial implementation of different components of policies, rules, or directives; and 3) exploitation of the regulatory vacuum and ambiguities (or 'playing the edge ball' in the literal translation of *da cabianqiu* in Chinese). *Biantong* however should be distinguished from informal state practices that are better characterised as 'illicit.' As Sun (2004) suggests, *biantong* does not necessarily entail outright violation or suspension of laws and regulations. Admittedly, some practices operate on the margin of the regulatory space and seek to expand the regulatory boundary. Yet, for the most part, *biantong* practices attempt to derive legitimacy by invoking existing laws and regulations, however remotely relevant these laws or regulations are. They are neither completely compliant with nor contradictory to existing rules and regulations.

Following this debate, this chapter examines the role of informality in mediating the process of making a master-planned new city in Yangzhou. The new city is a space of capital accumulation and testifies to the interest of the local governments in monetising land. In a crude way, I divide actors involved into three groups—developers, state actors, and affected residents. None of these groups should be considered to be coherent. Rather, within each group, actors may have sometimes conflicting interests and aspirations. The first two constituted the ad hoc project-based pro-growth coalition for the planning and construction of the new city. Relative to residents, given their command of resources, they were in a more dominant position. They were also more prepared and more apt at evading existing regulations. Informality then became an opportunity and a resource for them to accumulate profits from the urbanisation project.

The informality of the pro-growth coalition is central to this chapter. Complementing the extant literature, I will also look into political informality that emerges from state agents' multiple identities (Bénit-Gbaffou 2018). This perspective takes into account the embodied experiences of state agents. Whilst representing the state in public administration and governance, state actors are also members of families, communities, and networks of varying natures and therefore subject to extra-state values (à la Migdal (2001)). The multiple embeddedness of state agents may become an advantage for them in building networks among non-state actors, which can be important for carrying out everyday administration. It can further blur the boundary between the state and society. In many cases, this could give rise to clientelism or corruption. Alternatively, as illustrated below, it may be used by affected residents constrained by resources to improve their positions in the negotiations during land clearance.

Understanding the multiple embeddedness is particularly important to explain the behaviours and rationales of (quasi-)state agents deployed to the frontline to persuade rural residents to give up their homes and land for the planned new city, especially township and village cadres. Whereas the township is the lowest level of government in China, villages are not. Strictly speaking, village cadres are not civil servants or state officials. They are, supposedly, representatives of villagers elected to autonomously govern their villages, as mandated by the Organic Law of the Villagers' Committee of the People's Republic of China (first introduced in 1987 and amended in 1998 and again in 2010). Whilst the introduction of village elections was celebrated as a sign of grassroots democracy and civil society empowerment, in practice the Communist Party still exercises strong influence over village elections and administratively controls the operation of Villagers' Committees (He 2007). Village-level party branches often share offices with Villagers' Committees and influence personnel appointments and major decisions such as the use of village assets. Villagers' Committees also implement policies and carry out day-to-day administration of rural affairs. Thus, they are the 'governments next door' (Tomba 2014) in rural settings. Most village cadres are members of villages. In recent years, however, a growing number of college graduates are being recruited from outside villages to improve rural governance. In exchange for their services, these graduates are offered accelerated career promotions within the state bureaucracy. Thus, village cadres can still be seen as agents of the state. Their 'collusion' with rural residents throws the fissures within the state into sharp relief. It also further dissolves the binaries of formal/informal and licit/illicit.

Armed with these studies, I examine the mediation of political informality in urbanisation using a case from Yangzhou. I focus on the material aspects of urbanisation, namely the process of land clearance and real estate development. Since the early 2000s, local governments in Yangzhou have actively promoted several mega-urbanisation projects. These mega-urbanisation projects are sites of capital accumulation, enabling local governments to boost GDP growth and extract fiscal revenues from land and real estate development. Existing rural settlements were demolished to give way to urban expansion. Depending on the arrangements, affected rural residents were resettled in housing projects within the boundaries of these mega-urbanisation projects or offered compensation in cash so that they could choose where to make a new home. The project I examine below lies on the eastern side of Yangzhou (see Figure 35.1). It officially broke ground in 2006. Over the years, the planned area of this new city expanded from 8.5 km$^2$ in the original plan to 22.5 km$^2$ in order to balance the project's finances. I first show how informal practices contributed to the formation and maintenance of the pro-growth coalition and were common in the planning and construction of the new city. I then look from the perspectives of affected residents and examine their tactics in reworking the power relations to their advantage in the bargaining for higher compensation.

## INFORMALISATION OF THE PLANNING AND CONSTRUCTION OF A NEW CITY

A common method of urban expansion is debt financing, wherein local governments set up corporations using public assets (land in particular) to bypass fiscal regulations and borrow from the capital market (Wu 2022b). Such is the case for the urbanisation project in Yangzhou. Via its own investment corporations, the district government eventually partnered with a private developer and acquired 45 per cent equity in a jointly owned project company. The project company thus blurs the public/private boundary. Before the relationship between the private developer and the district government went sour, district government officials assigned to the project company and the senior manager of the private developer shared an office in the project company and jointly decided matters relating to the new city. Many decisions were communicated via verbal exchanges, without leaving any paper trails. Written agreements on the other hand were guarded as corporate secrets. Despite its joint ownership, the project company was not subject to the same rules applicable to public organisations. My requests for information on several land deals carried out by the project company under the public information disclosure regulations were rejected by the government agency in charge on the grounds that the operation of the project company was a private matter and not in the remit of existing regulations. In a sense, formal corporate structure and existing regulations shielded the operations of the project company from public scrutiny and were conducive to informal, illicit arrangements.

The project company's business covered two lines. The main one was to monopolise primary land development. This entailed property acquisitions, land clearance, and infrastructural development with the ultimate goal of preparing land for sale on the land market. The agreement between the private developer and the district government was that land revenues, less mandatory taxes and fees, would be returned to the project company in instalments once the land was sold. The other line was real estate development. In this instance, the project company served as a contractor and provided monies for the construction of commercial real estates (e.g., shopping malls and office towers) and public facilities (e.g., schools, libraries). Once these projects were completed, according to the agreement, the project company would both recover all the costs and make additional profits at a fixed rate of 12 per cent of the project costs before 2011 and 16 per cent thereafter (interview, 2019). At times, as the lawyer representing the private developer admitted, the private developer contributed financially to real estate projects within and outside the boundaries of the planned new city, purely as a 'favour' to the district government. A case in point is the construction of a high-end real estate complex (combining functions of catering, hotel, and conference facilities) next to the main road axis in the new city. This complex was intended to be used as a designated site to host political or economic elites and showcase the planned new city (interviews, 2017 and 2018).

However, these arrangements were in conflict with the prevailing regulations. At the time when the district government used land as investment in the project company, land was still owned by rural collectives and yet to be expropriated and purchased from rural households. Revenues generated from land sales are required to be managed by state authorities. They must also be used in specified ways, such as compensating existing land users and owners, subsidising agricultural and rural development, investing in the expansion of urban infrastructure and public housing, paying off employees of state-owned enterprises that are in financial insolvency or undergoing restructuring, and reimbursing costs of primary land development (The General Office of the State Council 2006). Moreover, it is legally mandatory for use rights of land intended for commercial, industrial, or tourism real estate development to be transferred via auctions and open bidding (Ministry of Land and Resources of the People's Republic of China 2002). Despite being partially owned by the district government, the project company was a corporate entity by legal status and therefore could not collect land revenues and planning gains. It did not acquire land use rights for commercial real estate projects through open bidding either.

The developer was not unaware of the shaky legal foundations of their informal, illicit arrangements with the district government. As the lawyer of the private developer acknowledged, some of the construction projects developed by the project company, either as a 'favour' to the district government or as part of the investment deal, were in fact 'illegal' in status as of 2020 because they had not yet acquired all legal documents (observation, 2021). If informal spaces are defined by the lack of legal titles, what the testimony of the representative suggests is that the state is also directly involved in the production of informal spaces.

The logical question then is why did private developers enter into such flawed, illicit agreements? First, the willingness of the private developers had a great deal to do with the fact that the deal was brokered informally by the then mayor of Yangzhou. As the manager of the private developer revealed in an interview in 2018, the CEO of the private developer and the then mayor of Yangzhou had interpersonal connections that dated back a considerable period. The former was a member of the Standing Committee of the Political Consultative Conference (a political advisory body for the Chinese government within the Chinese political system) in Nanjing, where the then mayor of Yangzhou also served in a leading position before being reassigned to Yangzhou. The CEO was invited by the mayor on a visit to attract investments. The investment deal was concluded subsequently.

Second, the developer profited from the informalisation of the planning and development of the new city. When the investment deal was concluded, there was no detailed planning for the planned new city. Combined with the then cosy relationships with government officials, this created an environment where existing rules and regulations could be flexibly suspended or implemented. One example is the enclosed green spaces. To prevent rural households from using yet-to-be-expropriated land for subsistence farming, which could damage the image of a modernist new city, the pro-growth coalition took away such land from rural households and temporarily used it as green spaces. With the help of the district government and its subordinating agencies, the project company offered rural households 'rent.' Careful characterisation of such monies as 'rent' rather than 'compensation' testifies to the shrewd mindset of the pro-growth coalition in *biantong*. Using the term 'compensation,' which is legally required in instances of state-led expropriation, would acknowledge the coercive nature of land-taking for green spaces and expose them to legal vulnerabilities.

Another example is the construction of resettlement sites. To avoid using too much land within the planned new city for resettlement apartments, which would diminish the profit margins of this urbanisation project, many resettlement apartment buildings were built adjacent to but outside the boundary of the planned new city. Contrary to what had been promised to many displaced households, these apartment buildings were built in higher density. Leaflets distributed to affected households showed apartment buildings with 13 floors at most, but upon completion, they ended up having 17 floors or more.

As a mode of power (Roy 2009), informality could enable the pro-growth coalition to accelerate accumulation of capital and profits by flexibly suspending the regulations and placing them above the law. However, it could also become their weakness. Due to the district government's failure to pay the project company in time, the project company sought to expand the project boundary westbound. This request was unsuccessful. Struggling with financial difficulties, the private developer eventually took the district government to court. As payments to the project company mixed 'costs' and 'profits,' which were not formally and explicitly defined, it became a point of contention as to what constituted 'costs' in financial accounting and how to calculate them correctly. The dispute between the private developer and the district government casts a shadow on the long-term prospect of this urbanisation project.

## INFORMAL POLITICS OF LAND DISPOSSESSION

At the time of land dispossession, discontented residents could potentially file a formal complaint with the court or with the Letter and Visit Offices (a communication channel between governments and citizens to address their grievances, although not always effectively). However, instead of pursuing formal avenues, most residents opted for informal bargains and tactics. These informal tactics contributed to diffusing the tension in dispossession.

To understand these informal practices, it is important to first delve into the logistics of land dispossession. To acquire land from rural households, the pro-growth coalition assembled an army of displacement crews, combining employees from private property valuation and displacement companies and cadres from involved rural villages and the township government. Employees of private companies were responsible for calculating compensation and keeping the paperwork in order. Proper paperwork was mandatory for auditing and inspection by higher-level authorities. Their calculation formed the basis of compensation packages. The cadres on the other hand were tasked to assist in compensation negotiation. There were two groups of cadres—cadres who were local residents and thus had a direct interest in land dispossession and those younger cohorts who were recruited through examinations from outside the villages or even Yangzhou. Each working group typically included at least one cadre

*Source:* Yunpeng Zhang.

*Figure 35.1   Building a new city in Yangzhou (2017)*

who was also a local resident. This intentional arrangement ensured that at least one member of a working group could speak the local dialect, possessed a tacit understanding of village politics, and/or had established interpersonal networks with to-be-displaced households. These locally embedded village cadres served as indispensable brokers in compensation negotiations and straddled between the state and society.

As neighbours, friends, relatives, family members, and frontline agents for the pro-growth coalition, local cadres' hybrid positions worked both for and against affected residents. In the case of Wu's family, for instance, when the negotiation reached an impasse because Wu's son disagreed with the compensation offer, the local cadre, who knew the power relations within Wu's family, deliberately chose a time when his son was absent and 'successfully' reached a deal with Wu and his wife. As the cadre recalled, 'Wu's son has a reputation for being difficult. We decided to exclude him in the end… So, I told him that we could never match the expectations of his son. The longer this negotiation dragged on, the worse the situation would become for them' (interview, 2018).

By contrast, in the case of Dong, the cadre, who was a neighbour of Dong, seemed more sympathetic. According to Dong, the cadre 'reclassified' trees in his backyard and the building materials of his house in the paperwork to ensure that he would qualify for a higher compensation than what was initially offered by the valuation company (interview, 2018). Such practices seemed to be common. As explained by a cadre, each working group could increase the compensation offer by a certain amount at their discretion (interview, 2018). Most cadres were prepared to exercise this discretion for three reasons. The primary reason was to expedite the process. Second, reimbursement of cadres' time was independent from the offers to households. Third, except for a few core rules, the process lacked fine-grained rules and many generic terms required subjective interpretation. However, discretionary offers by *biantong* could only be awarded for officially recognised items. In other words, informal arrangements, or *biantong*, need to be expressed formally and legitimately. Formality and informality become inter-penetrable. Despite being aware of these *biantong* practices and being frustrated by the inflated costs, the private developer, who financed the land clearance, was left with few options due to the existence of formal, documented evidence (interview, 2018).

Whilst most residents bargained for higher compensation on their own, some received additional support from external actors. The story of Chen's family exemplifies this situation (interview, 2018). At the time of land expropriation, his son worked for another state unit outside Yangzhou. His son requested leave to come back, but his employer rejected the request due to the nature of his job. Instead, the employer dispatched a staff member to Yangzhou who outranked the cadres involved in compensation negotiations. According to Chen's recollection, the employee representing his son's employer told those cadres that displacement was affecting his son's performance at work. The employee further stated that if tensions continued to escalate, the employer would have to report to upper-level authorities and intervene to protect the interests of Chen's son. The words of the employee seemed to be weighed in subsequent negotiation. Eventually, as Chen admitted, his family received a much higher offer compared to their neighbours.

In addition to state agents, a few residents also contacted violence specialists—local hooligans and gangsters—to negotiate on their behalf. To be clear, these violence specialists had little specialist knowledge of laws or regulations concerning displacement. In Wu's case, he hired them primarily for intimidation purposes and to counter coercive tactics employed by the displacement crew (interview, 2018). In the end, he did receive a slightly higher compensation. Yet, at the same time he had to pay a substantial amount to the violence specialists for their service, which Wu described as 'extortion.' Due to the illicit nature of his deal with violence specialists, he had to bear the costs. By contrast, through the unpaid 'favour' of violence specialists who Zhu referred to as 'buddies' from high school, Zhu received a much higher compensation package (interview, 2018).

The stories of Dong, Chen, Wu, and Zhu add nuance to the existing literature on contentious politics and informal state practices in China. First, whilst the institutional embeddedness of denizens can be exploited by state agents to ensure their acquiescence through coercion (O'Brien & Deng 2017), the multiple embeddedness of state agents can also become their weakness during displacements and work to the advantage of residents. Second, local state agents may outsource coercion to third parties, such as thugs or hooligans (Ong 2018), to pursue agendas that would otherwise not be tolerated by higher-level governments (Chen 2017). However, violence is not monopolised by the state and, as the cases above show, can be used by affected residents to squeeze more monies out of the growth coalition. These cases thus testify to the negotiability of informality on the everyday level (Rubin 2018). This said, one should not overlook that the commodification of violence often came at a hefty price. It may not only undermine the trust in the state but also worsen the conditions of residents, as exemplified by Wu's case. Additionally, it is important to recognise that residents were compelled to resort to commodified violence because of the organisation of land-taking and limited resources available to them.

## CONCLUSIONS

Since the 1990s, Chinese authorities have actively pursued urbanisation as land development. The existing literature has extensively discussed the mechanisms and consequences of China's urbanisation. This chapter has sought to foreground informal politics in China's urbanisation, using a mega-urbanisation project in Yangzhou as an example. By doing so, this chapter complements abstract theories of China's urbanisation as an outcome of capital switching to the secondary circuit (à la Harvey (1978)). Spatially fixing capitalist accumulation crises via the production of built environments is a politically mediated process and as such the outcome is contingent upon evolving relations, interactions, and transactions between different groups of actors involved.

Explicating the urban politics requires analyses to look beyond macro-level changes in land management, fiscal structure, financial government, public administration, or personnel appointment. By zooming into the practices of coalition-forming, city-making, and land-taking on a micro level, this chapter contributes to drawing out the messy entanglement of formal/informal and licit/illicit practices involved in building a new city that tend to be marginalised by macro-level accounts. Informal, illicit tactics were used by residents, who were constrained by resources, to squeeze more monies out of the pro-growth coalition. They were also critical to the formation of the pro-growth coalition and hardwired to the planning and construction of the new city, which enabled the political and economic elites to profiteer from urbanisation projects.

It is worth noting that informal/illicit practices such as secretive agreements, cronyism, illicit land uses, corruption, and excessive use of commodified violence are well-reported in urban development projects in other parts of China (Lin & Ho 2005, Zhu 2012). Studies in India and Italy have shown that the real estate sector has a notorious reputation for connections with organised crimes (Chiodelli 2019, Weinstein 2008). Informal planning and governing practices that enrich the elites have also been found to have gained popularity in Belgium (Ward 2022) and the Netherlands (Jaffe & Koster 2019). There is thus a converging trend of informalisation of urban politics globally. Rather than abandoning it, informality remains a useful concept to study urban development practices (Banks et al. 2020). In addition to its strength in uncovering survival tactics of the poor, it can sharpen critiques of the conditions that are conducive to informal, illicit practices that further the advantage of those already in power.

Moreover, this chapter sheds light on the contradictions within the Chinese state and the negotiability of state power. The comparative political economy and international relations literatures often depict the Chinese state as monolithic and coherent. However, seeing the state as constituted by the practices of state agents, this chapter's micro-level account reveals that state agents, embedded in relations of diverse natures, might follow logics and values beside those sanctioned by the state. By flexibilising the rules at their discretion (*biantong*), grass-roots state agents acted against the interest of the pro-growth coalition in profit generation. It is such informal practices on the everyday level that contribute to the resilience of the authoritarian political system in China. As Zhou (2011) reminds us, informal practices enable state actors to adapt formal rules and address context-specific problems. They also allow political bargaining, negotiation, and compromises to be made between the state and different groups of social actors.

Granted, the capacity to evade regulatory oversight and strategise on informality is unevenly distributed in society. Although informality can be harnessed by the powerful to their advantage, it can also become their weakness. By definition, informal, illicit arrangements entail legal risks for evading or outright violating state regulations. This risk exposure provides another means to hold dominant actors in urban development accountable. More research into political informality is thus needed to contribute to bringing about just urbanisation.

## REFERENCES

Andreas, J. & Zhan, S. (2016) Hukou and land: Market reform and rural displacement in China. *The Journal of Peasant Studies* 43(4): 798–827.
Banks, N., Lombard, M. & Mitlin, D. (2020) Urban informality as a site of critical analysis. *The Journal of Development Studies* 56(2): 223–238.
Bénit-Gbaffou, C. (2018) Unpacking state practices in city-making, in conversations with Ananya Roy. *Journal of Development Studies* 54(12): 2139–2148.
Brenner, N. & Schmid, C. (2014) The 'urban age' in question. *International Journal of Urban and Regional Research* 38(3): 731–755.
Brenner, N. & Schmid, C. (2015) Towards a new epistemology of the urban? *City* 19(2–3): 151–182.
Bromley, R. & Wilson, T. D. (2018) Introduction: The urban informal economy revisited. *Latin American Perspectives* 45(1): 4–23.
Chan, K. W. (2009) The Chinese hukou system at 50. *Eurasian Geography and Economics* 50(2): 197–221.
Chen, X. (2017) Origins of informal coercion in China. *Politics & Society* 45(1): 67–89.
Chien, S.-S. & Woodworth, M. D. (2018) China's urban speed machine: The politics of speed and time in a period of rapid urban growth. *International Journal of Urban and Regional Research* 42(4): 723–737.
China Statistics Bureau (2021) *China Statistics Yearbook*. Beijing: China Statistics Press.
Chiodelli, F. (2019) The dark side of urban informality in the Global North: Housing illegality and organized crime in Northern Italy. *International Journal of Urban and Regional Research* 43(3): 497–516.
Chiodelli, F. & Gentili, M. (2021) The many shades of grey in urban governance: How illegality shapes urban planning, policy and development. *Political Geography* 84: 102309.
Christophers, B. (2011) Revisiting the urbanization of capital. *Annals of the Association of American Geographers* 101(6): 1347–1364.
Coq-Huelva, D. (2013) Urbanisation and financialisation in the context of a rescaling state: The case of Spain. *Antipode* 45(5): 1213–1231.
Goodfellow, T. (2020) Political informality: Deals, trust networks, and the negotiation of value in the urban realm. *Journal of Development Studies* 56(2): 278–294.
Harvey, D. (1978) The urban process under capitalism: A framework for analysis. *International Journal of Urban and Regional Research* 2(1–3): 101–131.
Harvey, D. (2001) Globalization and spatial fix. *Geographische Revue* 2: 23–30.
He, B. (2007) *Rural Democracy in China: The Role of Village Elections*. Basingstoke: Palgrave Macmillan.
He, S. (2019) Three waves of state-led gentrification in China. *Tijdschrift voor economische en sociale geografie* 110(1): 26–34.
Hsing, Y.-T. (2010) *The Great Urban Transformation: Politics of Land and Property in China*. New York: Oxford University Press.
Huang, P. C. C. (2011) Chongqing: Equitable development driven by a 'third hand'? *Modern China* 37(6): 569–622.
Jaffe, R. & Koster, M. (2019) The myth of formality in the Global North: Informality-as-innovation in Dutch governance. *International Journal of Urban and Regional Research* 43(3): 563–568.
Jiang, Y., Waley, P. & Gonzalez, S. (2016) Shifting land-based coalitions in Shanghai's second hub. *Cities* 52: 30–38.

Lin, G. C. S. (2014) China's landed urbanization: Neoliberalizing politics, land commodification, and municipal finance in the growth of metropolises. *Environment and Planning A* 46(8): 1814–1835.
Lin, G. C. S. & Ho, S. P. S. (2005) The state, land system, and land development processes in contemporary China. *Annals of the Association of American Geographers* 95(2): 411–436.
Liu, J., & Fan, J. (2015) 《中国市制的历史演变与当代改革》. Nanjing: Southeast University Press.
Lund, C. (2006) Twilight institutions: Public authority and local politics in Africa. *Development and Change* 37(4): 685–705.
Migdal, J. S. (2001) *State in Society: Studying how States and Societies Transform and Constitute One Another*. Cambridge: Cambridge University Press.
Ministry of Land and Resources of the People's Republic of China (2002) 《招标拍卖挂牌出让国有建设用地使用权规定》.
Molotch, H. (1976) City as a growth machine – Toward a political-economy of place. *American Journal of Sociology* 82(2): 309–332.
O'Brien, K. J. & Deng, Y. (2017) Preventing protest one person at a time: Psychological coercion and relational repression in China. *China Review* 17(2): 179–201.
Ong, L. H. (2018) Thugs and outsourcing of state repression in China. *The China Journal* 80(1): 94–110.
Pan, F., Zhang, F., Zhu, S. & Wójcik, D. (2016) Developing by borrowing? Inter-jurisdictional competition, land finance and local debt accumulation in China. *Urban Studies* 54(4): 897–916.
Ren, X. (2011) *Building Globalization: Transnational Architecture Production in Urban China*. Chicago: University of Chicago Press.
Rithmire, M. E. (2015) *Land Bargains and Chinese Capitalism: The Politics of Property Rights under Reform*. New York: Cambridge University Press.
Roy, A. (2005) Urban informality: Toward an epistemology of planning. *Journal of the American Planning Association* 71(2): 147–158.
Roy, A. (2009) Why India cannot plan its cities: Informality, insurgence and the idiom of urbanization. *Planning Theory* 8(1): 76–87.
Rubin, M. (2018) At the borderlands of informal practices of the state: Negotiability, porosity and exceptionality. *The Journal of Development Studies* 54(12): 2227–2242.
Schindler, S. (2017) Towards a paradigm of Southern urbanism. *City* 21(1): 47–64.
Shepard, W. (2015) *Ghost Cities of China: The Story of Cities without People in the World's Most Populated Country*. London: Zed Books.
Smart, A. (2018) Ethnographic perspectives on the mediation of informality between people and plans in urbanising China. *Urban Studies* 55(7): 1477–1483.
Sorace, C. & Hurst, W. (2016) China's phantom urbanisation and the pathology of ghost cities. *Journal of Contemporary Asia* 46(2): 304–322.
Stone, C. N. (1989) *Regime Politics: Governing Atlanta, 1946–1988*. Lawrence: University Press of Kansas.
Stone, C. N. (1993) Urban regimes and the capacity to govern – A political-economy approach. *Journal of Urban Affairs* 15(1): 1–28.
Sun, L. (2004) 《转型与断裂: 改革以来中国社会结构的变迁》. Beijing: Tsinghua University Press.
Swider, S. C. (2015) *Building China: Informal Work and the New Precariat*. Ithaca and London: ILR Press.
The General Office of the State Council (2006) 《国务院办公厅关于规范国有土地使用权出让收支管理的通知》.
The State Council (2014) 《国家新型城镇化规划2014–2020年》.
Tomba, L. (2014) *The Government Next Door: Neighborhood Politics in Urban China*. Ithaca and London: Cornell University Press.
Tsai, K. S. & Naughton, B. (2015) Introduction: State capitalism and the Chinese economic miracle. In B. Naughton & K. S. Tsai (eds.) *State Capitalism, Institutional Adaptation, and the Chinese Miracle*. New York: Cambridge University Press, 1–24.
Varley, A. (2013) Postcolonialising informality? *Environment and Planning D: Society and Space* 31(1): 4–22.
Wang, L. (2020) China's new town movements since 1949: A state/space perspective. *Progress in Planning*: 100514.

Ward, C. (2022) Land financialisation, planning informalisation and gentrification as statecraft in Antwerp. *Urban Studies* 59(9): 1837–1854.

Weinstein, L. (2008) Mumbai's development mafias: Globalization, organized crime and land development. *International Journal of Urban and Regional Research* 32(1): 22–39.

Wu, F. (2018) Planning centrality, market instruments: Governing Chinese urban transformation under state entrepreneurialism. *Urban Studies* 55(7): 1383–1399.

Wu, F. (2022a) *Creating Chinese Urbanism: Urban Revolution and Governance Changes* (1st ed.). London: UCL Press.

Wu, F. (2022b) Land financialisation and the financing of urban development in China. *Land Use Policy* 112: 104412.

Wu, F., Zhang, F. & Liu, Y. (2021) Beyond growth machine politics: Understanding state politics and national political mandates in China's urban redevelopment. *Antipode* 54(2): 608–628.

Wu, Q., Edensor, T. & Cheng, J. (2018) Beyond space: Spatial (re) production and middle-class remaking driven by Jiaoyufication in Nanjing City, China. *International Journal of Urban and Regional Research* 42(1): 1–19.

Zhang, F., Wu, F. & Lin, Y. (2022) The socio-ecological fix by multi-scalar states: The development of 'Greenways of Paradise' in Chengdu. *Political Geography* 98.

Zhang, J. & Wu, F. (2008) Mega-event marketing and urban growth coalitions: A case study of Nanjing Olympic New Town. *Town Planning Review* 79(2–3): 209–226.

Zhang, T. (2002) Urban development and a socialist pro-growth coalition in Shanghai. *Urban Affairs Review* 37(4): 475–499.

Zhang, Y. (2018) Grabbing land for equitable development? Reengineering land dispossession through securitising land development rights in Chongqing. *Antipode* 50(4): 1120–1140.

Zhou, X. (2011) 《权威体制与有效治理：当代中国国家治理的制度逻辑》. *Open Times* 10: 67–85.

Zhu, J. N. (2012) The shadow of the skyscrapers: Real estate corruption in China. *Journal of Contemporary China* 21(74): 243–260.

# 36. University as the nexus between the urban and the social

*Do Young Oh*

Universities and other higher learning institutions have never been excluded from the sociological analysis of contemporary society. Louis Althusser (2014) conceptualised the university as an ideological state apparatus, contributing to the (re)production of bourgeois and capitalist society. For Althusser, the university is a practice reinforcing capitalist ideologies as the dominant state apparatus to reproduce capitalist relations of exploitation. To do so, the university focuses on transmitting knowledge, values, and beliefs that support the existing power structures through curriculum, assessment, and teaching methods (Althusser 2014). Bourdieu's (1984) theory of social class shares a similar notion. He diversified the class structure by introducing other class groups, such as intellectuals, the new bourgeoisie, and the new petite bourgeoisie, which have emerged in capitalist society. They do not hold economic capital but hold social and cultural forms of capital. The university is one of the core institutions where their institutionalised cultural and social capital is reproduced (Bourdieu 1986). In this regard, both authors understand the university as a core institution to reproduce social inequality.

These concepts have been further developed by an emerging field of research labelled 'critical university studies', mainly from the 1990s. Research from this field provides a rich theoretical and empirical analysis of universities' social, political, economic, and cultural dimensions. For example, Readings (1996) demonstrates that US universities have become increasingly instrumentalised and aligned with market forces. Slaughter and Rhoades (2004) support such an understanding in terms of the university's shift towards entrepreneurial practices, competition, and the commercialisation of research and education. From these studies, it can be understood that universities are increasingly operating as economic actors, pursuing profits, and engaging in market-oriented activities. However, most of these studies are limited in that they focus only on Anglophone universities. Recent research, such as that by Heller (2016) and Roth (2019), shows how the transformation of US universities is related to other existing processes, like American imperialism. Such work implies that the university is not a homogeneous entity, and that the geographical and historical context of the university must be taken into account.

In this regard, this chapter aims to conceptualise the university as a locally embedded urban institution related to various socioeconomic and political processes. While these analyses are undertaken at an abstract level, there have been more grounded studies on how universities have legitimised inequality in multiple ways. Roth (2019), for example, showed how universities reinforce the existing social stratification in the US.

Despite the well-known anti-urban bias of Anglophone universities, medieval universities such as in Bologna and Paris were largely urban institutions, followed by early modern universities such as in Leiden, Geneva, and Edinburgh (Bender 1988). For Oxford and Cambridge, they also inevitably maintained close but ambivalent ties to their towns to flourish together (Cobban 1988). In the US, universities were mobilised by the state to alleviate social problems of cities through the Urban Grant University Program (Addie 2017). Today's universities are understood to be a critical component of the competitiveness of global cities such as New York and London (Addie 2019). On the other hand, by analysing urban redevelopment projects in Columbus, Ohio, Bose (2015) investigated how a public research university in the US has become an entrepreneurial subject in a neoliberal city. These examples from different time periods give an idea of the diverse and complex relationships between universities and cities.

This chapter aims to extend the discussion on university–urban relations to the non-Western world following, for example, Perry and Wiewel's (2005) conclusions. They expanded their focus to international cases by investigating various university–urban relationships from Seoul, South Korea, to Jerusalem, Israel (Wiewel & Perry 2008). New perspectives to understand urban universities outside the US followed. For example, in China, where the higher education sector is rapidly growing, Li et al. (2014) show that universities are mobilised by the local state to accelerate the uneven development of cities. Kleibert et al. (2021) examine international branch campuses as transnational urban actors. Collins (2010) conceptualises South Korean students in Auckland, New Zealand, as transnational urban agents. As I have suggested elsewhere (Oh 2022a), such a study can provide an opportunity to understand how global and local interests shape universities and their surrounding urban environments in various ways.

In this regard, the rest of this chapter focuses on conceptualising and investigating various university–urban relations, considering their geographically and historically specific contexts by using different theories including the theory of capital circulation. In the following section I discuss the validity of the growth machine theory to explore the role of universities in urban politics. The next section presents the multi-scalar nature of the university beyond the city. The subsequent section then focuses on the new urban politics approach to understand the relationship between globalised cities and universities in relation to the built environment. An alternative view is provided by the theory of capital accumulation and circulation, which sees universities as key social infrastructure to reproduce current and future surplus value extraction. This approach is presented in the fourth section, while the fifth adds the ideological, elitist, and contradictory expressions of class struggles within universities. The sixth section then highlights the importance of the built environment in analysing the roles of universities. The seventh section introduces 'studentification' as an example of diverse ways in which universities are involved in urban processes. Finally, before the conclusion, I highlight the need to diversify an analysis of universities beyond Anglophone cases to postcolonial universities and explore the possibilities for the decolonisation of the university.

## THE UNIVERSITY AND URBAN POLITICS

Universities have not been the core interest of urban sociologists, but there is a growing interest in the various roles of the university in cities. For example, Zukin (1982) showed how New York University facilitated the gentrification process of Lower Manhattan. Domhoff (1978) examined Yale University's influential role in New Haven by refuting Dahl's (1961) prominent research that underestimated Yale's role in the city's urban politics. Castells' (1977) work also includes a discussion of how US universities, such as the University of Chicago and the University of Pennsylvania, directed the urban renewal programmes funded by the US federal government to transform their neighbourhoods into elite-oriented spaces. Such studies show an important role of the universities in reproducing inequality in cities and their relations to other urban issues such as migration, social networks, economic development, and gentrification. However, universities' activities have not been frequently conceived in connection with wider urbanisation processes and the transformation of societies at large.

Logan and Molotch's (1987) urban growth machine theory was one of the early attempts to critically understand the role of the university in the urban process. The core idea of the growth machine can be summarised in two ways: collaborative speculation to produce the preconditions for accumulation and risk sharing supported by the state, finance capital, and the media (Harvey 1989). The theory was developed in the 1970s by Molotch (1976) as a tool to understand the growth dynamics of cities, such as the shaping of land-use patterns and the distribution of resources. According to this argument, a coalition is formed in a city for pursuing economic growth by promoting high-density land use (Logan & Molotch 1987). This enables property owners to increase rent collection, while associated profits can be used for achieving growth. Every coalition member shares an interest in local growth and its effects on land values. Various actors and organisations in cities are identified as land-based interests. The 'rentier' class, who benefit from economic rent or unearned income generated by urban development and growth, including property developers and banks, is centred in a growth coalition. Auxiliary players, including the media, sports teams, and the chamber of commerce, support the rentier class to achieve their material goals. Public officials also play a significant role in a growth coalition, supporting the material interests of the rentier class.

In the growth machine theory, the university is considered as one of the auxiliary players (Logan & Molotch 1987), although it might play a more significant role in a city than the theory originally claimed. The university is induced to join a growth coalition by other actors, such as bankers and newspapers, by acting like a growth 'statesman' instead of being an advocate for a certain type of growth (Molotch 1976: 316). The reason for the university to join the growth coalition is that the university needs more students to sustain its own expansion plans. As a part of a growth coalition, the university is understood as a body pursuing its material goals and trying to maximise its benefits. The theory tends to conceptualise the university as a secondary player supporting the rentier class in a city, defining the university as a passive actor in the growth coalition.

The growth machine theory is considered to have limitations due to its inherent bias toward the urban development experiences of the US during the post-war period. Since the theory is based on the 'machine politics', which derived from the fragmented political conditions of the US in the 19th century while cities were experiencing rapid expansion, it focuses on hierarchical and disciplined party politics in terms of their roles and functions in the urban process. Still, the growth machine theory can be a useful framework to understand the dynamics among urban growth actors including the university, and it also explains the emergence of the university in urban politics. For example, in China, more than 100 university towns have been built through collaborations between local municipalities and universities as a property-driven economic development strategy (Li et al. 2014). Although the role of the central government is essential for the development of university towns in China, as Shen (2022) shows, it can be observed that the local growth coalition in Chinese cities bear some similarities to those in the US. Thus, the theory may help to understand university–urban relations in other parts of the world, including the rise of university towns in China.

## GLOBALISED CITIES AND THE UNIVERSITY

The emerging roles of the university in cities are closely related to the belief that the university can provide a competitive advantage for its host city. Cities and regions have become a collective unit due to the increasing interurban competition resulting from globalisation and financialisation (Harvey 1989). It is believed that fostering favourable environments for production and consumption can lead to securing their advantageous positions in interurban competition. Convention centres, sports stadiums, and large-scale shopping malls are examples showing the new patterns of development as well as a new accumulation strategy defined as flexible accumulation (Harvey 1987). The university is also one of the critical elements of cities to foster their competitiveness by supposedly improving the quality of the labour power and providing efficiency and depth to local social and physical infrastructures (Harvey 1989). The uneven geographical development resulting from increasing interurban competition is related to the role of the university in the city as well. Some powerful cities like New York and London have acquired centralised control and management over other parts of the world (Sassen 2012). Cultural and innovative powers such as those fermenting within the university walls can also be instruments for control and management (Harvey 1989), leading to uneven geographical development.

Increasing interurban competition at various scales is key to explaining the emerging position of the university within the ruling urban coalitions. The presence of the university is now considered a critical precondition for more profitable accumulation under the knowledge-based economy. This has been possible because of the belief that knowledge capital, derived from universities, has a close relationship with economic growth and wealth creation (Cooke 2002, Etzkowitz et al. 2000, Porter 1990). As Castells (1986) argues, this resulted from the experience of a major structural crisis in the world economy during the 1970s and 1980s. The need for restructuring capitalism emerged due to its crisis. Shortly after its emergence, a knowledge economy expanded its influence all over the world. Globalisation, information and communication technologies, and knowledge and networks have become important keywords for understanding this new economy. This also has affected the transformation of universities all over the world, including the vocabulary used in teaching and research and the expected employability of the students, but also justified their international expansion and the material construction of campuses.

This phenomenon often transcends national borders and progresses into transnational cooperation. As of 2023, 333 international branch campuses are operating in 83 countries, and the largest importers of foreign universities are China and the United Arab Emirates (C-BERT 2023). Nevertheless, these 'transnational education zones' demonstrate underlying contradictions regarding promoting a knowledge economy through universities (Rottleb & Kleibert 2022). Foreign universities are often located in a special zone promoted by the state as an exceptional space with fewer regulatory and cultural restrictions. They are also closely related to urban development strategies, as we see large-scale urban development projects driven by education functions, such as Education City in Qatar, Uniciti in Mauritius, and EduCity in Malaysia (Kleibert et al. 2021). In this regard, universities can also be conceptualised as transnational urban actors. However, despite the state's efforts, the contribution of these foreign universities to the knowledge economy of hosting countries is unclear, and they instead tend to play a role in reproducing existing social structures and inequalities, at both local and global scales (Rottleb & Kleibert 2022).

Overall, the city expects to benefit from the university through consumption and reinvestment activities within the city. Such a belief has led to the active spatial expansion of universities and the emerging position of universities within their host cities. The major difference with other built forms is that the university engages with multiple circuits of capital in a complex way. In this regard, the spatial expansion of universities within cities need not be overlooked as an auxiliary activity of their cities. Still, theories about the university and its contribution to regional economic development can partly explain the increasingly influential presence of the university in cities and regions, but they fall short of fully addressing the relationship between the university and the city itself. In theories of regional development, cities and regions are considered to be mediums for promoting regional and national economic growth. The reason that cities and regions are important is largely because geographical and cognitive proximity are understood to be accelerating knowledge production (Capello et al. 2013). In this process, the built environment is regarded as a by-product of economic activities and plays a passive role in the process.

## THE EMERGING UNIVERSITY–URBAN RELATIONSHIPS

Despite the widespread belief about the university's role in economic development, the university needs to be understood as a land-based interest. The existence of universities does not always result in innovative activities (Castells & Hall 1994, Scott & Storper 1987). In fact, such a notion is difficult to identify and test, as argued by Scott and Storper (1987), but the university utilises the belief that it can bring innovation and wealth to the city, as much of the above literature suggests. The construction of new university facilities for supporting a new mode of knowledge production can end up being a speculative real estate development project, as Felsenstein (1994) has argued. In this process, knowledge and innovation production may remain just rhetoric to justify real estate development projects conducted by the university and private interests (Harloe & Perry 2004). In this regard, the university has become an active land-based interest that negotiates its benefits from the government or private firms by utilising an illusion in the positive role of the university in the city and the region. In deindustrialised cities in the US such as Baltimore and Philadelphia, the university, together with the medical sector, replaces the role of the private sector to play a leadership role in city affairs (Ehlenz 2016, Stoker et al. 2015).

The 'new urban politics' is one of the key theories to investigate the way that the university engages with the urban process. The new urban politics understands urbanisation as a multi-scalar process wherein different levels of actors are involved (Jonas & Wilson 1999). Cox (1993, 1995) particularly stresses that global-level influences promote local economic development by attracting mobile capital instead of the narrow focus of the growth machine theory that has local politics as its centre. Furthermore, the new urban politics not only focuses on diverse urban actors from different levels but also emphasises the need to understand the internal political dynamics within a globalising city, which the globalisation literature tends to overlook (Ancien 2011, MacLeod 2011). In this regard, the university can be conceptualised as one of the urban actors collaborating with the state, the private sector, and global partners to promote local economic development and participate in urban development projects. Such activities are also related to the effort to integrate the university and the city in the global economy (Benneworth et al. 2010). As Cox (2011) and MacLeod and Jones (2011) admit, the existing studies of new urban politics mostly focus on the US context, but an increasing number of studies, including those of Jessop and Sum (2000) and Olds (1995), show their usefulness for understanding the nexus of variegated geographical contexts and politics on various scales (Ancien 2011).

The built environment is a core element of the new urban politics approach and the policies it informs. This would explain how the built environment of the university plays a key role in the urban process. Groups of policies try to enhance competitive advantages through improving and adapting the built environment in a city following the new urban politics approach (Swyngedouw et al. 2002). The policies for promoting new accumulation strategies aim to enhance investments in the built environment and restructure the labour market for accelerating the circulation of capital through state intervention. Swyngedouw et al. (2002) investigated large-scale urban development projects in Western Europe as cases of the new urban politics, and five out of six major urban development projects were found to include university buildings and research facilities for promoting the economic growth of their cities. Such projects tend to be beneficial to the dominant classes in cities and to promote socioeconomic polarisation rather than social cohesion, aggravating the living conditions of vulnerable social groups. Similar cases can be found not only in globalising Western European cities but also elsewhere, like in Abu Dhabi (Ponzini 2011) and Shanghai (Chen et al. 2009). However, much of the literature only focuses on the state and its policy: universities are only considered an additional element of development projects.

## THE UNIVERSITY IN THE PROCESS OF CAPITAL CIRCULATION

Theories discussed above, including urban politics and regional economic development, are helpful to explain the increasingly influential presence of the university in cities, but they fall short of fully addressing the complex relationship between the university and the city itself. These theories consider the built environment as a by-product of economic activities. This view contrasts with Harvey's (1978) argument that the built environment is forming a large part of the process of capital accumulation. The built environment and the production process have an interdependent relationship in enabling the accumulation process and addressing the inherent overaccumulation problems of capitalism. In this regard, emerging built forms resulting from new modes of accumulation need to be considered as a result of the interplay of different circuits of capital. Such built forms then affect existing urban space and lead to the social and political transformation of cities, as argued by O'Mara (2007). The emerging landscape of the knowledge economy may help the economic growth of cities but accelerate gentrification as a socio-spatial process of class struggle. This integrated relationship between the university and the city tends to be overlooked in many discussions.

To offer a holistic approach to understanding the complicated relationships between the university and the city, Harvey's (1978) theory of capital circulation is useful. The university is not directly engaged in production but enhances the conditions for producing surplus value in various ways as a social infrastructure, such as promoting research and development and improving the qualities of labour power (Harvey 1982). In this regard, capital is channelled to the university for upgrading labour forces and for offering new managerial techniques and technologies. It requires immobile, long-term, and large-scale investments. Even though the university does not produce anything in most cases, such investment is necessary for the state and the capitalist class to increase productivity to compete with others. The investment in the university is expected to be compensated eventually by providing means to produce more surplus value. By doing so, the university offers a competitive advantage to its host city and region by attracting productive capital (Harvey 1982: 403). In particular, the function of the university does not wear out like other physical infrastructures. The university thus can produce a geographical concentration of high-quality conditions for increasing surplus value production. Harvey (1989: 147) cited Route 128 and Silicon Valley as examples. This is not always the case because not every university has the capacity to produce such conditions, but such an idea implies that the university can be an important factor in the uneven geographical development of cities and regions. It also suggests that an investigation of the relationship between production and consumption alone cannot explain diverse patterns of urbanisation without considering reproduction.

The university is where diverse capital and revenue investments are circulated. Harvey (1982: 404) argued that the investment in social infrastructures is mainly undertaken by the state as a form of tax, but the forms of investment in the university are more diverse because universities' historical and geographical contexts are diverse. As shown above, in some countries, the higher education sector is funded more by private firms, financial institutions, and families. One common form of investment in the university is 'location rent' as defined by Harvey (1982: 403). Private firms share their surplus value with the university on the condition of accessing benefits from the university with higher priority. Harvey (1982: 404) argued that technology and labour are mobile, but this argument can only be partially accepted. In the same book, Harvey (1982: 418) himself admitted that the geographical concentration of capital and accumulation results from the collective provision of physical and social infrastructures. Walker (2000) also argued that the immobility of technologically sophisticated labour is due to existing barriers and accumulated advantages. The university enjoys its monopoly status by offering firms advanced means of production as well as reserve workers an opportunity to increase their future wages. Since the university is expected to increase the overall accumulation of society, the university can utilise fictitious capital, which is money based on future surplus value production. Fictitious capital enables university investment in other circuits of capital, such as the built environment, for further accumulation. The following section focuses on the university's investment in the built environment to explore the various roles of the university in its host city.

## THE UNIVERSITY AS SOCIAL INFRASTRUCTURE

For improving the overall productivity of society, the ideological control of society also needs to be undertaken. Such roles of the university can be located in the tertiary circuit of capital as categorised by Harvey (1978). He identifies two different kinds of investments in the tertiary circuit: investment in science and technology, as discussed above, and investment as a form of social expenditure, such as education, health, and welfare. Harvey (1978, 1982) also argued that such investments tend to be made by the state or its agent using the tax on surplus value because they must be long-term and large-scale and the result is often uncertain. Even though Harvey (1978) paid much less attention to the tertiary circuit in his explanation of capital circuits, as pointed out by Tretter (2016), the position of the university in the circuits of capital requires special attention considering its emerging position in cities and regions.

Investments in social infrastructures have been made in order to absorb the inevitable struggles and paradoxes in the accumulation process as a compensatory investment (King 1989, Soederberg 2015). They also work for ideological control and the repression of society (Harvey 1982: 401). Readings (1996) argued that the traditional function of the university was to nurture elite citizens. The university functions to solidify national cultures as a socio-political mission with the support of the state (Readings 1996, Scott 2006). One of the recent examples is the US university during the Cold War period. Chomsky (1997) once described how the Massachusetts Institute of Technology was operated with the support of the Pentagon: nearly 90 per cent of the academic budget came from the Pentagon in the 1960s. This was not only for science and engineering departments, and the political science department was also openly funded by the Central Intelligence Agency. Several government projects were implemented by social scientists to serve the interests of the state by promoting a pro-American ideology not only in the US but also in the other parts of the world (Simpson 1998). Such investment of the state is not directly related to production but obviously intended as a stabiliser of society.

However, these political functions of the university do not always work due to their underlying internal contradiction. Social infrastructures need to fulfil different class interests for the legitimation of the state and the dominant class. The university thus cannot be exclusive to the dominant class but also needs to serve the interest of the working class. In this regard, social infrastructures can be a general field of class struggle where different classes project their needs, even though they are mostly funded by the state and the capitalist class (Harvey 1982). This condition of the university means that the space of the university can be the centre of organised resistance against the dominant class, such as in the events of May 1968 in Paris and the anti-Vietnam War movement in the US in the 1960s. The university was in the field of class struggle not only in the West but also elsewhere. Oh (2022b) showed how university students were the centre of the social movement to fight against military regimes from the 1960s in South Korea. Similar cases can be found in other places like sub-Saharan Africa (Nkinyangi 1991) and Indonesia (Aspinall 1995).

## THE BUILT ENVIRONMENT OF THE UNIVERSITY

Universities are locally embedded institutions even though their economic and political functions cover national, regional, and local scales (Harvey 1989). In this regard, the university can be one of the noteworthy actors showing how different processes of capitalism have affected the urban process in relation to a specific historical and geographical context. Investigating different universities and constructing them as a group of specific actors in urban development processes can help investigate the dynamics of capitalism by 'reflecting daily life as in a mirror' (Harvey 1989: 10). In this regard, the peculiarity of conceptualising the built environment of the university in circuits of capital needs to be discussed to offer an alternative concept of the built environment of the university. This step is necessary because the theory of capital circulation helps in understanding concrete phenomena of time and space and offers a useful framework for an analysis of the urban process.

The built environment in the circuits of capital plays diverse roles to accommodate and produce surplus value. The built environment is a complicated concept that consists of different elements, such as factories, offices, shops, schools, and parks (Harvey 1978, 1982). It is utilised for various essential activities of society such as production, exchange, circulation, and consumption, which is the distinctive feature of the built environment. It is also characterised by its immobility because it cannot be moved once it is created: it can only be destroyed or become obsolete. Based on Harvey's (1978) categorisation, the built environment can be divided into structures for consumption and production. The built environment for consumption acts as a physical framework for consumption and reproduction activities, including housing, parks, and walkways. The built environment for production is operated as an aid for the production process. Factories and offices are examples of this. As Harvey pointed out, the built environment can neither be defined as a homogeneous concept nor as a process, but it can be labelled as part of the secondary circuit of capital to understand the circulation process of capital. The surplus from the primary circuit of capital is transferred to and invested in fixed capital and consumption funds for absorbing and reproducing the surplus from the primary circuit. This is an important process for maintaining capitalism because it enables the process of capital accumulation to continue, but investment in the built environment is normally a large-scale and long-term process, so there are barriers for individual capitalists to invest. In this regard, the state and financial institutions mediate this transfer process by utilising fictitious capital and implementing supportive policies.

The built environment of the university has unique characteristics: it does not only serve for the reproduction of society but also serves production. Such functions work in a complex way when compared to other kinds of built environments, such as offices, houses, and roads. The unique characteristics of the university suggest that the role of the university and its campus in the urbanisation process needs to be understood beyond its involvement in the tertiary circuit. The university thus needs to be conceptualised as an institution engaged in multiple circuits of capital, which differs from the traditional understanding of the university. It is also considered an ecosystem that consists of its own circuits of capital while interacting with other capitalists in different circuits of capital. In this regard, the built environment of the university should be understood as a multi-faceted process, wherein various levels of actors compete with and affect each other, which also greatly influencing the urban environment.

Emerging socio-political changes in society such as flexible accumulation and entrepreneurial cities are also closely related to the changing roles of the built environment of the university in the urban process. Such a phenomenon is closely linked to the emergence of new accumulation strategies in some parts of the world after experiencing the global deflation of the 1970s and the dollar deflation in the early 1980s. In this process, the rise of the 'entrepreneurial city' and an increase in inter-urban competition have been observed (Harvey 1987). The university is now increasingly participating in the primary circuit of capital, which is mobilised by the capitalist class or engaged by itself as an individual capitalist in the urbanisation process (Castells & Hall 1994, Massey & Wield 1992, Quintas et al 1992). The university is also actively engaged in the secondary circuit of capital, which can be defined by the term 'edifice complex', which describes the university's intention to build more buildings and facilities, including sports and cultural facilities, for its own sake (Coffield & Gaither 1976, Schimmel 1997).

Still, an analysis of the built environment of the university needs to be based on geographical and historical contexts. Harvey (2008) used the examples of Columbia University and the University of Baltimore in the United States to argue that universities became powerful institutions for shaping much of the urban fabric to suit their needs. Moss (2011) analysed various university expansion projects in New York and claimed that universities nowadays actively engage in urban development processes by utilising various planning and zoning tools as much as possible. Universities also become a part of neighbourhood development processes by carrying out real estate development-based projects (Coffey & Dierwechter 2005, Rodin 2007). While these cases from the US are highly related to the shift to a regime of flexible accumulation, universities could have different motivations to be involved in urban development in other contexts. For example, Oh and Shin (2023) showed that East Asian universities are participating in speculative urban development projects for different motivations based on their developmental legacies. In this regard, universities' engagement with the built environment should be understood as a nuanced process.

## VARIOUS URBAN PROCESSES RELATED TO THE UNIVERSITY

The university is not a homogeneous entity, as it has multiple stakeholders, such as faculty members, students, funding agencies, board members, managerial and administrative staff, and alumni. Thus, university–urban relations need to be understood from various perspectives based not only on their geographical and historical contexts but also their multifaceted social dimensions. While the way each stakeholder engages with the urban environment differently is beyond this chapter's focus, it is worthwhile to consider how students, the largest constituents of the university by volume, can be contextualised in the university–urban relations. In the UK context, it is considered that the increasing student population has influences on neighbourhood transformation in terms of social, economic, cultural, and physical aspects. This process is often defined as 'studentification', which extends the term gentrification (Smith & Holt 2007). The increasing student population may thus become a gentrifier of a region, which leads to the displacement of existing residential groups, who are mostly low-income populations, while changing the landscape of the region (Smith 2005).

Student-driven urban transformation processes are related to various external forces such as the financialisation of the higher education sector (e.g. students' debts) and the housing market, international migration, government policies, and local politics. Thus, more careful approaches are required to understand this process. Nearly two decades ago Chatterton and Hollands (2003) noted the growing trend for student cities like Leeds and Bristol to be more corporatised and commercialised. Kallin and Shaw (2019) furthermore showed a rising tension between the growing student population and existing residents in Edinburgh. However, in global cities like London where there are various influential urbanisation actors, universities and student accommodation providers do not possess the same bargaining power as in smaller cities despite London boasting the largest student population in the UK. As of 2019, London's student population amounted to 374,670, which was 4.2 per cent of the overall London population (HESA 2019). This was supported by my interviews with university estate directors of three major London universities. According to one interview I conducted in 2013, the City of Westminster, where there are several influential political and economic institutions, does not consider the university as an extraordinary institution within the city. In this regard, the idea of 'studentification' (Smith 2005) may not be a suitable term to understand the process related to student accommodation in large cities like London.

Student housing in large cities provides an opportunity to understand broader processes, such as financialisation. Financialisation, as an emerging socio-economic process, enables 'profit without producing' by facilitating financial systems (Lapavitsas 2013). The mechanism of finance to extract financial profits becomes increasingly important due to the limitations of increasing productivity growth, as we have seen in recent decades. In this process, the realm of finance has stretched to non-financial corporations and institutions by forcing them to participate in financial markets actively. In February 2020, the UK witnessed its largest-ever private property deal, amounting to GBP 4.7 billion. Goldman Sachs, a global investment bank headquartered in the US, along with the health research charity Wellcome Trust, jointly sold a student accommodation firm that currently owns 28,000 beds in the UK to Blackstone, a New York-based private equity firm (The Guardian 2020). Blackstone is considered the world's largest corporate landlord, and the firm has been criticised by a UN rapporteur as being a contributor to the ongoing global housing crisis by breaking up established communities and fuelling soaring rents and evictions (The Guardian 2019). This case helps us understand increasing financialisation in a global city like London.

Research on student housing is also concentrated in the Western context even though the urban process related to student accommodations outside the Anglophone sphere is considerably different. In Seoul, where there are 563,889 university students among its 9.7 million overall population, the existence of financial capital related to the construction and operation of student accommodation remains largely unnoticed. Instead, the national government has been seeking to invest substantial public funds to build new affordable student accommodations. For example, between 2018 and 2022, the government sought to invest GBP 393 million to build 23,300 student beds in the country. However, in the end several projects were unable to proceed, primarily due to opposition from petty landlords who were operating student rental units. For example, one private university had to reduce the capacity of the new student accommodation by a third due to the opposition of local landlords. This failure of state intervention is closely related to the historical contexts of the higher education sector in South Korea, largely driven by private interests (Oh 2021). Such a case shows that more heterogeneous understandings of student accommodations, as diverse, complicated, interactive, and multi-scalar processes, are needed.

## THE POSTCOLONIAL URBAN UNIVERSITY

The theory of capital circulation provides an overview of the university–urban relationship in contemporary society, but the theory is not sufficient to explain variegated university–urban relationships based on their geographical and historical contexts (Oh 2022a). Such a point is particularly relevant to the university when considering the institutional continuity of the university as the oldest institution in the West next to the Roman Catholic Church (Bender 1988). In this regard, universities can be expected to reflect various socioeconomic and political transformations over a long period of time, including the pre-modern era. The recent investigation of land-grant universities in the US and their land holdings by the Pulitzer Center highlights such an aspect. Through the 1862 Morril Act, universities received more than 40,000 square kilometres of land confiscated from tribal nations, not only as university campuses but also for financial endowments (Lee & Ahtone 2020). In this regard, the exploitation of indigenous communities can be understood as the cornerstone of the prosperity of US universities today. Baldwin (2021) further examined how urban universities in the US have been actively displacing African Americans in their neighbourhoods.

Colonial universities were also established in different parts of the world, including India, Singapore, Burma, and Nigeria. Their complex origins and roles are difficult to understand with the theory of capital circulation, as backed by Chattopadhyay's (2012) critique of the theory. These institutions need to be understood as a space where multiple processes, such as colonialism, capitalism, industrialisation, and Westernisation, are interacting. In this regard, as contended by Yeoh, universities, particularly outside the West, are not only a 'product of capitalist logic', but also an 'area of conflict between social groups which have differing vested interests in the city' (Yeoh 1996: 9). Oh (2022a) showed that varied global and local interests are key to understanding colonial universities and their surrounding urban environments in Korea and Singapore, and their different colonial legacies are closely related to variegated contemporary urban processes. Livsey (2014) showed that the campus of the University College Ibadan, a colonial university in Nigeria, was a symbol of modernity in the city and then became a critical institution for the decolonisation of the country. Such scholarship sheds light on how universities have become an important element of historical and contemporary urban formation.

The recent movement of 'decolonising the university' brings up more possibilities to diversify the research on the urban university. Recent student-led movements in the UK have sparked a broader movement challenging the legacy of colonialism within universities (Moosavi 2020). To fight against not only the colonial past but also the current neoliberal university system shaped by global capitalism and transnational elites, Mbembe (2016: 36) calls for a 'geographical imagination' that extends beyond the boundary of the nation state to decolonise the university. Such a movement coincides with arguments by postcolonial urban scholars such as Robinson (2002, 2016) and Roy (2016) calling for comparative urban research from the Global South to decolonise urban studies. There is emerging scholarship considering such an aspect. For example, Al-Saleh and Vora (2020) conceptualised US branch campuses in Qatar's Education City as institutionalised sites of imperial citizenship formation. Still, it is rare to find research focusing on diverse university–urban relationships based on their colonial legacies and contemporary development processes outside North America and Western Europe. Such a trend is similar to the 'decolonial turn', which tends to stay within Western academia (Moosavi 2020).

## CONCLUSIONS

To conclude, this chapter aimed to conceptualise the diverse university–urban relations beyond a conventional focus on universities' knowledge and innovation production functions for economic development. This chapter resonates with recent attempts to put 'universities at the centre of metropolitan transformation and cities' (Winling 2018: 2), but to do so, their complex structure and broader impacts need to be considered when discussing the transformation of the higher education system and universities themselves. Constantly changing socioeconomic and political contexts also need to be carefully considered, as universities and urban spaces are in 'constant negotiation', as argued by Haar (2011: xxv). For example, in the Tokyo Metropolitan Area in the first half of the 20th century, several universities moved to newly made suburban college towns developed by private rail companies. However, recently several suburban universities have been trying to return to the city centre to attract more students (Asahi Shimbun 2022). To explore the possibilities that these new university-led urban development processes contribute to dealing with society's pressing social and economic issues, further in-depth studies on various types of universities in different geographical contexts are required.

This chapter also calls for more active scholarship investigating various functions of the university as a globally linked but locally embedded urban institution beyond the West. While this chapter tried to provide diverse cases related to university–urban relations beyond the West, it failed to do so sufficiently, as studies outside North America and Western Europe are extremely rare. Investigating more diverse university–urban relationships in developing cities, where the urbanisation process is largely concentrated, can construct richer stories when considering their colonial legacies and geographically uneven contemporary urban processes. It can also promote a more plural and situated aspect of the urbanisation process while constructing active dialogues with other parts of the world. Finally, such an attempt can lead us to shift to 'universities in urban society', as argued by Addie (2017), for imagining a more progressive production of urban space and urban knowledge.

## REFERENCES

Addie, J. -P. D. (2017) From the urban university to universities in urban society. *Regional Studies* 51(7): 1089–1099.
Addie, J, -P. D. (2019) Urban(izing) university strategic planning: An analysis of London and New York City. *Urban Affairs Review* 55(6): 1612–1645.
Al-Saleh, D. & Vora, N. (2020) Contestations of imperial citizenship: Student protest and organizing in Qatar's Education City. *International Journal of Middle East Studies* 52(4): 733–739.
Althusser, L. (2014) *On the reproduction of capitalism: Ideology and ideological state apparatuses*. London; New York: Verso.
Ancien, D. (2011) Global city theory and the new urban politics twenty years on. *Urban Studies* 48(12): 2473–2493.
Asahi Shimbun (2022) Universities in Japan continue trend of moving to urban areas. *Asahi Shimbun* 7 June. Retrieved from: https://www.asahi.com/ajw/articles/14625000 (accessed 30 June 2023).
Aspinall, E. (1995) Students and the military: Regime friction and civilian dissent in the late Suharto period. *Indonesia* 59: 21–44.
Baldwin, D. L. (2021) *In the shadow of the ivory tower: How universities are plundering our cities*. New York: Bold Type Books.
Bender, T. (1988) Introduction. In T. Bender (ed.) *The university and the city: From medieval origins to the present*. Oxford: Oxford University Press, 3–10.
Benneworth, P., Charles, D. & Madanipour, A. (2010) Building localized interactions between universities and cities through university spatial development. *European Planning Studies* 18(10): 1611–1629.
Bose, S. (2015) Universities and the redevelopment politics of the neoliberal city. *Urban Studies* 52(14): 2616–2632.
Bourdieu, P. (1984) *Distinction: A social critique of the judgement of taste*. Cambridge, MA: Harvard University Press.
Bourdieu, P. (1986) The forms of capital. In J. G. Richardson (ed.) *Handbook of Theory and Research for the Sociology of Education*. Westport, CT: Greenwood Press, 241–258.
Capello, R., Olechnicka, A. & Gorzelak, G. (eds.) (2013) *Universities, cities and regions: Loci for knowledge and innovation creation*. Oxford: Routledge.
Castells, M. (1977) *The urban question: A Marxist approach*. Cambridge, MA: MIT Press.
Castells, M. (1986) High technology, world development, and structural transformation: The trends and the debate. *Alternatives* 11(3): 297–343.
Castells, M. & Hall, P. (1994) *Technopoles of the world: The making of 21st century industrial complexes*. London: Routledge.
Chatterton, P. & Hollands, R. (2003) *Urban nightscapes: Youth cultures, pleasure spaces and corporate power*. London: Routledge.
Chattopadhyay, S. (2012) Urbanism, colonialism and subalternity. In T. Edensor & M. Jayne (eds.) *Urban theory beyond the West: A world of cities*. London: Routledge, 90–107.

Chen, X., Wang, L. & Kundu, R. (2009) Localizing the production of global cities: A comparison of new town developments around Shanghai and Kolkata. *City and Community* 8(4): 433–465.
Chomsky, N. (1997) The Cold War and the university. In A. Schiffrin (ed.) *The Cold War and the university: Toward an intellectual history*. New York: The New Press, 171–194.
Cobban, A. B. (1988) *The medieval English universities: Oxford and Cambridge to c. 1500*. Aldershot: Scolar Press.
Coffey, B. & Dierwechter, Y. (2005) The urban university as a vehicle for inner-city renewal. In D. C. Perry & W. Wiewel (eds.) *The university as urban developer: Case studies and analysis*. Armonk, NY: M.E. Sharpe, 80–97.
Coffield, W. & Gaither, G. (1976) The edifice complex: Problems and prospects for capital outlay in higher education. *Journal of Education Finance* 2(2): 135–155.
Collins, F. L. (2010) International students as urban agents: International education and urban transformation in Auckland, New Zealand. *Geoforum* 41(6): 940–950.
Cooke, P. (2002) Regional innovation system: General findings and some new evidence from biotechnology clusters. *Journal of Technology Transfer* 27(1): 133–145.
Cox, K. R. (1993) The local and the global in the new urban politics: A critical view. *Environment and Planning D: Society and Space* 11(4): 433–448.
Cox, K. R. (1995) Globalisation, competition and the politics of local economic development. *Urban Studies* 32(2): 213–224.
Cox, K. R. (2011) Commentary. From the new urban politics to the 'new' metropolitan politics. *Urban Studies* 48(12): 2661–2671.
C-BERT (2023) C-BERT International Campus Listing [data originally collected by Kevin Kinser and Jason E. Lane]. Retrieved from: http://cbert.org/intl-campus/ (accessed 30 June 2023).
Dahl, R. A. (1961). *Who governs? Democracy and power in an American city*. New Haven, CT: Yale University Press.
Domhoff, G. W. (1978) *Who really rules? New Haven and community power re-examined*. New Brunswick, NJ: Transaction Books.
Ehlenz, M. M. (2016) Neighborhood revitalization and the anchor institution. *Urban Affairs Review* 52(5): 714–750.
Etzkowitz, H., Webster, A., Gebhardt, C. & Terra, B. R. C. (2000) The future of the university and the university of the future: Evolution of ivory tower to entrepreneurial paradigm. *Research Policy* 29(2): 313–330.
Felsenstein, D. (1994) University-related science parks – 'Seedbeds' or 'enclaves' of innovation? *Technovation* 14(2): 93–110.
Haar, S. (2011) *The city as campus: Urbanism and higher education in Chicago*. Minneapolis, MN: University of Minnesota Press.
Harloe, M. & Perry, B. (2004) Universities, localities and regional development: The emergence of the 'Mode 2' university? *International Journal of Urban and Regional Research* 28(1): 212–223.
Harvey, D. (1978) The urban process under capitalism: A framework for analysis. *International Journal of Urban and Regional Research* 2(1–3): 101–131.
Harvey, D. (1982) *The limits to capital*. Oxford: Basil Blackwell.
Harvey, D. (1987) Flexible accumulation through urbanization: 'Post-modernism' in the American city. *Antipode* 19(3): 260–286.
Harvey, D. (1989) From managerialism to entrepreneurialism: The transformation in urban governance in late capitalism. *Geografiska Annaler. Series B, Human Geography* 71(1): 3–17.
Harvey, D. (2008) The right to the city. *New Left Review* 53: 23–40.
Heller, H. (2016) *The capitalist university: The transformations of higher education in the United States, 1945–2016*. London: Pluto Press.
HESA (2019) Table 11 – HE student enrolments by domicile and region of HE provider 2014/15 to 2018/19. Retrieved from: https://www.hesa.ac.uk/data-and-analysis/students/table-11 (accessed 31 January 2022).
Jessop, B. & Sum, N.-L. (2000) An entrepreneurial city in action: Hong Kong's emerging strategies in and for (inter)urban competition. *Urban Studies* 37(12): 2287–2313.
Jonas, A. E. G. & Wilson, D. (1999) The city as a growth machine. In A. E. G. Jonas & D. Wilson (eds.) *The urban growth machine: Critical perspectives two decades later*. Albany, NY: SUNY Press, 3–18.

Kallin, H. & Shaw, M. (2019) Escaping the parasite of the student flat: Reflections on an experiment in co-operative housing. *Radical Housing Journal* 1(1): 223–226.
King, R. J. (1989) Capital switching and the role of ground rent: 1. Theoretical problems. *Environment and Planning A: Economy and Space* 21(4): 445–462.
Kleibert, J. M., Bobée, A., Rottleb, T. & Schulze, M. (2021) Transnational education zones: Towards an urban political economy of 'education cities'. *Urban Studies* 58(14): 2845–2862.
Lapavitsas, C. (2013) *Profiting without producing: How finance exploits us all*. London: Verso.
Lee, R. & Ahtone, T. (2020) Land-grab universities. *High Country News* 52(4). Retrieved from: https://www.hcn.org/issues/52.4/indigenous-affairs-education-land-grab-universities (accessed 31 January 2022).
Li, Z., Li, X. & Wang, L. (2014) Speculative urbanism and the making of university towns in China: A case of Guangzhou University Town. *Habitat International* 44: 422–431.
Livsey, T. (2014) 'Suitable lodgings for students': Modern space, colonial development and decolonization in Nigeria. *Urban History* 41(4): 664–685.
Logan, J. R. & Molotch, H. L. (1987) *Urban fortunes: The political economy of place*. Berkeley, CA: University of California Press.
MacLeod, G. (2011) Urban politics reconsidered: Growth machine to post-democratic city? *Urban Studies* 48(12): 2629–2660.
MacLeod, G. & Jones, M. (2011) Renewing urban politics. *Urban Studies* 48(12): 2443–2472.
Massey, D. & Wield, D. (1992) Science parks: A concept in science, society, and 'space' (a realist tale). *Environment and Planning D: Society and Space* 10(4): 411–422.
Mbembe, A. J. (2016) Decolonizing the university. New directions. *Arts and Humanities in Higher Education* 15(1): 29–45.
Molotch, H. L. (1976) The city as a growth machine: Toward a political economy of place. *American Journal of Sociology* 82(2): 309–332.
Moosavi, L. (2020) The decolonial bandwagon and the dangers of intellectual decolonisation. *International Review of Sociology* 30(2): 332–354.
Moss, M. L. (2011) Class struggle. *Architect's Newspaper* 28 July. Retrieved from: https://web.archive.org/web/20120113071550/http://archpaper.com/news/articles.asp?id=5557 (accessed 31 January 2022).
Nkinyangi, J. A. (1991) Student protests in sub-Saharan Africa. *Higher Education* 22(2): 157–173.
Oh, D. Y. (2021) Verticalization process of universities: Focusing on the cases of physical expansion activities of private universities and their foundations in South Korea from the late 1990. *Space & Environment* 31(1): 102–138.
Oh, D. Y. (2022a) The university and East Asian cities: The variegated origins of urban universities in colonial Seoul and Singapore. *Journal of Urban History* 48(2): 336–360.
Oh, D. Y. (2022b) University, landed class, and land reform: Transwar origins of private universities in South Korea, 1920–1960. In R. Hofmann & M. Ward (eds.) *Transwar Asia: Ideology, Practices, and Institutions, 1920–1960*. London: Bloomsbury Academic, 101–122.
Oh, D. Y. & Shin, H. B. (2023) University as real estate developer: Comparative perspectives from the Global East. *Geoforum* 144: 103764.
Olds, K. (1995) Globalization and the production of new urban spaces: Pacific Rim megaprojects in the late 20th century. *Environment and Planning A: Economy and Space* 27(11): 1713–1743.
O'Mara, M. P. (2007) Landscapes of knowledge and high technology. *Places* 19(1): 48–53.
Perry, D. C. & Wiewel, W. (eds.) (2005) *The university as urban developer: Case studies and analysis*. Armonk, NY: M.E. Sharpe.
Ponzini, D. (2011) Large scale development projects and star architecture in the absence of democratic politics: The case of Abu Dhabi, UAE. *Cities* 28(3): 251–259.
Porter, M. E. (1990) The competitive advantage of nations. *Harvard Business Review* 68(March/April): 73–93.
Quintas, P., Wield, D. & Massey, D. (1992) Academic-industry links and innovation: Questioning the science park model. *Technovation* 12(3): 161–175.
Readings, B. (1996) *The university in ruins*. Cambridge, MA: Harvard University Press.
Robinson, J. (2002) Global and world cities: A view from off the map. *International Journal of Urban and Regional Research* 26(3): 531–554.

Robinson, J. (2016) Comparative urbanism: New geographies and cultures of theorizing the urban. *International Journal of Urban and Regional Research* 40(1): 187–199.

Rodin, J. (2007) *The university and urban revival: Out of the ivory tower and into the streets.* Philadelphia: University of Pennsylvania Press.

Roth, G. (2019) *The educated underclass: Students and the promise of social mobility.* London: Pluto Press.

Rottleb, T. & Kleibert, J. M. (2022) Circulation and containment in the knowledge-based economy: Transnational education zones in Dubai and Qatar. *Environment and Planning A: Economy and Space* 54(5): 930–948.

Roy, A. (2016) Who's afraid of postcolonial theory? *International Journal of Urban and Regional Research* 40(1): 200–209.

Sassen, S. (2012) *Cities in a world economy.* 4th ed. Thousand Oaks, CA: SAGE Publications.

Schimmel, K. S. (1997) The edifice complex: Reliance on new sports stadiums to solve urban problems. *Sporting Traditions* 14(1): 146–155.

Scott, A. J. & Storper, M. (1987) High technology industry and regional development: A theoretical critique and reconstruction. *International Social Science Journal* 39: 215–232.

Scott, J. C. (2006) The mission of the university: Medieval to postmodern transformations. *The Journal of Higher Education* 77(1): 1–39.

Shen, J. (2022) Universities as financing vehicles of (sub)urbanisation: The development of university towns in Shanghai. *Land Use Policy* 112: 104679.

Simpson, C. (1998) Universities, empire, and the production of knowledge: An introduction. In C. Simpson (ed.) *Universities and Empire: Money and Politics in the Social Sciences During the Cold War.* New York: The New Press, xi–xxxiv.

Slaughter, S. & Rhoades, G. (2004) *Academic capitalism and the new economy: Markets, state, and higher education.* Baltimore, MD: Johns Hopkins University Press.

Smith, D. P. (2005) 'Studentification': The gentrification factory? In R. Atkinson & G. Bridge (eds.) *Gentrification in a global context: The new urban colonialism.* London: Routledge, 72–89.

Smith, D. P. & Holt, L. (2007) Studentification and 'apprentice' gentrifiers within Britain's provincial towns and cities: Extending the meaning of gentrification. *Environment and Planning A: Economy and Space* 39(1): 142–161.

Soederberg, S. (2015) Subprime housing goes south: Constructing securitized mortgages for the poor in Mexico. *Antipode* 47(2): 481–499.

Stoker, R. P., Stone, C. N. & Horak, M. (2015) Contending with structural inequality in a new era. In C. N. Stone & R. P. Stoker (eds.) *Urban Neighborhoods in a New Era: Revitalization Politics in the Postindustrial City.* Chicago: University of Chicago Press, 209–250.

Swyngedouw, E., Moulaert, F. & Rodriguez, A. (2002) New geographies of power, exclusion and injustice neoliberal urbanization in Europe: Large-scale urban development projects and the new urban policy. *Antipode* 34(3): 542–577.

The Guardian (2019) UN accuses Blackstone Group of contributing to global housing crisis. *The Guardian* 26 March. Retrieved from: https://www.theguardian.com/us-news/2019/mar/26/blackstone-group-accused-global-housing-crisis-un (accessed 31 January 2022).

The Guardian (2020) Blackstone pays record £4.7bn for student housing firm iQ. *The Guardian* 26 February. Retrieved from: https://www.theguardian.com/business/2020/feb/26/blackstone-pays-iq-student-housing-firm-goldman-sachs-wellcome (accessed 31 January 2022).

Tretter, E. M. (2016) *Shadows of a sunbelt city: The environment, racism, and the knowledge economy in Austin.* Athens, GA: University of Georgia Press.

Walker, R. A. (2000) The geography of production. In E. Sheppard & T. J. Barnes (eds.) *A Companion to Economic Geography.* Oxford: Blackwell, 111–132.

Wiewel, W. & Perry, D. C. (eds.) (2008) *Global universities and urban development: Case studies and analysis.* Armonk, NY: M.E. Sharpe.

Winling, L. C. (2018) *Building the ivory tower: Universities and metropolitan development in the twentieth century.* Philadelphia: University of Pennsylvania Press.

Yeoh, B. S. A. (1996) *Contesting space: Power relations and the urban built environment in Colonial Singapore.* Oxford: Oxford University Press.

Zukin, S. (1982) *Loft living: Culture and capital in urban change.* Baltimore: Johns Hopkins University Press.

# 37. Looking forward: a research agenda for contemporary urban sociology
*Mika Hyötyläinen and Miguel A. Martínez*

The definition of urban sociology seems often just out of reach and as Savage and Ward put it 30 years ago, it 'has often been a source of despair to its practitioners and advocates' (Savage & Ward 1993). Partly out of the continued desperation in defining the subject, handbooks such as this one are compiled to illuminate the matter. Handbooks in social sciences generally collect texts that editors view as important into a type of directory of key subjects in their field. These texts reflect the types of research the editors think have left a significant legacy in the discipline as well as research that they hope future scholars would also engage with in more detail. The handbook is then a directory of exemplary work to learn from and be inspired by. In concluding this collection of such texts, we hope to indicate, first, what new and important perspectives, research agenda even, the present collection offers in comparison to previous such attempts; second, what lessons we can draw from these contributions in order to help define the discipline; and third, which relevant fields of research have been omitted and, however, would require more attention.

A brief exploration of relatively recent collections and companion titles shows that there is Paddison's (2001) *Handbook of Urban Studies*, the multi-edition *The City Reader* (LeGates & Stout 2020), and a wealth of other readers and handbooks on specific urban topics, such as gentrification (Lees et al. 2008), urban design (Larice & Macdonald 2012), segregation (Musterd 2020), and urban planning and urban issues in specific contexts, such as China (Yep et al. 2019), Africa (Silva 2020), and Southeast Asia (Padawangi 2019). The list goes on. However, perhaps the closest comparison to be drawn with this *Handbook* is the *Urban Sociology Reader* (Lin & Mele 2013). Lin and Mele's reader provides both reprints of urban sociology classics and contemporary ethnographies and case studies to illustrate the enduring importance of certain topics in urban sociology for an audience not so familiar with the discipline. Now, what Saskia Sassen (2007) pointed out regarding 21st century urban sociology still holds: that is, the social life of cities continues to correspond to old, familiar trends, so it follows that much of urban sociology's research traditions and its many subfields remain relevant and continue to make up the core of the discipline.

The major difference between the *Urban Sociology Reader* and the present volume is that this *Handbook* expects from its audience a prior engagement with the topics and knowledge of the classic debates. To some extent, this is a handbook of pressing current issues in urban sociology. To indicate what new, important perspective is offered here, we can add that many scholars at the early stage of their careers are also introduced and engage with urban sociological approaches. Furthermore, the *Handbook* provides a platform for researchers beyond the Anglophone world working from the Global South and the peripheries of the Global North. However, urban sociology will not, of course, reinvent itself by simply moving to another context or by handing the torch to the next generation of scholars. As is presented in this chapter, this *Handbook* covers many topics that are already familiar to most urban scholars, such as segregation, gentrification, capitalist urbanisation, neighbourhood effects, the right to the city, the global city, and the housing question, to name a few.

One problem shared by readers and handbooks that hope to give a general overview of a subject is that they often try to include every perspective on the multitude of issues tackled by scholars in said field. In attempting to provide an overview of everything, the editors do not disclose their own theoretical positions. This *Handbook* stands out rather by offering in the beginning a neat approach within which the chapters of the book engage their various topics while also enjoying full discretion. By recalling the introductory chapter, a twofold approach to urban sociology is thus fleshed out in order to underpin the whole collection of contributions.

First, the book urges to focus the purpose of urban sociology on exploring the social production of urban space. This goes back to the spatial turn in social sciences in the 1960s. Its theoretical roots can be unearthed in the works of political geographers, economists, and sociologists, including the likes of Henri Lefebvre, Manuel Castells, David Harvey, Doreen Massey, Edward Soja, Sharon Zukin, Anne Haila, Janet Abu-Lughod, Saskia Sassen, and John Urry. In their works, space is understood as a product of social interactions and, in particular, a product of the relations between labour and capital. Instead of a container fixed in time with some stagnant nature, urban space is socially produced by the actions of different social groups and, especially, by the hegemonic practices of businesses. As these relations and actions are power-laden, unequal, and hierarchical, particular attention here is to be paid to the spatio-temporal conditions and contextual constraints regarding the relations between people and spaces. In this task, urban sociologists must question and make transparent their own practical alliances with specific social groups and reflect on the consequences of the knowledge that is produced and vice versa.

Second, this *Handbook* has argued for an interdependent approach to critical urban sociology in line with the implications of the mentioned spatial turn. An interdependent approach, as presented in Chapter 2, is aware of the connections between epistemology and politics and reflective of the prospects and limitations exerted by the second over the first. It thus entails an urban sociology that pursues the emancipation of the oppressed and contributes to progressive politics while maintaining social scientific integrity and rigour. This reflexive and self-critical epistemology also links the chapters in this *Handbook*, which could rightly deserve the title of 'Handbook of Critical Urban Sociology.' In this vein, the contributions to this *Handbook* are examples of work at the cutting edge of critical urban sociology.

While drawing on the rich studies that comprise this book, this concluding chapter is less an attempt to recapitulate all that has been said in the preceding chapters and more an effort to detect some of the continuing and novel trends as well as the vexed issues of cities and urbanisation in the early 21st century previously discussed. We also aim to suggest topics and questions that were not tackled in this *Handbook* but that are deserving of attention now and in the coming future.

# TOWARD A CRITICAL URBAN SOCIOLOGY

In 2015 Aldon Morris published a book that should, in our opinion, introduce an important caveat to the curriculum of every undergraduate course in urban sociology. Titled *The Scholar Denied: W. E. B. Du Bois and the Birth of Modern Sociology*, the book explores how the work of Black American sociologist W. E. B. Du Bois has been systematically erased from the history of sociology by influential white sociologists, such as the likes of Robert Park. The erasing and suppressing of the relevance and importance of Du Bois solidified the Chicago school as the birthplace of contemporary American sociology. The works of feminist and socially engaged sociologists such as Jane Addams (Deegan 1988) experienced a similar suppression, even when also developed in the same metropolitan area of Chicago. To this day Chicago is where our teachings of the history of urban sociology tend unquestioningly to begin.

However, according to the account of Morris, it was Du Bois, who worked at Atlanta University, a historically Black university serving Atlanta's Black community, who first developed empirical, scientific sociology in the United States. Du Bois wanted to not only understand but to correct social problems and injustices through his work. The most pressing injustice of his time, and one that has not been corrected since, was systemic racism at the heart of the American experiment. Du Bois's key text is *The Philadelphia Negro* (1996), a book that provides an in depth, data-based, and systematic investigation of Black life in Philadelphia's Seventh Ward neighbourhood, focusing on topics such as migration, religion, crime, family, health, and education. Du Bois and what Morris calls the Atlanta school of sociology were then precursors to the urban ecological musings of the Chicago school, pioneering many of the elements later identified with the Chicago school, particularly the development of the city as the spatial setting and subject for a serious, urban social science.

Morris does not only accuse white American sociologists of the 1920s of suppressing the importance of Du Bois but of perpetuating a racist approach to social science. Morris holds no punches and writes 'Robert Park's sociology portrayed African Americans as an inferior race. Indeed, the image of blacks emerging from Park's sociology is one of a population handicapped by a double heritage of biological and cultural inferiority' (Morris 2015: 119). The type of Black advancement supported by Du Bois, closely entwined with labour struggles and a wish to overthrow the Jim Crow legislation, found strong conservative opposition that came to be personified in Booker T. Washington, a Black industrialist who embraced race inequality. It is safe to say that the American elites found in Washington a much more suited candidate for developing 'race relations' than in Du Bois.

Montalva Barba, in this *Handbook*, takes his cue from the work of Morris and explores in detail how racism has been embedded in urban sociology not just in the Chicago school but throughout the discipline's centenarian history. Moving forward, as Montalva Barba suggests, we should develop and embrace global critical race theorising in line with, reconnecting to, and building on Du Boisian urban sociology. This approach would be underpinned by a deep acknowledgement and analysis of how white supremacy operates globally, with a focus on its interconnectivities and engaged with the inherently racist structures of state and economic institutions. It would also investigate the ideological, discursive, and representational scaffoldings that uphold national and global racial systems and orderings of globalisation, colonisation, and settler colonialism. Angelcos's chapter on the ghetto concept and Roitman and Walters's chapter on the informality concept add complementary scrutiny to the transfer of academic categories that need to be critically questioned before possible mobilisation in urban research, especially in the Global South context.

A recent entry in the debates on and critiques of mainstream urban sociological knowledge production is Loïc Wacquant's book *The Invention of the 'Underclass'* (2022). Wacquant shows how persistent racial stigmas and othering are in the rhetoric and conceptual tools of social sciences. Wacquant dissects the historical development of the toxic concept of the underclass that enjoyed great academic and popular use over a period of three decades to the extent that it had a major consequence on knowledge production regarding urban inequality and marginalisation. According to Wacquant, the underclass concept dominated discussions on race and poverty for 30 years in the US (1970–1997) and was even exported to Europe to try and make sense of the issues on this side of the Atlantic. The underclass concept was born as a structural explanation for poverty by the Swedish Gunnar Myrdal. It then became a behavioural concept to understand the lives and lifestyles of the black, urban poor. Finally, it took on a neo-ecological character in the investigations of William Julius Wilson.

Wacquant captures and analyses the development of a concept that attempted to describe the new reality of the isolated cadres of the Black population and its perceived anti-social behaviour from the perspective of the white middle class, which depicted poor Black people as responsible for their own predicaments. He asks: where did this concept arrive from as it circulated in academia, media, and policy? Essentially there were three historical forces that led to the concept's use. First, there was an American anti-urbanism, rooted in the agrarian settler colonialism from the 1830s onward, with the notion of the 'wicked city' or the metropolis as a deprived location of class conflict, ethnic promiscuity, vice, and negligence as compared to the virtuous features of the rural experience. Second, historical racial uprisings and Black rural–urban migration and revolts in the cities coloured the anti-urbanism. Third, its roots were in the 1970s class, racial, and anti-statist (restrictive welfare, expansive *prisonfare*) phenomena and processes. The underclass was both an instrument of mainstream knowledge production that catered to the prejudices of the white middle class and a symbolic tool for denigrating their perceived other and distancing themselves from it.

In this vein, in 2011 the urban sociologist Sharon Zukin discussed the importance of disciplinary self-critique in order to explore how tightly the subject areas explored by sociologists are directed from above. According to her (Zukin 2011: 13):

> Sociologists like architects are servants of power. Just as architects depend on the deep pockets of clients, so sociologists depend on the state for research funds, social recognition, and 'policy relevance.' […] 'Problem' populations are sociologists' bread and butter whether they are deviants and delinquents, ethnic minorities or immigrants, or the working class and poor. The presence of these populations opens the gates to government intervention in 'problem areas' and funds for research. But to qualify for funding sociologists must define these groups at least implicitly as problematic.

Here a key difference between what we understand as critical urban sociology—exemplified in the many works in this *Handbook*—and mainstream urban sociology is made visible. Critical sociologists will emphasise the rigorous analysis of the production of space. Mainstream urban scholars are often inclined to the kind of spatial and social fetishism favoured by policy elites: they prioritise the question of how space supposedly affects social life and behaviour instead of the socially unjust dynamics of capitalist urbanisation.

Recently, pleas for a more reflective and self-critical urban sociology have begun to circulate. Tom Slater (2013), for example, is known for his work in exorcising the ghosts of spatial fetishism, particularly the strand of neighbourhood effects research. The superficially persuasive argument of neighbourhood effects studies, suggests Slater, is that 'where you live affects your life chances.' Due to the popularity and success of this territorial fetishism in urban sociology, an analytic hegemony in urban studies now rests on the following premise: 'neighbourhoods matter and shape the fate of their residents (and their young residents most acutely), therefore, urban policies must be geared towards poor neighbourhoods, seen as incubators of social dysfunction' (Slater 2013: 368). Slater calls for urgently flipping the argument on its head and studying the urban question from the premise that 'your life chances affect where you live,' hence putting the emphasis on the myriad of inequalities that shape and dictate peoples' lives and places in the city. Yip's chapter in this *Handbook* expands this discussion further and discusses the reasons for and problems with the continued policy-driven endeavour to chart generalisable and quantifiable neighbourhood effects.

In one of his latest publications, Slater (2021) has also called on scholars to engage critically with urban research in general. There is in Slater's words, a 'heteronomy' of urban research that guides and influences the kind of questions mainstream urban sociology tends to ask these days. This heteronomy is, again, about the two-pronged nature of urban studies as both knowledge production and strategic ignorance production.

With the concept of heteronomy Slater refers to the condition of scholars being constrained in their research by vested-interest funding institutions and employers such as state foundations, university research centres, urban think tanks, and consultancy firms. Often such entities will be in a place of power to influence the questions and categories of scholars, guiding their work towards what they perceive to be important topics. Hence, critical urban studies would strive to prevent the subordination of scholarly work to policy, institutional, and corporate agendas. It would couple epistemological and social critiques, explore alternatives to the status quo, and formulate research-driven ideas, as opposed to policy-driven and private company-driven urban research.

By retracing the history of urban sociology and producing analyses of contemporary knowledge production that rest on past conceptual work, we can better develop and deploy concepts more carefully. We can better understand what kind of knowledge drives policies and also what alternative policy could, in turn, be in place otherwise. This work should not be taken lightly as concepts are abstractions of the social reality we hope to understand, and they come to both frame but also inhibit alternative ways for understanding the world. Based on these premises, we move now to explore several themes that might have been further developed than was possible in this *Handbook*.

## ECONOMIC RESTRUCTURING, INDUSTRIAL RELOCATION, URBAN GROWTH, AND SHRINKING CITIES

The continuous, intensifying global economic restructuring, relocating of productive and extractive industries to one context and the remodelling of local economies based on services and finance in another, and the various consequences such processes have for cities and their residents continue to be at the core of urban sociological inquiry. Such processes leave visible marks on large cities. It is large cities that have also remained in the focus of the sociological research literature. Changes in the economy, labour market, and migration flows have generated profound transformations in the social fabric of cities. However, as capitalism and urbanisation intensify, they force urban sociologists to also recalibrate their research questions regarding, for example, the significance of traditional urban hierarchies and classifications (see Díaz-Parra and Roca's chapter on class perspectives, Yrigoy's focus on labour exploitation, and Socoloff's chapter on economic elites leading real estate production in Argentina as illustrations of this debate).

Economic restructuring has been a key topic in urban sociology for decades. The continuing decline of manufacturing in the Global North brought by the moving of production to countries with weaker labour and environmental protection and lower salary expenses has immense effects on cities and urban life in both contexts. In the Global South and East, the explosive industrialisation to meet both domestic and international demand has led to a matching explosive urbanisation. China has embraced urbanisation to an even greater extent than the capitalist North and West as a spatial fix to the great capital accumulation brought by industrialisation. A growing Chinese urban middle class and its consumer power have made Chinese megacities into a global force. Meanwhile, the country has poured more concrete into urban territories and infrastructure in the past 20 years than Western cities during the past two centuries (Forrest et al. 2020, Yep et al. 2019). Zhang's chapter in this *Handbook* gives a hint on the macro and micro social processes that produce this urban space and change in China.

Fix in this book also points out how the global city thesis has been used by scholars as an analytical concept to abstract from and explain the emerging urban hierarchies of the time. However, urban planners and managers took the notion as a recipe for urban competitiveness and prosperity in the international, inter-urban competition. Mainstream urban thinking thus promoted the normative project of world-city-building. Academic debates and urban policies were soon affected by the discourse on the importance of cities becoming competitive in the world economy. In the Global North, the corresponding switch to a service economy extensively reorganised and continues to reorganise the urban labour force, employment, and earning distribution, and indeed the economic foundations of cities. The diffusion of the normative global city paradigm from the North to the South stimulates management models, promoted by international consultants who distribute supposedly successful growth recipes, as the São Paulo case examined by Fix illustrates. These recipes are in high demand from municipal authorities hoping to devise strategies for local economic development and competitiveness. So-called 'strategic planning of cities' was disseminated by multiparty local agencies and international consulting companies and became a kind of 'prescription for success' (Martínez 1999). However, urban sociologists must continue to separate analytical concepts and critical analyses from the allure of drawing up recipes for cities that fuel capitalist and authoritarian urbanisation and risk, increasing social inequalities. Çelik's chapter is also helpful in this respect as it provides a critical review of the main theoretical approaches to studying urban politics in general and the local state in particular. Lima's and Bródy's contributions add more specific illustrations of cases in Ireland and Hungary where the neoliberal mantras of urban competition have severely affected the chances of local residents to have a say in regeneration plans.

Economic restructuring and the following management models not only rearrange the economy of some cities but the intensifying urban competition also kills off others. Old manufacturing and extractive industry towns slowly disappear as the companies that birthed them in one period move out in another. The term 'shrinking cities' was introduced 36 years ago by Häussermann and Siebel who wrote about the deindustrialising Ruhr area in Germany. The Ruhr experienced an industrial boom in the 1960s and early 1970s. However, by the late 1980s productivity had dwindled due to technological development and international competition (Häussermann & Siebel 1988, Olsen 2013). De-industrialisation, growing unemployment, declining household incomes, increasing welfare dependence, outmigration leading to population loss and ageing, and a lack of resources underpin urban shrinkage.

Contextual variation exists in urban shrinkage. In Finland, regional inequalities between growing urban centres and shrinking industrial towns are becoming severe. Homeowners in shrinking cities in Finland have found their property values plummet, owner occupation has become a liability, and residents are stuck in place. In post-socialist Eastern Europe the transition to a market economy met with fertility decline and outmigration in small and mid-sized industrial towns. In the United States, manufacturing jobs have also disappeared from major metropolises, such as the auto-manufacturing industry's disappearance that all but wiped out Detroit. In such cases, as Olsen (2013) points out, the dislocations in the former industrial heartlands have been profound. Resource extraction and the cities developed around such industries also play a major role in China's economic development. Various economic, social, and environmental issues like resource depletion, pollution, lack of welfare, and growing unemployment pose challenges to Chinese cities. Further economic restructuring implemented by the central government is perceived as a way forward from such challenges and towards growth (Yep et al. 2019). In many instances growth still appears as the guiding rationale of major cities.

However, just as the global city became a prescription for success, urban consultants recently began to promote shrinking as a road to prosperity. This strategy, which the economist Edward Glaeser (2011) calls 'shrinking to greatness,' is an attempt to get rid of excess buildings, avoid construction-driven approaches to urban regeneration, and focus on 'human capital' (or the 'creative class' à la Florida), reframing shrinkage as an opportunity. Even demolitions of old working-class estates and the forced displacement of their dwellers can fall under the umbrella of such an approach, as justified in many so-called urban regeneration plans. Some planners have taken on Glaeser's ideas and promote shifting ideas in planning practice to recognise that urban prosperity might be removed from a singular focus on growth (Hollander & Németh 2011). In the city of Dresden, the strategic plan no longer sees growth as imperative but prioritises instead the development of services and population stability in a revitalised and compact urban centre (Wiechmann 2009, Olsen 2013). Hirt and Beauregard (2021) also criticise the compartmentalisation of cities in scholarship into successful growing cities and failing shrinking cities. Planners and policymakers, they note, are informed by the scholarly literature and will associate top-down categories of cities with their own cities. Urban growth is associated with density, vibrancy, and environmental sustainability, whereas urban shrinkage is associated with a host of distressful socio-economic conditions, when neither necessarily hold true universally. Debates on urban degrowth (as Çelik and, to some extent, Vidal when examining housing cooperativism suggest in their respective chapters) will certainly be more central concerns of urban scholars in the coming future (Savini et al. 2022).

A critical sociological light must continue to be directed at economic restructuring and distribution of manufacturing and extractive industries, as well as the growing dependence on rentier incomes and service economies, including their devastating ecological and labour implications (as for the latter, Martínez et al. (2021) as well as Boersma's chapter in this *Handbook* on domestic workers in Hong Kong and Grazioli's discussion of international migrants' rights to inhabit the city help understand this issue). Whether promoting growth or embracing shrinkage, what city managers, planners, and consultants omit from their normative agendas should be the bread and butter of urban sociologists: contributing serious analyses and explanation of first how the social production of space under capitalism inevitably leads to the uneven ebb and flow of urban growth and decline, paying attention to its contextual nuances, and second how people living in cities now and in the future will be affected by this uneven process of creation and destruction. Urban sociologists should not take for granted that growth has superior social outcomes or that a shrinking city will ultimately lead to social decline, nor retreat to best practice evidence-making like Glaeser's 'shrinking to greatness' thesis but critically unpack the very underlying structural dynamics of uneven development and its consequences. One area in which such analyses are being undertaken that has received little attention in this *Handbook* is the sphere of work in the city.

## URBAN LABOUR MARKETS, PLATFORM ECONOMY, AND GIG WORK

In the Global North, deindustrialisation and the transfer of extractive and manufacturing businesses overseas is coupled with the weakening power of labour unions. Built around protecting the interests of those working in such traditional occupations, unions now see declining memberships and narrowing of negotiating room. In the labour markets of the Global North, including those social democratic welfare-state contexts where the agreements and consensus between labour and capital have been long-standing, de-regulation now favours capital while union protection is weak, and the social safety networks of the welfare state are often erased by austerity politics (Wacquant 2008). Guy Standing (2011) wrote more than a decade ago about the combination of these events leading to a growth in employment precarity. Full-time, secure, and properly reimbursed employment opportunities are increasingly few and far between. Accordingly, one issue deserving more attention than was given room for in this handbook is the developing and changing urban labour market (Greenberg & Lewis 2017) and the platform economy.

Part and parcel of urban labour market transformation is the rise in so-called platform and sharing economies in major cities. Touted as forms of flexible micro-entrepreneurship, platform work has immense ramifications for the precariousness of labour and long-lasting impacts on cities and their residents. The platform economy 'represents an important and strategically consequential branch of global capitalism, not least because of the Schumpeterian creative destruction—or disruption, in the contemporary parlance—it has imposed across much of the economic landscape' (Vallas & Schor 2020: 273). Platform companies are reliant on dense concentrations of both workers and customers and so they thrive in big cities. Platforms represent a distinct type of governance mechanism, different from markets, hierarchies, or networks, and therefore pose a unique set of problems for regulators and workers, but also for social scientists.

Gig and platform labour are linked to growing inequality and insecurity while they boost capital accumulation for platform companies, which escape many traditional employer regulations. Gig workers are reported to operate without health insurance, paid leave, and stable salaries (Berg & Johnston 2019). Gig industries use penalising mechanisms of surveillance and control. Furthermore, gig workers assume personal responsibility for costs and risks and conform to the violent temporality of customer demand, reducing the autonomy that platform companies love to advertise to potential employees (Vallas & Schor 2020).

Platform companies can be analysed as a form of rentier capitalism. After any initial investment in the platform, the companies can expand with very little investment in any future value production. Instead, via the monopoly ownership of the platform, they can extract revenue, or rent, from the users of that platform. Those users, like food delivery workers or taxi drivers, are depicted as independent contractors or entrepreneurs. In reality, they are a flexible pool of labour whose work is subjected to the extractive logic of the company. Online platforms and digital companies are adjusting who captures value and where. However, they are also rearranging the social life of cities, often intensifying inequalities and anonymity. Many daily human connections are digitised, but also the divide between the consumers and workers is concealed. As Baber (2023) argues, labour precarity is obscured when services are designated as a 'sharing economy.' Furthermore, an important question is how the 'sharing economy' should be 'understood as a labour practice, within the context of the commodification of the city and displacement of lower income residents' (Kerzhner 2019: 428).

In this book, for instance, Gil explores Airbnb landlordism as a new, noxious form of assetised housing provision that has particularly insidious ramifications within cities. This platform-based company has been around for more than a decade, yet it is only in recent years that local decisionmakers and legislators have grown aware of the harms of a lack of regulation over the company's operational logics. Beyond the questions of urban political economy and assetisation, Airbnb has raised sociological questions regarding 'individual physical and emotional labour, unequal dispersion of benefits and impacts on long-term employment and social mobility' (Kerzhner 2019: 428). Platform work and gigs promise flexibility around the workers' schedules, like childcare, education, or health needs, or in the case of Airbnb around the notion of housing as basic need. However, instead of labour security, workers often find themselves juggling multiple precarious gigs, struggling to make up a monthly salary from small income streams, and find themselves with diminishing time for other pursuits, such as the abovementioned childcare, education, or health needs. However, as new platform industries are being invented, flexi-work practices continue to thrive (Peck & Theodore 2001). As several authors have pointed out, the gig economy grows much faster than regulation can keep up with.

Urgent topics for urban sociologists to investigate are, therefore, the struggles, successes, and organisation of labour protests and movements against platform companies. They tend to have a distinctly urban characteristic and regulatory struggles against platform companies have often sparked from city courts. In recent years, for example, taxi drivers around the world have protested ride-hailing apps, causing traffic slowdowns in London, Warsaw, Hong Kong, Paris, and Berlin. 'Proponents of the platform apps point to consumer convenience and lower (albeit heavily subsidised) costs, blaming the excessive regulation of the taxicab industry for its stagnation, but rarely speak to the cost for driver workers. Meanwhile, the ride-hail companies are fighting legal challenges around the world over using "freelance" contracts to circumvent labour laws' (Bates 2019: 423). Furthermore, explosive developments in AI and robotics are projected to have immense ramifications for the organisation of work and the workplace; indeed, the very nature of work is bound to change. What will become of the creative classes, IT workers, and gig labour as the tech revolution progresses? Visual, text, audio, and other content production can be increasingly outsourced to purpose-designed bots, adding to the precarisation of creative labour and content production, including academic work.

In stark contrast with platform and gig work, urban sociologists have studied, for example informal street vending work carried out by people of (either internal or international) immigrant backgrounds who struggle to find entry to the city's harsh official labour markets. Chapters in this *Handbook* by Udelsmann Rodrigues, Van Stapele and Kiriro, Campos, and Roitman and Walters pay some attention to these usually informal activities in Global South cities, but street vending is a common place in the Global North as well (Agyeman et al. 2017). Working in public spaces subject to crime and arrests, street vendors' legitimacy, practices, and belonging in the city are constantly questioned and criticised. Low-income immigrant operators in cities across the world are often dehumanised, viewed as encroachments on public spaces, but affluent native-born and white vendors are welcomed as rightful citizens of the city and its business classes. Branding and the selling of more upmarket items desirable to elite palates are used to distinguish these vendors from the traditional vendors. For the higher-income gourmet vendors, the street is a place to play around with concepts and attract investors for a presumed transition to a storefront restaurant. Likewise, the ongoing transformations—often in the form of increasing commodification—of outdoor and traditional food markets demand a careful examination of this essential urban infrastructure (González 2017, Venkov 2016).

Finally, and in connection to the next suggested topic for further research, deserving of more attention are analyses of the gendered dynamics of precarisation of the labour market. One recent example of such work comes from Centeno Maya et al. (2022). They investigate the gendered inequalities in the food delivery business. They contribute to understanding of the labour conditions, reasons behind choosing delivery work, and the many pros and cons women find in working for food delivery platforms. Does platform delivery work resolve or rather reproduce labour market inequalities for women workers (Centeno Maya et al. 2022)? Food delivery can be located also under the field of sociology of mobilities, a topic that will also need more urban sociological research in the future. Platform-based courier services and other gig work may also find an interesting analytical entry point in the urban mobilities literature.

## SOCIOLOGY OF MOBILITIES

Urban sociology brings space to the analysis of social phenomena. Underpinning studies is often the notion that social phenomena are shaped by and shape their rather stationary relationship to spaces and places. There is a degree to which urban sociology views cities and the world as made up of rather stagnant social structures, classes, and groups. When exploring the social production of space, in the final analysis, urban spaces are often reduced to containers for social phenomena. Cities and societies come to be seen according to their geographical position, but 'much of the social mobility literature regarded society as a uniform surface and failed to register the geographical intersections of region, city and place, with the social categories of class, gender and ethnicity' (Urry 2000: 3). Moreover, the world is viewed as organised into sovereign states ruling over confined territories (Agnew 2017: 30–31).

However, one argument that did not receive much attention in this *Handbook* is that as much as social relationships are characterised by space and spatiality, movement and the experience of being in transit should also be analysed as kinetic features of social lives, inequalities, and hierarchies. As discussed in the previous sections, when industries relocate, the movement of people and resources intensifies. The world is on the move, writes Vannini (2010). Sheller and Urry, for instance, observe how 'asylum seekers, international students, terrorists, members of diasporas, holidaymakers, business-people, sports stars, refugees, backpackers, commuters, the early retired, young mobile professionals, prostitutes, armed forces; these and many others fill the world's airports, buses, ships, and trains. The scale of this traveling is immense' (Sheller & Urry 2006: 207).

Particularly through the influential works of John Urry and Mimi Sheller, mobility became a keyword in sociology. Mobilities include the vast movement of people, material, and capital across the world. Mobilities studies can also include wireless and portable communication technology use, the social organisation of transportation and communication infrastructures, and regional and transnational flows of information (Vannini 2010). Mobilities also refer to local and mundane processes of the movement of objects and resources, for example in the city, the daily commutes and transportation, and people's movement in and through public spaces (see Figure 37.1). As Hannam et al. (2006) point out, the mobilities literature can be of great relevance as 'issues of movement, of too little movement or too much or of the wrong sort or at the wrong time, are central to many lives, organisations and governments' (Hannam et al. 2006: 1).

*Source:* Miguel A. Martínez.

*Figure 37.1* Tokyo (2014)

Yet travel and the movement of people and things have for sociologists been secondary phenomena at best, a set of supportive technological processes that assist causally more powerful economic, social, and political phenomena. Movement has customarily been thought of as a shift between two locations of meaning and significance and the temporal aspect of mobility as 'dead time' (Vannini 2010). Distinct from traditional sociological theory, mobilities theorisations deal with how movement itself is or should be conceptualised. Movement is put forth as experiences, representations, and infrastructures related to journeys. Mobilities studies investigate how movement is understood and experienced, and the social lives that develop through and around it.

Sheller (2014: 791) writes that the purpose of mobilities research is to bring together 'some of the more purely "social" concerns of sociology (inequality, power, hierarchies) with the "spatial" concerns of geography (territory, borders, scale) and the "cultural" concerns of anthropology or communication research (discourses, representations, schemas), while inflecting each with a relational ontology of the co-constitution of subjects, spaces, and meanings.' Especially for the critical realists among urban sociologists, this relational ontology of the mobilities paradigm may still offer interesting inroads to analysis.

Thinking of the previous section's labour issues in the heavily reorganising global economy, the mobility of workers is often at the spotlight of this field of research. Labour market migration is argued to affect the future of cities in profound ways. As noted above, shrinking cities suffer from ongoing population decline. Whether labour market conditions work as pull or push factors and to what extent following mobilities account for urban development is an important issue to be studied more. An urban sociology of mobilities can engage with various factors that affect migration decisions, such as labour market conditions, employment and wage levels, local urban amenities, the attractiveness of environments, consumer facilities, and public goods (Arntz 2010). However, it can also be concerned with the structural inequalities in whether households are able to make migration decisions and relocate to more favourable sites or are stuck in unfavourable circumstances. This requires a research methodology moving away from the binary model of migration that sees migrant workers as either rural or urban populations towards linking migration patterns with larger social and economic structures and examining the dynamic relations between them (Massey 1990).

Gonick in this *Handbook*, for example, connects migration mobility with crucial issues of private property markets such as homeownership. Gonick uses the word 'navigation' many times to illustrate the experience of migrants on often exclusionary and penalising housing markets. At the same time the road to homeownership is seen as rite of passage, where owner occupation is seen as the destination of an immigrant's settlement, a way to achieve a dreamed social inclusion in the destination society because, as Gonick has it, 'it suggests permanence, stability, and successful entry into the mainstream against forms of economic marginalization, racialization, and discrimination.'

The climate crisis should also force us to reconsider the possibility of international travel and movement on the contemporary scale. Can we sustain current levels of movement of people and goods in the future? Moreover, the rapid development in AI and robotics may have drastic ramifications for the purposes and ways that people and things move and hence the approach of mobilities within urban sociology. Furthermore, when the housing and property markets attempt to answer to an increasingly transient world, the outcomes are often dubious for local populations. Temporary accommodations offered through platforms and short-term rentals in apartment hotels have an effect of increasing overall rents. Units that could have affordably served the local population are turned into expensive temporary lodgings for visitors and so-called 'global nomads,' those on the move.

## THE ENDURING HOUSING QUESTIONS

According to Mary Pattillo, 'W.E.B. Du Bois captured a wealth of meaning when he wrote, "The size and arrangements of a people's homes are no unfair index of their condition" [...] Du Bois's word "arrangements" stands in for an assortment of physical, spatial, social, political, economic, and symbolic forces that are manifested through an analysis of homes and housing, and sociologists and others have taken up this wide array of topics in their research' (Pattillo 2013: 510). Housing and the production, organisation, and management of residential space in cities affect the urban population universally. The development of the built environment in cities is by and large about the development of dwellings and residential spaces. The economics, politics, ideas, and ideologies that drive this development show great variation and nuance across contexts. As Mary Pattillo, citing Du Bois, in the above quotation states, sociologists have tackled these and many other issues as they relate to housing. Pattillo herself has written a neat overview of the history of sociological investigations regarding housing, running from the analyses of Du Bois on housing and rent in the late 1800s in Atlanta's Black neighbourhoods and Charles Booth's statistical investigations of housing in London during the same period through Chicago school studies to their later displacement by the neighbourhood as a more favoured unit of analysis in sociology. In similar fashion other topics like racial conflict, families, social movements, urban politics, or financial institutions have dominated over the housing question and it has moved to the pages of political economy journals and its own separate spheres of interdisciplinary housing studies focused more on policy (Pattillo 2013). However, this does not mean that sociologists would not have their work cut out for them in the field of housing research.

Housing is of course not merely shelter but also a place of privacy, of domestic work, and of social and family life. Sociologists may be interested in the actions of households that inhabit the houses, the social relations of housing markets, and the socio-cultural and demographic aspects of housing consumption. They may also explore the institutional and legal frameworks of housing provision, including the local, national, and supranational policies and regulations that define responsibilities over housing provision. Finally, housing is an increasingly important node in the circulation of capital, a major expense for most and an instrument of speculation and rent extraction for some. Against the convictions of housing economists who assume that housing markets are like any other markets pivoting on an equilibrium of supply and demand, sociologists draw from the political economy of housing the understanding that houses are monopolistic commodities tied to place and embedded in markets that do not function as any other markets. Critical sociologists acknowledge how market expansion into the domains of land and housing is an evolving feature of capitalism and is by no means self-evident (Haila 2016). Such theoretical deliberations would warrant more attention that has been provided in this *Handbook*. More research should be done on the fact that markets in general are socio-political creations, and their dynamics are not to be taken for granted as natural laws. A critical housing sociology will thus unpack the commodity form of housing and land (Hyötyläinen & Beauregard 2023).

How societies respond to their populations' housing needs changes through history. In the West, over the past two centuries we have seen a development from tenant settlements for factory workers to middle-class homeowner cities (see Kohl's chapter for a broader analysis). The contemporary age is characterised by rentier cities and renting is once again on the rise after houses suitable for first time buyers have been bought up by professional investors and rented out. Homeownership rates in cities have plunged after the 2008 Global Financial Crisis. Growth in the private rental market has been analysed as the consequence of the return of the private landlord and the development of rentier capitalism and the assetisation of housing (Aalbers et al. 2020, Christophers 2020). Private rental real estate has come to play an increasingly prevalent role even in the Nordic welfare state context. Yrigoy's chapter also provides a wider lens on these topics by suggesting a tight link between financialisation and rentierism with processes of labour exploitation.

Housing tenure then is another social arrangement that might be given more attention by critical sociologists, as the chapter by Kohl indicates. Tenure is not a neutral arrangement but reflects wider political economic tendencies and priorities. The lives of individuals and the urban structures can both be impacted by housing tenure arrangements. As Kohl notes 'Tenant cities have higher mobility and may face cost-of-living crises and corresponding protests more easily, whereas homeowner cities may be more immobile and face foreclosure crises and tax protests. The concentration of rental ownership among fewer landlords in turn reveals the monopolistic nature of urban markets much more clearly and also changes urban protest dynamics.'

The search for and analyses of alternative forms of housing tenure and provision has been a growing feature of sociological work on housing. In this volume, for example, Vidal explores the notion of housing cooperatives as urban commons. Housing cooperatives are thus proposed as an instrument of urban commoning practised to confront and criticise the continuous process of enclosure in the city. Vidal suggests that when housing cooperatives are embedded in institutional frameworks that at the same time make use of the state's redistributive capacities, but also cater to various stakeholders while providing them autonomy against the state and market forces of enclosure, they may provide partially decommodified housing alternatives. Collectively governed cooperative housing communities can potentially engage with, learn from, and help develop further practices and movements reclaiming the commons and not merely a right to housing but the right to the city.

Another alternative lens for the housing question has been developed in much of the urban scholarship on postcolonial contexts of the Global South. In countries like India and Indonesia, industrialisation has seen the proliferation not of a state-planned and regulated urbanisation but of an informal urbanisation. Millions of people migrating from rural areas to cities to work in manufacturing and extractive industries find themselves dependent on informal housing and neighbourhoods for dwelling and services (Padawangi 2019). Given the highly limited capacity of the state to build and provide new housing for the growing urban population, informal settlements have become the housing alternative of the new urban masses in so-called developing countries. On urban peripheries and in the openings between developed parts of cities, informal residential space mushrooms, providing homes for millions and often electricity, water, and information networks. Life is of course precarious in informal settlements and households are subject to evictions, land grabs, and housing demolitions. Housing informality hinges on deep, structural urban inequality. However, as various contributors to this volume have shown (e.g. Campos, Angelcos, and Roitman and Walters in the Global South and Grazioli and Polanska in the Global North) precarious dwellers can also unfold their collective agency in order to autonomously ameliorate their living conditions and even contest the unjust structures and powerholders that reproduce those very conditions.

Indeed, closely linked to the housing question are nefarious urban inequalities that are related to the differentiation of residential spaces, housing displacement, and evictions but

*Source:* Miguel A. Martínez.

*Figure 37.2    Social housing estates in San Giovanni A Teduccio neighbourhood, Naples (2022)*

also more mundane experiences of the inadequacy and crowdedness of dwelling space and a continuous sense of insecurity over one's home (see Figure 37.2). Urban sociology and the sociology of housing are, therefore, intimately connected and will keep jointly flourishing as a key focus of research.

## SEGREGATION AND THE PROBLEM OF SOCIAL MIX POLICIES

The concern over urban inequality originally launched the whole discipline of urban sociology, so the questions of territorial divisions and divisions of people in cities have puzzled urban researchers ever since. Some scholars (Brenner et al. 2009) trace the *prehistory* of urban studies back to Friedrich Engels's *Condition of the Working Class in England* published in 1845, in which Marx's companion, frustrated by the sordid conditions of life in the working-class quarters of industrial English cities, criticised industrial capitalism for urban inequality and its incapability of solving the housing question.

Since the dawn of urban sociology socio-spatial differentiation and the study of the city as a 'social mosaic' have been one of its central concerns. Socio-spatial differences are expressed with notions of forced and self-segregation, ghettoisation, housing discrimination, socio-spatial injustice and inequality, disinvestment and degraded habitats, gated communities, and so on. However, unlike Engels, for whom the urban question was a class question, an unfortunate feature of mainstream European segregation work in recent decades has been the utter dismissal of class from segregation analysis. As Díaz-Parra and Roca in this book note, if we disregard the class-based process that generates socio-spatial segregation, we will lose the explanatory and emancipatory potential of class theory. Indeed, segregation research far too easily recoils into naive empiricism and positivism, particularly when scholars choose to ignore its connection to capitalist urbanisation, uneven development, and class struggles. Very deliberately, class is dismissed from many urban analyses as a central dynamic of inequality. The working class has in the long term been made 'unfashionable, inscrutable, unnoticed if not invisible' (Wacquant 2008: 200). Studies of segregation, urban poverty, violence, and street crime, for instance, have replaced traditional research on working-class neighbourhoods in urban studies in general, as the 'language of class has been supplanted by the tropes of the "underclass" in the United States and "exclusion" in Western Europe wherever working-class neighborhoods have undergone involution' (Wacquant 2008: 200).

Take, for example, the hometown of this concluding chapter's first author. Helsinki is widely known and celebrated for its tenure-mix policies and for avoiding the most extreme forms of segregation of income and language groups so familiar in other European urban contexts. The tenure-mixing policies in Helsinki have traditionally been practised to ensure that households with various employment, educational, and ethnic backgrounds can find housing in various neighbourhoods. Of course, this has not always succeeded. For example, in the southern neighbourhoods of central Helsinki one will find enclaves of wealthy households, whereas certain peripheral social housing neighbourhoods have seen concentrations of language minorities and the working class. However, in recent years the tenure-mix policies have clearly taken on features familiar from international experiences with tenure and social mixing. They are being practised with the goal of dispersing and diluting concentrations of working-class and immigrant-background households to try and rejuvenate social housing estates by introducing more owner occupation and attract middle-class households. In essence, the welfare ideals of equality and universal access of yesteryear appear to be changing to state-led gentrification and social-control policies (Hyötyläinen 2020). Social mixing is revealed as a liberal policy instrument, favoured and applied by city managers across the Global North. It has also attracted much attention and critique from scholars.

As Bacqué and Charmes in this volume argue:

> Many studies have examined the impact of poverty concentration in a neighbourhood by analysing different registers: the behaviour of individuals at different periods of life, with a focus on delinquent behaviour; the state of health; children's level of 'development' and success at school; and access to employment and professional insertion for young people and adults. [...] However, it is still difficult to identify which of these effects are specifically linked to the neighbourhood, and which stem from the social characteristics of individuals and families.

As a consequence, urban sociology has to disentangle the weight of different components of socio-spatial phenomena by also revealing the political implications, and side effects, of spatial determinism and fashionable urban policies such as those promoting 'social mixture' (see Figure 37.3).

Social mix has also become a euphemism for gentrification. Here, gentrification is not just a by-product of the inherently unjust housing market and capitalist urbanisation but is deliberately being used as a policy tool and mechanism to replace poor and non-native speaking populations with higher-income and native-speaking households. Social mix is a way to put a positive spin on the influx of relatively affluent households to working-class neighbourhoods. Social mix hides relations of domination and power that are at the core of these residential dynamics. It also prevents the empowerment and political mobilisation of working-class residents. Considering such neighbourhoods as ghettoes that must be eradicated is a deliberate failure to recognise their inhabitants as legitimate political actors; it is a refusal to draw on the social and political dynamics that shape them. It also obscures the fact that working-class neighbourhoods can be political bases. Joining together with peers can actually help build a common discourse and a common experience. It can improve visibility in the public political arena and is a way to acknowledge differences (Davies & Imbroscio 2010). In particular, chapters by Kadıoğlu, Sakızlıoğlu, Holm, and Caciagli provide a rich range of insights about the social dimensions of gentrification that debunk the myths of social mix and suggest further avenues for urban sociological research.

*Source:* Miguel A. Martínez.

*Figure 37.3  Varazhdane Park in Sofia (2022)*

## GENTRIFICATION AND HOUSING DISPLACEMENT

American sociologist Matthew Desmond's celebrated work *Evicted* (2016) aroused sociological imaginations and brought housing displacement into the radar of mainstream social sciences. However, critical urban scholars had already been researching evictions and displacement for decades (Martínez 2019, 2020). The fact that the loss of home endures as a major experience of the urban working-class, racialised, and marginalised households everywhere has not escaped those scholars dedicating their work to understanding the place of home and residential space in the housing market and the capitalist urbanisation process. One persistent process reflecting urban inequality under capitalism, directly linked to uneven investments in residential space and often with the social outcome of class displacement, is gentrification.

What might a sociological contribution to gentrification research entail in this era of gentrification having arguably become a ubiquitous global urban strategy and a planetary phenomenon (Lees et al. 2016)? Holm in this *Handbook* points out that we should keep the focus on the core political economic aspects of the process so as not to lose the concept to ambiguity. These elements are firstly the investment, disinvestment, and reinvestment of capital in urban space. The core of the political economic process underpinning gentrification was of course best depicted by Neil Smith as the rent gap theory and is also investigated in depth by Kadıoğlu in another chapter of this *Handbook* focused on Berlin and Stockholm. The second aspect is the direct or indirect displacement of working-class households and their replacement by high-income groups. The nuances of displacement were famously captured by Peter Marcuse (1985) and much of the work on gentrification is motivated by a concern with social justice based on criticism of the various expressions of unwanted working-class socio-spatial displacement. As Slater (2021) has pointed out, even though gentrification has been found in nearly every corner of the world, we should still keep studying it to keep the focus on the violence of people losing their homes. Holm suggests, however, that often gentrification research can become a checklist of this series of aspects, which are collected to present a strong gentrification diagnosis in a distinct context without providing any new, deeper understanding of gentrification.

Holm then fleshes out a sociological contribution to gentrification research and suggests it might consist of the following further elements: a) an analysis of the social order that becomes visible in gentrification processes; b) an analysis of the agency of the individual, collective, and institutional actors; and c) an analysis of state interventions and social movements in gentrification processes.

What Holm means by investigating the social order would entail exploring the rent gap in looking for the principles of investment decisions in gentrification processes (economics), but also analysing the power relations between different groups in displacement (politics) and examining the normative ideas that are made visible in gentrification processes and make them possible in the first place (law and culture). Second, Holm calls for more agency-oriented analyses of gentrification. These would explore and unpack moving decisions by households, investment and disinvestment decisions by property owners, and even state administrative decisions for or against policy mechanisms of social protection, but also investment incentives in gentrifying neighbourhoods. Caciagli's chapter in this book is also illustrative of such work, as she turns the lens on exploring a specific faction of the middle class according to their life stages and dilemmas in relation to their school choices in the ongoing gentrification of a neighbourhood of Milan.

Polanska in another chapter explores not just the experience of but the active opposition to home evictions in Sweden. Polanska analyses both the destruction of home and the experience of displacement, but also the question of how home comes to be given meaning and politicised by those at risk of displacement. The destructive side of the displacement process is often the topic of focus, but Polanska hopes to both conceptualise the processes of the destruction and include in the analysis the re-creation of home. What is the role homemaking plays in the negotiation for people's place and position in society, their political engagement and agency, specifically in the face of the destructive forces jeopardising the home? Indeed, residents are often portrayed as passive victims of eviction and displacement, but the perspective Polanska offers is an attempt to also account for how the destruction of home encounters very active resistance and collective protest, indeed very active resident subjects struggling for their homes and in doing so also for much more.

Defending the home and one's right to stay put is such a universal political struggle that grassroots tenants' groups have built coalitions and networks across the whole country. As Polanska observes, '[a]long with resistance to extensive renovations resulting in steep rent increases, Swedish tenants have in the last decade engaged in protesting against conversions of public housing, privatization of public property, poor maintenance/disinvestment in rental housing, and most recently proposals to introduce market rents in new construction and rent increases through the reorganization of the model for rent setting.'

Finally, as each instance of gentrification takes place in a distinct institutional context, a systematic analysis of the concrete local political arrangements in which, for example, property titles are granted and secured and locational investment potentials exploited would be useful. However, on the other hand, different contexts also allow for exploring nuanced cases of protest and social movements against gentrification, helping to understand struggles and conflicts but also possible successes in protecting residents, their homes, and neighbourhoods (Mayer 2016).

## RENTIER CAPITALISM AND THE ASSETISATION OF CITIES

Following the twofold purpose and approach of urban sociology put forth in the introductory chapter—the analysis of the social production of space and the emancipatory and progressive political objective—a topic of investigation that should receive all the attention it can be afforded is the development of the built environment under capitalism and the class struggle inherent to its social organisation.

As Swyngedouw (2018: 3) suggests,

> planetary urbanization with its multiple internal inequities and embedding within the combined and uneven geographical development of world capitalism is not only the geographical imprint of the deepening and widening of capitalist socio-ecological relations and accumulation dynamics; it is one of the driving forces through which the accumulation process proceeds. In other words, urbanization is an "active moment" in the development of capitalism. At the same time, cities have historically also been both the theatre of class struggle and the terrain that required repossessing from the dispossessing class dynamics that underpin the accumulation process.

The chapter by Rousseau develops this approach and uses the global and more-than-urban spread of the Covid-19 pandemic as a case in point.

More the field of expertise for political economists, urban sociologists have also engaged with serious work on how capitalism in its mutations affects the social production of space. This is a process riddled with inequalities and conflicting interests, especially in the contemporary era of deep assetisation of land and its appurtenances. In a volatile global financial market, the built environment is a safe investment. Land, real estate, and infrastructure have become privileged areas for the reproduction of financial capital. Meanwhile, local governments attempt to increasingly design their policies and steer legislation in ways that attract mobile capital to compete in the global urban sphere.

Real estate is today being targeted to satisfy investors' interests in exchange values rather than meet the use value and needs of the users of urban space. Other trends include real estate services internationalisation and asset management services (Christophers 2023) to serve institutional investors and assist in merging local real estate markets into international real estate investment networks. In this *Handbook* Socoloff illustrates how an urban sociologist might engage in an analysis of the ramifications of global real estate finance. She pays particular attention to the types of actors involved in what she calls an increasingly 'financialised' regime of urban development. Through the examination of a case study in Argentina, where during recent decades speculative real estate development has become a dominant way of spatial production, she shows how closely knit social networks of economic elites operate in their investments, impacting suppliers and their strategies and determining the locations of urban developments.

Socoloff thus argues that the increasing financialisation of the economy poses new challenges for urban sociologists. She suggests including in our analyses financial data and specialised press information and conducting studies of developers' and investors' strategies in order to demonstrate 'the intertwined relationship between large developers, (trans)national elites, financialization, and the expanding web of associated firms that operate across borders.' Indeed, sociological analyses can engage with further questions regarding the key players in the process where cities are objects of accumulation for traditional elites, but also novel agents and flows of capital. In this regard, more studies on the upper classes and super-rich people's socio-spatial practices to produce urban spaces, and their strategies to hide in privileged enclaves and enjoy high mobility across the globe with its subsequent extreme environmental impacts, certainly deserve further investigation (Andreotti et al. 2015, Atkinson 2021, Forrest et al. 2017). Despite all the reasonable criticism that Pahl's sociology of the urban managers received (Saunders 1986), there is still wide room to investigate their collusion with the socio-spatial making of the economic elites and their regular resort to global hubs such as tax havens, not to mention their unlimited accumulation of real estate properties and their operations of land grabbing and profiting from the privatisation of state assets and public goods. This approach would include a sociology of specific professionals involved in the real estate business, such as architects and urban planners, lawyers, mediating agents, banks' staff, private investors, local state officers, political representatives, police authorities, and even artists.

## SOCIALLY SHAPED CITIES

In recent theoretical debates, the physical limits of cities have been often questioned and calls for multi-scalar research, in spatial, social, and political dimensions, are now a commonplace in urban scholarship, not least across many chapters of this *Handbook*. However, the production, experience, and representation of urban life are always at the core of urban sociology, regardless of the continuous negotiations and conditions that erect different socio-spatial boundaries. In this regard, the relations between urban and non-urban spaces according to the representations and practices of different social groups, the expansion and role of metropolitan regions at a global scale of flows, and even the social significance of world regions and continents to understand the development of capitalist urbanisation processes and current expressions of class struggles will certainly continue to demand a central interest for urban sociologists. The case of the social, political, and urban dimensions of university campuses is, for instance, investigated in Oh's chapter.

This *Handbook* has presented many facets of how cities are socially shaped such as how it occurs in processes of citizen participation in urban planning matters (chapters by Çelik, Lima, Bródy, and Zhang, for example), in gender inequalities and expressions through socio-spatial processes (chapters by Sakızlıoğlu, Valdivia and Ortiz Escalante, Dagkouli-Kyriakoglou, and Boersma, in particular), and in conflicts related to social control and broken solidarities in urban settings (in the chapters by Sequera, Buchholz and Kuzmanić, and Van Stapele and Kiriro). Far from being exhaustive, we believe that these topics will continue to raise important academic and political debates, albeit demanding more clarification, worldwide and comparative evidence, as well as more conclusive explanations.

In terms of theory, it is obvious that some scholars have achieved more prominent influence in recent urban sociology scholarship than others. For instance, the works of Pierre Bourdieu (as here reviewed by Borges Pereira in his chapter) and Henri Lefebvre (as used by Grazioli and Rousseau in their respective chapters) are quite alive in the theoretical frameworks of many non-Anglophone scholars, despite the traditional dominance of other US and UK academic stars in other competing books. As noted before, the influence of more subaltern figures in the field of sociology who also had straightforward engagements with anti-racism and feminist politics suggests, nonetheless, that the theoretical canon of critical urban sociology still needs to be enriched and become more integrated when it comes to accounting for the main social structures of inequality and oppression. For example, issues of disability and age (childhood, youth, adulthood, old age) in relation to the urban space have hardly been empirically investigated and thus have not left any key trace in the theorising of current urban sociology.

Following the reflections triggered by the initial preparation of this *Handbook* and the different contributions collected here, we are aware that a research agenda for urban sociology still has to pay attention to many other forgotten or here only superficially touched topics. The list is too large so we will just conclude with a mention of four groups of topics in which others may develop their investigations further.

In the socio-spatial and economic realm, the role of outdoor markets, food markets, local retailing, shopping streets, shopping malls, and street vending seems a very underdeveloped field of studies with a sociological lens. Moreover, the consumption of both local and long-distance goods and the socio-ecological impacts of urban lifestyles, not to mention their class distinction features, are always urgently demanding a sociological re-examination, especially in times of climate crisis. This stretches to the consumption and supply of energy and other resources through key urban infrastructures (water, waste, transport, wires, etc.) beyond the avenues opened by the splintering urbanism approach and the simplified focus on the notion of infrastructures, which sometimes is merely used to replace the study of social relations and practices. Their privatisation, commodification, quality, and contestation by social movements aiming at keep them as essential commons have been central aspects over the development of neoliberal capitalism.

Social controversies about the built heritage and the cultural and economic value of architecture are also an important subject of research, especially in cities going through war, military occupation, natural disasters, and reconstruction. In all cases—in both ordinary and extraordinary times—sociologists investigate how social structures, social groups, and social relations are related to residential locations, mobility across different urban and extra-urban spaces, access to services and jobs, consumption, social reproduction, etc., not only at the macro scales of urban life but also in the meso and micro spheres of daily life, including social practices at night.

The phenomenon of urban tourism and its consequences has grown as an academic discipline itself, but less explored is the proliferation of online images about cities and social activities in urban life. This increase in urban imaginaries is even more important in times of expanding securitisation trends by which even taking pictures of the police is becoming forbidden and punished. Racial profiling and the criminalisation of vulnerable social groups can make authorities less accountable if the state control over sharing images and internet communication is tightened. The same applies to the urban expressions of gender and diverse sexual identities and orientations, for which the internet often enables both online reproduction of forms of oppression and their own communicative means to articulate emancipatory discourses. Not less significant is the contribution made by artists, art museums and galleries, art fairs, public art, and graffiti, for example, to shaping the cultural sphere of urban social life, sometimes in close relation with 'art-washing' phenomena associated with gentrification, mega-events, and mega-projects that nurture capital accumulation.

A final set of socio-spatial phenomena that have been traditionally on the margins of mainstream urban sociology refers to urban activism, protests, struggles, and movements (Mayer 2016, Pickvance 2003, Yip et al. 2019). These are manifested in, for example: the self-organisation of residents and neighbourhoods against perceived threats or while recreating their own urban landscape; their practices of social reciprocity, sharing, solidarity, and care in neighbourhoods and residential blocks, but also in other urban spaces, etc.; the survival strategies of marginalised social groups such as homeless people, waste pickers, etc.; and participatory initiatives led by urban grassroots groups promoting commoning and anti-capitalist and socialist prefiguring of collective practices in relation to housing, real estate development, environmentally friendly urbanisation, redistributive measures, direct democracy, etc. As shown in some previous chapters of this *Handbook* (by Valdivia and Ortiz Escalante, Van Stapele and Kiriro, Grazioli, and Campos, for instance), activist-research projects and the researchers' engagement with grassroots struggles may enhance not only the alliances that can help these movements thrive but also provide a deeper and more rigorous sociological knowledge of the processes at stake.

# REFERENCES

Aalbers, M. et al. (2020) The financialization of housing in capitalism's peripheries. *Housing Policy Debate* 30(4): 481–485.

Agnew, J. (2017) *Globalization and Sovereignty: Beyond the Territorial Trap*. Lanham: Rowman & Littlefield.

Agyeman, J. et al. (eds.) (2017) *Food Trucks, Cultural Identity, and Social Justice. From Loncheras to Lobsta Love*. Cambridge, MA: MIT.

Andreotti, A. et al. (2015) *Globalised Minds, Roots in the City: Urban Upper-middle Classes in Europe*. Chichester: Wiley Blackwell.

Arntz, M. (2010) What attracts human capital? Understanding the skill composition of interregional job matches in Germany. *Regional Studies* 44(4): 423–441.

Atkinson, R. (2021) *Alpha City. How London was Captured by the Super-Rich*. London: Verso.

Baber, A. (2023) Labour market engineers: Reconceptualising labour market intermediaries with the rise of the gig economy in the United States. *Work, Employment and Society*. https://doi.org/10.1177/09500170221150087.

Bates, L. (2019) Gigs, side hustles, freelance: What work means in the platform economy city. *Planning Theory & Practice* 20(3): 423–424.

Berg, J. & Johnston, H. (2019) Too good to be true? A comment on Hall and Krueger's analysis of the labor market for Uber's driver-partners. *ILR Review* 72(1): 39–68.

Brenner, N. et al. (2009) Cities for people, not for profit. *City* 13(2–3): 176–184.

Centeno Maya, L. A. et al. (2022) Food delivery workers in Mexico City: A gender perspective on the gig economy. *Gender & Development* 30(3): 601–617.

Christophers, B. (2020) *Rentier Capitalism: Who Owns the Economy, and Who Pays for It?* London: Verso.

Christophers, B. (2023) *Our Lives in Their Portfolios: Why Asset Managers Own the World*. London: Verso.

Davies, J. & Imbroscio, D. (eds.) (2010) Urban Politics. Los Angeles: Sage.

Deegan, M. J. (1988) *Jane Addams and the Men of the Chicago School, 1892–1918*. New Brunswick, NJ: Transaction.

Desmond, M. (2016) *Evicted: Poverty and Profit in the American City*. New York: Crown.

Du Bois, W. E. B. (1996 [1899]) *The Philadelphia Negro: A Social Study*. Philadelphia: University of Pennsylvania Press.

Forrest, R. et al. (2017) *Cities and the Super-Rich: Real Estate, Elite Practices and Urban Political Economies*. New York: Palgrave Macmillan.

Forrest, R. et al. (2020) *The City in China: New Perspectives on Contemporary Urbanism*. Bristol: Bristol University Press.

Glaeser, E. (2011) *The Triumph of the City. How Urban Spaces Make Us Human*. London: Macmillan.

González, S. (ed.) (2017) *Contested Markets, Contested Cities: Gentrification and Urban Justice in Retail Spaces*. New York: Routledge.

Greenberg, M. & Lewis, P. (eds.) (2017) *The City is the Factory: New Solidarities and Spatial Strategies in an Urban Age*. Ithaca, NY: Cornell University Press.

Haila, A. (2016) *Urban Land Rent: Singapore as a Property State*. Chichester: John Wiley & Sons

Hannam, K. et al. (2006) Mobilities, immobilities and moorings. *Mobilities* 1(1): 1–22.

Häußermann, H. & Siebel, W. (1988) Die schrumpfende Stadt und die Stadtsoziologie. *Soziologische Stadtforschung* 78–94.

Hirt, S. & Beauregard, R. (2021) Must shrinking cities be distressed cities? A historical and conceptual critique. *International Planning Studies* 26(1): 1–13.

Hollander, J. B. & Németh, J. (2011) The bounds of smart decline: A foundational theory for planning shrinking cities. *Housing Policy Debate* 21(3): 349–367.

Hyötyläinen, M. (2020) 'Not for normal people': The specialization of social rental housing in Finland. *ACME: An International Journal for Critical Geographies* 19(2): 545–566.

Hyötyläinen, M. & Beauregard, R. (eds.) (2023) *The Political Economy of Land. Rent, Financialization and Resistance*. Abingdon: Routledge.

Kerzhner, T. (2019) Labour, gender and making rent with Airbnb. *Planning Theory & Practice* 20(3): 428–431.
Larice, M. & Macdonald, E. (2012) *The Urban Design Reader*. London: Routledge.
Lees. L. et al. (2008) *Gentrification*. New York, NY: Routledge.
Lees, L. et al. (2016) *Planetary Gentrification*. Cambridge: Polity.
LeGates, R. & Stout, F. (eds.) (2020) *The City Reader*. New York, NY: Routledge.
Lin, J. & Mele, C. (eds.) (2013) *The Urban Sociology Reader*. Abingdon: Routledge.
Marcuse, P. (1985) Gentrification, abandonment, and displacement: Connections, causes, and policy responses in New York City. *Journal of Urban & Contemporary Law* 28: 195–240.
Martínez, M. A. (1999) La traslación de estrategias empresariales al territorio: problemas de la planificación estratégica en el urbanismo. *Política y Sociedad* 31: 93–116.
Martínez, M. A. (2019) Bitter wins or a long-distance race? Social and political outcomes of the Spanish housing movement. *Housing Studies* 34(10): 1588–1611.
Martínez, M. A. (2020) *Squatters in the Capitalist City. Housing, Justice, and Urban Politics.* New York, NY: Routledge.
Martínez, M. A. et al. (2021) *Reclaiming Space for Workers in the 21st Century: A Literature Review on Worker Centres*. Beirut: International Labour Organisation. https://www.ilo.org/newdelhi/whatwedo/publications/WCMS_800626/lang--en/index.htm.
Massey, D. S. (1990) Social structure, household strategies, and the cumulative causation of migration. *Population Index* 56(1): 3–26.
Mayer, M. (2016) Neoliberal urbanism and uprisings across Europe. In M. Mayer et al. (eds.) *Urban Uprisings. Challenging Neoliberal Urbanism in Europe*. New York, NY: Palgrave MacMillan, 57–92.
Morris, A. (2015) *The Scholar Denied: W. E. B. Du Bois and the Birth of Modern Sociology.* Los Angeles: University of California Press.
Musterd, S. (2020) *Handbook of Urban Segregation*. Cheltenham, UK and Northampton, MA, USA: Edward Elgar Publishing.
Olsen, A. K. (2013) Shrinking cities: Fuzzy concept or useful framework? *Berkeley Planning Journal* 26(1): 107–132.
Padawangi, R. (ed.) (2019) *Routledge Handbook of Urbanization in Southeast Asia*. New York, NY: Routledge.
Paddison, R. (ed.) (2001) *Handbook of Urban Studies.* London: Sage.
Pattillo, M. (2013) Housing: Commodity versus right. *Annual Review of Sociology* 39: 509–531.
Peck, J. & Theodore, N. (2001) Exporting workfare/importing welfare-to-work: Exploring the politics of Third Way policy transfer. *Political Geography* 20(4): 427–460.
Pickvance, C. (2003) From urban social movements to urban movements: A review and introduction to a symposium on urban movements. *International Journal of Urban and Regional Research* 27(1): 102–109.
Sassen, S. (2007) *A Sociology of Globalization*. New York, NY: W. W. Norton & Co.
Saunders, P. (1986) *Social Theory and the Urban Question*. (2nd edition). Abingdon: Routledge.
Savage, M. & Warde, A. (1993) *Urban Sociology, Capitalism and Modernity*. London: Macmillan.
Savini, F. et al. (2022) *Post-Growth Planning: Cities Beyond the Market Economy*. New York, NY: Routledge.
Sheller, M. (2014) The new mobilities paradigm for a live sociology. *Current Sociology* 62(6): 789–811.
Sheller, M. & Urry, J. (2006) The new mobilities paradigm. *Environment and Planning A* 38: 207–226.
Silva, C. N. (ed.) (2020) *Routledge Handbook of Urban Planning in Africa*. New York, NY: Routledge.
Slater, T. (2013) Your life chances affect where you live: A critique of the 'cottage industry' of neighbourhood effects research. *International Journal of Urban and Regional Research* 37(2): 367–387.
Slater, T. (2021) *Shaking up the City. Ignorance, Inequality, and the Urban Question*. Oakland, CA: University of California Press.
Standing, G. (2011) *The Precariat: The New Dangerous Class*. London: Bloomsbury.
Swyngedouw, E. (2018) The urbanization of capital and the production of capitalist natures. In M. Vidal et al. (eds.) *The Oxford Handbook of Karl Marx*. Oxford: Oxford University Press, 1–20.
Urry, J. (2000) *Sociology beyond Societies. Mobilities for the Twenty-First Century*. London: Routledge.
Vallas, S. & Schor, J. B. (2020) What do platforms do? Understanding the gig economy. *Annual Review of Sociology* 46: 273–294.

Vannini, P. (2010) Mobile cultures: From the sociology of transportation to the study of mobilities. *Sociology Compass* 4(2): 111–121.
Venkov, N. (2016) Conspiracy narratives at the women's market. http://seminar-bg.eu/spisanie-seminar-bg/special-issue-3/item/451-conspiracy-narratives-at-the-womens-market.html.
Wacquant, L. (2008) *Urban Outcasts: A Comparative Sociology of Advanced Marginality*. Cambridge: Polity.
Wacquant, L. (2022) *The Invention of the 'Underclass': A Study in the Politics of Knowledge*. Cambridge: Polity.
Wiechmann, T. (2009) Conversion strategies under uncertainty in post-socialist shrinking cities: The example of Dresden in Eastern Germany. In K. Pallagst et al. (eds.) *The Future of Shrinking Cities: Problems, Patterns and Strategies of Urban Transformation in a Global Context.* Berkeley, CA: University of California Press, 5–15.
Yep, R. et al. (2019) *Handbook on Urban Development in China*. Cheltenham, UK and Northampton, MA, USA: Edward Elgar Publishing.
Yip, N. M. et al. (eds.) (2019) *Contested Cities and Urban Activism*. Singapore: Palgrave-McMillan.
Zukin, S. (2011) Is there an urban sociology? Questions on a field and a vision. *Sociologica* 3: 1–17.

# Index

Aalbers, M. B. 65, 72, 113, 173, 178, 363
Abellán, J. 113
Abramo, P. 71, 541
Abrutyn, S. 151
Abu Dhabi 572
Abu-Lughod, J. 584
academic curating 12–13
accommodation challenge 513–14
Accra–Lagos corridor 225–6
accumulation economy 544
Acuto, M. 543
Adam, B. 511
Addams, J. 27, 585
Addie, J. -P. D. 579
Adorno, T. 38
advanced capitalism 493, 496
affordable housing 398–9, 401, 403, 408
Affori, school choices and gentrification 289–96 286
Africa 539, 548, 583
agency, in gentrification processes 179–80
Airbnb 380, 384, 385, 387, 391
    international growth 389
    landlordism 591
    and short-term rentals (STRs) 381, 383, 388, 394
Alford, R. 7
Algeria 120–22, 130
    colonial domination in 121, 122, 130
    crisis of traditional agriculture 121
Alihan, M. A. 138
Allen, A. 541
Allende, S. 307
Al-Saleh, D. 578
Althusser, L. 67, 220, 567
American anti-urbanism 586
Amsterdam 85, 98
    Eye Film Museum 4
    homeownership rates 100
anarchist practice 213–14
Anderson, B. 204
Anderson, E. 263
Andersson, R. 140
Angelcos, N. 305
Angelo, H. 223
Angola 314, 316, 318, 320
    hyper-marginalisation in cities 320–22
    population in 321
Annunziata, S. 181

ANRU *see* National Urban Renewal Agency (ANRU)
Appadurai, A. 336
Arantes, O. 86, 87
Arboleda, M. 223
Argentina 367–71, 373, 602
    business groups 360, 361, 363–8, 372–3
    Caputo group 368, 372
    elite in 367–8, 373
    financing strategy 372
    IRSA-Cresud group 365, 367, 368, 372, 374
    Pampa groups 365, 367–8
    real estate investment trusts (REITs) 363, 364, 372
    real estate market 365, 367
    top ten developers in 365–73
Aronowitz, S. 205
Arrighi, G. 113
Arua (Uganda) water crisis 547
Asia 91, 101, 509, 548
Asociación Nacional de Deudores Habitacionales (Andha Chile) 306, 308
asset economy 384–9, 394
asset price Keynesianism 382
Athens 11
    homosexual geographies 448–9
    housing problems 449–50, 453
Atkinson, R. 174, 414, 429
Ávila, D. 533
Ayuso, I. 439

Baber, A. 591
Baca, B. 423
Bachelard, G. 121
Bairro Costa do Sol 321
Bajos de Mena 304–8
Balakrishnan, S. 225
balanced community 253–5
Baldwin, D. L. 577
Ball, S. J. 288
Baltimore 83, 571
Banco Hipotecario Nacional 365
Bangladesh 22, 538, 546
Banks, N. 556
Barcelona 472–4, 476, 478, 481, 485–6, 528
    cooperative housing 478, 480, 482–3
    model 80, 87
Barnsbury 175
Barrow, H. 136

Bartra 403, 409
basic services, and infrastructure 540–41
Baumann, H. 512
Baum, H. 211
Bayat, A. 544
Beall, J. 350
Beauregard, R. 169, 589
Belgium 101, 563
Bell, W. 138
Bergamo 228, 512
Berlin 18, 100, 174, 269–70, 275, 591, 600
    construction site in 173
    homeownership rates in 98, 100
    housing policy protests 175
    Neukölln 275–7
Bernt, M. 176, 272, 273
Berry, B. 140
Beswick, J. 61
Bhattacharyya, R. 544
*biantong* practices 556–7, 560, 562
Bilge, S. 343
biopolitics
    dissuasive actions 532
    government and 531
    in public space 530–34
    securitarian policies
    preventive actions 533–4
    punitive actions 532–3
Bishop, B. 263
black ghetto 300
Blackman, L. 417
Blázquez, N. 348
Bloch, E. 205
Blokland, T. 35, 525
Boersma, M. K. 515
Bologna 567
Bonilla-Silva, E. 155
Booth, C. 65, 68, 595
Borja, J. 86, 87
Bose, S. 568
Boston 257, 259–60, 301
Boterman, W. R. 192, 292
Boudreau, J.-A. 539, 542
boundaries of neighbourhood 143
Bourassa, S. C. 271
Bourdieu, P. 41, 67, 120–23, 125, 177, 255, 287, 435, 477, 495, 603
    class theory 67
    sociological research in Porto 127–31
    theory of social class 567
    urban sociology 4
    urban theory and methods 8, 126–7
Brazil 21, 80, 82, 85, 86, 89, 94, 174, 299, 302, 310, 457–8, 460, 466, 468–9
    City Statute 462

    consequences of global financial crisis 461
    economic policies 461
    economy 86, 89, 91
    FDI and economy 90
    land occupations 460
    neoliberalism 89
    privatisation 91, 94
    social movement in 463
    socioeconomic shifts 460–62
    squatting movements 460–61
    urban legislation 91
    urban squatting 458
Bremen (Germany) 99
Brenner, N. 42, 58, 59, 222, 223, 225, 226–8, 231
Brickell, K. 414
Bridge, G. 192
Brill, M. 525
Bristol 174
Bryant, R. 327, 332, 333, 336
Budapest 21, 493, 497
    authoritarian turn of 501–3
    citizen participation in 498–504
    civic mobilisation 499
    construction workers at Bálna 502
    foreign capital investment 499
    market economy 499
    social urban rehabilitation 499–501
    urban regeneration in 498–501, 503–4
    Urban Rehabilitation Fund 498, 501
Buenos Aires 19, 85, 360, 366, 368, 373
    real estate market in 365, 367, 368
building occupations 460–66, 469
Burawoy, M. 26, 40
bureau repression 533
Burgess, E. W. 27, 138–9, 144, 154
Burma 577
business groups 360, 361, 363–7, 372–3
Butler, T. 174, 175, 177

Caciagli, C. 292
Cairo 30, 541
Calatrava, S. 91
Calbet i Elias, L. 273, 280
Caldeira, T. 301, 310
Camarero, H. 67
Campos, C. 464
Canguilhem, G. 121
Cantillon, R. 111
capital
    accumulation 112, 228, 360, 475, 554, 555, 572–3, 575
    labor/labour and 50, 75, 271, 554, 584, 590
capital circulation 554, 568
    university in 572–5, 577, 578

capitalism 57, 71, 75, 80, 93, 111, 140, 153, 156, 158, 219, 341, 474–5, 493, 494, 499
  contemporary 381
capitalist
  exploitation 38, 115, 153
  societies, role of the state in 56–7
  urbanization theory 71
capitalocene 219, 227, 231, 232
Caputo group 368, 372
Caputo, N. 368
Carabanchel 435, 436
Cardoso, J. Á. 461
care 341, 344–5, 354
  global crisis of 342, 344
  global transfer of 511, 513, 519
  reproduction and 342
  tasks 344, 351–2
  work 50
Carrero, R. 544, 547
Cartier, M. 126
Cassirer, E. 121
Castells, M. 27, 33–4, 68, 73, 86, 87, 180, 238, 299, 302, 308, 314–15, 493, 523, 568, 570, 584
Castoriadis, C. 214
Catalan Neighborhood Law 353
Catalonia 351, 480, 482
  cooperative housing sector 473
  housing associations 477
Caulfield, J. 271
Cayton, H. 300
Çelik, Ö 61
centrality 463
  conceptualisation of 238
  right to 242–3, 247
Centro Empresarial Nações Unidas (CENU) 90, 94
Certificate of Additional Building Rights (CEPAC) 92
Chamboredon, J. -C. 123, 124, 253, 255–7
Chatterton, P. 576
Chattopadhyay, S. 578
cheap labour 140, 229
Chesky, B. 380
Chesnais, F. 88, 89
Chicago 585
Chicago school 154, 155, 158, 159, 161
  of neo-classical economics 135
Chicago school of sociology 68, 135–8, 144, 146, 147, 176, 493, 523, 525, 585
  criticism of 136, 140
  neighbourhood and 137–8
Chile 306, 307, 309–10
  ghetto in 305
  *pobladores* of 18, 307

urban landscape of 299
urban poverty in 303–4
Chilean urban sociology 299, 300, 309
  ghetto in 302–4
China 22, 227–8, 552–3, 583, 588, 589
  capital circulations in 554, 555
  universities 570
  university towns in 569
  urban politics 555
  Villagers' Committee 557
China's urbanisation 552, 563, 588
  beyond the capital/state dichotomy 553–5
  *biantong* practices 556–7, 562
  demolition of rural settlements 554–5, 558
  development rights transfer 554–5
  growth coalitions in 555–8, 560–61
  growth or city-making coalitions in 555–8, 560–61
  *hukou* system 553
  illicit practices 556, 558, 559, 562, 563
  informality 556
  land management reform 554
  laws/policies or regulations 556–7
  multiple embeddedness of state agents 557
  planning and construction, informalisation of 558–60
  political informality 556–8
  regulatory changes 554
  state–capital approaches 553–5
Chiodelli, F. 552, 556
Chomsky, N. 574
Choplin, A. 225–6
Christian, M. 160
Christophers, B. 115, 178, 273, 277, 279, 280
*citadins* 236, 237, 239, 243–4, 247
cities 33, 98, 100, 104, 106, 107, 508, 525, 587–8
  assetisation of 602
  defined 30
  everyday lives of 519
  as fix and social capital 70–73
  global 588, 589
  in Global South 539–40, 543, 545, 547, 548
  homeownership in 99–104
  rentier 98, 100, 105–7
  shrinking 588–90, 594
  socially shaped 603–4
  as social mosaic 68–70
  social production of 30–31
  strategic planning of 588
  suburbanisation of 104
  temporalities in 510
  tenant 98, 106, 107, 596
  tenement- and non-tenement 99
citizen participation 402, 406, 408, 492
  in Budapest 498–504

political economy 493, 494, 497
  in public policy-making 495
  responsibility 494, 495
  structure–agency debate 493–6
  in urban regeneration 494–8
City Statute, Brazil 462
Ciudad Vieja district 484
Clark, K. 300
Clark, T. N. 151, 152
class 598
  conflict 66, 74, 76
  of cooperative housing 478
  labor and 76
  organization, space in 73–5
  perspectives 65, 66, 74, 75
  politics 74, 75
  in production of space and urban policy 70–73
  segregation 316
  social 66–70, 75
  struggles 38, 601
  theory 57, 58, 66–8, 71, 75–6
climate change 314
  crisis 594
  exacerbating marginalisation 317–18
  Global South 314
  of hazards 319–20
  hyper-marginalisation by 314, 319–22
  justice 317
  local economies and livelihoods, effect on 321
  socioeconomic impacts of 315
  urban impacts 315
  urban precarity and 315–18, 320
Clinton, B. 257
CLT model *see* community land trust (CLT) model
Cobos, P. 68, 71, 72
Cockburn, C. 50
Cocola-Gant, A. 383
cold spots 530
collaborative decision-making 400, 401, 408
  in urban planning 406
  urban regeneration and 399–401, 409
Col·lectiu Punt 6 19, 343, 344, 346–8, 351
collective action 546–7
Collins, F. L. 568
Collins, H. 343
Colombia 299
colorblind urbanism 151, 152
commodification 176, 180
  of housing 452
  pressures 473, 481–3
communities 203–4, 476–7, 545–8
  consultation 400–401

organizations 303, 307
  participation 349, 350, 398, 401, 406
  unionism 74
  weakened structures 403–4
community disintegration, urban regeneration and 403–6
community land trust (CLT) model 483
competitive advantage 570, 572, 573
conceptual enrichment 280
condominium ownership 104
Connell, R. W. 152
consultation process, fragmentation of 405
cooperative association 477
cooperative housing 472–3, 475–8, 486, 596
  accessing and scaling of sector 478–81
  capital in 477
  class character of 478
  community in 476–7, 480
  cooperative groups 480
  initiatives 484
  limits of 486
  in making and remaking of the city 483–5
  private 479–82, 484
  resilient to enclosure 481, 486
Copenhagen 472, 474, 476, 478, 485–6
  private housing cooperatives 479–80, 484–5
  rental housing in 480, 485
Cordeiro, H. 85
corporate restructuring 363
Cortese, T. T. P. 400
Costa Rica 299
Coulton, C. 143
COVID-19 pandemic 226–8, 305, 331, 383
  in Madrid 439
  urbanisation of inequalities 228–30
Cox, K. R. 571
CPTED *see* crime prevention through environmental design (CPTED)
Crang, M. 519
creative
  class 286
  economy 545
  *kampung* 545
creativity, and innovation 544–5
crime 326
  in Mathare 329–32
  and policing 327
  prevention 533–4
  urban public spaces 527, 530
crime prevention through environmental design (CPTED) 533
critical
  approach 9–12, 33–4, 44
  realism 39
  theory 37–9, 208

urban sociology 26, 40, 44, 136, 328, 329, 337, 584–7
urban studies 41–3, 222, 232
critical race theory (CRT) 151, 160–61
CRT *see* critical race theory (CRT)
cultural political economy 496–7
cultural-race 160
cultural turn (CT) 151, 153, 158–9, 288

Da Costa, W. M. 71
Dagkouli-Kyriakoglou, M. 390
Dahl, R. A. 51, 568
Dandara land occupation 465, 467
Dardot, P. 477
Darke, J. 342
Davidson, M. 174, 175, 414
Davis, D. E. 539, 542
Davis, M. 138, 527, 532, 542
DCC *see* Dublin City Council (DCC)
De Angelis, M. 476
*Death and Life of Great American Cities* (Jacobs) 253
De Backer, M. 523
debt financing 61, 558
decolonising the university 578
defensible space 534
de-hierarchizing planning process 346–7
de-industrialisation 158, 588
de Lauwe, C. 255
Del Valle, T. 345
democratisation/democratization 60–61, 308, 423, 495
demolition of rural settlements 554–5, 558
Dempsey, N. 143, 144
De Narváez, F. 368, 372
Denmark 273, 478–9, 481, 483, 486
    common housing 477, 480–81
    cooperative housing 472, 479
    privatisation of common housing 481–2
    'right to buy' scheme 481
de-patriarchalizing urban planning 347, 350
Deranty, J. P. 208
deregulation 434–5
Desmond, M. 429, 430, 600
destruction of homes 414–15, 601
developers
    rescaling of 361–3
    top ten in Argentina 365–73
development 319
    coalitions 495
    of neighbourhood 321
    rights transfer 554–5
    urban 72, 176, 273, 290, 498
Dewaele, A. 238
Dhaka 540, 546

informal settlements in 540–41
Dharavi slum (Mumbai) 542, 544, 547
dialectical materialism 39
digital platforms 383, 385, 390, 391
digital polyplatform rentierism 383, 390
Di Masso, A. 525, 527
direct displacement 391, 392
disciplining effect, on domestic workers 517–19
disengagement politics 421
displacement 167–71, 174, 178, 181, 197, 391, 412–13, 423, 450
    and destruction of homes 414–15
    dispossession and 391–3
    emotional burden of 193
    housing 391, 600–601
    of lower-class residents 192
    pressure 391–2
    state intervention and 172
    of tenants 391–2, 413
    through renovation in Sweden 415–16
    urban upgrading and 175–7
    violence of 416–17
dispositifs 531–4
dispossessions 190, 192, 194–8, 412–13
    emotional burden of 193
    of land, informal politics of 560–62
    urban inequalities and 188
dissuasive actions 532
distribution, of surplus value 111–12, 115, 117
division of labor/labour 513
    economic 30
    gendered 170, 189, 192, 341, 354
    intellectual 82
domestic workers, Filipina 21, 509, 589
    accommodation challenge 513–14
    dis-orientation 517
    earning money, unpredictable 516
    employment of 513
    legal case 518
    lived time of 513, 516
    premature termination 517–18
    public spaces usage of 514–15
    regulations 512, 513–514, 518, 519
    restrictions 514, 517
    spatialities/spatial 513–15, 520
    temporalities/temporal 513–15, 519–20
    two-year contracts 515–17
    uncertain migration trajectories 515–17
    working hours 513, 519
Domhoff, G. W. 568
domicide 414
Domínguez, M. 530
double globalization effect 174
Drake, S. C. 300
Dresden 589

drought 320–21
drug-trafficking agents 466
Dublin 20, 398–9, 401–3, 405, 407
    gentrification 407
    public–private partnership (PPP) 399, 403, 405
    working-class displacement 407
Dublin City Council (DCC) 399, 401, 402, 404, 405, 407
Du Bois, W. E. B. 151–3, 585, 595
Durán, M. A. 341
Durkheim, E. 6–7, 31, 121, 152, 153, 178, 202, 204–6, 214

Eckstein, S. 543
ecofeminism 344
economic
    conditions 493–4
    development 571–2
    growth 494
    informality 540
    restructuring 587–9
Ekström, M. 422
Elias, N. 531
elite, in Argentina 367–8, 373
elite theory of state 54–6
elitism 50–51
    upper classes 287
embedded racism 159–61
    in human ecology frame 155–6
    in political economy 156–7
    in theories 152–4
    in urban cultural turn approach 158–9
    in urban sociology 161
    in urban theorizing 159–61
    world-systems and global (WGS) theory 157–8
employment
    contracts 515–17
    precarity 590
empowerment 428, 431, 437–8
    women's 467
Engels, F. 6, 10, 27, 37, 65, 69, 71, 73, 156, 597, 598
England 301, 528
entrepreneurial cities 575
entrepreneurialism 52–4, 59
environmental inequality 320
epistemology 36–8, 44, 197–8
Epstein G. 113
ethnography 286, 289, 290, 294, 430, 431
    analysis 120–28, 130
    homeownership 429–33, 439
EU funds 499–500

Eugenia, Maria (immigrant), homeownership 428, 433–40
Eurocentrism 151, 153, 157, 342
European cities 98, 100
    homeownership rate 100–101
European Court of Human Rights 238
European Union (EU) 494
Europe, private rental share 105
Evans, J. 400
everyday life 510
    organisational rites and 245–7
    spatialities of 513–15
    temporalities in 511–15, 520
everyday state 556
exclusionary
    displacement 391, 392
    public space 527
exploitation
    capitalist 38, 115, 153
    labor/labour 15–16, 38, 110, 115–17, 554, 596
    rentierism and financialization 113
extended urbanisation 222, 224, 229, 230
    from Global South 225–6

Fainstein, S. S. 84, 527
Falú, A. 345
family 444, 446
    in Greece 447
    heteropatriarchal 447, 451
    home 447, 451
    housing 444
    role of 446
family-farming rates 101
Farrell, J. 223
Fattah, K. N. 546
FDI *see* foreign direct investment (FDI)
Feagin, J. 40
Federici, S. 341
Felsenstein, D. 571
feminism 344, 348, 354
    Col·lectiu Punt 6 19, 343, 344, 346–8, 351
    participatory methods 348–54
    planning 343–50, 353
    poverty 342
    sociology 188–90
    territorializing 348
    theory 188, 190–92
    urbanism 341, 353–4
Ferreira, J. S. W. 86
feudalism 59, 111
field of power, and housing policy 128–9
Fields, D. 383
Filipina domestic workers *see* domestic workers, Filipina

finance
    Marx, K. 114–15
    and rent 111–13
    in urban settings 115–17
financialization 2.0 372
financialization/financialisation 72, 82, 85, 110–13, 115, 117, 273, 362–3, 373, 374, 384, 390, 391, 393, 412–13, 452, 453, 576–7, 602
    financing and 372
    hyper- 236, 240
    Marxian turn of 110, 112–13
    municipal 61–2
    process 361, 363, 365, 372–4
    real estate 360–61, 364–5
    rental housing 393
    and rentier capitalism 381–3
    rentierism and 110, 112–13, 115, 117
Finland, regional inequalities 589
Fiori, J. L. 89, 95
Fix, M. 81, 93
flexible accumulation 570, 575–6
flooding 320–22
Florida, R. 72, 262
food delivery platforms 592
forced displacement 445
forced relocation 413, 414, 418, 451
foreclosure 438
foreign capital 494
foreign direct investment (FDI) 91
foreign universities 570
Forester, J. 212
formality, and informality 542–3
Foucault, M. 202, 208, 327, 335, 494, 524, 530–32
foundations of sociology 152–4
Fourcaut, A. 261
Fox O'Mahony, L. 412
fragmentation of consultation process 405
France 33, 101, 106, 120–23, 130, 219–21, 224, 227–30, 252–61, 264, 301, 361, 435
    epidemiological research 227
    family farming in 101
    ghetto in 299
Frankfurt school critical theory 38, 206, 214
Fraser, N. 194, 207, 261
Freire, P. 464
Friedland, R. 7
Friedmann, J. 82, 83, 85
Friedrichs, J. 144–5
FUCVAM *see* Uruguayan Federation of Mutual-Aid Housing Cooperatives (FUCVAM)
Fujita, K. 69
Fullilove, M. T. 414

Gabor, D. 105
Gaboury, J. 451
Gago, V. 385
Galster, G. C. 143, 145–7
Gans, H. 31, 253–5, 257, 258, 262
Gargiulo, E. 244
GCRR *see* global critical race and racism (GCRR)
Gebbia, J. 380
Gehl, J. 523, 527
*Gemeinschaft* 153
Gemzøe, L. 527
gender 444–5
    heteronormativity 445, 450–52
    inequalities 592
    relations 451
    roles 444, 447, 450
Gentili, M. 552
gentrification 172, 175–7, 193, 258, 263, 269–72, 275–7, 281, 289, 296, 392, 398, 400, 473, 483–6, 498, 500, 572, 576, 599–601
    analysis of agency in 179–80
    critical engagement with 192–3
    literature 188, 199
    middle class and school choices 287–9
    in Milan (Italy) 289–96
    processes 212
    rent gap closure and 274
    systemic crisis of social reproduction 194–8
    theoretical lens 273, 287–9
    transnational 449–50
    in urban sociology 199
gentrification research 167
    definitions of 168–70
    demand-side 170, 177
    explanation of 170–72
    multiple spatial manifestations of 173–6
    new questions in 172–3
    production-oriented 170
    role of sociology in 176–7
    social reproduction 192–3
    sociological approaches to 178–81
    urban policy 170, 171
geographical political economy 554
geoprevention paradigm 533
Germany 99, 105–6, 116, 220, 228, 273–5, 588
    homeownership rates in cities 100
*Gesellschaft* 153
Ghertner, A. 176, 272
ghetto 299–300, 305–7, 309–10, 403
    in American urban sociology 300–302
    in Latin American and Chilean urban sociology 302–4
    popular mobilization beyond the 304–7
Ghetto Foundation 326, 327, 333, 334

ghettoization 303
ghettoized poverty 299
Ghetto Youth 326–8, 334–6
Ghosh, S. 227
gig labour 590–91
gig work 590–91
Gilbert, A. 302
Gil, J. 383
Glaeser, E. 262, 588, 589
Glass, R. 27, 167, 168, 173, 285
global capitalism 158
    temporalities under 510–14, 519
global city 80, 81, 86, 588, 589
    as aspiration 82–5
    São Paulo 85–8
global critical race and racism (GCRR) 159–61
global housing crisis 429
globalisation 85, 88–90, 161, 174, 497
    capitalism during 93
    concept of 80, 81
    in Global South 225
    inequalities under 511
Global North 12, 14, 22, 84, 98, 113, 157, 158, 194, 219, 221–3, 230, 272, 342, 363, 412, 423, 457, 459, 461, 538, 539, 548, 583, 588, 590, 591, 596, 598
    farm ownership in 101
    labour 590
    urban squatting 459–60
global racial politics 161
Global South 8, 12, 14, 17, 19, 21, 22, 28, 35, 41, 113, 156–8, 176, 194, 219, 221–3, 225, 226, 230, 231, 238, 299, 310, 363, 459, 538, 578, 583, 588, 591, 596
    cities in 539–40, 543, 545, 547, 548
    climate change 314
    colonial 539
    disasters and crises 547–8
    economic informality 540
    extended urbanisation in 221, 223, 225–6, 231
    and Global North divide 13, 84
    hyper-marginalisation in 315, 319–20, 322–3
    industrial labour 539
    informality in 539
    informal settlements in 540–48
    of land and housing 541
    land use 543
    urban planning in 539
    urban precarity and 315–18
    urban squatting 459–60
global transfer of care 511, 513, 519
glocal social movements 34
Godschalk, D. 400
Goetz, W. 82

Goffman, E. 126
Goh, K. 223
Goldthorpe, J. H. 67
Gomez, D. 291
Gotanda, N. 160
Gothenburg 418
Gottdiener, M. 140
governmental/governmentality 30, 50, 462, 494, 531, 533, 542, 547
    agents 238
    crime prevention and control measures 345
    funding from agencies 161
    rationalities 494, 531
    system 52
    transnational 243
Grander, M. 416
gray spaces 542
Grazioli, M. 242, 246
Great Britain 99–100, 261, 263
Greece 20, 384, 444, 445, 450, 452–3
    Article 21 of the Constitution 447
    Athens 10–11, 238, 448–9
    boundaries in the HOME 450–51
    commodification of housing 452
    family in 447
    financial crisis 449
    forced translocations on 451
    heteropatriarchal family 447, 451
    homelessness 445
    homeownership 446, 449
    homosexual geographies 448–9
    housing policies 444
    housing problems 449–50, 453
    housing support 450–53
    LGBTQ+ 447, 449, 451, 452
    Orthodox Church 447–8
    rent gaps 450–51
    tenants in 449, 450
    welfare system 451
Greenberg, M. 75
green gentrification 193
Greenland 98
growth coalition 555–8, 560–61, 569
growth machine theory 54–6, 59, 61, 83–4, 92, 156, 569, 571

Haar, S. 578
Habermas, J. 51, 208, 209
habitability 236, 238, 242
Hackworth, J. 172
Haila, A. 31, 110, 584
Häkli, J. 417
Halbwachs, M. 123
Hall, P. 82
Hammel, D. 274

Hamnett, C. 270
Hannam, K. 593
Hannerz, U. 138
Haraway, D. 189, 348
Hardin, G. 474
Harding, A. 35, 54
Harding, S. G. 348
Harloe, M. 28
Harris, C. I. 157
Harvey, D. 27, 68, 71–4, 83, 114–15, 139, 156, 225, 361, 412, 475, 493, 554, 572–3, 575, 584
Häußermann, H. 588
Haussmann, G. 65
Hawley, A. H. 137, 147
HEA *see* human ecology approach (HEA)
Healey, P. 51–2
Hearne, R. 404, 405
Hegel G. W. F. 206
Heidegger, M. 332
Heller, H. 567
Helsinki 598
Herrero, Y. 344
heteronomy 587
heteronormativity 445, 450–52
heteropatriarchal family 447, 451
Hilferding, R. 111, 112
hinterland 222, 224, 226, 228, 230
Hirt, S. 589
historical comparison 99
Holgersson, H. 274
Hollands, R. 576
Holloway, J. 474, 476
home
    destruction of 414–15, 601
    family 447, 451
homelessness 445
homemaking 239, 413, 417, 422, 601
homeownership 98, 382, 428–31, 438, 444, 446, 449, 478
    agony of 435–7
    in cities 99, 104
    ethnographic analysis 429–33, 439
    ethnography 430, 431
    Eugenia, Maria (immigrant) 428, 433–40
    inequalities 430
    promise of 434–5
    quantitative regional studies on 99
    rates 98–101, 104, 105, 596
    rise of 98–100
    urban 100–105
homosexuality 448–9
Hong Kong 21, 85, 141, 509, 589, 591
    accommodation in 513–14
    domestic workers 589

employment policy 519
Filipina domestic workers in *see* domestic workers, Filipina
labour regimes 520
migrant domestic workers in 513–20
migration policies 515–16, 519
plan to stay, of domestic workers 516–17
public spaces 514
public space use on Sundays 514–15
regime 513, 520
temporalities of 517
working time regulations 514
Honneth, A. 202, 203, 206–9, 214
hooks, b. 159, 190
HOPE VI programmes 257–8, 261
Horizontal Property Law in 1983 481
Horkheimer, M. 38
hot spots 530
housing 169, 174, 177, 289, 382, 389, 394, 429–30, 446–7, 476–7, 595–7
    activism 437–8
    affordable 398, 399, 401, 403, 408
    assetisation 381, 383, 392–3, 596
    associations 477, 481
    cooperative *see* cooperative housing
    crisis 237, 240–44
    critical sociology 595
    displacement 391, 600–601
    family 444
    financialization 113, 363, 390, 393
    as generally idle resource 386–7
    global commodification of 240
    immigrants and 431
    informal 596
    injustice 468
    insecurity 239
    issues 10
    land occupations for 460–66
    limitations in 253
    markets 113, 273
    movements 437–8
    as permanently idle resource 388
    policy 128–9, 175, 256, 299
    political economy of 178, 595
    rental *see* rental housing
    and rentier capitalism 381–3
    rights 437
    social mix 252, 260, 262, 264
    and squatting movements 247
    support 450–53
    as temporarily idle resource 386–8
    tenure 99, 596
housing cooperatives *see* cooperative housing
Howard, E. 65
Hoyt, H. 68

Hsing, Y.-T. 554
*hukou* system 553
human ecology approach (HEA) 151, 153–5, 160
    embedded racism in 155–6
    Marxist political economy 156
    political economy 156–7
    urban cultural turn approach 158–9
    world-systems and global (WGS) theory 157–8
Hungary 21, 493, 497, 499–500, 588
Husby (Stockholm) 277–80
Husserl, E. 121
hyper-financialisation 236, 240
hyperghetto 301
hyper-marginalisation 314, 322–3
    in Angolan and Mozambican cities 320–22
    by climate change 314, 319–22
    in Global South cities 315, 319–20, 322–3
    segregation and 316–17
hyper-segregation 314, 316

Ibadan 578
Ibañez, B. 65
imagined communities 204
immigrants
    homeownership 428, 432, 433–40
    Maria Eugenia's story of 433–40
    mortgage problems 428, 432–3, 436–8
    population 439
immigration 431–2, 440
    housing law for 435
India 225, 229, 272, 556, 563, 577, 596
Indonesia 22, 513, 546, 574, 596
    domestic workers 513
    informal settlements in 223, 538, 545–6
    slum tourism 545
industrial
    production 10–11
    relocation 587
industrialisation 98, 588
inequalities
    gender 592
    under globalisation 511
    school 286, 290, 296–7
    social 124, 135, 228, 511, 512
    socio-spatial 289
    spatial 314, 319, 322
    urban 314–17, 319, 597
    urban space and 188, 189, 314
informality/informal 556–7, 596
    collective action 546–7
    community organisation 546
    concept 539–40
    economy 538, 540, 543–5
    financial assistance to residents 547

    formality and 542–3
    in Global South 539
    as governmental tool 542
    housing 596
    labour 540, 542
    of land and housing 541
    land market 541
    political 556–8
    resistance and 546–7
    savings groups 547
    social configurations of 543–8
    social networks 544
    space 546–7
    spatial 541
informal settlements 538, 552, 596
    community organisation 546–7
    creativity and innovation 544–5
    in Dhaka 540–41, 546
    Dharavi slum (Mumbai) 542, 544, 547
    to disasters and crises 547–8
    in Global South 540–48
    in Indonesia 223, 538, 545–6
    in Jakarta 223
    to necessity 544
    responsive adaptation
    social resistance 545–6
innovation, creativity and 544–5
institutionalist approach 474
insurgent 545
    movements 213
    practices 212–14
    self-confidence 211–13
    spatial practices 457, 468
integration 431, 435, 440
interdependence of science and politics 37
interests 110, 111, 117
    and economic rent 111
    rate of 114
    rent and 112
intersectionality 343
    climate vulnerability 320
    feminist perspective 346
    participatory planning 349–53
inter-urban competition 570, 575
invaded spaces 527
invented space 528, 530
investment
    decisions 360, 600
    social infrastructures 574
    in university 572–3
Ireland 101, 398, 401, 402, 404, 406, 408, 409, 588
IRSA-Cresud group 365, 367, 368, 372, 374
Islington 168
Israel 101, 512

homeownership rates 101
Istanbul 56, 86, 188, 195, 197–8
Italy 17, 33, 226, 228, 286, 288–9, 512, 563

Jacobs, J. 253, 525–7, 534
Jacobs, K. 429
Jaeggi, R. 212
Jäger, J. 72
Jakarta 540, 546
    informal settlements in 223
Jameson, F. 90
Japan 101, 174
Jaramillo, S. 71
Jelinek C. 499
Jenks, M. 143, 144
Jerusalem 512, 568
Jessop, B. 71, 497, 572
Jones, M. R. 58, 571
Jones, P. 400

Kabeer, N. 351
Kaika, M. 193
Kalijawi 546–7
Kallecki, M. 111
Kallin, H. 276, 280, 576
Kallio, K. P. 417
Kalyukin, A. 103
Kanai, J. M. 223, 225
Kant, I. 209
Karsten, L. 192
Kasarda, J. 140
Katz, C. 194
Kellecioğlu, I. 275
Keller, S. 138
Kempt 383
Kennedy, M. 169
Kenya 19, 328–30, 335
Kerameikos 449
Keynes, J. M. 110, 111, 112
Kholodilin, K. 104, 106
Kilian, T. 523, 530
Kiriro, S. 330
Kleibert, J. M. 568
Knight, D. M. 327, 332, 333, 336
Knowles, C. 512
Knox, P. L. 85
Kohl, S. 103–6
Kokoreff, M. 299
Korail (Dhaka), informal settlements in 540–41
Korea 578
    South 568, 574, 577
Krijnen, M. 273
Krippner, G. 113
Kropotkin, P. 213

labor/labour 7, 12, 21, 33, 59, 111, 114, 117, 271, 478, 482, 511, 512, 572–3, 587–9
    and capital relations 50, 75, 271, 554, 584, 590
    cheap 140, 229
    and class conflict 76
    conflict 73–5
    division of 513
    economic 30
    empirical studies 136
    exploitation 15–16, 38, 110, 115–17, 554, 596
    flexibilisation 81, 94, 509, 513, 591
    gendered 170, 189, 192, 341, 354
    gender inequalities 592
    gig 590–91
    Global North 590
    and housing, dualism 446
    industrial, in Global South 539
    informal 540, 542, 544, 552
    intellectual 82
    market 144, 314, 445
    Marx, K. and 115
    migration 520, 587, 594
    movements 73–4, 310, 591
    platform 590
    precariousness of 287, 590–92
    social reproduction 198, 354
    spatialities and temporalities 520
    urban 590–92
    women's participation 194, 513
Laferté, G. 126
Lagos 30, 540
Lambeth 50
land
    dispossession, informal politics of 560–62
    and housing, informality of 541
    invasion 541
    occupation 460–66, 541
Landes 219
land occupations
    for housing 460–66, 469
    in RMBH 464–5
land rents 111, 113–17
    and rentierism 110
land-use
    conflicts 406–8
    regulations, violation of 541
Lapavitsas, C. 115
Larsen, H. G. 485
Latina 435
Latin America 18, 81, 84, 87, 101, 303, 304, 309–10, 461, 548
    concept of ghetto in 302–4
    developers in

geographical expansion of 368
and Global South 310
real estate financialization 365
role of 364–5
top ten 365–73
urban sociology 361
Laval, C. 477
Lazarsfeld, P. 40
Leadership in Energy and Environmental Design (LEED) 197
Lees, L. 170, 173–5
Lefebvre, H. 8, 28, 33, 67–8, 71, 75, 156, 219–22, 226, 230–32, 236–9, 242–8, 255, 258, 462–3, 511, 523, 584, 603
  critiques of structuralism 69
Le Galès, P. 35, 495–6
Lemaire, M. 123, 124, 253, 255–7
Leonard, P. 169
Lesutis, G. 236, 239
Lewis, J. 367
Lewis, O. 302
Lewis, P. 75
Ley, D. 270, 271, 273
LGBTQ+ 444–5, 447, 449
  boundaries 451–2
  community 192
  forced translocations on 451
  Greece 447, 449, 451, 452
  homelessness 445
  Orthodox Church against 448
  suppression of the freedom 451
Linebaugh, P. 478
Lin, J. 583
LIS *see* Luxembourg Income Study (LIS)
Lisbon, public space 526
Listerborn, C. 422
lived space 511, 523
lived time 511–12
  of domestic workers 513, 516
  of Filipina domestic workers 513
live-in rule 514
Livsey, T. 578
Li, Z. 568
Lizardo, O. 151
local scale 50, 52, 54, 56, 61
local state 55–7, 59, 60, 62
  theory 50–53, 55, 61
Lofland, L. 527
Logan, J. R. 28, 55, 84, 569
London 50, 65, 84, 168, 174–6, 229, 285, 568, 570, 576, 591
Los Angeles 85, 90, 138
lost space 526
lost unity, and lost control 203–4
Loukaitou-Sideris, A. 527

low-income
  groups, limited benefits for 257–8
  neighborhoods 299–300, 304, 309–10, 336
  urban settlements 328–31
  workers 511
Low, S. M. 528
Lozano, A. 348
Luanda (Angola) 19, 314, 315, 317, 318, 322
  climate change impacts 319
  flooded neighbourhood in 318
  hyper-marginalisation in 320–22
  low-income poor settlements 320
  urban growth 320
  urban population 317, 320
Lukacs, G. 205, 206
Luke, N. 193
Lund Hansen, A. 485
Luxembourg Income Study (LIS) 106

McCabe, B. J. 430
machine politics 569
McKenzie, R. D. 136
MacLaran, A. 406
Maclennan, D. 142
MacLeod, G. 571
McNamara, B. 405
Macri, M. 367, 368
Madden, D. 69–70, 73, 74, 414
Madrid (Spain) 20, 389, 428, 432–4, 438
  archival and ethnographic work in 432–3
  COVID-19 pandemic 439 in
  homeownership 432, 434–9
  immigrants
  Maria Eugenia's story of 433–40
  meeting of the PAH 433
  population 439
  public space 528
  rental market 434–5, 438–9
  Santa Ana Square 529
Magdolna Quarter Programme 500
Maget, M. 123
Malang 545
Malo, M. 533
Malone, K. 523
Maloutas, T. 69
Malthus, T. 111
managerialism 50, 52–4, 527, 528
Manley, D. 144
Maputo (Mozambique) 19, 314, 315, 319, 322
  climate change impact 319
  hyper-marginalisation in 320–22
  resident of Bairro Costa do Sol 321
  urban growth 320
  urban population 318
Marcuse, H. 38

Marcuse, P. 69–70, 73, 74, 85, 169, 172, 391, 414, 450, 600
marginalisation 314–16
    climate change and 315
    in Global South 317
    hyper- *see* hyper-marginalisation
marginality theory 302
marginalized spaces and lives 196–7
Maricato, E. 82, 86
Marom, N. 126
Marques, E. 85
Martínez, M. A. 4, 11, 56, 70, 129, 141, 173, 191, 278, 302, 366, 433, 461, 463, 475, 484, 502, 526, 529, 593, 597, 599
Marxian/Marxist/Marxism 7, 38, 42, 57, 67, 116, 220, 231, 478
    class strategies 69
    financialization 69
    rentierism 69, 110, 112–13
    structural 51, 56–7, 59, 67, 71, 86, 496
    theory
        on urbanisation 86
        of urban politics 56
        urban sociology 33–5, 65
    of value 71
Marxist political economy (MPE) 156, 157, 159
Marx, K. 6–7, 31, 37–8, 50, 110, 111–12, 116, 121, 152, 153, 156, 597
    rent and finance in 114–15
Masclet, O. 126
Massey, D. 32, 71, 73, 511, 519, 584
Mathare
    crime in 330–32
    policing young and poor men in 328–30
    stealing in 331
    urban futures in 332–6
    violent policing in 328–9
    youth in 326–37
Matsuda, M. 161
Maya, C. 592
Mayer, M. 26, 35, 73, 463, 496
Mazzucato, M. 110, 113
Mbembe, A. J. 578
MCA *see* multiple correspondence analysis (MCA)
Mead, G. H. 206
megafires 219, 231
mega-urbanisation projects 558
Mele, C. 583
Merla, L. 512
Merrifield, A. 222, 231, 238, 463, 524
Metaxourgeio 449
methodological individualism 179
metropolis 525
Mexico 91, 302, 540

Mexico City 85
Miao, J. T. 53–4
Michael, J. 287
Michaud, A. 345
microphysics of power 530
middle-class 168–71, 174, 175, 177, 179, 182, 286, 287, 290, 291
    cultural hegemony 256
    families 286, 288, 289, 291, 293
    norms and values 299
    parents 288, 294, 295
    and school choices 287–91, 295, 296
    white 291
migration
    labour market 520, 587, 594
    temporalities of 512–13
    uncertain trajectories 515–17
Milan (Italy) 18, 228, 286, 601
    gentrification in 289–96
    square in gentrified area of 292
    tenancy rates in 100
Mills, C. W. 40, 421
Minsky, H. 113
Minton, A. 530
Miranda, R. 308
Mitchell, D. 530
MLB *see* Movimento de Luta nos Bairros (MLB)
mobilities, urban sociology of 592–4
mobilization 419–21, 423
    civic 499
    political 130, 259, 261, 599
    popular 304–7
Molotch, H. L. 28, 55, 84, 569
Montevideo 472–4, 476, 479, 482, 484–6
    FUCVAM estates in 484
    housing cooperatives in 483, 485
Moraes, A. C. R. 71
Morange, M. 238
Moreira, G. L. 466
Morris, A. 584–5
mortgage 428, 433–5, 437, 438, 440
    payments 436–7
mortification 440
Moses, R. 65
Mösgen, A. 274
Moss, M. L. 575
Movement for the Right to Habitation 237, 239–42
    citizens to *citadins* 243–4
    organisational rites and everyday life 245–7
    right to centrality 242–3
Movimento de Luta nos Bairros (MLB) 463
Movimento dos Trabalhadores Rurais sem Terra (MST) 468
Mozambique 314, 316, 318, 320

hyper-marginalisation in cities 320–22
   population in 321
MPE *see* Marxist political economy (MPE)
MST *see* Movimento dos Trabalhadores Rurais sem Terra (MST)
Müller, F. 412, 421
multiple correspondence analysis (MCA) 124, 128
multispatial metagovernance 361–3
multi-stakeholder organisational structures 481, 486
Mumbai 540, 547
   Dharavi slum 542, 544, 547
Mumford, L. 1, 33, 65
municipalism 60–61, 476, 486
municipalist vanguardism 480
Murphy, E. 403
Murray, C. 382
Musil, J. 158
Musterd, S. 140
Myanmar 513

Nairobi 19, 35, 326, 329, 331, 333
Nandy, A. 161
Naples 597
National Urban Renewal Agency (ANRU) 258, 261
natural space 31
neighbourhood effects 155, 69, 135–6, 141, 155, 255, 261, 440
   and Chicago school of urban ecology 137–8
   complication and confusion 140–45
   urban ecological and 138–40
neighbourhoods 168–72, 174–7, 179–81, 188, 195, 197–8, 204, 286, 287, 289–91, 293–6, 303, 307, 310, 349, 413, 414, 419, 422, 423
   critical 305
   gentrifying 192–4, 196, 291
   low-income 299–301, 304, 309
   social mix of 290
   urban transformations in 392
   working class 229, 230, 258, 260, 261, 263, 264, 301, 401, 598
neo-Lefebvrian 221, 231
neoliberalism 59, 89, 207, 342, 381, 407, 495–7, 531, 532, 539
   capitalism 510
   urban 71, 190
   urbanism/urbanization 32–4, 59, 71, 72, 224, 236, 239, 413, 423
neo-Marxist
   approach 66, 146, 474, 475
   political economy 151, 153
neo-Weberian approach 66

Nepal, earthquake in 547
Netherlands 563
networking, squatting 465–7
Neukölln (Berlin) 275–7
Neurath, O. 38–9
Neuwirth, R. 546
Newman, O. 534
new municipalism, and degrowth debates 60–61
new urbanism 257, 263
new urban poverty 303
new urban sociology 33–4, 43, 135, 136, 139, 140, 146, 303, 314, 322
New York 65, 84, 169, 174–5, 253, 257, 368, 568, 570, 575
NGOs 546
Nigeria 577, 578
Niguarda 294
Nijman, J. 544
normative concept 252, 253, 259, 262, 263, 265
Norris, M. 404
North America 219, 578, 579
Norway 101, 116, 126
nuclear family, internal disintegration of 302

O'Devaney Gardens community 398–9, 401–8
   research and case study 401–3
Oh, D. Y. 574, 576, 578
Ohmae, K. 88
Oldenburg, R. 524
Olds, K. 572
Olsen, A. K. 589
O'Mara, M. P. 572
Oreopoulos, P. 144
organic community 203–4
organisational rites 245–7
orientations 332–7, 421
   critical 41, 43
   global 222
   methodological 128
   radical 41, 43, 335
   sexual 189, 444, 446
   temporal dis- 515–17
   urban futures 336–7
   youth 327–8, 333
Oslo 98
Ossowski, S. 67
Ostrom, E. 474
OUC *see* Urban Operation Consortium (OUC)

Paddison, R. 583
PAH *see* Platform for People Affected by Mortgages (PAH)
Pahl, R. 28, 53, 602
Pain, R. 414, 416
Palestinians, daily lives of 512

Pampa Energía 372
Pampa groups 365, 367–8
pandemics 221, 225–7
    and megafires 231
    urbanisation of inequalities 228–30
Paris 123–4, 126, 228–30, 256, 259, 496, 567, 574, 591
    École Normale Supérieure in 121
    'Haussmannisation' of 220
    homeownership rates in 98
    tenancy rates 100
Park, R. E. 27, 68, 135–7, 139, 154, 162, 585
participatory
    methodology 343, 348
    practices 499–501, 503
    processes 349–53
participatory planning 349
    intersectional feminist perspective 349–53
Pasquali, P. 123
Paton, K. 193
Pattillo, M. 429, 430, 440, 595
Peake, L. 190
Peck, J. 59, 493
peer-to-peer (p2p) 380, 384
Penny, J. 61
Pentagon 574
Pereira, B. 86
Pérez Orozco, A. 344
Perry, D. C. 568
Phelps, N. A. 53–4
Philadelphia 100, 571, 585
Philippines 513, 516–18
    domestic workers 513
physical space 4–6, 32, 120, 125, 126, 128
    production and reproduction of 130
    social and 120–27
Piketty, T. 110, 113, 115, 179, 260
Pinçon, M. 256
Piñera, S. 306
placing people, at the center of urban decisions 344–5
planetary gentrification 71, 229, 483
planetary urbanisation 219–21, 225, 229–32, 236, 239, 330
    Covid-19 226–8
    theory, reloaded 221–3, 225–8, 231
planning ethics 203
    self-critical 211–12
platform
    capitalism 383
    economy 590–91
    real estate 383, 388–90, 393
Platform for People Affected by Mortgages (PAH) 428, 432, 433, 437
platform labour 590

platform-scale rent gaps 384
pluralism 50–52
*poblaciones callampas*, defined 310
*pobladores*, defined 310
*pobladores* movement 300, 302, 303, 310
    resurgence of 307–9
Polanska, D. V. 20, 420–22, 601
policing 328
    crime and 327, 333
    in Mathare 328–30
political
    informality 556–8
    reflexivity 44
political economy 111, 380, 385, 394, 493, 494
    citizen participation 493, 494, 497
    cultural 496–7
    embedded racism in 156–7
    geographical 554
    of globalisation 89
    of housing 595
political subjectivity 203, 206, 212–14, 416–17
    material and spatial dimensions 420–22
    political dimension 420–22
    social dimension of 418–20
    tenants 417–20, 424
politics 43
    of scale 493
    science and 36–7, 44
    urban 56–7, 60
    university and 568–9
popular
    mobilization 304–7
    politics 302, 307, 310
Porteous, J. D. 414
Porto 90, 120, 127, 128, 130, 131
    Bouça cooperative housing in 129
    Bourdieu's sociological research in 127–30
    mobilisation of Bourdieu's framework 120
Portugal 120, 127, 219, 384
postcolonial urban university 577–8
postmodernism 158
post-racial urbanism 152
post-Soviet countries, homeownership rates in 104
poverty 301, 319–21, 323, 539, 540, 548
    urban 299–304, 309
power 530–31
    recognition and 208–9
    relations 512
PPPs *see* public–private partnerships (PPPs)
precariousness of labor/labour 287, 590–92
premature termination 517–18
preventive urbanism 533–4
private housing cooperatives 479–82, 484

privatisation/privatization 32, 89, 229, 231, 277, 423, 461, 474, 498, 524, 601, 602, 604
   in Brazil 91, 94
   and managerialism in urban public space 528–30
   of rental housing 415, 419–20
   of a Swedish suburb 415
   Uruguay 481
property 472, 475, 479, 481–2
   rights 475
protest 175, 180–82
Proudhon, P.-J. 10, 111
Psyrri 449
p2p *see* peer-to-peer (p2p)
public
   sociology 40–41
   spaces 514–15
public–cooperative nexus 476, 477, 486
public participation, in urban regeneration 399, 400
public policies 252
   as ideal 262–4
   instruments 495
   as political stake 259–62
public–private partnerships (PPPs) 53, 87, 94
   redevelopment model 399–406
public spaces, urban 523, 524
   biopolitics in 530–34
   changes and fragmentation 527
   conflict and struggle 525
   crime 527, 530
   critical views of 526–8
   depoliticisation 531
   exclusionary 527
   of fear 530
   insecurity 525, 530
   laws and regulations 532–3
   managerialism 527, 528
   parks 528
   policies 532–4
   prevention 533–4
   privatisation 528–30
   romanticisation 524–6
   security 527, 528
   spatial segregation 527
   strangers in 525–7
   surveillance 527, 528
   uncivic behaviour 525
Puente Alto 304, 306
Puerto Madero 368, 372
punitive actions 532–3
Putnam, R. 254

Qatar 98, 570, 578
qualitative data analysis 399
quantitative easing policies 372
quasi-permanent settlements 541
Quesnay, F. 111
Quijano, A. 84, 219–20

Rabat 226
race-neutrality 151, 152
racial
   inequalities 316
   segregation 260, 300, 309
   stigmatisation 270, 275
   uprisings 586
racism 151, 585
   critical race and global critical race 160–61
   embedded *see* embedded racism
   theoretical themes and 152–4
Ranci, C. 297
Rannila, P. 415
Rasse, A. 304
rational choice theory 179
Readings, B. 567, 574
real estate 602
   in Buenos Aires 365, 367, 368
   financialization 360
   in Latin America 364–5
   platform 383, 388–90, 393
   speculation 461, 462
real estate investment trusts (REITs) 107, 363, 364, 372, 382
real estate market, in Buenos Aires 365, 367, 368
Recio, R. 542
Reclus, É. 65
recognition and power 208–9
refurbishment 485
regeneration 407, 408
   urban *see* urban regeneration
REITs *see* real estate investment trusts (REITs)
reloaded planetary urbanisation theory 221–3, 225–8, 231
relocation of residents 405–6
Relph, E. 143
renovation 279, 484, 601
   planned 418
   resistance against 416–17, 419–20
   in Sweden 415–16, 418, 421–3
renoviction 413, 415, 416, 422
rent
   finance and 111–13
   Marx, K. 114–15
   as unearned income 111–12
   in urban settings 115–17
rental housing 171, 173, 434–5, 479–80, 595–6, 601
   financialisation 393
   increase of rent 419, 420

privatization of 415, 419
    Sweden 415–16
rental market, in Madrid 434–5, 438–9
rent gaps 170, 172, 449–50
    consumption and production 270–72
    Husby (Stockholm) 277–80
    Neukölln (Berlin) 275–7
    short-term rentals (STRs) 393
    theory 112, 269–70, 273, 274, 279, 281, 384
rentier capitalism 386, 596, 601–2
    financialisation and 381–3
rentier cities 98, 100, 105–7
rentierism 106, 110–17
    financialization and 110, 112–13, 115, 117
    land rents and 110
    Marxian turn of 110, 112–13
Ren, X. 147
reproduction 575
    and care 342
    of physical space 130
    social *see* social reproduction
rescaling 363, 494, 497
    of developers 361–3, 373
    of the state 59
    of urban governance 362
research
    agenda 161, 603
    O'Devaney Gardens case study 401–3
    and policies in Brazil 80
research programme 120, 126
    in Porto city 127–30
resettlement apartment buildings 560
resistance, and informal settlements 545–6
responsive adaptation
    to disasters and crises 547–8
    to necessity 544
Rhoades, G. 567
rhythmanalysis 511–12
Ricardo, D. 110, 111
Richard, Å. 421
right
    to buy scheme 481
    to centrality 242–3, 247
    to the city 236–9, 242, 243, 247, 258, 460, 465
    to private property 461–5
Rio de Janeiro 85–7, 540
RMBH (Metropolitan Region of Belo Horizonte) 458, 469
    collectives and groups for legal advice 466
    integration with local communities 465–6
    land occupations for housing 460–66, 469
    land occupations in 464–5
    presence of religious entities 466
    right to private property 462–5

squatters' networks 465–7
squatting movement in 463
urban squatting in 460–69
Roberts, P. 399
Robinson, J. 85, 578
robust foundation, of emotional care 214
Rodrigues, C. U. 318
Rodríguez, J. P. 308–9
Rogers, D. 383
Rome (Italy) 246
    Article 5 243–4
    housing crisis 240
    housing rights movements 237, 241
    Movement for the Right to Habitation *see* Movement for the Right to Habitation
    squatted social centre and houses in 246
    squatting action in 238, 242
    urban squatters 244
Rose, D. 192, 270, 271
Rose, N. 531
Rosen, E. 429, 430
Rosenlund, L. 126
Rossi, U. 236, 362
Roth, G. 567
Roy, A. 330, 539, 541, 556, 578
Rufino, B. 365
Ruhr area 588
rural settlements, demolition of 554–5, 558
Russia 91, 103
    homeownership rate 103
Ruto, W. 333
Ryan-Collins, J. 382
Ryan, É. 403

Sachar, A. 85
Sadowski, J. 383
Salcedo, R. 304
San Francisco 380
San Giovanni A Teduccio, social housing estates in 597
Santiago 304, 307
    graffiti 305
Santo André 87
Santos, M. 85
Sanyal, K. 544
São Paulo 80, 81, 85–8, 92, 94–5, 469, 588
    Jardim Edith favela in 93
    largest business centre in 81
    *see also* global city
Sarkissian, W. 263
Sassen, S. 34–5, 72, 80, 82–5, 87, 95, 583–4
    global city 157
Saudi Arabia 116
Saunders, P. 5, 31, 32, 147
Sayad, A. 121

Sayer, A. 113
Scandinavian cities, homeownership rates 103–4
Schatzki, T. R. 332, 334
Schindler, S. 225, 554
Schmid, C. 222, 223, 225, 226, 228, 231
school
    decisions 291, 294
    and gentrification in Milan (Italy) 289–96
    inequalities 286, 290, 296, 297
    Italian school regime 290
    middle class and 287–91, 295, 296
    performance 295
    polarization of children in 292, 296
    relationship with neighborhood 294–5
    segregation 287–9, 295–6
    and socio-spatial inequalities 289
Schreiber, Z. J. 367
Schteingart, M. 65
Schwabe's law 100
science and politics 36–7, 44
scientific curating 13
Scotland 100, 144
    ownership rate in cities 100
Scott, A. J. 74, 571
segregation 598
    class-based 316
    of groups and social class 68–70
    and hyper-marginalisation 316–17
    racial 260, 300, 309
    school 287–9, 295–6
    urban 68, 69, 252, 256, 261, 317
    work 598
selection effect issues 143–4
self-critical planning ethics 211
self-critical theory 208
self-governance 531
self-help housing 541
Sennett, R. 523, 524
Seoul 35, 85, 568, 577
Seville, Miraflores park in 70
sexual division of labor 341, 354
Shanghai 572
shared space
    shared experience in 202
    shared values in 214
sharing economy 381, 384–9, 394, 591
Sharma, S. 511
Shaw, J. 383
Shaw, M. 576
Shaw, W. S. 161
Sheller, M. 592–4
Shen, J. 569
Sheppard, E. 544
Shin, H. B. 576

short-term rentals (STRs) 380–81, 384, 386–94, 449
    Airbnb and 381, 383, 388, 394
    converting houses into assets 383–4
    Covid-19 effects on 389–91
    social impact of 391–3
shrinking cities 588–90, 594
Siebel, W. 588
Sigler, T. 449
Silva, I. 302
Silver H. 495
Simmel, G. 202, 204–6, 214, 525, 2057
Simone, A. 236
Singapore 577, 578
Slater, T. 42, 127, 151, 161, 173, 274, 280, 586–7, 600
Slaughter, S. 567
Sloane, D. 139, 147, 148
slum 538, 543
    clearance protest 546
    Dharavi (Mumbai) 542, 544, 547
    life 543
    tourism 545
Small, A. W. 154
Small, M. 301
Smith, A. 110, 111
Smith, D. M. 140, 209
Smith, N. 68, 72, 112, 113, 172, 174, 269–74, 277, 384, 528, 600
Smith, S. E. 414
Smit, S. 512
sociability 127–8
social
    abstraction 205
    activism 458
    agency 29–30
    change 29
    class formation 120–21
    cohesion 204, 263
    conflict 44, 50–51, 54, 56–8, 61, 202, 206, 523, 527
    context 52, 153, 328
    control 70, 214, 258, 260, 486, 534, 603
    disintegration 303, 304, 309
    disorganization 154, 301, 302
    diversity 71, 205, 256, 259, 263, 264
    housing policies 129
    inequalities 124, 135, 228, 511, 512
    mosaic 68–70, 76
    organisation 546–8
    organization 342
    and physical space 120–27
    and political structures 269, 275, 280
    processes 3, 6, 26, 29, 44
    psychology 206

relations 29, 512
  and spatial movements 203
  structures 3, 5, 6, 26, 29–30, 34, 37, 44, 67–8, 182
  theory 66, 67
  urban rehabilitation 499–501
social class 66, 67, 75
  and segregation of groups 68–70
social distance, spatial proximity and 255–7
social housing 257, 403, 406–8
  estates, regeneration of 400–401
social infrastructure 572
  investment in 573
  university as 573–4
social mix 252, 258, 259, 281, 290, 598–9
  ideal of 252, 262–4
  of neighborhood 290
  policies 136, 252, 253, 257
  as political stake 259–62
  social sciences and 253–8
social movements 65, 73, 111, 180, 202–3, 206, 223, 231, 244, 264, 437–8, 458, 462–4, 467–8
  unions and 75
  *see also* squatting movements
social order, in gentrification processes 178–9
social reproduction 74, 188
  as feminist urban theory 190–92, 198
  gentrification research 192–3
  of labor 198, 354
  systemic crisis of, gentrification 194–8
social science 2–3, 37–9
  critical 39
  and social mix 253–8
social space 120, 124, 126, 128, 130, 131
  class theory and 75
  and physical space 125
social will, and social form 204–6
society, community and 203–4
socio-economic inequalities 130, 285, 287
  in Brazil 461
sociological theories 6–8, 167, 179, 182
sociology
  role in gentrification research 176–7
  urban *see* urban sociology
socio-spatial
  differentiation 598
  inequalities 289
  phenomena 5–6, 8, 10–11, 31–3, 44, 598, 604
  segregation 65, 66, 68–70, 75, 76, 126, 288, 598
  structure 65–9
  transformation 222, 288, 296
socio-symbolic topology 123–5

Sofia, Varazhdane park in 599
Soja, E. 73, 209, 584
Sorkin, M. 528
Sørvoll, J. 103, 478
South Africa 299, 316, 319, 321
Southeast Asia 171, 583
Southern Europe 219, 447
Southern European welfare regime 446
South Korea 568, 574, 577
Souza, M. L. 458, 467
space 4–6
  in class organization 73–5
  public *see* public spaces, urban
  urban *see* urban space
Spain 460
  homeownership 432
  housing 432
  immigrants in 428, 431–2, 434–8
  legislation of mortgage markets 434
  rental housing market 434–5
  urban rents 434
spatial/spatiality/spatialities 75, 84, 510, 512, 539
  of domestic workers 513–15, 520
  of everyday life 513–15
  inequalities 314, 319, 322
  informality 541
  of labour 520
  proximity, and social distance 255–7
  regulations 513–14, 519
  segregation 316
  selectivity 58
Speyer, T. 90
Spire, A. 238
Springer, S. 214
squatters
  networks 465–7
  settlements 541
squatting movements 239, 459–61, 463, 467, 468
  housing rights and 247
squatting, urban 457–8
  global North and South 459–60
  in RMBH 460–68
SRA *see* strategic relational approach (SRA)
Standing, G. 113, 590
state
  elite theory of 54–6
  hegemony 58
  policy formulation 58
  role in capitalist societies 56–7
statehood, and collective actors 180–81
status-race 160
Stavanger 126
Stavrides, S. 246, 477
Stockhammer, E. 113
Stockholm 18, 269, 270, 275, 277–80, 419, 600

demonstration against privatization 419, 420
first of May demonstration in 191
Husby 277–80
Stoker, G. 55, 56
Stone, C. N. 55, 556
Storper, M. 74, 571
strategic
    planning of cities 80, 588
    urban planning 86, 87, 94
strategic relational approach (SRA) 51, 57–9
street vending 591–2
STRs *see* short-term rentals (STRs)
structuralism 67–9
structuralist theory 56–60
structural Marxism 51, 56–7, 59, 67, 71, 86, 496
structural selectivity of the state 57–8
structural violence 301
structure-agency, citizen participation in 493–6
student housing 576–7
studentification 576
subaltern
    critical science 37
    urbanism 225
sub-Saharan Africa 319, 574
Sultana, F. 540
Sum, N.-L. 497, 572
Sun, L. 556
super-gentrification 174, 175, 274
surplus value, distribution of 111–12, 115, 117
Sweden 273, 277–9, 413, 601
    housing regulation 416
    renovation in 415–16, 418, 421–3
    rental housing 415–16
    resistance against 416–17, 419–20
Swyngedouw, E. 493, 572, 601
Sykes, H. 399
symbolisation 126, 129–30
Syriza 448


Tarlabaşı 188, 195–8
Tavares, M. C. 89, 95
Taylor, P. J. 85
temporal/temporality/temporalities 117, 213, 280, 334–5, 351, 416, 508–9
    of customer demand 590
    defined 510
    disciplining effect of 517–19
    dis-orientation 517
    domestic workers 513–15, 519–20
    of everyday life 511–15, 520
    under global capitalism 510–14, 519
    infrastructures 511, 520
    measures 512
    of migration 512–13
    regulations 512, 514, 518

restrictions 514, 517
of social institutions 512
time as 510
temporarily idle resource
    function of 388–9
    housing as 386–8
temporary employment 515–17, 519
Tenancy Act, Spanish 389, 390
tenancy rates 100
tenants 98, 100, 106, 413, 415–16, 601
    cities 98, 106, 107, 596
    displacement 391–2
    in Greece 449, 450
    material and spatial dimensions 422–3
    mobilization 421, 423
    political dimension 420–22
    political subjectivity 417–22, 424
    in rental housing 479–80
    resistance against renovations 416–17, 419–20
    social dimension 418–20
    solidarity with neighbors 418–19
    threat of losing home 421, 424
    union 418, 419, 421–2
tenure-mix policies 598
Teresa, B. 273, 280
territorial
    fetishism 586
    stigma 129–30, 270, 275, 280, 301, 303, 436–8
territorializing feminism 348
territorial stigma 436
Thailand 513
Theodore, N. 59
theoretical approaches 7, 65–6, 68
    capital 57, 58
    class 57–8, 66–8, 71–2, 75–6
    structural 178
theorization
    of finance, Marx, K. 112
    urban *see* urban theorization
theory, sociological 6–8
third spaces 524
Thompson, E. P. 67, 71, 73
Thompson, M. 60, 476
Thörn, C. 274, 421–2
Thörn, H. 422
Tibbalds, F. 526
Tickell A. 493
time
    daily time of migrant workers 512–13
    deficit/poverty 511, 514, 518–19
    disciplining effect 517–19
    domestic workers 514–19
    in everyday life 511–13

frames for earning money 516
lived *see* lived time
maintenance 511
as money 510
under neoliberal capitalism 510
regulations 514, 518
role of global capitalism in 510–13, 519
social inequalities and 511
in social processes 508–10
and space 34, 510–11, 514, 519
in temporal infrastructures 511
as temporality 510
uncertain migration trajectories and 517
Tokyo 84, 578, 593
Tonkiss, F. 544
Tönnies, F. 153, 202–4, 206, 214, 525
Topalov, C. 32, 33, 35, 71, 361
Toronto 99, 100, 144
Torres, H. 85
total ethnographic analysis 120–23
Touraine, A. 73
trade unionism 74
Trancik, R. 526
transdisciplinarity 1–3
transformative urban planning 343, 349
transnational
　education zones 570
　gentrification 449–50
trans-scalar 236, 243
Tretter, E. M. 573
Tulumello, S. 383
Turchin, P. 229
Turin, tenancy rates in 100
Turkey 174
Turner, J. 7
two-year contracts 515–17

Uganda 547
uncertain migration trajectories 515–17
underclass 69, 140, 261, 586, 598
un-homing 414
　threats of 423
United Arab Emirates 570
United Kingdom (UK) 33, 116, 141, 532, 576–8
United Nations' Declaration of Human Rights 238
United States (US) 69, 83, 89, 91, 152, 154, 157, 228, 254, 309–10, 555, 568, 571, 578, 585, 586, 589
　concept of the ghetto 301, 302
　HOPE VI programmes in 257–8, 261
　housing 257, 260
　tenement- and non-tenement cities in 99
　underclass in 598
　universities 568, 575–7

urban poverty in 299, 309
urban sociology 152
White racial domination 160
universal morality 214
university 567–8
　built environment of 572, 574–6
　in capital circulation process 572–5, 577, 578
　circuits of capital 574–5
　class struggle 574
　consumption and production 575
　economic development role 571–2
　edifice complex 575
　financialisation for 576–7
　globalised cities and 570–71
　growth machine theory 569, 571
　investment in 572–3
　knowledge and innovation 571, 578
　knowledge economy 570
　new urban politics 571–2
　political functions of 574
　promoting a knowledge economy 570
　as social infrastructure 573–4
　spatial expansion of 571
　student accommodation/housing 576–7
　studentification 576
　as transnational urban actors 570
　in urban development processes 575–6
　and urban politics 568–9
　urban process 569, 571, 576–7
university–urban relations 568, 571–2, 576–8
urban
　centrality 238–9, 242–3
　citizenship 243, 244
　competition 54, 570, 588
　conflict 66, 73, 209–11, 214
　contestations 495–6
　disaster governance 317–18
　entrepreneurialism 53, 80, 89, 362
　ghettos 299–307, 309, 403
　growth 320, 589
　growth machine theory 54–6, 59, 61, 83, 84, 92, 156, 555, 569, 571
　homeownership 98, 100–105
　housing 476
　inequalities 314–17, 319, 597
　informality 538, 539, 542
　labour market 590–92
　life 11, 123, 525
　movements 302, 307, 309
　neoliberalism 71, 190
　pluralism 50–52
　political economy 100, 497
　poverty 299–304, 309, 320
　proletariat 475, 478
　regime theory 54–6, 555

renewal 258, 484, 485
rentierism 98
rites 245–6
safety 345
segregation 68–9, 252, 256, 261, 317
sociability 127–8, 130
social ecology 136–8, 140
social movements 236, 238, 240, 247, 302
social sciences 1–3, 113
spatialities 84, 510
speculation 54
tourism 604
transformation 272, 285, 286, 288, 392
urban commons 60, 472, 473, 477–8, 483, 485, 486, 596
   through cooperativism 474–6
urban cultural turn (CT) 158–9
   embedded racism in 158–9
urban development 72, 176, 273, 290, 498
   coalitions 495
urban ecology 139, 146, 147
   and neighbourhood effects 138–40
urban futures 327, 328, 337
   in Mathare 332–6
   orientations 336–7
urbanisation 30–31, 72, 122, 485, 553
   on homeownership 99
   of inequalities 228–30
   political informality in Yangzhou (China) 557–8
   processes 220, 222, 223, 225, 226
   social class and 75
   structuralist Marxist theory on 86
urbanism 30–31, 221, 226
   neoliberal 32–3
urban life worlds 327, 328, 336–7
urban managerialism 53–4
   Rex and Moore's concept of 53
Urban Operation Consortium (OUC) 87–8, 91, 92
urban planning 51, 80, 398–400, 406, 408
   model 86
   processes 341–5, 348, 350
urban policy 362, 483, 494
   class in production of space and 70–73
urban politics 56–7, 60
   university and 568–9
urban precarity, and climate change 315–18
urban process 205, 394
   university 569, 571, 576–7
urban public spaces *see* public spaces, urban
urban redevelopment, participation in 406–7
urban regeneration 398, 408
   in Budapest 498–501, 503–4
   citizen participation in 494–8

   and collaborative decision-making 399–401, 409
   and community disintegration 403–6
   planning 406
   political complexity of 400
   public participation in 399–401
urban–rural homeownership gap 101–2
urban sociology 3–5, 27–8, 35–6, 72, 73, 126, 152, 155, 159, 182, 288, 300, 303, 308, 310, 314, 342, 353, 354, 583
   American, concept of ghetto in 300–302
   approaches 33–4, 44
   contemporary context 35
   critical 26, 40, 44, 136, 328–9, 337, 584–7
   defined 32
   embedded racism in 161
   feminist perspectives 190
   French schools of 35
   gentrification literature 199
   ghetto in 309
   Marxist 33–5, 65
   of mobilities 592–4
   physical space 5–6
   reforms 35, 36
   research 33–5
   rise of the new 33–4
   social production of cities 30–31
   social structures and processes 28–30
   spatiotemporal phenomena and contexts 31–3
urban space 4–6, 26, 69, 342, 400, 510
   capitalist production of 66
   and inequalities 188, 189, 314
   segregation of groups in 68–70
urban squatting 457–8
   Global North and South 459–60
   in RMBH 460–69
urban study, Bourdieu's sociology 126–7
urban theorization 112–13, 151, 156, 159
   embedded racism in 159–61
   Marxian, rent and finance 112–13
Urry, J. 584, 592, 593
Uruguay 368, 372, 374, 478–83
   cooperative housing 472, 479, 481
   privatisation 481
Uruguayan Federation of Mutual-Aid Housing Cooperatives (FUCVAM) 473, 479, 480–82, 484

Vainer, C. 86
Valentine, G. 254
Vallecas 437, 439
Van Ham, M. 141–2, 144
Vanhanen, T. 101–2
van Kempen, R. 85

Vannini, P. 592
Vasishth, A. 139, 147, 148
Veblen, T. 111
Vegliò, S. 219
Vekemans, R. 302
Venice 100, 228, 300
Vesterbro 484
Via Fabriano 290, 292–4
Via Iseo 293–4
Via Scialoia 290, 292, 293
Vice, S. 211
video surveillance 532
Vincent, C. 288
violence
　of displacement 415–17
　housing 415
　against women 345
Vora, N. 578

Wachsmuth, D. 273, 449
Wacquant, L. 8, 41–2, 126, 127, 300–303, 309–10, 436, 585–6
Walker, R. A. 573
Wallace, R. 227
wall of money 116, 117
Walters, P. 546
Walzer, M. 209
Ward, C. 65, 72, 213
Washington, B. T. 585
weakened community structures 403–4
Weberian approach 7
Weber, M. 6–7, 27, 31, 54, 121, 152, 153, 179, 205, 228, 494
Weinstein, L. 556
Weisler, A. 273
Western Europe 572, 578, 579, 598
Westminster 576
WGS theory see world-systems and global (WGS) theory
White middle- and upper-class standards 154
White supremacy 154, 155, 158, 161, 585
　and capitalism 157, 158
　global 158–60
　racism and 151, 157, 160
　Whiteness and 151, 152, 154, 155, 161
　White privilege and 159
Whyte, W. F. 138, 253, 255
Wiewel, W. 568
Williams, R. 74
Wilson, D. 300, 302
Wilson, W. J. 142, 299, 303, 309, 586
Winnicott, D. 206

Wirth, L. 300, 523
women's participation 194, 513
　in community organizations 307
　in labor 194, 513
working-class 289–90, 478, 598
　communities 193, 261
　displacement 600
　identity 308
　migrants 229
　movements 310
　neighbourhoods 229, 230, 258, 260, 261, 263, 264, 401, 598
　women 193, 342
World Social Forum (WSF) 90
world-systems and global (WGS) theory 151, 153, 157–8
　embedded racism in 157–8
World Trade Centre (WTC) 90
Wright, E. O. 67
Wright, M. 274
WSF see World Social Forum (WSF)
WTC see World Trade Centre (WTC)
Wu, C. 151, 152
Wyly, E. 39, 173

Yangzhou (China) 552, 553, 557, 558, 563
　building a new city in 561
　construction of resettlement sites 560
　land dispossession, informal politics of 560–62
　planning and construction, informalisation of 558–60
　political informality 557–8
Yeoh, B. S. A. 578
Yiftachel, R. 540
Yogyakarta 546
Yonkers 257, 259
Young, I. M. 209
young urban professional parents (YUPPs) 192
youth 326–31, 333, 334, 336, 337
　orientations 327–8, 333
Yu, H. 155, 156

Zanten, A. V. 290
Zeublin, C. 300
Zhang, Y. 561
Zhou, X. 563
Zorbaugh, H. 137
Zuberi, T. 155
Zukin, S. 34, 36, 158, 177, 271, 528, 529, 568, 584, 586